BELL ON
MISSISSIPPI FAMILY LAW

SECOND EDITION

by
Deborah H. Bell

Professor of Law
University of Mississippi

THE NAUTILUS PUBLISHING COMPANY
OXFORD, MISSISSIPPI
www.nautiluspublishing.com

BELL ON MISSISSIPPI FAMILY LAW

Citations to cases and statutes are current through December 31, 2010.

Copyright © 2011, 2017, Deborah H. Bell. Portions of Chapters I, VI, and X were published previ-ously in the Mississippi Law Journal in *Family Law at the Turn of the Century*, 71 Miss. L. J. 781 (2002); *Child Support Orders: The Common Law Framework*, 69 Miss. L. J. 1063 (2000); *Child Support Orders: The Federal-State Partnership*, 69 Miss. L.J. 597 (1999); and *Equitable Distribution: Implementing the Marital Partnership Theory*, 67 Miss. L.J. 115 (1997).

All rights reserved. No part of this publication may be reproduced or used in any form without written consent of the publisher or author. This publication is designed to provide accurate and authoritative information in regard to the subject matter covered. It is sold with the understanding that the author is not engaged in rendering legal, accounting, or other professional services.

Printed in the United States of America.

Library of Congress Cataloging-in-Publication Data

Bell, Deborah H. (1953 -
  Bell on Mississippi Family Law/By Deborah H. Bell
  2nd Edition
  ISBN 0-9722520-9-6/Paperback: 978-1-936946-87-7

To subscribe to the annual supplement or to order additional copies, contact:

The Nautilus Publishing Company
426 South Lamar Blvd., Suite 16, Oxford, MS 38655
Tel: 662-513-0159 • Fax: 662-234-9266
E-mail: dbell@msfamilylaw.com • Web: www.msfamilylaw.com

For
Mississippi's chancellors and family law attorneys

iv

PREFACE

Family law today bears little resemblance to the system in place several decades ago. Then, exit from marriage was carefully guarded — proof of narrow, specific fault grounds dominated divorce litigation. Men and women were not considered equal partners in marriage or upon divorce. Financial considerations at divorce were simple; property was awarded to the spouse with title, generally the husband, and an "innocent" wife received alimony for the remainder of her unmarried life. The maternal preference ruled custody decisions.

In the last three decades, Mississippi discontinued gender distinctions in family law rules, adopted no-fault divorce, discarded the title system for a marital property system, recognized two new forms of alimony, and abandoned the maternal preference for a rule of parental equality. Today, divorce is almost a matter of right. Divorce litigation focuses on complex financial issues and custody battles between parents on equal legal footing.

Modern custody suits regularly present issues that were rare or unthinkable thirty years ago — children's relationships with ex-stepparents and siblings, rights between unmarried parents with no relationship and unmarried parents with long-term commitments, grandparents' rights of visitation, same-sex couples as parents, disputes between biological fathers and legal fathers, and disputes between surrogates and intended parents. Awareness of child abuse and sexual assault and family violence has prompted state and federal measures that affect divorce, custody, and visitation orders.

One of the most dramatic changes in family law has occurred in the last decade. Six states have redefined marriage to include same-sex couples and eight have extended marriage-like rights through civil unions or domestic partnerships. At the same time, a majority of states have not only banned same-sex marriage but also deny recognition to same-sex marriages valid in other states, giving rise to significant issues of interstate enforcement.

The source of family law rules has shifted as well. Family law was traditionally regarded as the exclusive province of the individual states. The overriding theme of judicial discretion kept regulation at a minimum. Today, substantial portions of family law are governed by uniform acts and federal law. The four uniform acts adopted by the legislature align Mississippi with other states and make available a national body of caselaw interpreting the Acts. Family law actions are affected by federal regulation of bankruptcy, taxation, retirement benefits, the military, international adoption, child abduction, and domestic violence.

This book is intended to provide family law attorneys and judges with the substantive state and federal law applicable to most domestic relations cases. The book attempts to provide a comprehensive review of Mississippi law on each topic, combined with an overview of federal regulation and a survey of trends in other states. The organization was designed to facilitate use as a quick reference as well as for linear reading. The author invites comments and suggestions on content and organization for inclusion in yearly supplements and future editions.

D.H.B.
July 27, 2011

vi

ACKNOWLEDGEMENTS

The author wishes to thank Dean Sam Davis, Dean Richard Gershon, and Law Librarian Kris Gilliland of the University of Mississippi School of Law for their support for and encouragement of this project over the last two years, and my colleagues and students for their friendship, patience, and advice. Law students from the classes of 2010, 2011, and 2012 provided invaluable assistance for this Second Edition by tirelessly proofing and rechecking footnotes: Madeline Bobo, Angela Broun, Katie Bryant, Betsey Clemence, Brent Cole, Catherine Anne Daley, Alexis Farmer, Megan Felker, Trey Gunn, Bradley Hiatt, Diana Hodges, Lacy Hollins, Bryan Jones, Philip Levy, Joey Songy, Matt Roberts, Betsey Sawyer, Brett Thomas, Mark Woods, and Meaghan Ybos. Particular thanks go to Sarah Beth Miller, Class of 2011, who provided oversight for consistency in style and citation and organized the overwhelming task of rechecking thousands of footnotes, and to Genie Leslie for final proofing and creation of the Table of Cases. A special thanks to Carroll Chiles, Associate Publisher for the Nautilus Publishing Company, who worked long hours to polish and format this edition, without losing her good humor. And thanks to my husband and publisher, Neil White, who endured discussions of family law minutae and debates about chapter organization.

SUMMARY OF CONTENTS

PREFACE v

ACKNOWLEDGEMENTS vii

TABLE OF CONTENTS xi

PART ONE: RIGHTS BETWEEN PARTNERS

I	THE MARRIAGE RELATIONSHIP	1
II	RIGHTS BETWEEN UNMARRIED PARTNERS	41
III	ANNULMENT	57
IV	GROUNDS FOR DIVORCE	67
V	DOMESTIC VIOLENCE	111
VI	PROPERTY DIVISION	129
VII	RETIREMENT BENEFITS	197
VIII	DIVISION OF CLOSELY HELD BUSINESSES	217
IX	ALIMONY	229
X	ATTORNEYS' FEES	301

PART TWO: THE PARENT-CHILD RELATIONSHIP

XI	PATERNITY	313
XII	CHILD CUSTODY AND VISITATION	329
XIII	CHILD SUPPORT	413
XIV	ENFORCEMENT OF DECREES	475
XV	ASSISTED REPRODUCTION TECHNOLOGY	503
XVI	TERMINATION OF PARENTAL RIGHTS	519
XVII	ADOPTION	531

PART THREE: JURISDICTION, PRACTICE, AND PROCEDURE

XVIII	JURISDICTION	551
XIX	PROCEDURE	585
XX	ETHICAL ISSUES	633
XXI	BANKRUPTCY AND FAMILY LAW	645
XXII	TAX EFFECTS OF PAYMENTS AND TRANSFERS PURSUANT TO DIVORCE	655
XXIII	MARITAL AGREEMENTS	667

x

TABLE OF CONTENTS

PART ONE: RIGHTS BETWEEN PARTNERS

I MARRIAGE

§ 1.02 Overview.. 1

§ 1.02 The right to marry: General considerations.................................. 2

    [1] Constitutional limits of state regulation 2
    [2] Presumptions regarding marriage... 2
    [3] Conflicts of law 3

§ 1.03 Regulation of entry into marriage.. 3

    [1] Persons eligible to marry 3
        [a] Kinship 3
        [b] Bigamous marriages.. 4
        [c] Age.. 5
        [d] Same-sex marriages 5
        [e] Mental and physical capacity 6
    [2] Formal requirements.. 7
        [a] Common law marriage 8
        [b] Ceremonial marriage 9
            [i] License... 9
            [ii] Solemnization 9
            [iii] Failure to comply with requirements 9
    [3] Consent to marry 10
        [a] Fraud... 10
            [i] The "essentials" test.. 10
            [ii] The "but for" test 11
        [b] Duress.. 11
        [c] Limited-purpose marriage. 11
        [d] Marriage in jest 12

§ 1.04 Rights and duties within marriage: Legal status of women...................... 12

    [1] Common law rights and duties... 13
    [2] The Married Women's Property Acts 13
    [3] Constitutional constraints.. 13
    [4] The marital unity fiction 14

§ 1.05 Property rights between spouses... 14

    [1] Ownership, use, and control. 14

xi

TABLE OF CONTENTS

[2] Homestead property 15
   [a] Transfer without consent 15
   [b] Homestead rights at death 15
   [c] Homestead exemption 15
[3] Joint ownership... 16
   [a] Joint title presumption 16
   [b] Presumption of tenancy in common 16
   [c] Tenancy in common 17
   [d] Joint tenancy.. 17
   [e] Tenancy by the entirety 17
   [f] The right to partition 18
   [g] Effect of divorce on common ownership................................. 18

§ 1.06 RIGHTS OF INHERITANCE BETWEEN SPOUSES 18

[1] Through intestacy 18
[2] Under a will 19
[3] One-year allowance 19

§ 1.07 THE DUTY OF SUPPORT 19

[1] Support in the intact family 20
   [a] Direct support 20
   [b] The doctrine of necessaries 20
[2] Separate maintenance 21

§ 1.08 CONTRACTS AND CONVEYANCES BETWEEN SPOUSES 21

[1] Contracts for labor or services 22
[2] Conveyances... 22
   [a] Priority of bona fide purchasers 22
   [b] Priority of general creditors 23
   [c] Fraudulent transfers 24

§ 1.09 TORT ACTIONS 24

[1] Tort actions between spouses 24
   [a] Tort immunity... 24
   [b] Tort actions for domestic violence 25
[2] Tort actions against third parties 25
   [a] Loss of consortium 25
      [i] Nature of action 25
      [ii] Relation to injured spouse's suit.. 26
      [iii] Statute of limitations 26
   [b] Wrongful death actions 26

TABLE OF CONTENTS

[3] Heart balm actions 26
    [a] Alienation of affection 27
    [b] Criminal conversation 28
    [c] Breach of promise to marry 28

§ 1.10 EVIDENTIARY RULES 29

[1] Competency to testify 29
[2] Marital privilege 29

§ 1.11 CRIMES BETWEEN SPOUSES - MARITAL RAPE 30

§ 1.12 MEDICAL DECISION-MAKING 30

[1] Abortion and spousal consent requirements 30
[2] Healthcare directives and surrogates 31

§ 1.13 CHOICE OF RESIDENCE 32

§ 1.14 SEPARATE MAINTENANCE 32

[1] History and overview 33
    [a] Judicial authority 33
    [b] Gender equality 33
    [c] Scope 34
[2] Basis for award 34
[3] Amount of award 35
    [a] Factors 35
    [b] Application 36
    [c] Direct payments to third parties 36
    [d] Attorneys' fees and temporary support 37
[4] Property division and lump sum alimony 37
    [a] Equitable distribution 37
    [b] Lump sum support 37
    [c] Partition of jointly owned property 38
[5] Child custody and support 38
[6] Order to reconcile 38
[7] Modification and termination 38
[8] Res judicata effect at divorce 39

II RIGHTS BETWEEN UNMARRIED PARTNERS

§ 2.01 HISTORY AND OVERVIEW: LEGALITY 41

[1] Common law marriage 42

TABLE OF CONTENTS

[2] Cohabitation as a crime 42
[3] Sexual conduct as a crime 42
[4] Constitutionality 42
[5] Practical effects of criminalization 43

§ 2.02 FINANCIAL RIGHTS BETWEEN COHABITANTS 43

[1] Void marriages: The putative spouse doctrine 44
[2] Cohabitation between former spouses 44
    [a] Division of assets 44
    [b] Reimbursement for domestic services 45
[3] "Mere" cohabitants 45
[4] Rights based on express agreement 46
[5] Alimony 46

§ 2.03 OTHER BENEFITS 47

§ 2.04 THE AMERICAN LAW INSTITUTE PROPOSAL 47

§ 2.05 PATERNITY AND CHILD SUPPORT 48

§ 2.06 CUSTODY 48

[1] Between unmarried parents 48
[2] Effect of cohabitation on custody 48

§ 2.07 ADOPTION 49

§ 2.08 SAME-SEX PARTNERS: THE DIVISION BETWEEEN STATES 49

[1] Recognition of same-sex rights 49
[2] Nonrecognition of rights 50
[3] Federal law: Nonrecognition 50

§ 2.09 INTERSTATE RECOGNITION 51

[1] The common law rule 51
[2] Constitutionality 51
[3] Interstate divorce 52
    [a] Mini-DOMA states 52
    [b] Other states 52
    [c] Dissolving civil unions 52
    [d] Recognition of separation agreements 52
    [e] Extension of state benefits to same-sex couples 53

TABLE OF CONTENTS

§ 2.10 ADOPTION..**53**

    [1] Constitutionality of adoption prohibition...54
    [2] Full faith and credit 54

§ 2.11 PARENTAL RIGHTS BASED ON RELATIONSHIP..........................**54**

§ 2.12 CUSTODY ACTIONS...**55**

    [1] Jurisdiction 55
    [2] Role of sexual orientation in custody actions 55

§ 2.13 CONCLUSION **55**

III ANNULMENT

§ 3.01 HISTORY AND OVERVIEW..**57**

    [1] History 57
    [2] Mississippi 57

§ 3.02 THE VOID/VOIDABLE CLASSIFICATION **58**

    [1] Distinctions between void and voidable marriages...........................58
    [2] Classification 58

§ 3.03 GROUNDS FOR ANNULMENT...**59**

    [1] Void marriages...59
        [a] Bigamy 59
        [b] Kinship within the prohibited degree..59
    [2] Voidable marriages 60
        [a] Incurable impotency and [b] lack of physical capacity 60
        [c] Mental illness or retardation...60
        [d] Pregnancy of the wife by another 60
        [e] Minority..60
        [f] Lack of consent...60
        [g] Failure to obtain a license 60

§ 3.04 DEFENSES TO ANNULMENT **61**

    [1] Statute of limitations 61
    [2] Ratification 61
    [3] Laches..61
    [4] Estoppel 62

TABLE OF CONTENTS

§ 3.05 PARTIES WHO MAY CHALLENGE **62**

    [1] Third persons 62
    [2] Spouses 62

§ 3.06 EFFECT OF ANNULMENT **63**
    [1] Property and support rights 63
    [2] Children of annulled marriage 64
    [3] Retroactivity 64

§ 3.07 JURISDICTION AND PROCEDURE **64**

IV GROUNDS FOR DIVORCE

§ 4.01 HISTORY AND OVERVIEW **67**

    [1] English divorce law 67
    [2] Early American divorce law 67
    [3] Early Mississippi divorce law 67
    [4] Early twentieth century: Fault-based divorce 68
    [5] Divorce reform: Irreconcilable differences 68
    [6] Divorce reform in Mississippi 69
    [7] Jurisdiction 69

§ 4.02 FAULT-BASED GROUNDS FOR DIVORCE **70**

    [1] General considerations 70
        [a] No default judgment 70
        [b] Burden of proof 71
        [c] Corroboration 71
        [d] Divorce granted to the most innocent party 72
        [e] Findings of fact 72
        [f] Standard of review 73
    [2] Natural impotency 73
    [3] Adultery 73
        [a] Findings of fact 74
        [b] Direct proof 74
        [c] Circumstantial proof 74
        [d] Post-separation adultery 76
        [e] Same-sex relationships 76
        [f] Condonation 76
        [g] Remarriage may be barred 77
    [4] Sentenced to any penitentiary 77
    [5] Desertion for one year 77

xvi

TABLE OF CONTENTS

[a] Continuous for one year 77

[b] "Willful and obstinate" 78

    [i] Intent to abandon the marriage 78

    [ii] Without spouse's consent 79

[c] Rejection of reconciliation offer 79

[d] Constructive desertion 80

    [i] Refusal to have sex 80

    [ii] Dispute over location of residence 81

[e] Effect of separate maintenance decree 81

[6] Habitual drunkenness 81

[7] Habitual and excessive use of opium, morphine, or other like drug 82

[a] Habitual and excessive use 82

[b] "Other like drug" 82

[c] Use of prescription drugs 83

[d] Use must continue at time of suit 83

[8] Habitual, cruel, and inhuman treatment: Overview 83

[a] The defendant's conduct: Cruelty defined 83

[b] Causal connection 85

[c] Timing 86

[d] Corroboration 87

[e] Burden of proof 88

[f] Standard of review 88

[9] Habitual, cruel, and inhuman treatment: Specific conduct 89

[a] Physical violence 89

    [i] Pattern of violence or one or more incidents of severe violence 89

    [ii] Isolated acts of violence 89

[b] Verbal or emotional abuse 90

    [i] Unfounded accusations 91

    [ii] Refusal to have sexual relationship 91

    [iii] Aberrant sexual behavior 91

    [iv] Hiding child 92

[c] Factors in combination 92

[d] Revolting and unnatural conduct 94

[e] Incompatibility 95

[10] Mental illness at the time of the marriage 96

[a] Must exist at time of marriage 96

[b] Lack of knowledge 97

[c] Ratification 97

[11] Bigamy 97

[12] Pregnancy of the wife at the time of the marriage 97

[13] Kinship within the prohibited degree 98

[14] Incurable mental illness 98

§ 4.03 DEFENSES TO FAULT-BASED DIVORCE **99**

xvii

TABLE OF CONTENTS

[1] Knowledge of condition 99
[2] Ratification 99
[3] Mental illness 99
[4] Recrimination 100
[5] Reformation or repentance 101
[6] Condonation 101
    [a] Of adultery 101
    [b] Of continuing offenses 102
    [c] Voluntariness of condonation. 102
    [d] Conditional nature of condonation 103
[7] Connivance 103
[8] Collusion 103
[9] Res judicata 104
[10] The Servicemembers Civil Relief Act 104

§ 4.04 IRRECONCILABLE DIFFERENCES DIVORCE **105**

[1] Personal jurisdiction 105
[2] Consent 106
    [a] Voluntariness 106
    [b] Withdrawal of contest or denial 106
[3] Pleadings must be on file for sixty days 107
[4] Requirements for submission of agreement 107
    [a] Agreement must be in writing 107
    [b] Submission of issues to court 108
[5] No divorce before all matters resolved 108
[6] Proceedings 109
[7] Judgment 109

§ 4.05 REVOCATION OF DIVORCE **109**

V DOMESTIC VIOLENCE

§ 5.01 HISTORY AND OVERVIEW **111**

§ 5.02 PROTECTION ORDERS **112**

[1] Jurisdiction and venue 112
[2] Parties 112
[3] Basis for petition 113
[4] Procedure 113
    [a] Contents of petition 113
    [b] Notice and hearing 113
    [c] Emergency orders: Justice, municipal and county courts 114
    [d] Temporary orders: Justice and municipal courts 114

TABLE OF CONTENTS

[e] Permanent orders: County and chancery courts.................................114
[f] Custody and support in protection orders.................................114
[5] Judgments.................................114
   [a] Mutual orders 114
   [b] Findings of fact 115
   [c] Time.................................115
   [d] Attorneys' fees 115
[6] Enforcement 115
   [a] Arrest.................................115
   [b] Remedies for violation 115
[7] Modification 115
[8] Interstate order enforcement.................................115
[9] Firearms prohibitions 116
[10] Safety and lethality assessments 116

§ 5.03 GROUNDS FOR DIVORCE 116

[1] Habitual, cruel, and inhuman treatment 117
   [a] Repeated or severe violence.................................117
   [b] Isolated acts of violence.................................117
[2] Impact on plaintiff.................................118
[3] Corroboration 119
[4] Condonation 119

§ 5.04 FINANCIAL AWARDS IN DIVORCE 121

§ 5.05 CUSTODY OF CHILDREN.................................121

[1] Presumption against custody to violent parent.................................121
[2] Violent behavior under *Albright*.................................122
[3] Domestic violence as basis for loss of custody 122
[4] Joint custody.................................123
[5] Custody and visitation restrictions 123

§ 5.06 MEDIATION.................................124

§ 5.07 TORT ACTIONS BASED ON DOMESTIC VIOLENCE 124

[1] Interspousal tort immunity 124
[2] Causes of action.................................125
[3] Relationship to divorce action.................................125
[4] Statute of limitations 126

§ 5.08 AGREEMENTS BETWEEN SPOUSES.................................126

xix

TABLE OF CONTENTS

[1] Property settlement agreements 126
[2] Conveyances between spouses 127

§ 5.09 FALSE ALLEGATIONS OF ABUSE 127

VI PROPERTY DIVISION

§ 6.01 HISTORY AND OVERVIEW 129

[1] The title system 130
[2] Community property 130
[3] Property division reform 130
[4] Creation of equitable distribution 131
[5] Equitable distribution in Mississippi 131
   [a] Judicial adoption: *Ferguson v. Ferguson* 131
   [b] The Mississippi system 132
      [i] Steps in equitable distribution 132
      [ii] Presumption in favor of marital property 132
      [iii] Division factors 133
      [iv] Presumption of equal homemaker contribution 133

§ 6.02 CLASSIFICATION: THE BASIC SYSTEM 133

[1] Failure to classify or error in classification 133
[2] Marital property defined 134
[3] "During the marriage" 134
   [a] Beginning date 134
   [b] Ending date 135
[4] Date asset is "acquired" 137
   [a] Community property: Transfer of title 137
   [b] Equitable distribution: Creation of equity 137
[5] Through a spouse's efforts 138

§ 6.03 SEPARATE PROPERTY 138

[1] Gifts and inheritances 138
   [a] Joint gifts 139
   [b] Interspousal gifts 139
[2] Property acquired prior to marriage or after the cut-off date 140
[3] Property excluded by agreement 140
[4] Income and appreciation from separate property 140
   [a] The active-passive test 140
   [b] Burden of proof 141
   [c] Proving causation 142

TABLE OF CONTENTS

§ 6.04 EXCHANGES OF PROPERTY **143**

[1] The exchange rule 143
[2] Burden of proof 144
[3] Assets purchased with both separate and marital funds 144
[4] Tracing in accounts 144
    [a] Total recapitulation method 145
    [b] Clearinghouse method 145
    [c] De minimus rule 146
    [d] Mississippi rule 146

§ 6.05 CONVERSION OF SEPARATE PROPERTY TO MARITAL **146**

[1] Conversion by implied gift or family use 146
    [a] Conversion by implied gift 146
    [b] The Mississippi family-use doctrine 147
[2] Conversion by joint titling 148
    [a] The joint-title presumption 148
    [b] In equitable distribution 149
[3] Conversion by commingling 149
    [a] Conversion by untraceable commingling 149
    [b] Commingling in Mississippi 150

§ 6.06 SPECIFIC TYPES OF PROPERTY **152**

[1] Personal injury awards 152
[2] Workers' compensation awards 153
[3] Disability benefits 153
[4] Professional degrees and practices 154
    [a] Professional degrees 154
    [b] Professional practices 155
[5] Attorneys' fees 155
[6] Patents, copyrights, and trademarks 156
[7] Assets acquired with loan proceeds 156
[8] Life insurance proceeds and policies 157
[9] Trust interest and income 157
    [a] Spouse as settlor of trust 157
    [b] Spouse as beneficiary of trust 158
    [c] Self-settled trusts 158
[10] Marital home 159
[11] Lottery and gambling proceeds 160
[12] Closely owned businesses 160
[13] Retirement benefits 160

§ 6.07 VALUATION **161**

TABLE OF CONTENTS

[1] The measure of value 161

[2] Findings of fact regarding value 161

[3] Burden of proof 162

[4] Date of valuation 163

    [a] Temporary support order 163

    [b] Premarital assets 164

    [c] Valuation on remand 164

[5] Proof of value 164

    [a] Expert testimony 164

    [b] Testimony of the parties or other lay witnesses 165

    [c] Financial statements 165

    [d] Buy-sell agreements 166

[6] Retirement benefits 166

[7] Closely held businesses 166

§ 6.08 DIVISION OF MARITAL PROPERTY 166

[1] Basic principles of division 167

    [a] No division of separate assets 167

    [b] Equal division not required 167

    [c] Division of each asset not required 167

    [d] Division factors 168

    [e] Presumption of equal contribution 168

    [f] Relationship to alimony award 168

    [g] Findings of fact 168

    [h] Standard of review 169

[2] The *Ferguson* factors 150

    [a] Contribution to accumulation of assets. 171

        [i] Homemaker contribution 171

        [ii] Financial contribution 173

        [iii] Contribution to education and training 174

        [iv] Contribution to marital stability 174

    [b] Need 175

    [c] Spouse's separate estate 175

    [d] Elimination of need for alimony 176

    [e] Fault as factor 176

    [f] Prior use or distribution of assets 177

        [i] Dissipation of assets 177

        [ii] Disposition by agreement 179

    [g] Emotional value of assets 179

    [h] Tax consequences 180

[3] Award of marital home 180

[4] Assignment of debt 181

TABLE OF CONTENTS

§ 6.09 RIGHTS OF THIRD PARTIES.. 184

[1] Impact on third-party interests 184
[2] Joinder 184
[3] Third-party equitable lien... 185
[4] Constructive trust 185
[5] Children's assets 186
[6] Corporate entities 186

§ 6.10 FRAUDULENT CONVEYANCES.. 186

[1] Factors 187
[2] Application 187
[3] Transfer to satisfy antecedent debt 188

§ 6.11 UNDUE INFLUENCE 188

§ 6.12 THE MECHANICS OF DIVISION 189

[1] Transfer of title 189
[2] Monetary award.. 189
[3] Sale of assets and division of proceeds 189
[4] Partition in kind 190
[5] Continued joint ownership 190
[6] Equitable credit.. 191
[7] Reimbursement for marital contribution to separate property 191
[8] Judgment against spouse 191
[9] Reserved jurisdiction 191
[10] Security for payment 192
[11] Constructive trust 192

§ 6.13 MODIFICATION AND ENFORCEMENT 192

[1] Modification 192
[2] Clarification 193
[3] Frustration of purpose 193
[4] Waiver.. 194
[5] Enforcement 194
[6] Relief based on fraud... 194

§ 6.14 EFFECT OF BANKRUPTCY.. 195

VII RETIREMENT BENEFITS

§ 7.01 TERMINOLOGY.. 197

TABLE OF CONTENTS

[1] Defined benefit plan..197
[2] Defined contribution plan..197
[3] Participant..197
[4] Alternate payee..198
[5] Immediate offset..198
[6] Deferred distribution..198
[7] Vested pension...198
[8] Mature pension..198

§ 7.02 THE EQUITABLE DISTRIBUTION PROCESS 198

[1] Valuation..199
[2] Classification..199
[3] Division and distribution..200

§ 7.03 DEFINED CONTRIBUTION PLANS 201

[1] Valuation..201
[2] Classification..201
[3] Division and distribution..202
[4] Taxes..202

§ 7.04 DEFINED BENEFIT PLANS 203

[1] Date-of-retirement approach 203
　　[a] Valuation..203
　　[b] Classification..203
　　[c] Division and distribution..204
　　　　[i] Immediate award 204
　　　　[ii] Deferred distribution 204
[2] Date-of-divorce approach..204
　　[a] Valuation..204
　　[b] Classification..205
　　[c] Distribution..205
　　　　[i] Immediate award 205
　　　　[ii] Deferred distribution 205
[3] Comparison of methods 206
[4] Other approaches...206
[5] Mississippi...207

§ 7.05 OTHER RETIREMENT BENEFITS 207

§ 7.06 PRIVATE RETIREMENT BENEFITS UNDER ERISA 207

xxiv

TABLE OF CONTENTS

[1] Federal regulation 208
[2] The Qualified Domestic Relations Order 208
  [a] Requirements..208
  [b] Method of division. 208
    [i] Shared interest 209
    [ii] Separate interest..209
  [c] Qualified joint and survivor annuity 209
  [d] Other considerations 209
  [e] Approval 210
  [f] Enforcement..210

§ 7.07 MILITARY RETIRED PAY 210

[1] Military retirement 210
  [a] Retroactivity 211
  [b] Jurisdiction 211
  [c] Division 212
    [i] Direct payment...212
    [ii] Payment by member 212
    [iii] Survivor benefits...212
[2] Military disability benefits...212
  [a] Contract provisions to divide disability.......................213
  [b] Disability in lieu of retirement 213

§ 7.08 NON-MILITARY FEDERAL RETIREMENT BENEFITS 214

§ 7.09 IRAS...214

§ 7.10 SOCIAL SECURITY 215

§ 7.11 STATE BENEFITS 215

§ 7.12 UNVESTED PENSIONS 216

VIII DIVISION OF CLOSELY HELD BUSINESSES

§ 8.01 FORM OF OWNERSHIP...217

§ 8.02 JOINDER OF BUSINESS ENTITY OR PARTNERS..............................217

§ 8.03 CLASSIFICATION: SEPARATE AND MARITAL PORTIONS 218

[1] Marital property interest..218
  [a] Acquired through marital efforts or funds....................218
  [b] Acquired with joint loans or loans secured by marital assets 218

xxv

TABLE OF CONTENTS

[c] Separate funds commingled with marital funds..219
[2] Separate property interest..219
[3] Mixed asset...220
  [a] Acquired both during and outside of marriage..220
  [b] Appreciated value of separate property business...220
[4] Burden of proof...221

§ 8.04 VALUATION 222

[1] Revenue Ruling 59-60..222
[2] Valuation methods 222
  [a] Asset-based approach 222
  [b] Market-based approach 223
  [c] Income-based approach 223
  [d] Discounts 224
[3] Goodwill in businesses...224

§ 8.05 DIVISION 225

[1] Lump sum award 225
[2] Offset with other property 226
[3] Equitable liens 226
[4] Division of jointly owned business 226

§ 8.06 PIERCING THE CORPORATE VEIL 227

§ 8.07 FRAUDULENT TRANSFERS...227

IX ALIMONY

§ 9.01 HISTORY AND OVERVIEW...229

[1] History 229
[2] The transition to modern alimony 230
  [a] Gender neutrality...231
  [b] The role of fault..231
  [c] Forms of alimony 231
    [i] Rehabilitative alimony..231
    [ii] Transitional alimony..232
    [iii] Permanent alimony..232
  [d] Relationship to equitable distribution 232
[3] Modern theories of alimony 232
[4] Alimony guidelines..233
  [a] State and local guidelines..233
  [b] American Law Institute proposal..234

xxvi

TABLE OF CONTENTS

[c] AAML recommended guidelines 235
   [i] Amount of award 235
   [ii] Duration 235
   [iii] Deviation factors 235
   [iv] Examples.. 235
   [v] Application 235
[5] Alimony in Mississippi... 236
   [a] Traditional alimony 236
   [b] Transition to modern alimony 237
[6] General considerations 238
   [a] When available 238
   [b] Jurisdiction 238
   [c] Temporary alimony 238
   [d] Relationship to equitable distribution 239
[7] Overview 239

§ 9.02 TYPES OF ALIMONY 240

[1] Permanent alimony... 240
   [a] Purpose 240
   [b] Factors 240
   [c] Vesting 241
   [d] Amount 241
   [e] Modification 241
   [f] Conversion 241
   [g] Termination 241
     [i] At remarriage 242
     [ii] At the payee's death... 242
     [iii] At the payor's death 242
[2] Lump sum alimony.. 243
   [a] History 243
   [b] Modern lump sum alimony 244
     [i] Purpose 244
     [ii] Replacement for permanent or rehabilitative support 244
     [iii] Supplement to permanent or rehabilitative alimony 244
     [iv] Based on substantial contribution.................................... 245
     [v] Alimony as lump sum questioned...................................... 245
   [c] Factors 246
   [d] Vesting.. 246
   [e] Modification 247
   [f] Termination 247
   [g] Payment in installments 247
[3] Rehabilitative alimony 248
   [a] Purpose 248
   [b] Factors 249

xxvii

TABLE OF CONTENTS

[c] Vesting 249
[d] Modification 249
[e] Conversion to periodic 249
[f] Extension 249
[g] Termination 250
[4] Reimbursement alimony 250
[a] Purpose 250
[b] Factors 251
[c] Characteristics 251
[d] Amount 251

§ 9.03 HYBRID AND AMBIGUOUS AWARDS 251

[1] Traditional approach 252
[2] Hybrids created by agreement 253
[3] A word of caution 253
[4] Ambiguity: Alimony, property division, or child support 254

§ 9.04 TEST FOR AWARDING ALIMONY 254

[1] The *Armstrong* factors 255
[2] Findings of fact 255
[3] Overview of factor discussion 256
[4] Factors related to financial disparity 257
[a] Income of the parties 257
[i] Income included 257
[ii] Imputed income 257
[iii] Deductions from income 258
[b] Earning capacity 259
[c] Standard of living of the marriage and at the time of the order 259
[d] Reasonable expenses of the parties 260
[e] Free use of home and car 261
[f] Presence or absence of children in the home requiring childcare 262
[g] Obligations of the parties 262
[h] Assets of the parties 263
[i] Recipient's assets 263
[ii] Payor's assets 264
[5] Factors related to reducing disparity 264
[a] Length of marriage 265
[b] Health 266
[i] Payee's health 266
[ii] Payor's health 267
[c] Age 267
[d] Fault 268
[i] Payee's fault 268

xxviii

TABLE OF CONTENTS

[ii] Fault of payor...269
[iii] In irreconcilable differences divorce...269
[e] Dissipation of assets...269
[f] Other factors 270
   [i] Sacrificing employment opportunities for marriage-related
   reasons 270
   [ii] Support during schooling 270
[6] Tax consequences 270

§ 9.05 FACTORS GOVERNING LUMP SUM AWARDS RECOGNIZING CONTRIBUTION 271

[1] Substantial contribution to accumulation of the payor's assets by quitting work
to become a homemaker or assisting in business 271
[2] A long marriage 272
[3] Financial disparity 272
[4] Other considerations..273
   [a] Payor's assets 273
   [b] Payor's instability...273

§ 9.06 ANALYSIS OF REPORTED ALIMONY AWARDS 1994-2009 273

[1] Role of financial disparity 273
   [a] No financial disparity 274
   [b] Financial disparity 274
[2] Awards of permanent alimony based on length of marriage.........................274
   [a] Marriages over twenty years 276
   [b] Marriages ten to nineteen years 276
   [c] Marriages under ten years 277
[3] Amount of permanent awards 277
   [a] Marriages over twenty years 277
   [b] Marriages ten to nineteen years 278
   [c] Marriages under ten years 279
[4] Awards of rehabilitative alimony 279
   [a] Length of award 280
   [b] Amount of award..280
[5] Lump sum awards 280
[6] Summary...281

§ 9.07 THIRD-PARTY PAYMENTS AS ALIMONY..281

[1] Payment of medical expenses 281
[2] Mortgage payments 282
[3] Other payments...282
[4] Disguised alimony 283

xxix

TABLE OF CONTENTS

§ 9.08 MECHANICS OF AWARD **283**

[1] Form of award 283
   [a] Type of alimony... 283
   [b] Payee 283
   [c] Variation in amount 283
      [i] Escalation clauses 283
      [ii] Variation tied to anticipated change 284
[2] Reserved jurisdiction 284
[3] Source of payments 285
[4] Security for award 285
   [a] Equitable liens 285
   [b] Penalty provisions 285
   [c] Life insurance 285
   [d] Bond 286
[5] Drafting considerations 286
   [a] Specificity regarding type of alimony 286
   [b] Effect of standard provisions 286

§ 9.09 MODIFICATION **286**

[1] Types of alimony 286
   [a] Permanent alimony... 286
   [b] Rehabilitative alimony 287
   [c] Lump sum alimony.. 287
   [d] Reimbursement alimony 287
   [e] Third-party payments 287
[2] Test for modification... 288
   [a] Material change... 288
   [b] Occurring since the decree.. 288
   [c] Foreseeability 288
   [d] Comparison of financial circumstances.......................... 289
   [e] Application of *Armstrong* factors. 289
[3] Restrictions on modification.. 289
   [a] Original decree must provide for alimony 290
   [b] No modification of arrearages... 290
   [c] No out-of-court modification 290
   [d] No prospective modification by payor in arrears............ 290
[4] Circumstances that are not a material change 291
   [a] New debt... 291
   [b] Payor's remarriage and new family 291
[5] Petition to increase alimony 291
   [a] Payee's inability to meet reasonable needs 292
      [i] Poor health 292
      [ii] Decreased value of award.. 292

xxx

TABLE OF CONTENTS

[iii] Loss of income 292
[b] Payor's ability to pay increased amount 292
[6] Petition to reduce alimony 293
[a] Payor's decreased resources 293
[i] Involuntary income reduction 293
[ii] Involuntary expenses 294
[b] Payee's increased resources 294
[i] Increase in income or earning capacity 294
[ii] Receipt of Social Security benefits 294
[iii] Payee's reduced expenses 295
[c] Impact on financial disparity 295
[7] Effective date of modification 296

§ 9.10 TERMINATION BASED ON MATERIAL CHANGE IN CIRCUMSTANCES 296

§ 9.11 TERMINATION BASED ON COHABITATION 296

[1] History 296
[2] Current tests 297
[a] Cohabitation and presumed support 297
[b] *De facto* marriage 298
[c] Agreement of the parties 298
[d] Effective date 298

§ 9.12 EFFECT OF BANKRUPTCY 299

X ATTORNEYS' FEES

§ 10.01 FEE AWARDS BASED ON NEED 301

[1] Chancellor discretion 302
[2] Findings of fact regarding need 302
[3] Determining need. 302
[a] Inability to pay 302
[b] Financial disparity 303
[c] Proof of inability to pay 304
[4] Fault 304

§ 10.02 AMOUNT OF AWARD 304

[1] Factors 304
[2] Evidence of fees 305
[3] Findings of fact regarding amount 305
[4] Reduction of fees 306

xxxi

TABLE OF CONTENTS

§ 10.03 AWARDS BASED ON DEFENDANT BEHAVIOR 306

[1] Dilatory tactics.. 306
[2] Contempt actions... 307
[3] Unfounded allegations of abuse 308
[4] Frivolous litigation 308

§ 10.04 PROCEDURE 308

[1] Notice of hearing 308
[2] Payment to litigant.. 308

§ 10.05 APPEAL 309

[1] Fees on appeal 309
[2] Reversal of property division requires reversal of attorneys' fees................ 309

PART TWO: THE PARENT-CHILD RELATIONSHIP

XI PATERNITY

§ 11.01 HISTORY AND OVERVIEW 313

[1] Nonmarital children... 313
[2] Children of marriage 314
[3] Voluntary acknowledgment... 314

§ 11.02 JURISDICTION AND VENUE 314

§ 11.03 PARTIES 315

[1] Action by child 315
[2] Action by DHS 315
[3] Action by biological father 315
[4] Action by legal father 315

§ 11.04 PROCEDURE 316

[1] Appointment of a guardian ad litem... 316
[2] No right to jury trial... 316
[3] Service of process.. 316
[4] Time of trial 316
[5] Genetic tests.. 316
  [a] Refusal to cooperate 316

xxxii

TABLE OF CONTENTS

[b] Testing facility 317
[c] Challenge to report 317
[d] Test costs 317
[e] In acknowledgment proceedings 317
[6] Rebuttable presumption of paternity 317
[7] Expert testimony 317
[8] Witnesses 318
[a] Notice 318
[b] Testimony 318
[c] False claims 318
[9] Burden of proof 318
[10] Appeals 318

§ 11.05 DEFENSES 319

[1] Statute of limitations 319
[a] Paternity and support 319
[b] Suit to establish filiation only 319
[c] Suit to establish paternity by deceased 319
[2] Laches 320
[3] Res judicata and collateral estoppel 320

§ 11.06 ORDER OF PATERNITY 320

[1] Order of filiation 320
[2] Child support 320
[a] Order for back support 321
[b] Lump sum settlement 321
[3] Custody and visitation 321
[4] Security 322
[5] Costs 322

§ 11.07 LEGAL VS. BIOLOGICAL FATHERS 322

[1] Presumption of legitimacy 322
[2] Rebuttal 322
[3] Suits to disestablish defendant's paternity 323
[a] Other states 323
[b] Mississippi – the *in loco parentis* test 323
[c] Defenses to suit by mother 324
[4] Plaintiffs' suits to disestablish paternity 325
[5] Estoppel to disestablish 326
[6] Paternity fraud 326

§ 11.08 MODIFICATION AND ENFORCEMENT OF PATERNITY AWARDS 326

xxxiii

TABLE OF CONTENTS

XII CHILD CUSTODY AND VISITATION

§ 12.01 History and overview 329

[1] History 329
[2] Modern custody law 330
[3] Overview...330
[4] Custody presumptions 330
    [a] Parental equality...330
    [b] Presumption in favor of a natural parent 331
    [c] Presumption against custody to violent parent 331
    [d] Presumption in favor of joint custody upon request......................332
[5] Types of custody..332
[6] Types of custody proceedings 333
    [a] Divorce 333
    [b] Annulment...333
    [c] Separate maintenance..333
    [d] Petition for custody 333
    [e] Habeas corpus actions 334
    [f] Paternity...335
    [g] Adoption and termination of parental rights.................................335
    [h] Youth court proceedings..335
    [i] Civil protection orders 336
[7] Jurisdiction 336
[8] Temporary custody 336
[9] Emergency proceedings 337
[10] Effect of out-of-court agreement..337
[11] Appeal of custody orders 338
[12] Allegations of abuse or neglect in chancery proceedings 338

§ 12.02 Custody actions between parents...339

[1] The best interests test...339
[2] Custody actions between unmarried parents..340

§ 12.03 Application of the Albright factors 340

[1] Findings of fact..341
[2] Age, health, and sex of child 342
[3] Continuing care prior to separation..344
[4] Parenting skills 346
[5] Capacity to provide primary childcare and employment responsibilities......348
[6] Physical and mental health and age of parents...................................349
    [a] Physical health...349

xxxiv

TABLE OF CONTENTS

[b] Mental health..350
[c] Alcohol and drug use..351
[d] Age...351
[7] Emotional ties of the parent and child...352
[8] Moral fitness...352
[a] Sexual conduct...352
[b] Same-sex relationships...354
[c] Other..354
[9] Home, school, and community record of the child..............................355
[10] Preference of a child twelve or older..356
[11] Stability of the home environment and employment of each parent..........357
[a] Home environment...357
[b] Stability of employment...360
[12] Other relevant factors..360
[a] Separation of siblings...360
[b] Parental interference..361
[c] Religion..362
[d] Military service..362

§ 12.04 JOINT CUSTODY 363

[1] Forms of joint custody...364
[a] Joint legal custody..364
[b] Joint physical custody..364
[c] Ambiguous custody provisions...365
[2] When joint custody may be awarded...365
[a] By agreement...365
[b] By court order..365
[3] Factors...366
[a] Parental fitness..366
[b] Ability to cooperate...366
[c] Proximity..367
[d] Domestic violence...367
[4] Joint physical custody vs. sole custody and visitation........................368

§ 12.05 RESTRICTIONS AND CONDITIONS ON CUSTODY 369

§ 12.06 CUSTODY BETWEEN PARENTS AND THIRD PARTIES 369

[1] Presumption in favor of parents...369
[2] Third parties who may qualify as "parents".......................................370
[3] Standard for awarding third-party custody..371
[a] Unfitness and immoral conduct..371
[b] Abandonment..372
[c] Constructive abandonment...372

xxxv

TABLE OF CONTENTS

[d] Desertion 372

[e] Relinquishment of legal custody 373

[4] Natural parent visitation 373

[5] Modification of third-party custody 374

§ 12.07 CUSTODY ACTION BETWEEN TWO THIRD PARTIES 374

§ 12.08 VISITATION 374

[1] Noncustodial parent's rights...375

[2] Scope of visitation 375

[3] Responsibility for transportation 377

[4] Restrictions on visitation 377

[a] Abusive behavior 378

[b] Family or spousal violence 379

[c] Dangerous conduct...379

[d] Emotional abuse 379

[e] Potential kidnapping...380

[f] Imprisonment 380

[g] Mental health...380

[h] Poor parenting or household conditions 381

[i] Sexual conduct 381

[j] Activities 381

[k] Child's wishes 382

[5] Custodial parent interference with visitation 382

§ 12.09 THIRD-PARTY VISITATION 383

[1] Constitutionality 383

[2] Grandparent visitation in Mississippi..383

[a] Statutory requirements 383

[b] Constitutionality..384

[3] Additional factors 384

[4] Application 384

[a] Type 1 visitation 384

[b] Type 2 visitation 385

[5] Scope of visitation 385

[6] Procedure...386

[a] Venue 386

[b] Parties 386

[c] Attorneys' fees...386

[d] Modification and termination..386

[7] Grandparent visitation rights after adoption 386

[a] Rights of natural grandparents 387

[b] Rights of adoptive grandparents 387

xxxvi

TABLE OF CONTENTS

[8] Family visitation during military service 387

[9] Other third-party visitation 387

§ 12.10 APPOINTMENT OF GUARDIAN AD LITEM 388

[1] Mandatory appointment 388

[2] Discretionary appointment 388

[3] Duty of the guardian ad litem 389

    [a] Guardian as arm of the court 389

    [b] Guardian as the child's attorney 390

[4] Findings of fact 390

[5] Weight accorded guardian's report 391

[6] Fees 391

§ 12.11 MODIFICATION OF CUSTODY ORDERS 391

[1] Jurisdiction 391

    [a] Modification within the state 391

        [i] Continuing exclusive jurisdiction 391

        [ii] Emergency habeas jurisdiction 392

    [b] Interstate modification 392

[2] General considerations 392

    [a] Pleadings 392

    [b] Findings of fact 393

    [c] Burden of proof 393

    [d] Evidence of pre-decree conduct 393

[3] Maintaining stability 394

[4] Effect of nonpayment of child support 395

[5] Test for modification: Adverse material change 395

    [a] Material change 395

    [b] Adverse effect 397

    [c] Child's best interests 398

[6] Combined circumstances as material change 398

[7] Danger of physical or sexual abuse 398

[8] Custodial parent's remarriage 399

[9] Relocation 399

[10] Child's choice 401

[11] Custodial parent's cohabitation or sexual behavior 402

[12] Lack of cooperation by custodial parent 402

[13] Friction between child and custodial parent 403

[14] Child's behavior 404

[15] *De facto* change in custody 404

[16] Military service 405

[17] Improvement in noncustodial parent's circumstances 405

[18] Alternate test for modification: Ongoing adverse circumstances 405

xxxvii

TABLE OF CONTENTS

[19] Modification of joint custody 406
  [a] One parent's relocation 407
  [b] Based on inability to cooperate 407
  [c] Child reaching school age 408
  [d] Disruptive to children 408
  [e] Modification of joint legal custody 408
[20] Modification of visitation 408

§ 12.12 ENFORCEMENT 409

[1] Contempt 409
  [a] Custodial parent 409
  [b] Noncustodial parent violation 410
  [c] Joint custodian 410
[2] Bond 410

XIII CHILD SUPPORT

§ 13.01 HISTORY AND OVERVIEW 413

[1] History 413
  [a] The common law duty of support 413
  [b] Pre-guideline statutes 414
  [c] Federal involvement 414
[2] General considerations 415
  [a] Types of support actions 415
  [b] Jurisdiction and venue 415
  [c] Temporary support 416
  [d] Department of Human Services' role 416
    [i] Assignment of rights 416
    [ii] Scope of DHS litigation 417
    [iii] Distribution of support funds 417
    [iv] DHS liability for negligence 417

§ 13.02 CHILDREN ENTITLED TO SUPPORT 417

[1] Children of intact families 418
[2] Children of separated or divorced parents 418
[3] Children of unmarried parents 419
[4] Disabled adult children 419

§ 13.03 PERSONS RESPONSIBLE FOR SUPPORT 420

[1] Natural parents 420
[2] Adoptive parents 421

xxxviii

TABLE OF CONTENTS

[3] Stepparents 421
[4] Persons in *loco parentis* to child 421

§ 13.04 CALCULATING SUPPORT UNDER THE GUIDELINES **422**

[1] The Mississippi guidelines 422
    [a] Steps in determining basic support 422
    [b] Findings of fact 422
[2] Determining gross income 424
    [a] Overtime and second jobs 424
    [b] Payor's federal and state benefits 425
    [c] Federal and state benefits payable to a child 425
    [d] Alimony and child support 426
    [e] Current spouse's income 426
    [f] Employment benefits 427
    [g] Fluctuating income 427
    [h] Other income 427
[3] Gross income from self-employment 427
    [a] Business vs. personal expenses 427
    [b] Depreciation 428
    [c] Tax returns 428
[4] Imputing earning capacity 429
    [a] Findings of fact 429
    [b] Good faith/voluntariness test 430
        [i] Voluntary quit 430
        [ii] Voluntary unemployment 431
        [iii] Discharge from employment 431
        [iv] Reduced earnings based on illness 432
        [v] Resignation to pursue schooling 432
        [vi] Resignation to care for children 432
        [vii] Imprisonment 433
[5] Imputing hidden income 433
    [a] Based on transfer of income 433
    [b] Based on transfer of assets. 433
    [c] Based on inconsistent lifestyle or other evidence 433
    [d] Tax returns 434
[6] Adjustments to gross income 434
    [a] Mandatory deductions. 434
    [b] Voluntary deductions 434
    [c] Support for other children 435
        [i] Court-ordered child support 435
        [ii] Earlier-born children living in payor's home 435
        [iii] Later-born children living in the payor's home 435
[7] Applying the statutory percentage 436
[8] Adjusted gross income above $50,000 or below $5,000 436

xxxix

TABLE OF CONTENTS

§ 13.05 DEVIATION FROM THE GUIDELINES **436**

[1] Deviation criteria 437
[2] Extraordinary medical or educational expenses 437
   [a] Medical expenses 437
   [b] Educational expenses 437
[3] Shared custody or extensive visitation 438
[4] Reduced visitation 440
[5] Expenses of older children 440
[6] Child's income 440
[7] Childcare expenses 441
[8] Fluctuating income 441
[9] Deviation during college support 441
[10] Other 441
[11] Deviations reversed 441
[12] No order of support. 442
[13] Support from custodial parent 442

§ 13.06 SUPPORT AWARDS OUTSIDE THE STATUTORY PRESUMPTION **442**

[1] Yearly adjusted income above $50,000 442
[2] Yearly adjusted income below $5,000 443

§ 13.07 ADD-ONS TO BASE SUPPORT **443**

[1] Health insurance and medical expenses 444
[2] Life insurance 445
[3] College expenses 445
   [a] Award at divorce 446
   [b] Award in modification proceeding 446
   [c] Child's relationship with parents 446
   [d] Aptitude for college 446
   [e] Scope of college support 447
   [f] Division of expenses between parents 447
   [g] Reduction of basic support during college 447
   [h] Performance requirements 448
   [i] College support after majority 448
      [i] Implied agreements for post-majority support 449
      [ii] Scope 449
      [iii] Duration 449
   [j] Education accounts 450
[4] Other 450

§ 13.08 AWARD OF THE DEPENDENCY EXEMPTION **450**

TABLE OF CONTENTS

[1] Court-ordered transfer 451
[2] Support deviation based on transfer 451

§ 13.09 TERMINATION OF THE SUPPORT OBLIGATION 451

[1] At majority.. 451
[2] Upon emancipation.. 452
[3] Based on parental agreement.. 453
[4] Based on interference with visitation 453
[5] Based on a child's hostility.. 454
[6] At adoption or upon termination of parental rights........... 455
[7] At payor's death... 455
[8] Upon parents' remarriage to each other 455
[9] Upon disestablishment of paternity................................... 455

§ 13.10 MECHANICS OF THE AWARD... 455

[1] Designation of payee 455
[2] Escalation clauses.. 456
  [a] Percentage-of-income awards 456
  [b] Awards tied to child's age 457
  [c] Mississippi.. 457
[3] Income withholding.. 458
  [a] For public assistance recipients.................................... 458
  [b] In other cases... 458
  [c] Limits on wage withholding.. 458
  [d] Priority of child support withholding orders.................. 459
[4] Security for payment 459
  [a] Bond 459
  [b] Insurance 459
[5] Lump sum payment 460
[6] Definiteness 460
[7] Source of payments 460
[8] Qualified domestic relations order 460

§ 13.11 MODIFICATION.. 461

[1] Role of child support guidelines.. 461
  [a] Presumptions linked to guidelines 461
  [b] Mississippi presumptions... 461
  [c] Guidelines determine amount of support....................... 462
[2] Aspects of order subject to modification 462
[3] The material change in circumstances test.......................... 462
  [a] Material change 462

xli

TABLE OF CONTENTS

[b] Occurring since the decree 463

[c] Foreseeability 463

[d] Circumstances that are not a material change 464

[4] Limits on modification 464

[a] Modification of arrearages 464

[b] Modification by private agreement 464

[c] Modification by payor in arrears: The clean hands doctrine 465

[5] Petition to increase child support 466

[a] Payor's increase in income 466

[b] Increase in costs for older children 467

[c] Inflation 467

[d] Parties' relative financial position 468

[e] Other considerations 468

[6] Petition to reduce support 468

[a] Reduction in income 468

[b] Custodial parent's remarriage 469

[c] Emancipation 469

[d] Based on a change in custody 470

[7] Modification related to college expenses 471

[a] Award of college expenses 471

[b] Modification of basic support 471

[8] Amount of modified award 472

[9] Effective date of modification 473

§ 13.12 ABATEMENT OF SUPPORT 473

§ 13.13 EFFECT OF BANKRUPTCY 474

XIV ENFORCEMENT OF DECREES

§ 14.01 OVERVIEW 475

[1] Nature of proceeding 475

[2] Interstate enforcement actions 475

[3] Role of the Department of Human Services 475

§ 14.02 ESTABLISHING DEFAULT: NONPAYMENT OF SUPPORT 476

[1] Proof of arrearage 476

[2] Interest on arrearages 476

[3] Temporary support arrearages 477

[4] Credit against amount due 477

[a] Credit against property division arrearage 477

[b] Credit against alimony arrearages 477

[c] Credit against child support 478

xlii

TABLE OF CONTENTS

[i] Based on change in custody 478
[ii] For direct expenditures 479
[5] Credit for payments after emancipation 479
  [a] Per-child order 479
  [b] Undivided order 480
[6] Credit for third-party payments 480
[7] Credit for Social Security benefits 480
[8] Credit for custodial parent's debt to payor 481

§ 14.03 ESTABLISHING NONCOMPLIANCE WITH OTHER PROVISIONS 481

[1] Property division 481
[2] Child custody and visitation 481
  [a] Interference with visitation 481
  [b] Violation of visitation restrictions 482
  [c] Removal of child 482
[3] Other provisions 482

§ 14.04 DEFENSES TO JUDGMENT FOR DEFAULT 483

[1] Out-of-court modification 483
[2] Laches and estoppel 483
[3] Clean hands doctrine 484
[4] Res Judicata 485
[5] Statute of limitations 485
  [a] Alimony 485
  [b] Child support 485
  [c] Property division 486

§ 14.05 CONTEMPT 486

[1] Types of contempt 487
  [a] Civil contempt 487
  [b] Criminal contempt 487
[2] Defenses to contempt 488
  [a] Inability to pay 488
    [i] Evidence sufficient 489
    [ii] Evidence insufficient 489
    [iii] Inability to pay at time of agreement 490
  [b] Lack of willfulness 490
  [c] Ambiguity 491
  [d] Performance impossible 492
  [e] Payment or compliance 492
  [f] Payee's fault 492
  [g] Clean hands/estoppel 492

xliii

TABLE OF CONTENTS

[h] Incompetency 493
[i] Acting on advice of counsel or other authority................................ 493
[j] Judgment wrong... 493
[k] Judgment invalid 494

§ 14.06 ENTRY OF JUDGMENT 494

[1] Judgment for arrearages 494
    [a] Court may not forgive arrearages.. 494
    [b] Court may not suspend collection.. 494
[2] Income-withholding orders 495
[3] Order for asset transfer 495
[4] Imposition of equitable lien 496
[5] Requirement of bond 496
[6] Sanctions for contempt 496
    [a] Plaintiff's right to sanctions 496
    [b] Incarceration... 497
    [c] Attorneys' fees 498

§ 14.07 COLLECTION OF JUDGMENT 498

[1] Execution on judgment... 499
[2] Lien on workers' compensation benefits.. 499
[3] Seizure of financial accounts.. 499
[4] Seizure of tax rebates in IV-D cases... 499
[5] Seizure of retirement funds 499
[6] Entry of QDRO 500

§ 14.08 OTHER ENFORCEMENT TOOLS... 500

[1] License Revocation 500
[2] Report to credit bureau 500
[3] Criminal prosecution 500
[4] Parent locator services... 501
[5] Interstate enforcement 501

XV ASSISTED REPRODUCTION TECHNOLOGY

§ 15.01 INTRODUCTION 503

§ 15.02 TERMINOLOGY AND BASICS 503

§ 15.03 LEGAL STATUS OF THE EMBRYO... 504

§ 15.04 DIVISION OF EMBRYOS AT DIVORCE 505

TABLE OF CONTENTS

§ 15.05 USE OF EMBRYOS AFTER DEATH: THE POSTHUMOUSLY CONCEIVED CHILD **506**

[1] Inheritance 506
[2] Mississippi 507
[3] Social Security 507

§ 15.06 PARENTAL RIGHTS: DONORS AND INTENDED PARENTS **508**

[1] Husband's rights and duties 508
[2] Unmarried partner's rights and duties 509
[3] Same-sex partners 510
[4] Donor's rights 510
    [a] Donors for assisted conception 510
    [b] Known donors 510

§ 15.07 SURROGACY **511**

[1] Types of surrogacy arrangements 511
[2] The ABA Model Act 511
    [a] Alternative A: Judicially-approved agreement 512
    [b] Alternative B: Self-executing agreement 512
[3] State statutes 513
    [a] Recognizing surrogacy 513
    [b] Prohibiting surrogacy 514
    [c] Indirectly addressing surrogacy 514
[4] Decisional law 515
[5] Disputes between intended parents and surrogates 516
    [a] Gestational surrogacy 516
    [b] Traditional surrogacy 517

§ 15.08 EMBRYO DONATION AND ADOPTION **518**

XVI TERMINATION OF PARENTAL RIGHTS

§ 16.01 JURISDICTION AND VENUE 519

§ 16.02 PARTIES 520

[1] Plaintiff and defendant 520
[2] Guardian ad litem 520

§ 16.03 SERVICE OF PROCESS 521

§ 16.04 GROUNDS FOR INVOLUNTARY TERMINATION 521

xlv

TABLE OF CONTENTS

[1] Desertion or abandonment 522
   [a] Abandonment 522
   [b] Desertion 523
[2] Failure to contact 523
[3] Abuse 523
[4] Agency custody 524
[5] Ongoing parental behavior 524
[6] Extreme antipathy.. 525
[7] Felonious assault or sexual assault 526
[8] Abuse and neglect.. 526
[9] Voluntary relinquishment 527

§ 16.05 TRIAL 527

[1] Time of trial 527
[2] Burden of proof 527
[3] Right to counsel.. 527
[4] Alternatives to termination 527

§ 16.06 ORDER OF TERMINATION....................................... 528

[1] Placement 528
[2] Parental visitation 528
[3] Inheritance 529
[4] Child support 529

§ 16.07 APPEALS.. 529

XVII ADOPTION

§ 17.01 JURISDICTION AND VENUE 531

[1] Jurisdiction 531
[2] Venue 531
[3] Relationship to termination proceedings........................... 532
[4] Jurisdiction in interstate actions 532

§ 17.02 PARTIES.. 532

[1] Who may adopt... 532
[2] Necessary parties 533
   [a] Natural parents 533
   [b] Physical and legal custodians................................. 533
   [c] Child 534

xlvi

TABLE OF CONTENTS

[3] Grandparents 534

§ 17.03 APPOINTMENT OF GUARDIAN AD LITEM...534

[1] Mandatory appointment 534
[2] Discretionary appointment 534
[3] Guardian for minor parent..535

§ 17.04 PROCEDURE...535

[1] Rule 81...535
[2] Consent 535
[3] Petition..535
[4] Investigation 536

§ 17.05 UNCONTESTED ADOPTIONS 536

[1] Parties who must consent 536
  [a] Mother and legal father 536
  [b] Unmarried father 537
  [c] Child over fourteen..537
  [d] Grandparents/other custodians 537
  [e] Department of Human Services 537
[2] Procedure for consent...537
  [a] Surrender of child to home...537
  [b] Consent to private adoption 538
[3] Requirements...538
[4] Revocation of consent 538

§ 17.06 PETITION FOR DETERMINATION OF FATHER'S RIGHTS 539

§ 17.07 CONTESTED ADOPTION 539

[1] Test 540
[2] Enumerated grounds...540
  [a] Abandonment 540
  [b] Desertion 541
  [c] Abuse..541
  [d] Failure to provide...541
  [e] Condition making parent unable to provide.................................542
  [f] Conduct posing a substantial risk of harm 542
  [g] Grounds in termination statute...542
  [h] Other unfitness 542
[3] Procedure..543
  [a] Burden of proof...543

xlvii

TABLE OF CONTENTS

[b] Paternity 543
[c] Hearings.. 543

§ 17.08 FINAL DECREE **543**

[1] Interlocutory decree.................................... 543
[2] Provisions and effect 543
    [a] Inheritance rights.................................... 543
    [b] Termination of parental rights.................. 544
    [c] Grant of parental rights 544
    [d] Child's name 544
    [e] Grandparent visitation rights.................. 544
[3] Variations 544
    [a] Natural parent visitation 544
    [b] Adoption by unrelated parties 544
[4] Confidentiality 544

§ 17.09 ACTIONS TO SET ASIDE ADOPTION **545**

[1] Six-month statute of limitations 545
[2] Challenge to consent 546
[3] Challenge to jurisdiction 546

PART THREE: JURISDICTION, PRACTICE, AND PROCEDURE

XVIII JURISDICTION

§ 18.01 COURTS WITH JURISDICTION **551**

[1] Chancery court authority........................... 551
[2] Family law exception to federal court jurisdiction. 552
[3] Youth court jurisdiction: Abuse and neglect 552

§ 18.02 OVERVIEW OF JURISDICTION **553**

[1] Subject matter jurisdiction........................ 553
[2] Personal jurisdiction. 554
[3] Service of process..................................... 554

§ 18.03 JURISDICTION OVER DIVORCE **555**

[1] Subject matter jurisdiction........................ 555
    [a] Temporary absence................................. 556
    [b] Change of domicile 556

xlviii

TABLE OF CONTENTS

[2] Venue 557
   [a] Venue as jurisdictional 557
   [b] Location of venue 557
[3] Personal jurisdiction 558
[4] Service of process 558

§ 18.04 JURISDICTION OVER FINANCIAL AWARDS 559

[1] Subject matter jurisdiction 559
[2] Personal jurisdiction: Minimum contacts 559
   [a] Contacts sufficient 560
   [b] Contacts insufficient 560
[3] Personal jurisdiction: Defendant served in state 561
[4] Waiver of personal jurisdiction 561
[5] Jurisdiction over property located in state 562
[6] Jurisdiction to divide military pensions 562
[7] Jurisdiction to award child support 562

§ 18.05 JURISDICTION TO DETERMINE CUSTODY 562

[1] Subject matter jurisdiction 562
[2] Personal jurisdiction 563
[3] Service of process 563

§ 18.06 INTERSTATE CONFLICTS OVER INITIAL DIVORCE ORDERS 563

[1] Concurrent actions in two states 563
[2] Full faith and credit 564
[3] Foreign decrees 565

§ 18.07 JURISDICTION TO MODIFY 566

[1] Modification within a state 566
[2] Interstate modification 567
   [a] Modification of child support 567
   [b] Modification of alimony 567
   [c] Modification of custody 567

§ 18.08 THE UNIFORM INTERSTATE FAMILY SUPPORT ACT 568

[1] Personal jurisdiction 568
[2] The two-state procedure 569
[3] Retroactive application 570
[4] Modification under UIFSA 570
   [a] Modification of child support 570

xlix

TABLE OF CONTENTS

[i] Continuing exclusive jurisdiction...570
[ii] Consent to transfer jurisdiction 571
[iii] Assumption of jurisdiction after all parties have moved......................571
[b] Modification of alimony 573
[5] Enforcement under UIFSA...573
[a] Registration 574
[b] Registering state's authority..574
[c] Income withholding and administrative enforcement................................574

§ 18.09 THE UNIFORM CHILD CUSTODY JURISDICTION ENFORCEMENT ACT 575

[1] Scope of the UCCJEA..575
[2] UCCJEA affidavit..576
[3] Interstate cooperation 576
[4] Subject matter jurisdiction...576
[a] Child's home state 576
[b] Significant connections 577
[c] Emergency jurisdiction 577
[d] No other state has jurisdiction...577
[5] Defenses to initial jurisdiction..577
[a] Inconvenient forum defense..578
[b] Petitioner's conduct...578
[6] Waiver of subject matter jurisdiction 578
[7] Concurrent actions in two states..579
[8] Personal jurisdiction 579

§ 18.10 JURISDICTION TO MODIFY CUSTODY 580

[1] Continuing exclusive jurisdiction...580
[2] Modification in second state..581
[a] Inconvenient forum 581
[b] Emergency..581
[c] No significant connection..582

§ 18.11 INTERSTATE ENFORCEMENT OF CUSTODY DECREES 582

[1] Registration..582
[2] Enforcement 582

§ 18.12 OTHER JURISDICTIONAL ACTS 583

XIX PROCEDURE

§ 19.01 PARTIES TO THE ACTION 585

TABLE OF CONTENTS

[1] Divorce 585
[2] Property division 585
    [a] Joint ownership with third party 586
    [b] Transfer of assets to third party 586
    [c] Third-party interest 586
[3] Custody 586
[4] Child support 587
[5] Married minors 588
[6] Mentally incompetent spouse 588
[7] Pro se parties 588
[8] Prisoners 589

§ 19.02 PLEADINGS 589

[1] Complaint or petition 589
    [a] Request for divorce 589
        [i] Grounds for fault-based divorce 590
        [ii] Irreconcilable differences divorce 590
    [b] Request for property division, alimony or child support 590
        [i] Request for alimony 590
        [ii] Child support 591
        [iii] Form of support 591
    [c] Custody 592
    [d] Trial by consent/failure to object 592
    [e] Attorneys' fees 592
[2] Responsive pleadings 592
    [a] Preserving objections to jurisdiction 592
    [b] Affirmative defenses 593
    [c] Failure to answer 593
[3] Rule 8.05 financial statement 594
[4] UCCJEA affidavit 594

§19.03 SERVICE OF PROCESS 595

[1] Form of summons 595
[2] Manner of service 595
    [a] On resident defendant 595
    [b] On nonresident defendants 596
    [c] Service by publication 596
    [d] Service on mentally incompetent party 597
    [e] Waiver of process 597
[3] Inadequate process or service of process 597
[4] Preserving objections to process 598

§ 19.04 PRE-TRIAL PROCEEDINGS 590

li

TABLE OF CONTENTS

[1] Temporary orders.. 590
[2] Discovery... 600
[3] Continuances 601
[4] Motions... 601
    [a] Motion to recuse.. 601
    [b] Motion for summary judgment 602
    [c] Dismissal under Rule 41(b).. 602

§ 19.05 TRIAL.. 602

[1] Proceedings... 602
[2] No default; requirement of proof 603
[3] Limits on testimony 603
[4] Stipulations.. 603

§ 19.06 EVIDENCE.. 604

[1] Testimony of children.. 604
    [a] Tender years exception 604
    [b] Statement for purpose of medical diagnosis.................................... 605
    [c] Other hearsay exceptions 605
    [d] Testimonial statements 606
    [e] Testimony through closed-circuit television 606
    [f] In-chambers interview with child 606
[2] Expert testimony.. 606
[3] Medical testimony: Physician/patient privilege 607
    [a] Scope of privilege... 607
    [b] Waiver of privilege... 608
        [i] By parent in proceedings involving children 608
        [ii] By party alleging habitual, cruel, and inhuman treatment 608
        [iii] By child 609
[4] Medical records 609
    [a] HIPAA... 609
    [b] Procedure for determining privilege... 610
    [c] Authentication of records 610
[5] Court-ordered mental or physical examination................................... 610
[6] Priest/penitent privilege... 610
[7] Guardian ad litem testimony 611
[8] Journals... 611

§ 19.07 JUDGMENT... 611

[1] Findings of fact and conclusions of law.. 611
    [a] Required findings 611

TABLE OF CONTENTS

[b] Requested findings 612
[c] Adoption of one party's proposed findings and conclusions 612
[2] Time of decision 612
[3] Consent judgments 613
[4] Retention of jurisdiction 613
[5] Specific provisions 614
[6] Modification of bench opinion 614
[7] Finality 614
[8] Death of spouse before entry of judgment 614
[9] Offer of judgment 614
[10] Entry of judgment nunc pro tunc 615

§ 19.08 POST-JUDGMENT MOTIONS 615

[1] Reopening judgment within ten days 615
[2] Relief from judgment 616
  [a] Clerical mistakes 616
  [b] Misconduct, mistake, newly discovered evidence 616
  [c] Relief from judgment after six months 617
    [i] Void provisions 617
    [ii] Any other reason justifying relief 617
    [iii] Fraud on the court 618

§ 19.09 APPEALS 619

[1] Appealable orders 619
[2] Time of appeal 620
[3] Stay pending appeal 621
[4] Standard of review 622
[5] Appeal of consent judgment 622
[6] Briefs on appeal 623
  [a] Appellee's failure to file brief 623
  [b] Lack of citation 623
  [c] Untranscribed proceedings 623
  [d] Waiver 623
[7] Reversal 624
  [a] Reversal of divorce 624
  [b] Reversal of financial award 624
  [c] Remand 624
  [d] Harmless error 625
[8] Certiorari to Mississippi Supreme Court 625
[9] Agreement not to appeal 625
[10] Attorneys' fees on appeal 625
[11] Right to appeal *in forma pauperis* 625
[12] Dismissal of appeal 626
  [a] Fugitive dismissal rule 626

liii

TABLE OF CONTENTS

[b] Dismissal for mootness 626

§ 19.10 PETITIONS FOR MODIFICATION AND ENFORCEMENT 626

§ 19.11 RULE 81(d) PROCEDURES 627

[1] Scope of rule 627
[2] Pleadings 627
  [a] Initial pleading 627
  [b] Responsive pleadings 627
[3] Service of process 628
  [a] Form of summons 628
  [b] Manner of service 629
  [c] Waiver of service of process 629
  [d] Service in contempt proceedings in pending action 629
[4] Hearing 630
[5] Continuance 630
[6] Continuance by order of Chancery Clerk 630

§ 19.12 MEDIATION 630

§ 19.13 EFFECT OF BANKRUPTCY PROCEEDINGS 631

§ 19.14 SERVICEMEMBERS CIVIL RELIEF ACT 631

[1] Appearance by defendant 631
[2] Defendant does not appear 631

XX ETHICAL ISSUES IN FAMILY LAW PRACTICE

§ 20.01 CONFLICTS OF INTEREST 633

[1] Dual Representation 633
[2] Avoiding the appearance of dual representation 633
[3] Prior representation 634
[4] Subsequent representation 635
[5] Prior participation as judge 635
[6] Participation as a mediator 635

§ 20.02 CONFIDENTIALITY 635

§ 20.03 ATTORNEYS' FEES 636

[1] Fees 636
[2] Retainers 636

TABLE OF CONTENTS

[a] General retainers 636
[b] Special retainers 636
[c] Advance payment retainers 636

§ 20.04 ATTORNEY LIENS 637

[1] Consensual liens 637
[2] Judgment liens 637
[3] Common law liens.. 637
[4] Client files... 638

§ 20.05 THIRD-PARTY FEE PAYMENT 638

§ 20.06 LIMITED REPRESENTATION 638

§ 20.07 NON-LEGAL ADVICE 639

§ 20.08 CONDUCT DURING REPRESENTATION 639

[1] False Statements 639
[2] Client's criminal or fraudulent behavior 639
[a] Past conduct.. 640
[b] Future conduct... 640
[c] Assisting future conduct 640
[d] Mandatory reporting 640

§ 20.09 SURVEILLANCE 640

[1] Interspousal wiretapping 641
[2] Attorney use of and advice regarding wiretapping 642
[3] Interception of electronic mail 642
[a] Use of common computer 642
[b] Stored emails 643
[c] Exclusion from evidence....................................... 643
[d] Use of spyware 643

§ 20.10 NO DUTY OF CONTINUING REPRESENTATION 643

XXI BANKRUPTCY AND FAMILY LAW

§ 21.01 BANKRUPTCY BASICS.. 645

[1] Liquidation 645
[2] Reorganization... 646
[3] The automatic stay... 646

lv

TABLE OF CONTENTS

§ 21.02 THE BANKRUPTCY REFORM ACT OF 2005: AN OVERVIEW 646

    [1] The "domestic support obligation" 646
    [2] The automatic stay 647
    [3] Dischargeability 647
    [4] Priority 647
    [5] Effective date 647

§ 21.03 THE AUTOMATIC STAY AND FAMILY LAW OBLIGATIONS 647

    [1] Original orders 647
    [2] Modification of custody, alimony, or support 648
    [3] Property division 648
    [4] Collection of support payments 649
        [a] Currently-due payments 649
        [b] Collection of arrearages 649
    [5] Enforcement of judicial liens 650
    [6] Contempt actions 650
    [7] Other enforcement tools 650

§ 21.04 DISCHARGEABILITY 650

    [1] Alimony and child support 651
    [2] Property division 651
    [3] Payment of debts 651
    [4] Attorneys' fees 651

§ 21.05 DISTINGUISHING PROPERTY DIVISION PAYMENTS AND SUPPORT 652

§ 21.06 ASSETS OF THE NONDEBTOR SPOUSE AND THE BANKRUPTCY ESTATE 652

    [1] Bankruptcy filed during marriage 652
    [2] Bankruptcy filed during pending divorce 652
    [3] Bankruptcy filed after judgment of divorce 653
    [4] Joint debts 653

§ 21.07 THE TRUSTEE'S AVOIDANCE POWER 653

XXII TAX EFFECTS OF PAYMENTS AND TRANSFERS PURSUANT TO DIVORCE

§ 22.01 ALIMONY 655

    [1] Code requirements for alimony 655
        [a] Payment in cash 655

TABLE OF CONTENTS

[b] Payment to a spouse or on behalf of a spouse 655
   [i] Payment of life insurance premiums 656
   [ii] Payments related to residence 656
[c] Pursuant to a divorce decree or separation agreement................. 656
[d] Not designated as non-alimony... 656
[e] While the parties are not members of the same household.......... 657
[f] Not for the support of a child.. 657
[g] Does not survive the death of the payee 657
[2] Relationship to state law on alimony 658
[a] Traditional forms of alimony 658
[b] Hybrid alimony 658
[3] Problem areas 658
[a] Front-loaded alimony payments.. 658
[b] Underpayment of support 659

§ 22.02 Child support payments and related deductions............................ 659

[1] Code requirements.. 659
[2] Child-related deductions.. 659
[a] Dependency exemptions 659
[b] Child tax credit.. 660
[c] Educational credits 660
[d] Childcare credit 660
[e] Medical expense deductions 660

§ 22.03 Transfers of property.. 660

[1] Code treatment of transfers 661
[a] Non-recognition of gain or loss... 661
[b] Transferee's basis in property 661
[2] Property division payments as deductible alimony...................... 661
[3] Specific types of transfers 661
[a] Marital residence 661
[b] Pensions and IRAs 662
[c] Assignment of asset income 662
[d] Interest on installment payments 663
[e] Closely held corporations... 663

§ 22.04 Payments related to litigation 663

§ 22.05 Other divorce-related tax considerations 664

[1] Filing status 664
[a] During separation 664
[b] After divorce... 664

lvii

TABLE OF CONTENTS

[2] Tax refunds 664
[3] Tax liability 664
[4] Innocent spouse relief 665
[5] Estate and gift tax consequences 665

XXIII MARITAL AGREEMENTS

§ 23.01 MARITAL AGREEMENTS 667

[1] History 667
[2] Mississippi 668

§ 23.02 REQUIREMENTS 668

[1] Consideration 669
[2] Voluntariness 669
[3] Full and fair disclosure 669
[4] The role of independent counsel 669
[5] Procedural fairness 670
[6] Substantive fairness and unconscionability 670
[7] Interpretation of agreements 671

§ 23.03 STATUTE OF FRAUDS 671

§ 23.04 SCOPE OF ENFORCEABLE AGREEMENTS 672

§ 23.05 SETTLEMENT AGREEMENTS AS POSTMARITAL AGREEMENTS 672

§ 23.06 BREACH 672

§ 23.07 WAIVER 673

§ 23.08 SETTLEMENT AGREEMENTS 673

[1] Nature of agreement 673
[2] Requirements 674
[3] Formalities 674
  [a] In general 674
  [b] Irreconcilable differences divorce 675

§ 23.09 ENFORCEABILITY: BINDING EFFECT ON PARTIES 675

[1] General rule 675
[2] Mississippi: Withdrawal of consent to no-fault divorce 675
[3] Mississippi: Withdrawal of consent to other agreements 676

TABLE OF CONTENTS

§ 23.10 COURT APPROVAL AND INCORPORATION INTO DECREE **676**

[1] Court approval 677
   [a] Property division 677
   [b] Child custody and support 677
   [c] Alimony 678
[2] Out-of-court agreements 678
[3] Incorporation into decree 678

§ 23.11 DEFENSES TO ENFORCEMENT **678**

[1] Fraud, misrepresentation, or concealment 679
[2] Duress, undue influence, or overreaching 679
[3] Unconscionability 680
[4] Agreement void as against public policy 681
[5] Clarification 681
[6] Mistake 681
[7] Frustration of purpose 682
[8] Equitable principles 682

§ 23.12 ENFORCEMENT AND MODIFICATION **682**

[1] Enforcement 682
[2] Modification of consent decree 682

§ 23.13 CONSTRUCTION **683**

§ 23.14 SPECIFIC PROVISIONS **684**

[1] Custody of children 684
[2] Child support 684
[3] Alimony 684
[4] Property division 685
[5] Jurisdiction 686
[6] General release and waiver 686

§ 23.15 DEATH OF A SPOUSE **686**

[1] Agreements not contingent on divorce 686
[2] Agreements contingent on divorce 687

§ 23.16 RECONCILIATION **687**

lix

PART ONE

RIGHTS BETWEEN PARTNERS

I
THE MARRIAGE RELATIONSHIP

Marriage is both a contract between individuals and a state-regulated status. The state controls eligibility to marry and prescribes the necessary formalities. Spouses are bound automatically by legal rights and obligations peculiar to marriage – the union creates new property, inheritance, and support rights. Dissolution of marriage triggers even more intensive state oversight. Spouses may not exit marriage without judicial approval. State oversight of support obligations and child custody continues after divorce.

Marital rights and duties have been substantially altered as legal distinctions based on gender have been discarded. The early common law viewed a married woman as a legal non-entity, stripping her of rights to control her own property. Her legal identity was merged into that of her husband. Today, family law distinctions based on gender have largely disappeared; rights of support, property, and inheritance between spouses are reciprocal. Tort actions related to marriage have also been revised to reflect the modern notion of spouses as two persons under the law.

The no-fault divorce movement of the late twentieth century changed the nature of marriage in most states, allowing parties to exit marriage at will, albeit with financial consequences. To protect financially vulnerable homemakers, states adopted a new system of marital property that is triggered at divorce.

The most dramatic development affecting the institution of marriage has occurred in the last fifteen years. Six states have recognized same-sex marriage, challenging the traditional definition of marriage as a union between a man and a woman. Other states have responded by reaffirming the traditional definition and refusing full faith and credit to same-sex unions. The debate prompted congressional action to endorse state refusals to recognize same-sex unions and has sparked proposals to amend the United States Constitution and various state constitutions.

§ 1.01 OVERVIEW

This chapter begins with a discussion of constitutional limits on state regulation, presumptions related to marriage, and the extent to which states extend full faith and credit to conflicting marital rules. Section 1.03 discusses entry into marriage – eligibility to marry, formal requirements, and the necessity of consent. Section 1.04 briefly describes changes in the marital status of women. The subsequent sections examine the rights and duties of spouses – property, inheritance, support, contract, and torts – as well as evidentiary rules affecting spouses, crimes between spouses, medical decision-making, and spouses' choice of residence. The final section discusses financial support between separated spouses.

§ 1.02   **MISSISSIPPI FAMILY LAW**

§ 1.02 THE RIGHT TO MARRY: GENERAL CONSIDERATIONS

The power to regulate entry into marriage lies with the individual states; however, state requirements are affected by constitutional constraints, common law presumptions favoring marriage, and resolution of conflicts between state laws.

[1] Constitutional limits of state regulation. Federal constitutional law sets the parameters for state regulation of marriage. Marriage – "the relationship that is the foundation of the family in our society"[1] – is a fundamental right protected by the Constitution. State regulation that significantly interferes with the right to marry must advance important state interests and be closely tailored to meet only those interests.[2] Applying strict scrutiny to marriage entry requirements, the United States Supreme Court has struck down laws prohibiting interracial marriage[3] and barring delinquent child support payors from marriage.[4] Not all state marriage regulations are subject to strict scrutiny, however – regulations that do not significantly interfere with the right to marry are tested under the rational relationship test.[5] For example, parental consent requirements have been upheld as rationally related to the legitimate interest in preventing unstable marriages.[6]

[2] Presumptions regarding marriage. Several evidentiary presumptions affect resolution of marriage issues. These include the presumption that parties are eligible to marry,[7] that parties complied with formal marriage requirements,[8] and that the person officiating was authorized to perform marriages.[9] Probably the most frequently cited is the presumption that a person's most recent marriage is valid, based on the assumption that no one would marry if a valid marriage already existed.[10] One leading authority describes the various rules as a single presumption – that a purported marriage is valid.[11] The presumptions all place the burden of proof on one who attacks the validity of a marriage.[12] As explained by the Mississippi Supreme Court, the law "will indulge

---

[1] Zablocki v. Redhail, 434 U.S. 374, 386 (1978).

[2] Zablocki v. Redhail, 434 U.S. 374, 388 (1978).

[3] Loving v. Virginia, 388 U.S. 1, 12 (1967).

[4] Zablocki v. Redhail, 434 U.S. 374, 390-91 (1978). Applying strict scrutiny, the Colorado high court held that a state cannot constitutionally prohibit marriage between adopted siblings. Israel v. Allen, 577 P.2d 762, 764 (Colo. 1978) (prohibition does not further state interest in family harmony).

[5] Zablocki v. Redhail, 434 U.S. 374, 386 (1978) ("We do not mean to suggest that every state regulation which relates in any way to the incidents of or prerequisites for marriage must be subjected to rigorous scrutiny.").

[6] Moe v. Dinkins, 669 F.2d 67, 68 (2d Cir. 1982) (restrictions on right of minors to marry properly tested by rational relationship, rather than strict scrutiny).

[7] HOMER H. CLARK, JR., THE LAW OF DOMESTIC RELATIONS IN THE UNITED STATES § 2.7, at 70-71 (2d ed. 1988).

[8] See Walker v. Matthews, 3 So. 2d 820, 824 (Miss. 1941) ("The law has wisely provided that marriage may be proved by general reputation, cohabitation, and acknowledgment; when these exist, it will be inferred that a religious ceremony has taken place; and this proof will not be invalidated because evidence cannot be obtained of the time, place, and manner of the celebration of the marriage.") (quoting Travers v. Reinhardt, 205 U.S. 423, 437 (1907)).

[9] See Smith v. Weir, 387 So. 2d 761, 763 (Miss. 1980) ("Where there is proof of a marriage ceremony, the law will presume the capacity of the parties, consent of the parties, and all essentials to the validity of the marriage."); CLARK, JR., supra note 7, § 2.7, at 71. See generally Annotation, Presumptions Flowing from Marriage, 34 A.L.R. 464 (1925).

[10] See discussion infra § 1.03[1][b].

[11] CLARK, JR., supra note 7, § 2.7, at 70-71.

[12] See Pigford Bros. Constr. Co. v. Evans, 83 So. 2d 622, 625 (Miss. 1955).

THE MARRIAGE RELATIONSHIP   § 1.02[3]

every reasonable presumption" in favor of marriage: "A contrary rule would be dangerous to society."[13]

[3] Conflicts of law. Conflicts of law issues related to marriage are inevitable in a highly mobile society. Generally, states will recognize a marriage that was valid in the state in which the marriage occurred. Two exceptions apply: A state may refuse to recognize a marriage that violates a significant public policy of that state. In addition, a state may deny full faith and credit to its own residents who marry in another state to evade home state laws.[14] Conflicts of law rules have become a critical aspect of family law as the debate over recognition of same-sex marriages continues.[15]

Mississippi follows the general rule extending full faith and credit to out-of-state marriages that do not violate significant public policy.[16] Mississippi courts have extended recognition to common law marriages not valid under Mississippi law,[17] and to marriages between parties not eligible to marry in Mississippi.[18] The Mississippi legislature has provided, however, that same-sex marriages violate state policies. Full faith and credit will not be extended to marriages between persons of the same sex.[19] Also, no recognition will be given to a marriage incestuous under Mississippi law if residents have attempted to evade the law by marrying elsewhere and returning to Mississippi to live.[20]

§ 1.03 REGULATION OF ENTRY INTO MARRIAGE

A marriage is not valid unless the parties (1) are eligible to marry under state law; (2) comply with formal prerequisites for marriage; and (3) enter the marriage voluntarily. Failure to comply with these requirements opens the marriage to annulment by the parties or, in some instances, by others.

[1] Persons eligible to marry. Mississippi law regulates the right to marry based upon kinship, existing marriage, age, gender, and mental and physical capacity.

[a] Kinship. No one may marry his or her parent, grandparent, stepparent or stepgrandparent, adoptive parent, sibling, half-sibling, aunt, uncle, first cousin, or his

---

[13] Walker v. Matthews, 3 So. 2d 820, 824 (Miss. 1941); *see* Hull v. Rawls, 27 Miss. 471, 473 (1854) (where marriage was solemnized, "every presumption must be indulged in favor of its validity").

[14] Leszinske v. Poole, 798 P.2d 1049, 1054 (N.M. Ct. App. 1990). The *Leszinske* court noted that "the two exceptions are actually one" in contemporary conflicts theory. *Id.* (citing RESTATEMENT (SECOND) OF CONFLICT OF LAWS § 283 (1971)); *see also* Hesington v. Hesington's Estate, 640 S.W.2d 824, 826 (Mo. Ct. App. 1982) (citing RESTATEMENT (SECOND) OF CONFLICT OF LAWS § 283 (1971)); *In re* Lenherr's Estate, 314 A.2d 255, 258 (Pa. 1974) (same).

[15] *See* discussion *infra* § 1.03[1][d].

[16] Miller v. Lucks, 36 So. 2d 140, 142 (Miss. 1948) (recognizing marriage between Caucasian and African-American for purposes of allowing one spouse to inherit property located in Mississippi, where couple never lived in Mississippi).

[17] *See* George v. George, 389 So. 2d 1389, 1391 (Miss. 1980) (recognizing common law marriage in Georgia).

[18] *See* Miller v. Lucks, 36 So. 2d 140, 142 (Miss. 1948) (recognizing marriage between Caucasian and African-American for purposes of allowing one spouse to inherit property located in Mississippi, where couple never lived in Mississippi).

[19] MISS. CODE ANN. § 93-1-1(2) (2004).

[20] MISS. CODE ANN. § 93-1-3 (2004).

§ 1.03[1][b]   **MISSISSIPPI FAMILY LAW**

or her child's widow or widower.[21] A marriage that is incestuous is void[22] and may be annulled[23] or dissolved through divorce.[24] The state will not recognize a marriage contracted in another state by Mississippi residents in an attempt to avoid incest prohibitions under Mississippi law.[25] In contrast to the treatment of children of other invalid marriages, children of an incestuous marriage are labeled illegitimate even if the parties entered the marriage in good faith.[26]

[b] Bigamous marriages. A marriage is void if one of the parties is already legally married.[27] Bigamous marriages may be set aside by annulment[28] or dissolved by divorce.[29] Although bigamous marriages are labeled void, children of bigamous marriages are considered legitimate.[30]

The strong presumptions in favor of marriage may cloak an otherwise bigamous second marriage with validity. The most recent marriage contracted by a party is presumed to be valid.[31] Challenges to validity typically arise when successive spouses claim death benefits or inheritance rights as the legal husband or wife of a deceased. The burden rests on the first spouse to prove a negative – that the first marriage was never dissolved.[32] The first spouse must prove that divorce was not granted in any jurisdiction in which either of the first spouses lived after the marriage.[33] Proof by a first

---

[21] Miss. Code Ann. § 93-1-1 (2004). The statute prohibits marrying one's deceased child's former spouse, but does not prohibit the reverse. *See* State v. Winslow, 45 So. 2d 574, 576 (Miss. 1950) (dismissing criminal prosecution of man who married mother-in-law; statute prohibits mother-in-law from marrying child's widower, but not vice-versa). Note also that the statute does not prohibit marrying one's child's divorced spouse, nor does it prohibit marriage between stepsiblings.

[22] Miss. Code Ann. § 93-1-1 (2004); *see* Weeks v. Weeks, 654 So. 2d 33, 35 (Miss. 1995) (marriage between uncle and niece void). It is a crime punishable by up to ten years in prison for persons prohibited by kinship to marry, cohabit, or have a sexual relationship. Miss. Code Ann. § 97-29-5 (2006).

[23] Miss. Code Ann. § 93-7-1 (2004).

[24] Miss. Code Ann. § 93-5-1 (2004).

[25] Miss. Code Ann. § 93-1-3 (2004).

[26] Miss. Code Ann. § 93-7-5 (2004).

[27] Miss. Code Ann. § 93-7-1 (2004). Bigamy is a crime punishable by up to ten years in prison. Miss. Code Ann. § 97-29-13 (1994). Mississippi's "Enoch Arden" statute exempts from prosecution one whose husband or wife has been absent for seven years. Miss. Code Ann. § 97-29-15 (2010). Enoch Arden statutes do not validate the later marriage; they simply provide a defense to criminal prosecution for bigamy. *See* Clark, Jr., *supra* note 7, § 2.6, at 67. *But see* Harper v. Fears, 151 So. 745, 747 (Miss. 1934) (where wife remarried based on first husband's presumed death, then asserted right to inherit upon his death, his absence for the statutory period validated the later marriages).

[28] Miss. Code Ann. § 93-7-1 (2004).

[29] Miss. Code Ann. § 93-5-1 (2004).

[30] Miss. Code Ann. § 93-7-5 (2004).

[31] "The presumption of the validity of the last marriage has been held to be the strongest presumption known to the law; and in the absence of additional facts or circumstances it must prevail over all conflicting presumptions, such as presumptions as . . . to the validity . . . of a prior marriage." Whitman v. Whitman, 41 So. 2d 22, 25 (Miss. 1949) (omission in opinion) (quoting 55 C.J.S. *Marriage* § 43 (1948)).

[32] Aldridge v. Aldridge, 77 So. 150, 150 (Miss. 1918); *see* McAllum v. Spinks, 91 So. 694, 697 (Miss. 1922); *see also* Anderson-Tully Co. v. Wilson, 74 So. 2d 735, 737 (Miss. 1954) (presumption applies "to a subsequent common law marriage, as well as to a subsequent ceremonial marriage").

[33] In *Pigford Brothers Construction Co. v. Evans*, 83 So. 2d 622, 625 (Miss. 1955), the court recommended offering evidence "to show where each party to the prior marriage had resided up to the time of the second marriage, and then to procure from the clerk of the proper court in each such county a certificate of search showing that no divorce or annulment had been granted."

For a convoluted set of circumstances illustrating the presumption, see *Dale Polk Construction Co. v. White*, 287 So. 2d 278 (Miss. 1973). In that case, a woman sought workers' compensation benefits from her third, common law husband's estate. Her second husband was still living, but her first husband was deceased. Proof did not establish

THE MARRIAGE RELATIONSHIP   § 1.03[1][c]

wife that her marriage was never dissolved in Mississippi was insufficient, because she did not prove that the deceased lived in Mississippi the entire relevant period.[34] If a first marriage is still valid when a second marriage takes place, subsequent divorce between the first spouses does not make the second, bigamous marriage valid.[35]

[c] Age. Mississippi law prohibits marriage by a female under the age of fifteen or a male under the age of seventeen.[36] Historically, men and women have been permitted to marry at different ages.[37] Today gender-based age requirements for marriage are highly suspect; the Supreme Court has held other family law gender distinctions unconstitutional.[38] The Illinois Supreme Court held a similar statute unconstitutional, finding no justification for allowing men and women to marry at different ages.[39]

The age requirement may be waived by a chancery, circuit, or county court judge in the county in which either party resides on a showing that good cause exists and that the parents consent to the marriage.[40] Marriage of an underage party is voidable rather than void and may be annulled.[41] It is unclear, however, whether annulment may be at the request of either spouse or only the underage spouse. According to the leading family law treatise, a spouse of legal age cannot annul a marriage based on the other's minority.[42] The Mississippi statute, however, provides that annulment may be filed within six months of the time the impediment is or could have been discovered, suggesting the possibility of suit by the older spouse.[43] The marriage may not be attacked collaterally[44] or by third parties.[45] The marriage may be ratified by the underage spouse.[46]

[d] Same-sex marriages. The traditional definition of marriage[47] was challenged

---

[34] whether she was divorced from her first husband, so the second marriage was presumed valid. Proof established that she was never divorced from her second, living husband, so the second marriage was valid and the third bigamous. *See also* Smith v. Weir, 387 So. 2d 761, 763 (Miss. 1980); Walker v. Matthews, 3 So. 2d 820, 825 (Miss. 1941).

[34] Vaughn v. Vaughn, 16 So. 2d 23, 24 (Miss. 1943).

[35] *See* J.W. BUNKLEY & W.E. MORSE, AMIS ON DIVORCE & SEPARATION IN MISSISSIPPI § 1.02, at 24 (1957) (no presumption that second ceremonial marriage has followed first, invalid ceremonial marriage after removal of impediment). However, in states where common law marriages are recognized, an invalid marriage may become a valid common law marriage when the impediment to marriage is removed. *See* discussion *infra* § 1.03[2][a].

[36] MISS. CODE ANN. § 93-1-5(d) (2004).

[37] *See* Hunt v. Hunt, 161 So. 119, 120 (Miss. 1935) (common law age of consent for female was twelve); CLARK, JR., *supra* note 7, § 2.10, at 88 (common law age of consent was twelve for girls, fourteen for boys).

[38] *See* Orr v. Orr, 440 U.S. 268, 280, 283 (1979) (invalidating state law providing alimony for women but not for men; old notions do not justify gender-based distinctions in family law).

[39] *See* Phelps v. Bing, 316 N.E.2d 775, 776-77 (Ill. 1974); *cf.* Stanton v. Stanton, 421 U.S. 7, 14 (1975) (higher age of majority for men unconstitutional in connection with obligation to support children; not justified by gender-based sex roles).

[40] MISS. CODE ANN. § 93-1-5 (2004).

[41] MISS. CODE ANN. § 93-7-3 (2004).

[42] *See* CLARK, JR., *supra* note 7, § 2.10, at 95.

[43] *See* MISS. CODE ANN. § 93-7-3 (2004).

[44] *See* Doss v. State, 126 So. 197, 198-99 (Miss. 1930) (twelve-year-old wife's marriage could be annulled only in chancery court suit, not in collateral proceeding).

[45] Courts in other states have held that parents may not sue to set aside an underage child's marriage in the absence of specific statutory authority. *See* CLARK, JR., *supra* note 7, § 2.10, at 95 n.62 (cases); Annotation, *By and in Whose Name Suit to Annul Infant's Marriage Must Be Brought*, 150 A.L.R. 609 (1944).

[46] MISS. CODE ANN. § 93-7-3 (2004).

[47] *See* JOHN DE WITT GREGORY, PETER N. SWISHER & SHERYL L. WOLF, UNDERSTANDING FAMILY LAW § 2.04, at 35 (2d ed. 2001) (marriage traditionally defined as union between man and woman).

§ 1.03[1][e]　　　　　　　　　　　　　**MISSISSIPPI FAMILY LAW**

in 1993 when the Hawaii Supreme Court held that same-sex marriage prohibitions should be tested by strict scrutiny under the Hawaii Constitution as a sex-based classification.[48] On remand, the trial court found no compelling state interest underlying the prohibition and held that Hawaii was required to recognize same-sex marriages.[49] The Hawaii legislature responded by recognizing domestic partnerships with some, but not all, of the rights inherent in marriage.[50] Shortly after, Congress passed the Defense of Marriage Act[51] recognizing the right of states to refuse recognition of same-sex marriages and defining marriage for federal purposes as a union of a man and a woman.[52] A majority of state legislatures enacted corresponding statutes banning same-sex marriage.[53] Many states, including Mississippi, also denied full faith and credit to same-sex marriages valid in other states.[54]

At the same time, an increasing number of states have provided same-sex partners with marriage-like rights through domestic partnership and civil unions.[55] And in six states, same-sex couples may marry, with all the rights and privileges accorded heterosexual spouses.[56]

The move to recognize same-sex unions and the redefinition of traditional marriage is certainly the most significant development in family law since the adoption of no-fault divorce, and possibly since the emancipation of women.[57] The status of same-sex partners is discussed in detail in Chapter II.

[e] Mental and physical capacity. Parties to a marriage must have the mental capacity to consent to marry.[58] A marriage may be annulled if one of the parties is incom-

---

[48] *See* Baehr v. Lewin, 852 P.2d 44, 47 (Haw. 1993).

[49] Baehr v. Miike, No. 91-1394, 1996 WL 694235, at *21 (Haw. Cir. Ct. Dec. 3, 1996). Following the *Baehr* decision, Hawaii's legislature enacted legislation explicitly prohibiting same-sex marriages, but recognizing domestic partnerships. HAW. REV. STAT. § 572-1.

[50] *See* HAW. REV. STAT. §§ 572C-1 to 572C-7.

[51] 28 U.S.C. § 1738C (2006) (no state required to recognize another state's laws treating relationship between persons of same sex as marriage).

[52] The validity of the Defense of Marriage Act is criticized in numerous articles. *See, e.g.,* Larry Kramer, *Same-Sex Marriage, Conflict of Laws, and the Unconstitutional Public Policy Exception,* 106 YALE L.J. 1965 (1997); Scott Ruskay-Kidd, Note, *The Defense of Marriage Act and the Overextension of Congressional Authority,* 97 COLUM. L. REV. 1435 (1997). *But see* Ralph U. Whitten, *The Original Understanding of the Full Faith and Credit Clause and the Defense of Marriage Act,* 32 CREIGHTON L. REV. 255 (1998) (arguing for constitutionality of the Act). *See generally* Robin Cheryl Miller and Jason Binimow, *Marriage Between Persons of the Same Sex – United States and Canadian Cases,* 1 A.L.R. FED. 2d 1.

[53] *See* GREGORY ET. AL, *supra* note 47, § 2.08, at 48-49.

[54] MISS. CODE ANN. § 93-1-1 (2004); *cf.* Estate of Reaves v. Owen, 744 So. 2d 799, 802 (Miss. Ct. App. 1999) (acknowledging prohibition while refusing to find agreement between parties void simply because it was connected to termination of homosexual relationship; contract provided for payment of $59,000 for injuries resulting from altercation).

[55] See *infra* § 2.08[1].

[56] *See* N.H. REV. STAT. ANN. § 457:1-a (2009); VT. ST. ANN. tit. 15, § 8 (2009); Kerrigan v. Comm'r of Pub. Health, 957 A.2d 407 (Conn. 2008) (declined to follow by State v. Jenkins, 3 A.3d 806 (Conn. 2010)); Varnum v. Brien, 763 N.W.2d 862 (Iowa 2009); *In re* Op. of Justices to the Senate, 802 N.E.2d 565, 570 (Mass. 2004).

[57] *See, e.g.,* John G. Culhane, *Uprooting the Arguments Against Same-Sex Marriage,* 20 CARDOZO L. REV. 1119 (1999). Many commentators also oppose recognizing same-sex marriages. *See, e.g.,* Gerard V. Bradley, *Same-Sex Marriage: Our Final Answer?,* 14 NOTRE DAME J.L. ETHICS & PUB. POL'Y 729 (2000).

[58] The Mississippi licensing statute provides that a license may not be issued to anyone who is "drunk or a person with mental illness or mental retardation, to the extent that the clerk believes that the person does not understand the nature and consequences of the request." MISS. CODE ANN. § 93-1-5 (Supp. 2010).

THE MARRIAGE RELATIONSHIP

§ 1.03[2]

petent at the time of the marriage, provided suit is filed by one of the parties within six months.[59] The marriage cannot be attacked collaterally by third parties.[60] In addition, a marriage may be dissolved by divorce if one of the parties was incompetent at the time of the marriage and the other was unaware of the disability.[61] The annulment statute also permits annulment based upon lack of consent due to "lack of understanding."[62]

The Mississippi Supreme Court has stated that while a precise test for sufficient mental capacity to marry is not possible, "there ought to be enough of capacity to comprehend the subject, and the duties and responsibilities of the new relation."[63] Parties are generally presumed competent to enter into a contract; however, if proof shows that one of the parties was declared permanently incompetent before the marriage, it is presumed that the disability continued. The party asserting the validity of the marriage must prove that the disability did not exist at the time of the marriage.[64]

Spouses must also be physically capable of entering the marriage relationship. A marriage may be annulled based upon incurable impotency or if one of the parties is "physically incapable of entering the marriage relationship."[65] No Mississippi cases were found defining either term. Generally, impotence refers to inability to engage in intercourse and not to sterility or infertility.[66] In the case of physical incapacity, suit for annulment must be filed within six months of the time the incapacity was discovered or should have been discovered. The incapacity may be ratified.[67] No time limit is set for annulment based upon incurable impotency, nor does the statute mention ratification as a defense to annulment based upon impotency. Natural impotency is also a ground for divorce.[68]

[2] Formal requirements. The formal requirements for entry into marriage are governed by state statute. Today, most states, including Mississippi, recognize only ceremonial marriages pursuant to a license. However, common law marriages prior to 1956 are still valid in Mississippi, as are common law marriages validly contracted in other states. Thus, common law marriage rules may continue to affect inheritance, entitlement to benefits such as workers' compensation, and other rights based on the

---

[59] MISS. CODE ANN. § 93-7-3 (Supp. 2010). A marriage may be annulled based upon the "adjudicated mental illness or incompetence of either or both parties." The action may be brought by a guardian or next friend but must be brought within six months of the marriage. *Id.*

[60] Ellis v. Ellis, 119 So. 304, 305 (Miss. 1928) (marriage voidable, but not void, and therefore could be attacked only during lifetime of parties); *see* White v. Williams, 132 So. 573, 575 (Miss. 1931) (discussing potential for fraud by one who marries insane person but finding greater danger in allowing heirs to attack marriage after death on basis of insanity).

[61] MISS. CODE ANN. § 93-5-1 (Supp. 2010) provides for divorce based upon "mental illness or intellectual disability at the time of marriage, if the party complaining did not know of that infirmity."

[62] MISS. CODE ANN. § 93-7-1 (2004).

[63] Parkinson v. Mills, 159 So. 651, 655 (Miss. 1935) (quoting Smith v. Smith, 47 Miss. 211, 216 (1872)); *see* Haralson v. Haralson, 362 So. 2d 190, 192 (Miss. 1978) (finding sufficient mental capacity).

[64] Parkinson v. Mills, 159 So. 651, 654 (Miss. 1935).

[65] MISS. CODE ANN. § 93-7-1 (2004).

[66] CLARK, JR., *supra* note 7, § 2.12, at 100. *See generally* David B. Perlmutter, Annotation, *Incapacity for Sexual Intercourse as Ground for Annulment*, 52 A.L.R.3d 589 (1974) (collecting cases on wide range of incapacities).

[67] MISS. CODE ANN. § 93-7-3 (2004); *see* Parkinson v. Mills, 159 So. 651, 656 (Miss. 1935) (recommending that courts look carefully for ratification if incompetent person has recovered and continued in marriage without seeking annulment).

[68] MISS. CODE ANN. § 93-5-1 (2004).

§ 1.03[2][a]   MISSISSIPPI FAMILY LAW

marriage relationship.

   [a] **Common law marriage.** Although ceremonial marriage has been required
in England since 1753, many American states recognized common law marriages until
recently.[69] The Mississippi legislature abolished common law marriages in 1956.[70] Any
marriage contracted after that date must meet statutory requirements for licensing and
solemnization; however, non-ceremonial common law marriages contracted prior to
1956 remain valid.[71] In addition, Mississippi grants full faith and credit to a common
law marriage valid in the state where the marriage was contracted.[72]
   A valid common law marriage is based upon the parties' agreement to be married,
followed by cohabitation.[73] In this context, cohabitation means a "public assumption
by a man and woman of the marital relation, and dwelling together as such, thereby
holding themselves out to the public as being man and wife."[74] The party seeking to
establish a common law marriage has the burden of proof. And if one of the spouses is
deceased, the elements of common law marriage must be shown by clear, consistent,
and convincing evidence.[75] If an alleged common law spouse later enters a ceremonial
marriage, that act is considered evidence that he or she lacked intent to contract the earlier common law marriage.[76] The Mississippi Supreme Court has held that a common
law marriage that is bigamous because of a prior marriage may become valid when the
first marriage ends. The common law spouses must have entered the bigamous marriage in good faith and continue to hold themselves out as husband and wife after the
first marriage ends.[77] If, however, the parties knew the marriage was bigamous, a new
agreement is necessary for a valid common law marriage to occur.[78]

_____

   [69] In 1753, Lord Hardwicke's Act was passed in England requiring that all marriages comply with Church of
England rules for entry into marriage—announcement of the bans, a license, and a ceremony. *See* CLARK, JR., *supra*
note 7, § 2.1, at 23, § 2.4, at 45.
   [70] Marriage at common law was first recognized in Mississippi in 1856, and its validity recognized in the 1869
Constitution. The provision recognizing common law marriage was omitted from the 1890 Constitution, but in 1906,
the legislature restored it. From then until 1956, when it was abolished by statute, marriage at common law was recognized in Mississippi. *See* BUNKLEY & MORSE, *supra* note 35, § 1.02(4), at 14-15.
   [71] MISS. CODE ANN. § 93-1-15 (2004).
   [72] George v. George, 389 So. 2d 1389, 1390 (Miss. 1980) (recognizing common law marriage in Georgia); *see*
Walker v. Matthews, 3 So. 2d 820, 824 (Miss. 1941). Some courts have recognized formation of a valid common law
marriage where the parties live in one state but visit a state that recognizes common law marriages and hold themselves
out in that state as husband and wife. *See* GREGORY ET AL., *supra* note 47, § 2.05[A], at 38 & n.105 (suggesting these
decisions typically were in cases where parties had, in good faith, lived together for years as husband and wife).
   [73] Vetrano v. Gardner, 290 F. Supp. 200, 205 (N.D. Miss. 1968) (finding a lack of evidence that parties intended
common law marriage); Stutts v. Estate of Stutts, 194 So. 2d 229, 231 (Miss. 1967); Sims v. Sims, 85 So. 73, 75 (Miss.
1920) (conduct implies intent).
   [74] Hunt v. Hunt, 161 So. 119, 121 (Miss. 1935).
   [75] Ladnier v. Estate of Ladnier, 109 So. 2d 338, 342 (Miss. 1959) (claim of common law marriage "is regarded
with suspicion and will be closely scrutinized").
   [76] Enis v. State, 408 So. 2d 486, 488 (Miss. 1981).
   [77] Johnson v. Johnson, 17 So. 2d 805, 806 (Miss. 1944) (invalid ceremonial marriage became valid common
law marriage upon death of husband's first wife; no new agreement to marry necessary); Sims v. Sims, 85 So. 73, 75
(Miss. 1920) (ceremonial second marriage became valid as common law marriage upon termination of first marriage
by divorce).
   [78] Green v. Ribicoff, 201 F. Supp. 721, 723-24 (S.D. Miss. 1961) (where relationship began as adulterous in
intent, it will be presumed to continue as adulterous relationship); Nichols v. Sauls, 165 So. 2d 352, 358 (Miss. 1964)
(bigamous second marriage did not become valid marriage upon first wife's death "without any additional overt act
of marriage," where both parties knew of first marriage); Thompson v. Clay, 82 So. 1, 2 (Miss. 1919) ("changing the

8

THE MARRIAGE RELATIONSHIP

§ 1.03[2][b]

In contrast to its informal beginning, a common law marriage may be dissolved only through formal divorce proceedings.[79] The marriage is not dissolved simply because the parties live separately, even for many years.

[b] Ceremonial marriage. In order to enter a valid ceremonial marriage, the parties must acquire a license and solemnize the marriage through a ceremony.

[i] License. Applicants for a marriage license must file a written, sworn application with the circuit clerk of any county,[80] stating their names, ages, and addresses and the names and addresses of their parents.[81] The application must remain on file for three days unless the waiting period is waived by a judge. Parties must also submit proof of age and a medical certificate dated within thirty days of application showing they do not have syphilis.[82]

[ii] Solemnization. No marriage is valid in Mississippi unless, after the parties obtain a license, a ceremony is performed by "an authorized person."[83] Authorized persons include a minister, rabbi, or spiritual leader of any religious body authorized by that religion and in good standing, any justice of the Mississippi Supreme Court, any Mississippi Court of Appeals, circuit court, chancery court or county court judge, and any justice court judge or county supervisor performing a ceremony within his or her county.[84] A marriage performed by a justice court judge outside of his jurisdiction was found void.[85]

[iii] Failure to comply with requirements. A marriage may be annulled if the parties fail to comply with the statutory licensing requirements.[86] Mere irregularities or omissions in a license do not affect validity of a marriage.[87] Furthermore, failure to comply with licensure provisions does not affect the validity of a marriage solemnized

---

relation from illegal to legal requires something more than the mere continuance of the living together after all the difficulties in the way of marriage are removed").

[79] Barton v. State, 143 So. 861, 862 (Miss. 1932) ("nothing less than a decree of divorce pronounced by a court of competent jurisdiction can dissolve the relation"), *quoted in* Martin v. Martin's Estate, 63 So. 2d 827, 830 (Miss. 1953); BUNKLEY & MORSE, *supra* note 35, §1.02(4), at 18.

[80] If the female applicant is under the age of twenty-one, the application must be filed in the county in which she resides. MISS. CODE ANN. § 93-1-5(a) (2004).

[81] MISS. CODE ANN. § 93-1-5 (2004).

[82] If either party is under twenty-one, the clerk must notify the parent, guardian, or next of kin of each applicant. MISS. CODE ANN. § 93-1-5(b) (2004). "Any interested party" may protest issuance of the license on grounds that a party is a minor, not mature, or not capable of assuming the responsibilities of marriage. MISS. CODE ANN. § 93-1-7 (2004).

[83] MISS. CODE ANN. § 93-1-15 (2004). The leading treatise on American domestic relations notes the apparent absence of any requirement that the parties to a marriage ceremony be in the same place, raising the possibility of marriage by conference call. *See* CLARK, JR., *supra* note 7, § 2.3, at 38; *cf.* Great N. Ry. Co. v. Johnson, 254 F. 683, 684-85 (8th Cir. 1918) (upholding common law marriage by correspondence where widow sought to file wrongful death suit: "[w]hy should the physical presence of the parties be essential to the legality of this contract, any more than of any other?").

[84] MISS. CODE ANN. § 93-1-17 (2004). In *In re Will of Blackwell*, 531 So. 2d 1193, 1196 (Miss. 1988), a Universal Life minister who received a certificate of authorization by mail qualified as a religious or spiritual leader under the statute.

[85] Pittman v. Pittman, 909 So. 2d 148, 152 (Miss. Ct. App. 2005).

[86] MISS. CODE ANN. § 93-7-3 (2004).

[87] MISS. CODE ANN. § 93-1-13 (2004).

§ 1.03[3]   MISSISSIPPI FAMILY LAW

in a ceremony and followed by cohabitation.[88] However, complete failure to obtain a license, as opposed to a failure to meet some of the license requirements, is not cured by ceremony and cohabitation. A woman who entered a ceremonial marriage and cohabited with her "husband" was not entitled to his workers' compensation benefits even though they applied for, but never obtained, a license.[89] A reading of the statute implies that the reverse is also true – no marriage results if a couple obtains a license and cohabits but does not solemnize the relationship in a ceremony.

[3] Consent to marry. In addition to meeting eligibility requirements and complying with formal prerequisites for marriage, both parties must consent to enter the marriage free of duress or coercion. Lack of consent arises when one party is defrauded or coerced into entering marriage, or if one or both enter the marriage as a joke. Furthermore, consent may be lacking if one or both agree to go through a marriage ceremony without intending to live as husband and wife.

[a] Fraud. A marriage may be set aside if one party has been fraudulently induced to enter the marriage. Suit must be filed within six months of the time the fraud was or should have been discovered. The marriage may be ratified by the defrauded party.[90]

[i] The "essentials" test. Courts have employed two tests for determining whether one spouse's misrepresentations are sufficient to set aside a marriage for fraud. The older, narrower view requires that fraud go to the "essence" of marriage, meaning that it must relate to the sexual obligations of marriage.[91] Applying this test, courts have annulled marriages for misrepresentations about impotency,[92] sterility,[93] venereal disease,[94] willingness to have children,[95] and willingness to consummate the marriage.[96] Annulment is granted for fraud under this test if a wife was pregnant by another at the time of the marriage[97] but not because she misrepresented that she was pregnant when, in fact, she was not.[98]

Under the essentials test, misrepresentations about personal characteristics are not a reason for annulment.[99] The Massachusetts Supreme Court, introducing the essentials

---

[88] MISS. CODE ANN. § 93-1-9 (2004); *see* Hunt v. Hunt, 161 So. 119, 121-22 (Miss. 1935) (marriage pursuant to invalid license, followed by ceremony and cohabitation, valid even in absence of consummation).

[89] So. Cent. Heating & Plumbing Co. v. Dependents of Campbell, 219 So. 2d 140, 142 (Miss. 1969).

[90] MISS. CODE ANN. § 93-7-3 (2004).

[91] CLARK, JR., *supra* note 7, § 2.15, at 110. The test was announced in *Reynolds v. Reynolds*, 85 Mass. 605, 608 (1862) (granting annulment for wife's concealment of pregnancy by another at time of marriage).

[92] Aufort v. Aufort, 49 P.2d 620, 620 (Cal. Dist. Ct. App. 1935).

[93] Turner v. Avery, 113 A. 710, 710-11 (N.J. Ch. 1921).

[94] Watson v. Watson, 143 S.W.2d 349, 350 (Mo. Ct. App. 1940).

[95] Zoglio v. Zoglio, 157 A.2d 627, 629 (D.C. 1960); Stegienko v. Stegienko, 295 N.W. 252, 254 (Mich. 1940).

[96] Hyslop v. Hyslop, 2 So. 2d 443, 445 (Ala. 1941); Millar v. Millar, 167 P. 394, 396 (Cal. 1917).

[97] Lyman v. Lyman, 97 A. 312, 315 (Conn. 1916); Winner v. Winner, 177 N.W. 680, 682 (Wis. 1920).

[98] Mobley v. Mobley, 16 So. 2d 5, 7 (Ala. 1943); Gondouin v. Gondouin, 111 P. 756, 756 (Cal. Dist. Ct. App. 1910); Husband v. Wife, 262 A.2d 656, 657 (Del. Super. Ct. 1970); Brandt v. Brandt, 167 So. 524, 525 (Fla. 1936); Hill v. Hill, 398 N.E.2d 1048, 1052-53 (Ill. App. Ct. 1979); Levy v. Levy, 34 N.E.2d 650, 652 (Mass. 1941); *see* W.J. Dunn, Annotation, *Antenuptial Knowledge Relating to Alleged Grounds as Barring Right to Annulment*, 15 A.L.R.2d 706 (1951).

[99] *See, e.g.,* Woy v. Woy, 737 S.W.2d 769, 774 (Mo. Ct. App. 1987) (nondisclosure of premarital lesbian activity

THE MARRIAGE RELATIONSHIP

§ 1.03[3][a][ii]

test, stated, "any error or misapprehension as to personal traits or attributes, or concerning the position or circumstances in life of a party, is deemed wholly immaterial, and furnishes no good cause for divorce."[100]

[ii] The "but for" test. The broader approach, used primarily in New York, allows annulment if fraud was material – if the defrauded party would not have entered the marriage but for the fraudulent misrepresentation.[101] Under the "but for" test, New York courts have annulled marriages based upon misrepresentations about age,[102] disease,[103] and love and affection.[104]

No Mississippi annulment cases based upon fraud were found. However, Mississippi law specifically provides that a wife's pregnancy by another at the time of marriage, without her husband's knowledge, is a ground for both annulment[105] and divorce.[106]

[b] Duress. A marriage may be set aside by annulment if one of the parties entered the marriage under duress or force. Suit must be filed within six months of the marriage. The marriage may be ratified by the party acting under duress.[107]

Mississippi courts require proof by clear and convincing evidence that the duress "dominated throughout the transaction so as to disable the one influenced from acting as a free agent at the time of the marriage."[108] The Mississippi Supreme Court upheld annulment of a marriage because the husband consented to marry in the presence of the woman's father and brothers, who accompanied him to the ceremony armed with deadly weapons.[109] However, the court found that marriage was voluntary when a man arrested on statutory rape charges was released upon his agreement to marry the girl.[110]

[c] Limited-purpose marriage. Parties who marry for a limited purpose, such as legitimizing a child or securing immigration status, without intending to live as husband and wife, may later challenge the marriage based on lack of consent. Courts

---

and drug use); Wells v. Talham, 194 N.W. 36, 37, 40 (Wis. 1923) (wife reneged on second, Catholic ceremony and had concealed her prior divorce before second marriage).

[100] Reynolds v. Reynolds, 85 Mass. 605, 607 (1862) (parties should take upon themselves to learn the characteristics of persons they intend to marry). The court recognized that some authorities believed that questions as to the chastity of the woman should be exempted from this rule but concluded that misrepresentations about chastity, "as with other personal qualities," should not be the basis for annulment for fraud. *Id.* at 608.

[101] CLARK, JR., *supra* note 7, § 2.15, at 111.

[102] Tacchi v. Tacchi, 195 N.Y.S.2d 892, 894-95 (N.Y. Sup. Ct. 1959).

[103] Sobol v. Sobol, 150 N.Y.S. 248, 250-51 (N.Y. Sup. Ct. 1914) (tuberculosis).

[104] Schinker v. Schinker, 68 N.Y.S.2d 470, 472 (N.Y. App. Div. 1947). One authority suggests that courts have tended to expand annulment for fraud. CLARK, JR., *supra* note 7, § 2.15, at 110-11.

[105] MISS. CODE ANN. § 93-7-3 (2004).

[106] MISS. CODE ANN. § 93-5-1 (2004).

[107] MISS. CODE ANN. § 93-7-3 (2004).

[108] Main v. Main, 74 So. 138, 141 (Miss. 1917) (quoting Beeks v. Beeks, 63 So. 444, 445 (Fla. 1913)).

[109] Marsh v. Whittington, 40 So. 326, 326 (Miss. 1906).

[110] Zeigler v. Zeigler, 164 So. 768, 769 (Miss. 1935). The court looked to *Rogers v. Rogers,* 118 So. 619 (Miss. 1928), in which the court found no duress where a man consented to marry after being arrested for capital rape and advised that he would probably be hanged if he declined: "In that case the court said that the seducer had done no more than he ought to have done." *Zeigler,* 164 So. at 769.

§ 1.03[3][d]   MISSISSIPPI FAMILY LAW

frequently refuse to annul a marriage if the limited purpose was legal and did not violate public policy.[111] For example, courts have rejected attempts to annul marriages contracted to legitimize a child.[112] With regard to marriages for the purpose of obtaining benefits, employment, or immigration status, courts' responses vary. Some marriages have been held invalid for lack of consent,[113] while others have been upheld.[114]

The validity of marriage entered into for immigration purposes is governed by the Immigration Marriage Fraud Amendments Act of 1986, which provides for a two-year conditional residency after marriage of an alien to a United States citizen.[115]

[d] Marriage in jest. If parties marry as a joke, some courts will grant an annulment, particularly if the marriage has not been consummated.[116] Others will not annul marriages entered into in jest.[117] The Georgia Supreme Court refused to annul the marriage of two teenagers who married on a dare and "in a spirit of misguided fun and jest;" the parties were old enough to marry, there was no fraud, and marriages "cannot be set aside lightly and without cause."[118] The Mississippi annulment statute does not mention limited-purpose marriages or marriages in jest, nor does the wording of the statute appear to cover either.[119]

§ 1.04 RIGHTS AND DUTIES WITHIN MARRIAGE: LEGAL STATUS OF WOMEN

Under the common law, a married woman's legal identity was merged into her husband's. The resulting structure of marital rights and duties has gradually been dismantled, beginning with the Married Women's Property Acts in the 1800s and continuing into the last few decades. Today, most property, inheritance, and other marital

---

[111] *See* Schibi v. Schibi, 69 A.2d 831, 833 (Conn. 1949) (marriage to legitimate child); Bishop v. Bishop, 308 N.Y.S.2d 998, 1000-01 (N.Y. Sup. Ct. 1970) (same). *But see* Stone v. Stone, 32 So. 2d 278, 279 (Fla. 1947) (en banc) (sham marriage without intent to consummate was against public policy). For a general discussion of cases, see A. Della Porta, Annotation, *Validity of Marriage as Affected by Intention of Parties That It Should Be Only a Matter of Form or Jest*, 14 A.L.R.2d 624 (1950).

[112] *See, e.g.*, Erickson v. Erickson, 48 N.Y.S.2d 588, 589 (N.Y. Sup. Ct. 1944). *But see* Conley v. Conley, 14 Ohio Supp. 22, *available at* 1943 WL 6289, at *3 (Ohio Com. Pl. May 1, 1943) (where parents lived apart after wedlock, child's best interests served by annulment).

[113] The cases holding marriage invalid primarily involve attempts to achieve immigration status. *See, e.g.*, United States v. Lutwak, 195 F.2d 748, 753 (7th Cir. 1952) (holding that "sham marriage . . . can have no validity"), *aff'd*, 344 U.S. 604 (1953). *But see* United States v. Diogo, 320 F.2d 898, 909 (2d Cir. 1963) (refusing to hold marriage either void or fraudulent).

[114] *See* Hanson v. Hanson, 191 N.E. 673, 674 (Mass. 1934) (employment and increase in income); Delfino v. Delfino, 35 N.Y.S.2d 693, 693 (N.Y. Sup. Ct. 1942) (to preserve wife's reputation); De Vries v. De Vries, 195 Ill. App. 4, 5-6 (1915) (release from employment contract).

[115] *See* Pub. L. No. 100-525, 102 Stat. 2616 (1988) & Pub. L. No. 99-639, 100 Stat. 3537 (1986) (codified in scattered sections of 8 U.S.C. 1186a); Eileen P. Lynskey, Comment, *Immigration Marriage Fraud Amendments Act of 1986: Till Congress Do Us Part*, 41 U. MIAMI L. REV. 1087 (1987).

[116] *See* Davis v. Davis, 175 A. 574, 577 (Conn. 1934) (intent crucial in marriage as in other contracts); Meredith v. Shakespeare, 122 S.E. 520, 526 (W. Va. 1924); *see also* A. Della Porta, Annotation, *Validity of Marriage as Affected by Intention of Parties That It Should Be Only a Matter of Form or Jest*, 14 A.L.R.2d 624 (1950).

[117] *See* Hand v. Berry, 154 S.E. 239, 240 (Ga. 1930); Lannamann v. Lannamann, 89 A.2d 897, 897 (Pa. Super. Ct. 1952) (marriage valid in absence of duress or fraud).

[118] Hand v. Berry, 154 S.E. 239, 240 (Ga. 1930).

[119] *See* MISS. CODE ANN. § 93-7-3 (2004) (annulment where parties are "incapable, from want of age or understanding, of consenting" or "where the consent of either party shall have been obtained by force or fraud").

THE MARRIAGE RELATIONSHIP   § 1.04[1]

rights and duties apply equally to women and men.

[1] Common law rights and duties. At common law, women became legal non-entities upon marriage. The "disability of coverture" deprived married women of the power to contract, to sue and be sued, and to manage and control their own property.[120] A woman's husband had the right to use and manage her property and to receive all income from the property. A married woman was not legally capable of making a contract. Her earnings belonged to her husband.[121]

Spousal duties were tied to gender – a husband owed his wife a duty of support, and she had a duty to provide services to her husband.[122] Laws of inheritance provided unequal estates for husband and wife. A wife received dower, a life estate in one-third of her husband's real property, while a husband received curtesy, a life estate in all property owned by his wife.[123] Husband and wife were regarded as one person in law.[124] Accordingly, spouses could not sue one another in tort[125] or testify against each other in court.[126]

[2] The Married Women's Property Acts. By the end of the nineteenth century, most state legislatures had enacted Married Women's Property Acts removing the disability of coverture. The Mississippi legislature was one of the leaders in this reform, providing in 1839 that married women could own real and personal property.[127] The Mississippi Constitution of 1890 stated even more broadly, "Married women are hereby fully emancipated from *all* disability on account of coverture."[128] The current version of the emancipation statute provides that married women have the same rights as unmarried women to own property, to contract, and to sue and be sued.[129]

[3] Constitutional constraints. Married Women's Property Acts abolished disabilities related to property and contract rights. The Acts did not affect common law rules prohibiting tort actions between husband and wife.[130] Nor did they alter unequal marital support obligations[131] or remedy disparate inheritance rights.[132] These aspects of marriage remained unequal in most states until Supreme Court decisions in the

---

[120] *See* CLARK, JR., *supra* note 7, § 7.1, at 286-88.

[121] *See* CLARK, JR., *supra* note 7, § 7.1, at 287.

[122] *See* Miller v. Miller, 298 So. 2d 704, 707 (Miss. 1974) (discussing historic duty of wife to provide services); Henderson v. Henderson, 43 So. 2d 871, 872 (Miss. 1950) (husband's duty to support wife).

[123] *See* GREGORY ET AL., *supra* note 47, § 3.05[A], at 70.

[124] According to Blackstone, the common law treatment of married women was based on the legal fiction that the husband and wife were one person; thus, the woman's legal existence "is suspended during the marriage, or at least is incorporated and consolidated into that of the husband." 1 WILLIAM BLACKSTONE, COMMENTARIES 442, *quoted in* BUNKLEY & MORSE, *supra* note 35, §13.00, at 259.

[125] *See* discussion *infra* § 1.09[1].

[126] *See* discussion *infra* § 1.10.

[127] *See* BUNKLEY & MORSE, *supra* note 35, § 13.01 at 260.

[128] MISS. CONST. (1890) Art. IV, § 94 (emphasis added).

[129] MISS. CODE ANN. § 93-3-1 (2004) (disabilities of coverture "totally abrogated").

[130] Austin v. Austin, 100 So. 591, 592 (Miss. 1924).

[131] *See* BUNKLEY & MORSE, *supra* note 35, § 13.04, at 266; Galtney v. Wood, 115 So. 117, 121 (Miss. 1928).

[132] *See* MISS. CODE ANN. § 93-3-5 (2004) (abolishing dower and curtesy); Wolcott v. Wolcott, 184 So. 2d 381, 382 (Miss. 1966) (dower and curtesy abolished by statute).

§ 1.04[4]   **MISSISSIPPI FAMILY LAW**

1970s established that gender-based distinctions in family law are, for the most part, unconstitutional.[133] In response to Supreme Court pronouncements, the Mississippi legislature equalized statutory support rights by providing for gender-neutral alimony.[134] However, court decisions still often refer to separate maintenance, a judicial remedy for lack of support, as a remedy for wives.[135]

[4] The marital unity fiction. Other aspects of marriage have changed as the legal fiction that husband and wife are "one" has diminished. Courts have rejected the notion of marital unity as a reason for banning tort actions between spouses.[136] Similarly, spouses are no longer deemed incompetent to testify against each other for all purposes.[137]

§ 1.05 PROPERTY RIGHTS BETWEEN SPOUSES

Property rights between spouses in an intact marriage do not differ greatly from property rights between unrelated individuals. With the exception of homestead property, each party has full use and control of his or her own property. Although joint ownership is more commonly used by spouses, all the forms of joint ownership except tenancy by the entirety can be used by unrelated individuals. Upon divorce, however, property rights become dramatically different from those of unrelated persons.

[1] Ownership, use, and control. Mississippi, along with the majority of states, follows the title system for determining property rights between spouses during a marriage.[138] The title system allocates ownership, use, and control of property to the spouse who holds title.[139] With the exception of homestead property, a non-owning spouse has no voice in the owner's disposition or use of property.[140] The property of one spouse is also free from claims of the other's creditors. A married person has complete autonomy in disposing of property at death, subject to a surviving spouse's statutory share under descent and distribution statutes.[141]

If a couple divorces, however, their property rights are no longer governed by the title system. Equitable distribution, formally adopted in Mississippi in 1994, allows division of property earned by either spouse during the marriage, regardless of who

---

[133] *See* Orr v. Orr, 440 U.S. 268, 282-83 (1979) (invalidating state law providing alimony for women but not for men; old notions do not justify gender-based distinctions in family law).

[134] *See* MISS. CODE ANN. § 93-5-23 (2004) ("maintenance and alimony of the wife or the husband"); Robinson v. Robinson, 554 So. 2d 300, 306 (Miss. 1989) (statute amended in 1985).

[135] *See* discussion *infra* § 1.07[2].

[136] *See* discussion *infra* § 1.09[1].

[137] *See* discussion *infra* § 1.10.

[138] *See* BRETT TURNER, EQUITABLE DISTRIBUTION OF PROPERTY § 1.02, at 4 (2d ed. 1994).

[139] *See* GREGORY ET AL., *supra* note 47, § 3.02, at 66. Until passage of the Married Women's Property Act, a married woman's property belonged to her husband, who had authority to control, manage, and dispose of the property. *See* CLARK, JR., *supra* note 7, § 7.2, at 293-94.

[140] *See* Jones v. Somerville, 28 So. 940, 940 (Miss. 1900) (recognizing husband's right to convey two-thirds of estate to his daughter prior to his death; conveyance to prevent wife from inheriting is not fraud on marital rights).

[141] *See* Jones v. Somerville, 28 So. 940, 940 (Miss. 1900) (married persons differ in property rights from others only in that each inherits from the other in the absence of a will and can renounce a will and take a child's share).

THE MARRIAGE RELATIONSHIP § 1.05[2]

holds title.[142] A spouse may receive assets at divorce that belonged solely to the other during marriage.

In contrast, the eight community property states recognize marital property during the intact marriage and at death, as well as upon divorce. Each spouse is considered to own one-half of all property earned by the other during marriage.[143]

[2] Homestead property. Homestead property – the land and buildings owned and occupied as a family's residence[144] – is exempted from operation of the title system in several respects. A spouse who does not own the family homestead is protected against transfer of the home during marriage or at the owner's death and from seizure of the home by the owner's creditors.

[a] Transfer without consent. A spouse who is sole owner of a marital homestead cannot act alone to convey, mortgage, or otherwise encumber the property as long as the couple is living together.[145] The non-owning spouse receives no ownership rights – only a veto power over transfer.[146] A sale, lease, mortgage, deed of trust, or other interest is void without the non-owning spouse's consent to the transaction.[147] The right to object is lost by a spouse who abandons the home[148] but not by one who is wrongfully ousted.[149]

[b] Homestead rights at death. At the death of a spouse holding homestead title, the surviving spouse receives a life estate in the homestead until remarriage.[150]

[c] Homestead exemption. Homestead exemption laws protect the marital home from sale by creditors. The first $75,000 in equity in the marital home is exempt from claims of the owner's creditors.[151] Each homestead has only one exemption: if creditors of joint-owner spouses seek execution, the maximum exemption is $75,000.[152] However, the full exemption is available in an action by one spouse's creditors, even

---

[142] *See* Ferguson v. Ferguson, 639 So. 2d 921, 927 (Miss. 1994).

[143] *See* J. Thomas Oldham, Divorce, Separation & the Distribution of Property § 3.03[5], at 3-11 (2001).

[144] *See* Miss. Code Ann. § 85-3-21 (1999) (up to 160 acres).

[145] Miss. Code Ann. § 89-1-29 (1999). The statute sets out a procedure for obtaining judicial approval for conveyance or encumbrance if the non-owning spouse is incompetent. *Id.* The statute also provides that spousal consent is not necessary for a purchase money mortgage where the farmer's home administration is the mortgagee. *Id.*

[146] *See* Hughes v. Hahn, 46 So. 2d 587, 590 (Miss. 1950); *see also* Countrywide Home Loans v. Parker, 975 So. 2d 233, 234 (Miss. 2008) (deed of trust on deceased wife's house held invalid because non-owner husband did not sign deed of trust on homestead property); Alexander v. Daniel, 904 So. 2d 172, 179-80 (Miss. 2005) (husband's homestead conveyance without wife's consent was invalid; consequently, tax sale for nonpayment of taxes by purchaser was invalid).

[147] Hendry v. Hendry, 300 So. 2d 147, 149 (Miss. 1974); Yazoo Lumber Co. v. Clark, Jr., 48 So. 516, 517 (Miss. 1909).

[148] *See* Etheridge v. Webb, 50 So. 2d 603, 609 (Miss. 1951); Philan v. Turner, 13 So. 2d 819, 821 (Miss. 1943).

[149] Philan v. Turner, 13 So. 2d 819, 821 (Miss. 1943) (woman who left home because of husband's abuse can veto conveyance); *see* Robbins v. Berry, 57 So. 2d 576, 579-80 (Miss. 1952) (same); Scott v. Scott, 19 So. 589, 589 (Miss. 1896) (same).

[150] Miss. Code Ann. § 91-1-23 (2004).

[151] Miss. Code Ann. § 85-3-21 (1999). The homestead exemption extends to land up to 160 acres and value up to $75,000. The exempt value is determined by deducting all existing liens and encumbrances, including tax liens, so that the $75,000 applies to equity in the residence. *Id.*; *see* Joe T. Dehmer Distribs., Inc. v. Temple, 826 F.2d 1463, 1467 (5th Cir. 1987) (conveyance of homestead up to amount of exemption cannot defraud creditors).

[152] *See* Joe T. Dehmer Distribs., Inc. v. Temple, 826 F.2d 1463, 1469 (5th Cir. 1987).

§ 1.05[3]   **MISSISSIPPI FAMILY LAW**

if the property is jointly owned.[153] On the other hand, if an owning spouse has abandoned the property with the other's consent, the absent spouse's one-half interest can be attached by creditors, even if the co-owner spouse continues to reside in the homestead.[154]

[3] Joint ownership. Married persons frequently hold title to property as co-owners. Common ownership forms include tenancy in common, joint tenancy, and tenancy by the entirety. The choice of common ownership form has significant legal consequences: tenancy by the entirety and joint tenancy are characterized by a right of survivorship not applicable to tenancy in common. And both spouses must consent to alter a tenancy by the entirety, while the other two forms can be severed by the unilateral act of one spouse.

    [a] Joint title presumption. If an owning spouse transfers property into the joint names of both spouses, the law presumes the owner intended a gift of one-half of the property. The presumption may be rebutted by clear and convincing evidence that the joint titling was for some other purpose such as convenience.[155]

    [b] Presumption of tenancy in common. At common law, a conveyance to two or more persons created a joint tenancy, while a conveyance to husband and wife created a tenancy by the entirety.[156] In 1880 the Mississippi legislature reversed the common law presumption, providing that "conveyances . . . to husband and wife, shall . . . create estates in common . . . unless it manifestly appears . . . that it was intended to create an estate in joint tenancy or entirety."[157] Creation of a tenancy by the entirety or a joint tenancy requires precise drafting. Tenancy by the entirety is properly created by a conveyance to husband and wife "as joint tenants in entirety and not as tenants in common, but to the survivor."[158] A conveyance to spouses "as joint tenants, not as tenants in common, but with the right of survivorship" created a joint tenancy, rather than

---

[153] *See* Chapman v. White Sewing-Mach. Co., 28 So. 735, 736 (Miss. 1900).

[154] *See* Merch. Nat'l Bank v. Se. Fire Ins. Co., 751 F.2d 771, 777 (5th Cir. 1985).

[155] The presumption was applied and rebutted in *Sarver v. Sarver*, 687 So. 2d 749, 753-54 (Miss. 1997) (wife convinced husband to convey to her property intended for children, upon her promise to deed property to them on his death), *overruled on other grounds by* Pearson v. Pearson, 761 So. 2d 157 (Miss. 2000). It should be noted that the Mississippi Supreme Court has held that the presumption does not apply in division of marital assets between divorcing parties. Pearson v. Pearson, 761 So. 2d 157, 163 (Miss. 2000).

[156] *See* Wolfe v. Wolfe, 42 So. 2d 438, 439 (Miss. 1949) (restrictive or explanatory words necessary at common law to create tenancy in common); Conn v. Boutwell, 58 So. 105, 106 (Miss. 1912) (under statute of 1857, conveyance to husband and wife was conveyance to one person; the survivor took the interest of the other at death; neither could transfer their interest during life).

[157] MISS. CODE ANN. § 89-1-7 (1994). The statute had been amended many years earlier to abolish the general presumption in favor of joint tenancies, but the Mississippi court held that the earlier amendment did not apply to the presumption in favor of tenancies by the entirety. *See* Hemingway v. Scales, 42 Miss. 1, 13 (Miss. 1868) ("conveyance to husband and wife is not, in a legal sense, a conveyance to two persons, but to those who, for this purpose, are accounted but one person in law"). In 1880, the statute favoring tenancies in common was amended to include conveyances between husband and wife. *See* Conn v. Boutwell, 58 So. 105, 106 (Miss. 1912) (intended to place husband and wife on same footing with others with regard to conveyances).

[158] *See* Cuevas v. Cuevas, 191 So. 2d 843, 846 (Miss. 1966) (setting aside husband's attempted transfer of one-half interest to girlfriend).

THE MARRIAGE RELATIONSHIP §1.05[3][c]

a tenancy by the entirety.[159] The Mississippi Supreme Court found intention to create a joint tenancy in a conveyance to husband and wife "and to the survivor of them"[160] but a tenancy in common where the conveyance was to husband and wife "jointly."[161]

[c] Tenancy in common. Spouses who hold property as tenants in common may freely transfer or mortgage their share of the property. In addition, each may transfer the interest by will or allow it to pass by inheritance. One who purchases or inherits a spouse's one-half interest becomes a tenant in common with the other spouse.[162]

[d] Joint tenancy. Joint tenancy interests are subject to a right of survivorship. When one joint tenant dies, the surviving owner becomes the sole owner by operation of law.[163] An attempt to transfer a joint tenancy interest to a third person by will is ineffective.[164] A spouse may, however, transfer a joint tenancy interest during life. Transfer severs the joint tenancy, destroys the right of survivorship, and creates a tenancy in common between the transferee and the remaining owner.[165]

[e] Tenancy by the entirety. Only married persons may own property as tenants by the entirety.[166] Ownership by entirety provides benefits similar to homestead laws.[167] Property held by the entirety cannot be transferred, mortgaged, or otherwise severed except by consent of both spouses.[168] Creditors of one spouse have no claim on property held in tenancy by the entirety.[169]

Like joint tenancy, tenancy by the entirety carries with it a right of survivorship. Unlike joint tenancy, one spouse cannot destroy the right of survivorship by transferring an interest prior to death.[170] Spouses may sever a tenancy by entirety through a joint conveyance, or, in some instances, by separate deeds pursuant to agreement.[171] Both a joint tenancy and tenancy by the entirety can be severed if one spouse deeds the

---

[159] *See* Ayers v. Petro, 417 So. 2d 912, 913 (Miss. 1982) (amendment to statute intended to put husband and wife on same footing as others).

[160] *See* Wolfe v. Wolfe, 42 So. 2d 438, 439 (Miss. 1949) (right of survivorship indicates joint tenancy).

[161] *See* Doran v. Beale, 63 So. 647, 648 (Miss. 1913) (word "jointly" is consistent with tenancy in common ownership); *see also* Ferrara v. Walters, 919 So. 2d 876, 882 (Miss. 2005) (deed to husband and wife presumed to be conveyance of tenancy in common; no reference to survivorship).

[162] *See* Ferrara v. Walters, 919 So. 2d 876, 882-83 (Miss. 2005) (deceased husband's one-half interest in land held as tenant in common with wife was inherited by his heirs; wife continued to own one-half interest plus interest she inherited from her husband); *see also* Joseph William Singer, Introduction to Property § 8.2.1, at 335-36 (2001).

[163] Vaughn v. Vaughn, 118 So. 2d 620, 622 (Miss. 1960) ("distinguishing characteristic of a joint tenancy is the right of survivorship").

[164] Richardson v. Miller, 48 Miss. 311 (1873).

[165] Ayers v. Petro, 417 So. 2d 912, 914 (Miss. 1982) (upholding transfer by ex-husband of his one-half interest in property held with ex-wife as joint tenants); *see* Shepherd v. Shepherd, 336 So. 2d 497, 499 (Miss. 1976) (joint tenancy may be severed by agreement or by implication).

[166] Ayers v. Petro, 417 So. 2d 912, 914 (Miss. 1982).

[167] *See* Gregory et al., *supra* note 47, § 3.04, at 68 (tenancy by the entirety preserves assets from transfer by either of the spouses and from the claims of creditors of one of the spouses).

[168] *See* Ayers v. Petro, 417 So. 2d 912, 914 (Miss. 1982); Cuevas v. Cuevas, 191 So. 2d 843, 846 (Miss. 1966) (setting aside husband's transfer to his girlfriend of one-half interest in property owned as tenant by the entirety).

[169] *See* Gregory et al., *supra* note 47, § 3.04, at 69.

[170] Ayers v. Petro, 417 So. 2d 912, 914 (Miss. 1982).

[171] *See In re* Estate of Childress, 588 So. 2d 192, 197 (Miss. 1991) (tenancy by entirety severed where husband conveyed one-half to wife for life, then to grandson, and wife conveyed one-half to grandson, reserving life estate).

§ 1.05[3][f]   MISSISSIPPI FAMILY LAW

property to the other.[172]

[f] The right to partition. Commonly owned property, other than property held as tenants by the entirety,[173] may be partitioned at the request of one of the spouses during the marriage.[174] Until 2009, the right to partition applied to jointly owned homestead property.[175] In 2009, the Mississippi legislature amended the partition statutes to provide that homestead property owned by a married couple can only be partitioned by agreement.[176]

[g] Effect of divorce on common ownership. A tenancy by the entirety, available only to married persons, cannot survive divorce. If parties continue after divorce to hold title in common, ownership must be converted to a tenancy in common or joint tenancy. The Mississippi Supreme Court takes the minority position[177] that, in the absence of agreement otherwise, a tenancy by the entirety becomes a joint tenancy upon divorce.[178]

§ 1.06 RIGHTS OF INHERITANCE BETWEEN SPOUSES

Modern laws of descent and distribution provide a surviving spouse with a statutory share of the deceased spouse's estate. The statutory share may not be avoided by omitting a spouse from a will.

[1] Through intestacy. In Mississippi, the common law estates of dower and curtesy have been replaced by statutes specifying the estate inherited by a husband or wife upon their spouse's death.[179] In the absence of a will, an estate is divided equally between the deceased's children and spouse.[180] If there are no children or heirs of children, a surviving spouse inherits the entire estate.[181] In addition to a child's share of the estate, a surviving spouse receives a life estate in homestead property owned by the

---

[172] MISS. CODE ANN. § 89-1-7 (1999). The statute was amended in 1993 to clarify that a deed from one spouse to the other severs the tenancy, in response to *In re Estate of Childress*, 588 So. 2d 192, 197 (Miss. 1991) (discussing whether both spouses must join in conveyance to one spouse alone; holding that a spouse who transfers to the other is estopped from objecting to severance by one tenant alone).

[173] *See supra* § 1.05[3][e].

[174] *See* Lenoir v. Lenoir, 611 So. 2d 200, 204 (Miss. 1992) (estranged wife could seek partition of three jointly owned properties, including homestead, six years after leaving home); Trigg v. Trigg, 498 So. 2d 334, 336 (Miss. 1986).

[175] *See* Trigg v. Trigg, 498 So. 2d 334, 336 (Miss. 1986); Miller v. Miller, 838 So. 2d 295, 298 (Miss. Ct. App. 2002) (divorce not res judicata as to partition action); *cf.* Myers v. Myers, 881 So. 2d 180, 183 (Miss. 2004) (husband did not abandon request for partition by agreeing to proceed in action for separate maintenance rather than divorce). *But cf.* Thweatt v. Thweatt, 4 So. 3d 1085, 1090 (Miss. Ct. App. 2009) (husband who acted fraudulently and deceived wife not entitled to partition).

[176] MISS. CODE ANN. § 11-21-1 (Supp. 2010).

[177] Ayers v. Petro, 417 So. 2d 912, 914 (Miss. 1982).

[178] *See* Shepherd v. Shepherd, 336 So. 2d 497, 499 (Miss. 1976) (finding no evidence that parties intended a tenancy in common to result from the divorce); *see also* Tommy E. Furby, Note, *Property – Tenancy by the Entirety – Effect of Divorce on Tenancy by the Entirety in Mississippi*, 48 MISS. L.J. 352, 359 (1977).

[179] *See* MISS. CODE ANN. § 93-3-5 (2004); Wolcott v. Wolcott, 184 So. 2d 381, 383 (Miss. 1966); BUNKLEY & MORSE, *supra* note 35, § 13.01, at 261 (dower and curtesy abolished in Mississippi).

[180] MISS. CODE ANN. § 91-1-7 (2004). The share of a deceased child is divided equally among his descendants. *Id.*

[181] MISS. CODE ANN. § 91-1-7 (2004).

THE MARRIAGE RELATIONSHIP   § 1.06[2]

decedent.[182] The homestead right lasts so long as the survivor remains unmarried[183] and is available whether or not the surviving spouse actually lives on the property.[184]

[2] Under a will. A spouse is free to transfer property at death through a will to anyone of his or her choosing,[185] but a surviving spouse who receives less than a statutory child's share may renounce the will. The survivor must elect to renounce the will within ninety days of probate if the will included an inadequate provision for the spouse.[186] If a will makes no provision at all for the surviving spouse, renunciation is automatic. No action by the survivor is required.[187] A spouse may not defeat a survivor's homestead right by willing homestead property to a third person. The surviving spouse still takes a life estate in the homestead,[188] even without renouncing the will.[189] The right to renounce is linked to the surviving spouse's independent means. A spouse whose separate estate is equal to a child's share of the deceased's estate may not renounce the will.[190]

[3] One-year allowance. Executors and administrators of estates are instructed to set aside an amount sufficient for one year's support for a spouse and children who were dependent on the deceased.[191] The allowance may be claimed whether the supporting spouse died intestate or with a will.[192] The allowance is not available to a spouse who was living apart from the decedent or who was not being supported by the decedent at the time of death.[193]

§ 1.07 THE DUTY OF SUPPORT

Under the common law, a husband had a duty to support his wife. A wife's corresponding duty was to provide services to her husband without compensation.[194] At

---

[182] MISS. CODE ANN. § 91-1-23 (2004) (exempt property inherited by surviving spouse and others may not be partitioned so long as widowhood lasts and property is occupied or used by widow).

[183] *See* Cheeks v. Herrington, 523 So. 2d 1033, 1035 (Miss. 1988) (upon remarriage widow's right to prevent partition of homestead is terminated).

[184] Wright v. Coleman, 102 So. 774, 775 (Miss. 1925) (homestead cannot be partitioned so long as surviving spouse uses income for support); Tiser v. McCain, 74 So. 660, 661 (Miss. 1917).

[185] *See* Jones v. Somerville, 28 So. 940, 940 (Miss. 1900) (spouses have "absolute, independent, and separate dominion over and power of disposition of property"; rejecting wife's claim that husband's transfer of property to daughter prior to death defrauded wife).

[186] MISS. CODE ANN. § 91-5-25 (2004). *But see* Wolcott v. Wolcott, 184 So. 2d 381, 384 (Miss. 1966) (ninety-day period does not bar election by mentally incompetent surviving spouse without guardian; statute contemplates that widow is capable of "electing").

[187] MISS. CODE ANN. § 91-5-27 (2004).

[188] Mills v. Mills, 279 So. 2d 917, 924 (Miss. 1973); Biggs v. Roberts, 115 So. 2d 151, 154 (Miss. 1959).

[189] Rush v. Rush, 360 So. 2d 1240, 1244 (Miss. 1978) (wife who failed to renounce will within required period still entitled to homestead).

[190] MISS. CODE ANN. § 91-5-29 (2004).

[191] MISS. CODE ANN. § 91-7-135 (2004).

[192] Whitehead v. Kirk, 64 So. 658, 658 (Miss. 1914).

[193] *In re* Estate of Marshall, 138 So. 2d 482, 483-84 (Miss. 1962).

[194] Henderson v. Henderson, 43 So. 2d 871, 872 (Miss. 1950) ("One of the most fundamental duties growing out of the law of domestic relations is the duty of the husband to support the wife."); *cf.* Miller v. Miller, 298 So. 2d 704, 707 (Miss. 1974) (notion that wife owes husband services without compensation in return for support has been eroded by the passage of time and has "strictly limited validity and application, if it continues to have any at all"), *overruled on other*

§ 1.07[1]   **MISSISSIPPI FAMILY LAW**

one time, Mississippi law provided criminal sanctions against a husband who deserted or refused to support his wife.[195] Mississippi law currently criminalizes non-support of children, but not non-support of a spouse.[196] Today, the duty of support is enforceable only through a separate maintenance action between separated spouses. Until recently, however, the doctrine of necessaries allowed third-party enforcement of the support duty during an intact marriage.

The historic gender-based division of support and services is clearly unconstitutional in light of the Supreme Court's decision in *Orr v. Orr.*[197] The Mississippi Supreme Court has removed gender inequality in the doctrine of necessaries but has yet to officially abandon gender distinctions in separate maintenance actions.

[1] Support in the intact family. In the intact family, the duty of support is more an aspiration than an enforceable obligation. Between cohabiting spouses, the duty has historically been enforced only indirectly through the doctrine of necessaries.

[a] Direct support. In spite of considerable lip service to a husband's duty of support,[198] courts have rarely enforced the duty directly within the intact marriage. Refusal to intervene in the intact family is based on deference to family privacy and reluctance to become involved in day-to-day domestic disputes. In the often-cited case of *McGuire v. McGuire*, the Nebraska court refused to order the husband, a man of considerable wealth, to provide basic conveniences to his wife such as indoor plumbing. The court held that public policy required a hands-off approach in an intact marriage, even if the husband's attitude "leaves little to be said in his behalf."[199] No Mississippi case was found in which the court required a husband living with his wife to provide her with support.

[b] The doctrine of necessaries. While neither spouse is generally liable for the other's debts,[200] the common law allowed suit against a husband by merchants who provided basic necessities to his wife.[201] In Mississippi, a merchant could recover under the doctrine by proving that a husband failed to provide his wife with necessaries

---

grounds by Pearson v. Pearson, 761 So. 2d 157 (Miss. 2000).

[195] Miss. Laws of 1920, Chp. 212, § 1. The court interpreted this statute as requiring that the wife be left in a condition of extreme want, without resources for the basic necessities of life. *See* Moorman v. State, 93 So. 368, 368 (Miss. 1922) (dismissing indictment because deserted wife had forty acres, milk cows, and other stock).

[196] Parents may be prosecuted for abandonment or neglect under MISS. CODE ANN. § 97-5-3 (1994) ("Any parent who shall desert or wilfully neglect or refuse to provide for the support . . . [is] guilty of a felony."). Prior to 1995, the statute required a showing that the children were left "in destitute and necessitous circumstances." *See* Knowles v. State, 708 So. 2d 549, 552 n.1 (Miss. 1998); Bryant v. State, 567 So. 2d 234, 235 (Miss. 1990).

[197] 440 U.S. 268, 272 (1979) (invalidating state law providing alimony for women but not for men; old notions do not justify gender-based distinctions in family law).

[198] *See* Henderson v. Henderson, 43 So. 2d 871, 872 (Miss. 1950) (husband's obligation to provide a home measured by living standards of persons of "their social rank and standard of living, within the means and earning power of the husband").

[199] McGuire v. McGuire, 59 N.W.2d 336, 342 (Neb. 1953).

[200] *See* Skehan v. Davidson Co., 145 So. 247, 248 (Miss. 1933) (husband is not liable for debts for goods furnished on wife's credit alone). *But see* Putt v. Ray Sewell Co., 481 So. 2d 785, 786 (Miss. 1985) (one spouse may be held liable for debts incurred by the other in connection with a joint venture).

[201] CLARK, JR., *supra* note 7, § 6.3, at 265.

THE MARRIAGE RELATIONSHIP   § 1.07[2]

"convenient and suitable to their station in life."[202] In fact, a wife was not even legally liable for her own purchases of necessaries unless they were clearly furnished on her individual credit.[203]

In 1993, the Mississippi Supreme Court abolished the doctrine of necessaries.[204] A husband argued that imposing liability on him for his former wife's hospital bills constituted gender-based discrimination. The court noted that some states remedied gender inequality in the doctrine by extending the duty to both spouses.[205] The Mississippi Supreme Court opted instead to abolish the doctrine. As a result, spouses in Mississippi have no liability for the other's debts in the absence of an express agreement to assume the obligation.[206]

[2] Separate maintenance. When spouses separate, courts may enforce the spousal duty of support through an award of separate maintenance. Chancellors' authority to order separate maintenance was recognized in 1874. The Mississippi Supreme Court held that equity jurisdiction included the power to award support to a wife whose husband abandoned her without fault on her part.[207] Writers on the topic uniformly agree that separate maintenance must be available to both husband and wife to meet constitutional requirements.[208] Recent Mississippi separate maintenance cases still refer to the "husband's" duty of support;[209] however, the supreme court has acknowledged in dicta that a unilateral duty to support is constitutionally suspect.[210] Separate maintenance is discussed in detail in Section 1.14 of this chapter.

§ 1.08 CONTRACTS AND CONVEYANCES BETWEEN SPOUSES

Contracts and conveyances between husband and wife have been valid and en-

---

[202] Skehan v. Davidson Co., 145 So. 247, 248 (Miss. 1933) (husband not liable for debt contracted by wife without his knowledge or use of his credit in the absence of proof of lack of support); *see* Woolbert v. Lee Lumber Co., 117 So. 354, 359 (Miss. 1928) (recognizing husband's duty to provide necessaries but finding that a $16,000 home was not a necessary where the homestead exemption was only $3,000).

[203] *See* McLemore v. Riley's Hosp., 20 So. 2d 67, 68-69 (Miss. 1944) (woman treated at her husband's request was not personally liable for an emergency room bill: "To bind her personally, it must be made to appear that necessaries were supplied on her individual credit, where credit is given . . . to [both] husband and wife, the wife is not liable.").

[204] Govan v. Medical Credit Servs., Inc., 621 So. 2d 928, 930-31 (Miss. 1993).

[205] Govan v. Medical Credit Servs., Inc., 621 So. 2d 928, 931 (Miss. 1993) (citing cases from Louisiana and Ohio).

[206] The court acknowledged a strong public policy favoring "mutual duties of support" but also recognized the importance of individual autonomy. The court noted that otherwise, one spouse could deplete the resources of the other. Govan v. Medical Credit Servs., Inc., 621 So. 2d 928, 930-31 (Miss. 1993).

[207] Garland v. Garland, 50 Miss. 694, 1874 WL 4630, at *14 (1874) (based in part on statutory authorization to make orders related to maintenance of wife in divorce proceedings).

[208] *See* SHELTON HAND, MISSISSIPPI DIVORCE, ALIMONY, AND CHILD CUSTODY, § 2-11, at 37 n.7 (5th ed. 1998); CLARK, JR., *supra* note 7, § 6.4 , at 268.

[209] *See* Stanford v. Stanford, 734 So. 2d 359, 360 (Miss. Ct. App. 1999) ("wife is entitled to be maintained in the same standard of living"); Wilbourne v. Wilbourne, 748 So. 2d 184, 187-88 (Miss. Ct. App. 1999) (same). To date, the Mississippi court has not awarded separate maintenance to a husband deserted by his wife. *But see* Steen v. Steen, 641 So. 2d 1167, 1171 (Miss. 1994) (husband who did not want divorce was granted medical insurance for children and costs of court, in place of separate maintenance).

[210] In *Robinson v. Robinson*, 554 So. 2d 300, 306 (Miss. 1989), the court refused to address a husband's equal protection challenge since no separate maintenance was awarded. The court did state that *Orr v. Orr* and the resulting statutory amendment for alimony was "inapplicable" to a case where divorce is not granted, and that, in the proper case, "the governmental objectives in separate maintenance suits will have to be addressed." *Id.*

§ 1.08[1]   **MISSISSIPPI FAMILY LAW**

forceable since women were emancipated from the disabilities of coverture in 1880.[211] Because of the potential for abuse, however, some interspousal agreements and transfers are prohibited or closely reviewed to protect the rights of third parties. Contracts between spouses for labor and services are void, but business partnership agreements are enforceable. Interspousal conveyances are carefully scrutinized and may be subordinated to creditors' claims.

[1] Contracts for labor or services. In some states, contracts to pay for performance of spousal duties, such as childcare or housework, are not enforceable.[212] The Mississippi code provides that contracts for work and labor between husband and wife are void,[213] in part to protect third-party creditors.[214] Thus, a wife's contract retaining her lawyer/husband and pledging real property as payment was void.[215] The prohibition does not extend to business partnerships between husband and wife.[216] When a wife claimed assets of the couple's business titled in her husband's name, he argued that their agreement was void because it was based on her labor. The court held that the agreement was based upon an enforceable partnership entitling the wife to division of partnership assets.[217] Similarly, the statute did not prohibit an accounting and contribution action between spouses who owned real property as tenants in common.[218]

[2] Conveyances. In the absence of statutory authority to the contrary, conveyances between husband and wife are governed by the same rules as conveyances between unrelated individuals.[219] Both the general recording statute and prohibition against fraudulent conveyances apply to interspousal transfers. Interspousal gifts are subject to some restrictions not applicable to other conveyances.

A recorded conveyance between spouses is generally valid and enforceable. An unrecorded conveyance is subject to the rights of subsequent bona fide purchasers and lien creditors. An unrecorded conveyance not supported by consideration is also subject to the rights of general creditors.

[a] Priority of bona fide purchasers. The general rule preferring subsequent bona fide purchasers over holders of unrecorded conveyances applies to spouses. Any

---

[211] *See* Wyatt v. Wyatt, 32 So. 317, 318 (Miss. 1902) ("Since the adoption of the Code of 1880, . . . the validity of a contract between [spouses] cannot be questioned in judicial tribunals of this state; and such contracts may be enforced by one against the other."); *see also* Jones v. Jones, 55 So. 361, 361 (Miss. 1911) (after removal of disabilities of coverture, married woman can enter into partnership with husband).

[212] *See* GREGORY ET AL., *supra* note 47, § 4.04, at 102 (courts reason that the agreement is based upon a preexisting duty and therefore lacks consideration).

[213] MISS. CODE ANN. § 93-3-7 (2004).

[214] *See* Martin v. First Nat'l Bank, 164 So. 896, 899-900 (Miss. 1936) ("men and women living together as husband and wife could so easily, on account of their relation to each other, concoct contracts for work and labor . . . to the hurt of the public").

[215] *See* Martin v. First Nat'l Bank, 164 So. 896, 900-01 (Miss. 1936).

[216] *See* Horton v. Boatright, 97 So. 2d 637, 641 (Miss. 1957) (enforcing accounting with respect to partnership).

[217] *See* McGehee v. McGehee, 85 So. 2d 799, 804 (Miss. 1956).

[218] *See* Horton v. Boatright, 97 So. 2d 637, 641 (Miss. 1957) (application of income from joint operation of property applied to debts and liens does not contravene statute).

[219] Detrio v. Boylan, 190 F.2d 40, 43 (5th Cir. 1951) (noting, however, that such conveyances must be "carefully scrutinized on account of the temptation to give an unfair advantage to the wife over other creditors").

THE MARRIAGE RELATIONSHIP § 1.08[2][b]

unrecorded transfer of land from one spouse to the other will be junior in priority to a subsequent purchaser or lien creditor who was not aware of the conveyance.[220] The rule applies even if the interspousal conveyance was for good consideration. However, the statute's protection for creditors does not extend to general creditors without a lien on the property in question.[221]

[b] Priority of general creditors. In addition to the general recording rules, Mississippi law protects general creditors against an unrecorded interspousal conveyance if the conveyance was a gift. The relevant statute provides that conveyances between husband and wife without consideration are not valid against "any third person" unless the conveyance is in writing, acknowledged, and recorded.[222] In contrast to the general recording statute, "third parties" include general creditors without a lien against the property.[223] However, the protection extends only to creditors or those who claim an interest in the property.[224] The statute does not protect potential heirs seeking to set aside an unrecorded gift of land to the deceased's wife.[225]

It is irrelevant whether the creditor's claim arose before or after the interspousal transfer. Thus, a husband's unrecorded gift to his wife was invalid against a subsequent creditor whose claim arose after the transfer was made but before it was recorded.[226] The court explained the reason underlying the stricter rule for spouses: "The evil sought to be guarded against was the frequent perpetration of frauds by pretended transfers of property between husbands and wives, and the very great difficulty of detecting them."[227]

The statutory protection for general creditors applies only to gifts. Conveyances between spouses for consideration are valid against general creditors even if made and recorded after the creditor's interest arose.[228] A husband's transfer of land to his wife in satisfaction of a debt was valid against a general creditor whose debt arose before the transfer. The court noted that a debtor has a right, outside bankruptcy, to prefer one creditor over another, even if the creditor is his wife. However, there must be clear and convincing proof of the existence of a valid debt, the basis for and amount of the debt,

---

[220] *See* MISS. CODE ANN. § 89-5-5 (1999) ("Every conveyance, . . . shall take effect, as to all creditors and subsequent purchasers for a valuable consideration without notice, only from the time when delivered to the clerk to be recorded.").

[221] *See* Laurel Oil & Fertilizer Co. v. Horne, 57 So. 624, 625-26 (Miss. 1912) (lien creditor only); Loughridge v. Bowland, 52 Miss. 546, 558 (Miss. 1876) (creditor must have right to proceed against property in question before he can object to the conveyance).

[222] *See* MISS. CODE ANN. § 93-3-9 (2004) (possession by the grantee does not give notice to third parties).

[223] *See* Morgan v. Sauls, 413 So. 2d 370, 375 (Miss. 1982) (legislature imposed more stringent rule on transfers between spouses).

[224] *See* Fed. Credit Co. v. Scoggins, 130 So. 153, 154 (Miss. 1930).

[225] *See* Self v. King, 87 So. 489, 490 (Miss. 1921) (heirs are not creditors, purchasers, or persons with a claim to the property; they stand in the shoes of the deceased).

[226] Hudson v. Allen, 313 So. 2d 401, 403 (Miss. 1975) (emphasizing that the deed to the wife was without consideration); *see* McCrory v. Donald, 80 So. 643, 645 (Miss. 1919) (deed to wife without consideration void where recorded after debt arose).

[227] Hudson v. Allen, 313 So. 2d 401, 403 (Miss. 1975).

[228] Barbee v. Pigott, 507 So. 2d 77, 83-85 (Miss. 1987); *see* Hudson v. Allen, 313 So. 2d 401, 402-03 (Miss. 1975) (emphasizing that the deed to the wife was without consideration); Rollings v. Rosenbaum, 148 So. 384, 385 (Miss. 1933); Burks v. Moody, 106 So. 528, 529 (Miss. 1926).

§ 1.08[c]   **MISSISSIPPI FAMILY LAW**

and that the conveyance was in consideration of the debt.[229]

   [c] Fraudulent transfers. The Mississippi Uniform Fraudulent Conveyances Act provides that a transfer intended to defraud creditors is fraudulent as against a creditor, whether the creditor's claim arose before or after the transfer.[230] The statute contains a list of factors that courts should consider in determining whether a transfer was fraudulent. One factor is whether the transfer was to an insider, including a relative.[231] A transfer to a good faith purchaser for value is not fraudulent.[232] However, where there is a transfer to an insider for an antecedent debt, at a time when the debtor was insolvent, and the insider was aware of the insolvency, there "will be a strong presumption of fraud."[233]

   The Mississippi Supreme Court, interpreting the prior fraudulent transfers act, held that a transfer between husband and wife will not be presumed fraudulent simply because the grantor had outstanding debts; however, "[t]ransactions between husband and wife will be viewed with suspicion and, to prevent fraud as to creditors, they will be closely scrutinized to see that they are fair and honest."[234]

§ 1.09 TORT ACTIONS

   At common law, the status of marriage both created and destroyed rights of action in tort. Because of the notion of marital "oneness," marriage negated any right in one spouse to sue the other in tort for injuries. At the same time, the union created marital rights and obligations; injury to those rights by a third person gave rise to a cause of action in tort.

   [1] Tort actions between spouses. Litigation of property rights between spouses was authorized more than one hundred years ago with passage of the Married Women's Property Acts. In contrast, personal injury suits between spouses were barred until fairly recently.[235] Tort immunity was justified as a means of preserving marital harmony and preventing fraud by spouses on insurance companies.[236] Growing dissatisfaction with the doctrine in the last few decades finally resulted in its abrogation in most states.

   [a] Tort immunity. In 1988, the Mississippi Supreme Court abolished inter-

---

[229] Barbee v. Pigott, 507 So. 2d 77, 87 (Miss. 1987).

[230] MISS. CODE ANN. § 15-3-107 (2010).

[231] MISS. CODE ANN. § 15-3-101(g)(i)(1) (2010).

[232] MISS. CODE ANN. § 15-3-113(1) (2010).

[233] MISS. CODE ANN. § 15-3-107(2)(n), (3) (2010).

[234] Fid. & Deposit Co. v. Lovell, 108 F. Supp. 360, 363-64 (S.D. Miss. 1952) (finding transfer to wife shortly after claims filed against husband, without consideration and recording, fraudulent).

[235] *See* McNeal v. Adm'r of Estate of McNeal, 254 So. 2d 521, 522-23 (Miss. 1971) (one spouse has no right of action against the other to recover damages for personal injuries caused by the other); Ensminger v. Campbell, 134 So. 2d 728, 732 (Miss. 1961) (wife had no cause of action against former husband's estate for injuries in automobile accident); Ensminger v. Ensminger, 77 So. 2d 308, 309 (Miss. 1955) (wife's suit for injuries caused by husband's negligent operation of automobile, dismissed as no liability exists between husband and wife for personal tort).

[236] *See* GREGORY ET AL., *supra* note 47, § 7.02, at 194.

THE MARRIAGE RELATIONSHIP   § 1.09[1][b]

spousal tort immunity, permitting a woman's damages suit against her ex-husband based on physical abuse during the marriage.[237] The court stated that (1) the notion of marital "oneness" is no longer a viable legal concept; (2) the argument that marital tort suits will endanger domestic tranquility is "illusory"; and (3) permitting suits between spouses will no more promote fraud than in other litigation.[238] Accordingly, spouses may sue one another for both intentional torts and negligent acts.

[b] Tort actions for domestic violence. In recent years, victims of domestic violence have sought personal injury damages in suits based on assault, battery, and intentional infliction of emotional distress.[239] The relationship between these suits and divorce actions raises difficult procedural issues. These actions are discussed in detail in Chapter V.

[2] Tort actions against third parties. A spouse who has lost conjugal rights may have a cause of action against a third party who caused the loss. Actions against third parties range from modern wrongful death actions to the historic common law "heart balm" actions.

[a] Loss of consortium. Loss of consortium is an action for loss of a spouse's services and companionship as a result of injuries caused by a third person. Prior to 1968, Mississippi followed the common law rule that only a husband had a cause of action for loss of consortium.[240] The Mississippi Code was amended in 1968 to provide for a wife's cause of action for loss of consortium as a result of her husband's injury.[241]

[i] Nature of action. The action grows out of the loss of conjugal rights, defined as the "society, companionship, love, affection, aid, services, support, sexual relations and the comfort of [a spouse] . . . the right to live together in the same house, to eat at the same table, and to participate together in the activities, duties, and responsibilities necessary to make a home."[242] Damages are limited to recovery for loss of society and companionship, sexual relationship, and physical assistance.[243] The action does not include damages for loss of financial assistance or medical costs since the

---

[237] Burns v. Burns, 518 So. 2d 1205, 1209 (Miss. 1988) (marital harmony already destroyed; possibility of fraud exists in all lawsuits).

[238] Burns v. Burns, 518 So. 2d 1205, 1208-10 (Miss. 1988).

[239] *See generally* Clare Dalton, *Domestic Violence, Domestic Torts and Divorce: Constraints and Possibilities*, 31 NEW ENG. L. REV. 319 (1997); Douglas D. Scherer, *Tort Remedies for Victims of Domestic Abuse*, 43 S.C. L. REV. 543 (1992); George L. Blum, *Intentional Infliction of Distress in Marital Context*, 110 A.L.R. 5th 371 (2009).

[240] *See* Simpson v. Poindexter, 133 So. 2d 286, 288 (Miss. 1961); Nash v. Mobile & O.R. Co., 116 So. 100, 101-02 (Miss. 1928); *cf.* Brahan v. Meridian Light & Ry. Co., 83 So. 467, 467 (Miss. 1919) (husband's right to action for loss of consortium); Palmer v. Clarksdale Hosp., 57 So. 2d 476, 478 (Miss. 1952) (same), *overruled on other grounds by* McCoy v. Colonial Baking Co., 572 So. 2d 850 (Miss. 1990).

[241] *See* MISS.CODE ANN. § 93-3-1 (2004) ("A married woman shall have a cause of action for loss of consortium through negligent injury of her husband.").

[242] Tribble v. Gregory, 288 So. 2d 13, 16 (Miss. 1974), *overruled on other grounds by* Choctaw, Inc. v. Wichner, 521 So. 2d 878 (Miss. 1988).

[243] Am. Nat'l Ins. Co. v. Hogue, 749 So. 2d 1254, 1262 (Miss. Ct. App. 2000).

§ 1.09[2][a][ii]   **MISSISSIPPI FAMILY LAW**

injured spouse's action includes recovery for those items.[244]

    [ii] Relation to injured spouse's suit. A suit for loss of consortium is a derivative action; it depends on the right of the injured spouse to recover.[245] Defenses applicable to the injured spouse's suit, such as contributory negligence[246] or assumption of the risk,[247] also apply to the uninjured spouse's suit. Similarly, an unfavorable judgment for the injured spouse collaterally estops the uninjured spouse from prosecuting a consortium action.[248] On the other hand, a favorable judgment for the injured spouse does not ensure a recovery for loss of consortium. Recovery by the injured spouse establishes negligence but does not necessarily establish that the uninjured spouse suffered damages.[249] An action for loss of consortium survives the plaintiff's death.[250]

    [iii] Statute of limitations. Courts have reached different results as to the appropriate statute of limitations for loss of consortium claims. Some hold that because the action is derivative, loss of consortium is barred when the statute runs on the injured spouse's claim.[251] Others have applied the general statute of limitations to the loss of consortium claim even though the injured spouse's suit is covered by a specific statute of limitations.[252]

    [b] Wrongful death actions. One whose spouse dies as the result of a third person's actions may bring a wrongful death suit for damages that could have been recovered by the decedent and for medical and funeral expenses.[253] Damages resulting from the wrongful death of a spouse are divided equally between the deceased's spouse and children.[254] If the deceased has no children, all damages are awarded to the surviving spouse.[255]

    [3] Heart balm actions. The common law "heart balm" torts of alienation of affection and criminal conversation originated in the notion that wives were the chattel of

---

    [244] Tribble v. Gregory, 288 So. 2d 13, 16-17 (Miss. 1974).

    [245] Lindsey v. Sears Roebuck & Co., 846 F. Supp. 501, 507 (S.D. Miss. 1993) ("loss of consortium claim is wholly dependent upon a recovery of the primary claim of the injured spouse").

    [246] *See* Choctaw, Inc. v. Wichner, 521 So. 2d 878, 879 (Miss. 1988); Palmer v. Clarksdale Hosp., 57 So. 2d 476, 479 (1952).

    [247] *See* Byrd v. Matthews, 571 So. 2d 258, 260 (Miss. 1990).

    [248] In *McCoy v. Colonial Baking Co.,* 572 So. 2d 850, 853-54 (Miss. 1990), the court overruled its "outdated" position that loss of consortium was not barred by failure of the injured spouse's action. Some states require that both spouses sue in the same action. *See* CLARK, JR., *supra* note 7, § 11.3, at 392.

    [249] *See* Alldread v. Bailey, 626 So. 2d 99, 102-03 (Miss. 1993); *see also* Purdon v. Locke, 807 So. 2d 373, 377 (Miss. 2001) (evidence sufficient for jury to find loss of consortium); Am. Nat'l Ins. Co. v. Hogue, 749 So. 2d 1254, 1263 (Miss. Ct. App. 2000) (if evidence of loss of consortium is uncontradicted, some damages, even if minimal, are due).

    [250] Flight Line, Inc. v. Tanksley, 608 So. 2d 1149, 1169 (Miss. 1992) (action may be brought by estate).

    [251] *See* Kolar v. Chicago, 299 N.E.2d 479, 482 (Ill. App. Ct. 1973) (citing cases).

    [252] *See* Amer v. Akron City Hosp., 351 N.E.2d 479, 484 (Ohio 1976).

    [253] MISS. CODE ANN. § 11-7-13 (2004); *cf.* Burns v. Burns, 31 So. 3d 1227, 1232 (Miss. Ct. App. 2009) (premarital agreement did not bar husband from participating in a wrongful death settlement stemming from deceased wife's accident).

    [254] MISS. CODE ANN. § 11-7-13 (2004) ("children" includes descendants of a deceased child; descendants take the share of the deceased child by representation). In the case of nonmarital children and a natural father, the survivor must establish a right to inherit from the deceased under MISS. CODE ANN. § 91-1-15 (2004).

    [255] MISS. CODE ANN. § 11-7-13 (2004).

THE MARRIAGE RELATIONSHIP   § 1.09[3][a]

their husbands.[256] Alienation of affection actions are brought against a third party who deprives the plaintiff of the spouse's affections, while suits for criminal conversation seek recovery for a third party's adultery with the plaintiff's spouse. Mississippi has abolished the tort of criminal conversation but continues to recognize the action for alienation of affection.

The action for breach of promise to marry provided recovery for loss of reputation, social status, and support when a woman's fiancée refused to go through with the wedding. Although no breach of promise cases have been reported for fifty years in Mississippi, the action has not been abolished.

[a] **Alienation of affection.** The tort of alienation of affection allows a plaintiff whose spouse's affections have been diverted to recover damages from the responsible third party. To succeed, the plaintiff must show (1) wrongful conduct by the third party; (2) loss of the spouse's affection; and (3) a causal connection between the conduct and the loss.[257] The plaintiff must prove that the spouse was induced to abandon the relationship through active interference on the part of the defendant. A plaintiff proved active interference by showing that the defendant had an adulterous relationship with his wife and provided her with substantial sums of money, even though the defendant and wife testified that the marriage was "over" before the affair. The jury awarded him $750,000.[258]

Adultery is not a necessary element of the tort, but proof of adultery gives rise to a presumption of malice, which permits punitive damages.[259] A plaintiff proved alienation without proof of adultery by showing that the defendant provided the plaintiff's husband with a free vehicle, a place in her home to live, financed his divorce, and provided him with other funds.[260]

Damages for alienation of affection include damages for loss of consortium as well as physical and emotional injuries. A plaintiff may also recover for other expenses caused by the defendant's conduct, including lost wages, medical bills, private investigator's fees, and attorneys' fees.[261]

---

[256] Saunders v. Alford, 607 So. 2d 1214, 1215 (Miss. 1992).

[257] Saunders v. Alford, 607 So. 2d 1214, 1215 (Miss. 1992). Evidence of the plaintiff's prior affair is admissible as proof that the loss of affection was caused by the plaintiff's, rather than the defendant's, actions. Bland v. Hill, 735 So. 2d 414, 419 (Miss. 1999) (admitting evidence of affair ten years earlier).

[258] Fitch v. Valentine, 959 So. 2d 1012 (Miss. 2007). *But see* Pierce v. Cook, 992 So. 2d 612, 615 (Miss. 2008) (defendant's affair with plaintiff's wife began after plaintiff decided to remain in California rather than return to Mississippi where his wife lived); *cf.* Children's Medical Group v. Philips, 940 So. 2d 931 (Miss. 2006) (trial court did not err in denying hospital's motion to dismiss husband's alienation of affection action against hospital that employed wife and wife's lover).

[259] Walter v. Wilson, 228 So. 2d 597, 598 (Miss. 1969). Adultery must be alleged in the complaint or evidence of adultery will be excluded. Bland v. Hill, 735 So. 2d 414, 419 (Miss. 1999). In a recent case, *Gorman v. McMahon*, 792 So. 2d 307, 313 (Miss. Ct. App. 2001), the court seemed to assume causation upon proof of adultery. The court found "of no relevance" to the claim the allegation that defendant Gorman did not initiate the affair. The affair occurred while the wife was married and "served to transfer any affections that Louise harbored for Charles to Gorman." *Id.*

[260] Kirk v. Koch, 607 So. 2d 1220, 1224 (Miss. 1992) (upholding verdict of $50,000 for wronged wife).

[261] Gorman v. McMahon, 792 So. 2d 307, 314 (Miss. Ct. App. 2001). The plaintiff suffered depression and physical problems as a result of the affair and divorce, which led to loss of wages, medical bills, and private investigator and attorneys' fees in the divorce. *Id.* The court considered an alienation of affection action by a wife against her father-in-law in *Tucker v. Tucker*, 19 So. 955, 956 (Miss. 1896). The court held that the father-in-law was not liable in tort for encouraging his son to end the relationship where the father's motives were his son's well-being rather than malice. *Id.*

§1.09[3][b]   **MISSISSIPPI FAMILY LAW**

The applicable statute of limitations is the general three-year statute rather than the one-year statute applicable to some intentional torts.[262] The statute of limitations on an action for alienation of affection begins to run when the loss of affection "is finally accomplished."[263] The court rejected a husband's arguments that the action accrued in 2003 when he learned of his wife's affair and filed for divorce – the critical period is when the spouse having the affair becomes alienated, not when the innocent spouse learns of the affair.[264]

In a 2007 case, the Mississippi Supreme Court refused to join the majority of states that have abolished the tort "[i]n the interest of protecting the marriage relationship and providing a remedy for intentional conduct which causes a loss of consortium."[265]

[b] Criminal conversation. The tort of criminal conversation arose from a single act of adultery with a married person. It was designed to protect a spouse's right to an exclusive sexual relationship within marriage.[266] While the Mississippi Supreme Court affirmed the continuing vitality of alienation of affection suits,[267] it abolished the tort of criminal conversation in 1992.[268] As reasons for its holding, the court noted that (1) no defenses are available against the claim; (2) the action may provide a windfall to a plaintiff whose marriage is already destroyed; and (3) rights of consortium are already protected by the tort of alienation of affection.[269]

[c] Breach of promise to marry. The old tort of breach of promise to marry has been abolished in many states. In states that still recognize the action, damages may be available for mental suffering, as well as for financial loss, including expenditures in anticipation of the wedding. The Supreme Court of Washington held that a plaintiff could not recover for lost social position or the financial value of the anticipated marriage but could recover for foreseeable expenditures in reliance on the promise and for mental anguish, loss of reputation, and injury to health.[270] The South Carolina Supreme Court reaffirmed the viability of the action in 1983, allowing damages for mental an-

---

[262] *See* Carr v. Carr, 784 So. 2d 227, 230 (Miss. Ct. App. 2000) (applying three-year statute of Miss. CODE ANN. § 15-1-49); Brister v. Dunaway, 115 So. 36, 38 (Miss. 1927) (then six-year general statute of limitations), *overruled by* Saunders v. Alford, 607 So. 2d 1214 (Miss. 1992).

[263] Overstreet v. Merlos, 570 So. 2d 1196, 1198 (Miss. 1990) (cause of action is not barred because of divorce action).

[264] Hancock v. Watson, 962 So. 2d 627 (Miss. Ct. App. 2007) (wife's affections may not have been alienated – she remained with husband after the affair and had two more children with him).

[265] Fitch v. Valentine, 959 So. 2d 1012 (Miss. 2007). Justice Dickinson specially concurred, stating that the tort, established to protect a man's property interest in his wife, has no modern purpose and does more harm than good. *Id.* at 1030 (Dickinson, J., specially concurring); *cf.* Baker, Donelson, Bearman, Caldwell & Berkowitz, P.C. v. Seay, 42 So. 3d 474, 487-89 (Miss. 2010) (attorney's affair with client's wife did not breach fiduciary duty to client).

[266] *See* Walter v. Wilson, 228 So. 2d 597, 598 (Miss. 1969) ("husband is entitled to the services and companionship and consortium of his wife"), *overruled by* Saunders v. Alford, 607 So. 2d 1214 (Miss. 1992). Since the wife was considered the husband's property, adultery with her was a violation of his property rights. *Saunders*, 607 So. 2d at 1216.

[267] *See* Bland v. Hill, 735 So. 2d 414, 418 (Miss. 1999) (abolishing tort would send message that marriage relationship is devalued); *see also* Overstreet v. Merlos, 570 So. 2d 1196, 1198 (Miss. 1990); Camp v. Robert, 462 So. 2d 726, 726 (Miss. 1985), *overruled by* Saunders v. Alford, 607 So. 2d 1214 (Miss. 1992).

[268] Saunders v. Alford, 607 So. 2d 1214, 1219 (Miss. 1992).

[269] Saunders v. Alford, 607 So. 2d 1214, 1219 (Miss. 1992).

[270] Stanard v. Bolin, 565 P.2d 94, 97-98 (Wash. 1977).

THE MARRIAGE RELATIONSHIP   § 1.10

guish as well as for financial loss and expenditures in anticipation of a wedding.[271] And an Ohio court held that although the heart balm statute abolished recovery for mental suffering and damage to reputation, a jilted fiancée could recover for financial losses under an unjust enrichment theory.[272]

Although no case has been reported in Mississippi in a half-century, the action has not been abolished. The only reported Mississippi cases deal with the defense that the plaintiff is lacking in chastity. In 1928, the Mississippi Supreme Court held that "if the defendant should ascertain that his proposed bride is indelicate, immodest, and indecent in her conduct and speech, the probabilities are that the relation to be assumed would be so unbearable as that the defendant, having breached his contract on that account, ought not to suffer so much damages as in a case where he simply violated his obligation and breached his contract without such persuading, moving, mitigating circumstances."[273]

§ 1.10 Evidentiary rules

Two rules of evidence prevent spouses from testifying against each other. First, the common law rule that spouses are not competent witnesses against each other prohibits testimony in trial or discovery except in limited circumstances. Second, the marital privilege prevents a spouse from testifying regarding confidential communications.

[1] Competency to testify. By statute, spouses "shall not be competent as a witness and shall not be required to answer interrogatories or to make discovery of any matters" in any action where one is a party litigant without the consent of both spouses.[274] Notwithstanding the general prohibition, spouses may testify against each other "in all controversies between them." In addition, spouses may be compelled to testify against each other in any prosecution for a criminal act against a child, for contributing to the neglect or delinquency of a child, for desertion or nonsupport of a child under the age of sixteen, or for abandonment of a child.[275]

Unless one of the exceptions applies, a spouse's testimony is admissible only if both spouses agree. One spouse's consent to waive the privilege is not sufficient.[276] The rule does not prohibit former spouses from testifying against each other, even with regard to matters that occurred during marriage, so long as the testimony does not reveal privileged communications.[277]

[2] Marital privilege. The marital privilege prevents a spouse from testifying

---

[271] Bradley v. Somers, 322 S.E.2d 665, 666-67 (S.C. 1984).

[272] Wilson v. Dabo, 461 N.E.2d 8, 9 (Ohio Ct. App. 1983). For a full survey of cases, see *Measure and Elements of Damages for Breach of Contract to Marry*, 73 A.L.R. 2d 553 § 20.

[273] Carney v. McGilvray, 119 So. 157, 160 (Miss. 1928); *see* Freed v. Killman, 6 So. 2d 909, 909-10 (1942) (court did not err in allowing testimony of plaintiff's chastity; lack of chastity may be considered in mitigation of damages in a breach of marriage suit).

[274] Miss. Code Ann. § 13-1-5 (2002).

[275] Miss. Code Ann. § 13-1-5 (2002); *see* Miss. R. Evid. 601.

[276] Outlaw v. State, 43 So. 2d 661, 664 (Miss. 1949).

[277] Holden v. State, 399 So. 2d 1343, 1345 (Miss. 1981) (ex-wife could testify in criminal trial regarding husband's actions during marriage).

§ 1.11   MISSISSIPPI FAMILY LAW

regarding confidential communications,[278] even after the marriage is terminated by divorce.[279] A communication is deemed confidential "if it is made privately by any person to his or her spouse and is not intended for disclosure to any other person."[280] Thus, a communication made in the presence of a third party is not intended to be confidential.[281] An exception is made if a spouse is charged with a crime against a minor child, a crime against a person who lives in either spouse's household, or a crime against the other spouse's person or property.[282] The privilege may be claimed by the spouse making or receiving the confidence and can be waived if both spouses consent.[283]

§ 1.11 CRIMES BETWEEN SPOUSES: MARITAL RAPE

Marital rape was not a crime under the common law. A man could not be guilty of raping his wife because "the wife hath given herself up in this kind unto her husband, which she cannot retract."[284] All states now recognize marital rape as a crime, although a number of states impose limits on the action such as requiring aggravating circumstances.[285]

Mississippi has abolished the marital exemption for forcible rape or rape accomplished by administration of drugs.[286] But the exemption still prohibits prosecution of a cohabiting spouse for the crime of sexual battery.[287]

§ 1.12 MEDICAL DECISION-MAKING

Two very different circumstances raise issues regarding a spouse's right to make medical decisions for the other: when a husband wishes to veto a wife's choice to abort a fetus and when a spouse becomes incompetent to make medical decisions. United States constitutional law governs a wife's right to choose abortion, while other medical decision-making between spouses is controlled by state law.

[1] Abortion and spousal consent requirements. The Supreme Court established

---

[278] "The spousal privilege has ancient roots and prohibited a wife from testifying against her husband based upon the concept that husband and wife were one entity. Since the woman held no separate legal existence in medieval times, "the husband was that entity." Shell v. State, 554 So. 2d 887, 893 (Miss. 1989) (quoting Trammel v. United States, 445 U.S. 40, 44 (1980)), *overruled by* Shell v. State, 595 So. 2d 1323 (Miss. 1992).

[279] Dycus v. State, 396 So. 2d 23, 28 (Miss. 1981) (marital communications made with expectation of privacy may not be revealed after divorce). In *Fisher v. State*, 690 So. 2d 268, 272 (Miss. 1996), the court noted the difference between Rule 601 spousal immunity and the marital privilege – the non-offender spouse may be called to testify in a criminal trial but the defendant spouse may still invoke marital privilege if the exceptions of Rule 504 do not apply.

[280] MISS. R. EVID. 504.

[281] *See* Roland v. State, 882 So. 2d 262, 265-66 (Miss. Ct. App. 2004) (wife could testify to statements of husband in presence of man he later killed; not confidential); *see also* Fanning v. State, 497 So. 2d 70, 74 (Miss. 1986).

[282] MISS. R. EVID. 504(d) (also including a crime against a third person in the course of committing a crime against a minor child or someone residing in one spouse's household).

[283] Martin v. State, 773 So. 2d 415, 417-18 (Miss. Ct. App. 2000) (husband waived privilege by calling wife to testify).

[284] *See* 1 HALE, HISTORY OF PLEAS OF THE CROWN, 629, *quoted in* ELLMAN ET AL., FAMILY LAW, 175 (3d ed. 1988).

[285] ELLMAN ET AL., *supra* note 284, at 176.

[286] *See* MISS. CODE ANN. § 97-3-65(4)(b) (2006).

[287] MISS. CODE ANN. § 97-3-99 (2006) (defined as sexual intercourse without consent, as opposed to rape – forcible intercourse without consent).

THE MARRIAGE RELATIONSHIP   § 1.12[2]

a woman's right to choose abortion in *Roe v. Wade*,[288] holding that the right to privacy and freedom from bodily intrusion was not overridden by the state's interest in protecting life until the third trimester of pregnancy.[289] The Supreme Court subsequently struck down a Missouri statute requiring a husband's consent to a first-trimester abortion. Although it recognized the profound effects of a woman's abortion on her husband and on their marriage, the Court nonetheless held that a woman's privacy right outweighs her husband's interest in preventing an abortion.[290] Statutes requiring pre-abortion notice to the husband also violate a wife's right to privacy.[291]

Mississippi statutes do not require spousal consent or notification as a prerequisite to an abortion.[292] A husband is, however, provided a statutory action against a physician who performs an illegal, partial-birth abortion on his wife. The statute authorizes recovery of damages for psychological and physical injuries caused by the abortion and for statutory damages equal to three times the cost of the abortion.[293]

[2] Healthcare directives and surrogates. At common law and under the United States Constitution, an individual has a right to refuse life-preserving treatment.[294] If an individual lacks capacity to make healthcare decisions, however, the right of privacy does not allow a spouse to make decisions for the patient. If a healthcare provider refuses to follow a spouse's instructions, some authorization is necessary in the absence of a power of attorney.[295]

Mississippi law, modeled on the Uniform Health Care Directives Act, provides statutory authorization for spouses and other family members to assert the wishes of incompetent patients.[296] Under the Act, an individual may execute a healthcare directive stating specific wishes regarding medical treatment[297] and appointing an agent for healthcare decisions.[298] If the designated agent is a spouse, divorce or annulment automatically revokes the directive unless the divorce decree or healthcare directive provides otherwise.[299]

An agent's authority begins when the maker becomes incapacitated, as determined

---

[288] 410 U.S. 113 (1973).

[289] *Roe v. Wade* was subsequently modified in *Planned Parenthood v. Casey,* 510 U.S. 1309 (1994), which rejected the trimester approach and the strict scrutiny/compelling interest approach. The *Casey* court asked instead, "Does the particular state regulation place a substantial burden on the woman's right?" *Id.* at 1310.

[290] Planned Parenthood v. Danforth, 428 U.S. 52, 70 (1976).

[291] *See* Planned Parenthood v. Casey, 505 U.S. 833, 893-94 (1992). The Court struck down spousal notification requirements but upheld the requirement of a twenty-four hour waiting period. *Id.* at 885-87.

[292] *See* MISS. CODE ANN. § 41-41-33 (2009). The Mississippi constitution also guarantees freedom from bodily intrusion as part of the right of privacy and includes the woman's right to decide to have an abortion. The Mississippi court has adopted the less stringent *Casey* "substantial burden" test and held that a twenty-four hour waiting period and a requirement that two parents consent to a minor's abortion does not place an undue burden on the right. Pro-Choice Miss. v. Fordice, 716 So. 2d 645, 655-58 (Miss. 1998).

[293] *See* MISS. CODE ANN. § 41-41-73(3) (2009).

[294] *See* James F. Childress, *Refusal of Life-Saving Treatment by Adults*, 23 J. FAM. L. 191 (1984).

[295] *See* GREGORY ET AL., *supra* note 47, § 7.05, at 202 (must prove patient's wishes by clear and convincing evidence).

[296] *See* MISS. CODE ANN. § 41-41-203 (2009).

[297] MISS. CODE ANN. § 41-41-205(2) (2009).

[298] Health-care decisions include: (1) choice of health-care providers and institutions; (2) choice of tests, surgical procedures, medication, and orders not to resuscitate; and (3) directions to provide, withhold or withdraw artificial nutrition and hydration and other forms of healthcare. MISS. CODE ANN. § 41-41-203(h) (2009).

[299] MISS. CODE ANN. § 41-41-207(4) (2009).

§ 1.13   **MISSISSIPPI FAMILY LAW**

by the maker's primary physician.[300] The decision-making authority is automatically revoked when incapacity ends.[301] The agent is to make healthcare decisions in accordance with directives set out by the maker. If there are no specific directives, an agent is to make decisions based on the patient's best interests, considering the patient's values.[302] No judicial approval is necessary.[303]

In the absence of a healthcare directive, the Act authorizes surrogates to make healthcare decisions for a patient who lacks capacity. The Act provides a list of surrogates in order of preference, with the patient's spouse as the first choice of a surrogate.[304] An individual may disqualify certain persons from taking decision-making power as a surrogate by stating their disqualification in a healthcare directive.[305]

§ 1.13 CHOICE OF RESIDENCE

At common law, the right to choose a marital domicile belonged to the husband. The wife had a duty to follow him unless his choice was unreasonable or the move would endanger her health or well-being.[306] As late as 1949, the Mississippi Supreme Court suggested in dicta that a wife's unreasonable refusal to make her home in the city of her husband's choosing could constitute desertion.[307] Modern United States Supreme Court decisions[308] should invalidate common law rules placing choice of residence with the husband. In one of the few cases addressing the issue, the Louisiana Supreme Court held that a state statute requiring a wife to abide by her husband's choice of domicile was unconstitutional as a denial of equal protection.[309]

§ 1.14 SEPARATE MAINTENANCE

The common law action for separate maintenance provided support for a wife whose husband abandoned her without fault on her part. With the widespread adoption of no-fault divorce, the action is primarily of historical interest in most states. However, in the few states without no-fault divorce, couples may live separately for many years with no realistic prospect of divorce.[310] For that reason, separate maintenance remains

---

[300] MISS. CODE ANN. § 41-41-205(5) (2009).

[301] MISS. CODE ANN. § 41-41-205(5) (2009).

[302] MISS. CODE ANN. § 41-41-205(7) (2009).

[303] MISS. CODE ANN. § 41-41-205(8) (2009).

[304] MISS. CODE ANN. § 41-41-211 (2009). *But cf. In re* Estate of Ellis, 23 So. 3d 589, 599-00 (Miss. Ct. App. 2009) (not error to appoint a woman's granddaughter as conservator rather than her husband).

[305] MISS. CODE ANN. § 41-41-211(8) (2009).

[306] Ouzts v. Carroll, 199 So. 76, 77-78 (Miss. 1940) (finding husband acted without malice in seizing property owned by wife who would not follow him to chosen domicile); *see* Bilbo v. Bilbo, 177 So. 772, 776 (Miss. 1938) (woman's legal residence becomes that of her husband when she marries).

[307] *See* Starr v. Starr, 39 So. 2d 520, 522 (Miss. 1949) (rejecting husband's claim for divorce based on cruelty); *see also* Serio v. Serio, 94 So. 2d 799, 802 (Miss. 1957) (quoting *Ouzts* for proposition that wife has duty to abide by husband's reasonable choice of residence).

[308] *See* Orr v. Orr, 440 U.S. 268, 282-84 (1979) (invalidating state law providing alimony for women but not for men; old notions do not justify gender-based distinctions in family law).

[309] Crosby v. Crosby, 434 So. 2d 162, 163 (La. Ct. App. 1983) ("The very wording of [the statute] denies women equal protection of the laws.").

[310] Unless both parties agree to divorce, the party desiring divorce must be able to prove one of the twelve fault-based grounds for divorce. *See* discussion of Mississippi divorce grounds *infra* § 4.01[6].

THE MARRIAGE RELATIONSHIP §1.14[1]

a viable marital action in Mississippi.[311] Today, separate maintenance should be available to a husband or wife who is financially dependent on the other, and who is not substantially at fault in the separation.

[1] History and overview. Traditionally, a separate maintenance decree ordered a husband who abandoned his wife to provide her with adequate support. The Mississippi Supreme Court described the order as a "judicial command to the husband to resume cohabitation with his wife, or in default thereof, to provide suitable maintenance of her until such time as they may be reconciled."[312] Some states provide for support during separation through a decree of legal separation, or divorce from bed and board.[313] An order of legal separation specifically decrees that the parties will live separately, while a separate maintenance award orders the payor to return home or provide support.[314] Mississippi law does not provide for legal separation.[315]

[a] Judicial authority. The power of chancellors to order separate maintenance was first recognized in 1874. The Mississippi Supreme Court held that equity jurisdiction permitted an award to a wife abandoned by her husband without fault on her part. The court's holding was based in part on an 1874 divorce statute authorizing courts to "make all orders touching the care, custody and maintenance of the children of the marriage, and also touching the maintenance and alimony of the wife."[316] The court also held that a petition for separate maintenance may be filed independently of a divorce action or as an alternative to a request for divorce.[317]

[b] Gender equality. Family law experts uniformly agree that separate maintenance must be available to both husband and wife.[318] United States Supreme Court decisions in the 1970s established that gender-based distinctions in family law are, for the most part, unconstitutional.[319] Recent Mississippi separate maintenance cases still refer to the "husband's" duty of support;[320] however, the Mississippi Supreme Court has

---

[311] Separate maintenance cases still regularly make their way to the appellate courts. *See, e.g.*, Myers v. Myers, 881 So. 2d 180, 183 (Miss. 2004); Killen v. Killen, 54 So. 3d 869, 871-72, 874 (Miss. Ct. App. 2010) (separate maintenance properly awarded to wife who left home at her husband's request for a divorce and in fear of his temper); Diehl v. Diehl, 29 So. 3d 153, 156 (Miss. Ct. App. 2010) (wife not at fault; husband left her, taking funds from a joint account); Brown v. Brown, 817 So. 2d 588, 592 (Miss. Ct. App. 2002); Crenshaw v. Crenshaw, 767 So. 2d 272, 276 (Miss. Ct. App. 2000); Wilbourne v. Wilbourne, 748 So. 2d 184, 187 (Miss. Ct. App. 1999); Stanford v. Stanford, 734 So. 2d 359, 361 (Miss. Ct. App. 1999).

[312] Kennedy v. Kennedy, 650 So. 2d 1362, 1367 (Miss. 1995); *see also* Gray v. Gray, 484 So. 2d 1032, 1033 (Miss. 1986) (finding $250 a month inadequate support); McIntosh v. McIntosh, 977 So. 2d 1257, 1267 (Miss. Ct. App. 2008); Pool v. Pool, 989 So. 2d 920, 927 (Miss. Ct. App. 2008).

[313] *See* CLARK, JR., *supra* note 7, § 6.5, at 268 (noting that about one-half of states authorize legal separations).

[314] *See* CLARK, JR., *supra* note 7, § 6.5, at 267-68 (noting that there is actually little difference between the two orders).

[315] *See* Godwin v. Godwin, 758 So. 2d 384, 389 (Miss. 1999) (Prather, C.J., concurring in part and dissenting in part).

[316] *See* Garland v. Garland, 50 Miss. 694, 1874 WL 4630, at *14 (1874). The court relied on the same wording in the divorce statute in 1994 as authority for judicial recognition of equitable distribution. *See* Ferguson v. Ferguson, 639 So. 2d 921, 928 (Miss. 1994).

[317] *See* Garland v. Garland, 50 Miss. 694, 1874 WL 4630, at *7 (1874).

[318] *See, e.g.*, HAND, *supra* note 208, § 2-11, at 37 n.7; CLARK, JR., *supra* note 7, § 6.4, at 268.

[319] *See* Orr v. Orr, 440 U.S. 268, 282-83 (1979).

[320] *See* Stanford v. Stanford, 734 So. 2d 359, 360 (Miss. Ct. App. 1999) ("wife is entitled to be maintained in the

§ 1.14[1][c]   **MISSISSIPPI FAMILY LAW**

acknowledged in dicta that a unilateral duty to support is constitutionally suspect.[321]

[c] Scope. Separate maintenance orders may include a basic support award, orders for payment of specific expenses, child support, attorneys' fees, and temporary support. Some relief available at divorce is not available in a separate maintenance action – a court may not order relief that exceeds property rights between spouses during marriage. For example, a court may not award one spouse property owned solely by the other or order payment of lump sum support.[322]

[2] Basis for award. Separate maintenance is properly awarded to a recipient who is financially dependent on his or her spouse and who was not substantially at fault in the separation.[323] In addition, the petitioner must show willful abandonment and a failure to provide support.[324] The recipient need not be "totally blameless," so long as his or her conduct did not materially contribute to the separation.[325] Separate maintenance was denied when a wife's unfounded accusations, extreme threats, and persistent nagging were partly to blame for the separation.[326] And a husband whose religion was the source of marital discord was properly denied separate maintenance. After changing churches, he became controlling, demanded to be treated as the head of the household, and told his wife she was in danger of hellfire.[327]

Awards have been upheld, however, even though the marriage was admittedly argumentative and "unpleasant" on both sides, particularly if the husband left his wife for another woman.[328] A wife who was not "blameless" was nonetheless entitled to

---

same standard of living"); Wilbourne v. Wilbourne, 748 So. 2d 184, 187-88 (Miss. Ct. App. 1999) (same). To date, the Mississippi court has not awarded separate maintenance to a husband deserted by his wife. *But cf.* Steen v. Steen, 641 So. 2d 1167, 1171 (Miss. 1994) (husband who did not want divorce granted medical insurance for the children and costs of court in place of separate maintenance).

[321] In *Robinson v. Robinson*, 554 So. 2d 300, 306 (Miss. 1989), the court refused to address a husband's equal protection challenge since his wife was denied separate maintenance. The court did state that *Orr v. Orr* and the resulting statutory amendment for alimony was "inapplicable" to a case where divorce is not granted, and that, in the proper case, "the governmental objectives in separate maintenance suits will have to be addressed." *Id.*

[322] *See* discussion *infra* § 1.14[4].

[323] Thompson v. Thompson, 527 So. 2d 617, 621 (Miss. 1988); Bridges v. Bridges, 330 So. 2d 260, 262 (Miss. 1976).

[324] McIntosh v. McIntosh, 977 So. 2d 1257, 1268 (Miss. Ct. App. 2008).

[325] King v. King, 152 So. 2d 889, 890 (Miss. 1963) (rejecting analogy to rule that wife at fault may be entitled to alimony); *see* Robinson v. Robinson, 554 So. 2d 300, 304 (Miss. 1989). *But cf.* Brown v. Brown, 817 So. 2d 588, 592 (Miss. Ct. App. 2002) (remanded for chancellor to determine whether the wife should receive separate maintenance where there was no evidence "that the separation was *completely* her fault" (emphasis added)).

[326] Lynch v. Lynch, 616 So. 2d 294, 296 (Miss. 1993) (wife alienated husband and children, threatened suicide, accused husband of affairs); *see* Robinson v. Robinson, 554 So. 2d 300, 304 (Miss. 1989) (separate maintenance denied where wife's desire to live beyond husband's salary and intense arguments contributed to separation); G.B.W. v. E.R.W., 9 So. 3d 1200, 1207-08 (Miss. Ct. App. 2009) (husband not entitled to separate maintenance; wife granted divorce based on cruelty).

[327] Forthner v. Forthner, 52 So. 3d 1212, 1214, 1220 (Miss. Ct. App. 2010) (conduct not sufficient to constitute habitual cruelty).

[328] *See* Kergosien v. Kergosien, 471 So. 2d 1206, 1211 (Miss. 1985) (wife who argued with husband entitled to separate maintenance); Tackett v. Tackett, 967 So. 2d 1264 (Miss. Ct. App. 2007) (wife partly to blame for arguments, but husband left and refused to go to counseling); Brown v. Brown, 817 So. 2d 588, 592 (Miss. Ct. App. 2002) (court on remand should consider separate maintenance since separation was not "completely" wife's fault); Crenshaw v. Crenshaw, 767 So. 2d 272, 276 (Miss. Ct. App. 2000) (wife need not be perfect; separate maintenance properly awarded to wife whose husband had affair and left home); Wilbourne v. Wilbourne, 748 So. 2d 184, 187-88 (Miss. Ct. App. 1999) (finding wife did not materially contribute to separation); Shorter v. Shorter, 740 So. 2d 352, 355 (Miss. Ct. App. 1999)

THE MARRIAGE RELATIONSHIP   § 1.14[3]

separate maintenance – it was clear that her husband intended to leave the marriage and had no intention of reconciling, while it was equally clear that she was willing to work on the marriage.[329]

Fault sufficient to deny a wife's separate maintenance request is not identical to fault justifying a divorce. For example, a wife's conduct was not sufficient to constitute habitual, cruel, and inhuman treatment; however, because her conduct did materially contribute to the parties' separation, she was denied separate maintenance.[330] In one unusual case, a chancellor found that a wife was not entitled to separate maintenance but ordered her husband to continue paying her temporary support as an equitable measure.[331]

[3] Amount of award

[a] **Factors.** The goal of separate maintenance is to provide the normal support a spouse would have received in the intact marriage, without "unduly depleting" the other's estate.[332] To determine an appropriate amount of separate maintenance, a court applies the same factors used to determine permanent alimony:[333] (1) the health, earning capacity, entire source of income, and taxes of both husband and wife; (2) the reasonable needs of the petitioner and any child of the marriage; (3) the defendant's necessary living expenses; (4) resources available to the petitioner such as free use of home, furnishings, or automobile; and (5) other relevant facts and circumstances.[334] In at least one case, the court imputed income to a payor, awarding support based upon a husband's earning ability rather than his actual earnings.[335]

Because separate maintenance is based on continuation, rather than termination, of the marriage, a recipient may be entitled to support at a higher level than after divorce – separate maintenance requires support at the standard of living of the marriage, while in many divorces alimony is aimed at assisting the recipient to reenter the workforce.[336] For example, a court did not err in awarding a wife of twenty months one-half of her husband's net income as separate maintenance. She was in poor health, with a much

---

(wife need not be perfect; conduct did not materially contribute to separation); *see also* Diehl v. Diehl, 29 So. 3d 153, 156 (Miss. Ct. App. 2010) (wife not at fault; husband left her, taking funds from a joint account).

[329] Pool v. Pool, 989 So. 2d 920, 927-28 (Miss. Ct. App. 2008); *see also* Killen v. Killen, 54 So. 3d 869, 871-72, 874 (Miss. Ct. App. 2010) (separate maintenance properly awarded to wife who left home at her husband's request for a divorce and in fear of his temper); McIntosh v. McIntosh, 977 So. 2d 1257, 1268 (Miss. Ct. App. 2008).

[330] Robinson v. Robinson, 554 So. 2d 300, 304 (Miss. 1989).

[331] Miley v. Daniel, 37 So. 3d 84, 86 (Miss. Ct. App. 2009) (husband, who died while her appeal was pending, did not cross-appeal).

[332] *See* Thompson v. Thompson, 527 So. 2d 617, 622 (Miss. 1988); Diehl v. Diehl, 29 So. 3d 153, 156 (Miss. Ct. App. 2010); Pool v. Pool, 989 So. 2d 920, 927 (Miss. Ct. App. 2008); Honea v. Honea, 888 So. 2d 1192 (Miss. Ct. App. 2004).

[333] The modern factors for alimony were first set out in *Brabham v. Brabham*, 84 So. 2d 147, 153 (Miss. 1955). The factors were restated in *Armstrong v. Armstrong*, 618 So. 2d 1278, 1280 (Miss. 1993).

[334] *See* Crenshaw v. Crenshaw, 767 So. 2d 272, 276 (Miss. Ct. App. 2000) (citing *Brabham*, 84 So. 2d 153).

[335] *See* Crenshaw v. Crenshaw, 767 So. 2d 272, 277 (Miss. Ct. App. 2000) (husband capable of earning $9 per hour actually earning $5.50 delivering pizza; ordered to pay $1,086 a month from current salary of $2,300/month). For a discussion of cases imputing income in alimony cases, see *infra* § 9.04[4][a].

[336] For a discussion of rehabilitative alimony, see *infra* § 9.02[3]. *But cf.* Brown v. Brown, 817 So. 2d 588, 592 (Miss. Ct. App. 2002) (noting that there is little difference between the two awards; same principles apply to amount awarded).

35

§ 1.14[3][b]   **MISSISSIPPI FAMILY LAW**

lower income and earning capacity, and had no separate assets.[337] And a court properly awarded a wife $1,800 in separate maintenance without taking into account her separate funds of $67,000 and the fact that she allowed an adult daughter to live rent free in a separate property condominium. Her ability to provide for her daughter and her separate savings were part of the marital standard of living.[338]

[b] **Application.** The Mississippi Supreme Court upheld a separate maintenance award of 41% of a husband's gross monthly salary as support for his wife and children.[339] And 58% of a husband's adjusted income was properly awarded to maintain the family "in the same manner as if the husband and wife were cohabiting."[340] An award of $250 a month from a husband with savings of $140,000 and retirement income of $1,200 a month was inadequate separate maintenance.[341] A wife with income of $1,446 and expenses of $2,712 was properly awarded $500 a month and use of the home and car. Her husband (with income of $3,367 a month) was also ordered to pay homeowners', health, and car insurance, property taxes, and a portion of medical expenses and home and car repairs.[342] And a sixty-year-old wife of nineteen years, with income of $1,200 a month, was awarded $1,800 a month in separate maintenance from a husband with net monthly income of $5,500 and expenses of $2,387.[343] The supreme court held an award of separate maintenance excessive, however, when the husband was left with approximately fifty dollars a month after paying support.[344]

[c] **Direct payments to third parties.** Separate maintenance may take the form of payments directly to third parties. Courts have ordered defendants to pay medical insurance and out-of-pocket medical and dental expenses,[345] mortgage payments,[346] and to provide transportation and pay automobile expenses.[347] In addition, a court may award a recipient occupancy of the marital home even if it is titled in the other's name.[348]

---

[337] Tackett v. Tackett, 967 So. 2d 1264 (Miss. Ct. App. 2007).

[338] Diehl v. Diehl, 29 So. 3d 153, 156 (Miss. Ct. App. 2010) (wife not at fault; husband left her, taking funds from a joint account).

[339] *See* Robinson v. Robinson, 554 So. 2d 300, 305 (Miss. 1989).

[340] *See* Stanford v. Stanford, 734 So. 2d 359, 361-63 (Miss. Ct. App. 1999) (husband with monthly gross income of $12,758 and adjusted monthly income of $8,881 ordered to pay total of $5,176 in separate maintenance, child support, and mortgage payment).

[341] Gray v. Gray, 484 So. 2d 1032, 1033 (Miss. 1986).

[342] Pool v. Pool, 989 So. 2d 920, 923, 929 (Miss. Ct. App. 2008).

[343] Diehl v. Diehl, 29 So. 3d 153, 156 (Miss. Ct. App. 2010).

[344] *See* Williams v. Williams, 528 So. 2d 296, 297-98 (Miss. 1988) (award of $1,250 in maintenance and child support against husband with monthly income of $1,300 excessive).

[345] *See* Kennedy v. Kennedy, 662 So. 2d 179, 180 (Miss. 1995) (but requiring reduction of overall amount of award); Pool v. Pool, 989 So. 2d 920, 923 (Miss. Ct. App. 2008) (husband was ordered to pay homeowners', health, and car insurance, property taxes, and a portion of medical expenses and home and car repairs).

[346] *See* Stanford v. Stanford, 734 So. 2d 359, 360 (Miss. Ct. App. 1999) (husband ordered to pay mortgage of $2,544/month); Wilbourne v. Wilbourne, 748 So. 2d 184, 186 (Miss. Ct. App. 1999) (wife given possession of marital home; husband ordered to pay mortgage).

[347] *See* Kennedy v. Kennedy, 662 So. 2d 179, 180 (Miss. 1995); Wilbourne v. Wilbourne, 748 So. 2d 184, 186 (Miss. Ct. App. 1999) (transportation provided by husband).

[348] Kennedy v. Kennedy, 662 So. 2d 179, 181 (Miss. 1995). A court cannot, however, order that title to the home be transferred to a non-owning spouse. *See* Daigle v. Daigle, 626 So. 2d 140, 146 (Miss. 1993); Thompson v. Thompson, 527 So. 2d 617, 622-23 (Miss. 1988).

THE MARRIAGE RELATIONSHIP   § 1.14[3][d]

[d] Attorneys' fees and temporary support. A court may award suit money, attorneys' fees, and maintenance *pendente lite* in a separate maintenance action.[349] As in divorce actions, attorneys' fees awards must be based on need; a court erred in awarding fees in the absence of proof that a wife could not pay her attorney.[350]

[4] Property division and lump sum alimony

[a] Equitable distribution. The principles of equitable distribution do not apply except at divorce. A separate maintenance order cannot "confer [on the wife] any greater right than [she would have had] if cohabitation had continued."[351] With the exception of homestead property, a spouse has no right during marriage to property titled in the other's name.[352] Thus, a court may not divest one spouse of title to property as part of separate maintenance.[353] However, a lien may be imposed on a spouse's property to secure payment of a separate maintenance award.[354] And while a spouse who is sole owner of the marital home may not be divested of title, a court may award occupancy to the non-owning spouse.[355] Furthermore, other than homestead property,[356] a court may order division of jointly titled property or property titled in one spouse's name, to the extent that the other claims an interest apart from equitable distribution principles.[357]

[b] Lump sum support. An award of lump sum separate maintenance exceeds the authority of the court. As a nonmodifiable, vested right to payment, lump sum support is inconsistent with separate maintenance, which ceases if the payor returns to the recipient.[358]

---

[349] *See* Thompson v. Thompson, 527 So. 2d 617, 621-22 (Miss. 1988) (alimony *pendente lite* and attorneys' fees); Johnston v. Johnston, 179 So. 853, 854 (Miss. 1938) (same); Miley v. Daniel, 37 So. 3d 84, 86 (Miss. Ct. App. 2009) (award of temporary support); Crenshaw v. Crenshaw, 767 So. 2d 272, 277 (Miss. Ct. App. 2000) (attorneys' fees).

[350] Daigle v. Daigle, 626 So. 2d 140, 147 (Miss. 1993); Pool v. Pool, 989 So. 2d 920, 929 (Miss. Ct. App. 2008) (chancellor did not err in awarding wife attorneys' fees of $5,000 in a separate maintenance action based on need).

[351] Thompson v. Thompson, 527 So. 2d 617, 622 (Miss. 1988).

[352] *See* discussion of marital property rights *supra* § 1.05 (spouse must consent to transfer of homestead owned by the other).

[353] *See* Daigle v. Daigle, 626 So. 2d 140, 146 (Miss. 1993) (error for chancellor to divest husband of real property and profit-sharing funds); Bridges v. Bridges, 330 So. 2d 260, 264 (Miss. 1976) (husband cannot be ordered to sell the existing marital home and build another home for his wife); *cf.* Kennedy v. Kennedy, 662 So. 2d 179, 181 (Miss. 1995) (refusal to modify prior order would result in impermissible assets transfer since the husband's separate maintenance obligation exceeded his actual income necessitating sale of assets).

[354] *See* Daigle v. Daigle, 626 So. 2d 140, 147 (Miss. 1993) (lien on husband's assets warranted in light of his financial ventures); Shorter v. Shorter, 740 So. 2d 352, 354 (Miss. Ct. App. 1999) (lien to secure separate maintenance and child support).

[355] *See* Kennedy v. Kennedy, 662 So. 2d 179, 181 (Miss. 1995).

[356] See *infra* § 1.14[4][c].

[357] *See* Drummonds v. Drummonds, 156 So. 2d 819, 822 (Miss. 1963) (allowing division of jointly owned property); Duvall v. Duvall, 80 So. 2d 752, 756 (Miss. 1955) (emphasizing that property division is not permitted apart from equitable ownership).

[358] *See* Williams v. Williams, 528 So. 2d 296, 298 (Miss. 1988) (reversing award of $10,000 in lump sum maintenance); *see also* Weiss v. Weiss, 579 So. 2d 539, 541-42 (Miss. 1991) (distinguishing alimony and separate maintenance).

§ 1.14[4][c]   MISSISSIPPI FAMILY LAW

[c] Partition of jointly owned property. A chancellor may partition jointly owned property in a separate maintenance action. Spouses have an absolute right to partition jointly held property during marriage and therefore as part of separate maintenance.[359] Until recently, that right included a jointly owned homestead.[360] In 2009, the partition statute was amended to provide that jointly owned homestead property may only be partitioned by agreement.[361] Partition may not be ordered unless requested by one of the parties.[362]

[5] Child custody and support. A chancellor may determine custody and visitation[363] and order payment of child support in a separate maintenance action.[364] Child support is governed by the statutory guidelines.[365] While claims for child support and spousal support may be combined in one action, child support is an obligation independent of the separate maintenance action.[366] The Mississippi Supreme Court emphasized that a separate maintenance allowance and child support should be set out as separate and distinct obligations.[367] If the spouse receiving separate maintenance is the noncustodial parent, he or she may still be required to provide child support to the custodial spouse.[368]

[6] Order to reconcile. While an order of separate maintenance is designed to encourage a payor to reconcile with the recipient, a court lacked authority to enjoin a husband from living with another woman. A separate maintenance order directs the payor to resume living with the recipient or provide support; it cannot require them to live together.[369]

[7] Modification and termination. An order of separate maintenance may be modified based on a material change in circumstances arising after the original decree.[370] A chancellor erred in refusing to modify a separate maintenance award when

---

[359] *See* discussion of marital property rights *supra* § 1.05[3][f].

[360] Myers v. Myers, 881 So. 2d 180, 183 (Miss. 2004) (husband did not abandon request for partition by agreeing to proceed in action for separate maintenance rather than divorce).

[361] MISS. CODE ANN. § 11-21-1 (Supp. 2010).

[362] Bowen v. Bowen, 688 So. 2d 1374, 1382 (Miss. 1997) (wife should have requested partition to require sale).

[363] *See* Steen v. Steen, 641 So. 2d 1167, 1169 (Miss. 1994) (custody to wife); Johnston v. Johnston, 179 So. 853, 853-54 (Miss. 1938) (custody awarded to wife).

[364] *See* Robinson v. Robinson, 554 So. 2d 300, 304-05 (Miss. 1989); Boyett v. Boyett, 119 So. 299, 300-01 (Miss. 1928).

[365] *See* Stanford v. Stanford, 734 So. 2d 359, 362 (Miss. Ct. App. 1999) (child support guidelines applied to determine payment in separate maintenance action; husband ordered to pay 20% of adjusted gross income for two children).

[366] *See* Robinson v. Robinson, 554 So. 2d 300, 304-05 (Miss. 1989) (court reversed award of separate maintenance to wife who substantially contributed to marriage breakup but permitted award of child support); Boyett v. Boyett, 119 So. 299, 301 (Miss. 1928).

[367] *See* Robinson v. Robinson, 554 So. 2d 300, 304-05 (Miss. 1989).

[368] *See* Steen v. Steen, 641 So. 2d 1167, 1171 (Miss. 1994) (husband who did not want divorce granted a form of separate maintenance; case remanded to determine what child support he should pay to wife who had custody).

[369] *See* Wilbourne v. Wilbourne, 748 So. 2d 184, 187-88 (Miss. Ct. App. 1999) (reversal of order enjoining husband and threatening him with contempt if he continued to live with girlfriend).

[370] Landrum v. Landrum, 498 So. 2d 1299, 1299 (Miss. 1986) (change warranting modification); Riley v. Riley, 884 So. 2d 791, 793 (Miss. Ct. App. 2004) (custody order in separate maintenance can be modified based on material change in circumstances; modification not justified by father's religious conversion).

THE MARRIAGE RELATIONSHIP   § 1.14[8]

a husband was forced to retire early because of physical inability to perform his job.[371] However, a chancellor properly denied modification based on a husband's $400 a month income reduction. His new job included medical and dental insurance; in addition, his mortgage payments on his wife's behalf were reduced by $250 a month when she moved to a less expensive home.[372] A custody order in a separate maintenance proceeding is a final order and may be modified only upon proof of a material change in circumstances.[373]

Separate maintenance terminates if the parties reconcile[374] or if the payor makes a good faith offer of reconciliation that the recipient refuses.[375] The court of appeals held that a husband's statement, "you don't want me moving back in", made while discussing divorce, and while he was living with his girlfriend, was not a good faith reconciliation offer. A good faith offer to reconcile should include at least some expression of regret or repentance.[376]

Authorities generally state that divorce terminates a decree of separate maintenance,[377] as does the death of either of the spouses.[378] In a 2007 case, the court of appeals held that separate maintenance ordered in Mississippi in 1992 was properly terminated retroactive to the date of a 1995 United Kingdom divorce decree because the decree was a material change in circumstances.[379] In another case, the Mississippi Supreme Court held that divorce was a material change in circumstances warranting recharacterization of separate maintenance as alimony.[380]

[8] Res judicata effect at divorce. An order of separate maintenance may be res judicata as to some issues in a subsequent divorce. For example, a husband's suit for divorce based on desertion may be barred by a prior separate maintenance award based on a finding that his wife did not desert him.[381]

---

[371] Kennedy v. Kennedy, 650 So. 2d 1362, 1369 (Miss. 1995) (reduction in husband's income warranted reduction in separate maintenance; order designed to provide standard of living parties would have had in marriage).

[372] Watkins v. Watkins, 942 So. 2d 224, 229-30 (Miss. Ct. App. 2006).

[373] Riley v. Riley, 884 So. 2d 791, 793 (Miss. Ct. App. 2004) (modification not justified by father's religious conversion).

[374] Weiss v. Weiss, 579 So. 2d 539, 542 (Miss. 1991) (distinguishing alimony and separate maintenance); Day v. Day, 501 So. 2d 353, 357 (Miss. 1987) (husband made good faith offer of reconciliation); CLARK, JR., *supra* note 7, § 6.4, at 267.

[375] *See* Shorter v. Shorter, 740 So. 2d 352, 356 (Miss. Ct. App. 1999) (finding husband had no intention of returning to wife).

[376] Watkins v. Watkins, 942 So. 2d 224, 228-29 (Miss. Ct. App. 2006); *see also* Watkins v. Watkins, 957 So. 2d 440, 443-44 (Miss. Ct. App. 2007) (rejecting husband's argument that reconciliation was made impossible by wife's aiming gun at him; no proof he was attempting to reconcile).

[377] *See* CLARK, JR., *supra* note 7, § 16.3, at 639; C. T. Foster, Annotation, *Decree of Divorce a Vinculo as Affecting Prior Award of Alimony or Support Ordered or Decreed in a Suit for Divorce a Mensa et Thoro or for Separate Maintenance*, 166 A.L.R. 1004 (1947).

[378] *See* HAND, *supra* note 208, § 2-13, at 40.

[379] Ferguson v. Ferguson, 947 So. 2d 1015, 1017 (Miss. Ct. App. 2007).

[380] *See* Chapel v. Chapel, 876 So. 2d 290, 295 (Miss. 2004); Lofton v. Lofton, 924 So. 2d 596, 599, 604 (Miss. Ct. App. 2006) (Mississippi separate maintenance order converted to permanent alimony after divorce granted in Florida).

[381] *See* Etheridge v. Webb, 50 So. 2d 603, 607 (Miss. 1951) (excluding evidence of desertion prior to separate maintenance decree); Wilson v. Wilson, 22 So. 2d 161, 163 (Miss. 1945) (reversing husband's divorce based on desertion; prior order of separate maintenance to wife was necessarily based on finding that wife had not deserted husband); *see also* Maxey v. Maxey, 120 So. 179, 180 (Miss. 1929) (wife denied separate maintenance held not entitled to alimony based on estoppel by judgment; law at time of decision provided that wife at fault was not entitled to alimony).

40

II
RIGHTS BETWEEN UNMARRIED PARTNERS

Nonmarital cohabitation has increased dramatically in the last few decades. In a forty-year period, from 1960 to 2000, the number of cohabitant households increased 1,000%, from 500,000 to 4.9 million.[1] In 2009, for the first time, fewer than half of United States households included a married couple.[2] Many cohabitations are of short duration, leading to marriage or ending when the relationship dissolves. But a significant minority (one study suggests 10%) involve long-term partnerships.[3] The increase in cohabitation has promoted proposals to extend property division and spousal support to "marriage-like" relationships. To date, Mississippi courts have denied rights to cohabitants who have never been married. However, persons who cohabit with a former spouse or who entered into an invalid marriage may be awarded jointly accumulated assets or compensation for domestic services. The increase in nonmarital births is even more striking than increased cohabitation. In 2008, 41% of births in the United States were to unmarried women.[4] Today, rights of custody and child support between unmarried parents are almost identical to the rights between married parents.

In most states, partners of the same sex are limited to the rights available to unmarried partners or cohabitants. Six states now permit same-sex marriage and a number of states provide marriage-like rights through civil unions. But in most states, including Mississippi, same-sex marriage is specifically banned.

The first half of this chapter discusses the historical treatment of cohabitation and the extent to which traditional rules have been altered. The second half of the chapter reviews the current state of the law regarding same-sex marriage and civil unions and the extent to which rights offered by one state are enforceable in others. The chapter also reviews child custody, adoption, and support issues peculiar to same-sex couples.

§ 2.01 HISTORY AND OVERVIEW: LEGALITY

Through the mid-twentieth century, many states recognized a form of marriage based on cohabitation. Couples who lived together and held themselves out as married were considered common law spouses, with all the rights and duties of marriage. In contrast, cohabitation without a "holding out" as married was not only prohibited but proscribed as criminal. Many states also classified all nonmarital sex as criminal, whether heterosexual or between same-sex partners. Most states have

---

[1] CYNTHIA GRANT BOWMAN, UNMARRIED COUPLES, LAW, AND PUBLIC POLICY, at 97 (Oxford 2010).

[2] BOWMAN, *supra* note 1, at 1.

[3] BOWMAN, *supra* note 1, at 26.

[4] Pew Research Center, *The New Demography of American Motherhood*, *available at* http://pewresearch.org (Aug. 19, 2010).

§ 2.01[1]   **MISSISSIPPI FAMILY LAW**

repealed these statutes. However, Mississippi laws still classify cohabitation and sodomy as criminal acts.

[1] Common law marriage. Until the mid-twentieth century, many states recognized common law marriage – an agreement between cohabitants who held themselves out as a married couple. Common law spouses had the same rights and duties as parties to a ceremonial marriage. Divorce through a court action was required to dissolve the relationship.[5] Common law marriages were recognized in Mississippi until 1956.[6] The state continues to grant full faith and credit to common law marriages valid in the state where the marriage was contracted.[7] Today, common law marriages are valid in only eleven states.[8]

[2] Cohabitation as a crime. Until recently, cohabitation that did not qualify as common law marriage was criminalized in most states. Many of these statutes were repealed by the 1980s.[9] Mississippi remains one of the seven states in which cohabitation is still criminalized by statute.[10] Under the Mississippi statute, the crime may be proved by cohabitation combined with "circumstances which show habitual sexual intercourse."[11] The last reported appellate case involving a prosecution under the statute was in 1958.[12]

[3] Sexual conduct as a crime. In addition to criminalizing cohabitation, many states had statutes providing that sex outside of marriage was a crime.[13] In Mississippi, however, nonmarital sex was considered a crime only if combined with cohabitation.[14] Most states also criminalized sexual conduct between same-sex partners until the 1980s. Mississippi law still provides that sodomy is a crime.[15]

[4] Constitutionality. Decisions of the United States Supreme Court in the 1960s and 1970s raised serious questions about the constitutionality of statutes criminalizing nonmarital sexual conduct and cohabitation. After right to privacy decisions such as *Roe v. Wade*[16] and *Griswold v. Connecticut*,[17] many states repealed

---

[5] Barton v. State, 143 So. 861, 862 (Miss. 1932) ("nothing less than a decree of divorce pronounced by a court of competent jurisdiction can dissolve the relation"), *quoted in* Martin v. Martin's Estate, 63 So. 2d 827, 830 (Miss. 1953).

[6] *See* J.W. Bunkley & W.E. Morse, Amis on Divorce & Separation in Mississippi § 1.02 (4), at 14-15 (1957).

[7] George v. George, 389 So. 2d 1389, 1390 (Miss. 1980) (recognizing common law marriage in Georgia); *see* Walker v. Matthews, 3 So. 2d 820, 824 (Miss. 1941).

[8] Bowman, *supra* note 1, at 26.

[9] Bowman, *supra* note 1, at 12-13 (noting also that most states criminalized sex outside of marriage).

[10] Bowman, *supra* note 1, at 16 (seven states as of 2009).

[11] Miss. Code Ann. § 97-29-1 (2004) (penalty of $500 and six months in prison).

[12] See Annotations to Miss. Code Ann. § 97-29-1 (2004).

[13] Bowman, *supra* note 1, at 16.

[14] *See* Saunders v. Alford, 607 So. 2d 1214, 1219 (Miss. 1992).

[15] Miss. Code Ann. § 97-29-59 (2004) ("Every person who shall be convicted of the detestable and abominable crime against nature committed with mankind or with a beast, shall be punished by imprisonment in the penitentiary for a term of not more than ten years.").

[16] 410 U.S. 113 (1973).

[17] 381 U.S. 479 (1965).

RIGHTS BETWEEN UNMARRIED PARTNERS § 2.01[5]

fornication and cohabitation statutes. Some state courts held that fornication statutes violated the privacy right articulated by the Supreme Court.[18]

The constitutionality of criminalizing private sexual conduct was resolved in 2003 in *Lawrence v. Texas*. The Supreme Court struck down a Texas sodomy law, holding that a homosexual couple had a constitutional right of privacy to engage in consensual sexual conduct within the privacy of their home.[19] Arguably, the decision also makes cohabitation prohibitions unconstitutional, although differences can be drawn between private sexual conduct and living together openly.[20]

[5] Practical effects of criminalization. It is well documented that cohabitation statutes are rarely, if ever, enforced. However, a 1981 study illustrated that, while the crime is not enforced per se, a criminal statute may be used to affect the rights of cohabitants in other settings such as divorce or custody.[21] For example, a husband seeking custody against his estranged wife might have her arrested under a cohabitation statute to gain an advantage in a custody action.

The last appellate cases involving prosecution under the Mississippi cohabitation statute are from the 1950s. However, the fact that cohabitation is criminalized is clearly a factor in appellate courts' refusal to recognize property rights between cohabitants.[22] In addition, cohabitation may weigh against a parent in a custody action.[23]

§ 2.02 FINANCIAL RIGHTS BETWEEN COHABITANTS

The 1976 California case *Marvin v. Marvin* received nationwide attention because it suggested that a homemaker cohabitant might be awarded assets based on an "implied contract" or "tacit understanding" between the parties – in effect extending property division to persons who live together in a marriage-like relationship.[24] A few states, following California's lead, permit property division based on implied contract, but most refuse to divide assets in the absence of an express contract or actual joint financial contribution to the accumulation of assets.[25]

Mississippi appellate courts do not recognize marriage-like rights between "mere" cohabitants. The courts have, however, approved division of assets between parties to a void marriage and between cohabitants who were formerly married.

---

[18] *See, e.g.,* State v. Saunders, 381 A.2d 333, 339 (N.J. 1977).

[19] Lawrence v. Texas, 539 U. S. 558 (2003).

[20] BOWMAN, *supra* note 1, at 18; *see* Lawrence H. Tribe, *"The Fundamental Right" That Dare Not Speak Its Name*, 117 HARV. L. REV. 1893 (2004).

[21] Martha L. Fineman, *Law and Changing Patterns of Behavior: Sanctions on Non-Marital Cohabitation*, 1981 Wis. L. Rev. 275 (1981).

[22] *See, e.g.,* Davis v. Davis, 643 So. 2d 931, 936 (Miss. 1994).

[23] See *infra* § 2.06[2].

[24] Marvin v. Marvin, 557 P.2d 106, 122 (Cal. 1976).

[25] *See* cases collected in George L. Blum, Annotation, *Property Rights Arising From Relationship of Couple Cohabiting without Marriage*, 69 A.L.R.5TH 219 (1999); Goode v. Goode, 396 S.E.2d 430, 435-36 (W. Va. 1990) (allowing recovery); Watts v. Watts, 405 N.W.2d 303, 310-11 (Wis. 1987) (allowing recovery). *But see* Hewitt v. Hewitt, 394 N.E.2d 1204, 1211 (Ill. 1979) (not allowing property division between cohabitants).

43

§ 2.02[1]   **MISSISSIPPI FAMILY LAW**

The threshold requirement for application of these doctrines appears to be some form of marriage, even if it was bigamous. Mississippi cases do indicate, however, that an express agreement between cohabitants would be enforceable.

[1] Void marriages: The putative spouse doctrine. In most states, a party to an invalid marriage may have rights to property division under the putative spouse doctrine. Usually, a putative marriage arises when one or both of the parties is unaware of an impediment to the marriage.[26] The doctrine is most commonly used to permit equitable division of property accumulated during the purported marriage. However, some courts have extended the doctrine to allow rights of inheritance, alimony, and to provide access to government benefits.[27]

The Mississippi Supreme Court recognized the putative spouse doctrine to justify an award of assets to a woman who married in good faith, unaware that her husband was already married. The court noted that she had worked long hours to help build his business and that assets titled in his name had been accumulated by their joint efforts. The decision also appears to hold that in Mississippi, a putative spouse is not entitled to alimony, which must be based on a valid marriage.[28]

In a 2010 case, the Mississippi Court of Appeals held that the putative spouse doctrine does not require a good faith belief that the marriage is valid. A wife of thirty-seven years who was a homemaker and cared for the couple's four children was entitled to equitable distribution of assets even though her marriage was annulled as bigamous. She had never divorced her first husband. The court emphasized that her efforts as a homemaker assisted her partner's acquisition of assets: "Fannie's domestic efforts enabled, or at least assisted in allowing, Eddie to work outside the home as the primary breadwinner."[29]

[2] Cohabitation between former spouses

    [a] Division of assets. Mississippi appellate courts have approved division of assets between cohabitants who were once married. When a formerly married couple resumed cohabitation for twenty years after their divorce, the supreme court held that division of assets was proper, stating that "our law authorizes and sanctions an equitable division of property accumulated by two persons as a result of their joint efforts. This would be the case were a common law business partnership breaking up. It is equally the case where a man and woman, who have accumulated property in the course of a non-marital cohabitation, permanently separate." The court went on to emphasize that nonfinancial contributions should be considered:

---

[26] HOMER H. CLARK, JR., THE LAW OF DOMESTIC RELATIONS IN THE UNITED STATES § 2.4, at 55 (2d ed. 1988).

[27] CLARK, *supra* note 26, § 2.4, at 56.

[28] Chrismond v. Chrismond, 52 So. 2d 624, 630 (Miss. 1951); *see also* Pittman v. Pittman, 909 So. 2d 148, 150, 152 (Miss. Ct. App. 2005) (void marriage treated as joint venture between parties; reversed because trial court did not consider couple's settlement agreement).

[29] Cotton v. Cotton, 44 So. 3d 371, 375 (Miss. Ct. App. 2010).

RIGHTS BETWEEN UNMARRIED PARTNERS   § 2.02[2][b]

"[W]here one party to the relationship acts without compensation to perform work or render services to a business enterprise or performs work or services generally regarded as domestic in nature, these are nevertheless economic contributions."[30] The language of the opinion appeared to encompass all cohabitants. However, later decisions limited the holding to formerly married cohabitants or couples who entered an invalid marriage.

[b] Reimbursement for domestic services. The court of appeals articulated a new theory for recovery by a formerly married homemaker cohabitant in 2003. The court held that a woman who lived with her ex-husband for eleven years after their divorce was entitled to reimbursement for her domestic services. The court relied on dicta from earlier cases stating that domestic services are economic contributions to the accumulation of assets.[31] The court affirmed the chancellor's award compensating the woman for the market value of her services as a caregiver.[32] The court rejected her former husband's argument that the award amounted to "palimony": "Steve and Debra were more than "pals" by virtue of their previous marriage, their having a second child during their post-divorce period of cohabitation, their holding themselves out to the public as being husband and wife . . . . but for want of obtaining another marriage license, they lived in the same relationship in which they had lived from 1973 through 1994.[33]

[3] "Mere" cohabitants. Cohabitants who were not formerly married are not entitled to equitable distribution of property. The Mississippi Supreme Court denied a request for property division by a homemaker who cohabited in a "marriage-like relationship" for thirteen years and who had a child with her partner. The woman, Elvis, argued that she was entitled to an equitable share of the $5 million in assets accumulated by her partner during their cohabitation. She argued that the couple had an oral agreement or "understanding" that she was responsible for homemaking while he was responsible for financial matters. The court held that the assets were not accumulated by the joint efforts of the parties.[34] Similarly, the court reversed a chancellor's equitable division of property based solely on long-term cohabitation: "[T]he legislature has not extended the rights enjoyed by married people to those who have chosen merely to cohabit or carry on an affair."[35] And in one case, the supreme court held that a woman was not entitled to an equitable lien on a home

---

[30] *See* Pickens v. Pickens, 490 So. 2d 872, 875 (Miss. 1986); *see also* Jernigan v. Jernigan, 697 So. 2d 387 (Miss. 1997) (wife who cohabited with ex-husband for twelve years and contributed income and labor to home titled in his name entitled to some share of equity).

[31] *See* Woolridge v. Woolridge, 856 So. 2d 446, 452 (Miss. Ct. App. 2003) (quoting Pickens v. Pickens, 490 So. 2d 872, 875 (Miss. 1986)) (emphasis added).

[32] Woolridge v. Woolridge, 856 So. 2d 446, 453 (Miss. Ct. App. 2003).

[33] Woolridge v. Woolridge, 856 So. 2d 446, 453 (Miss. Ct. App. 2003).

[34] Davis v. Davis, 643 So. 2d 931, 936 (Miss. 1994) (the court emphasized that the woman, Elvis, had a chance to marry her millionaire cohabitant and turned him down).

[35] Malone v. Odom, 657 So. 2d 1112, 1117 (Miss. 1995) (reversing equitable lien granted to woman on house she occupied for years, titled in name of cohabitant).

§ 2.02[4]   MISSISSIPPI FAMILY LAW

owned by her deceased cohabitant, even though she contributed financially to the purchase of the house. The court stated that extending marital rights to cohabitants "essentially would resurrect the old common-law marriage doctrine which was specifically abolished by the Legislature."[36] Property division was also denied to a woman who cohabited with her partner and the father of her children for fourteen years, even though she managed a restaurant owned by him and contributed her income to household expenses. The decision appears to be based in part on the fact that she was paid $240 a week for her services in the restaurant, and in part on the fact that the couple never participated in a marriage ceremony. The court rejected her argument that she was entitled to a constructive trust on the home titled in his name because she contributed financially by paying utility bills and making improvements to the home (purchasing paint and flooring).[37]

The "mere" cohabitant cases distinguish cases involving formerly married cohabitants. In one case, for example, the supreme court noted that "Lori and David chose 'merely to cohabit.' They were never married or purported to be married."[38] The state's criminalization of cohabitation appears to be a factor in some of the decisions. In *Davis v. Davis,* for example, the court cited the cohabitation statute, noting that "cohabitation remains a crime against public morals and decency."[39]

[4] Rights based on express agreement. In most states, an express agreement for division of assets accumulated during cohabitation is enforceable.[40] Two cases suggest that the Mississippi courts would follow this rule. The Mississippi Supreme Court held that a woman was entitled to a quantum meruit recovery from her cohabitant's estate – she provided homemaking services for him for twenty-four years based upon his promise that she would receive all of his property at his death. The court stated, "when one has provided services for the other in reasonable reliance upon a promise . . . the promisee may recover of and from the estate on a quantum meruit basis."[41] The Mississippi Supreme Court also enforced an agreement between a same-sex couple for financial payments upon their separation. The court rejected the argument that the agreement was unenforceable as against public policy, stating, "No authority states that a contract between two unmarried persons is illegal. . . .the law of this State does not support any finding of illegality with regard to this contract."[42]

[5] Alimony. Even courts that permit property division between cohabitants

---

[36] *In re* Estate of Alexander, 445 So. 2d 836, 839 (Miss. 1984); *cf.* Dean v. Kavanaugh, 920 So. 2d 528, 534-35 (Miss. Ct. App. 2006) (long-term cohabitation does not create confidential relationship giving rise to presumption of undue influence).

[37] Nichols v. Funderburk, 881 So. 2d 266, 271 (Miss. Ct. App. 2003), *affirmed,* 883 So. 2d 554 (Miss. 2004).

[38] Nichols v. Funderburk, 881 So. 2d 266, 271 (Miss. Ct. App. 2003), *affirmed,* 883 So. 2d 554 (Miss. 2004).

[39] Davis v. Davis, 643 So. 2d 931, 934 (Miss. 1994).

[40] BOWMAN, *supra* note 1, at 47-48.

[41] Williams v. Mason, 556 So. 2d 1045, 1049 (Miss. 1990).

[42] *In re* Estate of Reaves, 744 So. 2d 799, 802 (Miss. Ct. App. 1999).

RIGHTS BETWEEN UNMARRIED PARTNERS   § 2.03

rarely award support similar to alimony.[43] The Mississippi Supreme Court has stated that alimony is available only upon proof of a valid marriage.[44] Furthermore, alimony is unavailable if a marriage occurred but was later annulled.[45] In one case that seems to stand alone, the supreme court upheld an award of thirty-six months of payments to a woman in ill health when her husband under a void marriage left her. The court noted that the case was unusual, and that the woman would otherwise be destitute.[46]

§ 2.03 OTHER BENEFITS

A few states have extended other benefits to cohabitants. For example, in a few states, cohabitants may receive workers' compensation benefits.[47] To date, no Mississippi case has recognized benefits other than division of assets as described above. The Mississippi Supreme Court reversed a chancellor's grant of a life estate in homestead to a woman who lived with the owner for more than thirty years. In the absence of an agreement that she would be compensated for her care of him, equity could not provide a remedy.[48] The supreme court has also rejected the claim of an unmarried cohabitant seeking workers' compensation benefits as a dependent widow.[49]

§ 2.04 THE AMERICAN LAW INSTITUTE PROPOSAL

In its recent articulation of family law principles, the American Law Institute proposes extending equitable distribution to "domestic partners" – persons of the opposite or same sex who live together in a marriage-like relationship for a significant period of time.[50] Explaining the proposal, the drafters discuss the increasing number of unmarried couples in long-term relationships,[51] the importance of a fair resolution between economically interdependent partners, and the significance to

---

[43] *See, e.g.,* Marvin v. Marvin, 176 Cal. Rptr. 555, 558-59 (Cal. Ct. App. 1981) (no obligation to provide for former cohabitant "in need").

[44] Pickens v. Pickens, 490 So. 2d 872, 875 (Miss. 1986).

[45] Aldridge v. Aldridge, 77 So. 150, 150-51 (Miss. 1918) (alimony may not be granted to woman whose marriage was declared void because of existing prior marriage); Sims v. Sims, 85 So. 73, 74 (Miss. 1920); Reed v. Reed, 37 So. 642, 642 (Miss. 1905).

[46] Taylor v. Taylor, 317 So. 2d 422, 423 (Miss. 1975). The court of appeals later characterized the *Taylor* order as a division of property *See* Pickens v. Pickens, 490 So. 2d 872, 875 (Miss. 1986). In another case, the court distinguished *Taylor* as an award based on a good faith marriage. *See* Malone v. Odom, 657 So. 2d 1112, 1117 (Miss. 1995). A 2010 case interpreted the payment as equitable distribution rather than alimony, and held that the award was consistent with the rule that a putative spouse need not have acted in good faith. *See* Cotton v. Cotton, 44 So. 3d 371 (Miss. Ct. App. 2010).

[47] BOWMAN, *supra* note 1, at 70-71 (California and Oregon).

[48] *In re* Estate of Alexander, 445 So. 2d 836, 840 (Miss. 1984) (provision of relief a matter for legislative, not judicial action).

[49] Dale Polk Constr. Co. v. White, 287 So. 2d 278, 280 (Miss. 1973).

[50] *See* AMERICAN LAW INSTITUTE, PRINCIPLES OF THE LAW OF FAMILY DISSOLUTION: ANALYSIS AND RECOMMENDATIONS § 6.01 (2002) [A.L.I. PRINCIPLES] (leaving to states the designation of a "significant" time period justifying property division).

[51] A.L.I. PRINCIPLES, *supra* note 50, § 6.03, Reporter's Notes, cmt a, at 929.

§ 2.05   **MISSISSIPPI FAMILY LAW**

society of preventing one partner's dependence on public assistance.[52] The American Law Institute principles also recommend that compensatory spousal payments, the proposed replacement for alimony awards, be extended to domestic partners.[53]

§ 2.05 PATERNITY AND CHILD SUPPORT

A nonmarital child's relationship to his or her father is typically established through a paternity action. In Mississippi, these actions are governed by the Mississippi Uniform Law on Paternity.[54] In addition, paternity may be established through a voluntary acknowledgment of paternity that has the same legal effect as an adjudication of paternity.[55] Today, a nonmarital child's right to parental support is almost identical to that of a child of marriage. The Paternity Act provides that the father of a child born out of wedlock "is liable to the same extent as the father of a child born of lawful matrimony."[56] The establishment of paternity is discussed in Chapter XI. Child support between unmarried parents is discussed in detail in Chapter XIII.

§ 2.06 CUSTODY

[1] Between unmarried parents. The father of an extra-marital child has the same rights to custody as the father of a child born of a marriage. The Mississippi Supreme Court has consistently rejected unmarried mothers' arguments that the test for custody between spouses – the best interests of the child test – does not apply between unmarried parents.[57] Once a man acknowledges a child or is adjudicated a child's father, he is on an equal footing with the mother with regard to parental rights.[58] Rights between unmarried parents are discussed in Chapter XII.[59]

[2] Effect of cohabitation on custody. For many years, a custodial parent who cohabited was at great risk of losing custody in a modification action.[60] In 1985, the Mississippi Supreme Court held that custody decisions may not be based on sexual behavior alone.[61] On the other hand, cohabitation may be considered as one of sev-

---

[52] A.L.I. PRINCIPLES, *supra* note 50, § 6.02, cmt.

[53] *See* A.L.I. PRINCIPLES, *supra* note 50, § 6.06.

[54] MISS. CODE ANN. §§ 93-9-1 to -49 (2004); *see* Dunn v. Grisham, 157 So. 2d 766, 768 (Miss. 1963) (Act applicable to children born prior to passage; constitutional prohibition of ex post facto laws not applicable to civil proceeding).

[55] MISS. CODE ANN. § 93-9-9 (4)(a)-(b) (2004).

[56] MISS. CODE ANN. § 93-9-7 (2004). At least as early as 1906, fathers of illegitimate children were required to support their children in Mississippi. Section 268, Code of 1906 (Hemingway's Code, § 217), required the father to provide support "When any single woman shall be delivered of a bastard," *cited in* Crum v. Brock, 101 So. 704, 705 (Miss. 1924) (holding that a widow was a "single woman" for purposes of the statute).

[57] Hayes v. Rounds, 658 So. 2d 863, 865 (Miss. 1995) (rejecting mother's argument that the father had to prove she had abandoned the child or was unfit).

[58] Law v. Page, 618 So. 2d 96, 101 (Miss. 1993).

[59] See *infra* § 12.02[2].

[60] See *infra* § 12.03[8][a].

[61] Carr v. Carr, 480 So. 2d 1120, 1123 (Miss. 1985); *see also* Moak v. Moak, 631 So. 2d 196, 197 (Miss. 1994); McAdory v. McAdory, 608 So. 2d 695, 701-02 (Miss. 1992).

RIGHTS BETWEEN UNMARRIED PARTNERS §2.07

eral factors that prove a material change in combination with others. Modification was proper based on a mother's cohabitation, frequent moves, relocation to Colorado, failure to provide medical care, and marriage to a man her child feared.[62]

§ 2.07 ADOPTION

Until fairly recently, unmarried fathers were largely disregarded in adoption proceedings. Until 2002, an unmarried father had no statutory right to be notified of or to object to an adoption. In 1998, the Mississippi Supreme Court held that the state's adoption statute was unconstitutional as applied to an unmarried father who had established a substantial relationship with his child.[63] The statute was amended in 2002 to reflect the court's decision. Under the amended statute, an unmarried father may not object to adoption unless, within thirty days after the child's birth, he has demonstrated "a full commitment to the responsibilities of parenthood."[64]

§ 2.08 SAME-SEX PARTNERS: THE DIVISION BETWEEEN STATES

The national debate over same-sex marriage began in earnest in 1996, when the Hawaii Supreme Court held that a ban on same-sex marriage violated that state's constitution. Six years later, the Vermont Supreme Court held that same-sex couples are constitutionally entitled to the same legal benefits as married couples, although the court did not require that the benefits be provided through marriage.[65] Four years later, the Massachusetts Supreme Judicial Court was the first state appellate court to hold that a civil union providing same-sex partners with the same rights and duties as marriage violated the state constitution.[66] Today, slightly over one-fourth of the states recognize same-sex marriage, civil unions, or domestic partnerships, while, at the other extreme, the remaining states ban same-sex marriage. The sharp divide between states creates a host of legal issues regarding interstate recognition of marriage under the Full Faith and Credit Clause.

[1] Recognition of same-sex rights. Today, same-sex couples may marry in six states – Connecticut, Iowa, Massachusetts, New Hampshire, New York, and Vermont. The right to marry was provided by legislative action in three states[67] and

---

[62] See Stark v. Anderson, 748 So. 2d 838, 843 (Miss. Ct. App. 1999); *see also* Sullivan v. Beason, 37 So. 3d 706, 708-09 (Miss. Ct. App. 2010) (custody transfer based on mother's three post-separation relationships, including one with a married man, and domestic violence in the home); Graves v. Haden, 52 So. 3d 407, 409 (Miss. Ct. App. 2010) (modifying custody of well-adjusted child based on mother's cohabitation, frequent moves, and relationships), *cert. denied*, 50 So. 3d 1003 (Miss. 2011); Richardson v. Richardson, 790 So. 2d 239, 243 (Miss. Ct. App. 2001) (mother lived for two years with abusive boyfriend, had child by him, and interfered with children's contact with father).

[63] Smith v. Malouf, 722 So. 2d 490 (Miss. 1998).

[64] MISS. CODE ANN. § 93-17-5(3) (2004). See § 17.05[1][b] for a full discussion of the rights of unmarried fathers.

[65] *See* Baker v. State, 744 A.2d 864, 886 (Vt. 1999). The Vermont legislature later provided for same-sex marriage by statute. *See* 2009 Vt. Act 3.

[66] *In re* Op. of Justices to the Senate, 802 N.E.2d 565, 570 (Mass. 2004).

[67] *See* N.H. REV. STAT. ANN. § 457:1-a (2009); The New York Marriage Equality Act (2011 Sess. Law News of N.Y. Ch. 95 (A. 8354)) of June 24, 2011, effective July 24, 2011; VT. ST. ANN. tit. 15, § 8 (2009).

§ 2.08[2]   **MISSISSIPPI FAMILY LAW**

through court decisions in three.[68] In addition, nine states currently offer same-sex couples marriage-like rights through civil unions or domestic partnerships.[69] And in 2011, Illinois extended civil union rights to heterosexual as well as homosexual couples.[70]

[2] Nonrecognition of rights. At the other end of the spectrum, in the last fifteen years a majority of states have enacted statutes or constitutional amendments banning same-sex marriage. Many of these statutes (called mini-DOMAs) also deny full faith and credit to same-sex marriages valid in other states.[71] In 1997, the Mississippi Code was amended to provide: "Any marriage between persons of the same gender is prohibited and null and void from the beginning. Any marriage between persons of the same gender that is valid in another jurisdiction does not constitute a legal or valid marriage in Mississippi. Any attempt to evade section 93-1-1 by marrying out of this state and returning to it shall be within the prohibitions of said section."[72] The Mississippi Constitution similarly states: "Marriage may take place and may be valid under the laws of this state only between a man and a woman. A marriage in another state or foreign jurisdiction between persons of the same gender, regardless of when the marriage took place, may not be recognized in this state and is void and unenforceable under the laws of this state." [73]

[3] Federal law: Nonrecognition. The anti-gay marriage statutes were bolstered by Congress' passage of the Defense of Marriage Act (DOMA) in 1996.[74] DOMA recognizes the right of states to refuse recognition to same-sex marriages. In addition, the Act defines marriage for federal purposes as a union of a man and a woman.[75] Thus, same-sex couples with a valid marriage under state law are not entitled to federal benefits such as Social Security or Veteran's Benefits, or to recognition as married taxpayers. In 2010, a federal district court in Massachusetts held that the Act violated the due process clause by defining marriage for federal purposes as between a man and a

---

[68] Kerrigan v. Comm'r of Pub. Health, 957 A.2d 407 (Conn. 2008) (declined to follow by State v. Jenkins, 3 A.3d 806 (Conn. 2010); Varnum v. Brien, 763 N.W.2d 862 (Iowa 2009); *In re* Op. of Justices to the Senate, 802 N.E.2d 565, 570 (Mass. 2004).

[69] National Conference of State Legislatures, *Civil Unions,* available at http://www.ncsl.org (last visited July 26, 2011).

[70] The Illinois Religious Freedom Protection and Civil Union Act (RFPCU), Public Act 096-1513 (2011) (effective June 1, 2011). The Act recognizes civil unions, affording unionized parties "the same legal obligations, responsibilities, protections and benefits as are afforded to spouses." Parties may be "of either the same or opposite sex." *Id.*

[71] *See* JOHN DE WITT GREGORY, PETER N. SWISHER & SHERYL L. WOLF, UNDERSTANDING FAMILY LAW § 2.08, at 48-49 (2d ed. 2001).

[72] MISS. CODE ANN. § 93-1-1 (2004).

[73] MISS. CONST. art. 14, § 263A (2004).

[74] 28 U.S.C. § 1738C (2006).

[75] PL 104-199 (HR 3396) *codified at* 1 U.S.C 7. The validity of the Defense of Marriage Act is criticized and defended in numerous articles. *See, e.g.,* Larry Kramer, *Same-Sex Marriage, Conflict of Laws, and the Unconstitutional Public Policy Exception,* 106 YALE L.J. 1965 (1997); Scott Ruskay-Kidd, Note, *The Defense of Marriage Act and the Overextension of Congressional Authority,* 97 COLUM. L. REV. 1435 (1997). *But see* Ralph U. Whitten, *The Original Understanding of the Full Faith and Credit Clause and the Defense of Marriage Act,* 32 CREIGHTON L. REV. 255 (1998) (arguing for constitutionality of the Act). *See generally* Robin Cheryl Miller and Jason Binimow, *Marriage Between Persons of the Same Sex – United States and Canadian Cases,* 1 A.L.R. FED. 2d 1.

RIGHTS BETWEEN UNMARRIED PARTNERS   § 2.09

woman.[76]

§ 2.09 INTERSTATE RECOGNITION

These diametrically opposed state laws raise complicated questions regarding the enforcement of same-sex marriages across state lines. A similar conflict arises with regard to adoption by same-sex couples, with some states allowing and others prohibiting adoption by persons of the same sex. As couples move from one state to another, family law attorneys and judges will be faced with new challenges to determine the validity of civil unions, marriages, contracts, and family arrangements regarding children.

[1] The common law rule. As a general rule, states will recognize a marriage that is valid in the state in which it was contracted unless the marriage violates a significant public policy of that state. Mississippi follows the general rule extending full faith and credit to out-of-state marriages that do not violate fundamental public policy. Mississippi courts have extended recognition to marriages between parties not eligible to marry in Mississippi. In *Miller v. Lucks*, the court recognized a marriage between a Caucasian and African-American for purposes of allowing one spouse to inherit property located in Mississippi, emphasizing that because the couple never lived in Mississippi their marriage did not violate the purpose of the law.[77] And in another case, the supreme court enforced marriage rights based on a common law marriage under Georgia law even though Mississippi does not permit marriage by common law.[78]

However, states reserve the right to deny recognition based on public policy and to deny recognition to residents who attempt to evade state law by marrying in another state. For example, no recognition will be given to a marriage incestuous under Mississippi law if residents have attempted to evade the law by marrying elsewhere and returning to Mississippi to live.[79]

The question of interstate recognition will arise primarily in two contexts – (1) whether a couple legally married in another state may divorce in a nonrecognition state and (2) whether a married same-sex couple is entitled to state benefits in a nonrecognition state.

[2] Constitutionality. One federal court has addressed the constitutionality of statutes denying recognition to same-sex marriages from other states. The court held that the Full Faith and Credit Clause does not require states to recognize marriages that violate public policy of the state. The federal district court for the northern district of Florida held that Florida was not required to recognize or apply Massachusetts' same-sex marriage law, which conflicted with Florida's express, statutory public policy of opposing same-sex marriage.[80]

---

[76] Gill v. Office of Personnel Management, 699 F. Supp. 2d 374 (D. Mass. 2010); Massachusetts v. U.S. Dep't of Health and Human Serv., 698 F. Supp. 2d 234 (D. Mass. 2010).

[77] 36 So. 2d 140 (Miss. 1948).

[78] George v. George, 389 So. 2d 1389, 1391 (Miss. 1980).

[79] MISS. CODE ANN. § 93-1-3 (2004).

[80] Wilson v. Ake, 354 F. Supp. 2d 1298 (M.D. Fla. 2005); *see Life After DOMA*, 17 DUKE J. GENDER L. & POLICY

§ 2.09[3]   **MISSISSIPPI FAMILY LAW**

[3] Interstate divorce. The difference in state recognition of same-sex marriage creates a dilemma in a mobile society. Jurisdiction for divorce is based on one spouse's residence in a state.[81] A couple married in a recognition state, but who have moved to a nonrecognition state, may be unable to obtain a divorce anywhere. For example, the Massachusetts Supreme Court held that two women who moved to Florida shortly after marrying in Massachusetts could not be divorced in Massachusetts.[82]

[a] Mini-DOMA states. In states with mini-DOMAs, courts are not required to recognize same-sex marriages valid in another state.[83] For example, the Texas Supreme Court held that Texas statutes prohibiting same-sex marriage and refusing full faith and credit established a public policy that prohibited the state from opening its courts to a couple married in Massachusetts.[84]

[b] Other states. In states that do not recognize same-sex marriage, but which have not passed mini-DOMAs, enforcement will depend upon a state's application of common law rules. Prior to its recognition of same-sex marriage, a New York court held that a couple legally married in Canada could file for divorce in New York. The court rejected the defendant's argument that the marriage was void because New York did not recognize same-sex marriages. The court held that New York's public policy exception applied only to polygamy and incest.[85] However, a New York couple who married in Massachusetts with the intention of living in New York were not entitled to divorce in New York. The Massachusetts statute does not extend marriage to nonresidents whose marriage would be void in their states of residence.[86]

[c] Dissolving civil unions. Dissolving a civil union may be even more difficult. The Supreme Court of Connecticut held that the state's divorce statutes did not confer subject matter jurisdiction to dissolve a Vermont civil union, even though the petitioner was a Connecticut resident. Nothing enumerated in the statute as a "family matter" could be construed to include a civil union between persons of the same sex.[87] A New York court, in contrast, held that a family court could hear an action to dissolve a Vermont civil union of a couple domiciled in New York.[88]

[d] Recognition of separation agreements. Unmarried couples, including same-sex partners, may arrange their financial affairs by agreement. The Mississippi Supreme Court held that a contract between same-sex partners arising out of the rela-

---

399 (2010) (noting difference between nonrecognitiion of sister state statutes and nonrecognition of judgments).

[81] See *infra* § 18.03.

[82] Cerutti-O'Brien v. Cerutti-O'Brien, 928 N.E.2d 1002 (Mass. Ct. App. 2010).

[83] Wilson v. Ake, 354 F. Supp. 2d 1298 (M.D. Fla. 2005).

[84] *In re* Marriage of J.B. and H.B., 326 S.W. 3d 654 (Tex. 2010).

[85] Beth R. v. Donna M., 853 N.Y.S. 2d 501 (N.Y. Sup. Ct. 2008).

[86] Gonzalez v. Green, 831 N.Y.S. 2d 856 (N.Y. Sup. 2006).

[87] Rosengarten v. Downes, 802 A. 2d 170 (Conn. 2002). This was before Connecticut adopted its own civil union statute. *See also* Chambers v. Ormiston, 935 A. 2d 956 (R.I. 2007) (statute empowering family courts to determine "all petitions for divorce from the bond of marriage" does not encompass a petition filed by a same-sex couple who were married in Massachusetts).

[88] Dickerson v. Thompson, 897 N.Y.S. 2d 298 (N.Y. App. Div. 2010).

RIGHTS BETWEEN UNMARRIED PARTNERS   § 2.09[3][e]

tionship was enforceable. Upon termination of their relationship, the two men entered into an agreement providing for the payment of $59,000 by one of the men, along with the return of certain personal property. When the payee died, the payor stopped making payment to his estate, even though the contract called for payments to survive his death. The court rejected the estate's argument that the agreement was unenforceable as against public policy: "Unless a contract is illegal or against public policy, parties have the right to enter into contracts concerning their property and interests therein and the right to rely upon the mutually agreed upon terms and conditions of the contract." The court held that, although the state does not recognize "palimony," same-sex couples have the right to contract with regard to their affairs.[89]

[4] Extension of state benefits to same-sex couples. In states with mini-DOMAs, benefits will not be extended to same-sex couples. In states that do not expressly prohibit recognition, the response has been varied. A New York court held that an employee of a community college who entered a valid Canadian marriage was entitled to health benefits for her same-sex partner. The court noted that New York has recognized marriages solemnized outside of New York unless they are prohibited by statute or are prohibited by "natural law." The court concluded that a same-sex marriage does not violate the natural law exception.[90]

In contrast, a New Jersey court refused to extend property rights to a couple married in Canada, because New Jersey does not recognize marriage between persons of the same sex. But the court noted that New Jersey will recognize civil unions from other states, according them the same rights as New Jersey domestic partners.[91]

A couple is not entitled to rights based on the law of the state in which they were joined. A couple joined in a Vermont Civil Union and a Canadian marriage argued that they should be entitled to hold property as tenants by the entirety in New Jersey. New Jersey law at that time recognized domestic partnerships, but did not afford this particular property right to domestic partners. The court held that while New Jersey recognized civil unions and domestic partnerships from other states, it is not required to provide rights not available to domestic partners under New Jersey law.[92]

§ 2.10 ADOPTION

In some states, same-sex couples may adopt a child. In others, same-sex adoption is specifically prohibited. In addition, some states that prohibit same-sex adoption also refuse recognition to same-sex adoptions from other states. Mississippi's adoption statutes provide, "Adoption by couples of the same gender is prohibited."[93] Federal courts have affirmed constitutionality of prohibiting same-sex adoption, but agree that states must recognize same-sex adoptions valid in other states.

---

[89] Estate of Reaves v. Owen, 744 So. 2d 799, 802 (Miss. Ct. App. 1999).

[90] Martinez v. County of Monroe, 850 N.Y.S. 2d 740 (N.Y. App. Div. 2008).

[91] Hennefeld v. Township of Montclair, 22 N.J. Tax 166, 2005 WL 646650 (2005).

[92] Hennefeld v. Township of Montclair, 22 N.J. Tax 166, 2005 WL 646650 (2005).

[93] MISS. CODE ANN. 93-17-3 (Supp. 2010).

§ 2.10[1]   **MISSISSIPPI FAMILY LAW**

[1] Constitutionality of adoption prohibition. In 2004, the Eleventh Circuit up-held held Florida's prohibition on adoption by a person who is "actively" homosexual. The court held that the statute is rationally related to the state's interest in assuring an optimal home environment for children. In contrast, the Arkansas Supreme Court held that the state's prohibition on gay foster parents was unconstitutional. The court affirmed the trial court's finding that the regulation did not promote the "health, safety, or welfare of children."[94]

[2] Full faith and credit. Two federal courts have held that statutes denying recognition to valid out-of-state same-sex adoptions are unconstitutional. The Tenth Circuit held unconstitutional an Oklahoma statute denying full faith and credit to out-of-state, same-sex adoptions. The Court held that the Full Faith and Credit Clause of the Constitution requires recognition of judgments from other states, including decrees of adoption, without regard to the public policy of the recognizing state. The court noted that the Supreme Court has interpreted the Full Faith and Credit Clause to provide a greater protection to judgments than to statutes, which may be denied enforcement if the statute contravenes a significant policy of the state in which enforcement is sought.[95] Similarly, the Court of Appeals for the Fifth Circuit held that Louisiana could not deny recognition of a New York decree of adoption in favor of same-sex parents.[96]

§ 2.11 PARENTAL RIGHTS BASED ON RELATIONSHIP

In some states, even in the absence of adoption, a same-sex partner may claim rights as a parent when the couple separates. Courts have varied with regard to the rights of a same-sex partner of a woman who gives birth through assisted reproduction. In some states, same-sex partners have been accorded rights as intended parents, or based on a court's finding that they have acted *in loco parentis* or as a de facto parent.[97] In others, courts have denied visitation to same-sex partners, finding that extension of visitation is a matter for the legislature,[98] or that the de facto parent doctrine does not apply to same-sex couples.[99]

---

[94] Lofton v. Secretary of the Department of Children and Family Services, 35877 F. 3d 8041275 (11th Cir., 2004). *But cf.* Department of Human Services and Child Welfare Agency Review Bd. v. Howard, 238 S.W.3d 1 (Ark. 2006).

[95] Finstuen v. Crutcher, 496 F. 2d 1139 (10th Cir. 2007),

[96] Adar v. Smith, 597 F.3d 697, 719 (5th Cir. 2010), *rev'd in part,* 639 F. 3d 146 (5th Cir. 2010) (en banc) (state must recognize adoption, but need not change child's birth certficate).

[97] *See, e.g.*, Charisma R. v. Kristina S., 44 Cal. Rptr. 3d 332 (Cal. Ct. App 2006) (same-sex partners may have parental rights when a child was received into the home and held out as a natural child); E.N.O. v. L.M.M., 711 N.E.2d 886, 892 (Mass. 1999), *cert. denied,* L.M.M. v. E.N.O., 528 U.S. 1005 (1999) (applying "de facto" parent test); T.B. v. L.R.M., 874 A.2d 34, 38 (Pa. Super. Ct. 2005), *appeal denied,* T.B. v. L.R.M., 890 A.2d 1060 (Pa. 2005) (The trial court erred in denying visitation to former same-sex partner who had *in loco parentis* standing to child.); L.S.K. v. H.A.N., 813 A.2d 872, 878 (Pa. Super. Ct. 2002) (former same-sex partner of biological mother was required to pay child support for five children born through artificial insemination during the relationship); Rubano v. DiCenzo, 759 A.2d 959, 976 (R.I. 2000) (biological mother equitably estopped from denying former same-sex partner parental rights to child born by artificial insemination; de facto parent).

[98] Janis C. v. Christine T., 742 N.Y.S.2d 381, 383 (N.Y. App. Div. 2002), *rev'g* J.C. v. C.T., 711 N.Y.S.2d 295 (N.Y. Fam. Ct. 2000).

[99] Jones v. Barlow, 154 P.3d 808, 813-14 (Utah 2007) (*in loco parentis* standing does not extend to former same-sex partner seeking visitation rights with child conceived by artificial insemination); *In re* Thompson, 11 S.W.3d 913, 923 (Tenn. Ct. App. 1999).

RIGHTS BETWEEN UNMARRIED PARTNERS § 2.12

§ 2.12 Custody actions

[1] Jurisdiction. Couples with connections with two states may find themselves forum shopping if one of the states views same-sex parenthood more favorably than the other. These disputes will be decided under the UCCJEA, which governs custody disputes between states. The UCCJEA is discussed in detail in Chapter XVIII.

A dispute involving Virginia and Vermont parties illustrates application of the Act. A lesbian couple was married in Vermont but lived in Virginia, where one of them had a child by artificial insemination. Her partner participated in the birth and acted as a mother to the child. The couple moved to Vermont in 2002, where they separated after a year. The child's biological mother moved back to Virginia and, two months later, filed a petition in Vermont to dissolve the union and for determination of parental rights. The Vermont court awarded her temporary custody and her partner visitation. Jurisdiction was appropriate in Vermont, which was the child's home state under the UCCJEA.

The mother then filed suit in Virginia, where she secured an order stating that her former partner had no rights with regard to the child. The Vermont court subsequently refused to recognize the Virginia order, based on application of the UCCJEA, which provided Vermont with continuing exclusive jurisdiction over the case.[100] A state will usually be required to recognize a custody decision of another state with UCCJEA juridiction.

[2] Role of sexual orientation in custody actions. In Mississippi, a parent's same-sex relationship may not be the sole reason for denying custody to that parent. However, a parent's same-sex relationship may be one of several factors on which custody is based. Custody actions involving a gay or lesbian parent are discussed in detail in Chapter XII.[101]

§ 2.13 Conclusion

The law regarding same-sex marriage and adoption is rapidly evolving on a state and federal level. But because of the deeply held differences in views, the uncertainty surrounding interstate enforcement will likely continue for many years. Same-sex couples in nonrecognition states are best served by executing agreements that effectuate their wishes rather than relying on interstate enforcement. Similarly, long-term cohabitants who wish to secure property rights growing out of the relationship should execute contracts that specifically set out their intentions with regard to the division of assets upon separation or death.

---

[100] Miller-Jenkins v. Miller-Jenkins, 912 A.2d 951 (Vt. 2006).
[101] See *infra* § 12.03[8][b] (original custody award); § 12.08[4][i] (modification of custody).

56

III
ANNULMENT

While a divorce terminates a valid marriage, an annulment declares that a marriage never existed. As a result, financial remedies for divorcing parties – alimony and equitable distribution – are generally not available in connection with annulment. Matters regarding children, however, are governed by the same rules whether a marriage is terminated by divorce or annulled. Modern annulment actions are governed by statute. However, historical common law distinctions between void and voidable marriages continue to influence the grounds for and defenses to annulment.

§ 3.01 History and overview

[1] History. It is questionable whether early American courts had the power to annul marriages. This country's courts derived their authority from England's civil courts, which had no power to annul marriages prior to 1857. Jurisdiction over annulments rested in the English ecclesiastical courts.[1] Nonetheless, most American courts were willing to use their inherent equitable powers to declare marriages null. Today, courts are authorized by statute to declare annulment, with grounds varying from state to state.[2] Even so, historical distinctions that arose under English ecclesiastical law continue to dictate some aspects of annulment.[3]

[2] Mississippi. Until the mid-twentieth century, annulment was strictly a judicial remedy in Mississippi, based somewhat uncertainly on the power of English ecclesiastical courts.[4] In 1962, the Mississippi legislature enacted a statute setting out nine grounds for annulling a marriage.[5] Unfortunately, the statute fails to address several critical issues and creates some distinctions that are difficult to fathom.[6] Very few recorded Mississippi cases address annulment under the statute or based on judicial authority.

Under the current statute, marriages may be annulled based on (1) bigamy; (2) kinship within the prohibited degrees; (3) incurable impotency; (4) adjudicated mental illness or incompetence of either or both parties; (5) failure to meet licensure requirements, if no cohabitation occurs; (6) incapacity to consent due to age or lack of understanding; (7) physical incapacity to enter into the marriage state; (8) lack of consent due to force or fraud; and (9) pregnancy of the wife by another at the time of marriage without the husband's knowledge.[7]

---

[1] Homer H. Clark, Jr., The Law of Domestic Relations in the United States § 3.1, at 125 (2d ed. 1988).

[2] Clark, Jr., *supra* note 1, § 3.2, at 126-27.

[3] *See* discussion of the void/voidable distinction *infra* § 3.02.

[4] *See* J.W. Bunkley & W.E. Morse, Amis on Divorce & Separation in Mississippi § 2.04, at 33-34 (1957).

[5] *See* Miss. Code Ann. § 93-7-1 (2004). According to Bunkley and Morse, the statute confused rather than clarified the action. Bunkley & Morse, *supra* note 4, § 2.06, 13-14 (Supp. 1980).

[6] *See* discussion of defenses to annulment *infra* § 3.04.

[7] Miss. Code Ann. §§ 93-7-1, -3 (2004).

§ 3.02   MISSISSIPPI FAMILY LAW

§ 3.02   The void/voidable classification

Historically, marriages prohibited by canonical law were considered void, while marriages that violated civil impediments were voidable.[8] The distinction has blurred considerably but still holds some significance in American law. Void marriages – those that violate the most serious state prohibitions – are *void ab initio*, or void for all purposes. Marriages violative of less serious prohibitions are voidable – valid for all purposes unless annulled by the parties.[9] Because a void marriage can never be legal, annulment is technically not necessary, although the action provides formal recognition of invalidity.[10] In contrast, a voidable marriage must be set aside through an annulment action. Otherwise, it is valid for all purposes.[11]

[1] Distinctions between void and voidable marriages. A void marriage cannot be ratified by the parties and may be challenged at any time, even after their deaths. Third parties may attack a void marriage in collateral proceedings, even after the deaths of the parties.[12] In contrast, a voidable marriage may be ratified by the parties, typically by continuing the marriage relationship after the impediment is removed or becomes known.[13] Furthermore, suits to annul voidable marriages may be brought only by one of the parties to the marriage.[14] Voidable marriages may not be attacked after the death of one of the parties[15] or in a collateral proceeding.[16]

[2] Classification. In Mississippi, only incestuous marriages and bigamous marriages are classified as void.[17] Violation of other prohibitions results in a voidable marriage.[18] Some of the common law consequences of the void/voidable distinction

---

[8] While the void/voidable distinction has been retained, impediments to marriage are not always placed in the same category as at common law. For example, incestuous marriages were voidable at common law, while marriages lacking in consent were void. Today, the opposite is true. *See* CLARK, JR., *supra* note 1, § 2.1, at 23.

[9] *See* CLARK, JR., *supra* note 1, § 3.2, at 127; JOHN DE WITT GREGORY, PETER N. SWISHER & SHERYL L. WOLF, UNDERSTANDING FAMILY LAW § 2.08[A], at 46-47 (2d ed. 2001).

[10] *See* BUNKLEY & MORSE, *supra* note 4, § 2.03, at 33; J. THOMAS OLDHAM, DIVORCE, SEPARATION, & THE DISTRIBUTION OF PROPERTY § 2.02[10], at 2-7 (2001).

[11] *See* Ervin v. Bass, 160 So. 568, 569 (Miss. 1935) ("A marriage, the consent to which has been induced by force or coercion, is not void, but voidable. In consequence it remains of full legal effect and valid for all purposes until dissolved by the decree of a competent court.") (quoting Ellis v. Ellis, 119 So. 304, 305 (Miss. 1928)).

[12] BUNKLEY & MORSE, *supra* note 4, § 2.07, at 48-49; *see* GREGORY ET. AL, *supra* note 9, § 2.08[A], at 47.

[13] GREGORY ET. AL, *supra* note 9, § 2.10[B], at 62; *see* BUNKLEY & MORSE, *supra* note 4, § 2.07, at 48 (spouse who continues cohabitation after discovery of invalidating facts loses right to set aside voidable marriage); CLARK, JR., *supra* note 1, § 2.15, at 114 (continuing marriage relationship after knowledge of fraud is defense to annulment action).

[14] *See* Ellis v. Ellis, 119 So. 304, 305 (Miss. 1928) ("If the parties who are alone recognized by the statutes as entitled to have the marriage annulled do not, during its existence, see fit to avoid it, a stranger to the marriage should not be permitted to question its validity in a collateral proceeding.") (quoting *In re* Gregorson's Estate, 116 P. 60, 63 (Cal. 1911)).

[15] *See* Ervin v. Bass, 160 So. 568, 569 (Miss. 1935).

[16] *See* Doss v. State, 126 So. 197, 199-00 (Miss. 1930) (twelve-year-old wife could not testify in abduction and rape trial against husband; marriage could be annulled only in suit in chancery court, not in collateral proceeding).

[17] *See* MISS. CODE ANN. §§ 93-1-1, 93-7-1 (2004). The annulment statute was not amended to include the 1997 prohibition on same-sex marriages, which are also void by statute. *See* MISS. CODE ANN. § 93-3-1(2) (2004). Prior versions of the Mississippi Code classified marriages between the races as void. *See* Ellis v. Ellis, 119 So. 304, 305 (Miss. 1928).

[18] *See* MISS. CODE ANN. § 93-7-3 (2004).

ANNULMENT   § 3.03

have been altered by statute. For example, Mississippi now recognizes the legitimacy of children of void bigamous marriages. However, children of incestuous marriages remain illegitimate.[19]

§ 3.03 GROUNDS FOR ANNULMENT

The Mississippi statute establishes two grounds that create a void marriage and seven circumstances under which a marriage is voidable.

[1] Void marriages. A marriage that is void because of bigamy or kinship may be set aside by either spouse or collaterally attacked by third parties.[20]

[a] Bigamy. A marriage is void if one of the parties is already legally married.[21] Bigamous marriages may be set aside by annulment[22] or dissolved by divorce.[23] Either spouse may obtain an annulment of a bigamous marriage.[24] However, only an innocent spouse may obtain a divorce based on bigamy.[25] Although bigamous marriages are labeled void, children of bigamous marriages are considered legitimate.[26]

[b] Kinship within the prohibited degree. No one may marry his or her parent, grandparent, stepparent or stepgrandparent, adoptive parent, sibling, half-sibling, aunt, uncle, first cousin, or his or her child's widow or widower.[27] A marriage that is incestuous is void[28] and may be annulled[29] or dissolved through divorce[30] by either party. Children of an incestuous marriage are labeled illegitimate even if the parties entered the marriage in good faith.[31]

---

[19] *See* MISS. CODE ANN. § 93-7-5 (2004).

[20] See discussion *supra* § 3.02.

[21] MISS. CODE ANN. § 93-7-1 (2004). Bigamy is a crime punishable by up to ten years in prison. MISS. CODE ANN. § 97-29-13 (2006). Mississippi's "Enoch Arden" statute exempts from prosecution one whose husband or wife has been absent for seven years. MISS. CODE ANN. § 97-29-15 (2006). Enoch Arden statutes do not validate the later marriage; they simply provide a defense to criminal prosecution for bigamy. *See* CLARK, JR., *supra* note 1, § 2.6, at 67. *But see* Harper v. Fears, 151 So. 745, 747 (Miss. 1934) (where wife remarried based on first husband's presumed death, then asserted right to inherit upon his death, his absence for the statutory period validated the later marriages). *See* discussion *supra* § 1.03[1][b].

[22] MISS. CODE ANN. § 93-7-1 (2004).

[23] MISS. CODE ANN. § 93-5-1 (2004).

[24] MISS. CODE ANN. § 93-7-1 (2004).

[25] *See* discussion *infra* § 4.02[11].

[26] MISS. CODE ANN. § 93-7-5 (2004).

[27] MISS. CODE ANN. § 93-1-1 (2004). The statute prohibits marrying one's deceased child's former spouse, but does not prohibit the reverse. *See* State v. Winslow, 45 So. 2d 574, 576 (Miss. 1950) (dismissing criminal prosecution of man who married mother-in-law; statute prohibits mother-in-law from marrying child's widower, but not vice versa). Note also that the statute does not prohibit marrying one's child's divorced spouse, nor does it prohibit marriage between stepsiblings. *See* discussion *supra* § 1.03[1][a].

[28] MISS. CODE ANN. § 93-1-1 (2004); *see* Weeks v. Weeks, 654 So. 2d 33, 35 (Miss. 1995) (marriage between uncle and niece void). It is a crime punishable by up to ten years in prison for persons prohibited by kinship to marry, cohabit, or have a sexual relationship. MISS. CODE ANN. § 97-29-5 (2006).

[29] MISS. CODE ANN. § 93-7-1 (2004).

[30] MISS. CODE ANN. § 93-5-1 (2004).

[31] MISS. CODE ANN. § 93-7-5 (2004).

59

§ 3.03[2]   MISSISSIPPI FAMILY LAW

[2] Voidable marriages. As a general rule, only spouses may set aside a voidable marriage.[32] However, the Mississippi statute does not clearly indicate which spouse may seek annulment of a voidable marriage.[33] It is also unclear the extent to which defenses apply to some of the voidable grounds.[34]

[a] Incurable impotency and [b] lack of physical capacity. A marriage may be annulled based upon "incurable impotency" existing at the time of the marriage ceremony.[35] Natural impotency is also a ground for divorce.[36] The Mississippi annulment statute also states that a marriage may be set aside if one of the parties is "physically incapable of entering the marriage relationship."[37]

[c] Mental illness or retardation. A marriage may be annulled based upon the "adjudicated mental illness or incompetence of either or both parties" at the time of the marriage. Suit may be brought by a guardian or next friend of the mentally ill or incompetent spouse.[38] A marriage may also be dissolved by divorce if (1) one or both spouses was mentally ill or mentally disabled at the time of marriage, and the other was unaware of the condition, or (2) a spouse with incurable mental illness has been confined to a mental institution for three or more years.[39] The annulment statute also provides that a marriage may be annulled if a party was incapable of consenting to the marriage "from want of . . . understanding."[40]

[d] Pregnancy of the wife by another. A husband may annul a marriage or obtain a divorce if his wife was pregnant by another at the time of the marriage without his knowledge of the pregnancy.[41]

[e] Minority. A marriage may be annulled based on a spouse's minority.[42]

[f] Lack of consent. Annulment may be granted to a party whose consent to a marriage was obtained through force or fraud.[43]

[g] Failure to obtain a license. If the parties failed to comply with marriage licensure provisions, an annulment may be granted unless the parties cohabited after the purported marriage.[44]

---

[32] *See* discussion *supra* § 3.02.
[33] *See* discussion *supra* § 3.02.
[34] *See* discussion *infra* § 3.04.
[35] MISS. CODE ANN. § 93-7-3 (2004). *See* discussion *supra* § 1.03[1][e].
[36] MISS. CODE ANN. § 93-5-1 (2004).
[37] MISS. CODE ANN. § 93-7-3(d) (2004). *See* discussion *supra* § 1.03[1][e].
[38] MISS. CODE ANN. § 93-7-3 (Supp. 2010).
[39] MISS. CODE ANN. § 93-5-1 (Supp. 2010).
[40] MISS. CODE ANN. § 93-7-3(d) (2004).
[41] MISS. CODE ANN. § 93-7-3(e) (2004) (annulment); MISS. CODE ANN. § 93-5-1 (2004) (divorce).
[42] MISS. CODE ANN. § 93-7-3(d) (2004). *See* discussion *supra* § 1.03[1][c].
[43] MISS. CODE ANN. § 93-7-3(d) (2004). *See* discussion of marriage based on lack of consent *supra* § 1.03[3].
[44] MISS. CODE ANN. § 93-7-3(c) (2004). *See* discussion of licensure requirements *supra* § 1.03[2].

ANNULMENT

§ 3.04

§ 3.04 Defenses to annulment

There are four defenses to annulment under Mississippi law: running of the statute of limitations, ratification, laches, and estoppel.

[1] Statute of limitations. Under the Mississippi statute, annulment actions based on age, mental or physical incapacity, lack of consent due to fraud or duress, or the wife's pregnancy by another must be brought within six months of the time the ground is or should have been discovered.[45] Suit to annul based on mental illness or lack of capacity must be brought within six months of the marriage.[46] The statute does not set a limitations period for actions based on failure to meet licensure requirements or impotency.[47] Void marriages – bigamous or incestuous marriages – may be annulled at any time.[48]

[2] Ratification. The Mississippi statute recognizes ratification as a defense to some, but not all, annulment actions. Annulments based on age, lack of mental or physical capacity, lack of consent due to fraud or duress, or pregnancy of the wife by another are subject to the defense of ratification.[49] Ratification typically occurs when a spouse continues cohabitation with knowledge of an impediment.[50] The statute does not mention ratification of marriages invalid because of impotency,[51] mental illness,[52] or failure to meet licensure requirements.[53]

No Mississippi annulment cases directly addressing ratification were found. In a case that predated the statute, the supreme court recognized the defense in dicta.[54] The supreme court has also applied the ratification defense in a divorce action based on mental illness at the time of the marriage.[55]

[3] Laches. The Mississippi Supreme Court recognized laches as a defense to annulment in one case involving a void marriage. The deceased's first wife sought to

---

[45] Miss. Code Ann. § 93-7-3 (2004).

[46] Miss. Code Ann. § 93-7-3 (Supp. 2010); *see* Haralson v. Haralson, 362 So. 2d 190, 191 (Miss. 1978) (sister's suit as guardian for brother barred because not brought within six months of marriage).

[47] *See* Miss. Code Ann. § 93-7-3 (2004).

[48] *See* discussion *supra* § 3.02.

[49] *See* Miss. Code Ann. § 93-7-3 (2004).

[50] *See* Kibler v. Kibler, 24 S.W.2d 867, 868 (Ark. 1930) (ratification by continuing marriage after majority); McLarty v. McLarty, 433 S.W.2d 722, 724 (Tex. Civ. App. 1968) (ratification by cohabiting after learning of fraud).

[51] Other states permit ratification as a defense to annulment based on impotency. *See, e.g.,* Donati v. Church, 80 A.2d 633, 634 (N.J. Super. Ct. App. Div. 1951) (continuing marriage with knowledge of impotency).

[52] *But cf.* McIntosh v. McIntosh, 117 So. 352, 352 (Miss. 1928) (applying ratification defense to divorce action based on mental illness at the time of the marriage).

[53] *See* Miss. Code Ann. § 93-7-3 (2004). The Mississippi Supreme Court in *Marsh v. Whittington*, 40 So. 326, 326 (Miss. 1906) acknowledged the defense of ratification – "there was no subsequent ratification" – in affirming a chancellor's holding that a marriage was invalid because the husband was accompanied to the wedding by armed in-laws.

[54] *See* Parkinson v. Mills, 159 So. 651, 656 (Miss. 1935) (suggesting that courts look carefully for ratification if mentally ill person has recovered and continued in marriage without seeking annulment) (case predates statute, which does not appear to permit ratification of condition).

[55] *See* McIntosh v. McIntosh, 117 So. 352, 352 (Miss. 1928) ("The law requires the party injured, under such circumstances, promptly to elect whether he will abide by the relation, or whether he will disavow and dissolve it . . . .") (also predating annulment statute).

§ 3.04[4]   MISSISSIPPI FAMILY LAW

annul his subsequent, bigamous marriage by proving that their divorce was invalid. The court held that her suit was barred by laches because she waited fifty years until his death to challenge the validity of their divorce. All potential witnesses involved in the divorce action were dead. In addition, the decedent's second wife of fifty years and their eight children would be unjustly injured if the suit were permitted.[56]

[4] Estoppel. A spouse who enters a second marriage without obtaining a divorce may be estopped from seeking to annul the second marriage on the basis of bigamy. For example, a man who deserted his first wife and married without obtaining a divorce could not annul the second marriage in order to inherit from his first wife.[57] Estoppel has also been used to overcome a husband's objection to his first wife's testimony in a criminal trial.[58]

Estoppel is not a defense to an action to annul an incestuous marriage.[59] For example, a husband of nine years successfully attacked the validity of a separate maintenance award to his wife, who was also his niece. Their years of cohabitation did not prevent setting aside the marriage: "public policy prevents the validation of a void marriage by the doctrine of estoppel."[60]

§ 3.05 PARTIES WHO MAY CHALLENGE

Third parties may challenge the validity of a void marriage. In other cases, the right to challenge the marriage is reserved to one or both spouses.

[1] Third persons. The Mississippi annulment statute does not specify who may bring an action to annul or challenge the validity of a marriage. The few cases to address the issue follow the general rule that third parties may attack void marriages, while voidable marriages may be challenged only by the parties to the marriage. In 1931, the Mississippi Supreme Court refused to allow a deceased, allegedly incompetent man's siblings to set aside his marriage in hopes of inheriting his estate. The court held that mental illness makes a marriage voidable, precluding suit by third parties.[61]

[2] Spouses. Either spouse may obtain an annulment of a bigamous or incestuous

---

[56] Stanley v. Stanley, 29 So. 2d 641, 644-45 (Miss. 1947) (first wife lived in same community with husband and second wife).

[57] Williams v. Johnston, 114 So. 733, 734 (Miss. 1927); *see* Minor v. Higdon, 61 So. 2d 350, 357 (Miss. 1952); Walker v. Matthews, 3 So. 2d 820, 826 (Miss. 1941) (woman estopped from claiming as heir of alleged common law first husband); Joy v. Miles, 199 So. 771, 771 (Miss. 1941) (woman estopped from claiming as heir of first husband whether or not she knew first divorce was ineffective); Williams v. Johnston, 114 So. 733, 734 (Miss. 1927) (desertion of wife and second marriage estopped husband from inheriting from first, legal wife).

[58] *See* Enis v. State, 408 So. 2d 486, 488 (Miss. 1981) (entry into ceremonial marriage inconsistent with claim of valid common law marriage).

[59] *See* BUNKLEY & MORSE, *supra* note 4, § 2.07, at 49 (it is in the public interest to dissolve void marriage).

[60] Weeks v. Weeks, 654 So. 2d 33, 37 (Miss. 1995).

[61] *See* Case v. Case, 150 So. 2d 148, 153 (Miss. 1963) (family members could not collaterally attack marriage after death of allegedly mentally ill spouse); White v. Williams, 132 So. 573, 575 (Miss. 1931) (discussing admitted potential for fraud by one who marries mentally ill person, but finding greater danger in allowing heirs to attack marriage after death); Ellis v. Ellis, 119 So. 304, 305 (Miss. 1928) (marriage was voidable, but not void, and therefore could be attacked only during lifetime of parties).

ANNULMENT

§ 3.06

marriage.[62] The Mississippi statute does not address whether one or both spouses can annul a voidable marriage. A review of authorities suggests that only the innocent party should be allowed to annul for fraud or duress.[63] Similarly, it would seem that only the husband should be entitled to annul a marriage for his wife's pregnancy by another. According to one authority, a spouse of legal age cannot annul a marriage based on the other's minority.[64] The language of the Mississippi statute, however, suggests the possibility of suit by the spouse of legal age, stating that annulment may be filed within six months of the time the impediment "is or should have been discovered."[65] Some courts have held that either party may annul a marriage based on impotence.[66] Unless the failure to comply with licensure requirements was fraudulent on the part of one party, annulment on that basis should be available to both spouses.

§ 3.06 EFFECT OF ANNULMENT

A spouse's obligation of support survives divorce in the form of alimony and equitable distribution of property. Because annulment declares that a marriage never existed, spouses to an annulled marriage may not be awarded alimony or an equitable distribution of property.

[1] Property and support rights. Spouses of an annulled marriage are not entitled to spousal support in the form of alimony.[67] Their rights with regard to property division are generally the same as those of cohabitants.[68] In many states, however, the putative spouse doctrine extends property rights to spouses who married in good faith, without knowledge that the marriage was invalid. A 2010 decision of the Mississippi Court of Appeals expanded this doctrine, affirming equitable division of assets to a purported wife who knew that her marriage was bigamous.[69]

Even though permanent alimony may not be granted in an annulment, some courts will award temporary alimony to a financially dependent spouse if there are genuine issues regarding the validity of the marriage.[70]

---

[62] MISS. CODE ANN. § 93-7-1 (2004) (either spouse may obtain a declaration of nullity based on a bigamous marriage). *But see* Callahan v. Callahan, 381 So. 2d 178, 179 (Miss. 1980) (citing Case v. Case, 150 So. 2d 148 (Miss. 1963)) (relying on cases that predate statute).

[63] *See* CLARK, JR., *supra* note 1, § 2.14, at 103 (party against whom force was used entitled to annulment).

[64] *See* CLARK, JR., *supra* note 1, § 2.10, at 95 (purpose of law was to protect underage party). Clark also states that unless the statute so provides, parents may not sue in their own names to set aside the marriage of an underage child. *Id.*

[65] MISS. CODE ANN. § 93-7-3 (2004).

[66] *See* Sarda v. Sarda, 153 A.2d 305, 308 (D.C. 1959) ("psychogenic" impotence); D v. C, 221 A.2d 763, 765-66 (N.J. Ch. 1966) (wife unaware of her vaginismus before wedlock); Gabriel v. Gabriel, 79 N.Y.S.2d 823, 825 (N.Y. App. Div. 1948) (denying annulment where proof not clear and convincing); Anon. v. Anon., 126 N.Y.S. 149, 149 (N.Y. Sup. Ct. 1910); *see also* David B. Perlmutter, Annotation, *Incapacity for Sexual Intercourse as Ground for Annulment*, 52 A.L.R.3d 589 (1973).

[67] *See* Aldridge v. Aldridge, 77 So. 150, 150-51 (Miss. 1918) (no alimony); *see also* BUNKLEY & MORSE, *supra* note 4, § 2.05, at 36.

[68] *See* discussion of rights of unmarried partners, *supra* § 2.02.

[69] Cotton v. Cotton, 44 So. 3d 371, 373-76 (Miss. Ct. App. 2010) (wife, who never divorced her first husband, received an equitable distribution of assets upon annulment of second, thirty-seven-year marriage).

[70] CLARK, JR., *supra* note 1, § 3.4, at 138 (spouse seeking temporary alimony must not be seeking annulment). While no case was found granting temporary alimony in Mississippi, the court recognized the possibility in *Parkinson*

§ 3.06[2]   MISSISSIPPI FAMILY LAW

[2] Children of annulled marriage. Custody and support of children of an annulled marriage are governed by the same rules that apply to children of divorce.[71] With
the exception of marriages annulled because of incest, children of annulled marriages
are considered legitimate if they were born after the ceremony.[72] The statute does not,
however, extend legitimacy to children of a couple who simply cohabited with no attempt to contract a marriage.[73]

[3] Retroactivity. Because an annulment declares that a marriage never existed,
courts have held that annulments "relate back," erasing any legal effect of the marriage.[74] Some courts apply the relation-back doctrine to revive public benefits payable
on the basis of a prior marriage.[75] Arguably, the doctrine should revive alimony payable
from a prior marriage as well. The majority of courts, however, refuse to apply the doctrine to revive a former spouse's financial obligations.[76] The Mississippi Supreme Court
held that alimony payments did not resume upon annulment of a second marriage; by
remarrying, the wife elected to look to her new husband "as the man from whom she
would receive her support."[77]

§ 3.07 JURISDICTION AND PROCEDURE

For a court to have jurisdiction over an annulment, at least one of the parties must
be domiciled in the forum state.[78] In a 1923 case, the Mississippi Supreme Court refused to hear an action to annul a marriage solemnized in Mississippi between spouses
domiciled in Alabama, even though the court had personal jurisdiction over the parties.
The court held that only a state in which one spouse is domiciled has jurisdiction over
the marriage status.[79] Jurisdiction lies with the chancery courts of the state.[80]
    A complaint for annulment may be filed in the defendant's county of residence,
the county where the marriage license was issued, or the plaintiff's county of residence

---

v. Mills, 159 So. 651, 656 (Miss. 1935) (denying temporary alimony and attorneys' fees where wife knew husband was
mentally ill, lived with him only a few days, and never looked to him for support).

    [71] See MISS. CODE ANN. § 93-7-7 (2004) ("[T]he chancery court may, in its discretion, . . . make all orders touching
the care, custody, and maintenance of the children of the marriage; and the court may, afterwards, on complaint, change
the judgment and make from time to time such new judgment as the case may require.").

    [72] See MISS. CODE ANN. § 93-7-5 (2004). The statutory concept of "legitimacy" has little meaning for the purposes
of family law today. The legal rights of children to support, and of parents to custody, are not affected by the statutory
categorization.

    [73] See Stutts v. Estate of Stutts, 194 So. 2d 229, 232 (Miss. 1967) (statute "contemplates more than a mere adulter-
ous or illicit relationship").

    [74] See CLARK, JR., supra note 1, § 3.5, at 143.

    [75] See Folsom v. Pearsall, 245 F.2d 562, 567 (9th Cir. 1957) (Social Security benefits); Means v. Indus. Comm'n,
515 P.2d 29, 32 (Ariz. 1973) (workers' compensation); Eureka Block Coal Co. v. Wells, 147 N.E. 811, 812 (Ind. App.
1925) (relation back for purposes of workers' compensation); First Nat'l Bank in Grand Forks v. N.D. Workmen's Comp.
Bureau, 68 N.W.2d 661, 664 (N.D. 1955) (relation back for purposes of workers' compensation); S. Ry. Co. v. Baskette,
133 S.W.2d 498, 502-03 (Tenn. 1939).

    [76] See cases cited in Ferdinand S. Tinio, Annotation, Annulment of Later Marriage as Reviving Prior Husband's
Obligations Under Alimony Decree or Separation Agreement, 45 A.L.R.3d 1033 (1972), and C.S. Parnell, Annotation,
Alimony as Affected by Wife's Remarriage, in Absence of Controlling Specific Statute, 48 A.L.R.2d 270 (1956).

    [77] Bridges v. Bridges, 217 So. 2d 281, 281 (Miss. 1968).

    [78] See CLARK, JR., supra note 1, § 3.2.

    [79] Antoine v. Antoine, 96 So. 305, 306 (Miss. 1923).

    [80] Case's Will v. Case, 150 So. 2d 148, 151 (Miss. 1963).

ANNULMENT   **§ 3.07**

if the defendant is a nonresident of Mississippi.[81] The procedural rules applicable to divorce actions govern annulment actions, including service of process.[82]

---

[81] MISS. CODE ANN. § 93-7-9 (2004).
[82] MISS. CODE ANN. § 93-7-11 (2004).

IV
GROUNDS FOR DIVORCE

Until the mid-twentieth century, American law barred divorce in all but the most extreme cases. Social changes in the 1950s and 60s created a demand for divorce that transformed the fault-based system within a decade. Today, most states offer a no-fault system with few legal barriers to divorce.[1] Mississippi divorce law was liberalized in 1976 to add irreconcilable differences as a ground for divorce. However, the legislature rejected the unilateral no-fault system adopted in most states – spouses can divorce on irreconcilable differences only if both consent to be divorced. As a result, the traditional fault-based grounds for divorce remain an important part of modern Mississippi divorce proceedings.

§ 4.01 HISTORY AND OVERVIEW

[1] English divorce law. The history of divorce in England is inextricably linked to the church. Marriage in medieval England was a sacrament that could not be dissolved by divorce. A spouse could secure a legal separation or "divorce from bed and board" for a few serious marital offenses but could not remarry.[2] England remained a relatively divorceless society until 1857. Passage of the Matrimonial Causes Act in that year placed divorce jurisdiction in civil rather than ecclesiastical courts and permitted divorce based on adultery.[3] It was not until 1937 that other fault-based grounds for divorce were recognized in England.[4]

[2] Early American divorce law. Divorce laws varied significantly from state to state through the nineteenth century. Southern states were more likely to allow divorce only by private legislative bill, while northern states were more likely to authorize judicial fault-based divorce.[5] By the late 1800s, most states provided for judicial dissolution of marriages based on legislatively-approved grounds for divorce.[6] Some states also provided for divorce from bed and board or judicially recognized separation.[7]

[3] Early Mississippi divorce law. In the early nineteenth century, divorce was available in Mississippi on fault grounds, but only if two-thirds of the legislature

---

[1] *See* JOHN DE WITT GREGORY, PETER N. SWISHER & SHERYL L. WOLF, UNDERSTANDING FAMILY LAW § 8.01, at 224 (2d ed. 2001) (in less than one decade of divorce reform, divorce rate doubled).

[2] GREGORY, ET AL., *supra* note 1, § 8.01, at 222.

[3] *See* IRA MARK ELLMAN, PAUL M. KURTZ & ELIZABETH S. SCOTT, FAMILY LAW 187 (1998) (citing LAWRENCE M. FREIDMAN, A HISTORY OF AMERICAN LAW, 204-207 (2d ed. 1985)) (noting that the very wealthy could occasionally obtain a legislative bill of divorce, but the average between 1800 and 1836 was three a year).

[4] HOMER H. CLARK, JR., THE LAW OF DOMESTIC RELATIONS IN THE UNITED STATES § 12.1, at 408 (2d ed. 1988).

[5] ELLMAN ET AL., *supra* note 3, at 188-90.

[6] CLARK, JR., *supra* note 4, § 12.1, at 408-09.

[7] CLARK, JR., *supra* note 4, § 65, at 268 n.14.

§ 4.01[4]   MISSISSIPPI FAMILY LAW

approved the divorce.[8] By 1869 legislative approval was replaced by judicial oversight.[9] Section 90 of the current Mississippi Constitution authorizes the legislature to make general laws regarding divorce[10] and places exclusive jurisdiction over divorce cases in the state's chancery courts.[11]

Until 1871, Mississippi also recognized divorce from bed and board in cases of extreme cruelty and drunkenness. With the merger of these grounds into the fault-based statute, absolute divorce became the only form of divorce recognized in Mississippi.[12] The legislature eventually settled on twelve fault-based grounds for absolute divorce, which have not been altered since 1932.[13]

[4] Early twentieth century: Fault-based divorce. The fault-based system of divorce remained largely unchanged until the latter half of the twentieth century. The system incorporated the notion that divorce should be available only to an innocent spouse based on serious unforgiven wrongdoing. A plaintiff had to prove that the defendant's conduct came within narrowly defined statutory grounds. Default judgments were barred. Even in uncontested cases, plaintiffs were required to appear before the court with strict, corroborated proof.[14] Common law defenses created additional impediments to ending a marriage. For example, the defense of condonation barred divorce if a spouse continued to live in the home after learning of the other's adultery.[15] The doctrine of recrimination took the requirement of an innocent spouse to an illogical extreme, denying divorce if both parties proved grounds.[16]

[5] Divorce reform: Irreconcilable differences. By the mid-twentieth century, a nationwide reform movement demanded overhaul of divorce laws. The strict limitations on divorce had prompted much-criticized collusion between spouses and attorneys to fabricate divorce grounds. While some spouses perjured themselves to obtain divorces, others opted for migratory divorce, traveling to jurisdictions with short residency requirements to obtain a divorce.[17]

State courts responded to the gap between social reality and divorce law by lenient application of divorce grounds – divorces based on cruelty were often granted on evidence that simply showed incompatibility.[18] The Mississippi courts were no exception. Cases from the 1960s and 1970s show courts increasingly granting divorce based on habitual cruel and inhuman treatment. Although the supreme court continued to

---

[8] J.W. BUNKLEY & W.E. MORSE, AMIS ON DIVORCE & SEPARATION IN MISSISSIPPI § 3.01, at 55 (1957) (citing MISS. CONST. of 1817, art. VI, § 7).

[9] BUNKLEY & MORSE, *supra* note 8, § 3.01, at 55 (citing MISS. CONST. of 1869, art. IV, § 22).

[10] MISS. CONST. art. IV, § 90.

[11] MISS. CONST. art. VI, § 159.

[12] BUNKLEY & MORSE, *supra* note 8, § 3.02, at 56 (citing MISS. CODE (1871), ch. 23, art. IV, §§ 1767-77).

[13] Incurable insanity was added to the statute in 1932. BUNKLEY & MORSE, *supra* note 8, § 3.15, at 134; *see* MISS. CODE ANN. § 93-5-1 (2004) for the current version of the statute.

[14] *See* CLARK, JR., *supra* note 4, § 14.4, at 539.

[15] *See* Thames v. Thames, 100 So. 2d 868, 869 (Miss. 1958) (resumption of cohabitation alone condones the marital offense).

[16] *See* discussion of recrimination *infra* § 4.03[4].

[17] *See* CLARK, JR., *supra* note 4, § 12.1, at 409-10 (Alabama at one time had a one-day residency requirement).

[18] ELLMAN ET AL., *supra* note 3, at 193-94.

GROUNDS FOR DIVORCE

§ 4.01[6]

articulate the traditional test for cruelty, divorces were often affirmed on grounds much closer to modern irretrievable breakdown.[19]

In 1969, California became the first state to enact no-fault divorce legislation, starting a trend that quickly swept the nation.[20] On the heels of the California act, the Commissioners on Uniform State Laws produced the Uniform Marriage and Divorce Act, which provided for divorce upon a finding that a marriage was irretrievably broken.[21] By 1985, every state in the country had enacted some form of no-fault or irreconcilable differences divorce.[22] Most no-fault statutes permit divorce if one spouse proves that the marriage is irretrievably broken, in effect permitting unilateral divorce.[23]

[6] Divorce reform in Mississippi. In 1976, the Mississippi legislature joined the divorce reform movement, enacting an irreconcilable differences divorce statute.[24] The Act initially required that both spouses agree to be divorced and also agree on custody, property division, and support issues. The statute was later amended so that parties who could not agree on financial and custody terms could submit disputed issues to the court.[25]

Mississippi is among a small minority of states that do not permit unilateral no-fault divorce based on one spouse's proof of irreconcilable differences.[26] Unless both parties consent, the traditional fault-based system applies, with its strict requirements of proof, corroboration, and common law defenses. Recent appellate court decisions reveal that a number of divorces still proceed on fault-based grounds, and a significant number are denied for failure to meet the system's strict requirements.[27] In 2007, a concurring judge urged the legislature to reconsider a true no-fault divorce statute, after a husband of two years was denied a divorce and ordered to pay his wife one-half of his net income as separate maintenance.[28]

[7] Jurisdiction. The jurisdictional requirements for fault-based divorce and irreconcilable differences divorce differ. Both require that one of the parties have been domiciled within the state for six months. However, a divorce based on fault may be granted without personal jurisdiction over the defendant. In contrast, a divorce based

---

[19] *See* discussion *infra* § 4.02[8][a].

[20] GREGORY ET AL., *supra* note 1, § 8.01, at 223-24.

[21] CLARK, JR., *supra* note 4, § 12.1, at 410.

[22] GREGORY ET AL., *supra* note 1, § 8.01[B], at 224.

[23] *See* ELLMAN ET AL., *supra* note 3, at 206 (discussing studies in California, Nebraska, and Iowa – survey of 10,000 divorce cases failed to show a single case where divorce was denied when one spouse desired divorce).

[24] *See* MISS. CODE ANN. § 93-5-2 (2004).

[25] *See* MISS. CODE ANN. § 93-5-2 (2004).

[26] *See* ELLMAN ET AL., *supra* note 3, at 216.

[27] *See* Talbert v. Talbert, 759 So. 2d 1105 (Miss. 1999) (no divorce where husband belittled his wife, screamed at her, and committed a few acts of violence early in the twenty-seven year marriage); Wilbourne v. Wilbourne, 748 So. 2d 184 (Miss. 1999) (no divorce although the marriage "was unpleasant and the parties were incompatible," and arguments "on occasion involved physical violence"); Mitchell v. Mitchell, 767 So. 2d 1037 (Miss. Ct. App. 2000) (marriage might be irreconcilable, the parties incompatible, and the wife argumentative, but those facts do not amount to proof of cruelty); Ayers v. Ayers, 734 So. 2d 213 (Miss. Ct. App. 1999) (no divorce where husband rarely talked to his wife or requested sex, she was uncomfortable in his church, she was "sensitive and prone to tears").

[28] Tackett v. Tackett, 967 So. 2d 1264, 1268-69 (Miss. Ct. App. 2007) (Irving, J., concurring) (divorce denied; wife's lack of interest in sex and constant arguing over money not sufficient evidence of cruelty).

§ 4.02   MISSISSIPPI FAMILY LAW

on irreconcilable differences may be granted only if both parties are before the court. The jurisdictional requirements for divorce are discussed in detail in Chapter XVIII.

§ 4.02 FAULT-BASED GROUNDS FOR DIVORCE

The continuing strong public policy against divorce is reflected in the limited grounds for divorce enumerated by the Mississippi legislature, as well as the courts' strict application of the grounds. Two grounds deal with sexual misconduct or infidelity – adultery and a wife's pregnancy by another at the time of the marriage. Five involve non-sexual misconduct that seriously affects the marriage relationship – habitual cruel and inhuman treatment, habitual drunkenness, habitual drug use, desertion, and imprisonment. Three grounds recognize conditions that make the traditional marriage relationship impossible – natural impotency, mental illness or mental retardation at the time of the marriage, and institutionalization for mental illness during the marriage. The remaining two grounds incorporate the state's ban on bigamous and incestuous marriages. Adultery and habitual cruel and inhuman treatment are by far the most commonly cited grounds for divorce. Most grounds, such as imprisonment, natural impotency, incest, bigamy, pregnancy, prohibited kinship, and mental illness, appear infrequently in reported cases or not at all. The remaining three – habitual drunkenness, habitual drug use, and desertion – appear only slightly more often.

The Mississippi Supreme Court insists on strict compliance with the statutory grounds, disavowing judicial authority to alter any aspect of the grounds. Refusing to dissolve an admittedly dead marriage, the supreme court stated, "Divorce is a creature of statute; it is not a gift to be bestowed . . . . [T]he statutes must be strictly followed as they are in derogation of the common law."[29] Even seemingly common sense extensions of the grounds are rejected. The supreme court denied divorce to a woman whose husband was incarcerated in a federal penitentiary because the statute provided for divorce against a spouse incarcerated in "the" penitentiary, not "a" penitentiary.[30]

[1] General considerations. Because of the public interest in preserving marriage, courts are more engaged in suits for divorce than in most civil actions. As the state's representative, the court has a duty "to fully inquire into the facts and circumstances"[31] before permitting divorce. As a result, rules governing divorce require strict proof of grounds, prohibit default judgments, and insist on identification of an "innocent" party.

[a] No default judgment. No divorce may be taken by default.[32] Rule 55 of the Mississippi Rules of Civil Procedure prohibits judgment in a divorce action "unless the claimant establishes his claim or rights to relief by evidence."[33] Even if a defendant fails

---

[29] *See* Kergosien v. Kergosien, 471 So. 2d 1206, 1210 (Miss. 1985).

[30] *See* Daughdrill v. Daugdrill, 178 So. 106 (Miss. 1938). More recently, the court has reversed divorces granted under the irreconcilable differences statute for failure to comply with the exact dictates of the statute. *See infra* § 4.04.

[31] Rawson v. Buta, 609 So. 2d 426, 430 (Miss. 1992).

[32] MISS. CODE ANN. § 93-5-7 (2004).

[33] MISS. R. CIV. P. 55.

GROUNDS FOR DIVORCE   § 4.02[1][b]

to answer and defend, a plaintiff must prove the elements of the case to the court's satisfaction.[34] However, a chancellor may dispense with financial statements and findings of fact in an uncontested case – the defendant "had the opportunity to have his day in court and has chosen not to take advantage of it."[35]

[b] Burden of proof. The party seeking a divorce bears the burden of proof.[36] In order to obtain a divorce on most of the listed grounds, the plaintiff must prove the grounds by clear and convincing evidence.[37] In 1974, however, the Mississippi Supreme Court lowered the standard in cases based on habitual cruel and inhuman treatment, which may now be proved by a preponderance of the evidence.[38]

[c] Corroboration. In 1941 the Mississippi Supreme Court held that a divorce plaintiff's testimony must be supported by corroborating evidence. The evidence should convince a prudent person that the plaintiff's testimony is true and not "the exaggerated product" of the desire for divorce.[39] Corroboration is excused if it is not reasonably possible because of the nature of the defendant's conduct or the parties' isolation. Corroboration was excused in one case because the plaintiff's inability to produce evidence was caused by the defendant's intimidation and threats to witnesses.[40] Without corroboration, however, cross-examination or questioning by the court should be "searching" to ensure that grounds for divorce exist.[41] Divorce has been denied in a number of cases for lack of evidence corroborating a plaintiff's testimony.[42]

Corroborating evidence may be provided through the testimony of friends and

---

[34] *See* Lindsey v. Lindsey, 818 So. 2d 1191 (Miss. 2002); Rawson v. Buta, 609 So. 2d 426, 430-31 (Miss. 1992) (complainant's proof requirement does not become lighter because the defendant fails to answer); Luse v. Luse, 992 So. 2d 659, 662 (Miss. Ct. App. 2008) (proof of grounds for divorce required even in uncontested actions).

[35] Luse v. Luse, 992 So. 2d 659, 663-64 (Miss. Ct. App. 2008). See Chapter XIX, *infra,* for a more detailed discussion of procedural issues.

[36] Burnette v. Burnette, 271 So. 2d 90, 93 (Miss. 1973).

[37] Anderson v. Anderson, 200 So. 726, 727 (Miss. 1941) (evidence must "convince the chancellor clearly and conclusively that the asserted facts are true in all essential respects"); *see* Brooks v. Brooks, 652 So. 2d 1113, 1116 (Miss. 1995) (adultery); Hill v. United Timber & Lumber Co., 68 So. 2d 240 (Miss. 1953) (clear and convincing evidence required to overcome presumption of validity of second marriage; would apply in divorce based on bigamy); Ward v. Dulaney, 23 Miss. 410, 414 (1852) (clear and satisfactory proof necessary to prove insanity for annulment action); Pool v. Pool, 989 So. 2d 920, 925 (Miss. Ct. App. 2008) (adultery); Brewer v. Brewer, 919 So. 2d 135, 138 (Miss. Ct. App. 2005) ("Adultery as a ground for divorce must be proved by clear and convincing evidence.").

[38] *See* Wires v. Wires, 297 So. 2d 900, 902 (Miss. 1974); *see also* Fulton v. Fulton, 918 So. 2d 877, 880 (Miss. Ct. App. 2006) (same); Cochran v. Cochran, 912 So. 2d 1086, 1089 (Miss. Ct. App. 2005) (burden of proof is by a preponderance of the evidence).

[39] *See* Anderson v. Anderson, 200 So. 726, 728 (Miss. 1941).

[40] *See* Shelton v. Shelton, 477 So. 2d 1357 (Miss. 1985).

[41] Anderson v. Anderson, 200 So. 726, 727 (Miss. 1941); *see also* Miss. Unif. Chan. Ct. R. 8.03 (substantial corroborating evidence required in uncontested divorces other than irreconcilable differences divorce).

[42] *See* Hassett v. Hassett, 690 So. 2d 1140, 1146 (Miss. 1997) (wife's testimony regarding sexual abuse not corroborated); Chamblee v. Chamblee, 637 So. 2d 850, 860 (Miss. 1994) (wife's testimony of physical abuse not corroborated); Gardner v. Gardner, 618 So. 2d 108, 114 (Miss. 1993) (same); Reed v. Reed, 839 So. 2d 565, 571 (Miss. Ct. App. 2003) (testimony of physical abuse not sufficiently corroborated); *see also* Stennis v. Stennis, 464 So. 2d 1161, 1161 (Miss. 1985) (wife's allegations of drunkenness not corroborated).

§ 4.02[1][d]   **MISSISSIPPI FAMILY LAW**

family,[43] private investigators,[44] taped recordings of conversations,[45] medical or mental health professionals,[46] the defendant's testimony,[47] or testimony of the defendant's paramour.[48] Corroboration may not be provided through hearsay testimony – the facts must be within the witness's personal knowledge. For example, a witness's testimony that a husband told him about a lack of sexual relations in his marriage was inadmissible hearsay.[49]

[d] Divorce granted to the most innocent party. Fault-based divorce is grounded in the notion of an innocent party. With the exception of incestuous marriages,[50] only the injured party may seek a divorce on the statutory grounds.[51] If both parties prove grounds for divorce, the court must identify the party whose conduct caused the separation or whose fault was greater and grant divorce to the other.[52] For example, a chancellor properly granted divorce to a wife based on her husband's cruelty – the marriage breakdown was caused by his conduct rather than her post-separation adultery.[53] Similarly, divorce was properly granted to a wife based on her husband's adultery during the marriage, rather than on her post-separation adultery.[54] Only one spouse can be found guilty of habitual, cruel, and inhuman treatment.[55] If both parties prove cruelty, divorce must be granted against the spouse who was more at fault.[56]

[e] Findings of fact. A court should make specific findings of fact supporting the grant of a divorce. However, a grant of divorce may be affirmed in the absence of

---

[43] *See* Sproles v. Sproles, 782 So. 2d 742, 747 (Miss. 2001) (abuse corroborated by mother and neighbor); Devereaux v. Devereaux, 493 So. 2d 1310, 1312 (Miss. 1986) (corroboration by son and daughter); Cassell v. Cassell, 970 So. 2d 267, 271 (Miss. Ct. App. 2007) (corroborated by son's testimony); Peters v. Peters, 906 So. 2d 64 (Miss. Ct. App. 2004) (corroboration by children).

[44] *See* Hassett v. Hassett, 690 So. 2d 1140, 1147-48 (Miss. 1997) (investigator followed wife and friend to hotel).

[45] *See* Rushing v. Rushing, 724 So. 2d 911, 914-15 (Miss. 1998) (recording of conversations between wife and paramour); Rodriguez v. Rodriguez, 2 So. 3d 720, 724-725 (Miss. Ct. App. 2009) (wife introduced taped telephone conversations and diaries to prove husband's adultery).

[46] *See* Faries v. Faries, 607 So. 2d 1204, 1209 (Miss. 1992) (social worker corroborated impact on health).

[47] *See* Rushing v. Rushing, 724 So. 2d 911, 914 (Miss. 1998) (counsel for wife conceded proof of adultery); McKee v. Flynt, 630 So. 2d 44, 48-49 (Miss. 1993) (husband admitted two incidents of violence; testimony of witnesses who observed bruises and scratches on plaintiff; emotional abuse); Jordan v. Jordan, 510 So. 2d 131, 132 (Miss. 1987) (wife described encounter with another man); Cain v. Cain, 795 So. 2d 614, 616 (Miss. Ct. App. 2001) (wife stipulated that she had affair).

[48] *See* Ferguson v. Ferguson, 639 So. 2d 921, 931 (Miss. 1994) (testimony of paramour directly established adulterous relationship); Martin v. Martin, 566 So. 2d 704, 706 (Miss. 1990) (wife and paramour admitted relationship in open court); Harmon v. Harmon, 757 So. 2d 305, 308 (Miss. Ct. App. 1999) (husband's friend testified regarding three-year relationship).

[49] Shorter v. Shorter, 740 So. 2d 352, 358 (Miss. Ct. App. 1999); *see also* Fleming v. Fleming, 56 So. 2d 35, 40 (Miss. 1952) (testimony by plaintiff that friends told him of his wife's extramarital affair inadmissible).

[50] Either party to an incestuous marriage may be granted a divorce. *See* MISS. CODE ANN. § 93-5-1 (2004).

[51] *See* MISS. CODE ANN. § 93-5-1 (2004) ("Divorces from the bonds of matrimony may be decreed to the injured party.").

[52] Boutwell v. Boutwell, 829 So. 2d 1216, 1224 (Miss. 2002).

[53] Boutwell v. Boutwell, 829 So. 2d 1216, 1224 (Miss. 2002); Garriga v. Garriga, 770 So. 2d 978, 983-84 (Miss. Ct. App. 2000).

[54] Harmon v. Harmon, 757 So. 2d 305, 308-09 (Miss. Ct. App. 1999); *see also* Dickerson v. Dickerson, 34 So. 3d 637, 642-43 (Miss. Ct. App. 2010).

[55] Hinton v. Hinton, 179 So. 2d 846, 848 (Miss. 1965) (contradictory to say that conduct of both parties caused separation; both cannot be innocent and guilty at the same time).

[56] Hyer v. Hyer, 636 So. 2d 381, 383-84 (Miss. 1994); Hinton v. Hinton, 179 So. 2d 846, 848 (Miss. 1965).

GROUNDS FOR DIVORCE   **§ 4.02[1][f]**

findings if the record includes "substantial, credible" evidence to support the grant of divorce.[57]

[f] Standard of review. In most cases, a chancellor's grant of divorce will not be reversed absent an abuse of discretion.[58] However, a finding regarding habitual, cruel, and inhuman treatment is viewed as a determination of law and is reviewed de novo on appeal.[59]

[2] Natural impotency. A plaintiff may obtain a divorce by proving that the defendant is "naturally impotent."[60] The impotent spouse cannot sue for divorce, but may seek an annulment of the marriage based on "incurable" impotency.[61] The only Mississippi case to discuss the ground provides little guidance on the test for natural impotency. A couple was unable to have intercourse during the four months they lived together, because the wife suffered from a physical condition that made intercourse painful. The court simply stated that these facts were insufficient to grant divorce based on natural impotency.[62]

Other state courts have defined impotency as an incurable inability to engage in sexual intercourse,[63] rather than inability to procreate.[64] Some courts have also held that the condition must exist at the time of the marriage as well as at the time of separation,[65] even when the applicable statute did not impose that requirement.[66] At least one court has held that a spouse with an incurable sexually transmitted disease was impotent because the condition made her incapable of healthy sexual intercourse.[67] Because of the nature of the ground, the only corroborating evidence may be testimony of the defendant or of a physician. A New Jersey court held that a defendant's refusal to submit to a court-ordered physical examination was sufficient corroboration of his wife's testimony regarding his impotence.[68]

[3] Adultery. An innocent spouse may obtain a divorce based on adultery,[69]

---

[57] *See* Cassell v. Cassell, 970 So. 2d 267, 271 (Miss. Ct. App. 2007) (record included corroborated testimony that husband called wife names, cursed her, and threw things at her).

[58] McAdory v. McAdory, 608 So. 2d 695, 699 (Miss. 1992).

[59] Kumar v. Kumar, 976 So. 2d 957, 960-63 (Miss. Ct. App. 2008) (wife's evidence of cruelty was sufficient; chancellor applied an incorrect standard of law in denying divorce).

[60] MISS. CODE ANN. § 93-5-1 (2004).

[61] *See* discussion *supra* § 3.03[2][a].

[62] Sarphie v. Sarphie, 177 So. 358, 358 (Miss. 1937) (wife pursued treatment for condition during cohabitation).

[63] *See* Long v. Long, 13 S.E.2d 349, 350 (Ga. 1941) (showing that couple did not consummate marriage in three weeks of cohabitation insufficient to prove incurable impotency); Smith v. Smith, 229 S.W. 398, 398-99 (Mo. Ct. App. 1921) (incurable impotency not proven where couple engaged in intercourse).

[64] *See* Smith v. Smith, 229 S.W. 398, 399 (Mo. Ct. App. 1921) ("The ability to become a parent is never an essential element in marriage . . . ."); Reed v. Reed, 177 S.W.2d 26, 27 (Tenn. Ct. App. 1943); *see also* cases collected in M.L. Cross, Annotation, *What Constitutes Impotency as Grounds for Divorce*, 65 A.L.R. 2d 776 (1959).

[65] *See* Cott v. Cott, 98 So. 2d 379, 380 (Fla. Ct. App. 1957) (must exist at time of marriage but need not exist from birth); Reed v. Reed, 177 S.W.2d 26, 27 (Tenn. Ct. App. 1943) (temporary impotence not sufficient).

[66] *See* Bascomb v. Bascomb, 25 N.H. 267, 1852 WL 2138 (1852) (husband could not obtain divorce from wife unable to have intercourse after bearing four children; natural impotence, taken from English law, requires impotence at the time of the marriage).

[67] *See* Ryder v. Ryder, 28 A. 1029, 1030 (Vt. 1892).

[68] *See* Bissell v. Bissell, 117 A. 252, 254 (N.J. Ch. 1922).

[69] MISS. CODE ANN. § 93-5-1 (2004).

73

§ 4.02[3][a]   **MISSISSIPPI FAMILY LAW**

defined as "voluntary sexual intercourse of a married person with a person other than the offender's spouse."[70] A single act of adultery is grounds for divorce.[71]

[a] Findings of fact. In divorce actions based on adultery, courts must make specific findings of fact. A bare conclusion that a party committed adultery is insufficient.[72] Failure to make findings, or verbatim adoption of one party's proposed facts, shifts appellate review from the deferential manifest-error standard[73] to de novo review.[74]

[b] Direct proof. Adultery may be established by a defendant's admissions[75] or by other testimony directly establishing the conduct, including testimony of the defendant's paramour.[76] Taped recordings of conversations may be admissible to prove adultery.[77] No corroboration is needed if the defendant admits adultery.[78]

[c] Circumstantial proof. Because of the secretive nature of the conduct, direct proof of adultery is not required.[79] Adultery may be proven circumstantially by showing (1) a spouse's generally adulterous nature, which may be either infatuation with another or a proclivity to adultery,[80] and (2) a reasonable opportunity to satisfy the infatuation or proclivity.[81] Circumstantial proof must be clear and convincing[82] and

---

[70] Owen v. Gerity, 422 So. 2d 284, 287 (Miss. 1982).

[71] Talbert v. Talbert, 759 So. 2d 1105, 1110 (Miss. 1999).

[72] Lister v. Lister, 981 So. 2d 340, 344 (Miss. Ct. App. 2008) (court must make findings of fact); Curtis v. Curtis, 796 So. 2d 1044, 1049 (Miss. Ct. App. 2001); Dorman v. Dorman, 737 So. 2d 426, 429-30 (Miss. Ct. App. 1999) (chancellor applied recrimination doctrine after concluding, without specific findings, that both committed adultery).

[73] *See* McAdory v. McAdory, 608 So. 2d 695, 699 (Miss. 1992) (appellate court will not disturb chancellor's findings "unless manifestly wrong, clearly erroneous, or an erroneous legal standard was applied").

[74] Brooks v. Brooks, 652 So. 2d 1113, 1118 (Miss. 1995); *see* Curtis v. Curtis, 796 So. 2d 1044, 1049 (Miss. Ct. App. 2001) (credibility issues are still resolved consistently with the chancellor's judgment).

[75] *See* Rushing v. Rushing, 724 So. 2d 911, 914 (Miss. 1998); Martin v. Martin, 566 So. 2d 704, 706 (Miss. 1990) (wife and paramour admitted relationship in open court); Jordan v. Jordan, 510 So. 2d 131, 132 (Miss. 1987) (wife described encounter with another man); Oberlin v. Oberlin, 29 So. 2d 82, 83 (Miss. 1947) (counsel for defendant stipulated to cohabitation); Cain v. Cain, 795 So. 2d 614, 616 (Miss. Ct. App. 2001) (wife stipulated that she had affair).

[76] *See* Ferguson v. Ferguson, 639 So. 2d 921, 930-31 (Miss. 1994) (testimony of paramour directly established adulterous relationship); Martin v. Martin, 566 So. 2d 704, 706 (Miss. 1990) (wife and paramour admitted relationship in open court); Harmon v. Harmon, 757 So. 2d 305, 308 (Miss. Ct. App. 1999) (husband's friend testified regarding three-year relationship).

[77] *See* Ferguson v. Ferguson, 639 So. 2d 921, 931 (Miss. 1994) (recordings properly admitted where paramour knew device was attached to phone); Rodriguez v. Rodriguez, 2 So. 3d 720, 724-725 (Miss. Ct. App. 2009) (wife introduced taped telephone conversations and diaries to prove husband's adultery).

[78] Sproles v. Sproles, 782 So. 2d 742, 746 (Miss. 2001) (rejecting husband's argument that court should have permitted testimony to corroborate wife's admission of post-separation adultery).

[79] Dillon v. Dillon, 498 So. 2d 328, 330 (Miss. 1986) (direct evidence not required due to "secretive" nature of adultery).

[80] *See* Hulett v. Hulett, 119 So. 581, 588 (Miss. 1928) (wife's invitation to man to come to her house while her husband was away so she could "see what was in him" showed adulterous inclination when viewed with other evidence).

[81] *See* Hensarling v. Hensarling, 824 So. 2d 583, 594 (Miss. 2002); McAdory v. McAdory, 608 So. 2d 695, 699 (Miss. 1992); Lister v. Lister, 981 So. 2d 340, 344 (Miss. Ct. App. 2008); Myers v. Myers, 741 So. 2d 274, 279 (Miss. Ct. App. 1998).

[82] Brooks v. Brooks, 652 So. 2d 1113, 1116-17 (Miss. 1995) (chancellor erred in granting divorce upon finding adultery by a preponderance of the evidence); Pool v. Pool, 989 So. 2d 920, 925-27 (Miss. Ct. App. 2008) (burden of proof clear and convincing evidence); Spence v. Spence, 930 So. 2d 415, 418-19 (Miss. Ct. App. 2005) (proof of husband's close friendship with neighbor did not satisfy clear and convincing test); Brewer v. Brewer, 919 So. 2d 135, 139 (Miss. Ct. App. 2005) (chancellor incorrectly stated that the burden of proof for adultery is a preponderance of the

GROUNDS FOR DIVORCE   § 4.02[3][c]

must exclude any other reasonable explanation for the behavior.[83] In the absence of direct proof of adultery, facts that support a finding of adultery include: unexplained overnight stays with a suspected paramour,[84] giving or receiving gifts,[85] physical affection toward[86] or admissions of affection for another,[87] secretive behavior,[88] and frequent telephone calls[89] or letters to a suspected paramour.[90] Evidence that tends to show "an adulterous disposition" is admissible even if unrelated to the particular alleged act of adultery.[91]

The supreme court found sufficient evidence of adultery based on proof that a husband gave expensive gifts to his friend, was physically affectionate with her, slept in the same bed with her, and admitted he loved her.[92] In contrast, evidence that a wife received telephone calls from men, was paged late at night, and occasionally stayed in hotels was insufficient to prove adultery.[93] Similarly, photographs of a wife and co-worker arm-in-arm at work and a photograph of the co-worker partially clad in the marital bed did not prove adultery. Testimony of the wife and witnesses attributed the photographs to job-related "horseplay" and explained that another co-worker took the

---

evidence, however, the proof established adultery by clear and convincing evidence).

[83] Brooks v. Brooks, 652 So. 2d 1113, 1116 (Miss. 1995) (evidence must be inconsistent with theory of innocence); Dillon v. Dillon, 498 So. 2d 328, 330 (Miss. 1986) (same); Pool v. Pool, 989 So. 2d 920, 925 (Miss. Ct. App. 2008) (evidence that wife spent three nights in male friend's home was subject to another reasonable explanation – that friend was ill); Lister v. Lister, 981 So. 2d 340, 344 (Miss. Ct. App. 2008) (can be proved circumstantially, but must be inconsistent with reasonable theory of innocence); Spence v. Spence, 930 So. 2d 415, 419 (Miss. Ct. App. 2005) (evidence of husband's relationship with neighbor could reasonably be interpreted as the conduct of two close friends); Mitchell v. Mitchell, 767 So. 2d 1037, 1041 (Miss. Ct. App. 2000) (other explanations for wife's behavior).

[84] See Arthur v. Arthur, 691 So. 2d 997, 1001 (Miss. 1997) (spent several nights with friend); Hassett v. Hassett, 690 So. 2d 1140, 1144 (Miss. 1997) (private investigator observed wife spending two nights in Holiday Inn room with friend); Holden v. Frasher-Holden, 680 So. 2d 795, 799 (Miss. 1996) (friend stayed in husband's trailer; her clothes and personal items kept there); Brooks v. Brooks, 652 So. 2d 1113, 1118 (Miss. 1995) (slept in same bed); Curtis v. Curtis, 796 So. 2d 1044, 1050 (Miss. Ct. App. 2001) (husband left marital home and moved in with woman); Reynolds v. Reynolds, 755 So. 2d 467, 469 (Miss. Ct. App. 1999) (spent several nights with friend).

[85] See Brooks v. Brooks, 652 So. 2d 1113, 1118 (Miss. 1995) (gifts of jewelry and clothing, paid friend's rent); Hodge v. Hodge, 186 So. 2d 748, 751 (Miss. 1966) (accepted valuable gifts).

[86] See Holden v. Frasher-Holden, 680 So. 2d 795, 799 (Miss. 1996) (arm around friend at car show); Brooks v. Brooks, 652 So. 2d 1113, 1118 (Miss. 1995) ("touching, kissing, and embracing"); Hodge v. Hodge, 186 So. 2d 748, 751 (Miss. 1966) ("constant association" with another man); Reynolds v. Reynolds, 755 So. 2d 467, 469 (Miss. Ct. App. 1999) (testimony that husband danced frequently with friend, paid much attention to her, and "seemed to be taken" with her).

[87] See Arthur v. Arthur, 691 So. 2d 997, 1001 (Miss. 1997) (husband admitted affection for friend); Holden v. Frasher-Holden, 680 So. 2d 795, 797 (Miss. 1996) (husband admitted "close friendship" and feelings of affection); Hodge v. Hodge, 186 So. 2d 748, 751 (Miss. 1966) (wife admitted she would marry friend if divorced).

[88] See Hassett v. Hassett, 690 So. 2d 1140, 1143 (Miss. 1997) (wife concealed existence of post office box where she received letters from friend).

[89] See Arthur v. Arthur, 691 So. 2d 997, 1001 (Miss. 1997) (telephoned friend several times a week); Holden v. Frasher-Holden, 680 So. 2d 795, 796 (Miss. 1996) (wife discovered number on phone bills).

[90] See Hassett v. Hassett, 690 So. 2d 1140, 1143 (Miss. 1997) (wife received fifteen affectionate cards from friend); Holden v. Frasher-Holden, 680 So. 2d 795, 797 (Miss. 1996) (cards from friend addressed to "my husband to be").

[91] See Hulett v. Hulett, 119 So. 581, 587 (Miss. 1928) (evidence of sexually suggestive conversation between wife and stranger); see also Talbert v. Talbert, 759 So. 2d 1105, 1110 (Miss. 1999) (wife's letters to her psychologist discussing fantasies of adulterous affairs were relevant because they "may prove her inclination to commit adultery").

[92] Brooks v. Brooks, 652 So. 2d 1113, 1119 (Miss. 1995); see also Lister v. Lister, 981 So. 2d 340, 344-45 (Miss. Ct. App. 2008) (adultery proved by evidence that husband and secretary took trips together, stayed together for five days; that husband provided her with substantial funds, allowed her to live in a mobile home owned by his company, and helped pay her divorce attorneys' fees).

[93] Mitchell v. Mitchell, 767 So. 2d 1037, 1041 (Miss. Ct. App. 2000) (wife explained that she stayed in hotels on occasions when her husband was abusive).

§ 4.02[3][d]   **MISSISSIPPI FAMILY LAW**

latter photograph.[94] Evidence that a wife went "skinny-dipping" with a man was not evidence of adultery.[95] And evidence that a husband hugged and kissed a female friend did not prove adultery. Their behavior was consistent with the conduct of close friends who provided emotional support for each other.[96] Cohabitation alone does not constitute adultery. A chancellor erred in granting a divorce based on a husband's cohabitation, without evidence of a sexual relationship.[97]

[d] Post-separation adultery. Divorce may be granted based on a spouse's sexual conduct during separation. There is no requirement that the plaintiff show a causal connection between adultery and separation.[98] However, if the adulterous spouse proves conduct that was the actual cause of the separation, divorce should be granted on those grounds. Thus, divorce was properly granted to a wife based on her husband's habitual, cruel, and inhuman treatment rather than on her post-separation adultery.[99]

[e] Same-sex relationships. The Mississippi appellate courts have not addressed whether sexual acts between persons of the same sex can constitute adultery. A number of courts have held that homosexual acts constitute adultery, rejecting a narrow or technical definition of "sexual intercourse."[100] However, one court held that a wife's lesbian relationship was not adultery, defining adultery as "sexual intercourse" and excluding relationships between two women.[101] The Mississippi Supreme Court has held that a same-sex relationship may be a factor in finding habitual, cruel, and inhuman treatment.[102]

[f] Condonation. Condonation, one of the defenses generally applicable in divorce actions, has particular significance in actions based on adultery. A spouse who resumes a sexual relationship after learning of the other's adultery may have condoned, or forgiven, the offense. Condonation bars divorce based on adultery unless the adul-

---

[94] McAdory v. McAdory, 608 So. 2d 695, 700 (Miss. 1992).

[95] Dickerson v. Dickerson, 34 So. 3d 637, 643 (Miss. Ct. App. 2010).

[96] Spence v. Spence, 930 So. 2d 415, 418-19 (Miss. Ct. App. 2005); *see also* Pool v. Pool, 989 So. 2d 920, 926 (Miss. Ct. App. 2008) (husband's evidence that wife spent three nights with male friend not sufficient without some evidence of infatuation).

[97] Atkinson v. Atkinson, 11 So. 3d 172, 177 (Miss. Ct. App. 2009) (opportunity for adultery to exist, but no evidence of inclination).

[98] Talbert v. Talbert, 759 So. 2d 1105, 1110-11 (Miss. 1999); Lister v. Lister, 981 So. 2d 340, 344-45 (Miss. Ct. App. 2008) (no requirement that adultery occur prior to separation); Pucylowski v. Pucylowski, 741 So. 2d 998, 1000-01 (Miss. Ct. App. 1999).

[99] Boutwell v. Boutwell, 829 So. 2d 1216, 1224 (Miss. 2002); *see* Garriga v. Garriga, 770 So. 2d 978, 983-84 (Miss. Ct. App. 2000) (same); *cf.* Dickerson v. Dickerson, 34 So. 3d 637, 642-43 (Miss. Ct. App. 2010) (wife who had post-separation affair granted divorce based on husband's adultery before separation).

[100] *See* Owens v. Owens, 274 S.E.2d 484, 485-86 (Ga. 1981); Adams v. Adams, 357 So. 2d 881 (La. Ct. App. 1978); S.B. v. S.J.B., 609 A.2d 124, 126 (N.J. Super. Ct. Ch. Div. 1992) (effect of same-sex extramarital relationship just as devastating as heterosexual relationship); R.G.M. v. D.E.M., 410 S.E.2d 564, 566-67 (S.C. 1991) (wife's lesbian relationship was adultery).

[101] Glaze v. Glaze, 46 Va. Cir. 333, 334 (Va. Cir. Ct. 1998) ("Sexual intercourse cannot occur between two women."). For a survey of cases discussing same-sex relationships as adultery, see J.M. Zitter, Annotation, *Homosexuality as Ground for Divorce*, 96 A.L.R. 5th 83 (2002) (majority holding that same-sex relationship can be adultery).

[102] *See* Morris v. Morris, 783 So. 2d 681, 690 (Miss. 2001); Crutcher v. Crutcher, 38 So. 337 (Miss. 1905).

GROUNDS FOR DIVORCE   § 4.02[3][g]

tery recurs.[103]

[g] Remarriage may be barred. Chancellors are authorized by statute to bar a party guilty of adultery from remarriage. After one year, the party may petition the court to remove the disability based on "satisfactory evidence of reformation" or good cause.[104]

[4] Sentenced to any penitentiary. Divorce may be granted to a plaintiff whose spouse is sentenced to "any penitentiary" without being pardoned before incarceration.[105] The statute, which previously referred to "*the* penitentiary," was amended to the present wording after the Mississippi Supreme Court denied divorce to a woman whose husband was sentenced to federal prison.[106]

[5] Desertion for one year. A spouse's "willful, continued and obstinate desertion for the space of one year" is grounds for divorce.[107] The period of time required for divorce based on desertion has been reduced gradually from five years in 1840 to three years, then two, and finally to one year in 1938.[108]

The essence of desertion is one spouse's abandonment of the marriage without the other's consent. To prove desertion, a plaintiff must show that (1) the defendant was absent for one year; (2) the defendant intended to abandon the marriage; and (3) the plaintiff did not consent to the separation. A good-faith reconciliation offer by a deserting spouse interrupts the one-year period. A deserted spouse's unreasonable refusal of a good-faith offer to return may provide the spouse offering reconciliation with grounds for divorce based on desertion. Divorce may also be granted for constructive desertion – conduct of one spouse so extreme that it drives the other away.

[a] Continuous for one year. Desertion must be continuous for the space of one year. If spouses separate, reconcile, and separate again, the two periods of separation may not be combined to satisfy the time requirement.[109] For example, a couple's ten-day reconciliation interrupted the running of the statutory period even though the total time of separation was longer than one year.[110] Some courts hold that sexual inti-

---

[103] Brewer v. Brewer, 919 So. 2d 135, 139 (Miss. Ct. App. 2005) (affair condoned by husband; yet where wife resumed affair, wife could no longer successfully claim condonation as a defense); *see infra* § 4.03[6][a].

[104] MISS. CODE ANN. § 93-5-25 (2004); *see* Boone v. Downey, 259 So. 2d 710 (Miss. 1972) (discussing 1956 divorce in which adulterous wife was barred from remarriage).

[105] MISS. CODE ANN. § 93-5-1 (2004); *see* Avery v. Avery, 864 So. 2d 1054, 1055 (Miss. Ct. App. 2004) (wife granted divorce based on husband's conviction and five-year sentence to Mississippi penitentiary); *cf.* Fisher v. Fisher, 944 So. 2d 134, 135, 137 (Miss. Ct. App. 2006) (prison inmate sought divorce based on desertion; wife did not visit prison or return phone calls or letters for ten years).

[106] *See* Daughdrill v. Daughdrill, 178 So. 106, 107 (Miss. 1938) ("The safe, sound construction of this statute is that it means that the offending party in divorce suits must have been sent to the penitentiary of the state of Mississippi . . . .").

[107] MISS. CODE ANN. § 93-5-1 (2004).

[108] *See* BUNKLEY & MORSE, *supra* note 8, § 3.11(1), at 90.

[109] CLARK, JR., *supra* note 4, § 13.3, at 501; *see* Annotation, *Individual Acts of Cohabitation Between Husband and Wife as Breaking Continuity of Abandonment, Desertion, or Separation, or as Condonation Thereof*, 155 A.L.R. 132 (1945).

[110] Gaillard v. Gaillard, 23 Miss. 152, 153 (1851) (applying three-year statute).

§ 4.02[5][b]   **MISSISSIPPI FAMILY LAW**

macy during separation does not interrupt the running of the one-year period if the deserting spouse has no intention of returning to the marriage.[111] In rare cases, even cohabitation may not interrupt the desertion period. Divorce based on desertion was granted to a husband whose wife returned home on her lawyer's advice but who lived separately in the house and was paid by her husband for childcare.[112]

Some courts hold that a deserted spouse's suit for divorce signals acceptance of the separation and therefore stops the time from running.[113] The Mississippi Supreme Court has held, however, that the statute continues in spite of litigation by either spouse – a deserted husband's divorce action did not interrupt the running of the one-year period against his wife.[114] Similarly, a deserting wife's separate maintenance suit against her husband did not toll the statute; she had no intention of returning to him.[115]

[b] "Willful and obstinate." To qualify as desertion, a spouse's absence must be accompanied by an intent to abandon the marriage. Furthermore, a separation between spouses who intend to end their marriage does not constitute desertion.

[i] Intent to abandon the marriage. Desertion must be willful and obstinate, that is, with an intent to abandon the marriage.[116] Absence for legitimate reasons is not desertion.[117] A husband's lengthy absence from Mississippi to find work in Florida was not desertion because he intended to return to his family.[118] A legitimate absence becomes desertion, however, if the absent spouse decides not to return.[119] Under those circumstances, the period of desertion should be computed from the time the intent is formed.[120]

A defendant's articulated reason for an extended absence will be rejected if found to be a pretext. For example, divorce was properly granted based on a wife's return to Mississippi from her marital home in California. The court did not believe her alleged health reasons for living in Mississippi.[121] In addition, refusal to return home except on

---

[111] *See* Campbell v. Campbell, 19 So. 2d 354, 354 (Ala. 1944) (couple spent one night at her parents' house and one in a road house; desertion continued because wife never altered intent); Sabia v. Sabia, 84 A.2d 559, 561 (N.J. 1951) (wife's premeditated act of sexual intercourse to bar cause of action did not interrupt time period); *see also* Parker v. Parker, 55 N.W.2d 183, 186 (Iowa 1952) (return for a few days, without intent to reconcile, did not break period of desertion).

[112] Graves v. Graves, 41 So. 384, 384 (Miss. 1906) ("[D]esertion . . .may be as complete under the same shelter as if oceans rolled between.").

[113] *See* CLARK, *supra* note 4, § 13.3, at 501-02.

[114] Lynch v. Lynch, 63 So. 2d 657, 662 (Miss. 1953).

[115] Richey v. Richey, 185 So. 2d 431, 432 (Miss. 1966).

[116] *See* 24 AM. JUR. 2D *Divorce and Separation* § 63 (2008).

[117] *See* Wilson v. Wilson, 22 So. 2d 161, 163 (Miss. 1945) (separate maintenance suit applying rules of desertion); CLARK, JR., *supra* note 4, § 13.3, at 505; *see also* Gottlieb v. Gottlieb, 448 S.E.2d 666, 670 (Va. Ct. App. 1994) (impact of marriage on health justified absence).

[118] Walton v. Walton, 25 So. 166, 168 (Miss. 1899). The court stated: "[T]he agent of his country in diplomatic service in foreign lands, the merchant in the prosecution of his business on the islands of the sea and to better his fortunes, and the traveler for pleasure, or in the interest of science in the polar regions, are each and all living with their wives and in their homes." *Id.*

[119] Walton v. Walton, 25 So. 166, 168 (Miss. 1899) (absent husband deserts only when he intends to sever the relationship).

[120] *Cf.* Criswell v. Criswell, 182 So. 2d 587, 589 (Miss. 1966) (one-year period computed from first date of refusal to reconcile).

[121] Carter v. Carter, 97 So. 2d 529 (Miss. 1957) (desertion proved where wife left husband in California and moved

GROUNDS FOR DIVORCE

§ 4.02[5][b][ii]

unreasonable conditions constitutes intent to abandon the marriage. A wife's insistence that she would return home only if she could bring her mother to live with her was unreasonable. Her absence was desertion.[122]

[ii] Without spouse's consent. Desertion requires a wronged party; separation by agreement or acquiescence is not desertion. Before the era of irreconcilable differences, this rule prevented collusive divorce between parties who could not prove any of the statutory grounds.[123] The evidence must show that one spouse intended to leave the marriage while the other stood ready to reconcile.[124] However, an agreed separation may become desertion if one party makes a good-faith offer of reconciliation that the other refuses.[125]

[c] Rejection of reconciliation offer. A good-faith offer of reconciliation by a deserter stops the period of desertion. If the abandoned spouse unjustifiably refuses the offer for a one-year period, the spouse offering to return may obtain a divorce based on desertion.[126] The offer must be unqualified. A wife's offer to return was not in good faith. It was conditioned on allowing her son – who tried to kill her husband – to visit in their home.[127] A husband's offer to return if "some changes" were made, combined with a threat to move in unless his wife agreed to a divorce, was not a good-faith, unconditional offer.[128]

The innocent spouse must be given sufficient time to consider and reply to the offer, and the deserter must respond to any reasonable concerns. A deserted wife's insistence that her husband free himself of his "trouble" – a mistress – before returning home was a reasonable request and not a refusal of his offer.[129] And when a wife sent her reconciliation offer through the local sheriff, her husband's request for time to discuss the offer with his lawyer was not an unqualified refusal.[130]

The duty to reconcile does not extend beyond the one-year period. Once the statutory period has run, the innocent spouse may obtain a divorce even though the deserter

---

to Mississippi where she remained for five years).

[122] Lynch v. Lynch, 63 So. 2d 657, 662-63 (Miss. 1953) (both parties claimed desertion; court held that husband's refusal to allow mother-in-law to move in was reasonable and not conduct sufficient to allow wife to claim constructive desertion).

[123] Fulton v. Fulton, 36 Miss. 517, 525, 1858 WL 4618 (1858) ("[O]therwise, parties to the matrimonial contract . . . would have it in their power to attain their object, by a voluntary separation . . . .").

[124] Criswell v. Criswell, 182 So. 2d 587, 588 (Miss. 1966) (no desertion by wife just because parties separated).

[125] Criswell v. Criswell, 182 So. 2d 587, 588-89 (Miss. 1966); Fulton v. Fulton, 36 Miss. 517, 528, 1858 WL 4618 (1858).

[126] Fulton v. Fulton, 36 Miss. 517, 528-29, 1858 WL 4618 (1858); see Criswell v. Criswell, 182 So. 2d 587, 588 (Miss. 1966) (one-year period computed from first date of refusal to reconcile).

[127] Fulton v. Fulton, 36 Miss. 517, 528-29, 1858 WL 4618 (1858); see also Marble v. Marble, 457 So. 2d 1342, 1343 (Miss. 1984) (wife not entitled to separate maintenance when her offer to return to her husband was qualified by her requirement that her husband receive counseling by therapist of her choice).

[128] Criswell v. Criswell, 182 So. 2d 587, 589 (Miss. 1966); see also Day v. Day, 501 So. 2d 353, 357 (Miss. 1987) (husband showed up unannounced at wife's house and proposed to move back in, without overtures of reconciliation or expressing regret).

[129] McLemore v. McLemore, 163 So. 500, 501 (Miss. 1935) (wife granted divorce based on husband's desertion).

[130] Thrasher v. Thrasher, 91 So. 2d 543, 544 (Miss. 1956) (wife stopped by house twice when husband was away, but otherwise never followed up on offer to return).

§ 4.02[5][d]   MISSISSIPPI FAMILY LAW

offers to reconcile.[131]

[d] **Constructive desertion.** A spouse who abandons home to escape abusive conduct may qualify as the deserted, rather than the deserting, party. In 1949, the Mississippi Supreme Court held that constructive desertion occurs if an innocent spouse is driven away by conduct that makes the marriage unendurable or dangerous to life, health, or safety.[132] In effect, conduct that would qualify as habitual, cruel, and inhuman treatment becomes constructive desertion when the innocent spouse leaves the home rather than remaining.[133] Proof that the offending spouse intended to drive the innocent spouse away is not required. It is sufficient that the separation was a natural consequence of the defendant's conduct.[134] The plaintiff must provide corroborating evidence of the alleged misconduct.[135]

The doctrine of constructive desertion, like the ground of habitual, cruel, and inhuman treatment, is to be used only "in extreme cases."[136] For example, a husband was not justified in leaving the marital home based on his spouse's alleged inability to communicate.[137] Similarly, a wife was not justified in abandoning her husband when he refused to allow her mother to live permanently in their home.[138] In contrast, a wife's daily, unfounded accusations of alcoholism and adultery for more than a decade were sufficient to constitute constructive desertion.[139] And a wife was justified in leaving a husband whose complete refusal to work left the family without adequate food and shelter and dependent on friends.[140]

[i] **Refusal to have sex.** An "inexcusable, long-continued" refusal of sexual relations can constitute constructive desertion.[141] A wife's refusal to have sexual relations for eight years was sufficiently long-continued to amount to constructive desertion.[142] However, a court properly denied a divorce because testimony regarding

---

[131] Lynch v. Lynch, 63 So. 2d 657, 663 (Miss. 1953) ("[W]hen the desertion has ripened into a ground for divorce, the day of repentance is ended . . . .").

[132] Griffin v. Griffin, 42 So. 2d 720, 722 (Miss. 1949); *see also* Benson v. Benson, 608 So. 2d 709, 711 (Miss. 1992) (chancellor erred in denying divorce on constructive desertion based on finding that husband's life was not endangered; court should have considered second part of test); Day v. Day, 501 So. 2d 353 (Miss. 1987) (affirming chancellor's finding of no constructive desertion); Shorter v. Shorter, 740 So. 2d 352, 358 (Miss. Ct. App. 1999) (rejecting constructive desertion argument of husband who left home to live with another woman).

[133] SHELTON HAND, MISSISSIPPI DIVORCE, ALIMONY, AND CHILD CUSTODY § 4-9 n.71 (5th ed. 1998); *see* Hoskins v. Hoskins, 21 So. 3d 705, 710 (Miss. Ct. App. 2009) (noting that the two grounds are alike, except that for constructive desertion, the plaintiff must leave the marital home for one year); Shorter v. Shorter, 740 So. 2d 352, 358 (Miss. Ct. App. 1999).

[134] Griffin v. Griffin, 42 So. 2d 720, 722 (Miss. 1949).

[135] *See* Hoskins v. Hoskins, 21 So. 3d 705, 710 (Miss. Ct. App. 2009) (failure to corroborate proof supporting constructive desertion).

[136] Griffin v. Griffin, 42 So. 2d 720, 722 (Miss. 1949). For an unusual application of the doctrine, see Deen v. Deen, 856 So. 2d 736 (Miss. Ct. App. 2003) (affirming grant of divorce based on wife's constructive desertion of blind husband after she left him with sister and refused to come get him).

[137] Grant v. Grant, 765 So. 2d 1263, 1267 (Miss. 2000).

[138] Lynch v. Lynch, 63 So. 2d 657, 662 (Miss. 1953).

[139] Lynch v. Lynch, 616 So. 2d 294, 297 (Miss. 1993).

[140] Griffin v. Griffin, 42 So. 2d 720, 722 (Miss. 1949).

[141] *See* Handshoe v. Handshoe, 560 So. 2d 182, 184 n.5 (Miss. 1990); Shorter v. Shorter, 740 So. 2d 352, 358 (Miss. Ct. App. 1999) (but evidence insufficient to prove constructive desertion).

[142] Handshoe v. Handshoe, 560 So. 2d 182, 184 n.5 (Miss. 1990).

GROUNDS FOR DIVORCE   § 4.02[5][d][ii]

lack of sexual relations was conflicting.[143] Divorce on the basis of habitual, cruel, and inhuman treatment may also be granted for refusal of sexual relations.[144]

[ii] Dispute over location of residence. At one time, a wife was legally bound to follow her husband to the residence of his choosing. Her refusal to do so was desertion,[145] unless the husband's choice was unreasonable or unsafe.[146] In 1949, the Mississippi Supreme Court suggested in dicta that a wife's unreasonable refusal to make her home in the city of her husband's choosing could be considered desertion.[147]

United States Supreme Court decisions on gender distinctions in family law should invalidate common law rules placing choice of residence with the husband.[148] The Louisiana Court of Appeals has addressed this issue, holding that a statute requiring a wife to abide by her husband's choice of domicile was unconstitutional.[149] If one spouse chooses to move for legitimate reasons and urges the other to follow, and the other refuses to follow for legitimate reasons, the best approach may be to hold that neither is guilty of desertion.

[e] Effect of separate maintenance decree. The outcome of a divorce based on desertion may be controlled by a prior order of separate maintenance. For example, a separate maintenance order was res judicata as to a husband's claim of desertion.[150] An order of separate maintenance necessarily establishes that the recipient was not at fault in the separation and therefore could not have been guilty of desertion at the time of the order.[151] The bar extends only to facts prior to the separate maintenance order. If the payor made a good-faith attempt to reconcile after the separate maintenance order, the recipient's rejection of the offer could be constructive desertion.[152]

[6] Habitual drunkenness. One spouse's habitual drunkenness is cause for divorce.[153] The ground was first recognized in 1857 as a basis for divorce from bed and board. It was made a ground for absolute divorce in 1871.[154] The few cases involving

---

[143] Shorter v. Shorter, 740 So. 2d 352, 358 (Miss. Ct. App. 1999).

[144] *See* discussion *infra* § 4.02[9][b][ii].

[145] *Cf.* Suter v. Suter, 16 So. 673, 674 (Miss. 1894) (denying divorce to wife who refused to live with husband in New Orleans).

[146] *See* Wright v. Wright, 2 Miss. Dec. 67, 1883 WL 6853, at *4 (1883) ("[A] woman with a comfortable home of her own is [not] bound to abandon it at the command of a vagrant and wholly impecunious husband and follow him into a wandering and homeless existence.").

[147] *See* Starr v. Starr, 39 So. 2d 520, 522 (Miss. 1949) (rejecting husband's claim for divorce based on cruelty); *see also* Serio v. Serio, 94 So. 2d 799, 802 (Miss. 1957) (quoting *Ouzts* for proposition that wife has duty to abide by husband's reasonable choice of residence).

[148] *See* Orr v. Orr, 440 U.S. 268, 282-84 (1979) (invalidating state law providing alimony for women but not for men; old notions do not justify gender-based distinctions in family law).

[149] Crosby v. Crosby, 434 So. 2d 162, 163 (La. Ct. App. 1983); *see* 24 Am. Jur. 2d *Divorce and Separation* § 71 (2008).

[150] *See* Wilson v. Wilson, 32 So. 2d 686, 688 (Miss. 1947); Rylee v. Rylee, 108 So. 2d 161, 162 (Miss. 1926); *cf.* Etheridge v. Webb, 50 So. 2d 603, 606 (Miss. 1951) (separate maintenance decree res judicata on issues of abandonment to determine homestead rights).

[151] Van Norman v. Van Norman, 38 So. 2d 452, 454 (Miss. 1949).

[152] Day v. Day, 501 So. 2d 353, 356 (Miss. 1987).

[153] Miss. Code Ann. § 93-5-1 (2004).

[154] *See* Bunkley & Morse, *supra* note 8, § 3.12, at 106; *see also* Waskam v. Waskam, 31 Miss. 154, 155 (1856) (per curiam).

§ 4.02[7]   **MISSISSIPPI FAMILY LAW**

divorce on this ground offer little guidance on the necessary proof. Divorce was granted based on proof that a husband's habit of drinking a case of beer each night caused him to become abusive, threatening, and critical.[155] In contrast, a husband's consumption of four or five beers a night, without evidence of an impact on the marriage or his work, did not warrant divorce.[156] By analogy to the closely-related ground of habitual drug use, a plaintiff should prove that the defendant was habitually, or frequently, drunk, that the drinking adversely affected the marriage, and that the habit continued at the time of the divorce trial.[157]

[7] **Habitual and excessive use of opium, morphine, or other like drug.** A court may grant divorce based on a spouse's habitual and excessive use of "opium, morphine, or other like drugs."[158] Habitual drug use was added to the divorce statute in 1892.[159]

[a] **Habitual and excessive use.** Habitual use is shown by proof that a defendant uses drugs "customarily and frequently" rather than for "occasional indulgence." A husband's daily use of drugs over a four-year period satisfied the requirement of habitual use.[160]

The term excessive implies abuse of drugs. The plaintiff must show that the user is so addicted "that he cannot control his appetite for drugs."[161] For example, a husband's misrepresentations to physicians to obtain multiple prescriptions was proof of his loss of control and excessive use of drugs.[162]

[b] **"Other like drug."** The phrase "other like drug" means that the drug must produce an effect similar to that of opium or morphine, causing the user to act irresponsibly or recklessly. Similar effects may be shown by proof that the drug affects the user's ability to work or perform marital duties or causes behavior that makes the marriage repugnant to the plaintiff. Family testimony that a husband's excessive prescription drug use caused extremes of hyperactivity or stupidity, loss of social relationships, and inability to work more than a few hours a week was sufficient proof of similar adverse effects.[163]

---

[155] Sproles v. Sproles, 782 So. 2d 742, 745 (Miss. 2001) (husband pointed a gun at wife, threatened to kill her, accused her of infidelity; divorce also based on habitual, cruel, and inhuman treatment).

[156] Culver v. Culver, 383 So. 2d 817, 817-18 (Miss. 1980) (wife alleged change in personality; son and friends testified no effect on work or family).

[157] *See infra* § 4.02[7].

[158] MISS. CODE ANN. § 93-5-1 (2004).

[159] BUNKLEY & MORSE, *supra* note 8, § 3.13, at 110.

[160] Ladner v. Ladner, 436 So. 2d 1366, 1375 (Miss. 1983); *see also* Ashburn v. Ashburn, 970 So. 2d 204, 207-08, 215 (Miss. Ct. App. 2007) (proof that wife abused illegal and prescription drugs for over a decade).

[161] Ladner v. Ladner, 436 So. 2d 1366, 1375 (Miss. 1983).

[162] Ladner v. Ladner, 436 So. 2d 1366, 1374-75 (Miss. 1983); *see also* Ashburn v. Ashburn, 970 So. 2d 204, 208 (Miss. Ct. App. 2007) (proof that wife abused illegal and prescription drugs for over a decade, forged prescriptions, overdosed, and entered rehabilitation three times); Lawson v. Lawson, 821 So. 2d 142, 145 (Miss. Ct. App. 2002) (wife obtained multiple prescriptions).

[163] Ladner v. Ladner, 436 So. 2d 1366, 1374-75 (Miss. 1983) (drugs used included Dalmane, Libriam, Ativan, Nolundar, Mellaril, Sinequan, Vivactil, Talwin, and Tylenol No. 3 with Codeine); *see also* Lawson v. Lawson, 821 So. 2d 142, 145 (Miss. Ct. App. 2002) (drug use, including Darvocet, Lortab, Hydrocodone, and Tylenol No. 3 with Codeine, negatively affected marriage).

GROUNDS FOR DIVORCE

§ 4.02[7][c]

[c] Use of prescription drugs. Habitual use of drugs as prescribed is not grounds for divorce even if the defendant becomes dependent on the drugs. But divorce may be granted when a spouse's initial, legitimate use of prescription drugs becomes misuse.[164] A husband was properly granted a divorce from his wife, who became addicted to prescribed drugs by procuring multiple prescriptions without disclosure to her doctors.[165]

[d] Use must continue at time of suit. Proof of prior habitual drug use is not sufficient; the use must continue at the time of suit. A wife's eight-year drug habit, continuing from the date of marriage until after separation, was not grounds for divorce because she conquered the habit before suit was filed.[166]

[8] Habitual, cruel, and inhuman treatment: Overview. From 1822 to 1871, Mississippi courts were authorized to grant divorce from bed and board based on extreme cruelty. The 1871 Code eliminated divorce from bed and board. In its place, the legislature authorized a new ground for divorce – habitual, cruel, and inhuman treatment "marked by physical violence."[167] The requirement of physical violence was eliminated in 1892,[168] permitting divorce characterized by emotional cruelty alone.[169]

Divorce on this ground "requires a dual focus: upon the conduct of the offending spouse and the impact of that conduct upon the plaintiff."[170] A plaintiff must (1) show conduct by the defendant that meets the stringent test for cruelty; (2) prove a causal connection between the conduct and the plaintiff's physical or mental health; and (3) provide independent corroborating evidence of the conduct.

Habitual, cruel, and inhuman treatment is by far the most commonly used fault-based ground for divorce. It is also probably the most difficult to define. The outcome of a particular case depends upon the nature, frequency, intensity, and timing of the defendant's conduct. Actions that would not in themselves support divorce may be sufficient in combination to qualify as habitual, cruel, and inhuman. And conduct that would be considered cruel directed at one plaintiff may have little effect on another.

This section provides a general discussion of the test for habitual, cruel, and inhuman treatment, followed by examples of specific conduct found to meet or fail the test.

[a] The defendant's conduct: Cruelty defined. The Mississippi Supreme

---

[164] Ladner v. Ladner, 436 So. 2d 1366, 1374 (Miss. 1983) (unfairly harsh to penalize party for a habit caused by conditions over which party had no control) (citing Rindlaub v. Rindlaub, 125 N.W. 479 (N.D. 1910)); Lawson v. Lawson, 821 So. 2d 142, 145 (Miss. Ct. App. 2002).

[165] Lawson v. Lawson, 821 So. 2d 142, 145 (Miss. Ct. App. 2002) (wife obtained two to three prescriptions per week); *see also* Ashburn v. Ashburn, 970 So. 2d 204, 207-08 (Miss. Ct. App. 2007) (proof that wife abused illegal and prescription drugs for over a decade).

[166] Smithston v. Smithston, 74 So. 149, 151 (Miss. 1916) (distinguishing divorce based on adultery, cruelty, or desertion; statute allows divorce for drug use only if ongoing).

[167] *See* BUNKLEY & MORSE, *supra* note 8, § 3.14, at 112.

[168] *See* BUNKLEY & MORSE, *supra* note 8, § 3.14, at 112.

[169] *See* Humber v. Humber, 68 So. 161, 163 (Miss. 1915) (no longer necessary to show physical assault).

[170] Bias v. Bias, 493 So. 2d 342, 345 (Miss. 1986); *see* Faries v. Faries, 607 So. 2d 1204, 1208-09 (Miss. 1992).

§ 4.02[8][a]   MISSISSIPPI FAMILY LAW

Court's definition of habitually cruel and inhuman conduct has not changed substantially since 1930. However, its application of the standard has varied considerably over the years. The court announced the well-known test in *Russell v. Russell*: "[C]onduct only as endangers life, limb, or health, or creates a reasonable apprehension of danger thereto, thereby rendering the continuance of the marital relation unsafe for the unoffending spouse, or such unnatural and infamous conduct as would make the marital relation revolting to the unoffending spouse and render it impossible for him or her, as the case may be, to discharge the duties thereof . . . ."[171] The definition includes two types of conduct – that which endangers the other spouse and that which is unnatural and revolting. Most cases involve conduct that endangers the physical, mental, or emotional health of the plaintiff. Actual danger is not required; the test is met if the plaintiff reasonably fears danger.[172] If divorce is based on the second prong of the test, fear of danger is not required. The court of appeals rejected a husband's argument that divorce should have been denied because his conduct did not create a reasonable apprehension of danger – the divorce was based on "unnatural and revolting" conduct that made the marriage unendurable.[173]

As the demand for divorce grew in the mid-twentieth century, courts began to grant divorces under circumstances closer to incompatibility than extreme cruelty.[174] The Mississippi Supreme Court was no exception. In spite of continuing reference to the *Russell* standard, the Mississippi Supreme Court adopted a more liberal attitude toward divorce on this ground. In a number of cases, divorce was affirmed based on conduct falling short of dangerous or unnatural.[175]

In 1984, the Mississippi Supreme Court announced a return to the more stringent traditional application of the test.[176] The court held that divorce would be granted based only on conduct so extreme that the plaintiff would risk "life, limb, or health" by continuing the marriage.[177] In subsequent years, the court made good its promise, denying divorces when the real underlying problem was incompatibility.[178] A 1989 case is illustrative – divorce was denied a couple whose marriage was a "shambles," who "genuinely hate each other," and who agreed only on the fact that both wanted to be divorced.[179]

---

[171] Russell v. Russell, 128 So. 270, 272 (Miss. 1930); *see also* Kumar v. Kumar, 976 So. 2d 957, 961 (Miss. Ct. App. 2008); Cassell v. Cassell, 970 So. 2d 267, 270 (Miss. Ct. App. 2007).

[172] *See* McNeill v. McNeill, 87 So. 645, 646 (Miss. 1921) ("[I]t is not necessary that danger to life or health shall in fact exist; but if the acts of cruelty are such as to create in the mind of the complainant a reasonable apprehension of such danger, relief should be granted.").

[173] *See* Peters v. Peters, 906 So. 2d 64 (Miss. Ct. App. 2004) (conduct included choking wife, throwing items at her, accusing her of adultery, threatening suicide, and closing her accounts). See *infra* § 4.02[9][d], for a discussion of cases relying on "unnatural conduct" as habitual, cruel, and inhuman treatment.

[174] CLARK, JR., *supra* note 4, § 13.4, at 506.

[175] *See* Wires v. Wires, 297 So. 2d 900, 901-02 (Miss. 1974) (husband granted divorce because his wife was jealous and accused him of philandering, would not let his daughter-in-law visit, and bickered so much his son left home; also reducing burden of proof from clear and convincing to preponderance of the evidence).

[176] Gallaspy v. Gallaspy, 459 So. 2d 283, 285 (Miss. 1984) (if cruelty is to remain a ground, the proof must support the charge); *see also* Kergosien v. Kergosien, 471 So. 2d 1206, 1210 (Miss 1985).

[177] Marble v. Marble, 457 So. 2d 1342, 1343 (Miss. 1984) (denying divorce even though "it is evident [the couple] can no longer live together"); *see* Jackson v. Jackson, 922 So. 2d 53, 56 (Miss. Ct. App. 2006) (stating test for habitual, cruel, and inhuman treatment).

[178] *See* discussion of incompatibility *infra* § 4.02[9][e].

[179] *See* Wilson v. Wilson, 547 So. 2d 803, 804-05 (Miss. 1989); *see also* Tackett v. Tackett, 967 So. 2d 1264, 1267

GROUNDS FOR DIVORCE § 4.02[8][b]

[b] Causal connection. Prior to 1986, a plaintiff was required to show that the defendant's conduct was the proximate cause of the separation.[180] Today, a plaintiff must show a causal connection between the defendant's conduct and physical or emotional harm to the plaintiff.[181] A chancellor did not err in granting divorce based in large part on a husband's conduct after the couple's separation.[182] The impact of a defendant's conduct on the plaintiff is determined under a subjective test – one spouse "might be severely affected and harmed by treatment considered minor by [another]."[183]

Proving an impact on the plaintiff is particularly critical in cases that do not involve physical violence. Divorce is more likely to be granted based on emotional cruelty if the plaintiff offers corroborated evidence of an impact on physical or mental health.[184] For example, a chancellor properly granted divorce upon a finding that a wife's depression resulted from her husband's extreme criticism, controlling behavior, neglect of the family, sexual rejection of her, and open discussion of encounters with other women.[185] In contrast, a husband was denied divorce because there was no proof that his wife's financial mismanagement, disappearances, and alleged mistreatment of their children impaired his health "even slightly."[186] A wife was denied divorce in part because she

---

(Miss. Ct. App. 2007) (divorce denied; wife's lack of interest in sex and constant arguing over money was not sufficient evidence of cruelty).

[180] *See* Fournet v. Fournet, 481 So. 2d 326, 329 (Miss. 1985).

[181] Bias v. Bias, 493 So. 2d 342, 345 (Miss. 1986) ("proximate cause of harm to the health and physical well being of the plaintiff"); *see* Faries v. Faries, 607 So. 2d 1204, 1209 (Miss. 1992); Peters v. Peters, 906 So. 2d 64 (Miss. Ct. App. 2004); Rakestraw v. Rakestraw, 717 So. 2d 1284, 1288 (Miss. Ct. App. 1998). *But see* Cochran v. Cochran, 912 So. 2d 1086, 1090 (Miss. Ct. App. 2005) (stating that a plaintiff must show a causal connection between the defendant's conduct and the separation, and the conduct must be related in time to the separation).

[182] G.B.W. v. E.R.W., 9 So. 3d 1200, 1205 (Miss. Ct. App. 2009) (post-separation conduct included breaking into house and physically restraining wife and threatening to set personal effects on fire; also noting that pre-separation conduct was probably sufficient to support ground).

[183] Faries v. Faries, 607 So. 2d 1204, 1209 (Miss. 1992); *see* Morris v. Morris, 783 So. 2d 681, 688 (Miss. 2001); Holladay v. Holladay, 776 So. 2d 662, 676 (Miss. 2000); *cf.* Peters v. Peters, 906 So. 2d 64 (Miss. Ct. App. 2004) (corroboration by children; also noting that it would be hard to imagine what caused separation other than husband's conduct – choking wife, throwing objects at her, and accusing her of adultery).

[184] *See* Bodne v. King, 835 So. 2d 52, 55 (Miss. 2003) (wife suffered depression and was treated by a psychiatrist); Holladay v. Holladay, 776 So. 2d 662, 676 (Miss. 2000) (wife sought counseling for abuse); Robison v. Robison, 722 So. 2d 601, 603 (Miss. 1998) (abuse resulted in wife's treatment for depression); Bullock v. Bullock, 699 So. 2d 1205, 1210 (Miss. 1997) (incessant degrading and insulting behavior had serious impact on plaintiff's health); Parker v. Parker, 519 So. 2d 1232, 1234 (Miss. 1988) (physician testified to wife's hospitalization and treatment for severe anxiety caused by husband's conduct); Sandifer v. Sandifer, 61 So. 2d 144, 144 (Miss. 1952) (wife's threats affected elderly husband); Cassell v. Cassell, 970 So. 2d 267, 271 (Miss. Ct. App. 2007) (wife suffered anxiety and depression and was treated by therapist); Richardson v. Richardson, 856 So. 2d 426, 430-31 (Miss. Ct. App. 2003) (wife suffered from depression and loss of self-esteem and took medication as a result of husband's conduct); Mitchell v. Mitchell, 823 So. 2d 568, 571 (Miss. Ct. App. 2002) (wife suffered depression requiring medication; testimony of nurse and social worker); Keller v. Keller, 763 So. 2d 902, 909 (Miss. Ct. App. 2000) (both mother and son sought psychiatric treatment as a result of abuse); Moore v. Moore, 757 So. 2d 1043, 1049 (Miss. Ct. App. 2000) (resulting depression requiring medication); *cf.* Horn v. Horn, 909 So. 2d 1151, 1156 (Miss. Ct. App. 2005) (divorce granted based on physical and emotional abuse; wife lost twenty-five pounds and developed spastic colon).

[185] *See* Robison v. Robison, 722 So. 2d 601, 603 (Miss. 1998); *see also* McIntosh v. McIntosh, 977 So. 2d 1257, 1264-65 (Miss. Ct. App. 2008) (husband's sister testified that he was depressed and suffered from high blood pressure as a result of wife's conduct); Kumar v. Kumar, 976 So. 2d 957, 960, 962-63 (Miss. Ct. App. 2008) (wife lived in fear and tried to commit suicide twice).

[186] Kergosian v. Kergosian, 471 So. 2d 1206, 1210 (Miss. 1985) (wife mishandled finances, often disappeared and could not be found, locked husband out of the house, told child she hated him, slapped another child, and complained to children that she had to care for them); *see also* Anderson v. Anderson, 54 So. 3d 850, 853 (Miss. Ct. App. 2010) (husband offered no evidence that wife's behavior affected his physical or mental health); Hoskins v. Hoskins, 21 So. 3d 705, 708-709 (Miss. Ct. App. 2009) (wife offered no medical testimony or records to prove impact on health; no cor-

§ 4.02[8][c]   MISSISSIPPI FAMILY LAW

presented no medical proof of nervousness, sleeplessness, or high blood pressure.[187] The plaintiff must also establish that the defendant's conduct was a likely cause of the physical or emotional symptoms.[188] Medical testimony that a wife suffered from gastro-intestinal illness, without a link to her husband's behavior, was insufficient.[189]

[c] **Timing.** Divorce may be granted based on conduct occurring during marriage or after separation. However, the timing of the defendant's conduct may affect the court's assessment of habitual, cruel, and inhuman treatment. Divorces have been denied because a defendant's actions were too remote from the date of suit. For example, several acts of violence early in a twenty-seven-year marriage did not constitute habitual, cruel, and inhuman treatment.[190] Divorces have also been denied because the allegedly cruel conduct occurred only recently in a long marriage. For example, divorce was denied in part because a wife's allegations of emotional cruelty pertained only to conduct occurring in the last four years of a thirty-six-year marriage.[191] On the other hand, conduct occurring after separation may contribute to a finding of habitual, cruel, and inhuman treatment.[192] A husband's continuing harassment and abuse of his estranged wife after her first, unsuccessful divorce attempt was sufficient to constitute habitual, cruel, and inhuman treatment when combined with his conduct before their separation.[193] And the Mississippi Supreme Court has recognized that in unusual circumstances, conduct occurring solely after separation might be sufficient to constitute

---

roboration of claimed cruelty, even though adult children lived with the couple); Brown v. Brown, 817 So. 2d 588, 591 (Miss. Ct. App. 2002) (wife's arguments and physical attacks had no mental or physical effect on husband); Pucylowski v. Pucylowski, 741 So. 2d 998, 999 (Miss. Ct. App. 1999) (wife's public fits of rage, threats to leave, and ridiculing his religion at most interfered with husband's ability to sleep).

[187] Hoskins v. Hoskins, 21 So. 3d 705, 708-10 (Miss. Ct. App. 2009). *But cf.* Stein v. Stein, 11 So. 3d 1288, 1291 (Miss. Ct. App. 2009) (divorce granted even though no medical testimony offered; wife testified that physician cut back on depression and blood pressure medication when she left home).

[188] *See* Potts v. Potts, 700 So. 2d 321, 323 (Miss. 1997) (wife did not seek treatment for alleged nervous condition); Reed v. Reed, 839 So. 2d 565, 571 (Miss. Ct. App. 2003) (wife testified that she "almost" had a nervous breakdown but never sought treatment; no medical evidence linking high blood pressure and a "bad heart" to mistreatment).

[189] Hodge v. Hodge, 837 So. 2d 786, 788 (Miss. Ct. App. 2003); *see also* Tedford v. Tedford, 856 So. 2d 753 (Miss. Ct. App. 2003) (wife failed to show that depression was caused by her husband's conduct).

[190] Talbert v. Talbert, 759 So. 2d 1105, 1109 (Miss. 1999) (no divorce where husband belittled his wife, screamed at her, and committed a few acts of violence early in the twenty-seven year marriage; conduct did not recur); *see also* Bland v. Bland, 620 So. 2d 543, 545 (Miss. 1993) (one act of violence ten years prior to divorce action); Scott v. Scott, 69 So. 2d 489, 494 (Miss. 1954) (all testimony related to acts of violence more than four years prior to divorce). *But see* Stein v. Stein, 11 So. 3d 1288, 1292 (Miss. Ct. App. 2009) (acts of physical violence in 1987 and 1991, combined with verbal abuse throughout marriage, sufficient to support divorce); McIntosh v. McIntosh, 977 So. 2d 1257, 1264-66 (Miss. Ct. App. 2008) (husband granted divorce even though much of wife's financial mismanagement occurred early in marriage).

[191] Tedford v. Tedford, 856 So. 2d 753 (Miss. Ct. App. 2003); *see also* Reed v. Reed, 839 So. 2d 565, 567 (Miss. Ct. App. 2003) (divorce denied; allegations of four acts of physical abuse in last two months of nineteen-year relationship; wife stated couple had good relationship prior to two months before separation).

[192] Richard v. Richard, 711 So. 2d 884, 890 (Miss. 1998); *see also* Morris v. Morris, 783 So. 2d 681, 687-88 (Miss. 2001); Gregory v. Gregory, 881 So. 2d 840 (Miss. Ct. App. 2003) ("The court should consider the offending conduct, even if it occurred during separation . . . . Something that occurs during separation could factually be found to have eliminated whatever opportunity might have existed that the spouses could be reconciled . . . .").

[193] Bias v. Bias, 493 So. 2d 342, 345 (Miss. 1986); *see also* Horn v. Horn, 909 So. 2d 1151, 1157 (Miss. Ct. App. 2005) (acts of physical violence after wife requested divorce could be considered; no requirement that conduct cause separation).

GROUNDS FOR DIVORCE   **§ 4.02[8][d]**

cruelty.[194] Pre-marital violence does not provide grounds for divorce,[195] but a court may admit testimony regarding pre-marital abuse to show the effect of later conduct on the plaintiff.[196]

[d] Corroboration. A plaintiff's testimony must be supported by independent evidence unless corroboration is not reasonably possible because of the nature of the conduct or the parties' isolation.[197] A chancellor properly denied divorce based on the uncorroborated testimony of a wife who worked and was in contact with others on a daily basis.[198] Corroborating testimony has been provided by family and friends,[199] medical personnel or other professionals,[200] or testimony of the defendant.[201] The corroborating evidence need not be sufficient in itself to establish the ground – it need only provide enough supporting facts for a court to conclude that the plaintiff's testimony is

---

[194] *See* Day v. Day, 501 So. 2d 353, 355 (Miss. 1987) ("[T]here is no reason on principle why the fact that the parties have not been living together should render it legally impossible to establish cruel and inhuman treatment."); Bias v. Bias, 493 So. 2d 342, 344 (Miss. 1986) (continuing harassment and abuse during separation).

[195] Cochran v. Cochran, 912 So. 2d 1086, 1090-91 (Miss. Ct. App. 2005) (rejecting evidence of physical assaults and cruelty prior to marriage, when offered as basis for divorce rather than to prove wife's reasonable fear of husband's later cruelty).

[196] *See* Holladay v. Holladay, 776 So. 2d 662, 676 (Miss. 2000) (severe beating prior to marriage relevant to plaintiff's state of mind and impact of later violence); *cf.* Moses v. Moses, 879 So. 2d 1043 (Miss. Ct. App. 2004) (wife not entitled to divorce based on the fact that she contracted a sexually transmitted disease from her husband; she knew of the condition prior to marriage).

[197] Andersen v. Andersen, 200 So. 726, 728 (Miss. 1941) (corroboration of husband's testimony necessary, where parties lived in crowded area and conduct would likely have been observed); *see* Hassett v. Hassett, 690 So. 2d 1140, 1146 (Miss. 1997) (wife's testimony regarding sexual abuse not corroborated); Chamblee v. Chamblee, 637 So. 2d 850, 860 (Miss. 1994) (wife's testimony of physical abuse not corroborated); Gardner v. Gardner, 618 So. 2d 108, 114 (Miss. 1993) (same); Heatherly v. Heatherly, 914 So. 2d 754, 757 (Miss. Ct. App. 2005) (court erred in granting a divorce based upon habitual cruelty in the absence of any corroborating evidence); Reed v. Reed, 839 So. 2d 565, 571 (Miss. Ct. App. 2003) (no corroboration of physical violence).

[198] Cochran v. Cochran, 912 So. 2d 1086, 1089 (Miss. Ct. App. 2005) (without corroboration, cross-examination must be searching and convince the chancellor that the allegations are true); *see also* Hoskins v. Hoskins, 21 So. 3d 705, 708-11 (Miss. Ct. App. 2009) (divorce denied; no corroboration of claimed cruelty, even though adult children lived with the couple).

[199] *See* Sproles v. Sproles, 782 So. 2d 742, 747 (Miss. 2001) (corroboration by mother and neighbor); Devereaux v. Devereaux, 493 So. 2d 1310, 1312 (Miss. 1986) (corroboration by son and daughter); Price v. Price, 22 So. 3d 331, 333 (Miss. Ct. App. 2009) (husband's evidence of abuse corroborated by teenaged son's testimony); Oswalt v. Oswalt, 981 So. 2d 993, 996 (Miss. Ct. App. 2007) (mother's testimony regarding violence); Cassell v. Cassell, 970 So. 2d 267, 271 (Miss. Ct. App. 2007) (testimony of son); Jackson v. Jackson, 922 So. 2d 53, 56 (Miss. Ct. App. 2006) (wife's testimony corroborated by children); Fulton v. Fulton, 918 So. 2d 877, 880-81 (Miss. Ct. App. 2006) (corroboration by family and friends); Horn v. Horn, 909 So. 2d 1151, 1156 (Miss. Ct. App. 2005) (wife's testimony corroborated by her sister's testimony and photographs of bruises); Peters v. Peters, 906 So. 2d 64 (Miss. Ct. App. 2004) (corroboration by children). *But see* Chamblee v. Chamblee, 637 So. 2d 850, 860 (Miss. 1994) (neighbor's testimony that she had seen bruises on wife's arms but did not know cause not sufficient corroboration of wife's allegations of three incidents of violence during marriage).

[200] *See* Faries v. Faries, 607 So. 2d 1204, 1208 (Miss. 1992) (social worker corroborated effect on plaintiff); Kumar v. Kumar, 976 So. 2d 957, 962 (Miss. Ct. App. 2008) (corroboration by family testimony, photographs, and medical records); *cf.* Hodge v. Hodge, 837 So. 2d 786, 788 (Miss. Ct. App. 2003) (physician testified regarding physical symptoms but failed to establish causal link).

[201] *See* Shavers v. Shavers, 982 So. 2d 397, 404-05 (Miss. 2008) (wife's testimony of abuse corroborated by husband's testimony that he struck her, even though he disputed the circumstances); McKee v. Flynt, 630 So. 2d 44, 48 (Miss. 1993) (husband admitted two incidents of violence); Gatlin v. Gatlin, 234 So. 2d 634, 635 (Miss. 1970) (husband's evidence corroborated by wife's testimony regarding violent arguments between the two); *cf.* Kumar v. Kumar, 976 So. 2d 957, 964 (Miss. Ct. App. 2008) (wife's testimony corroborated by admissions of husband because of his failure to respond).

§ 4.02[8][e]   MISSISSIPPI FAMILY LAW

true.[202] For example, a wife's testimony of her husband's physical and emotional abuse was corroborated by a social worker's testimony that the plaintiff's depression and low self-esteem were indicative of a victim of spousal abuse.[203] Similarly, a wife's testimony of numerous incidents of physical violence was adequately corroborated by her daughter's testimony that she saw her father strike her mother twice.[204] Photographs taken by a plaintiff's father, combined with his testimony, provided sufficient corroboration of a wife's testimony of numerous incidents of serious physical violence.[205] And the court of appeals affirmed divorce based on a husband's physical abuse of his wife, even though no one witnessed the abuse. Family members testified that they observed her bruises and scratches, and she sought psychiatric treatment as a result of the abuse.[206]

In contrast, a plaintiff's allegations of several incidents of physical violence were not sufficient to support divorce; she did not produce any corroborating witnesses, and several witnesses, including her husband, contradicted her testimony.[207] A single photograph of bruises on a wife's arms, without corroborating testimony by the photographer, friends, or neighbors, was not sufficient to support divorce based on her allegations of violence.[208] The court of appeals reversed a divorce for lack of corroboration, even though the wife had obtained a protective order against her husband. Her testimony of physical and sexual abuse was not sufficiently corroborated by police reports and the petition for protective order, because both were based on her testimony.[209]

[e] Burden of proof. To be granted divorce based on habitual, cruel, and inhuman treatment, the plaintiff must prove the ground by a preponderance of the evidence.[210]

[f] Standard of review. The question of whether habitual, cruel, and inhuman treatment has been proven is a question of law that is reviewed de novo upon appeal. The court of appeals held that a wife's evidence of cruel treatment was sufficient and therefore the chancellor applied an incorrect standard of law in finding that she did not prove habitual, cruel, and inhuman treatment.[211]

---

[202] Andersen v. Andersen, 200 So. 726, 728 (Miss. 1941).

[203] *See* Faries v. Faries, 607 So. 2d 1204, 1208 (Miss. 1992).

[204] Devereaux v. Devereaux, 493 So. 2d 1310, 1312 (Miss. 1986); *see also* Moore v. Moore, 757 So. 2d 1043, 1049 (Miss. Ct. App. 2000).

[205] Labella v. Labella, 722 So. 2d 472, 474 (Miss. 1998); *see also* McKee v. Flynt, 630 So. 2d 44, 48-49 (Miss. 1993) (husband admitted two incidents of violence; testimony of witnesses who observed bruises and scratches on plaintiff; combined with emotional abuse); Kumar v. Kumar, 976 So. 2d 957, 962 (Miss. Ct. App. 2008) (corroboration by family testimony, photographs, and medical records); Oswalt v. Oswalt, 981 So. 2d 993, 995-96 (Miss. Ct. App. 2007) (photographs combined with mother's testimony). *But see* Rawson v. Buta, 609 So. 2d 426, 432 (Miss. 1992) (two photographs of bruises on wife's arm, with no other corroborating testimony, insufficient; court noted that there might be rare circumstances where photographs alone were sufficient corroboration).

[206] Langdon v. Langdon, 854 So. 2d 485 (Miss. Ct. App. 2003); *see also* Fulton v. Fulton, 918 So. 2d 877, 880 (Miss. Ct. App. 2006) (corroborating witnesses saw bruises and saw plaintiff upset after altercation).

[207] *See* Gardner v. Gardner, 618 So. 2d 108, 114 (Miss. 1993).

[208] Rawson v. Buta, 609 So. 2d 426, 432 (Miss. 1992).

[209] Ladner v. Ladner, 49 So. 3d 669, 672 (Miss. Ct. App. 2010) (also stating that testimony that the son feared his father did not prove abuse of the mother).

[210] Kumar v. Kumar, 976 So. 2d 957, 961 (Miss. Ct. App. 2008).

[211] Kumar v. Kumar, 976 So. 2d 957, 960-63 (Miss. Ct. App. 2008); *see also* Anderson v. Anderson, 54 So. 3d 850, 851 (Miss. Ct. App. 2010) (whether cruelty standard is met is a question of law).

GROUNDS FOR DIVORCE §4.02[9]

[9] Habitual, cruel, and inhuman treatment: Specific conduct

[a] **Physical violence.** One spouse's physical violence toward the other presents a clear case of habitual, cruel, and inhuman treatment. Evidence that a defendant engaged in an ongoing pattern of physical or emotional abuse or one or more incidents of severe violence will support a grant of divorce. Minor physical contact or isolated acts of violence do not necessarily support divorce on this ground.

[i] **Pattern of violence or one or more incidents of severe violence.** Divorce will be granted on a showing of repeated episodes of violence by one spouse against the other.[212] For example, a chancellor properly granted divorce based on evidence of ten episodes of physical violence and numerous incidents of emotional abuse over a thirteen-year marriage.[213] In addition, one or more incidents of severe violence will support grant of a divorce.[214]

[ii] **Isolated acts of violence.** Isolated acts of physical violence may also support a grant of divorce, particularly when combined with other factors such as verbal or emotional abuse and threats.[215] For example, divorce was properly granted to a

---

[212] *See* Holladay v. Holladay, 776 So. 2d 662, 665-66 (Miss. 2000) (repeated episodes of physical violence throughout marriage); Labella v. Labella, 722 So. 2d 472, 473-74 (Miss. 1998) (ten episodes of violence); Devereaux v. Devereaux, 493 So. 2d 1310, 1312 (Miss. 1986) (between fifteen and twenty incidents of violence); Langdon v. Langdon, 854 So. 2d 485 (Miss. Ct. App. 2003) (at least three incidents of violence, one requiring hospitalization for a week).

[213] *See* Labella v. Labella, 722 So. 2d 472, 473-74 (Miss. 1998); *see also* Kumar v. Kumar, 976 So. 2d 957, 961-63 (Miss. Ct. App. 2008) (divorce based on proof of incidents of physical violence, verbal abuse, and transmission of STD to wife); Fulton v. Fulton, 918 So. 2d 877, 879-80 (Miss. Ct. App. 2006) (pattern of physical abuse by husband, including one event for which he was prosecuted and pled guilty and one in which he stood by while his girlfriend's friends beat his wife and injured her severely).

[214] *See* Sandifer v. Sandifer, 61 So. 2d 144, 144 (Miss. 1952) (threats to shoot husband or poison food); Serton v. Serton, 819 So. 2d 15, 18 (Miss. Ct. App. 2002) (husband threatened wife's life, pressed a gun to her neck, and beat and raped her in front of their two children); *cf.* Smith v. Smith, 994 So. 2d 882, 884-85 (Miss. Ct. App. 2008) (divorce granted to husband based on wife's stabbing him on Christmas; grant of divorce not an issue on appeal).

[215] *See* Sproles v. Sproles, 782 So. 2d 742, 745 (Miss. 2001) (husband drank a case of beer a night, was abusive, threatened wife's life, treated her in dehumanizing ways); Holladay v. Holladay, 776 So. 2d 662, 676-77 (Miss. 2000) (husband locked his wife out and away from her frightened child and closed her checking account; violence required two police interventions); Robison v. Robison, 722 So. 2d 601, 603 (Miss. 1998) (husband restricted his wife's social life, told her she was undesirable, discussed sexual relations with other women, rarely had sex with her, threw her off the bed the last three times he did have sex with her, and neglected the family financially); Price v. Price, 22 So. 3d 331, 332 (Miss. Ct. App. 2009) (wife physically attacked husband on a family vacation, destroyed his personal effects, threw things, and pled guilty to falsely applying for credit cards in his name); Stein v. Stein, 11 So. 3d 1288, 1292 (Miss. Ct. App. 2009) (acts of physical violence in 1987 and 1991, combined with verbal abuse throughout marriage, sufficient to support divorce); Goellner v. Goellner, 11 So. 3d 1251, 1257 (Miss. Ct. App. 2009) (outbursts of anger, abusive and vulgar language, and physical altercations); Atkinson v. Atkinson, 11 So. 3d 172, 174 (Miss. Ct. App. 2009) (husband choked his wife, put a knife to her chest, cursed at her and abused her verbally, and threatened to hit her with a rake and to rape her); Horn v. Horn, 909 So. 2d 1151, 1157 (Miss. Ct. App. 2005) (physical abuse combined with verbal and emotional abuse); Wright v. Wright, 823 So. 2d 586, 587 (Miss. Ct. App. 2002) (husband was jealous and suspicious, had problems managing anger, and physically assaulted his wife more than once); Garriga v. Garriga, 770 So. 2d 978, 983 (Miss. Ct. App. 2000) (husband was violent and adulterous, drank to excess, forced wife to have sexual relations, left her in a parking lot late at night, and would not allow her to choose her own clothes); Keller v. Keller, 763 So. 2d 902, 904, 909 (Miss. Ct. App. 2000) (committed at least one act of physical violence, refused to have sex for the last year of marriage, beat his wife's son from first marriage, and demanded that she "get rid" of the child by giving up custody); Moore v. Moore, 757 So. 2d 1043, 1049 (Miss. Ct. App. 2000) (emotional and verbal abuse, four instances of physical abuse, and resulting depression requiring medication); Mixon v. Mixon, 724 So. 2d 956, 960 (Miss. Ct. App. 1998) (several

§ 4.02[9][b]   MISSISSIPPI FAMILY LAW

wife whose husband choked her, threw objects at her, accused her of adultery, and uni-laterally closed her checking accounts and canceled her credit cards.[216]

The Mississippi Supreme Court has stated, however, that "[p]hysical violence in the marriage does not create a per se ground for a divorce."[217] Minor physical contact that does not rise to the level of genuine violence does not always warrant a grant of divorce. For example, divorce has been denied in spite of a physical altercation in which both parties were involved.[218] Similarly, divorce was denied when the alleged physical violence resulted in a scratch on the plaintiff's arm.[219]

The supreme court has also stated that while a single incident of violence is not ordinarily sufficient to grant divorce, one event may be so extreme and life-threatening as to constitute cruelty.[220] A chancellor erred in denying divorce to a woman whose husband attempted to shoot her – the assault alone was sufficient to grant divorce.[221]

[b] Verbal or emotional abuse. Although physical violence is no longer required for divorce based on habitual cruelty,[222] a defendant's conduct must "rise above the level of unkindness or rudeness or mere incompatibility or want of affection."[223] It is difficult to quantify the non-physical conduct that will support divorce based on habitual, cruel, and inhuman treatment. Conduct that appears similar may result in a denial or grant of divorce, depending on the frequency and severity of the conduct, the presence or absence of other conduct, and the impact on the plaintiff. A husband's controlling behavior, criticism, and name-calling was not sufficient to grant a divorce in one case,[224] while similar conduct was sufficient in another.[225]

Certain behaviors may alone be sufficient. Courts have held that a spouse's constant unfounded accusations, long-continuing refusal of sex, aberrant sexual behavior, or concealment of a child may support grant of a divorce even in the absence of other harmful conduct. More typically, however, emotional cruelty consists of a combination of behaviors that, taken together, meet the definition of habitual, cruel, and inhuman.

---

incidents of physical violence combined with verbal abuse, accusations, and acts of destruction).

[216] Peters v. Peters, 906 So. 2d 64 (Miss. Ct. App. 2004); *see also* Oswalt v. Oswalt, 981 So. 2d 993, 996 (Miss. Ct. App. 2007) (husband threatened suicide and threatened wife with gun, in addition to belittling her).

[217] *See* Reed v. Reed, 839 So. 2d 565, 570 (Miss. Ct. App. 2003).

[218] *See* Wilbourne v. Wilbourne, 748 So. 2d 184, 187 (Miss. 1999) (no divorce although the marriage "was unpleasant and the parties were incompatible;" arguments "on occasion involved physical violence"); Bowen v. Bowen, 688 So. 2d 1374, 1377-78 (Miss. 1997) (no divorce where husband inferred that wife was lesbian, called her names, and struck her twice during an altercation in which she also struck and bit him).

[219] *See* Steen v. Steen, 641 So. 2d 1167, 1170 (Miss. 1994) (physical contact included pinching and scratch on arm from door jamb).

[220] *See* Rawson v. Buta, 609 So. 2d 426, 431 (Miss. 1992).

[221] *See* Ellzey v. Ellzey, 253 So. 2d 249, 250 (Miss. 1971) (reversing chancellor who found the incident insufficient to grant divorce); *see also* Gatlin v. Gatlin, 234 So. 2d 634, 635 (Miss. 1970) (wife's shooting at husband would have been sufficient to grant divorce).

[222] *See* Morris v. Morris, 783 So. 2d 681, 688 (Miss. 2001).

[223] Hassett v. Hassett, 690 So. 2d 1140, 1146 (Miss. 1997).

[224] *See* Morris v. Morris, 804 So. 2d 1025 (Miss. 2002); *see also* Tedford v. Tedford, 856 So. 2d 753 (Miss. Ct. App. 2003).

[225] *See* Scally v. Scally, 802 So. 2d 128, 131 (Miss. Ct. App. 2001) (husband was "moody, controlling, dominating, and verbally abusive;" wife testified that his actions affected her health and caused her to fear for her safety); *see also* Cassell v. Cassell, 970 So. 2d 267, 271 (Miss. Ct. App. 2007) (husband called wife names, cursed her, and threw things at her).

GROUNDS FOR DIVORCE   § 4.02[9][b][i]

[i] Unfounded accusations. Habitual accusations of infidelity may constitute cruelty even in the absence of other conduct, if the accusations are clearly unfounded.[226] Divorce was justified by a wife's daily, unfounded accusations of adultery over many years, affecting the husband's physical health.[227] Similarly, a wife's constant accusations of incest between a father and daughter, in the daughter's hearing, were sufficient to grant a divorce.[228] However, a husband's insinuations that his wife was lesbian did not support divorce.[229]

Accusations made in good faith, although ultimately disproved, are not sufficient. A wife's good-faith accusation that her husband sexually molested their son did not establish habitual, cruel, and inhuman treatment, even though the evidence ultimately did not support the charge. Her charges were based on suspicious behavior by the child and her allegations were supported by expert testimony.[230] And a wife's accusations of adultery, even if wrong, were not unfounded; her minister husband received emails from women he met on dating websites and sent a sexually explicit email to an employee.[231]

[ii] Refusal to have sexual relationship. An "inexcusable, long-continued refusal of sexual relations" may warrant divorce on the grounds of habitual, cruel, and inhuman treatment, but the facts must be extreme.[232] A wife's refusal to have a sexual relationship with her husband for eight years was sufficiently extreme to permit a divorce based on cruelty.[233] Refusal to have sex for four months was not sufficient,[234] nor were periodic refusals to have sex for as much as a month at a time.[235]

[iii] Aberrant sexual behavior. In several cases, the supreme court has indicated that sexual behavior that is considered aberrant may constitute "brutal and unfeeling" conduct under the first prong of the test for cruelty.[236] The Mississippi Supreme Court affirmed divorce to a wife whose husband demanded that she participate in aberrant sexual behavior on at least three occasions. The court found that his conduct "substantially impaired her health, and created a reasonable apprehension of

---

[226] Thames v. Thames, 100 So. 2d 868, 870 (Miss. 1958) (husband's continued accusations of infidelity and statements that child was not his).

[227] Hibner v. Hibner, 64 So. 2d 756, 756, 758 (Miss. 1953).

[228] Richard v. Richard, 711 So. 2d 884, 888 (Miss. 1998) (other behavior also supported divorce) (dicta).

[229] Bowen v. Bowen, 688 So. 2d 1374, 1376 (Miss. 1997) (wife told husband she would choose friend over husband, but denied lesbian relationship).

[230] Gregory v. Gregory, 881 So. 2d 840 (Miss. Ct. App. 2003) ("[H]onestly made claims, even when found to have been erroneous, do not constitute habitual, cruel, and inhuman treatment.").

[231] Anderson v. Anderson, 54 So. 3d 850, 854 (Miss. Ct. App. 2010) (he explained that the website activity was "research" for counseling his congregation).

[232] Sarphie v. Sarphie, 177 So. 358, 359 (Miss. 1937); *see* Shorter v. Shorter, 740 So. 2d 352, 357 (Miss. Ct. App. 1999) (upholding chancellor's denial of a divorce where there was conflicting testimony regarding the lack of sexual relations between the parties).

[233] Culver v. Culver, 383 So. 2d 817, 817 (Miss. 1980).

[234] Sarphie v. Sarphie, 177 So. 358, 359 (Miss. 1937).

[235] Crenshaw v. Crenshaw, 767 So. 2d 272, 275 (Miss. Ct. App. 2000); *see also* Lewis v. Lewis, 602 So. 2d 881, 883 (Miss. 1992) (wife not entitled to divorce where lack of sexual relationship was due to prostate trouble).

[236] For cases discussing aberrant sexual behavior as a basis for divorce under the second type of cruelty, see *infra* § 4.02[9][d].

§ 4.02[9][b][iv]   MISSISSIPPI FAMILY LAW

continuing danger." [237] Divorce has also been granted based on a husband's desire to dress in women's clothing during sex.[238] In 2009, the court of appeals held that a husband's sexual demands on his wife met the requirements of both types of cruelty, stating that "a single act of sexual abuse may be sufficient to support a divorce based on the ground of habitual cruel and inhuman treatment."[239]

[iv] **Hiding child.** A wife's conduct in hiding a child from his father for the better part of a year was sufficient in itself to grant divorce based on habitual, cruel, and inhuman treatment.[240]

[c] **Factors in combination.** Habitual, cruel, and inhuman treatment may be found from a combination of factors that, taken alone, would not be sufficient to grant divorce. Cruelty "may consist of a series of acts, some of the same nature and some of different natures, but which, when taken together, tend to cause pain and suffering on the part of the innocent spouse."[241] The cumulative impact of such conduct over a long period of time may constitute cruelty, while similar conduct for a shorter time, or with fewer factors present, may not be cruelty.[242]

The following conduct has been discussed as supporting a finding of cruelty in combination with other conduct: abusive language,[243] constant criticism,[244] dehu-

---

[237] *See* Stockton v. Stockton, 203 So. 2d 806, 807 (Miss. 1967) (husband wanted to use whips and involve another man); *see also* Crutcher v. Crutcher, 38 So. 337, 337 (Miss. 1905) (husband's conviction for pederasty as cruelty creating reasonable apprehension of communication of disease).

[238] *See* Cherry v. Cherry, 593 So. 2d 13, 17-18 (Miss. 1991).

[239] Jones v. Jones, 43 So. 3d 465, 476-79 (Miss. Ct. App. 2009) (sexual behavior combined with verbal abusive and controlling behavior).

[240] Michael v. Michael, 650 So. 2d 469, 472 (Miss. 1995); *cf.* McIntosh v. McIntosh, 977 So. 2d 1257, 1260-61 (Miss. Ct. App. 2008) (wife's telling husband that premarital child was dead rather than adopted part of evidence of habitual, cruel, and inhuman treatment).

[241] Savell v. Savell, 240 So. 2d 628, 629 (Miss. 1970).

[242] *See* Jackson v. Jackson, 922 So. 2d 53, 56 (Miss. Ct. App. 2006) (husband's conduct over many years, including failure to visit home during long absences, lack of support, excessive drinking, verbal abuse, and condescension, sufficient in combination); Horn v. Horn, 909 So. 2d 1151, 1156-57 (Miss. Ct. App. 2005) (divorce granted on cruelty grounds where husband was verbally abusive, enraged by minor incidents, refused to speak to wife for days, closed her up in the bathroom, falsely accused her of infidelity, called her insulting names, stated that he wished she would die, threatened to burn her, and became physically abusive after she stated that she wanted a divorce; "unrelenting" nature of the conduct proved that the conduct was habitual); Rakestraw v. Rakestraw, 717 So. 2d 1284, 1286, 1289 (Miss. Ct. App. 1998) (combined effect of practices over twenty-year relationship). *But see* Anderson v. Anderson, 54 So. 3d 850, 854-55 (Miss. Ct. App. 2010) (wife's yelling, accusations, and threats did not constitute cruelty).

[243] *See* Savell v. Savell, 240 So. 2d 628, 629 (Miss. 1970); Sandifer v. Sandifer, 61 So. 2d 144, 144 (Miss. 1952); Goellner v. Goellner, 11 So. 3d 1251, 1258 (Miss. Ct. App. 2009) (outbursts of anger, abusive and vulgar language, and physical altercations); Kumar v. Kumar, 976 So. 2d 957, 964 (Miss. Ct. App. 2008); Cassell v. Cassell, 970 So. 2d 267, 271 (Miss. Ct. App. 2007) (husband called wife names, cursed her, and threw things at her); Stone v. Stone, 824 So. 2d 645, 647 (Miss. Ct. App. 2002).

[244] *See* Rakestraw v. Rakestraw, 717 So. 2d 1284, 1286 (Miss. 1998); Jackson v. Jackson, 922 So. 2d 53, 56 (Miss. Ct. App. 2006) (condescension toward wife); Stone v. Stone, 824 So. 2d 645, 647 (Miss. Ct. App. 2002); Robison v. Robison, 722 So. 2d 601, 603 (Miss. Ct. App. 1998).

GROUNDS FOR DIVORCE   § 4.02[9][c]

manizing treatment,[245] degrading sexual behavior,[246] outbursts of temper,[247] throwing things,[248] alcohol or drug problems,[249] failing to assist in any household chores,[250] lack of affection[251] or emotional support,[252] willful failure to support,[253] extreme money mismanagement,[254] indictment for murder,[255] filing assault charges against the other,[256] suicide attempts,[257] abusive conduct toward children,[258] use of child pornography,[259] threatening the other with guns,[260] forcing a wife to abort or threats to abort a pregnancy,[261] questioning paternity of children,[262] obsessive or addictive behavior,[263]

---

[245] Sproles v. Sproles, 782 So. 2d 742, 747 (Miss. 2001); Bullock v. Bullock, 699 So. 2d 1205, 1210 (Miss. 1997); *see also* Muhammed v. Muhammed, 622 So. 2d 1239, 1241-42, 1250 (Miss. 1993) (divorce granted to a wife who found her husband's decision to live in an extremely restrictive Black Muslim community intolerable; women treated as subordinate).

[246] Jones v. Jones, 43 So. 3d 465, 476 (Miss. Ct. App. 2009) (a single act of sexual abuse may constitute cruelty). *See also* cases cited in § 4.02[9][b][3] *supra*.

[247] Boutwell v. Boutwell, 829 So. 2d 1216, 1220 (Miss. 2002); Goellner v. Goellner, 11 So. 3d 1251, 1257 (Miss. Ct. App. 2009) (outbursts of anger, abusive and vulgar language, and physical altercations); Stone v. Stone, 824 So. 2d 645, 647 (Miss. Ct. App. 2002).

[248] *See* Price v. Price, 22 So. 3d 331, 332 (Miss. Ct. App. 2009) (divorce granted to husband; wife physically attacked him on a family vacation, destroyed his personal effects, threw things, and pled guilty to falsely applying for credit cards in his name); Cassell v. Cassell, 970 So. 2d 267, 271 (Miss. Ct. App. 2007) (husband called wife names, cursed her, and threw things at her); Rakestraw v. Rakestraw, 717 So. 2d 1284, 1286 (Miss. Ct. App. 1998); *cf.* Peters v. Peters, 906 So. 2d 64 (Miss. Ct. App. 2004) (throwing objects combined with physical violence).

[249] *See* Boutwell v. Boutwell, 829 So. 2d 1216, 1220 (Miss. 2002); Sproles v. Sproles, 782 So. 2d 742, 747 (Miss. 2001); Savell v. Savell, 240 So. 2d 628, 629 (Miss. 1970); Jackson v. Jackson, 922 So. 2d 53, 56 (Miss. Ct. App. 2006) (excessive drinking four or five nights a week); Garriga v. Garriga, 770 So. 2d 978 (Miss. Ct. App. 2000).

[250] Richard v. Richard, 711 So. 2d 884, 887-88 (Miss. 1984); Rakestraw v. Rakestraw, 717 So. 2d 1284, 1285-86 (Miss. Ct. App. 1998).

[251] Stone v. Stone, 824 So. 2d 645, 647 (Miss. Ct. App. 2002).

[252] *See* Robison v. Robison, 722 So. 2d 601, 603 (Miss. 1998); McIntosh v. McIntosh, 977 So. 2d 1257, 1262 (Miss. Ct. App. 2008) (wife refused to attend social events with husband, who was a high school principal); Rakestraw v. Rakestraw, 717 So. 2d 1284, 1286 (Miss. Ct. App. 1998).

[253] *See* Robison v. Robison, 722 So. 2d 601, 603 (Miss. 1998); Savell v. Savell, 240 So. 2d 628, 629 (Miss. 1970); Jackson v. Jackson, 922 So. 2d 53, 56 (Miss. Ct. App. 2006) (long-term lack of support for wife and children); Rakestraw v. Rakestraw, 717 So. 2d 1284, 1285 (Miss. Ct. App. 1998) (husband held thirty-five jobs during marriage and left family without any kitchen appliances).

[254] Price v. Price, 22 So. 3d 331, 332 (Miss. Ct. App. 2009) (wife pled guilty to falsely applying for credit cards in husband's name); McIntosh v. McIntosh, 977 So. 2d 1257, 1260-67 (Miss. Ct. App. 2008) (wife stole checks and savings bonds from her husband and forged his signature, purchased items on a credit card and returned them for cash, failed to file tax returns, and lied about her actions).

[255] Bodne v. King, 835 So. 2d 52, 59 (Miss. 2003).

[256] Bodne v. King, 835 So. 2d 52, 59 (Miss. 2003).

[257] Morris v. Morris, 783 So. 2d 681, 690 (Miss. 2001); *cf.* Jenkins v. Jenkins, 55 So. 3d 1094, 1095 (Miss. Ct. App. 2010) (suicide attempt combined with locking family out of home, threatening to jump from car, and disabling wife's car); Oswalt v. Oswalt, 981 So. 2d 993 (Miss. Ct. App. 2007) (suicide threats combined with physical violence); Peters v. Peters, 906 So. 2d 64 (Miss. Ct. App. 2004) (same).

[258] Keller v. Keller, 763 So. 2d 902, 904 (Miss. Ct. App. 2000) (also insisted that wife send son away and verbally abused wife).

[259] *See* Bodne v. King, 835 So. 2d 52, 59 (Miss. 2003) (husband also indicted for three murders). *But cf.* Hodge v. Hodge, 837 So. 2d 786, 788 (Miss. Ct. App. 2003) (alleged use of pornography did not support divorce); Tedford v. Tedford, 856 So. 2d 753 (Miss. Ct. App. 2003) (alleged use of computer to view pornography did not support grant of divorce).

[260] Jones v. Jones, 532 So. 2d 574, 576 (Miss. 1988); Sandifer v. Sandifer, 61 So. 2d 144, 144 (Miss. 1952).

[261] Smith v. Smith, 614 So. 2d 394, 395-96 (Miss. 1993); Stein v. Stein, 11 So. 3d 1288, 1291 (Miss. Ct. App. 2009) (two incidents of physical violence, forced abortion, screaming, name-calling, and threats to kill wife).

[262] Rakestraw v. Rakestraw, 717 So. 2d 1284, 1286 (Miss. Ct. App. 1998).

[263] Richard v. Richard, 711 So. 2d 884, 888 (Miss. 1998).

§ 4.02[9][d]   MISSISSIPPI FAMILY LAW

false accusations,[264] controlling behavior,[265] extreme jealousy,[266] statements about a spouse's undesirability or one's sexual attraction to others,[267] refusal to have sex,[268] unexplained absences,[269] and refusal to evict a violent adult child.[270]

A pattern of adultery during marriage may be a factor in finding habitual, cruel, and inhuman treatment, even if the adultery has been condoned.[271] However, two extramarital affairs alone did not constitute cruelty.[272] A same-sex relationship during marriage may, with other conduct, support a finding of habitual, cruel, and inhuman treatment.[273]

[d] **Revolting and unnatural conduct.** The second type of cruelty – conduct "so unnatural and infamous as to make the marriage revolting to the non-offending spouse," – appears much less frequently as a basis for divorce. Several of the cases involve sexual conduct considered aberrant and degrading.[274] In a 2009 case, the court of appeals stated, "Sexual indignity can rise to the level of being so repugnant to the non-offending spouse so as to render impossible the discharge of marital duties, thereby defeating the whole purpose of the marriage."[275]

The court of appeals found a husband's refusal to live with his wife after they married to be sufficiently unnatural to grant her a divorce.[276] A wife's stealing from her husband, lying to him about the birth of a child, and abusive behavior while he

---

[264] Sproles v. Sproles, 782 So. 2d 742, 745 (Miss. 2001); Richard v. Richard, 711 So. 2d 884, 888 (Miss. 1998); *cf.* Peters v. Peters, 906 So. 2d 64 (Miss. Ct. App. 2004) (combined with physical violence).

[265] Holladay v. Holladay, 776 So. 2d 662, 677 (Miss. 2000); Robison v. Robison, 722 So. 2d 601, 603 (Miss. 1998); Stein v. Stein, 11 So. 3d 1288, 1291 (Miss. Ct. App. 2009) (two incidents of physical violence, forced abortion, screaming, name-calling, and threats to kill wife); Scally v. Scally, 802 So. 2d 128, 131 (Miss. Ct. App. 2001); Garriga v. Garriga, 770 So. 2d 978, 982-83 (Miss. Ct. App. 2000).

[266] McBroom v. McBroom, 58 So. 2d 831, 831 (Miss. 1952).

[267] Robison v. Robison, 722 So. 2d 601, 603 (Miss. 1998); Smith v. Smith, 614 So. 2d 394, 395 (Miss. 1993) (expression of unresolved feelings for first husband).

[268] Robison v. Robison, 722 So. 2d 601, 603 (Miss. 1998); Keller v. Keller, 763 So. 2d 902, 908 (Miss. Ct. App. 2000). *But see* Tedford v. Tedford, 856 So. 2d 753 (Miss. Ct. App. 2003) (limited sexual contact did not support divorce based on habitual cruel and inhuman treatment when there was conflicting testimony and couple had sex three months before separating).

[269] Jackson v. Jackson, 922 So. 2d 53, 57 (Miss. Ct. App. 2006) (unexplained absences combined with other factors).

[270] Ferro v. Ferro, 871 So. 2d 753 (Miss. Ct. App. 2004) (husband properly granted divorce based on habitual, cruel, and inhuman treatment based on his wife's refusal to evict her thirty-six-year-old son from their home; son was unemployed, recently charged with grand larceny, drank daily, and physically assaulted his stepfather).

[271] *See* Fisher v. Fisher, 771 So. 2d 364, 368 (Miss. 2000) (combined with physical violence); Kumar v. Kumar, 976 So. 2d 957, 961-63 (Miss. Ct. App. 2008) (divorce granted in part based on husband's adultery and transmission of STD to wife); *cf.* Ferguson v. Ferguson, 639 So. 2d 921, 931 (Miss. 1994) (evidence of adultery as part of cruelty not admissible where husband did not plead adultery as part of conduct supporting divorce on the ground of cruelty).

[272] *See* Bland v. Bland, 620 So. 2d 543, 545 (Miss. 1993) (court reversed divorce on grounds of cruelty upon proof of extramarital relationship; should have been granted on basis of adultery). *But see* Rush v. Rush, 914 So. 2d 322, 324 (Miss. Ct. App. 2005) (wife granted divorce on habitual cruelty based on husband's adultery and cohabitation).

[273] *See* Morris v. Morris, 783 So. 2d 681, 689 (Miss. 2001) (rejecting Crutcher v. Crutcher, 38 So. 337 (Miss. 1905), which held that a homosexual relationship alone could constitute cruelty); Robison v. Robison, 722 So. 2d 601 (Miss. 1998).

[274] *See* Cherry v. Cherry, 593 So. 2d 13, 17-18 (Miss. 1991) (husband dressed in women's clothing); Stockton v. Stockton, 203 So. 2d 806, 807 (Miss. 1967) (husband wanted to use whips; involve another man); Crutcher v. Crutcher, 38 So. 337, 337 (Miss. 1905) (husband's conviction for pederasty as cruelty).

[275] Jones v. Jones, 43 So. 3d 465, 476-79 (Miss. Ct. App. 2009) (sexual behavior combined with verbally abusive and controlling behavior).

[276] Pace v. Pace, 16 So. 3d 734 (Miss. Ct. App. 2009).

GROUNDS FOR DIVORCE § 4.02[9][e]

appeared to be having a heart attack were considered sufficiently unnatural and repugnant to grant divorce. [277] And a wife was granted divorce on this ground based on her husband's indictment for murder and arrest for use of child pornography.[278]

[e] Incompatibility. Inability to live together as husband and wife is not grounds for divorce.[279] As the Mississippi Supreme Court has noted, the parties may be miserable, the marriage incompatible, and the problems insurmountable, without satisfying the standard for habitual cruelty.[280] Divorce was denied even though a marriage was "troubled and possibly irreparable."[281] The Mississippi appellate courts have refused to approve divorce based in part on quarreling,[282] yelling,[283] constant nagging,[284] name-calling,[285] "boorish, obnoxious, and selfish" or embarrassing behavior,[286] extreme criticism,[287] controlling behavior,[288] intense arguments,[289] weight gain and lack of

---

[277] McIntosh v. McIntosh, 977 So. 2d 1257, 1267 (Miss. Ct. App. 2008); *see also* Peters v. Peters, 906 So. 2d 64 (Miss. Ct. App. 2004) (conduct included choking wife, throwing items at her, accusing her of adultery, threatening suicide, and closing her accounts). *But cf.* Killen v. Killen, 54 So. 3d 869 (Miss. Ct. App. 2010) (wife's refusal to attend brother-in-law's funeral and embarrassment at being in public with husband was not sufficiently "revolting").

[278] Bodne v. King, 835 So. 2d 52, 59 (Miss. 2003) (husband also filed assault charges against wife).

[279] Stennis v. Stennis, 464 So. 2d 1161, 1162 (Miss. 1985).

[280] Wilbourne v. Wilbourne, 748 So. 2d 184, 187 (Miss. 1999) (no divorce although the marriage "was unpleasant and the parties were incompatible;" arguments "on occasion involved physical violence"); *see* Talbert v. Talbert, 759 So. 2d 1105, 1108 (Miss. 1999) (no divorce where husband belittled his wife, screamed at her, and committed a few acts of violence early in the twenty-seven year marriage); Potts v. Potts, 700 So. 2d 321, 322 (Miss. 1997) (husband stormed out when angry and moved into another room); Bowen v. Bowen, 688 So. 2d 1374, 1376-78 (Miss. 1997) (no divorce where husband inferred that wife was lesbian, called her names, struck her twice during an altercation in which she also struck and bit him, and once put a gun in his mouth); Wilson v. Wilson, 547 So. 2d 803, 804-05 (Miss. 1989) (court noted that couple genuinely hated each other and could not agree on the day of the week); Robinson v. Robinson, 554 So. 2d 300, 303 (Miss. 1989) (another case "in our developing litany where one spouse seeks a divorce on the basis of cruel and inhuman treatment but the problem is fundamental incompatibility"); Kergosian v. Kergosian, 471 So. 2d 1206, 1208 (Miss. 1985) (wife often disappeared, locked husband out of house, told child she hated him, slapped another child, threw toys out in the yard, and complained to children that she had to take care of them); Mitchell v. Mitchell, 767 So. 2d 1037, 1043 (Miss. Ct. App. 2000) (divorce denied although the marriage might be irreconcilable, the parties incompatible, and the wife argumentative); Ayers v. Ayers, 734 So. 2d 213, 214-16 (Miss. Ct. App. 1999) (no divorce where husband rarely talked to his wife or requested sex, and where wife was uncomfortable in his church and was "sensitive and prone to tears").

[281] Anderson v. Anderson, 54 So. 3d 850, 855 (Miss. Ct. App. 2010).

[282] *See* Stringer v. Stringer, 46 So. 2d 791, 791-92 (Miss. 1950); Killen v. Killen, 54 So. 3d 869, 873 (Miss. Ct. App. 2010) (fact that marriage "had grown unpleasant and argumentative" did not support divorce); Tackett v. Tackett, 967 So. 2d 1264, 1267 (Miss. Ct. App. 2007) (divorce denied; wife's lack of interest in sex and constant arguing over money not sufficient evidence of cruelty); Spence v. Spence, 930 So. 2d 415, 420 (Miss. Ct. App. 2005) (court erred in granting divorce when only evidence was that both spouses argued frequently).

[283] Anderson v. Anderson, 54 So. 3d 850, 854 (Miss. Ct. App. 2010).

[284] Taylor v. Taylor, 108 So. 2d 872, 873-74 (Miss. 1959) (reversing grant of divorce against wife who did not like house, husband's friends or his job, causing husband weight loss and problems at work).

[285] Morris v. Morris, 804 So. 2d 1025, 1028 (Miss. 2002).

[286] Talbert v. Talbert, 759 So. 2d 1105, 1109 (Miss. 1999); *see* Anderson v. Anderson, 54 So. 3d 850 (Miss. Ct. App. 2010).

[287] Talbert v. Talbert, 759 So. 2d 1105, 1109 (Miss. 1999).

[288] Morris v. Morris, 804 So. 2d 1025, 1029 (Miss. 2002).

[289] Steen v. Steen, 641 So. 2d 1167, 1170 (Miss. 1994); Daigle v. Daigle, 626 So. 2d 140, 144 (Miss. 1993) ("constant bickering"); Wilson v. Wilson, 547 So. 2d 803, 804 (Miss. 1989) (arguments and criticism over finances; accusations of infidelity); Moses v. Moses, 879 So. 2d 1043 (Miss. Ct. App. 2004) (husband tape-recorded his wife's telephone conversations in 1995; smashed her cell phone); Brown v. Brown, 817 So. 2d 588, 590 (Miss. Ct. App. 2002); Crenshaw v. Crenshaw, 767 So. 2d 272, 275 (Miss. Ct. App. 2000) (friction and general disagreements).

§ 4.02[10]   MISSISSIPPI FAMILY LAW

attention to personal appearance,[290] lack of communication,[291] poor housekeeping,[292] incompatibility,[293] difference in religious views,[294] lack of sex,[295] and financial irresponsibility.[296]

[10] Mental illness at the time of the marriage. The eighth ground for divorce, added in 1857, was "[i]nsanity or idiocy at the time of marriage, if the party complaining did not know of such infirmity."[297] In 2008, the Mississippi legislature amended this ground to replace the terms "insanity or idiocy" with "mental illness or mental retardation." It was amended again in 2010 to replace "mental retardation" with "intellectual disability."[298] Divorce based on mental illness at the time of the marriage is available only to the sane spouse; however, the marriage may be annulled on the petition of a guardian or next friend for the incompetent spouse.[299]

The Mississippi Supreme Court has stated that a precise test for mental capacity sufficient to enter marriage is not possible. The court noted, however, that "there ought to be enough of capacity to comprehend the subject, and the duties and responsibilities of the new relation."[300]

[a] Must exist at time of marriage. A plaintiff must overcome the presumption that parties have the capacity to contract by showing that the defendant lacked capacity on the date of the marriage. Intermittent bouts of mental illness do not create a presumption of lack of capacity at the critical moment.[301] Proof that a wife had periods of mental illness both prior to and after marriage was not sufficient to overcome the presumption of capacity on the date of marriage.[302] However, proof of "complete and permanent insanity" before marriage created a presumption that the condition continued, shifting the burden of proof to the defendant to show a lucid interval on the date of the marriage. In an annulment action, a physician's testimony that a husband was permanently incompetent prior to the marriage was sufficient to prove lack of capacity

---

[290] Skelton v. Skelton, 111 So. 2d 392, 393 (Miss. 1959) (rejecting husband's suit for divorce based on wife's weight gain from 165 to 210; he bought beer for her, and she was not small when they married).

[291] Morris v. Morris, 804 So. 2d 1025, 1029 (Miss. 2002); Fournet v. Fournet, 481 So. 2d 326, 327 (Miss. 1985); Ayers v. Ayers, 734 So. 2d 213, 215 (Miss. Ct. App. 1999).

[292] Marble v. Marble, 457 So. 2d 1342, 1343 (Miss. 1984).

[293] Morris v. Morris, 804 So. 2d 1025, 1027-28 (Miss. 2002); Robinson v. Robinson, 554 So. 2d 300, 303 (Miss. 1989); Wilson v. Wilson, 547 So. 2d 803 (Miss. 1989); Gallaspy v. Gallaspy, 459 So. 2d 283, 286 (Miss. 1984); Mitchell v. Mitchell, 767 So. 2d 1037, 1043 (Miss. Ct. App. 2000); Wilbourne v. Wilbourne, 748 So. 2d 184, 187 (Miss. Ct. App. 1999).

[294] Marble v. Marble, 457 So. 2d 1342, 1343 (Miss. 1984).

[295] Ayers v. Ayers, 734 So. 2d 213, 214 (Miss. Ct. App. 1999).

[296] Wilson v. Wilson, 547 So. 2d 803, 804 (Miss. 1989); Kergosien v. Kergosien, 471 So. 2d 1206, 1210 (Miss. 1985).

[297] Miss. Code Ann. § 93-5-1 (2004). Prior to 1857, insanity at the time of marriage was a ground for annulment only. *See* Bunkley & Morse, *supra* note 8, § 3.05, at 60.

[298] See Miss. Code Ann. § 93-5-1 (Supp. 2010).

[299] Miss. Code Ann. § 93-7-3 (2004).

[300] Parkinson v. Mills, 159 So. 651, 654 (Miss. 1935) (quoting Smith v. Smith, 47 Miss. 211, 216, 1872 WL 6164, at *3 (1872)); *see* Haralson v. Haralson, 362 So. 2d 190, 192 (Miss. 1978) (finding sufficient mental capacity).

[301] *See* Lambert v. Powell, 24 So. 2d 773, 775 (Miss. 1946) (discussing mental capacity at time of executing document).

[302] Smith v. Smith, 47 Miss. 211, 217-18 (1872).

GROUNDS FOR DIVORCE   § 4.02[10][b]

on the date of marriage.[303]

[b] Lack of knowledge. Premarital knowledge of the mental incapacity bars divorce; the plaintiff is assumed to accept the condition going into the marriage.[304] Knowledge must be actual and not inferred. A wife had no premarital knowledge of her husband's mental illness based on his parents' comments that he had been thrown by a mule, was "a little off" sometimes, and might not be able to provide for her.[305]

[c] Ratification. A spouse's failure to seek a divorce within a reasonable time after learning of the condition indicates acceptance of the condition. A husband who learned of his wife's mental illness shortly after their marriage, but who stayed with her through twenty years and the birth of four children, was barred from obtaining a divorce.[306]

[11] Bigamy. Divorce may be granted to an innocent spouse based on the defendant's "[m]arriage to some other person at the time of the pretended marriage between the parties."[307] A bigamous marriage may also be annulled at any time by either spouse and may be collaterally attacked by third parties.[308] Divorce on this ground is not available to the bigamist's first spouse. A husband whose wife entered a second marriage after they separated was not entitled to divorce on this ground.[309]

The law presumes that the most recent marriage contracted by a party is valid.[310] A party seeking divorce for bigamy must prove that the defendant was previously married and that the first marriage was never dissolved.[311] The Mississippi Supreme Court recommended that the plaintiff obtain a certificate from the proper court clerk in every jurisdiction in which either of the parties to the first marriage lived, stating that the marriage was never dissolved in that jurisdiction.[312]

[12] Pregnancy of the wife at the time of the marriage. The tenth fault-based ground for divorce is "pregnancy of the wife by another person at the time of the mar-

---

[303] *See* Parkinson v. Mills, 159 So. 651, 654 (Miss. 1935) (annulment action brought by guardian).

[304] Wilson v. Wilson, 61 So. 453, 454 (Miss. 1913).

[305] *See* Wilson v. Wilson, 61 So. 453, 454 (Miss. 1913).

[306] McIntosh v. McIntosh, 117 So. 352, 352 (Miss. 1928) ("[L]aw requires the party injured, under such circumstances, promptly to elect whether he will abide by the relation, or whether he will disavow and dissolve it . . . .").

[307] MISS. CODE ANN. § 93-5-1 (2004). Bigamy is a crime punishable by up to ten years in prison. MISS. CODE ANN. § 97-29-13 (2010). Mississippi's "Enoch Arden" statute exempts from prosecution one whose husband or wife has been absent for seven years. MISS. CODE ANN. § 97-29-15 (2010). Enoch Arden statutes do not validate the later marriage; they simply provide a defense to criminal prosecution for bigamy. *See* CLARK, JR., *supra* note 4, § 2.6, at 67.

[308] *See supra* § 3.02.

[309] Harmon v. Harmon, 757 So. 2d 305, 309 (Miss. Ct. App. 1999) (second husband, not first, has grounds).

[310] Whitman v. Whitman, 41 So. 2d 22, 25 (Miss. 1949). The court stated: "[T]he presumption of the validity of the last marriage has been held to be the strongest presumption known to the law; and in the absence of additional facts or circumstances it must prevail over all conflicting presumptions, such as presumptions as . . . to the validity . . . of a prior marriage." *Id.* (quoting 55 C.J.S., *Marriage* § 43 (1948)) (ellipses in opinion).

[311] Fleming v. Fleming, 56 So. 2d 35, 39 (Miss. 1952) (husband properly denied divorce based on bigamy when he failed to prove that first husband was alive at time of second marriage and that marriage was never dissolved).

[312] Pigford Bros. Constr. Co. v. Evans, 83 So. 2d 622, 625 (Miss. 1955); *see* Dale Polk Constr. Co. v. White, 287 So. 2d 278, 279 (Miss. 1973); *see also* Smith v. Weir, 387 So. 2d 761, 763 (Miss. 1980); Walker v. Matthews, 3 So. 2d 820, 825 (Miss. 1941).

§ 4.02[13]   **MISSISSIPPI FAMILY LAW**

riage, if the husband did not know of such pregnancy."[313] A husband may also obtain an annulment based on this ground.[314] The supreme court held in a 1959 case that divorce was not available to a husband who knew his future wife was pregnant but who believed he was the child's father: "Having married her with knowledge that she was unchaste he must take the risk and is bound by his bargain."[315]

[13] Kinship within the prohibited degree. If spouses are related in a degree designated by statute as incestuous, either of them may obtain a divorce.[316] Annulment is also available to either spouse.[317] No case was found granting divorce based on kinship; however, a recent case refused to award separate maintenance to a woman married for nine years to her uncle, based on the invalidity of the marriage.[318] Children of an incestuous marriage are declared illegitimate by statute even if the parties entered into the marriage in good faith.[319]

[14] Incurable mental illness. "Incurable insanity" was added as a divorce ground in 1932.[320] In 2008, the Mississippi legislature amended this ground, replacing the term "incurable insanity" with "incurable mental illness."[321] A plaintiff may secure a divorce from a spouse who has been confined in an institution for treatment for at least three years immediately preceding the action.[322] The petition must be supported by the examination and testimony of two physicians that the defendant is currently mentally ill.[323] The physicians' affidavits create a presumption of incurable mental illness justifying divorce.[324]

Process must be served on the superintendent of the hospital in which the defendant is a patient as well as the next blood relative and guardian.[325] If the defendant has no guardian, the court must appoint a guardian ad litem. The guardian ad litem, relative, and superintendent of the institution are entitled to appear and be heard in the case.[326]

The statute provides that divorce does not alter the plaintiff's obligation to support the institutionalized spouse "in any way." The court has discretion to order the plaintiff

---

[313] MISS. CODE ANN. § 93-5-1 (2004).

[314] *See* MISS. CODE ANN. § 93-7-3 (2004).

[315] Burdine v. Burdine, 112 So. 2d 522, 523 (Miss. 1959).

[316] *See* MISS. CODE ANN. § 93-5-1 (2004). No one may marry his or her parent, grandparent, stepparent or stepgrandparent, adoptive parent, sibling, half-sibling, aunt, uncle, first cousin, or his or her child's widow or widower. MISS. CODE ANN. § 93-1-1 (2004).

[317] MISS. CODE ANN. § 93-7-1 (2004). It is a crime punishable by up to ten years in prison for persons prohibited by kinship to marry, cohabit, or have a sexual relationship. MISS. CODE ANN. § 97-29-5 (1994).

[318] *See* Weeks v. Weeks, 654 So. 2d 33, 36 (Miss. 1995) (couple advised by pastor that they could marry).

[319] MISS. CODE ANN. § 93-7-5 (2004).

[320] BUNKLEY & MORSE, *supra* note 8, § 3.15, at 134.

[321] See MISS. CODE ANN. § 93-5-1 (Supp. 2010).

[322] MISS. CODE ANN. § 93-5-1 (2004). A trial release recommended by a physician, which proves unsuccessful, followed by reconfinement, is counted as part of the three year period. *Id.*

[323] MISS. CODE ANN. § 93-5-1 (2004) (one must be the superintendent of the state hospital or the veterans hospital in which the patient is confined, or a member of the staff of the hospital where the spouse is confined).

[324] MISS. CODE ANN. § 93-5-1 (2004).

[325] MISS. CODE ANN. § 93-5-1 (2004). Service on out-of-state hospitals by publication is combined with sending a copy by registered mail to the superintendent of the hospital. *Id.*

[326] MISS. CODE ANN. § 93-5-1 (2004).

GROUNDS FOR DIVORCE   § 4.03

to enter a bond for support for the remainder of the defendant's life unless the defendant's estate is sufficient to provide support.[327]

§ 4.03 DEFENSES TO FAULT-BASED DIVORCE

[1] Knowledge of condition. A plaintiff's actual knowledge of a spouse's condition at the time of the marriage may bar divorce on that ground. The Mississippi statute specifically provides that premarital knowledge of a wife's pregnancy by another or knowledge of a spouse's mental illness bars divorce on those grounds.[328] The supreme court has also suggested that premarital knowledge of other conditions such as habitual drunkenness, drug use, imprisonment, or impotency may bar divorce.[329]

Mere suspicion of a spouse's condition or habit is not sufficient, nor is it enough to show that the plaintiff had information that would have revealed the ground if diligently pursued.[330] For example, knowledge that a husband was a social drinker at the time of marriage does not imply knowledge that one is marrying a "habitual drunkard."[331]

[2] Ratification. With regard to grounds involving conditions at the time of marriage, the defense of ratification may bar divorce by a spouse who fails to act within a reasonable time after learning of the condition. Failure to act promptly indicates acceptance of the condition. For example, a husband who learned of his wife's mental illness shortly after the marriage, but who remained with her for twenty years was barred from obtaining a divorce.[332] No other cases were found discussing ratification as a defense to divorce.[333]

[3] Mental illness. In a 1925 case, the Mississippi Supreme Court held that a mentally ill wife could not be guilty of desertion or habitual, cruel, and inhuman treatment: "[T]he act was the result of insanity, and not an habitually cruel and inhuman act of a sane person, [or] . . . the willful and obstinate act of a sane person."[334] Courts also generally hold that mental illness is a defense to divorce on the ground of adultery.[335]

The mental illness must be so severe that the defendant is unable to distinguish

---

[327] MISS. CODE ANN. § 93-5-1 (2004).

[328] *See* MISS. CODE ANN. § 93-5-1 (2004).

[329] Kincaid v. Kincaid, 43 So. 2d 108, 109 (Miss. 1949).

[330] Kincaid v. Kincaid, 43 So. 2d 108, 109 (Miss. 1949). For a general discussion, see W. J. Dunn, Annotation, *Antenuptial Knowledge Relating to Alleged Grounds as Barring Right to Divorce*, 15 A.L.R. 2d 670 (1951).

[331] Kincaid v. Kincaid, 43 So. 2d 108, 109 (Miss. 1949) (court acknowledged general rule but limited consideration of knowledge defense to habitual drunkenness); *see* cases cited in Dunn, *supra* note 330.

[332] McIntosh v. McIntosh, 117 So. 352, 352 (Miss. 1928) ("[L]aw requires the party injured, under such circumstances, promptly to elect whether he will abide by the relation, or whether he will disavow and dissolve it . . . .").

[333] The Mississippi statutes on annulment appear to recognize ratification of some, but not all, grounds for annulment. *See supra* § 3.05[2].

[334] Walker v. Walker, 105 So. 753, 756 (Miss. 1925); *see* McIntosh v. McIntosh, 117 So. 352, 353 (Miss. 1928) ("[A]n act of cruelty committed during the insanity of the party committing the act is not cruelty . . . , because the mind of the person perpetrating such act is incapable of willful or deliberate conduct . . . .").

[335] *See, e.g.,* Nichols v. Nichols, 31 Vt. 328, 331 (1858) ("[G]eneral insanity is a full defence for all acts which by the statute are grounds of granting divorce."); P.H. Vartanian, Annotation, *Insanity as Affecting Right to Divorce or Separation on Other Grounds,* 19 A.L.R. 2d 144, § 4 (1951).

§ 4.03[4]   MISSISSIPPI FAMILY LAW

right and wrong.[336] A Connecticut court rejected a defendant's argument that her paranoia caused the extreme jealousy on which her husband's divorce action was based. The court noted that in most cases where mental illness has barred divorce, the defendant was "indubitably" insane and usually committed to an institution.[337] The Mississippi Supreme Court appeared to adopt this position without directly addressing the issue. The court affirmed a grant of divorce based on habitual, cruel, and inhuman treatment to a husband whose wife was severely emotionally disturbed, even though much of her behavior stemmed from her emotional disturbance and paranoia.[338]

[4] Recrimination. Until 1964, the doctrine of recrimination required that a chancellor deny divorce if both parties proved grounds.[339] An adulterous husband and his wife who deserted him were both denied divorce – neither was an innocent party.[340] Similarly, divorce was denied to a man whose wife deserted him eighteen years earlier, because he remarried based on advice that he was legally entitled to do so.[341] In order for conduct to trigger recrimination, it must rise to the level of conduct warranting a grant of divorce.[342] Evidence that a wife sat on a man's lap and allowed "boudoir photographs" of herself to be taken was not sufficient to deny divorce based on recrimination.[343]

Today, a chancellor may grant a divorce even though the evidence establishes recrimination. The current statute authorizes chancellors to use or ignore the doctrine.[344] However, the Mississippi Supreme Court held that a chancellor erred in applying recrimination to deny divorce to a woman guilty of post-separation adultery; her husband's fault clearly caused the separation.[345]

---

[336] *See* Cosgrove v. Cosgrove, 217 N.E.2d 754, 756 (Mass. 1966) ("[D]efence of insanity will not prevail if the offending spouse was capable of understanding the nature and consequences of his acts."); Vartanian, *supra* note 335, § 4.

[337] Dochelli v. Dochelli, 6 A.2d 324, 325-26 (Conn. 1939) (no evidence that defendant's paranoia prevented her from distinguishing right and wrong).

[338] Morris v. Morris, 783 So. 2d 681, 689-90 (Miss. 2001) ("[I]t is the repeated evidence in this case that this woman is severely and emotionally disturbed that renders this an excellent case on the facts in which to grant a divorce on the ground of habitual cruel and inhuman treatment.").

[339] *See* Parker v. Parker, 519 So. 2d 1232, 1235 (Miss. 1988) (policies underlying rule included preserving stability of marriage, deterring immorality, protecting wife economically, and preventing bad marriage risks from reentering the marriage market). A somewhat related defense, provocation, appeared in several cases in the 1920s and 30s. *See* Long v. Long, 135 So. 204, 204 (Miss. 1931) (denying divorce based on provocation where both parties provoked acts of cruelty; court noted that the "honors are even" when both parties are offenders); Ammons v. Ammons, 109 So. 795, 795 (Miss. 1926) ("[C]omplainant . . . must be free from provoking the defendant into the acts which constitute the alleged grounds for divorce."). In one extreme case, the court suggested that a husband's physical violence was excused by his wife's cursing his family. *See* Price v. Price, 179 So. 855, 857-58 (Miss. 1938) (court upheld chancellor's denial of divorce to a woman whose husband beat her "unmercifully" because her "vile epithets" directed at his family provoked his actions).

[340] Oberlin v. Oberlin, 29 So. 2d 82, 83 (Miss. 1947) ("[O]ne who comes into its courts complaining of a mote in the eye of his spouse must beware lest there appear a disfiguring beam in his own.").

[341] Dunn v. Dunn, 125 So. 562, 563 (Miss. 1930).

[342] Oberlin v. Oberlin, 29 So. 2d 82, 83 (Miss. 1947).

[343] Cherry v. Cherry, 593 So. 2d 13, 18 (Miss. 1991).

[344] *See* Miss. Code Ann. § 93-5-3 (2004); Dickerson v. Dickerson, 34 So. 3d 637, 642-43 (Miss. Ct. App. 2010); Ware v. Ware, 7 So. 3d 271, 273 (Miss. Ct. App. 2008).

[345] Parker v. Parker, 519 So. 2d 1232, 1236 (Miss. 1988) (policies impractical in modern society); *see* Jenkins v. Jenkins, 55 So. 3d 1094, 1095-97 (Miss. Ct. App. 2010) (wife granted divorce based on cruelty in spite of post-separation affair); Harmon v. Harmon, 757 So. 2d 305, 309 (Miss. Ct. App. 1999) (wife's post-separation, bigamous marriage did not prevent granting her divorce based on adultery); *cf.* Hyer v. Hyer, 636 So. 2d 381, 384 (Miss. 1994) (divorce should

GROUNDS FOR DIVORCE §4.03[5]

[5] Reformation or repentance. Divorce should not be granted on the basis of habitual drunkenness or habitual drug use if the defendant has reformed and discontinued the habit.[346] Repentance or reformation is not a defense to divorce based on adultery or cruelty. However, if the innocent spouse accepts the repentance and forgives adultery, divorce may be barred by the defense of condonation.[347] Also, while reformation does not bar divorce based on cruelty, a court may deny divorce if the conduct has discontinued and the acts of cruelty are remote in time from the divorce suit.[348] Although reconciliation offers during the one-year statutory period are a defense to desertion, repentance after the one-year period comes too late.[349]

[6] Condonation. Condonation, or forgiveness, may be a defense to divorce. Condonation may result from express forgiveness, such as a reconciliation, or may be implied when an innocent spouse continues the marital relationship after learning of the offense.[350] Condonation is an affirmative defense that must be specifically pled. A chancellor erred in denying a husband's divorce based on condonation when the wife failed to assert the defense in her pleadings.[351] Condonation is presumed to be conditioned on the wrongdoer's continued good behavior.

[a] Of adultery. Condonation of adultery was once implied merely because a couple cohabited after the innocent spouse knew of the adultery.[352] The Mississippi fault grounds statute still incorporates the old rule, providing that adultery is not a ground for divorce if the parties cohabit after knowledge by the complainant.[353] A later-enacted statute is directly contradictory: "It shall be no impediment to a divorce that the offended spouse did not leave the marital domicile."[354] Applying the latter statute, the Mississippi Supreme Court held that no condonation occurs if an innocent spouse who continues to live with the other does not resume sexual relations.[355] It should be noted, however, that the court has also urged lawyers to "advise and warn [their clients]

---

be granted to party less at fault); Hinton v. Hinton, 179 So. 2d 846, 847-48 (Miss. 1965) (same).

[346] *See supra* § 4.02[7][d].

[347] *See* discussion *infra* § 4.03[6].

[348] *See* discussion *supra* § 4.02[8][c].

[349] *See* Lynch v. Lynch, 63 So. 2d 657, 663 (Miss. 1953).

[350] *See* Thames v. Thames, 100 So. 2d 868, 870 (Miss. 1958) (any conduct prior to reconciliation condoned); Fulton v. Fulton, 918 So. 2d 877, 881 (Miss. Ct. App. 2006) (divorce properly denied based on condonation – the wife ended her affair, confessed to her husband, and the couple resumed sexual relations for at least eight months).

[351] Ashburn v. Ashburn, 970 So. 2d 204, 215 (Miss. Ct. App. 2007) (but court did note cases stating that court may recognize the defense on its own).

[352] Armstrong v. Armstrong, 32 Miss. 279, 1856 WL 4020 (1856).

[353] Miss. Code Ann. § 93-5-1 (2004).

[354] Miss. Code Ann. § 93-5-4 (2004).

[355] Cheatham v. Cheatham, 537 So. 2d 435, 442 (Miss. 1988) (wife slept in same bed with husband for several weeks after learning of adultery; stated that she remained to obtain evidence); *see* Cherry v. Cherry, 593 So. 2d 13, 17-18 (Miss. 1991) (wife entitled to divorce; no condonation simply because she continued cohabitation with knowledge of husband's sexual problems and the fact that he dressed in women's clothes); Wood v. Wood, 495 So. 2d 503, 505 (Miss. 1986); Lawrence v. Lawrence, 956 So. 2d 251, 257 (Miss. Ct. App. 2006) (resuming residence does not constitute condonation); Fulton v. Fulton, 918 So. 2d 877, 881 (Miss. Ct. App. 2006) (merely resuming cohabitation does not condone affair, but resumption of sexual relationship does). *But see* Jethrow v. Jethrow, 571 So. 2d 270, 274 (Miss. 1990) (noting that Miss. Code Ann. § 93-5-4 technically applies only in irreconcilable differences divorces).

§ 4.03[6][b]   MISSISSIPPI FAMILY LAW

about the undesirability of continuing to live in the same household following filing of suit."[356]

Condonation of adultery requires knowledge of the offending conduct.[357] It also requires forgiveness. A chancellor properly rejected the condonation defense of a wife – it was clear that the husband did not forgive her and planned to seek a divorce, even though he spent a night with her after their separation.[358]

[b] Of continuing offenses. The defense of condonation is not applied in the same manner to continuing offenses. A plaintiff's continued cohabitation in the face of ongoing marital misconduct such as habitual cruelty, drunkenness, or drug addiction is not considered condonation: "The effort to endure unkind treatment as long as possible is commendable and the patient endurance by the wife of her husband's ill-treatment should not be allowed to weaken her right to a divorce."[359]

However, a spouse who resumes cohabitation after separation may have condoned conduct prior to the separation. The Mississippi Supreme Court has held that habitual, cruel, and inhuman treatment is condoned when an innocent spouse resumes cohabitation after a separation and no further acts of cruelty occur.[360] In some cases involving domestic violence, however, a battered spouse's return home may be viewed as involuntary; if so, it should not be considered condonation of prior abuse.[361]

[c] Voluntariness of condonation. Condonation requires voluntariness. No condonation of adultery occurred when the wife was not a willing participant in sex.[362] Similarly, reconciliation based on fraud, force, or duress is not condonation. A husband's attempts to lure his wife into reconciliation in order to move venue to another county were ineffective.[363]

---

[356] Jethrow v. Jethrow, 571 So. 2d 270, 274 (Miss. 1990) (if finances are reason for continued cohabitation, parties should seek temporary support).

[357] Ware v. Ware, 7 So. 3d 271, 273-74 (Miss. Ct. App. 2008) (not clear whether husband knew of affair; he had been told by wife's lover, but wife continued to deny the affair); Stribling v. Stribling, 906 So. 2d 863, 868 (Miss. Ct. App. 2005) (no condonation of affairs of which husband had no knowledge).

[358] Ware v. Ware, 7 So. 3d 271, 274-75 (Miss. Ct. App. 2008); *see also* Lawrence v. Lawrence, 956 So. 2d 251, 258 (Miss. Ct. App. 2006) (just engaging in the act of sex "does not seal the defense of condonation").

[359] Smith v. Smith, 40 So. 2d 156 (Miss. 1949) (reconciliation after cruelty should not be viewed in same way as reconciliation after adultery); *see* Cherry v. Cherry, 593 So. 2d 13, 17-18 (Miss. 1991) (wife did not condone husband's wearing women's clothes by continuing to live with him for three years); Manning v. Manning, 133 So. 673, 674 (Miss. 1931) (condonation not usually applicable to cruelty; if condonation does occur, it is conditioned on behavior ending).

[360] *See* Chaffin v. Chaffin, 437 So. 2d 384, 386 (Miss. 1983); Stribling v. Stribling, 215 So. 2d 869, 870 (Miss. 1968) (wife condoned husband's acts of violence, which caused permanent physical damage, by reconciling and resuming cohabitation); Thames v. Thames, 100 So. 2d 868, 870 (Miss. 1958) (husband's conduct prior to separation condoned by reconciliation); Scott v. Scott, 69 So. 2d 489, 494 (Miss. 1954); Kumar v. Kumar, 976 So. 2d 957, 962 (Miss. Ct. App. 2008) (spouse does not condone cruelty by continuing to cohabit but may condone conduct if the parties separate and then reconcile; abuse recurred, so grounds were revived); *cf.* Langdon v. Langdon, 854 So. 2d 485 (Miss. Ct. App. 2003) (condonation of two incidents of violence by separation and reconciliation; but divorce granted because violence recurred, removing condonation). *But cf.* Ashburn v. Ashburn, 970 So. 2d 204, 215 (Miss. Ct. App. 2007) (where husband returned to wife after separation, court cited cases stating that condonation is generally not applied to continuing offenses).

[361] *See infra* § 4.03[6][c].

[362] Harmon v. Harmon, 757 So. 2d 305, 309 (Miss. Ct. App. 1999) (chancellor did not err in granting divorce based on finding that wife did not consent and therefore did not condone adultery).

[363] Lee v. Lee, 232 So. 2d 370, 373 (Miss. 1970) ("It is necessary also that the condonation be free and voluntary. If it is induced by fraud, fear, or force, it is of no effect.").

GROUNDS FOR DIVORCE

§ 4.03[6][d]

In an 1856 case, the Mississippi Supreme Court stated that continued cohabitation by a wife should be considered under a more lenient rule because of the wife's dependence on her husband and his authority over her.[364] Although this view of marriage roles is outdated, the case arguably stands as authority that courts should be less inclined to find condonation where one spouse remains in or returns to the home because of financial dependence or emotional control by the other.

[d] Conditional nature of condonation. Condonation is conditional, based upon the future good behavior of the guilty spouse. Divorce for adultery was properly granted even though a couple continued a sexual relationship; the wife resumed her adulterous affair the day after condonation occurred.[365] If the conduct recurs, the innocent spouse may obtain a divorce based in part upon conduct prior to condonation.[366] In one case, however, a wife was foreclosed from relying on acts prior to separation by her written agreement dismissing litigation and stating specifically that all prior acts were condoned.[367]

[7] Connivance. Connivance is one spouse's consent to the other's wrongful conduct. The defense of connivance arises from the fault-based notion of a wronged spouse; one who does not object to known misconduct has not been wronged. Connivance may be express or implied "by silence or feigned ignorance."[368] Connivance does not appear as a successful defense to divorce in Mississippi appellate cases. For example, no connivance occurred when a wife continued to live with her husband for several weeks while obtaining evidence of adultery through a private investigator.[369]

[8] Collusion. Collusion, particularly in connection with adultery, was once a common method of obtaining divorce. Prior to no-fault divorce, spouses desperate to terminate a marriage sometimes conspired to fabricate divorce grounds. Collusion might consist of an agreement to create divorce grounds, perjury regarding facts supporting

---

[364] *See* Armstrong v. Armstrong, 32 Miss. 279, 289 (1856).

[365] Lindsey v. Lindsey, 818 So. 2d 1191,1195 (Miss. 2002); *see also* Chaffin v. Chaffin, 437 So. 2d 384, 386 (Miss. 1983) (cohabitation condoned prior acts, but when wife resumed behavior, prior offenses were revived); Ashburn v. Ashburn, 970 So. 2d 204, 215 (Miss. Ct. App. 2007) (wife's drug use continued after condonation); Lawrence v. Lawrence, 956 So. 2d 251, 257 (Miss. Ct. App. 2006) (condonation is like "temporary probation" — the defense does not apply unless the wrongdoer meets the conditions of the forgiveness); Brewer v. Brewer, 919 So. 2d 135, 138 (Miss. Ct. App. 2005) (affair condoned by husband; yet where wife resumed affair, wife could no longer successfully claim condonation as a defense).

[366] *See* Wood v. Wood, 495 So. 2d 503, 505 (Miss. 1986) (divorce need not be based solely on facts after behavior recurs); Smith v. Smith, 40 So. 2d 156 (Miss. 1949); Ashburn v. Ashburn, 970 So. 2d 204, 215 (Miss. Ct. App. 2007) (divorce based on habitual drug use proven by drug use before and after condonation); Lawrence v. Lawrence, 956 So. 2d 251, 257 (Miss. Ct. App. 2006) (prior and subsequent conduct can be combined to meet grounds for divorce if conduct recurs).

[367] *See* Starr v. Starr, 39 So. 2d 520, 522-23 (Miss. 1949).

[368] Cheatham v. Cheatham, 537 So. 2d 435, 441 (Miss. 1988). The defense of connivance, which originated in English ecclesiastical courts, "is that if one spouse corruptly consents to adultery committed by the other, he is not entitled to a divorce for that adultery." *See* M. L. Cross, *What Amounts to Connivance by One Spouse at Another's Adultery*, 17 A.L.R. 2d 342, § 1 (1951).

[369] Cheatham v. Cheatham, 537 So. 2d 435, 441 (Miss. 1988) (spouse may not make opportunities for the other to commit adultery, but may "leave her free to follow opportunities which she has herself made").

§ 4.03[9]   **MISSISSIPPI FAMILY LAW**

divorce, or an agreement not to contest a divorce.[370] As a result, ferreting out collusive divorces was an integral part of judicial oversight of the divorce process.[371]

The Mississippi statute provides that adultery is a ground for divorce unless "it was committed by collusion of the parties for the purpose of procuring a divorce."[372] Except in irreconcilable differences divorces, parties must still provide an affidavit stating that the parties have not colluded to obtain a divorce.[373] The doctrine has little remaining relevance, since spouses who desire a divorce may agree to be divorced on irreconcilable differences.[374] The continuing statutory bar against collusion does not prevent a party from admitting adultery and agreeing to a divorce on that basis.[375]

[9] Res judicata. The doctrine of res judicata applies in divorce actions as in other civil cases. In the context of divorce grounds, a judgment denying a divorce is res judicata as to whether grounds were proven based on the facts known at the time of trial. In cases in which the cumulative effect of conduct is relevant, however, evidence admitted in an earlier divorce action is admissible. For example, a spouse who was denied divorce based on habitual, cruel, and inhuman treatment could introduce evidence from a prior action to show that the defendant's cumulative conduct supported divorce at the time of the second action.[376]

A prior divorce action on one ground may also preclude subsequent divorce on other grounds if the evidence was available at the time of the earlier action. However, if the plaintiff was not aware of the conduct at the time of the earlier action, res judicata does not preclude the second action. Evidence of adultery that predated a first divorce action was admissible; the wife was not aware at that time of her husband's opportunity to commit adultery.[377]

[10] The Servicemembers Civil Relief Act. Effective December 19, 2003, the Servicemembers Civil Relief Act[378] completely revised the Soldiers' and Sailors' Relief Act of 1918,[379] the federal law establishing procedures for civil suits involving persons in the military. Under the Act, a divorce action against a servicemember may be stayed under certain circumstances. The Act is discussed in detail in Chapter XIX.

---

[370] *See* Gurley v. Gorman, 102 So. 65, 66 (Miss. 1924) (agreement not to contest divorce was collusive; agreement void).

[371] *See* Crosby v. Hatten, 56 So. 2d 705, 706 (Miss. 1952) (chancellor denied divorce because parties colluded to obtain divorce on basis of habitual, cruel, and inhuman treatment; wife could set aside husband's deed conveying homestead property in spite of collusion).

[372] MISS. CODE ANN. § 93-5-1 (2004).

[373] MISS. CODE ANN. § 93-5-7 (2004).

[374] *See* MISS. CODE ANN. § 93-5-2 (2004).

[375] *See* Rushing v. Rushing, 724 So. 2d 911, 914 (Miss. 1998) (wife agreed to divorce after court admitted taped recordings of her conversations with friend); Cain v. Cain, 795 So. 2d 614 (Miss. Ct. App. 2001) (no fraud where wife stipulated to affair).

[376] *See* Bias v. Bias, 493 So. 2d 342, 344 (Miss. 1986) (citing BUNKLEY & MORSE, *supra* note 8, § 16.06, at 13-14).

[377] Myers v. Myers, 741 So. 2d 274, 279 (Miss. Ct. App. 1998).

[378] 50 U.S.C. App. § 501 (2006).

[379] 50 U.S.C. App. § 101.

GROUNDS FOR DIVORCE

§ 4.04

§ 4.04 IRRECONCILABLE DIFFERENCES DIVORCE

Most states have adopted a true no-fault ground for divorce, allowing divorce based upon proof by one of the parties that the couple has irreconcilable differences, that the marriage is irretrievably broken or the parties "incompatible," or that the parties have lived apart for a required period of time. Mississippi, along with a few other states, adopted a version of irreconcilable differences divorce that requires that the parties agree to be divorced. Divorce in Mississippi is not available based on one party's proof that the marriage is irretrievably broken.

The Mississippi legislature first authorized irreconcilable differences as a separate ground for divorce in 1976. The statute allowed a court to grant irreconcilable differences divorce if the parties agreed to be divorced and had reached agreement on all related matters. No divorce could be granted if one of the parties contested the divorce or if the parties could not agree on all aspects of the dissolution.[380] The Mississippi Supreme Court enforced the statute as written, but several members of the court urged that the requirement of complete agreement made irreconcilable differences divorce difficult and created a potential tool for blackmail.[381] In 1990, the statute was amended to permit divorce when the parties consent to an irreconcilable differences divorce and agree in writing to submit custody or financial matters to the court. The amended statute has been strictly construed. The Mississippi Supreme Court requires exact compliance with the statutory procedures.[382]

The following requirements must be met for a court to grant divorce based on irreconcilable differences: (1) the court must have personal jurisdiction over the parties; (2) the parties must consent to divorce and withdraw any contest or denial; (3) a pleading requesting irreconcilable differences divorce must have been on file for sixty days; (4) the parties must agree on all issues or must agree in writing to submit issues to the court; and (5) all matters related to the divorce must be settled prior to judgment.

[1] Personal jurisdiction. As a general rule, a court may grant divorce to a plaintiff domiciled in the state without acquiring personal jurisdiction over the defendant.[383] Because Mississippi's no-fault divorce requires consent of both spouses, divorce based on irreconcilable differences may be granted "only upon the joint complaint of the husband and wife or a complaint where the defendant has been personally served with process or where the defendant has entered an appearance by written waiver of process."[384]

---

[380] *See* Gallaspy v. Gallaspy, 459 So. 2d 283, 284 (Miss. 1984) (both parties desired divorce but could not agree on property division and support; irreconcilable differences divorce not available).

[381] *See* Wilson v. Wilson, 547 So. 2d 803, 805 (Miss. 1989) ("However viable a theory of freedom of contract in other contexts, it is an oxymoron in divorce cases."); Alexander v. Alexander, 493 So. 2d 978, 980 (Miss. 1986) (Robertson, J., concurring).

[382] *See* Massengill v. Massengill, 594 So. 2d 1173, 1175 (Miss. 1992) ("Divorce in Mississippi is a creature of statute . . . . The chancellor, therefore, may exercise only such authority in the granting of a divorce as he has been given by the legislature."); Engel v. Engel, 920 So. 2d 505, 509 (Miss. Ct. App. 2006) (divorce reversed because strict requirements of statute not followed).

[383] *See* discussion of divorce jurisdiction *infra* § 18.03 (financial issues may not be addressed without personal jurisdiction).

[384] MISS. CODE ANN. § 93-5-2(1) (2004).

§ 4.04[2]   MISSISSIPPI FAMILY LAW

[2] Consent. Consent is essential to obtain a divorce based on irreconcilable differences.[385] The agreement must be entered voluntarily. The parties' consent can be manifested at the outset of an action by filing a joint complaint, or later by withdrawing a contest of the action and submitting a written agreement. The requirement of consent is not met by separate pleadings requesting irreconcilable differences divorce as an alternative to fault grounds.[386]

Proceedings initiated by consent can later be contested. The consent in a joint complaint is withdrawn and divorce contested if one party files a complaint for divorce based on fault[387] or files an express withdrawal of the joint complaint.[388]

[a] Voluntariness. The cornerstone of no-fault divorce in Mississippi is voluntariness. The Mississippi Court of Appeals has noted, however, that reluctance about the decision does not destroy consent: "Wavering on whether a divorce should be entered may often occur and does not invalidate the divorce. . . . What is important is that the agreement be validly expressed on the day that the chancellor is considering the issue."[389] For example, a husband's unhappiness with his options – to agree to divorce or possibly remain married – did not negate his agreement on the day of trial to be divorced on irreconcilable differences.[390] In at least one case, however, the Mississippi Supreme Court reversed a divorce because a pro se defendant's consent did not appear to be voluntary.[391]

[b] Withdrawal of contest or denial. No consent exists if either party has contested a fault-based ground for divorce, or denied the other's right to a divorce. However, the parties may convert a fault-based action to an irreconcilable differences divorce by submitting a written agreement stating that all contests and denials are withdrawn. The irreconcilable differences statute provides that divorce can be granted only if the contest or denial has been withdrawn by leave of court.[392] For example, divorce should not have been granted when the parties agreed to divorce on irreconcilable differences but failed to state that the wife withdrew her answer and counterclaim.[393]

---

[385] *See* Johnson v. Johnson, 21 So. 3d 694, 697 (Miss. Ct. App. 2009) (reversing a chancellor's grant of irreconcilable differences divorce in a case in which the parties never agreed to irreconcilable differences divorce).

[386] *See* Massengill v. Massengill, 594 So. 2d 1173, 1178 (Miss. 1992) (filing of cross-complaint was contest which was not withdrawn by leave of court); *see also* Alexander v. Alexander, 493 So. 2d 978 (Miss. 1986) (divorce on irreconcilable differences improperly granted where husband contested divorce based on adultery); *cf.* Gardner v. Gardner, 618 So. 2d 108, 112-13 (Miss. 1993) (no consent where both alleged irreconcilable differences as alternative; wife's pleadings did not admit husband's right to divorce on this ground, but merely stated that irreconcilable differences existed).

[387] *See* Grier v. Grier, 616 So. 2d 337, 340 (Miss. 1993) (filing of second complaint voids joint complaint).

[388] *See* McCleave v. McCleave, 491 So. 2d 522, 523 (Miss. 1986).

[389] Sanford v. Sanford, 749 So. 2d 353, 356 (Miss. Ct. App. 1999); *see also* Harvey v. Harvey, 918 So. 2d 837, 839 (Miss. Ct. App. 2005) (rejecting husband's argument that he objected to divorce; wavering on whether to agree to divorce does not invalidate a divorce).

[390] Cobb v. Cobb, 29 So. 3d 145, 151 (Miss. Ct. App. 2010).

[391] Sanford v. Sanford, 749 So. 2d 353 (Miss. Ct. App. 1999) (unrepresented wife, whose first language was not English, nodded her head in agreement to the court's questioning about consent, but also repeatedly objected to the divorce; some evidence that she mistakenly believed that she had no option but to agree).

[392] Heatherly v. Heatherly, 914 So. 2d 754, 758 (Miss. Ct. App. 2005); *see also* Engel v. Engel, 920 So. 2d 505 (Miss. Ct. App. 2006) (divorce improperly granted; husband failed to withdraw fault grounds).

[393] Heatherly v. Heatherly, 914 So. 2d 754, 758 (Miss. Ct. App. 2005). *But cf.* Breland v. Breland, 920 So. 2d 510,

GROUNDS FOR DIVORCE § 4.04[3]

Two recent cases have greatly reduced the importance of this provision. The cases establish different rules for withdrawing consent – one when the parties agreed to divorce and submit issues to the court (subsection (3) of the statute), and another when the parties resolve all issues and submit their agreement to the court (subsection (2)). In 2009, the Mississippi Supreme Court held that when parties consent to divorce but submit some issues to the court for trial, explicit withdrawal of contests or denials is not required. The court reasoned that subsection (5) of the statute[394] makes a subsection (3) agreement an implicit withdrawal of contests and denials.[395] Then, in 2010, the court of appeals held that failure to withdraw contests or denials in a divorce under subsection (2) is harmless error if the objecting party's substantive rights are not affected.[396] Thus, it appears that failure to withdraw contests or denials will not affect the validity of a divorce in most cases.

[3] Pleadings must be on file for sixty days. A complaint requesting irreconcilable differences divorce must be on file for sixty days before divorce can be granted.[397] The filing may be a joint complaint of the parties or the complaint of one of the parties asserting irreconcilable differences as a sole ground for divorce or as an alternative to fault-based grounds.[398] A complaint requesting divorce on fault grounds alone will not support a later agreement to divorce based on irreconcilable differences, even if the fault-based complaint has been on file for sixty days.[399] In computing the sixty-day period, the last day is counted, so that a divorce may be granted on the sixtieth day from filing.[400]

[4] Requirements for submission of agreement. Parties may agree to all terms of divorce and submit the agreement to the court for approval, or may agree to be divorced on irreconcilable differences and specify issues for resolution by the court. The agreement must be in writing and, if issues are submitted to the court, must include certain language set out in the statute.

[a] Agreement must be in writing. The Mississippi Supreme Court insists on strict compliance with the statutory requirements for a written agreement. The writing must be sufficiently complete to show the parties' agreement. A handwritten agreement

---

512 (Miss. Ct. App. 2006) (statute only requires withdrawal of "contest" – a complainant's uncontested fault grounds need not be withdrawn).

[394] MISS. CODE ANN. § 93-5-2(5) (2004) ("*Except as otherwise provided in subsection (3)* of this section, no divorce shall be granted on the ground of irreconcilable differences where there has been a contest or denial.") (emphasis added).

[395] Irby v. Estate of Irby, 7 So. 3d 223, 236-40 (Miss. 2009); *see also* O'Neal v. O'Neal, 17 So. 3d 572, 575-78 (Miss. 2009); Cossey v. Cossey, 22 So. 3d 353, 356-57 (Miss. Ct. App. 2009) (following *Irby*); *cf.* Sellers v. Sellers, 22 So. 3d 299, 302-06 (Miss. Ct. App. 2009) (following *Irby*, but disagreeing with reasoning).

[396] Cobb v. Cobb, 29 So. 3d 145, 151-52 (Miss. Ct. App. 2010) (husband's substantive rights were not affected because he clearly agreed to divorce).

[397] MISS. CODE ANN. § 93-5-2(4) (2004).

[398] MISS. CODE ANN. § 93-5-2(6) (2004).

[399] Perkins v. Perkins, 787 So. 2d 1256, 1263-64 (Miss. 2001); *cf.* Tyrone v. Tyrone, 32 So. 3d 1206, 1212-14 (Miss. Ct. App. 2009) (reversing a chancellor's grant of divorce; at the time of grant, all requests for irreconcilable differences divorce had been dismissed and only separate maintenance requests were pending).

[400] *In re* Robbins, 744 So. 2d 394, 396 (Miss. Ct. App. 1999) (citing MISS. R. CIV. P. 6).

§ 4.04[4][b]   **MISSISSIPPI FAMILY LAW**

is sufficient,[401] but incomplete handwritten attorney's notes were not sufficient even though signed by the parties.[402] In several cases, a grant of divorce has been reversed because the parties' agreement was presented orally or dictated into the court record rather than memorialized in writing.[403] However, in 2008, the court of appeals declined to reverse a judgment based upon an agreement that was read into the record. The court relied upon a modification case holding that an agreement dictated into the record is effective.[404]

    [b] Submission of issues to court. Parties who cannot agree to all terms may agree to divorce and to submit other terms to the court. The agreement must (1) be in writing, (2) be signed personally by the parties, (3) specifically state the issues for submission to the court, (4) state that the parties voluntarily consent to court decision of the specified issues, and (5) state that the parties understand that the court's decision will be a binding judgment.[405] The court of appeals reversed a grant of divorce because the agreement to submit issues to the court did not state specifically that "the parties voluntarily consent to permit the court to decide" the listed issues. Nor did it state that "the parties understand that the decision of the court shall be a binding and lawful judgment."[406]

    After the parties have submitted issues to the court and proceedings, including motions, have begun, consent may not be withdrawn without leave of court.[407]

    [5] No divorce before all matters resolved. The irreconcilable differences statute provides that no divorce shall be granted until all custody, child support, and property rights between the parties have been agreed upon and found to be adequate or resolved by the court.[408] In contrast to its strict reading of the statute's writing requirements, the Mississippi Supreme Court has upheld divorces granted before all issues were resolved. Under a strict reading of the statute, a chancellor erred in granting an irreconcilable differences divorce and reserving decision on other issues for thirty days unless the parties reached agreement. However, since the agreement was actually filed, approved, and included in the judgment, the complaining husband could show no prejudice.[409]

---

    [401] White v. Smith, 645 So. 2d 875, 876 (Miss. 1994) (parties submitted handwritten consent to divorce during trial).

    [402] Joiner v. Joiner, 739 So. 2d 1043, 1045 (Miss. Ct. App. 1999).

    [403] *See, e.g.,* Cassibry v. Cassibry, 742 So. 2d 1121, 1125 (Miss. 1999); *cf.* Cook v. Cook, 725 So. 2d 205, 207 (Miss. 1998) (oral modification of agreement in irreconcilable differences divorce not valid).

    [404] Bougard v. Bougard, 991 So. 2d 646, 649-50 (Miss. Ct. App. 2008) (the agreement stated that the parties intended to be bound by the agreement even if they did not sign a written order).

    [405] MISS. CODE ANN. § 93-5-2(3) (2004); *see* Massengill v. Massengill, 594 So. 2d 1173, 1175 (Miss. 1992).

    [406] Engel v. Engel, 920 So. 2d 505, 509-10 (Miss. Ct. App. 2006) (also reversing because husband did not withdraw fault grounds; court noted that error might have been harmless, but reversed since husband did not file brief in response to wife's appeal).

    [407] MISS. CODE ANN. § 93-5-2(3) (2004); *see* McDuffie v. McDuffie, 21 So. 3d 685, 689 (Miss. Ct. App. 2009) (chancellor did not err in denying husband's request to withdraw consent after his wife admitted adultery in court).

    [408] MISS. CODE ANN. § 93-5-2(3) (2004).

    [409] Rounsaville v. Rounsaville, 732 So. 2d 909, 911 (Miss. 1999) (husband who agreed to order sought to reverse divorce after ex-wife remarried); *see also* Johnston v. Johnston, 722 So. 2d 453, 457 (Miss. 1998) (harmless error where court took support and property issues under advisement while granting divorce).

GROUNDS FOR DIVORCE   § 4.04[6]

[6] Proceedings. A joint complaint of husband and wife for divorce solely on the ground of irreconcilable differences is taken as proved and judgment may be entered without proof or testimony.[410] Rule 8.04 of the Uniform Rules of Chancery Practice provides that attorneys must appear with the file to obtain a chancellor's approval and signature and must be prepared to respond to the court's questions.[411]

If the parties are not represented by attorneys, appearance is not required by the rules or by statute; however, a chancellor has discretion to require that the parties appear. The Mississippi Supreme Court held that a court abused its discretion in requiring appearance by indigent pro se parties who agreed to all terms; the husband was incarcerated and the wife lived in California.[412]

[7] Judgment. The irreconcilable differences statute provides that an agreement may be incorporated into a judgment only if the court "finds that such provisions are adequate and sufficient."[413] The Mississippi Supreme Court reversed a divorce in part because the record was silent regarding the chancellor's review and approval.[414] In 2008, however, the court of appeals held that a chancellor's failure to state that an agreement was "adequate and sufficient" did not invalidate the agreement – the question is whether, in fact, the agreement is adequate.[415] A court is not required to make the specific findings of fact required in contested actions.[416]

Even if the agreement provides that it is binding between the parties, a chancellor has discretion to disapprove or modify the agreement.[417] Agreements in contemplation of irreconcilable differences divorce are void unless presented to the court. A divorcing couple's private agreement, in conflict with their agreement presented to the court, was not binding – enforcement of a secret agreement would contradict public policy.[418]

§ 4.05 REVOCATION OF DIVORCE

A judgment of divorce may be revoked upon the joint application of the divorced spouses.[419] However, the revocation does not relate back to the date of divorce. A wife's alleged sexual relationship during the period between divorce and reconciliation was not grounds for a second divorce based on adultery. Furthermore, property divided and awarded to the wife in the first divorce did not revert to her husband as a result of the

---

[410] MISS. CODE ANN. § 93-5-2(4) (2004).

[411] MISS. UNIF. CHAN. CT. R. 8.04.

[412] *See* Bullard v. Morris, 547 So. 2d 789, 791 (Miss. 1989).

[413] MISS. CODE ANN. § 93-5-2 (2004); *see* Ash v. Ash, 877 So. 2d 458, 460 (Miss. Ct. App. 2003) (irreconcilable differences divorce agreement must be approved by chancellor).

[414] *See* Perkins v. Perkins, 787 So. 2d 1256, 1264 (Miss. 2001) (requirement of review "clearly anticipates more than just a mere recitation of the obligatory words of the statute").

[415] *In re* Dissolution of the Marriage of De St. Germain, 977 So. 2d 412, 417 (Miss. Ct. App. 2008); *see also* Cobb v. Cobb, 29 So. 3d 145, 149-50 (Miss. Ct. App. 2010) (question is whether agreement is in fact adequate and sufficient).

[416] Perkins v. Perkins, 787 So. 2d 1256, 1265 (Miss. 2001).

[417] Grier v. Grier, 616 So. 2d 337, 340 (Miss. 1993). *See infra* § 23.10.

[418] *See* Sullivan v. Pouncey, 469 So. 2d 1233, 1234 (Miss. 1985) (parties ordered to return payments already made under agreement to restore the status quo).

[419] *See* Miss. Code Ann. § 93-5-32 (2004).

§ 4.05   **MISSISSIPPI FAMILY LAW**

revocation.[420] In a case of first impression, the Mississippi Supreme Court held in 2010 that a joint application for revocation may be granted upon satisfactory proof of reconciliation, even though one of the spouses dies while the application is pending.[421]

---

[420] Devereaux v. Devereaux, 493 So. 2d 1310 (Miss. 1986).

[421] Carlisle v. Allen, 40 So. 3d 1252, 1255-61 (Miss. 2010).

V
DOMESTIC VIOLENCE

Domestic violence alters the dynamics in family law matters. Procedures are now available to obtain swift and detailed orders of protection against domestic violence. On the other hand, an order of protection is no guarantee of safety. An attorney for a victim of violence must weigh securing an order of protection while moving forward in litigation that may exacerbate conflict. The attorney must be aware of grounds for divorce based on violence, as well as potential barriers to divorce. Domestic violence triggers special rules regarding child custody where the batterer is the other parent. Care should be taken to fashion custody awards that protect a victim from ongoing contact with a batterer-coparent. However, abuse by a current spouse or partner may cause a victim to lose custody to a noncustodial parent or third party. And, because a divorcing client may have tort claims against a spouse, the attorney should consider the effect of divorce settlement on potential tort claims.

§ 5.01 HISTORY AND OVERVIEW

Awareness of domestic violence as a serious social problem is fairly recent. Before 1970 there were five brief social science studies on the topic, all implying that the problem was caused by the victim's provocation of the abuser.[1] And almost two hundred years ago, the Mississippi Supreme Court explicitly recognized a husband's right to inflict physical violence on his wife. In a case involving assault and battery, the Mississippi Supreme Court expressed its "abhorrence" for the practice of spousal abuse but noted that "Family broils and dissensions cannot be investigated before the tribunals of the country, without casting a shade over the character of those who are unfortunately engaged in the controversy." Accordingly, the court held that a man should be allowed to "moderately chastise" his wife to "screen from public reproach" and prevent "vexatious prosecutions."[2]

The 1970s brought increased focus on the problem of violence in intimate relationships. Over the next few decades, considerable resources were expended to create a network of domestic violence shelters, to educate law enforcement and healthcare providers about violence, and to develop resources to assist victims of violence. A number of groups and organizations provide information and assistance to victims and those who represent them.[3]

In 2005, the American Bar Association Commission on Domestic Violence and its partner organizations developed *Standards of Practice for Lawyers Representing Victims of Domestic Violence, Sexual Assault and Stalking in Civil Protection Order*

---

[1] Joan Zorza, *Batterer Psychopathology: Questions and Implications*, National Battered Women's Law Project (1993), *reprinted in* NANCY D.K. LEMON, DOMESTIC VIOLENCE LAW 78 (Thomson West 2d ed. 2005).

[2] Bradley v. State, 1 Miss. (Walker) 156 (1824), *overruled by* Harris v. State, 14 So. 266 (Miss. 1894).

[3] Forms and information are available from the Mississippi Attorney General's Office of Domestic Violence, *http://www.ago.state.ms.us/index.php/sections/victims/domestic_violence; see also http://www.mcadv.org/* (Mississippi Coalition Against Domestic Violence); *http://www.ncadv.org/* (National Coalition Against Domestic Violence).

111

§ 5.02   **MISSISSIPPI FAMILY LAW**

Cases. The Standards, adopted by the ABA in 2007, address best practices for lawyers in civil protection cases from several perspectives. The Standards outline the knowledge and skills necessary for assisting victims to obtain a protection order. The Standards also discuss other legal needs that a protection order client may have, including housing, employment, benefits, and immigration issues. The standards, which are aspirational rather than mandatory, provide useful information to any lawyer representing a client who has suffered domestic violence.[4]

§ 5.02 PROTECTION ORDERS

In the last twenty years, state legislatures have passed a series of laws providing increasingly strong protection for victims of violence in the form of protection orders. In Mississippi, protection orders are available to victims of domestic violence as part of a divorce or through an independent action. The order may be obtained through any of four court systems, and may include several forms of relief. An abuser may be ordered to refrain from contact with the victim. The petitioner may be awarded possession of the home, temporary custody and child support, and damages. Mississippi has also adopted a uniform act addressing interstate recognition of protection orders. The major provisions of the Protection from Domestic Abuse Act are set out below.

[1] Jurisdiction. Jurisdiction over in-state protection orders has been altered several times in the last few years. Currently, the Act provides for jurisdiction in chancery court, county court, justice court or municipal court.[5] However, justice and municipal courts are limited in the scope of relief that they can provide. Orders from these courts last for a maximum of thirty days and cannot address child custody and support.[6]

In interstate cases, jurisdiction over custody aspects of an order for protection are governed by the Uniform Child Custody Jurisdiction and Enforcement Act. If no custody order is outstanding, jurisdiction to award custody generally lies in the child's home state.[7] However, a state that lacks home state jurisdiction may enter an order of temporary emergency custody upon a showing that the child is physically in the state and the child or a parent has been abused.[8] If a custody order is outstanding, the state that issued the order maintains exclusive jurisdiction to modify custody unless all parties have moved from the state;[9] however, a similar exception exists if the child is physically in another state and the parent has been physically abused. The court in which the child and parent are located may issue a temporary emergency order.[10]

[2] Parties. Under the Mississippi statute, protection orders are available to a

---

[4] AMERICAN BAR ASSOCIATION, STANDARDS OF PRACTICE FOR LAWYERS REPRESENTING VICTIMS OF DOMESTIC VIOLENCE, SEXUAL ASSAULT AND STALKING IN CIVIL PROTECTION (2007) (ABA STANDARDS).

[5] MISS. CODE ANN. §§ 93-21-3(c), -5(1) (Supp. 2010) (requiring record in justice and municipal court).

[6] See *infra* § 5.02[5][d].

[7] See *infra* § 18.09[4][a].

[8] See *infra* § 18.09[4][c] for a discussion of the emergency exception.

[9] See *infra* § 18.10[1].

[10] See *infra* § 18.10[2][b].

DOMESTIC VIOLENCE   § 5.02[3]

wide range of persons. Protection orders may be obtained against current or former spouses and cohabitants, including same-sex cohabitants. The Act has been extended to provide protection to persons currently or formerly in a dating relationship. The Act defines dating relationship as a romantic or intimate relationship between two persons, to be determined by the length and type of the relationship and the frequency of interaction.[11] Protection orders may also be obtained against a co-parent or current or former household members related by blood or marriage.[12]

[3] Basis for petition. Domestic violence for purposes of a protection order includes causing or attempting to cause bodily injury, placing the petitioner in fear of imminent serious bodily injury, criminal sexual conduct against a minor, stalking, cyberstalking, and the sexual crimes of statutory rape, drugging, spousal rape, and sexual battery.[13]

[4] Procedure

[a] Contents of petition. The petition must include information regarding the parties' relationship and any divorce or custody proceedings, must describe the abuse, and, if emergency relief is requested, explain why it is needed. Although parties are to state their address and county of residence, that information may be disclosed to the court orally and in camera to protect the petitioner. The petition should be signed under oath.[14] The Domestic Violence Division of The Attorney General's Office has developed forms for use in filing protection orders.[15]

[b] Notice and hearing. The Act provides that petitions for protection orders are to be handled as priority cases on a court's docket.[16] After a petition is filed, the court must hold a hearing within ten days. By a 2009 amendment to the statute, the defendant must be notified by personal service of process. However, the hearing may proceed in the absence of a defendant who has been notified.[17] In a hearing for emergency relief, notice is not required.

[c] Emergency orders: Justice, municipal and county courts. A victim may obtain an *ex parte* emergency order in justice, municipal, or county court. but not in

---

[11] Miss. Code Ann. § 93-21-3(d) (Supp. 2010) (excluding a casual relationship or "ordinary fraternization").

[12] Miss. Code Ann. § 93-21-3(a) ("spouses, former spouses, persons living as spouses or who formerly lived as spouses, persons having a child or children in common, other individuals related by consanguinity or affinity who reside together or who formerly resided together or between individuals who have a current or former dating relationship").

[13] Miss. Code Ann. § 93-21-3(a) (Supp. 2010); *see* Wolfe v. Wolfe, 49 So. 3d 650 (Miss. Ct. App. 2010) (husband's conduct – touching wife's stomach, pinning her between car and door, and threatening to keep son, not sufficient evidence of serious bodily injury or fear of serious injury).

[14] Miss. Code Ann. § 93-21-9 (Supp. 2010).

[15] *http://www.ago.state.ms.us/index.php/sections/victims/domestic_violence.*

[16] Miss. Code Ann. § 93-21-7(1) (Supp. 2010).

[17] Miss. Code Ann. § 93-21-11 (Supp. 2010).

113

§ 5.02[4][d]   MISSISSIPPI FAMILY LAW

chancery court.[18] The matter is to be handled in an "expedited manner."[19] The order may be entered without notice to the defendant upon a showing that the petitioner, a minor child, or one who is incompetent is in immediate danger of abuse. The order is effective for ten days, and may be extended to a maximum of twenty days.[20] The *ex parte* order may restrain the defendant from abuse of the petitioner, grant possession of the parties' residence, require that the respondent maintain a certain distance from and avoid contact with the petitioner or other household members, and prohibit the transfer of jointly owned assets.[21]

[d] Temporary orders: Justice and municipal courts. Justice courts and municipal courts are limited to entering thirty-day temporary orders, even after notice to the defendant. The relief available in a temporary order is the same as the relief available in an emergency order.[22]

[e] Permanent orders: County and chancery courts. After a hearing with notice to the defendant, a permanent protection order may be issued by a chancery or county court ordering the respondent to cease abuse and to maintain a certain distance from, and refrain from contacting the petitioner and other household members. The permanent order may include an award of possession of the residence and an order of temporary custody, visitation, and child support. The court may order payments to remedy direct injuries stemming from the abuse, including medical expenses, out-of-pocket expenses, attorneys' fees, and moving expenses. The order may also require the defendant to undergo counseling or other medical treatment and to refrain from disposing of assets.[23]

[f] Custody and support in protection orders. Child custody and support may be included in protection orders ordered by a chancery or county court. Justice and municipal courts are not authorized to address these issues. By a 2009 amendment to the statute, a chancery or county court's award of custody or child support in a protection order is valid for a maximum of 180 days. After that time, custody and support revert to the pre-order status.[24]

[5] Judgments

[a] Mutual orders. In the past, courts hearing allegations of domestic violence often entered mutual orders – orders restraining both parties from abuse and from contacting the other. The Mississippi statute now provides that a court may restrain

---

[18] MISS. CODE ANN. § 93-21-7(2) (Supp. 2010). However, the Act also provides that nothing in the Act precludes a chancery court from entering an emergency order when it deems one necessary under the circumstances. *Id.* § 93-21-7(4).

[19] MISS. CODE ANN. § 93-21-13(1) (Supp. 2010).

[20] MISS. CODE ANN. § 93-21-13(1)(c)(1) (Supp. 2010).

[21] MISS. CODE ANN. §§ 93-21-15(1)(a) (Supp. 2010).

[22] See *infra* § 5.02 [5][c].

[23] MISS. CODE ANN. § 93-21-15 (Supp. 2010). An order may not affect title to real property. *Id.* § 93-21-17(3).

[24] MISS. CODE ANN. § 93-21-15(2)(c) (Supp. 2010).

DOMESTIC VIOLENCE   § 5.02[5][b]

both parties only if both filed a petition seeking relief and only if the court makes an on-the-record finding that both were "principal aggressors" and that neither acted in self-defense.[25]

[b] Findings of fact. The court's order should contain findings of fact regarding the abuse and contain provisions specifically describing the prohibited conduct. [26]

[c] Time. The court has discretion to set an appropriate length of time for the order. The order should state the expiration date.[27]

[d] Attorneys' fees. Upon a finding that abuse has occurred, a court may order the defendant to pay costs and attorneys' fees. If the court finds that the petitioner's allegations are without merit, attorneys' fees may be awarded against the petitioner.[28]

[6] Enforcement

[a] Arrest. Law enforcement officials have authority to make warrantless arrests based upon probable cause to believe that a protection order violation has occurred within the last twenty-four hours.[29]

[b] Remedies for violation. Violation of a restraining order may be a misdemeanor, punishable by imprisonment for six months, a fine of $1,000, or both. Or, the court may find the defendant in contempt for violation of the order. The defendant may not be convicted for a misdemeanor and found in contempt.[30]

A contempt action based on violation of a protection order must follow the requirements of Rule 81(d) of the Mississippi Rules of Civil Procedure for contempt matters. A Mississippi court lacked jurisdiction to incarcerate a husband for violation of an Ohio order, because the action was not initiated with a Rule 81 summons.[31]

[7] Modification. A court may amend, modify, or terminate a protection order upon the filing of a petition by one of the parties, notice to the defendant, and a hearing.[32] A protection order may only be amended by court order.[33]

[8] Interstate order enforcement. In 2004, Mississippi adopted the Uniform Interstate Enforcement of Domestic Violence Protection Orders Act. The Act provides

---

[25] Miss. Code Ann. § 93-21-15(3) (Supp. 2010).

[26] Miss. Code Ann. § 93-21-15(3) (Supp. 2010).

[27] Miss. Code Ann. § 93-21-15(2)(b) (Supp. 2010).

[28] Miss. Code Ann. § 93-21-7(3) (Supp. 2010).

[29] Miss. Code Ann. § 93-21-21 (Supp. 2010); *see also* Miss. Code Ann. § 93-21-28 (Supp. 2010) (victim of violence may request law enforcement assistance in leaving home, obtaining transportation to hospital or shelter, and in returning to retrieve personal belongings; order of protection not necessary).

[30] Miss. Code Ann. § 93-21-21 (Supp. 2010).

[31] Wolfe v. Wolfe, 49 So. 3d 650 (Miss. Ct. App. 2010) (if jurisdiction had been obtained, husband's conduct of touching wife's stomach and pinning her to car would have been a violation of the order).

[32] Miss. Code Ann. § 93-21-15(6) (Supp. 2010).

[33] Miss. Code Ann. § 93-21-17(2) (Supp. 2010).

115

§ 5.02[9]   MISSISSIPPI FAMILY LAW

for enforcement of foreign protection orders that comply with the Act's requirements.[34] The foreign order must comply with the issuing state's jurisdictional requirements and must have included notice to the respondent. A Mississippi court may also enforce custody and visitation provisions of a protection order issued in compliance with the foreign state's jurisdictional rules on custody. However, the court may not enforce support provisions of another state's protection order under this Act.[35]

[9] Firearms prohibitions. Under federal law, a person convicted of domestic violence is prohibited from possession of a firearm. The prohibition applies to anyone who is subject to a court order restraining them from "harassing, stalking, or threatening" an intimate partner or the partner's child, or engaging in conduct that would place an intimate partner in reasonable fear of bodily injury to the partner or child. However, the Act also requires that the order was issued after actual notice and a hearing at which the defendant had an opportunity to participate. In addition, the order must include a finding that the defendant is a credible threat to the plaintiff's physical safety and must explicitly prohibit use of force or threats of force.[36]

[10] Safety and lethality assessments. A victim's decision to leave an abuser, to file for divorce, or to seek a protection order may put her or him in even greater danger. It is widely accepted that physical violence often escalates when a partner leaves an abuser. A protection order will not always be the best solution for a particular client. Advocacy organizations encourage attorneys representing victims of abuse to advise their clients of this danger and to direct them to law enforcement or trained counselors who may assist them in assessing the potential danger of initiating litigation.[37] The National Coalition Against Domestic Violence offers safety plan information, including home and workplace safety, internet safety, and identity protection.[38]

§ 5.03 GROUNDS FOR DIVORCE

An attorney representing a domestic violence survivor should be aware of peculiarities in Mississippi divorce law. Mississippi law provides divorce grounds based on physical violence, but common law requirements and defenses can present barriers to a grant of divorce. True no-fault divorce is not available in Mississippi. Spouses can agree to divorce based on irreconcilable differences. However, an abuser will often refuse to agree to divorce to maintain control of his or her spouse. Without an agreed divorce, the victim must be able to prove one of the twelve fault-based grounds for divorce, requiring additional resources, time, and probably creating additional opportunities for contact with the abuser.

---

[34] MISS. CODE ANN. § 93-22-5 (2004); *see also id.* § 93-21-16 (2004).

[35] MISS. CODE ANN. § 93-22-5 (2004).

[36] 18 U.S.C. § 922(d)(8).

[37] ABA STANDARDS , *supra* note 4, at 43.

[38] *http://www.ncadv.org/* (under "protect yourself" tab). A Danger Assessment Tool for assessing homicide risk, developed by Dr. Jacquelyn Campbell, is available at *http://www.dangerassessment.org/WebApplication1/default.aspx.* *Broken link.*

DOMESTIC VIOLENCE   § 5.03[1]

Physical violence will almost always provide grounds for divorce under the fault-based ground of habitual, cruel and inhuman treatment. However, the common law defense of condonation can bar divorce for a victim of violence who leaves home and then returns to the abuser. In addition, the requirement of corroboration of divorce grounds can be a problem – the plaintiff must provide corroborating proof of conduct that is often secretive.[39]

[1] Habitual, cruel, and inhuman treatment. In order to obtain a divorce on this ground a plaintiff must (1) show conduct by the defendant that meets the test for cruelty; (2) prove a causal connection between the conduct and the plaintiff's physical or mental health; and (3) provide independent corroborating evidence of the conduct.

[a] Repeated or severe violence. Evidence of repeated violence throughout a marriage, or of several severe episodes of violence, is certainly grounds for divorce based on habitual, cruel, and inhuman treatment.[40] A chancellor properly granted divorce based on evidence of fifteen to twenty episodes of physical violence in a marriage.[41] In addition, one or more incidents of severe violence will support grant of a divorce.[42] A wife was granted divorce based upon proof of three incidents of violence, one requiring a week of hospitalization.[43]

[b] Isolated acts of violence. A single act of violence may be sufficiently severe to support divorce.[44] The Mississippi Supreme Court reversed a chancellor's denial of divorce to a woman whose husband tried to shoot her – the assault alone was grounds for divorce.[45] Less severe isolated acts of violence combined with other conduct, such as verbal threats and emotional abuse, may be sufficient to prove cruelty. In a number of cases, divorce has been granted upon a showing of a pattern of verbal and physical abuse.[46]

---

[39] See *supra* § 4.02 for a discussion of fault-based grounds.

[40] Devereaux v. Devereaux, 493 So. 2d 1310, 1312 (Miss. 1986) (between fifteen and twenty incidents of violence); *see* Holladay v. Holladay, 776 So. 2d 662, 665-66 (Miss. 2000) (repeated episodes of physical violence throughout marriage);

[41] *See* Labella v. Labella, 722 So. 2d 472, 473-74 (Miss. 1998); *see also* Kumar v. Kumar, 976 So. 2d 957, 961-63 (Miss. Ct. App. 2008) (divorce based on proof of incidents of physical violence, verbal abuse, and transmission of STD to wife); Fulton v. Fulton, 918 So. 2d 877, 879-80 (Miss. Ct. App. 2006) (pattern of physical abuse by husband, including one event for which he was prosecuted and pled guilty and one in which he stood by while his girlfriend's friends beat his wife and injured her severely).

[42] *See* Sandifer v. Sandifer, 61 So. 2d 144, 144 (Miss. 1952) (threats to shoot husband or poison food); Serton v. Serton, 819 So. 2d 15, 18 (Miss. Ct. App. 2002) (husband threatened wife's life, pressed a gun to her neck, and beat and raped her in front of their two children); *cf.* Smith v. Smith, 994 So. 2d 882, 884-85 (Miss. Ct. App. 2008) (divorce granted to husband based on wife's stabbing him on Christmas; grant of divorce not an issue on appeal).

[43] Langdon v. Langdon, 854 So. 2d 485 (Miss. Ct. App. 2003).

[44] *See* Rawson v. Buta, 609 So. 2d 426, 431 (Miss. 1992).

[45] *See* Ellzey v. Ellzey, 253 So. 2d 249, 250 (Miss. 1971); *see also* Gatlin v. Gatlin, 234 So. 2d 634, 635 (Miss. 1970) (wife's shooting at husband would have been sufficient to grant divorce).

[46] *See* Sproles v. Sproles, 782 So. 2d 742, 745 (Miss. 2001) (husband drank a case of beer a night, was abusive, threatened wife's life, treated her in dehumanizing ways); Holladay v. Holladay, 776 So. 2d 662, 676-77 (Miss. 2000) (husband locked his wife away from her frightened child and closed her checking account; violence required two police interventions); Stein v. Stein, 11 So. 3d 1288, 1292 (Miss. Ct. App. 2009) (acts of physical violence in 1987 and 1991, combined with verbal abuse throughout marriage, sufficient to support divorce); Goellner v. Goellner, 11 So. 3d 1251, 1257 (Miss. Ct. App. 2009) (outbursts of anger, abusive and vulgar language, and physical altercations); Atkinson v.

§ 5.03[2]   MISSISSIPPI FAMILY LAW

The Mississippi Supreme Court has stated, however, that "[p]hysical violence in the marriage does not create a per se ground for a divorce."[47] For example, divorce was denied in spite of a physical altercation in which both parties were involved.[48]

The timing of domestic violence may be significant. Conduct that might be sufficient if recent may be insufficient if a long time has passed with no other incidents of violence. Several acts of violence early in a twenty-seven-year marriage did not constitute habitual, cruel, and inhuman treatment.[49] Violence that occurred before the parties married is not grounds for divorce. A wife was denied divorce based on corroborated episodes of premarital violence. She alleged, but could not corroborate, violence after the couple married.[50] However, a court may admit testimony regarding premarital abuse to show the effect of later conduct on the plaintiff.[51]

[2] Impact on plaintiff. To obtain a divorce based on habitual cruelty, the plaintiff must show a causal connection between the defendant's conduct and physical or emotional harm to the plaintiff.[52] In cases involving serious physical abuse, the impact on the plaintiff is obvious. Cases involving physical abuse often grant divorce without discussing the requirement of impact on the plaintiff. In cases involving more isolated incidents combined with verbal abuse, however, it may be important to provide evidence of the impact on the plaintiff.[53]

Atkinson, 11 So. 3d 172, 174 (Miss. Ct. App. 2009) (husband choked his wife, put a knife to her chest, cursed at her and abused her verbally, and threatened to hit her with a rake and to rape her); Oswalt v. Oswalt, 981 So. 2d 993, 996 (Miss. Ct. App. 2007) (husband threatened suicide and threatened wife with gun, in addition to belittling her); Horn v. Horn, 909 So. 2d 1151, 1157 (Miss. Ct. App. 2005) (physical abuse combined with verbal and emotional abuse); Wright v. Wright, 823 So. 2d 586, 587 (Miss. Ct. App. 2002) (husband was jealous and suspicious, had problems managing anger, and physically assaulted his wife more than once); Garriga v. Garriga, 770 So. 2d 978, 983 (Miss. Ct. App. 2000) (husband was violent and adulterous, drank to excess, forced wife to have sexual relations); Keller v. Keller, 763 So. 2d 902, 904, 909 (Miss. Ct. App. 2000) (committed at least one act of physical violence, refused to have sex for the last year of marriage, beat his wife's son from first marriage, and demanded that she "get rid" of the child by giving up custody); Moore v. Moore, 757 So. 2d 1043, 1049 (Miss. Ct. App. 2000) (emotional and verbal abuse, four instances of physical abuse, and resulting depression requiring medication); Mixon v. Mixon, 724 So. 2d 956, 960 (Miss. Ct. App. 1998) (several incidents of physical violence combined with verbal abuse, accusations, and acts of destruction).

[47] *See* Reed v. Reed, 839 So. 2d 565, 570 (Miss. Ct. App. 2003).

[48] *See* Wilbourne v. Wilbourne, 748 So. 2d 184, 187 (Miss. 1999) (no divorce although the marriage "was unpleasant and the parties were incompatible;" arguments "on occasion involved physical violence"); Bowen v. Bowen, 688 So. 2d 1374, 1377-78 (Miss. 1997) (no divorce where husband inferred that wife was lesbian, called her names, and struck her twice during an altercation in which she also struck him); Steen v. Steen, 641 So. 2d 1167, 1170 (Miss. 1994) (physical contact included pinching and scratch on arm from door jamb).

[49] Talbert v. Talbert, 759 So. 2d 1105, 1109 (Miss. 1999) (no divorce where husband belittled his wife, screamed at her, and committed a few acts of violence early in the twenty-seven year marriage; conduct did not recur); *see also* Bland v. Bland, 620 So. 2d 543, 545 (Miss. 1993) (one act of violence ten years prior to divorce action); Scott v. Scott, 69 So. 2d 489, 494 (Miss. 1954) (all testimony related to acts of violence more than four years prior to divorce). *But see* Stein v. Stein, 11 So. 3d 1288, 1292 (Miss. Ct. App. 2009) (acts of physical violence in 1987 and 1991, combined with verbal abuse throughout marriage, sufficient to support divorce).

[50] Cochran v. Cochran, 912 So. 2d 1086, 1090-91 (Miss. Ct. App. 2005) (rejecting evidence of physical assaults and cruelty prior to marriage, when offered as basis for divorce rather than to prove wife's reasonable fear of husband's later cruelty).

[51] *See* Holladay v. Holladay, 776 So. 2d 662, 676 (Miss. 2000) (severe beating prior to marriage relevant to plaintiff's state of mind and impact of later violence).

[52] Bias v. Bias, 493 So. 2d 342, 345 (Miss. 1986) ("proximate cause of harm to the health and physical well being of the plaintiff"); *see* Faries v. Faries, 607 So. 2d 1204, 1209 (Miss. 1992); Peters v. Peters, 906 So. 2d 64 (Miss. Ct. App. 2004); Rakestraw v. Rakestraw, 717 So. 2d 1284, 1288 (Miss. Ct. App. 1998).

[53] See *supra* § 4.02[8][b] for a discussion of the requirement of impact on the plaintiff.

DOMESTIC VIOLENCE

§ 5.03[3]

[3] Corroboration. Domestic violence often occurs in private, behind closed doors. An abuser may inflict violence only on a romantic partner or spouse; a perpetrator of domestic violence is not necessarily violent outside the home.[54] The Mississippi fault-based system of divorce requires that a plaintiff provide independent, corroborating evidence of grounds for divorce, including physical abuse. Divorce has been denied to plaintiffs who allege, but cannot corroborate, abuse. In a 2010 case, the court of appeals reversed a divorce for lack of corroboration, even though the wife had obtained a protection order against her husband and even though police had been called to her home twice. Her testimony of physical and sexual abuse was not sufficiently corroborated by police reports and the petition for protection order, because both were based on her testimony.[55] Similarly, a wife who provided corroboration of premarital violence was denied a divorce – she could not corroborate her allegations of violence during their short marriage.[56] However, corroboration need not rise to the level of proof required to obtain a divorce – it need only provide enough supporting facts for a court to conclude that the plaintiff's testimony is true.[57] In one case, a wife's testimony of her husband's physical and emotional abuse was corroborated by a social worker's testimony that the plaintiff's depression and low self-esteem were indicative of a victim of spousal abuse.[58]

The requirement of corroboration may be waived if corroboration is not reasonably possible because of the nature of the conduct or the parties' isolation.[59] However, this test was interpreted to require corroborating evidence from a plaintiff who worked outside the home and was therefore in daily contact with others.[60]

[4] Condonation. The common law defense of condonation, or forgiveness, may be critical for a petitioner who leaves an abusive spouse, returns, and then makes the decision to leave permanently. The defense, primarily applicable to adultery, is based on the notion of marital forgiveness. Condonation is implied when a spouse continues a marital relationship after learning of an offense, such as adultery.[61] If an offense has been condoned, divorce is no longer available on that ground. However, condonation

---

[54] See Cheryl Hanna, *The Paradox of Hope: The Crime and Punishment of Domestic Violence*, William & Mary L. Rev. 1505, 1564-66 (1998) (discussing study indicating that only 25% of batterers exhibit violence outside the home).

[55] Ladner v. Ladner, 49 So. 3d 669, 672 (Miss. Ct. App. 2010) (also stating that testimony that the son feared his father did not prove abuse of the mother).

[56] Cochran v. Cochran, 912 So. 2d 1086, 1090-91 (Miss. Ct. App. 2005).

[57] Andersen v. Andersen, 200 So. 726, 728 (Miss. 1941).

[58] *See* Faries v. Faries, 607 So. 2d 1204, 1208 (Miss. 1992); see *supra* §4.02[8][d] for a discussion of corroboration of cruelty.

[59] Andersen v. Andersen, 200 So. 726, 728 (Miss. 1941) (corroboration of husband's testimony necessary, where parties lived in crowded area and conduct would likely have been observed); *see* Hassett v. Hassett, 690 So. 2d 1140, 1146 (Miss. 1997) (wife's testimony regarding sexual abuse not corroborated); Chamblee v. Chamblee, 637 So. 2d 850, 860 (Miss. 1994) (wife's testimony of physical abuse not corroborated); Gardner v. Gardner, 618 So. 2d 108, 114 (Miss. 1993) (same); Reed v. Reed, 839 So. 2d 565, 571 (Miss. Ct. App. 2003) (no corroboration of physical violence).

[60] Cochran v. Cochran, 912 So. 2d 1086, 1089 (Miss. Ct. App. 2005) (without corroboration, cross-examination must be searching and convince the chancellor that the allegations are true); *see also* Hoskins v. Hoskins, 21 So. 3d 705, 708-11 (Miss. Ct. App. 2009) (divorce denied; no corroboration of claimed cruelty, even though adult children lived with the couple).

[61] *See* Thames v. Thames, 100 So. 2d 868, 870 (Miss. 1958) (any conduct prior to reconciliation condoned); Fulton v. Fulton, 918 So. 2d 877, 881 (Miss. Ct. App. 2006) (divorce properly denied based on condonation – the wife ended her affair, confessed to her husband, and the couple resumed sexual relations for at least eight months).

§ 5.03[4]   **MISSISSIPPI FAMILY LAW**

is conditioned on a wrongdoer's continued good behavior. If the offense occurs again, the ground for divorce is revived.[62]

The Mississippi Supreme Court has emphasized that the defense of condonation does not usually apply to habitual cruelty in the same manner as to adultery: "The effort to endure unkind treatment as long as possible is commendable and the patient endurance by the wife of her husband's ill-treatment should not be allowed to weaken her right to a divorce."[63]

However, the defense does apply to a spouse who resumes cohabitation after separation. In a series of cases beginning in 1954, the Mississippi Supreme Court has held that habitual, cruel, and inhuman treatment is condoned when an innocent spouse resumes cohabitation after a separation and no further acts of cruelty occur.[64]

For many reasons – financial, emotional, for reasons related to children - victims may leave home and return several times before finally making a break from an abusive relationship.[65] Based on this rule as stated, a spouse who leaves home and then returns has forfeited grounds for divorce based on abuse. She or he must wait for violence to recur, or divorce will be denied. Attorneys should advise clients that a return home may cost them their divorce grounds unless they remain until violence recurs.

Arguably, however, a battered spouse's return home can be viewed as involuntary; if so, the return should not be considered condonation of the prior abuse. Condonation requires voluntariness. For example, the supreme court held that a wife did not condone her husband's adultery by resuming a sexual relationship with him, if she was not a willing participant.[66] Similarly, reconciliation based on fraud, force, or duress is not a voluntary condonation. A husband's attempts to lure his wife into reconciliation in order to move venue to another county were ineffective. The supreme court stated that "It is necessary also that the condonation be free and voluntary. If it is induced by fraud, fear, or force, it is of no effect."[67] In an 1856 case, the Mississippi Supreme Court stated that continued cohabitation by a wife should be considered under a more lenient rule because of the wife's dependence on her husband and his authority over her.[68] Although this view of marriage roles is outdated, the case arguably stands as authority that courts should be less inclined to find condonation where one spouse remains in or returns to the home because of financial dependence or emotional control by the

---

[62] See *supra* §4.03[6] for a discussion of condonation in general.

[63] Smith v. Smith, 40 So. 2d 156 (Miss. 1949); *see* Manning v. Manning, 133 So. 673, 674 (Miss. 1931) (condonation not usually applicable to cruelty).

[64] *See* Chaffin v. Chaffin, 437 So. 2d 384, 386 (Miss. 1983); Stribling v. Stribling, 215 So. 2d 869, 870 (Miss. 1968) (wife condoned husband's acts of violence, which caused permanent physical damage, by reconciling and resuming cohabitation); Thames v. Thames, 100 So. 2d 868, 870 (Miss. 1958) (husband's conduct prior to separation condoned by reconciliation); Scott v. Scott, 69 So. 2d 489, 494 (Miss. 1954); Kumar v. Kumar, 976 So. 2d 957, 962 (Miss. Ct. App. 2008) (spouse does not condone cruelty by continuing to cohabit but may condone conduct if the parties separate and then reconcile; abuse recurred, so grounds were revived); *cf.* Langdon v. Langdon, 854 So. 2d 485 (Miss. Ct. App. 2003) (condonation of two incidents of violence by separation and reconciliation; but divorce granted because violence recurred, removing condonation).

[65] ABA STANDARDS, *supra* note 4, at 44 (noting that a victim may leave and return numerous times before finding the "financial, emotional, and social resources" to leave).

[66] Harmon v. Harmon, 757 So. 2d 305, 309 (Miss. Ct. App. 1999) (chancellor did not err in granting divorce based on finding that wife did not consent and therefore did not condone adultery).

[67] Lee v. Lee, 232 So. 2d 370, 373 (Miss. 1970).

[68] *See* Armstrong v.Armstrong, 32 Miss. 279, 289 (1856).

DOMESTIC VIOLENCE   § 5.04

other.

§ 5.04 FINANCIAL AWARDS IN DIVORCE

In Mississippi, marital misconduct is a factor for consideration in property division and in alimony.[69] A chancellor may consider marital misconduct to the extent that it "places a burden on the stability and harmony" of the marriage.[70] In 1998, the court of appeals held that fault may be considered as a factor even in irreconcilable differences divorces.[71] Most Mississippi cases discussing fault in property division and alimony involve adultery or dissipation of assets. In one case, however, a husband's ongoing abuse was a factor in awarding more than half of the marital assets to a wife of many years.[72]

Because fault is a factor in financial awards in Mississippi, a judgment of divorce may preclude a later tort recovery. This possibility should be considered if a divorcing victim of violence anticipates filing suit for damages after the divorce proceedings are concluded.[73]

§ 5.05 CUSTODY OF CHILDREN

An abuser will often use custody as a weapon for maintaining control over a victim. Custody disputes between parents are ordinarily based on a presumption of parental equality, and decided by application of a factor-based best interests test. However, in cases involving a parent with a history of violence, the usual test does not apply. Instead, there is a presumption that a parent with a history of family violence should not be awarded custody. Even if the presumption is not invoked, a parent's violent nature may weigh against him or her in a factor-based custody dispute. On the other hand, a custodial parent's violent relationship with a third party may provide grounds for modification of custody to the other parent.

In addition to being aware of custody rules related to domestic violence, it is important to understand the special jurisdictional rules applicable to interstate custody actions involving domestic violence. Attorneys should also consider the possibility of child abduction and procedures available to protect against child-snatching.[74]

[1] Presumption against custody to violent parent. In 2003, the Mississippi legislature created a rebuttable presumption that custody should not be granted to a

---

[69] *See* Carrow v. Carrow, 642 So. 2d 901, 904 (Miss. 1994) (wife's post-separation adultery a proper factor for consideration in property division); Driste v. Driste, 738 So. 2d 763, 766 (Miss. Ct. App. 1998) (fault is factor in property division in irreconcilable differences divorce).

[70] Phillips v Phillips, 45 So. 3d 684, 697 (Miss. Ct. App. 2010) (quotation omitted) (court did not err in disregarding wife's post-separation affair).

[71] *See* Driste v. Driste, 738 So. 2d 763, 768 (Miss. Ct. App. 1999).

[72] King v. King, 946 So. 2d 395, 403-04 (Miss. Ct. App. 2006) (greater share to wife who was verbally and physically abused during forty-four year marriage; husband dissipated half of couple's assets).

[73] See *infra* § 5.07.

[74] ABA STANDARDS, *supra* note 4, at 23.

121

§ 5.05[2]   MISSISSIPPI FAMILY LAW

parent with a history of family violence.[75] A "history" of family violence includes a pattern of violence or one incident resulting in serious bodily injury.[76] If the presumption is raised and not rebutted, custody should be awarded to the nonviolent parent without consideration of the *Albright* factors. The presumption applies only in the case of serious domestic violence. The court of appeals rejected a mother's argument that a chancellor should have applied the presumption: "General yelling and screaming" – involving occasional slapping and one incident of choking without injuries – did not constitute a pattern of family violence.[77]

The presumption may be rebutted by showing that, notwithstanding the violence, the child's best interests are served by placing custody with the parent accused of violence. Factors that may be considered as rebuttal evidence include adverse circumstances of the nonviolent parent, such as mental illness or substance abuse; the violent parent's completion of a treatment or substance abuse program or parenting class; compliance with a restraining order; and whether the violence has discontinued.[78]

[2] Violent behavior under *Albright*. Even if evidence of violence is not sufficient to invoke the presumption against custody, a parent's violent behavior weighs against him or her in custody. In deciding custody between parents, Mississippi courts examine factors set out in *Albright v. Albright* for determining the child's best interests.[79] Violent behavior has weighed against parents under the factor of physical and mental health. A mother who screamed at her boys, disciplined them excessively and threw one of them on the floor during a physical attack on the father, was denied custody.[80] A mother was favored under this factor over the father, who was verbally and physically abusive, had a volatile temper, and suffered from anxiety.[81] Similarly, a father's verbal and physical abuse of his children's mother was a factor in awarding custody to her.[82] And a father who failed to take responsibility for his physical attacks on his wife was rated unfavorably on the factor of parenting skills.[83]

[3] Domestic violence as basis for loss of custody. In several cases, a custodial parent has lost custody based on domestic violence in a current relationship. Custody was modified from a mother based in large part on her violent relationship with her second husband. Police were called to the home when he destroyed property in the house. He threatened to kill himself, shooting a gun into the air outside his parents'

---

[75] *See* MISS. CODE ANN. § 93-5-24 (2004).

[76] MISS. CODE ANN. § 93-5-23 (2004).

[77] C.W.L. v. R.A., 919 So. 2d 267, 272 (Miss. Ct. App. 2005); *see also* Cockrell v. Watkins, 936 So. 2d 970, 973 (Miss. Ct. App. 2006) (three incidents between parents did not constitute history of family violence).

[78] MISS. CODE ANN. § 93-5-23 (2004). If both parents have a history of violence, the court may (1) award custody to the parent least likely to continue violent behavior; (2) order a treatment program for the custodial parent; and/or (3) award custody to a third party and limit access to the violent parent(s). *Id.*

[79] Albright v. Albright, 437 So. 2d 1003, 1005 (Miss. 1983).

[80] Gilliland v. Gilliland, 969 So. 2d 56, 61-62 (Miss. Ct. App. 2007).

[81] Horn v. Horn, 909 So. 2d 1151, 1160 (Miss. Ct. App. 2005).

[82] Brock v. Brock, 906 So. 2d 879, 885 (Miss. Ct. App. 2005).

[83] Franks v. Franks, 873 So. 2d 135, 139 (Miss. Ct. App. 2004) (father blamed his former wife for his physical assault on her, his verbal abuse, the fact that he could not clean the house, and that he watched pornography).

DOMESTIC VIOLENCE   § 5.05[4]

home in the presence of the children.[84] Similarly, a mother's home environment was considered less stable than the father's; she was seeking a divorce from her second husband, who had a drug problem and was subject to a restraining order.[85]

The custody presumption may work against a victim of violence who remains in the marital home. A teenage girl's maternal grandparents prevailed in a custody action against her parents, who were married and living together. The father had a history of violence against the mother and once struck his daughter. The chancellor held that the parents failed to rebut the presumption against awarding custody to a parent with a history of family violence.[86]

[4] Joint custody. Joint custody is generally considered inappropriate in cases involving domestic violence. Parents' ability to work cooperatively is an important factor to consider in awarding joint custody.[87] A guardian ad litem recommended against joint custody in a case involving domestic violence, stating that the husband's control issues would prevent smooth decision-making.[88] Linda Elrod, one of the leading writers on child custody, states emphatically that the evidence argues against granting joint custody in cases of domestic violence.[89] In Mississippi, the presumption against custody to a parent with a history of violence should prevent joint custody awards in cases involving serious family violence.

[5] Custody and visitation restrictions. Chancery courts have substantial discretion to fashion custodial arrangements, including imposing restrictions on parents who pose a danger to a child or other parent. A court may award visitation to a parent with a history of family violence only if the court finds that "adequate provision for the safety of the child and the parent who is a victim of domestic or family violence can be made." To protect the custodial parent and child, the court may order exchanges in a protected setting, order supervised visitation, restrict overnight visitation, or require a bond for the child's safe return. If visitation is to be supervised by a member of the noncustodial parent's family, the court must set conditions to be followed during visitation. The court may order the batterer to attend counseling sessions as a condition of visitation or to refrain from alcohol or drug consumption for twenty-four hours prior to visitation.[90] A custodial father was ordered to attend anger management classes,

---

[84] Sullivan v. Beason, 37 So. 2d 706 (Miss. Ct. App. 2010); *see also* McSwain v. McSwain, 943 So. 2d 1288, 1291-92 (Miss. 2006) (en banc); Weeks v. Weeks, 989 So. 2d 408, 413 (Miss. Ct. App. 2008) (custody to father over mother whose live-in boyfriend assaulted her in front of children); White v. Thompson, 822 So. 2d 1125, 1128 (Miss. Ct. App. 2002) (fact that a mother and her current husband had filed and withdrawn divorce pleadings, and evidence of violence in their home were part of the reasons for denying her custody); Richardson v. Richardson, 790 So. 2d 239, 242-43 (Miss. Ct. App. 2001) (mother lived for two years with abusive boyfriend).

[85] *See* Massey v. Huggins, 799 So. 2d 902, 907 (Miss. Ct. App. 2001); *see also* Mixon v. Sharp, 853 So. 2d 834, 840 (Miss. Ct. App. 2003) (stability of home environment favored father; mother married three times, was unemployed, arrested, and in abusive relationship).

[86] J.P. v. S.V.B., 987 So. 2d 975, 980-83 (Miss. 2008) (mother was not considered suitable for custody because she resided with the father and rationalized his behavior).

[87] See *infra* § 12.04[3].

[88] Horn v. Horn, 909 So. 2d 1151, 1159-60 (Miss. Ct. App. 2005) (awarding custody to mother in part based on father's violence).

[89] LINDA ELROD, CHILD CUSTODY PRACTICE AND PROCEDURE § 5.14 (2010).

[90] MISS. CODE ANN. § 93-5-24 (6)(d) (2004).

§ 5.06   MISSISSIPPI FAMILY LAW

based on evidence that he screamed at his wife in front of the children, and on at least one occasion, at his sons.[91]

§ 5.06 MEDIATION

Courts and attorneys in Mississippi are increasingly turning to mediation to resolve family law disputes, from divorce and financial matters to custody and child support. Attorneys handling cases involving domestic violence should be aware of the debate over the appropriateness of mediation in cases of violence.[92] In some states, mediation in domestic violence cases is prohibited by statute or court rule. Other states permit mediation upon a victims's request for mediation, while others provide specific precautions to be followed in mediating domestic violence cases.[93] No Mississippi rule or statute addresses this issue.

§ 5.07 TORT ACTIONS BASED ON DOMESTIC VIOLENCE

In recent years, victims of domestic violence have sought personal injury damages in suits based on assault and battery and on intentional infliction of emotional distress.[94] In many cases, a suit for damages may be futile – the defendant may lack the resources to support an award. And, in many cases, the emotional cost and potential danger of continuing contact necessitated by a civil suit may offset any potential recovery. However, if suit is a realistic possibility, an attorney handling a divorce for a victim of violence must consider the interrelationship between the two suits. A divorce judgment may bar subsequent recovery in a tort suit.

[1] Interspousal tort immunity. Personal injury suits between spouses were barred until fairly recently.[95] Tort immunity was justified as a means of preserving marital harmony and preventing fraud by spouses on insurance companies.[96] Growing dissatisfaction with the doctrine in the last few decades finally resulted in its abrogation in most states. In 1988, the Mississippi Supreme Court abolished interspousal tort immunity, permitting a woman's damages suit against her ex-husband based on physical abuse during the marriage.[97] The court stated that (1) the notion of marital

---

[91] Gilliland v. Gilliland, 969 So. 2d 56, 63, 71 (Miss. Ct. App. 2007).

[92] See Joanne Fuller and Rose Mary Lyons, *Mediation Guidelines*, 33 WILLIAMETTE L. REV. 922 (1997) (discussing arguments for and against mediation in domestic violence cases).

[93] Holly Joyce, *Mediation and Domestic Violence: Legislative Responses*, 14 J. AM. ACAD. MATRIM. LAW 447 (1997).

[94] *See generally* Clare Dalton, *Domestic Violence, Domestic Torts and Divorce: Constraints and Possibilities*, 31 NEW ENG. L. REV. 319 (1997); Douglas D. Scherer, *Tort Remedies for Victims of Domestic Abuse*, 43 S.C. L. REV. 543 (1992); George L. Blum, *Intentional Infliction of Distress in Marital Context*, 110 A.L.R. 5th 371 (2009).

[95] *See* McNeal v. Adm'r of Estate of McNeal, 254 So. 2d 521, 522-23 (Miss. 1971) (one spouse has no right of action against the other to recover damages for personal injuries caused by the other); Ensminger v. Campbell, 134 So. 2d 728, 732 (Miss. 1961) (wife had no cause of action against former husband's estate for injuries in automobile accident); Ensminger v. Ensminger, 77 So. 2d 308, 309 (Miss. 1955) (wife's suit for injuries caused by husband's negligent operation of automobile dismissed as no liability exists between husband and wife for personal tort).

[96] *See* JOHN DE WITT GREGORY, PETER N. SWISHER & SHERYL L. WOLF, UNDERSTANDING FAMILY LAW § 7.02, at 194 (2d ed. 2001).

[97] Burns v. Burns, 518 So. 2d 1205, 1209 (Miss. 1988) (marital harmony already destroyed; possibility of fraud

DOMESTIC VIOLENCE   § 5.07[2]

"oneness" is no longer a viable legal concept; (2) the argument that marital tort suits will endanger domestic tranquility is "illusory;" and (3) permitting suits between spouses will no more promote fraud than in other litigation.[98]

[2] Causes of action. Spouses have sought recovery based on the tort of assault and battery[99] and based on intentional infliction of emotional distress.[100]

[3] Relationship to divorce action. Some courts have permitted a spouse to seek tort damages in a divorce action; others require a separate action.[101] The Mississippi Supreme Court held that while a tort suit properly belongs in circuit court, a chancellor did not err in considering a claim for assault and battery submitted to the court by both parties.[102]

In jurisdictions where fault is relevant in divorce, property division, or alimony, res judicata may bar a subsequent suit for damages.[103] Because fault is a consideration even in irreconcilable differences divorce in Mississippi, [104] a suit delayed until after divorce may be barred. In addition, a standard release-of-claims provision in a settlement agreement may waive the right to pursue tort damages.[105] The Mississippi Court of Appeals dismissed a plaintiff's damages action against her ex-husband for physical abuse. The court held that her personal injury claim was barred by a provision in their divorce settlement agreement that "each party releases the other party from all claims

---

exists in all lawsuits).

[98] Burns v. Burns, 518 So. 2d 1205, 1208-10 (Miss. 1988).

[99] See, e.g., Drumright v. Drumright, 821 So. 2d 1021, 1028 (Miss. Ct. App. 2001) (reversing $25,000 award for inadequate proof of damages).

[100] See, e.g., Curtis v. Firth, 850 P. 2d 749 (Idaho 1993); Feltmeier v. Feltmeier, 798 N.E.2d 75 (Ill. 2003) (public policy does not prohibit allowing spousal suit for IIED); cf. Giovine v. Giovine, 663 A. 2d 109 (N.J. Super Ct. App. Div. 1995) (tort action of domestic violence).

[101] See Nash v. Overholser, 757 P.2d 1180, 1181 (Idaho 1988) (joinder permitted but not required), *rejected on other grounds by* State v. Guzman, 842 P.2d 660 (Idaho 1992); Stuart v. Stuart, 421 N.W. 2d 505, 508 (Wis. 1988) (same). *But see* Simmons v. Simmons, 773 P.2d 602, 604-05 (Colo. Ct. App. 1988) ("sound policy considerations preclude either permissive or compulsory joinder of interspousal tort claims [with divorce actions]"); Aubert v. Aubert, 529 A.2d 909, 911-12 (N.H. 1987) (divorce court without jurisdiction to award personal injury damages); Walther v. Walther, 709 P.2d 387, 388 (Utah 1985) (same). *Contra* Tevis v. Tevis, 400 A.2d 1189, 1196 (N.J. 1979) (must be joined).

[102] Drumright v. Drumright, 821 So. 2d 1021, 1028 (Miss. Ct. App. 2001) (reversing $25,000 award for inadequate proof of damages). *But cf.* Little v. Collier, 759 So. 2d 454, 458 (Miss. Ct. App. 2000) (father's suit against child's mother for intentional infliction of emotional distress for alienating child proper in circuit, not chancery court).

[103] See Smith v. Smith, 530 So. 2d 1389, 1390 (Ala. 1988) (suit barred because payment of medical bills central to negotiated settlement); Kemp v. Kemp, 723 S.W.2d 138, 140 (Tenn. Ct. App. 1986) (suit barred by res judicata; husband ordered to pay medical bills stemming from abuse); Brinkman v. Brinkman, 966 S.W.2d 780, 783 (Tex. Ct. App. 1998) (res judicata barred tort action where wife sought disproportionate share of assets based on violence). *But see* McCoy v. Cook, 419 N.W.2d 44, 46 (Mich. Ct. App. 1988) (property division based in part on fault did not bar suit); *cf.* Nash v. Overholser, 757 P.2d 1180, 1181 (Idaho 1988) (suit for assault and battery not barred by divorce which did not address issue), *rejected on other grounds by* State v. Guzman, 842 P.2d 660 (Idaho 1992); Stuart v. Stuart, 421 N.W.2d 505, 507 (Wis. 1988) (claims not barred by no-fault divorce).

[104] See Driste v. Driste, 738 So. 2d 763, 765 (Miss. Ct. App. 1998).

[105] See Overberg v. Lusby, 727 F. Supp. 1091, 1094 (E.D. Ky 1990) (release of all claims barred tort action for infliction of sexually transmitted disease), *aff'd*, 921 F.2d 90 (6th Cir. 1990); Jackson v. Hall, 460 So. 2d 1290, 1291 (Ala. 1984) (boilerplate provision barred action for assault and battery); Cerniglia v. Cerniglia, 679 So. 2d 1160, 1164 (Fla. 1996) (same). *But cf.* Gaber v. Gaber, 32 P.3d 921, 925 (Or. Ct. App. 2001) (genuine question of fact whether claim barred by agreement to release all claims "arising out of or in any way connected with [the parties'] marriage to each other").

§ 5.07[4]   MISSISSIPPI FAMILY LAW

or demands."[106]

[4] Statute of limitations. The statute of limitations may vary depending on
the cause of action. In Mississippi, the statute of limitations for assault and battery
actions is one year.[107] Earlier decisions of the Mississippi Supreme Court and Court
of Appeals differed on the limitations period for intentional infliction of emotional
distress.[108] The issue was resolved in 2010 when the Mississippi Supreme Court held
that intentional infliction of emotional distress actions are governed by the one-year
statute of limitations.[109] The point at which the statute begins to run can be critical. If
each incidence of violence is considered a separate tort triggering the statutory period,
damages cannot be recovered for injuries outside the brief statute of limitations.[110] If
domestic violence is viewed as a continuing tort, with the statute triggered by the last
action of violence, damages can be recovered for the entire course of conduct.[111] In a
similar context, the Mississippi Court of Appeals held that a father's suit against his son
for intentional infliction of emotional distress was a continuing tort with the statute of
limitations running from the date of the last injury.[112]

§ 5.08 AGREEMENTS BETWEEN SPOUSES

[1] Property settlement agreements. A victim of domestic violence may agree
to divorce or custody and child support on onerous terms in order to secure a spouse's
agreement to irreconcilable differences divorce. An unfair agreement may be set aside
under some circumstances, including duress and overreaching. A petition to set aside
an agreement on these grounds must be filed within six months of judgment.[113] To
prove duress, the petitioner must show that his or her consent to the agreement was
the result of the other spouse's wrongful conduct.[114] For example, a custody agreement
was properly set aside on the basis of duress – a child's father held him for nine days
and threatened to abscond to Mexico unless the mother signed the agreement.[115] The
Mississippi Supreme Court held in 2005 that a party may also set aside a divorce
settlement agreement based on overreaching. Overreaching occurs when one party

---

[106] Martinez v. Martinez, 860 So. 2d 1247, 1250 (Miss. Ct. App. 2003).

[107] MISS. CODE ANN. § 15-1-35 (1994).

[108] *See* Hubbard v. Miss. Conference of the United Methodist Church, 138 F. Supp. 780, 780 (S.D. Miss. 2001)
(noting conflicting decisions of Mississippi Supreme Court and Court of Appeals; following supreme court). *Compare*
Norman v. Bucklew, 684 So. 2d 1246, 1248 (Miss. 1996) (three-year statute of limitations) *with* Air Comfort Sys., Inc. v.
Honeywell, Inc., 760 So. 2d 43, 47 (Miss. Ct. App. 2000) (one-year statute). *See also* MISS. CODE ANN. § 15-1-49 (1994)
(general statute of limitations).

[109] Jones v. Fluor Daniel Servs. Corp., 32 So. 3d 417, 423 (Miss. 2010).

[110] *See* Nash v. Overholser, 757 P.2d 1180, 1180-81 (Idaho 1988) (four of five incidents of violence barred by
statute of limitations on assault).

[111] One court held that the statute of limitations may be tolled upon a showing that the victim suffered from
battered women's syndrome and was unable to bring the action. *See* Giovine v. Giovine, 663 A.2d 109, 115-16 (N.J.
App. Div.1995). One court has held that a suit for intentional infliction of emotional distress for domestic violence is a
continuing tort, with the statute of limitations running from the last occurrence. *See* Curtis v. Firth, 850 P.2d 749, 756
(Idaho 1993).

[112] McCorkle v. McCorkle, 811 So. 2d 258, 264 (Miss. Ct. App. 2001).

[113] *See infra* § 19.08.

[114] LAURA W. MORGAN & BRETT R. TURNER, ATTACKING AND DEFENDING MARITAL AGREEMENTS § 4.05 (2001).

[115] *In re* Filiation of M.D.B., 914 So. 2d 316, 318-19 (Miss. Ct. App. 2005) (en banc).

DOMESTIC VIOLENCE

§ 5.08[2]

takes unfair advantage of another, which may occur through abuse of superior bargaining power. An agreement may be one-sided or unfair without rising to the level of overreaching. The complaining party must show that he or she "had no meaningful choice."[116] Agreements may also be set aside within six months after judgment based on a showing of undue influence. The plaintiff must prove that he or she was so dominated by the other that the agreement was not voluntary.[117]

[2] Conveyances between spouses. A conveyance may be set aside if a court finds that one spouse unduly influenced the other to make the conveyance. A divorcing wife's conveyance of marital assets to her daughter, at her husband's insistence, was properly set aside. The minister husband controlled and abused his wife during their long marriage. When he was convicted of tax fraud and sexual battery and sentenced to sixty years, he instructed his wife to sign a quitclaim deed conveying the marital land, home, and buildings to his daughter. The chancellor found that there was a fiduciary duty between the husband and wife and that she signed the documents under undue influence.[118]

§ 5.09 FALSE ALLEGATIONS OF ABUSE

With every attempt to provide a solution, the law creates a tool for misuse. Parties to divorce or custody actions may make false allegations of domestic violence in order to create divorce grounds, to invoke a presumption against custody, or to gain another advantage in a divorce or other family law matter. False allegations of abuse may subject a party to sanctions, including costs and attorney's fees.[119] In addition, false allegations of abuse may weigh against a parent in a custody action. In a 2010 case, a father was awarded custody, based in part on the fact that the mother took their child to another state and obtained a protection order based on false allegations, preventing the father from contacting her or the child.[120]

---

[116] Lowrey v. Lowrey, 919 So. 2d 1112, 1119-22 (Miss. Ct. App. 2005) (overreaching may be asserted under Miss. R. Civ. P. 60(b) as "other misconduct").

[117] MORGAN & TURNER, *supra*, note 114, § 4.051.

[118] King v. King, 946 So. 2d 395, 402 (Miss. Ct. App. 2006) (wife signed documents immediately after trial and without reading them).

[119] MISS. CODE ANN. §§ 93-5-24(9)(c) (Supp. 2010).

[120] T.K. v. H.K., 24 So. 3d 1055 (Miss. Ct. App. 2010).

VI
PROPERTY DIVISION

In one of the most significant family law developments of the century, common law states abolished the method historically used to divide property between divorcing couples. Under the old common law system, assets were awarded to the spouse who held title. The new system – equitable distribution – disregards title, allowing courts to divide property acquired during marriage as a result of either spouse's efforts.

In 1994, the Mississippi Supreme Court judicially adopted equitable distribution. Over the last sixteen years, the state's appellate courts grappled with the complex issues that accompany the system, generating a substantial body of case law on the classification and division of marital assets. For the most part, Mississippi law mirrors national trends in equitable distribution. In at least two aspects, however, Mississippi has diverged from the national consensus. In most states, a spouse may "trace" and claim separate property that has been commingled with marital property. In Mississippi, once separate property has been mixed with marital property or funds, it is converted to marital. Mississippi cases on valuation of businesses similarly have diverged from the majority, refusing to recognize goodwill in the valuation of businesses for purposes of equitable distribution.

Divisions of property under equitable distribution bear little resemblance to those under the old title system. Adoption of the system has radically altered divorce practice as well, often requiring experts for business and pension valuation, introducing protracted financial discovery, and raising issues of fraudulent transfers and dissipation of assets.

This chapter examines the transition from the title system to equitable distribution and describes the basic system for classifying a couple's assets as separate or marital. The chapter then discusses assets that present unique problems in classification. The chapter concludes with a discussion of the division process. Classification and division of retirement benefits and closely held businesses are discussed in Chapters VII and VIII.

§ 6.01 HISTORY AND OVERVIEW

Until the mid-1900s, two opposing theories of marital property controlled property division at divorce.[1] Community property states divided assets earned during marriage equally, without regard to title. But in common law states, property was simply awarded to the spouse who held title. Today, all common law states have abandoned the title system for equitable distribution, a marital property system modeled on – but distinct from – community property.

---

[1] J. THOMAS OLDHAM, DIVORCE, SEPARATION & THE DISTRIBUTION OF PROPERTY §3.01, at 3-1 to 3-2 & § 3.03[1], at 3-7 (2010). *See generally* Harriet Spiller Daggett, *Division of Property Upon Dissolution of Marriage*, 6 LAW & CONTEMP. PROBS. 225 (1939).

§ 6.01[1]   MISSISSIPPI FAMILY LAW

[1] The title system. The title system viewed marriage as a union of economically separate individuals, with spouses acquiring property for themselves rather than for the marriage.[2] When a couple divorced, each spouse was awarded the property titled in his or her name.[3] Courts had no authority to divest title from an owner. It was not uncommon for most of a family's assets to be titled in the husband's name alone. As a result, women frequently left a marriage with few assets.[4] For example, a wife who worked long hours on a family farm was denied any interest in the farm at divorce because it was titled in her husband's name.[5] To remedy economic imbalance, a court could award alimony to a wife without sufficient assets and income to support herself, but only if she was not at fault in the divorce.[6]

[2] Community property. The community property system views spouses as an economic unit.[7] Income earned by either spouse is marital, as is property acquired with a spouse's earnings. Each owns one-half of all property classified as marital; title is irrelevant.[8] In contrast, property acquired through gift or inheritance, or owned prior to the marriage, is the separate property of the owner.[9] Thus, spouses equally own the products of their efforts during marriage but maintain separate ownership of any other property.

[3] Property division reform. By the middle of the twentieth century, critics attacked the title system as unfair to homemakers. They argued that homemakers' valuable contributions were ignored by a system that awarded all property to wage earners.[10] Furthermore, critics dismissed alimony as an ineffective means of post-divorce support. There was no guarantee of collection. Support was only available if a wife did not "cause" the divorce.[11] There seems to have been fairly wide agreement that the title system worked to a traditional wife and homemaker's disadvantage.[12]

In response to these concerns, some legislatures began to chip away at the title system, passing statutes that allowed divorce courts to award a wife assets to which she had made direct contribution.[13] In other states, courts developed judicial remedies to

---

[2] LESLIE J. HARRIS & LEE TEITELBAUM, FAMILY LAW 8 (1996).

[3] BRETT R. TURNER, EQUITABLE DISTRIBUTION OF PROPERTY § 1.02, at 4 (2d ed. 1994); Harris ET AL., *supra* note 2, at 329.

[4] Bea Ann Smith, *The Partnership Theory of Marriage: A Borrowed Solution Fails*, 68 TEX. L. REV. 689, 697 n.47 (1990).

[5] *See* Hinton v. Hinton, 179 So. 2d 846, 848 (Miss. 1965); *see also* Murdoch v. Murdoch, [1975] 1 S.C.R. 423 (Can.) (holding wife not entitled to share of ranch titled in husband's name even though she worked on ranch, including having primary responsibility during almost half of year), *reprinted in* HARRIS ET AL., *supra* note 2, at 14.

[6] OLDHAM, *supra* note 1, § 3.02[1], at 3-3.

[7] *See* AMERICAN LAW INSTITUTE, PRINCIPLES OF THE LAW OF FAMILY DISSOLUTION: ANALYSIS AND RECOMMENDATIONS § 4.02 cmt., at 646 (2002) [ALI PRINCIPLES] (recognizing past dichotomy between majority of states and eight states following community property principles); William A. Reppy, Jr., *Major Events in the Evolution of American Community Property Law and Their Import to Equitable Distribution States*, 23 FAM. L.Q. 163, 164-65 (1989) (recognizing that nine states follow a community property regime).

[8] TURNER, *supra* note 3, § 1.02, at 5.

[9] *See* Reppy, *supra* note 7, at 165; TURNER, *supra* note 3, § 1.02, at 5.

[10] OLDHAM, *supra* note 1, § 3.02[2][b], at 3-4.

[11] *See* discussion *infra* § 9.01[4][a].

[12] OLDHAM, *supra* note 1, § 3.02[2], at 3-4 to 3-6.

[13] TURNER, *supra* note 3, § 1.02, at 6.

PROPERTY DIVISION   § 6.01[4]

accomplish the same result. By the mid-1960s, a substantial number of states permitted discretionary division of assets between spouses without regard to title.[14] Following the no-fault divorce revolution of the 1970s, the trend toward discretionary property division turned into a wholesale overhaul of marital property law.[15]

[4] Creation of equitable distribution. The common law states ultimately addressed concerns about the title system by developing a third marital property system, a hybrid between title and community property. The new system, equitable distribution, borrowed the marital partnership theory from community property law, but applied it only at divorce. Today, no state uses the title system at divorce.[16]

Equitable distribution classifies all assets acquired through a spouse's labor as marital.[17] Assets acquired before marriage, or through gift or inheritance, remain the owner's separate property.[18] Courts may divide marital assets between divorcing spouses in a fair and equitable manner – equal division is not required.

In contrast to community property, however, equitable distribution applies only if a couple divorces. There is no marital property in an intact marriage – spouses have no interest in assets owned by the other, with the exception of homestead property.[19]

[5] Equitable distribution in Mississippi

[a] Judicial adoption: *Ferguson v. Ferguson.* The transition to equitable distribution in Mississippi fit the national pattern. As in other states, the transition was tentative, initially involving a discretionary remedy rather than a legal right. Over twenty years, a series of decisions by the Mississippi Supreme Court substantially eroded the title system.[20] The transition was complete in 1994, when the Mississippi Supreme Court decided *Ferguson v. Ferguson.*[21]

The Fergusons' circumstances were typical of cases that prompted development of equitable distribution across the country. The couple separated after twenty-four years

---

[14] TURNER, *supra* note 3, § 1.02, at 6.

[15] Brett Turner, one of the leading authorities on equitable distribution, suggests that the rapid change from the title system to equitable distribution was accelerated by the rising divorce rate of the 1960s and changing social expectations about women in the workforce, among other things. See TURNER, *supra* note 3, § 1.02, at 6-10.

[16] The initial catalyst for the rapid changes was the Uniform Marriage and Divorce Act, which proposed two alternative marital property regimes—a community property system and an all property equitable distribution system. UNIF. MARRIAGE & DIVORCE ACT § 307 (amended 1973), 9A U.L.A. 288-89 (1998) (UMDA). The UMDA was not widely adopted, but it sparked a national debate that resulted in the passage of equitable distribution statutes in almost all states. TURNER, *supra* note 3, § 1.02, at 14.

[17] *See* Robert J. Levy, *An Introduction to Divorce-Property Issues*, 23 FAM. L.Q. 147, 148 (1989) (discussing purposes served by defining property for division at divorce). A minority of states follow equitable distribution systems in which courts may divide all property owned by either spouse. Reppy, *supra* note 7, at 166; OLDHAM, *supra* note 1, § 3.03[2], at 3-4 to 3-5. A table listing all property equitable distribution states is set out in Joseph W. McKnight, *Defining Property Subject to Division at Divorce*, 23 FAM. L.Q. 193, 196-97 (1989).

[18] McKnight, *supra* note 17, at 193-94. Professor Levy suggests that separate property exceptions reflect "essentially commonsense extrapolations of fairness notions and beliefs about spouses' expectations." Levy, *supra* note 17, at 152.

[19] *See* discussion of property rights between married persons *supra* § 1.05.

[20] *See generally* Thomas W. Crockett & Walter P. Neeley, *Mississippi's New Equitable Distribution Rules: The Ferguson Guidelines and Valuation*, 15 MISS. C. L. REV. 415, 416-24 (1995) (including good discussion of decisions marking shift from title system to equitable distribution).

[21] 639 So. 2d 921 (Miss. 1994).

§ 6.01[5][b]   MISSISSIPPI FAMILY LAW

of marriage and the birth of two children.[22] She was a homemaker and wage-earner. His salary was almost four times hers. And, with the exception of the marital home and cars, he held title to all the family's assets. The court discussed at length the title system's failure to recognize the contributions of homemakers and the unfairness of property divisions under the title system.[23] The court also acknowledged the gradual erosion of title system principles: "This Court has been in a transitory state regarding the division of marital assets. . . . With this opinion, this Court adopts guidelines for application of the equitable distribution method of division of marital assets."[24]

In most states, equitable distribution was legislatively adopted. The Mississippi court based judicial adoption on chancery courts' statutory authority to "make all orders . . . touching the maintenance and alimony of the wife or the husband, or any allowance to be made to her or him."[25] The court also emphasized that it did not intend to create a community property regime: "[N]o right to property vests by virtue of the marriage relationship alone prior to entry of a judgment or decree granting equitable or other distribution . . . . Thus the rights of alienation and the laws of descent and distribution are not affected by our recognition of marital assets."[26]

[b] The Mississippi system

[i] Steps in equitable distribution. The *Ferguson* decision outlined the steps to be followed in making an equitable distribution of property: Courts are to (1) classify assets as marital or separate; (2) value assets, using expert testimony if necessary; (3) divide marital property equitably, based on factors set out in the decision; and (4) award alimony if needed after division of assets.[27]

[ii] Presumption in favor of marital property. The first step in equitable distribution is classification of all assets as separate or marital. In *Hemsley v. Hemsley*,[28] the companion case to *Ferguson*, the supreme court adopted a presumption that any property acquired during marriage is marital. The burden of proof is on a spouse claiming a separate property interest in a particular asset.[29]

---

[22] Ferguson v. Ferguson, 639 So. 2d 921, 929 (Miss. 1994). The Fergusons also litigated custody of their son, Bubba. Billy sought custody based upon Bubba's expressed desire to live with him. *Id.* There was proof, however, that Billy let Bubba chew tobacco, ride a four-wheeler alone, carry a .357 magnum pistol, and had promised him a truck. The court upheld the chancellor's award of custody to Linda. *Id.* at 932.

[23] Ferguson v. Ferguson, 639 So. 2d 921, 926 (Miss. 1994).

[24] Ferguson v. Ferguson, 639 So. 2d 921, 925 (Miss. 1994).

[25] *See* MISS. CODE ANN. § 93-5-23 (2004).

[26] Ferguson v. Ferguson, 639 So. 2d 921, 928 (Miss. 1994).

[27] Ferguson v. Ferguson, 639 So. 2d 921, 928 (Miss. 1994); *see* Dorsey v. Dorsey, 972 So. 2d 48, 52 (Miss. Ct. App. 2008); Spahn v Spahn, 959 So. 2d 8, 12 (Miss. Ct. App. 2006) (classification is first step in equitable distribution); Striebeck v. Striebeck, 911 So. 2d 628, 632 (Miss. Ct. App. 2005) (en banc) (court classifies, then divides assets; alimony considered only after property division).

[28] Hemsley v. Hemsley, 639 So. 2d 909, 914 (Miss. 1994).

[29] *See* Hemsley v. Hemsley, 639 So. 2d 909, 914 (Miss. 1994); Everett v. Everett, 919 So. 2d 242, 247 (Miss. Ct. App. 2005) (stocks in husband's name classified as marital; husband failed to prove stocks were purchased with separate funds); *cf.* Horn v. Horn, 909 So. 2d 1151, 1165 (Miss. Ct. App. 2005) (presumption places burden of proof on party seeking separate treatment of debt).

PROPERTY DIVISION   **§ 6.01[5][b][iii]**

[iii] **Division factors**. The Mississippi Supreme Court did not adopt a presumption of equal division. Courts have discretion to make a fair division, based on the following factors: (1) substantial contribution to property accumulation, including direct or indirect economic contribution, contribution to marital and family stability, and contribution to the education or training of the wage-earning spouse; (2) spousal use or disposition of assets and distribution by agreement; (3) the market and emotional value of assets; (4) the value of each spouse's separate estate; (5) tax consequences and legal consequences to third parties; (6) the extent to which property division can eliminate the need for alimony; (7) the needs of each spouse; (8) other factors which should be considered in equity. In addition, the court noted that it would require findings of fact by chancellors applying the eight factors governing division.[30]

[iv] **Presumption of equal homemaker contribution.** Although there is no presumption that equal division of assets is required, the Mississippi Supreme Court did adopt a presumption that a homemaker's contributions to accumulation of assets equal those of a wage earner.[31]

§ 6.02 CLASSIFICATION: THE BASIC SYSTEM

Classification of assets as separate or marital is the first step in equitable distribution. All assets are presumed to be marital; a party seeking separate classification must prove that an asset was owned before marriage, was acquired with separate funds, was a gift or inheritance, or was properly excluded by a valid agreement. Even then, a separate asset commingled with marital property or used extensively by the family may become marital. In addition, if the value of separate property has appreciated through a spouse's efforts, the appreciated value will be marital.

[1] **Failure to classify or error in classification.** A chancellor's failure to classify assets is reversible error.[32] Similarly, a court's failure to classify debt alleged to be marital is reversible error.[33] However, if the parties themselves omit an asset from the action, title remains with the owning spouse[34] unless the omission is considered fraudulent.[35] As a general rule, an error in classification requires that the case be reversed and

---

[30] Ferguson v. Ferguson, 639 So. 2d 921, 928-29 (Miss. 1994).

[31] See discussion *infra* § 6.08[1][e].

[32] Smith v. Smith, 856 So. 2d 717, 719 (Miss. Ct. App. 2003); *see* Hopkins v. Hopkins, 703 So. 2d 849, 850 (Miss. 1997) (failure to classify and divide wife's pension); Reddell v. Reddell, 696 So. 2d 287, 288 (Miss. 1997) (court's failure to mention wife's pension, clearly a marital asset); Thompson v. Thompson, 894 So. 2d 603 (Miss. Ct. App. 2004) (failure to classify husband's businesses).

[33] *See* Owens v. Owens, 950 So. 2d 202, 217 (Miss. Ct. App. 2006).

[34] Newman v. Newman, 558 So. 2d 821, 823 (Miss. 1990); McIntosh v. McIntosh, 977 So. 2d 1257, 1270 (Miss. Ct. App. 2008) (refusing to reverse on basis that husband's pension was not listed as asset; contributions were listed in income section of 8.05; wife had obligation to bring asset to trial court's attention); Parker v. Parker, 929 So. 2d 940, 945 (Miss. Ct. App. 2005) (rejecting husband's argument that trial court erred in omitting $100,000 death benefit; benefit was not asserted at trial); *cf.* Phillips v. Phillips, 904 So. 2d 999, 1002 (Miss. 2004) (not error to omit wife's pension from distribution where parties stipulated that husband's pension was only asset for distribution). *But see* White v. White, 868 So. 2d 1054, 1057 (Miss. Ct. App. 2004) (court erred in failing to address husband's National Guard retirement, where one of husband's exhibits mentioned that he had been in the Guard).

[35] See *infra* § 6.10.

133

§ 6.02[2]   MISSISSIPPI FAMILY LAW

remanded for division based on proper classification.[36] In a few cases, however, division has been affirmed in spite of a classification error, because the overall division was considered fair.[37] For example, a court's failure to classify a husband's $30,000 pension was error, but the division was affirmed because his wife received approximately two-thirds of the marital assets.[38]

[2] Marital property defined. In *Hemsley*, the supreme court defined marital property as "[a]ssets acquired or accumulated during the course of a marriage" other than assets "attributable to one of the parties' separate estates prior to the marriage or outside the marriage."[39] *Ferguson* established that gifts and inheritances received during marriage are separate property.[40] Subsequent cases developed the notion of a mixed asset, partly separate and partly marital. For example, if a spouse's labor during marriage increases the value of separate property, that portion of the asset value is marital; the rest remains separate.[41] Similarly, a pension acquired both before and during marriage is a mixed asset, with both separate and marital portions.[42]

These holdings may be summarized in a fairly simple definition: *Marital property is any property acquired or value created by a spouse's efforts during marriage.* Applying the definition requires that a court (1) identify the relevant beginning and ending dates of marriage; (2) determine the date each asset was acquired; and (3) determine whether a particular asset or portion of an asset was the result of a spouse's efforts.

[3] "During the marriage." Courts must identify the date on which an asset was acquired and the beginning and ending dates for accumulation of marital property. The process is not as simple as the definition suggests. An asset is not necessarily "acquired" on the day title passes to the owner. And the actual dates of the marriage may not be the relevant beginning and ending dates. The wedding ceremony usually signals the beginning of marital property accumulation. But the cutoff date may be as early as a temporary support order or as late as the date of divorce.

[a] Beginning date. In most states, marital asset accumulation begins on the date of marriage.[43] In a few states, however, assets acquired during premarital cohabitation are marital property.[44] Some states also classify property bought in contemplation

---

[36] *See* Redd v. Redd, 774 So. 2d 492, 496 (Miss. Ct. App. 2000) (court misclassified horses as husband's separate property); *see also* Kilpatrick v. Kilpatrick, 732 So. 2d 876, 882 (Miss. 1999); Magee v. Magee, 661 So. 2d 1117, 1124 (Miss. 1995); Striebeck v. Striebeck, 911 So. 2d 628, 633 (Miss. Ct. App. 2005) (en banc) (court's error in failing to classify contingent fees as marital required reversal); Pittman v. Pittman, 791 So. 2d 857, 871 (Miss. Ct. App. 2001).

[37] *See* Messer v. Messer, 850 So. 2d 161, 167-70 (Miss. Ct. App. 2003) (involving a failure to classify eight acres as marital due to commingling).

[38] *See* Tillman v. Tillman, 716 So. 2d 1090, 1095 (Miss. 1998).

[39] Hemsley v. Hemsley, 639 So. 2d 909, 915 (Miss. 1994).

[40] *See* Ferguson v. Ferguson, 639 So. 2d 921, 928 (Miss. 1994).

[41] *See* Carrow v. Carrow, 642 So. 2d 901, 906 (Miss. 1994).

[42] *See* Arthur v. Arthur, 691 So. 2d 997, 1003-04 (Miss. 1997).

[43] OLDHAM, *supra* note 1, § 6.07[1], at 6-31; *see, e.g.,* COLO. REV. STAT. § 14-10-113 (2001); MINN. STAT. ANN. § 518.54 (West Supp. 2002); Mo. ANN. STAT. § 452.330 (West Supp. 2002).

[44] *See., e.g., In re* Marriage of Dubnicay, 830 P.2d 608, 610 (Or. Ct. App. 1992); *In re* Marriage of Burton, 758 P.2d 394, 395 (Or. Ct. App. 1988). The ALI Principles provide for marital property classification for assets acquired during a period of cohabitation. ALI PRINCIPLES, *supra* note 7, § 4.03, at 91-92. However, a majority of courts have classified such

134

PROPERTY DIVISION   **§ 6.02[3][b]**

of marriage as marital.[45]

Mississippi follows the general rule that property acquired before marriage is separate. The supreme court overruled a court of appeals decision classifying property acquired during premarital cohabitation as marital.[46] No Mississippi decision was found directly discussing property acquired in contemplation of marriage.[47]

[b] Ending date. Establishing the ending date for marital property accumulation has proven more difficult than identifying the beginning date. Courts and legislatures use no fewer than six different cutoff dates: (1) the date of actual separation;[48] (2) the date of a legal separation agreement or order;[49] (3) the date of filing for divorce;[50] (4) the date of a divorce hearing;[51] (5) the date of divorce;[52] and (6) a date fixed by the court in its discretion.[53]

In Mississippi, an order of separate maintenance or temporary support ends marital property accumulation as a matter of law. The Mississippi Supreme Court held in 1999 that any property acquired after entry of a separate maintenance order is separate property. The order "creates a point of demarcation with respect to the parties and their estates."[54] Accordingly, a husband's deferred compensation plan, acquired after a separate maintenance order, was his separate property.[55] Two years later, the court of appeals extended the rule to temporary support orders. The court held that the portion of a husband's business interest acquired before a temporary support order was marital;

---

property as separate. *See* Crouch v. Crouch, 410 N.E.2d 580, 582 (Ill. App. Ct. 1980); Grishman v. Grishman, 407 A.2d 9, 11-12 (Me. 1979); McIver v. McIver, 374 S.E.2d 144, 149-51 (N.C. Ct. App. 1988).

[45] *See In re* Marriage of Altman, 530 P.2d 1012, 1013 (Colo. App. 1974); *In re* Marriage of Jacks, 558 N.E.2d 106, 108-09 (Ill. App. Ct. 1990); Stallings v. Stallings, 393 N.E.2d 1065, 1067 (Ill. App. Ct. 1979); F.W.H. v. R.J.H., 666 S.W.2d 910, 912 (Mo. Ct. App. 1984); Coney v. Coney, 503 A.2d 912, 917 (N.J. Super. Ct. Ch. Div. 1985). Turner suggests, however, that marital classification in most of these cases would also be the result under the implied gift rule. TURNER, *supra* note 3, § 5.11, at 180-81. For a discussion of implied gift, see *infra* § 6.05[1].

[46] *See* Bunyard v. Bunyard, 828 So. 2d 775, 777 (Miss. 2002) (but holding that property was nonetheless marital based on commingling); *see also* Gregg v. Gregg, 31 So. 3d 1277, 1282-83 (Miss. Ct. App. 2010) (house and business owned by wife prior to marriage was her separate property); Spahn v. Spahn, 959 So. 2d 8, 12 (Miss. Ct. App. 2006) (warehouse owned by husband prior to marriage was separate); Seymour v. Seymour, 960 So. 2d 513, 518 (Miss. Ct. App. 2006) (stock owned by husband before marriage was separate property); Fitzgerald v. Fitzgerald, 914 So. 2d 193, 197 (Miss. Ct. App. 2005) (rental houses owned by husband prior to marriage properly classified as separate).

[47] In *Neville v. Neville,* 734 So. 2d 352, 357 (Miss. Ct. App. 1999) the court held that a husband's family heirloom, given to his wife as an engagement ring, was separate because it was acquired before marriage. Arguably, this decision implicitly rejects the "in contemplation of marriage" exception.

[48] *See* Waggoner v. Waggoner, 531 N.E.2d 1188, 1189 (Ind. Ct. App. 1988); King v. King, 481 A.2d 913, 915 (Pa. Super. Ct. 1984); Price v. Price, 355 S.E.2d 905, 909 (Va. Ct. App. 1987).

[49] *See* COLO. REV. STAT. § 14-10-113(2)(c) (2001); KY. REV. STAT. ANN. § 403.190(2)(c) (LexisNexis 1999).

[50] *See* Schanck v. Schanck, 717 P.2d 1, 3 (Alaska 1986); Ducharme v. Ducharme, 535 N.Y.S.2d 474, 476 (N.Y. App. Div. 1988).

[51] *See* OHIO REV. CODE ANN. § 3105.17.1(A)(2) (Anderson 2000); TENN. CODE ANN. § 36-4-21(b)(1)(A) (2001).

[52] *See In re* Marriage of Brooks, 486 N.E.2d 267, 271 (Ill. App. Ct. 1985); *In re* Marriage of Goforth, 459 N.E.2d 1374, 1381 (Ill. App. Ct. 1984); Taylor v. Taylor, 736 S.W.2d 388, 391 (Mo. 1987).

[53] FLA. STAT. ANN. § 61.075(6) (West 1997).

[54] Godwin v. Godwin, 758 So. 2d 384, 386 (Miss. 1999). *But cf.* Marshall v. Marshall, 979 So. 2d 699 (Miss. Ct. App. 2007) (marital property accumulation continued where seven-year-old divorce filing and temporary support order were dismissed and wife filed new divorce action).

[55] Godwin v. Godwin, 758 So. 2d 384, 386-87 (Miss. 1999); *see* Hensarling v. Hensarling, 824 So. 2d 583, 591 (Miss. 2002) (husband's contributions to savings account after separate maintenance order was entered were his separate property).

§ 6.02[3][b]   MISSISSIPPI FAMILY LAW

the portion earned after the order was separate.[56] The rule applies only to value newly created after a support order, such as earned income or active appreciation; an asset acquired after a support order but with income earned before the order is marital.[57] A temporary support order also marks the end of accumulation of marital debt. A chancellor properly classified $10,000 in credit card debt, incurred after a temporary support order was entered, as the wife's separate property debt.[58]

When an asset appreciates in value after a temporary support order, the court must determine whether the increase was "active" – caused by the efforts of one of the spouses – or "passive" – caused by other forces. Active appreciation will be the separate property of the owning spouse. For example, a husband's contributions to his savings account after a support order were his separate property.[59] Similarly, the post-support-order growth in value of a husband's plastic surgery clinic was his separate property.[60] Passive appreciation will take the classification of the underlying asset. Thus, interest accrued after a support order on the marital portion of a retirement account was marital property.[61] The court of appeals reversed a chancellor's separate property classification of $2 million of post-support order appreciation of a husband's business. The wife presented evidence that the growth was passive, caused by an increase in scrap metal prices. The court of appeals stated that if the increase was passive, it was marital to the extent that the business was marital.[62]

In the absence of a support order, marital property accumulation continues until divorce.[63] The court of appeals reversed separate property designation of a business interest earned before a support order was entered: "Until the formality of the court order on temporary support or separate maintenance, the effect of each spouse's earnings remains the same as if the couple were still physically and even happily residing in the marital home."[64] A husband's attorneys' fees earned during separation were

---

[56] See Pittman v. Pittman, 791 So. 2d 857, 863-64 (Miss. Ct. App. 2001) (stating that both separate maintenance and temporary support orders "are practical recognitions that the spouses are not [sic] longer living together as husband and wife"); see also Fogarty v. Fogarty, 922 So. 2d 836, 839 (Miss. Ct. App. 2006) (assets acquired after entry of temporary support order were nonmarital).

[57] See Godwin v. Godwin, 758 So. 2d 384, 386-87 (Miss. 1999); Pittman v. Pittman, 791 So. 2d 857, 863 (Miss. Ct. App. 2001); see also Wilson v. Wilson, 811 So. 2d 342, 346 (Miss. Ct. App. 2001) (reversing separate property designation of assets acquired by the wife after separation; impossible to tell from record whether items were purchased solely with funds earned after separation).

[58] Hults v. Hults, 11 So. 3d 1273, 1281 (Miss. Ct. App. 2009).

[59] Hensarling v. Hensarling, 824 So. 2d 583, 591-92 (Miss. 2002). See infra § 6.03[4] for a discussion of the active-passive rule.

[60] Wells v. Wells, 35 So. 3d 1250 (Miss. Ct. App 2010).

[61] Hensarling v. Hensarling, 824 So. 2d 583, 591-92 (Miss. 2002).

[62] Fleishhacker v. Fleishhacker, 39 So. 3d 904, 913 (Miss. Ct. App. 2009).

[63] Cases appear to hold that, as a matter of law, property acquired during separation is marital unless a support order has been entered. See Doyle v. Doyle, 55 So. 3d 1097, 1107 (Miss. Ct. App. 2010) (lawnmower purchased during separation was marital); Deal v. Wilson, 922 So. 2d 24, 28 (Miss. Ct. App. 2005) (property acquired by wife during separation properly classified as marital; no evidence that funds used were separate); Goodson v. Goodson, 910 So. 2d 35, 39 (Miss. Ct. App. 2005) (automobile purchased during separation was marital); Stone v. Stone, 824 So. 2d 645, 647-48 (Miss. Ct. App. 2002) (husband's contributions to credit union account after separation were marital property where no order for separate maintenance was entered). However, a few earlier cases suggested that the issue was a question of fact for the chancellor to decide. See Aron v. Aron, 832 So. 2d 1257, 1258-59 (Miss. Ct. App. 2002) (stating that in the absence of a support order, a chancellor has discretion to classify post-separation assets as separate or marital); Graham v. Graham, 767 So. 2d 277, 281 (Miss. Ct. App. 2000) (approving marital classification of post-separation property because parties were still financially interdependent; suggests fact-based test).

[64] Pittman v. Pittman, 791 So. 2d 857, 866 (Miss. Ct. App. 2001); see also Striebeck v. Striebeck, 911 So. 2d 628,

PROPERTY DIVISION

§ 6.02[4]

marital property – no temporary support order had been entered.[65] And a wife's severance package, paid during the couple's separation, was marital in the absence of a temporary support order.[66] However, in dividing the marital assets, a court may award one spouse a greater share based on his or her greater contribution during separation.[67] And in a few cases, courts have accomplished an unequal division by valuing an asset as of the date of separation, effectively awarding post-separation appreciation to the owning spouse.[68]

[4] Date asset is "acquired." Courts must also determine whether a particular asset was acquired within the relevant dates. For purposes of equitable distribution, an asset is acquired as payment is made, rather than when the owner receives title. As a result, in most states, a single asset may be classified as partly separate and partly marital, depending on the source and timing of payments.

[a] Community property: Transfer of title. Under community property rules, an asset is acquired when the owner receives title.[69] This seemingly reasonable rule can produce unfair results: real property purchased two years before marriage but financed over ten years would be classified as separate, even though eight years of mortgage payments were made with marital funds.[70]

[b] Equitable distribution: Creation of equity. In equitable distribution states, an asset purchased over time is viewed as acquired in increments. Acquisition occurs as payment is made and equity created. The result may be a mixed asset, partly marital and partly separate.[71] Mississippi appellate courts follow this approach with regard to pensions and other employment benefits acquired both before and dur-

---

633 (Miss. Ct. App. 2005) (en banc) (contingency fee earned during separation should have been included in marital assets). *But cf.* Sullivan v. Sullivan, 990 So. 2d 783, 786 (Miss. Ct. App. 2008) (court valued marital asset as of date when wife left husband ($206,647) rather than at date of trial ($320,000), treating subsequent growth as husband's separate property).

[65] Striebeck v. Striebeck, 5 So. 3d 450, 452 (Miss. Ct. App. 2008) (awarding wife $75,000 of $360,000 award).

[66] Wheat v. Wheat, 37 So. 3d 632, 639 (Miss. 2010).

[67] *See, e.g.,* Amacker v. Amacker, 33 So. 3d 493, 496 (Miss. Ct. App. 2009) (camp house purchased by husband after separation was marital property, but awarded to husband; wife made little contribution); Striebeck v. Striebeck, 911 So. 2d 628, 632-33 (Miss. Ct. App. 2005) (en banc) (although marital property accumulation continues during separation, court may find that one spouse is entitled to greater share of post-separation marital assets). On the other hand, some courts find that one spouse's childcare during separation substantially contributed to the other's post-separation earnings. *See* Grishman v. Grishman, 407 A.2d 9, 11-12 (Me. 1979); McIver v. McIver, 374 S.E.2d 144 (N.C. Ct. App. 1988); *In re* Marriage of Burton, 758 P.2d 394, 395 (Or. Ct. App. 1988).

[68] *See* Hensarling v. Hensarling, 824 So. 2d 583, 591-92 (Miss. 2002) (but referring in one place in the opinion to the date of separation rather than the date of a separate maintenance order); Cossey v. Cossey, 22 So. 3d 353, 360 (Miss. Ct. App. 2009). See § 6.07[4][a] *infra*.

[69] TURNER, *supra* note 3, § 5.09, at 147. The fact that classification impacts the rights of creditors during the course of the marriage makes it important that assets be easily and permanently identified as separate or marital in community property states. *Id. See also* OLDHAM, *supra* note 1, § 3.03[5], at 3-11 to 3-17.

[70] Community property states deal with the unfairness described by a system of reimbursement to the marital estate. *See* Joan M. Krauskopf, John D. Montgomery & Steven Windsor, *Principles of Property Distribution, in* 3 FAMILY LAW AND PRACTICE, Ch. 37, § 37.04[4], at 3787 (Arnold Rutkin ed. 1985).

[71] *See* Frank G.W. v. Carol M.W., 457 A.2d 715, 717-19 (Del. 1983); Harper v. Harper, 448 A.2d 916, 918 (Md. 1982); *see also* Jackson v. Jackson, 765 S.W.2d 561, 563 (Ark. 1989); Thomas v. Thomas, 377 S.E.2d 666, 669 (Ga. 1989). The ALI Principles adopt a similar pro-rata rule. ALI PRINCIPLES, *supra* note 7, § 4.06, at 132 & 141 cmt. b; *see also* TURNER, *supra* note 3, § 5.10, at 166-67.

§ 6.02[5]   MISSISSIPPI FAMILY LAW

ing marriage. For example, only the portion of a husband's severance package earned during his brief marriage was marital property; the portion earned during his previous twenty-five years of employment was separate.[72] However, other assets purchased over time are often classified as all marital, based on a broad commingling rule.[73]

[5] Through a spouse's efforts. Only assets acquired as a result of one of the spouses' efforts during the marriage are marital. Assets acquired through gift or inheritance are the separate property of the owner.[74] This applies equally to initial acquisition of an asset and to growth of the asset. To the extent that an asset appreciates during the marriage as a result of one or both spouse's efforts, the appreciation is marital.[75]

§ 6.03 SEPARATE PROPERTY

Assets owned before marriage or acquired after the cutoff date for marital property are the separate property of the owner. In addition, gifts and inheritances are classified as separate. Under the exchange rule, when separate property is exchanged for another asset, the newly acquired asset is also separate.[76] However, income from and appreciation of separate property may be marital or separate, depending on the cause of the income or appreciation. And, separate property that has been commingled with marital property or used for family purposes may be converted to marital.[77] Property that would otherwise be marital may be excluded from marital assets by a valid pre- or postnuptial agreement.[78]

[1] Gifts and inheritances. Only assets produced by a spouse's efforts belong to the marital estate. Property acquired by inheritance or gift belongs to the individual owner.[79] A family business, gifted to a husband in the last years of the marriage, was his separate property.[80] The spouse requesting separate property classification has the burden of proving that the asset was a gift or inheritance.[81] Disputes over initial clas-

---

[72] Prescott v. Prescott, 736 So. 2d 409, 412 (Miss. Ct. App. 1999); *see also* Phillips v. Phillips, 904 So. 2d 999 (Miss. 2004) (portion of pension earned during marriage is marital); Mabus v. Mabus, 890 So. 2d 806, 825 (Miss. 2003) (one-third of husband's pension classified as marital, where five of fifteen years he worked for the state were during marriage); Arthur v. Arthur, 691 So. 2d 997, 1003-04 (Miss. 1997) (holding pension acquired in part prior to marriage is only partly marital property); Dye v. Dye, 22 So. 3d 1241, 1245 (Miss. Ct. App. 2009) (error to classify retirement account accumulated partly before marriage as all marital).

[73] *See* discussion of commingling *infra* § 6.05[3].

[74] Ferguson v. Ferguson, 639 So. 2d 921, 927 (Miss. 1994).

[75] *See infra* § 6.03[4].

[76] *See infra* § 6.04[3].

[77] *See infra* § 6.05.

[78] *See* Chapter XXIII *infra*.

[79] Ferguson v. Ferguson, 639 So. 2d 921, 928 (Miss. 1994); Gregg v. Gregg, 31 So. 3d 1277, 1282-83 (Miss. Ct. App. 2010) (wife's $300,000 inheritance was separate property); Dorsey v. Dorsey, 972 So. 2d 48, 58 (Miss. Ct. App. 2008) (inter vivos gifts are separate property); Parker v. Parker, 929 So. 2d 940, 944 (Miss. Ct. App. 2005) (inheritance not a marital asset); Everett v. Everett, 919 So. 2d 242, 248 (Miss. Ct. App. 2005) (wife's inheritance classified as separate); *cf.* Shoffner v. Shoffner, 909 So. 2d 1245, 1250-51 (Miss. Ct. App. 2005) (husband's anticipated inheritance of father's construction business properly disregarded in equitable distribution).

[80] McKissack v. McKissack, 45 So. 3d 716, 718-22 (Miss. Ct. App. 2010).

[81] Everett v. Everett, 919 So. 2d 242, 247 (Miss. Ct. App. 2005) (stocks in husband's name classified as marital;

PROPERTY DIVISION   **§ 6.03[1][a]**

sification of gifts often focus on whether a gift was intended for one or both spouses.

    [a] Joint gifts. Whether a gift was made to one or both spouses is determined by the donor's intent.[82] To ascertain intent, courts look to the donor's statements,[83] whether the gift was delivered jointly,[84] whether the gift was jointly titled,[85] the couple's tax treatment of the gift,[86] their statements regarding the gift,[87] and the relationship between the donor and the spouses.[88] Because of the presumption in favor of marital property, a spouse seeking separate classification bears the burden of proof. For example, a wife's parents' contribution to the couple's home was a gift to the marriage, absent clear proof otherwise.[89] A gift made jointly to both spouses is generally considered marital property rather than a gift of a separate one-half interest to each.[90]

    [b] Interspousal gifts. Treatment of interspousal gifts varies from state to state. In the absence of a controlling statute, classification is usually determined by the donor's intent.[91] The Mississippi Supreme Court has indicated that the nature of the

---

husband failed to prove stocks purchased with separate funds).

    [82] TURNER, *supra* note 3, § 5.17, at 204.

    [83] *See In re* Marriage of Eklund, 768 P.2d 340, 342 (Mont. 1989) (admitting evidence of donors' statements regarding their intent to make gift solely to husband even though letters were addressed to both spouses); Stainback v. Stainback, 396 S.E.2d 686, 689-90 (Va. Ct. App. 1990) (holding that donor's testimony sufficiently proved intent to make gift to donee alone).

    [84] *See* Vogel v. Vogel, 549 N.Y.S.2d 438, 440 (N.Y. App. Div. 1989) (gifts delivered to husband individually instead of to spouses jointly).

    [85] *See* O'Neal v. O'Neal, 703 S.W.2d 535, 538 (Mo. Ct. App. 1985) (requiring clear and convincing evidence to prove conveyance by deed intended for one spouse only); Niles v. Niles, 550 N.Y.S.2d 208, 209 (N.Y. App. Div. 1990) (conveyance to spouses as joint tenants was marital property); Osguthorpe v. Osguthorpe, 804 P.2d 530, 535-36 (Utah Ct. App. 1990) (checks made payable jointly to both spouses constituted marital property).

    [86] *See* Portuondo v. Portuondo, 570 So. 2d 1338, 1340 (Fla. Dist. Ct. App. 1990) (analyzing tax treatment of gifts to determine if gift was made to one spouse or to both); Dotsko v. Dotsko, 583 A.2d 395, 400 (N.J. Super. Ct. App. Div. 1990) (analyzing tax consequences of gift to conclude donor did not intend to make gift to both spouses).

    [87] *See* Nolden v. Nolden, 448 N.W.2d 892, 893-94 (Minn. Ct. App. 1989) ($10,000 gift was nonmarital property based on recipient spouse's testimony that gift was given expressly to her); Maher v. Maher, 533 N.Y.S.2d 961, 961-62 (N.Y. App. Div. 1988) ($14,000 gift was nonmarital based on testimony of plaintiff's sister that their father intended gift only to plaintiff).

    [88] Gifts to a spouse from a parent or relative are more likely to be treated as separate. *See In re* Marriage of Martens, 406 N.W.2d 819, 822 (Iowa Ct. App. 1987) (relationship between donor and donee should be considered when determining if gift is marital or separate property); *see also* Angel v. Angel, 562 S.W.2d 661, 664 (Ky. Ct. App. 1978) (wife's receipt of her father's property properly classified as nonmarital property). In the case of family heirlooms, it is even more likely that a gift will be treated as the separate property of the related spouse. *See* Elliott v. Elliott, 621 S.W.2d 305, 307-08 (Mo. Ct. App. 1981) (holding that family heirlooms and antiques acquired by wife from her parents were nonmarital property). In one case, the Mississippi Supreme Court held that payments by a husband's father and employer were income, not gifts. *See* Hankins v. Hankins, 729 So. 2d 1283, 1287 (Miss. 1999) (citing *Hemsley* presumption in favor of marital property).

    [89] Watson v. Watson, 882 So. 2d 95, 105-06 (Miss. 2004); *see also* Henderson v. Henderson, 757 So. 2d 285, 290-91 (Miss. 2000) (finding that investment accounts given to the wife individually were her separate property); Ferguson v. Ferguson, 639 So. 2d 921, 928 (Miss. 1994) (gifts to "an individual spouse" are separate, implying that joint gifts are marital).

    [90] *See In re* Marriage of Vrban, 359 N.W.2d 420, 428 (Iowa 1984); Calloway v. Calloway, 832 S.W.2d 890, 892-93 (Ky. Ct. App. 1992) (gift given to and enjoyed by both spouses jointly was marital property); Forsythe v. Forsythe, 558 S.W.2d 675, 679 (Mo. Ct. App. 1977) (gift acquired by spouses jointly was subject to division as marital property); Ackley v. Ackley, 472 N.Y.S.2d 804, 806 (N.Y. App. Div. 1984) (gift of property to both spouses is marital property). Viewing a joint gift as two separate gifts of a one-half interest would require equal division. Classifying a joint gift as marital allows equitable division.

    [91] *See* OLDHAM, *supra* note 1, § 6.02[3], at 6-11 to 6-12.

139

§ 6.03[2]   **MISSISSIPPI FAMILY LAW**

gift is a critical factor in determining intent. The court suggested that highly personal gifts are more likely to be separate, while impersonal gifts such as stocks and bonds are more likely to be marital.[92] For example, a husband's gift to his wife of a diamond ring and a belly button ring were her separate property, given the intimate nature of the gift.[93] The court of appeals held that a husband's transfer of separate property mineral interests to his wife, in her name alone, was her separate property, based in part on the husband's testimony that he intended for it to be hers.[94]

[2] Property acquired prior to marriage or after the cut-off date. Property owned by a spouse prior to marriage or acquired after the cut-off date for accumulation of marital assets is the separate property of the owner.[95]

[3] Property excluded by agreement. Parties may provide by premarital agreement for separate treatment of assets that would otherwise be classified as marital.[96] In addition, a postmarital agreement or division of assets may result in separate classification.[97]

[4] Income and appreciation from separate property. Separate property may produce income or appreciate in value during marriage. Classification depends on the reason for the appreciation or income production.

[a] The active-passive test. Most courts classify the appreciated value of a separate asset by examining the reason for appreciation. If the increase resulted from a spouse's efforts, the appreciation is "active" or marital. Appreciation resulting from other causes – "passive" appreciation – remains separate.[98] The Mississippi Supreme Court adopted the active-passive test in the first year of equitable distribution; the appreciated value of a husband's Corvette collection was marital because the couple's renovation and repair work caused the increased value.[99] Mississippi also uses the active-passive test to classify income from separate property. For example, income produced by a husband's separate investments remained separate; no active effort was involved in their growth.[100] Similarly, the $170,000 growth during marriage in a

---

[92] Ferguson v. Ferguson, 639 So. 2d 921, 929 (Miss. 1994); *see also* Brown v. Brown, 797 So. 2d. 253, 256 (Miss. Ct. App. 2001).

[93] Oswalt v. Oswalt, 981 So. 2d 993 (Miss. Ct. App. 2007).

[94] Larue v. Larue, 969 So. 2d 99, 105 (Miss. Ct. App. 2007) (but gift was commingled and therefore marital when he transferred mineral interests to his wife and children, had the children reconvey their interests to him, and then conveyed a portion of that interest to his wife).

[95] *See* discussion *supra* § 6.02[3].

[96] *See* discussion *infra* § 23.02.

[97] *See* discussion *infra* § 23.02.

[98] TURNER, *supra* note 3, § 5.22, at 233 n.462.

[99] Carrow v. Carrow, 642 So. 2d 901, 906 (Miss. 1994) (much of collection's $400,000 value resulted from work on the cars; wife sanded and fiberglassed cars as well as performing domestic chores to free husband's time to work on cars); *see also* Craft v. Craft, 825 So. 2d 605, 608-09 (Miss. 2002) (applying active-passive test); A & L, Inc. v. Grantham, 747 So. 2d 832, 839-40 (Miss. 1999) (same); Spahn v. Spahn, 959 So. 2d 8, 13 (Miss. Ct. App. 2006) (husband's premarital construction business properly classified as marital; wife assisted in the company and contributed to growth).

[100] Franks v. Franks, 759 So. 2d 1164, 1166-68 (Miss. 1999) (couple lived on her $23,000 salary and his $12,000 salary during the marriage, while the husband reinvested income from gifts from his parents to build a separate estate of

PROPERTY DIVISION §6.03[4][b]

husband's retirement account was separate; the account was fully funded prior to the marriage.[101]

In a few states appreciation is classified as marital only if the non-owning spouse's efforts caused the increase in value.[102] The majority of states, however, classify appreciation and income as marital if either spouse caused the increase. Early Mississippi cases on the issue vacillated between the two approaches.[103] In subsequent cases, the appellate courts endorsed the majority approach, stating that any appreciation attributable to an owner's efforts is a marital asset.[104] De minimus efforts do not require marital classification. A wife's management of family finances, including her husband's investments, did not require marital classification of the appreciated value of his investments.[105]

[b] Burden of proof. Usually, the spouse seeking separate classification of an asset has the burden of proof. With regard to separate property appreciation, however, most courts require the non-owning spouse to prove that marital contributions were made to the asset and that it increased in value. The burden then shifts to the owning

---

over a million dollars; resulting estate was separate); *see also* Haney v. Haney, 788 So. 2d 862, 865-66 (Miss. Ct. App. 2001) (appreciation on husband's investment accounts during marriage deemed separate). *But cf.* Gregg v. Gregg, 31 So. 3d 1277, 1281 (Miss. Ct. App. 2010) (growth of husband's retirement account during marriage classified as marital, even though all but one year of contributions made prior to marriage).

[101] Wheat v. Wheat, 37 So. 3d 632, 639 (Miss. 2010).

[102] OLDHAM, *supra* note 1, § 6.04[2], at 6-19 & § 6.04[3], at 6-22; *see* S.C. CODE ANN. § 20-3-630 (Supp. 2010) (appreciation is marital property only when increase was due to efforts of non-owning spouse); *see also* Lowdermilk v. Lowdermilk, 825 P.2d 874, 878 (Alaska 1992) ("time and energy . . . caring for the couple's child and keeping the family home . . . made some direct contribution" to separate property car business); Nell v. Nell, 560 N.Y.S.2d 426, 426 (N.Y. App. Div. 1990) (work and creative talents contribute to appreciation of value of husband's separate condo).

In a very small number of states, both spouses must actively contribute. OLDHAM, *supra* note 1, § 6.04[3], at 6-22 n.15; *see* Loyacono v. Loyacono, 618 So. 2d 896, 897 (La. Ct. App. 1993) (uncompensated "common labor or industry" of spouses counts as spousal efforts; house repairs); MacDonald v. MacDonald, 559 A.2d 780, 781 (Me. 1989) (growth in car dealership was "attributable to marital efforts"); Ford v. Ford, 766 P.2d 950, 952 (Okla. 1988) (efforts need not be in form of monetary contribution or actual physical labor; rather, raising children counts as spousal effort in distribution of closely held corporation).

[103] See Carrow v. Carrow, 642 So. 2d 901, 907 (Miss. 1994) (requiring efforts of non-titled spouse); Waring v. Waring, 722 So. 2d 723 (Miss. Ct. App. 1998) (efforts of either spouse).

[104] *See* Craft v. Craft, 825 So. 2d 605, 609 (Miss. 2002) (appreciation during marriage as result of husband's efforts deemed marital property); A & L, Inc. v. Grantham, 747 So. 2d 832, 839 (Miss. 1999) (same, but also based on piercing the corporate veil principles); Hankins v. Hankins, 866 So. 2d 508, 511 (Miss. Ct. App. 2004) (increase in chicken farm value deemed marital); *see also* Pearson v. Pearson, 761 So. 2d 157, 165 (Miss. 2000) (distinguishing *Grantham* as involving active appreciation by husband owner's efforts). *But cf.* Smith v. Smith, 994 So. 2d 882, 886 (Miss. Ct. App. 2008) (awarding wife $5,000 for improvements to husband's separate property, without determining whether her efforts contributed to appreciation); Elam v. Hinson, 932 So. 2d 76, 80 (Miss. Ct. App. 2006) (wife's contribution to growth of husband's inherited family business was minimal; not entitled to lump sum alimony representing share of business).

[105] Mabus v. Mabus, 890 So. 2d 806, 825-27 (Miss. 2003); *see also* Hankins v. Hankins, 729 So. 2d 1283, 1286-87 (Miss. 1999) (rejecting husband's argument that wife's separate real estate was converted to marital property because he had planted some trees on the property); Gregg v. Gregg, 31 So. 3d 1277, 1281 (Miss. Ct. App. 2010) (husband's maintenance of wife's separate property house and business was not significant enough to convert them to marital); Dorsey v. Dorsey, 972 So. 2d 48, 51 (Miss. Ct. App. 2008) (wife's uncompensated bookkeeping did not convert business to marital property); Ory v. Ory, 936 So. 2d 405, 411 (Miss. Ct. App. 2006) (en banc) (wife's separate property land not converted because husband planted seedlings and hauled dirt onto land; no evidence that the value increased during marriage); Elam v. Hinson, 932 So. 2d 76, 80 (Miss. Ct. App. 2006) (wife's contribution to growth of husband's inherited family business was minimal; not entitled to lump sum alimony representing share of business). *But cf.* Faerber v. Faerber, 13 So. 3d 853, 859 (Miss. Ct. App. 2009) (chancellor should have considered wife's homemaker contributions to growth of husband's business).

§ 6.03[4][c]   MISSISSIPPI FAMILY LAW

spouse to prove that the appreciation was caused by other forces.[106] Mississippi appears to follow the rule that the separate property owner bears the burden of proving that appreciation was passive. The Mississippi Supreme Court held that a husband business owner had the burden of proving the value of his business at the time of the marriage and of proving the cause of the increase in value during the marriage.[107] Furthermore, a recent case appears to hold that the owning spouse has the burden of proving the value of the business at the time of marriage in order to have the premarital portion of the asset classified as separate.[108]

[c] Proving causation. Upon finding that a spouse's efforts contributed to appreciation, courts often classify the entire appreciated value as marital.[109] In some cases, however, marital efforts may cause only a portion of the increase – part may be attributable to market forces or the efforts of other key personnel. In a 2009 case, the court of appeals recognized that a business's appreciation may be passive even though a spouse is actively involved in the business. A husband's separate property business appreciated by $2 million after a temporary support order was entered. The court of appeals remanded the case for the chancellor to determine whether the appreciation was caused by the husband's efforts or by the market for scrap metal. Because a support order had been entered, any active appreciation after that date would be separate, while any passive appreciation would take the classification of the business, which was primarily marital.[110] Significantly, the decision may allow owners to argue that appreciation during marriage should be classified as passive, notwithstanding their active efforts.[111]

Breaking down active and passive portions of appreciation for a single asset is a difficult task and in many cases, may not warrant the expense of expert proof. Community property states have developed two formulas for apportioning appreciation between passive and active forces in the absence of expert proof of the actual causes of appreciation. The *Van Camp* formula provides that a marital estate should be com-

---

[106] TURNER, *supra* note 3, § 5.22, at 236. *See* Seymour v. Seymour, 960 So. 2d 513, 518-19 (Miss. Ct. App. 2006) (stock owned by husband before marriage was separate property; no proof of increase in value); *cf.* Bowen v. Bowen, 982 So. 2d 385, 395 (Miss. 2008) (premarital investment account treated as partly marital without proof of exact amount of contribution during marriage; older parties both had failing memories; neither presented proof of value at time of marriage of ten years).

[107] A & L, Inc. v. Grantham, 747 So. 2d 832, 839 (Miss. 1999); *see also* Flechas v. Flechas, 791 So. 2d 295, 303 (Miss. 2001) (burden on husband to prove marital portion of premarital pension); Stewart v. Stewart, 2 So. 3d 770, 775 (Miss. Ct. App. 2009) (husband's premarital business properly classified as all marital; burden was on him to prove no appreciated value); *cf.* Parker v. Parker, 980 So. 2d 323, 327 (Miss. Ct. App. 2008) (three acres of separate property adjoining marital estate of eighty-five acres assumed to be used by wife; burden on husband to prove no family use or commingling). *But see* Waring v. Waring, 747 So. 2d 252 (Miss. 1999) (burden on non-owning spouse).

[108] Stewart v. Stewart, 2 So. 3d 770, 774-75 (Miss. Ct. App. 2009).

[109] *See, e.g.,* Craft v. Craft, 825 So. 2d 605, 608-09 (Miss. 2002); A & L, Inc. v. Grantham, 747 So. 2d 832, 839 (Miss. 1999); Hankins v. Hankins, 866 So. 2d 508, 511 (Miss. Ct. App. 2004).

[110] Fleishhacker v. Fleishhacker, 39 So. 3d 904, 913 (Miss. Ct. App. 2009). A reading of Mississippi cases prior to *Fleishhacker* suggests that a finding of active efforts results in classification of all appreciation as marital. However, no case was found in which it appeared that a party presented expert proof to identify passive and active portions of appreciation.

[111] The court of appeals held that the appreciation during marriage and before the support order was active and therefore marital. However, it did not appear that any evidence was presented that appreciation before the support order was caused by passive forces. Fleishhacker v. Fleishhacker, 39 So. 3d 904, 913 (Miss. Ct. App. 2009).

PROPERTY DIVISION   § 6.04

pensated for the reasonable value of a spouse's efforts to improve separate property. If the appreciated value exceeds reasonable compensation, the excess belongs to the separate property owner.[112] If the contributing spouse was compensated at a reasonable rate during marriage, the entire appreciated value is separate.[113] In contrast, the *Pereira* formula assumes that a separate property owner is entitled to a reasonable rate of return on the asset. If the appreciated value exceeds a reasonable return, the excess is marital property.[114] The *ALI Principles of the Law of Family Dissolution* suggest measuring separate and marital portions of appreciation with a formula similar to *Pereira*.[115]

§ 6.04 EXCHANGES OF PROPERTY

An asset acquired in exchange for separate property is separate. However, because all property is presumed to be marital, a separate property owner must trace an asset to its separate property source. Tracing can be a one-step process or extremely complicated. In Mississippi, owners are permitted to trace some, but not all, assets to separate funds.

[1] The exchange rule. Property acquired by a spouse retains the classification of the property for which it was exchanged.[116] The exchange rule applies to purchases, direct trades, a rollover of accounts – any transaction in which an owner relinquishes funds or property in return for other property.[117] The Mississippi Supreme Court recognized the exchange rule in the first year of equitable distribution, holding that automobiles purchased with a husband's inheritance were separate property.[118] Similarly, insurance proceeds from a husband's separate property retained their separate character when used to build a house.[119] Funds received from a separate property stock repurchase, then loaned to a third party, repaid, and put into certificates of deposit,

---

[112] *See* Van Camp v. Van Camp, 199 P. 885, 888-89 (Cal. 1921). The *Van Camp* and *Pereira* formulas are discussed in detail in TURNER, *supra* note 3, § 5.22, at 246.

[113] A few equitable distribution states seem to follow this approach. *See* McNaughton v. McNaughton, 538 A.2d 1193, 1197 (Md. Ct. Spec. App. 1988) (husband "always received a fair and reasonable salary, full benefits and profit sharing as compensation for his work for these corporations"); Hoffman v. Hoffman, 676 S.W.2d 817, 825-26 (Mo. 1984) (finding husband was compensated for efforts; wife "failed by any proof to establish the value of the husband's services to the corporation or that he had indeed sacrificed payment of marital funds, by way of salary or dividends, in order to increase the value of the corporation's stock").

[114] Pereira v. Pereira, 103 P. 488, 491 (Cal. 1909); *see In re* Marriage of Folb, 126 Cal. Rptr. 306, 312-14 (Cal. Ct. App. 1975) (applying 12% rate of return to commercial real estate investments; 7% to cash), *overruled on other grounds by In re* Marriage of Fonstein, 552 P.2d 1169, 1175 n.5 (Cal. 1976); Gillespie v. Gillespie, 506 P. 2d 775 (N. Mex. 1973) (applying a rate of return based upon the prime rate prevailing during the marriage plus two percentage points; the rate of interest that would have been charged for a loan).

[115] The American Law Institute Principles suggest that a spouse who devotes substantial time to manage separate property is entitled to a sum equal to a return on similar capital "if invested in assets of relative safety requiring little management." Any excess over this amount is marital. ALI PRINCIPLES, *supra* note 7, § 4.04, at 112.

[116] *See* J. Thomas Oldham, *Tracing, Commingling, and Transmutation,* 23 FAM. L. Q. 219, 220 (1989) (item purchased with separate property remains separate).

[117] TURNER, *supra* note 3 § 5.23, at 257-58 (property must be of "roughly equivalent" value).

[118] Carrow v. Carrow, 642 So. 2d 901, 907 (Miss. 1994).

[119] Brooks v. Brooks, 757 So. 2d 301, 304 (Miss. Ct. App. 1999); *see also* Delk v. Delk, 41 So. 3d 738, 741-42 (Miss. Ct. App. 2010) (insurance proceeds replaced condominium destroyed in Katrina); Lewis v. Lewis, 54 So. 3d 233, 241-42 (Miss. Ct. App. 2009) (lot acquired in exchange for husband's separate property should not have been classified as marital), *rev'd in part on other grounds,* 54 So. 3d 216 (Miss. 2011).

143

§ 6.04[2]   **MISSISSIPPI FAMILY LAW**

remained the husband's separate property.[120] And two promissory notes from the sale of a husband's business were properly classified as marital.[121]

[2] Burden of proof. Any asset owned by a spouse is presumed to be marital.[122] To overcome this presumption, an owner requesting separate property classification has the burden of tracing the asset to a separate property source.[123]

[3] Assets purchased with both separate and marital funds. Tracing is relatively simple when separate property is the only consideration for newly acquired property. The process becomes more difficult when an asset is purchased with both separate and marital funds. In most states, if the separate contribution is properly traced, the newly acquired property will be a mixed asset, partly marital and partly separate.[124] If the contribution cannot be traced, the asset is classified as marital.

Without specifically referring to "tracing," the Mississippi appellate courts apply the exchange rule to some mixed assets. The court has consistently classified pensions acquired before and during marriage as a mixed asset.[125] Businesses have also been treated as mixed assets, with spouses allowed to identify separate and marital portions of the business.[126] With respect to marital homes, real property, and accounts, however, the courts have usually held that commingling converts the entire value to marital property.[127] Some cases disregard the strict commingling rule. A chancellor properly classified the value of a marital home at the time of the marriage as separate and the remaining value as marital, since the couple made payments on the home during the marriage from a joint account.[128]

[4] Tracing in accounts. Most courts permit a spouse to identify separate funds commingled in an account with marital funds, using various presumptions to trace the funds. Clear evidence of intent to the contrary may alter the presumptions.[129]

---

[120] McKissack v. McKissack, 45 So. 3d 716, 718-23 (Miss. Ct. App. 2010).

[121] Parker v. Parker, 929 So. 2d 940, 944 (Miss. Ct. App. 2005); *see also* Oswalt v. Oswalt, 981 So. 2d 993 (Miss. Ct. App. 2007) (jeep owned by husband's business but purchased with marital funds was marital asset).

[122] Yancey v. Yancey, 752 So. 2d 1006, 1011-12 (Miss. 1999).

[123] Oldham, *Tracing, supra* note 116, at 221-22; *see* Parker v. Parker, 929 So. 2d 940, 944-45 (Miss. Ct. App. 2005) (investment account containing marital funds commingled with inheritance classified as marital; no evidence to distinguish separate and marital funds).

[124] *See* BRETT R. TURNER, EQUITABLE DISTRIBUTION OF PROPERTY § 5.59, at 609, § 5.60, at 615 (3d ed. 2005).

[125] *See, e.g.,* Arthur v. Arthur, 691 So. 2d 997, 1003 (Miss. 1997) (wife entitled to equitable distribution of pension earned during marriage, but not to value of pension at time of marriage); Dye v. Dye, 22 So. 3d 1241, 1244-45 (Miss. Ct. App. 2009) (error to classify retirement account accumulated partly before marriage as all marital); Barnett v. Barnett, 908 So. 2d 833, 839 (Miss. Ct. App. 2005) (chancellor properly classified an IRA owned by the husband before marriage as partly marital and partly separate); Prescott v. Prescott, 736 So. 2d 409, 412 (Miss. Ct. App. 1999) (reversing trial court's designation of pension as all marital property, where husband worked for company thirty-two years prior to seven-year marriage).

[126] *See* A & L, Inc. v. Grantham, 747 So. 2d 832, 839 (Miss. 1999) (premarital value separate; appreciation during marriage is deemed marital); Hankins v. Hankins, 866 So. 2d 508, 511 (Miss. Ct. App. 2004) (same).

[127] *See* discussion *infra* § 6.06[10]. Even without the broad commingling rule, a separately owned marital home would be converted to marital under the family-use doctrine. *Id.*

[128] Oswalt v. Oswalt, 981 So. 2d 993 (Miss. Ct. App. 2007); *see also* Brock v. Brock, 906 So. 2d 879, 887-88 (Miss. Ct. App. 2005) (recognizing tracing rule in connection with marital home).

[129] *See* OLDHAM, *supra* note 1, § 11.032[2], at 11-30; Becker v. Becker, 639 So. 2d 1082, 1084 (Fla. Dist. Ct. App. 1994) (commingling funds in money market account converted to marital with the exception of separate rental funds;

PROPERTY DIVISION

§ 6.04[4][a]

Some courts presume that a withdrawal for family purposes uses marital funds and a withdrawal for separate property purposes uses separate funds.[130] If all withdrawals can be identified as separate or marital using this method, the remaining balance can be classified by subtracting separate withdrawals from separate deposits, and marital withdrawals from marital deposits.[131]

[a] **Total recapitulation method.** If all withdrawals are not clearly identifiable as described above, some courts apply the "total recapitulation" approach. This approach also presumes that marital funds are used for marital expenses. Using this method, the court totals marital withdrawals and deposits for the duration of the account. If total marital withdrawals exceed deposits, any remaining funds are the separate property of the owning spouse.[132] Similarly, any assets purchased from the account are separate, since all marital funds were expended on marital expenses.[133]

[b] **Clearinghouse method.** The clearinghouse approach allows separate classification of assets purchased through a one-time deposit and withdrawal of separate funds.[134] For example, an Illinois court held that a wife's lump sum pension, deposited

---

husband and wife agreed funds were deposited and then used to make mortgage payments on the rental property); *In re* Higgins, 507 N.W.2d 725, 727 (Iowa Ct. App. 1993) (husband's inherited funds deposited in the wife's credit union account were separate despite commingling; purpose was to earn interest on the funds, and there was no evidence of intent to make a gift to the marital estate); Wadlow v. Wadlow, 491 A.2d 757, 762 (N.J. Super. Ct. App. Div. 1985) (commingled funds remained separate when both parties admitted they were "not intended as a gift").

[130] *See* TURNER, *supra* note 3, § 5.23, at 271.

[131] OLDHAM, *supra* note 1, § 11.03[1][a], at 11-24, 11-25.

[132] OLDHAM, *supra* note 1, § 11.03[1][c], at 11-27 to 11-29.

[133] *See* Houska v. Houska, 512 P.2d 1317, 1319 (Idaho 1973) (approving total recapitulation method of tracing separate and community funds); Weilmunster v. Weilmunster, 858 P.2d 766, 776 (Idaho Ct. App. 1993) (total recapitulation to show that marital expenses exceeded marital deposits, therefore other purchases were separate; no need to show that marital funds exhausted at exact moment of purchase); Zemke v. Zemke, 860 P.2d 756, 762-64 (N. Mex. Ct. App. 1993) (marital deposit of $721,000 and marital expenses of $748,000; asset purchases from account from separate funds; also relying on husband's testimony of intent to keep separate); *see also* Porter v. Porter, 195 P.2d 132, 134 (Ariz. 1948) (husband's salary and separate funds commingled, but community expenses greatly exceeded community income).

The California and Nevada courts have refused to apply this method, requiring instead that the spouse seeking separate property classification show that, at the time of the purchase, all community funds were expended. *See* See v. See, 415 P.2d 776, 779-80 (Cal. 1966) (if community and separate funds in account, asset is partly separate and partly marital); Malmquist v. Malmquist, 792 P.2d 372, 381 (Nev. 1990) (stating in passing that separate but commingled funds may be traced by "proof that *at the time of the purchase* all community income was exhausted by family expenses" (emphasis added)). However, the California court's reason for rejecting total recapitulation relates to aspects of community property not applicable to equitable distribution.

In Texas, Missouri, and Virginia, courts have approved direct tracing, but the cases do not necessarily indicate that total recapitulation would be rejected. *See* Friedman v. Friedman, 965 S.W.2d 319, 328 (Mo. Ct. App. 1998) (funds considered separate where the husband's expert directly traced the amount of separate funds in the account at each purchase); Harris v. Ventura, 582 S.W.2d 853, 855 (Tex. Civ. App. 1979) (separate funds were adequately directly traced; no discussion of whether this was the only means of tracing); Welder v. Welder, 794 S.W.2d 420, 428 (Tex. Ct. App. 1990) (court approved a detailed, item by item analysis of bank accounts to show that purchases were made with separate funds); Hurt v. Hurt, 433 S.E.2d 493, 498 (Va. Ct. App. 1993) (husband maintained system of ledgers that accounted for family and business expenses separately).

[134] *See* Frerichs v. Frerichs, 704 S.W.2d 258, 261-62 (Mo. Ct. App. 1986) (horses purchased with funds from commingled account were separate, when husband paid $10,000 from account to purchase horses, and deposited $10,000 of separate funds the following day); *see also* Brehm v. Brehm, 762 So. 2d 1259 (La. Ct. App. 2000) (separate funds deposited close in time to purchase of asset); Hunt v. Hunt, 952 S.W.2d 564, 567 (Tex. Ct. App. 1997) (commingled insurance funds used to purchase motor home); Holden v. Holden, 520 S.E.2d 842, 843 (Va. Ct. App. 1999) (husband deposited funds from sale of comic book collection into joint account several months prior to purchase of house).

§ 6.04[4][c]   MISSISSIPPI FAMILY LAW

in a joint account and withdrawn three months later, remained separate. The close proximity of time, the equivalence of the amount, and the owner's statement of intention showed that the account was being used as a clearinghouse for a particular purpose.[135]

[c] De minimus rule. If tracing is not possible, the entire account is usually classified as marital.[136] However, some courts apply a de minimus rule, refusing to convert separate property commingled with a relatively small amount of marital property.[137] The Mississippi Supreme Court held that a husband's separate rental properties were not converted to marital simply because he deposited some rental funds in a joint account and paid expenses with the funds.[138]

[d] Mississippi rule. In most cases involving mixed-asset accounts, the Mississippi Supreme Court has stated that commingling converts funds to marital, appearing to foreclose tracing in accounts.[139] However, the court of appeals appeared to use the clearinghouse rule to trace separate funds in one case. A certificate of deposit purchased with a wife's inheritance was classified as separate even though she deposited the funds in a marital account and then withdrew them to purchase the certficate of deposit. The court noted that there was no evidence that she intended to use the funds for family purposes.[140]

§ 6.05 CONVERSION OF SEPARATE PROPERTY TO MARITAL

Separate property may be converted to marital through actions of the owning spouse. Conversion may occur when an owning spouse commingles separate assets with marital, allows extensive family use of the asset, or, in most states, jointly titles the asset. Mississippi rules on separate property conversion depart significantly from the approach taken in most states. The Mississippi courts have abandoned one generally accepted method of conversion, while greatly expanding the other two.

[1] Conversion by implied gift or family use. The majority "implied gift" rule recognizes conversion of separate property to marital based on an owner's intent, determined by examining a number of factors. In Mississippi, one of those factors – family use – has become the basis for an independent method of conversion.

[a] Conversion by implied gift. In many states, conversion by implied gift

---

[135] *In re* Marriage of Raad, 704 N.E.2d 964 (Ill. App. Ct. 1998).

[136] *In re* Marriage of Raad, 704 N.E.2d 964 (Ill. App. Ct. 1998).

[137] OLDHAM, *supra* note 1, § 11.03[1][d], at 11-29, 11-30.

[138] Bresnahan v. Bresnahan, 818 So. 2d 1113, 1117-18 (Miss. 2002).

[139] See Johnson v. Johnson, 650 So. 2d 1281, 1286 (Miss. 1994) (wife's separate funds deposited into marital account became marital); Oswalt v. Oswalt, 981 So. 2d 993 (Miss. Ct. App. 2007) (husband's $198,000 separate property commingled into joint account properly classified as marital; chancellor considered separate property contribution in division).

[140] Oliver v. Oliver, 812 So. 2d 1128, 1135 (Miss. Ct. App. 2002). The case involved inheritance rather than equitable distribution, but was analyzed under equitable distribution principles. *See also* Brock v. Brock, 906 So. 2d 879, 887-88 (Miss. Ct. App. 2005).

PROPERTY DIVISION § 6.05[1][b]

occurs when an owner's actions show an intention to give an asset to the marital estate.[141] Courts analyze several factors to determine intent, including statements by the owner,[142] family use of the asset,[143] the manner in which title is held, and whether the asset was commingled with marital assets.[144]

[b] **The Mississippi family-use doctrine.** Mississippi courts have created a unique conversion rule by focusing on a single element of the implied gift theory – family use. The court of appeals first announced the rule in 2000, holding that a husband's separate property furnishings became marital when they were placed in the home and used by the family.[145] The court expanded on the doctrine a year later, holding that a wife's family china, silver, and antiques became marital through family use. The court indicated that conversion could be avoided by storing the assets or placing them in a room accessible only to the owner.[146] Use of income from separate property for family use does not, however, convert the asset itself to marital property. The court of appeals reversed a chancellor's marital classification of certificates of deposit based on the family-use doctrine. Use of a portion of the separate property certificates of deposit for family purposes did not convert the remaining funds into marital.[147]

The family-use doctrine will almost always convert a separately owned marital home to marital property.[148] In several cases, however, a separately owned marital home

---

[141] *See* TURNER, *supra* note 3, § 5.24, at 277-78.

[142] *In re* Nicks, 531 N.E.2d 1069, 1072 (Ill. App. Ct. 1988) (statement by husband that he put title in joint tenancy because his wife said she had never owned anything and because "[s]he wanted to be proud of something she owned"); McCulloch v. McCulloch, 435 N.W.2d 564, 568 (Minn. Ct. App. 1989) (statement of husband that "[s]he would own the house equally with [himself]") (alteration in original); Westbrook v. Westbrook, 364 S.E.2d 523, 527 (Va. Ct. App. 1988) (statements by owning spouse: "I agree we own the house together," and "It's my understanding that in Virginia that, you know, that's marital property").

[143] *See* Burgess v. Burgess, 710 P.2d 417, 420-21 (Alaska 1985) (premarital property used as marital residence created marital interest in accumulated equity); *In re* Marriage of Tatham, 527 N.E.2d 1351, 1361 (Ill. App. Ct. 1988) (sailboat given to husband prior to marriage considered marital because it was intended for family use and enjoyment); Boyce v. Boyce, 694 S.W.2d 288, 290 (Mo. Ct. App. 1985) (Ford Mustang owned by husband prior to marriage was marital property; his wife drove it every day after their marriage). TURNER, *supra* note 3, § 5.24, at 283.

[144] TURNER, *supra* note 3, § 5.24, at 283.

[145] Brame v. Brame, No. 98-CA-00502-COA, 2000 Miss. App. LEXIS 142, at *9 (Miss. Ct. App. 2000) (piano, clock, and furniture became marital when commingled in the marital home, taking on the "new persona of full family use"), *rev'd in part*, 796 So. 2d 970 (Miss. 2001); *see also* King v. King, 760 So. 2d 830, 836 (Miss. Ct. App. 2000) (marital home "used by the family becomes a marital asset, losing its identity as a separate estate").

[146] Pittman v. Pittman, 791 So. 2d 857, 862-63 (Miss. Ct. App. 2001) (also rejecting wife's argument that house was partly her separate property, in absence of evidence that she alone used a portion of house); *see also* Stewart v. Stewart, 864 So. 2d 934, 937-38 (Miss. 2003) (furniture brought into marital home converted to marital); Smith v. Smith, 994 So. 2d 882, 886 (Miss. Ct. App. 2008) (husband's separate property vehicles used by family became marital property); *cf.* Parker v. Parker, 980 So. 2d 323, 327 (Miss. Ct. App. 2008) (three acres of separate property adjoining marital estate of eighty-five acres assumed to be used by wife; burden on husband to prove no family use or commingling). *But cf.* Dorsey v. Dorsey, 972 So. 2d 48, 52 (Miss. Ct. App. 2008) (wife's testimony that children rode four-wheelers on separate property land did not convert property to marital); Gutierrez v. Bucci, 827 So. 2d 27, 37-38 (Miss. Ct. App. 2002) (fact that wife occasionally rode husband's motorcycle did not convert it to marital).

[147] McKissack v. McKissack, 45 So. 3d 716, 718-22 (Miss. Ct. App. 2010); *see* Boutwell v. Boutwell, 829 So. 2d 1216, 1222 (Miss. 2002) (income from separate promissory note did not convert note to marital asset); Pearson v. Pearson, 761 So. 2d 157, 163-64 (Miss. 2000) (same); Sanderson v. Sanderson, 824 So. 2d 623, 626-27 (Miss. Ct. App. 2002) (rejecting wife's argument that the husband's separate property stock was converted to a marital asset because he used some of the income for marital purposes, but also holding that stock was to be considered in determining amount of alimony).

[148] *See* Bowen v. Bowen, 982 So. 2d 385, 395 (Miss. 2008) (family use converted premarital marina to marital asset because couple lived at marina); Stewart v. Stewart, 864 So. 2d 934, 938-39 (Miss. 2003) (but allowing unequal division

§ 6.05[2]   **MISSISSIPPI FAMILY LAW**

has been awarded to the owner without discussion of the family-use doctrine.[149] And in a 2007 case, the marital home was classified as partly marital and partly separate in spite of family use.[150] In a 2010 case, the court of appeals also affirmed a mixed-asset approach, holding that a wife's premarital home was marital based on family use, but valuing the marital portion by subtracting the value of the home at the time the couple moved into it from the value at the time of sale.[151] And a wife's Memphis home was not converted to marital by the couple's brief occupancy before they purchased a home. She was responsible for all payments on the home during the four-year marriage.[152]

The family-use doctrine places Mississippi in a distinct minority. Two of the leading commentators on property division strongly criticize conversion based on family use without reference to intent. Both suggest that the approach encourages hoarding behavior and runs counter to most spouses' expectations.[153]

[2] Conversion by joint titling. In most states, an asset becomes marital if the owner titles it in the name of both spouses. The Mississippi Supreme Court held in 1999 that the joint-title presumption does not apply in equitable distribution.

[a] The joint-title presumption. Common law states have long employed a presumption that any owner who retitles property jointly with another intends to give the transferee a one-half interest in the property.[154] In Mississippi, the presumption has been applied to inter vivos transfers between spouses and other family members[155] as well as unrelated persons.[156]

The presumption of a gift can be rebutted by clear and convincing evidence that

---

between spouses who shared home for only one year); Boutwell v. Boutwell, 829 So. 2d 1216, 1221-22 (Miss. 2002); McDuffie v. McDuffie, 21 So. 3d 685, 691 (Miss. Ct. App. 2009) (home owned by husband prior to marriage properly classified as marital); Faerber v. Faerber, 13 So. 3d 853, 861 (Miss. Ct. App. 2009) (error to classify marital home used by family as husband's separate property); Stewart v. Stewart, 2 So. 3d 770, 773-74 (Miss. Ct. App. 2009) (husband's premarital home converted to marital through family use); Fogarty v. Fogarty, 922 So. 2d 836, 840 (Miss. Ct. App. 2006) (husband's separate property home classified as marital based on family use and commingling; couple lived in the home and added a carport); Hankins v. Hankins, 866 So. 2d 508, 511-12 (Miss. Ct. App. 2004); Lockert v. Lockert, 815 So. 2d 1267, 1269-70 (Miss. Ct. App. 2002). *But see* Wilson v. Wilson, 820 So. 2d 761, 763 (Miss. Ct. App. 2002) (error to classify home as marital where wife lived in home only three years and made no financial contributions). A number of states classify homes as marital even if they were separately owned by one spouse. TURNER, *supra* note 3, § 5.24, at 280.

[149] *See* Duncan v. Duncan, 915 So. 2d 1124, 1127 (Miss. Ct. App. 2005) (en banc) (marital home owned by wife prior to marriage awarded to her either as separate property or because husband made no contribution; no discussion of family use); Brock v. Brock, 906 So. 2d 879, 887-88 (Miss. Ct. App. 2005) (home inherited by wife classified as separate; no mention of family use even though couple lived in home several times during marriage); *cf.* Jordan v. Jordan, 963 So. 2d 1235, 1247-48 (Miss. Ct. App. 2007) (marital home financed by husband's parents properly awarded to husband; wife's economic and homemaker contributions were limited); Jackson v. Jackson, 922 So. 2d 53, 58 (Miss. Ct. App. 2006) (en banc) (permissible to classify furniture given to wife by her children as separate property; husband did not live in the home for most of the marriage and, at trial, disavowed any interest in the items).

[150] Oswalt v. Oswalt, 981 So. 2d 993 (Miss. Ct. App. 2007).

[151] Delk v. Delk, 41 So. 3d 738, 741-42 (Miss. Ct. App. 2010).

[152] Doyle v. Doyle, 55 So. 3d 1097, 1109 (Miss. Ct. App. 2010).

[153] Oldham, *Tracing, supra* note 116, at 220 (encourages "selfish and antisocial behavior"); TURNER, *supra* note 3, § 5.24, at 282.

[154] Oldham, *Tracing, supra* note 116, at 236.

[155] *See* Johnson v. Johnson, 550 So. 2d 416, 420 (Miss. 1989) (husband presumed to make gift of one-half interest in house to wife; presumption may be overcome by "substantial evidence to the contrary").

[156] *Cf.* Madden v. Rhodes, 626 So. 2d 608, 618 (Miss. 1993) (presumption of gift of one-half of contents of safe deposit box to hospice volunteer rebutted; statutory presumption for safe deposit boxes).

PROPERTY DIVISION § 6.05[2][b]

no gift was intended. For example, the presumption was rebutted by proof that a wife convinced her husband to convey property intended for his children to her, based on her promise to convey the property to the children on his death.[157] Couples frequently title property jointly to obtain tax benefits or for estate planning purposes. Some courts reject efforts to set aside joint title by a spouse who used the form of ownership to obtain legal benefits.[158]

[b] In equitable distribution. Most equitable distribution states apply the joint-title presumption at divorce. Courts typically hold that joint titling indicates a gift to the marital estate rather than of an undivided one-half interest in the property. Thus, instead of each spouse owning a separate one-half interest, the property may be equitably divided.[159] However, a growing number of states reject the joint-title presumption for purposes of equitable distribution.[160]

The Mississippi Supreme Court applied the joint-title presumption in the early years of equitable distribution.[161] But in 2000, the court held the presumption inapplicable in divorce actions, on the basis that title is irrelevant in equitable distribution. The court rejected a wife's argument that three jointly titled homes purchased with her husband's separate property were marital assets.[162]

[3] Conversion by commingling. In most states, separate property becomes marital when it is so commingled with marital property that the owner cannot trace the separate funds. In Mississippi, commingling converts separate property to marital even if the separate property is identifiable.

[a] Conversion by untraceable commingling. It is a basic rule of equitable

---

[157] Sarver v. Sarver, 687 So. 2d 749, 755 (Miss. 1997) (wife convinced husband property would be tied up in probate if willed to children), *overruled in part by* Pearson v. Pearson, 761 So. 2d 157, 163 (Miss. 2000); *see also* Devore v. Devore, 725 So. 2d 193, 196-97 (Miss. 1998) (presumption rebutted where wife did not fulfill agreement on which joint titling was based).

[158] *See* Lynam v. Gallagher, 526 A.2d 878, 884 (Del. 1987); Ball v. Ball, 335 So. 2d 5, 7 (Fla. Dist. Ct. App. 1976); Alwell v. Alwell, 471 N.Y.S.2d 899, 901-02 (N.Y. App. Div. 1984); Brown v. Brown, 507 A.2d 1223, 1225-26 (Pa. Super. Ct. 1986); *cf.* McGee v. McGee, 726 So. 2d 1220, 1225 (Miss. Ct. App. 1998) (court refused to set aside interest in house transferred to daughter for purpose of shielding assets); Simmons v. Simmons, 724 So. 2d 1054, 1059-60 (Miss. Ct. App. 1998) (same; transfer of motorcycle to grandmother); *see also* cases cited in TURNER, *supra* note 3, § 5.18, at 212-215.

[159] TURNER, *supra* note 3, § 5.18, at 209; *see* Farmer v. Farmer, 398 So. 2d 723, 726 (Ala. Civ. App. 1981) (wife's $17,000 contribution to purchase price of house was contribution to marital estate; division was subject to discretion of court); Lynam v. Gallagher, 526 A.2d 878, 884 (Del. 1987) (husband's transfer of stock to wife as joint tenants created rebuttable presumption that he intended it as gift of marital property to be divided according to court's discretion); Carter v. Carter, 419 A.2d 1018, 1022 (Me. 1980) (real property transferred from husband to himself and his wife as joint tenants was marital property).

[160] *See* TURNER, *supra* note 124, § 5.43, at 479 (3d ed.).

[161] *See* Sarver v. Sarver, 687 So. 2d 749, 755 (Miss. 1997) (presumption rebutted), *overruled in part by* Pearson v. Pearson, 761 So. 2d 157, 163 (Miss. 2000); Myrick v. Myrick, 739 So. 2d 432, 434 (Miss. Ct. App. 1999) (wife's separate property personal injury settlement converted into marital property when she placed her husband's name on account); *cf.* Devore v. Devore, 725 So. 2d 193, 197 (Miss. 1998) (divesting wife of jointly titled property; husband transferred property based on her promise to stay with him and "make me a wife"; her failure to fulfill agreement justified divesting her of the title).

[162] Pearson v. Pearson, 761 So. 2d 157, 163 (Miss. 2000); *see also* Delk v. Delk, 41 So. 3d 738, 741-42 (Miss. Ct. App. 2010) (wife's premarital condominium not converted to marital by joint titling). *But see* Atkinson v. Atkinson, 11 So. 3d 172, 178 (Miss. Ct. App. 2009) (wife's separate property land converted to marital when she titled it in joint names).

§ 6.05[3][b]   MISSISSIPPI FAMILY LAW

distribution that property retains its character even though it takes another form. Most states permit an owner to trace commingled separate funds. If the separate funds can be identified, the asset is classified as mixed, partly marital and partly separate.[163] If tracing is not possible, the marital property presumption applies and the entire asset is classified as marital. Conversion is not caused by the act of commingling but by inability to trace and identify the separate property.[164]

[b] Commingling in Mississippi. The Mississippi Supreme Court allows tracing of commingled separate funds in some, but not all, assets. The court has stated very broadly that the act of commingling converts separate funds to marital,[165] without predicating conversion on inability to trace. For example, the court stated that when a wife deposited separate funds in a marital account "she converted these nonmarital assets to marital assets."[166] Similarly, a husband's $70,000 inheritance, used as a down payment on the home, "was co-mingled and became a part of the marital estate."[167] And a husband's use of his salary to make mortgage payments on separate property real estate "changed their character from non-marital to marital."[168]

---

[163] *See* discussion of tracing *supra* at § 6.04.

[164] *See* Porter v. Porter, 195 P.2d 132, 138 (Ariz. 1948) ("[C]ommingling alone is not sufficient to stamp the whole with the community status, but only when the commingling results in . . . loss of identity . . . ."); McKay v. McKay, 8 S.W.3d 525 (Ark. 2000); Hicks v. Hicks, 27 Cal. Rptr. 307, 314 (Cal. Dist. App. 1962) ("[M]ere commingling of separate with community funds in a bank account does not destroy the character of the former . . . ."); Becker v. Becker, 639 So. 2d 1082, 1084 (Fla. Dist. Ct. App. 1994); Weilmunster v. Weilmunster, 858 P. 2d 766, 771 (Idaho Ct. App. 1993); *In re* Higgins, 507 N.W.2d 725, 726 (Iowa Ct. App. 1993); Brehm v. Brehm, 762 So. 2d 1259, 1264 (La. Ct. App. 2000) (mixing community and separate funds does not convert entire account into community if separate funds can be identified); Nash v. Nash, 388 N.W.2d 777, 781 (Minn. Ct. App. 1986) ("Simply routing the funds through a joint account does not transform nonmarital property into marital property."); Friedman v. Friedman, 965 S.W.2d 319 (Mo. App. 1998) (using indirect tracing to show amount of separate funds in account at each purchase); *In re* Marriage of Zahm, 978 P.2d 498, 504 (Wash. 1999) (marital property presumption can be rebutted by showing commingled, separate property; applied even to joint account).

[165] *See* Henderson v. Henderson, 703 So. 2d 262, 265 (Miss. 1997) ("[T]he money received from Mary's parents, which was initially non-marital property, became marital property when Mary commingled it with the marital assets."); Maslowski v. Maslowski, 655 So. 2d 18, 20 (Miss. 1995) (commingling occurs when there is "a combination of marital and non-marital property which loses its status as non-marital as a result").

[166] Johnson v. Johnson, 650 So. 2d 1281, 1286 (Miss. 1994); *see also* Oswalt v. Oswalt, 981 So. 2d 993 (Miss. Ct. App. 2007) (husband's $198,000 separate property commingled into joint account properly classified as marital; chancellor considered separate property contribution in division). *But cf.* Doyle v. Doyle, 55 So. 3d 1097, 1107 (Miss. Ct. App. 2010) (rejecting wife's argument that husband's separate property check was converted to marital when she took it without permission and put it into a marital account).

[167] Singley v. Singley, 846 So. 2d 1004, 1011 (Miss. 2002). However, the trial court can adjust the *Ferguson* distribution "because of the factors surrounding the source and application of the $70,000." *Id.*; *see also* Stewart v. Stewart, 2 So. 3d 770, 773 (Miss. Ct. App. 2009) (funds from sale of husband's premarital home lost separate property character when commingled with marital funds to purchase new home).

[168] Gutierrez v. Bucci, 827 So. 2d 27, 38 (Miss. Ct. App. 2002) (but not error to award $5,000 equity in properties to husband in light of wife's dissipation of assets); *see also* Irby v. Estate of Irby, 7 So. 3d 223, 234 (Miss. 2009) (wife's premarital home properly classified as marital; mortgage paid with marital funds); Faerber v. Faerber, 13 So. 3d 853, 860-61 (Miss. Ct. App. 2009) (error to classify marital home as husband's separate property; wife contributed funds and sweat equity to building of home); Lewis v. Lewis, 54 So. 3d 233, 240-41 (Miss. Ct. App. 2009) (separate rental properties properly classified as marital; husband did not identify source of mortgage payments, which exceeded rental income), *rev'd in part on other grounds*, 54 So. 3d 216 (Miss. 2011); Messer v. Messer, 850 So. 2d 161, 168-69 (Miss. Ct. App. 2003) (husband's separate property (real estate) converted to marital because couple paid taxes from joint account); *cf.* Spahn v. Spahn, 959 So. 2d 8, 12 (Miss. Ct. App. 2006) (premarital warehouse not converted; husband maintained separate account into which he deposited warehouse income and from which he paid expenses). *But see* Smith v. Smith, 994 So. 2d 882, 886 (Miss. Ct. App. 2008) (wife's improvements to husband's separate property did not convert to marital; wife awarded $5,000 as equitable payment for her work); Dorsey v. Dorsey, 972 So. 2d 48, 52 (Miss. Ct. App. 2008)

PROPERTY DIVISION § 6.05[3][b]

The wording of these cases, taken literally, puts Mississippi in a small minority with regard to tracing rules.[169] Despite the broad language, however, many of the cases can be explained by reference to other conversion rules. Several cases involve jointly titled property and were decided before the court abandoned the joint-title presumption.[170] Others involve the marital home, which is independently converted to marital property through the family-use doctrine.[171] And in a few cases, the separate funds had already been spent on marital expenses and dedicated to the marital estate by choice.[172] Others, however, are clearly a product of the strict commingling rule.[173]

A few recent cases have suggested a move away from the strict commingling rule. The court of appeals appeared to adopt the majority tracing rule with regard to a wife's separate property interest in a home. The court rejected her husband's argument that the house was converted to marital by commingling because he paid taxes and made repairs on the house. The court stated that separate property is transmuted into marital by commingling only when assets are so mixed that the separate property cannot be traced: "the key to . . . transmutation by commingling is whether the marital interests can be identified."[174] And in a 2007 case, the court of appeals affirmed a chancellor's classification of the marital home and a mobile home as "mixed assets." The equity owned by the husband at the time of marriage was his separate property, while the remaining balance of the value was marital. Similarly, a mobile home purchased by his wife with money from her parents was her separate property; however, $2,000 of marital funds used for the purchase were classified as marital.[175] And in a 2010 case, the court of appeals affirmed a chancellor's valuation of a home as a mixed asset. The home, which was converted to marital by family use, was separate to the extent of its value at the time the couple moved in. The marital portion was the appreciated value.[176] In other cases, however, the court has continued to apply the broad commingling

---

(marital funds used to pay expenses on separate property "were 'easily traceable' and not 'so commingled as to have become unidentifiable'"; property remained separate).

[169] Turner devotes several pages in his treatise to a discussion of Mississippi's "unitary property" approach to commingling. He states, "The holding of these cases is not presently the law in any state other than Mississippi." *See* TURNER, *supra* note 124, App. A, Mississippi (3d ed.).

[170] *See* Bullock v. Bullock, 699 So. 2d 1205, 1210-11 (Miss. 1997); Henderson v. Henderson, 703 So. 2d 262, 264-65 (Miss. 1997); Heigle v. Heigle, 654 So. 2d 895, 897 (Miss. 1995); Myrick v. Myrick, 739 So. 2d 432, 434 (Miss. Ct. App. 1999) (jointly titled account).

[171] *See* Bullock v. Bullock, 699 So. 2d 1205, 1210-11 (Miss. 1997); Henderson v. Henderson, 703 So. 2d 262, 264-65 (Miss. 1997) (jointly titled marital home); Maslowski v. Maslowski, 655 So. 2d 18, 23 (Miss. 1995); Belding v. Belding, 736 So. 2d 425, 432 (Miss. Ct. App. 1999); James v. James, 724 So. 2d 1098, 1102-03 (Miss. Ct. App. 1998).

[172] *See* Heigle v. Heigle, 654 So. 2d 895, 897 (Miss. 1995); Johnson v. Johnson, 650 So. 2d 1281, 1286 (Miss. 1994)*; see also* Jones v. Jones, 995 So. 2d 706, 714 (Miss. 2008) ($691,000 from books written prior to marriage was separate property but was commingled and became marital).

[173] *See, e.g.,* Lewis v. Lewis, 54 So. 3d 233, 240-41 (Miss. Ct. App. 2009) (separate rental properties properly classified as marital; husband did not identify source of mortgage payments, which exceeded rental income), *rev'd in part on other grounds,* 54 So. 3d 216 (Miss. 2011); Messer v. Messer, 850 So. 2d 161, 168-69 (Miss. Ct. App. 2003) (husband's separate property (real estate) converted to marital because couple paid taxes from joint account).

[174] Brock v. Brock, 906 So. 2d 879, 887-88 (Miss. Ct. App. 2005); *see also* Dorsey v. Dorsey, 972 So. 2d 48, 52 (Miss. Ct. App. 2008) (marital funds used to pay expenses on separate property "were 'easily traceable' and not 'so commingled as to have become unidentifiable'"; property remained separate); Oliver v. Oliver, 812 So. 2d 1128, 1134-35 (Miss. Ct. App. 2002).

[175] Oswalt v. Oswalt, 981 So. 2d 993 (Miss. Ct. App. 2007).

[176] Delk v. Delk, 41 So. 3d 738, 740-41 (Miss. Ct. App. 2010).

§ 6.06   MISSISSIPPI FAMILY LAW

rule.[177]

In contrast, tracing is permitted in some contexts. For example, pensions acquired partly before and partly during marriage are classified as mixed assets in spite of the commingling of separate and marital funds.[178] And separate, premarital businesses that actively appreciate during marriage are treated as a mixed asset.[179]

Brett Turner, author of a leading national treatise on equitable distribution, characterizes the Mississippi commingling rule as a return to the "unitary property" system tried and rejected by two states in the early years of equitable distribution. He notes that Virginia and Illinois abandoned the unitary system, in part because experts concluded that the system made settlement of property division more difficult.[180]

§ 6.06 SPECIFIC TYPES OF PROPERTY

Some forms of property, such as personal injury awards, are not easily classified as either marital or separate. Others, such as goodwill, are completely excluded from equitable distribution in Mississippi. And still other forms of property are governed by rules unique to the particular asset. This section outlines the rules applicable to specific types of property in equitable distribution.

[1] Personal injury awards. Most courts classify personal injury awards as a mixed asset, using a method called the analytical approach.[181] To the extent the award compensates for pain and suffering, it is the separate property of the injured spouse. Compensation for items that were costs to the marriage, such as lost wages or medical expenses, are marital property.[182] A minority of states classify the pain and suffering component of personal injury awards as marital property, treating the injured spouse's health as a marital asset.[183]

Mississippi follows the majority approach.[184] In *Tramel v. Tramel*, the supreme court reversed a chancellor's order awarding a wife 40% of her husband's personal

---

[177] *See* Ory v. Ory, 936 So. 2d 405, 412 (Miss. Ct. App. 2006) (en banc) (chancellor erred in crediting wife for contributing $16,000 in personal injury funds to marital home; funds were commingled and lost separate classification); Fogarty v. Fogarty, 922 So. 2d 836, 840 (Miss. Ct. App. 2006) (husband's separate property classified as marital based on family use and commingling; couple lived in the home and added a carport; Dobbs v. Dobbs, 912 So. 2d 491, 492-93 (Miss. Ct. App. 2005) (rejecting husband's argument that he should be credited with mortgage payments made prior to marriage; home was properly classified as marital).

[178] *See* discussion *supra* § 6.05[3].

[179] *See supra* § 6.03[4].

[180] TURNER, *supra* note 124, App. A, Mississippi (3d ed.). According to Turner, they believed that when separate property is converted to marital by commingling, judges often use their discretion in the division stage to divide the asset unequally, causing "rampant inconsistency" and making resolution more difficult because of the unpredictability of results.

[181] OLDHAM, *supra* note 1, § 8.01, at 8-6.

[182] *See* Jurek v. Jurek, 606 P.2d 812, 814 (Ariz. 1980); Campbell v. Campbell, 339 S.E.2d 591, 593 (Ga. 1986); Weakley v. Weakley, 731 S.W.2d 243, 246 (Ky. 1987); Ward v. Ward, 453 N.W.2d 729, 732 (Minn. Ct. App. 1990); Landwehr v. Landwehr, 545 A.2d 738, 742-43 (N.J. 1988).

[183] *See In re* Marriage of Fjeldheim, 676 P.2d 1234, 1236 (Colo. Ct. App. 1983) (holding that personal injury settlement for pain and suffering is marital property); Boyce v. Boyce, 541 A.2d 614, 615 (D.C. 1988) (same); Maricle v. Maricle, 378 N.W.2d 855, 857 (Neb. 1985) (same); Kozich v. Kozich, 580 A.2d 390, 393 (Pa. Super. Ct. 1990) (same); Marsh v. Marsh, 437 S.E.2d 34, 36 (S.C. 1993) (same).

[184] The Mississippi Supreme Court adopted the majority view in a pre-*Ferguson* case. *See* Regan v. Regan, 507 So. 2d 54, 56-57 (Miss. 1987) (rejecting a wife's claim to her husband's personal injury award).

PROPERTY DIVISION   § 6.06[2]

injury recovery. The supreme court classified awards allocable to pain, suffering, and disfigurement as the injured spouse's separate property; awards for loss of consortium as the separate property of the non-injured spouse, awards for lost wages and medical expenses during the marriage as marital property; and awards for post-divorce wages and medical expenses as the injured spouse's separate property.[185]

In practice, the rule is difficult to apply.[186] A personal injury award is rarely divided neatly into the *Tramel* categories. Furthermore, a personal injury settlement agreement designating specific amounts for each category would be suspect if the injured spouse anticipated divorce when the document was executed.

In two cases, the Mississippi Court of Appeals found that the entire remaining proceeds from personal injury settlements represented pain and suffering and belonged solely to the injured spouse. In one case, pre-settlement advances representing the marital portion – lost wages and medical expenses – had already been spent by the family for living expenses.[187] In the other, the husband presented no proof that marital funds were used to pay his injured wife's medical bills, so there was no need to reimburse the marital estate from the recovery.[188]

[2] Workers' compensation awards. States tend to classify workers' compensation awards under the same rule used to classify personal injury awards. States that use the analytical approach classify workers' compensation payments for pain, suffering, or disfigurement as the injured employee's separate property.[189] States following the minority rule treat the entire workers' compensation award as marital, with the exception of recovery for post-divorce wages and expenses.[190] In keeping with this practice, the Mississippi Court of Appeals held that workers' compensation benefits should be classified under the analytical approach set out in *Tramel*.[191]

[3] Disability benefits. Classification of disability benefits has proven more difficult than personal injury and workers' compensation awards. Some aspects of disabil-

---

[185] Tramel v. Tramel, 740 So. 2d 286, 289-91 (Miss. 1999); *see also* Myers v. Myers, 741 So. 2d 274, 280 (Miss. 1998) (reversing chancellor's classification of personal injury award as all separate property).

[186] In *Tramel*, the court noted that the personal injury award did not specify amounts for each of the elements, and remanded the case to the chancellor to "perform the alchemy of turning gross sums into clear, detailed portions." Tramel v. Tramel, 740 So. 2d 286, 289-91 (Miss. 1999).

[187] Tynes v. Tynes, 860 So. 2d 325, 330-31 (Miss. Ct. App. 2003) ($47,688 in pre-settlement advances were marital; remaining $800,043 represented damages for pain and suffering).

[188] Langdon v. Langdon, 854 So. 2d 485, 491-93 (Miss. Ct. App. 2003) ($200,000 payment awarded to wife; although she incurred $72,000 in medical bills, her attorney was holding $40,000 for potential claims). *But see* Ory v. Ory, 936 So. 2d 405, 412 n.5 (Miss. Ct. App. 2006) (en banc) (dicta appears to place burden on injured spouse to prove personal injury award was nonmarital under analytical approach).

[189] *See In re* Marriage of Smith, 817 P.2d 641, 644 (Colo. Ct. App. 1991) (holding that workers' compensation benefits that compensated for loss of earning during the marriage were marital property but benefits were not marital property if compensating for loss of post-dissolution earning capacity); Weisfeld v. Weisfeld, 513 So. 2d 1278, 1280-81 (Fla. Dist. Ct. App. 1987) (holding that workers' compensation benefits paid to injured party for personal loss were sole property of that party and damages paid for economic loss during marriage were marital property).

[190] *See* Goode v. Goode, 692 S.W.2d 757, 759 (Ark. 1985) (classifying workers' compensation claims as marital property); *In re* Marriage of Lukas, 404 N.E.2d 545, 552 (Ill. App. Ct. 1980) (stating that parties treated workers' compensation funds as marital property).

[191] *See* Wesson v. Wesson, 818 So. 2d 1272, 1278 (Miss. Ct. App. 2002) (reserving jurisdiction to apply *Tramel* rules to future workers' compensation benefits).

§ 6.06[4]   **MISSISSIPPI FAMILY LAW**

ity benefits suggest marital classification. Disability benefits are often earned through employment during marriage or purchased with marital funds. Furthermore, disability benefits may replace marital retirement benefits. In other respects, disability benefits resemble separate property. Some payments compensate for pain and suffering. Benefits may replace post-divorce lost wages rather than retirement benefits.

Some courts hold, based on a strict reading of the state's applicable statute, that disability benefits earned through employment during marriage, or purchased with marital funds, are marital.[192] For example, the Arkansas Supreme Court held that a husband's disability benefits acquired during marriage were marital, even though the benefits replaced post-divorce wages and were separate from retirement benefits.[193] Other courts look to the loss compensated rather than the manner in which the benefits were acquired. In these states, disability benefits are classified by analogy to personal injury benefits – to the extent they replace post-divorce, non-retirement wages and expenses, or compensate for pain and suffering, they are the disabled spouse's separate property. For example, a husband's pre-retirement disability benefits, which were subject to termination based on recovery, were his separate property. Even though the benefits were obtained through employment during the marriage, the payments replaced post-divorce wages.[194] The Arizona Court of Appeals applied this approach to classify disability benefits as a mixed asset. The court held that 86% of a husband's disability benefit was actually deferred compensation, while the remainder was a true disability benefit, representing personal loss.[195] No Mississippi case was found addressing this issue.

To the extent that disability benefits are a direct replacement for marital retirement benefits, the benefits should be marital.[196] The California Supreme Court rejected a husband's argument that disability benefits of 75% of his base pay, in lieu of retirement benefits of 65% of base pay, were his separate property; to permit conversion of marital benefits to separate property by unilateral election would "negate the protective philosophy" of the community property system.[197]

[4] Professional degrees and practices

[a] Professional degrees. In the early years of equitable distribution, some parties argued that a professional degree earned during marriage was "property" and the resulting flow of income a divisible asset. With limited exceptions,[198] courts rejected

---

[192] *See* Morrison v. Morrison, 692 S.W.2d 601, 603 (Ark. 1985); Grace Ganz Blumberg, *Marital Property Treatment of Pensions, Disability Pay, Workers' Compensation, and Other Wage Substitutes: An Insurance, or Replacement, Analysis*, 33 UCLA L. Rev. 1250, 1269-70 (1986).

[193] Dunn v. Dunn, 811 S.W.2d 336, 338-39 (Ark. Ct. App. 1991).

[194] *See In re* Marriage of Anglin, 759 P.2d 1224, 1229 (Wash. Ct. App. 1988).

[195] Villasenor v. Villasenor, 657 P.2d 889, 892 (Ariz. Ct. App. 1982) (community property state); *see* Gilbert v. Gilbert, 442 So. 2d 1330, 1332 (La. Ct. App. 1983) (benefits more in nature of retirement than compensation for disability); *In re* Marriage of Huteson, 619 P.2d 991, 994 (Wash. Ct. App. 1980) (disability benefits acquired before husband had vested interest in retirement solely to compensate for future lost wages; separate property of husband); *see also* Blumberg, *supra* note 192, at 1271.

[196] *See* Turner, *supra* note 3, § 6.16, at 384-85.

[197] *In re* Marriage of Stenquist, 582 P.2d 96, 98-99 (Cal. 1978).

[198] *See* O'Brien v. O'Brien, 489 N.E.2d 712, 716-19 (N.Y. 1985).

154

PROPERTY DIVISION   § 6.06[4][b]

the attempt to characterize a degree or license as divisible marital property.[199] The Mississippi Supreme Court agreed with the majority, refusing to classify a wife's nursing degree as marital property. The court held that marital property does not include "intellectual or technical mental enhancement gained during the course of a marriage."[200] The court did, however, adopt reimbursement alimony as a means of recognizing the contribution of a spouse to the education and training of the other.[201]

[b] Professional practices. A professional practice is marital property to the extent that it is built during marriage. The Mississippi Supreme Court stated that the "facilities, equipment, fixtures, furniture, [and] accounts receivable" of a professional practice may be assets subject to equitable distribution.[202]

As a general rule, the valuation of a business in divorce proceedings may include a figure for enterprise goodwill that is not based on the individual owner's reputation and skill.[203] Most states extend this rule to division of professional practices.[204] Some courts hold, however, that the non-owning spouse must affirmatively prove that the goodwill is enterprise, rather than individual goodwill.[205] However, a few courts, including Mississippi, adopt a bright-line rule that professional goodwill is not divisible at all.[206] The Mississippi Supreme Court acknowledged that some courts view enterprise goodwill attributable to factors such as location or supplier relationships, as independent of personal goodwill. The court concluded, however, that enterprise and personal goodwill are too intertwined to be divided in a professional practice.[207]

[5] Attorneys' fees. As a general rule, fees earned by an attorney for work performed during marriage are marital property. Courts disagree with regard to classification of contingent fees in pending cases. A minority of courts hold that unvested contingent fees are not marital property.[208] But in most states, a contingent fee received after divorce may be marital property in proportion to the percentage of work per-

---

[199] *See* Hughes v. Hughes, 438 So. 2d 146, 149 (Fla. Dist. Ct. App. 1983); Inman v. Inman, 648 S.W.2d 847, 852 (Ky. 1982); Hubbard v. Hubbard, 603 P.2d 747, 750 (Okla. 1979).

[200] Guy v. Guy, 736 So. 2d 1042, 1044 (Miss. 1999).

[201] Guy v. Guy, 736 So. 2d 1042, 1044 (Miss. 1999).

[202] Mace v. Mace, 818 So. 2d 1130, 1133 (Miss. 2000) (declining to rule on issue of goodwill, which was not before the court).

[203] TURNER, *supra* note 124, § 6.73, at 396, 409 (3d ed.).

[204] *See, e.g.,* Mitchell v. Mitchell, 732 P.2d 208, 211-12 (Ariz. 1987); Howell v. Howell, 523 S.E.2d 514, 520 (Va. Ct. App. 2000).

[205] *See* Wilson v. Wilson, 741 S.W.2d 640, 647 (Ark. 1987) (medical practice); Thompson v. Thompson, 576 So. 2d 267, 269 (Fla. 1991); Butler v. Butler, 663 A.2d 148, (Pa. 1995) (accounting firm).

[206] TURNER, *supra* note 124, § 6.73, at 405 (3d ed.) (stating that Mississippi is the only state to clearly distinguish between enterprise and individual goodwill and exclude both); *see In re* Marriage of Zells, 572 N.E.2d 944, 945-46 (Ill. 1991) (law practice); Travis v. Travis, 795 P.2d 96, 100 (Okla. 1990) (law practice); Hazard v. Hazard, 833 S.W.2d 911, 915 (Tenn. Ct. App. 1991) (medical practice).

[207] Watson v. Watson, 882 So. 2d 95, 105-06 (Miss. 2004). The *Watson* decision removed any lingering doubts left by *Singley v. Singley,* in which the court left open the question of whether enterprise goodwill could be included in valuing a solo professional practice at divorce. *See* Singley v. Singley, 846 So. 2d 1004, 1010 n.2 (Miss. 2002). The exclusion of goodwill from valuation of professional practices was later extended to all business valuations at divorce. *See infra* § Chapter VIII.

[208] *See* Goldstein v. Goldstein, 414 S.E.2d 474, 475 (Ga. 1992); Beasley v. Beasley, 518 A.2d 545, 555 (Pa. Super. Ct. 1986).

§ 6.06[6]   **MISSISSIPPI FAMILY LAW**

formed during the marriage.[209] Division is usually accomplished by the court's reservation of jurisdiction to divide the award. The percentage to which each spouse is entitled
may be fixed at the time of divorce or delayed until the fees are actually received.[210] The
Mississippi Supreme Court recognizes that contingent fees received during marriage
may be marital property,[211] but has yet to discuss the proper method for classifying and
dividing fees in pending cases.

[6] Patents, copyrights, and trademarks. Intellectual property may be marital to
the extent the work necessary to acquire the interest was performed during the marriage.[212] For example, future royalties from books written by a wife during the marriage
were marital property.[213] If the work was performed in part before the marriage[214] or
will require efforts after the marriage,[215] courts have treated the patent or copyright as
a mixed asset.

[7] Assets acquired with loan proceeds. Classification of assets acquired with
loan funds typically depends on whether both spouses are liable for the loan and
whether the loan is secured by separate or marital property. Loan proceeds will be
classified as separate if the loan was secured with separate property and repaid with
separate funds, the non-owning spouse was not liable on the loan, and if the borrower
intended the property to remain separate.[216] In some states, property secured by separate assets is classified as separate even if the non-owning spouse signed a promissory
note as guarantor.[217]

The Mississippi Court of Appeals has addressed classification of loan proceeds
in two cases. The court held that a vacant lot purchased by a wife with her separate

---

[209] See Garrett v. Garrett, 683 P.2d 1166, 1170 (Ariz. Ct. App. 1983); McDermott v. McDermott, 986 S.W.2d 843, 848 (Ark. 1999); Metzner v. Metzner, 446 S.E.2d 165, 173 (W. Va. 1994).

[210] See TURNER, supra note 3, § 5.09, at 158.

[211] See Kilpatrick v. Kilpatrick, 732 So. 2d 876, 882 (Miss. 1999) (reversing chancellor's property division for fail-ure to make findings regarding $800,000 in attorneys fees received by husband); Striebeck v. Striebeck, 5 So. 3d 450, 453 (Miss. Ct. App. 2008) (attorneys' fees earned during separation were marital; rejecting argument that fees were separate because wife's contributions were early in marriage); Striebeck v. Striebeck, 911 So. 2d 628, 633 (Miss. Ct. App. 2005) (en banc) (chancellor erred in excluding husband's contingency fee earned during separation from marital assets).

[212] See In re Marriage of Hienze, 631 N.E.2d 728, 731 (Ill. App. Ct. 1994); Hazard v. Hazard, 833 S.W.2d 911, 916 (Tenn. Ct. App. 1991); Moon v. Moon, 790 P.2d 52, 57 (Utah Ct. App. 1990).

[213] Jones v. Jones, 995 So. 2d 706, 710 (Miss. 2008) (but awarding royalties to wife).

[214] See McDougal v. McDougal, 545 N.W.2d 357, 363 (Mich. 1996).

[215] In re Marriage of Heinze, 631 N.E.2d 728, 731 (Ill. App. Ct. 1994); In re Marriage of Monslow, 912 P.2d 735, 747 (Kan. 1996).

[216] See Gudelj v. Gudelj, 259 P.2d 656, 661 (Cal. 1953) (proceeds separate if lender relies primarily on separate property; but finding no evidence that the lender was relying on husband's separate property); Horton v. Horton, 480 So. 2d 258, 259 (Fla. Dist. Ct. App. 1986) (husband put up separately owned home as collateral); Welder v. Welder, 794 S.W.2d 420, 426 (Tex. App. 1990) (question is whether spouse intended to secure loan with separate assets only); Mortenson v. Trammell, 604 S.W.2d 269, 276 (Tex. App. 1980) (loan proceeds separate where lender was limited to separate collateral); Harris v. Ventura, 582 S.W.2d 853, 857 (Tex. App. 1979) (property deemed husband's separate property because secured with separately owned note).

[217] See Porter v. Porter, 195 P.2d 132, 139 (Ariz. 1948) (court rejected the wife's argument that property purchased with separate funds became marital because she signed the note and mortgage); Hicks v. Hicks, 27 Cal. Rptr. 307, 313 (Cal. Dist. Ct. App. 1962) (loans obtained with separate collateral were separate funds, even though owner's wife signed promissory note); Gilman v. Gilman, 526 S.E.2d 763, 770 (Va. Ct. App. 2000) (real estate purchase with loan secured by husband's separate stock classified as separate, even though wife cosigned).

PROPERTY DIVISION

§ 6.06[8]

property as collateral was her separate property at divorce.[218] Similarly, property acquired by a husband for use in his separate business, through loans on which only he was liable, was separate property.[219] In contrast, a husband's premarital business was converted to marital in part because the marital home was used as collateral for a loan benefitting the business.[220] However, use of a wife's separate property to secure marital debt did not convert her property to marital.[221] An asset acquired with separate loan funds may become marital through commingling or family use.[222]

Payments due to one or both spouses as a lender are marital if the loaned funds were marital. Payments pursuant to a couple's loan to friends were properly classified as marital, in the absence of proof that separate funds were used to make the loan.[223]

[8] Life insurance proceeds and policies. A life insurance policy with cash surrender value is marital property if payments were made with marital funds, and separate property if payments were made with separate funds.[224] If both marital and separate funds were used, the policy would be partly separate and partly marital if the separate funds were properly traced.[225] For purposes of equitable distribution, the value of a life insurance policy is the cash surrender value of the policy, not the amount ultimately payable to the beneficiary.[226] The Mississippi appellate courts have not directly addressed this issue. However, the supreme court reversed a chancellor's separate classification of an insurance policy and remanded the case for findings regarding the source of payments, suggesting its adherence to the general rule.[227]

A spouse who receives life insurance proceeds as a policy beneficiary does not, except in unusual circumstances, earn the funds. Life insurance proceeds received by a spouse are generally treated as a gift and classified as separate property.[228]

[9] Trust interest and income

[a] Spouse as settlor of trust. Whether a trust established by a spouse for third

---

[218] Langdon v. Langdon, 854 So. 2d 485, 493 (Miss. Ct. App. 2003) (no marital funds used for payments; no commingling).

[219] Hankins v. Hankins, 866 So. 2d 508, 511-12 (Miss. Ct. App. 2004) (even the fact that his wife loaned him funds to use in the business did not convert the business to marital property; relationship was treated as a debtor-creditor relationship; loans were repaid).

[220] Faerber v. Faerber, 13 So. 3d 853, 859-60 (Miss. Ct. App. 2009) (husband's girlfriend forged wife's name on loan documents).

[221] Jones v. Jones, 904 So. 2d 1143 (Miss. Ct. App. 2004).

[222] See supra § 6.05.

[223] Yancey v. Yancey, 752 So. 2d 1006, 1011-12 (Miss. 1999); see also Parker v. Parker, 929 So. 2d 940, 944 (Miss. Ct. App. 2005) (promissory notes from sale of husband's marital business properly classified as marital).

[224] Wright v. Wright, 779 S.W.2d 183, 184 (Ark. Ct. App. 1989); Kambur v. Kambur, 652 So. 2d 99, 102-03 (La. Ct. App. 1995); Mount v. Mount, 476 A.2d 1175, 1181 (Md. Ct. Spec. App. 1984).

[225] See In re Marriage of Henke, 728 N.E.2d 1137, 1147 (Ill. App. Ct. 2000). In Mississippi, however, the commingling rule could convert the asset to all marital. See supra § 6.05.

[226] In re Marriage of Foottit, 903 P. 2d 1209, 1213 (Colo. Ct. App. 1995); Davis .v Davis, 775 S.W.2d 942, 944 (Ky. Ct. App. 1989); Kambur v. Kambur, 652 So. 2d 99, 104 (La. Ct. App. 1995); Mount v. Mount, 476 A.2d 1175, 1181 (Md. Ct. Spec. App. 1984); Dixon v. Dixon, 919 P.2d 28, 30-31 (Okla. Civ. App. 1996).

[227] See Traxler v. Traxler, 730 So. 2d 1098, 1104-05 (Miss. 1998).

[228] See In re Marriage of Goodwin, 606 N.W.2d 315, 319 (Iowa 2000); Odle v. Eastman, 453 S.E.2d 598, 602 (W. Va. 1994).

157

§ 6.06[9][b]   MISSISSIPPI FAMILY LAW

parties is considered property in equitable distribution depends upon whether the trust is revocable. A revocable trust is considered the property of the settlor, while an irrevocable trust belongs to the beneficiary. Thus, a spouse who creates a revocable trust still owns the trust assets – the beneficiary's interest is speculative because of the right to revoke. Assets in a revocable trust should be classified as they would have been in the absence of the trust.[229] Upon divorce, trust assets that would otherwise be marital may be divided equitably.[230]

On the other hand, an irrevocable trust created by a spouse belongs to the beneficiary; trust assets should not be included in the marital estate.[231] However, some courts have held that the value of marital assets placed in a trust established during marriage may be treated as marital property at divorce and the value distributed, even in the absence of proof of an intent to avoid the spouse's claim.[232] In a related context, the Mississippi Court of Appeals suggested that funds transferred to children's educational accounts, but used for other purposes, may be marital property.[233]

[b] Spouse as beneficiary of trust. A beneficiary spouse's interest in a revocable trust created by a third party is not "property" for purposes of equitable distribution.[234] Nor is the possibility of inheritance considered a marital asset.[235] On the other hand, a spouse's beneficial interest in a vested, irrevocable trust is property belonging to that spouse and must be classified as marital or separate. The interest will generally be separate property, since trust interests are usually gifts.[236] For example, a husband's interest in a family land partnership that held title to the marital home was found to be his separate property.[237]

Most courts hold that an unvested interest in an irrevocable trust is too speculative to qualify as "property" for purposes of equitable distribution, and therefore need not be classified as separate or marital.[238]

[c] Self-settled trusts. An irrevocable trust created by a spouse for himself or herself will generally take the classification of the assets transferred into the trust.[239] Self-settled trusts have traditionally been considered against public policy as a means of removing assets from the reach of the settlor's creditors, including a divorcing

---

[229] *See* Skokos v. Skokos, 968 S.W.2d 26, 31 (Ark. 1998); Heinrich v. Heinrich, 609 So. 2d 94, 95-96 (Fla. Dist. Ct. App. 1992).

[230] *See In re* Marriage of Malquist, 739 P.2d 482, 484 (Mont. 1987); Lynch v. Lynch, 522 A.2d 234, 235 (Vt. 1987); Kelln v. Kelln, 515 S.E.2d 789, 796 (Va. Ct. App. 1999).

[231] *See* Galachiuk v. Galachiuk, 691 N.Y.S.2d 828, 829 (N.Y. App. Div. 1999).

[232] OLDHAM, *supra* note 1, § 8.05[4], at 8-61-61; *see* Riechers v. Riechers, 679 N.Y.S.2d 233 (N.Y. Sup. Ct. 1998). *But see* Skokos v. Skokos, 968 S.W.2d 26, 36 (Ark. 1998) (requiring proof of fraud in order to set aside trust in favor of children).

[233] *See* Thompson v. Thompson, 894 So. 2d 603 (Miss. Ct. App. 2004).

[234] *See* Rubin v. Rubin, 527 A.2d 1184, 1187 (Conn. 1987).

[235] MISS. CODE ANN. §§ 93-5-2, -23 (Supp. 2010) (providing that interest as heir of living person or under a third-party will is not an "asset" for divorce purposes).

[236] TURNER, *supra* note 124, § 6.93, at 480 (3d ed.); *see* Mason v. Mason, 895 S.W.2d 513, 520 (Ark. 1995); McGinley v. McGinley, 565 A.2d 1220, 1225 (Pa. Super. Ct. 1989).

[237] Owen v. Owen, 22 So. 3d 386, 389-90 (Miss. Ct. App. 2009).

[238] TURNER, *supra* note 124, § 6.94, at 484-85 (3d ed.).

[239] TURNER, *supra* note 124, § 6.94, at 482 (3d ed.).

PROPERTY DIVISION   **§ 6.06[10]**

spouse.[240]

   [10] Marital home. Under basic rules of equitable distribution, an asset is marital to the extent it was purchased or improved with marital funds or efforts, and separate to the extent that equity is attributable to separate funds.[241] In Mississippi, however, the marital home is rarely classified as a separate or mixed asset. Under the Mississippi family-use doctrine, any separate property used extensively by a family is converted to a marital asset. In addition, the commingling of separate and marital funds in the purchase and upkeep of a home usually converts the entire property to a marital asset.[242] A few recent court of appeals decisions appear to reject the strict commingling rule.[243] In other cases, however, the traditional Mississippi commingling rule has been applied.[244] In several cases, marital homes have been treated as separate property without discussion of the family-use doctrine.[245]
   Marital homes have been classified as separate in a few cases involving short marriages in which the non-owning spouse contributed little or nothing to the home purchase or improvement.[246] In other cases involving short marriages, homes have been classified as marital, but divided unequally in light of the owner's separate property contribution. For example, a court erred in failing to credit a husband of five years with some amount in recognition of his premarital ownership of the lot on which the home was built.[247] And a court did not err in classifying a home as marital but awarding a

---

[240] See Restatement (Third) of Trusts § 58, which provides that: "A restraint on the voluntary and involuntary alienation of a beneficial interest retained by the settlor of a trust is invalid." A growing minority of states now permit self-settled trusts. However, the statutory scheme may except claims by divorcing spouses and children for support and property division. See 2007 ABA Section of Taxation Panel, 2007 ABATAX-CLE 0929036.

[241] See discussion supra § 6.04.

[242] See, e.g., Stewart v. Stewart, 864 So. 2d 934, 938 (Miss. 2003) (family use); Boutwell v. Boutwell, 829 So. 2d 1216, 1221 (Miss. 2002) (family use); Singley v. Singley, 846 So. 2d 1004, 1011-12 (Miss. 2002) (commingling); Bullock v. Bullock, 699 So. 2d 1205, 1210-11 (Miss. 1997) (commingling); Henderson v. Henderson, 703 So. 2d 262, 264-65 (Miss. 1997) (commingling); Maslowski v. Maslowski, 655 So. 2d 18, 23 (Miss. 1995) (commingling); Hankins v. Hankins, 866 So. 2d 508, 511-12 (Miss. Ct. App. 2004) (family use); King v. King, 760 So. 2d 830, 836 (Miss. Ct. App. 2000) (family use); Belding v. Belding, 736 So. 2d 425, 432 (Miss. Ct. App. 1999) (commingling).

[243] See Brock v. Brock, 906 So. 2d 879, 887-88 (Miss. Ct. App. 2005); see also Delk v. Delk, 41 So. 3d 738, 740-41 (Miss. Ct. App. 2010) (treating premarital home used for family purposes as mixed asset); Oliver v. Oliver, 812 So. 2d 1128, 1134-35 (Miss. Ct. App. 2002).

[244] See Ory v. Ory, 936 So. 2d 405, 412 (Miss. Ct. App. 2006) (en banc) (chancellor erred in crediting wife for contributing $16,000 personal injury funds to marital home; funds were commingled and lost separate classification); Fogarty v. Fogarty, 922 So. 2d 836, 840 (Miss. Ct. App. 2006) (husband's separate property classified as marital based on family use and commingling; couple lived in the home and added a carport; cf. Jordan v. Jordan, 963 So. 2d 1235, 1247-48 (Miss. Ct. App. 2007) (marital home financed by husband's parents properly awarded to husband; wife's economic and homemaker contributions were limited).

[245] See Duncan v. Duncan, 915 So. 2d 1124, 1127 (Miss. Ct. App. 2005) (marital home owned by wife prior to marriage awarded to her either as separate property or because husband made no contribution; no discussion of family use); Brock v. Brock, 906 So. 2d 879, 887-88 (Miss. Ct. App. 2005) (home inherited by wife classified as separate; no mention of family use even though couple lived in home several times during marriage).

[246] See Wilson v. Wilson, 820 So. 2d 761, 763 (Miss. Ct. App. 2002) (error to classify husband's premarital home as marital property; wife made no financial contribution and lived in the home only five years); Uglem v. Uglem, 831 So. 2d 1175, 1177-78 (Miss. Ct. App. 2002) (separate funds used to construct home remained separate after two-year marriage; premarital agreement significant, but result held equitable without agreement). But see Stewart v. Stewart, 864 So. 2d 934, 938 (Miss. 2003) (home classified as marital and divided unequally after one year of cohabitation).

[247] See Drumright v. Drumright, 812 So. 2d 1021, 1025-26 (Miss. Ct. App. 2001) (fairness required some credit, although not necessarily dollar-for-dollar); see also Singley v. Singley, 846 So. 2d 1004, 1008 (Miss. 2002) (error to divide marital home equally in light of husband's $70,000 contribution and wife's adultery).

§ 6.06[11]   MISSISSIPPI FAMILY LAW

husband eighty percent of the value based on his premarital ownership.[248] Division of the marital home is discussed in more detail in Section 6.08[3].

[11] Lottery and gambling proceeds. Winnings from lotteries and gambling are typically classified based on the funds used to purchase the lottery ticket. If marital funds were used, the winnings are marital.[249] The Mississippi Court of Appeals held that a chancellor erred in failing to classify lottery winnings, but did not address whether the proceeds were separate or marital.[250] Courts often divide lottery winnings equally between divorcing spouses, rejecting the winning spouse's argument that purchasing the ticket was an extraordinary contribution.[251] However, if the winnings were received after the parties separated, courts have sometimes awarded most or all of the winnings to the owning spouse.[252]

[12] Closely owned businesses. Closely owned businesses present unique challenges in equitable distribution. Businesses may be mixed assets, owned before marriage or gifted to the owner, but actively appreciating during the marriage. Valuation is critical and difficult, requiring courts to value an asset unlikely to be sold and closely linked to the owner's management. Mississippi courts have added an additional twist to valuation, requiring the exclusion of goodwill from all business valuations in divorce. Division of closely owned businesses is discussed in detail in Chapter VIII.

[13] Retirement benefits. Retirement benefits, often one of divorcing parties' primary assets, are governed by federal law in addition to state family law doctrines. Special rules govern the classification, valuation, and division of retirement benefits. These rules are discussed in detail in Chapter VII.

---

[248] Stewart v. Stewart, 864 So. 2d 934, 939 (Miss. 2003); *see also* Lindsey v. Lindsey, 749 So. 2d 77, 80 (Miss. 1999) (approving award of one-fifth of home value to wife); Bullock v. Bullock, 699 So. 2d 1205, 1211 (Miss. 1997) (error to divide equally where husband contributed $35,000 in separate property during nine-year marriage); Curry v. Curry, 45 So. 3d 724, 727-28 (Miss. Ct. App. 2010) (awarding husband 30% of wife's premarital home); Berryman v. Berryman, 907 So. 2d 958 (Miss. Ct. App. 2004) (not error to award all of equity to wife, who contributed approximately that amount to acquisition), *aff'd*, 907 So. 2d 944 (Miss. 2005) (en banc). *But see* A & L, Inc. v. Grantham, 747 So. 2d 832, 840 (Miss. 1999) (equal division not error, in spite of husband's separate contribution, after eight-year marriage); Lockert v. Lockert, 815 So. 2d 1267, 1269-70 (Miss. Ct. App. 2002) (wife's separate property home converted to marital during nineteen-year marriage; wife awarded larger share of overall marital estate).

[249] *See In re* Marriage of Swartz, 512 N.W.2d 825, 826 (Iowa Ct. App. 1993); Alston v. Alston, 629 A.2d 70, 74 (Md. 1993); Ullah v. Ullah, 555 N.Y.S.2d 834, 835 (N.Y. App. Div. 1990); Mayes v. Stewart, 11 S.W.3d 440, 457 (Tex. App. 2000).

[250] *See* Kalman v. Kalman, 905 So. 2d 760 (Miss. Ct. App. 2004) (reversing for "determination under the applicable case law" whether winnings were separate or marital).

[251] *See* TURNER, *supra* note 3, § 6.24, at 434-435; *In re* Marriage of Swartz, 512 N.W.2d 825, 826-27 (Iowa Ct. App. 1993) (equal division fair); Ullah v. Ullah, 555 N.Y.S.2d 834, 835-36 (N.Y. App. Div. 1990) (same).

[252] *See* Alston v. Alston, 629 A.2d 70, 76 (Md. 1993) (error to divide post-separation lottery winnings equally); Holliday v. Holliday, 651 A.2d 12, 15 (N.H. 1994) (court did not err in awarding all lottery winnings to husband; winnings acquired three years after separation following a short marriage).

PROPERTY DIVISION

§ 6.07

§ 6.07 VALUATION

Establishing the value of divorcing parties' assets is one of the basic steps in equitable distribution.[253] Failure to value assets may be reversible error.

[1] The measure of value. Assets of divorcing parties are measured by fair market value[254] – the price a willing buyer would pay to a willing seller if both were adequately informed about the transaction.[255] Except in unusual cases, liquidation value is not the proper measure of value.[256]

Disputes arise over whether the fair market value of an asset should be reduced to reflect costs of sale and taxes. Most courts hold that fees and taxes should not be deducted unless the asset will actually be sold.[257] The Mississippi Supreme Court held that it was error to reduce the marital home value by 6% to reflect a hypothetical sales commission where parties did not plan to sell.[258]

If the asset involves a stream of payments after divorce, such as a retirement benefit, the proper valuation is the present value of the anticipated stream of benefits. The Mississippi Supreme Court held that a chancellor should have valued a husband's retirement benefit by present value, rather than the total amount of the anticipated stream of income.[259]

[2] Findings of fact regarding value. Mississippi appellate courts have reversed a number of decisions for failure to value marital assets or because values were out-of-date or untrustworthy.[260] However, some decisions have been affirmed even though an asset was not valued.[261] In some cases, an estimate of value may be appropriate if the parties fail to present evidence of value. The court of appeals affirmed a chancellor's

---

[253] *See* Ferguson v. Ferguson, 639 So. 2d 921, 929 (Miss. 1994).

[254] Ferguson v. Ferguson, 639 So. 2d 921, 929 (Miss. 1994); *see* Heigle v. Heigle, 771 So. 2d 341, 346 (Miss. 2000); Ward v. Ward, 825 So. 2d 713, 716 (Miss. Ct. App. 2002); Drumright v. Drumright, 812 So. 2d 1021, 1025 (Miss. Ct. App. 2001).

[255] *See* Redd v. Redd, 774 So. 2d 492, 495 (Miss. Ct. App. 2000) (quoting expert: "[F]air market value is 'the most likely price at which the business would change hands between a willing buyer and a willing seller.'").

[256] TURNER, *supra* note 124, § 7.7, at 650 (3d ed.).

[257] TURNER, *supra* note 124, § 7.8, at 653-655 (3d ed.).

[258] Scott v. Scott, 835 So. 2d 82, 87 (Miss. Ct. App. 2002).

[259] Lowrey v. Lowrey, 25 So. 3d 274, 291-92 (Miss. 2009).

[260] *See* Bresnahan v. Bresnahan, 818 So. 2d 1113, 1119 (Miss. 2002) (remand appropriate where value of disputed items were either out of date or untrustworthy); Richardson v. Richardson, 912 So. 2d 1079, 1082 (Miss. Ct. App. 2005) (court erred in assigning "seemingly arbitrary" value of $850 to each head of cattle; remanded for findings with regard to value); Horn v. Horn, 909 So. 2d 1151, 1162-63 (Miss. Ct. App. 2005) (reversing property division for failure to value assets; only evidence was couple's conflicting statements of value); Aron v. Aron, 832 So. 2d 1257, 1260 (Miss. Ct. App. 2002) (reversed for specific findings regarding marital asset values); Scott v. Scott, 835 So. 2d 82, 87 (Miss. Ct. App. 2002) (use of 1970 values error); Ward v. Ward, 825 So. 2d 713, 718 (Miss. Ct. App. 2002) (failure to value ten horses, saddles, tack, a mobile home, and vehicles); Wilson v. Wilson, 811 So. 2d 342, 346 (Miss. Ct. App. 2001) (reversing for failure to value front end loader, trailer, and subsoiler); King v. King, 760 So. 2d 830 (Miss. Ct. App. 2000). *But cf.* Bresnahan v. Bresnahan, 818 So. 2d 1113, 1119-20 (Miss. 2002) (chancellor warranted in accepting old appraisals of wife's furs and jewelry to balance claim that other valuations were inflated).

[261] *See* East v. East, 775 So. 2d 741, 744-45 (Miss. Ct. App. 2000) (awarding wife $31,500 and husband $6,650 plus his retirement account which was not valued); *cf.* Rodriguez v. Rodriguez, 2 So. 3d 720, 725 (Miss. Ct. App. 2009) (affirming chancellor's award even though certain assets not valued; court awarded assets as requested by parties).

§ 6.07[3]   MISSISSIPPI FAMILY LAW

$10,000 estimate of value where no other evidence was available.[262] Similarly, when the parties provided inadequate proof of value, a chancellor's valuation with "some evidentiary support" was upheld.[263] A chancellor did not err in valuing a marital home by dividing the parties' appraised values. Taking the average of the two appraisals was a fair manner of arriving at a valuation.[264]

In other cases, a court's estimate of value has been reversed. A court erred in estimating a husband's separate property interest at between $250,000 and $400,000, based solely on the income generated by the property.[265] In two 2009 cases, the court of appeals appeared to require a more rigorous examination of the value of closely held businesses. A chancellor erred in valuing a closely held business based on financial statements presented by a wife who could not explain the basis of the value.[266] And a chancellor erred in accepting a husband's business valuation without examining the evidence to determine whether personal and business expenses and assets had been commingled.[267]

[3] Burden of proof. The Mississippi appellate courts have not directly addressed whether a party seeking division of an asset has the burden of proving value.[268] In at least one case, the supreme court affirmed a chancellor's refusal to award a wife any interest in her husband's farm property because she failed to introduce any evidence of value.[269] In other cases, however, division has been reversed for failure to value assets.[270] In some cases involving mixed assets with multiple valuation dates, the spouse seeking to classify a portion of the asset as separate may have the burden of proving

---

[262] Messer v. Messer, 850 So. 2d 161, 170 (Miss. Ct. App. 2003).

[263] Dunaway v. Dunaway, 749 So. 2d 1112, 1121 (Miss. Ct. App. 1999); *see also* Wilson v. Wilson, 975 So. 2d 261, 264 (Miss. Ct. App. 2007) (court properly valued corporation based on balance sheet provided by wife, even though underlying documentation missing); Studdard v. Studdard, 894 So. 2d 615 (Miss. Ct. App. 2004) (chancellor did not err in basing value on parties' financial statements; they offered no appraisals and no experts); *cf.* Jones v. Jones, 904 So. 2d 1143 (Miss. Ct. App. 2004) (failure to explicitly value personal property awarded to each party not error; court had values in financial statements).

[264] McKnight v. McKnight, 951 So. 2d 594, 596 (Miss. Ct. App. 2007).

[265] Johnston v. Johnston, 722 So. 2d 453, 459 (Miss. 1998); *see also* Goodson v. Goodson, 910 So. 2d 35, 37-38 (Miss. Ct. App. 2005) (remanding for specific valuation of wife's painting business; chancellor found only that business was worth "at least $100,000" based on yearly income).

[266] Lewis v. Lewis, 54 So. 3d 233, 238-40 (Miss. Ct. App. 2009), *rev'd in part on other grounds*, 54 So. 3d 216 (Miss. 2011). *But cf.* Irby v. Estate of Irby, 7 So. 3d 223, 235 (Miss. 2009) (chancellor did not err in accepting husband's testimony valuing marital business; no other evidence of value was offered); Wilson v. Wilson, 975 So. 2d 261, 264 (Miss. Ct. App. 2007) (court properly valued corporation based on balance sheet provided by wife, even though underlying documentation missing).

[267] Faerber v. Faerber, 13 So. 3d 853, 860 n.2 (Miss. Ct. App. 2009) (tax returns in evidence showed business deductions that may have been personal expenses paid by the company).

[268] Turner states that courts vary in their approach to this issue, with some requiring a party seeking division to offer proof of value and others remanding for a determination of value. TURNER, *supra* note 124, § 7.1, at 613-14 (3d ed.).

[269] *See* Carnathan v. Carnathan, 722 So. 2d 1248, 1252 (Miss. 1998). *But see* McDuffie v. McDuffie, 21 So. 3d 685, 690-91 (Miss. Ct. App. 2009) (chancellor did not err in ordering all personal property sold and proceeds divided to avoid "further wasting of the legal systems's valuable resources" where neither party presented evidence of the value). In another case, however, a chancellor erred in ordering a couple's property sold and divided as a remedy for their failure to provide values. Parker v. Parker, 980 So. 2d 323, 326-27 (Miss. Ct. App. 2008).

[270] Horn v. Horn, 909 So. 2d 1151, 1162-63 (Miss. Ct. App. 2005) (reversing property division for failure to value assets; only evidence was couple's conflicting statements of value); Ward v. Ward, 825 So. 2d 713, 718 (Miss. Ct. App. 2002) (failure to value ten horses, saddles, tack, a mobile home, and vehicles); Wilson v. Wilson, 811 So. 2d 342, 346 (Miss. Ct. App. 2001) (reversing for failure to value front-end loader, trailer, and subsoiler).

PROPERTY DIVISION   § 6.07[4]

one or more of the valuation dates.[271]

[4] Date of valuation. The proper date for valuation is a matter within the chancellor's discretion.[272] With the exceptions noted below, assets should generally be valued as close to the trial date as feasible.[273] A court erred in using 1970 values in a 2000 divorce action.[274] And a home should have been valued after post-hurricane repairs were made, rather than by using an earlier valuation.[275]

Some assets require valuation at an earlier date such as the date of a temporary support order. Assets classified as "mixed" may require two and, in some cases, three valuation dates. And in some cases, valuation after divorce may be required, when the value of an asset to be divided between the parties drops in value.

[a] Temporary support order. If a temporary support order or separate maintenance order has been entered, marital property accumulation ends on that date in Mississippi. Subsequent increases in value attributable to a spouse's efforts are separate property. Passive increases in value after that date will take the character of the asset as of the date of the temporary support order.[276] For example, a husband's contributions to an investment account after a separate maintenance order were his separate property, while interest increases on the marital share were marital property.[277] In these cases, assets may need to be valued both at the date of the temporary support order and the date of trial.

In a few cases, chancellors have valued an asset on the date of separation even in the absence of a temporary support order, as a means of recognizing one spouse's sole contribution to the asset. A chancellor did not err in valuing a wife's retirement as of the time of the couple's separation and the husband's retirement as of the time of the divorce hearing six years later. Upon separation, the husband discontinued contributions to retirement, while the wife continued making contributions to hers.[278] Similarly, the court of appeals affirmed an order valuing a husband's retirement account on the date that his wife left him and their children for a man she met in a bar.[279]

---

[271] *See supra* § 6.03[4][b].

[272] Hensarling v. Hensarling, 824 So. 2d 583, 591 (Miss. 2002); MacDonald v. MacDonald, 698 So. 2d 1079, 1086 (Miss. 1997) (declining to set valuation date as a matter of law; chancellor did not err in valuing business as of date of divorce rather than separation); Holdeman v. Holdeman, 34 So. 3d 650 (Miss. Ct. App. 2010); Bullock v. Bullock, 733 So. 2d 292, 298-99 (Miss. Ct. App. 1998) (same).

[273] TURNER, *supra* note 3, § 7.02; *see* Bresnahan v. Bresnahan, 818 So. 2d 1113, 1119 (Miss. 2002) (remand appropriate where value of disputed items were either out-of-date or untrustworthy); Heigle v. Heigle, 771 So. 2d 341, 350 (Miss. 2000) (chancellor erred in valuing business as of 1998, the date of remand, rather than 1992, the effective date of divorce).

[274] Scott v. Scott, 835 So. 2d 82, 87 (Miss. Ct. App. 2002).

[275] Saucier v. Saucier, 830 So. 2d 1261 (Miss. Ct. App. 2002).

[276] *See supra* § 6.03[4].

[277] *See* Hensarling v. Hensarling, 824 So. 2d 583, 591-92 (Miss. 2002) (but referring in one place in the opinion to the date of separation rather than the date of a separate maintenance order).

[278] Cossey v. Cossey, 22 So. 3d 353, 360 (Miss. Ct. App. 2009). The case does not state whether the account appreciated apart from the wife's additional contributions.

[279] Sullivan v. Sullivan, 990 So. 2d 783 (Miss. Ct. App. 2008) (two-thirds of assets awarded to husband whose wife left him and their children for man she met in a bar).

163

§ 6.07[4][b]   MISSISSIPPI FAMILY LAW

[b] Premarital assets. Two valuation dates may be needed for premarital assets. For example, if a premarital asset has actively appreciated in value during marriage, the asset should be valued at the date of marriage and the date of trial.[280] If a temporary support order is also involved, three measures of value may be required. A 2009 case involving premarital ownership of a business, a temporary support order, and post-support order appreciation illustrates the need for multiple valuation dates. A husband's separate property business appreciated during marriage through his efforts. After a temporary support order was entered in the couple's divorce, the business appreciated passively, according to the wife's expert. To properly divide the asset, the court would need a valuation at the date of marriage, the date of the temporary support order, and the date of trial.[281]

[c] Valuation on remand. To the extent that an asset has appreciated post-divorce because of one spouse's efforts, that asset should be valued as of the date of divorce. The Mississippi Supreme Court held that a husband's one-half interest in the marital home should be valued at the time of divorce and not, as he argued, several years after the case had been appealed and retried. His wife lived in the home and had made all payments since the divorce.[282] However, if a marital asset has appreciated passively since divorce, the growth should be included in the valuation on remand.[283]

[5] Proof of value. Value may be proven by expert testimony, lay witnesses, or documents such as financial statements. Expert opinion is not required with regard to some assets, but may be critical to an accurate valuation of others, such as closely held businesses.

[a] Expert testimony. Whether to require expert testimony on the value of an asset is a matter generally within the court's discretion. However, the Mississippi Supreme Court has stated that in some divorce cases, the complexity of valuation issues requires expert testimony. The court reversed and remanded a chancellor's valuation of a husband's medical practice based on his testimony alone.[284] Similarly, the court of appeals reversed a chancellor's valuation of a business based on a financial statement offered by the wife but which she could not explain.[285] The court of appeals also

---

[280] *See* A & L, Inc. v. Grantham, 747 So. 2d 832, 839 (Miss. 1999) (business classified as all marital because husband failed to introduce proof of value at the time of the marriage).

[281] Fleishhacker v. Fleishhacker, 39 So. 3d 904, 911 (Miss. Ct. App. 2009) (case remanded for determination of value at date of marriage and whether post-support order appreciation was passive or active).

[282] Henderson v. Henderson, 757 So. 2d 285, 293 (Miss. 2000); *see also* Yelverton v. Yelverton, 26 So. 3d 1053, 1057 (Miss. 2010) (value of husband's business on remand to be determined as of date of divorce); Lowrey v. Lowrey, 25 So. 3d 274, 286 (Miss. 2009) (chancellor erred in valuing husband's assets as of date of remand rather than at the time of divorce).

[283] TURNER, *supra* note 124, at § 7.6, at 648-49 (3d ed.). *But cf.* Lowrey v. Lowrey, 25 So. 3d 274, 286, 291-92 (Miss. 2009) (chancellor erred in valuing husband's assets as of date of remand rather than at the time of divorce; not clear whether growth was passive or active).

[284] Mace v. Mace, 818 So. 2d 1130, 1134 (Miss. 2002); *see also* Heigle v. Heigle, 771 So. 2d 341, 349 (Miss. 2000) (not abuse of discretion to appoint expert).

[285] Lewis v. Lewis, 54 So. 3d 233, 239-40 (Miss. Ct. App. 2009), *rev'd in part on other grounds*, 54 So. 3d 216 (Miss. 2011). *But see* Irby v. Estate of Irby, 7 So. 3d 223, 235 (Miss. 2009) (chancellor did not err in accepting husband's testimony valuing marital business; no other evidence of value was offered).

PROPERTY DIVISION

§ 6.07[5][b]

held that a chancellor should have closely examined a husband's business valuation for commingling of personal and business assets.[286] In contrast, a chancellor's refusal to appoint an expert to value household belongings was not error; the valuation issues were not complicated.[287] And a court properly valued a couple's homes and retirement accounts based on their estimates.[288]

A party without sufficient resources to retain a separate expert may request court appointment of an expert, with the costs to be shared or born by the higher-income spouse.[289] Business valuation may be provided by accountants as well as certified business valuation experts. A trial court erred in excluding an accountant's testimony regarding the value of his client's dental practice, since the rules of evidence permit testimony by a lay person familiar with value.[290] A court may order valuation of properties even in the absence of a request by the parties.[291]

[b] Testimony of the parties or other lay witnesses. In the absence of expert testimony, other evidence of value may be presented, including testimony of the parties[292] or other lay witnesses familiar with the value of the property.[293] A building was valued below the figure used in financial statements, based on the husband's testimony that the foundation needed repair.[294] However, the opinion must have some basis in fact. A court properly rejected a husband physician's opinion that his practice was worth six times the monthly net income of the practice, based on a formula he read in a medical journal.[295]

[c] Financial statements. A court may adopt values set out in a party's financial statements. A husband's prior financial statements were properly used to value dairy cattle even though he testified that the actual value was lower.[296] When no other evidence of value is presented, a court may also base its valuation on a party's Rule

---

[286] Faerber v. Faerber, 13 So. 3d 853, 859 (Miss. Ct. App. 2009).

[287] Wells v. Wells, 800 So. 2d 1239, 1243 (Miss. Ct. App. 2001).

[288] *See* Sandlin v. Sandlin, 699 So. 2d 1198, 1203 (Miss. 1997); *cf.* Smith v. Smith, 25 So. 3d 369, 376 (Miss. Ct. App. 2009) (not error to use marital home value of $600,000, agreed to by husband in deposition, even though home had been on market for nine months with no offer above $500,000).

[289] *See* Mace v. Mace, 818 So. 2d 1130, 1134 (Miss. 2002) (chancellor may appoint expert to assist with complex valuation); Heigle v. Heigle, 771 So. 2d 341, 349 (Miss. 2000) (expert fees may be awarded based on showing that one party is unable to pay; reversed for findings); Rush v. Rush, 932 So. 2d 800, 803 (Miss. Ct. App. 2005) (expert appointed by court), *rev'd in part on other grounds,* 932 So. 2d 794 (Miss. 2006) (en banc); Rush v. Rush *ex rel.* Mayne, 914 So. 2d 322, 326 (Miss. Ct. App. 2005) (en banc) (court did not accept husband's $3,500 valuation of mobile home; ordered appraisal).

[290] *See* Singley v. Singley, 846 So. 2d 1004, 1010 (Miss. 2002).

[291] Parker v. Parker, 980 So. 2d 323, 333 (Miss. Ct. App. 2008); Miss. R. Evid. 706(a).

[292] *See* Mace v. Mace, 818 So. 2d 1130, 1134 (Miss. 2002). In one case, the court rejected expert valuation in favor of the lay opinion of one of the parties. *See* Dunn v. Dunn, 911 So. 2d 591, 599 (Miss. Ct. App. 2005) (court did not err in accepting husband's testimony regarding land value over unrealistic appraisal).

[293] *See* Miss. R. Evid. 702.

[294] Watson v. Watson, 882 So. 2d 95, 106 (Miss. 2004) (valued at $120,000 rather than $150,000 figure in financial statements); *see also* Marshall v. Marshall, 979 So. 2d 699 (Miss. Ct. App. 2007) (court did not err in establishing value that took into account needed repairs); Carroll v. Carroll, 976 So. 2d 880 (Miss. Ct. App. 2007) (party who failed to comply with discovery could not complain that valuation was based on testimony of parties).

[295] *See* Mace v. Mace, 818 So. 2d 1130, 1134 (Miss. 2002).

[296] *See* Dunaway v. Dunaway, 749 So. 2d 1112, 1118 (Miss. Ct. App. 1999).

§ 6.07[5][d]   **MISSISSIPPI FAMILY LAW**

8.05 Financial Statement.[297] And a court's use of tax appraisals for valuation was appropriate; the parties relied on the figure at trial.[298] Similarly, a chancellor properly relied on values in a husband's recent bankruptcy petition in the absence of other evidence.[299] However, the Mississippi Supreme Court rejected a wife's argument that financial statements were a better indicator of value than expert testimony. The court noted the importance of expert testimony in establishing fair market value.[300] And the court of appeals reversed a court's determination of business value based on financial statements produced by a wife who could not explain the basis of the value.[301]

      [d] Buy-sell agreements. Divorce courts are not bound by values set out in partnership or corporate buy-sell agreements, but will frequently give deference to them, particularly where the agreement was entered prior to marital breakdown and not for the purpose of defrauding the other spouse.[302]

      [6] Retirement benefits. Valuation of retirement benefits is addressed in detail in Chapter VII.

      [7] Closely held businesses. Valuation of closely held businesses is addressed in Chapter VIII.

§ 6.08 DIVISION OF MARITAL PROPERTY

In the final stage of equitable distribution, marital assets are divided equitably between the parties. In contrast to the rule-oriented classification stage, the division stage is characterized by judicial discretion. Judges are charged with reaching a fair result in each case based on general factors set out in *Ferguson v. Ferguson*.[303] If the court has properly classified the parties' assets and made the required findings with regard to each division factor, the resulting award is rarely reversed.[304]

A court's division of assets is based on the unique circumstances of each couple – it is impossible to develop a formula for division. A particular *Ferguson* factor may strongly influence division of assets in one case and play an insignificant role in another.

---

[297] *See* Common v. Common, 42 So. 3d 59, 62-63 (Miss. Ct. App. 2010) (court did not err in using 8.05 values absent more reliable evidence); King v. King, 946 So. 2d 395, 403 (Miss. Ct. App. 2006) (value based on wife's Rule 8.05 financial statements; husband presented no evidence of value and did not submit financial statements); Jackson v. Jackson, 922 So. 2d 53, 58 (Miss. Ct. App. 2006) (en banc) (value of three automobiles based on wife's Rule 8.05 financial statement; no other evidence of value); Seymour v. Seymour, 960 So. 2d 513, 518 (Miss. Ct. App. 2006) (not error to value stock at $157,500 based on husband's Rule 8.05 statement).

[298] Sullivan v. Sullivan, 942 So. 2d 305, 307 (Miss. Ct. App. 2006).

[299] *See* Christopher v. Christopher, 766 So. 2d 119, 122 (Miss. Ct. App. 2000).

[300] *See* Redd v. Redd, 774 So. 2d 492, 494-95 (Miss. Ct. App. 2000).

[301] Lewis v. Lewis, 54 So. 3d 233, 239-40 (Miss. Ct. App. 2009), *rev'd in part on other grounds*, 54 So. 3d 216 (Miss. 2011).

[302] Scalchunes v. Scalchunes, 520 N.Y.S.2d 812 (N.Y. App. Div. 1997) (error for court to substitute its own valuation over buy-sell agreement executed prior to marital discord).

[303] Ferguson v. Ferguson, 639 So. 2d 921 (Miss. 1994).

[304] *See* TURNER, *supra* note 3, § 8.01, at 550 (even if a uniform rule for division could be stated, the variety of fact patterns would make it fairly useless).

PROPERTY DIVISION   § 6.08[1]

[1] Basic principles of division. Equitable distribution allows division of assets classified as marital. The system does not require equal division or division of each asset. Rather, the overall division must be equitable.

    [a] No division of separate assets. Only property classified as marital may be divided between divorcing parties. A court may not divest a spouse of title to separate property.[305] However, a spouse's separate estate may be a factor in determining each party's fair share of marital property. In addition, separate property may serve as security for property division payments.

    [b] Equal division not required. Some states have adopted a presumption that marital property should be divided equally.[306] However, the Mississippi appellate courts have repeatedly emphasized that equitable does not mean equal.[307] Chancellors have discretion to award more assets to a spouse in recognition of greater contribution, to address greater need, based on dissipation of assets, or in light of other *Ferguson* factors.[308]

    [c] Division of each asset not required. There is no requirement that each individual asset be divided between the parties. Courts frequently award a primary asset such as a business, home, or pension to one party, with the other receiving assets or payments comparable in value. A husband was not entitled to a share of the marital home simply because his wife received one-half of his pension.[309] And the supreme court rejected a wife's argument that the marital home was treated as separate because it was awarded solely to her husband – each party received an equal share of the total asset value.[310]

---

[305] *See* Ferguson v. Ferguson, 639 So. 2d 921, 929 (Miss. 1994).

[306] *See* TURNER, *supra* note 3, § 8.02, at 554 (a "respectable" minority presume equal division is fair; party seeking unequal division must rebut presumption; also noting that some states establish an equal division "starting point").

[307] *See, e.g.,* Jones v. Jones, 995 So. 2d 706, 715 (Miss. 2008); Ferguson v. Ferguson, 639 So. 2d 921, 927 (Miss. 1994) ("[T]here is no automatic right to an equal division of jointly-accumulated property, but rather, the division is left to the discretion of the court."); Owen v. Owen, 12 So. 3d 603, 606-07 (Miss. Ct. App. 2009) (wife awarded 75% of her retirement account based in part on greater emotional attachment to the plan); Marshall v. Marshall, 979 So. 2d 699 (Miss. Ct. App. 2007); Dobbs v. Dobbs, 912 So. 2d 491, 493 (Miss. Ct. App. 2005) (court did not err in awarding the wife 55% of marital assets; no requirement of equal division); Wells v. Wells, 800 So. 2d 1239, 1243-44 (Miss. Ct. App. 2001) (equal division not required; wife made greater contribution to stability and her need was greater).

[308] *See* Bresnahan v. Bresnahan, 818 So. 2d 1113, 1119 (Miss. 2002) (finding no error in chancellor's decision to award husband more of estate where husband was deemed major contributor to accumulation of assets, even though wife worked and was homemaker) (slightly under $1 million estate); Adair v. Adair, 735 So. 2d 383, 384 (Miss. 1999) (chancellor did not err in awarding wife small percentage of marital estate, considering husband's frugality compared with her "spendthrift ways" and chancellor's finding that her contributions were "minimal"); Brown v. Brown, 574 So. 2d 688, 691 (Miss. 1990) (chancellor decides division based on actual contributions of the parties); Brabham v. Brabham, 950 So. 2d 1098, 1102 (Miss. Ct. App. 2007) (awarding greater share of assets to husband who provided most of financial support and did most of household chores).

[309] Wells v. Wells, 800 So. 2d 1239, 1242 (Miss. Ct. App. 2001).

[310] Collins v. Collins, 722 So. 2d 596, 600 (Miss. 1998); *see also* Hunt v. Asanov, 975 So. 2d 899, 904-05 (Miss. Ct. App. 2008) (upholding division of marital corporation; 25% to wife, 75% to husband); Wilson v. Wilson, 975 So. 2d 261, 264 (Miss. Ct. App. 2007) (rejecting wife's argument that court classified business as separate because it was awarded solely to husband); Shoffner v. Shoffner, 909 So. 2d 1245, 1250 (Miss. Ct. App. 2005) (rejecting wife's argument that she received no interest in marital home; her share was offset by dissipated retirement funds).

§ 6.08[1][d]   **MISSISSIPPI FAMILY LAW**

[d] Division factors. In *Ferguson v. Ferguson*, the Mississippi Supreme Court set out eight factors to guide chancellors in dividing marital property. To reach a fair division, courts are to consider: (1) substantial contribution to property accumulation, including indirect economic contribution, contribution to family stability, and contribution to the education or training of the wage-earning spouse; (2) spousal use or disposition of assets and distribution by agreement; (3) the market and emotional value of assets; (4) the value of each spouse's separate estate; (5) tax consequences and legal consequences to third parties; (6) the extent to which property division can eliminate the need for alimony; (7) the needs of each spouse; and (8) other factors which should be considered in equity.[311] Later in 1994, the supreme court clarified the role of marital fault in property division, holding that fault remains a factor for consideration but that division should not be designed to punish a party for fault.[312] The *Ferguson* listing is not exclusive; a chancellor may consider other factors.[313]

[e] Presumption of equal contribution. Although there is no presumption that assets should be divided equally, the Mississippi Supreme Court did adopt a presumption that a homemaker's contributions to accumulation of assets equal those of a wage-earner.[314]

[f] Relationship to alimony award. The fairness of property division can be determined only in conjunction with alimony. As the Mississippi Supreme Court stated in *Ferguson*, "Alimony and equitable distribution are distinct concepts, but together they command the entire field of financial settlement of divorce. Therefore, where one expands, the other must recede.[315]

[g] Findings of fact. Chancellors must make specific findings of fact and conclusions of law with regard to the division factors.[316] A chancellor need not address each factor, only those relevant to the particular case.[317] But an award will be reversed if the appellate court finds that factors other than those identified by the chancellor are significant.[318] For example, an award representing a wife's share of a business was re-

---

[311] Ferguson v. Ferguson, 639 So. 2d 921, 928 (Miss. 1994).

[312] Carrow v. Carrow, 642 So. 2d 901, 904 (Miss. 1994) ("[M]arital misconduct is a viable factor entitled to be given weight by the chancellor . . . .").

[313] Johnson v. Johnson, 823 So. 2d 1156, 1160 (Miss. 2002).

[314] Helmsley v. Helmsley, 639 So. 2d 909, 915 (Miss. 1994).

[315] *See* Ferguson v. Ferguson, 639 So. 2d 921, 929 (Miss. 1994).

[316] Ferguson v. Ferguson, 639 So. 2d 921, 928 (Miss. 1994); *see* Gray v. Gray, 909 So. 2d 108, 110-11 (Miss. Ct. App. 2005) (reversed for failure to make *Ferguson* findings of fact); Thompson v. Thompson, 894 So. 2d 603 (Miss. Ct. App. 2004) (reversing for failure to make findings under *Ferguson*).

[317] *See* Sproles v. Sproles, 782 So. 2d 742, 748 (Miss. 2001); Spahn v. Spahn, 959 So. 2d 8, 14 (Miss. Ct. App. 2006) (chancellor did not consider all factors, but considered those that were relevant); Rush v. Rush *ex rel.* Mayne, 914 So. 2d 322, 325 (Miss. Ct. App. 2005) (en banc) (chancellor need only consider relevant factors); Dunn v. Dunn, 911 So. 2d 591, 596 (Miss. Ct. App. 2005) (not every *Ferguson* factor need be considered); Glass v. Glass, 857 So. 2d 786, 790 (Miss. Ct. App. 2003); Tynes v. Tynes, 860 So. 2d 325, 329 (Miss. Ct. App. 2003); Thompson v. Thompson, 815 So. 2d 466 (Miss. Ct. App. 2002).

[318] *See* Owen v. Owen, 798 So. 2d 394, 399 (Miss. 2001) (wife's domestic contributions should have been given more consideration).

168

PROPERTY DIVISION   § 6.08[1][h]

versed because the chancellor did not specifically address tax consequences or need for financial security.[319] In a 2010 case, the Mississippi Court of Appeals held that, in order to award a spouse survivor benefits from the other's retirement, the court must make findings with regard to the beneficiary's contributions to the retirement account.[320]

The trial court must conduct a *Ferguson* analysis even when the parties agree to property division and submit only the issue of alimony to the court.[321] In addition, if division is to be accomplished in part by a lump sum award, the chancellor should use the *Ferguson* factors to analyze the need for a lump sum award.[322] However, a chancellor need not make *Ferguson* findings in an uncontested proceeding[323] or in a judgment based upon the parties' agreement.[324]

Awards have been reversed and remanded for additional findings because a court stated that it reviewed the *Ferguson* factors without making specific findings regarding the factors.[325] However, failure to provide a factor-by-factor analysis of facts does not necessarily require reversal; a recitation of facts prior to discussion of the *Ferguson* factors may suffice.[326] And in one case, the court of appeals affirmed division of assets based on a listing of the factors followed by a discussion of the contribution of the parties to each asset.[327]

[h] Standard of review. An appellate court's review of a chancellor's actual division of marital assets is extremely deferential. A court's division of assets will not be reversed "unless the chancellor was manifestly wrong, clearly erroneous or an erroneous legal standard was applied."[328] Appeals based solely on the unfairness of a

---

[319] Louk v. Louk, 761 So. 2d 878, 883 (Miss. 2000).

[320] Pierce v. Pierce, 42 So. 3d 658, 662-63 (Miss. Ct. App. 2010).

[321] Cosentino v. Cosentino, 912 So. 2d 1130, 1133 (Miss. Ct. App. 2005) (factor six – the extent to which property division eliminates the need for alimony – and factor seven – the parties' financial needs – should have been considered in making alimony award).

[322] Dickerson v. Dickerson, 34 So. 3d 637, 646-47 (Miss. Ct. App. 2010) (court should not use *Cheatham* factors; however, case will not be reversed if substantial evidence supports award). *See* discussion at § 9.02[2][b][v] *infra*.

[323] Luse v. Luse, 992 So. 2d 659, 663 (Miss. Ct. App. 2008).

[324] Bougard v. Bougard, 991 So. 2d 646, 649 (Miss. Ct. App. 2008); *cf.* Seghini v. Seghini, 42 So. 3d 635, 641 (Miss. Ct. App. 2010) (failure to make findings not reversible error; couple had few assets and agreed on division of most assets).

[325] *See* Fisher v. Fisher, 771 So. 2d 364, 369 (Miss. 2000); Heigle v. Heigle, 771 So. 2d 341, 346-47 (Miss. 2000); Sandlin v. Sandlin, 699 So. 2d 1198, 1204 (Miss. 1997); Daniels v. Daniels, 950 So. 2d 1044 (Miss. Ct. App. 2007); *see also* Lauro v. Lauro, 847 So. 2d 843, 846-47 (Miss. 2003) (reversed for failure to make findings classifying marital property or explaining division of the assets); Johnson v. Johnson, 823 So. 2d 1156, 1161-62 (Miss. 2002) (no findings of fact to support extremely unequal division of household furnishings); Chmelicek v. Chmelicek, 51 So. 3d 1000 (Miss. Ct. App. 2010); Goodson v. Goodson, 816 So. 2d 420, 425 (Miss. Ct. App. 2002) (chancellor listed and divided items, but did not make *Ferguson* findings to support decision); *cf.* Segree v. Segree, 46 So. 3d 861, 865-66 (Miss. Ct. App. 2010) (reversed; *Ferguson* not mentioned; no findings of fact regarding division).

[326] Palmer v. Palmer, 841 So. 2d 185, 190 (Miss. Ct. App. 2003); *cf.* Duncan v. Duncan, 915 So. 2d 1124, 1127 (Miss. Ct. App. 2005) (en banc) (award of the only marital asset to wife upheld even though the court made no findings of fact; evidence supported award).

[327] Morris v. Morris, 5 So. 3d 476 (Miss. Ct. App. 2008); *see also* Sullivan v. Sullivan, 43 So. 3d 536, 540-41 (Miss. Ct. App. 2010) (court's discussion of facts provided sufficient foundation to support property division); Smith v. Smith, 994 So. 2d 882, 887 (Miss. Ct. App. 2008) (court did not cite *Ferguson*, but made findings regarding contribution, dissipation and emotional attachment).

[328] *See* Spahn v. Spahn, 959 So. 2d 8, 12 (Miss. Ct. App. 2006) (court does not conduct a new *Ferguson* analysis, but reviews for abuse of discretion); Lauro v. Lauro, 924 So. 2d 584, 590 (Miss. Ct. App. 2006) (property division reviewed under abuse of discretion standard); Rush v. Rush *ex rel.* Mayne, 914 So. 2d 322, 325 (Miss. Ct. App. 2005) (en banc) (appellate court does not reweigh *Ferguson* factors); Dunn v. Dunn, 911 So. 2d 591, 595-96 (Miss. Ct. App. 2005)

169

§ 6.08[2]   MISSISSIPPI FAMILY LAW

particular division are rarely successful. Most reversals of property division are based on an error of law or failure to make the required findings. Two cases were found in which equal division was reversed as substantively unfair. In one, the court held that a wife's extreme marital fault required unequal division.[329] In another, failure to recognize a husband's separate property contribution to marital assets after a short marriage required reversal.[330] Two cases were also found in which unequal division was reversed as substantively unfair. In the early years of equitable distribution, a court erred in awarding a wife who committed adultery only 5% of marital assets.[331] In another case, a court erred in dividing assets unequally based almost exclusively on the husband's financial contribution.[332] In contrast, awards or denials of alimony are much more likely to be reversed as substantively unfair.[333]

[2] The *Ferguson* factors. Each couple's circumstances present unique facts for analysis under the *Ferguson* factors. In many cases, analysis of the factors leads to an equal division of assets. Assets have been divided equally between spouses after brief marriages[334] and at the termination of lengthy marriages.[335] Equal division has been ordered even though one spouse was considered at fault.[336] And each spouse has been awarded half of marital property in cases involving small estates and estates with substantial assets.[337]

In a number of cases, however, unequal division has been affirmed. Courts have ordered unequal division to address financial need, to reward greater contribution, to account for dissipation, or because one spouse has substantial separate property. It is not uncommon for a one-third to two-third division to be affirmed as fair.[338] However,

---

(appellate court does not conduct new *Ferguson* analysis); Barnett v. Barnett, 908 So. 2d 833, 837-38 (Miss. Ct. App. 2005) (appellate court reviews division of assets under manifest error standard if chancellor used proper legal standards); Thompson v. Thompson, 815 So. 2d 466, 468 (Miss. Ct. App. 2002).

[329] *See* Singley v. Singley, 846 So. 2d 1004 (Miss. 2002) (numerous affairs during marriage affected stability).

[330] *See* Bullock v. Bullock, 699 So. 2d 1205 (Miss. 1997) (four-year marriage; husband owned house prior to marriage).

[331] *See* Davis v. Davis, 638 So. 2d 1288 (Miss. 1994).

[332] *See* Owen v. Owen, 798 So. 2d 394 (Miss. 2001).

[333] *See* discussion of alimony awards *infra* § 9.06.

[334] *See* Rogers v. Morin, 791 So. 2d 815, 819 (Miss. 2001) (five years); Parsons v. Parsons, 678 So. 2d 701, 704 (Miss. 1996) (three years); Burnham-Steptoe v. Steptoe, 755 So. 2d 1225, 1229 (Miss. Ct. App. 1999) (four years).

[335] *See* Godwin v. Godwin, 758 So. 2d 384, 386 (Miss. 1999) (thirty-seven years); Hemsley v. Hemsley, 639 So. 2d 909, 914 (Miss. 1994); Duncan v. Duncan, 815 So. 2d 480, 484 (Miss. Ct. App. 2002).

[336] *See* Henderson v. Henderson, 757 So. 2d 285, 293 (Miss. 2000) (husband committed adultery); Vaughn v. Vaughn, 798 So. 2d 431, 435 (Miss. 2001) (same); Godwin v. Godwin, 758 So. 2d 384, 386 (Miss. 1999) (same); Voda v. Voda, 731 So. 2d 1152, 1156 (Miss. 1999) (same); Bullock v. Bullock, 699 So. 2d 1205, 1209 (Miss. 1997) (husband found guilty of habitual, cruel, and inhuman treatment); Wallmark v. Wallmark, 863 So. 2d 68, 71 (Miss. Ct. App. 2003) (husband committed adultery); Duncan v. Duncan, 815 So. 2d 480, 484 (Miss. Ct. App. 2002) (same).

[337] *See* Davis v. Davis, 832 So. 2d 492, 502 (Miss. 2002) ($3.45 million); Rogers v. Morin, 791 So. 2d 815 (Miss. 2001) ("[B]oth parties were practically bankrupt . . . ."); Selman v. Selman, 722 So. 2d 547 (Miss. 1998) (approximately $15,000); Phelps v. Phelps, 937 So. 2d 974 (Miss. Ct. App. 2006); Johnson v. Johnson, 852 So. 2d 681 (Miss. Ct. App. 2003) (approximately $800,000); Gable v. Gable, 846 So. 2d 296 (Miss. Ct. App. 2003) (slightly over $100,000); Driste v. Driste, 738 So. 2d 763 (Miss. Ct. App. 1999) (approximately $50,000); Russell v. Russell, 733 So. 2d 858, 861 (Miss. Ct. App. 1999) (substantial assets).

[338] *See* Hensarling v. Hensarling, 824 So. 2d 583, 589-90 (Miss. 2002) (two-thirds to higher-income spouse); Dickerson v. Dickerson, 34 So. 3d 637, 645 (Miss. Ct. App. 2010) (60% to lower-income spouse); Klauser v. Klauser, 865 So. 2d 363, 365 (Miss. Ct. App. 2003) (two-thirds to lower-income spouse); Franklin v. Franklin, 864 So. 2d 970, 976 (Miss. Ct. App. 2003) (two-thirds to higher-income spouse); Weeks v. Weeks, 832 So. 2d 583, 585 (Miss. Ct. App. 2002)

PROPERTY DIVISION § 6.08[2][a]

only a few reported cases involve an award in which the disparity exceeds one-third of the assets.[339] The following discussion focuses primarily on the extent to which a particular factor influenced an unequal division of assets.

[a] Contribution to accumulation of assets. A spouse's contribution to marital asset accumulation is probably the single most important factor guiding property division. Consideration is not limited to economic contribution. A party's indirect contributions – childcare, homemaker services, contribution to family stability, support for training or education – are equally important.[340] It is for this reason, perhaps, that in many cases assets are divided equally between spouses.

[i] Homemaker contribution. The Mississippi Supreme Court held in *Hemsley,* the companion case to *Ferguson,* that a homemaker's contributions to marital asset accumulation are presumed to equal those of a wage earner.[341] The presumption can be rebutted by showing that a homemaker spouse did not make significant indirect contributions.[342] A chancellor did not err in awarding only 22% of assets to a homemaker husband whose author wife earned 96% of the family income. The court found that his domestic contributions were limited and that neither contributed to marital stability.[343]

Failure to recognize and apply this presumption requires reversal. For example, a court erred in finding that a wife who performed all household chores had made few indirect contributions to the marriage.[344] Similarly, the supreme court reversed an

---

(two-thirds to higher-income spouse); Lockert v. Lockert, 815 So. 2d 1267, 1270 (Miss. Ct. App. 2002) (two-thirds to higher-income spouse); Buckley v. Buckley, 815 So. 2d 1260, 1264 (Miss. Ct. App. 2002) (two-thirds to higher-income spouse); Cork v. Cork, 811 So. 2d 427, 429 (Miss. Ct. App. 2001) (two-thirds to higher-income spouse); *see also* Mabus v. Mabus, 890 So. 2d 806, 825-26 (Miss. 2003) (60% to lower-income spouse).

[339] In three cases involving limited marital assets, the primary asset was awarded to the lower-income spouse. *See* Franks v. Franks, 759 So. 2d 1164, 1169 (Miss. 1999) (marital home awarded to wife); Atkinson v. Atkinson, 11 So. 3d 172, 178 (Miss. Ct. App. 2009) (marital home and 32.5 acres, the only marital asset, awarded to wife); Bumpous v. Bumpous, 770 So. 2d 558, 559 (Miss. Ct. App. 2000) (restaurant awarded to wife). In three cases involving dissipation, the majority of assets were awarded to the innocent spouse. *See* Love v. Love, 687 So. 2d 1229, 1232 (Miss. 1997); Childs v. Childs, 806 So. 2d 273, 275 (Miss. Ct. App. 2000); Wolfe v. Wolfe, 766 So. 2d 123, 126 (Miss. Ct. App. 2000). And in three cases, a higher-income spouse was awarded 75% of assets. *See* Jones v. Jones, 995 So. 2d 706 (Miss. 2008) (awarding 78% of assets to wife who earned 96% of income during marriage); Ford v. Ford, 795 So. 2d 600, 602 (Miss. Ct. App. 2001) (wife awarded 25% of assets did not appeal); Redd v. Redd, 774 So. 2d 492, 494-95 (Miss. Ct. App. 2000) (noting that award of 23% of $4 million estate to wife was not necessarily error; remanded for other reasons).

[340] Chamblee v. Chamblee, 637 So. 2d 850, 863-64 (Miss. 1994); *see also* Hensarling v. Hensarling, 824 So. 2d 583, 590 (Miss. 2002) (equitable does not mean equal); Savelle v. Savelle, 650 So. 2d 476, 478 (Miss. 1995) (Mississippi is not a community property state); Dillon v. Dillon, 498 So. 2d 328, 330 (Miss. 1986) (same).

[341] Hemsley v. Hemsley, 639 So. 2d 909, 915 (Miss. 1994).

[342] *See* Chamblee v. Chamblee, 637 So. 2d 850, 864 (Miss. 1994) (court need not award 50% of assets to wife who does not substantially contribute); John R. Dowd, Note, *Defining the Doctrine of Equitable Distribution in Mississippi: A Rebuttable Presumption That Homemaking Services are as Valuable To the Acquisition of Marital Property as Breadwinning Services*, 16 Miss C. L. Rev. 479, 482 (1996) (simply because one has been a homemaker does not guarantee a finding of equal contribution); *cf.* Brown v. Brown, 574 So. 2d 688, 691 (Miss. 1990) (chancellor decides division based on actual contributions of the parties); Jordan v. Jordan, 963 So. 2d 1235, 1247-48 (Miss. Ct. App. 2007) (marital home financed by husband's parents properly awarded to husband; wife's economic and homemaker contributions were limited).

[343] Jones v. Jones, 995 So. 2d 706, 713 (Miss. 2008).

[344] *See* King v. King, 760 So. 2d 830, 837 (Miss. Ct. App. 2000) (domestic contributions are of equal value to financial contributions; chancellor failed to give proper weight to the wife's non-economic contributions).

§ 6.08[2][a][i]   **MISSISSIPPI FAMILY LAW**

award of most marital assets to a husband – the award focused on the wife's adultery, ignoring her substantial contributions as a homemaker.[345] Awarding 60% of assets to a husband based on financial contribution, without considering his wife's homemaker contributions, was error.[346] And a chancellor's failure to consider a disabled husband's domestic contributions was error. The court awarded a greater share of assets to the wage-earner wife based on her greater financial contribution, without considering the husband's contributions in the home.[347]

The presumption does not require equal division. Awards of less than 50% of assets to a homemaker have been affirmed if the court properly considered homemaker contribution and the resulting division was equitable.[348] The Mississippi Court of Appeals held that an award of two-thirds of a $5 million dollar marital estate to a husband did not overlook the non-economic contributions of his wife of twenty years.[349] Similarly, a court did not err in awarding a homemaker wife only one-third of the marital estate, particularly since she received debt-free assets.[350]

King v. King – a case that was appealed twice – illustrates the interaction of the homemaker presumption and the deferential standard of review. The court of appeals reversed an award in favor of a husband wage earner because the chancellor did not consider his wife's indirect contributions.[351] On remand, the chancellor found that the wife's contributions were equally valuable, but nonetheless awarded her husband a greater share of assets. The court of appeals affirmed the second award, noting that the chancellor considered the wife's contributions on remand, that equal division is not required, and that the appellate review standard is extremely deferential.[352]

In other cases, homemakers have been awarded a greater share of assets based on contribution and need. A court properly awarded a greater share of assets to a homemaker wife – her needs were greater than her husband's, her earning ability was lower, and her contribution to family stability was substantial.[353] Similarly, a chancellor properly awarded a homemaker wife of twenty years 65% of the couple's assets.[354] And a homemaker's significant domestic contributions entitled her to an award of one-half of the couple's $1 million dollar marital estate, even though the assets were acquired with the husband's earnings and through gifts from his family.[355]

---

[345] Davis v. Davis, 638 So. 2d 1288, 1293 (Miss. 1994).

[346] *See* Owen v. Owen, 798 So. 2d 394, 399-400 (Miss. 2001); *see also* Hankins v. Hankins, 729 So. 2d 1283, 1287-88 (Miss. 1999) (dismissing husband's argument that his wife's contributions should be valued at minimum wage).

[347] Owens v. Owens, 950 So. 2d 202, 214 (Miss. Ct. App. 2006).

[348] *See* King v. King, 862 So. 2d 1287, 1289 (Miss. Ct. App. 2004); Franklin v. Franklin, 864 So. 2d 970, 976 (Miss. Ct. App. 2003); Weeks v. Weeks, 832 So. 2d 583, 586 (Miss. Ct. App. 2002).

[349] *See* Weeks v. Weeks, 832 So. 2d 583, 586 (Miss. Ct. App. 2002) (but court should have awarded periodic alimony, considering her ill health and earning potential); *see also* Redd v. Redd, 774 So. 2d 492, 494-96 (Miss. Ct. App. 2000) (23% of $5 million marital estate to wife of thirty years in divorce based on husband's physical abuse reversed to include omitted assets; court of appeals noted that 23% award not necessarily error in light of deferential review standard).

[350] *See* Franklin v. Franklin, 864 So. 2d 970, 976 (Miss. Ct. App. 2003).

[351] *See* King v. King, 760 So. 2d 830, 837 (Miss. Ct. App. 2000).

[352] *See* King v. King, 862 So. 2d 1287 (Miss. Ct. App. 2004) (husband was granted divorce based on desertion).

[353] Wells v. Wells, 800 So. 2d 1239, 1243-44 (Miss. Ct. App. 2001).

[354] Buckley v. Buckley, 815 So. 2d 1260, 1264 (Miss. Ct. App. 2000) (appealed on issue of alimony; reversed for failure to award alimony in addition to unequal division).

[355] Tatum v. Tatum, 54 So. 3d 855, 860-62 (Miss. Ct. App. 2010).

PROPERTY DIVISION   § 6.08[2][a][ii]

[ii] **Financial contribution**. Financial contribution to asset accumulation is an important factor in property division. If both spouses are wage earners, with neither providing a greater share of homemaking services, courts have in some cases based an unequal award primarily on financial contribution. For example, the court of appeals affirmed an award of two-thirds of marital assets to a higher-income wife based explicitly on her greater financial contribution.[356] A husband who worked throughout the marriage and did most of the household chores was properly awarded a greater share of the marital assets.[357] And a wife who earned 96% of the family's income was awarded the greater share of marital assets based on her contribution; her husband did not work during most of the marriage, spent more than she did, and made limited domestic contributions.[358] In a case involving two wage earners who kept their finances separate, the chancellor divided the couple's condominium equity based on the percentages that each had contributed to its upkeep.[359]

On the other hand, the contribution of a higher-salaried spouse may be negated by lack of frugality. A court properly awarded a greater share of assets to a husband who saved while his wife spent, even though her earnings were slightly higher.[360] And the lower-income of two wage earners may receive a greater share of assets based on need. The court of appeals affirmed an award of two-thirds of marital assets to a teacher wife, rejecting her veterinarian husband's argument that the award was inequitable.[361]

Financial contribution may also include a contribution of separate property. In Mississippi, separate property is frequently converted into marital property through application of the family use and commingling rules.[362] In the division stage of equitable distribution, a court may consider the extent to which a spouse's separate property increased the marital estate.[363] If the separate contribution benefitted or improved a particular asset, the court may award a greater percentage of that asset to the contribut-

---

[356] Lockert v. Lockert, 815 So. 2d 1267, 1270 (Miss. Ct. App. 2002); *see also* Bresnahan v. Bresnahan, 818 So. 2d 1113, 1119 (Miss. 2002) (husband awarded 55% of assets; both worked, husband earned more, wife also committed adultery); Parks v. Parks, 914 So. 2d 337, 339-40, 343 (Miss. Ct. App. 2005) (en banc) (wife awarded 75% of home equity based on her higher earnings, his accumulation of debt, and her payment of mortgage during marriage); Jones v. Jones, 904 So. 2d 1143 (Miss. Ct. App. 2004) (wife awarded greater share based on greater financial contribution). *But see* Morris v. Morris, 5 So. 3d 476, 493 (Miss. Ct. App. 2008) (husband was not automatically entitled to a larger share based on the fact that his contributions were greater than those of his working wife); Deal v. Wilson, 922 So. 2d 24, 28 (Miss. Ct. App. 2005) (rejecting wife's argument that she should have received 62.95% of marital assets because she earned 62.95% of marital income; husband supported her during medical school).

[357] Brabham v. Brabham, 950 So. 2d 1098, 1102 (Miss. Ct. App. 2007).

[358] Jones v. Jones, 995 So. 2d 706 (Miss. 2008) (awarding most of assets to wife).

[359] Delk v. Delk, 41 So. 3d 738, 740-41 (Miss. Ct. App. 2010) (rejecting husband's argument that the court focused too exclusively on financial contribution).

[360] Love v. Love, 687 So. 2d 1229, 1232 (Miss. 1997).

[361] Klauser v. Klauser, 865 So. 2d 363, 365 (Miss. Ct. App. 2003); *see also* Goellner v. Goellner, 11 So. 3d 1251, 1264 (Miss. Ct. App. 2009) (rejecting husband's argument that his wife was not entitled to one-half of the assets because she worked outside the home at low wages).

[362] *See* discussion *supra* § 6.05.

[363] *See* Maslowski v. Maslowski, 655 So. 2d 18, 24 (Miss. 1995) (court may recognize separate property contribution to home; remanding for findings of fact); Gregg v. Gregg, 31 So. 3d 1277, 1280-81 (Miss. Ct. App. 2010) (awarding wife greater share of real estate purchased primarily with her separate property contribution); James v. James, 736 So. 2d 492, 494-95 (Miss. Ct. App. 1999) (awarding $12,000 to husband in recognition of separate property contribution not error); *cf.* Bates v. Bates, 755 So. 2d 478, 482 (Miss. Ct. App. 1999) (greater share to husband who owned substantial separate assets commingled in marital estate); Welch v. Welch, 755 So. 2d 6, 10 (Miss. Ct. App. 1999) (greater share to husband who contributed marital funds to improve wife's separate property).

§ 6.08[2][a][iii]   **MISSISSIPPI FAMILY LAW**

ing spouse. In several cases involving short marriages, spouses have been awarded an additional amount to reflect separate property contribution to the marital home.[364] For example, a court erred in awarding a wife of five years a 50% interest in her husband's premarital home.[365] And the marital home was properly awarded to a wife of six years who contributed all but $3,000 of the $148,000 equity in the home.[366] On the other hand, equal division has been upheld in a number of cases in spite of one spouse's separate property contribution to the marital home.[367] A wife was entitled to equal division of marital assets of one million dollars, even though they were acquired in part through the husband's separate property assets and income.[368] An asset acquired during separation may be awarded to the spouse who made the primary financial contribution.[369]

[iii] Contribution to education and training. One spouse's support for the other's education and training is a relevant factor in property division. A court did not err in dividing substantial assets equally between a physician husband and the wife who supported him through medical school and contributed to family stability.[370] Similarly, a husband who supported his wife through four years of school was awarded 60% of marital assets in recognition of his support for her training.[371]

[iv] Contribution to marital stability. Substantial contribution to accumulation of marital assets may include one spouse's contribution to family stability and harmony.[372] A wife's contribution to family stability supported an award to her of 50% of marital assets of $2.44 million. She provided support for her husband to build his

---

[364] See Lindsey v. Lindsey, 749 So. 2d 77, 80 (Miss. 1999) (husband who paid one-third of mortgage before marriage awarded greater share); Tillman v. Tillman, 716 So. 2d 1090, 1095 (Miss. 1998) (wife who made separate property contribution to home awarded 70% value of marital home); Gregg v. Gregg, 31 So. 3d 1277, 1280-81 (Miss. Ct. App. 2010) (husband awarded greater share of marital home that he owned prior to marriage).

[365] Drumright v. Drumright, 812 So. 2d 1021, 1026 (Miss. Ct. App. 2001) (95% of payments made prior to marriage); see also Bullock v. Bullock, 699 So. 2d 1205, 1210-11 (Miss. 1997) (error to award wife 50% of home owned by husband prior to marriage); cf. Curry v. Curry, 45 So. 3d 724, 727-28 (Miss. Ct. App. 2010) (husband awarded 20% of value of wife's premarital home).

[366] Berryman v. Berryman, 907 So. 2d 958, 959-60 (Miss. Ct. App. 2004), aff'd, 907 So. 2d 944 (Miss. 2005) (en banc).

[367] See Ory v. Ory, 936 So. 2d 405, 412 (Miss. Ct. App. 2006) (en banc) (reversing chancellor's equitable credit to wife for separate property contribution to marital home); Fogarty v. Fogarty, 922 So. 2d 836, 840 (Miss. Ct. App. 2006) (husband's separate property classified as marital based on family use and commingling; couple lived in the home and added a carport); Dobbs v. Dobbs, 912 So. 2d 491, 492-93 (Miss. Ct. App. 2005) (rejecting husband's argument that he should be credited with mortgage payments made prior to marriage); Belding v. Belding, 736 So. 2d 425, 432 (Miss. Ct. App. 1999) (home owned by wife prior to marriage divided equally; marital funds used to pay mortgage during marriage).

[368] Tatum v. Tatum, 54 So. 3d 855, 860-62 (Miss. Ct. App. 2010).

[369] See Amacker v. Amacker, 33 So. 3d 493, 495-96 (Miss. Ct. App. 2009) (camp house purchased by husband after separation was marital property, but awarded to husband; wife made little contribution); Striebeck v. Striebeck, 911 So. 2d 628, 632-33 (Miss. Ct. App. 2005) (en banc) (although marital property accumulation continues during separation, court may find that one spouse is entitled to greater share of post-separation marital assets).

[370] Russell v. Russell, 733 So. 2d 858, 861 (Miss. Ct. App. 1999); see also Deal v. Wilson, 922 So. 2d 24, 28 (Miss. Ct. App. 2005) (rejecting wife's argument that she should have received 62.95% of marital assets because she earned 62.95% of marital income; husband supported her during medical school).

[371] See Sproles v. Sproles, 782 So. 2d 742 (Miss. 2001); see also Lauro v. Lauro, 924 So. 2d 584, 590-91 (Miss. Ct. App. 2006) (wife who supported husband through school awarded greater share of marital assets).

[372] Ferguson v. Ferguson, 639 So. 2d 921, 928 (Miss. 1994).

PROPERTY DIVISION   § 6.08[2][b]

medical practice and moved to allow him to obtain necessary training.[373] Similarly, a chancellor did not err in awarding the greater share of assets to a wife who contributed more to family stability, even though both she and her husband contributed to asset accumulation.[374] On the other hand, a spouse's disruption of family stability may be a negative factor in property division. For example, a court properly awarded one-third of marital assets to a homemaker wife based in part on behavior that contributed to the instability of the marriage.[375]

[b] Need. One spouse may be awarded a greater share of marital assets based on need, even though both spouses contributed equally to asset accumulation.[376] For example, a wife was awarded the only significant marital asset – a family restaurant – based on her financial need.[377] Similarly, a court properly awarded a greater share of assets to a homemaker with limited income, based on financial need and her contribution to family stability.[378] The court of appeals affirmed an award of two-thirds of marital assets to a teacher, rejecting her higher-income husband's argument that the unequal award in her favor was inequitable.[379]

[c] Spouse's separate estate. Courts are to consider the separate estate of each spouse in dividing marital assets. An award to a husband of two-thirds of marital property was not error, even though he had substantial income. His wife had a separate estate of over $1 million, while he had almost no separate property.[380] Similarly, a husband's substantial separate estate supported an award of 60% of marital assets to

---

[373] Davis v. Davis, 832 So. 2d 492, 501-02 (Miss. 2002).

[374] Wells v. Wells, 800 So. 2d 1239, 1243-44 (Miss. Ct. App. 2001) (wife also had greater need).

[375] *See* Weeks v. Weeks, 832 So. 2d 583, 586 (Miss. Ct. App. 2002); *see also* Jones v. Jones, 995 So. 2d 706, 713 (Miss. 2008) (22% of assets to homemaker husband who made limited domestic contributions and who did not contribute to marital stability); Sullivan v. Sullivan, 990 So. 2d 783 (Miss. Ct. App. 2008) (two-thirds of assets awarded to husband whose wife left him and their children for man she met in a bar); Brabham v. Brabham, 950 So. 2d 1098, 1102 (Miss. Ct. App. 2007) (chancellor properly awarded a greater share of assets to a husband whose wife had an affair, made false accusations against him, abused alcohol, and refused to have a sexual relationship with him for three years).

[376] Wells v. Wells, 800 So. 2d 1239, 1243-44 (Miss. Ct. App. 2001) (wife awarded equal share of retirement and all of marital home, based on greater need and contribution to stability of home).

[377] Bumpous v. Bumpous, 770 So. 2d 558 (Miss. Ct. App. 2000); *see also* Larue v. Larue, 969 So. 2d 99, 109-10 (Miss. Ct. App. 2007) (greater share of assets to elderly wife from husband in nursing home); Graham v. Graham, 948 So. 2d 451, 453-54 (Miss. Ct. App. 2006) (jointly owned convenience store awarded to wife who worked in store; no other source of income); Seymour v. Seymour, 960 So. 2d 513, 519 (Miss. Ct. App. 2006) (wife with three children and $18,000 income awarded most of $155,400 marital assets; husband had $157,000 separate property business and income of $50,000); Lauro v. Lauro, 924 So. 2d 584, 590-91 (Miss. Ct. App. 2006) (wife with no income awarded more than husband at fault with high income).

[378] See Wells v. Wells, 800 So. 2d 1239 (Miss. Ct. App. 2001); *see also* Owens v. Owens, 950 So. 2d 202, 214 (Miss. Ct. App. 2006) (error to award greater share to wife without considering disabled husband's need); Patterson v. Patterson, 917 So. 2d 111, 119 (Miss. Ct. App. 2005) (husband received $59,200 in marital assets, while lower-income wife received $71,900); Rush v. Rush *ex rel.* Mayne, 914 So. 2d 322, 325-26 (Miss. Ct. App. 2005) (en banc) (greater share to disabled wife living on Social Security income of $550 per month). *But see* Everett v. Everett, 919 So. 2d 242, 249 (Miss. Ct. App. 2005) (equal division of assets; rejecting husband's argument that he deserved greater share of assets based on age and poor health); Klauser v. Klauser, 865 So. 2d 363 (Miss. Ct. App. 2003) (award of two-thirds); Thompson v. Thompson, 815 So. 2d 466 (Miss. Ct. App. 2002).

[379] Klauser v. Klauser, 865 So. 2d 363, 365 (Miss. Ct. App. 2003).

[380] Welch v. Welch, 755 So. 2d 6, 10 (Miss. Ct. App. 1999) (husband had also contributed to her separate property during marriage by paying taxes; she was awarded $2,000 per month alimony).

§ 6.08[2][d]   MISSISSIPPI FAMILY LAW

his wife.[381] An award of the only marital asset – the home – to a wife was proper; her husband had substantial separate property investments.[382] And a court should have considered the value of a wife's interest in insurance policies with a cash surrender value of $295,000 and possible future value of $762,337.[383] However, a wife's anticipated inheritance was not part of her separate estate for purposes of the *Ferguson* analysis – a possible inheritance is merely an expectancy.[384]

[d] Elimination of need for alimony. Courts are also directed to consider whether a particular award may eliminate the need for alimony. An award of 60% of marital assets to a wife was justified in part because the award helped alleviate the need for alimony.[385] The court of appeals upheld an order requiring a husband to pay mortgage debt, but dividing profits from the sale of the marital home equally; unequal division eliminated the necessity of continuing support payments to his wife.[386]

[e] Fault as factor. Mississippi is in a minority of states in which marital misconduct is a factor for consideration in property division.[387] A chancellor may consider marital misconduct to the extent that it "places a burden on the stability and harmony" of the marriage.[388] In an irreconcilable differences divorce, a chancellor may limit testimony related to fault, so that the proceeding does not become a contested divorce.[389] Fault may occasionally be so extreme as to require unequal division. In a rare reversal of an equal division of assets, the supreme court held that a chancellor erred in awarding 50% of marital assets to a wife who had eight affairs in a fifteen-year period.[390] A

---

[381] Mabus v. Mabus, 890 So. 2d 806, 825-26 (Miss. 2003) (award of 60% of marital assets of approximately $485,000 to wife based on disparity of separate estates); *see also* Dickerson v. Dickerson, 34 So. 3d 637, 643-45 (Miss. Ct. App. 2010) (60% of $86,000 in marital assets to wife based in large part on husband's separate property valued at $215,000).

[382] Franks v. Franks, 759 So. 2d 1164 (Miss. 1999); *see also* Seymour v. Seymour, 960 So. 2d 513, 519 (Miss. Ct. App. 2006) (wife with three children and $18,000 income awarded most of $155,400 marital assets).

[383] Striebeck v. Striebeck, 911 So. 2d 628, 635 (Miss. Ct. App. 2005) (en banc) (wife's assets should have been considered for purpose of awarding alimony).

[384] Parker v. Parker, 929 So. 2d 940, 946 (Miss. Ct. App. 2005) ("[A]n expectancy of an inheritance is not an asset."); *see also* MISS. CODE ANN. §§ 93-5-2, -23 (Supp. 2010) (interest as heir of living person, or under third-party will, not to be considered as factor in financial awards at divorce).

[385] Mabus v. Mabus, 890 So. 2d 806, 826 (Miss. 2003); *see also* Humphries v. Humphries, 904 So. 2d 192, 197-98 (Miss. Ct. App. 2005) (award of debt to husband obviated need for alimony award).

[386] *See* Thompson v. Thompson, 815 So. 2d 466, 469 (Miss. Ct. App. 2002) (also considering husband's use and expenditure of other marital assets which offset his contribution).

[387] *See* Carrow v. Carrow, 642 So. 2d 901, 904 (Miss. 1994) (wife's post-separation adultery a proper factor for consideration in property division); Sullivan v. Sullivan, 990 So. 2d 783 (Miss. Ct. App. 2008) (two-thirds of assets awarded to husband whose wife left him and their children for man she met in a bar); Brabham v. Brabham, 950 So. 2d 1098, 1102 (Miss. Ct. App. 2007) (greater share of assets to a husband whose wife had an affair, made false accusations against him, abused alcohol, and refused to have a sexual relationship with him for three years); Seymour v. Seymour, 960 So. 2d 513, 519 (Miss. Ct. App. 2006) (adultery as factor in awarding most of assets to wife); Deal v. Wilson, 922 So. 2d 24, 28 (Miss. Ct. App. 2005) (wife's adultery properly considered in dividing assets equally between husband and higher-income wife); Welch v. Welch, 755 So. 2d 6, 9 (Miss. Ct. App. 1999) (not error to consider wife's material contribution to separation); Driste v. Driste, 738 So. 2d 763, 766 (Miss. Ct. App. 1998) (fault is factor in property division in irreconcilable differences divorce). *See* TURNER, *supra* note 124, § 8.24, at 892 (3d ed.) (a minority of states consider non-economic fault).

[388] Phillips v Phillips, 45 So. 3d 684, 697 (Miss. Ct. App. 2010) (quotation omitted) (court did not err in disregarding wife's post-separation affair).

[389] Driste v. Driste, 738 So. 2d 763, 766 (Miss. Ct. App. 1998) (but excluding all evidence of adultery was error).

[390] Singley v. Singley, 846 So. 2d 1004, 1008 (Miss. 2002) (noting that equitable distribution envisions partners

PROPERTY DIVISION § 6.08[2][f]

chancellor properly awarded two-thirds of marital assets to a man whose wife left him and their children for a man she met in a bar. The chancellor did not err in placing great emphasis on the affair, which had a "tremendous" impact on family stability.[391] On the other hand, cases have been affirmed in which the spouse at fault received a greater share of assets than the innocent spouse.[392] A wife who stabbed her husband on Christmas day was properly awarded half of the marital assets. The divorce was based on a single incident and did not involve a pattern of conduct that strained the marriage.[393]

[f] Prior use or distribution of assets. Division of assets is to be made in light of the "degree to which each spouse has expended, withdrawn or otherwise disposed of marital assets and any prior distribution of such assets by agreement, decree or otherwise."[394]

[i] Dissipation of assets. One spouse's dissipation of marital assets should be considered in equitable distribution.[395] A husband's expenditure of funds on his girlfriend constituted dissipation.[396] However, a husband did not dissipate assets by taking his girlfriend on fishing tournament trips that he would have attended anyway.[397] A spouse's dissipation of assets through gambling may be considered in dividing assets.[398] A wife who lost hundreds of thousands of dollars in gambling was not entitled to any award of marital assets if her losses exceeded one-half of the value of the marital as-

---

"pulling equally together"); *see also* Watson v. Watson, 882 So. 2d 95, 105-06 (Miss. 2004) (chancellor "obviously ignored conduct" by dividing assets equally between a wife of twenty-one years, in ill health, and her husband who left her for a younger woman); King v. King, 946 So. 2d 395, 403-04 (Miss. Ct. App. 2006) (greater share to wife who was verbally and physically abused during forty-four year marriage; husband dissipated half of couple's assets); Lauro v. Lauro, 924 So. 2d 584, 590 (Miss. Ct. App. 2006) (wife awarded greater share, based in part on husband's affair which caused marriage breakup); Jackson v. Jackson, 922 So. 2d 53, 59-60 (Miss. Ct. App. 2006) (en banc) (awarding wife greater share based in part on husband's fault, including cruelty, failure to support, and dissipation of assets).

[391] Sullivan v. Sullivan, 990 So. 2d 783, 786 (Miss. Ct. App. 2008).

[392] *See* Mabus v. Mabus, 890 So. 2d 806, 825-26 (Miss. 2003) (wife who committed adultery awarded 60% of assets; award eliminated need for alimony); Sproles v. Sproles, 782 So. 2d 742, 748-49 (Miss. 2001) (60% to husband guilty of habitual cruelty, but who supported wife through school); Turpin v. Turpin, 699 So. 2d 560, 563 (Miss. 1997) (two-thirds to husband guilty of habitual cruelty, based on his greater financial contributions and poor health); Redd v. Redd, 774 So. 2d 492, 494-95 (Miss. Ct. App. 2000) (75% of $4 million estate to husband guilty of habitual cruelty).

[393] Smith v. Smith, 994 So. 2d 882, 887 (Miss. Ct. App. 2008); *see also* Rodriguez v. Rodriguez, 2 So. 3d 720, 729 (Miss. Ct. App. 2009) (chancellor did not err in disregarding husband's fault; two affairs early in a thirty-seven-year marriage did not affect the stability of the marriage).

[394] Ferguson v. Ferguson, 639 So. 2d 921, 928 (Miss. 1994).

[395] *See* Childs v. Childs, 806 So. 2d 273 (Miss. Ct. App. 2000); Wolfe v. Wolfe, 766 So. 2d 123 (Miss. Ct. App. 2000).

[396] Dunaway v. Dunaway, 749 So. 2d 1112, 1119 (Miss. Ct. App. 1999); *see also* Lauro v. Lauro, 924 So. 2d 584, 590 (Miss. Ct. App. 2006) (husband dissipated assets by liquidating an IRA, selling a vehicle, paying his girlfriend's rent, and taking her on trips); Garriga v. Garriga, 770 So. 2d 978, 984 (Miss. Ct. App. 2000) (funds used by the wife for gifts or travel for a post-separation, extra-marital relationship were dissipated). *But cf.* Barnett v. Barnett, 908 So. 2d 833, 842 (Miss. Ct. App. 2005) (court did not err in failing to charge husband with expenditures on girlfriend, where wife presented no documentary evidence of amount or type of expenditures).

[397] Hults v. Hults, 11 So. 3d 1273, 1282 (Miss. Ct. App. 2009) (nor did he dissipate assets by buying a lot to build a house with her; he lived with his parents and would need a home).

[398] Jones v. Jones, 995 So. 2d 706, 714 (Miss. 2008) (husband's greater expenditure of funds a factor in unequal division); Craft v. Craft, 825 So. 2d 605, 611 (Miss. 2002) (chancellor took into account husband's dissipation of assets through gambling). *But cf.* Larue v. Larue, 969 So. 2d 99, 109-10 (Miss. Ct. App. 2007) (chancellor did not err in refusing to treat wife's gambling losses as dissipation; the couple gambled together, and the husband "pouted" if she would not accompany him).

§ 6.08[2][f][i]   MISSISSIPPI FAMILY LAW

sets.[399] Dissipation may be caused by one party's misconduct, even if the financial loss was not intentional. When a husband who violated a non-compete clause was forced to cancel promissory notes received for the sale of his business, the court properly treated his conduct as dissipation of a marital asset.[400] The fact that one spouse spent more than the other, while not ordinarily dissipation, has been considered as a factor in equitable distribution. The court noted, in awarding a greater share of assets to a wife, that she earned most of the family income while her husband spent substantially more of the income.[401]

The dissipating spouse may be required to reimburse the other for one-half the value of the dissipated funds.[402] A court erred, however, in awarding the innocent spouse an amount equal to 100% of the dissipated funds.[403] In the alternative, a court may include the dissipated funds as part of the marital estate and consider them as part of the dissipating spouse's share of assets.[404] For example, a wife's share of marital assets included $47,000 in funds withdrawn from accounts at the time of separation.[405] And a wife whose husband dissipated $265,000 in assets was awarded most of the remaining $334,000 in assets.[406]

Use of assets for ordinary and reasonable living expenses during separation is not dissipation. Funds used by a husband to support both households during separation were properly excluded from marital property.[407] Similarly, a wife who used her husband's weekly disability check to support herself and her children during separation

---

[399] Lowrey v. Lowrey, 25 So. 3d 274, 291 (Miss. 2009).

[400] Parker v. Parker, 929 So. 2d 940, 944 (Miss. Ct. App. 2005) (notes were considered awarded to husband).

[401] Jones v. Jones, 995 So. 2d 706, 714 (Miss. 2008) (husband's greater expenditure of funds a factor in unequal division).

[402] See Stribling v. Stribling, 906 So. 2d 863, 870 (Miss. Ct. App. 2005) (husband awarded $221,000 in lump sum alimony equal to one-half of net profits from wife's sale of marital assets); Dunaway v. Dunaway, 749 So. 2d 1112, 1119 (Miss. Ct. App. 1999).

[403] Dunaway v. Dunaway, 749 So. 2d 1112, 1119 (Miss. Ct. App. 1999); see also Garriga v. Garriga, 770 So. 2d 978, 984 (Miss. Ct. App. 2000) (funds used by the wife for gifts or travel for a post-separation, extra-marital relationship were dissipated and should be reimbursed to the marital estate or set-off from distribution).

[404] See Parker v. Parker, 929 So. 2d 940, 944 (Miss. Ct. App. 2005) (promissory notes cancelled by husband were considered awarded to husband); Shoffner v. Shoffner, 909 So. 2d 1245, 1250 (Miss. Ct. App. 2005) (court properly awarded wife dissipated retirement funds and husband marital home); Coggin v. Coggin, 837 So. 2d 772, 775 (Miss. Ct. App. 2003) (no error in awarding wife 80% of marital assets based on husband's depletion of retirement and insurance assets during separation); Buckley v. Buckley, 815 So. 2d 1260, 1265 (Miss. Ct. App. 2002) (chancellor credited wife with $6,700 as part of equitable distribution to reflect funds withdrawn from account); cf. Rush v. Rush ex rel. Mayne, 914 So. 2d 322, 326 (Miss. Ct. App. 2005) (en banc) (greater share to wife based in part on husband's attempted dissipation of assets).

[405] A & L, Inc. v. Grantham, 747 So. 2d 832, 842 (Miss. 1999); see also Wells v. Wells, 35 So. 3d 1250, 1253 (Miss. Ct. App. 2010) ($6,300 withdrawn by wife treated as part of her share of marital assets); Rodriguez v. Rodriguez, 2 So. 3d 720, 726-27 (Miss. Ct. App. 2009) (wife's withdrawal of $36,000 in marital funds for attorneys' fees and living expenses treated as dissipation); Strong v. Strong, 981 So. 2d 1052, 1055 (Miss. Ct. App. 2008) (marital funds transferred by wife to her mother should have been assigned to wife in division); Jones v. Jones, 904 So. 2d 1143 (Miss. Ct. App. 2004) (rejecting wife's argument that $17,000 in savings withdrawn by her was not dissipated; funds were used to pay her divorce attorney and redecorate a house in which she alone lived); cf. Parker v. Parker, 980 So. 2d 323, 328 (Miss. Ct. App. 2008) (wife entitled to one-half of full value of assets sold by husband at less than fair market value).

[406] King v. King, 946 So. 2d 395, 404 (Miss. Ct. App. 2006) (wife was also verbally and physically abused during the forty-four year marriage).

[407] Pittman v. Pittman, 791 So. 2d 857, 865 (Miss. Ct. App. 2001); see also Stein v. Stein, 11 So. 3d 1288, 1293-94 (Miss. Ct. App. 2009) (single purchase of a dress wife never wore, three bounced checks, and use of funds for alcohol rehabilitation were not dissipation).

PROPERTY DIVISION   **§ 6.08[2][f][ii]**

was not required to reimburse him.[408]

   [ii] Disposition by agreement. A couple's prior distribution of assets by agreement is relevant to classification and division of property. A chancellor properly treated investment accounts as a husband's separate property – the accounts contained the husband's share of marital funds that the couple agreed to divide equally. His wife had already received her equitable share of the funds.[409] And a court properly awarded all farm property to a husband; his wife previously conveyed her interest in the farm to him as satisfaction for dissipated assets that exceeded the value of her interest.[410] However, a chancellor properly disregarded a couple's exchange of deeds shortly before separation. The transfer, initiated by the husband, left the wife with substantially less than she would have received otherwise.[411]

   [g] Emotional value of assets. In determining the disposition of particular assets, a court may consider the emotional value of property. For example, a court erred in awarding a husband a home situated on land belonging to his wife's family.[412] However, a family connection to a particular asset should not override the importance of an economically fair division. The court of appeals upheld an award giving a wife a restaurant established by her husband's parents. The husband's emotional connection to the business was less important than her need for a means of support.[413]

---

   [408] Turnley v. Turnely, 726 So. 2d 1258, 1266 (Miss. Ct. App. 1998); *see also* Herron v. Herron, 936 So. 2d 956, 959-60 (Miss. Ct. App. 2006) (husband's withdrawal of $3,500 to pay marital credit card debt not dissipation); Stribling v. Stribling, 906 So. 2d 863, 872 (Miss. Ct. App. 2005) (no dissipation where disabled husband cashed $26,000 certificate of deposit but used funds for living expenses while divorce was pending); *cf.* Rush v. Rush, 932 So. 2d 800, 807-08 (Miss. Ct. App. 2005) (wife's four unsuccessful business ventures and one-time loss of $10,000 in internet stock trading was not dissipation; husband was aware of and consented to the business ventures, and the stock market loss was a one-time incident), *rev'd in part on other grounds*, 932 So. 2d 794 (Miss. 2006) (en banc). *But see* Rodriguez v. Rodriguez, 2 So. 3d 720, 726-27 (Miss. Ct. App. 2009) (wife's withdrawal of $36,000 in marital funds for attorneys' fees and living expenses treated as dissipation).

   [409] Thompson v. Thompson, 816 So. 2d 417, 419 (Miss. Ct. App. 2002); *see also* Striebeck v. Striebeck, 911 So. 2d 628, 632 (Miss. Ct. App. 2005) (en banc) (prior to divorce, the parties agreed that certain assets that would otherwise be marital would be the separate property of each, including retirement accounts, automobiles, investment accounts, furnishings, and other personal property).

   [410] Childs v. Childs, 806 So. 2d 273, 275 (Miss. Ct. App. 2000) (dissipated assets four times value of farm property).

   [411] Phillips v Phillips, 45 So. 3d 684, 698 (Miss. Ct. App. 2010) (wife quitclaimed property with equity of $50,000 to husband, in return for a one-third interest in a half acre of property purchased for $800).

   [412] *See* Scott v. Scott, 835 So. 2d 82, 86-87 (Miss. Ct. App. 2002) (also based on need); *see also* Jones v. Jones, 995 So. 2d 706, 714 (Miss. 2008) (marital home awarded to husband with greater emotional attachment); Owen v. Owen, 12 So. 3d 603, 606-07 (Miss. Ct. App. 2009) (wife awarded 75% of her retirement account based in part on greater emotional attachment to the plan); Atkinson v. Atkinson, 11 So. 3d 172, 178 (Miss. Ct. App. 2009) (marital home and 32.5 acres awarded to wife; land was a gift from her parents); Sullivan v. Sullivan, 990 So. 2d 783, 786 (Miss. Ct. App. 2008) (wife with emotional attachment to home awarded house); Jackson v. Jackson, 922 So. 2d 53, 59-60 (Miss. Ct. App. 2006) (en banc) (awarding wife greater share based on financial contribution, husband's fault, and emotional attachment to home); Deal v. Wilson, 922 So. 2d 24, 27 (Miss. Ct. App. 2005) (wife with greater attachment to one of two farms properly awarded farm); Everett v. Everett, 919 So. 2d 242, 246 (Miss. Ct. App. 2005) (marital home purchased by husband's father, awarded to husband); Sandlin v. Sandlin, 906 So. 2d 39 (Miss. Ct. App. 2004) (chancellor did not err in awarding marital home entirely to wife; the home was once her grandparents', was a gift from her father, and was located near her family). *But cf.* Owens v. Owens, 950 So. 2d 202, 213 (Miss. Ct. App. 2006) (error to award marital home to wife based on fact that she raised children there; so did the husband).

   [413] Bumpous v. Bumpous, 770 So. 2d 558, 560 (Miss. Ct. App. 2000) (court also noted that the husband's parents had tried to sell the business on the open market before their son and daughter-in-law purchased).

§ 6.08[2][h]   MISSISSIPPI FAMILY LAW

[h] Tax consequences. Courts are to consider the tax consequences of awards in determining an equitable distribution.[414] However, a court need not factor in tax consequences with respect to property that the recipient is unlikely to liquidate. A court did not err in awarding a wife liquid assets with no tax consequences while her husband received non-liquid assets – he was unlikely to liquidate the marital home and business.[415] In contrast, a court properly ordered the parties to share the tax burden of liquidating a husband's pension.[416] Some courts factor in estimated taxes in valuing a pension that will be offset by other property, rather than divided between the spouses.[417]

[3] Award of marital home. The marital home is a unique and important family asset. In many cases, it is the primary asset. Courts may award ownership of the home to one spouse[418] or order continued joint ownership with possession by one spouse. If the parties are to continue joint ownership, the court may award the mortgage deduction to the party who will make the payments on the home.[419] A court may also order a home sold immediately and the proceeds divided between the parties or applied to debt.[420]

Because of the Mississippi family-use and commingling doctrines, the marital home is usually classified as a marital asset, even if it was separately owned by one spouse prior to the marriage or if the value was enhanced by one spouse's separate property contribution.[421] In some cases, a greater share of the home's value has been awarded to a spouse who made a substantial separate property contribution. In other cases the value of the home is divided equally in spite of one spouse's separate property contribution.[422]

The Mississippi Supreme Court has stated that it is generally better to award the home to a custodial parent.[423] However, an award to a husband who conducted his business from the home was proper even though his ex-wife was the custodial parent of their children.[424] Homes have also been awarded based on need[425] and emotional

---

[414] See Louk v. Louk, 761 So. 2d 878, 883 (Miss. 2000) (reversing in part for failure to consider tax consequences).

[415] Davis v. Davis, 832 So. 2d 492, 502 (Miss. 2002).

[416] Phillips v. Phillips, 904 So. 2d 999 (Miss. 2004). *But cf.* Jones v. Jones, 904 So. 2d 1143 (Miss. Ct. App. 2004) (no tax consequences where account could be rolled over through use of qualified domestic relations order).

[417] *See* TURNER, supra note 124, § 8.29, at 925 (3d ed.).

[418] *See, e.g.,* Weston v. Mounts, 789 So. 2d 822, 826 (Miss. Ct. App. 2001) (marital home awarded to wife, who was to pay husband $26,500 for his interest); Burnham-Steptoe v. Steptoe, 755 So. 2d 1225, 1235 (Miss. Ct. App. 1999) (husband required to purchase wife's one-half interest).

[419] Rodriguez v. Rodriguez, 2 So. 3d 720, 728 (Miss. Ct. App. 2009).

[420] *See* Garriga v. Garriga, 770 So. 2d 978 (Miss. 2000) (appropriate to order home and furnishings sold and proceeds divided); Drumright v. Drumright, 812 So. 2d 1021, 1027 (Miss. Ct. App. 2001); Curtis v. Curtis, 796 So. 2d 1044, 1051 (Miss. Ct. App. 2001) (court did not err in ordering sale of marital home but not of adjoining property).

[421] *See* discussion *supra* § 6.06[10].

[422] *See* discussion *supra* § 6.08[2][a][ii].

[423] *See* Hankins v. Hankins, 729 So. 2d 1283, 1287 (Miss. 1999).

[424] *See* Burnham-Steptoe v. Steptoe, 755 So. 2d 1225, 1235 (Miss. Ct. App. 1999) (husband required to purchase wife's one-half interest); *see also* Boykin v. Boykin, 445 So. 2d 538, 539 (Miss. 1984) (award of home to wife not error even though husband had custody of children).

[425] *See* Scott v. Scott, 835 So. 2d 82, 87-88 (Miss. Ct. App. 2002) (also based on fact that house was located on land previously owned by wife).

PROPERTY DIVISION

§ 6.08[4]

attachment.[426]

A court may award possession to one spouse with the property to be sold and equity divided on a specified date or occurrence. The supreme court rejected an ex-husband's claim that he had an absolute right to partition jointly owned property – the chancellor had discretion to grant his wife exclusive use of the home for so long as she remained unmarried.[427] Similarly, a chancellor's order that a wife have exclusive use of the marital home and adjoining twenty acres until the child's majority was not error.[428] And an agreement that the wife would have use and possession of the jointly owned marital home was an implied agreement not to partition. The court of appeals rejected the husband's argument twenty years later that the agreement exceeded a reasonable time.[429] In one case, the court awarded the home to the husband but allowed the wife to live in the home rent-free for two years.[430]

A court may order equity in the home equally divided even though one spouse makes mortgage payments during the continued joint ownership. The court of appeals upheld an order allowing a wife to purchase her husband's equity in the home for $25,000, but requiring that he pay the remaining mortgage debt in lieu of alimony.[431] On the other hand, equal division of sale proceeds was reversed where a wife awarded the marital home made 80% of mortgage payments. The court noted, however, that because she benefitted by occupying the house, she need not receive credit for all payments.[432]

An order awarding possession to one spouse and requiring the other to make mortgage payments may be an award of alimony or part of property division.[433] Because of the tax consequences and the effect on future modification of the award, an order should clearly state whether it is intended as property division or alimony.

[4] Assignment of debt. Debts are classified similarly to assets for purposes of equitable distribution. As with marital property, a temporary support order marks the end of accumulation of marital debt.[434] Debts are ordinarily assumed to be marital. The

---

[426] *See* Scott v. Scott, 835 So. 2d 82, 86-87 (Miss. Ct. App. 2002) (court erred in awarding the marital home, located on land inherited by the wife, to her husband; also based on need).

[427] Sartin v. Sartin, 405 So. 2d 84, 86 (Miss. 1981); *see also* Kelley v. Kelley, 953 So. 2d 1139, 1141 (Miss. Ct. App. 2007) (court awarded possession to wife until remarriage or child's emancipation). *But cf.* Mosby v. Mosby, 962 So. 2d 119, 124 (Miss. Ct. App. 2007) (former wife entitled to partition jointly owned home twenty-six years after divorce, when husband conveyed his one-half to his current wife).

[428] Regan v. Regan, 507 So. 2d 54, 57 (Miss. 1987); *see also* Selman v. Selman, 722 So. 2d 547, 552 (Miss. 1998) (wife to have possession until child reached twenty-one; then divided equally, even though wife ordered to make mortgage payments); Johnson v. Johnson, 650 So. 2d 1281, 1288 (Miss. 1995) (husband ordered to pay mortgage until child reached twenty-one, at which time he could continue payments or deed his one-half interest to ex-wife).

[429] Hawkins v. Hawkins, 45 So. 3d 1212, 1216-17 (Miss. Ct. App. 2010) (husband ordered to pay mortgage on home).

[430] Fogarty v. Fogarty, 922 So. 2d 836, 840 (Miss. Ct. App. 2006); *see also* Larue v. Larue, 969 So. 2d 99, 108 (Miss. Ct. App. 2007) (court did not err in awarding each elderly spouse one-half of equity in home, but allowing wife to occupy for the remainder of her life).

[431] *See* Thompson v. Thompson, 815 So. 2d 466, 469 (Miss. Ct. App. 2002).

[432] *See* Trovato v. Trovato, 649 So. 2d 815, 817-18 (Miss. 1995).

[433] *See* discussion *infra* § 9.07[2].

[434] Hults v. Hults, 11 So. 3d 1273, 1281-82 (Miss. Ct. App. 2009) (chancellor properly classified $10,000 in credit card debt, incurred after a temporary support order, as the wife's separate debt).

§ 6.08[4]   **MISSISSIPPI FAMILY LAW**

spouse seeking separate classification of a debt bears the burden of proof.[435] Debts incurred by a spouse before marriage or for individual purposes are usually separate.[436] A $100,000 mortgage, secured by a wife to pay personal tax debt, was properly assigned to her.[437]

Debts incurred for the benefit of the marriage are marital.[438] However, marital classification does not require that both spouses agreed to or were aware of specific purchases. For example, a court did not err in ordering a husband to pay his wife's accounts – he was aware of her debts and did nothing to prevent her from amassing additional debt.[439] A husband was properly ordered to pay one-half of the debt associated with a business his wife established during the marriage.[440] However, a $336,000 judgment for unpaid taxes was a husband's separate debt. He was solely in charge of finances and did not consult with his wife about management of the businesses. Immediately after his incarceration, she applied for a tax ID number in an attempt to comply with the law.[441]

Student loans may be partly marital if the proceeds were used for living expenses. For example, a husband's student debt was marital to the extent funds were used for household expenditures.[442] They may also be marital if the marriage benefitted from the student spouse's increased earnings.[443]

A spouse seeking payment of debt as part of equitable distribution must provide some evidence of the debt and its amount. Listing creditors and amounts in a financial statement was insufficient without supporting evidence in the form of statements or clear testimony.[444] The court must address responsibility for debts alleged to be marital

---

[435] Doyle v. Doyle, 55 So. 3d 1097, 1107-08 (Miss. Ct. App. 2010) (husband alleged that wife used credit card for her family but failed to support allegations); Shoffner v. Shoffner, 909 So. 2d 1245, 1251 (Miss. Ct. App. 2005) (party seeking separate classification of debt has the burden of proof); Horn v. Horn, 909 So. 2d 1151, 1165 (Miss. Ct. App. 2005) (credit card debt properly treated as marital in absence of proof by husband that debt was separate).

[436] TURNER, *supra* note 3, § 6.29; *see* Fitzgerald v. Fitzgerald, 914 So. 2d 193, 197 (Miss. Ct. App. 2005) (mortgage debt incurred to pay husband's premarital IRS obligation should have been classified as separate); Humphries v. Humphries, 904 So. 2d 192, 197-98 (Miss. Ct. App. 2005) ($100,000 debt on marital business assigned to husband; loan used in part to pay his $50,000 pre-marital debt; he also withdrew $54,000 from company). *But cf.* Barnett v. Barnett, 908 So. 2d 833, 841 (Miss. Ct. App. 2005) (husband's $2,000 post-separation debt, used to purchase furnishings for his apartment, was a necessary marital expenditure because wife retained all home furnishings).

[437] Curry v. Curry, 45 So. 3d 724, 727-28 (Miss. Ct. App. 2010).

[438] *See* Doyle v. Doyle, 55 So. 3d 1097, 1107-08 (Miss. Ct. App. 2010) (husband properly ordered to pay a portion of wife's credit card debt used for marital expenses); Larue v. Larue, 969 So. 2d 99, 108 (Miss. Ct. App. 2007) (loan from wife's daughter to couple to pay tax debts was for benefit of marriage); Shoffner v. Shoffner, 909 So. 2d 1245, 1251 (Miss. Ct. App. 2005) (credit card debt for automobile maintenance, family gifts, meals, and other family expenses properly classified as marital; irrelevant that cards were in husband's name only); Prescott v. Prescott, 736 So. 2d 409, 418 (Miss. Ct. App. 1999) (chancellor properly ordered husband to pay wife's credit card debt for items purchased for home).

[439] Burge v. Burge, 851 So. 2d 384, 388 (Miss. Ct. App. 2003); *see also* Barnett v. Barnett, 908 So. 2d 833, 841 (Miss. Ct. App. 2005) (marital classification does not require proof that debtor consulted with spouse regarding purchase, if prior consultation was not the couple's practice).

[440] Burnham-Steptoe v. Steptoe, 755 So. 2d 1225, 1234 (Miss. Ct. App. 1999); *see also* Irby v. Estate of Irby, 7 So. 3d 223 (Miss. 2009) (federal taxes of $104,130 from the husband's business were marital debt).

[441] King v. King, 946 So. 2d 395, 400-01, 404 (Miss. Ct. App. 2006).

[442] Kay v. Kay, 12 So. 3d 622, 627 (Miss. Ct. App. 2009); *see also* Lowrey v. Lowrey, 25 So. 3d 274, 290 (Miss. 2009) (debts incurred for goals other than the general welfare of the marriage are considered separate); Harbit v. Harbit, 3 So. 3d 156, 161 (Miss. Ct. App. 2009) (debt on wife's premarital vehicle classified as marital; vehicle was used as collateral for loan to pay marital debts incurred while husband was unemployed).

[443] TURNER, *supra* note 124, § 6.97, at 515-16 (3d. ed.).

[444] Glass v. Glass, 857 So. 2d 786, 789 (Miss. Ct. App. 2003) (chancellor did not err in refusing to divide debt).

PROPERTY DIVISION

§ 6.08[4]

– a chancellor erred in refusing to address division of a couple's credit card debt on the basis that he had insufficient evidence to do so.[445]

If debt is secured by a marital asset, courts typically include only the net value of the asset in the marital estate and order payment of the secured debt by the spouse awarded the asset.[446] However, a court may also order payment of secured debt by the other spouse or order that proceeds from the sale of other assets be applied to the debt. A court properly ordered marital property sold and the proceeds applied to secured debt, so that the wife could take the encumbered property free of liens.[447] And a husband was properly ordered to pay the $57,000 mortgage on a home awarded to the wife. The debt was used for his business.[448]

Treatment of unsecured debt varies. In some cases, debt is calculated as part of the overall net distribution of assets. For example, the court of appeals affirmed a division in which the court awarded each spouse one-half of the value of marital assets, assigned each one-half of the debt, and ordered the husband to make an equalizing payment reflecting the net amount due his wife.[449] In others, property division and debt division are treated separately. A court may divide the equity in assets and assign debt separately. If marital debt is not calculated in the net division of assets, it may be treated as a factor in property division. For example, awarding a wife 35% of marital assets was not error because her husband was awarded most of the marital debt.[450] Unsecured marital debt may be divided equally between the parties[451] or one party may be assigned a greater share of debt.[452] A court did not err in assigning all marital debt to a husband whose income was triple that of his wife and who had more separate property assets.[453]

---

[445] Owens v. Owens, 950 So. 2d 202, 217 (Miss. Ct. App. 2006).

[446] *See, e.g.,* Barnett v. Barnett, 908 So. 2d 833, 843 (Miss. Ct. App. 2005) (chancellor properly assigned mortgage debt to wife who was awarded marital home); Langdon v. Langdon, 854 So. 2d 485, 494 (Miss. Ct. App. 2003) (husband ordered to pay debt associated with business assigned to him); Dunaway v. Dunaway, 749 So. 2d 1112, 1116 (Miss. Ct. App. 1999) (court did not err in ordering husband to pay most marital debt, where he was awarded the business with which most of the debts were associated). *But cf.* Humphries v. Humphries, 904 So. 2d 192, 197-98 (Miss. Ct. App. 2005) ($100,000 debt on marital business assigned to husband; loan used in part to pay his $50,000 pre-marital debt, and he also withdrew $54,000 from company).

[447] Dunaway v. Dunaway, 749 So. 2d 1112 (Miss. Ct App. 1999).

[448] Walker v. Walker, 36 So. 3d 483, 490-91 (Miss. Ct. App. 2010).

[449] *See* Burnham-Steptoe v. Steptoe, 755 So. 2d 1225, 1235 (Miss. Ct. App. 1999) (deducting debts from marital property); *see also* Patterson v. Patterson, 917 So. 2d 111, 119 (Miss. Ct. App. 2005) (equity in marital estate calculated by subtracting debt from assets).

[450] *See* Franklin v. Franklin, 864 So. 2d 970, 976 (Miss. Ct. App. 2003); *see also* Brabham v. Brabham, 950 So. 2d 1098, 1102 (Miss. Ct. App. 2007) (chancellor properly awarded a greater share of assets to a husband who was also ordered to pay most of marital debts).

[451] Deal v. Wilson, 922 So. 2d 24, 27 (Miss. Ct. App. 2005) (debts divided equally).

[452] Dickerson v. Dickerson, 34 So. 3d 637, 643-45 (Miss. Ct. App. 2010) (husband ordered to pay all marital debt of $14,000); Shoffner v. Shoffner, 909 So. 2d 1245, 1248 (Miss. Ct. App. 2005) (husband ordered to pay two-thirds of marital debt).

[453] Larue v. Larue, 969 So. 2d 99, 108 (Miss. Ct. App. 2007); *see also* Walker v. Walker, 36 So. 3d 483, 490-91 (Miss. Ct. App. 2010) (not error to assign all debt to husband; debt was associated with his business and his income was greater).

§ 6.09   MISSISSIPPI FAMILY LAW

§ 6.09 Rights of third parties

In some cases, third parties may share an interest in assets subject to property division. Spouses may own property with other individuals, have an interest in a corporation or partnership, or be the beneficiary of a trust interest. As a general rule, a third party's interest and ownership in a marital asset is not directly affected by equitable distribution, and does not require joinder of that party in a divorce action. However, if one spouse seeks division of a third-party interest, that individual or corporation must be joined in the action.

[1] Impact on third-party interests. Only assets belonging to the spouses may be divided in divorce proceedings, absent unusual circumstances. One spouse's part interest in property or share in a corporation may be included in equitable distribution without affecting the rights of a third-party co-owner.[454] It is the spouse's interest or shares in the asset that is divided – not the asset or business itself.

The Mississippi Supreme Court stated in *Ferguson* that the impact on third parties should be considered in dividing marital assets.[455] Courts typically award a co-owned marital asset to the owner, with an award of other property or a lump sum payment to the non-owner. However, courts have discretion to award a non-owning spouse an interest in a co-owned asset, unless the transfer is prohibited or preempted by a buy-sell agreement.[456] However, most courts have advised against leaving divorcing spouses as co-owners.[457] Leaving a divorcing spouse as co-owner of property with third parties would seem equally ill-advised in most cases.

Transfers by spouses are subject to the rules of fraudulent transfer. A fraudulent transfer to a third party may be set aside and the asset treated as marital.[458]

[2] Joinder. Equitable distribution may be accomplished without joining a third party who owns property with a divorcing spouse. For example, a wife was properly awarded a share of her husband's 75% interest in a pawn shop, to be paid through a lump sum award, without joining the partnership or the husband's partner. The supreme court noted that the award divided her husband's interest in the business, not the business assets. The decision did not affect the status of the partnership or the rights of other partners.[459] Similarly, imposition of an equitable lien on a wife's one-half interest

---

[454] McGee v. McGee, 726 So. 2d 1220 (Miss. Ct. App. 1998); MacDonald v. MacDonald, 698 So. 2d 1079, 1085 (Miss. 1997) (court also found that business really belonged to husband; partner father never participated in business or benefitted from business); *see also* Rush v. Rush, 932 So. 2d 800, 804 (Miss. Ct. App. 2005) (value of husband's one-third interest in business included in marital assets without joining partners).

[455] Ferguson v. Ferguson, 639 So, 2d 921 (Miss. 1994).

[456] Turner, *supra* note 124, § 9.6.

[457] *See infra* § 8.05[4].

[458] *See infra* § 6.10.

[459] MacDonald v. MacDonald, 698 So. 2d 1079, 1085 (Miss. 1997); *see also* Rush v. Rush, 932 So. 2d 800, 804 (Miss. Ct. App. 2005) (value of husband's one-third interest in business included in marital assets without joining partners), *rev'd in part on other grounds*, 932 So. 2d 794 (Miss. 2006) (en banc); *cf.* Strong v. Strong, 981 So. 2d 1052, 1055 (Miss. Ct. App. 2008) (marital funds in certificate of deposit transferred by wife to mother could not be divided without joining mother, but court could classify as marital and assign to wife).

184

PROPERTY DIVISION

§ 6.09[3]

in property did not require joinder of her daughter, who owned the other one-half.[460]

If, however, a spouse seeks division of assets titled in the name of a third party, the third party must be joined in the action. A court erred in awarding a wife use of an automobile belonging to her husband's company without joining the corporation as a party.[461] Similarly, an ex-husband's corporation was a necessary party to his suit to modify his ex-wife's employment contract with his company.[462]

[3] Third-party equitable lien. A third party may be granted an equitable lien on property owned by one or both spouses. For example, granting a divorcing wife's mother an equitable lien on the marital home to secure a $50,000 loan related to the home was not error.[463] Similarly, the supreme court affirmed a chancellor's grant of an equitable lien to a divorcing husband's parents to secure repayment of their loan to build the couple's home.[464] Conversely, a husband was awarded a $10,000 lien on his in-laws' home to recover his share of a $20,000 contribution to renovate the home.[465]

[4] Constructive trust. A constructive trust may be imposed to protect the interest of a spouse in property titled in the name of another. Similarly, a constructive trust may be imposed on a spouse's property to protect a third party's interest. A constructive trust arises when "one party holds funds which in equity and good conscience should be possessed by another."[466] Courts may impose a constructive trust "to prevent fraud, overreaching, or other wrongful act by which one person has obtained legal title to property rightfully belonging to another." A type of constructive trust, sometimes called a resulting trust, may be imposed to reflect the actual understanding of the parties to a transaction.[467]

Clear and convincing proof is necessary to establish a constructive trust.[468] For example, an investment account in a husband's name was properly classified as marital, even though he testified that the funds belonged to his mother and were transferred to him to allow her to apply for Medicaid. His was the only name on the account, state-

---

[460] McGee v. McGee, 726 So. 2d 1220 (Miss. Ct. App. 1998).

[461] Skinner v. Skinner, 509 So. 2d 867, 870 (Miss. 1987) (also error to allow her to obtain $160 per month of goods at drugstore belonging to corporation).

[462] East v. East, 493 So. 2d 927, 933 (Miss. 1986) (employment contract entered as part of parties' divorce agreement); *see also* Grogan v. Grogan, 641 So. 2d 734, 739 (Miss. 1994) (wife attempting to set aside transfer joined husband's two corporations and his brother to whom he sold the corporations the day before a temporary restraining order prohibiting sale became effective). *But cf.* Dye v. Dye, 22 So. 3d 1241, 1245-47 (Miss. Ct. App. 2009) (tractors and other equipment kept and used at the marital home and insured by the parties were properly classified as marital, even though husband testified that they belonged to his father); Burns v. Burns, 789 So. 2d 94 (Miss. Ct. App. 2000) (not necessary to join third party claimed by husband to be equitable owner of stocks titled in husband's name; chancellor found that stocks belonged to husband).

[463] Dudley v. Light, 586 So. 2d 155, 159-60 (Miss. 1991).

[464] Neyland v. Neyland, 482 So. 2d 228, 230-31 (Miss. 1986).

[465] Phelps v. Phelps, 937 So. 2d 974, 977 (Miss. Ct. App. 2006).

[466] Mizell v. Mizell, 708 So. 2d 55, 62 (Miss. 1998) (quoting Planter's Bank & Trust v. Skylar, 555 So. 2d 1024, 1034 (Miss. 1990)) (internal quotations omitted).

[467] Nichols v. Funderburk, 881 So. 2d 266, 273 (Miss. Ct. App. 2003) (no constructive trust imposed where cohabitant worked in restaurant belonging to boyfriend and purchased carpet and paint to improve home belonging to him); Simmons v. Simmons, 724 So. 2d 1054, 1057 (Miss. Ct. App. 1998).

[468] Mizell v. Mizell, 708 So. 2d 55, 62 (Miss. 1998).

§ 6.09[5]   MISSISSIPPI FAMILY LAW

ments were sent to him, and he commingled his own funds in the account.[469] Use of the trust is an equitable remedy and may be subject to equitable defenses. The court of appeals rejected a wife's claim that she and her husband owned a motorcycle titled by them in his grandmother's name to avoid tax seizure – the clean-hands doctrine barred her from claiming title to the vehicle.[470]

[5] Children's assets. Property transferred from parents to minor children may qualify as third-party property excluded from the marital estate. According to Brett Turner, if a gift is properly made and observed under the Uniform Gift to Minors Act, there should be a strong presumption of ownership by the child.[471]

Courts may order that property titled in a parent's name be used for a child's benefit, based on the parents' prior agreement. An investment account in the husband's name, established by the parents for their children's college education, should have been classified as marital property with the stipulation that the funds be used only for the children's college expenses.[472]

[6] Corporate entities. Assets owned by a corporation, partnership, or trust are third-party property, even if one spouse is the sole owner of the corporation or partnership, or the sole beneficiary of the trust. The asset to be classified and divided is the stock, partnership interest, or beneficial interest in the entity.[473] However, courts may divide corporate assets upon a finding that the entity is the alter ego of the owner or by "piercing the corporate veil."[474]

§ 6.10 FRAUDULENT CONVEYANCES

Equitable distribution applies only at divorce; during an intact marriage, each spouse holds title to assets free of claims of the other spouse.[475] The Mississippi Supreme Court emphasized in adopting the new system that "no right to property vests by virtue of the marriage relationship alone prior to entry of a judgment or decree granting equitable or other distribution pursuant to dissolution of the marriage. Thus the rights of alienation and the laws of descent and distribution are not affected by our recognition of marital assets."[476] A spouse may not, however, transfer assets to a third party in an attempt to defeat the other's marital share. General principles of fraudulent conveyance apply to pre-divorce transfers by spouses.

The Mississippi legislature in 2006 adopted the Uniform Fraudulent Transactions

---

[469] Barnett v. Barnett, 908 So. 2d 833, 840-41 (Miss. Ct. App. 2005).

[470] Simmons v. Simmons, 724 So. 2d 1054, 1059-60 (Miss. Ct. App. 1998); *cf.* Palmer v. Palmer, 654 So. 2d 1, 4 (Miss. 1995) (applying doctrine to protect wife's community interest in property purchased in Mississippi by husband using community funds); Brabham v. Brabham, 84 So. 2d 147, 151 (Miss. 1955) (discussing but refusing to apply doctrine).

[471] TURNER, *supra* note 124, § 5.15, at 305-06 (3d ed.).

[472] Barnett v. Barnett, 908 So. 2d 833, 839-40 (Miss. Ct. App. 2005) (noting that parents could petition for release of account if children did not attend college).

[473] TURNER, *supra* note 124, § 5.16, at 311-12 (3d ed.).

[474] See *infra* Chapter VIII for a more detailed discussion of business interests.

[475] *See* discussion *supra* § 1.05[1].

[476] Ferguson v. Ferguson, 639 So. 2d 921, 928 (Miss. 1994).

PROPERTY DIVISION   § 6.10[1]

Act (UFTA) which replaced the earlier Fraudulent Conveyances Act (FCA). The previous Act provided that a gift or conveyance of property for the purpose of delaying or defrauding creditors was void.[477] Applying this statute, the Mississippi Supreme Court affirmed an order setting aside a husband's conveyance of substantial property to his father two days after the couple separated: "A wife, in respect of her right to maintenance or alimony, is within the protection of statutes or the rule avoiding conveyances or transfers in fraud of creditors . . . irrespective of whether the conveyance or transfer was made before, and in anticipation of the wife's suit for maintenance or alimony, or pending the suit, or after a decree has been made in the wife's favor."[478] However, a transfer for adequate consideration and not for the purpose of defrauding one's spouse is valid.[479] The new UFTA also provides that a transfer intended to defraud creditors is fraudulent,[480] but that a transfer to a good faith purchaser for value is valid.[481]

[1] Factors. Under the old FCA, certain "badges of fraud" were to be considered in determining whether a transfer was fraudulent.[482] Factors set out in the new UFTA are similar to those under the FCA. Courts are to consider whether: the transfer was to an insider; the debtor retained possession or control of the property; the transfer was concealed; the debtor was threatened with suit before the transfer; the transfer was of substantially all the debtor's assets; the debtor absconded or concealed assets; the consideration was "reasonably equivalent" to actual value; the debtor was insolvent; the transfer occurred shortly before or after a substantial debt was incurred; the transfer was to a lienor who transferred the assets to an insider.[483] The UFTA also includes additional factors related to a debtor who is insolvent.[484]

[2] Application. Applying the criteria under the FCA, a chancellor properly set aside a husband's blanket conveyance of assets to his brother and sister. The transaction did not include a price. Furthermore, the siblings did not live in the area and had no connection with the corporations transferred to them.[485] Similarly, a husband's conveyance of property to his sister was a fraudulent transfer designed to prevent his wife's claim to the assets as marital property; there was no consideration for the transfer, and the husband continued to possess the property after the transfer.[486] However, a father's pre-divorce transfer of a four-wheeler and a camper to his son was not fraudulent. The

---

[477] MISS. CODE ANN. § 15-3-3 (2003).

[478] Blount v. Blount, 95 So. 2d 545, 552 (Miss. 1957).

[479] MISS. CODE ANN. § 15-3-5 (2003).

[480] MISS. CODE ANN. § 15-3-107 (Supp. 2010).

[481] MISS. CODE ANN. § 15-3-113(1) (Supp. 2010).

[482] A & L, Inc. v. Grantham, 747 So. 2d 832, 843 (Miss. 1999). They included: (1) inadequate consideration; (2) conduct out of the ordinary course of business; (3) an absolute conveyance as security for a loan; (4) secrecy; (5) the transferor's insolvency; (6) a transfer of all the grantor's property; (7) retention of possession by the grantor; (8) failure to list the property covered by the conveyance; (9) the relationship of the transferor and transferee; and (10) whether the transfer was to someone with no apparent use for the property. *Id.*; *see* McNeil v. McNeil, 607 So. 2d 1192, 1195 (Miss. 1992).

[483] MISS. CODE ANN. § 15-3-107 (Supp. 2010).

[484] MISS. CODE ANN. § 15-3-107 (2)(l), (m), (n) (Supp. 2010).

[485] A & L, Inc. v. Grantham, 747 So. 2d 832, 843 (Miss. 1999) (corporations and siblings made parties to the action).

[486] Myers v. Myers, 741 So. 2d 274, 281 (Miss. Ct. App. 1998).

§ 6.10[3]   MISSISSIPPI FAMILY LAW

father testified that the camper was for the son to live in and that the four-wheeler was bought by his son but titled in the father's name, because the son was too young to hold title.[487] And a husband's transfer of $154,000 to his mother from the sale of a gravel business was not fraudulent. He purchased the business from his parents five years earlier for $450,000, as evidenced by a contract and amortization table. The amount transferred was the amount remaining on the debt.[488] A spouse must support allegations of fraud with evidence. When a wife's grandfather foreclosed on the marital home and purchased it, the husband's allegations of fraud should have been supported with testimony or other evidence.[489]

Transfers to, rather than from, a spouse, may be recharacterized based on fraud. The supreme court held that a chancellor erred in restricting an ex-wife's attempts to determine through discovery whether corporate "loans" to her ex-husband were actually income, a portion of which she was entitled to under the divorce decree.[490]

[3] Transfer to satisfy antecedent debt. A transfer to relatives for an antecedent debt will be set aside unless there is clear proof of a bona fide indebtedness, that the creditor intends to enforce the debt, and that the debt was not materially less than the value of the property conveyed. A chancellor properly set aside an ex-husband's transfer of property to his mother and sister for an alleged debt of less than half the value of the property.[491] In contrast, no fraud was found where an ex-husband's father exercised his right to repurchase his son's share of their business based on the son's financial mismanagement. As consideration for the transfer, the father cancelled documented outstanding debts owed to him by his son.[492]

§ 6.11 UNDUE INFLUENCE

A conveyance may be set aside if a court finds that one spouse unduly influenced the other to enter an agreement or make a conveyance. The court of appeals affirmed a judgment setting aside a divorcing wife's conveyance of marital assets to her daughter, at her husband's insistence. The minister husband controlled and abused his wife during their long marriage. When he was convicted of tax fraud and sexual battery and sentenced to sixty years, he instructed his wife to sign a quitclaim deed conveying the marital land, home, and buildings to his daughter. The chancellor found that there was a fiduciary duty between the husband and wife and that she signed the documents

---

[487] Herron v. Herron, 936 So. 2d 956, 959 (Miss. Ct. App. 2006).

[488] Carroll v. Carroll, No. 2009-CA-00328-COA, 2010 WL 5093660, at *3 (Miss. Ct. App. Dec. 14, 2010). The chancellor mistakenly analyzed the transaction under the UFTA, which did not apply retroactively. However, the court of appeals held that the factors under the UFTA were sufficiently similar to the FCA to allow it to review the decision. *Id.*

[489] Seghini v. Seghini, 42 So. 3d 635, 642 (Miss. Ct. App. 2010) (husband had been ordered to pay wife $516 during separation to pay mortgage).

[490] West v. West, 891 So. 2d 203 (Miss. 2004).

[491] See Morreale v. Morreale, 646 So. 2d 1264, 1268-69 (Miss. 1994) (affirming chancellor's ruling setting aside ex-husband's transfer of property worth $165,000 to his mother and sister for an alleged antecedent debt of $60,000, as an attempt to avoid payment of support).

[492] McNeil v. McNeil, 607 So. 2d 1192, 1195 (Miss. 1992) (court found that father had always intended to collect debt); *see also* Carroll v. Carroll, No. 2009-CA-00328-COA, 2010 WL 5093660, at *3 (Miss. Ct. App. Dec. 14, 2010).

PROPERTY DIVISION   § 6.12

under undue influence.[493]

§ 6.12 THE MECHANICS OF DIVISION

Actual division of assets may be accomplished through transfer of title or an award of equalizing payments. Payments may be secured by equitable liens on a payor's marital or separate assets. In addition, a court may order property sold immediately and the proceeds divided, order continued joint ownership, or retain jurisdiction over assets not ripe for division.

[1] Transfer of title. If one spouse holds title to property awarded to the other in equitable distribution, the court may order a transfer of title to accomplish the division. In *Ferguson*, the Mississippi Supreme Court explained the essence of equitable distribution as "the authority of the courts to award property legally owned by one spouse to the other."[494]

[2] Monetary award. In some cases, the nature of the marital assets may preclude a fair physical division of property. In that case, one spouse may be awarded assets exceeding a fair share of the total and ordered to make equalizing payments to the other. For example, a business is usually awarded to the owner, who is ordered to pay the other for his or her share of the business.[495] The payment is typically called "lump sum alimony." This has created some confusion, since alimony based on need could be awarded in a lump sum payment.[496] The court of appeals rejected a husband's argument that an order that he pay $4,000 a month could only be alimony – chancellors have authority to order property division payments in installments.[497]

If a payor lacks sufficient funds to make an immediate payment, the court may order payment in installments. Installment payments may be secured by an equitable lien on property awarded to the payor or on the payor's separate property.[498] For example, a chancellor properly ordered a husband to pay his wife lump sum alimony of $28,000, payable in ninety installments of $312 a month.[499]

[3] Sale of assets and division of proceeds. Courts also have authority to order specific assets sold and the proceeds divided between the parties. A court's order that

---

[493] King v. King, 946 So. 2d 395, 402 (Miss. Ct. App. 2006) (wife signed documents immediately after trial and without reading them).

[494] Ferguson v. Ferguson, 639 So. 2d 921, 927 n.4 (Miss. 1994).

[495] *See* Waring v Waring, 722 So. 2d 723, 725-26 (Miss. Ct. App. 1998); *see also* Rush v. Rush, 932 So. 2d 800, 804 (Miss. Ct. App. 2005) (marital business awarded to husband; one-half of value to be paid to wife through lump sum payment), *rev'd in part on other grounds*, 932 So. 2d 794 (Miss. 2006) (en banc). See *infra* § 8.05[4] for discussion of division of jointly owned businesses.

[496] See East v. East, 775 So. 2d 741, 745 (Miss. Ct. App. 2000) (suggesting that courts use label "property division" rather than lump sum alimony).

[497] Wilkerson v. Wilkerson, 955 So. 2d 903, 910 (Miss. Ct. App. 2007).

[498] Waring v Waring, 722 So. 2d 723 (Miss. Ct. App. 1998); *see* Rush v. Rush, 932 So. 2d 800, 804 (Miss. Ct. App. 2005) (lump sum payment representing one-half of business value secured by equitable lien on home awarded to husband), *rev'd in part on other grounds*, 932 So. 2d 794 (Miss. 2006) (en banc).

[499] Common v. Common, 42 So. 3d 59 (Miss. Ct. App. 2010).

§ 6.12[4]   MISSISSIPPI FAMILY LAW

the parties sell the marital home and divide the proceeds was not error. The supreme court noted with approval, however, that the court provided a thirty-day window to permit the husband to arrange financing to purchase his wife's interest.[500]

The court of appeals affirmed an order that real property be sold and proceeds used to avert foreclosure of other properties while divorce was pending; a chancery court has inherent power to prevent "waste of the marital estate pending a final resolution of the marital relation."[501] Similarly, a court properly ordered marital property sold and the proceeds applied to debt on other property, so that the wife could take the encumbered property free of liens.[502] The court of appeals has held, however, that assets should only be ordered sold if sale is better for the parties – a court should not have ordered sale as a remedy for failure to value the property.[503]

[4] Partition in kind. If one party requests that a particular asset be partitioned in kind, it is error for a court to order sale unless there is proof that sale is the only feasible method of dividing the property.[504] The burden of proof is on the party seeking sale.[505] A court erred in ordering the sale and division of a couple's rental property business without a showing that partition in kind was not feasible.[506]

[5] Continued joint ownership. A court may order that the parties continue as joint owners of property. With regard to the marital home, a court may award one party exclusive use and possession for a period of time, leaving the property jointly titled for that period.[507] Or the court may award the home to one party with the other granted the right of possession for a specified period of time.[508] The usual right of owners to partition jointly held property is subject to a chancellor's authority to ensure adequate support for both spouses at divorce.[509]

Although less common, a court may also order that non-homestead property con-

---

[500] Johnson v. Johnson, 550 So. 2d 416, 420 (Miss. 1989); *see also* Herron v. Herron, 936 So. 2d 956, 958 (Miss. Ct. App. 2006) (chancellor ordered land, marital home, and personal property sold and proceeds divided); Drumright v. Drumright, 812 So. 2d 1021, 1027 (Miss. Ct. App. 2001) (affirming order for sale of home and furnishings); Curtis v. Curtis, 796 So. 2d 1044, 1052-53 (Miss. Ct. App. 2001) (court did not err in ordering sale of marital home but not of adjoining property).

[501] Garriga v. Garriga, 770 So. 2d 978, 982 (Miss. Ct. App. 2000).

[502] Dunaway v. Dunaway, 749 So. 2d 1112, 1114-15 (Miss. Ct. App. 1999); *see also* Rush v. Rush *ex rel.* Mayne, 914 So. 2d 322, 325 (Miss. Ct. App. 2005) (en banc) (court awarded equipment to disabled wife and ordered it sold and proceeds used for her support); Richardson v. Richardson, 912 So. 2d 1079, 1082 (Miss. Ct. App. 2005) (on remand, court could award wife cattle equal to one-third of herd's value or order cattle sold and award her one-third of sale price).

[503] Parker v. Parker, 980 So. 2d 323, 327 (Miss. Ct. App. 2008). *But see* McDuffie v. McDuffie, 21 So. 3d 685, 690 (Miss. Ct. App. 2009) (chancellor did not err in ordering all personal property sold and proceeds divided to avoid "further wasting of the legal system's valuable resources" where neither party presented evidence of the value).

[504] Garriga v. Garriga, 770 So. 2d 978, 984-85 (Miss. Ct. App. 2000).

[505] Overstreet v. Overstreet, 692 So. 2d 88, 90 (Miss. 1997).

[506] Garriga v. Garriga, 770 So. 2d 978, 982 (Miss. Ct. App. 2000).

[507] *See* Boykin v. Boykin, 565 So. 2d 1109, 1112-13 (Miss. 1990); Regan v. Regan, 507 So. 2d 54, 58 (Miss. 1987).

[508] *See* Fogarty v. Fogarty, 922 So. 2d 836, 840 (Miss. Ct. App. 2006) (marital home awarded to husband; wife to live rent-free in the home for two years).

[509] Sartin v. Sartin, 405 So. 2d 84, 86 (Miss. 1981); *see also* Regan v. Regan, 507 So. 2d 54, 57 (Miss. 1987) (rejecting husband's claim of right to partition twenty acres awarded to wife during child's minority). *See also supra* § 1.05[f] (recent statutory amendment restricting right to partition homestead).

PROPERTY DIVISION   § 6.12[6]

tinue in joint ownership. A chancellor did not err in leaving the parties as joint tenants of 110 acres of land with the right to dispose of the property by agreement or partition. The court found that continued ownership might be financially beneficial to the parties.[510] As a general rule, however, courts are reluctant to leave divorcing spouses as co-owners.[511]

[6] Equitable credit. A court may credit one party with an amount equal to property already received or dissipated by that party. A chancellor properly credited a wife with having already received marital property worth $12,000 to account for $12,000 in income that she withheld from her husband.[512]

[7] Reimbursement for marital contribution to separate property. The court of appeals approved an order awarding a husband separate property in accordance with a premarital agreement, but requiring him to reimburse his wife for her contributions to the mortgage on the property.[513] Similarly, a husband's premarital payment of a $49,000 lien on his wife's land was treated as a loan and reimbursed at divorce but did not convert the property to marital.[514] And in one case, a court properly awarded a wife a judgment for $6,000 for payment of her husband's attorneys' fees in a criminal action.[515]

[8] Judgment against spouse. In at least one divorce action, a wife was awarded a judgment against her husband for a loan that she made to him during the marriage. The court of appeals noted that, although chancellors are not usually asked to rule on such matters, the parties agreed to submit this issue to the court for decision.[516]

[9] Reserved jurisdiction. Certain marital assets may not be ripe for division at the time of trial. A court may reserve jurisdiction to divide these assets at a later date. The court may defer any decisions related to the asset, or may determine the percentages or amounts that should be awarded to each spouse when and if the asset is available for distribution. The reserved jurisdiction approach is particularly appropriate for unvested assets such as unvested pensions[517] or attorney contingency fees.[518] A chancellor properly reserved jurisdiction to divide an anticipated award of worker's compensation

---

[510] Messer v. Messer, 850 So. 2d 161, 170-71 (Miss. Ct. App. 2003) (based on testimony that the parties had purchased the land as an investment for their child's education).

[511] *See* TURNER, *supra* note 3, § 9.02, at 623; *cf.* Hunt v. Asanov, 975 So. 2d 899, 903 (Miss. Ct. App. 2008) (wife awarded 25% of corporation, but husband had alternative of buying out her share within thirty days to prevent discord).

[512] Collins v. Collins, 722 So. 2d 596, 600 (Miss. 1998). *But cf.* Bowen v. Bowen, 982 So. 2d 385, 396 (Miss. 2008) (husband was not entitled to equitable credit for payment of temporary alimony during the pendency of the divorce proceeding); Parker v. Parker, 929 So. 2d 940, 945 (Miss. Ct. App. 2005) (same).

[513] Uglem v. Uglem, 831 So. 2d 1175, 1177-78 (Miss. Ct. App. 2002) (husband's investment $127,000; wife made mortgage payments of $13,000); *see also* Smith v. Smith, 994 So. 2d 882, 886 (Miss. Ct. App. 2008) (wife's improvements to husband's separate property did not convert to marital even though property appreciated during marriage; wife awarded $5,000 as equitable payment for her work).

[514] Ory v. Ory, 936 So. 2d 405, 411 (Miss. Ct. App. 2006) (en banc).

[515] Avery v. Avery, 864 So. 2d 1054, 1057-58 (Miss. Ct. App. 2004).

[516] Duncan v. Duncan, 915 So. 2d 1124, 1128 (Miss. Ct. App. 2005) (en banc).

[517] *See* discussion *infra* § 7.12.

[518] *See* discussion *supra* § 6.06[5].

§ 6.12[10]   MISSISSIPPI FAMILY LAW

benefits to the husband.[519] Reserved jurisdiction may also be appropriate when assets cannot be valued and classified because of pending bankruptcy proceedings.[520] In one case, a chancellor properly retained jurisdiction to determine income pending an audit of the parties' business.[521]

[10] Security for payment. A chancellor may impose an equitable lien to secure property division payments. The lien may be imposed on marital assets awarded to the payor[522] or on separate assets.[523] A lien may be imposed even if the payor shares ownership of the encumbered property with a third person. A wife's one-half interest in property was properly subjected to a lien to secure her husband's share of equity, even though she owned the home jointly with her daughter.[524] An equitable lien may also be imposed to protect the interest of a third party.[525] In addition, upon proof that a party may leave the state to avoid payment, a spouse may be required to execute a bond conditioned on not leaving the state. The bond may be required before the final decree, and may be continued after the decree to ensure compliance.[526]

[11] Constructive trust. A court may impose a constructive trust to protect assets titled in one person's name, but that in fact belong to another.[527]

§ 6.13 MODIFICATION AND ENFORCEMENT

[1] Modification. A court's division of marital property is a nonmodifiable order.[528] A husband's agreement to provide a $150,000 life insurance policy for his wife as part of a property settlement rather than alimony was not modifiable.[529] Similarly, a husband's obligation to make mortgage payments as part of property division could not be modified and survived the wife's remarriage.[530]

---

[519] Wesson v. Wesson, 818 So. 2d 1272, 1278 (Miss. Ct. App. 2002).

[520] Heigle v. Heigle, 654 So. 2d 895, 898 (Miss. 1995) (chancellor erred in dividing assets of husband's business while bankruptcy involving the business was pending).

[521] Black v. Black, 741 So. 2d 299, 300 (Miss. Ct. App. 1999).

[522] Lindsey v. Lindsey, 612 So. 2d 376, 379-80 (Miss. 1992) (husband's one-half interest in marital home impressed with lien to secure $22,000 expended by wife on home); *see* Rush v. Rush, 932 So. 2d 800, 808 (Miss. Ct. App. 2005) (chancellor did not err in granting equitable lien on the marital home to secure husband's payment of wife's interest in business), *rev'd in part on other grounds,* 932 So. 2d 794 (Miss. 2006) (en banc).

[523] Lindsey v. Lindsey, 612 So. 2d 376, 379-80 (Miss. 1992); *see* Sarver v. Sarver, 687 So. 2d 749, 756 (Miss. 1997).

[524] McGee v. McGee, 726 So. 2d 1220, 1222-23 (Miss. Ct. App. 1998); *see also* Gray v. Gray, 745 So. 2d 234, 239 (Miss. 1999) (chancellor awarded husband real property but granted wife a 50% lien on property and ordered her ex-husband to manage the property – primarily rental units – and report to her periodically; remanded to determine whether 50% lien applied to the value of the property at the time of divorce or to the growing value of the property).

[525] *See supra* § 6.09[3].

[526] Blount v. Blount, 95 So. 2d 545, 562 (Miss. 1957) (husband disappeared shortly after divorce action filed and transferred property to father; court did not err in ordering husband jailed until bond executed).

[527] *See* discussion of constructive trust *supra* § 6.09[4].

[528] East v. East, 493 So. 2d 927, 931 (Miss. 1986); Lestrade v. Lestrade, 49 So. 3d 639, 644-45 (Miss. Ct. App. 2010) (reversing chancellor's "equitable modification" of couple's property division agreement); Hopson v. Hopson, 851 So. 2d 397, 399 (Miss. Ct. App. 2003).

[529] Geiger v. Geiger, 530 So. 2d 185, 187 (Miss. 1998) (dicta).

[530] Mount v. Mount, 624 So. 2d 1001, 1004 (Miss. 1993); *see also* Logue v. Logue, 106 So. 2d 498, 500 (Miss. 1958); Kelley v. Kelley, 953 So. 2d 1139, 1143 (Miss. Ct. App. 2007) (court erred in modifying couple's agreement

PROPERTY DIVISION   § 6.13[2]

[2] Clarification. A court may, however, clarify an ambiguous property division order. A court did not err in extending the time for one party's performance under a settlement agreement when there was a good-faith misunderstanding between the parties regarding the meaning of the agreement.[531] An ambiguous order regarding division of a husband's pension was clarified several years after the decree.[532] And a court had authority to clarify whether a complicated repayment formula in a judgment called for the husband to pay interest on $35,000.[533] However, a chancellor properly refused to reform a couple's three-year-old property settlement agreement to reflect the husband's mistaken understanding of the final agreement. The final agreement provided that the wife would receive 50% of the husband's "*FERS Retirement Annuity*" rather than (as an earlier exchanged proposal stated), 50% of husband's "*FERS Retirement Surviving Spousal Annuity.*"[534] Similarly, when a husband continued to work at seventy-one, a court erred in modifying the couple's agreement to allow the former wife to receive her share of retirement benefits. The agreement provided that she would receive one-half of her husband's retirement; it did not require that he retire at sixty-five.[535]

[3] Frustration of purpose. Courts may also fashion an equitable remedy if unforeseen circumstances frustrate the purpose of property division. For example, when a car on which the husband was to make payments was destroyed and his obligation satisfied with insurance proceeds, the court should have required him to make similar payments on another automobile.[536] And a husband was ordered to pay proceeds to his former wife when he received payment on an insurance policy covering property awarded to her.[537] A chancellor properly reformed a couple's agreement that each would receive a specific amount from a retirement account that lost substantial value before

---

regarding marital home obligations); Chroniger v. Chroniger, 914 So. 2d 311, 315 (Miss. Ct. App. 2005) (husband's obligation to pay wife one-half of his military retirement was part of property division and did not terminate upon cohabitation).

[531] Dalton v. Dalton, 852 So. 2d 586, 589 (Miss. Ct. App. 2002).

[532] Rogers v. Rogers, 919 So. 2d 184, 187-88 (Miss. Ct. App. 2005). A provision that the wife was to receive "one-half of the husband's 401k in the approximate sum of $69,000.00" meant $69,000 at the time of the divorce hearing, not when the qualified domestic relations order was entered several years later. Thus, any increase in value after the hearing belonged to the wife. *Id.; see also* Wood v. Wood (*In re* Dissolution of Marriage of Wood), 35 So. 3d 507, 513 (Miss. 2010) (provision for specific amounts to be awarded from "estimated" value of retirement account was ambiguous; court looked to extrinsic evidence). *But cf.* Lestrade v. Lestrade, 49 So. 3d 639, 644-45 (Miss. Ct. App. 2010) (reversing chancellor's modification of unambiguous retirement provision based on wife's "assumption" that husband would retire at sixty-five).

[533] Wilkerson v. Wilkerson, 955 So. 2d 903, 907-08 (Miss. Ct. App. 2007); *see also* Daley v. Carlton, 19 So. 3d 781, 783 (Miss. Ct. App. 2009) (clarifying that husband's obligation to satisfy mortgage included balloon payment not mentioned in agreement); Crisler v. Crisler, 963 So. 2d 1248, 1252 (Miss. Ct. App. 2007) (court clarified ambiguous provision regarding sale of property). *But cf.* Williams v. Williams, 37 So. 3d 1171, 1175-76 (Miss. 2010) (reversing chancellor's clarification of pension provision); Pratt v. Pratt 977 So. 2d 386, 389 (Miss. Ct. App. 2007) (husband not entitled to revision of property settlement agreement to conform to his understanding of pension division); Salemi v. Salemi, 972 So. 2d 1, 5 (Miss. Ct. App. 2007) (husband time-barred from seeking clarification of agreement nine years after judgment).

[534] Pratt v. Pratt, 977 So. 2d 386, 390-91 (Miss. Ct. App. 2007).

[535] Lestrade v. Lestrade, 49 So. 3d 639, 644-45 (Miss. Ct. App. 2010) (her assumption that he would retire at sixty-five was not a reason to modify).

[536] Morgan v. Morgan, 744 So. 2d 321, 325-26 (Miss. 1999).

[537] Sullivan v. Sullivan, 942 So. 2d 305, 307 (Miss. Ct. App. 2006) (property was destroyed after divorce); *cf.* Day v. Day, 28 So. 3d 672 (Miss. Ct. App. 2010) (wife not entitled to enforce provision for division of equity based on appraisal, when she delayed appraisal for one year by barring husband from house).

§ 6.13[4]   MISSISSIPPI FAMILY LAW

division. The court properly determined the percentages awarded to each and applied the percentages to the current value of the account.[538]

[4] Waiver. While property division provisions are not modifiable, a party's own failure to comply with a provision may constitute a waiver of a particular provision. A wife who failed to select an appraiser to establish the value of the marital home could not complain of division based on an appraiser selected by her husband.[539]

[5] Enforcement. A party's failure to comply with property division orders may be enforced through judgment and contempt. For example, an ex-husband who failed to maintain a life insurance policy as part of property division was properly held in contempt.[540] A former husband's default on property division installment payments justified imposition of an equitable lien to secure payment of the remaining installments.[541] Enforcement of judgments of divorce is discussed in Chapter XIV.

[6] Relief based on fraud. A judgment of divorce and property division may be reopened in some circumstances based on fraudulent concealment of assets. A chancellor should have held a former husband in contempt for failure to disclose substantial lottery winnings. Even though four years had passed since the judgment of divorce, the case was remanded for consideration of whether the winnings were marital assets.[542] However, not every failure to list an asset is fraudulent. The court of appeals rejected a former wife's attempt to set aside a seven-year-old property division that did not include her husband's post office pension. The pension was not listed under retirement accounts, but a notation was made by hand in the section for payroll deductions.[543]

In 2010, the Mississippi Supreme Court held that a property division may be set aside under Rule 60(b)(6) of the Mississippi Rules of Civil Procedure when one party intentionally makes a substantial misstatement on a Rule 8.05 Financial Statement. The husband's 8.05 statement valued his business at $100,000. One year later, in litigation with his business partners, his expert testified that it was worth $1 million. The court held that an intentional, substantial misstatement of value was fraud on the court, allowing the judgment to be set aside several years after entry.[544]

---

[538] Wood v. Wood (*In re* Dissolution of Marriage of Wood), 35 So. 3d 507, 514-16 (Miss. 2010) (rejecting wife's argument that husband delayed in dividing account; no proof that she provided him with the necessary account information).

[539] Weathersby v. Weathersby, 693 So. 2d 1348, 1352 (Miss. 1997) (parties may waive specific provisions by failing to carry out their own responsibilities).

[540] Martin v. Ealy, 859 So. 2d 1034, 1038 (Miss. Ct. App. 2003) (rejecting argument that insurance was to secure child support, rather than part of property division).

[541] *See* Alexander v. Alexander, 494 So. 2d 365, 368 (Miss. 1986) (judgment on husband's indebtedness to wife for her share of home and farm).

[542] Kalman v. Kalman, 905 So. 2d 760, 763-64 (Miss. Ct. App. 2004).

[543] Shaw v. Shaw, 985 So. 2d 346 (Miss. Ct. App. 2007); *see also* McIntosh v. McIntosh, 977 So. 2d 1257, 1270 (Miss. Ct. App. 2008) (refusing to reverse on basis that husband's pension was not listed as asset; contributions were listed in income section of 8.05).

[544] Trim v. Trim, 33 So. 3d 471, 478-79 (Miss. 2010).

PROPERTY DIVISION   § 6.14

§ 6.14 Effect of bankruptcy

Under the Bankruptcy Reform Act of 1994, payments and transfers pursuant to property division at divorce could be discharged in Chapter 7 bankruptcy proceedings. The Act required application of a balancing test to determine whether property division payments should be discharged.[545]

The Bankruptcy Abuse Prevention and Consumer Protection Act of 2005 substantially altered bankruptcy treatment of property obligations. Now, property division obligations may not be discharged in Chapter 7 bankruptcies. Under some circumstances, however, they may be discharged in Chapter 13 proceedings. The effect of bankruptcy on property division is discussed in detail in Chapter XXI.

---

[545] 11 U.S.C. § 523(a)(15) (2000).

196

VII
RETIREMENT BENEFITS

Dividing retirement benefits can be one of the most emotionally charged and legally complicated issues in divorce. In many cases, retirement benefits are one of the most valuable assets in the marital estate.[1] Retirement benefits are governed by both state and federal law, raise difficult valuation issues, and involve unique classification problems. Different rules may apply, depending on whether the plan is private, military, federal, state, or individual. In addition, the two primary types of plans – defined benefit and defined contribution – are valued, classified, and divided differently.[2] This chapter begins with an explanation of terms used in the equitable distribution of retirement benefits, followed by a discussion of the methods used to value, classify, and divide defined contribution and defined benefit plans. The remainder of the chapter briefly sets out rules specific to private, military, federal, and state retirement benefits.

§ 7.01 TERMINOLOGY

[1] Defined benefit plan. A defined benefit plan offers retirement benefits calculated by a formula; the value of the plan and the amount of benefits are not directly based on the amount of contributions.[3] For example, a defined benefit plan might provide employees with an annual benefit of 2% of the employee's highest annual salary for each year of employment. An employee who retired after twenty-five years at a salary of $100,000 would be entitled to an annual benefit of $50,000. Some plans also provide periodic cost-of-living increases after maturity.[4]

[2] Defined contribution plan. In contrast, benefits under defined contribution plans are based on the total amount of contributions and accrued earnings – the amount in the account at the time of retirement.[5]

[3] Participant. An employee spouse entitled to receive benefits under a plan gov-

---

[1] *See* David Gregory, *The Scope of ERISA Preemption of State Law: A Study in Effective Federalism*, 48 U. Pitt. L. Rev. 427, 435 (1987) ("Pension plans constitute the largest block of private capital in the United States, and 'represent the world's largest identifiable source of private wealth.'").

[2] Several excellent treatises and articles provide an in-depth analysis of pension valuation and division. *See* Thomas F. Burrage & Sandra Morgan Little, Divorce and Domestic Relations Litigation (2003); David Clayton Carrad, The Complete QDRO Handbook (3d ed. 2009); J. Thomas Oldham, Divorce, Separation & the Distribution of Property (2010); Gary. A Shulman & David I. Kelley, Dividing Pensions in Divorce (1999); Marvin Snyder, Value of Pensions in Divorce (3d ed. 1999); Brett Turner, Equitable Distribution of Property (2d ed. 1994); Elizabeth Barker Brandt, *Valuation, Allocation, and Distribution of Retirement Plans at Divorce: Where are We?*, 35 Fam. L. Q. 469, 471 (2001); Susan J. Prather, *Characterization, Valuation, and Distribution of Pensions at Divorce*, 15 J.Am Acad. Matrim. Law. 443, 445 (1998).

[3] Brandt, *supra* note 2, at 471; Marvin Snyder, *Challenges in Valuing Pension Plans*, 35 Fam. L.Q. 235, 235-36 (2001).

[4] Brandt, *supra* note 2, at 471.

[5] Snyder, *supra* note 3, at 236.

§ 7.01[4]   MISSISSIPPI FAMILY LAW

erned by ERISA is called a participant.

[4] Alternate payee. A non-employee spouse who receives benefits directly from a retirement plan under a Qualified Domestic Relations Order is called an alternate payee.[6]

[5] Immediate offset. A non-employee spouse's share of a retirement benefit may be awarded at the time of divorce through a lump sum payment or an award of other property of equal value. Under this method, the employee spouse retains sole ownership of the retirement benefit.[7]

[6] Deferred distribution. Division may be deferred until the participant reaches retirement age. For deferred distribution, private retirement benefits may be divided through a Qualified Domestic Relations Order [QDRO], non-military federal plans through a Court Order Acceptable for Processing [COAP], and military plans through a court order that meets the requirements of the applicable statutes.

Deferred distribution of private defined benefit plans may be accomplished by dividing each payment received during the participant's life between the participant and alternate payee – the shared interest approach – or by paying the alternate payee's share over his or her lifetime – the separate interest approach.[8] Deferred distribution of military and civil service benefits may be accomplished only through shared payments.[9]

[7] Vested pension. A pension vests when a participant is entitled to benefits whether or not employment continues.[10]

[8] Mature pension. A pension is matured when a participant is entitled to begin receiving benefits.[11]

§ 7.02 THE EQUITABLE DISTRIBUTION PROCESS

State law governs classification of retirement benefits as marital or separate. In the early years of equitable distribution, some courts held that pensions earned during marriage were separate property. Today, however, retirement benefits acquired during marriage are marital property in every state.[12]

The Mississippi Supreme Court allowed division of pensions between divorcing spouses even before equitable distribution was formally adopted.[13] Even so, employee spouses still occasionally attempt to exclude pensions from the marital estate, arguing

---

[6] 29 U.S.C. § 1056(d)(3)(K) (2006).

[7] *See* discussion *infra* § 7.03[3].

[8] *See* discussion *infra* § 7.04[1][c][ii].

[9] *See* discussion *infra* § 7.07[1][c][i].

[10] Brandt, *supra* note 2, at 470 n.4 (noting that most pensions vest in seven years).

[11] OLDHAM, *supra* note 2, § 7.10[4].

[12] *See* TURNER, *supra* note 2, § 6.09 (some courts still exclude unvested pensions from the marital estate).

[13] *See* Brown v. Brown, 574 So. 2d 688, 690 (Miss. 1990) (spouse's pension is personal property subject to division at divorce).

RETIREMENT BENEFITS

§ 7.02[1]

that the non-owning spouse made no direct contribution to the asset. Mississippi appellate courts have consistently rejected this argument.[14]

To divide retirement benefits at divorce, courts must (1) value the benefit; (2) classify separate and marital portions of the benefit; (3) divide the marital portion equitably between the parties; and (4) decide whether the non-employee spouse's share should be distributed immediately or deferred until retirement. All four steps are considerably more complicated with regard to defined benefit plans. This section outlines the four steps. Sections 7.03 and 7.04 apply the steps to defined benefit and defined contribution plans.

The process described in these three sections applies generally to division of all benefits – private, military, federal, and state. Private benefits are more likely to be provided through defined contribution plans, while government benefits are more likely to be provided as defined benefit plans. Specific rules applicable to private, military, and other governmental plans follow these sections.

[1] Valuation. The value of a defined contribution plan is the amount of funds in the plan on the valuation date.[15] Valuing a defined benefit plan is more complicated. The valuator must estimate the retirement stream of income and reduce the estimated payments to present value.[16] Because of the difficulty of valuing defined benefit pensions, some courts opt to defer distribution until retirement, avoiding the need to establish present value.

[2] Classification. Pensions, like marital homes, are not acquired in one transaction – their value is built over a number of years that may include periods before, during, and after marriage. Courts apply a pro rata approach to classify marital and separate portions of pensions.[17] The portion acquired during marriage is marital property; the portion acquired before marriage or after the relevant cut-off date is the participant's separate property.[18] The Mississippi Supreme Court uses this approach to divide pensions.[19] For example, a wife of fifteen years was not entitled to an equal division of her husband's retirement benefits accumulated over twenty-four years.[20]

---

[14] *See* Baker v. Baker, 807 So. 2d 476, 480 (Miss. Ct. App. 2001) (error to exclude husband's retirement account from marital property); *see also* Owen v. Owen, 798 So. 2d 394, 400 (Miss. 2001) (error to exclude husband's employee stock ownership plan and 401k plan from marital assets); Savelle v. Savelle, 650 So. 2d 476, 478 (Miss. 1995); Parker v. Parker, 641 So. 2d 1133, 113 (Miss. 1994); Pierce v. Pierce, 648 So. 2d 523, 525 (Miss. 1994); Draper v. Draper, 627 So. 2d 302, 305-06 (Miss. 1993).

[15] *See* discussion *infra* § 7.03[1].

[16] *See* discussion *infra* § 7.04[1][a].

[17] OLDHAM, *supra* note 2, § 7.10[5].

[18] *See* discussion of classification *infra* § 7.03[2] and § 7.04[1][b].

[19] *See* Draper v. Draper, 627 So. 2d 302, 306 (Miss. 1993) (award to wife of 35% of husband's retirement); Barnett v. Barnett, 908 So. 2d 833, 839 (Miss. Ct. App. 2005) (chancellor properly classified an IRA owned by husband before marriage as partly marital and partly separate); Murphy v. Murphy, 797 So. 2d 325, 331 (Miss. Ct. App. 2001) (wife awarded 33% of marital share of husband's civil service retirement).

[20] Arthur v. Arthur, 691 So. 2d 997, 1103-04 (Miss. 1997) (pension funds accumulated before marriage, as well as any interest on those funds, were the husband's separate estate and not subject to equitable distribution); *see also* Dye v. Dye, 22 So. 3d 1241, 1245 (Miss. Ct. App. 2009) (error to classify retirement account as all marital; husband worked for company for six years prior to marriage).

§ 7.02[3]   **MISSISSIPPI FAMILY LAW**

[3] Division and distribution. After a pension is valued and classified, the marital portion is divided between spouses based on state-established criteria for equitable distribution.[21] Although many pensions are divided equally, there is no automatic right to 50% of the marital share upon divorce.[22]

A non-employee spouse's share may be distributed at divorce or retirement.[23] If distribution occurs at divorce, the non-employee may be awarded a lump sum payment, or may receive other marital property to offset award of the pension to the employee spouse.[24] Or, distribution to the non-owning spouse may be delayed until benefits are actually available to the employee.[25] Deferred distribution may be preferable for dividing defined benefit plans – the complicated process of valuing the benefit is avoided.[26] If distribution is deferred, the benefits may be divided through a Qualified Domestic Relations Order or other order appropriate to the particular plan. As an alternative, a participant is sometimes ordered to make payments directly to the non-employee spouse.[27] The order or agreement should indicate clearly how division is to be accomplished and the amount or percentage each spouse is to receive.[28] When a retirement account's value dropped sharply after divorce, it was impossible for the spouses to receive the amounts set out in their agreement. The chancellor properly determined each spouse's percentage under the agreement and applied those percentages to the reduced amount.[29]

It is important to determine in advance of entering a QDRO whether a particular plan permits division prior to retirement. A divorcing couple agreed that the wife would receive one-half of the value of the husband's post office pension at the time of divorce. When the parties later learned that the plan did not allow immediate division, an amended QDRO was entered providing that she would receive one-half of the marital portion of the actual benefits when he retired.[30]

---

[21] *See* Ferguson v. Ferguson, 639 So. 2d 921, 929 (Miss. 1994).

[22] *See* Savelle v. Savelle, 650 So. 2d 476, 479 (Miss. 1995) (stating that automatic fifty-fifty split is not required); Pierce v. Pierce, 648 So. 2d 523, 526 (Miss. 1994) (holding no automatic right to fifty-fifty division of pension); Parker v. Parker, 641 So. 2d 1133, 1139 (Miss. 1994) (holding right vests only after chancellor makes equitable division); Almond v. Almond, 850 So. 2d 104, 107 (Miss. Ct. App. 2002); *cf.* Draper v. Draper, 627 So. 2d 302, 306 (Miss. 1993) (award to wife of 35% of husband's retirement); Baker v. Baker, 861 So. 2d 351, 353 (Miss. Ct. App. 2003) (award to wife of 30% of husband's pension as alimony not error); Murphy v. Murphy, 797 So. 2d 325, 331 (Miss. Ct. App. 2001) (wife awarded 33% of marital share of husband's civil service retirement).

[23] *See* Gemma v. Gemma, 778 P.2d 429, 431 (Nev. 1989) (explaining benefits of each approach).

[24] *See* Mabus v. Mabus, 890 So. 2d 806, 826 (Miss. 2003) (awarding lump sum equal to one-half of marital share); Kilpatrick v. Kilpatrick, 732 So. 2d 876, 881 (Miss. 1999) (each spouse awarded his own retirement plan as part of equitable distribution).

[25] *See* Holloman v. Holloman, 691 So. 2d 897, 900 (Miss. 1996) (QDRO used to divide defined contribution plan); Parker v. Parker, 641 So. 2d 1133, 1135-36 (Miss. 1994) (awarding wife a 30% interest in husband's profit-sharing plan to be set aside in separate account through QDRO).

[26] OLDHAM, *supra* note 2, § 7.10[5].

[27] *See* Warren v. Warren, 815 So. 2d 457, 460 (Miss. Ct. App. 2002) (wife ordered to pay husband $225.00 of monthly state retirement benefit; payment was non-modifiable property division, not alimony); *cf.* McDannell v. United States Office of Personnel Mgmt., 716 F.2d 1063, 1065-66 (5th Cir. 1983) (husband, as trustee of wife's share, to pay 25% of monthly benefit to wife).

[28] *See* Boykin v. Boykin, 565 So. 2d 1109, 1114-15 (Miss. 1990) (reversing chancellor's order placing lien on husband's civil service benefits; not clear from the order whether the lien secured alimony, awarded one-third of benefits to wife, or required husband to pay one-third to her).

[29] Wood v. Wood, 35 So. 3d 507, 515 (Miss. 2010) (recommending that parties use percentages to express their respective interests in an asset of fluctuating value).

[30] Salemi v. Salemi, 972 So. 2d 1, 6-7 (Miss. Ct. App. 2007) (dismissing husband's motion to clarify nine years

RETIREMENT BENEFITS § 7.03

Attorneys should ensure that the retirement plan paperwork necessary to effectuate the judgment is completed. The United States Supreme Court held that a retirement plan administrator properly released benefits to a deceased member's ex-wife as his listed beneficiary, even though she waived any interest in retirement benefits in their divorce agreement. The husband did not execute the required form changing his beneficiary. The Court did, however, leave open the question whether the estate could have sought recovery against the ex-wife to obtain the distributed benefits.[31]

§ 7.03 DEFINED CONTRIBUTION PLANS

The process of valuing and dividing defined contribution plans is relatively simple. As a result, these benefits are valued and spouses' interests are almost always separated at divorce.

[1] Valuation. The value of a defined contribution plan is the value of an employee's individual account on the valuation date. The value can usually be established without expert testimony through a participant statement showing the account balance on or near the relevant date.[32] The account balance should reflect both contributions to the account and accrued interest.

[2] Classification. Most courts classify marital and separate shares of a defined contribution plan by determining the amount of contributions made during and outside marriage and the accrued interest on each amount. In states such as Mississippi where passive income from separate property is separate,[33] the interest earned on pre-marital contributions should be separate property, while the interest earned on marital contributions is marital property.[34] Because marital property accumulation ends at a temporary support order, any contributions made after a temporary support order will be the employee spouse's separate property. However, passive growth after a temporary support order takes the classification of the account at the time of the support order.[35]

Determining the precise interest accrued on a pre-marital portion can be time-consuming. A less exact but simpler method is to identify the average growth of the account during marriage and to compound separate contributions by that figure to arrive at the separate portion of the total.[36]

Some courts calculate the separate share by subtracting the value of the account at the time of marriage from its value at the time of divorce; however, this method fails to recognize the passive increase of the premarital contributions.[37] In a 2010 case,

---

later).

[31] Kennedy v. DuPont Sav. and Inv. Plan, 129 S. Ct. 865, 869-70 (2009).

[32] Snyder, *supra* note 3, at 246.

[33] *See* discussion *supra* § 6.03[4].

[34] *See* Brandt, *supra* note 2, at 476; TURNER, *supra* note 2, § 6.10, at 336; *see also* Thomas v. Thomas, 4 S.W.3d 517, 524-25 (Ark. Ct. App. 1999); Blase v. Blase, 704 So. 2d 741, 742 (Fla. Dist. Ct. App. 1998); Alford v. Alford, 653 So. 2d 133, 135-36 (La. Ct. App. 1995) (remanded to determine separate and marital portions); Barkley v. Barkley, 694 N.E.2d 989, 992 (Ohio Ct. App. 1997).

[35] *See supra* § 6.02[3][b].

[36] SHULMAN & KELLEY, *supra* note 2, § 6.03[4], at 235-37.

[37] SHULMAN & KELLEY, *supra* note 2, at 233.

§ 7.03[3]   **MISSISSIPPI FAMILY LAW**

the Mississippi Court of Appeals appears to have used this approach, holding that the appreciated value of a husband's retirement account (from $38,000 to $86,000 over a thirteen-year marriage) was marital, even though all of the contributions but one year were made prior to the marriage. The court rejected his argument that the increase was passive.[38]

[3] Division and distribution. In the division stage, each spouse is awarded a share of the marital portion based on factors established for fair division of assets.[39] A non-employee spouse's share may be distributed immediately through a lump sum award or by awarding other marital property of equal value.[40] Or, distribution to the non-employee may be deferred by ordering the plan administrator to divide the existing account into two separate accounts.[41] Thereafter, each spouse's account accrues interest separately; future contributions do not benefit the non-employee spouse.[42] Whether a pension is distributed through offset, purchase, or separate accounts, both spouses' shares are identified and separated at the time of divorce, avoiding the post-divorce increase issues that plague division of defined benefit plans.

[4] Taxes. Under deferred distribution, creation of a new account for the non-employee at the time of divorce is not a taxable event.[43] Each spouse is taxed on amounts as they are actually distributed from their account.

If the non-employee receives a lump sum award or other marital property in offset, the award is part of property division and is not taxable.[44] The participant's share will be reduced by taxes as benefits are received.[45] Courts have differed as to whether an immediate award to the non-employee should be reduced to reflect the future tax effect on the employee. Some courts hold that future tax liability is too speculative to calculate[46] while others have discounted present value to reflect tax liability.[47]

---

[38] Gregg v. Gregg, 31 So. 3d 1277, 1281 (Miss. Ct. App. 2010); *see also* Doyle v. Doyle, 55 So. 3d 1097, 1110 (Miss. Ct. App. 2010) (wife awarded slightly more than half of value of husband's retirement accumulated during marriage).

[39] The Mississippi factors are set out in *Ferguson v. Ferguson*, 639 So. 2d 921, 928 (Miss. 1994).

[40] *See, e.g.*, Mabus v. Mabus, 890 So. 2d 806, 826 (Miss. 2003) (awarding lump sum equal to one-half marital share); *see also* Blase v. Blase, 704 So. 2d 741, 742 (Fla. Dist. Ct App. 1998).

[41] *See* Holloman v. Holloman, 691 So. 2d 897, 900 (Miss. 1996) (QDRO used to divide defined contribution plan); Parker v. Parker, 641 So. 2d 1133, 1135-36 (Miss. 1994) (awarding wife a 30% interest in husband's profit-sharing plan to be set aside in separate account through QDRO).

[42] TURNER, *supra* note 2, § 6.11.

[43] *See infra* § 22.03[3][b]; Jones v. Jones, 904 So. 2d 1143 (Miss. Ct. App. 2004) (rejecting wife's argument that division of retirement account would have tax consequences; division could be accomplished through QDRO).

[44] *See infra* § 22.03[1][a].

[45] *See* BURRAGE & LITTLE, *supra* note 2, at 137.

[46] *See* Barnes v. Barnes, 820 P.2d 294, 297 (Alaska 1991); *In re* Marriage of Marx, 159 Cal. Rptr. 215, 220 (Cal. Ct. App. 1979); King v. King, 719 So. 2d 920, 923 (Fla. Dist. Ct. App. 1998); Sherrod v. Sherrod, 709 So. 2d 352, 356 (La. Ct. App. 1998); Wilkins v. Wilkins, 432 S.E.2d 891, 897 (N.C. Ct. App. 1993) (error to discount for taxes; too speculative).

[47] *See* Dodson v. Dodson, 955 P.2d 902, 909-10 (Alaska 1998) (401k awarded to wife discounted by 31%); Day v. Day, 663 S.W.2d 719, 722 (Ark. 1984); Porter v. Porter, 526 N.E.2d 219, 227 (Ind. Ct. App. 1988); Freeman v. Freeman, 497 S.W.2d 97, 100 (Tex. Civ. App. 1973); *cf.* Brown v. Brown, 14 S.W.3d 704, 707 (Mo. Ct. App. 2000) (court has discretion to discount; court could consider discount for taxes where early withdrawal of funds was likely).

RETIREMENT BENEFITS   § 7.04

§ 7.04 DEFINED BENEFIT PLANS

The value of a defined benefit plan is not directly tied to contributions. Instead, it is the present value of the anticipated stream of income that a participant will receive. In addition, because value is not directly linked to pre- and post-marital contributions, courts have struggled to develop formulas to allocate separate and marital shares of defined benefit plans. Courts use two different methods to value and classify these accounts – the date-of-retirement method and the date-of-divorce method.

[1] Date-of-retirement approach

[a] Valuation. Placing a present value on benefits that have not yet matured is a multi-step process.[48] To determine the present value of an active employee's full anticipated retirement benefits, one must (1) predict retirement date, salary at retirement, and date of death; (2) using these figures, calculate the anticipated stream of income;[49] (3) reduce the stream of income to present value; and (4) discount present value for the statistical likelihood that the employee will die before retirement.[50] In addition to being highly speculative, this valuation includes estimated post-divorce salary increases. As a result, some courts reject this method, particularly for valuing unmatured pensions.[51]

[b] Classification. A marital or coverture fraction is generally used to identify separate and marital portions of defined benefit pensions. The date-of-retirement method divides years of employment service during marriage by total number of service years to retirement.[52] For example, the Arkansas Supreme Court held that a husband was entitled to one-half of the marital share of his wife's pension benefits. The marital share was 42.68%, determined by dividing 70, the number of months of employment during marriage, by 164, the total months of employment to retirement.[53] The court rejected her argument that he should have been limited to one-half of the amount she would have received had she retired at divorce, noting that when distribution of marital property is deferred, both spouses are entitled to share in the growth of

---

[48] Shulman & Kelley call this the "most valuable accrual rate." SHULMAN & KELLEY, *supra* note 2, § 7.18, at 160. It has also been called the "matured full benefit method." *See* Michael A. Stoller, *Estimating the Present Value of Pensions: Why Different Estimators Get Varying Results*, 2 DEC. J. LEGAL ECON. 49 (1992) (excellent article for variables in present value calculations, including salary projections, age of retirement, inclusion of post-retirement cost-of-living increases, and projected life expectancy).

[49] A good summary of the various approaches to predicting these variables is found in TURNER, *supra* note 2, § 6.12. Many courts use age sixty-five as the presumed date of retirement, while others have used the average retirement age for the particular company or the earliest possible date of retirement. If special circumstances exist, the court may use a date peculiar to the individual employee. *Id.*

[50] SHULMAN & KELLEY, *supra* note 2, § 7.6, at 146; *see* OLDHAM, *supra* note 2, § 7.10[6].

[51] *See* discussion *infra* § 7.04[3].

[52] *See* OLDHAM, *supra* note 2, § 7.10[5]; SHULMAN & KELLEY, *supra* note 2, § 18.3; TURNER, *supra* note 2, § 6.10; Thomas v. Thomas, 4. S.W.3d 517 (Ark. Ct. App. 1999) (marital share of monthly benefit equal to 7/33 of benefit, where spouses were married 7 of 33 years of employment service).

[53] Brown v. Brown, 962 S.W.2d 810, 812-13 (Ark. 1998); *see also* Askins v. Askins, 704 S.W.2d 632, 635-36 (Ark. 1986) (dividing military pension); Barbour v. Barbour, 464 A.2d 915, 921 (D.C. Cir. 1983) (dividing civil service benefits); Lynch v. Lynch, 665 S.W.2d 20, 24 (Mo. Ct. App. 1983); Fondi v. Fondi, 802 P.2d 1264, 1267 (Nev. 1990); Workman v. Workman, 418 S.E.2d 269, 272-74 (N.C. Ct. App. 1992); Bulicek v. Bulicek, 800 P.2d 394, 399 (Wash. Ct. App. 1990).

§ 7.04[1][c]   MISSISSIPPI FAMILY LAW

the marital portion.[54]

The Mississippi Court of Appeals has used a date-of-retirement marital fraction for deferred distribution. A wife was properly awarded 35% of the marital share of her husband's pension, calculated by dividing years of marriage by total years of service. The order instructed that the wife receive 35% of that amount of each payment.[55]

[c] Division and distribution

[i] Immediate award. Valuation is required if a non-employee spouse receives his or her share through a lump sum or offset for immediate distribution. The court must value the benefit as described above and apply the marital fraction to determine the marital share.[56] The non-employee's share is awarded through a lump sum payment or award of other assets. There seems to be general agreement, however, that this is not the best method to use – the date-of-divorce method is preferable if the non-employee spouse is to receive an immediate award.

[ii] Deferred distribution. If distribution is deferred until retirement, it is not necessary to calculate present value.[57] Instead, the court may order that the non-employee spouse receive a portion of the actual retirement benefit, based on a fixed amount, percentage, or formula provided by the court. For example, a court might order that a wife of ten years receive 50% of each payment received by the participant, multiplied by a fraction described as ten years divided by total years of employment service. If the participant worked an additional twenty years to retirement, she would receive one-half of one-third of each payment, or one-sixth.[58] Most courts appear to use the date-of-retirement fractional method for deferred distribution.

[2] Date-of-divorce approach. Some courts reject the date-of-retirement approach for immediate awards because the method includes post-divorce salary increases. Instead, these courts value and classify pensions as of the date of the divorce.[59]

[a] Valuation. Using this approach, present value is calculated using actual years in service and salary at the time of divorce, rather than estimated years to retirement and a predicted retirement salary. This method of valuation does not include estimated post-divorce salary increases. For example, under a plan providing benefits of 2% of a participant's highest salary for each year of employment, an employee with a

---

[54] Brown v. Brown, 962 S.W.2d 810, 812 (Ark. 1998); *see also* Stouffer v. Stouffer, 867 P.2d 226, 232 (Haw. Ct. App. 1994) (formula recognizes that each year of employment played an integral part in acquiring the right to the retirement payments).

[55] *See* Cork v. Cork, 811 So. 2d 427, 429 (Miss. Ct. App. 2001)*; see also* Salemi v. Salemi, 972 So. 2d 1, 6 (Miss. Ct. App. 2007) (using marital fraction to determine benefits to wife*); cf.* Lestrade v. Lestrade, 49 So. 3d 639, 645 (Miss. Ct. App. 2010) (enforcing husband's agreement that wife would receive one-half of his retirement even though partly separate; parties may agree to divide nonmarital assets).

[56] *See In re* Marriage of James, 950 P.2d 624, 627-28 (Colo. Ct. App. 1997).

[57] SHULMAN & KELLEY, *supra* note 2, at 281.

[58] *See* Thomas v. Thomas, 4 S.W.3d 517, 524 (Ark. Ct. App. 1999) (spouse to receive one-half of 7/33 of each payment).

[59] *See, e.g.,* Berry v. Berry, 647 S.W.2d 945, 946-47 (Tex. 1983).

RETIREMENT BENEFITS

§ 7.04[2][b]

divorce-date salary of $40,000 and ten years of employment would expect a retirement benefit of 20% of that amount, or $8,000. By predicting date of retirement and death, the valuator calculates a stream of income using these figures, and reduces it to present value.[60] It is error to value retirement for immediate offset without reducing to present value. The Mississippi Supreme Court held that a chancellor overstated the value of marital assets by valuing a husband's retirement account based on the total anticipated stream of income rather than reducing the stream to present value. [61]

[b] Classification. Under the date-of-divorce method, the marital portion is calculated by dividing years of service during the marriage by total years of service on the date of divorce, rather than by total years to retirement. For example, if a divorcing employee was married for the entire term of employment, the entire value of the pension is marital. The date-of-divorce method will usually increase the marital percentage, but lower the pension value.[62]

The Mississippi Supreme Court affirmed use of the date-of-divorce method for immediate offset in at least one case. However, the husband had terminated employment at the time of divorce, so the date-of-retirement method could not have been used. The husband worked for the state for a total of 14.25 years, five during the parties' marriage. The court calculated the marital share by multiplying the pension value by 5/14.25. The resulting amount, $18,253, was divided equally.[63]

[c] Distribution

[i] Immediate award. To make an immediate award under the date-of-divorce approach, present value is multiplied by the marital fraction or percentage. Each spouse is awarded an equitable share of the marital portion, and the non-employee spouse is awarded a lump sum payment or other marital assets equal to his or her share. For example, if a couple divorced after fifteen years of marriage, a husband's twenty years of accumulated benefits would be valued by calculating the benefits to which he would be entitled if he left employment on the date of divorce, and reducing those benefits to present value. The marital share of that value would be 15/20, or 75%.[64]

[ii] Deferred distribution. There is considerable disagreement over whether the date-of-divorce method should be used for deferred distribution of defined benefit plans. Most commentators argue that this approach denies the nonparticipant the benefit of post-divorce passive growth,[65] depriving him or her of the investment value of

---

[60] *See* Desfosses v. Desfosses, 815 P.2d 1094, 1099 (Idaho Ct. App. 1991) (dividing civil service benefits); OLDHAM, *supra* note 2, § 7.10[5]; SHULMAN & KELLEY, *supra* note 2, § 18.9; TURNER, *supra* note 2, § 6.10. Calculation of present value based on the date-of-divorce approach is explained in William M. Troyan, *An Update on Pension Valuations*, 31 FAM. L. Q. 5 (1997).

[61] Lowrey v. Lowrey, 25 So. 3d 274, 291 (Miss. 2009).

[62] *See* Berry v. Berry, 647 S.W.2d 945, 946-47 (Tex. 1983) (wife entitled to one-half the amount of pension her husband would have received had he terminated employment on the date of divorce – $110, rather than 26/38 of his retirement benefit on the date of retirement – approximately $300).

[63] *See* Mabus v. Mabus, 890 So. 2d 806, 826 (Miss. 2003) (method of valuing not clear).

[64] *See* Troyan, *supra* note 60, at 10.

[65] *See* OLDHAM, *supra* note 2, § 7.10[5]; SHULMAN & KELLEY, *supra* note 2, § 18.3-9; TURNER, *supra* note 2, §

205

§ 7.04[3]   MISSISSIPPI FAMILY LAW

the award.[66] According to one authority, an inflation factor should be added if a court uses a date-of-divorce approach for deferred distribution of these plans.[67]

[3] Comparison of methods. Critics of the date-of-retirement approach contend that the approach is too speculative when used for immediate distribution, requiring prediction of too many variables.[68] Those who favor the date-of-retirement method respond that defined benefit plans are a method of deferred compensation in which later increases are actually recognition for earlier years of service.[69] Furthermore, supporters criticize the date-of-divorce approach for deferred distribution because it fails to provide for post-divorce passive appreciation of the marital portion.[70] Some courts have attempted to accommodate concerns about including post-divorce merit increases by allowing an employee spouse to prove, at retirement, that some portion of the post-divorce increases were merit and not cost-of-living increases.[71]

There appear to be valid arguments supporting the use of either method for dividing pensions for immediate offset. However, for purposes of deferred distribution, there seems to be general agreement that the date-of-retirement approach is more accurate and that if the date-of-divorce approach is used, some inflation factor must be included.

[4] Other approaches. Commentators seem to agree that defined benefit pensions should be divided by one of the methods set out above, depending on whether the jurisdiction accepts the "deferred compensation" view of defined benefit plans or holds that no post-divorce increases may be distributed. Nonetheless, courts have also divided defined benefit plans by the following methods: (1) creating a marital fraction based on the ratio of marital contributions to total contributions;[72] (2) subtracting the value of a pension at marriage from value at the time of divorce;[73] (3) using the withdrawal value of the pension.[74] Most courts have rejected these methods, and commentators seem to

---

6.10.

[66] *See* SHULMAN & KELLEY, *supra* note 2, § 18.1, at 261-62 (date-of-divorce approach provides 100% of post-marital increase to employee spouse in deferred distribution). *But see* Grier v. Grier, 731 S.W. 2d 931, 932 (Tex. 1987) (applying date-of-divorce approach to deferred distribution to divide military pension).

[67] *See* OLDHAM, *supra* note 2, § 7.10[6].

[68] *See* SHULMAN & KELLEY, *supra* note 2, § 2.8 (acknowledging legitimate objections to use of approach for immediate distribution).

[69] *See* Stouffer v. Stouffer, 867 P.2d 226, 227 (Haw. Ct. App. 1994); Kelly v. Kelly, 702 A.2d 999, 1004 (Md. Ct. Spec. App. 1997) (unfair to award all post-divorce growth to employee; pay increases might relate to prior years service as much as to merit pay); Lynch v. Lynch, 665 S.W.2d 20, 24 (Mo. Ct. App. 1983); Brown v. Brown, 962 S.W.2d 810, 813 (Ark. 1998).

[70] *See In re* Marriage of Judd, 137 Cal. Rptr. 318, 322 (Cal. Ct. App. 1977) ("contributions in the early years of employment during the marriage, even though based on a smaller salary, may actually be worth more than contributions during the post-separation years, due to the longer period of accumulated interest and investment income prior to the commencement of benefit payments").

[71] *See* Croft v. Croft, 634 So. 2d 76, 77 (La. Ct. App. 1994) (employee spouse had burden of proving pay increase not due to cost-of-living increase, but to merit or achievement); Petschel v. Petschel, 406 N.W.2d 604, 607 (Minn. Ct. App. 1987); Gemma v. Gemma, 778 P.2d 429, 432 (Nev. 1989) (example of true merit increase might be pay increase based on advanced degree obtained after divorce).

[72] *See* Brandt, *supra* note 2, at 473.

[73] *See In re* Marriage of James, 950 P.2d 624, 627-28 (Colo. Ct. App. 1997) (trial court erred using subtraction method).

[74] SHULMAN & KELLEY, *supra* note 2, § 7.22, at 163 (using this value "severely shortchanged" non-owning spouse);

RETIREMENT BENEFITS

§ 7.04[5]

agree that they are not the most accurate means of valuing and allocating pensions.[75]

[5] Mississippi. The Mississippi Court of Appeals recognized competing approaches to defined benefit pension valuation without expressing a preference for one method over the other. Divorcing after a seven-year marriage, the parties disputed valuation of the husband's pension, accrued over thirty-eight years. His expert used a coverture fraction of 7/38, producing a marital share of $47,330.[76] His wife argued that the court should instead subtract the pension's value on the date of marriage from the current value, yielding a marital share of $152,000.[77] The court acknowledged competing concerns: the salary increases of later years were based in part on prior years of service, which "cannot be ignored." But the court also noted that the husband was "at his maximum value to the company" during the later, marital years. The court remanded, without specifying a particular method, for the chancellor to consider the "twin concerns" outlined in the opinion.[78]

§ 7.05 OTHER RETIREMENT BENEFITS

The rules applicable to division of pensions apply equally to other future employment benefits, including severance packages, deferred compensation plans, and profit-sharing and stock ownership plans.[79] Mississippi appellate courts have upheld equitable division of profit-sharing plans,[80] severance packages,[81] and employee stock ownership plans.[82] An agreement to divide equally "any and all retirement funds of any description" included a Savings and Investment 401k as well as a husband's retirement income plan.[83]

§ 7.06 PRIVATE RETIREMENT BENEFITS UNDER ERISA

Private retirement plans are regulated by federal law, which preempts most state regulation of retirement benefits. However, courts apply state law to determine whether a particular benefit is marital or separate property and to whom the asset should be awarded.

---

see Desfosses v. Desfosses, 815 P.2d 1094, 1098-99 (Idaho Ct. App. 1991) (error to value based on cash surrender value); Diefenthaler v. Diefenthaler, 580 N.E.2d 477, 483 (Ohio Ct. App. 1989) (rejecting valuation based on accumulated contributions).

[75] *See* TURNER, *supra* note 2, § 6.12.

[76] The post-divorce increase issue did not arise since the husband had already retired. *See* Prescott v. Prescott, 736 So. 2d 409, 413 (Miss. Ct. App. 1999).

[77] This method is criticized by commentators because it does not include interest on the premarital share. *See supra* note 73 and accompanying text.

[78] Prescott v. Prescott, 736 So. 2d 409, 413-14 (Miss. Ct. App. 1999).

[79] *See* TURNER, *supra* note 2, § 6.08, at 324.

[80] *See* Parker v. Parker, 641 So. 2d 1133, 1137 (Miss. 1994); Prescott v. Prescott, 736 So. 2d 409, 413 (Miss. Ct. App. 1999).

[81] *See* Wheat v. Wheat, 37 So. 3d 632, 637-38 (Miss. 2010); Prescott v. Prescott, 736 So. 2d 409, 413 (Miss. Ct. App. 1999).

[82] *See* Owen v. Owen, 798 So. 2d 394, 400 (Miss. 2001); Armstrong v. Armstrong, 836 So. 2d 794, 797-98 (Miss. Ct. App. 2002).

[83] Holloman v. Holloman, 691 So. 2d 897, 899-900 (Miss. 1996).

§ 7.06[1]   **MISSISSIPPI FAMILY LAW**

[1] Federal regulation. Most private pension plans are governed by the Employee Retirement Income Security Act of 1974 [ERISA],[84] which preempts state regulation of these pensions.[85] Qualification under ERISA benefits both employer and employee: an employer may deduct contributions and the employee is not taxed on investment growth until withdrawal.[86]

ERISA prohibits an employee from assigning pension benefits to a third person.[87] In the decade after ERISA's enactment, some courts held that the anti-assignment clause prohibited state courts from dividing regulated pensions at divorce.[88] In 1984, the Act was amended by the Retirement Equity Act [REA] to address this concern.[89] The amendment provides that divorce courts may divide qualified plan benefits through use of a Qualified Domestic Relations Order [QDRO].[90] The REA also provided protection for employees' families, requiring that pensions provide benefits payable for the joint lives of employee and spouse. Joint and survivor benefits can be replaced with a benefit for the employee's life alone only if the employee's spouse consents in writing.[91]

[2] The Qualified Domestic Relations Order. Deferred distribution of private pensions may be accomplished only through an order complying with federal requirements. ERISA permits a non-taxable transfer of pension rights to a divorcing spouse as an alternate payee, pursuant to a Qualified Domestic Relations Order [QDRO].[92]

[a] Requirements. To qualify as a QDRO, an order must be related to child support, alimony, or property division pursuant to state domestic relations law.[93] The order must also be one that grants an alternate payee rights to some portion of a participant's benefits. The alternate payee must be a spouse, former spouse, child, or other dependent of the participant. In addition, the order must include the participant and alternate payee's names and last known mailing addresses, the amount or percentage of benefits payable to the alternate payee or a formula for determining the amount or percentage, the effective period for payments, and the name of each plan affected. The document may not order payment of benefits in excess of the amount payable to the participant or benefits already assigned by another QDRO.[94]

[b] Method of division. QDROs may be categorized as shared interest or separate interest. A shared interest QDRO divides the actual payments to which a participant is entitled, while a separate interest QDRO divides the entire pension into two separate income streams. When a defined contribution plan is divided by QDRO, the

---

[84] 29 U.S.C. §§ 1001-1461 (1974).
[85] *See* Parker v. Parker, 641 So. 2d 1133, 1136 (Miss. 1994) (discussing enactment of ERISA and federal preemption).
[86] BURRAGE & LITTLE, *supra* note 2, at 136.
[87] *See* 29 U.S.C. §§ 1056(d)(1) - (d)(3)(A) (1974).
[88] *See* TURNER, *supra* note 2, § 6.07.
[89] *See* 29 U.S.C. § 1056(d)(3)(A) (1974).
[90] *See* 29 U.S.C. § 1056(d)(3)(A) (1974); I.R.C. § 401(a)(13)(B).
[91] *See* 29 U.S.C. § 1056(c)(2)(A) (1974); OLDHAM, *supra* note 2, § 7.10[4].
[92] 29 U.S.C. § 1056(d)(3)(B)(ii) (1974); I.R.C. § 401 (a)(13)(B).
[93] 29 U.S.C. § 1056(d)(3)(B)(ii) (1974).
[94] 29 U.S.C. § 1056(d)(3)(B) (1974); I.R.C. § 414; *see* Parker v. Parker, 641 So. 2d 1133, 1136 (Miss. 1994).

208

RETIREMENT BENEFITS

§ 7.06[2][b][i]

separate interest approach is generally used because of the simplicity of dividing the benefits. Both approaches are used to divide defined benefit plans.

[i] Shared interest. A QDRO may require that each benefit payment be divided between the participant and alternate payee, based on a formula, percentage, or fixed dollar amount payable to the alternate payee.[95] The alternate payee's benefits are linked to the participant's benefits, and cannot be provided at a different time or in a different form than paid to the participant.[96]

[ii] Separate interest. Defined contribution plans are usually divided by creating a separate account for the alternate payee.[97] The QDRO specifies the amount to be placed in a separate account. Any subsequent increase attributable to those funds belongs to the alternate payee.[98]

The alternate payee's share of defined benefit plans may also be set aside in a separate income stream. For example, if the alternate payee is awarded 25% of benefits, a separate income stream may be established that is the actuarial equivalent of twenty-five percent of the participant's benefits.[99] Under this method, payments may begin when the benefits mature, even if the participant has not retired.[100]

[c] Qualified joint and survivor annuity. Qualified plans must provide for a joint and survivor annuity payable to a participant and spouse, in an amount that is the actuarial equivalent of a benefit for the participant's life.[101] The payments are lower than under a single life annuity but continue after the participant's death.[102] A QDRO may preserve this right for a divorcing spouse, requiring that shared interest payments be based on a joint and survivor annuity rather than a single life annuity.[103] In addition, a divorcing spouse may be provided with a survivor annuity that will pay benefits in the event the participant dies prior to retirement.[104] The Mississippi Court of Appeals held in 2010 that a chancellor erred in awarding a wife of seven years survivor benefits without making findings of fact that the wife had contributed to the accumulation of the plan.[105]

[d] Other considerations. Complete analysis of the issues involved in negotiating and drafting QDROs is beyond the scope of this treatise. Among other issues,

---

[95] *See* Pamela Perdue, *Pension and Welfare Benefit Administration QDRO Guidelines*, SC58 ALI-ABA 419, 423 (1998).

[96] CARRAD, *supra* note 2, 8.5.

[97] Perdue, *supra* note 95, at 424.

[98] CARRAD, *supra* note 2, 8.5; *cf.* Rogers v. Rogers, 919 So. 2d 184, 188-89 (Miss. Ct. App. 2005) (increase in wife's share that accrued after divorce but before QDRO was entered, belonged to wife).

[99] *See* 29 U.S.C. § 1055(g) (1974); CARRAD, *supra* note 2, 6.3.E.

[100] CARRAD, *supra* note 2, 8.5, at 113.

[101] *See* 29 U.S.C. § 1055(c)(2)(A), (d) (1974).

[102] CARRAD, *supra* note 2, 2.3.G, at 24-25.

[103] *See* 29 U.S.C. § 1055(g) (1974).

[104] *See* 29 U.S.C. § 1055(a)(2) (1974).

[105] Pierce v. Pierce, 42 So. 3d 658, 662 (Miss. Ct. App. 2010) (wife did not work during marriage, and did not live with husband for most of marriage).

§ 7.06[2][e]   MISSISSIPPI FAMILY LAW

drafters should consider addressing division of increases after the court's order is entered but before the QDRO is approved, the division of cost-of-living increases, division of early retirement subsidies, allocation of tax liability, division of year-end contributions, the impact of a takeover by the Pension Benefit Guarantee Corporation, and indemnity in the event of plan nonpayment.[106] Clarity in drafting these provisions is critical. A significant number of post-divorce property division disputes center around interpretation of provisions to divide retirement accounts.[107] Several excellent treatises address QDRO drafting in detail.[108]

[e] **Approval.** The plan administrator must approve a QDRO within a reasonable period of time.[109] During this time, any benefits that would have been payable to the alternate payee must be segregated in a separate account.[110] If the QDRO is approved within eighteen months of the time the first payment would have been due under the QDRO, segregated amounts are payable to the alternate payee. If the order is not approved within eighteen months of that time, segregated amounts are paid to the participant.[111] This does not mean, however, that eighteen months is a reasonable period of time for the decision.[112]

[f] **Enforcement.** A court may order a party to enter a QDRO in accordance with a court-ordered or agreed division. A former husband who failed to disclose a second retirement account should have been ordered to enter a QDRO dividing the account equally, in compliance with a settlement agreement to provide his wife with one-half of all retirement benefits.[113] In one case, a wife's action to obtain a QDRO ten years after divorce was not barred by the state statute of limitations. Her failure to obtain a QDRO within seven years from the date of judgment was excused; the agreement placed the burden on her husband to divide benefits. Furthermore, her good faith reliance on statements of the plan administrator tolled the statute of limitations.[114]

§ 7.07 Military retired pay

[1] **Military retirement.** In 1981, the United States Supreme Court held in *McCarty v. McCarty* that federal preemption prevents state courts from classifying military retirement benefits as marital property.[115] Congress overruled the decision the follow-

---

[106] *See generally* CARRAD, *supra* note 2, for thorough coverage of each of these issues. This user-friendly work is an excellent and practical resource for analyzing pension division as well as drafting qualified orders.

[107] See *infra* § 23.14[4].

[108] *See* authorities cited *supra* note 2.

[109] 29 U.S.C. § 1056(d)(3)(G) (1974).

[110] 29 U.S.C. § 1056(d)(3)(H) (1974).

[111] 29 U.S.C. § 1056(d)(3)(H) (1974).

[112] Perdue, *supra* note 95, at 431.

[113] Holloman v. Holloman, 691 So. 2d 897, 901-02 (Miss. 1996); *see also* McDannell v. United States Office of Personnel Mgmt., 716 F.2d 1063, 1065-66 (5th Cir. 1983) (where husband failed to pay 25% to wife as required, wife should return to court to obtain QDRO), *discussed with approval in* Boykin v. Boykin, 565 So. 2d 1109, 1114 (Miss. 1990).

[114] Carite v. Carite, 841 So. 2d 1148, 1152 (Miss. Ct. App. 2002). There is no federal statute of limitations for obtaining a QDRO.

[115] McCarty v. McCarty, 453 U.S. 210, 232-35 (1981).

RETIREMENT BENEFITS
§ 7.07[1][a]

ing year with enactment of the Uniformed Services Former Spouses Protection Act.[116] The USFSPA permits, but does not require, states to treat military retirement as marital property.[117] Applying rules generally applicable to pensions, the great majority of states classify military retirement benefits as marital property to the extent the benefits were acquired during the marriage.[118] The Mississippi Supreme Court has consistently held that military retirement benefits may be divisible marital property.[119] However, it has also noted that neither state law nor the USFSPA require an equal division of benefits.[120]

[a] Retroactivity. The USFSPA was made retroactive to June 25, 1981, the day before the *McCarty* decision. As a result, cases decided under *McCarty*, but before the enactment of USFSPA are covered by the Act.[121] State courts have differed as to whether a decree entered after *McCarty* but before the USFSPA can be reopened. This issue was of greater significance immediately after the Act. After such a long passage of time, attempts to reopen a case from 1981-82 would likely be dismissed on the basis of laches.[122] Divorce decrees prior to June 25, 1981, cannot be reopened on the basis of the Act. The Mississippi Supreme Court has acknowledged that the USFSPA was amended in 1990 to specifically prohibit courts from reviewing pre-1981 decrees unless the decree reserved jurisdiction over the military benefits.[123]

[b] Jurisdiction. The USFSPA provides that a state may divide retirement benefits only if the member is domiciled or resides in the state or consents to jurisdiction.[124] The Mississippi Supreme Court applied this provision to decline jurisdiction over a serviceman who moved from the state fifteen years prior to the action, even though the parties lived in Mississippi during their marriage.[125]

Most courts have held that a member may not object to jurisdiction over military pensions while submitting to jurisdiction for resolution of other marital issues.[126] The Mississippi court in dicta appeared to endorse the view that a general appearance

---

[116] *See* 10 U.S.C. § 1408 (2000).

[117] *See* 10 U.S.C. § 1408(c)(2000) (applies to "disposable retired or retainer pay").

[118] *See* TURNER, *supra* note 2, § 6.13, at 376.

[119] *See* Rennie v. Rennie, 718 So. 2d 1091, 1096 (Miss. 1998) (approving award to wife of 32% of husband's Air Force retirement benefits); Hemsley v. Hemsley, 639 So. 2d 909, 913-14 (Miss. 1994) (citing USFSPA as authority for division; upholding 50% division of military retirement); Southern v. Glenn, 568 So. 2d 281, 284 (Miss. 1990) (determining "whether the spouse of a serviceman has a vested right in the military retirement pension is governed by the law of the state . . . of domicile during the term of active duty service"); Newman v. Newman, 558 So. 2d 821, 823 (Miss. 1990) ("military retirement pension . . . is subject to the personal property laws of the states"); Black v. Black, 741 So. 2d 299, 302 (Miss. Ct. App. 1999) (wife entitled to half of military pension, earned entirely during marriage).

[120] *See* Pierce v. Pierce, 648 So. 2d 523, 526 (Miss. 1994) (federal act simply removed bar to state division of benefits; state law requires equitable, not equal, distribution).

[121] 10 U.S.C. § 1408(c) (2000).

[122] *See* TURNER, *supra* note 2, § 6.04, at 307.

[123] *See* Hollyfield v. Hollyfield, 618 So. 2d 1303, 1305 (Miss. 1993) (rejecting wife's request to reopen 1979 divorce decree).

[124] 10 U.S.C. § 1408(c)(4) (2000).

[125] *See* Petters v. Petters, 560 So. 2d 722, 726 (Miss. 1990) (act places significant limits on state long-arm jurisdiction).

[126] *See* Judkins v. Judkins, 441 S.E.2d 139, 140 (N.C. Ct. App. 1994); Morris v. Morris, 894 S.W.2d 859, 861-62 (Tex. Ct. App. 1995); *In re* Marriage of Peck, 920 P.2d 236, 238-39 (Wash. Ct. App. 1996). *But see* Pender v. Pender, 945 S.W.2d 395, 397 (Ark. Ct. App. 1997) (consent to suit not consent to jurisdiction over retirement benefits).

§ 7.07[1][c]   **MISSISSIPPI FAMILY LAW**

would waive the provisions of the Act.[127] In order to ensure enforcement by the Defense Finance and Accounting Service, compliance with these federal jurisdictional requirements should be noted in the order for division.

If the divorcing service member is in active duty, proceedings must comply with the requirements of the Servicemember's Civil Relief Act dealing with default judgments.[128]

[c] Division

[i] **Direct payment.** The options for deferred distribution of military benefits are more limited than those for private plans. Military benefits may be paid directly to a non-owning spouse only if the couple was married for ten years of the member's military service.[129] Furthermore, if the direct payment system is used, the Act caps payments to former spouses at 50%,[130] and payments to former spouses or children at 65% of the member's retirement pay.[131] Direct payments may be made only through the shared interest approach, with the alternate payee's benefits linked to the date and form of payment to the member spouse.[132] To receive direct payment, the former spouse must submit the court order and a Department of Defense (DD) Form 2293.[133]

[ii] **Payment by member.** If the ten-year requirement is not met, a state court may not order direct payment by the federal government,[134] but may order the member spouse to make payments to the nonmember based on retirement benefits.[135] Furthermore, the 50% cap on an award of benefits does not apply to payments by the member spouse.[136]

[iii] **Survivor benefits.** A divorcing spouse may be awarded an annuity under the Survivor Benefit Plan in the event of the member's death.[137]

[2] Military disability benefits. Military disability benefits are not divisible in state court proceedings. Because federal law preempts state domestic relations law,

---

[127] The court in *Petters* states that since defendant "has made no appearance in this matter nor done anything else which might be construed as a present waiver, there is no basis upon we might find that within the meaning of Section 1408(c)(4)(C) he has consented to the jurisdiction of the Mississippi court." Petters v. Petters, 560 So. 2d 722, 726 (Miss. 1990).

[128] *See* discussion *infra* § 19.14.

[129] 10 U.S.C. § 1408(d)(2) (2000).

[130] 10 U.S.C. § 1408(e)(1) (2000).

[131] 10 U.S.C. § 1408(e)(1)(4)(b) (2000). Division is limited to "disposable retired pay." *Id.* § 1408(c).

[132] 10 U.S.C. § 1408(c)(3)(2000).

[133] CARRAD, *supra* note 2, 11.9, 11.14 (setting out the requirements for the DD 2293 and court order).

[134] 10 U.S.C. § 1408(d)(2) (2000).

[135] *See* Anciaux v. Anciaux, 666 So. 2d 577, 578 (Fla. Dist. Ct. App. 1996); Warren v. Warren, 563 N.E.2d 633, 634-35 (Ind. Ct. App. 1990); Warner v. Warner, 651 So. 2d 1339, 1340 (La. 1995).

[136] CARRAD, *supra* note 2, 11.6; *see* Maxwell v. Maxwell, 796 P.2d 403, 406 (Utah Ct. App. 1990); Forney v. Minard, 849 P.2d 724, 729 (Wyo. 1993). *But see In re* Marriage of Bowman, 972 S.W.2d 635, 639 (Mo. Ct. App. 1998).

[137] 10 U.S.C. § 1450(f) (2000); *see* CARRAD, *supra* note 2, 11.10 (survivor benefits end if a recipient under the age of 55 remarries; benefits resume if marriage ends in divorce).

RETIREMENT BENEFITS § 7.07[2][a]

military benefits are divisible only if an express provision is made to that effect.[138] In *Mansell v. Mansell*,[139] the United States Supreme Court held that the USFSPA was carefully worded to allow division of military retirement benefits only. Thus, state courts may not divide military disability or veteran's disability benefits.[140]

[a] Contract provisions to divide disability. Courts disagree as to whether *Mansell* invalidates a separation agreement providing for division of disability benefits. Some courts read *Mansell* narrowly as prohibiting only court-ordered division. These courts find that *Mansell* permits a spouse to voluntarily agree to divide military disability pay.[141] Others hold that *Mansell* is a bar to any division of disability benefits, whether court-ordered or by agreement.[142]

Even if military disability payments are not divisible as marital property, the income may be considered as an asset to the member spouse and factored into division of the marital estate.[143] However, it has been held to be error to make a specific offset to the non-military spouse that is equal to the benefits.[144]

[b] Disability in lieu of retirement. A difficult issue arises when a divorced member of services elects to forego retirement for non-divisible disability benefits. By doing so, the member deprives the former spouse of retirement benefits that were a part of equitable distribution. Under these circumstances, courts have reopened the entire decree,[145] ordered the member to continue to pay the amount that would have been provided under retirement benefits,[146] or required the member to indemnify the former spouse for the loss.[147] Courts have also held that the election is a change in circumstances justifying an alimony increase.[148] A few courts have held that the payee spouse is without recourse in the absence of an express indemnity provision.[149]

---

[138] Mansell v. Mansell, 490 U.S. 581, 588-92 (1989).

[139] 490 U.S. 581 (1989).

[140] *See* 10 U.S.C. §§ 1201-1221 (2000) (military disability benefits); 38 U.S.C. § 1131 (2000) (veteran's disability benefits).

[141] *See* Price v. Price, 480 S.E.2d 92, 93-94 (S.C. Ct. App. 1996) (upholding settlement agreement where husband agreed to pay wife percentage of military retirement pay which included disability pay).

[142] *See* Abernethy v. Fishkin, 699 So. 2d 235, 236 (Fla. 1997); Moon v. Moon, 795 S.W.2d 511, 514 (Mo. Ct. App. 1990).

[143] *See* TURNER, *supra* note 2, § 6.7, at 53 (3d ed. 2005); Miller v. Miller, 617 A.2d 375, 376-78 (Pa. Super. Ct. 1992) (court erred in dividing military benefits as marital property, but on remand, did not err in increasing wife's percentage of other marital assets).

[144] *See* Clauson v. Clauson, 831 P.2d 1257, 1264 (Alaska 1992); Jones v. Jones, 780 P.2d 581, 583 (Haw. Ct. App. 1989). For a listing of cases, *see* TURNER, *supra* note 2, § 6.10, at 70-71.

[145] *See* Torwich v. Torwich, 660 A.2d 1214, 1214 (N.J. Super. Ct. App. Div. 1995).

[146] *See In re* Marriage of Gaddis, 957 P.2d 1010, 1012 (Ariz. Ct. App. 1997).

[147] *See* Harris v. Harris, 991 P.2d 262, 266 (Ariz. Ct. App. 1999); Dexter v. Dexter, 661 A.2d 171, 174-75 (Md. Ct. Spec. App. 1995); Hisgen v. Hisgen, 554 N.W.2d 494, 497-98 (S.D. 1996); Owen v. Owen, 419 S.E.2d 267, 270-71 (Va. Ct. App. 1992).

[148] *See* Kramer v. Kramer, 567 N.W.2d 100, 113 (Neb. 1997).

[149] *See* Ashley v. Ashley, 990 S.W.2d 507, 509 (Ark. 1999); *In re* Marriage of Pierce, 982 P.2d 995, 998-99 (Kan. Ct. App. 1999).

§ 7.08 MISSISSIPPI FAMILY LAW

§ 7.08 NON-MILITARY FEDERAL RETIREMENT BENEFITS

Non-military federal retirement plans include the Federal Employees Retirement System and the Civil Service Retirement System.[150] These benefits are divisible in divorce proceedings based on state equitable distribution law.[151] The Mississippi Court of Appeals has recognized that federal civil service benefits may be divisible marital property.[152]

Federal regulations set out the form for ordering division of civil service benefits. The order must qualify as a Court Order Acceptable for Processing, or COAP; a QDRO is not the proper form for dividing civil service benefits.[153]

Unlike plans covered by ERISA, benefits are available only as a shared interest payment linked to the time and method of payment available to the employee.[154] Although payment is not available as a joint and survivor annuity, these plans do provide a Former Spouse Survivor Annuity (FSSA).[155] Benefits cease if a recipient under fifty-five remarries.[156] The cost of the annuity may be deducted from either the employee or former spouse's share of retirement benefits.[157]

Thrift Saving Plans established for federal employees may be divided in divorce proceedings through a Retirement Benefits Court Order.[158] Railroad retirement benefits are divided into two types of benefits – Tier I, which are not divisible at divorce; and Tier II, which may be divided.[159]

§ 7.09 IRAs

Individual Retirement Accounts may be divided at divorce pursuant to a court order or written agreement.[160] These accounts are not governed by ERISA and do not require a QDRO for division. If a non-owning spouse's share is rolled over into a separate IRA within sixty days of the order, the transfer is not a taxable event.[161] A

---

[150] CARRAD, *supra* note 2, 12.1.

[151] *See* 5 U.S.C. § 8345(j)(1) (2000); Leisure v. Leisure, 605 N.E.2d 755, 759 (Ind. 1993); UNITED STATES OFFICE OF PERSONNEL MANAGEMENT, RETIREMENT AND INSURANCE SERVICE, *HANDBOOK FOR ATTORNEYS ON COURT-ORDERED RETIREMENT, HEALTH BENEFITS, AND LIFE INSURANCE UNDER THE CSRS, FERS, FEHS AND FEGLI*, (RI 83-116 July 1997), *available at* http://www.opm.gov.

[152] *See* Murphy v. Murphy, 797 So. 2d 325, 330 (Miss. Ct. App. 2001) (awarded wife 33% of $13,000, the amount that husband's federal retirement account increased during the marriage); *cf.* Tynes v. Tynes, 860 So. 2d 325, 329 (Miss. Ct. App. 2003) (not error to exclude husband's Railroad Retirement Benefits, where court also excluded wife's PERS benefits; also noting that wife would receive divorced spouse's annuity from Railroad Retirement Board); Reynolds v. Reynolds, 755 So. 2d 467, 468 (Miss. Ct. App. 1999) (wife properly awarded 19%, or one-half, of marital share of husband's government pension, 38% of which was acquired during marriage).

[153] *See* 5 C.F.R.838.103; *In re* Marriage of Burns, 903 S.W. 2d 648, 651-52 (Mo. Ct. App. 1995); CARRAD, *supra* note 2, 12.2. The requirements and procedures for processing COAPs are found at 5 C.F.R. § 838.101-1018.

[154] *See* 5 C.F.R. § 838.103 (2002) (listing divisible benefits); *id.* § 838.302(b) (payments may not be ordered to continue after employee's death); CARRAD, *supra* note 2, 12.1.

[155] 5 C.F.R. § 838.103 (2002).

[156] 5 C.F.R. § 838.721(b)(1)(vi)(A)-(C) (2002).

[157] 5 C.F.R. § 838.807 (2002); CARRAD, *supra* note 2, 12.4.

[158] *See* 5 U.S.C. § 8435 (2000); 5 C.F.R. § 1653 (Part A) (2002) (separate federal guidelines for Thrift Saving Plan orders).

[159] *See* 20 C.F.R. § 295.2 (2002).

[160] 26 U.S.C. § 408(d)(6) (1974); *see* CARRAD, *supra* note 2, 13.1.

[161] 26 U.S.C. § 402(a)(5)(A) (1974).

RETIREMENT BENEFITS   § 7.10

leading authority on pension division recommends that the appropriate procedure is to divide the existing IRA into two accounts, then transfer the newly created account to the non-owning spouse.[162]

§ 7.10 SOCIAL SECURITY

Most courts hold that Social Security benefits are not divisible marital property.[163] The Social Security system has its own system of marital property. Any spouse or former spouse who was married to a covered employee for ten years is entitled to benefits based on their former spouse's employment if they have not been in the labor force for more than a specified amount of time.[164] However, most courts consider it proper to consider Social Security benefits in the division stage as a separate asset available to the owning spouse.[165]

§ 7.11 STATE BENEFITS

Mississippi employees are covered by the Public Employees Retirement System (PERS), a defined benefit plan. The Mississippi Supreme Court has recognized that a state pension is marital to the extent it was acquired during marriage. A husband's PERS account, acquired over fourteen and a quarter years, was 5/14.25 marital because the couple was married for five of his years of service.[166] Similarly, a wife was entitled to an award equaling one-half of the value of her husband's pension acquired during their ten years of marriage.[167]

Some state retirement plans specifically provide for direct division of benefits between divorcing spouses. In Mississippi, PERS benefits may be divided through a lump sum payment or offsetting award,[168] but not through direct payment by the state. In 1977, the Mississippi Supreme Court held that the PERS anti-assignment clause prohibited a chancellor from impressing a lien on a husband's retirement to secure alimony.[169] PERS does not provide procedures similar to a QDRO for direct division of

---

[162] See CARRAD, supra note 2, 13.1.

[163] See Mann v. Mann, 778 P.2d 590, 591 (Alaska 1989); Gross v. Gross, 8 S.W.3d 56, 58 (Ky. Ct. App. 1999); Thibodeaux v. Thibodeaux, 712 So. 2d 1024, 1028 (La. Ct. App. 1998); Olson v. Olson, 445 N.W.2d 1, 11 (N.D. 1989); see generally TURNER, supra note 2, § 6.06, at 317-18. But see In re Marriage of Gilmore, 943 S.W.2d 866, 875 (Mo. Ct. App. 1997).

[164] 42 U.S.C. § 416(d) (2004).

[165] See Gross v. Gross, 8 S.W.3d 56, 57 (Ky. Ct. App. 1999); David v. David, 954 S.W.2d 611, 616 (Mo. Ct. App. 1997). But see Cox v. Cox, 882 P.2d 909, 920 (Alaska 1994). Two decisions of the Mississippi courts suggest indirectly that Social Security benefits should be included in divisible marital property. See Traxler v. Traxler, 730 So. 2d 1098, 1102-03 (Miss. 1998) (harmless error to exclude Social Security benefits from marital property); Murphy v. Murphy, 797 So. 2d 325, 331 (Miss. Ct. App. 2001) (under Traxler, it was necessary to consider wife's future eligibility for Social Security as marital property).

[166] Mabus v. Mabus, 890 So. 2d 806, 826 (Miss. 2003).

[167] Phillips v. Phillips, 904 So. 2d 999 (Miss. 2004).

[168] See Mabus v. Mabus, 890 So. 2d 806, 826 (Miss. 2003) (awarding wife a share equal to one-half of the marital portion of state pension).

[169] See Hodges v. Hodges, 346 So. 2d 903, 904 (Miss. 1977); see also MISS. CODE ANN. § 25-11-129 (2004) (benefits exempt from "levy and sale, garnishment, attachment or any other process whatsoever, and shall be unassignable except as specifically otherwise provided"). It should be noted, however, that the court of appeals inferred that a QDRO could be used to divide a wife's PERS account. See Warren v. Warren, 815 So. 2d 457, 460 (Miss. Ct. App. 2002) (failure

§ 7.12   **MISSISSIPPI FAMILY LAW**

state retirement.[170]

§ 7.12 Unvested pensions

Until recently, courts disagreed as to whether non-vested pensions could constitute divisible marital property.[171] Today a majority of courts hold that they may be divided as a marital asset.[172] However, valuation of an unvested pension in equitable distribution is a problem. If a pension has not yet vested, the value must be discounted to reflect the likelihood that the employee will not serve enough creditable time for the pension to vest. Because this calculation is so speculative, most courts refuse to assign a present value to unvested pensions.[173] Although a few courts have actually developed formulas to account for this contingency, the approach taken by most courts is simply to defer division until the pension vests.[174] This issue has not yet been addressed by Mississippi courts.

---

to file QDRO to secure $225.00 payment from wife's PERS account did not prevent husband from obtaining payment directly from wife).

[170] *See* CARRAD, *supra* note 2, 13.3 (noting that some state systems provide for division, while others do not).

[171] *See* Burns v. Burns, 847 S.W.2d 23, 26 (Ark. 1993) (nonvested military benefits not subject to division; lacked characteristics of property); Hennessey v. Hennessey, 551 So. 2d 597, 598 (Fla. Dist. Ct. App. 1989) (nonvested pension plans were correctly considered as marital property); Poe v. Poe, 711 S.W.2d 849, 857 (Ky. Ct. App. 1986) (nonvested military pension was properly characterized as marital); Hatcher v. Hatcher, 343 N.W.2d 498, 503 (Mich. Ct. App. 1983) (party must first prove that pension had vested before it could be deemed marital property); Lemon v. Lemon, 537 N.E.2d 246, 249 (Ohio Ct. App. 1988) (unvested pension should be considered as marital property due to fact that it had value).

[172] OLDHAM, *supra* note 2, § 7.10[4].

[173] *See* TURNER, *supra* note 2, § 6.12, at 371.

[174] TURNER, *supra* note 2, § 6.09, at 332 (recommended method).

VIII
DIVISION OF CLOSELY HELD BUSINESSES

Closely held businesses are divided between spouses under the general rules of equitable distribution. However, division of businesses raises valuation and division issues unique to this asset. Valuation of closely held businesses requires an understanding of federal regulations and valuation methods peculiar to businesses. In addition, the corporate structure of a business may dictate the manner in which assets may be divided.

§ 8.01 FORM OF OWNERSHIP

A closely held business may be a sole proprietorship, partnership, limited liability partnership, corporation, limited liability corporation (LLC), or Subchapter S corporation. The form of business organization determines the type of asset available for equitable distribution. An owner of an unincorporated sole proprietorship owns the actual assets of the business – the accounts, inventory, real estate, and other assets. These assets may become part of the marital estate. In contrast, an owner of a partnership, LLC, or corporation holds a partnership interest, membership interest, or stock. The business entity owns the underlying assets. Absent unusual circumstances, a court may not divide assets belonging to a partnership or corporation. The divisible asset is the owning spouse's partnership interest, membership interest, or corporate stock.[1]

§ 8.02 JOINDER OF BUSINESS ENTITY OR PARTNERS

It is not necessary to join a divorcing spouse's business partners or the business entity simply because the spouse's interest is included in the marital estate. The divorcing owner's interest may be classified as marital and the non-owning spouse awarded an offsetting share without affecting the legal rights of other owners. A wife was properly awarded a share of her husband's 75% interest in a pawn shop, to be paid through a lump sum award, without joining the partnership or the husband's partner. The award divided her husband's interest in the business, not the business assets, and did not affect the status of the partnership or the rights of other partners.[2] However, joinder is necessary if one spouse seeks a transfer of partnership or corporate assets, to set aside the corporate form, or to otherwise directly affect third-party rights. A court erred in awarding a wife use of an automobile belonging to her husband's company without

---

[1] A & L, Inc. v. Grantham, 747 So. 2d 832, 839 (Miss. 1999) (no distribution of corporate assets unless court pierces the corporate veil); *see* Craft v. Craft, 825 So. 2d 605, 610 (Miss. 2002) (wife of one-half owner of partnership not entitled to partnership assets but to lump sum based on the increase in value of husband's interest in the partnership); Skinner v. Skinner, 509 So. 2d 867, 870 (Miss. 1987) (corporation is separate legal entity from owner).

[2] MacDonald v. MacDonald, 698 So. 2d 1079, 1085 (Miss. 1997) (court also found that business really belonged to husband; partner/father never participated in or benefited from business); *see also* Rush v. Rush, 932 So. 2d 800, 803 (Miss. Ct. App. 2005) (value of husband's one-third interest in business included in marital assets without joining partners), *rev'd in part on other grounds*, 932 So. 2d 794 (Miss. 2006).

§ 8.03   MISSISSIPPI FAMILY LAW

joining the corporation as a party.[3] Similarly, an ex-husband's corporation was a necessary party to his suit to modify his ex-wife's employment contract with his company.[4]

§ 8.03 CLASSIFICATION: SEPARATE AND MARITAL PORTIONS

A divorcing spouse's interest in a closely held business may be separate property, marital property, or a mixed asset – partly marital and partly separate. The general classification rules of equitable distribution are used to classify business interests.

[1] Marital property interest. A business interest is marital if the interest was acquired through a spouse's efforts during marriage or purchased with marital funds. A separate property business may also become marital as a result of commingling.

[a] Acquired through marital efforts or funds. An interest acquired during marriage through a spouse's efforts is marital. A husband's pawn shop built through his efforts during marriage was a marital asset.[5] A business interest is also marital if the owning spouse used marital funds to purchase the interest. A chancellor erred in classifying two corporations established with marital funds as separate.[6]

Similarly, appreciation caused by a spouse's efforts is marital property. The court of appeals reversed separate property classification of the $1.6 million increase in value of a husband's premarital business. Although he claimed the increase was a return on premarital investments, the court noted that most of his salary during the marriage was apparently reinvested in the company. Any company assets acquired through investment of his salary should have been classified as marital.[7]

A separate property business may become marital property if the non-owning spouse expends considerable time or effort in the business. A court did not err in awarding a wife a 25% interest in a Russian company owned by her husband. Both spouses were listed as incorporators and directors. The wife served as bookkeeper and accountant and provided skills as an industrial engineer while her husband provided technical and scientific contributions.[8]

[b] Acquired with joint loans or loans secured by marital assets. Classification of a business purchased or expanded with loan funds depends on liability and collateral for the loans. A transaction is viewed as a marital purchase if both spouses

---

[3] Skinner v. Skinner, 509 So. 2d 867, 870 (Miss. 1987) (also error to allow her to obtain $160 per month of goods at drugstore belonging to corporation).

[4] East v. East, 493 So. 2d 927, 933 (Miss. 1986) (employment contract entered as part of parties' divorce agreement); *see also* Grogan v. Grogan, 641 So. 2d 734, 739 (Miss. 1994) (wife attempting to set aside transfer joined husband's two corporations and his brother, to whom he sold the corporations the day before a temporary restraining order prohibiting sale became effective).

[5] MacDonald v. MacDonald, 698 So. 2d 1079, 1083-84 (Miss. 1997).

[6] Johnson v. Johnson, 877 So. 2d 485, 491-92 (Miss. Ct. App. 2003).

[7] Flechas v. Flechas, 791 So. 2d 295, 304 (Miss. Ct. App. 2001).

[8] Hunt v. Asanov, 975 So. 2d 899, 905-906 (Miss. Ct. App. 2008). *But cf.* Dorsey v. Dorsey, 972 So. 2d 48, 51-52 (Miss. Ct. App. 2008) (wife's testimony that she provided uncompensated bookkeeping assistance to the company did not cause the company to become marital).

DIVISION OF CLOSELY HELD BUSINESSES § 8.03[1][c]

are obligated on the loan or if the loan is secured by marital property.[9] An interest acquired during marriage through loans collateralized with separate property is classified as separate. Similarly, an interest is separate if it was purchased through loans on which only the owner was obligated. Property acquired by a husband for use in his separate business, through loans on which only he was liable, was separate property. Even the fact that his wife loaned him funds to use in the business did not convert the business to marital property.[10] However, a separately secured business may become marital through commingling or if marital funds were used to repay the loans.

[c] Separate funds commingled with marital funds. A separate business may be converted to a marital asset if business and marital funds are commingled. A husband's corporation was properly classified as marital in part because of the extensive commingling of business and marital funds.[11] A minimal amount of commingling does not require marital classification. A husband's separate property rental houses did not become marital simply because rental income was deposited in a marital account and funds from the account used to maintain the properties.[12] Furthermore, the fact that income from a separate business is used for marital purposes does not convert the business itself to a marital asset.[13]

[2] Separate property interest. A business interest owned prior to marriage is the separate property of the owning spouse, at least to the extent of its value at the time of the marriage.[14] Similarly, any business interest acquired during marriage by gift or inheritance is separate property.[15] A business interest purchased during marriage with separate funds is also classified as separate, based on the tracing rule that an asset retains the character of funds used to acquire the asset.[16]

---

[9] This rule is inferred from cases holding that property acquired through an individual loan or secured by separate collateral is separate. *See* Hankins v. Hankins, 866 So. 2d 508, 511-512 (Miss. Ct. App. 2004); Langdon v. Langdon, 854 So. 2d 485, 493 (Miss. Ct. App. 2003).

[10] *See* Hankins v. Hankins, 866 So. 2d 508, 511-512 (Miss. Ct. App. 2004) (relationship was treated as a debtor-creditor relationship; loans were repaid).

[11] *See* A & L, Inc. v. Grantham, 747 So. 2d 832, 838 (Miss. 1999) (also based on piercing corporate veil and active appreciation in value during marriage); *see also* Oswalt v. Oswalt, 981 So. 2d 993 (Miss. Ct. App. 2007) (business assets and funds extensively commingled with marital funds in joint account held to be marital). *But cf.* Dorsey v. Dorsey, 972 So. 2d 48, 52 (Miss. Ct. App. 2008) (separate property business not converted by use of some personal funds to pay business debts; payments were "easily traceable" and not "so commingled as to have become identifiable").

[12] Bresnahan v. Bresnahan, 818 So. 2d 1113, 1118 (Miss. 2002); *see also* Spahn v. Spahn, 959 So. 2d 8, 12 (Miss. Ct. App. 2006) (premarital warehouse not converted to marital; husband maintained separate account into which he deposited warehouse income and from which he paid expenses).

[13] *See* Pearson v. Pearson, 761 So. 2d 157, 164-65 (Miss. 2000) (rejecting wife's argument that use of separate property income to pay household expenses converted property to marital); *cf.* Boutwell v. Boutwell, 829 So. 2d 1216, 1221 (Miss. 2002) (income from separate property promissory note used for family purposes becomes marital, but post-divorce income from the note was separate property).

[14] Craft v. Craft, 825 So. 2d 605, 608-09 (Miss. 2002); Gregg v. Gregg, 31 So. 3d 1277, 1281 (Miss. Ct. App. 2010) (wife's premarital business classified as separate).

[15] *See* McKissack v. McKissack, 45 So. 3d 716, 718 (Miss. Ct. App. 2010) (business inherited by husband in last years of marriage classified as separate); *see also* Ferguson v. Ferguson, 639 So. 2d 921, 928 (Miss. 1994) (gifts are separate property); Dorsey v. Dorsey, 972 So. 2d 48, 52 (Miss. Ct. App. 2008) (husband's business – an inter vivos gift from his father – was separate property).

[16] *See* Carrow v. Carrow, 642 So. 2d 901, 907 (Miss. 1994) (automobiles purchased with inherited funds classified as separate).

§ 8.03[3]   **MISSISSIPPI FAMILY LAW**

[3] Mixed asset. A business may be classified as partly separate and partly marital.

[a] Acquired both during and outside of marriage. A business interest may be acquired or built over a period of time – before marriage, during marriage, and after the cutoff date for marital property accumulation.[17] Marital property accumulation ends when a court enters a temporary support order, a separate maintenance order, or an order of divorce.[18] Value created before marriage or after the cutoff date is the owner's separate property, while value created during marriage is marital.[19] For example, a husband's five percent interest in a family business, acquired as compensation for a year of work without pay, was a mixed asset. One third of the uncompensated work was accomplished while the parties were married and before a court's temporary support order ended the accumulation of marital property. The remainder of the uncompensated work was performed after the temporary support order. Thus, only one third of the interest was marital.[20]

[b] Appreciated value of separate property business. A business owned prior to marriage may be classified as mixed if its value appreciates during marriage. Mississippi follows the active-passive test for classifying the appreciated value of a separate asset. If the appreciation was caused by the owner's efforts during marriage, the appreciated value is marital. If appreciation was caused by other forces, such as inflation or third-party efforts, the entire asset remains separate.[21] Appreciation in a husband's separate business was marital "[t]o the extent that there was a substantial increase in value of the net assets of the corporations due at least in part to [the husband's] managerial efforts."[22] Similarly, the court of appeals held that a chancellor erred in classifying the full value of a premarital business as separate after finding that "the value of the business has increased due to [the husband's] significant efforts" during marriage.[23]

Until recently, courts appeared to assume that if an owner was actively involved

---

[17] *See* discussion *supra* § 6.02[3].

[18] *See* Pittman v. Pittman, 791 So. 2d 857, 865 (Miss. Ct. App. 2001).

[19] This assumes that the value created during marriage was the result of a spouse's active efforts or through the use of marital funds. *See* discussion *supra* § 6.03[4].

[20] Pittman v. Pittman, 791 So. 2d 857, 865-66 (Miss. Ct. App. 2001).

[21] *See* Carrow v. Carrow, 642 So. 2d 901, 907 (Miss. 1994).

[22] A & L, Inc. v. Grantham, 747 So. 2d 832, 839 (Miss. 1999).

[23] Johnson v. Johnson, 877 So. 2d 485, 491-93 (Miss. Ct. App. 2003). The business valuation expert provided proof of the value of the business at the time of the marriage and several months prior to trial. The difference was the marital portion of the business. *Id.* at 493; *see also* Craft v. Craft, 825 So. 2d 605, 609 (Miss. 2002) (but affirming because chancellor considered business assets in making lump sum alimony award); Spahn v. Spahn, 959 So. 2d 8, 13-14 (Miss. Ct. App. 2006) (husband's premarital construction business properly classified as marital; wife assisted in the company and contributed to growth); Hankins v. Hankins, 866 So. 2d 508, 511 (Miss. Ct. App. 2004) (husband's separately owned chicken farm did not become marital property in its entirety – only the appreciated value was marital). *But cf.* Gregg v. Gregg, 31 So. 3d 1277, 1281 (Miss. Ct. App. 2010) (husband's maintenance of wife's separate property business was not significant enough to convert them to marital); Elam v. Hinson, 932 So. 2d 76, 80 (Miss. Ct. App. 2006) (wife's contribution to growth of husband's inherited family business was minimal; not entitled to lump sum alimony representing share of business).

DIVISION OF CLOSELY HELD BUSINESSES   § 8.03[4]

in his business, any appreciation during marriage was active, and therefore, marital.[24] A 2009 court of appeals case opens the door for courts to engage in fact-finding to determine whether appreciation actually resulted from a spouse's active efforts or from outside forces. In *Fleishhacker v. Fleishhacker*, a wife argued that a $2 million appreciation in her husband's business after entry of a temporary support order[25] was passive, even though he was actively involved in the business. She argued that the appreciation was caused by a change in scrap metal prices. The court of appeals remanded for the chancellor to determine whether the appreciation was caused by his efforts in the business or by the market for scrap metal.[26] This case marks the first time that the Mississippi appellate courts have been confronted with expert proof that appreciation in a spouse's primary business was caused by forces other than the spouse's efforts. The decision allows chancellors to look to the actual causes of appreciation, rather than automatically assuming that a spouse's active involvement in a business causes appreciation.[27]

[4] Burden of proof. Ordinarily, the burden of proof is on a spouse claiming a separate property interest in a particular asset.[28] With regard to separate property appreciation, however, most courts require the non-owning spouse to prove that marital contributions were made to the asset and that it increased in value. The burden then shifts to the owning spouse to prove that the appreciation was caused by other forces.[29] Mississippi appears to follow the rule that the separate property owner bears the burden of proving that appreciation was passive. The Mississippi Supreme Court held that a husband/business owner had the burden of proving the value of his business at the time of the marriage and of proving the cause of the increase in value during the marriage.[30]

---

[24] See discussion *supra* at § 6.03[4].

[25] Appreciation caused by a spouse's efforts after the cut-off date for marital property accumulation belongs to that spouse. *See* Wells v. Wells, 35 So. 3d 1250, 1258 (Miss. Ct. App 2010) (increase in value of a husband's plastic surgery clinic, occurring after the court entered a temporary support order, was classified as the husband's separate property); *cf.* Hensarling v. Hensarling, 824 So. 2d 583, 591-92 (Miss. 2002) (husband's contributions to savings account, apparently after separate maintenance order, were his separate property, while interest accrued on the marital share during that period was marital); Vaughn v. Vaughn, 798 So. 2d 431, 435 (Miss. 2001) (even in absence of support order cutoff, wife not entitled to increase in value during separation because she did not contribute to the business during that time).

[26] Fleishhacker v. Fleishhacker, 39 So. 3d 904, 913 (Miss. Ct. App. 2009).

[27] If the post-support order appreciation was passive, it would be classified in the same separate and marital percentages as the business at the time of the support order. Fleishhacker v. Fleishhacker, 39 So. 3d 904, 913 (Miss. Ct. App. 2009).

[28] *See* Hemsley v. Hemsley, 639 So. 2d 909, 914 (Miss. 1994); Everett v. Everett, 919 So. 2d 242, 247 (Miss. Ct. App. 2005) (stocks in husband's name classified as marital; husband failed to prove stocks were purchased with separate funds); *cf.* Horn v. Horn, 909 So. 2d 1151, 1165 (Miss. Ct. App. 2005) (presumption places burden of proof on party seeking separate treatment of debt).

[29] BRETT TURNER, EQUITABLE DISTRIBUTION OF PROPERTY § 5.22 (2d ed. 1994); *see* Seymour v. Seymour, 960 So. 2d 513, 518-19 (Miss. Ct. App. 2006) (stock owned by husband before marriage was separate property; no proof of increase in value); *cf.* Bowen v. Bowen, 982 So. 2d 385, 395 (Miss. 2008) (premarital investment account treated as partly marital without proof of exact amount of contribution during marriage; older parties both had failing memories; neither presented proof of value at time of marriage of ten years); Parker v. Parker, 980 So. 2d 323, 327 (Miss. Ct. App. 2008) (separate property three acres adjoining marital estate of eighty-five acres assumed to be used by wife; burden on husband to prove no family use or commingling).

[30] A & L Inc. v. Grantham, 747 So. 2d 832, 839 (Miss. 1999); *see also* Flechas v. Flechas, 791 So. 2d 295, 303 (Miss. 2001) (burden on husband to prove marital portion of premarital pension); Stewart v. Stewart, 2 So. 3d 770, 774-75 (Miss. Ct. App. 2009) (husband's premarital business properly classified as marital; burden was on him to prove no appreciated value). *But see* Waring v. Waring, 747 So. 2d 252 (Miss. 1999) (burden on non-owning spouse).

§ 8.04   **MISSISSIPPI FAMILY LAW**

Furthermore, a recent case appears to hold that the owning spouse has the burden of proving the value of the business at the time of marriage in order to have that portion of the asset classified as separate.[31]

§ 8.04 VALUATION

According to one expert, determining the fair market value of a closely held business interest is one of the most challenging issues in equitable distribution.[32] Expert opinion is critical to an accurate evaluation of most closely held businesses. However, other evidence of value may be used if expert testimony is not available.

An expert valuing a closely held corporation will typically review factors set out by the Internal Revenue Service for valuing a business and then apply one or more of several generally accepted methods of valuation. The commonly used valuation methods assess value from three perspectives – business assets, business income, and comparable sales.

The Mississippi Supreme Court has taken a minority position with regard to valuation of businesses at divorce, holding that goodwill may not be valued and divided in equitable distribution.

[1] Revenue Ruling 59-60. Revenue Ruling 59-60, the commonly used guideline for valuing a closely held corporation, lists the following factors for consideration: (1) the nature and history of the business; (2) the general economic outlook and outlook for the specific industry; (3) the book value and financial condition of the company; (4) the earning capacity of the business; (5) the dividend-paying capacity of the business; (6) goodwill or other intangible value; (7) stock sales and the amount of stock to be valued; and (8) market price of similar stocks.[33]

[2] Valuation methods. In most states, a business valuator may use one or a combination of the following methods to value a closely held business.

[a] Asset-based approach. A business may be valued based on the net value of tangible and intangible assets – real estate, equipment, inventory, accounts, and goodwill.[34] An asset-based approach may be the best valuation tool for a capital-intensive business such as a real estate holding company. It may also be the best measure for an unprofitable business or one that would be considered for liquidation.[35] For example, a chancellor properly valued a distressed farming operation on an asset basis rather than as an ongoing concern. The business held substantial assets but was financially unsound, leading the husband to file bankruptcy shortly after divorce was filed. The court of appeals affirmed an asset-based valuation under these circumstances: "An individual operating an unprofitable business in a half-million dollar building cannot

---

[31] Stewart v. Stewart, 2 So. 3d 770, 775 (Miss. Ct. App. 2009).
[32] 3 FAMILY LAW AND PRACTICE Ch. 36, § 36.10, at 36-44 (Arnold H. Rutkin ed. 1999).
[33] Rev. Rul. 59-60, 1959-1 C.B. 237.
[34] *See* TURNER, *supra* note 29, § 7.07, at 530.
[35] *See* FAMILY LAW AND PRACTICE, *supra* note 32, § 36.11[1], at 36-55 n.11.

222

DIVISION OF CLOSELY HELD BUSINESSES § 8.04[2][b]

use the balance sheet of his poorly-conceived business venture to demonstrate that the building is without value."[36] The Mississippi Supreme Court recommended that valuation using the asset approach be based on the value of the business' assets as a group rather than individually.[37]

In most states, a company's net assets may include intangible assets such as goodwill and intellectual property rights. Goodwill is often measured by using the excess earnings method, comparing a company's earnings to the earnings of an average comparable business.[38] Considerable controversy has arisen nationally over inclusion of goodwill in the value of professional corporations.[39]

[b] Market-based approach. A business may be valued based on the sale of comparable businesses. Comparable sales comparisons may be the most effective way of determining fair market value. However, in the case of closely held corporations, data on similar sales is frequently not available.[40] As an alternative, an expert may use the comparable industry or guideline company method, comparing the business with publicly-traded companies whose business is comparable.[41]

[c] Income-based approach. A third recognized method values a business based on the company's estimated future earnings. Using this approach, a valuation expert reviews historic earnings and makes adjustments to develop "normalized" earnings. Among other adjustments, an expert will exclude one-time gains and losses that distort the income analysis.[42] In valuing a closely held corporation, salaries of owners and officers should also be excluded, except to the extent that they exceed the industry average. Earnings which exceed the industry average are included in the company's normalized earnings.[43]

Normalized earnings are then multiplied by a capitalization factor that reflects the risk of investing in the business. The resulting figure is the business' value.[44] For example, in the case of a competitive, established industrial business, an analyst might conclude that an investor would be willing to extend investment recovery over five years. A five-year investment recovery produces a capitalization rate of twenty percent and a multiplier of five. If the business' normalized annual earnings are $80,000, the value of the company would be five times those earnings, or $400,000.[45]

An income-based valuation typically requires expert testimony. The court of appeals held that a court properly valued a husband's business on an asset, rather than

---

[36] Dunaway v. Dunaway, 749 So. 2d 1112, 1117-18 (Miss. Ct. App. 1999); *see also* Dunn v. Dunn, 911 So. 2d 591, 598 (Miss. Ct. App. 2005) (chancellor did not err in adopting asset-based rather than income-based valuation; wife presented no evidence of normalized historic earnings, established client base, or other matters appropriate to income-based valuation) (case predated exclusion of goodwill from valuation in Mississippi).

[37] *See* Watson v. Watson, 882 So. 2d 95, 105 (Miss. 2004) (noting that value as a group may be higher).

[38] TURNER, *supra* note 29, § 7.07, at 533.

[39] *See* discussion *infra* § 8.04[3].

[40] TURNER, *supra* note 29, § 7.08, at 540.

[41] FAMILY LAW AND PRACTICE, *supra* note 32, § 36.11[2], at 36-56.

[42] TURNER, *supra* note 29, § 7.08, at 542.

[43] TURNER, *supra* note 29, § 7.08, at 543.

[44] TURNER, *supra* note 29, § 7.08, at 542.

[45] *See* BARTH H. GOLDBERG, VALUATION OF DIVORCE ASSETS, § 6.6 (1984).

§ 8.04[2][d]   **MISSISSIPPI FAMILY LAW**

income, basis. The only evidence submitted consisted of financial records submitted by the company's accountant. The wife presented no evidence of normalized historic earnings, an established client base, or other matters appropriate to an income-based valuation.[46]

[d] Discounts. Courts have approved the use of discounts to reflect risks inherent in a closely held business. If a business depends on the skill of one or a few key individuals, a key person discount may be used. A chancellor properly applied a key person discount to reflect a husband's role in his business.[47] If the block of stock being valued is less than a controlling interest, courts may also allow a minority interest discount to reflect the difficulty of selling a noncontrolling interest.[48]

Courts have also affirmed the use of marketability discounts in valuation of closely held businesses, recognizing there is often no ready market for sale of a closely held business. However, courts are divided as to whether a marketability discount is appropriate in a divorce action if sale of the business is not imminent. For example, the West Virginia Supreme Court held that a chancellor erred in rejecting a marketability discount to a husband's dental practice value on the basis that the practice would not be sold. In divorce, valuation is based on a theoretical sale, not on actual sale.[49] And the Colorado Court of Appeals held that failure to recognize lack of marketability in a closely held corporation "could unfairly penalize a party for ownership of shares that cannot be readily sold or liquidated."[50] A minority of courts have held that marketability discounts are not appropriate if the business will not be sold.[51]

[3] Goodwill in businesses. Ordinarily, a business valuation may include a figure for goodwill. Both the asset-based approach and the income approach place a value on earnings that exceed the average earnings for a similar business, known as goodwill. A majority of courts recognize goodwill as a part of valuation for purposes of equitable distribution.[52] However, the Mississippi appellate courts have taken a minority position, holding that valuation for a divorce action may not include a figure for goodwill. As a result, valuation is effectively limited to the net asset approach.

Some states exclude goodwill from divorce business valuation, but only with

---

[46] Dunn v. Dunn, 911 So. 2d 591, 598 (Miss. Ct. App. 2005).

[47] *See* Burnham-Steptoe v. Steptoe, 755 So. 2d 1225, 1235 (Miss. Ct. App. 1999) (also holding that key person discount may be used when key officer's salary has been removed from annual earnings).

[48] *See* Brett Turner, *Valuing Minority Interests in Close Corporations*, 20 EQUITABLE DISTRIBUTION JOURNAL No. 3 (March 2003).

[49] May v. May, 589 S.E.2d 536 (W. Va. 2003) (but rejecting the discount because of a lack of factual basis for the discount); *see also* Erp v. Erp, 976 So. 2d 1237-38 (Fla. Dist. Ct. App. 2008) (rejecting wife's argument that marketability discounts should never be applied in divorce proceedings). *See generally* Use of Marketability Discount, 16 A.L.R. 6th 693 (2010).

[50] *In re* Marriage of Thornhill, 200 P.3d 1083, 1087 (Colo. App. 2008), *rev'd in part on other grounds*, 232 P. 2d 782 (Colo. 2010).

[51] *See* Hoebelheinrich v. Hoebelheinrich, 600 S.E.2d 152, 156 n.2 (Va. Ct. App. 2004); Brown v. Brown, 792 A.2d 463 (N.J. App. Div. 2002); Drumheller v. Drumheller, 972 A.2d 176, 190 (Vt. 2009) (minority discount should not be applied unless business will be sold).

[52] *See, e.g.*, Mitchell v. Mitchell, 732 P.2d 208, 212 (Ariz. 1987); Wilson v. Wilson, 741 S.W.2d 640, 647 (Ark. 1987) (medical practice); Thompson v. Thompson, 576 So. 2d 267, 269 (Fla. 1991); Howell v. Howell, 523 S.E.2d 514, 518 (Va. Ct. App. 2000).

DIVISION OF CLOSELY HELD BUSINESSES   § 8.05

regard to professional practices. These courts hold that the connection between an individual professional's reputation and the success of a professional practice are too intertwined to be separated.[53] Other courts hold that even professional practices may include goodwill separate from the individual divorcing spouse.[54]

The Mississippi Supreme Court aligned with the minority in a 2000 case, holding that goodwill may not be included in valuing a solo professional corporation in divorce proceedings. The court concluded that enterprise and personal goodwill are too intertwined to be divided in a solo professional practice.[55] The holding was subsequently expanded to service businesses.[56] And in 2007, the exclusion of goodwill was extended to all business valuations in divorce. The supreme court reversed and remanded a chancellor's valuation of a husband's car dealership interest, stating that goodwill – whether personal or business enterprise – shall not be included in a business valuation in divorce proceedings.[57] Accordingly, the court of appeals held that a chancellor properly accepted a husband's expert valuation based on net asset value rather than the wife's valuation using the income/market approach, which included a figure for goodwill.[58]

§ 8.05 Division

Equitable distribution requires that a chancellor divide marital assets fairly between divorcing spouses. There is no requirement that each receive one-half of the marital assets.[59] Nor is there is a requirement that each individual asset be divided between the parties.[60] A marital property business is generally awarded to the owning or actively involved spouse. The non-owning spouse's share may be offset by an award of other marital assets[61] or lump sum alimony. Only in rare circumstances will courts award both spouses an interest in the same asset.

[1] Lump sum award. A court may award a marital business to the owning spouse and order the owner to make a lump sum payment in satisfaction of the non-owner's interest. If immediate payment in full would jeopardize operation of the business, a

---

[53] *See, e.g., In re* Zells, 572 N.E.2d 944, 946 (Ill. 1991) (law practice); Travis v. Travis, 795 P.2d 96, 100 (Okla. 1990) (law practice); Hazard v. Hazard, 833 S.W.2d 911, 914 (Tenn. Ct. App. 1991) (medical practice).

[54] Turner, *supra* note 29, § 6.73.

[55] *See* Watson v. Watson, 882 So. 2d 95, 105 (Miss. 2004). The *Watson* decision removed any lingering doubts left by *Singley v. Singley,* in which the court left open the question of whether enterprise goodwill could be included in valuing a solo professional practice at divorce. *See* Singley v. Singley, 846 So. 2d 1004, 1010 n.2 (Miss. 2002).

[56] Goodson v. Goodson, 910 So. 2d 35, 37-38 (Miss. Ct. App. 2005) (but noting that value is not limited to physical assets; may also include income, accounts, pending contracts, and customer lists); *see also* Fogarty v. Fogarty, 922 So. 2d 836, 839-40 (Miss. Ct. App. 2006) (sole proprietorship automobile body shop goodwill was not divisible asset). *But cf.* Rush v. Rush, 932 So. 2d 800, 804-05 (Miss. Ct. App. 2005) (multi-owner service business may include goodwill), *rev'd in part on other grounds,* 932 So. 2d 794 (Miss. 2006).

[57] Yelverton v. Yelverton, 961 So. 2d 19, 30 (Miss. 2007).

[58] Dorsey v. Dorsey, 972 So. 2d 48, 53 (Miss. Ct. App. 2008); *see also* Wise v. Wise, 37 So. 3d 95, 98 (Miss. Ct. App. 2010) (initial, market-based appraisal of $410,143 revised to remove goodwill; revised valuation was $80,000).

[59] *See* Ferguson v. Ferguson, 639 So. 2d 921, 927 (Miss. 1994).

[60] *See* Collins v. Collins, 722 So. 2d 596, 599 (Miss. 1998) (rejecting wife's argument that court treated the marital home as separate by awarding it solely to her husband, where each party received an equal share of value of the total assets).

[61] *See* Dunaway v. Dunaway, 749 So. 2d 1112, 1116 (Miss. Ct. App. 1999) (financially troubled dairy farm awarded to husband).

§ 8.05[2]   **MISSISSIPPI FAMILY LAW**

court should order payment in installments.[62] A chancellor erred in ordering immediate payment by a spouse who lacked substantial liquid assets to satisfy the award.[63]

[2] Offset with other property. A court may award the entire business to the owning spouse and award other assets to the non-owning spouse. For example, a wife who was awarded 40% of the couple's assets received the marital home and other assets, while the husband's 60% interest consisted of three corporations.[64]

[3] Equitable liens. A lump sum award may be secured by an equitable lien on the owner's business interest or on other property. A lump sum award for a wife's share of a business interest was properly secured with an equitable lien on the husband's 75% interest in the partnership. The lien was simply a charge on the property and did not divest the husband of title or transfer possession to her.[65]

[4] Division of jointly owned business. A business owned by both spouses is usually awarded to the more actively involved spouse. As one commentator notes, "it is highly undesirable to leave both parties as co-owners of the same asset" – particularly assets requiring ongoing cooperation.[66] For example, a wife was awarded a jointly owned restaurant she managed during the marriage, even though the business was originally her husband's parents'.[67] A jointly owned business may be awarded to the spouse with greater need for the income. A court properly awarded a convenience store, in which both spouses worked, to the wife. The husband was also a truck driver, while the wife had no other source of income.[68]

But it may be proper to award each spouse a share of a severable business. A husband was awarded the couple's company, Tim's, Inc., but was ordered to transfer one of the business's three convenience stores to the wife.[69] And the Mississippi Court of Appeals held that a chancellor erred in ordering a couple's rental real estate sold and divided. The property should have been partitioned in kind.[70] In one case, a court awarded a wife 25% of her husband's marital property business, but gave the husband the option of buying out her share within thirty days.[71]

---

[62] Aldridge v. Aldridge, 27 So. 2d 884, 885-86 (Miss. 1946) (approving lump sum payment of $7,500) (chancellor to weigh burden on payor against immediate benefit to payee); *see also* Rush v. Rush, 932 So. 2d 800, 808 (Miss. Ct. App. 2005) (marital business awarded to husband; one-half of value to be paid to wife through lump sum payment), *rev'd in part on other grounds,* 932 So. 2d 794 (Miss. 2006).

[63] Aldridge v. Aldridge, 27 So. 2d 884, 886 (Miss. 1946).

[64] *See* A & L, Inc. v. Grantham, 747 So. 2d 832, 837 (Miss. 1999).

[65] MacDonald v. MacDonald, 698 So. 2d 1079, 1085 (Miss. 1997); *see also* Rush v. Rush, 932 So. 2d 800, 808 (Miss. Ct. App. 2005) (lump sum payment representing one-half of business value secured by equitable lien on home characterized as husband's separate property), *rev'd in part on other grounds,* 932 So. 2d 794 (Miss. 2006).

[66] *See* TURNER, *supra* note 29, § 9.02, at 623. *But see* Humphries v. Humphries, 904 So. 2d 192, 196-98 (Miss. Ct. App. 2005) (husband and wife each awarded a one-half interest in four marital businesses).

[67] Bumpous v. Bumpous, 770 So. 2d 558, 560 (Miss. Ct. App. 2000).

[68] Graham v. Graham, 948 So. 2d 451, 453-54 (Miss. Ct. App. 2006).

[69] Wise v. Wise, 37 So. 3d 95, 101 (Miss. Ct. App. 2010).

[70] *See* Garriga v. Garriga, 770 So. 2d 978, 984-85 (Miss. Ct. App. 2000).

[71] Hunt v. Asanov, 975 So. 2d 899, 904 (Miss. Ct. App. 2008).

DIVISION OF CLOSELY HELD BUSINESSES   § 8.06

§ 8.06 PIERCING THE CORPORATE VEIL

The rule prohibiting division of corporate assets does not apply if the owner has disregarded the corporate form and treated the business as an alter ego. Under these circumstances, a court may set aside the corporate structure, or "pierce the corporate veil," recharacterizing corporate assets as individual. The Mississippi Supreme Court applied piercing rules to disregard the corporate structure of a husband's business. During the marriage, the couple routinely paid personal bills from corporate accounts and deposited personal funds into the accounts. They also used corporate funds to purchase and build their home. The court held that corporate entity may be disregarded when an owner conducts private and corporate business as if they were one. Because the corporations were clearly the husband's alter ego, the chancellor justifiably pierced the corporate veil and distributed corporate assets to the owner's wife.[72]

§ 8.07 FRAUDULENT TRANSFERS

General principles of fraudulent conveyances apply to both pre- and post-divorce transfers by spouses.[73] Under these rules, a divorcing spouse's fraudulent transfer of corporate interests to family members may be set aside.[74] These rules are equally applicable to a fraudulent transfer to, rather than from, a spouse. A chancellor erred in restricting an ex-wife's attempts to determine through discovery whether corporate "loans" to her ex-husband were actually income, a portion of which she was entitled to under the divorce decree. The court outlined factors used to determine whether a payment to a shareholder is a loan or a dividend: the shareholder's interest in the corporation, the corporation's dividend history, the size of the loan, whether a ceiling was placed on the loan amount, whether security was given for the loan, whether a maturity date was placed on the loan, whether the corporation sought repayment, whether the shareholder could repay the loan, and whether there was proof of an attempt to make payments.[75] By limiting discovery to depositions, the court below made it impossible to analyze these factors – "in contentious proceedings involving complex finances of such great magnitude, it is not sufficient to simply tell one party to rely on the self-interested assertions of their opponent and his witnesses."[76]

---

[72] *See* A & L, Inc. v. Grantham, 747 So. 2d 832, 842-43 (Miss. 1999) (husband paid ex-wife's alimony and children's tuition from corporate account).

[73] See discussion of fraudulent conveyances by spouses *supra* § 6.10.

[74] *See* A & L, Inc. v. Grantham, 747 So. 2d 832, 842-43 (Miss. 1999) (corporations and siblings made parties to the action).

[75] West v. West, 891 So. 2d 203 (Miss. 2004).

[76] West v. West, 891 So. 2d 203 (Miss. 2004).

228

IX
ALIMONY

More than any other area of family law, alimony is in a state of transition and uncertainty. The historical basis for alimony has been undermined by the shift to no-fault divorce and the blurring of gender roles. A new system has replaced alimony as the principal financial award at divorce. Alimony was once the sole means of financial redistribution at divorce; now, property division is the preferred system. Alimony underwent one period of reform in response to these changes – all states adopted some form of time-limited alimony, diminished the significance of marital fault in alimony awards, and made alimony available to men as well as women. But the reforms did not provide a modern conceptual basis for awarding alimony. In most states, judges awarding alimony are guided only by a list of general factors. The uncertainty surrounding alimony awards has sparked proposals for statutory alimony guidelines, and a few states are experimenting with this approach. In its comprehensive study of family law, the American Law Institute recommends sweeping reform that would replace alimony with "compensatory spousal payments" under state-enacted guidelines. However, in spite of its flaws, alimony remains an important piece of the overall financial award at divorce. Many couples lack sufficient assets to achieve the necessary financial balance through property division. And while post-divorce self-sufficiency may be encouraged, it is not a realistic possibility for many spouses, particularly those exiting a long marriage.

In the last fifteen years, Mississippi courts authorized time-limited rehabilitative alimony and reimbursement alimony to supplement traditional permanent and lump sum alimony. In addition, the courts endorsed a more contractual, less regulated approach to the forms of alimony. The options for modifying alimony awards were also expanded. As in most states, however, awards continue to be governed by general factors. Judges are provided with little guidance as to the type, amount, and duration of alimony appropriate in a particular case. Because alimony is in a state of transition, this chapter discusses, in some detail, national trends in alimony and proposals for reform. The chapter also includes an analysis of modern Mississippi alimony opinions, in an attempt to identify patterns in alimony awards.

§ 9.01 HISTORY AND OVERVIEW

[1] History. Alimony developed in England to provide a support remedy for a wife who obtained a legal separation from her husband. The award enforced an errant husband's marital duty to support his innocent wife. A wife who was at fault in the separation forfeited the right to support.[1] American states transported alimony into divorce law without reexamining the theoretical basis for the award. Courts usually repeated the rationale for awarding alimony during legal separation – the award

---

[1] *See* HOMER H. CLARK, JR., THE LAW OF DOMESTIC RELATIONS IN THE UNITED STATES § 16.1, at 619-20 (2d ed. 1988) (guilty wife not entitled to support).

§ 9.01[2]   MISSISSIPPI FAMILY LAW

enforced a husband's duty to support his innocent wife.[2]

Homer Clark, one of the foremost writers on family law, finds reliance on the marital support duty at divorce conceptually unsound. He suggests that the real underlying policy reasons for alimony include preventing dependency on the state, accomplishing divorce with a minimum of social and financial damage, providing a form of compensation for a wife's services during marriage, and recognizing damages for a husband's breach of the marital contract.[3] Another commentator suggests that alimony was awarded, in part, to punish a husband for leaving the marriage.[4]

The traditional form of support was permanent, or periodic, alimony – a regular monthly payment without a specified ending date. Permanent alimony mimicked the marital duty of support – payments could be modified if the parties' circumstances changed substantially, and the obligation terminated if either party died or the woman remarried.[5] The test for an award in most states – "need" – was subject to extreme variations in interpretation. Some courts viewed "need" at a subsistence level. Others aimed to provide the dependent spouse with a middle-class standard of living or attempted to replicate the marriage standard of living.[6] In some states, courts were permitted to substitute a lump sum payment for ongoing permanent support.[7]

Until the mid-twentieth century, alimony was the only means of post-divorce support for financially dependent wives. A divorcing wife was not entitled to an award of property accumulated during marriage if her husband held title to the property.[8] Furthermore, alimony was available only to a wife who was not at fault – a wife who committed adultery was usually denied an award of alimony and custody of her children.[9] Alimony could also be terminated because of a woman's post-divorce sexual conduct.[10]

[2] The transition to modern alimony. The traditional alimony model became increasingly obsolete in the wake of legal and social changes in the 1970s. As a result, alimony evolved from permanent support for an innocent wife to a gender-neutral award based primarily on income disparity, frequently for a limited period of time. At the same time, alimony shifted from the primary financial equalizer at divorce to a secondary remedy.

---

[2] CLARK, JR., *supra* note 1, § 16.4, at 642.

[3] CLARK, JR., *supra* note 1, § 16.4, at 642; *see also* JOHN DE WITT GREGORY, PETER N. SWISHER & SHERYL L. WOLF, UNDERSTANDING FAMILY LAW § 9.01, at 289 (2d ed. 2001).

[4] J. THOMAS OLDHAM, DIVORCE, SEPARATION, & THE DISTRIBUTION OF PROPERTY § 3.02[1], at 3-3 to 3-5 (2001).

[5] CLARK, JR., *supra* note 1, § 16.4, at 650.

[6] *See* AMERICAN LAW INSTITUTE, PRINCIPLES OF THE LAW OF FAMILY DISSOLUTION: ANALYSIS AND RECOMMENDATIONS § 5.02, cmt. a (2002) [Hereinafter A.L.I. PRINCIPLES] (discussing cases with divergent views of need).

[7] *See* 3 FAMILY LAW AND PRACTICE ch. 35, § 35.04, at 35-77 (Arnold Rutkin ed.) (but noting that lump sum awards are used infrequently).

[8] *See* Hinton v. Hinton, 179 So. 2d 846, 848 (Miss. 1965) (wife who worked on farm with husband not entitled to interest in land titled in his name).

[9] *See* Winfield v. Winfield, 35 So. 2d 443, 444 (Miss. 1948) (wife guilty of adultery not entitled to custody of children or alimony except in exceptional circumstances); *see also* King v. King, 191 So. 2d 409 (Miss. 1966) (same); Keyes v. Keyes, 171 So. 2d 489 (Miss. 1965) (same).

[10] *See* McHann v. McHann, 383 So. 2d 823, 826 (Miss. 1980) (terminating alimony payable to woman who had sexual relations with four men after divorce).

ALIMONY   § 9.01[2][a]

[a] Gender neutrality. In 1979, the United States Supreme Court held in *Orr v. Orr* that equal protection requires gender neutrality in family law matters.[11] In response to *Orr*, all states abandoned gender classifications for alimony. Alimony is now equally available to husbands and wives, although the vast majority of awards are still made to women as the lower-income spouse.[12] In one of the few reported cases involving an alimony award to a husband, the Mississippi Court of Appeals affirmed an award of $5,000 a month in permanent alimony to a disabled husband of twenty-two years.[13]

[b] The role of fault. In less than a decade after California initiated the no-fault divorce era, most states adopted some form of no-fault divorce.[14] The traditional rule basing alimony on fault was discarded soon after.[15] The majority of states completely eliminated fault as a factor in alimony awards, finding the traditional rule inconsistent with a no-fault basis for divorce.[16] In states where fault is still considered, it is generally one of a number of factors for consideration rather than a reason in itself to deny alimony.[17]

[c] Forms of alimony. One of the most distinctive features of the modern era of alimony has been the shift from permanent alimony to time-limited alimony. While permanent alimony is still awarded in some cases, courts and legislatures developed short-term rehabilitative and transitional alimony as an alternative, and often preferred, form of spousal support.

[i] Rehabilitative alimony. Social changes in gender roles led to an expectation that divorced spouses would become self-supporting if possible.[18] Accordingly, attention began to focus away from providing permanent support toward assisting an employable spouse to become self-supporting. Time-limited rehabilitative alimony developed to support a dependent spouse for a specified period of job training or search.[19] Rehabilitative awards are typically for a short period, rarely more than a few years. The amount of the award is not measured by the "standard of living of the marriage" test, but by the needs of the spouse pending completion of job training or education.[20] Mississippi adopted rehabilitative alimony in 1995.[21]

---

[11] *See* Orr v. Orr, 440 U.S. 268, 279 (1979) (invalidating state law providing alimony for women but not for men; old notions do not justify gender-based distinctions in family law).

[12] *See* GREGORY, ET. AL, *supra* note 3, § 8.01, at 243.

[13] Stribling v. Stribling, 906 So. 2d 863, 871 (Miss. Ct. App. 2005).

[14] *See supra* § 4.01[5].

[15] *See* Brenda L. Storey, *Surveying the Alimony Landscape*, 25 FAM. ADVOC. 10 (Spring 2003).

[16] *See* GREGORY, ET. AL, *supra* note 3, § 8.03, at 250 (twenty-nine states eliminated fault altogether); Storey, *supra* note 15.

[17] GREGORY, ET. AL, *supra* note 3, § 8.03, at 250 (few states still make fault an absolute bar).

[18] GREGORY, ET. AL, *supra* note 3, § 9.01, at 290.

[19] Brett Turner, *Rehabilitative Alimony Reconsidered: The "Second Wave" of Spousal Support Reform*, 10 DIVORCE LITIG. 185, 187 (1998).

[20] Jennifer L. McCoy, *Spousal Support Disorder: An Overview of Problems in Current Alimony Law*, 33 FLA. ST. U. L. REV. 501, 512 (2005).

[21] *See infra* § 9.02[3].

§ 9.01[2][c][ii]   **MISSISSIPPI FAMILY LAW**

[ii] Transitional alimony. In some cases, a short-term award may be appropriate even if the lower-income spouse is working and not in need of career rehabilitation. After the adoption of rehabilitative alimony, courts began to award time-limited alimony to a lower-income working spouse when the circumstances – usually a short marriage – did not warrant an award of permanent alimony. Some states label alimony for this purpose as "transitional" alimony,[22] others use "reorientation" or "bridge-the-gap" support.[23] In some states, including Mississippi, courts use the "rehabilitative" label even when the purpose is really short-term transitional support.[24] Transitional alimony, as its label suggests, is to allow the recipient to adjust to the financial realities of single life.[25]

[iii] Permanent alimony. Rehabilitative and transitional alimony did not replace permanent alimony. In most states, courts have discretion to award either type of alimony depending on the individual circumstances of the case. In some cases, both may be awarded. For example, a homemaker leaving a long marriage may be entitled to rehabilitative alimony to support a period of retraining, combined with an award of permanent alimony to remedy the income disparity expected to remain after retraining. In most states, courts have broad discretion with regard to the type, as well as the amount, of support to award.

[d] Relationship to equitable distribution. As the purpose and form of alimony was reshaped, its prominence in the divorce system changed as well. Beginning in the 1970s, common law states adopted equitable distribution, a property system requiring fair division of marital assets regardless of title.[26] A primary goal of equitable distribution was to alleviate the need for alimony, replacing ongoing financial entanglement between ex-spouses with a one-time property division.[27] Alimony became a tool for supplementing property division rather than the primary means of redistributing assets.

[3] Modern theories of alimony. The historic underpinnings of alimony – the husband's duty to support his wife for life – do not explain the continuing role of alimony in a gender-neutral era of no-fault divorce. In the 1970s, the Uniform Marriage and Divorce Act recharacterized alimony as "maintenance" and posited a needs-based rationale for the award.[28] The focus was on providing alimony for spouses with earning capacity insufficient to meet his or her reasonable needs.[29] In the 1990s, commentators proposed new theories to support the recognized need for alimony in some cases.

---

[22] *See infra* § 9.02[3].

[23] *See* Jesse J. Bennett, Jr., *Bridge-the-Gap Alimony: An Emerging Vehicle for Satisfying Short-term Need,* FLA. BUS. J., Nov. 1999, at 65; McCoy, *supra* note 20, at 512.

[24] Turner, *supra* note 19, at 195, 203 (noting that time-limited alimony is sometimes labeled rehabilitative even if not for purpose of support during rehabilitation).

[25] McCoy, *supra* note 20, at 513.

[26] *See supra* § 6.01.

[27] *See* Ferguson v. Ferguson, 639 So. 2d 921 (Miss. 1994).

[28] UNIF. MARRIAGE AND DIVORCE ACT § 308, 9 U.L.A. 147, 347.

[29] Mary Kay Kisthardt, *Re-thinking Alimony: The AAML's Considerations for Calculating Alimony, Spousal Support, or Maintenance,* 21 J. AM. ACAD. MATRIM. L. 61, 627-68 (2008).

ALIMONY

§ 9.01[4]

One approach, seen in the American Law Institute proposals discussed below, sought to justify alimony as compensation for loss of earning capacity caused by marital decisions.[30] Others proposed rationales based on contract or partnership law, while still others looked to public policy of preventing welfare dependency.[31] However, no widely accepted new theory of alimony has emerged. Courts continue to award alimony based on a set of factors that provide little real guidance, without articulating a modern theory to support the award.

[4] Alimony guidelines. In determining whether, for how long, and in what amount to award alimony, courts are guided only by general factors. One expert has noted that judges probably have more discretion in making alimony awards than in almost any other area of the law.[32] The American Law Institute noted that alimony awards nationwide are "hopelessly confused."[33] In the last decade, alimony guidelines have been proposed to eliminate some of the current uncertainty. The discussion below outlines the efforts of some groups to articulate standards for alimony awards. Whether guidelines will prove more effective than the use of discretionary factor-based awards remains to be seen.

Supporters of alimony guidelines focus on the same factors that prompted adoption of child support guidelines – lack of uniformity, uncertainty, and inconsistent and unfair results in alimony awards. They argue that the inconsistency and uncertainty make it difficult to negotiate and resolve cases out of court. Detractors note that alimony awards require consideration of a much wider and less quantifiable range of factors. While child support is based primarily on income, alimony is tied to marriage length, earning capacity, rehabilitation potential, and fault. Opponents also emphasize that there is a general consensus that parents should support their children to majority, but substantial disagreement about the proper amount and length of spousal support.[34]

[a] State and local guidelines. Frustration with the lack of standards for alimony awards prompted some states and local groups to experiment with alimony guidelines. In Maricopa County, Arizona, permanent alimony is presumptively appropriate after a twenty-year marriage if the recipient is fifty or older.[35] For shorter marriages, the guidelines recommend time-limited support equal to 30 to 50% of the marriage length.[36] In California, many counties follow discretionary guidelines that classify a marriage of less than ten years as a short marriage and presume that support should last for one-half the length of the marriage. As the marriage length increases, the alimony duration increases until it equals the length of the marriage. The guidelines

---

[30] Kisthardt, *supra* note 29, at 71.

[31] David A. Harcy, *Nevada Alimony: An Important Policy in Need of a Coherent Purpose*, 9 NEV. L. J. 325, 330 (2009).

[32] *See generally* Robert Kirkman Collins, *The Theory of Marital Residuals: Applying an Income Adjustment Calculus to the Enigma of Alimony*, 24 HARV. WOMEN'S L.J. 23 (2001); Marsha Garrison, *How do Judges Decide Divorce Cases? An Empirical Analysis of Discretionary Decisionmaking*, 74 N.C. L. REV. 401 (1996).

[33] A.L.I. PRINCIPLES, *supra* note 6, §§ 5.01-.05.

[34] Brett Turner, *Redefining Alimony in a Time of Transition*, 4 DIVORCE LITIG. 221 (Nov. 1992).

[35] Virginia R. Dugan & Jon A. Feder, *Alimony Guidelines: Do They Work?*, 25 FAM. ADVOC. 20 (Spring 2003).

[36] *See* A.L.I. PRINCIPLES, *supra* note 6, § 5.06, cmt. a (citing Fam. Ct. Dep't, Super. Ct. of Maricopa County, Ariz., Spousal Maint. Guidelines (approved April 19, 2000)).

§ 9.01[4][b]   MISSISSIPPI FAMILY LAW

also create a formula for determining the appropriate amount of support.[37] In Maine, only rehabilitative alimony may be awarded if the marriage lasted fewer than ten years. For marriages between ten and twenty years, support is provided for half the length of the marriage; in marriages over twenty years, judges have discretion to determine the award.[38] A Delaware statute provides that in marriages of less than twenty years, support should not last more than one-half the duration of the marriage.[39] The most restrictive jurisdiction is Texas, which allows support only after a ten-year marriage and then only up to $2,500 a month for a maximum of three years.[40]

Some guidelines also address the amount of support, often as a percentage of the parties' income disparity. For example, in some Kansas counties, guidelines provide for alimony equal to 25% of the income disparity up to a $50,000 difference, and 22% of the disparity above a $50,000 difference.[41] Guidelines recommended for one district in New Mexico create a formula similar to the American Academy of Matrimonial Lawyers recommendations discussed below.[42] Guidelines have also been used in Pennsylvania, Michigan, and Virginia.[43]

[b] American Law Institute proposal. In its comprehensive review of marital dissolution laws, the American Law Institute (ALI) proposes replacing alimony with "compensatory spousal payments."[44] The proposal discards the indefinite standard of "need." Disparity in income alone does not justify an award under the proposal – the disparity must be linked to the marriage. The ALI proposal identifies four circumstances in which income disparity is related to marriage dissolution: (1) a long marriage;[45] (2) one spouse's role as caretaker for children or disabled family;[46] (3) one spouse's sacrifice of premarital earning capacity for the marriage;[47] and (4) a spouse's unrecovered investment in the other's career.[48]

Under this proposal, the amount of an award under (1) and (2) is determined by a state-established formula tied to the length of the marriage (or childcare) and the disparity in incomes.[49] The proposal does not endorse equalizing incomes; awards are capped at 40% of the income disparity except in unusual circumstances.[50] The proposal also presumes that awards should be time-limited rather than indefinite, unless the

---

[37] Dugan & Feder, *supra* note 35, at 20; Kisthardt, *supra* note 29, at 73 (amount determined by subtracting 50% of the payee's net income from 40% of the payor's net income).

[38] ME. REV. STAT. ANN. tit. 19A, § 951A(2)(A)(1) (2004) (presumption rebuttable).

[39] DEL. CODE ANN. tit. 13, § 1512(d) (2003); *see also* KAN. STAT. ANN. § 60-1610(b)(2) (2003) (maximum support order of 121 months; may be renewed upon application to court).

[40] Dugan & Feder, *supra* note 35, at 20; *see* TEX. FAM. CODE ANN. §§ 8.051(2), 8.055(a)(1), 8.054(a)(1) (2010).

[41] *See* Kisthardt, *supra* note 29, at 76.

[42] Kisthardt, *supra* note 29, at 76 (30% of payor's gross income minus 50% of payee's if no children; 39% and 58% if children).

[43] Kisthardt, *supra* note 29, at 76.

[44] A.L.I. PRINCIPLES, *supra* note 6, § 5.04.

[45] A.L.I. PRINCIPLES, *supra* note 6, § 5.04.

[46] A.L.I. PRINCIPLES, *supra* note 6, § 5.05.

[47] A.L.I. PRINCIPLES, *supra* note 6, § 5.13 (does not include income disparity that existed at time of marriage).

[48] A.L.I. PRINCIPLES, *supra* note 6, § 5.13.

[49] A.L.I. PRINCIPLES, *supra* note 6, §§ 5.04, 5.06.

[50] A.L.I. PRINCIPLES, *supra* note 6, §§ 5.02, 5.04.

ALIMONY § 9.01[4][c]

marriage length and the recipient's age suggest otherwise.[51] The award under (3), available after a short marriage, is linked to lost premarital earning capacity rather than the marriage standard of living.[52]

[c] AAML recommended guidelines. In 2007, an American Academy of Matrimonial Lawyers Commission made recommendations for alimony guidelines after an extensive study of alimony trends, the ALI proposal, and state and local guidelines. The Commission concluded that alimony awards lack consistency, resulting in perceived unfairness and an inability to predict outcomes.[53] The Commission opted for a relatively simple formula that addresses both the amount and duration of alimony.

[i] Amount of award. The recommended presumptive amount of alimony is calculated by taking 30% of the payor's gross income, minus 20% of the payee's gross income, with the resulting total income to the payee not to exceed 40 % of the parties' combined gross incomes.

[ii] Duration. Under the AAML proposal, the duration of alimony is calculated by multiplying the marriage length by the following factors: 0-3 years of marriage (.3); 3-10 years of marriage (.5); 10-20 years of marriage (.75), over 20 years, permanent alimony.

[iii] Deviation factors. The recommended amount or duration may be varied based upon deviation factors, including: care for a dependent child or disabled adult child, pre-existing support obligations or court-ordered payment of debts or other obligations, unusual needs, age or health, sacrifice of career or support for the other's career, disproportionate property division, unusual tax consequences, or agreement of the spouses.[54]

[iv] Examples. In a case involving a payor with gross income of $90,000 and a payee with gross income of $30,000 leaving a fifteen-year marriage, the formula would provide for $1,500 a month in alimony for a period of eleven years and three months.[55] A payor with gross income of $60,000 leaving an eight-year marriage with a spouse who had gross income of $30,000 would pay $500 a month for four years.[56]

[v] Application. In 2009, a Maryland trial court consulted the AAML

---

[51] A.L.I. Principles, *supra* note 6, § 5.06 (term set by presumption governs in absence of written findings supporting deviation).

[52] A.L.I. Principles, *supra* note 6, § 5.13 (does not include income disparity that existed at time of marriage).

[53] Kisthardt, *supra* note 29, at 62.

[54] Kisthardt, *supra* note 29, Appendix A (citing AAML Comm'n Recommendations).

[55] (1) 30% of $90,000 = $27,000. (2) 20% of $30,000 = $6,000. (3) $27,000 - $6,000 = $21,000/year or $1,750/month. (4) [40% of $120,000] = $48,000 – $30,000 = $18,000 ($1,500/month). (5) 15 years x .75 = 11.25, or 11 years and 3 months.

[56] (1) 30% of $60,000 = $18,000. (2) 20% of $30,000 = $6,000. (3) $18,000 - $6,000 = $12,000. (4) [40% of $90,000] = $36,000 - $30,000 = $6,000 or $500/month. (4) 8 years x .5 = 4 years.

§ 9.01[5]   MISSISSIPPI FAMILY LAW

guidelines in addition to the state's statutory factors for an award of alimony. The court of appeals rejected the husband's argument that the trial court erred in consulting non-statutory guidelines: "We hold that, given the difficulty of translating predominantly qualitative factors into a numerical award, courts may consult guidelines developed by a reliable and neutral source that do not conflict with or undermine any of the considerations expressed in the statute."[57]

[5] Alimony in Mississippi. The development of alimony in Mississippi follows the national pattern. Alimony awards were based on the traditional model until the latter part of the twentieth century when the purpose, basis, and forms of alimony were reformulated. As in other states, the resulting system supplements traditional forms with new types of alimony and is probably less coherent than any other aspect of divorce law.

[a] Traditional alimony. Alimony awards were first authorized by statute in Mississippi in 1848.[58] The statute currently in force states simply that a court has power to make all orders regarding alimony as "may seem equitable and just" and afterwards to modify the decree "as the case may require."[59] As in most states, courts historically based the right to alimony on the "continuing legal duty of the husband to support his wife."[60]

Fault was the controlling factor in Mississippi alimony decisions until 1992.[61] The rule was never absolute; the Mississippi Supreme Court held as early as 1913 that a wife who had no means of support, who was ill and could not work, or who contributed to the accumulation of her husband's property should not be denied minimal support.[62] But the exception was to prevent destitution and not to match the marital standard of

---

[57] Boemio v. Boemio, 994 A.2d 911, 917 (Md. 2010). Application of the guidelines produced permanent alimony of $3,800/month for the wife; however, the court awarded $3,000 a month. *Id.*

[58] J.W. BUNKLEY & W.E. MORSE, AMIS ON DIVORCE & SEPARATION IN MISSISSIPPI § 6.01, at 181 (1957). Since 1848, the wording of the statute has remained almost unchanged with the exception of adding that a husband may receive alimony. *See* SHELTON HAND, MISSISSIPPI DIVORCE, ALIMONY, AND CHILD CUSTODY § 11-1, at 262 (4th ed. 1996) (statute amended in 1979).

[59] MISS. CODE ANN. § 93-5-23 (2004); *see* Helmsley v. Helmsley, 639 So. 2d 909, 912 (Miss. 1994) (rejecting husband's argument that irreconcilable differences statute does not authorize alimony award because the word "alimony" does not appear in statute); Taylor v. Taylor, 392 So. 2d 1145, 1148 (Miss. 1981) (same).

[60] Miller v. Miller, 159 So. 112, 119 (Miss. 1935); *see* Robinson v. Robinson, 72 So. 923, 923 (Miss. 1916) ("The allowance of alimony is justified by the natural obligation of the husband, as the bread winner of the family, to support his wife."); *see also* Felder v. Felder's Estate, 13 So. 2d 823, 828 (Miss. 1943) (alimony based on public policy, not contract; husband cannot use homestead exemption to avoid ex-wife's alimony claim).

[61] A 1990 case strongly endorsed the traditional rule: "[A] husband is entitled to have his wife receive her support in his home while she is discharging the duties of a wife as imposed under the marriage contract." Retzer v. Retzer, 578 So. 2d 580, 592-93 (Miss. 1990) (husband granted divorce based on adultery not required to pay lump sum alimony); *see* Russell v. Russell, 241 So. 2d 366, 367 (Miss. 1970) (reversing award of $500/month alimony following grant of divorce to husband); Winfield v. Winfield, 35 So. 2d 443, 444 (Miss. 1948) (wife guilty of adultery not entitled to custody of children or alimony except in exceptional circumstances); *see also* King v. King, 191 So. 2d 409, 411 (Miss. 1966) (same); Keyes v. Keyes, 171 So. 2d 489, 490 (Miss. 1965) (same).

[62] *See* Winkler v. Winkler, 61 So. 1, 2 (Miss. 1913) (upholding chancellor's award of alimony to mother of four whose husband obtained divorce based on desertion). *But see* Retzer v. Retzer, 578 So. 2d 580, 593 (Miss. 1990) (in all cases allowing alimony to prevent destitution, divorce was based on cruelty or desertion; alimony always denied where wife committed adultery).

ALIMONY   § 9.01[5][b]

living.[63]

Until the mid-twentieth century, the only guideline for the proper amount of alimony was the marital standard of living. In 1856, the supreme court stated: "There appears to be no fixed rule upon this subject, but it depends upon the discretion of the court . . . the only general rule being, that the wife is entitled to a support corresponding to her rank and condition in life and the estate of her husband."[64] In 1955, the supreme court delineated factors to guide chancellors in making alimony awards.[65] The factors direct attention to circumstances relevant to spousal support such as income and earning capacity, resources, and age and health, but do not provide guidelines or presumptions that suggest a particular result in a given case.

Mississippi courts have long had the option of ordering alimony paid periodically or in a non-modifiable lump sum settlement. Traditional permanent alimony was a regular, modifiable payment with no fixed ending date. Lump sum alimony was a one-time settlement of the support obligation that could not be modified or terminated.[66]

[b] Transition to modern alimony. Alimony law in Mississippi has altered significantly in the last twenty years. In response to United States Supreme Court decisions, the Mississippi legislature provided in 1979 that alimony is equally available to husbands and wives.[67] In 1992 the supreme court abandoned the "innocent spouse" rule, holding that marital fault is merely one factor for consideration in an alimony award.[68] Today, fault is a viable factor "when the misconduct places a burden on the stability and harmony of the marital and family relationship."[69]

With the adoption of equitable distribution in 1994, alimony became a secondary means of achieving financial equity after divorce.[70] If, after property division, each party's assets and income are sufficient to meet reasonable expenses, no further award is required. But if property division "leaves a deficit for one party," courts are to consider whether alimony should be awarded.[71]

---

[63] *See* Retzer v. Retzer, 578 So. 2d 580, 593 (Miss. 1990).

[64] *See* Armstrong v. Armstrong, 32 Miss. 279 (1856) (approving lump sum alimony equal to one-third of husband's estate).

[65] *See* Brabham v. Brabham, 84 So. 2d 147, 153 (Miss. 1955). The factors, very similar to those currently applied, include: "(1) the health of the husband and his earning capacity; (2) the health of the wife and her earning capacity; (3) the entire sources of income of both parties; (4) the reasonable needs of the wife; (5) the reasonable needs of the child; (6) the necessary living expenses of the husband; (7) the estimated amount of income taxes the respective parties must pay on their incomes; (8) the fact that the wife has the free use of the home, furnishings and automobile, and (9) such other facts and circumstances bearing on the subject." *Id.*

[66] *See* Miller v. Miller, 159 So. 112, 119-20 (Miss. 1935) (discussing 1856 recognition of lump sum alimony); *see also* Robinson v. Robinson, 72 So. 923, 924 (Miss. 1916) (lump sum payment as final settlement of obligations between parties); Guess v. Smith, 56 So. 166, 167 (Miss. 1911) (lump sum alimony not modifiable). *But see* discussion at § 9.02[2][b][v] *infra* (suggesting that true lump sum alimony no longer exists).

[67] *See* HAND, *supra* note 58, § 11-1, at 262; *see also* MISS. CODE ANN. § 93-5-23 (2004); Neville v. Neville, 734 So. 2d 352, 356, 358 (Miss. Ct. App. 1999) (chancellor awarded husband 120 months of rehabilitative alimony; court of appeals revised order to lump sum alimony).

[68] *See* Hammonds v. Hammonds, 597 So. 2d 653, 655 (Miss. 1992) (wife guilty of adultery entitled to sufficient alimony to prevent destitution; court found no reason to distinguish adultery and other fault); *see also* Driste v. Driste, 738 So. 2d 763, 765 (Miss. Ct. App.1998) (fault is factor for consideration in both alimony and equitable distribution even in irreconcilable differences divorce).

[69] Carrow v. Carrow, 642 So. 2d 901, 904-05 (Miss. 1994).

[70] *See* Ferguson v. Ferguson, 639 So. 2d 921 (Miss. 1994).

[71] Johnson v. Johnson, 650 So. 2d 1281, 1287 (Miss. 1994); *see also* Kilpatrick v. Kilpatrick, 732 So. 2d 876, 880

§ 9.01[6]　　　　　　　　　　MISSISSIPPI FAMILY LAW

The forms and purposes of alimony in Mississippi have also been substantially revised. In 1995, the supreme court recognized rehabilitative alimony – short term alimony to assist the recipient to become self-supporting.[72] Four years later, the court approved reimbursement alimony to compensate a spouse who supported the other through schooling.[73] The two new forms of alimony supplement the traditional forms rather than replacing them. In addition to adding new alimony forms, the court blurred the lines between permanent and lump sum alimony by offering parties greater freedom to tailor alimony awards to their needs.[74]

These developments place Mississippi's alimony system in line with national trends. Today, equitable distribution is the first step in financial adjustments at divorce. Courts may then supplement property division with permanent alimony, lump sum alimony, rehabilitative alimony, reimbursement alimony, a combination of awards, or an agreed hybrid payment. As in most states, there are no specific guidelines indicating what form of alimony should be awarded or the appropriate amount or duration of alimony.

[6] General considerations

[a] When available. Alimony may be awarded only between divorcing parties. Alimony may not be awarded to one whose marriage has been annulled.[75] Nor may alimony be awarded based on marriage-like cohabitation.[76]

[b] Jurisdiction. Chancery courts have jurisdiction to award alimony at divorce and retain continuing jurisdiction to modify some awards based on a material change in circumstances. A court must have personal jurisdiction over a defendant in order to address alimony and support. Jurisdiction to order and modify alimony is addressed in detail in Chapter XVIII.

[c] Temporary alimony. A court may award temporary alimony, or alimony pendent lite, while divorce or separate maintenance proceedings are pending. Temporary support may be ordered only if the parties are married and living apart, one has filed suit against the other for separate maintenance or divorce, and the court has jurisdiction over the action and personal jurisdiction over the defendant.[77] A final judgment of divorce terminates an obligation to pay temporary alimony, but does not eliminate the obligation to pay temporary alimony arrearages.[78] The supreme court held that a husband was not entitled to credit in property division for payment of tem-

---

(Miss. 1999).

[72] *See* Hubbard v. Hubbard, 656 So. 2d 124, 130 (Miss. 1995).

[73] *See* Guy v. Guy, 736 So. 2d 1042, 1046 (Miss. 1999).

[74] *See infra* § 9.03[2].

[75] *See supra* § 3.06[1].

[76] *See supra* § 2.02[5].

[77] Neely v. Neely, 52 So. 2d 501 (Miss. 1951).

[78] Prescott v. Prescott, 736 So. 2d 409, 416 (Miss. Ct. App. 1999); *cf.* Diehl v. Diehl, 29 So. 3d 153, 155 n.2 (Miss. Ct. App. 2010) (temporary alimony terminated when wife's complaint for divorce was dismissed). *But cf.* Clark v. Clark, 43 So. 3d 496, 503 (Miss. Ct. App. 2010) (temporary support continued after divorce action dismissed for lack of service of process).

ALIMONY

§ 9.01[6][d]

porary alimony. He cited no authority for the proposition that temporary support should be considered in equitable distribution.[79]

[d] Relationship to equitable distribution. One of the goals of adopting equitable distribution was to alleviate the need for alimony. If an award of marital property is sufficient to meet the parties' needs, no alimony should be awarded. Accordingly, spousal support should be considered only after division of marital property.[80] For the same reason, when a court's division of marital property is reversed, an accompanying award or denial of alimony must also be reversed.[81]

[7] Overview. The discussion of current Mississippi alimony rules is divided into three sections. Section 9.02 reviews the four types of alimony and the characteristics of each. Section 9.03 discusses the extent to which parties may vary alimony forms. As a general rule, an alimony award must comply with the set characteristics associated with that particular form. Recent decisions allow parties some flexibility to create hybrid alimony with mixed characteristics, but the exact parameters of hybrid agreements are not clear.

Sections 9.04 and 9.05 are discussions of factors articulated by the Mississippi Supreme Court to guide chancellors in making alimony awards. The alimony factors section is followed in section 9.06 with an analysis of actual alimony awards since 1994, based on the factors that appear most critical – disparity in income and length of marriage. Sections 9.07 and 9.08 discuss third-party payments as alimony and the mechanics of the alimony award, including provisions for security, variable payments and some drafting considerations. The chapter concludes with a section on modification of alimony awards. Enforcement of financial awards, including alimony, is discussed in Chapter XIV.

---

[79] Bowen v. Bowen, 982 So. 2d 385, 396 (Miss. 2008).

[80] Ferguson v. Ferguson, 639 So. 2d 921 (Miss. 1994); *see also* Lauro v. Lauro, 924 So. 2d 584, 588 (Miss. Ct. App. 2006) (alimony and property division considered together; where one expands, the other must recede); Striebeck v. Striebeck, 911 So. 2d 628, 635 (Miss. Ct. App. 2005) (en banc) (alimony considered only after property division); Cosentino v. Cosentino, 912 So. 2d 1130, 1132 (Miss. Ct. App. 2005) (alimony and property division are linked; alimony may be awarded only if property division leaves one party without adequate provision); Roberts v. Roberts, 924 So. 2d 550, 554 (Miss. Ct. App. 2005) (alimony not considered in a vacuum; must be viewed with equitable distribution); Marsh v. Marsh, 868 So. 2d 394, 398 (Miss. Ct. App. 2004) (alimony recedes when equitable distribution expands; alimony denied to wife who received two-thirds of large marital estate).

[81] Pierce v. Pierce, 42 So. 3d 658, 664 (Miss. Ct. App. 2010) (alimony and attorneys' fees reversed); Segree v. Segree, 46 So. 3d 861, 866 (Miss. Ct. App. 2010) (alimony and child support reversed); McKissack v. McKissack, 45 So. 3d 716, 723 (Miss. Ct. App. 2010) (award of alimony not error, but may need reconsideration in light of reversal of property division); Long v. Long, 928 So. 2d 1001, 1004 (Miss. Ct. App. 2006) (alimony award reversed because property division reversed); Lauro v. Lauro, 924 So. 2d 584, 588 (Miss. Ct. App. 2006) (periodic alimony, but not rehabilitative, must be reversed when property division is reversed); Gray v. Gray, 909 So. 2d 108, 112-13 (Miss. Ct. App. 2005) (because property division award reversed, chancellor should reconsider child support, alimony, and attorneys' fees); Fitzgerald v. Fitzgerald, 914 So. 2d 193, 198 (Miss. Ct. App. 2005) (periodic alimony award reversed because property division reversed); Hankins v. Hankins, 866 So. 2d 508, 511-512 (Miss. Ct. App. 2004); *see also* Lauro v. Lauro, 847 So. 2d 843 (Miss. 2003) (rule not applicable to rehabilitative alimony).

§ 9.02   **MISSISSIPPI FAMILY LAW**

§ 9.02 TYPES OF ALIMONY

Four distinct types of alimony are recognized in Mississippi – permanent, lump sum, rehabilitative, and reimbursement. The form in which alimony is awarded is critical – it determines whether the award can later be modified based on a change in circumstances; whether it terminates at the payor's death; whether it survives the payee's death; and whether it terminates if the payee remarries or cohabits. Until recently, permanent and lump sum alimony had fixed, opposing characteristics that could not be altered by agreement or court order. Now parties have increased flexibility in fashioning agreed awards. This section discusses the history and generally recognized characteristics of each of the four forms of alimony.

[1] Permanent alimony. Permanent alimony is the traditional ongoing monthly support payment awarded as a substitute for the marital support obligation. The characteristics of permanent alimony mimic those of the marital support duty – the award terminates at the death of either party or upon the payee's remarriage and can be modified based upon a change in circumstances. Historically, the characteristics of permanent and lump sum alimony could not be altered by court order or agreement.[82]

[a] Purpose. Traditional permanent alimony was based on a husband's continuing duty to support his innocent wife after dissolution of the marriage.[83] Today, permanent alimony may be awarded to either spouse, including one who was at fault in the divorce.[84] The purpose of alimony in the age of gender equality and no-fault divorce has not been clearly articulated.[85] Mississippi courts still express the purpose in traditional terms – to provide for a financially dependent spouse at the marital standard of living.[86]

[b] Factors. The factors governing permanent alimony awards include: (1) the parties' income and expenses; (2) the parties' health and earning capacity; (3) the needs of each party; (4) the obligations and assets of each party; (5) the length of the marriage; (6) the presence or absence of minor children in the home, and the need for child care; (7) the parties' ages; (8) the parties' standard of living during the marriage and at the time support is determined; (9) tax consequences of the spousal support order; (10) fault or misconduct; (11) dissipation of assets by either party; or (12) any other factor deemed to be "just and equitable."[87] A detailed analysis of the factors is set

---

[82] *See* Cleveland v. Cleveland, 600 So. 2d 193, 196-97 (Miss. 1992) (court-ordered permanent alimony of $600/month for seven years or until remarriage or death was held to be permanent and not subject to seven-year cut-off date; payments also increased to $1,000/month).

[83] Miller v. Miller, 159 So. 112, 119 (Miss. 1935); *see also* Robinson v. Robinson, 72 So. 923, 923 (Miss. 1916) ("The allowance of alimony is justified by the natural obligation of the husband, as the bread winner of the family, to support his wife.").

[84] *See* Hammonds v. Hammonds, 597 So. 2d 653, 655 (Miss. 1992).

[85] *See supra* § 9.01[3].

[86] *See* Beezley v. Beezley, 917 So. 2d 803, 807 (Miss. Ct. App. 2005) (periodic alimony awarded based on need); Johnson v. Johnson, 877 So. 2d 485, 498 (Miss. Ct. App. 2003); Weeks v. Weeks, 832 So. 2d 583, 587-88 (Miss. Ct. App. 2002).

[87] Armstrong v. Armstrong, 618 So. 2d 1278, 1280 (Miss. 1993) (modifying factors set out in Brabham v. Brabham,

240

ALIMONY § 9.02[1][c]

out in section 9.04.

[c] **Vesting.** Permanent alimony vests on the date each periodic payment becomes due.[88] A payment that is due and vested cannot be modified or forgiven and becomes a claim on the payor's estate.[89] Payments not yet due are not vested and can be modified or terminated.[90]

[d] **Amount.** With regard to the proper amount of permanent alimony, the appellate courts have stated that the general rule for calculating the amount of permanent alimony is that "the recipient should be entitled to a reasonable allowance that is commiserate with the standard of living to which they had become accustomed measured against the ability to pay."[91]

[e] **Modification.** Permanent alimony may be modified based upon a material change in circumstances since the date of the award.[92] The award may be increased, decreased, or terminated to reflect a change.[93] Modification is an essential characteristic of permanent alimony, which replaces "the inherently changing financial ability of the husband to support his wife."[94] Parties may not alter this characteristic by agreement.[95] For example, the supreme court permitted alimony modification based on an ex-wife's cohabitation even though the agreement prohibited modification without consent. [96]

[f] **Conversion.** Permanent alimony may be converted to rehabilitative upon a showing of a material change in circumstances. The court of appeals affirmed a chancellor's modification of permanent alimony to rehabilitative, based on the husband's significant loss of income and the wife's receipt of free housing from a male friend.[97]

[g] **Termination.** The duration of permanent alimony corresponds to the marital duty of support – the obligation terminates upon the payor's death, the recipient's death, or the recipient's remarriage.[98] The obligation may also be terminated

---

84 So. 2d 147, 153 (Miss. 1955)).

[88] Bowe v. Bowe, 557 So. 2d 793, 795 (Miss. 1990); Beezley v. Beezley, 917 So. 2d 803, 807 (Miss. Ct. App. 2005).

[89] McCardle v. McCardle, 862 So. 2d 1290, 1293 (Miss. Ct. App. 2004) (vested alimony arrearages survived payor's death and were payable from estate).

[90] Hubbard v. Hubbard, 656 So. 2d 124, 129 (Miss. 1995).

[91] Palculict v. Palculict, 22 So. 3d 293, 297 (Miss. Ct. App. 2009) (finding that there was no abuse of discretion in the chancellor's decision to award periodic alimony).

[92] Holley v. Holley, 969 So. 2d 842, 844 (Miss. 2007); Hubbard v. Hubbard, 656 So. 2d 124, 129 (Miss. 1995); Carroll v. Carroll, 976 So. 2d 880, 887 (Miss. Ct. App. 2007); Chroniger v. Chroniger, 914 So. 2d 311, 314-15 (Miss. Ct. App. 2005); see Beezley v. Beezley, 917 So. 2d 803, 807 (Miss. Ct. App. 2005); Grice v. Grice, 726 So. 2d 1242, 1251 (Miss. Ct. App. 1998).

[93] Bowe v. Bowe, 557 So. 2d 793, 794 (Miss. 1990).

[94] McDonald v. McDonald, 683 So. 2d 929, 931 (Miss. 1996).

[95] Taylor v. Taylor, 392 So. 2d 1145, 1147 (Miss. 1981); see McDonald v. McDonald, 683 So. 2d 929, 931 (Miss. 1996) (permanent alimony modifiable "regardless of any intent expressed by the parties to the contrary"). But see infra § 9.03 (discussing permissible alterations in alimony characteristics).

[96] See Ellis v. Ellis, 651 So. 2d. 1068, 1073-74 (Miss. 1995).

[97] Austin v. Austin, 981 So. 2d 1000, 1006 (Miss. Ct. App. 2007).

[98] Holley v. Holley, 969 So. 2d 842, 844 (Miss. 2007); Hubbard v. Hubbard, 656 So. 2d 124, 128-29 (Miss. 1995);

§ 9.02[1][g][i]   **MISSISSIPPI FAMILY LAW**

based upon the recipient's cohabitation or de facto marriage.[99]

[i] At remarriage. Permanent alimony terminates upon the recipient's remarriage. Alimony terminated because of remarriage is not reinstated if the second marriage ends in divorce or is annulled.[100]

[ii] At the payee's death. Permanent alimony terminates at the payee's death.[101] This particular characteristic is a critical component of the IRS definition of deductible alimony.[102]

[iii] At the payor's death. Termination at the payor's death is a traditional characteristic of permanent alimony. Unlike some features, however, this characteristic may be altered by agreement. In addition, drafters should be aware that use of standard provisions common in divorce agreements may unintentionally alter this characteristic.

Parties may agree to extend permanent alimony beyond a payor's death, making the payments a binding obligation on the payor's estate.[103] The Mississippi Supreme Court enforced an express agreement that a husband's estate would be obligated to pay alimony until the wife died or remarried.[104] In one case, the supreme court held that a husband and wife agreed to extend alimony beyond his death based on a standard settlement provision in their agreement. The agreement stated that alimony would terminate upon the wife's death but was silent regarding the effect of the husband's death. The court held that his estate was obligated to continue alimony payments to his ex-wife, based on a provision which stated that "[t]his agreement shall be binding upon the parties hereto, their administrators, executors and assigns."[105] However, alimony is not extended solely because an agreement fails to mention the payor's death as a terminating event – the omission must be paired with a clause making all obligations of the agreement binding on the estate.[106] As this decision illustrates, the impact of

---

Holleman v. Holleman, 527 So. 2d 90, 92 (Miss. 1988), *abrogated on other grounds by* Smith v. Smith, 607 So. 2d 122 (Miss. 1992); East v. East, 493 So. 2d 927, 931 (Miss. 1986); Maxcy v. Estate of Maxcy, 485 So. 2d 1077, 1078 (Miss. 1986); Carroll v. Carroll, 976 So. 2d 880, 887 (Miss. Ct. App. 2007); Chroniger v. Chroniger, 914 So. 2d 311, 314 (Miss. Ct. App. 2005); *cf.* Patterson v. Patterson, 915 So. 2d 496, 499 (Miss. Ct. App. 2005) (wife not entitled to recover arrearages under 1974 agreement that husband would pay alimony until wife's death; chancellor's order made alimony terminable at remarriage).

[99] See *infra* § 9.11.

[100] Bridges v. Bridges, 217 So. 2d 281, 283 (Miss. 1968) (annulment); Sides v. Pittman, 150 So. 211, 212 (Miss. 1933) (divorce) ("It is contrary to the principles of justice to require a former husband to support the wife of a later husband."); *cf.* Weathersby v. Weathersby, 693 So. 2d 1348, 1351 (Miss. 1997) (clause terminated alimony for cohabitation; could not later be reinstated through modification).

[101] Hubbard v. Hubbard, 656 So. 2d 124, 129 (Miss. 1995); Armstrong v. Armstrong, 618 So. 2d 1278, 1281 (Miss. 1993).

[102] *See infra* § 22.01[1][g].

[103] *In re* Estate of Kennington, 204 So. 2d 444, 450 (Miss. 1967); *see In re* Last Will and Testament of Sheppard, 757 So. 2d 173, 175 (Miss. 2000).

[104] *See In re* Estate of Kennington, 204 So. 2d 444, 450 (Miss. 1967) (but noting that the obligation should be reduced to a lump sum representing the present value of the payment).

[105] *See In re* Last Will and Testament of Sheppard, 757 So. 2d 173, 175 (Miss. 2000); *cf.* Smith v. Smith, 349 So. 2d 529, 530-31 (Miss. 1977) (agreement that trust funds secured alimony was not an implied agreement that alimony survived payor's death).

[106] *In re* Estate of Hodges, 807 So. 2d 438, 443 (Miss. 2002).

ALIMONY

§ 9.02[2]

standard provisions on all financial obligations should be carefully reviewed to avoid unintended consequences.

[2] Lump sum alimony. Lump sum alimony has an interesting history spanning a century and a half. Courts initially used it as a one-time settlement in lieu of permanent alimony. Mid-twentieth century, it began to function as a precursor of equitable distribution. And when equitable distribution was officially adopted in 1994, the term lump sum alimony was also applied to payments made as part of property division.

Since 1994, chancellors have continued to award alimony in lump sum form, usually in small amounts. Several recent appellate decisions, however, appear to hold that lump sum alimony no longer exists, and that lump sum payments in divorce are always a part of property division.[107]

Lump sum alimony is a fixed, certain sum that is vested at the time the order is entered. In contrast to permanent alimony, it cannot be modified, does not terminate at the payee's death or remarriage, and survives the payor's death as an obligation of the estate.

[a] History. As early as 1856, the Mississippi Supreme Court authorized courts to order payment of a lump sum in place of permanent alimony. A husband, who was ordered to pay his wife a sum equal to one-third of his estate, argued that the divorce statute did not authorize lump sum awards. The supreme court rejected his argument – courts have discretion to order a transfer of funds in full settlement of a recipient's claim for permanent support.[108]

In the mid-twentieth century, as a precursor to equitable distribution, courts began to award lump sum alimony to homemakers to recognize contribution. In 1973, the Mississippi Supreme Court followed suit, holding that a homemaker of twenty-four years, who substantially contributed to accumulation of her husband's wealth, was entitled to a lump sum award.[109] Similarly, a wife of many years who worked in her husband's business was entitled to an award that would not only provide basic support, but also reflect "her share in the jointly accumulated assets."[110] The award became, "in a sense[,] an award to a wife of a portion of her husband's estate."[111] During this period, in *Cheatham v. Cheatham*, the supreme court adopted factors for lump sum alimony that resemble the factors now used for equitable distribution.[112]

In 1994, the Mississippi Supreme Court abandoned the title system of property

---

[107] *See infra* § 9.02[b][v].

[108] *See* Armstrong v. Armstrong, 32 Miss. 279 (1856).

[109] *See* Jenkins v. Jenkins, 278 So. 2d 446, 449 (Miss. 1973). The court in *Retzer v. Retzer*, 578 So. 2d 580, 591 (Miss. 1990) cites *Jenkins* as a critical decision in limiting chancellors' discretion in awarding lump sum alimony.

[110] Clark v. Clark, 293 So. 2d 447, 449 (Miss. 1974); *see also* Cleveland v. Cleveland, 600 So. 2d 193, 197 (Miss. 1992) (wife cleaned and did laundry for chiropractic clinic, did all advertising, decorated, attended seminars, was at clinic daily); Tutor v. Tutor, 494 So. 2d 362, 365 (Miss. 1986) (award of $50,000 to wife of many years inadequate where husband had assets of $1 million; wife should receive at least $150,000); Schilling v. Schilling, 452 So. 2d 834, 835-36 (Miss. 1984) (award of one-third of $750,000 estate not excessive); Reeves v. Reeves, 410 So. 2d 1300, 1302-03 (Miss. 1982) (wife who worked in husband's business "entitled" to lump sum award representing share of assets; suggested award equaling 10% of estate).

[111] Retzer v. Retzer, 578 So. 2d 580, 590 (Miss. 1990).

[112] Cheatham v. Cheatham, 537 So. 2d 435, 438 (Miss. 1988).

§ 9.02[2][b]   MISSISSIPPI FAMILY LAW

and adopted equitable distribution for dividing marital assets at divorce. Under the new system, alimony became a means of adjusting financial inequities that remained after property division.[113] In a somewhat confusing development, however, the term "lump sum alimony" was also used to describe offsetting payments under the new system. For example, a $120,000 property division payment to a wife for her share of a business awarded to her husband was "lump sum alimony."[114] To alleviate confusion, the supreme court has suggested that parties use the label "property division" rather than "lump sum alimony" to designate payments used to divide marital assets.[115] Lump sum payments pursuant to property division are discussed in Chapter VI.

[b] Modern lump sum alimony

[i] **Purpose.** As true alimony and not property division, a lump sum payment has sometimes served as a substitute for part or all of a permanent or rehabilitative alimony award. In other cases, lump sum alimony appears to function as an equitable award to a spouse who made substantial long-term contributions to the marriage, but whose contributions cannot be rewarded through property division.[116]

[ii] **Replacement for permanent or rehabilitative support.** Lump sum alimony has replaced other alimony in some cases. A court properly awarded a wife $150,000 in lump sum alimony in lieu of permanent support; courts have discretion to design alimony "to bring finality to the economic relationship."[117] A small award of rehabilitative lump sum alimony and no other spousal support was properly awarded to a wife of ten years who dissipated assets.[118]

[iii] **Supplement to permanent or rehabilitative alimony.** More commonly, a lump sum award supplements permanent or rehabilitative alimony, replacing part rather than all of the ongoing support.[119]

---

[113] *See* Johnston v. Johnston, 722 So. 2d 453, 458 (Miss. 1998) (but reversing for inadequate valuation of husband's separate estate); Crowe v. Crowe, 641 So. 2d 1100, 1103 (Miss. 1994) (court may award lump sum alimony, permanent alimony, or both).

[114] *See* MacDonald v. MacDonald, 698 So. 2d 1079, 1080 (Miss. 1997); *see also* Tillman v. Tillman, 716 So. 2d 1090, 1093 (Miss. 1998) (wife received $18,000 lump sum alimony "equal to one-half of Wallace's salaried savings plan (401k)"); Weeks v. Weeks, 832 So. 2d 583, 586 (Miss. Ct. App. 2002) (award of $50,000 lump sum part of property division).

[115] *See* East v. East, 775 So. 2d 741, 745 (Miss. Ct. App. 2000) ("lump-sum alimony" which actually represents part of equitable distribution of marital estate should be labeled equitable distribution and not lump sum alimony). For an example of a case awarding lump sum alimony as property division and also as alimony, see *Long v. Long*, 734 So. 2d 206, 207 (Miss. Ct. App. 1999) (approximately $77,700 as part of property division and $20,000 as alimony).

[116] In recent cases, however, the appellate courts have questioned whether lump sum alimony is still a viable form of true alimony. See discussion *infra* § 9.02[b][v].

[117] Pearson v. Pearson, 761 So. 2d 157, 166 (Miss. 2000); *see also* Sanderson v. Sanderson, 824 So. 2d 623, 626 (Miss. 2002) ($200,000 lump sum alimony; reversed as inadequate after long marriage where husband's separate assets exceeded $1 million); Johnston v. Johnston, 722 So. 2d 453, 459 (Miss. 1998) (lump sum alimony awarded in lieu of permanent; reversed based on asset valuation).

[118] *See* Sarver v. Sarver, 687 So. 2d 749, 753 (Miss. 1997) (award of $2,500 lump sum alimony to assist wife in transition after divorce).

[119] *See, e.g.*, Mosley v. Mosley, 784 So. 2d 901, 903 (Miss. 2001) ($150/month permanent; $10,000 lump sum); Monroe v. Monroe, 745 So. 2d 249 (Miss. 1999) ($450/month permanent; $12,000 lump sum); Robison v. Robison, 722 So. 2d 601, 604 (Miss. 1998) ($250/month permanent; $250/month lump sum for forty months); Russell v. Russell, 733

ALIMONY

§ 9.02[2][b][iv}

[iv] Based on substantial contribution. Today, long term contributions to asset accumulation are compensated primarily through property division. Nonetheless, a homemaker's contribution has occasionally been recognized through an award of true alimony in a lump sum. For example, a homemaker wife of sixteen years was awarded $50,000 in lump sum alimony in addition to permanent alimony and an equal division of marital assets. She quit her nursing job to provide childcare, sacrificed her education and career for the family, and provided a stable home while her husband accumulated assets.[120] Lump sum awards also provide a means of rewarding contribution when the marital estate is small, but the other spouse has substantial separate income or assets.[121] A wife of twelve years was awarded $175,000 in lump sum alimony from a husband whose separate property business was valued at over a million dollars.[122] Similarly, a wife was awarded lump sum alimony of $75,000, including a cash payment and the husband's assumption of debt; the marital estate was modest but her husband had over a million dollars in separate property investments.[123]

[v] Alimony as lump sum questioned. After the adoption of equitable distribution, courts continued to occasionally award alimony in a lump sum form.[124] At least as late as 2004, courts appeared to use lump sum alimony as a form of true alimony. For example, a wife was awarded lump sum alimony in lieu of permanent alimony.[125] And a wife whose husband was incarcerated was awarded lump sum alimony payable over thirty-six months.[126] Several cases in recent years have suggested that lump sum payments as alimony are no longer recognized. In a 2005 case, the supreme court stated that "lump sum alimony is nothing more than a tool to assist a chancellor in equitable distribution."[127] And in 2010, the court of appeals noted that lump sum alimony is "[n]o more than equitable distribution in the form of cash." The court held that it is improper to award lump sum alimony based upon need and ability to pay

---

So. 2d 858, 860 (Miss. Ct. App. 1999) ($5,000/month permanent; $50,000 rehabilitative lump sum); Flechas v. Flechas, 724 So. 2d 948, 953-54 (Miss. Ct. App. 1998) ($750 rehabilitative; $18,000 lump sum; reversed as inadequate).

[120] Davis v. Davis, 832 So. 2d 492, 499-502 (Miss. 2002); *see also* Craft v. Craft, 825 So. 2d 605, 609 (Miss. 2002) (large lump sum in addition to property division to wife who worked, cared for husband's son, and provided homemaking services, where primary assets were classified as separate); A & L, Inc. v. Grantham, 747 So. 2d 832, 841(Miss. 1999) (affirming lump sum in form of release from tax liability in addition to property division to wife who quit lucrative job to move and support husband's business ventures); Stevens v. Stevens, 924 So. 2d 645, 647-48 (Miss. Ct. App. 2006) (lump sum award to wife who worked without pay in husband's business during marriage); Long v. Long, 734 So. 2d 206, 209 (Miss. Ct. App. 1999) ($20,000 lump sum alimony in addition to equal property division and permanent alimony, based on length of marriage and contribution).

[121] *See* Driste v. Driste, 738 So. 2d 763, 767 (Miss. Ct. App. 1998) (wife of eight years, who quit job and moved, contributed to marital estate, and assisted husband, was entitled to lump sum alimony); *see also* Crowe v. Crowe, 641 So. 2d 1100, 1103 (Miss. 1994) (small award in addition to permanent alimony to disabled wife of ten years who assisted husband in junking business); Flechas v. Flechas, 791 So. 2d 295, 298 (Miss. Ct. App. 2001) (lump sum alimony to wife of six years who left job and moved from another state to marry).

[122] Craft v. Craft, 825 So. 2d 605, 608-11 (Miss. 2002).

[123] Franks v. Franks, 759 So. 2d 1164, 1165 (Miss. 1999); *see also* Palculict v. Palculict, 22 So. 3d 293, 296-297 (Miss. Ct. App. 2009) (wife of nine years, who sacrificed career for husband and who contributed $80,000 separate property to the marriage, entitled to $60,000 in lump sum alimony; husband received only marital asset worth $21,000).

[124] *See* discussion *infra* § 9.06[5].

[125] White v. White, 868 So. 2d 1054 (Miss. Ct. App. 2004).

[126] Avery v. Avery, 864 So. 2d 1054 (Miss. Ct. App. 2004).

[127] Haney v. Haney, 907 So. 2d 948, 952 (Miss. 2005) (en banc); *see also* Yelverton v. Yelverton, 961 So. 2d 19, 25 n.6 (Miss. 2007) (*Cheatham* factors have been "consumed" by *Ferguson* factors).

§ 9.02[2][c]　　　　　　　　　　　　　　　**MISSISSIPPI FAMILY LAW**

alone, and stated that chancellors should consider the *Ferguson* factors, rather than the *Cheatham* factors, in awarding lump sum alimony.[128]

[c] Factors. A separate set of factors for lump sum alimony was announced in 1988 to support its use as an early form of equitable distribution. The factors were set out in *Cheatham v. Cheatham*: (1) substantial contribution to accumulation of the payor's assets by quitting work to become a homemaker or assisting in business; (2) a long marriage; (3) the recipient spouse has no separate income or the separate estate is meager by comparison; and (4) the recipient would lack financial security without the lump sum award.[129] Some opinions analyzing lump sum awards refer to the *Cheatham* factors; others cite the *Armstrong* factors used for permanent and rehabilitative alimony.[130]

[d] Vesting. An award of lump sum alimony is vested at the time the order is entered, even if payment is to be made in installments. The award is final and cannot be modified by either party. The supreme court noted in a 1911 case, "When alimony is commuted to a lump sum, to be paid presently . . . the court takes into consideration the possible remarriage of the wife to a husband able to support her, and any and all other contingencies which might arise."[131] Because the award is vested when ordered, payments cannot be made contingent on some event. A chancellor erred in awarding lump sum alimony payable in installments that would be waived for any month during

---

[128] Dickerson v. Dickerson, 34 So. 3d 637, 645 (Miss. Ct. App. 2010) (lump sum used to accomplish property division).

[129] Cheatham v. Cheatham, 537 So. 2d 435, 438 (Miss. 1988).

[130] Cases citing *Armstrong v. Armstrong*, 618 So. 2d 1278 (Miss. 1993) include: Mosley v. Mosley, 784 So. 2d 901, 909-10 (Miss. 2001) (affirming $10,000 award of lump sum in addition to permanent to working mother based primarily on disparity; fourteen-year marriage); Pearson v. Pearson, 761 So. 2d 157, 166 (Miss. 2000) (affirming $240,000 lump sum award for purpose of rehabilitation to wife of six years who contributed little to asset accumulation); Franks v. Franks, 759 So. 2d 1164, 1165 (Miss. 1999) (lump sum award of $75,000 to working wife, including cash payment and husband's assumption of debt after fourteen-year marriage); Kilpatrick v. Kilpatrick, 732 So. 2d 876, 882 (Miss. 1999) (reversing lump sum award to working payee as inadequate based on disparity in incomes); East v. East, 775 So. 2d 741, 746 (Miss. Ct. App. 2000) (affirming award of $10,000 lump sum alimony plus permanent alimony to disabled spouse after long marriage, based primarily on disparity). Cases citing *Cheatham v. Cheatham*, 537 So. 2d 435 (Miss. 1988) include: Davis v. Davis, 832 So. 2d 492, 494-95, 498-500 (Miss. 2002) (affirming $50,000 award of lump sum in addition to $4,000 permanent alimony to homemaker in ill health after eighteen-year marriage, based on homemaker contribution over sixteen years); Robison v. Robison, 722 So. 2d 601, 602, 604-05 (Miss. 1998) (affirming award of lump sum payable in installments in addition to permanent alimony to wife of twenty-one years based primarily on disparity); Sarver v. Sarver, 687 So. 2d 749, 757 (Miss. 1997) (affirming award of $2,500 as rehabilitative after ten-year marriage in spite of wife's dissipation of assets); Creekmore v. Creekmore, 651 So. 2d 513, 515-18 (Miss. 1995) ($24,000 lump sum award to wife of drug-addicted husband with separate estate inadequate after seven-year marriage, based primarily on disparity); Crowe v. Crowe, 641 So. 2d 1100, 1102-03 (Miss. 1994) (affirming $4,500 lump sum in addition to $300/month permanent to disabled wife after ten-year marriage); Stevens v. Stevens, 924 So. 2d 645, 649 (Miss. Ct. App. 2006); Long v. Long, 734 So. 2d 206, 207, 209-10 (Miss. Ct. App. 1999) (affirming $20,000 lump sum award in addition to permanent alimony to homemaker wife of twenty-eight years); Driste v. Driste, 738 So. 2d 763, 767-68 (Miss. Ct. App. 1998) (reversing as inadequate award of $20,000 lump sum in addition to $750/month rehabilitative for eighteen months to wife of eight years who quit work to assist husband in business); Flechas v. Flechas, 724 So. 2d 948, 953-54 (Miss. Ct. App. 1998) (reversing as inadequate award of $18,000 lump sum in addition to $750/month rehabilitative alimony for one year to wife of six years who quit job and moved to act as homemaker).

[131] Guess v. Smith, 56 So. 166, 167 (Miss. 1911); *see also* McDonald v. McDonald, 683 So. 2d 929, 931 (Miss. 1996) (award is not "in the nature of continuing support, but rather a property transfer which is vested in the recipient spouse at the time said alimony is awarded"); Miller v. Miller, 159 So. 112, 119-20 (Miss. 1935) (lump sum alimony is a settlement of all wife's claims against husband's estate).

ALIMONY § 9.02[2][e]

which the wife lived in the marital home.[132] The obligation does not terminate at remarriage and survives the death of either party as a debt of the payor's estate and an asset of the payee's estate.[133]

[e] Modification. In contrast to permanent alimony, lump sum alimony cannot be modified based on a change in the parties' circumstances[134] absent a contractual provision to that effect or fraud.[135] The payment is "a final settlement between the husband and wife . . . which cannot be changed or modified on the application of either party for any cause whatever."[136] The parties' post-divorce circumstances are irrelevant – a husband's decision to leave his medical practice to enroll in school did not affect his obligation to complete payment of lump sum installments.[137]

[f] Termination. Lump sum alimony does not terminate at the payor's death, even if the award is payable in installments. It is a binding obligation of the payor's estate.[138] Similarly, lump sum alimony does not terminate if the recipient remarries or dies. Any remaining installments are payable to the recipient's estate.[139] Nor does lump sum alimony terminate upon a recipient's cohabitation.[140]

[g] Payment in installments. In 1946, the Mississippi Supreme Court authorized payment of lump sum alimony in a series of installments. The court encouraged chancellors to order installment payments if immediate payment would unfairly burden a payor.[141] Courts should weigh the benefit of immediate payment to the recipient with the burden on the payor – ordering immediate payment by a payor who lacked substantial liquid assets was error.[142] Payment in installments does not alter the characteristics of lump sum alimony. The award still vests when it is ordered and cannot be modified.[143] Because lump sum installment payments may resemble permanent alimony, it is important to avoid ambiguity by labeling the payment as lump

---

[132] Faerber v. Faerber, 13 So. 3d 853, 862-863 n.12 (Miss. Ct. App. 2009).

[133] Hubbard v. Hubbard, 656 So. 2d 124, 129 (Miss. 1995).

[134] Hubbard v. Hubbard, 656 So. 2d 124, 129 (Miss. 1995); Armstrong v. Armstrong, 618 So. 2d 1278, 1281 (Miss. 1993); Carroll v. Carroll, 976 So. 2d 880, 887 (Miss. Ct. App. 2007); Beezley v. Beezley, 917 So. 2d 803, 806 (Miss. Ct. App. 2005); Chroniger v. Chroniger, 914 So. 2d 311, 314 (Miss. Ct. App. 2005).

[135] Norton v. Norton, 742 So. 2d 126, 129 (Miss. 1999) (holding modified by Dodson v. Singing River Hosp. Sys., 839 So. 2d 530 (Miss. 2003)).

[136] Wray v. Wray, 394 So. 2d 1341, 1344 (Miss. 1981).

[137] McDonald v. McDonald, 683 So. 2d 929, 934-35 (Miss. 1996); *see also* East v. East, 493 So. 2d 927, 931 (Miss. 1986) (lump sum alimony improperly labeled as permanent cannot be modified).

[138] Creekmore v. Creekmore, 651 So. 2d 513, 518 (Miss. 1995); Hubbard v. Hubbard, 656 So. 2d 124, 129 (Miss. 1995); Armstrong v. Armstrong, 618 So. 2d 1278, 1281(Miss. 1993).

[139] Wray v. Wray, 394 So. 2d 1341, 1344-45 (Miss. 1981) (overruling Aldridge v. Aldridge, 27 So. 2d 884, 879-80 (Miss. 1946), which held that installment payments terminate at recipient's death or remarriage); *see also* Maxcy v. Estate of Maxcy, 485 So. 2d 1077, 1078 (Miss. 1986); Carroll v. Carroll, 976 So. 2d 880, 887 (Miss. Ct. App. 2007).

[140] Chroniger v. Chroniger, 914 So. 2d 311, 315 (Miss. Ct. App. 2005) (three years of payments were lump sum alimony that did not terminate upon ex-wife's cohabitation).

[141] *See* Aldridge v. Aldridge, 27 So. 2d 884, 885-86 (Miss. 1946).

[142] Aldridge v. Aldridge, 27 So. 2d 884, 885-86 (Miss. 1946) (approving lump sum of $7,500).

[143] *See* McDonald v. McDonald, 683 So. 2d 929, 931 (Miss. 1996); Butler v. Hinson, 386 So. 2d 716, 717 (Miss. 1980) (lump sum alimony payable in installments was not terminable at wife's remarriage, even though chancellor stated he intended alimony to be permanent).

§ 9.02[3]   **MISSISSIPPI FAMILY LAW**

sum and stating a fixed total amount for the award.[144]

[3] Rehabilitative alimony. In 1995, the Mississippi Supreme Court recognized rehabilitative alimony as a separate form of spousal support.[145] Rehabilitative alimony closely resembles permanent alimony, but has a fixed ending date and is awarded for a different reason – to provide transitional support to a spouse who may reenter the workforce. Rehabilitative alimony has also been used to award time-limited support apart from rehabilitative purposes, functioning similarly to what some states label "transitional" or "time-limited" alimony.

[a] Purpose. Rehabilitative alimony is "an equitable mechanism which allows a party needing assistance to become self-supporting without becoming destitute in the interim."[146] Unlike permanent and lump sum alimony, rehabilitative alimony is not intended as an equalizer between the parties. Instead, it is designed to provide temporary support for a spouse who may become employed after a period of training or job search.[147] In several cases, the courts have stated that a rehabilitative award is to prevent a spouse from "being destitute" rather than to provide for the marriage standard of living.[148]

A review of rehabilitative alimony awards indicates that Mississippi courts also award rehabilitative alimony as transitional support for recipients who have already reached full earning capacity.[149] This use of the award is consistent with the national trend to award time-limited alimony except in long marriages.[150] In one case, the supreme court suggested that an award of rehabilitative alimony to a recipient working at full earning capacity may be error.[151] But the court of appeals rejected a husband's argument that an award of rehabilitative alimony to a working wife was error, noting that awards have been made to spouses already in the workforce.[152]

---

[144] *See infra* § 9.03 (discussion regarding ambiguous awards).

[145] *See* Hubbard v. Hubbard, 656 So. 2d 124, 129-30 (Miss. 1995); *see also* Waldron v. Waldron, 743 So. 2d 1064, 1065 (Miss. Ct. App. 1999). *But cf.* Gatlin v. Gatlin, 161 So. 2d 782, 783 (Miss. 1964) (eighteen months alimony resembling rehabilitative granted to wife at fault for a "period of readjustment").

[146] Hubbard v. Hubbard, 656 So. 2d 124, 130 (Miss. 1995).

[147] Hubbard v. Hubbard, 656 So. 2d 124, 130 (Miss. 1995); *see also* LeBlanc v. Andrews, 931 So. 2d 683, 686 (Miss. Ct. App. 2006) (purpose of rehabilitative alimony to allow party to become self-supporting); Roberts v. Roberts, 924 So. 2d 550, 554 (Miss. Ct. App. 2005) (rehabilitative alimony designed to allow recipient to return to workplace; properly awarded to wife with earning capacity equal to husband); Waldron v. Waldron, 743 So. 2d 1064, 1065 (Miss. Ct. App. 1999) (permanent alimony based on duty of support; rehabilitative designed to allow reentry into workplace); Flechas v. Flechas, 724 So. 2d 948, 954 (Miss. Ct. App. 1998).

[148] *See* Hubbard v. Hubbard, 656 So. 2d 124, 130 (Miss. 1995); Waldron v. Waldron, 743 So. 2d 1064, 1065 (Miss. Ct. App. 1999) (permanent alimony based on duty of support; rehabilitative designed to allow reentry into workplace); *cf.* Flechas v. Flechas, 724 So. 2d 948, 954 (Miss. Ct. App. 1998) (rehabilitative alimony not intended as an equalizer).

[149] *See infra* § 9.06[4].

[150] *See supra* § 9.01[3].

[151] *See* Holley v. Holley, 892 So. 2d 183, 186 (Miss. 2004) (remanding for findings of fact; suggesting that rehabilitative alimony to accountant wife may be wrong type of alimony); *see also* McIntosh v. McIntosh, 977 So. 2d 1257, 1272 (Miss. Ct. App. 2008) (wife's claim for alimony was flawed since she was employed full-time as a schoolteacher); Beezley v. Beezley, 917 So. 2d 803, 806 (Miss. Ct. App. 2005) (alimony provision not rehabilitative because wife did not intend to reenter workforce).

[152] Brady v. Brady, 14 So. 3d 823, 826 (Miss. Ct. App. 2009) (wife of seven months awarded $1,500 a month rehabilitative alimony, payable until thirty-six months after the marital home was sold).

ALIMONY § 9.02[3][b]

[b] Factors. An award of rehabilitative alimony is based on the same factors used to award permanent alimony: (1) the parties' income and expenses; (2) the parties' health and earning capacity; (3) the needs of each party; (4) the obligations and assets of each party; (5) the length of the marriage; (6) the presence or absence of minor children in the home, which may require child care; (7) the parties' ages; (8) the parties' standard of living during the marriage and at the time support is determined; (9) tax consequences of the spousal support order; (10) fault or misconduct; (11) dissipation of assets by either party; and (12) any other factor deemed to be "just and equitable."[153]

[c] Vesting. Rehabilitative alimony vests as it comes due.[154] A payment that is due and vested cannot be modified or forgiven and is a charge on the payor's estate.[155] Future payments are not vested and may be modified based on a change in circumstances.[156] Although payments are usually set for a fixed period, the court of appeals affirmed an award of rehabilitative alimony to last until thirty-six months after the marital home was sold.[157]

[d] Modification. Rehabilitative alimony may be modified based on a change in circumstances.[158] No Mississippi case was found in which rehabilitative alimony was modified during the term originally set for payment, probably because the awards are typically for no more than two or three years.[159]

[e] Conversion to periodic. The Mississippi Court of Appeals held in 2004 that rehabilitative alimony may be converted to permanent alimony,[160] The court reversed a chancellor's conversion for procedural reasons. However, the court held that a recipient of rehabilitative alimony may seek modification of the award to one for permanent alimony. Conversion to permanent alimony should be based upon a chancellor's written findings of a material change in the recipient's circumstances justifying conversion.[161]

[f] Extension. In holding that rehabilitative alimony may be converted to permanent, the court of appeals in dicta suggested that a chancellor may also reserve jurisdiction to extend rehabilitative alimony for an additional period. It is not clear from

---

[153] *See* Turnley v. Turnley, 726 So. 2d 1258, 1267 (Miss. Ct. App. 1998) (citing *Armstrong* factors as basis for awarding rehabilitative alimony); *see also* Flechas v. Flechas, 724 So. 2d 948, 951-52 (Miss. Ct. App. 1998).

[154] Turnley v. Turnley, 726 So. 2d 1258, 1266 (Miss. Ct. App. 1998).

[155] *See infra* § 9.09[3][b].

[156] Hubbard v. Hubbard, 656 So. 2d 124, 129-30 (Miss. 1995); Wolfe v. Wolfe, 766 So. 2d 123, 128-29 (Miss. Ct. App. 2000).

[157] Brady v. Brady, 14 So. 3d 823, 826 (Miss. Ct. App. 2009) (noting that award was "unconventional").

[158] Overstreet v. Overstreet, 692 So. 2d 88, 91-92 (Miss. 1997); Hubbard v. Hubbard, 656 So. 2d 124, 129-30 (Miss. 1995); Wolfe v. Wolfe, 766 So. 2d 123, 128-29 (Miss. Ct. App. 2000); Waldron v. Waldron, 743 So. 2d 1064, 1065 (Miss. Ct. App. 1999).

[159] *See infra* § 9.06[4].

[160] The chancellor awarded six months of rehabilitative alimony, reserving jurisdiction to revisit the award in six months. The conversion was initiated by the payee's motion for a review of the award, rather than by a petition for modification of the award. *See* Oster v. Oster, 876 So. 2d 428, 421-32 (Miss. Ct. App. 2004).

[161] *See* Oster v. Oster, 876 So. 2d 428, 431-32 (Miss. Ct. App. 2004). See *Rickenbach v. Kosinksi*, 32 So. 3d 732, 735-36 (Fla. Dist. App. 2010), for a detailed discussion of the Florida test for converting rehabilitative alimony to permanent.

§ 9.02[3][g]   **MISSISSIPPI FAMILY LAW**

the opinion whether rehabilitative alimony may also be extended in the absence of a reservation of jurisdiction. However, it would seem logical that if a material change can support conversion to permanent alimony, it could also support extension for a fixed period of time.[162]

[g] Termination. Rehabilitative alimony terminates upon the death of the payor or payee.[163] In several cases, the appellate courts stated that rehabilitative alimony also terminates upon remarriage of the payee.[164] However, in 1999 the court of appeals held that "automatic termination upon the recipient spouse's remarriage is not part of the current definition of rehabilitative periodic alimony."[165] Although termination upon remarriage is no longer a characteristic of rehabilitative alimony, a chancellor may expressly order that an award terminate upon remarriage.[166] Parties agreeing to payment of rehabilitative alimony should take care to state whether the award survives the recipient's remarriage. Presumably, rehabilitative alimony that survives remarriage would also survive cohabitation.

[4] Reimbursement alimony. The Mississippi Supreme Court added a fourth form of alimony in 1999. Reimbursement alimony is awarded to a spouse who supported the other through school and whose contribution cannot be recognized through property division. Reimbursement is made in the form of lump sum alimony – it is vested, is not modifiable, and does not terminate upon the parties' death or remarriage.

[a] Purpose. Reimbursement alimony may be awarded when parties divorce shortly after one spouse has supported the other through school and before the couple has accumulated assets reflecting the educational investment.[167] In *Guy v. Guy*, the supreme court rejected a husband's argument that his wife's nursing degree was marital property subject to equitable distribution. But the court acknowledged the potential injury to a spouse who receives a divorce complaint shortly after supporting the other through professional school. The supporting spouse "postponed, as it were, present consumption and a higher standard of living, for the future prospect of greater support and material benefits."[168] To remedy the loss, the supporting spouse may be reimbursed for direct expenditures toward education such as tuition and books, as well as the cost of housing, food, clothing, and other living expenses. The spouse seeking

---

[162] *See* Oster v. Oster, 876 So. 2d 428, 431-32 (Miss. Ct. App. 2004) (court had reserved jurisdiction; decision does not address modification if jurisdiction not reserved).

[163] Overstreet v. Overstreet, 692 So. 2d 88, 91 (Miss. 1997).

[164] *See* Bridges v. McCracken, 724 So. 2d 1086, 1087 (Miss. Ct. App. 1998); *see also* Overstreet v. Overstreet, 692 So. 2d 88, 91 (Miss. 1997); Neville v. Neville, 734 So. 2d 352, 358 (Miss. Ct. App. 1999) (modifiable and terminates at remarriage).

[165] Waldron v. Waldron, 743 So. 2d 1064, 1065 (Miss. Ct. App. 1999).

[166] *See* Waldron v. Waldron, 743 So. 2d 1064, 1065 (Miss. Ct. App. 1999).

[167] Guy v. Guy, 736 So. 2d 1042, 1046 (Miss. 1999). The role of fault in reimbursement alimony is not completely clear. The court at one point states that reimbursement can be ordered "where one spouse supports the other through school and *is then divorced* after the supported spouse earns a degree." *Id.* (emphasis added); *see also* Beezley v. Beezley, 917 So. 2d 803, 806 (Miss. Ct. App. 2005) (monthly support of $5,000 was not reimbursement alimony; almost twenty years since husband finished residency).

[168] Guy v. Guy, 736 So. 2d 1042, 1045 (Miss. 1999) (quoting Mahoney v. Mahoney, 453 A.2d 527, 533-34 (N.J. 1982)).

ALIMONY § 9.02[4][b]

reimbursement must provide more than simply an estimate of expenditures.[169]

[b] Factors. The court did not provide an explicit list of factors governing reimbursement alimony awards. However, the test appears to require: (1) a spouse's support of the other through school; (2) the expectation of increased earnings; and (3) a divorce that occurs shortly after schooling and before a financial return on the education is realized. The American Law Institute Principles of Family Dissolution suggests a similar award to compensate a spouse who provides support for training that substantially enhances the other's earning capacity, if the education was completed within a short period prior to divorce. The ALI proposal excludes educational support that does not enhance earning capacity.[170]

[c] Characteristics. The court in *Guy* remanded the case for a determination of the amount of lump sum alimony necessary to reimburse the supporting spouse.[171] Presumably, reimbursement alimony should have the characteristics of lump sum alimony – it should vest at the time of the order, be nonmodifiable, and should not terminate upon the death of either party or the recipient's remarriage.[172]

[d] Amount. The court in *Guy* stated that a supporting spouse may be reimbursed for direct expenditures toward education such as tuition and books as well as the costs of housing, food, clothing, and other living expenses. Under the American Law Institute proposal, a supporting spouse should be reimbursed for direct expenditures for education plus the student spouse's share of family expenses during the period of support, less any amount the student provided toward support. The proposal also states that the resulting amount should be adjusted for changes in the value of the dollar.[173] The ALI Principles provide that the award should be made in a lump sum payment or by adjusting equitable distribution. If either would be a substantial hardship on the payor, the award may be made in fixed, nonmodifiable, and nonterminable installment payments.[174]

§ 9.03 HYBRID AND AMBIGUOUS AWARDS

Historically, an alimony award could not combine characteristics of permanent and lump sum alimony, even if the court or parties clearly intended to structure a hybrid form. Recent decisions permit creation of some hybrid awards by agreement, but the extent to which the forms may be altered is unclear.

---

[169] Guy v. Guy, 736 So. 2d 1042, 1046 (Miss. 1999).
[170] A.L.I. PRINCIPLES, *supra* note 6, § 5.13.
[171] Guy v. Guy, 736 So. 2d 1042, 1046-47 (Miss. 1999).
[172] *See supra* § 9.02[2].
[173] A.L.I. PRINCIPLES, *supra* note 6, § 5.13.
[174] A.L.I. PRINCIPLES, *supra* note 6, §§ 5.13, 5.14.

§ 9.03[1]   MISSISSIPPI FAMILY LAW

[1] Traditional approach. Until recently, an alimony award could not contain elements of both permanent and lump sum alimony – ambiguous awards were labeled as either permanent or lump sum and then given the characteristics traditionally associated with that form. For example, court-ordered permanent alimony of $600 a month for seven years or until remarriage or death was held to be permanent and not subject to the seven-year cut-off date.[175] Cases typically state that ambiguous awards will be labeled permanent unless the order contains "clear and express" language indicating that the award is lump sum alimony.[176] On the other hand, courts have also stated that there is no set form for lump sum alimony[177] and that no technical words are required.[178] It is not even essential that the words "lump sum alimony" be used.[179]

For an ambiguous award to be classified as lump sum alimony, it is essential that the award can be calculated as an exact amount. An award of lump sum alimony in the amount of one-half of the husband's earnings was characterized by the supreme court as periodic alimony subject to modification – a fixed dollar amount is a critical feature of lump sum alimony.[180] A review of cases suggests that specifically stating the total dollar figure in the alimony provision may also be important to classifying an award as lump sum alimony. Ambiguous awards that did not specifically state the total amount were held to be permanent alimony, even though the total could be calculated.[181] In contrast, ambiguous awards that stated a total dollar amount and provided a fixed termination date were interpreted as lump sum alimony.[182] And in two cases, the fact that a specific dollar amount was listed supported a finding of lump sum alimony even though the award was labeled permanent.[183]

The purpose of an award may also be critical in classification. If an ambiguous award is clearly related to property division, it will be deemed lump sum. An award of

---

[175] *See* Cleveland v. Cleveland, 600 So. 2d 193, 196-97 (Miss. 1992).

[176] *See* Bowe v. Bowe, 557 So. 2d 793, 795 (Miss. 1990); Bonderer v. Robinson, 502 So. 2d 314, 316 (Miss. 1986); Sharplin v. Sharplin, 465 So. 2d 1072, 1073 (Miss. 1985); Wray v. Wray, 394 So. 2d 1341, 1345 (Miss. 1981); Chroniger v. Chroniger, 914 So. 2d 311, 315 (Miss. Ct. App. 2005) (ambiguous alimony award will be treated as periodic rather than lump sum).

[177] *See* Barrett v. United States, 74 F.3d 661, 665 (5th Cir. 1996) (holding that two payments ordered by court were lump sum).

[178] *See* Bowe v. Bowe, 557 So. 2d 793, 795 (Miss. 1990).

[179] Cunningham v. Lanier, 589 So. 2d 133, 137 (Miss. 1991); Bowe v. Bowe, 557 So. 2d 793, 795 (Miss. 1990); Smith v. Little, 834 So. 2d 54, 58 (Miss. Ct. App. 2002).

[180] West v. West, 891 So. 2d 203 (Miss. 2004).

[181] *See* Wray v. Wray, 394 So. 2d 1341, 1345 (Miss. 1981) (court-ordered award of $400/month for twenty-four months was permanent because total amount due was not stated; terminated upon remarriage). *But see* Dufour v. Dufour, 631 So. 2d 192, 195 (Miss. 1994) (award of $600/month "periodic transitional alimony" for thirty months, was lump sum rather than permanent alimony).

[182] *See* Bowe v. Bowe, 557 So. 2d 793, 795 (Miss. 1990) (court-ordered award of $5,000, to be paid in installments of $200, held to be lump sum alimony); Maxcy v. Estate of Maxcy, 485 So. 2d 1077, 1078 (Miss. 1986) (award of $16,000, payable in four installments, "constituting one-half of the assets" was clearly lump sum payment and could be recovered by wife's estate following her death).

[183] *See* Creekmore v. Creekmore, 651 So. 2d 513, 518 (Miss. 1995) (court-ordered "permanent" alimony of $12,000, payable in twenty-four monthly installments to terminate at payor's death, was actually lump sum alimony); Neville v. Neville, 734 So. 2d 352, 353, 357-58 (Miss. Ct. App. 1999) (award of "periodic rehabilitative alimony" of $1,400/month for ten years to survive remarriage was recast by court of appeals as lump sum alimony because clear purpose of award was equitable compensation rather than rehabilitation); *see also* Beezley v. Beezley, 917 So. 2d 803, 807 (Miss. Ct. App. 2005) (labels used by parties are not controlling); *cf.* Smith v. Little, 834 So. 2d 54, 58-59 (Miss. Ct. App. 2002) (husband's obligation to make payments on Jaguar used by wife until December 2007 unless she remarried, in which case payments would cease in December 2005, was held to be non-modifiable lump sum alimony).

ALIMONY   § 9.03[2]

$16,000, payable in four installments, "constituting one-half of the assets" was clearly a lump sum payment and could be recovered by the wife's estate following her death.[184] In contrast, a three-year award clearly intended as temporary support was rehabilitative and not lump sum alimony.[185]

Assigning a specific label to an ambiguous award usually provides a gap-filler for characteristics not addressed in the judgment. For example, the designation makes clear whether an award terminates at remarriage or survives the payor's death.[186] However, when an ambiguous award includes characteristics that conflict with the court's classification, those characteristics are disregarded under the traditional approach. A chancellor's award of "permanent" alimony of $12,000, to be paid over twenty-four months and terminable at the payor's death, was classified as lump sum alimony. As a result, the award survived the payor's death in spite of the chancellor's order to the contrary.[187] And an award of lump sum alimony of one-half of the payor's income was reclassified as permanent; the award was therefore modifiable even though the parties' agreement prohibited modification.[188]

[2] Hybrids created by agreement. Two decisions signal a shift in Mississippi appellate courts' willingness to recognize hybrid forms of alimony.[189] Divorcing spouses may now agree to lump sum alimony payable in installments that terminate at the death of the parties or upon remarriage. In one case, the supreme court upheld an agreement for lump sum alimony that would terminate at the payor's death.[190] In another, the court of appeals approved an agreement for lump sum alimony to terminate at the recipient's death or remarriage but which would survive the payor's death.[191] Nonetheless, the supreme court warned that while parties should be able to contract for alimony that suits their needs, "parties and judges should be mindful of the traditional characteristics of lump sum and [permanent] alimony in drafting."[192] The court reaffirmed that if the intent of the parties is unclear, payments will be presumed to be permanent alimony.[193]

[3] A word of caution. It is unclear to what extent the traditional characteristics of alimony may be altered. Parties may alter permanent alimony to survive the payor's

---

[184] Maxcy v. Estate of Maxcy, 485 So. 2d 1077, 1078 (Miss. 1986); *see also* Smith v. Little, 834 So. 2d 54, 59-60 (Miss. Ct. App. 2002) (payments related to house were clearly to equalize property settlement, not alimony).

[185] Wolfe v. Wolfe, 766 So. 2d 123, 129 (Miss. Ct. App. 2000) (also important that no fixed dollar amount was included).

[186] *See* Wray v. Wray, 394 So. 2d 1341, 1345 (Miss. 1981); *see also* Sharplin v. Sharplin, 465 So. 2d 1072, 1072-73 (Miss. 1985) (agreed alimony for thirty-six months deemed permanent; no lump sum stated).

[187] Creekmore v. Creekmore, 651 So. 2d 513, 518 (Miss. 1995) (payment of definite amount in specific installments was lump sum, not permanent alimony).

[188] West v. West, 891 So. 2d 203 (Miss. 2004).

[189] At least one earlier case upheld agreed hybrid alimony. An agreement for non-modifiable payments of $5,000/month to survive the husband's death or the wife's remarriage, but to terminate at her death, was upheld in *East v. East*, 493 So. 2d 927, 929, 932-33 (Miss. 1986).

[190] *See* McDonald v. McDonald, 683 So. 2d 929, 931-33 (Miss. 1996).

[191] *See* Elliott v. Rogers, 775 So. 2d 1285 (Miss. Ct. App. 2000).

[192] *See* MacDonald v. MacDonald, 683 So. 2d 929, 932 (Miss. 1996).

[193] *See* McDonald v. McDonald, 683 So. 2d 929, 933 (Miss. 1996).

§ 9.03[4]   MISSISSIPPI FAMILY LAW

death[194] but may not agree that it is nonmodifiable.[195] Parties may also create lump sum alimony that terminates at the death of either party or remarriage.[196] But a court may not award lump sum alimony that is contingent on a particular event.[197] Parties or courts may provide that rehabilitative alimony terminates at remarriage.[198] Beyond these already approved variations, parties should proceed with caution in creating hybrids. In addition, it is critical to specify the exact characteristics of a hybrid award. The agreement should indicate whether the provision can be modified[199] and whether it survives the payor's death, the payee's death, or the payee's remarriage.

[4] Ambiguity: Alimony, property division, or child support. In some cases, it is unclear whether a particular payment is intended to be alimony, part of property division, or child support. The classification will affect whether the payment is modifiable or terminates at death, remarriage, or cohabitation, and how it is treated for tax purposes. For example, a settlement agreement provided that, in addition to child support, the husband would pay to his former wife $5,000 a month "with no limitations." The provision stated that it was not alimony; yet, payments continued indefinitely. The provision appeared in the child support rather than property division section of agreement. The court of appeals held that the provision was ambiguous and required introduction of parole evidence regarding the parties' intent.[200]

§ 9.04 TEST FOR AWARDING ALIMONY

Since the mid-1950s, the Mississippi Supreme Court has provided a list of factors to guide chancellors in making alimony awards.[201] The alimony factors were most recently refined in 1993 in *Armstrong v. Armstrong.*[202] The *Armstrong* factors govern both permanent and rehabilitative alimony awards and in many cases are used to determine lump sum awards. The factors are stated generally, without guidance as to how the factors should be weighed to determine the appropriate type of award, the proper amount, and the proper duration.

---

[194] *See In re* Estate of Kennington, 204 So. 2d 444, 449 (Miss. 1967). *But see* East v. East, 493 So. 2d 927, 931 (Miss. 1986) ("The parties cannot by contract deprive, and it is doubtful if any court has the authority to deprive itself of the future authority to modify ordinary permanent alimony, *or make it continue beyond the remarriage of the wife or the death of the husband.*") (emphasis added).

[195] *See supra* § 9.02[1][e].

[196] *See* Elliott v. Rogers, 775 So. 2d 1285, 1289-90 (Miss. Ct. App. 2000).

[197] Faerber v. Faerber, 13 So. 3d 853, 862-863 (Miss. Ct. App. 2009).

[198] *See* Waldron v. Waldron, 743 So. 2d 1064, 1065 (Miss. Ct. App. 1999).

[199] One of the hybrid cases suggests in dicta that hybrid lump sum alimony may be modifiable under some circumstances. The court noted that an agreed lump sum award with some characteristics of permanent alimony is not generally modifiable but might be modifiable based on "equitable considerations" not presented in that case. *See* Elliott v. Rogers, 775 So. 2d 1285, 1289-90 (Miss. Ct. App. 2000).

[200] Beezley v. Beezley, 917 So. 2d 803, 807 (Miss. Ct. App. 2005); *see also* Carroll v. Carroll, 976 So. 2d 880, 887-88 (Miss. Ct. App. 2007) (award of $4,000 /month "until further court order" remanded for clarification whether part of property division or alimony); *cf.* Pierce v. Pierce, 42 So. 3d 658 (Miss. Ct. App. 2010) (provision for $700 a month in alimony until stepdaughter graduated would be interpreted by IRS as child support).

[201] The court first articulated alimony factors in *Brabham v. Brabham,* 84 So. 2d 147, 153 (Miss. 1955). Before *Brabham,* alimony was based primarily on fault and the marital standard of living. *See supra* § 9.01.

[202] Armstrong v. Armstrong, 618 So. 2d 1278 (Miss. 1993).

ALIMONY   § 9.04[1]

[1] The *Armstrong* factors. In awarding alimony, courts are to consider: (1) the parties' income and expenses; (2) the parties' health and earning capacity; (3) the needs of each party; (4) the obligations and assets of each party; (5) the length of the marriage; (6) the presence or absence of minor children in the home, which may require child care; (7) the parties' ages; (8) the parties' standard of living during the marriage and at the time support is determined; (9) tax consequences of the spousal support order; (10) fault or misconduct; (11) dissipation of assets by either party; and (12) any other factor deemed to be "just and equitable."[203]

[2] Findings of fact. Until recently, an alimony award not supported by findings of fact under *Armstrong* was likely to be reversed. The appellate courts held in a number of cases that failure to provide an on-the-record discussion of the factors governing permanent alimony was manifest error.[204] Similarly, failure to make findings of fact regarding rehabilitative alimony has caused reversal.[205] Findings of fact are also required in actions to modify alimony awards.[206] In addition, the court of appeals held that when divorcing parties agree to property division and submit the issue of alimony to the court, the court must conduct a *Ferguson* analysis prior to addressing the *Armstrong* alimony factors.[207]

Recently, however, the appellate courts have declined to reverse alimony decisions for failure to make *Armstrong* findings. In 2007, the court of appeals held "[w]hen the chancellor fails to address all factors on the record, we are not required to remand the case, and should not, so long as all facts are available to us so as to allow an equitable determination to be made."[208] The appellate courts have also stated that a chancellor

---

[203] Armstrong v. Armstrong, 618 So. 2d 1278 (Miss. 1993); *see* Barker v. Barker, 996 So. 2d 161, 163-64 (Miss. Ct. App. 2008) (*Armstrong* factors as basis for awarding rehabilitative alimony); Turnley v. Turnley, 726 So. 2d 1258, 1267 (Miss. Ct. App. 1998) (citing *Armstrong* factors as basis for awarding rehabilitative alimony); *see also* Flechas v. Flechas, 724 So. 2d 948, 951-52 (Miss. Ct. App. 1998).

[204] *See* Henderson v. Henderson, 703 So. 2d 262, 266 (Miss. 1997) (chancellor's award of $683 a month permanent alimony reversed for failure to make findings); Gray v. Gray, 909 So. 2d 108, 112 (Miss. Ct. App. 2005) (reversing award of alimony for failure to make specific fact findings); Weeks v. Weeks, 832 So. 2d 583, 587 (Miss. Ct. App. 2002); *see also* Haney v. Haney, 881 So. 2d 862 (Miss. Ct. App. 2003) (court's consideration of alimony must include analysis as well as findings of fact), *cert. granted*, 878 So. 2d 67 (Miss. 2004), *and aff'd in part, rev'd in part*, 907 So. 2d 948 (Miss. 2005); *see also* Smith v. Smith, 856 So. 2d 717, 719 (Miss. Ct. App. 2003) (reversing because court discussed factors in *Hemsley v. Hemsley*, 639 So. 2d 909 (Miss. 1994), which govern reasonableness of the amount of an award, rather than *Armstrong* factors, which control whether alimony should be awarded at all).

[205] *See* Holley v. Holley, 892 So. 2d 183, 186 (Miss. Ct. App. 2004); Flechas v. Flechas, 724 So. 2d 948, 954 (Miss. Ct. App. 1998).

[206] *See* Steiner v. Steiner, 788 So. 2d 771, 776 (Miss. 2001); Jones v. Jones, 917 So. 2d 95, 99-100 (Miss. Ct. App. 2005) (court erred in modifying decree to increase alimony without applying *Armstrong* factors).

[207] *See* Cosentino v. Cosentino, 986 So. 2d 1065, 1068 (Miss. Ct. App. 2008) (particularly, factor six, the extent to which property division eliminates the need for alimony, and factor seven, the parties' financial needs, should be considered); Cosentino v. Cosentino, 912 So. 2d 1130, 1132-33 (Miss. Ct. App. 2005). *But cf.* Tritle v. Tritle, 956 So. 2d 369, 380-81 (Miss. Ct. App. 2007) (court's discussion of parties' agreed property division before awarding alimony met requirement).

[208] Roberson v. Roberson, 949 So. 2d 866, 869 (Miss. Ct. App. 2007) (noting that failure to make findings "creates difficulty" for the court); *see also* Dorsey v. Dorsey, 972 So. 2d 48, 54 (Miss. Ct. App. 2008) (reversal not required if sufficient facts in record to support decision); Ghoston v. Ghoston, 979 So. 2d 719 (Miss. Ct. App. 2007) (same); Street v. Street, 936 So. 2d 1002, 1013 (Miss. Ct. App. 2006) (lack of *Armstrong* analysis does not require reversal where original judgment and amended judgment provided sufficient support for opinion); Stevens v. Stevens, 924 So. 2d 645, 648-49 (Miss. Ct. App. 2006) (unnecessary that court recite *Armstrong* factors if opinion clearly details facts related to each factor); Stribling v. Stribling, 906 So. 2d 863, 871 (Miss. Ct. App. 2005) (alimony award affirmed although no findings

§ 9.04[3]   MISSISSIPPI FAMILY LAW

need not individually list each factor, and may consider the factors as an "overall combination."[209] In one case, the court affirmed an alimony denial even in the absence of findings of fact, because the similar factors for equitable distribution were discussed thoroughly.[210] The supreme court has also stated that it will presume on appeal that a chancellor has considered all factors and, if the facts are available in the record, will review the facts without remanding for specific findings.[211] If the record is not sufficient for an independent review, the case will be reversed for failure to make findings.[212] For example, a denial of alimony was remanded for failure to make findings; the chancellor simply found that the wife was not working at full capacity and was receiving thirty to forty dollars a month from a man who stayed with her several nights a week.[213] And an award of alimony and child support was reversed for failure to make findings regarding the husband's income.[214]

[3] Overview of factor discussion. This discussion takes the liberty of rearranging the order in which the *Armstrong* factors are presented. The twelve factors are grouped into two subsets that address different aspects of alimony awards. The first set of factors assists courts in identifying a disparity in the parties' resources after equitable distribution – the parties' incomes, reasonable expenses, free use of home or car, custodial arrangements, assets, and earning capacity. The second set of factors guide courts in determining whether a disparity should be reduced by awarding alimony. These include marriage length, fault, dissipation of assets, age, health, and any other equitable concerns. A final factor – tax consequences – affects the actual value of the award.

If the first set of factors does not show a disparity, no alimony should be awarded. If a disparity exists, a court's analysis of the second set of factors may lead it to award permanent alimony, rehabilitative or limited term alimony, lump sum alimony, some combination of the three, or to deny alimony altogether.[215]

The factors are stated generally, without specific guidelines for the type and amount of alimony appropriate for certain circumstances. But distinct patterns can be

---

based on *Armstrong* factors; substantial evidence supported award); White v. White, 913 So. 2d 323, 325-26 (Miss. Ct. App. 2005) (affirming award; chancellor did not cite *Armstrong*, but clearly considered factors); Ferro v. Ferro, 871 So. 2d 753 (Miss. Ct. App. 2004) (on-the-record *Armstrong* analysis not required); Klauser v. Klauser, 865 So. 2d 363 (Miss. Ct. App. 2003); Palmer v. Palmer, 841 So. 2d 185, 188 (Miss. Ct. App. 2003) (requiring reversal in cases of manifest error); *cf.* Carroll v. Carroll, 976 So. 2d 880, 888 (Miss. Ct. App. 2007) (no need for on-the-record *Armstrong* analysis, but must reverse if clear that no analysis occurred, or record does not support); Thompson v. Thompson, 816 So. 2d 417, 420 (Miss. Ct. App. 2002) (requiring reversal only in cases of manifest error).

[209] Gable v. Gable, 846 So. 2d 296, 300 (Miss. Ct. App. 2003) (no specific mention of marital fault required); *see also* Blalack v. Blalack, 938 So. 2d 909, 912 (Miss. Ct. App. 2006) (chancellor not required to specifically mention alleged desertion; chancellor considers overall factors); Wells v. Wells, 800 So. 2d 1239, 1249 (Miss. Ct. App. 2001).

[210] Marsh v. Marsh, 868 So. 2d 394, 398 (Miss. Ct. App. 2004).

[211] *See* Voda v. Voda, 731 So. 2d 1152, 1155 (Miss. 1999).

[212] Godwin v. Godwin, 758 So. 2d 384, 387-88 (Miss. 1999) (reversing for failure to make findings regarding refusal to award permanent or lump sum alimony).

[213] *See* Pacheco v. Pacheco, 770 So. 2d 1007, 1010-11 (Miss. Ct. App. 2000); *see also* Chmelicek v. Chmelicek, 51 So. 3d 1000, 1008 (Miss. Ct. App. 2010) (reversed for findings; chancellor stated that he reviewed the factors, but did not provide analysis).

[214] Seghini v. Seghini, 42 So. 3d 635, 639-40 (Miss. Ct. App. 2010).

[215] *See* Harrell v. Harrell, 231 So. 2d 793, 797 (Miss. 1970) (holding no error to award $5,325 in lump sum alimony and $150/month in permanent alimony).

ALIMONY

§ 9.04[4]

seen in reported alimony cases, most noticeably based on marriage length. An analysis of actual awards since 1994 follows the discussion of factors.

[4] Factors related to financial disparity. Disparity in the parties' financial circumstances is the most frequently cited reason for an award of alimony. In *Johnson v. Johnson*, a companion case to *Ferguson*, the supreme court held that if the "division of marital property, considered with each party's nonmarital assets, leaves a deficit for one party, then alimony based on the value of nonmarital assets should be considered."[216] Whether one spouse is "left with a deficit" depends upon whether there is a financial disparity in the spouses' ability to meet their reasonable expenses.[217]

Financial disparity is determined by examining factors set out in *Armstrong v. Armstrong,* including income, earning capacity, assets, obligations, reasonable expenses, standard of living, and custodial arrangements. These factors are grouped together below.

[a] Income of the parties. In comparing parties' incomes, courts usually consider the net value of each party's actual or imputed income after taxes and mandatory deductions.

[i] Income included. Income should include all regular sources of income, whether from wages, investments, or other income.[218] Personal expenses paid by an employer or business should be added to wages to determine net income.[219] A court properly considered a wife's employer-provided health insurance when determining her need for alimony.[220] A chancellor may average income over a period of years to arrive at an accurate income. A chancellor properly averaged six years of income to calculate the income of a stockbroker whose annual earnings fluctuated with the market.[221]

[ii] Imputed income. A court will impute income to a party who is working below earning capacity or who has concealed income. Imputing income to

---

[216] Johnson v. Johnson, 650 So. 2d 1281, 1287 (Miss. 1994); *see also* Larue v. Larue, 969 So. 2d 99, 111 (Miss. Ct. App. 2007) (wife awarded alimony of $700/month, the amount by which the husband's income exceeded his expenses); Rush v. Rush *ex rel.* Mayne, 914 So. 2d 322, 327 (Miss. Ct. App. 2005) (en banc) (lower-income wife awarded $400/month, representing 28% of the disparity between her income of $550 and his of $2,000). *But cf.* Sandlin v. Sandlin, 906 So. 2d 39 (Miss. Ct. App. 2004) ("deficit alone is an inadequate basis on which to award alimony").

[217] *See, e.g.*, Pierce v. Pierce, 42 So. 3d 658, 663 (Miss. Ct. App. 2010) (alimony considered based on disparity of income and standard of living); George v. George, 22 So. 3d 424, 428 n.8 (Miss. Ct. App. 2009) (alimony is appropriate when a spouse has "a disparity of income and standard of living following the equitable division of assets"); Elliott v. Elliott, 11 So. 3d 784, 786-787 n.5 (Miss. Ct. App. 2009) (wife suffered a deficit in her ability to meet expenses after equitable division). *But see* Sellers v. Sellers, 22 So. 3d 299, 301 (Miss. Ct. App. 2009) (homemaker wife denied alimony; because she received 63% of the $304,230 marital assets, she was not "left with a deficit").

[218] *See* Tatum v. Tatum, 54 So. 3d 855, 864 (Miss. Ct. App. 2010) (considering husband's separate property income in determining alimony and child support). There is substantial caselaw regarding determination of income in the child support context, which may be used by analogy in alimony cases. *See infra* § 13.04[1] - [3].

[219] Franklin v. Franklin, 846 So. 2d 970, 980 (Miss. Ct. App. 2003); *cf.* Barnett v. Barnett, 908 So. 2d 833, 844-45 (Miss. Ct. App. 2005) (husband's expense account was properly considered as income for purposes of alimony award; amount was reported as income to IRS; husband was not required to use for business purposes).

[220] Elam v. Hinson, 932 So. 2d 76, 78 (Miss. Ct. App. 2006).

[221] Holley v. Holley, 969 So. 2d 842 (Miss. Ct. App. 2007).

§ 9.04[4][a][iii]   MISSISSIPPI FAMILY LAW

a potential recipient may result in an outright denial of alimony.[222] A wife who left a demanding but high-paying job for less stressful employment at a 50% pay cut was denied permanent alimony based in part on her higher earning capacity.[223] Or, if a disparity exists after imputing a higher income to a payee spouse, the court may award alimony in a lower amount.[224] Income may also be imputed to a payor based on earning capacity or hidden income. A court properly imputed additional income to a husband who claimed income of $800 a month – he had recently built an expensive home, owned a boat, and assisted his daughter in building a house.[225] And a disabled wife of eleven years was properly awarded permanent alimony of $300 a month from her unemployed husband. He chose not to work in order to take care of his mother, who did not need full-time care.[226] A chancellor did not err in awarding a wife of twenty-nine years $375 in alimony a month from her unemployed husband. He testified that he was capable of making $30,000 a year as a carpenter and had always been able to find work.[227]

    [iii] **Deductions from income.** Courts typically compare the parties' net income after mandatory deductions. Voluntary payments or withholdings should not be deducted. A court erred in comparing a wife's income after mandatory deductions with her husband's income after mandatory and voluntary deductions such as insurance, deferred compensation, and credit union deductions.[228]

    Child support should be deducted from a child support payor's income to arrive at net income for purposes of alimony, but should not be added to the custodial parent's net income. Child support covers additional costs incurred as a result of the children's presence in the home and should not be considered income to the custodial parent in determining whether a disparity exists.[229]

------

[222] *See* Mabus v. Mabus, 890 So. 2d 806, 823 (Miss. 2003) (ability to earn high income); Rogers v. Morin, 791 So. 2d 815, 827-28 (Miss. 2001) (imputing $1,535 income to wife; alimony denied); Roberts v. Roberts, 924 So. 2d 550, 554 (Miss. Ct. App. 2005) (no need for permanent alimony in light of division of assets and wife's earning capacity); Masino v. Masino, 829 So. 2d 1267, 1271-72 (Miss. Ct. App. 2002) (denial of alimony to wife who refused to work).

[223] *See* Craft v. Craft, 825 So. 2d 605, 611 (Miss. 2002); Dorsey v. Dorsey, 972 So. 2d 48, 54 (Miss. Ct. App. 2008) (alimony denied to wife who could increase income by working forty hours a week); *cf.* Hults v. Hults, 11 So. 3d 1273, 1280 (Miss. Ct. App. 2009) (forty-year-old wife and homemaker of twenty years who planned to return to school was properly denied permanent alimony and awarded five years of rehabilitative alimony of $900 a month).

[224] *See* Vaughn v. Vaughn, 798 So. 2d 431, 436 (Miss. 2001) (awarding $500 to wife capable of earning $15,000/year); Barnett v. Barnett, 908 So. 2d 833, 842 (Miss. Ct. App. 2005) (imputing earning capacity of $1,200 a month to wife who was working part-time earning $700 a month); Roberts v. Roberts, 924 So. 2d 550, 554 (Miss. Ct. App. 2005) (wife who worked part-time capable of earning amount equal to husband's; award of rehabilitative alimony appropriate); Moore v. Moore, 803 So. 2d 1214, 1219 (Miss. Ct. App. 2001) (wife could supplement alimony award with work).

[225] Clark v. Clark, 754 So. 2d 450, 458-59 (Miss. 1999) (imputing income to husband to support award of child support and alimony); *see also* Seymour v. Seymour, 960 So. 2d 513, 517 (Miss. Ct. App. 2006) (imputing unreported income from plumbing business); Rush v. Rush *ex rel.* Mayne, 914 So. 2d 322, 327 (Miss. Ct. App. 2005) (en banc) (imputing income of $2,000/month to self-employed carpenter, based on testimony that he could earn $17/hour).

[226] Beddingfield v. Beddingfield, 11 So. 3d 780, 783-784 (Miss. Ct. App. 2009).

[227] Roberson v. Roberson, 949 So. 2d 866, 871 (Miss. Ct. App. 2007); *cf.* Craft v. Craft, 32 So. 3d 1232, 1244 (Miss. Ct. App. 2010) (husband who lost $87,000 job through his own misconduct ordered to pay wife $100/month in permanent alimony, even though his current income was slightly lower than hers).

[228] Saucier v. Saucier, 830 So. 2d 1261, 1263-64 (Miss. Ct. App. 2002).

[229] Buckley v. Buckley, 815 So. 2d 1260, 1263 (Miss. Ct. App. 2002) (error to assume that equal amount of income is sufficient for mother with custody of two children and single father).

258

ALIMONY § 9.04[4][b]

[b] Earning capacity. If a disparity in income exists, courts also consider whether additional training or education will remove or reduce the disparity. If a lower-income spouse's earning capacity can be enhanced by a period of training, an award of rehabilitative rather than permanent alimony may be appropriate. For example, three years of rehabilitative alimony was properly awarded to a former teacher who could be re-certified in that period, providing her with an earning capacity equal to her husband's.[230] In a longer marriage it may be appropriate to combine rehabilitative with permanent alimony if a substantial disparity will exist even after the increase in income. Earning capacity may not be presumed; a court erred in finding that a wife could earn $25,000 a year without proof to that effect.[231] Vocational experts are often used to provide expert testimony regarding a spouse's earning potential.[232]

[c] Standard of living of the marriage and at the time of the order. The marriage standard of living affects a court's determination of the parties' reasonable expenses. Cases still frequently include a statement to the effect that an alimony recipient "is entitled to support corresponding to her rank and condition in life, and the estate of her husband."[233] The wrong standard was applied when a court held that a wife was entitled to a "semblance" of the marriage standard of living: "Our legal standard for the award of permanent periodic alimony is not to maintain a 'semblance' of the standard of living . . . . [T]he general rule . . . provides that the recipient should be entitled to a reasonable allowance that is commiserate [sic] with the standard of living to which they had become accustomed measured against the ability to pay."[234] A wife of twenty-four years was properly awarded $6,000 in alimony; without a substantial

---

[230] *See* Roberts v. Roberts, 924 So. 2d 550, 554 (Miss. Ct. App. 2005) (rehabilitative alimony designed to allow recipient to return to workplace; properly awarded to wife with earning capacity equal to husband); Hoggatt v. Hoggatt, 766 So. 2d 9 (Miss. Ct. App. 2000) (awarding three years rehabilitative alimony to wife of eighteen years who could resume teaching with equal earning capacity); *see also* Tatum v. Tatum, 54 So. 3d 855, 861 (Miss. Ct. App. 2010) (two years of rehabilitative alimony awarded to wife of six years in her early thirties, who could reenter the workforce with transitional help); Hults v. Hults, 11 So. 3d 1273, 1280 (Miss. Ct. App. 2009) (forty-year-old wife and homemaker of twenty years who planned to return to school was awarded five years of rehabilitative alimony of $900/month); McCarrell v. McCarrell, 19 So. 3d 168, 170 (Miss. Ct. App. 2009) (wife of twelve years awarded rehabilitative alimony for five years, to allow her to obtain her associate's degree); Roberts v. Roberts, 924 So. 2d 550, 554 (Miss. Ct. App. 2005) (rehabilitative alimony properly awarded to wife with earning capacity equal to husband); Wolfe v. Wolfe, 766 So. 2d 123, 128-29 (Miss. Ct. App. 2000) (awarding three years rehabilitative alimony to wife who recently earned degree); Turnley v. Turnley, 726 So. 2d 1258, 1266-67 (Miss. Ct. App. 1988) (awarding three years rehabilitative alimony to wife in school).

[231] Johnson v. Johnson, 877 So. 2d 485, 498 (Miss. Ct. App. 2003).

[232] *See* Brett Turner, *Vocational Evidence: A 2005 Update*, 17 Div. Lit. 157 (No. 10) (2005) (good overview of the use of vocational evidence).

[233] *See* Holley v. Holley, 969 So. 2d 842, 844 (Miss. 2007) (alimony should be commensurate with standard of living, considering husband's ability to pay); Brennan v. Brennan, 638 So. 2d 1320, 1324 (Miss. 1994) (requiring husband to support wife "in the manner to which she has become accustomed"); Roberson v. Roberson, 949 So. 2d 866, 871 (Miss. Ct. App. 2007) (alimony award of $375 would assist wife with income of $1,000/month to maintain standard of living of the marriage); Barnett v. Barnett, 908 So. 2d 833, 843-44 (Miss. Ct. App. 2005) (alimony should be awarded in amount commensurate with accustomed standard of living and considering obligor's ability to pay); *see also* Weeks v. Weeks, 832 So. 2d 583, 587-88 (Miss. Ct. App. 2002).

[234] Johnson v. Johnson, 877 So. 2d 485, 498 (Miss. Ct. App. 2003) (deeming award of $750/month permanent alimony inadequate to sustain wife accustomed to higher marriage standard of living); *see* Klauser v. Klauser, 865 So. 2d 363, 366 (Miss. Ct. App. 2003) (award should be commensurate with the accustomed standard of living, considering the higher income spouse's ability to pay).

259

§ 9.04[4][d]   **MISSISSIPPI FAMILY LAW**

award, she would not be able to maintain the marital standard of living.[235] Permanent alimony was properly awarded to a wife whose husband insisted that she not work and instructed her not to shop at budget stores because she was a doctor's wife.[236]

The marriage standard of living is a factor, not the actual measure of an award. It is generally understood that, because of duplicative living expenses, most spouses will have at least a slightly lower standard of living after divorce. The court determines what constitutes reasonable post-divorce expenses based on both the marriage standard of living and the funds available to the parties after divorce.[237] For example, an alimony award of $4,000 was proper, even though it might require the wife to live at a lower standard of living than the marriage. The court noted that in some cases, both spouses will live below the marriage standard of living after divorce.[238]

   [d] Reasonable expenses of the parties. Courts are to consider the reasonable expenses of each spouse in determining whether a disparity exists.[239] "Reasonable" is a relative term – items which are not strict necessities may be reasonable if they provide a standard of living similar to that of the marriage.[240] Even in higher income cases, however, a court may disregard expenses considered extravagant. A husband's monthly expenses for a condominium in Colorado and two country club memberships were not reasonable and necessary expenses for purposes of alimony analysis.[241] Claimed expenses for gifts, church, and travel were deemed unnecessary for a husband living on $2,700 a month.[242] Similarly, a wife's assertion that she needed approximately $3,200 a month for "clubs, social obligations, travel, recreation . . . lawn care . . . donations, hair care . . . vacation . . . dining out and entertaining friends" was "excessive" in 1995.[243] Housing expenses for a 3600-square-foot house were considered unreasonable for a woman living alone.[244] And reasonable expenses did not include funds to support a thirty-six-year-old adult child.[245]

In one case, a court seemed to consider a husband's need to build retirement funds as a "reasonable need." During the thirty-five-year marriage, the wife built a significant retirement working for the state, while he borrowed $100,000 from his account to send their children to college. She was denied alimony even though his income was double hers and he was at fault in the marriage breakup.[246]

Courts do not hesitate to scrutinize financial statements and discount inflated or undocumented expenses. A husband's claimed expenditures were discounted in part

---

[235] McKissack v. McKissack, 45 So. 3d 716, 718 (Miss. Ct. App. 2010) (husband's income $22,000/month).

[236] Lauro v. Lauro, 924 So. 2d 584, 589 (Miss. Ct. App. 2006).

[237] *See* Bridges v. McCracken, 724 So. 2d 1086, 1088 (Miss. Ct. App. 1998) (exemplifying that in many cases, both parties will live below the standard of living of the marriage after divorce).

[238] Wilson v. Wilson, 975 So. 2d 261, 266 (Miss. Ct. App. 2007).

[239] *See* Palmer v. Palmer, 841 So. 2d 185, 188-89 (Miss. Ct. App. 2003) (wife unable to pay necessaries); Wesson v. Wesson, 818 So. 2d 1272, 1275-76 (Miss. Ct. App. 2002) (wife unable to provide basics on $620/month).

[240] *See* Box v. Box, 622 So. 2d 284, 288-89 (Miss. 1993).

[241] *See* Box v. Box, 622 So. 2d 284, 288 (Miss. 1993).

[242] Parsons v. Parsons, 678 So. 2d 701, 702 (Miss. 1996).

[243] Brooks v. Brooks, 652 So. 2d 1113, 1123 (Miss. 1995).

[244] Henderson v. Henderson, 757 So. 2d 285, 294 (Miss. 2000) (denying alimony because wife could sell house and reduce expenses).

[245] Ferro v. Ferro, 871 So. 2d 753 (Miss. Ct. App. 2004).

[246] Meador v. Meador, 44 So. 3d 411, 419 (Miss. Ct. App. 2010) (also assumed an additional $96,000 in debt).

ALIMONY

§ 9.04[4][e]

because he presented no receipts or canceled checks.[247] A husband's claimed expenses were also deemed high in light of the fact that his live-in girlfriend was not contributing to household expenses.[248]

If a disparity in income exists but the lower-income spouse is able to meet reasonable expenses, no alimony should be awarded.[249] A disparity between wealthy parties did not justify alimony; the wife's assets and earning capacity were sufficient to meet her reasonable needs.[250]

On the other hand, a payor's ability to meet his expenses may justify a higher award of alimony. An award of almost half of a husband's net income was justified in part because he had sufficient remaining income to meet his reasonable expenses.[251] And a wife of eighteen years was properly awarded $250 a month in permanent alimony; her monthly income of $2,675 did not cover her expenses, while her former husband's monthly income of $3,497 slightly exceeded his expenses.[252]

A payor must be left with sufficient income to meet basic needs. A court erred in setting total child support and alimony awards in an amount exceeding the payor's disposable income after basic needs were met.[253] Similarly, a court erred in awarding a wife $2,500 in permanent alimony, $2,500 in child support, and $5,000 in lump sum alimony, from a payor with monthly income of $12,000 and expenses of $6,000.[254]

[e] Free use of home and car. One party's free use of the marital home or car is relevant in determining alimony[255] – eliminating these payments substantially reduces monthly expenses. Mortgage or car payments may be a form of alimony, or a part of property division.[256]

---

[247] Parsons v. Parsons, 678 So. 2d 701, 702 (Miss. 1996).

[248] Palmer v. Palmer, 841 So. 2d 185, 188-89 (Miss. Ct. App. 2003); *see also* Wilson v. Wilson, 975 So. 2d 261, 265-66 (Miss. Ct. App. 2007) (wife's claimed monthly expenses of $9,000 greatly exaggerated). *But cf.* Holley v. Holley, 969 So. 2d 842, 844 (Miss. 2007) (wife's expenses not exaggerated; "missing" $25,000/year explained by increased credit card debt and failure to pay ordinary expenses).

[249] Wells v. Wells, 35 So. 3d 1250, 1259 (Miss. Ct. App. 2010) (wife of eight years able to support herself "comfortably" as pediatric nurse; no alimony although significant financial disparity); Graham v. Graham, 767 So. 2d 277, 280 (Miss. Ct. App. 2000) ($33,000/year income; no evidence of need); Osborn v. Osborn, 724 So. 2d 1121, 1127 n.7 (Miss. Ct. App. 1998) (noting that wife's resources were only $140 short of listed expenses).

[250] Mabus v. Mabus, 890 So. 2d 806 (Miss. 2003).

[251] Russell v. Russell, 733 So. 2d 858, 861-62 (Miss. Ct. App. 1999) (net income of $11,150); *see also* Woodfin v. Woodfin, 26 So. 3d 389, 400 (Miss. Ct. App. 2010) (husband with income of $5,146 and expenses of $2,886 properly ordered to pay wife with net income of $800, $1,200 in child support and $700 in alimony); Wilson v. Wilson, 975 So. 2d 261, 266 (Miss. Ct. App. 2007) (wife awarded one-half of husband's reported income; remainder sufficient to meet his expenses); Parker v. Parker, 934 So. 2d 359, 361 (Miss. Ct. App. 2006) (affirming award of $1,500 to wife whose expenses exceeded income of $2,684, while husband's monthly expenses were less than his income); Rush v. Rush *ex rel.* Mayne, 914 So. 2d 322, 326-27 (Miss. Ct. App. 2005) (en banc) (husband with income of $2,000 and expenses of $1,600 able to pay $400/month alimony); Barnett v. Barnett, 908 So. 2d 833, 844 (Miss. Ct. App. 2005) (alimony and child support set in amount to leave husband with enough for reasonable expenses); *cf.* Parsons v. Parsons, 678 So. 2d 701, 703-05 (Miss. 1996) ($600 award not error where disabled husband had $1,400 in income and $1,100 in expenses); Bumpous v. Bumpous, 770 So. 2d 558, 561 (Miss. Ct. App. 2000) (husband still able to meet expenses after award).

[252] Stuart v. Stuart, 956 So. 2d 295, 298 (Miss. Ct. App. 2006).

[253] McEachern v. McEachern, 605 So. 2d 809, 814-15 (Miss. 1992).

[254] Yelverton v. Yelverton, 961 So. 2d 19, 28 (Miss. 2007).

[255] *See* Elam v. Hinson, 932 So. 2d 76, 78-79 (Miss. Ct. App. 2006) (alimony of $350/month adequate, considering that husband was to pay car note and wife had free use of the home); Armstrong v. Armstrong, 618 So. 2d 1278, 1281-82 (Miss. 1993).

[256] *See infra* § 9.07.

§ 9.04[4][f]   MISSISSIPPI FAMILY LAW

[f] Presence or absence of children in the home requiring childcare. The fact that a potential alimony recipient has custody of minor children is an important factor in determining income and reasonable expenses.[257] The responsibilities of childcare may limit a custodial parent's ability to produce income. For example, a mother's custody of school-age children supported an award of alimony even though the children were beyond an age requiring daycare. The court noted that the children "continue to require attention and supervision."[258] An award of one-half of a payor's net income as alimony and child support to a homemaker wife supporting six children was not unreasonable.[259] Furthermore, a working custodial parent may incur substantial expenses for childcare that are not covered by child support. The absence of children may also be significant in determining whether alimony should be awarded. In some cases, permanent alimony has been denied in part because there were no children of the marriage,[260] or because the potential alimony payor was the custodial parent.[261]

[g] Obligations of the parties. Parties' debt obligations are a relevant consideration in determining alimony. A wife was properly denied alimony from a husband with slightly higher income who was responsible for most of the marital debt.[262] And a husband of thirty-five years who committed adultery was not ordered to pay alimony to his wife, even though his income was double hers, in large part because he assumed $96,000 in debt for their sons' college educations.[263] However, a court may disregard short-term obligations.[264] A husband's short-term obligations of $686 a month did not prevent the court from ordering him to pay alimony since he would have sufficient income for a decent standard of living after the two loans were paid.[265]

---

[257] *See* Armstrong v. Armstrong, 618 So. 2d 1278, 1280 (Miss. 1993).

[258] Johnson v. Johnson, 877 So. 2d 485, 497 (Miss. Ct. App. 2003).

[259] Knutson v. Knutson, 704 So. 2d 1331, 1335 (Miss. 1997); *see also* Holley v. Holley, 969 So. 2d 842, 843-44 (Miss. 2007) (wife's custody of children a factor in alimony); Seymour v. Seymour, 960 So. 2d 513, 520 (Miss. Ct. App. 2006) (wife's custody of three children factor in permanent alimony award); *cf.* Barnett v. Barnett, 908 So. 2d 833, 844 (Miss. Ct. App. 2005) (rehabilitative alimony awarded in part based on need for childcare).

[260] *See* Pearson v. Pearson, 761 So. 2d 157, 160 (Miss. 2000) (no permanent alimony awarded to thirty-six-year-old wife after childless six-year marriage); Ericson v. Tullos, 876 So. 2d 1038, 1041 (Miss. Ct. App. 2004) (sixty-three-year-old quadriplegic husband was properly denied alimony from his forty-seven-year-old wife of nine years; marriage was of moderate length with no children); Ferro v. Ferro, 871 So. 2d 753 (Miss. Ct. App. 2004) (rehabilitative alimony proper after eight-year marriage with no children; wife had substantial experience as insurance agent and secretary; husband was retired); *cf.* Carnathan v. Carnathan, 722 So. 2d 1248 (Miss. 1998) (awarding only rehabilitative alimony where no children).

[261] *See* Masino v. Masino, 829 So. 2d 1267, 1270-71 (Miss. Ct. App. 2002) (fact that husband had custody of children was factor in denying alimony to wife); *cf.* Street v. Street, 936 So. 2d 1002, 1013 (Miss. Ct. App. 2006) (court did not err in amending alimony award when custody changed from mother to father; alimony award was based largely on presence of children in mother's home).

[262] Kay v. Kay, 12 So. 3d 622, 627-628 (Miss. Ct. App. 2009) (wife of fourteen years with income of $1,975 denied alimony from husband with income of $2,550 and most of marital debt).

[263] Meador v. Meador, 44 So. 3d 411, 420 (Miss. Ct. App. 2010) (also withdrew $100,000 to finance college, while she had built state retirement).

[264] *See* Bumpous v. Bumpous, 770 So. 2d 558, 561 (Miss. Ct. App. 2000) (finding short-term financial strain on husband was temporary).

[265] Magee v. Magee, 724 So. 2d 1034, 1043 (Miss. Ct. App. 1998); *see also* Traxler v. Traxler, 730 So. 2d 1098, 1104 (Miss. 1998) (finding monthly obligations of $1,000 to be short-term debt; not error to award alimony of $750); Palculict v. Palculict, 22 So. 3d 293, 296-297 (Miss. Ct. App. 2009) (rejecting husband's argument that his obligations for child support, permanent alimony, and lump sum alimony would exceed his income; short-term obligations may be

ALIMONY

§ 9.04[4][h]

A recipient spouse's substantial debt may be a reason for awarding alimony.[266]

[h] Assets of the parties. Examining the factors above reveals whether the parties' incomes are sufficient to meet their reasonable expenses. If not, the court must consider whether a party at a deficit has assets that may be used to meet expenses, and whether a higher-income party has assets that may be used to satisfy an award. The court should consider both assets received in equitable distribution and separate property assets. The Mississippi Supreme Court remanded an award of permanent alimony to an unemployed wife because the court failed to consider assets awarded to her in equitable distribution.[267] And a court erred in denying permanent alimony from a husband with separate assets of over a million dollars.[268]

[i] Recipient's assets. A potential recipient's substantial assets may justify denying or reducing alimony.[269] The Mississippi Supreme Court has emphasized that equitable distribution and alimony are linked – "where one expands, the other must recede."[270] Furthermore, if the "division of marital assets in conjunction with nonmarital assets will adequately provide for a party, alimony need not be awarded."[271] A spouse's assets may also be a reason for awarding rehabilitative rather than permanent alimony,[272] or for awarding less permanent alimony.[273] A disproportionate award of marital assets to a lower-income spouse may also be a reason to deny alimony.[274]

Assets must be substantial for a court to require their depletion. A spouse is not expected to liquidate modest assets received in equitable distribution to meet monthly living expenses. For example, $14,000 in additional marital assets to a wife employed at minimum wage was not a replacement for alimony.[275] Similarly, liquid assets of $77,000 were properly viewed as a reserve for retirement and unexpected expenses

---

disregarded).

[266] Stuart v. Stuart, 956 So. 2d 295, 298 (Miss. Ct. App. 2006) (wife of eighteen years with substantial credit card debt, awarded $250/month in permanent alimony; income of $2,675/month was insufficient to meet monthly expenses).

[267] Gambrell v. Gambrell, 650 So. 2d 517, 519-20 (Miss. 1995) (including among assets: car, coin collection, marital home, monthly notes with income of $350, and IRAs and cash worth approximately $10,000); *see also* Striebeck v. Striebeck, 911 So. 2d 628, 634-35 (Miss. Ct. App. 2005) (en banc) (wife's estate for alimony analysis should have included $34,055 property division payment representing her home equity; harmless error because home value also excluded from husband's estate).

[268] Sanderson v. Sanderson, 824 So. 2d 623 (Miss. 2002).

[269] *See* Mabus v. Mabus, 890 So. 2d 806, 823, 826 (Miss. 2003) (separate property and equitable distribution); Johnson v. Johnson, 852 So. 2d 681 (Miss. Ct. App. 2003) (equitable distribution).

[270] Ferguson v. Ferguson, 639 So. 2d 921, 927 (Miss. 1994).

[271] Marsh v. Marsh, 868 So. 2d 394, 398 (Miss. Ct. App. 2004) (alimony denied to wife who received two-thirds of large marital estate).

[272] *See* Henderson v. Henderson, 757 So. 2d 285, 294-95 (Miss. 2000); Hults v. Hults, 11 So. 3d 1273, 1280 (Miss. Ct. App. 2009) (forty-year-old wife and homemaker of twenty years was properly awarded five years of rehabilitative alimony of $900/month; she planned to return to school and received $414,000 in marital assets).

[273] *See* Rodriguez v. Rodriguez, 2 So. 3d 720, 729-730 (Miss. Ct. App. 2009) (fifty-nine-year-old homemaker wife of thirty-seven years awarded $300 in alimony; monthly amount was sufficient, considering her good health, willingness to work, and that she received substantial assets in the division of assets); Welch v. Welch, 755 So. 2d 6 (Miss. Ct. App. 1999).

[274] *See* Mabus v. Mabus, 890 So. 2d 806, 826 (Miss. 2003) (receiving 60% of marital estate); Pearson v. Pearson, 761 So. 2d 157, 164 (Miss. 2000) (awarding $150,000 lump sum alimony); Johnson v. Johnson, 852 So. 2d 681 (Miss. Ct. App. 2003).

[275] Buckley v. Buckley, 815 So. 2d 1260, 1266 (Miss. Ct. App. 2002).

§ 9.04[4][h][ii]   MISSISSIPPI FAMILY LAW

and not as a replacement for permanent alimony.[276] A wife was not required to use a $250,000 buy-out of her interest in the marital home for monthly expenses; she would need the funds to purchase another residence.[277] In contrast, a wife with substantial earning capacity and assets of over $800,000 was properly denied alimony.[278] And a homemaker wife who received $2.6 million in marital assets was denied alimony from a high-income husband.[279] However, the fact that a spouse may inherit from a living person, or is listed as a beneficiary in a third-party will, may not be considered in determining alimony.[280]

One spouse's substantial retirement may affect an award of alimony. A husband of thirty-five years who depleted his retirement to pay for children's college was not required to pay alimony to his lower-income wife, who had built substantial state retirement.[281]

[ii] **Payor's assets.** Even though a spouse's separate assets cannot be divided in equitable distribution, they may serve as the source for alimony payments.[282] A court erred in denying alimony to a wife of twenty-two years whose husband had substantial separate assets.[283] However, inequality of assets does not require an award of alimony to a spouse whose income is sufficient to meet reasonable needs. The fact that a retired husband had more separate property than his wife, who was still working, did not require an alimony award to her.[284] A payor spouse's potential inheritance may not be considered in determining alimony.[285]

[5] Factors related to reducing disparity. If the court finds no financial disparity between the parties, alimony should not be awarded.[286] If a disparity does exist, it may

---

[276] Long v. Long, 734 So. 2d 206, 209 (Miss. Ct. App. 1999).

[277] Johnson v. Johnson, 877 So. 2d 485, 496-97 (Miss. Ct. App. 2003).

[278] Mabus v. Mabus, 890 So. 2d 806 (Miss. 2003).

[279] Cosentino v. Cosentino, 986 So. 2d 1065, 1069 (Miss. Ct. App. 2008) (rejecting as speculative, chancellor's reasoning that wife "could easily outlive" her share of the marital estate).

[280] *See* Miss. Code Ann. §§ 93-5-2, -23 (Supp. 2010).

[281] Meador v. Meador, 44 So. 3d 411, 420-21 (Miss. Ct. App. 2010).

[282] Johnson v. Johnson, 650 So. 2d 1281, 1287 (Miss. 1994) (stating that if "division of marital property, considered with each party's nonmarital assets, leaves a deficit for one party, then alimony based on the value of nonmarital assets should be considered").

[283] Sanderson v. Sanderson, 824 So. 2d 623 (Miss. 2002); *see also* McKissack v. McKissack, 45 So. 3d 716, 723 (Miss. Ct. App. 2010) (alimony of $6,000 to wife whose husband had over $1 million in separate assets); Stevens v. Stevens, 924 So. 2d 645, 649 (Miss. Ct. App. 2006) (husband's assets were almost double those of wife); Parker v. Parker, 934 So. 2d 359, 361 (Miss. Ct. App. 2006) (affirming award of $1,500 to wife with $28,000 in assets from husband with $100,000 in assets).

[284] Prescott v. Prescott, 736 So. 2d 409, 414 (Miss. Ct. App. 1999) (wife's separate property about 20% of husband's); *see also* Wells v. Wells, 35 So. 3d 1250, 1259 (Miss. Ct. App 2010) (wife who was able to support herself comfortably as pediatric nurse denied alimony from physician husband with separate assets of $614,000); Sellers v. Sellers, 22 So. 3d 299 (Miss. Ct. App. 2009) (homemaker wife of many years denied alimony even though husband had $137,500 in separate assets and she had only $13,620; she received greater share of marital assets).

[285] *See* Miss. Code Ann. §§ 93-5-2, -23 (Supp. 2010).

[286] *See* Rogers v. Morin, 791 So. 2d 815, 828-29 (Miss. 2001) (no alimony; spouses had equal earning capacity); Love v. Love, 687 So. 2d 1229 (Miss. 1997) (wife earned more than husband); Dorsey v. Dorsey, 972 So. 2d 48, 54 (Miss. Ct. App. 2008) (if wife worked forty hours a week, income would equal husband's); Jackson v. Jackson, 922 So. 2d 53, 60 (Miss. Ct. App. 2006) (en banc) (neither party entitled to alimony given their age, poor health, and limited income); McLaurin v. McLaurin, 853 So. 2d 1279, 1283-84 (Miss. Ct. App. 2003) (allowing no alimony after forty-five-year marriage where wife had equal income and assets); Chesney v. Chesney, 828 So. 2d 219 (Miss. Ct. App. 2002) (reversing

ALIMONY § 9.04[5][a]

be remedied by an award of permanent, rehabilitative, or lump sum alimony. In some cases a court may find a disparity but conclude that the circumstances do not require an award. Courts are guided in this determination by a second subset of factors: the marriage length, the parties' age and health, marital fault, whether one spouse dissipated assets, and whether one spouse sacrificed earning capacity for the benefit of the marriage.

[a] Length of marriage. Marriage length may be the most critical factor in determining whether a disparity should be remedied by alimony. In many states that have adopted guidelines, marriage length determines both duration and amount of an alimony award.[287] And an analysis of Mississippi alimony awards reveals a distinct pattern of increasing the size and length of awards in longer marriages.[288] Mississippi courts cite the brevity of marriage as a significant factor in denials of alimony or awards of rehabilitative rather than permanent alimony. For example, rehabilitative rather than permanent alimony was appropriate following a four-year marriage.[289] Similarly, rehabilitative alimony for twenty-four months was proper after a three-year marriage between parties who were both financially insecure.[290] And rehabilitative lump sum alimony of $2,500 was properly awarded to a thirty-six-year-old wife leaving a short marriage.[291]

A lengthy marriage is frequently the primary factor supporting an award of permanent alimony.[292] A number of cases have been reversed because a financially dependent spouse was denied permanent alimony after a long marriage.[293] The court of appeals contrasted the importance of permanent alimony to an older spouse leaving

---

award of alimony where spouses' incomes were equal). Two exceptions would be where an award of reimbursement alimony is warranted, or where the other spouse has dissipated assets that were not offset in equitable distribution.

[287] *See supra* § 9.01[3].

[288] *See infra* § 9.06.

[289] Hubbard v. Hubbard, 656 So. 2d 124, 130 (Miss. 1995); *see also* Bowen v. Bowen, 982 So. 2d 385, 392 (Miss. 2008) (wife of eight years in ill health and unable to meet expenses awarded $430/month in rehabilitative alimony for five years and $60,000 in lump sum alimony); *cf.* Larney v. Record, 908 So. 2d 171, 174-75 (Miss. Ct. App. 2005) (low-income, disabled wife of fourteen months denied all alimony).

[290] Burnham-Steptoe v. Steptoe, 755 So. 2d 1225, 1230 (Miss. Ct. App. 1999); *see also* Tatum v. Tatum, 54 So. 3d 855, 863 (Miss. Ct. App. 2010) (homemaker wife of six years in her early thirties awarded rehabilitative alimony of $2,000/month for two years).

[291] Pearson v. Pearson, 761 So. 2d 157, 166 (Miss. 2000) (asserting there is no reason wife could not obtain education and become self-supporting with lump sum award); *see also* Sarver v. Sarver, 687 So. 2d 749, 757 (Miss. 1997) (stating that rehabilitative alimony assisted wife in getting new start); Ericson v. Tullos, 876 So. 2d 1038 (Miss. Ct. App. 2004) (sixty-three-year-old quadriplegic husband was properly denied alimony from his forty-seven-year-old wife of nine years; marriage was of moderate length with no children); *cf.* Wells v. Wells, 35 So. 3d 1250, 1258-59 (Miss. Ct. App. 2010) (wife of eight years, able to comfortably support herself, denied alimony from physician husband).

[292] *See, e.g.,* Holley v. Holley, 969 So. 2d 842, 843 (Miss. 2007) (permanent alimony appropriate after nineteen-year marriage); Sanderson v. Sanderson, 824 So. 2d 623, 626 (Miss. 2002) (reversing denial of permanent alimony to homemaker after twenty-two-year marriage); McKissack v. McKissack, 45 So. 3d 716, 723 (Miss. Ct. App. 2010) (permanent alimony after twenty-four-year marriage); Roberson v. Roberson, 949 So. 2d 866, 870 (Miss. Ct. App. 2007) (awarding permanent alimony to low-income wife of twenty-nine years); Long v. Long, 734 So. 2d 206, 209-10 (Miss. Ct. App. 1999) (awarding permanent alimony after twenty-eight-year marriage). *But cf.* Brabham v. Brabham, 950 So. 2d 1098, 1103 (Miss. Ct. App. 2007) (denying all alimony to a wife of fifteen years who refused to work outside or in the home, whose extreme behavior contributed to the marriage breakup, and who had an affair).

[293] *See* Sanderson v. Sanderson, 824 So. 2d 623, 626 (Miss. 2002) (twenty-two years); Buckley v. Buckley, 815 So. 2d 1260, 1264 (Miss. Ct. App. 2002) (twenty years); Weeks v. Weeks, 832 So. 2d 583, 586 (Miss. Ct. App. 2002) (twenty-two years); Pittman v. Pittman, 791 So. 2d 857, 861-62 (Miss. Ct. App. 2001) (twenty-one years).

§ 9.04[5][b]   MISSISSIPPI FAMILY LAW

a long marriage with meager job experience and to a young spouse departing an eight-year marriage with meaningful work experience.[294] Marriage length may also affect the amount of alimony awarded – an award leaving a wife of thirty years with less than half the monthly income of her husband was inadequate.[295] However, spouses in long marriages have been denied alimony if they are able to support themselves and pay for their reasonable needs.[296]

[b] Health. The health of both recipient and payor is a significant factor in alimony decisions.[297]

[i] Payee's health. A recipient's poor health may support an award of permanent alimony. For example, permanent alimony is rarely awarded in short marriages, but was awarded to a disabled wife after a ten-year, childless marriage.[298] Similarly, a chancellor erred in denying permanent alimony to a professionally-trained wife who suffered from manic-depressive illness.[299] However, a chancellor did not err in denying alimony to a disabled wife after the dissolution of a fourteen-month marriage.[300]

Poor health may also support a larger award than would otherwise be required. An alimony award of one-half of a husband's income to a disabled spouse was appropriate after a thirty-year marriage.[301] Similarly, denial of alimony to a disabled wife was

---

[294] Driste v. Driste, 738 So. 2d 763, 766 (Miss. Ct. App. 1999) (but reversing because amount of rehabilitative alimony to wife of eight years was inadequate).

[295] Baker v. Baker, 807 So. 2d 476, 480 (Miss. Ct. App. 2001).

[296] Meador v. Meador, 44 So. 3d 411, 419-21 (Miss. Ct. App 2010) (lower-income wife of thirty-eight years denied alimony).

[297] *See* Davis v. Davis, 832 So. 2d 492, 497-98 (Miss. 2002) (wife's recent injury and recurring depression supported alimony award); Hemsley v. Hemsley, 639 So. 2d 909, 912-13 (Miss. 1994) (factoring in husband's good health and wife's poor health in award of permanent alimony).

[298] *See* Crowe v. Crowe, 641 So. 2d 1100, 1102-03 (Miss. 1994); *see also* Palculict v. Palculict, 22 So. 3d 293 (Miss. Ct. App. 2009) (wife of nine years in remission from cancer properly awarded $1,500 permanent alimony); *cf.* Beddingfield v. Beddingfield, 11 So. 3d 780, 783-784 (Miss. Ct. App. 2009) (disabled wife of eleven years was properly awarded permanent alimony of $300/month from her unemployed husband, who chose not to work); Amacker v. Amacker, 33 So. 3d 493, 497 (Miss. Ct. App. 2009) (a temporarily disabled wife who would be able to return to work was not entitled to alimony from her disabled husband).

[299] Monroe v. Monroe, 612 So. 2d 353, 358-59 (Miss. 1992); *see also* Klumb v. Klumb, 194 So. 2d 221, 224 (Miss. 1967); George v. George, 22 So. 3d 424 428 (Miss. Ct. App. 2009) (permanent alimony of $1,000/month to a fifty-year-old wife of thirty-three years who had health problems); Larue v. Larue, 969 So. 2d 99, 110 (Miss. Ct. App. 2007) (permanent alimony awarded to seventy-year-old wife in ill health); Rush v. Rush *ex rel.* Mayne, 914 So. 2d 322, 326-27 (Miss. Ct. App. 2005) (en banc) (alimony award proper; disabled wife was left without ability to support herself); Stribling v. Stribling, 906 So. 2d 863, 871 (Miss. Ct. App. 2005) ($5,000/month in permanent alimony to disabled husband of twenty-two years); White v. White, 913 So. 2d 323, 326 (Miss. Ct. App. 2005) (wife of twenty-nine years, ill with cancer, properly awarded $500/month in permanent alimony); Curtis v. Curtis, 796 So. 2d 1044 (Miss. Ct. App. 2001); East v. East, 775 So. 2d 741 (Miss. Ct. App. 2000) (finding wife's disability significant factor in award); *cf.* Bowen v. Bowen, 982 So. 2d 385, 392-93 (Miss. 2008) (wife of eight years in ill health and unable to meet expenses awarded $430/month in rehabilitative alimony for five years and $60,000 in lump sum alimony); Stuart v. Stuart, 956 So. 2d 295, 298 (Miss. Ct. App. 2006) (wife of eighteen years, with health problems and substantial credit card debt, awarded $250/month in permanent alimony). *But see* Ericson v. Tullos, 876 So. 2d 1038 (Miss. Ct. App. 2004) (sixty-three-year-old quadriplegic husband was properly denied alimony from his forty-seven-year-old wife of nine years; marriage was of moderate length with no children).

[300] Larney v. Record, 908 So. 2d 171, 174-75 (Miss. Ct. App. 2005).

[301] East v. East, 775 So. 2d 741, 746 (Miss. Ct. App. 2000).

ALIMONY § 9.04[5][b][ii]

error even though she received a substantial award of marital property.[302] And a wife was awarded permanent alimony in part based on poor health, even though she had a year-long extramarital affair.[303] In contrast, the supreme court has affirmed denials of permanent alimony in part because the lower-income spouse was in good health and able to work,[304] even at the age of sixty-five.[305]

[ii] Payor's health. A potential payor's ill health or disability may be a reason to deny permanent alimony when it might otherwise be appropriate. A court's denial of permanent alimony to an older wife was appropriate in part because of her husband's ill health.[306] A husband's poor health was a factor in denying alimony to a wife of seventeen years[307] and in awarding only rehabilitative alimony after a twenty-three-year marriage.[308] However, poor health that does not affect a payor's income or ability to pay is irrelevant.[309] For example, a husband's chronic back pain and sleep apnea did not affect his earning capacity even though he was unable to drive and had to be chauffeured.[310]

[c] Age. A recipient's age may be a factor in awarding or denying permanent alimony. Several rare awards of permanent alimony after short marriages were to older spouses.[311] On the other hand, alimony has been denied to older women with substantial earning capacity or earning capacity comparable to their husbands.[312]

Courts have denied permanent alimony in part because the party requesting

---

[302] Weeks v. Weeks, 832 So. 2d 583, 587 (Miss. Ct. App. 2002).

[303] Ladner v. Ladner, 49 So. 3d 669, 672 (Miss. Ct. App. 2010).

[304] *See* Craft v. Craft, 825 So. 2d 605, 610-11 (Miss. 2002) (asserting wife's good health supported rehabilitative alimony award); Pearson v. Pearson, 761 So. 2d 157, 164 (Miss. 2000) (factoring in youth, health, and ability to work); *cf.* Rodriguez v. Rodriguez, 2 So. 3d 720, 729-730 (Miss. Ct. App. 2009) (fifty-nine-year-old homemaker wife of thirty-seven years awarded $300 in alimony; amount was sufficient, considering her good health, willingness to work, and that she received substantial assets).

[305] *See* Sarver v. Sarver, 687 So. 2d 749, 757 (Miss. 1997) (rehabilitative alimony to older wife who dissipated assets).

[306] *See* Sarver v. Sarver, 687 So. 2d 749, 757 (Miss. 1997) (awarding wife $2,500 in lump sum alimony); *see also* Chapel v. Chapel, 700 So. 2d 593, 598-99 (Miss. 1997) (awarding no alimony to younger wife from older husband in ill health); Amacker v. Amacker, 33 So. 3d 493, 497 (Miss. Ct. App. 2009) (a temporarily disabled wife who would be able to return to work was not entitled to alimony from her disabled husband). *But see* Parsons v. Parsons, 678 So. 2d 701, 703-05 (Miss. 1996) (upholding award of permanent alimony to sixty-year-old wife of man with Alzheimer's after three-year marriage).

[307] *See* Lindsey v. Lindsey, 749 So. 2d 77, 79-80 (Miss. 1999) (denying alimony; husband also awarded more in equitable distribution).

[308] *See* Wesson v. Wesson, 818 So. 2d 1272, 1275 (Miss. Ct. App. 2002) (husband disabled); *see also* Clower v. Clower, 988 So. 2d 441, 444-45 (Miss. Ct. App. 2008) (husband's age and poor health justified reducing award); *cf.* Barker v. Barker, 996 So. 2d 161, 163 (Miss. Ct. App. 2008) (wife of ten years, in ill health, awarded $200/month rehabilitative alimony for two years from husband also in ill health).

[309] Long v. Long, 734 So. 2d 206, 208-09 (Miss. Ct. App. 1999).

[310] Long v. Long, 734 So. 2d 206, 209 (Miss. Ct. App. 1999).

[311] *See* Watson v. Watson, 724 So. 2d 350, 354-55 (Miss. 1998) (award to sixty-year-old wife); Parsons v. Parsons, 678 So. 2d 701, 703-04 (Miss. 1996) (award of permanent alimony to sixty-year-old wife of man with Alzheimer's after three-year marriage); *see also* Larue v. Larue, 969 So. 2d 99, 110 (Miss. Ct. App. 2007) (permanent alimony awarded to seventy-year-old wife in ill health upon dissolution of second marriage); *cf.* Lawton v. Lawton, 905 So. 2d 723, 726 n.1 (Miss. Ct. App. 2004) ($500/month alimony to fifty-year-old wife of nine years, with high school education).

[312] *See* Mabus v. Mabus, 890 So. 2d 806, 823 (Miss. 2003) (fifty-year-old wife had capacity to earn substantial income); Sarver v. Sarver, 687 So. 2d 749, 757 (Miss. 1997) (sixty-five-year-old wife of ten years able to work).

§ 9.04[5][d]   **MISSISSIPPI FAMILY LAW**

alimony was young and able to work.[313] However, alimony has been awarded to younger women who were unable to work or where a significant disparity in income existed.[314] At least before retirement age, an individual's age may be less significant than the extent to which age affects earning capacity.

[d] Fault. Marital fault no longer bars an award of alimony. However, fault is still a factor for consideration, even in irreconcilable differences divorces. In 1992, the supreme court held that marital fault is merely one factor for consideration in an alimony award.[315] Today, fault is significant "when the misconduct places a burden on the stability and harmony of the marital and family relationship."[316]

[i] Payee's fault. Although a payee's marital fault is no longer a per se reason to deny alimony, it is still an important consideration. In some cases, alimony has been denied based in part on the recipient's fault. For example, a chancellor did not err in denying alimony to a wife of twenty-two years who committed adultery, even though her husband's income was three times the amount of her income.[317] In several cases, fault is mentioned as a supporting factor in denying alimony to wives with substantial earning capacity and separate assets.[318] Fault does not necessarily bar an award of alimony to a spouse in need. A low-income wife who committed adultery was awarded rehabilitative alimony from her disabled husband in spite of her fault.[319] And a wife of twenty-plus years was awarded permanent alimony even though she had an extramarital affair.[320] However, the court of appeals has emphasized that while a recipient's fault is not a total bar to alimony, it is awarded to a wrongdoer not to

---

[313] *See* Craft v. Craft, 825 So. 2d 605, 610-11 (Miss. 2002) (wife's good health and age, thirty-nine, supported rehabilitative alimony award); Hults v. Hults, 11 So. 3d 1273, 1280 (Miss. Ct. App. 2009) (forty-year-old wife and homemaker of twenty years who planned to return to work was properly denied permanent alimony and awarded five years of rehabilitative alimony of $900/month).

[314] *See* Creekmore v. Creekmore, 651 So. 2d 513, 517-18 (Miss. 1995) (thirty-year-old wife of seven years should receive lump sum award from drug-addicted husband with separate funds); Johnson v. Johnson, 877 So. 2d 485, 499 (Miss. Ct. App. 2003) (thirty-five-year-old wife in twelve-year marriage); *cf.* Craft v. Craft, 32 So. 3d 1232, 1244 (Miss. Ct. App. 2010) (wife of fifteen years, in her mid-thirties, with three children, earning $1,400/month, awarded $100/month in alimony from husband at fault in marriage breakup).

[315] *See* Hammonds v. Hammonds, 597 So. 2d 653, 655 (Miss. 1992) (wife guilty of adultery entitled to sufficient alimony to prevent destitution; court found no reason to distinguish adultery and other fault); *see also* Driste v. Driste, 738 So. 2d 763, 765 (Miss. Ct. App. 1998) (fault is factor for consideration even in irreconcilable differences divorce).

[316] Carrow v. Carrow, 642 So. 2d 901, 904-05 (Miss. 1994). *But see* Miller v. Miller, 874 So. 2d 469, 472 (Miss. Ct. App. 2004) (holding that fault is not a factor in an award of lump sum alimony paid as an "equalizer" because property distribution has left one spouse's assets out of balance to the other).

[317] Sandlin v. Sandlin, 906 So. 2d 39 (Miss. Ct. App. 2004) (wife would not be left destitute); *see also* Sullivan v. Sullivan, 990 So. 2d 783, 788 (Miss. Ct. App. 2008) (wife of twenty-eight years who left home to live with man she met at a bar denied alimony); McIntosh v. McIntosh, 977 So. 2d 1257, 1259, 1271 (Miss. Ct. App. 2008) (wife of twenty-seven years at fault in marriage breakup denied alimony); Brabham v. Brabham, 950 So. 2d 1098, 1103 (Miss. Ct. App. 2007) (denying all alimony to a wife of fifteen years who refused to work outside or in the home, whose extreme behavior contributed to the marriage breakup, and who had an affair).

[318] *See* Mabus v. Mabus, 890 So. 2d 806, 822 (Miss. 2003); Graham v. Graham, 767 So. 2d 277, 280-81 (Miss. Ct. App. 2000) (wife at fault with substantial income should be denied alimony).

[319] Turnley v. Turnley, 726 So. 2d 1258, 1266-67 (Miss. Ct. App. 1988); *see also* Rush v. Rush, 932 So. 2d 800, 807 (Miss. Ct. App. 2005), *rev'd in part on other grounds,* 932 So. 2d 794 (Miss. 2006) ($500/month in permanent alimony to wife of eighteen years in spite of post-separation adultery).

[320] Ladner v. Ladner, 49 So. 3d 669, 672 (Miss. Ct. App. 2010) (fault is merely one factor to consider).

ALIMONY   **§ 9.04[5][d][ii]**

replicate the marriage standard of living but to prevent destitution.[321]

      [ii] Fault of payor. A court may consider a payor's fault as a factor in awarding alimony. For example, a husband's adultery and transmission of a venereal disease to his wife was a significant factor in reversing a court's denial of permanent alimony.[322] The supreme court has stated, however, that a payor's fault is not a reason to increase an otherwise appropriate amount of alimony – alimony "is not a punishment."[323] For example, a husband who had several affairs was not required to pay alimony to a lower-income wife of thirty-five years who was able to support herself.[324] However, the fact that a chancellor commented on a husband's adultery in ruling on alimony did not prove that the award was a punishment for marital fault.[325]

      [iii] In irreconcilable differences divorce. In 1998, the court of appeals held that fault may be considered as an alimony factor even in irreconcilable differences divorces. The court did note that a chancellor may limit fault-related testimony to avoid converting the proceeding into a contested divorce.[326] Subsequently, the court of appeals reversed an award of alimony in an irreconcilable differences divorce for failure to consider the wife's desertion as a factor.[327]

      [e] Dissipation of assets. Dissipation of assets is an important factor in alimony decisions, particularly when a couple's marital assets are insufficient to remedy the dissipation. In several cases, a wife with no income was denied permanent alimony and granted limited rehabilitative or lump sum alimony based on her substantial dissipation of assets.[328] A wife who was able to work was denied all alimony based on dissipation

---

[321] Graham v. Graham, 767 So. 2d 277, 280-81 (Miss. Ct. App. 2000) (wife at fault with substantial income should be denied alimony).

[322] Buckley v. Buckley, 815 So. 2d 1260, 1265 (Miss. Ct. App. 2002); *see also* Holley v. Holley, 969 So. 2d 842, 843-44 (Miss. 2007) (husband's adultery factor in award of permanent alimony); Tatum v. Tatum, 54 So. 3d 855, 861 (Miss. Ct. App. 2010) (husband's adultery considered in award of rehabilitative alimony to wife of six years); Craft v. Craft, 32 So. 3d 1232, 1244 (Miss. Ct. App. 2010) (wife of fifteen years awarded $100/month in alimony from husband making $1,000/month, but who lost high-paying job through his misconduct); Tritle v. Tritle, 956 So. 2d 369, 377 (Miss. Ct. App. 2007) (chancellor did not err in considering husband's affair); Seymour v. Seymour, 960 So. 2d 513, 520 (Miss. Ct. App. 2006) (husband's adultery factor in alimony award); Lauro v. Lauro, 924 So. 2d 584, 589 (Miss. Ct. App. 2006) (permanent alimony awarded to wife of nine years whose husband had affair and dissipated assets); Stevens v. Stevens, 924 So. 2d 645, 649 (Miss. Ct. App. 2006) (substantial alimony to wife whose husband had affair); Patterson v. Patterson, 917 So. 2d 111, 113-14 (Miss. Ct. App. 2005) (husband's separation was a factor in alimony award to wife of twenty years; fault one factor among many); White v. White, 913 So. 2d 323, 325-26 (Miss. Ct. App. 2005) (wife of twenty-nine years, ill with cancer, awarded alimony from adulterous husband). *But cf.* Lawton v. Lawton, 905 So. 2d 723 (Miss. Ct. App. 2004) (wife's bingo habit and cigarette smoking not marital fault).

[323] Lauro v. Lauro, 847 So. 2d 843, 850 (Miss. 2003); *see* Welch v. Welch, 755 So. 2d 6, 15 (Miss. Ct. App. 1999).

[324] Meador v. Meador, 44 So. 3d 411, 420 (Miss. Ct. App 2010) (significant that wife had substantial retirement while fifty-eight-year-old husband had depleted his retirement to send sons to college).

[325] Wells v. Wells, 800 So. 2d 1239, 1245 (Miss. Ct. App. 2001) (rejecting husband's argument that chancellor punished him for adultery by awarding alimony).

[326] *See* Driste v. Driste, 738 So. 2d 763, 768 (Miss. Ct. App. 1999).

[327] *See* Graham v. Graham, 767 So. 2d 277, 280-81 (Miss. Ct. App. 2000). *But see* Burge v. Burge, 851 So. 2d 384, 387 (Miss. Ct. App. 2003) (fault should not be considered: "consent proceedings are by definition no-fault proceedings; any evidence showing that the divorce was the fault of either party is to be eschewed").

[328] *See* Pearson v. Pearson, 761 So. 2d 157, 165-66 (Miss. 2000) (awarding lump sum alimony); Sarver v. Sarver, 687 So. 2d 749, 756-57 (Miss. 1997) (awarding one-year rehabilitative alimony).

§ 9.04[5][f]   **MISSISSIPPI FAMILY LAW**

of assets.[329] And a wife who used the couple's scarce resources on bingo and cigarettes was awarded a lower amount of alimony based in part on her dissipation of marital assets. [330]

[f] Other factors. In addition to the enumerated factors, courts are to consider any other factor the court deems "just and equitable."[331]

[i] Sacrificing employment opportunities for marriage-related reasons. The *Armstrong* factors do not specifically list childcare or other marital contributions as factors affecting an alimony award. However, one spouse's sacrifice of employment or education to benefit the marriage is a commonly discussed reason for an award of alimony.[332] Marriage-related sacrifices may include staying home to care for children,[333] resigning a job to relocate,[334] or resigning work to remain at home at the other spouse's request.[335] A wife, who worked throughout the marriage in her husband's business without pay, was entitled to substantial permanent alimony as well as lump sum alimony.[336] Loss of earning capacity caused by marriage-related sacrifices may justify a substantial award of alimony even after a relatively short marriage.[337]

[ii] Support during schooling. Before reimbursement alimony was recognized as a distinct award, courts considered one spouse's support of the other through school as a significant factor in awarding alimony.[338] For example, an award of almost one-half of a husband's disposable income as alimony was not excessive; his wife supported him through medical school and gave up her career as a nurse to manage his medical practice.[339] Conversely, the fact that a higher-income husband supported his wife during school was a consideration in the amount of alimony he was required to pay.[340]

[6] Tax consequences. The tax consequences of an alimony award should be

---

[329] *See* Chapel v. Chapel, 700 So. 2d 593, 599-600 (Miss. 1997).

[330] *See* Lawton v. Lawton, 905 So. 2d 723 (Miss. Ct. App. 2004); *see also* Lauro v. Lauro, 924 So. 2d 584, 589 (Miss. Ct. App. 2006) (permanent alimony awarded to wife of nine years whose husband had affair and dissipated assets); *cf.* Elam v. Hinson, 932 So. 2d 76, 81 (Miss. Ct. App. 2006).

[331] Armstrong v. Armstrong, 618 So. 2d 1278 (Miss. 1993).

[332] The American Law Institute's proposal to reform spousal support laws suggests that alimony should be awarded *only* when disparity results from marital contributions. *See supra* § 9.01[3].

[333] Sanderson v. Sanderson, 824 So. 2d 623, 626-27 (Miss. 2002); Creekmore v. Creekmore, 651 So. 2d 513, 519-20 (Miss. 1995) (justifying lump sum award); Johnson v. Johnson, 877 So. 2d 485, 499 (Miss. Ct. App. 2003); Russell v. Russell, 733 So. 2d 858, 862 (Miss. Ct. App. 1999).

[334] Driste v. Driste, 738 So. 2d 763, 765 (Miss. Ct. App. 1999); Flechas v. Flechas, 724 So. 2d 948, 952 (Miss. Ct. App. 1998).

[335] *See* Parsons v. Parsons, 678 So. 2d 701, 703-04 (Miss. 1996); Larue v. Larue, 969 So. 2d 99, 110 (Miss. Ct. App. 2007) (permanent alimony awarded to seventy-year-old wife who quit work at husband's request; twenty-year marriage); Turnley v. Turnley, 726 So. 2d 1258, 1267 (Miss. Ct. App. 1998).

[336] Stevens v. Stevens, 924 So. 2d 645, 649 (Miss. Ct. App. 2006).

[337] *See* Driste v. Driste, 738 So. 2d 763, 765 (Miss. Ct. App. 1999); Flechas v. Flechas, 724 So. 2d 948, 952 (Miss. Ct. App. 1998).

[338] *See* Russell v. Russell, 733 So. 2d 858, 861-62 (Miss. Ct. App. 1999).

[339] Russell v. Russell, 733 So. 2d 858, 861-62 (Miss. Ct. App. 1999).

[340] Elam v. Hinson, 932 So. 2d 76, 80 (Miss. Ct. App. 2006).

ALIMONY

§ 9.05

considered in determining the parties' net incomes.[341] An award that meets the IRS definition of alimony will be deductible income to the payor, reducing the cost of the payment, and taxable income to the payee, reducing the net income available to the payee.[342]

§ 9.05 FACTORS GOVERNING LUMP SUM AWARDS RECOGNIZING CONTRIBUTION

In spite of the adoption of equitable distribution in 1994, lump sum awards continued to provide a means for rewarding contribution in cases where marital assets were not sufficient to do so. In those cases, courts typically used the factors set out in *Cheatham v. Cheatham* to recognize contribution to the marriage, rather than the *Armstrong* factors.[343] This discussion includes only cases in which lump sum alimony was based on substantial contribution. Lump sum awards that are truly alimony tend to be small awards supplementing permanent or rehabilitative alimony.[344] Recent cases, however, call into question the continued use of lump sum alimony outside of equitable distribution.[345]

[1] Substantial contribution to accumulation of the payor's assets by quitting work to become a homemaker or assisting in business. Spouses who contribute homemaking services at the expense of career or education have been awarded lump sum alimony. A homemaker wife of eighteen years was awarded $50,000 in lump sum alimony in addition to permanent alimony and an equal division of marital assets, in large part because of her contribution to the marriage. She quit her nursing job, sacrificing her education and career to provide childcare and a stable home, while her husband accumulated assets.[346] Similarly, a wife who worked without pay in her husband's business was entitled to permanent and lump sum alimony.[347] In contrast, a

---

[341] Armstrong v. Armstrong, 618 So. 2d 1278, 1280 (Miss. 1993).

[342] *See infra* § 22.01.

[343] Cheatham v. Cheatham, 537 So. 2d 435, 438 (Miss. 1988); *see* discussion *supra* § 9.02[2][b].

[344] *See* Mosley v. Mosley, 784 So. 2d 901, 909-10 (Miss. 2001); Monroe v. Monroe, 745 So. 2d 249, 250 (Miss. 1999) ($12,000); Robison v. Robison, 722 So. 2d 601, 604-05 (Miss. 1998) ($10,000 over forty months); Crowe v. Crowe, 641 So. 2d 1100, 1103 (Miss. 1994) ($4,500); Ford v. Ford, 795 So. 2d 600, 602 (Miss. Ct. App. 2001) ($6,500 as forgiven debt); East v. East, 775 So. 2d 741, 746 (Miss. Ct. App. 2000) ($10,000); Long v. Long, 734 So. 2d 206, 209-10 (Miss. Ct. App. 1999) ($20,000 lump sum in addition to $2,000/month permanent alimony).

[345] *See supra* § 9.02[b][v].

[346] Davis v. Davis, 832 So. 2d 492, 499 (Miss. 2002); *see also* Craft v. Craft, 825 So. 2d 605, 609 (Miss. 2002) (large lump sum in addition to property division to wife who worked and provided homemaking services, where primary assets were classified as separate); Sanderson v. Sanderson, 824 So. 2d 623, 629 (Miss. 2002) ($54,000 lump sum in addition to rehabilitative deemed inadequate to wife and homemaker of twenty-two years due to wife's contribution and economic disparity); A & L, Inc. v. Grantham, 747 So. 2d 832, 841 (Miss. 1999) (affirming $80,000 award in addition to property division to wife who quit lucrative job to move and support husband's business ventures); Long v. Long, 734 So. 2d 206, 209 (Miss. Ct. App. 1999) (court did not err in awarding $20,000 lump sum alimony in addition to equal property division and permanent alimony based on length of marriage and contribution); Russell v. Russell, 733 So. 2d 858, 862 (Miss. Ct. App. 1999) (affirming $50,000 lump sum award as rehabilitative in addition to substantial permanent alimony to homemaker wife of fifteen years); *cf.* Haney v. Haney, 881 So. 2d 862, 866 (Miss. Ct. App. 2003) (no real contribution just because wife performed clerical work for husband's business for a few months).

[347] Stevens v. Stevens, 924 So. 2d 645, 649 (Miss. Ct. App. 2006) (awarding lump sum alimony of $75,000); *see also* Palculict v. Palculict, 22 So. 3d 293, 296 (Miss. Ct. App. 2009) (wife of nine years, who sacrificed career for husband and who contributed $80,000 separate property to the marriage, entitled to $60,000 in lump sum alimony; husband received only marital asset worth $21,000).

§ 9.05[2]   **MISSISSIPPI FAMILY LAW**

wife whose husband supported her through school, and who kept her income for personal use, was not entitled to a lump sum award. Her contributions to the growth of his
family business were minimal.[348] Lump sum awards have also been made to spouses
who moved to provide homemaking services or assist in a spouse's business, even in
the absence of children and after relatively short marriages. A wife who quit her job to
move to another state and assist her wealthy husband was entitled to a substantial lump
sum award after an eight-year marriage.[349]

[2] A long marriage. Marriage length is important in determining whether lump
sum alimony should be awarded. A wife of twenty-one years was entitled to installment
lump sum alimony in addition to permanent alimony even though the award, combined
with child support, was two-thirds of the payor's income.[350] Lump sum alimony has
also been used to compensate marital contribution in shorter marriages. Lump sum
awards under *Cheatham* have been made to a spouse who quit work at the other's
request, even though the marriage did not exceed ten years.[351]

[3] Financial disparity. The remaining two *Cheatham* factors address financial
disparity: "the recipient spouse has no separate income or the separate estate is meager
by comparison" and "recipient would lack financial security without the lump sum
award."[352] While contribution and marriage length are important elements in a lump
sum award, the Mississippi Supreme Court has emphasized that the most important
element is financial disparity: "Disparity of the separate estates has continued to be
the most compelling factor."[353] Lump sum awards have often compensated contribution
in addition to addressing financial disparity.[354] However, they have also been used to
address financial disparity between parties to a short marriage even though the recipient
contributed little to asset accumulation. A disabled wife of ten years was awarded lump

---

[348] Elam v. Hinson, 932 So. 2d 76, 80 (Miss. Ct. App. 2006).

[349] *See* Driste v. Driste, 738 So. 2d 763, 767-68 (Miss. Ct. App. 1999) (award of $20,000 lump sum and $750
rehabilitative inadequate where husband had high income); *see also* Flechas v. Flechas, 724 So. 2d 948, 953-54 (Miss.
Ct. App. 1998) (award of one year rehabilitative and $18,000 lump sum inadequate for wife who quit job in Georgia,
moved to Mississippi, provided homemaking services, and cared for husband's son).

[350] Robison v. Robison, 722 So. 2d 601, 604 (Miss. 1998); *see also* Long v. Long, 734 So. 2d 206, 209-10 (Miss.
Ct. App. 1999) (affirming $20,000 lump sum award in addition to permanent alimony to homemaker wife of seventeen
years).

[351] *See* Driste v. Driste, 738 So. 2d 763, 767-68 (Miss. Ct. App. 1999) (six years); *see also* Sarver v. Sarver, 687
So. 2d 749, 756-57 (Miss. 1997) (ten years); Palculict v. Palculict, 22 So. 3d 293, 296 (Miss. Ct. App. 2009) (wife of
nine years, who sacrificed career for husband and who contributed $80,000 separate property to the marriage, entitled to
$60,000 in lump sum alimony); Flechas v. Flechas, 724 So. 2d 948, 953-54 (Miss. Ct. App. 1998) (eight years).

[352] Cheatham v. Cheatham, 537 So. 2d 435, 438 (Miss. 1988).

[353] Creekmore v. Creekmore, 651 So. 2d 513, 517 (Miss. 1995); *see* Tilley v. Tilley, 610 So. 2d 348, 352 (Miss.
1992); *cf.* Elam v. Hinson, 932 So. 2d 76, 81-82 (Miss. Ct. App. 2006) (lump sum not warranted; wife with $30,000
income would receive $1,650 for support payments, payment of car note, and free use of house).

[354] *See* Davis v. Davis, 832 So. 2d 492, 499-500 (Miss. 2002); Sanderson v. Sanderson, 824 So. 2d 623, 629
(Miss. 2002) ($54,000 lump sum in addition to rehabilitative alimony inadequate to wife and homemaker of twenty-two
years, emphasizing contribution and income disparity); Stevens v. Stevens, 924 So. 2d 645, 649 (Miss. Ct. App. 2006)
(awarding unemployed wife of fifteen years $5,000/month alimony and $75,000 lump sum alimony from husband with
$140,000/year income and greater assets); Long v. Long, 734 So. 2d 206, 209-10 (Miss. Ct. App. 1999) (affirming
$20,000 lump sum award in addition to permanent alimony to homemaker wife of seventeen years, emphasizing wife's
contribution and income disparity); Russell v. Russell, 733 So. 2d 858, 862 (Miss. Ct. App. 1999) (affirming $50,000
lump sum award as rehabilitative plus substantial permanent alimony to wife who supported husband through school).

ALIMONY § 9.05[4]

sum alimony of $4,500 in addition to permanent alimony despite conflicting evidence of contribution.[355]

[4] Other considerations

[a] Payor's assets. In determining whether to award alimony in a lump sum, a court must weigh the benefit of immediate payment to the recipient with the burden on the payor. Ordering payment at once from a payor without substantial liquid assets was error.[356] Courts should order installment payments if immediate payment would unfairly burden the payor.[357]

[b] Payor's instability. A lump sum award may be particularly appropriate if a payor with assets appears financially or personally unstable so that ongoing payments may be jeopardized. Remanding a case, the supreme court suggested lump sum alimony as an effective means of securing both spousal and child support from a drug-addicted husband with separate assets.[358]

§ 9.06 ANALYSIS OF REPORTED ALIMONY AWARDS 1994-2009

By 1995, the current Mississippi alimony system was in place. The Mississippi Supreme Court rejected the traditional emphasis on marital fault in 1992. Two years later, property division supplanted alimony as the primary financial adjustment at divorce. And the following year, judges were authorized to award time-limited rehabilitative alimony. This section analyzes reported appeals of alimony awards since 1994 in an attempt to identify patterns in modern awards. The study excludes cases with insufficient information to categorize the award and cases that were decided based on a legal issue rather than a factual analysis of the appropriateness of an award.

The study describes the type and amount of alimony awarded by length of marriage, dividing cases into those involving marriages ten years and under, marriages ten to nineteen years, and marriages twenty years and over. For cases with exact information on income, the study identifies the income disparity between the parties and describes the award as a percentage of the income disparity. The income disparity is calculated by subtracting any child support awarded from the payor's net income, then comparing the net incomes of the parties. For example, an alimony award of $2,000 per month to a payee with monthly net income of $1,000, from a payor with a net income of $5,000, would be fifty percent of the $4,000 disparity, equalizing the parties' incomes.

[1] Role of financial disparity. A court must find financial disparity to award alimony. A finding of disparity will usually, but not always, result in an award of one of the three types of alimony.

---

[355] Crowe v. Crowe, 641 So. 2d 1100, 1103 (Miss. 1994).
[356] Aldridge v. Aldridge, 27 So. 2d 884, 885-86 (Miss. 1946).
[357] Aldridge v. Aldridge, 27 So. 2d 884, 885-86 (Miss. 1946) (approving lump sum of $7,500).
[358] *See* Creekmore v. Creekmore, 651 So. 2d 513, 517-18 (Miss. 1995).

273

§ 9.06[1][a]   MISSISSIPPI FAMILY LAW

[a] No financial disparity. If no disparity existed or only a slight disparity was found, alimony was not awarded, even after long marriages.[359] Furthermore, even if a disparity in income was shown, no alimony was awarded if the lower-income spouse was able to meet reasonable needs.[360] A disparity at high-income levels did not necessarily result in an award; in some cases, spouses with substantial income and/or assets were denied alimony even though the other had higher income or assets.[361]

[b] Financial disparity. Alimony in some form was awarded in most cases where a substantial disparity was found. A substantial disparity in long marriages usually resulted in an award of permanent alimony.[362] After short marriages, financial disparity was more often addressed through rehabilitative alimony.[363] In some cases of disparity, alimony was denied based on dissipation of assets, marital fault, or because of the higher-income spouse's ill health or retirement.[364] All alimony was denied to a wife of fifteen years who made little direct or indirect contribution to the marriage, and whose extreme conduct contributed to the marriage breakdown.[365] And alimony has been denied in spite of financial disparity in income, when a spouse's assets were deemed sufficient to provide for her needs. The supreme court reversed an award of alimony to a wife who received $2.6 million in assets – there was no showing that the assets were not sufficient for her needs.[366]

[2] Awards of permanent alimony based on length of marriage. In the cases reviewed, permanent alimony was awarded or required on appeal in about twenty-five percent of the cases involving marriages under ten years,[367] half of marriages between

---

[359] *See* Selman v. Selman, 722 So. 2d 547 (Miss. 1998) (twenty-three-year marriage); McLaurin v. McLaurin, 853 So. 2d 1279 (Miss. Ct. App. 2003) (forty-five-year marriage); Chesney v. Chesney, 828 So. 2d 219 (Miss. Ct. App. 2002) (twenty-three-year marriage).

[360] *See* Graham v. Graham, 767 So. 2d 277 (Miss. Ct. App. 2000) (wife, at fault, lived during seven years of separation on her income).

[361] *See* Mabus v. Mabus, 890 So. 2d 806, 823 (Miss. 2003) (wife had high earning capacity and separate property); Cosentino v. Cosentino, 986 So. 2d 1065, 1070 (Miss. Ct. App. 2008).

[362] *See infra* § 9.06.

[363] *See infra* § 9.06; *see, e.g.*, Drumright v. Drumright, 812 So. 2d 1021 (Miss. Ct. App. 2001); Burnham-Steptoe v. Steptoe, 755 So. 2d 1225 (Miss. Ct. App. 1999) (rehabilitative alimony after four-year marriage even though extreme disparity in income).

[364] *See, e.g.*, Chapel v. Chapel, 700 So. 2d 593 (Miss. 1997) (awarding no alimony where wife dissipated assets); Sandlin v. Sandlin, 906 So. 2d 39, 40 (Miss. Ct. App. 2004) (wife committed adultery); Prescott v. Prescott, 736 So. 2d 409 (Miss. Ct. App. 1999) (alimony denied in part based on husband's retirement, where wife was working).

[365] Brabham v. Brabham, 950 So. 2d 1098, 1103 (Miss. Ct. App. 2007); *see also* Sandlin v. Sandlin, 906 So. 2d 39, 40-41 (Miss. Ct. App. 2004) (wife at fault denied alimony from higher-income husband).

[366] Cosentino v. Cosentino, 986 So. 2d 1065 (Miss. Ct. App. 2008); *see also* Marsh v. Marsh, 868 So. 2d 394, 398 (Miss. Ct. App. 2004) (wife with earning capacity and substantial assets denied alimony).

[367] Of the cases involving marriages under ten years, permanent alimony was awarded and affirmed in six cases. *See* Watson v. Watson, 724 So. 2d 350 (Miss. 1998); Parsons v. Parsons, 678 So. 2d 701 (Miss. 1996); Palculict v. Palculict, 22 So. 3d 293 (Miss. Ct. App. 2009); Lauro v. Lauro, 924 So. 2d 584, 588 (Miss. Ct. App. 2006); Burcham v. Burcham, 869 So. 2d 1058 (Miss. Ct. App. 2004); Lawton v. Lawton, 905 So. 2d 723 (Miss. Ct. App. 2004).

Permanent alimony was denied but rehabilitative or lump sum ordered in the majority of cases involving marriages under ten years. *See* Bowen v. Bowen, 982 So. 2d 385 (Miss. 2008); Pearson v. Pearson, 761 So. 2d 157 (Miss. 2000); Creekmore v. Creekmore, 651 So. 2d 513 (Miss. 1995); Brady v. Brady, 14 So. 3d 823 (Miss. Ct. App. 2009); Goellner v. Goellner, 11 So. 3d 1251 (Miss. Ct. App. 2009); LeBlanc v. Andrews, 931 So. 2d 683, 686 (Miss. Ct. App. 2006) (rehabilitative awarded after two-year marriage); Ferro v. Ferro, 871 So. 2d 753 (Miss. Ct. App. 2004); Drumright v. Drumright, 812 So. 2d 1021 (Miss. Ct. App. 2001); Burnham-Steptoe v. Steptoe, 755 So. 2d 1225 (Miss. Ct. App. 1999);

274

ALIMONY

§ 9.06[2]

ten and nineteen years,[368] and seventy percent of marriages twenty years and over.[369]

Driste v. Driste, 738 So. 2d 763 (Miss. Ct. App. 1999). Several cases were reversed because the amount of rehabilitative alimony awarded was inadequate; however, the court did not appear to hold that an award of permanent alimony was necessary. *See* Creekmore v. Creekmore, 651 So. 2d 513 (Miss. 1995); Driste v. Driste, 738 So. 2d 763 (Miss. Ct. App. 1999); Flechas v. Flechas, 724 So. 2d 948 (Miss. Ct. App. 1998).

In several cases, all alimony was denied. *See* Rogers v. Morin, 791 So. 2d 815 (Miss. 2001); Chapel v. Chapel, 700 So. 2d 593 (Miss. 1997); Love v. Love, 687 So. 2d 1229 (Miss. 1997); Larney v. Record, 908 So. 2d 171, 174-75 (Miss. Ct. App. 2005) (fourteen-month marriage); Ericson v. Tullos, 876 So. 2d 1038 (Miss. Ct. App. 2004); Masino v. Masino, 829 So. 2d 1267 (Miss. Ct. App. 2002); Prescott v. Prescott, 736 So. 2d 409 (Miss. Ct. App. 1999).

[368] Permanent alimony was awarded in a number of cases. *See* Holley v. Holley, 969 So. 2d 842 (Miss. 2007); Yelverton v. Yelverton, 961 So. 2d 19 (Miss. 2007) (permanent alimony awarded after sixteen-year marriage reversed as excessive); Mosley v. Mosley, 784 So. 2d 901 (Miss. 2001); Vaughn v. Vaughn, 798 So. 2d 431 (Miss. 2001); Monroe v. Monroe, 745 So. 2d 249 (Miss. 1999); Knutson v. Knutson, 704 So. 2d 1331 (Miss. 1997); Crowe v. Crowe, 641 So. 2d 1100 (Miss. 1994); Bedingfield v. Bedingfield, 11 So. 3d 780 (Miss. Ct. App. 2009); Smith v. Smith, 25 So. 3d 369 (Miss. Ct. App. 2009); Wilson v. Wilson, 975 So. 2d 261 (Miss. Ct. App. 2007); Phelps v. Phelps, 937 So. 2d 974, 976-77 (Miss. Ct. App. 2006); Blalack v. Blalack, 938 So. 2d 909, 911-12 (Miss. Ct. App. 2006); Elam v. Hinson, 932 So. 2d 76, 81 (Miss. Ct. App. 2006); Seymour v. Seymour, 960 So. 2d 513, 520 (Miss. Ct. App. 2006); Stevens v. Stevens, 924 So. 2d 645, 648-49 (Miss. Ct. App. 2006); Stuart v. Stuart, 956 So. 2d 295, 298-99 (Miss. Ct. App. 2006); Rush *ex rel.* Mayne, 914 So. 2d 322, 327 (Miss. Ct. App. 2005) (en banc); Rush v. Rush, 932 So. 2d 800, 807 (Miss. Ct. App. 2005) (en banc), *rev'd in part on other grounds*, 932 So. 2d 794 (Miss. 2006); Barnett v. Barnett, 908 So. 2d 833, 843-44 (Miss. Ct. App. 2005) (periodic plus rehabilitative and lump sum alimony awarded after twelve-year marriage); Burge v. Burge, 851 So. 2d 384 (Miss. Ct. App. 2003); Langdon v. Langdon, 854 So. 2d 485 (Miss. Ct. App. 2003); Gable v. Gable, 846 So. 2d 296 (Miss. Ct. App. 2003); Johnson v. Johnson, 877 So. 2d 485 (Miss. Ct. App. 2003); Russell v. Russell, 733 So. 2d 858 (Miss. Ct. App. 1999).

Permanent alimony was denied but rehabilitative or lump sum awarded in several cases. *See* Craft v. Craft, 825 So. 2d 605 (Miss. 2002); Henderson v. Henderson, 757 So. 2d 285 (Miss. 2000); Voda v. Voda, 731 So. 2d 1152 (Miss. 1999); Carnathan v. Carnathan, 722 So. 2d 1248 (Miss. 1998); Johnston v. Johnston, 722 So. 2d 453 (Miss. 1998); Sarver v. Sarver, 687 So. 2d 749 (Miss. 1997); McCarrell v. McCarrell, 19 So. 3d 168 (Miss. Ct. App. 2009); Barker v. Barker, 996 So. 2d 161 (Miss. Ct. App. 2008); Fogarty v. Fogarty, 922 So. 2d 836, 838, 841 (Miss. Ct. App. 2006); Spahn v. Spahn, 959 So. 2d 8, 10, 15 (Miss. Ct. App. 2006) ($56,835 lump sum alimony); Roberts v. Roberts, 924 So. 2d 550 (Miss. Ct. App. 2005); White v. White, 868 So. 2d 1054, 1056 (Miss. Ct. App. 2004) ($14,000 lump sum alimony); Ford v. Ford, 795 So. 2d 600 (Miss. Ct. App. 2001); Hoggatt v. Hoggatt, 766 So. 2d 9 (Miss. Ct. App. 2000); Wolfe v. Wolfe, 766 So. 2d 123 (Miss. Ct. App. 2000); Turnley v. Turnley, 726 So. 2d 1258 (Miss. Ct. App. 1988).

All alimony was denied in other cases. *See* Mabus v. Mabus, 890 So. 2d 806 (Miss. 2003); Lindsey v. Lindsey, 749 So. 2d 77 (Miss. 1999); Amacker v. Amacker, 33 So. 3d 493, 497 (Miss. Ct. App. 2009) (a temporarily disabled wife who would be able to return to work was not entitled to alimony from her disabled husband); Brabham v. Brabham, 950 So. 2d 1098 (Miss. Ct. App. 2007); Jones v. Jones, 904 So. 2d 1143 (Miss. Ct. App. 2004); Wallmark v. Wallmark, 863 So. 2d 68 (Miss. Ct. App. 2003).

[369] Permanent alimony was awarded in most cases. *See* Sanderson v. Sanderson, 824 So. 2d 623 (Miss. 2002); Kilpatrick v. Kilpatrick, 732 So. 2d 876 (Miss. 1999); Robison v. Robison, 722 So. 2d 601 (Miss. 1998); Tillman v. Tillman, 716 So. 2d 1090 (Miss. 1998); Traxler v. Traxler, 730 So. 2d 1098 (Miss. 1998); Brooks v. Brooks, 652 So. 2d 1113 (Miss. 1995); Brennan v. Brennan, 638 So. 2d 1320 (Miss. 1994); Hemsley v. Hemsley, 639 So. 2d 909 (Miss. 1994); Rodriguez v. Rodriguez, 2 So. 3d 720 (Miss. Ct. App. 2009); George v. George, 22 So. 3d 424 (Miss. Ct. App. 2009); Elliott v. Elliott, 11 So. 3d 784 (Miss. Ct. App. 2009); Cosentino v. Cosentino, 986 So. 2d 1065 (Miss. Ct. App. 2008) (reversed); Roberson v. Roberson, 949 So. 2d 866 (Miss. Ct. App. 2007); Larue v. Larue, 969 So. 2d 99 (Miss. Ct. App. 2007); Tritle v. Tritle, 956 So. 2d 369 (Miss. Ct. App. 2007); Parker v. Parker, 934 So. 2d 359, 360 (Miss. Ct. App. 2006); Dobbs v. Dobbs, 912 So. 2d 491, 493 (Miss. Ct. App. 2005); Patterson v. Patterson, 917 So. 2d 111, 119 (Miss. Ct. App. 2005); White v. White, 913 So. 2d 323, 326 (Miss. Ct. App. 2005); Seale v. Seale, 863 So. 2d 996 (Miss. Ct. App. 2004); Brennan v. Ebel, 880 So. 2d 1058 (Miss. Ct. App. 2004); Klauser v. Klauser, 865 So. 2d 363 (Miss. Ct. App. 2003); Palmer v. Palmer, 841 So. 2d 185 (Miss. Ct. App. 2003); Buckley v. Buckley, 815 So. 2d 1260 (Miss. Ct. App. 2002); Duncan v. Duncan, 815 So. 2d 480 (Miss. Ct. App. 2002); McIlwain v. McIlwain, 815 So. 2d 476 (Miss. Ct. App. 2002); Weeks v. Weeks, 832 So. 2d 583 (Miss. Ct. App. 2002); Baker v. Baker, 807 So. 2d 476 (Miss. Ct. App. 2001); Cork v. Cork, 811 So. 2d 427 (Miss. Ct. App. 2001); Curtis v. Curtis, 796 So. 2d 1044 (Miss. Ct. App. 2001); Moore v. Moore, 803 So. 2d 1214 (Miss. Ct. App. 2001); Pittman v. Pittman, 791 So. 2d 857 (Miss. Ct. App. 2001); East v. East, 775 So. 2d 741 (Miss. Ct. App. 2000); Long v. Long, 734 So. 2d 206 (Miss. Ct. App. 1999); Welch v. Welch, 755 So. 2d 6 (Miss. Ct. App. 1999); Magee v. Magee, 724 So. 2d 1034 (Miss. Ct. App. 1998).

Permanent alimony was denied but rehabilitative or lump sum awarded in several cases. *See* Hensarling v. Hensarling, 824 So. 2d 583 (Miss. 2002); Hults v. Hults, 11 So. 3d 1273 (Miss. Ct. App. 2009); Avery v. Avery, 864 So. 2d 1054 (Miss. Ct. App. 2004); Wesson v. Wesson, 818 So. 2d 1272 (Miss. Ct. App. 2002); Bumpous v. Bumpous, 770 So. 2d 558 (Miss. Ct. App. 2000); Osborn v. Osborn, 724 So. 2d 1121 (Miss. Ct. App. 1998).

§ 9.06[2][a]   MISSISSIPPI FAMILY LAW

[a] Marriages over twenty years. In most cases involving marriages over twenty years, a showing of financial disparity led to an award of some form of alimony.[370] Two wives who were at fault in the divorce were denied all alimony in spite of disparity.[371] And in one case, a wife was denied alimony because she had substantial earning capacity.[372] In most cases of significant disparity, permanent alimony was awarded rather than rehabilitative.[373] Four decisions were reversed for failure to award permanent alimony after a long marriage.[374]

[b] Marriages ten to nineteen years. Awards in the middle range were less consistent. Permanent alimony was awarded in about half of the cases. Rehabilitative or lump sum alimony was awarded in approximately one-third of the cases.[375] Alimony was denied altogether in 14% of the cases. All alimony was denied when there was no financial disparity between the parties[376] or when the lower-income spouse had high income, assets, or earning capacity.[377] And in one case, all alimony was denied to a wife of fifteen years who made almost no direct or indirect contribution to the marriage, and whose extreme behavior caused the marriage to end.[378]

Rehabilitative alimony was awarded to a wife whose husband was disabled and living on a small, fixed income,[379] and to a wife who had dissipated assets and whose husband was seriously ill.[380] Rehabilitative alimony was also awarded to spouses who

---

All alimony was denied in the following cases: Selman v. Selman, 722 So. 2d 547 (Miss. 1998); Sellers v. Sellers, 22 So. 3d 299 (Miss. Ct. App. 2009); McIntosh v. McIntosh, 977 So. 2d 1257 (Miss. Ct. App. 2008); Marsh v. Marsh, 868 So. 2d 394 (Miss. Ct. App. 2004); Sandlin v. Sandlin, 906 So. 2d 39 (Miss. Ct. App. 2004); Johnson v. Johnson, 852 So. 2d 681 (Miss. Ct. App. 2003); McLaurin v. McLaurin, 853 So. 2d 1279 (Miss. Ct. App. 2003); Chesney v. Chesney, 828 So. 2d 219 (Miss. Ct. App. 2002); Graham v. Graham, 767 So. 2d 277 (Miss. Ct. App. 2000).

[370] Alimony was denied in cases involving no financial disparity. *See* Selman v. Selman, 722 So. 2d 547 (Miss. 1998) (equal income); Johnson v. Johnson, 852 So. 2d 681 (Miss. Ct. App. 2003) (substantial separate assets); McLaurin v. McLaurin, 853 So. 2d 1279 (Miss. Ct. App. 2003) (equal income); Chesney v. Chesney, 828 So. 2d 219 (Miss. Ct. App. 2002) (equal income); Graham v. Graham, 767 So. 2d 277 (Miss. Ct. App. 2000) (wife had high, although not equal, income).

[371] McIntosh v. McIntosh, 977 So. 2d 1257, 1259, 1272 (Miss. Ct. App. 2008) (alimony denied to wife of twenty-seven years, at fault in marriage breakup, even though husband's salary was three times hers); Sandlin v. Sandlin, 906 So. 2d 39, 43 (Miss. Ct. App. 2004) (alimony denied to wife of twenty-two years who had affair but was not left destitute).

[372] Marsh v. Marsh, 868 So. 2d 394, 398 (Miss. Ct. App. 2004) (fifty-nine-year-old wife of thirty-six years denied alimony from husband with income of $56,000 a year).

[373] *See infra* § 9.06. *But see* Hensarling v. Hensarling, 824 So. 2d 583 (Miss. 2002); Hults v. Hults, 11 So. 3d 1273, 1280 (Miss. Ct. App. 2009) (awarding rehabilitative alimony to wife of twenty years who planned to return to school); Wesson v. Wesson, 818 So. 2d 1272 (Miss. Ct. App. 2002); Bumpous v. Bumpous, 770 So. 2d 558 (Miss. Ct. App. 2000); Osborn v. Osborn, 724 So. 2d 1121 (Miss. Ct. App. 1998). In *Wesson* and *Bumpous*, the husband, rather than the wife, appealed the decision. *Hensarling* and *Osborn* appear at odds with the results in most of the cases.

[374] *See* Sanderson v. Sanderson, 824 So. 2d 623 (Miss. 2002); Weeks v. Weeks, 832 So. 2d 583 (Miss. Ct. App. 2002); Buckley v. Buckley, 815 So. 2d 1260 (Miss. Ct. App. 2002); Pittman v. Pittman, 791 So. 2d 857 (Miss. Ct. App. 2001).

[375] *See* cases cited *supra* note 368.

[376] *See* Lindsey v. Lindsey, 749 So. 2d 77 (Miss. 1999) (income apparently equal); Amacker v. Amacker, 33 So. 3d 493, 497 (Miss. Ct. App. 2009) (husband disabled while wife was temporarily disabled and perceived to be able to go back to work); Wallmark v. Wallmark, 863 So. 2d 68 (Miss. Ct. App. 2003) (wife's income was 70% of husband's but she had free medical care).

[377] *See* Mabus v. Mabus, 890 So. 2d 806 (Miss. 2003) (high earning capacity and over $1 million in assets).

[378] Brabham v. Brabham, 950 So. 2d 1098, 1103 (Miss. Ct. App. 2007).

[379] *See* Turnley v. Turnley, 726 So. 2d 1258 (Miss. Ct. App. 1988) (award of rehabilitative alimony until husband's private disability benefits ceased); *see also* Barker v. Barker, 996 So. 2d 161 (Miss. Ct. App. 2008) (both spouses disabled).

[380] *See* Sarver v. Sarver, 687 So. 2d 749 (Miss. 1997) (award of $2,500 lump sum alimony to wife in good health

ALIMONY

§ 9.06[2][c]

planned to return to the workforce or had substantial earning capacity.[381] Similarly, rehabilititave alimony was proper for a wife who had a high earning capacity and received substantial assets.[382] Interestingly, while denials of permanent alimony were reversed in several cases involving long marriages, no case involving a mid-length marriage was reversed for failure to award permanent alimony.

[c] Marriages under ten years. Permanent alimony was awarded in only six of the twenty-four cases involving marriages under ten years.[383] Two recipients were at least sixty years old. One was unable to work. The other had discontinued work at her husband's request.[384] One was seriously ill.[385] In most, rehabilitative or lump sum alimony was awarded.[386] All alimony was denied when the court assumed equal earning capacity,[387] the husband was disabled,[388] or the lower-income spouse had dissipated assets.[389] All alimony was also denied after a fourteen-month marriage.[390]

[3] Amount of permanent awards. Just as permanent alimony was more frequently awarded after longer marriages, the amount of awards tended to be higher in cases involving longer marriages.

[a] Marriages over twenty years. In the cases reviewed, awards of permanent alimony in marriages over twenty years ranged in amount from 25% to 100% of the

---

and able to work).

[381] *See* Voda v. Voda, 731 So. 2d 1152 (Miss. 1999) (rehabilitative alimony to thirty-five-year-old wife of eleven years expected to have almost equal earning capacity); McCarrell v. McCarrell, 19 So. 3d 168, 170 (Miss. Ct. App. 2009) (wife planned to return to work); Roberts v. Roberts, 924 So. 2d 550 (Miss. Ct. App. 2005); Hoggatt v. Hoggatt, 766 So. 2d 9 (Miss. Ct. App. 2000) (rehabilitative alimony to homemaker wife of eighteen years during period needed for re-certification as teacher); Wolfe v. Wolfe, 766 So. 2d 123 (Miss. Ct. App. 2000) (wife earned degree and sought work, husband's income was low; wife received only marital asset).

[382] *See* Craft v. Craft, 825 So. 2d 605 (Miss. 2002) (awarding substantial lump sum alimony to wife with earning capacity of $65,000/year).

[383] *See* cases cited *supra* note 367.

[384] *See* Watson v. Watson, 724 So. 2d 350 (Miss. 1998) (sixty-year-old wife unable to work); Parsons v. Parsons, 678 So. 2d 701 (Miss. 1996) (sixty-year-old wife quit work at husband's request).

[385] Palculict v. Palculict, 22 So. 3d 293, 296 (Miss. Ct. App. 2009) (wife in remission from cancer).

[386] *See supra* note 367. *See* Bowen v. Bowen, 982 So. 2d 385, 392-93 (Miss. 2008) (wife of eight years in ill health and unable to meet expenses awarded $430/month in rehabilitative alimony for five years and $60,000 in lump sum alimony); Drumright v. Drumright, 812 So. 2d 1021 (Miss. Ct. App. 2001) (awarding five years rehabilitative alimony to wife of five years despite husband's high income); Burnham-Steptoe v. Steptoe, 755 So. 2d 1225 (Miss. Ct. App. 1999) (awarding $300/month rehabilitative alimony for two years to wife of four years). *But see* Lauro v. Lauro, 924 So. 2d 584, 586, 589 (Miss. Ct. App. 2006) (permanent alimony awarded after nine-year marriage). In two cases, the amount of rehabilitative alimony awarded was reversed as inadequate; in both cases the payor's income was high. *See* Driste v. Driste, 738 So. 2d 763 (Miss. Ct. App. 1999) (eighteen months of $750/month alimony inadequate for wife who quit job and moved); Flechas v. Flechas, 724 So. 2d 948 (Miss. Ct. App. 1998) (eighteen months of $750/month rehabilitative to wife of six years who moved was inadequate). Lump sum alimony was awarded to a thirty-year-old wife of seven years. Creekmore v. Creekmore, 651 So. 2d 513 (Miss. 1995) (amount inadequate); *see also* Pearson v. Pearson, 761 So. 2d 157 (Miss. 2000) ($150,000 lump sum from husband with $2 million in separate assets deemed inadequate for thirty-six-year-old wife of six years with no children).

[387] *See* Rogers v. Morin, 791 So. 2d 815 (Miss. 2001) (wife's imputed income almost equal to husband's); Love v. Love, 687 So. 2d 1229 (Miss. 1997) (incomes almost equal); Masino v. Masino, 829 So. 2d 1267 (Miss. Ct. App. 2002) (wife refused to work full-time). In another case, the husband was retired and the wife working. *See* Prescott v. Prescott, 736 So. 2d 409 (Miss. Ct. App. 1999).

[388] Ericson v. Tullos, 876 So. 2d 1038 (Miss. Ct. App. 2004).

[389] *See* Chapel v. Chapel, 700 So. 2d 593 (Miss. 1997) (wife dissipated $100,000 of husband's assets).

[390] Larney v. Record, 908 So. 2d 171 (Miss. Ct. App. 2005).

§ 9.06[3][b]   **MISSISSIPPI FAMILY LAW**

financial disparity between the parties.[391] In most cases, awards provided payees with an amount equal to less than half the income disparity.[392] In a few cases, however, awards left the payee with a higher net income than the payor.[393] Two awards were reversed as excessive. A monthly award of $7,200, which was more than the husband's monthly net income, was deemed an abuse of discretion.[394] Similarly, an award of $6,000 a month, 70% of the payor's $11,000 a month net income, was reversed.[395] On the other hand, awards of 70% and 83% of the financial disparity were approved in cases involving low-income families; the recipients were struggling to meet basic expenses.[396] And in one case, the court of appeals upheld an award of 100% of the income disparity to a disabled wife of many years.[397] No reported cases since 2004 have affirmed awards of more than 50% of the income gap.

   [b] Marriages ten to nineteen years. In cases involving marriages under twenty years, two awards equalized the parties' incomes.[398] One award provided a wife who supported her husband through school with 44% of the disparity between their incomes.[399] Other awards ranged from 6% to 38% of the disparity.[400] Two awards

---

   [391] *See supra* introduction to § 9.06 (explanation of percentage calculation).

   [392] *See* Tillman v. Tillman, 716 So. 2d 1090 (Miss. 1998) (31% award); Roberson v. Roberson, 949 So. 2d 866, 870 (Miss. Ct. App. 2007) (permanent alimony equaling 25% of disparity awarded after thirty-year marriage); Larue v. Larue, 969 So. 2d 99, 108, 110-11 (Miss. Ct. App. 2007) (permanent alimony equal to 15% of disparity, plus occupancy of home, awarded to wife of twenty-two years); Tritle v. Tritle, 956 So. 2d 369, 381 (Miss. Ct. App. 2007) (permanent alimony awarded to wife of twenty-one years); Parker v. Parker, 934 So. 2d 359, 361-62 (Miss. Ct. App. 2006) ($1,500 award; exact disparity unclear); Patterson v. Patterson, 917 So. 2d 111, 119 (Miss. Ct. App. 2005) ($2,000 award equal to 31% of income gap); White v. White, 913 So. 2d 323, 326 (Miss. Ct. App. 2005) ($500 award equal to 39% of income gap); McIlwain v. McIlwain, 815 So. 2d 476 (Miss. Ct. App. 2002) (25% award); Cork v. Cork, 811 So. 2d 427 (Miss. Ct. App. 2001) (33% award); Curtis v. Curtis, 796 So. 2d 1044 (Miss. Ct. App. 2001) (42% award); Magee v. Magee, 724 So. 2d 1034 (Miss. Ct. App. 1998) (29% award).

   [393] *See* Robison v. Robison, 722 So. 2d 601 (Miss. 1998) (awarding $250/month, 70% of disparity, to very low-income payee); Traxler v. Traxler, 730 So. 2d 1098 (Miss. 1998) (awarding $750/month, 83% of disparity); Hemsley v. Hemsley, 639 So. 2d 909 (Miss. 1994) (awarding $1,400/month, 57% of disparity); Palmer v. Palmer, 841 So. 2d 185 (Miss. Ct. App. 2003) (awarding $600/month, 52% of disparity); East v. East, 775 So. 2d 741 (Miss. Ct. App. 2000) (awarding $1,300, 100% of disparity, to disabled wife of many years).

   [394] Brooks v. Brooks, 652 So. 2d 1113 (Miss. 1995).

   [395] Duncan v. Duncan, 815 So. 2d 480 (Miss. Ct. App. 2002).

   [396] *See* Robison v. Robison, 722 So. 2d 601 (Miss. 1998) (awarding 70%); Traxler v. Traxler, 730 So. 2d 1098 (Miss. 1998) (awarding 83%).

   [397] East v. East, 775 So. 2d 741 (Miss. Ct. App. 2000).

   [398] Wilson v. Wilson, 975 So. 2d 261, 265 n.7 (Miss. Ct. App. 2007) (permanent alimony equaling 50% of income disparity, after eighteen-year marriage); Seymour v. Seymour, 960 So. 2d 513, 517, 520 (Miss. Ct. App. 2006) ($3,000 award equal to 54% of income gap).

   [399] Russell v. Russell, 733 So. 2d 858 (Miss. Ct. App. 1999) ($5,000/month award to wife, with children, from husband with high income; case preceded recognition of reimbursement alimony); *see also* Stevens v. Stevens, 924 So. 2d 645, 650 (Miss. Ct. App. 2006) ($5,000 award equal to 43% of disparity).

   [400] *See* Davis v. Davis, 832 So. 2d 492 (Miss. 2002) (awarding $4,000/month to wife from husband with $34,000/month income, which was 13% of disparity); Vaughn v. Vaughn, 798 So. 2d 431 (Miss. 2001) (awarding $500/month from husband with $8,000/month income, which was 10% of disparity); Knutson v. Knutson, 704 So. 2d 1331 (Miss. 1997) (awarding $1,000/month to wife from husband with $10,000/month income, which was 17% of disparity); Magee v. Magee, 661 So. 2d 1117 (Miss. 1995) (awarding $1,600/month to wife from husband with $5,500/month income, which was 29% of disparity); Crowe v. Crowe, 641 So. 2d 1100 (Miss. 1994) (awarding $300/month, 33% of difference between low-income parties); Smith v. Smith, 25 So. 3d 369 (Miss. Ct. App. 2009) ($2,000 a month, 12% of disparity); Phelps v. Phelps, 937 So. 2d 974, 977 (Miss. Ct. App. 2006) ($1,000 award equal to 35% of disparity); Blalack v. Blalack, 938 So. 2d 909, 911-12 (Miss. Ct. App. 2006) ($500 award equal to 14% of disparity); Elam v. Hinson, 932 So. 2d 76, 81-82 (Miss. Ct. App. 2006) ($350 award equal to 12% of disparity); Stuart v. Stuart, 956 So. 2d 295, 298-99 (Miss. Ct. App. 2006) ($250 award equal to 30% of disparity); Barnett v. Barnett, 908 So. 2d 833, 843-44 (Miss. Ct. App. 2005)

ALIMONY

§ 9.06[3][c]

were reversed as inadequate, both involving awards of less than $1,000 a month to parties whose spouses earned over $10,000 a month.[401] And one award was reversed as excessive when viewed in combination with other support awards. A chancellor erred in ordering $2,500 in permanent alimony, $2,500 in child support, and $5,000 in lump sum payments, from a payor with earning capacity of $12,000 a month.[402]

[c] Marriages under ten years. The six awards of permanent alimony after marriages of less than ten years provided the payees with one-fourth or less of the disparity between the parties' incomes.[403]

[4] Awards of rehabilitative alimony. A review of reported awards of rehabilitative alimony suggests that the award is used both for rehabilitation and as a form of time-limited alimony when permanent alimony is not warranted. In some cases, courts awarded rehabilitative alimony to a recipient who could reenter the workforce,[404] or increase earning capacity,[405] after a period of training or transition. In other cases, however, awards do not appear related to increasing earning capacity, but seemed to provide support for a limited period of adjustment after divorce.[406]

(award equal to 14% of income gap); Rush v. Rush *ex rel.* Mayne, 914 So. 2d 322, 327 (Miss. Ct. App. 2005) (en banc) ($400 award equal to 28% of income gap); Rush v. Rush, 932 So. 2d 800, 807 (Miss. Ct. App. 2005) ($500 award equal to 7% of income gap), *rev'd en banc in part on other grounds,* 932 So. 2d 794 (Miss. 2006); Burge v. Burge, 851 So. 2d 384 (Miss. Ct. App. 2003) (awarding $400/month to wife with $24,000/year income, which was 25% of disparity); Gable v. Gable, 846 So. 2d 296 (Miss. Ct. App. 2003) (awarding $500/month to wife from husband with $4,100/month income, which was 22% of disparity); Langdon v. Langdon, 854 So. 2d 485 (Miss. Ct. App. 2003) (awarding $300/month, which was 13% of disparity).

[401] *See* Monroe v. Monroe, 745 So. 2d 249 (Miss. 1999) ($450/month to disabled wife from husband with $130,000/year income deemed inadequate); Johnson v. Johnson, 877 So. 2d 485 (Miss. Ct. App. 2003) ($750/month to homemaker wife from husband with $12,000/month income deemed inadequate).

[402] Yelverton v. Yelverton, 961 So. 2d 19 (Miss. 2007) (sixteen-year marriage).

[403] *See* Watson v. Watson, 724 So. 2d 350 (Miss. 1998) (awarding $1,000/month, which was 25% of disparity); Parsons v. Parsons, 678 So. 2d 701 (Miss. 1996) (awarding $600/month, which was 22% of disparity); Palculict v. Palculict, 22 So. 3d 293 (Miss. Ct. App. 2009) ($1,500/month, 23% of disparity); Lauro v. Lauro, 924 So. 2d 584, 589 (Miss. Ct. App. 2006) ($3,000 award equal to 21% of income disparity); Burcham v. Burcham, 869 So. 2d 1058 (Miss. Ct. App. 2004) ($400/month, 9% of disparity); Lawton v. Lawton, 905 So. 2d 723 (Miss. Ct. App. 2004) ($500/month, 19% of disparity).

[404] *See* Carnathan v. Carnathan, 722 So. 2d 1248 (Miss. 1998) (stating that wife could work as legal secretary); Graham v. Graham, 948 So. 2d 451, 453-54 (Miss. Ct. App. 2006) (husband, co-owner of convenience store that was awarded to wife, awarded three months of rehabilitative alimony to find employment as truck driver); Hoggatt v. Hoggatt, 766 So. 2d 9 (Miss. Ct. App. 2000) (declaring wife could become re-certified to teach); Wolfe v. Wolfe, 766 So. 2d 123 (Miss. Ct. App. 2000) (showing wife completed degree and was seeking work); Driste v. Driste, 738 So. 2d 763 (Miss. Ct. App. 1999) (stating that wife who quit work needed support to reenter workforce); Flechas v. Flechas, 724 So. 2d 948 (Miss. Ct. App. 1998) (holding that former teacher needed assistance to relocate and begin work).

[405] *See* Roberts v. Roberts, 924 So. 2d 550, 554 (Miss. Ct. App. 2005) (rehabilitative alimony awarded; wife had equal earning capacity); *cf.* Craft v. Craft, 825 So. 2d 605 (Miss. 2002) (wife with higher earning capacity working at lower paying, less stressful job); LeBlanc v. Andrews, 931 So. 2d 683, 687 (Miss. Ct. App. 2006) (rejecting wife's argument that she should have received rehabilitative alimony in the form of cash rather than debt payment; wife was working at time of trial).

[406] *See* Henderson v. Henderson, 757 So. 2d 285 (Miss. 2000) (awarding rehabilitative alimony to recipient teaching school); Fogarty v. Fogarty, 922 So. 2d 836, 840 (Miss. Ct. App. 2006) (two years rehabilitative alimony awarded to disabled wife); Wesson v. Wesson, 818 So. 2d 1272 (Miss. Ct. App. 2002) (awarding rehabilitative alimony in the form of house payments to wife working at low wage job); Drumright v. Drumright, 812 So. 2d 1021 (Miss. Ct. App. 2001) (awarding $150/month for five years to working wife of five years); Osborn v. Osborn, 724 So. 2d 1121 (Miss. Ct. App. 1998) (awarding rehabilitative alimony to wife working at low wages). In a recent case, however, the supreme court suggested that rehabilitative alimony may be improper if the recipient is working at full capacity. *See* Holley v. Holley, 892 So. 2d 183 (Miss. 2004).

§ 9.06[4][a]   **MISSISSIPPI FAMILY LAW**

[a] **Length of award.** Most of the awards of rehabilitative alimony reviewed provided support for two to four years.[407] Five reported awards provided longer support.[408] Two awards of rehabilitative alimony for less than two years were reversed as inadequate, based on the combined effect of the short time period and the low amount awarded.[409]

[b] **Amount of award.** In most of the cases reviewed, the lower-income spouse was awarded an amount equal to 10% to 20% of the income gap between the parties.[410] In one case, the award represented 50% of the income disparity, equalizing the parties' incomes for two years.[411] Two awards providing spouses of wealthy payors with less than 10% of the disparity were reversed as inadequate.[412]

[5] **Lump sum awards.** In most of the cases reviewed, lump sum awards were relatively small awards supplementing permanent or rehabilitative alimony.[413] In some

---

[407] Examples of two-year awards of rehabilitative alimony include: Craft v. Craft, 825 So. 2d 605 (Miss. 2002); Carnathan v. Carnathan, 722 So. 2d 1248 (Miss. 1998); Barker v. Barker, 996 So. 2d 161, 163 (Miss. Ct. App. 2008) (wife of ten years, in ill health, awarded $200/month rehabilitative alimony for two years from husband also in ill health); Fogarty v. Fogarty, 922 So. 2d 836, 840 (Miss. Ct. App. 2006) (rehabilitative award of $200/month for two years); Wolfe v. Wolfe, 766 So. 2d 123 (Miss. Ct. App. 2000); Burnham-Steptoe v. Steptoe, 755 So. 2d 1225 (Miss. Ct. App. 1999). Examples of three-year awards of rehabilitative alimony include: Henderson v. Henderson, 757 So. 2d 285 (Miss. 2000); Roberts v. Roberts, 924 So. 2d 550, 554 (Miss. Ct. App. 2005) ($673/month in rehabilitative alimony for three years); Hoggatt v. Hoggatt, 766 So. 2d 9 (Miss. Ct. App. 2000); Osborn v. Osborn, 724 So. 2d 1121 (Miss. Ct. App. 1998); Turnley v. Turnley, 726 So. 2d 1258 (Miss. Ct. App. 1988). Examples of four-year awards of rehabilitative alimony include: Drumright v. Drumright, 812 So. 2d 1021 (Miss. Ct. App. 2001); Bumpous v. Bumpous, 770 So. 2d 558 (Miss. Ct. App. 2000). *But see* Graham v. Graham, 948 So. 2d 451, 453-54 (Miss. Ct. App. 2006) (husband, co-owner of convenience store that was awarded to wife, awarded three months of rehabilitative alimony to find employment as truck driver).

[408] Bowen v. Bowen, 982 So. 2d 385, 392-93 (Miss. 2008) (wife of eight years in ill health and unable to meet expenses awarded $430/month in rehabilitative alimony for five years and $60,000 in lump sum alimony); Hensarling v. Hensarling, 824 So. 2d 583 (Miss. 2002) (awarding six years rehabilitative alimony); Hults v. Hults, 11 So. 3d 1273 (Miss. Ct. App. 2009) ($900/month for five years); McCarrell v. McCarrell, 19 So. 3d 168 (Miss. Ct. App. 2009) ($1,800/month for five years); Ford v. Ford, 795 So. 2d 600 (Miss. Ct. App. 2001) (awarding five years rehabilitative alimony).

[409] *See* Driste v. Driste, 738 So. 2d 763 (Miss. Ct. App. 1999) (eighteen months deemed inadequate); Flechas v. Flechas, 724 So. 2d 948 (Miss. Ct. App. 1998) (one year deemed inadequate). *But see* Goellner v. Goellner, 11 So. 3d 1251 (Miss. Ct. App. 2009) ($300/month for 14 months); Ferro v. Ferro, 871 So. 2d 753 (Miss. Ct. App. 2004) (affirming one-year rehabilitative).

[410] *See* Bowen v. Bowen, 982 So. 2d 385, 393 (Miss. 2008) (10%); Johnston v. Johnston, 722 So. 2d 453 (Miss. 1998) (8%); Brady v. Brady, 14 So. 3d 823 (Miss. Ct. App. 2009) (20%); Hults v. Hults, 11 So. 3d 1273 (Miss. Ct. App. 2009) (20%); McCarrell v. McCarrell, 19 So. 3d 168 (Miss. Ct. App. 2009) (22%); Barker v. Barker, 996 So. 2d 161 (Miss. Ct. App. 2008) (12%); Drumright v. Drumright, 812 So. 2d 1021 (Miss. Ct. App. 2001) (varying between 2% and 10%); Ford v. Ford, 795 So. 2d 600 (Miss. Ct. App. 2001) (15%); Bumpous v. Bumpous, 770 So. 2d 558 (Miss. Ct. App. 2000) (13%); Hoggatt v. Hoggatt, 766 So. 2d 9 (Miss. Ct. App. 2000) (15%); Wolfe v. Wolfe, 766 So. 2d 123 (Miss. Ct. App. 2000) (11%); Burnham-Steptoe v. Steptoe, 755 So. 2d 1225 (Miss. Ct. App. 1999) (14%); Osborn v. Osborn, 724 So. 2d 1121 (Miss. Ct. App. 1998) (20%); Turnley v. Turnley, 726 So. 2d 1258 (Miss. Ct. App. 1988) (9%). At least one case was higher than 20%. *See* Craft v. Craft, 825 So. 2d 605 (Miss. 2002) (ranging between 29% to 38%).

[411] Carnathan v. Carnathan, 722 So. 2d 1248 (Miss. 1998).

[412] Driste v. Driste, 738 So. 2d 763 (Miss. Ct. App. 1999); Flechas v. Flechas, 724 So. 2d 948 (Miss. Ct. App. 1998).

[413] *See* Davis v. Davis, 832 So. 2d 492 (Miss. 2002) (awarding $50,000 lump sum alimony in addition to permanent); Mosley v. Mosley, 784 So. 2d 901 (Miss. 2001) (awarding $10,000 lump sum alimony in addition to permanent); Robison v. Robison, 722 So. 2d 601 (Miss. 1998) (awarding $250 lump sum alimony for forty months in addition to permanent); Crowe v. Crowe, 641 So. 2d 1100 (Miss. 1994) (affirming $4,500 lump sum alimony award in addition to $300/month permanent); East v. East, 775 So. 2d 741 (Miss. Ct. App. 2000) (awarding $10,000 lump sum in

ALIMONY

§ 9.06[6]

cases, lump sum alimony was awarded as a form of rehabilitative alimony.[414] Lump sum alimony took the form of release from debt in a few cases.[415] Larger lump sums were awarded primarily in cases in which the monied spouse's assets were separate property, so that contribution could not be recognized through property division.[416]

[6] Summary. Several caveats should be noted with regard to this study. The observations are based on reported appellate cases with sufficient data to analyze the type and amount of award. This is obviously a small percentage of the many cases in which alimony is an issue, and excludes cases that are settled or litigated but not appealed. Keeping that in mind, the following observations can be made from this sample of cases. *First,* income disparity is required for an award but does not automatically guarantee an award. *Second,* once a disparity is shown, the length of marriage is of great importance. Permanent alimony was typically awarded to remedy a disparity in marriages over twenty years; rehabilitative was awarded after marriages under ten years. The appellate courts reversed four cases for failure to award permanent alimony in marriages exceeding twenty years and did not reverse a single denial of permanent alimony in marriages of less than twenty years. *Third,* the amount of alimony awarded appears to increase with the length of the marriage. Awards ranged from one-fourth of the disparity in short marriages to awards that equalized or more than equalized incomes after long marriages.

§ 9.07 THIRD-PARTY PAYMENTS AS ALIMONY

One spouse may be ordered to make payments to a third party as part of property division or alimony. Payment of previously incurred debt is usually part of property division, while payment of future expenses is usually part of alimony. The nature of the payment will dictate tax treatment of the payment, as well as whether the payment can be modified and whether it terminates at death or remarriage.

[1] Payment of medical expenses. One spouse may be ordered to pay the other's medical insurance premiums and/or out-of-pocket medical expenses.[417] An order for

---

addition to permanent); Driste v. Driste, 738 So. 2d 763 (Miss. Ct. App. 1999) (awarding $20,000 lump sum alimony in addition to rehabilitative); Long v. Long, 734 So. 2d 206 (Miss. Ct. App. 1999) (awarding $20,000 lump sum alimony in addition to permanent).

[414] *See* Pearson v. Pearson, 761 So. 2d 157 (Miss. 2000) (awarding $240,000 as rehabilitative lump sum alimony in high-income case); Sarver v. Sarver, 687 So. 2d 749 (Miss. 1997) (awarding wife of ten years $2,500 as rehabilitative lump sum alimony).

[415] *See* A & L, Inc. v. Grantham, 747 So. 2d 832 (Miss. 1999) (deeming release from $80,000 tax liability as lump sum alimony); *see also* LeBlanc v. Andrews, 931 So. 2d 683, 686-87 (Miss. Ct. App. 2006) ($6,000 debt repayment as rehabilitative lump sum alimony); Ford v. Ford, 795 So. 2d 600 (Miss. Ct. App. 2001) (finding husband's payment of $6,500 in debt to be lump sum alimony).

[416] *See* Craft v. Craft, 825 So. 2d 605 (Miss. 2002) (awarding $175,000 to wife of thirteen years); Sanderson v. Sanderson, 824 So. 2d 623 (Miss. 2002) (awarding $200,000 to wife of twenty-two years from husband with $4 million separate property); Pearson v. Pearson, 761 So. 2d 157 (Miss. 2000) (awarding $150,000 to wife of six years from husband with $2 million separate property); Franks v. Franks, 759 So. 2d 1164 (Miss. 1999) (awarding $35,000 and $40,000 in debt payments to wife of fourteen years from husband with $1 million separate property).

[417] *See* Driste v. Driste, 738 So. 2d 763, 766 (Miss. 1999) (reversing chancellor's ruling that caselaw prohibited ordering one spouse to pay medical insurance premiums for other). *But cf.* Godwin v. Godwin, 758 So. 2d 384, 388

§ 9.07[2]   MISSISSIPPI FAMILY LAW

payment of future medical expenses must include a maximum amount. An order requiring a husband to pay one-half of all of his wife's future medical expenses was unenforceable – the court of appeals reasoned that an open-ended order constitutes a monthly modification of support without court approval.[418] The court of appeals also reversed an order requiring a husband to provide insurance or to pay all of his wife's medical bills if her health insurance became unavailable. A court may not require payment of a spouse's health insurance unless the costs are known.[419] In contrast, an order that a husband pay 25% of his wife's future medical expenses up to $250 a month was definite and enforceable.[420] And a court did not err in ordering a husband to provide COBRA coverage for his wife for the "maximum period allowed by law."[421]

[2] Mortgage payments. Mortgage payments assigned to one party in a divorce decree may be alimony,[422] part of property division,[423] or even a form of child support.[424] The court of appeals upheld an order that a husband pay his wife's mortgage and home insurance as a form of rehabilitative alimony.[425] In another case, a husband's obligation to make monthly payments on a home awarded to his wife was part of property division equalization and did not terminate when she remarried.[426] One spouse's tax return characterization of third-party payments may estop him or her from asserting another classification. A husband's argument that his monthly "house payments" to his ex-wife were child support, and therefore terminated on the child's emancipation, was rejected. He had reported the payment as alimony on tax returns for eighteen years.[427]

[3] Other payments. A chancellor may order one spouse to pay alimony in the form

---

(Miss. 1999) (denying medical coverage proper where wife's employment policy covered 80% of medical treatment); Spahn v. Spahn, 959 So. 2d 8, 14-15 (Miss. Ct. App. 2006) (chancellor not required to order that husband provide his wife with medical insurance); Glass v. Glass, 857 So. 2d 786, 791 (Miss. Ct. App. 2003) (chancellor not required to order husband to provide health insurance to disabled wife with Medicare coverage, who was also eligible for Medicaid).

[418] *See* Tillman v. Tillman, 791 So. 2d 285, 288 (Miss. Ct. App. 2001).

[419] Duncan v. Duncan, 815 So. 2d 480, 484 (Miss. Ct. App. 2002); *see also* Weeks v. Weeks, 29 So. 3d 80, 85 (Miss. Ct. App. 2009) (order that husband pay wife's monthly $516 premium, did not require him to pay increased premium of $639).

[420] Tillman v. Tillman, 791 So. 2d 285, 287 (Miss. Ct. App. 2001).

[421] Dye v. Dye, 22 So. 3d 1241 (Miss. Ct. App. 2009) (noting that thirty-six months was the maximum period); *see also* Goellner v. Goellner, 11 So. 3d 1251 (Miss. Ct. App. 2009) (husband to pay thirty-six months of health insurance premiums).

[422] *See* Jones v. Jones, 917 So. 2d 95, 102 (Miss. Ct. App. 2005) (divorce decree provision requiring husband to pay mortgage, taxes, and insurance on home awarded to wife was provision for alimony; obligation could be modified based on change in circumstances); Weston v. Mounts, 789 So. 2d 822, 827-28 (Miss. Ct. App. 2001) (ordering mortgage payments as alimony but allowing modification based on change in circumstances); *see also* Wilson v. Wilson, 810 So. 2d 615, 616-17 (Miss. Ct. App. 2002) (ordering payment of $1,500 house note as form of alimony).

[423] *See* Logue v. Logue, 106 So. 2d 498 (Miss. 1958) (holding mortgage payments to be property rights settlement, not alimony, and therefore not modifiable); Smith v. Little, 834 So. 2d 54, 60 (Miss. Ct. App. 2002) (finding payments on car and payments related to house not alimony but property division); *cf.* Mount v. Mount, 624 So. 2d 1001, 1004 (Miss. 1993) (ordering husband continue payment of monthly mortgage note as part of property division even though wife sold home).

[424] Johnson v. Johnson, 650 So. 2d 1281, 1284 (Miss. 1994) (ordering husband to make mortgage payments until children's majority as form of child support).

[425] *See* Wesson v. Wesson, 818 So. 2d 1272, 1277 (Miss. Ct. App. 2002) (payments to continue until the wife remarried or youngest child reached age twenty-one, whichever came first).

[426] Logue v. Logue, 106 So. 2d 498, 500 (Miss. 1958).

[427] Brown v. Brown, 724 So. 2d 874, 877 (Miss. 1998) (even though purpose of payments was ambiguous).

ALIMONY   **§ 9.07[4]**

of utility payments or payment of a utility allowance.[428] Alimony awards have also included orders to pay a spouse's car note, tag, insurance, and repairs.[429] In addition, payors have been ordered to pay alimony in the form of repayment of the recipient spouse's debts.[430] One agreement provided that a husband would "maintain memberships in two health clubs for his children, a social club for [his wife], maintain life insurance policies, vehicles, taxes on the former marital residence as well as a New Hampshire vacation home, and an annual vacation."[431]

[4] Disguised alimony. Alimony disguised as another form of payment will be treated as alimony. A husband's agreement to pay his wife $800 a month for ten years for consulting services was intended as lump sum alimony; the supreme court rejected his request to terminate the payments for lack of services.[432]

§ 9.08 MECHANICS OF AWARD

[1] Form of award

[a] Type of alimony. A court may award a single type of alimony or a combination of two or more forms of alimony.[433] A hybrid form of alimony, mixing the characteristics of two types, may be used under limited circumstances in an agreed order.[434]

[b] Payee. Alimony payments may include payments to third parties, as well as direct payments to the recipient.[435]

[c] Variation in amount. Alimony is typically awarded as a set amount payable in fixed monthly installments. However, parties may agree to alimony that fluctuates based on a cost-of-living index. In addition, a court may order that the amount of alimony increase or decrease based on specific anticipated changes in circumstances.

[i] Escalation clauses. The supreme court held that parties should be allowed broad latitude in fashioning alimony awards, including the use of an escalation clause tied to a cost-of-living index. The court upheld an agreement that a husband

---

[428] *See* Fisher v. Fisher, 771 So. 2d 364, 369 (Miss. 2000).

[429] *See* Wells v. Wells, 800 So. 2d 1239, 1241 (Miss. Ct. App. 2001); *see also* Elam v. Hinson, 932 So. 2d 76, 78 (Miss. Ct. App. 2006) (payment of car note as a form of alimony).

[430] LeBlanc v. Andrews, 931 So. 2d 683, 687 (Miss. Ct. App. 2006) (rehabilitative alimony in the form of payment of $6,000 in debt).

[431] *See* Nicholas v. Nicholas, 841 So. 2d 1208, 1210 (Miss. Ct. App. 2003).

[432] *See* Norton v. Norton, 742 So. 2d 126, 129-31 (Miss. 1999) (rejecting husband's attempt to terminate payments for lack of services as attempt to modify lump sum alimony).

[433] *See* Grogan v. Grogan, 641 So. 2d 734, 742 (Miss. 1994) (stating court can award lump sum, permanent, or both forms of alimony simultaneously); Jenkins v. Jenkins, 278 So. 2d 446, 449 (Miss. 1973) (stating same principle); Barnett v. Barnett, 908 So. 2d 833, 843-44 (Miss. Ct. App. 2005) (court awarded $400/month rehabilitative, $600/month permanent, and $5,000 lump sum alimony).

[434] *See supra* § 9.03.

[435] *See supra* § 9.07.

§ 9.08[1][c][ii]   **MISSISSIPPI FAMILY LAW**

would pay permanent alimony of $1,500 a month, to be adjusted annually to "increase or decrease directly in relation to . . . [the] Consumers Cost of Living Index."[436] Similarly, a chancellor properly enforced an agreement that a wife's alimony award would increase as the husband's net income increased, except for raises based on military rank or longevity. The agreement was enforceable as a contract without a showing of a material change in circumstances. Furthermore, the wife could seek recovery of amounts due prior to the filing of her petition.[437] However, use of an escalation clause does not prevent modification of permanent alimony based on a material change in circumstances.[438]

       [ii] Variation tied to anticipated change. An order may not provide that permanent alimony will terminate or the amount change upon a specific event or date unless the event or date relates to a specific anticipated change in the recipient's need. A court properly ordered that a husband's monthly $800 alimony payment would be reduced to $400 when his wife's mortgage payments ended.[439] However, a chancellor erred in ordering that alimony payments would be reduced from $2,400 to $900 after nine years without making specific findings of fact that the wife's income would increase at that point.[440]

Appellate courts have reversed orders altering support at retirement age unless the variation is linked to a change in income. A chancellor erred in ordering that a fifty-two-year-old wife's alimony would terminate at sixty-five in the absence of specific findings explaining the termination.[441] Similarly, a chancellor properly rejected a husband's argument that his permanent alimony obligation continue only until he reached retirement age.[442] However, the court of appeals approved an alimony award of $400 a month, to be replaced with thirty-five percent of a husband's pension when he retired.[443]

       [2] Reserved jurisdiction. A court may find that while existing circumstances do not require an award of alimony, evidence suggests that alimony may be appropriate in the future. However, a divorce decree that does not initially provide for alimony may not be later modified to award alimony based on changed circumstances. To preserve the option of a later award, some courts have awarded a nominal sum of alimony at divorce. More recently, courts have simply reserved jurisdiction to award alimony

---

[436] Speed v. Speed, 757 So. 2d 221, 223 (Miss. 2000).

[437] D'Avignon v. D'Avignon, 945 So. 2d 401, 404 (Miss. Ct. App. 2006) (increase to be in same percentage to husband's income as original alimony award; recovery limited by three-year contract statute of limitations).

[438] Speed v. Speed, 757 So. 2d 221, 225-26 (Miss. 2000); see also West v. West, 891 So. 2d 203 (Miss. 2004) (alimony based on escalation clause and labeled lump sum alimony reclassified as permanent; could be modified based on change in circumstances).

[439] Wells v. Wells, 800 So. 2d 1239, 1241 (Miss. Ct. App. 2001).

[440] Box v. Box, 622 So. 2d 284, 289 (Miss. 1993).

[441] Skinner v. Skinner, 509 So. 2d 867, 869 (Miss. 1987) ("The record discloses no extenuating circumstances to warrant termination of the payments at age 65.").

[442] Tutor v. Tutor, 494 So. 2d 362, 363 (Miss. 1987). However, alimony is automatically reduced when a recipient begins receiving Social Security benefits on the payor's account.

[443] See Cork v. Cork, 811 So. 2d 427, 429-30 (Miss. Ct. App. 2001) (husband was to make up difference as alimony if payment fell below $400); see also Hemsley v. Hemsley, 639 So. 2d 909, 915 (Miss. 1994) (affirming award of permanent alimony with instruction that alimony would automatically reduce in proportion to retirement benefits).

ALIMONY   § 9.08[3]

in the future.[444] The Mississippi Supreme Court urged the lower courts to adopt this more direct practice.[445] Reservation of jurisdiction is appropriate if a wage-earner spouse is currently unemployed or otherwise unable to pay alimony, if alimony is not feasible because of substantial post-marital debt, or if an employed spouse has medical problems that create a likelihood of future unemployment.[446]

[3] Source of payments. Alimony may be awarded even though payments will be made from a payor's non-marital assets or from income normally protected from seizure.[447] Courts have rejected payors' arguments that alimony may not be awarded if the only resource available for payment is non-assignable income. For example, alimony was properly awarded even though the payor's only source of income was veteran's disability income.[448]

[4] Security for award

[a] Equitable liens. An alimony award may be secured by an equitable lien on a payor's marital or separate estate.[449] A court's award of $16,000 in lump sum alimony, secured by a lien on property given to the husband by his mother, was proper.[450] An equitable lien does not divest the debtor of title, but is "merely a charge on the property for the purpose of security."[451] If the debtor spouse defaults, the charged property may be sold to satisfy the obligation.

[b] Penalty provisions. Parties may include a late payment fee to remedy payment delays. An agreed provision that alimony and child support payments made after the tenth of the month would be subject to a 10% late fee was not an unenforceable penalty.[452]

[c] Life insurance. A payor may be required to maintain life insurance in an amount sufficient to satisfy payment of alimony obligations that survive the payor's death.[453] The obligation to maintain insurance ends when alimony terminates.[454]

---

[444] *See* Brett Turner, *Redefining Alimony in a Time of Transition,* 4 DIVORCE LITIG. 247 (1992).

[445] *See* McNalley v. McNalley, 516 So. 2d 499, 502 (Miss. 1987).

[446] *See* Turner, *supra* note 444, at 248.

[447] Haney v. Haney, 788 So. 2d 862, 865 (Miss. Ct. App. 2001); Elliott v. Rogers, 775 So. 2d 1285, 1287-88 (Miss. Ct. App. 2000).

[448] Steiner v. Steiner, 788 So. 2d 771, 777-78 (Miss. 2001); *cf.* Rushing v. Rushing, 909 So. 2d 155, 158 (Miss. Ct. App. 2005) (although veteran's benefits cannot be subject of withholding order, court did not err in ordering payor in arrears to purge himself of contempt by executing voluntary wage assignment of veteran's benefits).

[449] Morgan v. Morgan, 397 So. 2d 894, 896-97 (Miss. 1981) (noting that the lien was not impressed upon payor's property until his conduct demonstrated he would not comply with the divorce decree's terms).

[450] Morgan v. Morgan, 397 So. 2d 894, 895 (Miss. 1981) (citing Smith v. Smith, 293 So. 2d 466 (Miss. 1974); Pierce v. Pierce, 267 So. 2d 300 (Miss. 1972)).

[451] MacDonald v. MacDonald, 698 So. 2d 1079, 1085 (Miss. 1997).

[452] Varner v. Varner, 666 So. 2d 493, 496 (Miss. 1995) (holding that amount must be "reasonable pre-estimate of damages").

[453] *See* Hodges v. Hodges, 807 So. 2d 438, 442-44 (Miss. 2002) (agreement to provide insurance policy up to $164,000, to be reduced as monthly alimony was paid, did not permit an ex-wife to retain an entire $200,000 insurance policy, even though she was the named beneficiary).

[454] *See* Patterson v. Patterson, 915 So. 2d 496, 500 (Miss. Ct. App. 2005); Beezley v. Beezley, 917 So. 2d 803,

§ 9.08[4][d]   MISSISSIPPI FAMILY LAW

[d] Bond. A chancery court may require that a payor provide bond or sureties to secure an award of alimony.[455]

[5] Drafting considerations

[a] Specificity regarding type of alimony. An agreement should state whether a payment is alimony, child support, or part of property division and should indicate which form of alimony is intended. The agreement should also state whether the payments are modifiable, tax-deductible, terminate upon death, or terminate upon remarriage.

[b] Effect of standard provisions. It is important to review alimony provisions in light of an agreement's standard provisions. For example, a provision that an agreement is binding on the parties' heirs and assigns may alter the characteristics of alimony payments or child support.[456]

§ 9.09 MODIFICATION

Permanent and rehabilitative alimony may be modified to reflect a change in circumstances that affects the payor's ability to pay or the recipient's need for alimony. Not all financial changes justify modification. A payor's voluntary financial choices such as supporting a new family or incurring new debt are not reasons for modification.

[1] Types of alimony. Permanent and rehabilitative alimony may be modified based on a material change in circumstances. As a general rule, lump sum and reimbursement alimony may not.

[a] Permanent alimony. Modification is an essential feature of permanent alimony.[457] Parties may not create nonmodifiable permanent alimony even by agreement.[458] For example, the supreme court granted an ex-husband's petition to modify alimony based on his former wife's cohabitation even though their agreement prohibited modification without consent.[459] Permanent alimony may be modified to increase the award, decrease the award, or terminate the award.[460] And, in a 2007 case, the court of appeals affirmed a chancellor's modification of permanent alimony to re-

---

807-08 (Miss. Ct. App. 2005) (insurance policy intended to replace permanent alimony at payor's death should terminate upon recipient's remarriage).

[455] *See* MISS. CODE ANN. § 93-5-23 (2004) ("[T]he court may, upon petition of the person to whom such payments are owing, or such person's legal representative, enter an order requiring that bond, sureties or other security be given . . .").

[456] *See* discussion *supra* § 9.02[1][g][iii].

[457] *See* Hubbard v. Hubbard, 656 So. 2d 124, 130 (Miss. 1995); Grice v. Grice, 726 So. 2d 1242, 1251 (Miss. Ct. App. 1998).

[458] *See* McDonald v. McDonald, 683 So. 2d 929, 931 (Miss. 1996) (permanent alimony modifiable regardless of "any intent expressed by the parties to the contrary"); Taylor v. Taylor, 392 So. 2d 1145, 1147 (Miss. 1981).

[459] *See* Ellis v. Ellis, 651 So. 2d 1068, 1073-74 (Miss. 1995).

[460] Clower v. Clower, 988 So. 2d 441, 444 (Miss. Ct. App. 2008).

ALIMONY

§ 9.09[1][b]

habilitative, based on the husband's significant loss of income and the wife's receipt of free housing from a male friend.[461]

[b] Rehabilitative alimony. Mississippi cases defining rehabilitative alimony state that rehabilitative alimony may be modified.[462] No Mississippi cases were found involving modification during the time set for the award, possibly because rehabilitative alimony is typically awarded for only a few years. However, the court of appeals did address whether rehabilitative alimony can be extended or converted to periodic alimony. The court held that rehabilitative alimony may be converted to permanent based upon a chancellor's written findings of a material change in the recipient's circumstances.[463] The decision also suggested that even if conversion to permanent alimony was not appropriate, the court might extend the rehabilitative alimony for an additional period.[464]

[c] Lump sum alimony. Lump sum alimony vests when the award is made and may not be altered based on changed circumstances.[465] Accordingly, a payor whose income decreased when he left his medical practice to enter school was not permitted to modify lump sum alimony.[466]

Recent decisions permitting parties to create hybrid forms of alimony have not addressed whether parties may create modifiable lump sum alimony.[467] In one decision, however, the supreme court stated in dicta that lump sum alimony is nonmodifiable absent a contractual provision to that effect.[468]

[d] Reimbursement alimony. Reimbursement alimony, awarded as compensation for supporting a spouse through school, is not modifiable. Reimbursement is accomplished through an award of lump sum alimony, which is vested at the time of the award.[469]

[e] Third-party payments. Third-party payments that are considered part of a permanent alimony obligation may be modified based upon a material change in circumstances. For example, a husband's duty to pay mortgage, taxes, and insurance on a home awarded to his former wife was a form of alimony and could be modified based

---

[461] Austin v. Austin, 981 So. 2d 1000, 1006 (Miss. Ct. App. 2007).

[462] *See* Overstreet v. Overstreet, 692 So. 2d 88 (Miss. 1997); Hubbard v. Hubbard, 656 So. 2d 124, 130 (Miss. 1995); Wolfe v. Wolfe, 766 So. 2d 123, 128 (Miss. Ct. App. 2000); Waldron v. Waldron, 743 So. 2d 1064, 1065 (Miss. Ct. App. 1999).

[463] *See* Oster v. Oster, 876 So. 2d 428, 431-32 (Miss. Ct. App. 2004). See *Rickenbach v. Kosinski*, 32 So. 3d 732, 735-36 (Fla. Dist. Ct. App. 2010) for a detailed discussion of the Florida test for converting rehabilitative alimony to permanent.

[464] *See* Oster v. Oster, 876 So. 2d 428, 432 (Miss. Ct. App. 2004).

[465] Hubbard v. Hubbard, 656 So. 2d 124, 129 (Miss. 1995); Armstrong v. Armstrong, 618 So. 2d 1278, 1281 (Miss. 1993).

[466] McDonald v. McDonald, 683 So. 2d 929, 933 (Miss. 1996); *see also* East v. East, 493 So. 2d 927, 932 (Miss. 1986) (lump sum alimony labeled as periodic cannot be modified).

[467] *See* discussion *supra* § 9.03.

[468] *See* Norton v. Norton, 742 So. 2d 126, 129 (Miss. 1999).

[469] *See* Guy v. Guy, 736 So. 2d 1042, 1046 (Miss. 1999).

287

§ 9.09[2]   **MISSISSIPPI FAMILY LAW**

on an unforeseeable material change.[470]

[2] Test for modification. A petitioner seeking to modify alimony must prove a material change in circumstances that was not foreseeable at the time of the decree. In addition, the petitioner must show that the change has affected the disparity between the parties' financial conditions. The original award may be increased or decreased to reflect the change. An agreed support order may be modified in the same manner as court-ordered support.[471]

[a] Material change. An alimony award may be modified upon a showing that the parties' circumstances have changed materially since the original decree.[472] The change must be clear and substantial.[473] Not every material change justifies modification.[474]

[b] Occurring since the decree. Modification must be based upon events occurring since the order awarding alimony.[475] Modification cannot be used to correct a perceived error in an earlier decree. A chancellor erred in modifying alimony and child support based on his view that the amount of support originally ordered was too high.[476] Similarly, the fact that a payor agreed to an amount that he could not afford is not a reason to modify.[477]

[c] Foreseeability. The change must be one that could not have been anticipated by the parties at the time of the earlier decree. Circumstances occurring shortly after the original decree are likely to be considered reasonably foreseeable.[478] A wife's receipt of $32,000 from sale of the marital home did not justify modifying alimony; the sale was contemplated in the divorce decree.[479] Similarly, a payor's request to decrease support based on his loss of severance pay was denied because he was aware at the time of the decree that the pay would terminate.[480] And a husband's request for

---

[470] Jones v. Jones, 917 So. 2d 95, 102 (Miss. Ct. App. 2005).

[471] Keller v. Keller, 230 So. 2d 808, 809 (Miss. 1970); Austin v. Austin, 981 So. 2d 1000, 1003-04 (Miss. Ct. App. 2007); cf. Towles v. Towles, 137 So. 2d 182, 184 (Miss. 1962) (while modification of agreed order does not require greater proof than modification of court-imposed order, chancellor correctly noted that husband knew his financial situation and agreed to pay alimony based on existing circumstances).

[472] See Weeks v. Weeks, 29 So. 3d 80, 90 (Miss. Ct. App. 2009); D'Avignon v. D'Avignon, 945 So. 2d 401, 414 (Miss. Ct. App. 2006); Dix v. Dix, 941 So. 2d 913, 916 (Miss. Ct. App. 2006); see also In re Profilet, 826 So. 2d 91, 95-96 (Miss. 2002); Magee v. Magee, 754 So. 2d 1275, 1279 (Miss. Ct. App. 1999).

[473] McKee v. McKee, 382 So. 2d 287, 288 (Miss. 1980); Austin v. Austin, 981 So. 2d 1000, 1005 (Miss. Ct. App. 2007).

[474] See infra § 9.09[4].

[475] Austin v. Austin, 981 So. 2d 1000, 1005 (Miss. Ct. App. 2007) (chancellor properly modified alimony and child support based upon husband's job loss, occurring after husband's previous petition for modification was denied); see In re Profilet, 826 So. 2d 91, 95 (Miss. 2002); Magee v. Magee, 754 So. 2d 1275, 1279 (Miss. Ct. App. 1999).

[476] Shaeffer v. Shaeffer, 370 So. 2d 240, 242 (Miss. 1979) (amounts were high but not unconscionable; did not amount to accident, mistake, or fraud permitting revision of judgment).

[477] Price v. Price, 5 So. 3d 1151 (Miss. Ct. App. 2009).

[478] Magee v. Magee, 754 So. 2d 1275, 1279 (Miss. Ct. App. 1999); cf. Roberts v. Roberts, 395 So. 2d 1035, 1037 (Ala. Civ. App. 1981) (assertion of changed circumstances six months after decree should be carefully scrutinized).

[479] Spradling v. Spradling, 362 So. 2d 620, 624 (Miss. 1978).

[480] Tingle v. Tingle, 573 So. 2d 1389, 1392 (Miss. 1990).

ALIMONY   § 9.09[2][d]

reduction based in part on his wife's receipt of disability benefits was properly denied. Their divorce agreement contemplated that she might receive disability.[481] A chancellor did not err in refusing to increase a wife's alimony award based upon health problems arising after the original award. Considering the extent of her health problems at the time of the decree, the two additional problems were not an unforeseeable material change in circumstances.[482] And an order increasing alimony based on a recipient's worsened mental condition was reversed to determine whether her mental deterioration was foreseeable at the time of divorce.[483]

[d] Comparison of financial circumstances. A payee's increased income or payor's loss of income may not qualify as a material change if the parties' relative financial positions are similar to those at divorce. In determining whether a material change has occurred, courts compare "the relative positions of the parties at the time of the request for modification in relation to their positions at the time of the divorce decree."[484] For example, a payor's request for modification based on his increased expenses and his ex-wife's increased income was denied – his monthly income still exceeded hers.[485] And a husband with current monthly income of $18,584 was not entitled to reduce his $3,250 a month alimony obligation to his former wife even though his income had dropped from its previous, higher level. Her income of $3,807 was not sufficient to meet her expenses.[486]

[e] Application of *Armstrong* factors. The court of appeals held that a chancellor modifying alimony must, in addition to considering the factors set out above, apply the *Armstrong* factors to determine the appropriate amount of alimony.[487]

[3] Restrictions on modification. Alimony may not be modified by an out-of-court agreement. In addition, neither the parties nor a court may modify amounts already due. Alimony may not be awarded initially in a modification action.

---

[481] Morris v. Morris, 8 So. 3d 917 (Miss. Ct. App. 2009) (husband's obligation not reduced even though income dropped from $158,000 to $90,000; his lifestyle had not been reduced).

[482] Weeks v. Weeks, 29 So. 3d 80 (Miss. Ct. App. 2009).

[483] *See In re* Profilet, 826 So. 2d 91, 96 (Miss. 2002) (wife had psychological problems at time of 1982 divorce, but was able to work; bipolar disorder worsened and she was unable to work in 1999).

[484] James v. James, 724 So. 2d 1098, 1102 (Miss. Ct. App. 1998); *see* Dix v. Dix, 941 So. 2d 913, 916 (Miss. Ct. App. 2006) (court must compare the disparity between the parties' current incomes with the disparity between their incomes at the time of divorce); Jones v. Jones, 917 So. 2d 95, 100-01 (Miss. Ct. App. 2005) (court erred in finding current financial disparity without comparing circumstances at time of divorce and at hearing).

[485] Steiner v. Steiner, 788 So. 2d 771, 777 (Miss. 2001) (although payments were "high" they were not unconscionable or oppressive); *see* Magee v. Magee, 754 So. 2d 1275, 1280 (Miss. Ct. App. 1999) (husband made $42,439 annually, after alimony payments, while wife made $37,800, including alimony payments).

[486] Justus v. Justus, 3 So. 3d 141 (Miss. Ct. App. 2009) (courts to consider relative positions at time of divorce and at time of modification).

[487] Jones v. Jones, 917 So. 2d 95, 99-100 (Miss. Ct. App. 2005); *see* discussion of *Armstrong* factors *supra* § 9.04; *cf.* Steiner v. Steiner, 788 So. 2d 771, 776 (Miss. 2001) (courts should apply factors to determine disparity); Dix v. Dix, 941 So. 2d 913, 916 (Miss. Ct. App. 2006) (petitioner must prove a material change in circumstances since the award of alimony, considering the factors enumerated in *Brabham v. Brabham*, 84 So. 2d 147, 153 (Miss. 1955)).

§ 9.09[3][a]   MISSISSIPPI FAMILY LAW

[a] Original decree must provide for alimony. Alimony may not be awarded for the first time in a modification proceeding, no matter how drastically the parties' circumstances have changed since the decree. Alimony may be addressed post-divorce only if the original decree awarded alimony or reserved jurisdiction to address alimony in the future.[488] An award of nominal alimony will support later modification; however, the supreme court recommended that courts simply reserve jurisdiction if circumstances suggest that alimony may be appropriate in the future.[489]

A decree awarding only lump sum alimony may not be modified to include permanent alimony unless the court reserved jurisdiction for that purpose.[490] The reverse is also true. A court's order modifying permanent alimony to require a lump sum payment of $10,000 to defray debts was reversed.[491]

[b] No modification of arrearages. Only payments not yet due may be modified. Vested payments of alimony cannot be modified or forgiven by the parties or by the court.[492] Each payment in arrears becomes a judgment against the payor.[493] A court properly rejected a husband's request to reduce alimony arrearages – unexpected circumstances may allow prospective modification, but do not excuse arrearages.[494]

[c] No out-of-court modification. A private, out-of-court agreement modifying alimony or child support is unenforceable.[495] Support orders may be modified only by another order of the court.[496] A court properly disregarded a wife's out-of-court letter stating that she would not hold her husband to make alimony payments as agreed.[497]

[d] No prospective modification by payor in arrears. Payors in arrears have been barred from seeking prospective modification by the clean hands doctrine: "a husband may not petition for modification of the original decree without showing either that he has performed it or that his performance has been wholly impossible."[498] A chancellor erred in ordering modification at the request of a payor who failed to prove that he was unable to make prior payments.[499]

In a 1992 case, however, the supreme court stated that a court's entry of judgment

---

[488] Gatlin v. Gatlin, 161 So. 2d 782, 783 (Miss. 1964) (court may, and in some cases, should, retain jurisdiction to determine whether alimony is needed in future).

[489] *See* McNalley v. McNalley, 516 So. 2d 499, 502 (Miss. 1987).

[490] Hopkins v. Hopkins, 379 So. 2d 314, 315 (Miss. 1980) (lump sum is a final settlement of alimony claims between husband and wife and cannot be modified).

[491] Austin v. Austin, 766 So. 2d 86, 89 (Miss. Ct. App. 2000) (lump sum alimony is fixed and nonmodifiable).

[492] Tanner v. Roland, 598 So. 2d 783, 786 (Miss. 1992); Gregg v. Montgomery, 587 So. 2d 928, 933 (Miss. 1991); Rubisoff v. Rubisoff, 133 So. 2d 534, 537 (Miss. 1961).

[493] Brand v. Brand, 482 So. 2d 236, 237 (Miss. 1986).

[494] Pope v. Pope, 803 So. 2d 499, 502 (Miss. Ct. App. 2002).

[495] Armstrong v. Armstrong, 618 So. 2d 1278, 1281 (Miss. 1993); Bell v. Bell, 572 So. 2d 841, 845 (Miss. 1990); East v. East, 493 So. 2d 927, 931 (Miss. 1986); Taylor v. Taylor, 392 So. 2d 1145, 1149 (Miss. 1981).

[496] Tillman v. Tillman, 809 So. 2d 767, 770 (Miss. Ct. App. 2002).

[497] Gregg v. Montgomery, 587 So. 2d 928, 933 (Miss. 1991).

[498] Kincaid v. Kincaid, 57 So. 2d 263, 265 (Miss. 1952) (payor must show "[t]hat he earned all he could, that he lived economically and paid all surplus money above a living on the alimony decreed to the wife"); *see* Hooker v. Hooker, 205 So. 2d 276, 278 (Miss. 1967) (citing Ramsay v. Ramsay, 87 So. 491 (Miss. 1921)).

[499] Taylor v. Taylor, 348 So. 2d 1341, 1343 (Miss. 1977).

ALIMONY   § 9.09[4]

for arrearages "cleansed" the payor's hands, allowing him to seek modification.[500] The court of appeals followed this approach in two subsequent cases, holding that modification could be ordered after the entry of a "cleansing" judgment even though the arrears had not yet been satisfied.[501] The clean hands doctrine did not bar modification by a husband who was not in contempt for willful nonpayment – he received $1,384 in Social Security, which was insufficient to pay monthly alimony of $2,000. In addition, he discontinued payment only upon filing the petition.[502]

[4] Circumstances that are not a material change. A payor's lifestyle choices generally do not permit modification of support obligations. Petitions to reduce support based on remarriage, the birth of additional children, or financial difficulty resulting from new debt will be denied.

[a] New debt. The fact that a support payor has difficulty making payments because of new debt is not a material change in circumstances.[503] Similarly, filing a bankruptcy petition does not constitute a material change in circumstances without a finding that the petition was filed in good faith. A husband's bankruptcy petition, filed one week after his motion to modify alimony was denied, was not a material change in circumstances.[504] And a husband was not entitled to modify alimony even though his monthly expenses exceeded his $18,000 a month income. In recent years, he made voluntary purchases such as a lake home, condominiums, and recreational vehicles.[505]

[b] Payor's remarriage and new family. A payor's remarriage and resulting increased expenses do not justify a reduction of alimony: "the claim of the divorced wife . . . on [the divorced husband's] earnings takes precedence over that of the second wife."[506] Similarly, the illness of an alimony payor's second wife was not a valid reason to reduce alimony awarded to a first wife.[507] A payor may not reduce support based on the birth of additional children in a second family.[508]

[5] Petition to increase alimony. Alimony may be increased if changed

---

[500] *See* Brennan v. Brennan, 605 So. 2d 749, 753 (Miss. 1992) (remanded to consider modification petition).

[501] *See* Cook v. Whiddon, 866 So. 2d 494, 499 (Miss. Ct. App. 2004); Lane v. Lane, 850 So. 2d 122, 127 (Miss. Ct. App. 2002) (alimony and child support modification); *cf.* Brawdy v. Howell, 841 So. 2d 1175, 1181 (Miss. Ct. App. 2003) (chancellor did not err in granting a modification of child support even though the father was in contempt for nonpayment, where he misunderstood the agreement and was not in "willful" contempt).

[502] Clower v. Clower, 988 So. 2d 441, 445 (Miss. Ct. App. 2008).

[503] *See* Yancey v. Yancey, 752 So. 2d 1006, 1010 (Miss. 1999); Rushing v. Rushing, 909 So. 2d 155, 159 (Miss. Ct. App. 2005) (payor's request to reduce alimony because of substantial debt properly denied); Magee v. Magee, 754 So. 2d 1275, 1280 (Miss. Ct. App. 1999) (personal bills cannot be used as a reason to reduce support).

[504] Varner v. Varner, 666 So. 2d 493, 497 (Miss. 1995).

[505] Justus v. Justus, 3 So. 3d 141 (Miss. Ct. App. 2009).

[506] De Marco v. De Marco, 24 So. 2d 358, 359 (Miss. 1946); *see* Rushing v. Rushing, 909 So. 2d 155, 159 (Miss. Ct. App. 2005) (payor's request to reduce alimony based on birth of additional children properly denied).

[507] Yancey v. Yancey, 752 So. 2d 1006, 1009-10 (Miss. 1999); *cf.* Goodin v. Department of Human Services, 772 So. 2d 1051, 1057 (Miss. 2000) (child support is not modifiable simply because the custodial parent has remarried and has obtained employment).

[508] James v. James, 724 So. 2d 1098, 1103-04 (Miss. Ct. App. 1998); *cf.* Bailey v. Bailey, 724 So. 2d 335, 337-39 (Miss. 1998) (child support modification).

§ 9.09[5][a]   MISSISSIPPI FAMILY LAW

circumstances affect a payee's ability to meet reasonable needs and the payor is financially able to provide increased support.

[a] Payee's inability to meet reasonable needs. An alimony payee's ability to meet reasonable needs may have changed because of illness or disability, loss of income, or the effect of inflation on the value of the award.

[i] Poor health. A payee's post-divorce illness or disability may support modification. Alimony was increased from $1,000 to $1,500 a month, based on a recipient wife's illness and inability to work.[509] Similarly, a $500 a month award was increased to $1,000 based on the recipient's illness.[510] However, the supreme court reversed and remanded a chancellor's order increasing a twenty-year-old award from $400 to $4,000 a month based on a payee's mental disability, because it was not clear whether the disability was foreseeable at the time of divorce.[511] And a former wife was not entitled to an increase. She offered no evidence to support her statement that health problems prevented her from working.[512]

[ii] Decreased value of award. A court may consider the impact of inflation in determining whether alimony should be increased.[513] The supreme court noted in approving an alimony increase that a 1975 award of $500 was comparable to $1,560 in 1999.[514]

[iii] Loss of income. A payee's involuntary loss of income and resulting inability to meet reasonable needs may justify increasing alimony. An alimony recipient who was unable to continue working because of illness was granted an increase in alimony.[515] If a payee's income loss is voluntary, income should be imputed based on earning capacity.[516]

[b] Payor's ability to pay increased amount. In addition to finding that the payee cannot meet reasonable needs, the court must find that the payor is financially able to provide increased support. In making this determination, the court compares the parties' current income disparity with the disparity of their incomes at divorce. If a substantial disparity remains, alimony may be increased even if the payor's income has recently decreased. A former husband's alimony obligation was increased by $500 a month in spite of his recent retirement – his income was still much higher than at the time of the original decree and substantially exceeded his former wife's current

---

[509] Grice v. Grice, 726 So. 2d 1242, 1245 (Miss. Ct. App. 1998) (modification in prior hearing not on appeal; case involved husband's petition to reduce modified amount).

[510] Austin v. Austin, 766 So. 2d 86, 91 (Miss. Ct. App. 2000).

[511] See In re Profilet, 826 So. 2d 91, 96 (Miss. 2002) (also suggesting that husband's increase in income might have been foreseeable).

[512] Weeks v. Weeks, 29 So. 3d 80 (Miss. Ct. App. 2009).

[513] See Spradling v. Spradling, 362 So. 2d 620, 624 (Miss. 1978) (noting effects of inflation since original decree; denying modification based on payee's employment).

[514] See Austin v. Austin, 766 So. 2d 86, 90 (Miss. Ct. App. 2000).

[515] Austin v. Austin, 766 So. 2d 86, 90 (Miss. Ct. App. 2000) (wife's cancer forced retirement).

[516] Cf. Martin v. Martin, 751 So. 2d 1132, 1135 (Miss. Ct. App. 1999) (wife with law degree able to earn more).

ALIMONY   **§ 9.09[6]**

income.[517] Similarly, a payor whose income decreased from $63,000 a year to $43,000 a year was not entitled to reduce alimony. He was still able to enjoy a decent standard of living and his yearly income after alimony payments exceeded his former wife's combined income and alimony by almost $5,000.[518]

[6] Petition to reduce alimony. A reduction in alimony may be based upon a change in the payor's circumstances, including an involuntary loss of income or increase in expenses. Or, reduction may be based upon the payee's improved circumstances. In addition to finding a material change, the court must find that the change substantially altered the parties' relative financial positions.

[a] Payor's decreased resources

[i] Involuntary income reduction. A payor's loss of income may support modification if the loss was involuntary and in good faith, was not foreseeable, and affects the payor's standard of living. A chancellor properly rejected the modification petition of a payor who quit work over a dispute with his supervisor and failed to secure employment at a level based on his education and job qualifications.[519] In contrast, a chancellor properly reduced alimony when a payor was fired and suffered a loss of two-thirds of his income.[520] Similarly, a husband's alimony was properly reduced when his income dropped from $100,000 a year to Social Security benefits of $1,384 a month. The court rejected his wife's argument that his poor decisions caused his income loss – there was no evidence that his decisions were in bad faith, or an attempt to cause the business to fail.[521] A court may average a payor's income to determine the proper amount of reduction. A chancellor did not err in averaging a surgeon's income over four years to determine that he had suffered an average reduction in income of 5.25 percent.[522] A temporary drop in income is not a reason to reduce alimony.[523]

A court may impute income to a payor who hides or diverts income or assets. For example, a husband who lost income was granted a smaller than requested reduction in alimony because he transferred income-producing assets to his second wife.[524] A payor who reports a reduction in income must show a corresponding reduction in standard of living. A payor who continued to purchase new vehicles and enjoy expensive club memberships was properly denied modification.[525] Modification was also denied to a

---

[517] Austin v. Austin, 766 So. 2d 86, 90 (Miss. Ct. App. 2000).

[518] Magee v. Magee, 754 So. 2d 1275, 1279-80 (Miss. Ct. App. 1999) (husband able to purchase new home, contribute to 401k plan).

[519] Yancey v. Yancey, 752 So. 2d 1006, 1010 (Miss. 1999); *see also* Towles v. Towles, 137 So. 2d 182, 184 (Miss. 1962) (no reduction where payor voluntarily sold business and continued as employee); Lane v. Lane, 850 So. 2d 122, 124 (Miss. Ct. App. 2002) (no reduction in alimony and child support where payor voluntarily retired). For cases discussing imputed income in original awards of alimony, see *supra* § 9.04[4][a]. For cases discussing imputed income in child support awards, see *infra* § 13.04[4].

[520] Austin v. Austin, 981 So. 2d 1000 (Miss. Ct. App. 2007).

[521] Clower v. Clower, 988 So. 2d 441, 444-45 (Miss. Ct. App. 2008).

[522] Burwell v. Burwell, 44 So. 3d 421, 424 (Miss. Ct. App. 2010).

[523] Dix v. Dix, 941 So. 2d 913, 916 (Miss. Ct. App. 2006) (one-year drop in payor's income not a material change in circumstances; payor's affluent lifestyle considered).

[524] *See* Seale v. Seale, 863 So. 2d 996, 998 (Miss. Ct. App. 2004).

[525] Grice v. Grice, 726 So. 2d 1242, 1252 (Miss. Ct. App. 1998); *see also* Justus v. Justus, 3 So. 3d 141 (Miss. Ct.

§ 9.09[6][a][ii]   MISSISSIPPI FAMILY LAW

payor whose income decreased but who simultaneously purchased an expensive new automobile.[526]

[ii] **Involuntary expenses**. Increased expenses due to causes beyond a payor's control may justify modification. A chancellor properly reduced a husband's alimony obligation from $1,250 to $850 to reflect his reduction in income as a result of illness.[527] However, a payor's petition to modify alimony based on disability-related expenses was denied. While his expenses had increased by $1,100, his income had increased by $1,900 and was still substantially greater than that of his former wife.[528] And a payor who incurs expenses voluntarily, or through his or her fault, is not entitled to reduce alimony. A chancellor properly denied a payor's request to modify his second wife's alimony because his first wife's alimony had been increased as a result of delinquency – the arrearages were his own fault.[529]

[b] Payee's increased resources

[i] **Increase in income or earning capacity.** An increase in a recipient's income may justify a reduction in alimony. A chancellor properly reduced alimony from $950 to $700 to reflect a recipient's increased monthly earnings of $250.[530] Income based on earning capacity may be imputed to a payee who is earning below actual potential. A court properly terminated alimony to a payee who earned a law degree and graduated high in her class, but who was earning only about one-third of her income potential.[531] On the other hand, a wife's "nominal" income at a part-time job was not a material change in circumstances justifying a downward modification in alimony. Her monthly expenses still exceeded her income.[532]

[ii] **Receipt of Social Security benefits.** An alimony payor is entitled to a reduction in alimony equal to the amount of Social Security benefits received by a payee on the payor's account. The Mississippi Supreme Court has held that an alimony payor in arrears is entitled to credit for derivative Social Security payments received by the payee. A court properly credited a former husband with $360 a month against arrears to reflect his ex-wife's receipt of benefits based on his employment.[533] No credit against arrearages was due, however, for benefits received by an alimony payee based

---

App. 2009) (denying modification to payor whose income had dropped to $18,000/month; he had purchased vacation homes and recreational vehicles in recent years); Morris v. Morris, 8 So. 3d 917 (Miss. Ct. App. 2009) (husband's $1,500/month alimony obligation not reduced even though income dropped from $158,000 to $90,000; he had country club membership, purchased two cars and two recreational vehicles, and had assets of $500,000).

[526] Holcombe v. Holcombe, 813 So. 2d 700, 705 (Miss. 2002).

[527] Seale v. Seale, 863 So. 2d 996, 999 (Miss. Ct. App. 2004) (but refusing greater reduction based on petitioner's transfer of assets to second wife).

[528] Steiner v. Steiner, 788 So. 2d 771, 777 (Miss. 2001).

[529] Rushing v. Rushing, 909 So. 2d 155, 159 (Miss. Ct. App. 2005).

[530] Tillman v. Tillman, 809 So. 2d 767, 771 (Miss. Ct. App. 2002).

[531] Martin v. Martin, 751 So. 2d 1132, 1135 (Miss. Ct. App. 1999) (wife also received almost $1 million in property settlement).

[532] Reid v. Reid, 998 So. 2d 1032, 1039, 1041 (Miss. Ct. App. 2008).

[533] Spalding v. Spalding, 691 So. 2d 435, 439 (Miss. 1997) (chancellor increased alimony from $250 to $450/month with a monthly offset of $360 in recognition of benefits).

ALIMONY § 9.09[6][b][iii]

on her own employment.[534]

[iii] Payee's reduced expenses. Reduction in a recipient's living expenses may justify a corresponding reduction in alimony. Alimony of $750 a month plus payment of a $1,500 mortgage note as alimony was properly reduced to an overall alimony payment of $1,225 a month when the recipient sold the family home and reduced her mortgage payments to $603 a month.[535] And alimony was properly reduced based upon a husband's decreased income and the wife's receipt of free housing from a male friend.[536]

[c] Impact on financial disparity. In addition to proving a change in one of the parties' circumstances, a payor must show that the change substantially alters the parties' relative financial positions. Alimony was properly modified when a payor's income reduction left him with less disposable income than the payee.[537] However, a chancellor properly refused to modify a $750 a month alimony payment even though the payor's income decreased from $73,720 to $36,972 a year. A monthly payment of that amount, to a wife of twenty-four years with income of $17,000, was not excessive.[538]

A payee's increased income is not automatically grounds for reduction. A chancellor properly refused to decrease alimony payable to a newly employed recipient. Her income after employment was still less than the payor's.[539] Similarly, alimony of $900 a month was not reduced when the payee obtained a teaching position earning $500 a month; the payor's yearly income was $53,000.[540] In contrast, modification was appropriate when an ex-wife's income increased to the point that her income and alimony combined exceeded her ex-husband's income.[541]

In some cases, a slight modification may be granted when a disparity exists. For example, a small reduction in alimony was appropriate when a payor's income fell from $9,000 to $5,000 a month and the payee's income increased from $1,333 to $2,000 a month. Reducing the award from $1,500 to $1,300 a month still left the ex-wife's

---

[534] *See* Seale v. Seale, 863 So. 2d 996, 998 (Miss. Ct. App. 2004).

[535] Wilson v. Wilson, 810 So. 2d 615, 616-17 (Miss. Ct. App. 2002) (sale of home was material change in circumstances).

[536] Austin v. Austin, 981 So. 2d 1000, 1006 (Miss. Ct. App. 2007).

[537] Nichols v. Nichols, 254 So. 2d 726, 727 (Miss. 1971) (wife's income with alimony was $1,800 more than ex-husband's).

[538] Brennan v. Ebel, 880 So. 2d 1058, 1063 (Miss. Ct. App. 2004) (also noting that payor's income had fluctuated up and down in previous years; alimony probably should have been higher in some previous years).

[539] Magee v. Magee, 754 So. 2d 1275, 1280 (Miss. Ct. App. 1999); *see also* Hockaday v. Hockaday, 644 So. 2d 446, 450 (Miss. 1994) (modification properly denied where income of both parties had increased, but husband's standard of living still exceeded ex-wife's); Dix v. Dix, 941 So. 2d 913, 917 (Miss. Ct. App. 2006) (former wife's employment as nurse not a reason to modify; comparing their annual incomes of $60,000 and $534,000); D'Avignon v. D'Avignon, 945 So. 2d 401, 406-07 (Miss. Ct. App. 2006) (wife's increased income of $75,000/year not reason to modify alimony; husband's income had also increased); Jones v. Jones, 917 So. 2d 95, 101 (Miss. Ct. App. 2005) (court erred in finding current financial disparity, but not comparing circumstances at time of divorce and at modification hearing); McCraw v. McCraw, 759 So. 2d 519, 521 (Miss. Ct. App. 2000) (part-time employment and receipt of $200/month from pension did not justify modification).

[540] Spradling v. Spradling, 362 So. 2d 620, 624 (Miss. 1978) (noting effects of inflation since original decree; denying modification based on payee's employment).

[541] Nichols v. Nichols, 254 So. 2d 726, 727 (Miss. 1971) (after alimony payment of $1,800, wife's income was $7,040 and husband's $5,160).

§ 9.09[7]   **MISSISSIPPI FAMILY LAW**

income substantially below her former husband's.[542] And in one case, the court reduced alimony in the same percentage as the payor's reduction in income.[543]

[7] Effective date of modification. Courts have discretion to order modification of alimony retroactive to the date a modification petition was filed.[544] A court did not err in making a reduction effective as of the date of filing.[545] On the other hand, a court has discretion to refuse a retroactive reduction.[546] The court of appeals held that a wife could seek amounts owing under an alimony escalation clause prior to the date of filing the petition, based on the contractual nature of the provision.[547]

§ 9.10 TERMINATION BASED ON MATERIAL CHANGE IN CIRCUMSTANCES

In 2007, the Mississippi Court of Appeals affirmed a chancellor's effective termination of periodic alimony by converting it to rehabilitative. The payor's annual income dropped from $322,000 to $114,000 when he was fired from his job. The chancellor reduced his alimony payments from $1,000 a month in periodic alimony, plus 35% of bonuses, to $650 a month of rehabilitative alimony for two years, retroactive to the date of the hearing.[548]

§ 9.11 TERMINATION BASED ON COHABITATION

The effect of a payee's relationship or cohabitation on alimony has changed substantially in twenty years.

[1] History. As late as 1980, the Mississippi Supreme Court upheld a chancellor's termination of alimony based on a wife's post-divorce "adultery."[549] Two years later, the court noted that post-divorce sexual conduct is fornication, not adultery. Nonetheless, the court continued to hold that post-divorce sexual conduct terminated alimony.[550] In 1994, the supreme court abandoned the traditional rule and held that neither sexual conduct nor cohabitation automatically terminates alimony. Instead, alimony should terminate if a payee's cohabitation is combined with mutual financial support.[551] Applying this test, a chancellor was to determine (1) whether cohabitation had occurred; and (2) whether the third party provided support to the recipient or

---

[542] *See* James v. James, 724 So. 2d 1098, 1104 (Miss. Ct. App. 1998).

[543] Burwell v. Burwell, 44 So. 3d 421 (Miss. Ct. App. 2010) (alimony reduced from $6,000/month to $5,685, based on 5.25% reduction in income).

[544] Cumberland v. Cumberland, 564 So. 2d 839, 847 (Miss. 1990) (contrasting alimony and child support); Shearer v. Shearer, 540 So. 2d 9, 12 (Miss. 1989).

[545] McHann v. McHann, 383 So. 2d 823, 826 (Miss. 1980) (payments falling due after petition filed are not "vested"); *see also* Clower v. Clower, 988 So. 2d 441, 443, 445 (Miss. Ct. App. 2008) (retroactive to date of filing); *cf.* Austin v. Austin, 981 So. 2d 1000, 1007 (Miss. Ct. App. 2007).

[546] Shearer v. Shearer, 540 So. 2d 9, 12 (Miss. 1989).

[547] D'Avignon v. D'Avignon, 945 So. 2d 401, 408 (Miss. Ct. App. 2006).

[548] Austin v. Austin, 981 So. 2d 1000, 1006 (Miss. Ct. App. 2007) (also based on wife's receipt of free housing from man with whom she was involved).

[549] *See* McHann v. McHann, 383 So. 2d 823, 826 (Miss. 1980).

[550] *See* Owen v. Gerity, 422 So. 2d 284, 287 (Miss. 1982) (proof failed to establish sexual relationship).

[551] Hammond v. Hammond, 641 So. 2d 1216 (Miss. 1994).

ALIMONY   § 9.11[2]

the recipient contributed to the third party's support.[552] Under this test, a chancellor properly terminated alimony payments to a woman who admitted that a man lived rent free in her home – she provided indirect support to him in the form of rent and utilities.[553]

[2] Current tests. Today, permanent alimony may be terminated based upon the recipient's cohabitation or de facto marriage. Lump sum alimony does not terminate upon cohabitation.[554]

[a] Cohabitation and presumed support. In 1997, the supreme court discarded the fact-based test for determining whether an alimony payee's cohabitation involves mutual financial support. The court reasoned that an alimony payor lacks the necessary information to prove mutual support between cohabitants. Accordingly, the court adopted a presumption that cohabitation is accompanied by financial support. A cohabiting payee must rebut the presumption by proving lack of mutual support.[555] A 2009 case suggests, however, that cohabitants will almost always engage in some form of mutual support. The court of appeals reversed a chancellor's finding of no mutual support between a former wife and the man with whom she lived. They bought groceries and cooked separately and did not share a bedroom or a social life, although they occasionally engaged in a sexual relationship. The court of appeals held that their relationship was the epitome of mutual support – he had a free place to live and she received the benefit of repairs and yard work that he provided.[556]

A short period of cohabitation may not trigger the presumption. A chancellor properly refused to reduce alimony to a recipient whose friend and two sons moved into her house for five weeks after a hurricane. Her friend did not share her bedroom, bought groceries only once, and moved when his home was repaired.[557] However, a chancellor properly terminated alimony after a former wife's five-month cohabitation and mutual support.[558] Cohabitation may occur even if both parties maintain separate residences. The court of appeals held that alimony was properly terminated for cohabitation when the recipient's friend had a key, stayed frequently in her home, assisted with maintaining and repairing the home, and received substantial support from her in the form of attorneys' fees and personal expenses.[559] In a factually unusual case,

---

[552] Ellis v. Ellis, 651 So. 2d 1068, 1072 (Miss. 1995).

[553] Anderson v. Anderson, 692 So. 2d 65, 72 (Miss. 1997) ("Where an alimony recipient spouse deliberately and purposefully avoids marriage merely to continue receiving alimony, equity should not require the paying spouse to endure supporting such misconduct.").

[554] Chroniger v. Chroniger, 914 So. 2d 311, 315 (Miss. Ct. App. 2005) (payments were lump sum alimony that did not terminate upon ex-wife's cohabitation).

[555] Scharwath v. Scharwath, 702 So. 2d 1210, 1211 (Miss. 1997); see Dill v. Dill, 908 So. 2d 198, 203 (Miss. Ct. App. 2005) (former wife's cohabitation for five months prior to remarriage justified termination of alimony as of date of cohabitation); cf. Rester v. Rester, 5 So. 3d 1132 (Miss. Ct. App. 2008) (finding cohabitation where payee's friend, who worked out-of-state for long periods, stayed with her when he returned home, kept his vehicle at her house, listed her address for his vehicle registration, put most of his furniture in storage, and had no other permanent place of residence); Alexis v. Tarver, 879 So. 2d 1078, 1080 (Miss. Ct. App. 2004).

[556] Wallace v. Wallace, 12 So. 3d 572 (Miss. Ct. App. 2009).

[557] Tillman v. Tillman, 809 So. 2d 767, 770 (Miss. Ct. App. 2002).

[558] Burrus v. Burrus, 962 So. 2d 618, 624-25 (Miss. Ct. App. 2006).

[559] Burrus v. Burrus, 962 So. 2d 618, 622-23 (Miss. Ct. App. 2006); see also Rester v. Rester, 5 So. 3d 1132 (Miss.

§ 9.11[2][b]   MISSISSIPPI FAMILY LAW

a chancellor properly conditioned an award of rehabilitative alimony on the wife's moving from her boyfriend's home and establishing her own residence.[560]

[b] De facto marriage. Alimony may also be terminated even in the absence of cohabitation if a court finds that a payee is avoiding marriage to continue alimony. Alimony was terminated to a payee who was engaged without immediate plans to marry, even though there was little evidence of mutual financial support, on the basis that she had entered a de facto marriage. The court found significant that the couple appeared to forego marriage to obtain the benefits of alimony, stating that "equity should not require the paying spouse to endure supporting such misconduct."[561]

The de facto marriage test was subsequently restated to include an element of financial support. The court of appeals stated that alimony may be terminated where a recipient and another person "so fashioned their relationship, to include their physical living arrangements and their financial affairs, that they could reasonably be considered as having entered into a de facto marriage." Applying this test, no de facto marriage existed based on proof that a woman spent several weekends with a man, that he stayed at her house overnight five or six times, and that he purchased groceries on those occasions.[562]

[c] Agreement of the parties. Divorcing spouses may agree that alimony will terminate if the recipient cohabits. In that case, the only question is whether cohabitation occurred.[563] The wording of the agreement is critical. The court of appeals reviewed a divorce agreement that provided that alimony would terminate if the wife was involved in a relationship "so as to afford said man sexual exclusivity and the benefits of marriage." Evidence showed that the wife was involved in a monogamous long-distance relationship, did not plan to marry, and was financially independent from her partner. The court stated that "the only issue properly before the court is whether the ex-spouse received financial support from the partner/cohabitant and not the moral aspects of such relationship." Because the evidence did not show any change in financial circumstances, the relationship did not afford her partner the benefits of marriage.[564]

[d] Effective date. A court may order termination retroactive to the effective

---

Ct. App. 2008) (ex-wife failed to rebut presumption; friend who lived with her bought groceries, contributed to utility bills, allowed her to use vehicle, bought flat-screen television and assisted in repairs on house).

[560] Alexis v. Tarver, 879 So. 2d 1078, 1082 (Miss. Ct. App. 2004) (holding that "renting" a trailer behind a boy-friend's house but continuing to share meals and car and to sleep in his house, was not sufficient to establish a separate residence).

[561] Martin v. Martin, 751 So. 2d 1132, 1136 (Miss. Ct. App. 1999) (even though there was no cohabitation, the court found evidence of mutual support because the defendant received discounts on her fiancée's "employee/family" discount at the department store where he worked; in addition, he performed errands and household duties).

[562] Pope v. Pope, 803 So. 2d 499, 504 (Miss. Ct. App. 2002); *see also* Burrus v. Burrus, 962 So. 2d 618, 623 (Miss. Ct. App. 2006) (alimony properly terminated; evidence showed that couple chose not to marry so that alimony would continue); Alexis v. Tarver, 879 So. 2d 1078, 1080 (Miss. Ct. App. 2004) (alimony terminates if recipient "becomes supported in a manner equivalent to marriage").

[563] Weathersby v. Weathersby, 693 So. 2d 1348, 1351 (Miss. 1997) (clause terminated alimony, which could not later be reinstated through modification).

[564] Byars v. Byars, 850 So. 2d 147, 148-49 (Miss. Ct. App. 2003).

ALIMONY

§ 9.12

date of the filing of the petition.[565]

§ 9.12 EFFECT OF BANKRUPTCY

Alimony obligations are not dischargeable in bankruptcy. Furthermore, the automatic stay does not apply to actions to establish or modify an order of alimony or child support. In Chapter 7 bankruptcy, the debtor's post-petition income is not part of the bankruptcy estate; thus, arrearages may be collected against future income. In Chapter 13 proceedings, claims for alimony and child support are treated as priority claims behind claims of administration but before tax obligations.[566]

---

[565] Wallace v. Wallace, 12 So. 3d 572 (Miss. Ct. App. 2009) (remanded to determine whether termination should be made retroactive).

[566] *See infra* Chapter XXI for a detailed discussion of bankruptcy rules.

300

X
ATTORNEYS' FEES

Under the American rule, each party in a civil action is responsible for his or her own legal fees. In divorce actions, however, courts are authorized to award attorneys' fees based on need. In addition, fees may be awarded upon successful prosecution of a contempt action, as a result of dilatory actions by one spouse, or when one party pursues a frivolous claim.

§ 10.01 FEE AWARDS BASED ON NEED

In divorce and other family law proceedings, courts may order one party to pay the other's attorneys' fees based on need.[1] The requesting party must prove that he or she is unable to pay fees and that the financial disparity between the parties justifies the award.[2] If the requesting spouse is capable of paying some of the amount charged, an award of a portion of the fee is appropriate.[3] Fees should not be awarded when neither party has the ability to pay attorneys' fees.[4] The inability-to-pay standard also applies in actions to modify decrees[5] and for separate maintenance.[6] Other fees, such as those charged by accountants, expert witnesses, and private investigators, are awarded under the same standard.[7] The inability-to-pay requirement does not apply in paternity actions. The paternity statutes provide that courts "shall" order payment of fees and costs in a successful paternity action.[8]

Courts have authority to award attorneys' fees pending litigation.[9] The Mississippi Supreme Court held in 1893 that counsel fees pending divorce should be awarded based on the "necessity of the case" and the reasonable cost of conducting the case. The court also suggested that fees could be awarded periodically as the litigation progresses, rather than making an initial award based on conjecture about the cost of suit.[10]

---

[1] Dillon v. Dillon, 498 So. 2d 328, 331 (Miss. 1986) (authority to award fees based on chancellor's broad discretion to make all orders regarding maintenance and alimony); *see also* Tynes v. Tynes, 860 So. 2d 325, 331 (Miss. Ct. App. 2003); Bates v. Bates, 755 So. 2d 478 (Miss. Ct. App. 1999). In at least one case, a spouse with higher income was awarded attorneys' fees, based on the court's finding that her actual expenses for herself and the children put her in a worse financial position than her lower-income husband. *See* Rayburn v. Rayburn, 749 So. 2d 185, 189 (Miss. Ct. App. 1999).

[2] Bates v. Bates, 755 So. 2d 478, 482 (Miss. Ct. App. 1999); *see* Pacheco v. Pacheco, 770 So. 2d 1007, 1012 (Miss. Ct. App. 2000).

[3] Mixon v. Mixon, 724 So. 2d 956, 964 (Miss. Ct. App. 1998).

[4] Masino v. Masino, 829 So. 2d 1267, 1274 (Miss. Ct. App. 2002).

[5] Lahmann v. Hallmon, 722 So. 2d 614, 623 (Miss. 1998); Setser v. Piazza, 644 So. 2d 1211, 1216 (Miss. 1994); Pearson v. Hatcher, 279 So. 2d 654, 656 (Miss. 1973). *But cf.* McCraw v. Buchanan, 10 So. 3d 979, 985-86 (Miss. Ct. App. 2009) (mother properly refused fees in unsuccessful custody dispute with paternal grandmother; attorneys' fees are not usually awarded in custody modification proceedings).

[6] *See* Daigle v. Daigle, 626 So. 2d 140, 147 (Miss. 1993) (error to award fees in absence of proof of inability to pay); Johnston v. Johnston, 179 So. 853, 854 (Miss. 1938) (same); Crenshaw v. Crenshaw, 767 So. 2d 272, 277 (Miss. Ct. App. 2000).

[7] *See* Garriga v. Garriga, 770 So. 2d 978 (Miss. Ct. App. 2000) (accountant fees).

[8] MISS. CODE ANN. § 93-9-45 (2004); *see* Daniels v. Bains, 967 So. 2d 77, 82 (Miss. Ct. App. 2007) (only requirement is that fees must be "reasonable"); Kelley v. Day, 965 So. 2d 749, 755 (Miss. Ct. App. 2007) (same).

[9] *See* Anderson v. Anderson, 162 So. 2d 853 (Miss. 1956); Bilbo v. Bilbo, 177 So. 772 (Miss. 1938).

[10] Parker v. Parker, 14 So. 459, 459 (Miss. 1893).

§ 10.01[1] MISSISSIPPI FAMILY LAW

[1] Chancellor discretion. Chancellors have broad discretion in determining whether attorneys' fees should be awarded.[11] An award or denial of fees will not be reversed unless the decision was manifest error.[12] A chancellor may award a portion of a litigant's fees. Even if a party shows inability to pay, the court has discretion to decline to award the full amount.[13]

[2] Findings of fact regarding need. The Mississippi Court of Appeals noted in a 1999 opinion: "Whether or not the chancellor must make an on the record determination that a party is unable to pay attorneys' fees is a matter of some contention."[14] In some cases, awards have been approved without a specific finding of need. For example, an award was affirmed without findings, based on a wife's testimony and a financial statement showing that her monthly expenses exceeded her net monthly income.[15] On the other hand, cases have been reversed for failure to make a finding of inability to pay, even though the requesting party testified to that effect.[16]

The court's finding should focus on inability to pay – the court of appeals reversed an award based upon a finding of income disparity, without an accompanying finding of inability to pay.[17] Noting the conflicting cases, the court of appeals held that an award may be affirmed even in the absence of a specific finding if the record contains substantial evidence to support the finding.[18]

[3] Determining need. It is difficult to define "need" for purposes of awarding fees. Each case varies, depending on the requesting party's income and assets, the amount of fees, and the relative financial disparity between the parties.

[a] Inability to pay. A party's ability to pay fees is based on his or her income,

---

[11] Smith v. Smith, 614 So. 2d 394, 398 (Miss. 1993); Dorsey v. Dorsey, 972 So. 2d 48, 55 (Miss. Ct. App. 2008); Lauro v. Lauro, 924 So. 2d 584, 591 (Miss. Ct. App. 2006) (attorneys' fees awards entrusted to discretion of court); Duncan v. Duncan, 915 So. 2d 1124, 1128 (Miss. Ct. App. 2005) (en banc); Tynes v. Tynes, 860 So. 2d 325, 331 (Miss. Ct. App. 2003); Pacheco v. Pacheco, 770 So. 2d 1007,1012 (Miss. Ct. App. 2000).

[12] Holloway v. Holloway, 865 So. 2d 382, 383 (Miss. Ct. App. 2003); *see* Watson v. Watson, 724 So. 2d 350, 357 (Miss. 1998) (error to award fees to wife of six years who was awarded alimony, the marital home, with mortgage, taxes, and insurance paid by her husband, plus 25% of his retirement accounts); Bates v. Bates, 755 So. 2d 478, 482 (Miss. Ct. App. 1999) (reversing denial of fees as abuse of discretion).

[13] Clower v. Clower, 988 So. 2d 441, 446 (Miss. Ct. App. 2008).

[14] Prescott v. Prescott, 736 So. 2d 409 (Miss. Ct. App. 1999).

[15] Wright v. Stanley, 700 So. 2d 274, 282 (Miss. 1997); *see also* Gray v. Gray, 909 So. 2d 108, 113 (Miss. Ct. App. 2005) (evidence supported chancellor's finding that wife with monthly income of $1,576 while attending college was unable to pay fees); Duncan v. Duncan, 915 So. 2d 1124, 1128 (Miss. Ct. App. 2005) (en banc) (proof of inability to pay satisfactory; wife had $20 left after paying monthly bills; forced to borrow from finance company); Rush v. Rush *ex rel.* Mayne, 914 So. 2d 322, 328 (Miss. Ct. App. 2005) (en banc) (proper to award fees to disabled wife who was clearly unable to pay).

[16] *See, e.g.,* Hankins v. Hankins, 729 So. 2d 1283, 1285 (Miss. 1999); Overstreet v. Overstreet, 692 So. 2d 88, 93 (Miss. 1997); Gambrell v. Gambrell, 650 So. 2d 517, 521 (Miss. 1995); *see also* Ladner v. Ladner, 49 So. 3d 669, 672-73 (Miss. Ct. App. 2010) (no finding regarding inability to pay); Tatum v. Tatum, 54 So. 3d 855, 866 (Miss. Ct. App. 2010) (only findings were that matter was complex and attorneys worked hard); Sessums v. Vance, 12 So. 3d 1146, 1149 (Miss. Ct. App. 2009) (reversed for failure to make findings of fact regarding ability to pay and reasonableness of award).

[17] Jones v. Jones, 917 So. 2d 95, 103-104 (Miss. Ct. App. 2005).

[18] Prescott v. Prescott, 736 So. 2d 409 (Miss. Ct. App. 1999) (but reversing award for specific findings; record contained substantial evidence that wife actually did have ability to pay).

ATTORNEYS' FEES §10.01[3][b]

expenses, and assets. Assets received by a spouse as part of equitable distribution may be considered in determining ability to pay.[19] However, a party should not be required to liquidate modest assets received in equitable distribution if the other spouse has the ability to pay the fees. A court properly awarded fees to a wife whose only income was her alimony, which was less than her expenses; she should not be required to liquidate her retirement account to pay the fees.[20] In another case, the supreme court held that a wife living on a teacher's salary should not be required to deplete $110,000 that she received from sale of the marital home, when her former husband was able to pay her attorneys' fees.[21] However, a chancellor properly refused an award of fees to a wife with $300,000 in assets and $70,000 in cash and certificates of deposit, even though her husband had more assets than she.[22]

[b] Financial disparity. Inability to pay does not in itself ensure an award of fees. The court must also consider the other party's financial resources and ability to

---

[19] *See* Hankins v. Hankins, 729 So. 2d 1283, 1286 (Miss. 1999) (reversing for chancellor to consider ability to pay, including $210,000 awarded in equitable distribution).

[20] Wells v. Wells, 800 So. 2d 1239, 1246 (Miss. Ct. App. 2000); *see also* Pool v. Pool, 989 So. 2d 920, 929 (Miss. Ct. App. 2008) (wife not required to use her only liquid asset, a $20,000 savings account, to pay attorneys' fees); Howard v. Howard, 968 So. 2d 961, 979 (Miss. Ct. App. 2007) (wife who earned $16,000 a year and had exhausted all resources to provide for children entitled to fees from husband who earned $120,000 a year); Carroll v. Carroll, 976 So. 2d 880, 888-89 (Miss. Ct. App. 2007) (affirming award of fees to wife who had no income at time of award; husband's delays and refusals to cooperate cause of some of the fees); *cf.* Stuart v. Stuart, 965 So. 2d 295, 299 (Miss. Ct. App. 2006) (affirming award; wife with monthly income of $2,675 and no liquid assets was unable to pay her attorneys' fees); Lauro v. Lauro, 924 So. 2d 584, 592 (Miss. Ct. App. 2006) (unemployed wife unable to pay fees).

[21] Adams v. Adams, 591 So. 2d 431 (Miss. 1991); *see also* McCarrell v. McCarrell, 19 So. 3d 168, 172-74 (Miss. Ct. App. 2009) (wife who worked part-time and who received marital assets of $15,000, did not have sufficient funds to pay her fees); Riddick v. Riddick, 906 So. 2d 813 (Miss. 2004) (rejecting argument that property received in divorce should be used to pay attorneys' fees in modification action); Hemsley v. Hemsley, 639 So. 2d 909, 915 (Miss. 1994) (wife whose expenses exceeded income not required to deplete $9,000 share of marital home to pay fees); Stewart v. Stewart, 2 So. 3d 770, 776 (Miss. Ct. App. 2009) (wife with annual income of $16,000, who received marital assets of $74,372, should not be required to deplete her equitable distribution award to pay her fees); Smith v. Smith, 25 So. 3d 369, 377 (Miss. Ct. App. 2009) (awarding fees to wife who received marital assets of $314,545, but who had no other source of income but alimony), *cert. denied*, 24 So. 3d 1038 (Miss. 2010); Larue v. Larue, 969 So. 2d 99, 111-112 (Miss. Ct. App. 2007) (court properly ordered husband to pay $7,000 of wife's attorneys' fees; rejecting argument that she should have liquidated only income-producing property to pay fees); East v. East, 775 So. 2d 741 (Miss. Ct. App. 2000) (disabled wife should not be required to pay attorneys' fees from lump sum alimony that was her only liquid asset).

[22] *See* Daigle v. Daigle, 626 So. 2d 140, 147 (Miss. 1993); *see also* Wells v. Wells, 35 So. 3d 1250, 1259-60 (Miss. Ct. App 2010) (fees denied to wife who received over $100,000 in the divorce settlement and worked part-time as a nurse practitioner); Hults v. Hults, 11 So. 3d 1273, 1277, 1282-83 (Miss. Ct. App. 2009) (fees properly denied to wife who received $414,000 in marital assets); Rodriguez v. Rodriguez, 2 So. 3d 720, 732 (Miss. Ct. App. 2009) (fees properly denied to wife who received $32,000 in cash and would receive $300,000 upon the sale of the marital home); Owen v. Owen, 22 So. 3d 386, 390, 393 (Miss. Ct. App. 2009) (attorneys' fees denied to wife who received $100,000 in cash, even though her husband's income was twice hers); Weeks v. Weeks, 29 So. 3d 80 (Miss. Ct. App. 2009) (wife with retirement assets of over one million dollars able to pay her own fees); Parker v. Parker, 980 So. 2d 323, 329-30 (Miss. Ct. App. 2008) (chancellor erred in awarding fees to a wife who received marital assets of $261,000 from a husband who received $35,000); McIntosh v. McIntosh, 977 So. 2d 1257, 1272 (Miss. Ct. App. 2008) (chancellor did not err in awarding wife who received net marital assets of $52,000 only $3,000 of her $12,000 attorneys' fees); Spahn v. Spahn, 959 So. 2d 8, 15 (Miss. Ct. App. 2006) (court did not err in refusing to award attorneys' fees to wife who received $56,000 in lump sum alimony, shares of stock, and an income-producing business); Seymour v. Seymour, 960 So. 2d 513, 521 (Miss. Ct. App. 2006) (reversing award of attorneys' fees to wife who received most of the $155,000 marital estate, including $16,000 investment account); Jones v. Jones, 917 So. 2d 95, 103-04 (Miss. Ct. App. 2005) (award of attorneys' fees reversed; wife with equity in home and retirement account of $62,000 could pay fees); Pacheco v. Pacheco, 770 So. 2d 1007 (Miss. Ct. App. 2000) (denial of fees to low-income wife who chose not to work full-time; received $40,000 in savings and $40,000 in retirement accounts in divorce).

§ 10.01[3][c]   **MISSISSIPPI FAMILY LAW**

pay. For example, the supreme court affirmed an award of fees to a wife whose monthly expenses exceeded her income, from a husband whose income was double hers.[23] In contrast, a court erred in awarding fees to a wife whose financial net worth exceeded that of her husband.[24] And an award of fees to a wife unable to pay was error when her elderly, disabled husband also lacked the ability to pay the fees.[25]

[c] Proof of inability to pay. A defendant must present some evidence of inability to pay. A wife who presented no evidence of her inability to pay fees was not entitled to an award.[26] And the court of appeals reversed an award of fees to a working wife from her unemployed husband. No evidence was introduced of the amount of her income or her inability to pay.[27]

[4] Fault. Attorneys' fees may be awarded to a spouse who is at fault in the divorce. A chancellor did not err in awarding a wife $7,294 of her attorneys' fees even though she left her husband for another man.[28]

§ 10.02 AMOUNT OF AWARD

[1] Factors. In *McKee v. McKee*, the Mississippi Supreme Court stated that an award of fees should be fair, should compensate only work actually performed, and should be based on a finding that the work was reasonably required and necessary.[29] The court established the following factors for consideration in determining the proper amount of fees to be awarded: (1) the parties' relative financial ability; (2) the skill and standing of the attorney; (3) the novelty and difficulty of the questions; (4) the degree of responsibility involved in management of the case; (5) time and labor; (6) the usual and customary charge in the community; and (7) preclusion of other employment as a result of accepting the case.[30] The amount awarded should be "no more than the amount necessary to compensate the attorney for the services he actually rendered."[31]

---

[23] Crowe v. Crowe, 641 So. 2d 1100, 1105 (Miss. 1994); *see also* Pool v. Pool, 989 So. 2d 920, 928-29 (Miss. Ct. App. 2008) (fees properly awarded to wife with monthly income of $1,446 and expenses of $2,712, from husband with monthly income of $3,367 and expenses of $2,266).

[24] Carpenter v. Carpenter, 519 So. 2d 891, 895 (Miss. 1988); *see also* Dorsey v. Dorsey, 972 So. 2d 48, 55 (Miss. Ct. App. 2008) (parties' incomes were not greatly disparate, and wife and husband had equal earning capacity). *But cf.* Scurlock v. Purser, 985 So. 2d 362, 364-65 (Miss. Ct. App. 2008) (award of partial attorneys' fees to a mother whose gross income exceeded the payors' income).

[25] Sarver v. Sarver, 687 So. 2d 749, 756 (Miss. 1997).

[26] Deen v. Deen, 856 So. 2d 736, 739 (Miss. Ct. App. 2003); *see also* Duncan v. Duncan, 915 So. 2d 1124, 1128 (Miss. Ct. App. 2005) (en banc) (party seeking fees has burden of proving inability to pay).

[27] Sullivan v. Sullivan, 43 So. 3d 536, 541 (Miss. Ct. App. 2010).

[28] Sullivan v. Sullivan, 990 So. 2d 783, 788 (Miss. Ct. App. 2008).

[29] McKee v. McKee, 418 So. 2d 764, 767 (Miss. 1982); *see also* Pool v. Pool, 989 So. 2d 920, 929 (Miss. Ct. App. 2008) (attorney's fee of $7,500, at the rate of $150 to $200 an hour, was reasonable).

[30] McKee v. McKee, 418 So. 2d 764, 767 (Miss. 1982); *see* Pacheco v. Pacheco, 770 So. 2d 1007, 1012 (Miss. Ct. App. 2000) (factors govern *amount* to be awarded, not question of *whether* fees should be awarded). *But see* Burham-Steptoe v. Steptoe, 755 So. 2d 1225, 1235 (Miss. Ct. App. 1999) (*McKee* factors are "criteria to be analyzed in determining whether to award attorneys fees").

[31] Bredemeier v. Jackson, 689 So. 2d 770, 778 (Miss. 1997).

ATTORNEYS' FEES   § 10.02[2]

[2] Evidence of fees. Ideally, an itemized statement should be submitted,[32] with accompanying testimony related to the *McKee* factors. If no evidence is presented to support an award, the award must be reversed. A chancellor erred in awarding fees based only upon a wife's statement that she owed her attorney $550.[33] While estimates of time are "frowned upon," courts may consider estimates if the attorney provides a clear explanation of the method of approximating the hours.[34] No itemized statement was required when an attorney testified that his hourly fee was $175, his minimum fee for a contempt proceeding $1,500, and that he actually spent more hours than the requested fee represented.[35] In contrast, an award of attorneys' fees was reversed because no itemized account of fees was introduced into evidence; the only testimony was that the fee charged was $1,500 and the requesting party stated that she was unable to pay that amount.[36]

[3] Findings of fact regarding amount. A chancellor's award or denial of fees should be supported by findings of fact regarding the *McKee* factors.[37] However, awards have been affirmed even though the court did not provide a factor-by-factor analysis. For example, an award of fees was affirmed based on a chancellor's statement that he reviewed the bill and found the rates to be reasonable in light of the nature and difficulty of the work.[38] Another award based on an itemized bill was affirmed even though the chancellor did not specifically review the *McKee* factors – the award appeared reasonable.[39] Similarly, a denial of attorneys' fees was affirmed in spite of failure to address the *McKee* factors; the record provided ample evidence of the wife's ability to pay.[40] And an award was affirmed because the wife's financial statements and affidavits, as well as the court's discussion of her financial situation, supported the award.[41]

---

[32] *See* Mabus v. Mabus, 910 So. 2d 486, 489-91 (Miss. 2005) (en banc) (attorneys submitted detailed itemized statements and affidavits setting out educational background, experience practicing law, experience practicing in domestic relations cases, regular hourly rate, rate actually charged, and usual and customary rates in area; attorneys also testified); Varner v. Varner, 666 So. 2d 493, 497 (Miss. 1995) (itemized account of fees); Howard v. Howard, 968 So. 2d 961, 980 (Miss. Ct. App. 2007) (statement broken down by the quarter-hour, with entries such as "phone call" and "work on case" was sufficiently definite to support award); Lahman v. Hallman, 722 So. 2d 614, 623 (Miss. Ct. App. 1998) (itemized statement introduced).

[33] Powell v. Powell, 644 So. 2d 269, 276 (Miss. 1994); *see also* Carpenter v. Carpenter, 519 So. 2d 891 (Miss. 1988); Suess v. Suess, 718 So. 2d 1126, 1129-30 (Miss. Ct. App. 1998) (fees properly denied, in part because no evidence presented under *McKee* factors).

[34] McKee v. McKee, 418 So. 2d 764, 767 (Miss. 1982).

[35] Watkins v. Watkins, 748 So. 2d 808, 813 (Miss. Ct. App. 1999).

[36] Turner v. Turner, 744 So. 2d 332, 338 (Miss. Ct. App. 1999).

[37] For a case in which the attorney properly presented evidence based on the factors, *see* Grice v. Grice, 726 So. 2d 1242 (Miss. Ct. App. 1999); *see also* Weeks v. Weeks, 29 So. 3d 80, 92-93 (Miss. Ct. App. 2009) (denial of fees remanded for failure to consider *McKee* factors).

[38] A & L, Inc. v. Grantham, 747 So. 2d 832, 845 (Miss. 1999).

[39] Varner v. Varner, 666 So. 2d 493, 497 (Miss. 1995); *cf.* Bounds v. Bounds, 935 So. 2d 407, 412 (Miss. Ct. App. 2006) (*McKee* analysis not required in contempt action).

[40] Tynes v. Tynes, 860 So. 2d 325, 331 (Miss. Ct. App. 2003) (wife had $5,000 to $6,000 in certificates of deposit); *see also* Pool v. Pool, 989 So. 2d 920, 928 (Miss. Ct. App. 2008) (chancellor's failure to cite *McKee* factors is grounds for reversal only if there is manifest error); *cf.* Harbit v. Harbit, 3 So. 3d 156, 163 (Miss. Ct. App. 2009) (analysis of the *McKee* factors was not required). Four judges dissented in part, stating that an award of attorneys' fees must be supported by an analysis of the *McKee* factors governing the reasonableness of an attorneys' fee award. *Id.* at 164 (Griffis, J., concurring in part, dissenting in part).

[41] Wells v. Wells, 800 So. 2d 1239 (Miss. Ct. App. 2001); *see also* Lahmann v. Hallmon, 722 So. 2d 614, 623 (Miss.

§ 10.02[4]   MISSISSIPPI FAMILY LAW

[4] Reduction of fees. The supreme court has stated that courts may not ignore substantial credible evidence and instead fix a fee that has no relationship to the evidence.[42]
A recent court of appeals case involving a trial court's award of fees in an amount substantially below the amount requested prompted a strong dissent. The majority opinion
held that a court did not err in awarding a wife $1,500 in fees, although she expended
almost $10,000 to prosecute a contempt action.[43] Four judges dissented, stating that
there was no evidence to contradict the reasonableness of the fee or the accuracy of the
attorney's records or to suggest that the time indicated was not spent on the contempt
motion. The dissent urged that adequate attorneys' fees should be awarded in enforcement proceedings: "[T]he integrity of the court's order is maintained only through the
full and complete enforcement of its judgment."[44]

§ 10.03 AWARDS BASED ON DEFENDANT BEHAVIOR

Fees may be awarded based on a party's wrongful conduct, without regard to inability to pay. Conduct justifying an award may include failure to comply with court
orders, dilatory tactics, false accusations, or frivolous claims.

[1] Dilatory tactics. A party who incurs legal fees as the result of another's conduct may be awarded fees without regard to need. The award is reimbursement for the
expenses caused by the payor's conduct.[45] Attorneys' fees have been awarded when
one party has prolonged litigation by concealing assets[46] or by refusing to comply with
discovery requests.[47] An award of $10,000 of a wife's $36,000 in attorneys' fees was
necessitated in part by numerous motions filed by her husband's two attorneys.[48] Similarly, a wife was properly awarded fees incurred as a result of her husband's failure to
comply with a temporary order and his denial of an extramarital affair.[49] However, the
award must be limited to the time and expense incurred as a result of the conduct.[50] The
supreme court reversed an award of $20,000 in attorneys' fees based on a husband's
concealment of assets; it was not clear which portion of the fees was attributable to
locating assets.[51] And a court erred in awarding fees in a greater amount than the re-

---

Ct. App. 1998) (award affirmed even though court did not specifically apply factors; appeared reasonable).

[42] Hensarling v. Hensarling, 824 So. 2d 583, 592 (Miss. 2002).

[43] Holloway v. Holloway, 865 So. 2d 382, 383 (Miss. Ct. App. 2003).

[44] Holloway v. Holloway, 865 So. 2d 382, 386 (Miss. Ct. App. 2003).

[45] *See In re* Spencer, 985 So. 2d 330, 337 (Miss. 2008) (awarding fees against attorney who filed frivolous pleadings); Chesney v. Chesney, 849 So. 2d 860, 863 (Miss. 2002); Dickerson v. Dickerson, 34 So. 3d 637, 648-49 (Miss. Ct.
App. 2010); Douglas v. Douglas, 766 So. 2d 68, 71 (Miss. Ct. App. 2000).

[46] Myers v. Myers, 741 So. 2d 274 (Miss. 1998).

[47] Russell v. Russell, 733 So. 2d 858, 862-63 (Miss. Ct. App. 1999) (defendant's recalcitrance was "persistent" and
caused "numerous unnecessary hearings").

[48] Stuart v. Stuart, 956 So. 2d 295, 299 (Miss. Ct. App. 2006); *see also* McDuffie v. McDuffie, 21 So. 3d 685, 692-
93 (Miss. Ct. App. 2009) (wife was properly awarded $5,000 against husband who prolonged litigation "on numerous
occasions").

[49] Chesney v. Chesney, 849 So. 2d 860, 863 (Miss. 2002); *see also* Lauro v. Lauro, 924 So. 2d 584, 591 (Miss. Ct.
App. 2006) (husband's failure to pay support during proceedings caused wife to incur additional fees).

[50] Garriga v. Garriga, 770 So. 2d 978 (Miss. Ct. App. 2000) (reversing because award did not appear to be limited
to fees caused by dilatory action).

[51] Hensarling v. Hensarling, 824 So. 2d 583, 593 (Miss. 2002).

306

ATTORNEYS' FEES   § 10.03[2]

cipient actually incurred in defending against frivolous pleadings.[52]

[2] Contempt actions. A petitioner who successfully prosecutes a contempt action is entitled to attorneys' fees without regard to inability to pay.[53] A chancellor need not engage in a *McKee* analysis to award fees in a successful contempt petition.[54] If the defendant is not held in contempt, fees should not be awarded.[55] However, fees may be awarded when a defendant avoids contempt by complying with a decree shortly before a hearing but after the petitioner has engaged an attorney and incurred legal fees.[56] A defaulting father should have been held in contempt for failure to obtain required life insurance for his children until six weeks after his wife filed a petition for contempt.[57] On the other hand, if the finding of no contempt is based on evidence other than the defendant's recent cure of default, fees should not be awarded.[58] Fees should not be awarded for a respondent's successful defense of a contempt proceeding. A court erred in awarding a wife fees for successfully defending her husband's contempt petition in the absence of a showing that the petition was frivolous.[59] A court may not award an amount that exceeds the attorney's actual charge as a punitive measure for contempt. A court erred in awarding fees in a contempt action in the amount of $3,500, when the

---

[52] *In re* Spencer, 985 So. 2d 330, 338 (Miss. 2008).

[53] *See* Mabus v. Mabus, 910 So. 2d 486, 491 (Miss. 2005) (en banc) (attorneys' fees awarded to father in contempt action against mother for failure to follow visitation order); Morreale v. Morreale, 646 So. 2d 1264, 1271 (Miss. 1994) (error to deny fees against defendant found to be in contempt); Mount v. Mount, 624 So. 2d 1001, 1005 (Miss. 1993); Howard v. Howard, 968 So. 2d 961, 978 (Miss. Ct. App. 2007); Bounds v. Bounds, 935 So. 2d 407, 411 (Miss. Ct. App. 2006) (successful contempt petitioner not required to prove inability to pay); Lauro v. Lauro, 924 So. 2d 584, 592 (Miss. Ct. App. 2006) (husband's failure to pay support during proceedings caused wife to incur additional fees); Faris v. Jernigan, 939 So. 2d 835, 840 (Miss. Ct. App. 2006) (mother who refused to return child from visitation in another state ordered to pay $40,000 in attorneys' fees); Chasez v. Chasez, 935 So. 2d 1058, 1063 (Miss. Ct. App. 2005) (attorneys' fees properly awarded in contempt proceedings covering four years); Rushing v. Rushing, 919 So. 2d 155, 158-59 (Miss. Ct. App. 2005) (chancellor properly ordered payment of attorneys' fees in former wife's successful petition for contempt for alimony arrearages); Stribling v. Stribling, 906 So. 2d 863, 872 (Miss. Ct. App. 2005) (affirming award of $24,901 for fees incurred by husband in contempt actions necessitated by wife's conduct); Durr v. Durr, 912 So. 2d 1033, 1040 (Miss. Ct. App. 2005) (affirming award of attorneys' fees in successful contempt action); *cf. In re* Hampton, 919 So. 2d 949, 958 (Miss. 2006) (award of attorneys' fees proper in criminal contempt action against attorney). *But cf.* Day v. Day, 28 So. 3d 672, 677 (Miss. Ct. App. 2010) (court denied fees even though husband found in contempt; chancellor had found that the protracted litigation was the result of "some failure on the part of each [party] to implement the [property settlement] agreement"); Suess v. Suess, 718 So. 2d 1126, 1129-30 (Miss. Ct. App. 1998) ("the fact that a successful petitioner is eligible for an award of fees in a contempt action does not automatically entitle him or her to an award"); *see also* Prescott v. Prescott, 736 So. 2d 409, 415 (Miss. Ct. App. 1999) ("We are reluctant to disturb a chancellor's discretionary determination whether or not to award attorneys' fees and the amount of the award.").

[54] Bounds v. Bounds, 935 So. 2d 407, 412 (Miss. Ct. App. 2006)

[55] Hensarling v. Hensarling, 824 So. 2d 583, 593 (Miss. 2002) (reversing in part for court to address contempt); A & L, Inc. v. Grantham, 747 So. 2d 832, 845 (Miss. 1999) (45% of fees incurred in attempting to set aside fraudulent conveyances); Bryant v. Bryant, 924 So. 2d 627, 633 (Miss. Ct. App. 2006) (petitioner in unsuccessful contempt action not entitled to fee award); Scroggins v. Riley, 758 So. 2d 467, 473 (Miss. Ct. App. 2000).

[56] Holloway v. Holloway, 865 So. 2d 382, 383 (Miss. Ct. App. 2003) (husband paid $500,000 in arrears after motion for contempt filed).

[57] Pipkin v. Dolan, 788 So. 2d 834 (Miss. Ct. App. 2001).

[58] *See* Douglas v. Douglas, 766 So. 2d 68, 72-73 (Miss. Ct. App. 2000). *But see* Dorr v. Dorr, 797 So. 2d 1008 (Miss. Ct. App. 2001) (stating that a child support payee who recovers arrearages in a contempt action is entitled to attorneys' fees without regard to whether the defendant's conduct was "willfully contemptuous") (citing Pearson v. Hatcher, 279 So. 2d 654 (Miss. 1973)). Judge Irving dissented, stating that the right to attorneys' fees was not automatic in an arrearage action without a finding of contempt or willful nonpayment. Dorr, 797 So. 2d at 1019 (Irving, J., dissenting).

[59] Young v. Deaton, 766 So. 2d 819, 823 (Miss. Ct. App. 2000).

§ 10.03[3]   MISSISSIPPI FAMILY LAW

attorney charged only $600.[60]

[3] Unfounded allegations of abuse. If a court finds that allegations of child abuse are unfounded, the alleging party should be ordered to pay costs and reasonable attorneys' fees associated with defending the allegation.[61] A chancellor did not err in ordering that a mother pay $40,000 in attorneys' fees expended by her husband when she refused to return a child from Georgia, made unfounded accusations against him, and turned the child over to Georgia's Child Protective Services.[62] A court properly ordered a mother to pay attorneys' fees when there was substantial evidence contradicting her allegations of abuse, even though the parties ultimately agreed that she would have custody.[63] And a court properly divided fees between parents who both made unproven allegations of abuse.[64] However, an award of fees was not justified when a mother's accusations of abuse, although disproved, were not unfounded; her claims were supported by expert testimony.[65]

Similarly, a party who makes completely unfounded accusations of domestic violence in an attempt to secure custody of a child should be assessed the other's attorneys' fees and costs incurred in defending the accusation.[66]

[4] Frivolous litigation. As in all civil actions, attorneys' fees may be awarded against a party or attorney who asserts a claim or defense that is without substantial justification, interposes a claim or defense for delay or harassment, or unnecessarily expands proceedings by other improper conduct including, but not limited to, abuse of discovery procedures.[67] An award must be accompanied by findings regarding the reason for the award, using the factors in the statute.[68]

§ 10.04 PROCEDURE

[1] Notice of hearing. Attorneys' fees may not be awarded in an ex parte hearing. The Mississippi Supreme Court reversed an award of attorneys' fees made in a posttrial hearing without notice to the defendant.[69]

[2] Payment to litigant. Fees should be awarded to the litigant, not to the litigant's attorney.[70] A motion for fees filed in the name of the plaintiff's attorneys, rather than in

---

[60] Mixon v. Mixon, 724 So. 2d 956 (Miss. Ct. App. 1998).

[61] MISS. CODE ANN. § 93-5-23 (2004).

[62] Faris v. Jernigan, 939 So. 2d 835, 840 (Miss. Ct. App. 2006).

[63] Rogers v. Morin, 791 So. 2d 815, 829 (Miss. 2001) (custody in issue for three years prior to agreement).

[64] Foster v. Foster, 788 So. 2d 779, 782-83 (Miss. 2001).

[65] Gregory v. Gregory, 881 So. 2d 840, 846 (Miss. Ct. App. 2003).

[66] MISS. CODE ANN. § 93-5-24(9)(c) (2004).

[67] MISS. CODE ANN. § 11-55-5(1) (2004); *see* Balius v. Gaines, 914 So. 2d 300, 309 (Miss. Ct. App. 2005) (attorneys' fees properly ordered where father's custody litigation was intended to financially harass mother; no need to prove disparity in income).

[68] Dep't of Human Servs. v. Shelby, 802 So. 2d 89 (Miss. 2001) (DHS' action to establish that a decree was void against public policy was substantively unsuccessful and untimely, but not frivolous).

[69] Griffin v. Griffin, 579 So. 2d 1266, 1268 (Miss. 1991) (defendant entitled to examine witnesses and question reasonableness of award); *see also* Powell v. Powell, 644 So. 2d 269, 276 (Miss. 1994).

[70] Massey v. Massey, 475 So. 2d 802, 806 (Miss. 1985).

ATTORNEYS' FEES   § 10.05

the party's name, was dismissed without prejudice to allow refiling in her name.[71] And a chancellor erred in awarding fees against an attorney, payable to the opposing party's attorney and guardian ad litem.[72]

§ 10.05 Appeal

[1] Fees on appeal. An appellate court may award a successful appellant attorneys' fees equal to one-half of the amount awarded in the trial court.[73] An exception is made when the appellant has been awarded alimony or assets in an amount sufficient to pay the fees.[74] Fees may not be awarded on appeal if they were not granted or requested at the trial level.[75] A wife was not entitled to an award on appeal in the amount of one-half of her trial attorneys' fees of $19,213.17. The amount was excessive for handling the appeal, and her attorney did not submit a statement of time expended on the appeal. An award of fees on appeal is discretionary with the appellate court, and should only compensate "for service actually rendered" based on a finding that fees were reasonable and necessary.[76]

[2] Reversal of property division requires reversal of attorneys' fees. All financial awards in family law actions are linked – property division, alimony, child support, and attorneys' fees. The supreme court held that when division of property is reversed on appeal, other financial awards, including an award of attorneys' fees, should also be reversed.[77] In at least one case, however, reversal of property division required reversal of alimony and child support, but not of attorneys' fees. The court of appeals stated that the record supported a finding of the wife's inability to pay her fees.[78]

---

[71] Blount v. Blount, 96 So. 2d 232, 232 (Miss. 1957).

[72] *In re* Spencer, 985 So. 2d 330, 338 (Miss. 2008).

[73] Grant v. Grant, 765 So. 2d 1263, 1268 (Miss. 2000); Williams v. Williams, 164 So. 2d 898 (Miss. 1964) (awarding successful appellant one-half of amount awarded at trial); Pool v. Pool, 989 So. 2d 920, 929 (Miss. Ct. App. 2008) (wife awarded one-half of amount of trial fees in appeal of separate maintenance award); Lauro v. Lauro, 924 So. 2d 584, 592 (Miss. Ct. App. 2006) (fees awarded to successful party on appeal usually half of amount at trial; fees on appeal based on need); Broome v. Broome, 832 So. 2d 1247, 1256 (Miss. Ct. App. 2002); Black v. Black, 741 So. 2d 299 (Miss. Ct. App. 1999); *cf.* Durr v. Durr, 912 So. 2d 1033, 1040-41 (Miss. Ct. App. 2005) (no requirement that successful party be awarded fees on appeal; denial of fees appropriate considering mother's seventeen-year delay in seeking enforcement of decree).

[74] McKee v. McKee, 418 So. 2d 764, 767 (Miss. 1982); *cf.* Riddick v. Riddick, 906 So. 2d 813 (Miss. 2004) (suggesting that an appellant may be required to deplete assets for attorneys' fees on appeal even though attorneys' fees were awarded based on need in trial).

[75] Rankin v. Bobo, 410 So. 2d 1326, 1329 (Miss. 1982).

[76] Howard v. Howard, 968 So. 2d 961, 980 (Miss. Ct. App. 2007).

[77] Lauro v. Lauro, 847 So. 2d 843 (Miss. 2003); *see also* Gray v. Gray, 909 So. 2d 108, 113 (Miss. Ct. App. 2005) (because equitable distribution was reversed on appeal, court should reconsider attorneys' fees award; however, court noted that evidence supported award); *cf.* Yelverton v. Yelverton, 961 So. 2d 19, 29-30 (Miss. 2007) (on remand of child support and alimony award, court could reconsider attorneys' fees even though not requested by appellant); Pierce v. Pierce, 42 So. 3d 658, 664 (Miss. Ct. App. 2010) (attorneys' fees "*may* be revisited" on remand when property division and alimony reversed).

[78] Segree v. Segree, 46 So. 3d 861, 868-69 (Miss. Ct. App. 2010) (affirming chancellor's award of attorneys' fees but declining to award attorneys' fees for appeal).

309

310

PART TWO

THE PARENT-CHILD RELATIONSHIP

XI
PATERNITY

At one time, nonmarital children were accorded few rights. Today, a nonmarital child's right to parental support is almost identical to that of a child of marriage. The child's right to support is established through a paternity action, governed by the Uniform Law on Paternity. With the introduction of highly accurate genetic tests, the traditional paternity action has become a relatively uncomplicated proceeding. At the same time, the availability of precise testing has prompted a new paternity suit that tests the limits of judicial ability to resolve family disputes. An increasing number of actions seek to establish that a man who believes himself to be a child's father is not, in fact, the child's biological father. These troubling actions require courts to balance competing claims based on biology, equity, and the child's best interest.

§ 11.01 HISTORY AND OVERVIEW

[1] **Nonmarital children.** Under the English common law, children born out of wedlock were denied the rights of support and inheritance accorded children of marriage. The law viewed nonmarital children as *filius nullius*, the children of no one, without the right to inherit from either parent.[1] Fathers were not required to support children born outside marriage. This disparate treatment was adopted in the United States, and, to some extent, continued until the second half of the twentieth century. In a series of decisions beginning in 1968, the United States Supreme Court eliminated much of the legal discrimination based on legitimacy.[2] Today, nonmarital children may inherit from either parent and are generally entitled to the same support and benefits as marital children.

A child's relationship to his or her father is typically established through a paternity action. In Mississippi, these actions are governed by the Mississippi Uniform Law on Paternity, adopted in 1962.[3] A court hearing a paternity action may resolve issues of custody and visitation as well as paternity and support.[4] Actions to establish paternity as part of an inheritance proceeding are governed by the statutes on wills and estates of decedents, and are not discussed in detail in this chapter.[5]

---

[1] *See* JOHN DE WITT GREGORY, PETER N. SWISHER & SHERYL L. WOLF, UNDERSTANDING FAMILY LAW § 5.03[A], at 113 (2d ed. 2001).

[2] *See* Clark v. Jeter, 486 U.S. 456, 463-64 (1988); Trimble v. Gordon, 430 U.S. 762, 776 (1977) (right to inherit from father); Gomez v. Perez, 409 U.S. 535, 537-38 (1973) (constitutional duty to support nonmarital child); Levy v. Louisiana, 391 U.S. 68, 71-72 (1968) (states may not exclude nonmarital children from suits for parent's wrongful death).

[3] MISS. CODE ANN. §§ 93-9-1 to -49 (2004); *see* Dunn v. Grisham, 157 So. 2d 766, 768 (Miss. 1963) (Act applicable to children born prior to passage; constitutional prohibition of ex post facto laws not applicable to civil proceeding).

[4] See *infra* § 11.06[3].

[5] Suits to establish paternity for purposes of inheritance must be filed within one year of the decedent's death or within ninety days of notice to creditors, whichever is less. The period is not tolled by a child's minority or by lack of notice. MISS. CODE ANN. § 91-1-15(3)(c) (2004). Paternity testing is not required in a suit under this statute. *See* Smith v. Bell, 876 So. 2d 1087 (Miss. Ct. App. 2004). Even after a declaration of paternity, a father who has not openly acknowledged and supported a child is barred from inheriting from the child. *See* MISS. CODE ANN. § 91-1-15(3)(d) (2004); Estate

313

§ 11.01[2]   MISSISSIPPI FAMILY LAW

[2] Children of marriage. One of the strongest presumptions under the common law is the presumption that a child born during marriage was fathered by the mother's husband.[6] At one time, the presumption was irrebuttable. In Mississippi, the presumption may be rebutted by proof beyond a reasonable doubt that the child was fathered by another.[7] The introduction of precise genetic tests has spawned a surprising number of cases challenging legal fatherhood. A mother, child, or biological father may seek to disestablish a presumed father's paternity. In other cases, a legal father seeks to disestablish his own paternity. These actions are also governed by the Uniform Law on Paternity.[8]

[3] Voluntary acknowledgment. Parents may sign a voluntary acknowledgment of paternity that has the same legal effect as an adjudication of paternity. The acknowledgment must include the notarized signatures of both parties and clearly inform the parties of the legal effect of the acknowledgment. An acknowledgment may be rescinded for sixty days after signing or until the date of a judicial proceeding related to the child to which the signer is a party, whichever occurs first. After that date, the acknowledgment may be challenged based on fraud, duress, or mistake.[9]

§ 11.02 JURISDICTION AND VENUE

Jurisdiction over paternity actions lies in chancery, circuit, or county court.[10] Youth courts have no jurisdiction over paternity actions.[11] An action may be brought in the county where the father lives or has property or where the mother or child resides. A father domiciled in Mississippi may remove the action to his county of residence by a motion filed within thirty days of service of process.[12] An action involving the Department of Human Services may be transferred to any county with venue upon DHS's written request.[13] In contrast to divorce actions, venue in paternity actions is not jurisdictional. Failure to object to improper venue is a waiver of the defect.[14]

In interstate cases, custody jurisdiction is governed by the Uniform Child Custody Jurisdiction and Enforcement Act. Jurisdiction over support is governed by the Uniform Interstate Family Support Act.[15]

---

of Patterson v. Patterson, 798 So. 2d 347, 349-50 (Miss. 2001) (father barred from inheriting; paternity established four days before death, but father knew of child's birth three years earlier).

[6] Rafferty v. Perkins, 757 So. 2d 992, 995 (Miss. 2000) (quoting Karenina v. Presley, 526 So. 2d 518, 523 (Miss. 1988)).

[7] Baker v. Williams, 503 So. 2d 249, 253 (Miss. 1987).

[8] See *infra* § 11.07.

[9] MISS. CODE ANN. § 93-9-9 (4)(a)-(b) (2004).

[10] MISS. CODE ANN. § 93-9-15 (2004) (defendant must defend the action in the court in which it is filed).

[11] Helmert v. Biffany, 842 So. 2d 1287, 1292 (Miss. 2003).

[12] MISS. CODE ANN. § 93-9-17(1) (2004).

[13] MISS. CODE ANN. § 93-9-17(2) (2004).

[14] Belk v. State Dep't of Pub. Welfare, 473 So. 2d 447, 451 (Miss. 1985).

[15] See *infra* §§ 18.08, 09.

PATERNITY § 11.03

§ 11.03 PARTIES

A paternity action may be initiated by a child, a public authority charged with the child's support, the child's mother, or the child's legal or biological father.[16]

[1] Action by child. A child may bring suit to establish paternity and obtain an order of support. For example, a child had standing, through her mother as next friend, to bring an action against her mother's ex-husband – her presumed father – and against her alleged father, to establish paternity.[17] Suits have also been filed on a child's behalf by a biological father seeking to establish his parentage of the child.[18] Although a child may bring suit through a parent as next friend, the supreme court has emphasized that the interests of each of these parties in a paternity action are distinct and separate.[19] Because of the conflicting interests in an action involving a legal and a biological father, the child's interest may be best served by appointment of a guardian ad litem as the child's next friend.[20]

[2] Action by DHS. The Department of Human Services is charged with establishing paternity for children who are recipients of public benefits. For a small fee, the department may also represent non-recipients in paternity and support actions.[21] In an action by DHS, the mother is not a necessary party.[22] The Department of Human Services may initiate a paternity action even if the action challenges the legitimacy of a child born during a marriage. The supreme court rejected an argument that DHS could not institute a paternity action on behalf of a child born during marriage but fathered by one other than the mother's husband.[23]

[3] Action by biological father. A man who believes that he is a child's biological father is entitled to bring an action to establish his paternity.[24] A court erred in dismissing a biological father's suit against a custodial father to establish his paternity of two of the four children of the defendant's marriage.[25]

[4] Action by legal father. A presumed or legal father may bring an action against the mother and/or the child's biological father to disestablish his own paternity and

---

[16] Miss. Code Ann. § 93-9-9 (2004).

[17] Baker v. Williams, 503 So. 2d 249, 252 (Miss. 1987).

[18] *See* Karenina v. Presley, 526 So. 2d 518, 522 (Miss. 1988).

[19] *See* Miss. Dep't of Human Servs. v. Sanford, 850 So. 2d 86, 89 (Miss. 2003).

[20] *See infra* § 13.07; *cf.* Rafferty v. Perkins, 757 So. 2d 992, 996 (Miss. 2000) (mother's suit on child's behalf to establish paternity in another, without consent of ex-husband with joint custody, should have been submitted for court approval).

[21] *See* Miss. Code Ann. §§ 43-19-31(c), -35(1) (2009); *see also* discussion of DHS's role in paternity and support litigation *supra* § 10.01[2][d].

[22] *See* McCollum v. State Dep't of Welfare, 447 So. 2d 650, 653 (Miss. 1984) (error to address visitation rights of father where mother was not a party).

[23] Miss. Dep't of Human Servs. v. Gaddis, 730 So. 2d 1116, 1118 (Miss. 1998).

[24] *See* Karenina v. Presley, 526 So. 2d 518, 522 (Miss. 1988); Baker v. Williams, 503 So. 2d 249, 252 (Miss. 1987).

[25] Ivy v. Harrington, 644 So. 2d 1218, 1223 (Miss. 1994) (putative father has standing under the Act).

315

§ 11.04   **MISSISSIPPI FAMILY LAW**

establish paternity in another.[26]

§ 11.04 PROCEDURE

[1] Appointment of a guardian ad litem. Courts have discretion to appoint a guardian ad litem in a paternity action. In an action to prove that a mother's husband was not her child's biological father, the supreme court strongly encouraged the appointment of a guardian ad litem to represent the child's interest, noting that the mother's interest "may not be co-extensive with the interest of the child."[27] And in a recent case requiring a best-interest analysis in these suits, the supreme court instructed a chancellor to appoint a guardian ad litem.[28]

[2] No right to jury trial. Until July 1, 2000, a defendant was entitled to a jury trial on the question of paternity. The statute now provides that there is no right to a jury trial in paternity actions.[29]

[3] Service of process. An action for paternity is a Rule 81 matter, which requires a special summons to the defendant. The procedures for Rule 81 matters are set out in Chapter XIX.[30]

[4] Time of trial. Unless the putative father consents, a paternity action may not be tried until after a child's birth.[31]

[5] Genetic tests. The Act requires that the court order the alleged father and child in a paternity action to submit to genetic tests upon the motion of either party.

[a] Refusal to cooperate. If a party refuses to be tested, the court may find against that party on the issue of paternity or enforce the order for tests.[32] The supreme court held that a chancellor erred in denying a plaintiff's motion for summary judgment on the issue of paternity when a defendant refused to be tested.[33] Similarly, a court erred in refusing to order tests upon the request of a putative father – a court has no discretion in whether blood tests should be ordered.[34] And a court erred in denying DHS's request for blood tests even though the request was not made until the day set for trial – the defendant did not suffer any prejudice, and the child's interest was best served by ordering the tests.[35]

---

[26] Williams v. Williams, 843 So. 2d 720, 722 (Miss. 2003); R.E. v. C.E.W., 752 So. 2d 1019, 1020-21 (Miss. 1999) (suit filed on behalf of child against mother, biological father, and himself).

[27] Baker v. Williams, 503 So. 2d 249, 252 (Miss. 1987); *see* Vronsky v. Presley, 526 So. 2d 518, 522 (Miss. 1988) (guardian ad litem appointed to replace putative father as next friend).

[28] Griffith v. Pell, 881 So. 2d 184, 188 (Miss. 2004).

[29] *See* MISS. CODE ANN. § 93-9-27(3) (2004).

[30] See *infra* § 19.11.

[31] MISS. CODE ANN. § 93-9-19 (2004) (court may take and preserve testimony during pregnancy).

[32] MISS. CODE ANN. § 93-9-21(2) (2004).

[33] W.H.W. v. J.J., 735 So. 2d 990, 992 (Miss. 1999).

[34] Ivy v. Harrington, 644 So. 2d 1218, 1221 (Miss. 1994).

[35] Dep't of Human Servs. v. Jones, 627 So. 2d 810, 812 (Miss. 1993); Dep't of Human Servs. v. Smith, 627 So. 2d

PATERNITY § 11.04[5][b]

A court may order blood tests to be performed on witnesses who testify to a sexual relationship with the mother during the period of conception, but may not compel compliance with the order. If a witness refuses to submit to tests, the court may exclude the testimony of that witness.[36]

[b] Testing facility. Genetic tests must be performed by a facility approved by the Department of Human Services. Approved facilities must be qualified to do business in Mississippi and be able to provide test results in less than two weeks.[37]

[c] Challenge to report. Any party may challenge an expert's report within thirty days after the report is mailed. Upon a challenge the court may, upon good cause, order a second test at the expense of the person challenging the report.[38]

[d] Test costs. The court has discretion to determine a reasonable fee for court-ordered tests and court-appointed expert witnesses. One party may be ordered to bear the costs or the parties may be required to share the costs in a percentage fixed by the court. The court may also order that test fees be included in the costs of the action.[39] However, an indigent defendant may not be required to bear the cost of testing in a state-initiated paternity action, even if the defendant requested the tests.[40]

[e] In acknowledgment proceedings. An alleged father who signs a voluntary acknowledgement of paternity has one year in which to request genetic testing through DHS.[41] A request for testing tolls the running of the one-year period to rescind the acknowledgment until the test results are revealed to the father.[42]

[6] Rebuttable presumption of paternity. A rebuttable presumption of paternity arises if the court finds, based on the tests and expert reports, a ninety-eight percent or greater possibility of paternity. The presumption may be rebutted by a preponderance of the evidence.[43]

[7] Expert testimony. The Act dispenses with the need for expert testimony regarding genetic tests.[44] However, upon a motion by one of the parties ten days prior

---

352, 353 (Miss. 1993).

[36] *In re* Estate of Chambers, 711 So. 2d 878, 882 (Miss. 1998).

[37] Miss. Code Ann. § 93-9-21(5) (2004) (DHS must prepare list of approved facilities and distribute list to chancellors); *see* Rafferty v. Perkins, 757 So. 2d 992, 994 (Miss. 2000) (chancellor ordered new trial because first blood tests not performed by approved facility).

[38] Miss. Code Ann. § 93-9-23(2) (2004); *see* McIntosh v. Dep't of Human Servs., 886 So. 2d 721 (Miss. 2004) (court properly refused request for retesting by defendant who offered no reason and made request nine years later).

[39] Miss. Code Ann. § 93-9-25 (2004).

[40] Little v. Streater, 452 U.S. 1, 9-10 (1981) (distinguishing privately initiated action).

[41] Miss. Code Ann. § 93-9-9(4)(d) (2004), as amended by Act effective July 1, 2011, ch. 530, 2011 Miss. Laws 1, 1 (West) (changing sixty-day period for requesting test to one-year period). See discussion of disestablishment *infra* § 11.07[4].

[42] Miss. Code Ann. § 93-9-9(4)(d) (2004), as amended by Act effective July 1, 2011, ch. 530, 2011 Miss. Laws 1, 1 (West).

[43] Miss. Code Ann. § 93-9-27(2) (2004).

[44] *See* Miss. Code Ann. § 93-9-9(1) (2004) (no need for third-party foundation testimony regarding birth certifi-

§ 11.04[8]   **MISSISSIPPI FAMILY LAW**

to hearing, the court may order the expert analyst to appear for cross-examination at the expense of the requesting party.[45] To establish paternity, it is not necessary that an expert state conclusively that the defendant is the child's father; instead, the expert typically testifies as to the statistical probability of paternity.[46]

[8] Witnesses

[a] Notice. A party who plans to call a witness to testify to a sexual relationship with the mother during the time of conception must give twenty days notice to all parties of the witness' name and address.[47]

[b] Testimony. Paternity may be proven by testimony rather than genetic tests. A court did not err in admitting a putative father's photographs of himself and the child's mother as a couple to prove his paternity.[48] In the absence of blood tests, paternity was proven by testimony that the mother and putative father lived together as husband and wife at the time of conception, that the putative father provided financial support for the child, and that he admitted paternity on several occasions.[49]

Evidence to disprove paternity may include testimony regarding a mother's sexual activity at the time of conception. However, testimony should be limited to the relevant time period. A chancellor erred in admitting testimony regarding a mother's sexual conduct from several months prior to conception through the entire period of pregnancy. The only proper evidence of a mother's sexual activity is during the period of possible conception. It was also error to admit evidence related to her relationship with a man excluded as the potential father.[50]

[c] False claims. A false claim regarding a father's identity is punishable as perjury.[51]

[9] Burden of proof. In an action brought during an alleged father's lifetime, paternity must be proved by a preponderance of the evidence.[52] After the alleged father's death, paternity must be proved by clear and convincing evidence.[53]

[10] Appeals. Appeal may be taken by any party or guardian ad litem by appealing directly to the supreme court within thirty days of entry of final judgment.[54] The

---

cates, fees, genetic tests and fees, or DHS attorneys' fees).

   [45] Miss. Code Ann. § 93-9-23(4) (2004).

   [46] *See In re* Estate of Chambers, 711 So. 2d 878, 882 (Miss. 1998).

   [47] Miss. Code Ann. § 93-9-21(3) (2004).

   [48] Groves v. Slaton, 733 So. 2d 349, 353 (Miss. Ct. App. 1999).

   [49] Harkins v. Fletcher, 499 So. 2d 773, 775 (Miss. 1986).

   [50] *In re* Estate of Chambers, 711 So. 2d 878, 883-84 (Miss. 1998). *But see* Dep't of Human Servs. v. Smith, 627 So. 2d 352, 353 (Miss. 1993) (questions related to mother's sexual activities during ten months prior to child's birth relevant and proper).

   [51] Miss. Code Ann. § 93-9-37 (2004).

   [52] Chisolm v. Eakes, 573 So. 2d 764, 766 (Miss. 1990).

   [53] Miss. Code Ann. § 91-1-15(3) (2004).

   [54] Miss. Code Ann. § 93-9-41 (2004). A putative father's appeal to circuit court was properly dismissed; the only

PATERNITY   § 11.05

appeal does not operate as a stay of execution unless the defendant provides security for support as well as security for the costs of appeal.[55]

§ 11.05 DEFENSES

Few defenses are available in a traditional suit to establish paternity. As a general rule, laches and estoppel will not bar a paternity suit. In a suit to disestablish a legal father's paternity, however, defenses of res judicata, collateral estoppel, and the child's best interest may affect the action. These defenses are discussed separately in § 11.07.

[1] Statute of limitations. A paternity action for the purpose of establishing support and a paternity action for the sole purpose of establishing filiation are governed by different statutes of limitations.

[a] Paternity and support. A suit to establish paternity may be brought at any time until a child is twenty-one or emancipated.[56] If support is sought from the estate of a deceased father, the action must be filed within one year of the father's death or within ninety days after notice to creditors, whichever is first.[57]

[b] Suit to establish filiation only. In a twenty-nine-year-old man's paternity suit against his alleged father, the court of appeals held that the general three-year statute of limitations applies to paternity actions for purposes other than securing child support. Under the Mississippi savings statute, the cause of action was tolled until the plaintiff reached the age of twenty-one. The right to bring a paternity action unrelated to support expired when he reached the age of twenty-four.[58] The court noted, however, that paternity could be resolved upon the alleged father's death, when suit could be brought within one year after his death or ninety days after publication of notice to creditors, whichever came first.[59]

[c] Suit to establish paternity by deceased. A suit to establish paternity for purposes of inheritance may not be brought more than one year after an alleged parent's death or ninety days after notice to creditors, whichever occurs first. The action is not tolled by the child's minority.[60] However, the statute was amended in 2008 to provide that the one-year limitation does not apply to suits to establish paternity for the purpose of receiving Social Security benefits.[61]

---

appeal is to the supreme court. Grisham v. Britfield, 391 So. 2d 107, 108 (Miss. 1980).

[55] MISS. CODE ANN. § 93-9-41 (2004).

[56] *See* MISS. CODE ANN. § 93-9-9 (Supp. 2010) (amending to extend DHS suit from 18 to 21).

[57] MISS. CODE ANN. § 93-9-13 (2004) (support is limited to amounts accrued before death).

[58] Autrey v. Parson, 864 So. 2d 294 (Miss. Ct. App. 2003) (action governed by MISS. CODE ANN. § 15-1-49 (2003)).

[59] Autrey v. Parson, 864 So. 2d 294 (Miss. Ct. App. 2003) (inheritance suit governed by MISS. CODE ANN. § 91-1-15 (2004)).

[60] MISS. CODE ANN. § 91-1-15(3)(c) (Supp. 2010).

[61] MISS. CODE ANN. § 91-1-15(5) (Supp. 2010).

§ 11.05[2]   MISSISSIPPI FAMILY LAW

[2] Laches. Laches is generally not a defense to a paternity action for support. For example, a court erred in dismissing DHS's suit based on a twelve-year delay in prosecuting the action. The supreme court held that a state-initiated paternity action brought within the statute of limitations is not barred by laches. In addition, even if the doctrine of laches applied, the defendant did not establish that he was unduly prejudiced by the delay.[62] Similarly, suit by a child, even through the mother as next friend, is not subject to a claim that the mother delayed in bringing suit. To impute the mother's conduct to her child would frustrate legislative intent to provide for the support of children.[63] And a biological father was not allowed to assert laches as a defense against a mother and her husband who delayed in asserting the child's true paternity. He was not injured by the delay.[64]

[3] Res judicata and collateral estoppel. Res judicata may bar suit by one party but not by another. A mother's second paternity action was barred by res judicata; her previous suit was dismissed with prejudice for her failure to cooperate with blood tests. However, her child's action was not barred by the doctrine of collateral estoppel; the mother's interest in the suit and the child's interest were not substantially identical.[65]

§ 11.06 ORDER OF PATERNITY

[1] Order of filiation. If the court finds that a party is the child's father, the court is to enter an order of filiation declaring paternity.[66]

[2] Child support. The Act provides that the father of a child born out of wedlock "is liable to the same extent as the father of a child born of lawful matrimony . . . for the education, necessary support and maintenance, and medical and funeral expenses of the child."[67] For example, a chancellor did not err in ordering a doctor to pay child support for a nonmarital child, including $1,200 a month in basic support, health insurance, all out-of-pocket medical and dental expenses, a life insurance policy of $500,000, and all college expenses. The court of appeals held that college support may be ordered in a paternity action for a young, nonmarital child, since the child's relationship with the payor may be nonexistent.[68] The father may be ordered to pay child support to the child's mother or to a person or entity designated as trustee.[69] A father may be ordered to provide health insurance for the child.[70]

---

[62] Dep't of Human Servs. v. Molden, 644 So. 2d 1230, 1231 (Miss. 1994); *see also* Dep't of Human Servs. v. Helton, 741 So. 2d 240, 243-44 (Miss. 1999) (court erred in dismissing DHS's suit for failure to prosecute after DHS requested eleven continuances; best interest of child outweighs defendant's right to prompt adjudication).

[63] McGlaston v. Cook, 576 So. 2d 1268, 1269 (Miss. 1991).

[64] R.E. v. C.E.W., 752 So. 2d 1019, 1023 (Miss. 1999).

[65] Miss. Dep't of Human Servs. v. Sanford, 850 So. 2d 86, 89 (Miss. 2003).

[66] MISS. CODE ANN. § 93-9-29(1) (2004).

[67] MISS. CODE ANN. § 93-9-7 (2004). In 1977, the Mississippi Supreme Court held that a statute limiting support for out-of-wedlock children to age sixteen was unconstitutional. Rias v. Henderson, 342 So. 2d 737, 740 (Miss. 1977).

[68] Daniels v. Bains, 967 So. 2d 77, 84 (Miss. Ct. App. 2007) (distinguishing cases that held support should not be ordered for young children since the parent-child relationship is a factor in ordering support).

[69] MISS. CODE ANN. § 93-9-29(2) (2004).

[70] MISS. CODE ANN. § 93-9-29 (2004).

PATERNITY

§ 11.06[2][a]

[a] Order for back support. Payment of back support is limited to support for one year prior to the action.[71] A putative father was properly ordered to pay support for one year prior to filing the action and during the two-year period in which the action was litigated.[72] However, a chancellor need not order a full year of back support. The court of appeals rejected a mother's argument that a chancellor erred in granting only three months of back support.[73] Back support need not be requested in the pleadings to be considered by the court.[74] A court may order back support even though the defendant paid some support pursuant to an out-of-court agreement. A chancellor properly ordered support for the year preceding the petition filing, giving the father credit for amounts actually paid during that year.[75]

[b] Lump sum settlement. Until highly reliable DNA tests were available, proof of paternity was often less than certain. Accordingly, the Mississippi legislature authorized lump sum settlements in paternity actions.[76] The statute remains in effect today. A mother who settled a 1977 paternity action for $18,000 was barred from bringing a second action against the alleged father. In light of the statutory authorization for lump sum settlements, the rule prohibiting waiver of a child's support right does not apply in paternity actions.[77] The court did note that settlement could be attacked on the basis of fraud or collusion.[78] DHS must be included in an agreement to settle support for a recipient of public benefits.[79]

[3] Custody and visitation. Custody and visitation may be addressed in an action to which the mother of the child is a party. In an action filed by DHS, the defendant father may file a complaint against the mother seeking custody or visitation and request that the actions be consolidated. A chancellor may hear the actions separately or in a single proceeding.[80] DHS is not authorized to handle custody and visitation matters in paternity and support proceedings.[81]

A nonmarital father's rights with regard to custody are the same as those of a married father. The supreme court has rejected arguments that an unmarried father may

---

[71] Miss. Code Ann. § 93-9-11 (2004).

[72] R.E. v. C.E.W., 752 So. 2d 1019, 1025-26 (Miss. 1999); *see also* McClee v. Simmons, 834 So. 2d 61, 64-65 (Miss. Ct. App. 2002) (back support properly based on father's current income; he presented no evidence of prior income and failed to respond to a subpoena of tax records).

[73] Burnett v. Burnett, 792 So. 2d 1016, 1019 (Miss. Ct. App. 2001) (one-year period is a maximum, not a minimum); *see also* Hill v. Brinkley, 840 So. 2d 778, 780 (Miss. Ct. App. 2003) (award of back support within discretion of chancellor).

[74] Parker v. Miss. Dep't of Human Servs., 827 So. 2d 18, 20 (Miss. Ct. App. 2002).

[75] Kelley v. Day, 965 So. 2d 749, 754 (Miss. Ct. App. 2007).

[76] Miss. Code Ann. § 93-9-49 (2004).

[77] Atwood v. Hicks, 538 So. 2d 404, 406 (Miss. 1989) (settlement provided $7,800 to mother for birth expenses and support to date, $7,200 to her attorney, and $3,000 in the guardianship estate). The court also relied on Miss. Code Ann. § 93-13-59 (2004) allowing guardians to compromise the doubtful claims of wards.

[78] Atwood v. Hicks, 538 So. 2d 404, 408 (Miss. 1989).

[79] Miss. Dep't of Human Servs. v. Barnett, 633 So. 2d 430, 436 (Miss. 1993) (error to deny DHS intervention until after settlement negotiated).

[80] *See* McCollum v. State Dep't of Welfare, 447 So. 2d 650, 653 (Miss. 1984).

[81] *See* Miss. Code Ann. § 43-19-35(3) (2009).

§ 11.06[4]   MISSISSIPPI FAMILY LAW

obtain custody only by proving the mother unfit or by proving a material change in circumstances.[82]

[4] Security. A court may order a father to provide security for support in an amount no more than three times the amount of support due yearly.[83]

[5] Costs. Upon a finding of paternity, court costs are to be assessed against the defendant, including attorneys' fees and expert witness fees.[84] Fees are to be awarded in a successful paternity action without regard to the petitioner's ability to pay. The only question is the reasonableness of the fees.[85] In a suit by a presumed father against a biological father, the biological father was properly ordered to pay attorneys' fees incurred by the presumed father in prosecuting the suit. In addition, the child's mother was to be reimbursed for fees incurred during the time she acted as the child's next friend.[86]

§ 11.07 LEGAL VS. BIOLOGICAL FATHERS

Genetic tests offer great accuracy in establishing paternity. Their use has also instigated one of the most difficult scenarios in modern family law – proof that a man's presumed child was fathered by another. The issue arises in two contexts – when a legal father seeks to terminate a relationship and support for a child and when a mother or biological father seeks to terminate a legal father's rights over his objection. As in any modern paternity action, the facts of paternity are not difficult to ascertain. The difficult questions are whether a paternity action should be barred by the child's best interest or by conduct of the mother, legal father, or biological father. And in recent years, this scenario has given rise to a new tort action by legal fathers – paternity fraud.

[1] Presumption of legitimacy. The presumption that a child born during marriage is the child of the married couple is "one of the strongest presumptions known to our law."[87] The presumption applies to a child conceived before marriage but born during marriage.[88]

[2] Rebuttal. The presumption of legitimacy may be rebutted by proof beyond a

---

[82] *See, e.g.,* Sauls v. Rainey, 919 So. 2d 182, 183-84 (Miss. Ct. App. 2005) (chancellor properly awarded custody of two-year-old girl to natural father based on proof that child's mother was actively using drugs); *see* discussion *supra* § 12.02[2].

[83] MISS. CODE ANN. § 93-9-31(1) (2004).

[84] MISS. CODE ANN. § 93-9-45 (2004).

[85] MISS. CODE ANN. § 93-9-45 (2004); *see* Kelley v. Day, 965 So. 2d 749, 755 (Miss. Ct. App. 2007); Daniels v. Bains, 967 So. 2d 77, 82 (Miss. Ct. App. 2007).

[86] R.E. v. C.E.W., 752 So. 2d 1019, 1027 (Miss. 1999).

[87] Rafferty v. Perkins, 757 So. 2d 992, 995 (Miss. 2000) (quoting Karenina v. Presley, 526 So. 2d 518, 523 (Miss. 1988)).

[88] Ivy v. Harrington, 644 So. 2d 1218, 1221 (Miss. 1994); Baker v. Williams, 503 So. 2d 249, 253 (Miss. 1987); *cf.* Wells v. Wells, 35 So. 3d 1250, 1252 (Miss. Ct. App. 2010) (husband was not considered father of younger child conceived through artificial insemination to which he did not consent).

PATERNITY

§ 11.07[3]

reasonable doubt that a child was fathered by another.[89] Prior to the widespread use of genetic tests, the presumption was rebutted by proof that the husband was impotent or had no access to the mother during the period of conception.[90] Today, the presumption is rebutted through the use of tests.[91] For example, the presumption was rebutted by proof that the mother's husband was out of the country at the time of conception as well as through blood tests proving conclusively that he could not be the child's father.[92] Similarly, the presumption was rebutted by blood tests proving conclusively that the mother's husband could not be the father and establishing a 99.94 percent likelihood that another was the father.[93]

[3] Suits to disestablish defendant's paternity. Suits by a mother or biological father to disestablish a legal or presumed father's paternity against his wishes pit nature against nurture. In some cases, the biological father seeks to be established as the child's father. In others, a mother seeks to sever ties between a child and her former husband or partner. Suit by the mother may be barred by equitable defenses.

[a] Other states. State courts have struggled to establish a disestablishment test that best serves the interest of the child. In some states, courts are directed to hold a best-interest hearing to determine whether a paternity action against a legal father should proceed.[94] In other states, the child's best interest is not a defense to a paternity proceeding, even if the action will sever bonds between a child and psychological parent.[95] In California, a legal father's paternity may not be challenged by any party after a child reaches the age of two.[96]

Some states have developed the narrow doctrine of "equitable fatherhood" to determine whether a woman's husband should be treated as a parent in law. Under that doctrine, a man may be declared a child's father notwithstanding biology, if he was married to the child's mother when the child was conceived and born, believed that he was the child's father, established an actual father-child relationship; and if equitable fatherhood is in the child's best interests.[97]

[b] Mississippi – the *in loco parentis* test. In 1988, the Mississippi Supreme Court refused to hear a best-interest defense to a paternity action against a legal father, stating that "positive law should not declare a fact that which natural law shows could

---

[89] Baker v. Williams, 503 So. 2d 249, 253 (Miss. 1987).

[90] Rafferty v. Perkins, 757 So. 2d 992, 997 (Miss. 2000) (McRae, J., dissenting).

[91] Ivy v. Harrington, 644 So. 2d 1218, 1221 (Miss. 1994).

[92] Karenina v. Presley, 526 So. 2d 518, 524 (Miss. 1988).

[93] Rafferty v. Perkins, 757 So. 2d 992, 995 (Miss. 2000).

[94] *See In re* Marriage of Ross, 783 P. 2d 331, 338-39 (Kan. 1989); McDaniels v. Carlson, 738 P. 2d 254, 261 (Wash. 1987).

[95] *See* Warren v. Joeckel, 656 P. 2d 329, 332 (Or. Ct. App. 1982); *In re* J.W.T., 872 S.W.2d 189, 197 (Tex. 1994).

[96] CAL. FAM. CODE § 7541(b) (2005). The 2000 version of the Uniform Parentage Act, adopted by four states, also requires that suit be brought within two years of a child's birth. In addition, the Act requires a best-interest analysis. UNIF. PARENTAGE ACT §§ 607(a), 608(b), 9B U.L.A. 295 (2000).

[97] *See* Gallagher v. Gallagher, 539 N.W. 2d 479, 481 (Iowa 1995); *see also* Atkinson v. Atkinson, 408 N.W. 2d 516, 519 (Mich. 1987) (recognizing equitable parent where husband and child acknowledge relationship, husband wants rights of parent and is willing to support child).

§ 11.07[3][c] MISSISSIPPI FAMILY LAW

not have been."[98] In 2004, however, the court adopted a unique approach to disestablishment cases, holding that courts should proceed to determine paternity, but that the rights of the presumed and biological fathers should be determined in a separate action. The court held that a presumed father may have rights even after his paternity is disproved. "Merely because another man was determined to be the minor child's biological father does not automatically negate the father-daughter relationship."[99] Similarly, identifying the biological father does not necessarily require that he be accorded visitation or custody rights.[100]

The court looked to the doctrine of *in loco parentis*, which provides that a person who assumes the status and obligations of a parent may have the rights and obligations of a parent.[101] The court remanded the case for a determination of custody and support under this doctrine. The court instructed the chancellor to appoint a guardian ad litem for the child and to make a determination of the child's best interest, using the *Albright* factors.[102]

Subsequently, the supreme court applied the *in loco parentis* doctrine to affirm a chancellor's award of custody to a divorcing husband, even though genetic testing showed that he was not the child's father. The court rejected the equitable fatherhood doctrine relied upon by the chancellor.[103] And in another case, the supreme court rejected a legal father's argument that the chancellor should have held a best-interest hearing before ordering genetic tests to determine whether his cousin was father of one of the children of his marriage. The supreme court looked to the mandatory language of the paternity statute, which provides that, upon a motion by any party, the court "shall" order genetic test.[104]

[c] Defenses to suit by mother. Judicial estoppel may bar suit by a mother who represented in divorce proceedings that a child was born of the marriage. However, her representations do not prevent her from testifying in an action by the biological father.[105] Res judicata may also bar suit by a mother against her former husband to disprove his paternity. However, neither res judicata nor collateral estoppel prevent suit by a child or biological father who were not parties to the divorce. The Mississippi Supreme Court rejected the notion that a mother's representations at divorce barred an action by or against the biological father.[106] Some states have applied the doctrine of

---

[98] Karenina v. Presley, 526 So. 2d 518, 524 (Miss. 1988); *see also* Rafferty v. Perkins, 757 So. 2d 992, 993 (Miss. 2000) (reversing court of appeals ruling that chancellor should consider whether it was in child's best interest to disestablish paternity of presumed father; issue not properly before the court).

[99] Griffith v. Pell, 881 So. 2d 184, 186 (Miss. 2004).

[100] Griffith v. Pell, 881 So. 2d 184, 186 (Miss. 2004).

[101] Griffith v. Pell, 881 So. 2d 184, 186 (Miss. 2004).

[102] Griffith v. Pell, 881 So. 2d 184, 188 (Miss. 2004); *see also In re* Guardianship of J.N.T., 910 So. 2d 631, 633-34 (Miss. Ct. App. 2005) (custody awarded to man who child believed to be her father, rather than to deceased mother's best friend).

[103] P.M. v. T.D.M., 932 So. 2d 760, 785 (Miss. 2006) (en banc).

[104] Thoms v. Thoms, 928 So. 2d 852, 854-55 (Miss. 2006).

[105] Ivy v. Harrington, 644 So. 2d 1218, 1222 (Miss. 1994).

[106] R.E. v. C.E.W., 752 So. 2d 1019, 1023 (Miss. 1999) (action by presumed father and mother not barred by collateral estoppel because of sworn statements in their divorce action that the child was of the marriage; putative father was not a party to the action, and the issue of paternity was not litigated in the action); *see also* Baker v. Williams, 503 So. 2d 249, 254-55 (Miss. 1987).

PATERNITY § 11.07[4]

equitable estoppel to bar a mother's suit to disestablish paternity.[107]

[4] Plaintiffs' suits to disestablish paternity. Actions by a legal or presumed father to disestablish his own paternity raise different concerns. Courts must balance the fairness of requiring a man to continue support for an unrelated child with the effect of terminating the child's relationship with his or her only known father. One commentator notes that the response of states to this dilemma has been "wildly inconsistent" – some courts refuse to allow adjudicated fathers to disestablish paternity while others allow disestablishment years after adjudication.[108]

In 2003, the Mississippi Supreme Court held that a man may not be required to continue support for a child who is not his, absent a voluntary, knowing assumption of the obligation. A man who acknowledged paternity of a nonmarital child was permitted to disestablish paternity nine years later, when genetic tests in a wrongful death action excluded him as a possible father. To require him to continue to pay support would be "profoundly unjust."[109] The court held that the issue was properly addressed through a Rule 60(b)(6) motion for relief.[110] Similarly, a court erred in requiring a divorced husband to continue paying child support after tests proved conclusively that he was not the child's father. [111]

In 2007 the Mississippi legislature codified this approach by amending the paternity statute to provide for disestablishment of paternity upon proof by DNA testing. The 2007 statute provided that upon DNA proof of non-paternity, "the court shall disestablish paternity and may forgive any child support arrears of the obligor for the child or children . . . if the court makes a written finding that . . . the forgiveness of the arrears is equitable under the circumstances."[112]

In 2011, however, the legislature again amended this statute. The amended statute provides nonmarital fathers with more limited rights than under the 2007 version. A legal father may file a petition in the court with jurisdiction over a child support order, alleging that evidence discovered since the establishment of paternity shows that he is not the child's father. In order to grant relief, the court must find that evidence of non-paternity came to the petitioner's attention after the paternity determination; that the testing was properly conducted; and that the petitioner did not prevent the biological father from asserting his rights. [113]

Paternity may not be set aside if the petitioner (1) married or lived with the mother and voluntarily assumed the parental obligation knowing that he was not the child's father; (2) signed the birth certificate or executed an acknowledgement of paternity and

---

[107] *See* Gallagher v. Gallagher, 539 N.W. 2d 479, 482 (Iowa 1995) (suit barred based on concealment, the father's lack of knowledge, intent that he act on the concealment, and reliance to his detriment).

[108] Ronald K. Henry, *The Innocent Third Party: Victims of Paternity Fraud*, 40 Fam. L.Q. 51, 52 (2006).

[109] M.A.S. v. Miss. Dep't of Human Servs., 842 So. 2d 527, 528 (Miss. 2003) (suit brought under Miss. R. Civ. P. 60(b)(6)).

[110] M.A.S. v. Miss. Dep't of Human Servs., 842 So. 2d 527, 530-31 (Miss. 2003) (rejecting court of appeals reasoning that petitioner delayed unreasonably in seeking relief).

[111] Williams v. Williams, 843 So. 2d 720, 721 (Miss. 2003) (the mother did not remember the biological father's name).

[112] Miss. Code Ann. § 93-11-71 (Supp. 2010).

[113] Act effective July 1, 2011, ch. 530, 2011 Miss. Laws 1, 1 (West) (to be codified at Miss. Code Ann. § 93-9-10(b)(i) (providing one year to request DNA test)).

325

§ 11.07[5]   MISSISSIPPI FAMILY LAW

did not withdraw consent within one year, unless he can prove fraud, duress, or mistake of fact; (3) signed a stipulated court-approved agreement of paternity; (4) was named father or ordered to pay support after declining genetic testing; or (5) failed to appear for a scheduled genetic testing required by court order. [114]

[5] Estoppel to disestablish. A man who holds himself out as a child's father, knowing that the child is not his, may not later seek to disestablish his paternity through genetic tests.[115] For example, a man who knew at divorce that he was not the father of a child born during the marriage was not entitled to disestablish paternity. One year prior to the divorce, he learned from a home paternity test that the child was not his. Nonetheless, he alleged in divorce pleadings that the child was his and agreed to pay child support and exercised visitation.[116]

[6] Paternity fraud. Men defrauded about the paternity of their presumed children have responded with suits against the mother for damages for paternity fraud. The Mississippi Court of Appeals held in 2008 that a man who is defrauded into believing that he is the father of another's child may be entitled to damages for fraud, including reimbursement for child support payments. The plaintiff must prove the elements of fraud - a material, false representation, the speaker's knowledge of its falsity or ignorance of its truth and her intention that the plaintiff act on the statement, the defendant's ignorance of its falsity, and reasonable reliance on the statement to his detriment.[117] The court also held that the general three-year statute of limitations began to run at the time when the plaintiff suspected that he was not the child's father.[118] In that case, however, the plaintiff failed to prove that he was "ignorant of the falsity" of the mother's statement that he was the father, and that he reasonably relied on her statement.[119] In contrast, a father who supported a child born during his marriage, with knowledge that the child was not his, was not entitled to reimbursement for child support; he entered into the obligation voluntarily, knowing he was not the child's father.[120]

§ 11.08 MODIFICATION AND ENFORCEMENT OF PATERNITY AWARDS

After paternity is established, a father's duty of support may be enforced in the same manner as any other child support award.[121] The Act also provides for the same continuing jurisdiction to modify and enforce orders as in the case of divorce.[122] Modi-

---

[114] Act effective July 1, 2011, ch. 530, 2011 MISS. LAWS 1, 1 (West) (to be codified at MISS. CODE ANN. § 93-9-10(b) (i) (providing one year to request DNA test)).

[115] M.A.S. v. Miss. Dep't of Human Servs., 842 So. 2d 527, 528 (Miss. 2003) (suit brought under Rule 60(b)(6)).

[116] Lee v. Lee, 12 So. 3d 548 (Miss. Ct. App. 2009).

[117] Dep't of Human Servs. v. Murphy, 997 So. 2d 983, 990 (Miss. Ct. App. 2008); *see also* McBride v. Jones, 803 So. 2d 1168, 1169-70 (Miss. 2002). *But cf.* Act effective July 1, 2011, ch. 530, 2011 MISS. LAWS 1, 1 (West) (to be codified at MISS. CODE ANN. § 93-9-10(b)(i)).

[118] Dep't of Human Servs. v. Murphy, 997 So. 2d 983, 992-93 (Miss. Ct. App. 2008).

[119] Dep't of Human Servs. v. Murphy, 997 So. 2d 983, 992-93 (Miss. Ct. App. 2008) (reversing award of $23,183.10 in reimbursement for child support payments).

[120] R.E. v. C.E.W., 752 So. 2d 1019, 1026 (Miss. 1999).

[121] MISS. CODE ANN. § 93-9-9(1) (2004).

[122] MISS. CODE ANN. § 93-9-15 (2004) ("The court has continuing jurisdiction to modify or revoke an order and to

PATERNITY § 11.08

fication and enforcement in interstate cases is governed by the Uniform Interstate Family Support Act, discussed in detail in Chapter XVIII.[123]

---

increase or decrease amounts fixed by order for future education and necessary support and maintenance.").

[123] See *infra* § 18.08.

328

XII
CHILD CUSTODY AND VISITATION

Modern custody dispositions are less predictable than those of thirty years ago. Then, fit mothers were invariably awarded custody. Today, parents are presumed to be equally entitled to custody. As a result, custody litigation is more complex, involving fact-intensive proof of the attributes, strengths, and weaknesses of each parent. Courts today recognize that children benefit from a continuing close relationship with both parents. As an alternative to the traditional award of sole custody, courts may order that parents share joint custody or may award a noncustodial parent extended visitation. Visitation arrangements have been further complicated by extension of visitation rights to grandparents and, in some states, other third parties. Unfortunately, the increased flexibility of custody rules has contributed to more frequent litigation. To alleviate the potentially damaging effects of parental conflict, courts may appoint guardians ad litem to represent children and may sanction parents who attempt to destroy a child's relationship with the other.

Even the definition of a legal parent is expanding and changing. The development of assisted reproduction technology has required courts to grapple with identifying the legal parents of children born through in vitro fertilization and surrogacy. Courts have developed conduct-based definitions of parenthood to address the difficult issues presented by paternity fraud cases. These concepts, such as equitable parent, or intended parent, are often broad enough to extend rights to persons other than parties to assisted reproduction and fathers defrauded about paternity.

§ 12.01 HISTORY AND OVERVIEW

[1] **History.** Until the mid-nineteenth century, children were regarded as property belonging to their father.[1] In the rare case of divorce or legal separation, custody was awarded to a father unless he was unfit.[2] In the nineteenth century the doctrine of *parens patriae* developed; during this period, children were viewed as wards of the court in need of protection.[3] Over time, the paternal preference was gradually replaced with a bias toward mothers as custodians. Courts and legislatures developed the tender-years doctrine – the notion that young children should be in their mother's custody.[4] In a complete reversal of early common law, a mother was awarded custody of young children unless she was proven to be unfit.[5] Marital fault was frequently equated with

---

[1] WILLIAM BLACKSTONE, COMMENTARIES ON THE LAW OF ENGLAND 452-53 (Lewis ed. 1898); *see also* Albright v. Albright, 437 So. 2d 1003, 1004 (Miss. 1983) ("At common law, a father had the absolute proprietary right to the custody of his legitimate minor children, and this right was incorporated into the jurisprudence of our country.").

[2] *See* Sinclair v. Sinclair, 86 N.Y.S. 539 (App. Div. 1904); Shelley v. Westbrooke, (1817) 37 Eng. Rep. 850 (Ch.) (denying custody to Percy Bysshe Shelley).

[3] *See* LINDA D. ELROD, CHILD CUSTODY PRACTICE AND PROCEDURE § 1:06 (Clark Boardman Callaghan ed. 1996) (children were no longer viewed as "miniature adults").

[4] *See* ELROD, *supra* note 3, § 1:06.

[5] *See* Albright v. Albright, 437 So. 2d 1003, 1005 (Miss. 1983) (rejecting rule).

§ 12.01[2]   MISSISSIPPI FAMILY LAW

unfitness; a mother who committed adultery was usually denied custody.[6] The maternal preference rule, adopted in Mississippi in 1879,[7] governed custody actions for the
next century.[8]

[2] Modern custody law. The 1970s saw a blurring of gender roles in the family.
Women entered the workforce in greater numbers, and fathers became more involved
in childcare. In the same decade, the United States Supreme Court held gender-based
family law distinctions unconstitutional.[9] As a result, the tender-years doctrine was
replaced by a presumption that fathers and mothers are equally entitled to custody
of their children. Today, all states have abandoned the maternal preference.[10] Modern
custody decisions are based on a child's best interest, determined by consideration of
judicially-enumerated factors.[11]

At the same time, the move from fault-based to no-fault divorce weakened the presumption that custody should be denied to a parent who was at fault in the divorce.
Fault was relegated to one of several factors for consideration. Since 1983, the Mississippi Supreme Court has held that a parent's marital fault may not be the sole reason
for a denial of custody.

The 1970s also brought an important development in the design of custody awards.
Historically, one parent was awarded sole legal and physical custody; the other was
awarded visitation. As fathers became more involved in childcare, joint custody developed as an alternative form of custody.

[3] Overview. This chapter begins with a review of presumptions that apply in
custody actions, the tests for determining custody, and the types of actions in which
custody is litigated. Sections 5.02 and 5.03 discuss custody actions between parents and
illustrate application of the factors used to award custody. Custody disputes between
parents and third parties are reviewed in Section 5.06. Sections 5.07 and 5.08 discuss
the visitation rights of parents and third parties. The final sections discuss modification
of custody orders and actions to enforce custody orders.

[4] Custody presumptions. The maternal preference has been abolished, but other
presumptions now influence the outcome of custody actions. These include the presumption of parental equality, the presumption in favor of joint custody upon parents'
request, the presumption against custody to a violent parent, and the presumption in
favor of a natural parent.

[a] Parental equality. It is presumed that mothers and fathers are equally enti-

---

[6] *See* Keyes v. Keyes, 171 So. 2d 489, 490 (Miss. 1965) (court properly found that mother was unfit custodian).

[7] *See* Johns v. Johns, 57 Miss. 530, 1879 WL 6488 (1879).

[8] *See* Albright v. Albright, 437 So. 2d 1003, 1005 (Miss. 1983) (age and sex of child just one factor to be considered in custody cases).

[9] *See* Orr v. Orr, 440 U.S. 268, 280, 283 (1979) (invalidating state law providing alimony for women but not for
men; old notions do not justify gender-based distinctions in family law).

[10] *See* ELROD, *supra* note 3, § 1:06.

[11] JOHN DE WITT GREGORY, PETER N. SWISHER & SHERYL L. WOLFE, UNDERSTANDING FAMILY LAW § 10.03[3], at 376
(2d ed. 1993).

330

CHILD CUSTODY AND VISITATION **§ 12.01[4][b]**

tled to custody of their children. In 1983, the Mississippi Supreme Court replaced the maternal preference with a presumption of parental equality.[12] The court's holding was based in part on a Mississippi statute providing that neither parent "has any right paramount to the right of the other concerning custody."[13] In 2000, the Mississippi legislature again underscored the importance of parental equality by providing that "[t]here shall be no presumption that it is in the best interest of a child that a mother be awarded either legal or physical custody."[14] Today, actual custody awards reflect an increasing acceptance of the notion of parental equality.[15]

[b] Presumption in favor of a natural parent. It is presumed that natural parents are a child's best custodians. Custody may be awarded to a third party over a parent's objection only if the parent is unfit or has abandoned the child. The presumption does not apply to a parent who has voluntarily relinquished legal custody of a child.[16]

[c] Presumption against custody to violent parent. In 2003, the Mississippi legislature created a rebuttable presumption that custody should not be granted to a parent with a history of family violence.[17] A "history" of family violence includes a pattern of violence or one incident resulting in serious bodily injury.[18] If the presumption is raised and not rebutted, custody should be awarded to the nonviolent parent without consideration of the *Albright* factors.

The presumption may be rebutted by showing that, notwithstanding the violence, the child's best interests are served by placing custody with the parent accused of violence. Factors that may be considered as rebuttal evidence include adverse circumstances of the nonviolent parent, such as mental illness or substance abuse; the violent parent's completion of a treatment or substance abuse program or parenting class; compliance with a restraining order; and whether the violence has discontinued.[19]

If both parents have a history of violence, the court may (1) award custody to the parent least likely to continue violent behavior; (2) order a treatment program for the custodial parent; and/or (3) award custody to a third party and limit access to the violent parent(s).[20] In an unusual application of this provision, a teenage girl's mater-

---

[12] *See* Albright v. Albright, 437 So. 2d 1003, 1005 (Miss. 1983); *see also* Blevins v. Bardwell, 784 So. 2d 166, 172-73 (Miss. 2001) (tender-years doctrine has continuing validity as a factor for consideration in custody matters).

[13] *See* Miss. Code Ann. § 93-13-1 (2004) (parents are "the joint natural guardians of their minor children and are equally charged with their care, nurture, welfare, and education, and the care and management of their estates").

[14] Miss. Code Ann. § 93-4-24(7) (2004); *see also* Miss. Code Ann. § 93-13-1 (2004) (if one parent dies, the other is the child's legal guardian).

[15] The number of recent cases awarding custody to fathers attests to the acceptance of fathers as equal parents. *See* cases cited *infra* § 12.03.

[16] *See infra* § 12.06[3].

[17] *See* Miss. Code Ann. § 93-5-24 (2004).

[18] Miss. Code Ann. § 93-5-23 (2004). The presumption applies only in the case of serious domestic violence. The court of appeals rejected a mother's argument that a chancellor should have applied the presumption: "general yelling and screaming" – involving occasional slapping and one incident of choking without injuries – did not constitute a pattern of family violence. C.W.L. v. R.A., 919 So. 2d 267, 272 (Miss. Ct. App. 2005); *see also* Brumfield v. Brumfield, 49 So. 3d 138, 142-43 (Miss. Ct. App. 2010) (single incident, in which husband shoved wife to floor and hit her with a belt, did not prove a history of violence); Cockrell v. Watkins, 936 So. 2d 970, 973 (Miss. Ct. App. 2006) (three incidents between parents did not constitute history of family violence).

[19] Miss. Code Ann. § 93-5-23 (2004).

[20] Miss. Code Ann. § 93-5-23 (2004).

§ 12.01[4][d]   MISSISSIPPI FAMILY LAW

nal grandparents prevailed in a custody action against her parents, who were married and living together. The father had a history of violence against the mother and once struck his daughter. The chancellor held that the parents failed to rebut the presumption against awarding custody to a parent with a history of family violence.[21]

The statute does not require specific pleading of the presumption, which applies in all actions where the custody of a child is in dispute. A chancellor erred by not making findings of fact with regard to whether a husband had a "history of family violence," even though the mother did not raise the presumption at trial.[22]

Courts are directed to order payment of all costs and attorneys' fees by a party who makes frivolous allegations of family violence.[23]

[d] Presumption in favor of joint custody upon request. If both parents request joint custody, it is presumed that joint custody is in the best interests of the child.[24]

[5] Types of custody. Custody of a child includes both physical and legal custody. Physical custody is the period of time during which a child resides with or is under the care of one of the parents, while legal custody means the decision-making rights related to a child's health, education, and welfare.[25]

Custody may be awarded solely to one parent or parents may be made joint custodians. Joint physical custody means that a child spends significant periods of physical custody with each parent. When joint legal custody is awarded, parents share decision-making rights with regard to the child.[26] A court may award joint physical and legal custody; joint physical custody, with sole legal custody in one parent; joint legal custody, with sole physical custody in one parent; or physical and legal custody to one parent.[27] A court may also order split custody, with children divided between parents.[28] However, there is a strong preference for keeping children in the same home.[29]

An award of "custody" to one parent, without specifying, is understood to include both legal and physical custody. The court of appeals rejected a mother's argument that an award of "custody" to the father was ambiguous with regard to legal custody.[30] Courts sometimes use labels other than "joint" and "sole" to describe custody. A court's award of "paramount" custody to a mother was not error – it was clear that the court intended to award her sole physical and legal custody.[31] Confusion may be cre-

---

[21] J.P. v. S.V.B., 987 So. 2d 975, 980-83 (Miss. 2008) (mother was not considered suitable for custody because she resided with the father and rationalized his behavior).

[22] Lawrence v. Lawrence, 956 So. 2d 251, 253 (Miss. Ct. App. 2006); *cf.* J.P. v. S.V.B., 987 So. 2d 975, 981-82 (Miss. 2008) (chancellor's application of presumption upheld even though he did not specifically consider each rebuttal factor).

[23] Miss. Code Ann. § 93-5-23 (2004).

[24] Miss. Code Ann. § 93-5-23 (2004).

[25] *See* Miss. Code Ann. § 93-5-24 (2004).

[26] *See* Miss. Code Ann. § 93-5-24 (2004).

[27] *See* Miss. Code Ann. § 93-5-24 (2004).

[28] *See* Sanderson v. Sanderson, 824 So. 2d 623, 624 (Miss. 2002) (joint legal custody, with physical custody of children split between parents).

[29] *See infra* § 12.03[12][a].

[30] Wheat v. Koustovalas, 42 So. 3d 606, 608 (Miss. Ct. App. 2010), *cert. denied*, 49 So. 3d 106 (Miss. 2010).

[31] Tritle v. Tritle, 956 So. 2d 369, 379 (Miss. Ct. App. 2007).

CHILD CUSTODY AND VISITATION   § 12.01[6]

ated, however, when parties are awarded "joint physical custody" with one party having "primary custody."[32]

[6] Types of custody proceedings. Unlike property division and alimony, which arise only in the context of divorce, custody of children may be litigated in a variety of proceedings and between parties other than spouses. The various actions in which custody may be litigated are set out below.

[a] Divorce. Chancellors are authorized to address the "care, custody and maintenance of the children of the marriage" in a divorce action and to subsequently modify and enforce the decree.[33] In addition, a court may award temporary custody while a divorce action is pending.[34] Custody may be ordered in a divorce action even though divorce is denied,[35] including an award of joint custody.[36] Furthermore, a chancellor who finds divorcing parents unfit as custodians may award custody to a third person.[37]

[b] Annulment. Chancery courts are similarly authorized to address all matters related to children in an annulment action. A court hearing an annulment action has continuing jurisdiction to modify and enforce the decree.[38]

[c] Separate maintenance. In Mississippi, a suit for separate maintenance may be filed independently of divorce or as an alternative to a request for divorce.[39] In a separate maintenance action, a court may determine custody and visitation[40] and order payment of child support.[41]

[d] Petition for custody. Until 1960, custody suits involving nonmarital children were usually brought through habeas proceedings. Court authority in these proceedings is more limited than in divorce actions; a habeas court does not retain con-

---

[32] *See* discussion *infra* § 12.04[1][c].

[33] Miss. Code Ann. § 93-5-23 (2004).

[34] Miss. Code Ann. § 93-5-17 (2004) (court has authority, upon reasonable notice, to hear complaints for temporary custody).

[35] Waller v. Waller, 754 So. 2d 1181, 1181 (Miss. 2000); Faries v. Faries, 607 So. 2d 1204, 1209-10 (Miss. 1992); Jellenc v. Jellenc, 567 So. 2d 847, 847-48 (Miss. 1990); Davis v. Davis, 12 So. 2d 435, 436 (Miss. 1943) (chancery court has equitable power to determine matters regarding children, granted by Mississippi constitution).

[36] *See* Miss. Code Ann. § 93-5-24(3) (2004) (provides for joint custody in irreconcilable differences divorces or "other cases, . . . in the discretion of the court"); Ayers v. Ayers, 734 So. 2d 213, 216-17 (Miss. Ct. App. 1999) (affirming award of joint legal custody between a separated couple).

[37] *See* Rodgers v. Rodgers, 274 So. 2d 671, 673 (Miss. 1973) (reversing award of custody to grandparent); Moody v. Moody, 211 So. 2d 842, 844 (Miss. 1968); Mann v. Mann, 904 So. 2d 1183, 1183-84 (Miss. Ct. App. 2004).

[38] Miss. Code Ann. § 93-7-7 (2004) ("the chancery court may, in its discretion, . . . as may seem equitable and just, make all orders touching the care, custody, and maintenance of the children of the marriage; and the court may, afterwards, on complaint, change the judgment and make from time to time such new judgment as the case may require").

[39] The remedy of separate maintenance was recognized in 1874 as part of the chancery court's equity jurisdiction. *See* Garland v. Garland, 50 Miss. 694, 1874 WL 4630, at *14 (1874).

[40] *See* Steen v. Steen, 641 So. 2d 1167, 1169 (Miss. 1994) (custody to wife); Johnston v. Johnston, 179 So. 853, 853-54 (Miss. 1938) (custody awarded to wife).

[41] *See* Robinson v. Robinson, 554 So. 2d 300, 304-05 (Miss. 1989); Boyett v. Boyett, 119 So. 299, 300-01 (Miss. 1928).

§ 12.01[6][e]   MISSISSIPPI FAMILY LAW

tinuing jurisdiction over the parties.[42] Recognizing the need for broader equitable jurisdiction, the Mississippi legislature authorized chancery courts to "entertain suits for the custody, care, support, and maintenance of minor children and . . . hear and determine all such matters."[43] Today, unmarried parents and third parties may petition for custody before a chancellor with authority to award custody, visitation, and child support,[44] and with continuing jurisdiction to modify and enforce the order.[45] Venue for the general petition for custody lies in the child's county of residence, the county where the party with actual custody resides, or the county in which the defendant resides.[46] These proceedings are governed by Rule 81(d) of the Mississippi Rules of Civil Procedure. Rule 81(d) procedures are discussed in detail in Chapter XIX.

[e] **Habeas corpus actions.** The writ of habeas corpus was for many years the only remedy for obtaining custody outside marriage.[47] Use of the writ in child custody actions began in the eighteenth century.[48] Initially, it was used only to enforce already determined legal rights to custody.[49] Gradually, the writ took on most of the characteristics of a modern custody action.[50] However, habeas courts did not have continuing jurisdiction to modify awards.[51] Today, the general petition for custody is used in lieu of the writ in most cases.

The statutory writ extends to all cases in which "the rightful custody of any person is withheld from the person entitled thereto."[52] Jurisdiction in habeas actions lies in county court,[53] circuit court, or chancery court.[54] Venue lies in the county where the children allegedly are being wrongfully detained.[55] While the writ cannot ordinar-

---

[42] *See, e.g.,* Mitchell v. Powell, 179 So. 2d 811 (Miss. 1965).

[43] Miss. Code Ann. § 93-11-65 (2004); *see* Mitchell v. Powell, 179 So. 2d 811, 817-18 (Miss. 1965) (chancellor erred in modifying habeas order, but appellate court treated proceeding as one under new statute); *see also* Homer H. Clark, Jr., The Law of Domestic Relations in the United States § 19.3, at 794 (2d ed. 1988) (listing modern statutes and cases providing for civil action).

[44] *See* Rutland v. Pridgen, 493 So. 2d 952, 954-55 (Miss. 1986) (court may grant custody to grandmother under this statute); Smith v. Watson, 425 So. 2d 1030, 1032 (Miss. 1983) (father's suit against nonresident mother under statute); Gladney v. Hopkins, 102 So. 2d 181 (Miss. 1958) (habeas action by maternal grandmother against paternal grandmother). A custody action has also been brought under this statute by a married parent. *See* Walters v. Walters, 519 So. 2d 427, 428 (Miss. 1988).

[45] *See, e.g.,* Mitchell v. Powell, 179 So. 2d 811 (Miss. 1965).

[46] Miss. Code Ann. § 93-11-65 (2004).

[47] *See* J.W. Bunkley & W.E. Morse, Amis on Divorce & Separation in Mississippi § 8.11, at 224 (1957); *see also* Mitchell v. Powell, 179 So. 2d 811 (Miss. 1965).

[48] Clark, Jr., *supra* note 43, § 19.3 (noting that the writ was well-established by the nineteenth century).

[49] The writ was traditionally used to enforce a legal right to custody and did not question the right to custody based on subsequent events. As an example of traditional use, see Pearson v. Pearson, 458 So. 2d 711, 712 (Miss. 1984) (custodial father filed habeas action to secure return of children wrongfully removed by mother). A habeas court could not consider changed circumstances. *See also* Bubac v. Boston, 600 So. 2d 951, 954-55 (Miss. 1992) (citing Gray v. Gray, 83 So. 725 (Miss. 1920)).

[50] *See* Clark, Jr., *supra* note 43, § 19.3, at 793; *see also* Smith v. Watson, 425 So. 2d 1030, 1033 (Miss. 1983); Boone v. Downey, 259 So. 2d 710, 711 (Miss. 1972).

[51] *See* Neal v. Neal, 119 So. 2d 273 (Miss. 1960); J.V. v. Barron, 332 N.W.2d 796, 799 (Wis. 1983); *see also* Mitchell v. Powell, 179 So. 2d 811 (Miss. 1965).

[52] Miss. Code Ann. § 11-43-1 (2004).

[53] Miss. Code Ann. § 9-9-23 (2002).

[54] *See* Miss. Code Ann. § 11-43-7 (2004). Appeal is directly to the supreme court. Miss. Code Ann. § 11-43-53 (2004).

[55] Neal v. Neal, 119 So. 2d 273, 275 (Miss. 1960); Logan v. Rankin, 94 So. 2d 330, 335 (Miss. 1957).

CHILD CUSTODY AND VISITATION § 12.01[6][f]

ily be used to modify custody,[56] the Mississippi Supreme Court in 1985 created a narrow exception to this rule. A noncustodial parent may use the proceeding to obtain temporary custody if the custodial parent has abandoned the child or become "altogether unfit" to have custody.[57] In a habeas action involving allegations of abuse, the court of appeals held that a chancellor did not err in holding an ex parte hearing under the authority of Rule 65(b).[58] Because habeas jurisdiction under these circumstances is temporary, the court's order should include an expiration date giving the parties a reasonable period of time to seek permanent modification in the court with continuing jurisdiction.[59] A custodial parent may also use a habeas corpus petition to enforce a custody order if the noncustodial parent wrongfully retains a child in another county.[60]

Because habeas is more limited in scope[61] and does not provide continuing jurisdiction over the order, a general petition for custody will usually be a more desirable vehicle for seeking custody.

[f] Paternity. A court may resolve custody between unmarried parents in connection with a paternity action.[62] For example, upon establishing his paternity, a father requested and was awarded custody of his son.[63]

[g] Adoption and termination of parental rights. Custody rights may also be determined in a third party's action to terminate parental rights or to adopt a child. A mother was properly granted custody in a suit that originated as an adoption action by grandparents.[64]

[h] Youth court proceedings. Youth courts are vested with exclusive jurisdiction over abused and neglected children.[65] Youth courts may address the custody of children in cases involving abuse and neglect arising in youth court.[66] However, when abuse allegations first arise in a chancery court custody action, the chancery court

---

[56] *See* Fulton v. Fulton, 218 So. 2d 866 (Miss. 1969) (father could seek modification in court issuing divorce decree, but could not seek modification through habeas proceedings); Neal v. Neal, 119 So. 2d 273, 275-76 (Miss. 1960) (issuing court has continuing exclusive jurisdiction to modify outstanding custody order).

[57] Wade v. Lee, 471 So. 2d 1213, 1215 (Miss. 1985) (father showed mother was intoxicated when she arrived to pick up child, was drug user and emotionally unstable); C.M. v. R.D.H., 947 So. 2d 1023, 1027 (Miss. Ct. App. 2007).

[58] C.M. v. R.D.H., 947 So. 2d 1023, 1028 (Miss. Ct. App. 2007).

[59] Wade v. Lee, 471 So. 2d 1213, 1217 (Miss. 1985).

[60] Pearson v. Pearson, 458 So. 2d 711, 712-13 (Miss. 1984) (custodial father filed habeas action to secure return of children wrongfully removed by mother).

[61] Mississippi cases conflict regarding the scope of a habeas court's authority to address other issues. *Compare* Wade v. Lee, 471 So. 2d 1213, 1217 (Miss. 1985) (habeas order included visitation) *with* Roach v. Lang, 396 So. 2d 11, 13 (Miss. 1981) (no power to address visitation and child support).

[62] *See* McCollum v. State Dep't of Pub. Welfare, 447 So. 2d 650, 653 (Miss. 1984).

[63] *See* Law v. Page, 618 So. 2d 96, 102 (Miss. 1993).

[64] *See* Naveda v. Ahumada, 381 So. 2d 147, 150 (Miss. 1980).

[65] *See* Miss. Code Ann. § 43-21-151(1) (2009) ("The Youth court shall have exclusive original jurisdiction in all proceedings concerning a delinquent child, a child in need of supervision, a neglected child, an abused child or a dependent child.").

[66] Custody awards in youth court proceedings are beyond the scope of this treatise. Youth courts have a variety of custody options available, including durable legal custody. *See* Miss. Code Ann. § 43-21-609 (2009) (describing options for custody of children in youth court neglect and abuse proceedings).

§ 12.01[6][i]   **MISSISSIPPI FAMILY LAW**

has jurisdiction to investigate the charges and determine custody.[67] Chancery courts are required to follow youth court procedures in proceedings involving allegations of abuse and neglect.[68]

[i] Civil protection orders. Chancery and county courts are authorized to award temporary custody in actions in which a parent seeks an order of protection from domestic violence.[69] The temporary custody may last for no longer than 180 days. After that period, the order expires and custody reverts to the pre-protection order arrangement.[70]

[7] Jurisdiction. Jurisdiction over interstate custody disputes is governed by the Uniform Child Custody Jurisdiction Enforcement Act and the Parental Kidnapping Prevention Act. Jurisdiction and venue for custody actions are addressed in detail in Chapter XVIII. Jurisdiction over children residing on tribal lands is governed by the Indian Child Welfare Act.[71] International child abductions are addressed under the Hague Convention on the Civil Aspects of International Child Abduction and the International Child Abduction Remedies Act.[72]

[8] Temporary custody. Courts are authorized to award temporary custody pending final resolution of a proceeding, including an action to modify custody.[73] A petition for temporary custody is governed by Rule 81(d) of the Rules of Civil Procedure.[74] A temporary award is not res judicata as to facts existing prior to the temporary order; courts undertake a comprehensive de novo review to determine permanent custody.[75] The supreme court rejected an argument that a material change in circumstances is required to deny permanent custody to a parent with temporary custody.[76] However, the court of appeals affirmed a chancellor's ruling that a three-year-old temporary custody order should be treated as a de facto permanent order, requiring the former custodial mother to prove a material change in circumstances since the father was awarded temporary custody. "[W]here a temporary order remains uncontested for a period of years, we find such orders to have acquired incidents of permanency . . . ."[77] Similarly,

---

[67] *See* Miss. Code Ann. § 43-21-151(1)(c) (2009).

[68] See *infra* § 5.02.

[69] Miss. Code Ann. § 93-21-15(2)(a)(iv) (Supp. 2010).

[70] Miss. Code Ann. § 93-21-15(2)(a)(iv) (Supp. 2010).

[71] 25 U.S.C. § 1911 (2006).

[72] International Child Abduction Remedies Act, 42 U.S.C. §§ 11601-11610 (2006); International Child Abduction, 22 C.F.R. §§ 94.1-94.8 (2006); *see* Elrod, *supra* note 3, § 15.20.

[73] Miss. Code Ann. § 93-5-17 (2004) (temporary custody order in divorce action); *see* Thompson v. Thompson, 799 So. 2d 919, 924 (Miss. Ct. App. 2001) (chancellor has equitable power to enter temporary order in modification action; temporary order treated as permanent because of four-year delay in permanent custody hearing); *cf.* Blevins v. Bardwell, 784 So. 2d 166, 171 (Miss. 2001) (award which appears permanent on its face will be treated as temporary if both parties agree it was intended to be temporary). *But cf.* MacDonald v. MacDonald, 876 So. 2d 296, 297-98 (Miss. 2004) (custody order treated as temporary and not appealable even though order stood for several years). Requests for temporary custody are governed by Rule 81(d) of the Mississippi Rules of Civil Procedure. *See infra* § 19.11.

[74] *See infra* § 19.11.

[75] Blevins v. Bardwell, 784 So. 2d 166, 170-71 (Miss. 2001).

[76] *See* Williams v. Williams, 656 So. 2d 325, 330 (Miss. 1995). However, the fact that one parent had temporary custody may be considered as a factor favoring that parent in the *Albright* analysis. *See* discussion *infra* § 12.03[3].

[77] Swartzfager v. Derrick, 942 So. 2d 255, 259 (Miss. 2006).

336

CHILD CUSTODY AND VISITATION   § 12.01[9]

a two-year-old order that did not set out specific triggers for reviewing custody was converted from a temporary to a permanent order.[78] A temporary custody order is not an appealable final order.[79]

[9] Emergency proceedings. Chancery courts have authority under Rule 65(b) of the Mississippi Rules of Civil Procedure to issue an ex parte order granting temporary custody under emergency circumstances. The petitioner must provide written certification describing attempts to contact the adverse party and the reason notice should not be required. The court must find from specific allegations that "immediate and irreparable harm will result otherwise."[80] Applying this test, the court of appeals held that a chancellor properly awarded custody to a grandmother without notice to the mother, based on allegations that the child had been sexually abused while in the mother's care.[81] In contrast, a mother's receipt of welfare funds was not the sort of "urgent and necessitous" circumstance requiring an emergency order for temporary custody.[82] After a restraining order has been entered, a hearing for preliminary injunction must be set as soon as possible.[83]

In 2009, the Mississippi legislature enacted the Uniform Child Abduction Protection Act, which allows a party to petition a court for abduction prevention measures. If abduction appears imminent a court may issue an ex parte order to law enforcement to take physical custody of the child. The defendant must be served when the child is taken or immediately after and given a hearing by the next judicial day.[84] Jurisdiction to make the determination is governed by the Uniform Child Custody Jurisdiction Enforcement Act. The temporary jurisdiction provisions of the UCCJEA apply if there is a credible threat of abduction.[85]

[10] Effect of out-of-court agreement. A court is not required to recognize an out-of-court custody agreement between parents. Chancery courts are responsible for determining the custody arrangement that will best suit a child's needs; parents may not avoid judicial oversight by a private agreement. A father's petition for custody was treated as an original custody action even though he had privately agreed that the mother would have custody of the child.[86] The court properly proceeded to an *Albright*

---

[78] Quadrini v. Quadrini, 964 So. 2d 576, 580-81 (Miss. Ct. App. 2007) (distinguishing orders that set date for review or specify events that will trigger review).

[79] Michael v. Michael, 650 So. 2d 469, 471 (Miss. 1995); *cf.* Quadrini v. Quadrini, 964 So. 2d 576, 581 (Miss. Ct. App. 2007) (temporary order converted to permanent is appealable).

[80] Miss. R. Civ. P. 65(b).

[81] E.J.M. v. A.J.M, 846 So. 2d 289, 294 (Miss. Ct. App. 2003); *see also* C.M. v. R.D.H., 947 So. 2d 1023, 1027 (Miss. Ct. App. 2007) (court properly held ex parte hearing based on allegations of abuse); Burrus v. Burrus, 962 So. 2d 618, 620 (Miss. Ct. App. 2006) (trial court entered a temporary, ex parte order removing children from custodial mother cohabiting with convicted sex offender).

[82] Robinson v. Robinson, 481 So. 2d 855, 856 (Miss. 1986).

[83] C.M. v. R.D.H., 947 So. 2d 1023, 1027 (Miss. Ct. App. 2007).

[84] Miss. Code Ann. § 93-29-1, -23 (Supp. 2010).

[85] Miss. Code Ann. § 93-29-9 (Supp. 2010). *See infra* §18.09 for a discussion of the UCCJEA.

[86] *See* White v. Thompson, 822 So. 2d 1125, 1128 (Miss. Ct. App. 2002); *see also* Beasley v. Beasley, 913 So. 2d 358, 363 (Miss. Ct. App. 2005) (rejecting argument that parties had agreed informally to joint custody; court had not approved agreement).

§ 12.01[11] MISSISSIPPI FAMILY LAW

analysis rather than treating the action as one for modification.[87] Similarly, a couple's post-nuptial agreement giving a father custody upon separation was void as against public policy.[88] And a custodial father's alleged promise to share time equally with a mother notwithstanding their divorce settlement agreement was not enforceable – it would be against public policy to allow parties to present one agreement to the court while secretly intending to be bound by another.[89] As with custody, courts are not bound by parties' agreements with regard to visitation. A court must review the agreement to determine whether it is in the best interests of the child.[90]

[11] Appeal of custody orders. Custody and visitation are matters within the discretion of the chancellor. A chancellor's award of custody and visitation will not be reversed absent a mistake of law or abuse of discretion.[91] However, an appellate court conducts a de novo review to determine whether the proper legal standard was applied.[92]

[12] Allegations of abuse or neglect in chancery proceedings. When allegations of abuse or neglect are made in a custody proceeding in chancery court, the court may assume jurisdiction if no youth court proceeding is pending.[93] The Uniform Rules of Youth Court Practice, effective January 1, 2009, made significant changes in chancery court proceedings involving allegations of abuse or neglect of a child.

When allegations of abuse or neglect arise in chancery court, the court must order an investigation by the designated Youth Court Intake Unit. Upon receiving the Unit's recommendation, the chancery court is to act on the recommendation without a hearing. At this point, the chancery court must decide whether to hear the case or transfer it to youth court.[94] If the chancery court keeps the case, it must follow *all* procedures required of a youth court under the rules.[95] All proceedings must be confidential.[96] Any subpoenas related to a child's records must be directed to the youth court for transfer to the chancery court.[97] The chancery court must conduct an in camera hearing to determine whether the records should be disclosed.[98]

---

[87] White v. Thompson, 822 So. 2d 1125, 1128 (Miss. Ct. App. 2002).

[88] *See* McKee v. Flynt, 630 So. 2d 44, 50 (Miss. 1993); *see also* McManus v. Howard, 569 So. 2d 1213, 1216 (Miss. 1990) (parents cannot agree that relocation by one parent triggers a change in custody).

[89] Wilburn v. Wilburn, 991 So. 2d 1185, 1193 (Miss. 2008).

[90] *See* Lowrey v. Lowrey, 919 So. 2d 1112, 1119 (Miss. Ct. App. 2005).

[91] *See* Tritle v. Tritle, 956 So. 2d 369, 373-74 (Miss. Ct. App. 2007) (in light of conflicting evidence on *Albright* factors, court could not say chancellor erred); Henderson v. Henderson, 952 So. 2d 273, 279 (Miss. Ct. App. 2006) (en banc) (visitation order will be reversed only if there is no credible evidence, the court has committed manifest error or has applied an erroneous legal standard); Ellis v. Ellis, 952 So. 2d 982, 989 (Miss. Ct. App. 2006) (chancellor reviews credibility of witnesses; court will not substitute judgment for chancellor, who "is in the best position to evaluate all factors relating to the best interests of the child") (quoting Barnett v. Oathout, 883 So. 2d 563, 566 (Miss. 2004) (en banc)).

[92] Potter v. Greene, 973 So. 2d 291, 293 (Miss. Ct. App. 2008).

[93] *See* § 18.01[3] *infra* for a discussion of jurisdiction between chancery and youth courts.

[94] U.R.Y.C.P. 8(c) (2011).

[95] U.R.Y.C.P. 8(c) Cmt. (2011).

[96] U.R.Y.C.P. 5 (2011) (except as provided by Miss. Code Ann. § 43-21-261(2009) or other law).

[97] U.R.Y.C.P. 6(a) (2011).

[98] U.R.Y.C.P. 6(a)(4) (2011) (youth court may conduct a hearing to determine whether the court or parties should be allowed access to records including youth court files, social records, law enforcement records, and agency records, as defined by Miss. Code Ann. § 43-21-251, -257 (2009)).

CHILD CUSTODY AND VISITATION § 12.02

Rule 13 of the Uniform Rules provides for appointment of a guardian ad litem to represent the child's best interest, to make recommendations, and to testify in court. The Rule also provides that if the child disagrees with the guardian's recommendation, the court shall also appoint an attorney to represent the child's preferences.[99]

§ 12.02 CUSTODY ACTIONS BETWEEN PARENTS

Custody between parents is based on the best interests of the child. Courts are guided by several presumptions in making this determination. These include the presumption that parents are equally entitled to custody, that a request by both parents for joint custody should be honored, and that a violent parent should not be awarded custody.[100] In some cases, third parties may be treated as parents and granted equal standing in a custody action.[101]

The Mississippi Supreme Court has enumerated factors that provide a guideline for analyzing a child's best interests. Nonetheless, the difficult question of custody between parents can never be reduced to a formula. Each case is different – judges are given great discretion to determine the arrangement that best serves the needs of a particular child.

[1] The best interests test. Courts in every state determine custody based on a child's best interests. As the Mississippi Supreme Court has repeatedly emphasized, "the polestar consideration in child custody cases is the best interest and welfare of the child."[102] At one time, the maternal preference provided a simple test for determining a child's best interests. If a mother was fit and a child was "of tender years," custody to the mother was presumed to serve the child's best interests. In 1983, in *Albright v. Albright*,[103] the Mississippi Supreme Court abandoned the maternal preference, holding that a child's age is but one of several factors for consideration in a custody award.

The court set out twelve factors for courts to weigh in awarding custody: (1) the age, health, and sex of a child; (2) which parent had continuing care of the child prior to separation; (3) which parent has the best parenting skills; (4) which has the willingness and capacity to provide primary child care; (5) the employment responsibilities of both parents; (6) the physical and mental health and age of parents; (7) emotional ties of the parent and child; (8) the parents' moral fitness; (9) the child's home, school, and community record; (10) the preference of a child at the age of twelve; (11) stability of the home environment and employment of each parent; and (12) other relevant factors.[104] The list is not exhaustive – courts may consider other relevant factors.[105] Chancellors have substantial discretion in making custody decisions, which are reviewed under the

---

[99] U.R.Y.C.P. 13(f) (2011).

[100] *See supra* § 12.01[4].

[101] *See infra* § 12.06[2].

[102] Albright v. Albright, 437 So. 2d 1003, 1005 (Miss. 1983).

[103] Albright v. Albright, 437 So. 2d 1003 (Miss. 1983).

[104] Albright v. Albright, 437 So. 2d 1003, 1005 (Miss. 1983).

[105] *See, e.g.,* Sellers v. Sellers, 638 So. 2d 481, 485 (Miss. 1994) (considering separation of siblings as factor); Brown v. Crum, 30 So. 3d 1254, 1259 (Miss. Ct. App. 2010) (chancellor may consider factors in addition to the *Albright* factors, such as credibility of witnesses and the weight of their testimony).

§ 12.02[2]   MISSISSIPPI FAMILY LAW

abuse of discretion standard. On appeal, the court need not reexamine all of the evidence, but must determine whether the chancellor's decision is supported by credible evidence in the record.[106]

[2] Custody actions between unmarried parents. The *Albright* best interests test governs custody determinations between unmarried parents. An unmarried father is "on equal footing" with a mother in an initial custody proceeding.[107] The Mississippi Supreme Court rejected an unmarried mother's argument that she was entitled to custody unless the child's father could prove that she had abandoned the child or was unfit.[108] In a similar case, the court held that an unmarried father did not have to prove a material change in circumstances to obtain custody of his child when no custody order had been entered.[109]

An unmarried father is entitled to an *Albright* custody analysis even if he has previously been adjudicated a child's father and ordered to pay child support. The court of appeals held that an unmarried father's suit for custody of his seven-year-old child should be treated as an original action for custody. The court rejected the mother's argument that she was implicitly granted custody in the earlier paternity and child support action. The court noted that DHS was the petitioner in the proceeding; the mother was not even a party. There was no indication that the court in the prior proceeding considered the *Albright* factors or awarded custody. The court also saw no reason that the father's seven-year delay in seeking custody should alter the settled rule.[110] In a 2008 case, a divided court of appeals rejected a mother's argument that a father had waived his right to seek custody under *Albright* because he did not pursue a relationship with the child for two years after the child's birth.[111] And in 2010, the court of appeals reaffirmed these holdings but noted that a judge may consider a father's delay in asserting his rights as a custody factor.[112]

§ 12.03 APPLICATION OF THE *ALBRIGHT* FACTORS

The *Albright* factors guide chancellors in reviewing evidence relevant to custody. They are not, as the supreme court has noted, "the equivalent of a mathematical formula."[113] Although chancellors are instructed to weigh parents' relative merits under each factor, a parent who "wins" on more factors is not necessarily entitled to custody.

---

[106] Funderburk v. Funderburk, 909 So. 2d 1241, 1243 (Miss. Ct. App. 2005).

[107] S.B. v. L.W., 793 So. 2d 656, 659 (Miss. Ct. App. 2001) (awarding custody to father) (citing Law v. Page, 618 So. 2d 96, 101 (Miss. 1993)).

[108] *See* Hayes v. Rounds, 658 So. 2d 863, 866 (Miss. 1995).

[109] *See* S.B. v. L.W., 793 So. 2d 656, 659 (Miss. Ct. App. 2001); *cf.* C.W.L. v. R.A., 919 So. 2d 267, 271 (Miss. Ct. App. 2005) (action treated as original custody proceeding even though prior paternity action awarded father reasonable visitation – paternity court did not award mother sole custody in previous action).

[110] Romans v. Fulgham, 939 So. 2d 849, 852-53 (Miss. Ct. App. 2006) (en banc); *see also* Brown v. Crum, 30 So. 3d 1254, 1259 (Miss. Ct. App. 2010) (father awarded custody).

[111] Williams v. Stockstill, 990 So. 2d 774, 776 (Miss. Ct. App. 2008) (four judges dissented, arguing for a change in the law).

[112] Reed v. Fair, 56 So. 3d 577, 583 (Miss. Ct. App. 2010); *see also* Curry v. McDaniel, 37 So. 3d 1225, 1227-30 (Miss. Ct. App. 2010) (father's custody petition filed six years after paternity and support order treated as original custody action).

[113] Lee v. Lee, 798 So. 2d 1284, 1288 (Miss. 2001).

CHILD CUSTODY AND VISITATION   § 12.03[1]

In some cases, one or two factors may control an award.[114] Furthermore, a chancellor's ultimate decision is guided by additional considerations – the credibility of witnesses, the weight of their testimony, and the weighing of evidence capable of more than one interpretation.[115]

[1] Findings of fact. A chancellor is required to make findings of fact with regard to each *Albright* factor. Failure to make the required findings is one of the most common reasons for reversal of a custody award. Ideally, the court should (1) list each factor; (2) if a factor is inapplicable, briefly state the reason the factor does not apply; (3) under each relevant factor, discuss the evidence as it relates to each parent; (4) under each factor, indicate which parent appears stronger; and (5) state which parent should be awarded custody, discussing the overall balance of the factors in light of the child's best interests.

Appellate courts have reversed awards with no *Albright* findings of fact[116] even though the court discussed the evidence presented at trial.[117] When a chancellor has explicitly considered some but not all of the factors, the outcome on appeal varies. For example, the court of appeals reversed a decision that did not address the child's age or the father's violent behavior and that stated some factors favored the father without explaining why.[118] Some custody decisions have been upheld even though the court did not consider all the factors.[119] If a factor is obviously irrelevant, a court may simply state that the factor is inapplicable without entering detailed findings to that effect.[120] Decisions that discuss the *Albright* factors without stating which parent is favored on each factor are likely to be affirmed if the court's discussion illustrates the reason for the ruling.[121] The court of appeals has indicated, however, that specific findings on each

---

[114] *See* Ellis v. Ellis, 952 So. 2d 982, 997 (Miss. Ct. App. 2006) (*Albright* test not a formula); Divers v. Divers, 856 So. 2d 370, 376 (Miss. Ct. App. 2003) (one factor may weigh so heavily that it controls award).

[115] *See* Johnson v. Gray, 859 So. 2d 1006, 1013-14 (Miss. 2003) (chancellor has ultimate discretion to weigh evidence).

[116] *See, e.g.,* Franklin v. Franklin, 864 So. 2d 970, 981-82 (Miss. Ct. App. 2003); Formigoni v. Formigoni, 733 So. 2d 868, 870-71 (Miss. Ct. App. 1999); Limbaugh v. Limbaugh, 749 So. 2d 1244 (Miss. Ct. App. 1999). *But cf.* Pearson v. Pearson, 11 So. 3d 178, 184 (Miss. Ct. App. 2009) (affirming custody award even though the chancellor did not label his discussion of facts using the *Albright* factors).

[117] *See* Powell v. Ayars, 792 So. 2d 240 (Miss. 2001) (reversing award because the chancellor stated that he applied the *Albright* factors without an on-the-record determination of factors, even though evidence relating to parenting skills and stability of the home environment discussed).

[118] *See* Fulk v. Fulk, 827 So. 2d 736, 739-40 (Miss. Ct. App. 2002); *see also* Hamilton v. Hamilton, 755 So. 2d 528 (Miss. Ct. App. 1999) (acknowledging that the chancellor discussed at least five of the factors, but reversing "for the purposes of addressing each of the *Albright* factors").

[119] *See* Sobeiske v. Preslar, 755 So. 2d 410, 411-12 (Miss. 2000) (affirming even though only factor discussed was geographical location; express consideration of every factor would be preferable); Richardson v. Richardson, 912 So. 2d 1079, 1081 (Miss. Ct. App. 2005) (custody award affirmed even though the court did not specifically address *Albright* factors; testimony and father's pleadings provided substantial evidence); *In re* Guardianship of J.N.T., 910 So. 2d 631, 632-33 (Miss. Ct. App. 2005) (though chancellor did not designate *Albright* factors, he clearly applied *Albright* factors).

[120] *See* Hensarling v. Hensarling, 824 So. 2d 583, 587 (Miss. 2002).

[121] *See* Alderson v. Alderson, 810 So. 2d 627, 629 (Miss. Ct. App. 2002) (chancellor enumerated each factor and the facts he considered pertinent; not necessary for the chancellor to state who prevailed under each factor); Myers v. Myers, 814 So. 2d 833, 835 (Miss. Ct. App. 2002) (not necessary that chancellor state which parent "wins" on each factor, where chancellor stated each factor and the evidence that related to each); Murphy v. Murphy, 797 So. 2d 325, 329-30 (Miss. Ct. App. 2001) (no error since chancellor recited evidence relevant to each factor and stated that she considered the *Albright* factors; more "preferable" to include precise findings).

§ 12.03[2]   **MISSISSIPPI FAMILY LAW**

factor are preferable.[122] In at least one case, an award was affirmed even though the court did not provide reasons for choosing one parent over the other, since the record supported the award.[123] However, a 2007 decision stated that a chancellor must articulate his or her rationale for the finding on each *Albright* factor and that failure to do so is reversible error.[124]

Specific *Albright* findings are required in actions to modify custody if the court has found an adverse material change in circumstances. In the absence of an adverse material change, an *Albright* analysis is unnecessary.[125] Specific findings are not required when parents enter an agreed consent judgment with regard to custody[126] or in an uncontested proceeding.[127] *Albright* findings are required to support an award of joint physical custody, but not to support an award of joint legal custody.[128]

[2] Age, health, and sex of child. At one time, mothers were presumed to be the best custodians of girls and young children. Today, a court may not base custody solely on a child's age and sex or on a presumption that mothers are superior custodians.[129] For example, a court erred in awarding custody of a two-year-old child to a mother solely because the father failed to prove that she was unfit.[130]

A court may, however, consider a child's age and sex as a factor favoring a mother. For example, the court of appeals rejected a father's argument that a chancellor resurrected the maternal preference by awarding custody of one- and three-year-old children to their mother. A chancellor may properly consider age and sex as a factor – "there is still a presumption that a mother is generally better suited to raise a young child."[131] Furthermore, a fit mother who has been a child's primary caretaker is likely to be awarded custody based in part on that factor[132] – a consideration entirely separate from the maternal preference.

The age of a child weighs in favor of a mother only in a child's early years. The Mississippi Court of Appeals stated that a child "is no longer of tender years when that child can be equally cared for by persons other than the mother. . . . [A] child of seven

---

[122] *See* Murphy v. Murphy, 797 So. 2d 325, 329-30 (Miss. Ct. App. 2001). *But cf.* Weeks v. Weeks, 989 So. 2d 408, 411 (Miss. Ct. App. 2008) (affirming the award even though chancellor did not state which parent prevailed on each factor).

[123] *See* M.C.M.J. v. C.E.J., 715 So. 2d 774, 776-77 (Miss. 1998).

[124] Norman v. Norman, 962 So. 2d 718, 721-22 (Miss. Ct. App. 2007).

[125] *See infra* § 12.11[2].

[126] Rushing v. Rushing, 724 So. 2d 911, 916-17 (Miss. 1998) (rejecting wife's argument that the chancellor's order should be overturned for failure to make specific findings of fact).

[127] Henrichs v. Henrichs, 32 So. 3d 1202, 1205 (Miss. Ct. App. 2009), *cert. denied*, 31 So. 3d 1217 (Miss. 2010) (where a party fails to defend their case in the chancery court, she is barred from doing so on appeal).

[128] Palculict v. Palculict, 22 So. 3d 293, 298 (Miss. Ct. App. 2009).

[129] *See* Albright v. Albright, 437 So. 2d 1003, 1005 (Miss. 1983).

[130] Pellegrin v. Pellegrin, 478 So. 2d 306, 307 (Miss. 1985); *see* Baneck v. Baneck, 455 So. 2d 766, 767-68 (Miss. 1984); Passmore v. Passmore, 820 So. 2d 747, 750-51 (Miss. Ct. App. 2002) (dicta).

[131] *See* Henderson v. Henderson, 952 So. 2d 273, 278 (Miss. Ct. App. 2006) (en banc) (mother of two- and three-year-old sons favored under age, health, and sex of the children and the continuity of care factors); Taylor v. Taylor, 909 So. 2d 1280, 1281 (Miss. Ct. App. 2005) (tender-years factor slightly favored mother of three-year-old boy); Horn v. Horn, 909 So. 2d 1151, 1159 (Miss. Ct. App. 2005) (doctrine favored mother of three-year-old child); Passmore v. Passmore, 820 So. 2d 747, 750-51 (Miss. Ct. App. 2002) (no error in finding that factor favored mother of one- and three-year-old children).

[132] *See infra* § 12.03[3].

CHILD CUSTODY AND VISITATION § 12.03[2]

is long past the age that requires this type of special care."[133] In several cases, the appellate courts have stated that a child of four is no longer of tender years.[134]

Recent cases indicate an increasing acceptance of involved fathers as primary custodians. A father who has been a child's primary caretaker may be awarded custody of very young children. For example, a father who had been the primary caretaker for a two-year-old child was awarded custody – under these circumstances the child's young age did not favor the mother.[135] Similarly, a chancellor properly awarded a father custody of a four-year-old girl who was more closely bonded to him, even though her age and sex favored her mother.[136] And in one case, a father was awarded custody of nine- and thirteen-year-old girls, in part because his female relatives lived nearby.[137]

An older child's same-sex parent may be considered the better custodian if all other factors are equal.[138] For example, a ten-year-old boy's age and sex favored his father, because of the importance of male guidance at that age.[139] Similarly, a father was considered the better custodian of a two-year-old son and his older brother; the sex of the boys outweighed their age in importance.[140] And a court awarded split custody, placing a twelve-year-old boy with his father and a fifteen-year-old girl with her mother, based on their age and sex and the stated preference of each.[141] A court awarded cus-

---

[133] Mercier v. Mercier, 717 So. 2d 304, 307 (Miss. 1998) (child of seven no longer considered of tender years); Gutierrez v. Bucci, 827 So. 2d 27, 31 (Miss. Ct. App. 2002) (child over seven "long past" the age of tender years); cf. Mixon v. Sharp, 853 So. 2d 834, 839 (Miss. Ct. App. 2003) (age of ten-year-old girl did not favor mother where custodial father was remarried with another daughter).

[134] See Lee v. Lee, 798 So. 2d 1284, 1289 (Miss. 2001); Woodham v. Woodham, 17 So. 3d 153, 156 (Miss. Ct. App. 2009) (doctrine not applicable to a four-year-old girl who was bottle fed, equally cared for by both parents, and received attention from her paternal grandmother and great-grandmother); see also Price v. McBeath, 989 So. 2d 444, 454 (Miss. Ct. App. 2008) (doctrine not applicable to a child of five); Gilliland v. Gilliland, 969 So. 2d 56, 66-67 (Miss. Ct. App. 2007) (awarding custody of five- and seven-year-old boys to father); Jordan v. Jordan, 963 So. 2d 1235, 1240 (Miss. Ct. App. 2007) (custody of ten-, six-, and five-year-olds to father); Street v. Street, 936 So. 2d 1002, 1010 (Miss. Ct. App. 2006) (at five, the boys "were not especially dependent" on their mother, and at seven, "the tender-years doctrine no longer applies"); In re Filiation of M.D.B., 914 So. 2d 316, 320 (Miss. Ct. App. 2005) (age of one-year-old child favored neither party). But cf. Beasley v. Scott, 900 So. 2d 1217, 1220 (Miss. Ct. App. 2005) (factor favored mother of four-year-old girl).

[135] Blevins v. Bardwell, 784 So. 2d 166, 172 (Miss. 2001) (but awarding the mother custody on other factors); see also Copeland v. Copeland, 904 So. 2d 1066 (Miss. 2004) (father who provided more care awarded custody of two-year-old son).

[136] Brewer v. Brewer, 919 So. 2d 135, 141 (Miss. Ct. App. 2005) (custody to father who was more responsive to child's needs); see also Montgomery v. Montgomery, 20 So. 3d 39, 44-45 (Miss. Ct. App. 2009) (custody of five-year-old male child favored father due to weakening of tender-years doctrine by Brewer); Gilliland v. Gilliland, 969 So. 2d 56, 66 (Miss. Ct. App. 2007) (awarding custody of five- and seven-year-old boys to father); Jordan v. Jordan, 963 So. 2d 1235, 1240 (Miss. Ct. App. 2007) (custody of ten-, six-, and five-year-olds to father).

[137] Marter v. Marter, 914 So. 2d 743, 749 (Miss. Ct. App. 2005); see also Ellis v. Ellis, 952 So. 2d 982, 997 (Miss. Ct. App. 2006) (age and sex of fourteen-year-old girl did not favor either party, particularly since the father had female relatives nearby).

[138] See Watts v. Watts, 854 So. 2d 11, 13 (Miss. Ct. App. 2003) (sex of thirteen- and nine-year-old girls favored mother); cf. Bass v. Bass, 879 So. 2d 1122, 1124 (Miss. Ct. App. 2004) (age of four-year-old boy favored mother; sex favored father).

[139] See Messer v. Messer, 850 So. 2d 161, 167 (Miss. Ct. App. 2003); see also Hassett v. Hassett, 690 So. 2d 1140, 1149 (Miss. 1997) (granting custody of six-year-old son to father because "child was entering an age when male guidance [was] needed").

[140] Steverson v. Steverson, 846 So. 2d 304, 306 (Miss. Ct. App. 2003) (custody to father even though age of youngest weighed in favor of mother); see also Webb v. Webb, 974 So. 2d 274, 277 (Miss. Ct. App. 2008) (father awarded custody of eighteen-month-old boy; tender-years factor less important with regard to male children); Gilliland v. Gilliland, 969 So. 2d 56, 67 (Miss. Ct. App. 2007) (suggesting that tender-years doctrine less important with regard to boys); Parker v. South, 913 So. 2d 339, 348 (Miss. Ct. App. 2005) (age and sex of nine-year-old boy favored father).

[141] Sandlin v. Sandlin, 906 So. 2d 39 (Miss. Ct. App. 2004).

§ 12.03[3]   MISSISSIPPI FAMILY LAW

tody of a twenty-one-month-old boy to his father, finding that while the boy's mother was favored because of his age, the father was favored because of his sex.[142] A mother of three girls was favored because of their sex.[143]

Overall, a child's age and sex appear to be less important than prior caretaking, strong parenting skills, and a stable home environment.[144] For example, a court did not err in awarding custody of ten- and six-year-old girls to a father who had been their primary caregiver prior to separation and who provided a more stable home environment than their mother.[145]

One parent's attention to a child's health may be considered under this factor or under parenting skills. A chancellor properly found for a father on this factor; the child's mother allowed Medicaid coverage to lapse for a child with health problems.[146] And a father who was willing to provide his sexually abused son with counseling was favored over a mother who seemed indifferent to the need for counseling.[147]

[3] Continuing care prior to separation. A parent who has been a child's primary caretaker may have a substantial advantage in a custody action. The factor is so significant that some states have replaced the maternal preference with a presumption in favor of the primary caretaker.[148] To determine who has been the primary caretaker, courts consider who bathed and dressed children, put them to bed, took them to school, prepared meals, arranged social activities and babysitters, dealt with medical care, purchased clothing, provided discipline, read to the children, played with them, and made educational arrangements.[149]

Although not explicitly weighted more heavily than other factors in Mississippi, a parent's role as primary caretaker is often the determining factor in a custody award. In several decisions awarding custody to fathers, courts relied heavily on the fact that the father had provided more childcare than the mother.[150] Custody has been awarded

---

[142] Klink v. Brewster, 986 So. 2d 1060, 1063-64 (Miss. Ct. App. 2008).

[143] Benal v. Benal, 22 So. 3d 369, 373 (Miss. Ct. App. 2009) (fourteen-, eleven-, and eight-year-old girls).

[144] *See* Holland v. Holland, 759 So. 2d 1271, 1272 (Miss. Ct. App. 2000) (custody to father even though age of younger child favored mother; moral fitness and home environment favored father); Limbaugh v. Limbaugh, 749 So. 2d 1244, 1246-47 (Miss. Ct. App. 1999) (custody of five- and nine-year-old girls awarded to father who lived in the marital home and had a work schedule that permitted more time with the children; mother had stayed with the children in a boyfriend's home overnight).

[145] Gutierrez v. Bucci, 827 So. 2d 27, 31-32 (Miss. Ct. App. 2002) (custody to father even though age and sex favored mother).

[146] Wheat v. Koustovalas, 42 So. 3d 606, 609 (Miss. Ct. App. 2010), *cert. denied*, 49 So. 3d 106 (Miss. 2010).

[147] Reed v. Fair, 56 So. 3d 577, 583 (Miss. Ct. App. 2010); *see also* McDonald v. McDonald, 39 So. 3d 868, 872, 882 (Miss. Ct. App. 2010) (favoring father who provided structured environment for boys with developmental problems and ADHD).

[148] ELROD, *supra* note 3, § 4:08 (West Virginia first state to use presumption); *cf.* Moak v. Moak, 631 So. 2d 196, 198 (Miss. 1994) (most factors being equal, custody awarded to mother as primary caretaker); Marshall v. Harris, 981 So. 2d 345, 347 (Miss. Ct. App. 2008) (custody properly awarded to mother who had been primary caregiver over father who divided time between Jackson and Port Gibson).

[149] ELROD, *supra* note 3, § 4:09; *see* Watts v. Watts, 854 So. 2d 11, 13 (Miss. Ct. App. 2003) (mother got children ready for school, took them to school and picked them up, participated in extracurricular activities, took them to the doctor); *cf.* Horn v. Horn, 909 So. 2d 1151, 1159 (Miss. Ct. App. 2005) (continuity of care weighed equally where parents shared custody during separation).

[150] *See* Messer v. Messer, 850 So. 2d 161, 166 (Miss. Ct. App. 2003) (father provided 75% of care prior to separation); Gutierrez v. Bucci, 827 So. 2d 27, 31-32 (Miss. Ct. App. 2002) (custody of six- and ten-year-old girls to father); Limbaugh v. Limbaugh, 749 So. 2d 1244, 1247 (Miss. Ct. App. 1999) (father provided more childcare, taking children

CHILD CUSTODY AND VISITATION   § 12.03[3]

to mothers who were primary caretakers in spite of adulterous affairs[151] or a bigamous second marriage.[152] The fact that a mother had been the primary caregiver was an important consideration in granting custody to her in spite of her past serious emotional problems.[153]

On the other hand, a primary caretaker may lose custody to a parent with stronger parenting skills or a more stable home environment.[154] A chancellor properly modified custody to a father even though continuity of care favored the mother; she had moved ten times in four years, and the child failed the first grade after attending three different schools.[155] A parent who claims to be the primary caretaker will not be favored if primary care was actually provided by a third party. The factor did not favor a mother who lived with her husband's parents, who provided primary childcare during his military service.[156]

In *Albright,* the supreme court directed chancellors to determine which parent had "the continuity of care *prior to the separation.*"[157] In several cases, however, custody has been awarded to a parent based in part on care during separation. The court of appeals held that the factor should not have favored a father who provided more care prior to separation. Instead, the factor favored the mother who had continuous care of the children during the parties' eighteen-month separation – the father did not seek to take custody or provide support during that period.[158] In another case, the court of appeals upheld a chancellor's award of custody to a father primarily because he was the children's caretaker during separation. In affirming the award, the court stated that periods of caretaking both prior to and after separation should be considered.[159] And

---

to school and picking them up when ill).

[151] *See* Brekeen v. Brekeen, 880 So. 2d 280, 287 (Miss. 2004); Brock v. Brock, 906 So. 2d 879, 886 (Miss. Ct. App. 2005) (despite her adultery, custody to mother who provided more childcare during marriage; no evidence that affair affected ability as a parent); Bass v. Bass, 879 So. 2d 1122 (Miss. Ct. App. 2004); Ivy v. Ivy, 863 So. 2d 1010, 1014 (Miss. Ct. App. 2004).

[152] Harmon v. Harmon, 757 So. 2d 305, 310 (Miss. Ct. App. 1999); *see also* Beasley v. Scott, 900 So. 2d 1217, 1220 (Miss. Ct. App. 2005) (continuity of care favored single mother who had sole care of child for first two and a half years of child's life, in spite of cohabitation, a DUI, use of alcohol and marijuana out of the child's presence, and an unstable employment history).

[153] *See* Passmore v. Passmore, 820 So. 2d 747, 751 (Miss. Ct. App. 2002) (mother's past depression under control).

[154] *See* Klink v. Brewster, 986 So. 2d 1060, 1064 (Miss. Ct. App. 2008) (mother who had provided primary care lost custody to father with stronger parenting skills; mother failed to provide medication, and child swallowed lighter fluid in her care); Price v. McBeath, 989 So. 2d 444, 453-59 (Miss. Ct. App. 2008) (custody to father; mother was favored on continuity of care, but child's age and sex, moral fitness, home record, stability of home and employment, and parenting skills, favored the father); Clay v. Clay, 837 So. 2d 215, 218 (Miss. Ct. App. 2003) (based in part on evidence of mother's unwillingness to get up in the night with a child and her readiness to leave him in the care of others).

[155] Brown v. White, 875 So. 2d 1116, 1119 (Miss. Ct. App. 2004); *see also* Jordan v. Jordan, 963 So. 2d 1235, 1241 (Miss. Ct. App. 2007) (custody to father with better parenting skills and more stable home environment, over mother who provided primary care during marriage).

[156] Divers v. Divers, 856 So. 2d 370, 374 (Miss. Ct. App. 2003); *see also* Sumrall v. Sumrall, 970 So. 2d 254, 257-58 (Miss. Ct. App. 2007) (mother favored over father whose parents provided care for child while he was with father). *But cf. In re* Filiation of M.D.B., 914 So. 2d 316, 320 (Miss. Ct. App. 2005) (factor favored mother who was primary caretaker for first four months of child's life even though couple with whom she lived shared care for next eight months).

[157] *See* Albright v. Albright, 437 So. 2d 1003, 1005 (Miss. 1983) (emphasis added).

[158] Watts v. Watts, 854 So. 2d 11, 13 (Miss. Ct. App. 2003) (father did not seek custody or provide financial support for year-and-a-half separation); *see also* Gantenbein v. Gantenbein, 852 So. 2d 63, 65-66 (Miss. Ct. App. 2002) (mentioning that in making award to mother, chancellor considered that father gave mother temporary custody).

[159] *See* Caswell v. Caswell, 763 So. 2d 890, 893 (Miss. Ct. App. 2000); *see also* Lowrey v. Lowrey, 25 So. 3d 274,

§ 12.03[4]   MISSISSIPPI FAMILY LAW

in a 2009 case, the court of appeals awarded custody to a father who had temporary custody, even though the mother was the primary caregiver for several years during the marriage. The court stated that caregiving after separation should be given equal consideration.[160]

When a custody award is reversed and remanded, the court on remand may consider who has been the primary caretaker prior to retrial. When a custody award to a father was appealed and remanded, the chancellor erred in failing to consider that the father had care of the children for the three years prior to retrial.[161]

[4] Parenting skills. The factor of parenting skills encompasses a parent's ability to provide physical care, emotional support, discipline, and guidance. Parents may be rated favorably on parenting skills based on a showing that they are attentive to a child's personal hygiene and medical needs,[162] engage the child in appropriate social and extracurricular activities,[163] are a good disciplinarian,[164] and spend their free time with the child.[165] Attention to a child's special needs is important. For example, the factor favored a father who sought counseling for a child who was experiencing emotional

---

296 (Miss. 2009) (custody to father who cared for three girls since the couple's separation); Copeland v. Copeland, 904 So. 2d 1066 (Miss. 2004); McCullough v. McCullough, 52 So. 3d 373, 380-81 (Miss. Ct. App. 2009) (custody of girls to father who had temporary custody prior to trial, even though mother was primary caregiver during marriage); Lawrence v. Lawrence, 956 So. 2d 251, 258-59 (Miss. Ct. App. 2006) (court erred in holding that factor favored father who was the primary caregiver on the date of separation, rather than mother who was primary caregiver during most of marriage and five-month separation); *cf.* Wells v. Wells, 35 So. 3d 1250, 1255 (Miss. Ct. App. 2010) (neither favored; mother was the primary caregiver of twins before separation, but parents shared equal custody during separation).

[160] Montgomery v. Montgomery, 20 So. 3d 39, 41-45 (Miss. Ct. App. 2009) (during the fifteen months that the father had temporary physical custody of the children, the mother moved three times); *cf.* Brumfield v. Brumfield, 49 So. 3d 138, 145-46 (Miss. Ct. App. 2010) (favoring father who was primary caregiver for last two years of marriage over mother who had been primary caregiver for four children prior to that).

[161] Jerome v. Stroud, 689 So. 2d 755, 757 (Miss. 1997); *see also* Vaughn v. Vaughn, 36 So. 3d 1261, 1267 (Miss. 2010) (on remand of three-year-old custody award to grandmother, court should consider the child's circumstances as of the date of remand); Richardson v. Richardson, 790 So. 2d 239 (Miss. Ct. App. 2001) (continuity of care favored father in modification action, since mother had permitted the children to live with him for the year preceding the hearing). It is also appropriate, on remand of a child custody decision, to consider any substantial change in circumstances of the parents that has arisen during the appeal. Hamilton v. Hamilton, 755 So. 2d 528, 530-31 (Miss. Ct. App. 1999); *see* Pace v. Owens, 511 So. 2d 489, 492 (Miss. 1987).

[162] *See* Price v. McBeath, 989 So. 2d 444, 455 (Miss. Ct. App. 2008) (custody to father who sought medical care for conditions mother ignored); Romans v. Fulgham, 939 So. 2d 849, 853 (Miss. Ct. App. 2006) (en banc) (favoring father who helped child with school work, was attentive to health and hygiene, involved the child in church, and provided more one-on-one time); Brewer v. Brewer, 919 So. 2d 135, 141 (Miss. Ct. App. 2005) (custody of four-year-old girl to father who was more attentive to needs); C.W.L. v. R.A., 919 So. 2d 267, 272 (Miss. Ct. App. 2005) (custody to father; in mother's care, child was dirty and often wore same clothes consecutive days); Hoggatt v. Hoggatt, 796 So. 2d 273, 274 (Miss. Ct. App. 2001) (persistent failure to attend to hygiene and medical needs); Stark v. Anderson, 748 So. 2d 838, 843 (Miss. Ct. App. 1999) (failure to provide adequate dental and medical care); Brawley v. Brawley, 734 So. 2d 237, 241-42 (Miss. Ct. App. 1999) (mother's failure to attend to child's hygiene and medical care one of reasons to modify custody).

[163] Mercier v. Mercier, 717 So. 2d 304, 307 (Miss. 1998).

[164] McCullough v. McCullough, 52 So. 3d 373, 381(Miss. Ct. App. 2009) (favoring father who was more attentive to the girls' medical needs, was a better disciplinarian, and was more emotionally supportive).

[165] *See* Copeland v. Copeland, 904 So. 2d 1066 (Miss. 2004) (factor of parenting skills favored father who spent time with children over mother who spent time with paramour); Romans v. Fulgham, 939 So. 2d 849, 853 (Miss. Ct. App. 2006) (en banc) (favoring father who helped child with school work, was attentive to health and hygiene, involved the child in church, and provided more one-on-one time); *In re* Filiation of M.D.B., 914 So. 2d 316, 320 (Miss. Ct. App. 2005) (mother who stayed home with child favored over father who stayed out all night fishing with friends). *But cf.* Lawrence v. Lawrence, 956 So. 2d 251, 261 (Miss. Ct. App. 2006) (court erred in finding this factor against mother who had a boyfriend; "no requirement that following a divorce the custodial parent remain single and devote his or her entire life only to the children").

346

CHILD CUSTODY AND VISITATION   § 12.03[4]

problems.[166] Similarly, custody of two boys was properly modified to their father, in part because he planned to enroll the younger child in an academic setting suited to his learning disability.[167] A child's tardiness and absences in one parent's care reflects negatively on parenting skills.[168] A chancellor did not err in awarding custody of two girls to their father; evidence showed that they attended school more regularly and were better behaved in his custody.[169] A father was awarded custody over a mother who was moody, impatient, aggressive, and a poor housekeeper.[170]

Failure to supervise or protect a child from danger reflects poor parenting skills. A mother was slightly favored on this factor because the father failed to put up fences to keep his children from wandering into a swimming pool.[171] A father's lack of supervision was a negative factor; he left a young teenager in charge of her brother and she was involved in an accident while driving him to the emergency room.[172] Custody was transferred to a father in part because the mother failed to take steps to protect a child who was touched inappropriately by a relative.[173] And the factor weighed against a father who accidentally dislocated a child's shoulder while disciplining him.[174] The factor may weigh against a parent who attempts to alienate a child from the other parent.[175] A court found that a father had better parenting skills based on the mother's refusal to follow visitation orders and her harassment of her husband during the separation.[176]

Parents have been rated negatively under parenting skills for making poor choices, such as moving out of state with a recent acquaintance and taking a six-year-old to a bar at night.[177] A father had superior parenting skills because he made major decisions with

---

[166] Mercier v. Mercier, 717 So. 2d 304, 307 (Miss. 1998).

[167] Cooper v. Ingram, 814 So. 2d 166 (Miss. Ct. App. 2002); *see also* McDonald v. McDonald, 39 So. 3d 868, 872, 882 (Miss. Ct. App. 2010) (custody modified to father who provided structured environment for sons with development problems and ADHD).

[168] J.P.M. v. T.D.M., 932 So. 2d 760, 773 (Miss. 2006) (en banc) (favoring father; child had a routine and performed well in school in his care, while her schedule with the mother was irregular: she was late for school and sometimes failed to have her homework done); Mercier v. Mercier, 717 So. 2d 304, 307 (Miss. 1998).

[169] Myers v. Myers, 814 So. 2d 833, 834-35 (Miss. Ct. App. 2002).

[170] Jordan v. Jordan, 963 So. 2d 1235, 1240 (Miss. Ct. App. 2007).

[171] *See* Passmore v. Passmore, 820 So. 2d 747, 751-52 (Miss. Ct. App. 2002) (also evidence that he regularly drank in front of children).

[172] *See* Mosley v. Mosley, 784 So. 2d 901, 907 (Miss. 2001) (unlicensed child had to drive brother to emergency room); *see also* Stewart v. Stewart, 937 So. 2d 487, 489 (Miss. Ct. App. 2006) (finding against father who took young child on a three-wheeler without a helmet after he had been drinking, and who occasionally spanked her and put pillows under the door to shut out the sound of her crying); Marter v. Marter, 914 So. 2d 743, 750 (Miss. Ct. App. 2005) (custody modified to father after mother's move, in part because mother left children alone in house).

[173] [169] Parker v. South, 913 So. 2d 339, 342 (Miss. Ct. App. 2005); *see also* C.W.L. v. R.A., 919 So. 2d 267, 270 (Miss. Ct. App. 2005) (custody to father; mother continued to expose child to relative who sexually abused her).

[174] Horn v. Horn, 909 So. 2d 1151, 1159 (Miss. Ct. App. 2005).

[175] Ellis v. Ellis, 952 So. 2d 982, 995-96 (Miss. Ct. App. 2006) (father had superior parenting skills over mother who attempted to alienate child from him).

[176] *See* Gutierrez v. Bucci, 827 So. 2d 27, 35-36 (Miss. Ct. App. 2002) (mother's behavior exposed daughters to scenes from which they should have been protected); *see also* Davis v. Davis, 17 So. 3d 114, 118 (Miss. Ct. App. 2009) (custody modified from a mother to a father based in part upon the mother's interference with visitation); Price v. McBeath, 989 So. 2d 444, 455 (Miss. Ct. App. 2008) (mother's refusal to allow father to see child for eighteen months could be considered as negative parenting skills).

[177] Parker v. South, 913 So. 2d 339, 348 (Miss. Ct. App. 2005); *see also* Davis v. Davis, 17 So. 3d 114, 118 (Miss. Ct. App. 2009) (father rated more highly than mother who wrote intimidating letter to daughter's friend); Street v. Street, 936 So. 2d 1002, 1010 (Miss. Ct. App. 2006) (mother found lacking on parenting skills when she violated court order by living with alcoholic and said that she did not know whether she could abide by the order).

§ 12.03[5]   **MISSISSIPPI FAMILY LAW**

his son as his first priority.[178] Similarly, a father was rated over a mother who repeatedly violated a court order to keep her children from her live-in boyfriend, a man accused of child molestation.[179] And a mother's coaching her son to lie to the court about her cohabitation was a factor in modifying custody.[180] A father's "inability to take responsibility for his own actions" also reflected negatively on his parenting skills and judgment.[181]

In several cases, a party's parenting skills have been questioned based on the care of children not before the court. The fact that a mother had a child who was cared for by someone else weighed against her,[182] as did a father's voluntary relinquishment of parental rights to other children.[183] Similarly, a mother rated poorly on this factor because the Department of Human Services had removed another child from her custody.[184] However, the court of appeals rejected a mother's argument that significant weight should be given to the fact that a father's rights had been terminated with regard to two children from another relationship – the event was remote in time, he regretted the termination, and he was in touch with the two children and their mother.[185]

[5] Capacity to provide primary childcare and employment responsibilities. This section combines the factors of capacity to provide childcare and employment responsibilities. Discussion of employment responsibilities generally focuses on the impact of a parent's job on provision of childcare. The fact that one parent's work schedule allows more time with children weighs in favor of that parent.[186] A homemaker-mother was favored over a working father because of her ability to provide primary childcare.[187] Similarly, a father was awarded custody in part because his employment allowed him to work from home and to provide primary care for a young child.[188]

---

[178] Hill v. Hill, 942 So. 2d 207, 213 (Miss. Ct. App. 2006).

[179] Mayfield v. Mayfield, 956 So. 2d 337, 343 (Miss. Ct. App. 2007); *see also* Woodham v. Woodham, 17 So. 3d 153, 159 (Miss. Ct. App. 2009) (custody to father; mother left the child with family to spend the night with her boyfriend).

[180] Pruett v. Prinz, 979 So. 2d 745, 750-51 (Miss. Ct. App. 2008).

[181] Franks v. Franks, 873 So. 2d 135, 139 (Miss. Ct. App. 2004) (father blamed his former wife for his physical assault on her, his verbal abuse, the fact that he could not clean the house, and that he watched pornography).

[182] *See* Fletcher v. Shaw, 800 So. 2d 1212, 1216 (Miss. Ct. App. 2001). *But cf.* Bass v. Bass, 879 So. 2d 1122, 1126 (Miss. Ct. App. 2004) (fact that ex-husband had custody of son from previous marriage was "an entirely separate matter").

[183] *See* Gantenbein v. Gantenbein, 852 So. 2d 63, 66-67 (Miss. Ct. App. 2002).

[184] *See* Mixon v. Sharp, 853 So. 2d 834, 839 (Miss. Ct. App. 2003).

[185] Parker v. South, 913 So. 2d 339, 349 (Miss. Ct. App. 2005).

[186] *See* Wells v. Wells, 35 So. 3d 1250, 1255 (Miss. Ct. App. 2010) (favoring physician father with flexible schedule and clinic near home over mother who traveled in several counties); Marter v. Marter, 914 So. 2d 743, 750 (Miss. Ct. App. 2005) (father's employment was more flexible and allowed more time with children); Brock v. Brock, 906 So. 2d 879, 884-85 (Miss. Ct. App. 2005) (father's unpredictable work schedule a factor in custody award to mother); Massey v. Huggins, 799 So. 2d 902, 906-07 (Miss. Ct. App. 2001); *see also* Moak v. Moak, 631 So. 2d 196, 198 (Miss. 1994) (father worked long shifts and nights; his elderly mother would have care of children); Ivy v. Ivy, 863 So. 2d 1010, 1014 (Miss. Ct. App. 2004) (factor favored mother where father worked long hours).

[187] *See* Cavett v. Cavett, 744 So. 2d 372, 377 (Miss. Ct. App. 1999); *see also* Webb v. Webb, 974 So. 2d 274, 278 (Miss. Ct. App. 2008) (factor favored father who used parents to provide childcare over mother who used babysitter).

[188] *See* Rinehart v. Barnes, 819 So. 2d 564, 565 (Miss. Ct. App. 2002); *see also* Copeland v. Copeland, 904 So. 2d 1066 (Miss. 2004) (factor favored parent whose mother cared for child during work hours over parent who put child in daycare); DeVito v. DeVito, 967 So. 2d 74, 76 (Miss. Ct. App. 2007) (factor favored father over mother who had to work two nights a week); Jordan v. Jordan, 963 So. 2d 1235, 1241 (Miss. Ct. App. 2007) (custody to father with flexible job, who lived near parents, over mother who lived in apartment and was seeking full-time employment); Bass v.

CHILD CUSTODY AND VISITATION   § 12.03[6]

The ability to take a preschool child to work with her weighed in favor of a mother.[189] With respect to school-age children, a mother who could pick children up after school and be home with them in the summer was favored on this factor.[190] Proximity of employment to home is also important. A father was favored on this factor because his employment was close to home while the mother's workplace was fifty miles from home.[191] Similarly, a mother was favored because the father's military career required long absences from home.[192] In a 2007 case, the court of appeals found that a father had greater capacity to provide childcare than a mother who exhibited emotional problems that affected her discipline of the children.[193] And a mother was favored over a father whose parents cared for his child while the boy was in his custody.[194]

The court of appeals noted that the "employment" factor has been used in two ways. A parent may be favored because he or she is a homemaker or has employment that is conducive to childcare. In other cases, a working parent may be favored over an unemployed parent based on employment stability.[195] However, a chancellor who found for a working mother over a disabled father erred under either approach – the father was able to provide full-time childcare and his lack of employment was not willful.[196]

[6] Physical and mental health and age of parents

[a] **Physical health.** Physical disability or poor health should not in itself be a reason to deny custody or to find against a parent on this factor unless the parent's ability to care for a child is affected. Custody was properly awarded to a disabled homemaker-father who had been a primary caretaker after his injury and whose physical condition did not affect his ability to provide childcare.[197] However, a court did not err in modifying custody from a legally blind mother who was involved in an accident

---

Bass, 879 So. 2d 1122, 1125 (Miss. Ct. App. 2004) (mother slightly favored because father spent some time traveling for training).

[189] *See* Hollon v. Hollon, 784 So. 2d 943, 948 (Miss. 2001).

[190] *See* Watts v. Watts, 854 So. 2d 11, 14 (Miss. Ct. App. 2003); *see also* Tritle v. Tritle, 956 So. 2d 369, 374 (Miss. Ct. App. 2007) (favoring mother whose work ended at 3:00 p.m. and who was off most of the summer). *But cf.* Montgomery v. Montgomery, 20 So. 3d 39, 45 (Miss. Ct. App. 2009) (fact that father worked the evening shift did not favor the mother, since she had held four different jobs in recent years).

[191] *See* Lee v. Lee, 798 So. 2d 1284, 1288 (Miss. 2001); *see also* Webb v. Webb, 974 So. 2d 274, 277-78 (Miss. Ct. App. 2008) (factor favored father who had same job for twenty years and lived three miles from work, over mother who lived in one town and worked in another).

[192] *See* Belding v. Belding, 736 So. 2d 425, 428 (Miss. Ct. App. 1999); *see also* Morris v. Morris, 5 So. 3d 476, 487-90 (Miss. Ct. App. 2008) (mother favored over father on active duty and subject to deployment); Franks v. Franks, 873 So. 2d 135 (Miss. Ct. App. 2004) (custody awarded to mother who worked day shift over father who worked seven days of twelve-hour night shifts, then seven days off; chancellor thought consistent routine more important than father's additional days with children).

[193] Gilliland v. Gilliland, 969 So. 2d 56, 69-70 (Miss. Ct. App. 2007).

[194] Sumrall v. Sumrall, 970 So. 2d 254, 257 (Miss. Ct. App. 2007).

[195] *See, e.g.,* Brown v. Crum, 30 So. 3d 1254, 1257 (Miss. Ct. App. 2010) (favoring employed father over mother who had no time frame for becoming employed).

[196] Owens v. Owens, 950 So. 2d 202, 210 (Miss. Ct. App. 2006). *But see* Tanner v. Tanner, 956 So. 2d 1106, 1108-09 (Miss. Ct. App. 2007) (court did not err in finding that this factor favored neither, even though employed father dropped child off at 5:00 a.m. at his mother's while disabled mother was at home and able to care for child); Mayfield v. Mayfield, 956 So. 2d 337, 344 (Miss. Ct. App. 2007) (factor favored steadily employed father over mother; rejecting mother's argument that chancellor was required to find for her because her job situation was more conducive to childcare).

[197] *See* Caswell v. Caswell, 763 So. 2d 890, 893 (Miss. Ct. App. 2000).

349

§ 12.03[6][b]   **MISSISSIPPI FAMILY LAW**

while driving her child. The court of appeals rejected her argument that the court found against her based on disability. The decision was based on her choices involving her disability, which endangered her child.[198]

[b] Mental health. Evidence of serious mental or emotional illness may support a denial of custody. A court properly awarded sole physical and legal custody to a father and supervised visitation to a mother who was suicidal, engaged in self-mutilation, and had violent thoughts toward her husband and child.[199] In a case involving a suicidal parent with borderline personality syndrome, the factor of mental health weighed so heavily in favor of the father that custody was awarded to him based on that factor alone.[200] And a chancellor properly awarded custody to a father based primarily on testimony related to the mother's emotional problems. She was extremely nervous, screamed at the boys, disciplined them excessively, threw one of them on the floor during a physical attack on the father, and exhibited extreme and bizarre behavior.[201]

In less severe cases, mental health may be one of several factors supporting an award of custody. Modification of custody was appropriate based on evidence that a mother moved repeatedly, held a series of short-term jobs, and exhibited paranoid behavior, while the father had a stable home and employment and extended family to assist him.[202] Custody was awarded to a father in part because the mother twice left the children with him while she traveled to meet a man she met through the Internet.[203]

On the other hand, the fact that a parent has experienced mental or emotional problems is not a bar to custody unless the parent's present ability to care for a child is affected. A mother was awarded custody in spite of a history of serious depression and one suicide attempt, based on expert testimony that she was receiving counseling and taking medication and that the illness would not interfere with her ability to care for her children.[204] Prior commitment to a mental facility for depression did not weigh against a mother who recovered from her illness.[205] And the fact that a mother once took Paxil

---

[198] Curry v. McDaniel, 37 So. 3d 1225, 1230 (Miss. Ct. App. 2010) (also faulting mother on attention to child's physical needs and health problems).

[199] Morris v. Morris, 783 So. 2d 681, 693 (Miss. 2001) (lesbian relationship also a factor); *see also* McSwain v. McSwain, 943 So. 2d 1288, 1293 (Miss. 2006) (en banc) (mother's depression and thoughts of suicide a factor in modification action).

[200] *See* Divers v. Divers, 856 So. 2d 370, 375 (Miss. Ct. App. 2003) (reversing a chancellor's award of custody to mother); *cf.* Pearson v. Pearson, 11 So. 3d 178, 185 (Miss. Ct. App. 2009) (finding for father on mental health factor, over mother who suffered from bipolar disorder and was taking medication for depression and anxiety).

[201] Gilliland v. Gilliland, 969 So. 2d 56, 61-62 (Miss. Ct. App. 2007).

[202] Fletcher v. Shaw, 800 So. 2d 1212, 1216 (Miss. Ct. App. 2001); *see also* Wheat v. Koustovalas, 42 So. 3d 606, 609 (Miss. Ct. App. 2010) (father favored over mother who was arrested for disorderly conduct and who used cocaine), *cert. denied*, 49 So. 3d 106 (Miss. 2010); Woodham v. Woodham, 17 So. 3d 153, 158 (Miss. Ct. App. 2009) (father favored over mother who combined alcohol with depression medication); Clay v. Clay, 837 So. 2d 215, 220 (Miss. Ct. App. 2003) (custody to father; mother married four times at thirty-three, suffered from some physical problems and obsession with dieting, and had questionable parenting skills).

[203] *See* Bower v. Bower, 758 So. 2d 405, 411-12 (Miss. 2000).

[204] *See* Passmore v. Passmore, 820 So. 2d 747, 751 (Miss. Ct. App. 2002) (father also showed some emotional instability); *see also* J.P.M. v. T.D.M., 932 So. 2d 760, 775 (Miss. 2006) (en banc) (father who had been treated for depression and alcohol addiction after his father's death, favored over mother who had recently used illegal drugs and had failed one drug test); Beasley v. Scott, 900 So. 2d 1217, 1221 (Miss. Ct. App. 2005) (mother's temporary use of antidepressants after child's birth did not weigh against her).

[205] *See* McCraw v. McCraw, 841 So. 2d 1181, 1184 (Miss. Ct. App. 2003). *But cf.* Pearson v. Pearson, 11 So. 3d 178, 185 (Miss. Ct. App. 2009) (finding for father on mental health factor, over mother who suffered from bipolar disor-

CHILD CUSTODY AND VISITATION   § 12.03[6][c]

for panic attacks was not a reason to find against her on this factor – it did not affect her ability to care for the children.[206]

A parent's treatment of a spouse may weigh against them under this factor. A mother was favored under this factor over the father, who was verbally and physically abusive, had a volatile temper, and suffered from anxiety.[207] And a father was rated more highly on mental health than a mother who interfered with his visitation and showed poor judgment by writing a "ranting" intimidating letter to her daughter's friend.[208]

[c] Alcohol and drug use. Parents have been rated poorly on mental health based on alcohol abuse,[209] use of illegal drugs, and abuse of prescription drugs.[210] In some cases, drug or alcohol use is considered under the factors of stability of the home environment or parenting skills.[211] An award of joint custody with paramount physical custody to a father was proper based on a mother's five-year history of prescription drug abuse.[212] And custody was properly modified to a father; the mother had been arrested, involved in several wrecks, and was violent when drinking.[213] Use of alcohol does not weigh heavily against a parent who uses but does not abuse alcohol.[214] And a father's nine-year-old cocaine conviction did not weigh heavily against him; he had matured, gone to school, and was not using drugs.[215]

[d] Age. Very few cases discuss parents' ages as an important factor. In one case, a thirty-three-year-old mother was rated more favorably on this factor than a fifty-nine-year-old father, but custody was awarded to the father nonetheless.[216]

---

der and was taking medication for depression and anxiety).

[206] Tritle v. Tritle, 956 So. 2d 369, 376-77 (Miss. Ct. App. 2007).

[207] Horn v. Horn, 909 So. 2d 1151, 1160 (Miss. Ct. App. 2005).

[208] Davis v. Davis, 17 So. 3d 114, 118 (Miss. Ct. App. 2009).

[209] *See* Watts v. Watts, 854 So. 2d 11, 14 (Miss. Ct. App. 2003) (mother awarded custody even though this factor weighed against her).

[210] *See* Jordan v. Jordan, 963 So. 2d 1235, 1243-44 (Miss. Ct. App. 2007) (mother's excessive use of prescription drugs discussed as factor in awarding custody to father); Gutierrez v. Bucci, 827 So. 2d 27, 34-35 (Miss. Ct. App. 2002).

[211] Lee v. Lee, 798 So. 2d 1284, 1288 (Miss. 2001) (father admitted using alcohol two to four nights a week, but no showing that it impaired ability to care for children).

[212] Lawson v. Lawson, 821 So. 2d 142 (Miss. Ct. App. 2002).

[213] Johnson v. Gray, 859 So. 2d 1006, 1014 (Miss. 2003) (mother's rehabilitation was recent and evidence was conflicting over whether the behavior would continue); *see also* McSwain v. McSwain, 943 So. 2d 1288, 1293 (Miss. 2006) (en banc) (custodial parent's post-divorce drug use constituted material change in circumstances, even though not continuing at time of modification hearing); J.P.M. v. T.D.M., 932 So. 2d 760, 775 (Miss. 2006) (en banc) (father who had been treated for depression and alcohol addiction after his father's death, favored over mother who had recently used illegal drugs and had failed one drug test); Bellais v. Bellais, 931 So. 2d 665, 671 (Miss. Ct. App. 2006) (en banc) (custody of girls awarded to father who had been convicted of simple assault and driving with a suspended license, over mother who used drugs during separation); Sauls v. Rainey, 919 So. 2d 182, 183 (Miss. Ct. App. 2005) (custody awarded to father based on proof that child's mother was actively using drugs, including ecstasy and cocaine); Parker v. South, 913 So. 2d 339, 342-43, 349-50 (Miss. Ct. App. 2005) (custody to father; mother was convicted of DUI and her boyfriend drove child while intoxicated).

[214] *See* Bower v. Bower, 758 So. 2d 405, 411-12 (Miss. 2000) (father who drank awarded custody over mother with alleged internet addiction).

[215] McDonald v. McDonald, 39 So. 3d 868, 882 (Miss. Ct. App. 2010).

[216] *See* Clay v. Clay, 837 So. 2d 215, 217-18 (Miss. Ct. App. 2003).

§ 12.03[7]   MISSISSIPPI FAMILY LAW

[7] Emotional ties of the parent and child. In most cases, courts find that children have close emotional ties to both parents. In some cases, however, the parent-child bond plays a significant role in a custody decision. For example, the close bond between a father and son was a primary reason for awarding custody to the father.[217] Similarly, custody of two boys was awarded to their father based upon a finding that the older boy was very close to his father and distant from his mother.[218]

[8] Moral fitness

[a] Sexual conduct. Until twenty years ago, a parent who committed adultery was considered unfit and not entitled to custody except in unusual circumstances.[219] Similarly, it was not uncommon for a court to modify custody based on a parent's post-divorce sexual conduct or cohabitation. In 1985, the Mississippi Supreme Court held that custody decisions may not be based on sexual behavior alone.[220] Instead, a parent's sexual conduct should be considered under the *Albright* factor of moral fitness along with other relevant factors.[221]

Today, a parent's adultery, cohabitation, or other sexual conduct is not in itself a reason to deny custody unless the conduct is shown to have an adverse impact on a child. For example, the court of appeals reversed an award of custody to a father. The court below focused too exclusively on the mother's adultery and ignored factors that favored her such as continuity of care and work schedule.[222] Similarly, a court erred in awarding custody to a father based on a mother's decision to be divorced to be with another man.[223]

But sexual conduct that directly affects parenting may be a significant factor in a custody decision. A court did not err in considering a mother's moral fitness as a strong factor after she followed her boyfriend, a convicted felon, to another state. [224] Similarly, a chancellor did not overemphasize the conduct of a mother who left her child with oth-

---

[217] *See* Torrence v. Moore, 455 So. 2d 778, 780 (Miss. 1984); *see also* Mayfield v. Mayfield, 956 So. 2d 337, 344-45 (Miss. Ct. App. 2007) (factor favored father; based in part on children's negative reaction to going to mother's house); Beasley v. Scott, 900 So. 2d 1217, 1221 (Miss. Ct. App. 2005) (factor favored mother of four-year-old girl).

[218] *See* Steverson v. Steverson, 846 So. 2d 304, 306 (Miss. Ct. App. 2003); *see also* Massey v. Huggins, 799 So. 2d 902, 909 (Miss. Ct. App. 2001) (oldest child had "significant emotional bond with father").

[219] *See* Keyes v. Keyes, 171 So. 2d 489, 490 (Miss. 1965) (court properly found that mother was unfit custodian); *see also* King v. King, 191 So. 2d 409, 410-11 (Miss. 1966) (same); Winfield v. Winfield, 35 So. 2d 443, 444 (Miss. 1948) (wife guilty of adultery not entitled to custody of children or alimony except in exceptional circumstances). *But see* Yates v. Yates, 284 So. 2d 46, 47 (Miss. 1973) (affirming custody award to adulterous mother based on ability to provide childcare).

[220] Carr v. Carr, 480 So. 2d 1120, 1123 (Miss. 1985); *see also* Moak v. Moak, 631 So. 2d 196, 197 (Miss. 1994); McAdory v. McAdory, 608 So. 2d 695, 701-02 (Miss. 1992).

[221] Carr v. Carr, 480 So. 2d 1120, 1123 (Miss. 1985).

[222] Brekeen v. Brekeen, 880 So. 2d 280, 285-86 (Miss. 2004); *see also* Brock v. Brock, 906 So. 2d 879, 886 (Miss. Ct. App. 2005) (despite her adultery, custody to mother who provided more childcare during the marriage; no evidence that affair affected ability as a parent). *But cf.* Thurman v. Johnson, 998 So. 2d 1026, 1028-30 (Miss. Ct. App. 2008) (award of custody to father upheld, even though moral fitness was only factor on which he was favored; mother's affair continued during divorce; she repeatedly violated court order prohibiting boyfriend from staying in home with children).

[223] Lackey v. Fuller, 755 So. 2d 1083, 1087 (Miss. 2000); *see also* McCraw v. McCraw, 841 So. 2d 1181, 1184 (Miss. Ct. App. 2003) (custody award to primary caretaker mother with flexible schedule, in spite of relationships with two men during separation; no evidence of harm to children from relationships).

[224] Bradley v. Jones, 949 So. 2d 802, 805 (Miss. Ct. App. 2006).

352

CHILD CUSTODY AND VISITATION   § 12.03[8][a]

ers to spend the night with her boyfriend. A parent's conduct associated with an affair, such as foregoing time with a child, is relevant to the determination of custody.[225] For example, a chancellor did not err in considering a mother's three sexual relationships during separation as a factor – the court did not punish her conduct, but faulted her for exposing her children to the affairs.[226]

A parent who is clearly the better custodian on other factors may be awarded custody notwithstanding cohabitation or an extramarital affair. A court properly awarded custody to a mother who was loving and attentive to her child's needs notwithstanding her adultery and the fact that she had four children by different men.[227] On the other hand, a parent's sexual conduct may be one of several factors supporting a denial of custody without an explicit showing of adverse impact.[228] Custody was awarded to a father who had remarried and established a stable home rather than to a mother who had lived with two men during separation, moved frequently, and who visited casinos.[229]

When both parents have engaged in affairs, neither parent should be favored on the factor of moral fitness.[230] However, a chancellor properly found for a father on this

---

[225] Woodham v. Woodham, 17 So. 3d 153, 157 (Miss. Ct. App. 2009); *see also* Montgomery v. Montgomery, 20 So. 3d 39, 43 (Miss. Ct. App. 2009) (custody to father over mother who moved out during an affair, leaving four children with her husband; chancellor did not impermissibly double count by finding against the mother on moral fitness and parenting skills because of affair).

[226] Brumfield v. Brumfield, 49 So. 3d 138, 148 (Miss. Ct. App. 2010) (partners included a married man and a man she met on the internet).

[227] Boaz v. Boaz, 817 So. 2d 627, 629 (Miss. Ct. App. 2002); *see also* Mosley v. Atterberry, 819 So. 2d 1268, 1273 (Miss. 2002) (no modification even though mother was pregnant at the time of the divorce and concealed the fact, and cohabited for several months immediately after the divorce); Beasley v. Scott, 900 So. 2d 1217, 1221-22 (Miss. Ct. App. 2005) (custody to mother even though the court found against her on moral fitness based on cohabitation, use of alcohol and marijuana out of the child's presence, and unstable employment history); Ivy v. Ivy, 863 So. 2d 1010, 1014 (Miss. Ct. App. 2004) (custody to primary caretaker-mother in spite of affairs).

[228] *See* Copeland v. Copeland, 904 So. 2d 1066 (Miss. 2004) (custody awarded to father over mother who had affair); Carr v. Carr, 480 So. 2d 1120, 1123 (Miss. 1985); McCullough v. McCullough, 52 So. 3d 373, 381-82 (Miss. Ct. App. 2009) (favoring father on moral fitness over mother who had been married twice before and who tended to get drunk and make passes at other men); Klink v. Brewster, 986 So. 2d 1060, 1064 (Miss. Ct. App. 2008) (mother who had four children by different fathers lost custody to father based on moral fitness, as well as parenting skills and stability of employment); Weeks v. Weeks, 989 So. 2d 408, 410-11 (Miss. Ct. App. 2008) (rejecting mother's argument that chancellor placed too much weight on affair); DeVito v. DeVito, 967 So. 2d 74, 76 (Miss. Ct. App. 2007) (not error to consider mother's admitted affair along with other factors; not error to disregard husband's alleged affair with no proof other than mother's allegations); Tritle v. Tritle, 956 So. 2d 369, 377 (Miss. Ct. App. 2007) (factor favored mother over father who had extramarital affair); *In re* Filiation of M.D.B., 914 So. 2d 316, 321 (Miss. Ct. App. 2005) (factor favored mother due to unmarried father's involvement with other women during the marriage).

[229] *See* Eason v. Kosier, 850 So. 2d 188, 190-91 (Miss. Ct. App. 2003); *see also* Jones v. Jones, 19 So. 3d 775, 779-80 (Miss. Ct. App. 2009) (father favored over mother who left family to be with man she met on internet); Webb v. Webb, 974 So. 2d 274, 278-79 (Miss. Ct. App. 2008) (father who viewed pornography favored over mother who had an affair and allowed man to be in the home with their children); Hill v. Hill, 942 So. 2d 207, 211 (Miss. Ct. App. 2006) (custody modified to father; mother involved with four men in three years, including one married man); Romans v. Fulgham, 939 So. 2d 849, 854 (Miss. Ct. App. 2006) (en banc) (favoring father over mother who had three children with different fathers); Parker v. South, 913 So. 2d 339, 344-45 (Miss. Ct. App. 2005) (two cohabitations combined with alcohol abuse, frequent moves, and other poor parenting choices, justified modification); Jernigan v. Jernigan, 830 So. 2d 651, 653 (Miss. Ct. App. 2002) (custody to father based on mother's cohabitation prior to marriage in addition to frequent moves, interference with noncustodial parent rights, and unfounded allegations of father's sexual abuse); Massey v. Huggins, 799 So. 2d 902, 906 (Miss. Ct. App. 2001) (court may properly consider a parent's cohabitation as a factor); Richardson v. Richardson, 790 So. 2d 239, 242-43 (Miss. Ct. App. 2001) (custody properly awarded to father where, among other things, mother lived with boyfriend and had a child with him).

[230] Lawrence v. Lawrence, 956 So. 2d 251, 256 (Miss. Ct. App. 2006) (court erred in finding against mother based on a post-separation affair, when the father was involved with a pregnant secretary during the marriage); *see also* Phillips

§ 12.03[8][b]   MISSISSIPPI FAMILY LAW

factor even though both parties had relationships during their separation. The father's girlfriend did not stay at his house during visitation, while the mother lived with a man accused of child molestation and repeatedly violated court orders to keep the children away from him.[231]

[b] Same-sex relationships. A parent's same-sex relationship may not be the sole reason for denying custody. As with other sexual conduct, however, it may be one of several factors on which an award is based.[232] The Mississippi Supreme Court reversed a custody award to a father based primarily on a mother's alleged homosexual relationship – a same-sex relationship may not be emphasized to the exclusion of other factors.[233] Subsequently, the court of appeals reversed a custody decision that placed undue emphasis on a mother's lesbian relationship, stating, "it is of no consequence that a mother was having an affair with a woman rather than a man."[234] However, if other factors also support denial of custody, an award will be affirmed even though the decision was based partly on the existence of a same-sex relationship. Custody was properly granted to a married father with a stable home and employment rather than to the mother, who was beginning a new and uncertain business, was living with a lesbian partner, and planned to relocate.[235] Similarly, custody was modified to a father because the mother lived with three different women, shared a bedroom with her current girlfriend, and watched sexual videos with her partner in the children's presence. The court of appeals noted that custody may be modified if a relationship is coupled with other behavior that is harmful to a child or if the relationship clearly endangers the child's well-being.[236] And a father's same-sex relationship was a factor in refusing to modify custody to him even though the child's mother was married to an alcoholic ex-felon who had been charged with domestic violence.[237]

[c] Other. A mother's foul language weighed against her in a court's *Albright* analysis, although custody was awarded to her.[238] A father was favored over a mother under the factor of moral fitness because of her drug use.[239] In one case, the fact that a

---

v. Phillips, 45 So. 3d 684, 688 (Miss. Ct. App. 2010) (mother had post-separation affair, but father had significant affair during marriage), *cert. denied*, 49 So. 3d 636 (Miss. 2010); *cf.* Sumrall v. Sumrall, 970 So. 2d 254, 258-59 (Miss. Ct. App. 2007) (neither parent favored; mother lived with two men during couple's long separation, but father impregnated mother when she was sixteen and he was twenty-two).

[231] Mayfield v. Mayfield, 956 So. 2d 337, 343 (Miss. Ct. App. 2007); *see also* Williams v. Stockstill, 990 So. 2d 774, 776 (Miss. Ct. App. 2008) (married father of nonmarital child favored over child's mother, who was under house arrest on drug charges).

[232] S.B. v. L.W., 793 So. 2d 656, 661 (Miss. Ct. App. 2001).

[233] *See* Hollon v. Hollon, 784 So. 2d 943, 952 (Miss. 2001) (chancellor failed to consider that mother was primary caretaker).

[234] Fulk v. Fulk, 827 So. 2d 736, 740-41 (Miss. Ct. App. 2002) (quoting Plaxico v. Michael, 735 So. 2d 1036, 1039-40 (Miss. 1999)).

[235] S.B. v. L.W., 793 So. 2d 656, 661 (Miss. Ct. App. 2001) (evidence also showed lack of financial and emotional stability); *see also* White v. Thompson, 569 So. 2d 1181, 1184 (Miss. 1990) (custody to father based on mother's lesbian relationship, neglect, and drug use).

[236] Davidson v. Coit, 899 So. 2d 904, 909-10 (Miss. Ct. App. 2005).

[237] *See* Weigand v. Houghton, 730 So. 2d 581, 586-87 (Miss. 1999) (only factors weighing in mother's favor were church attendance and father's homosexuality).

[238] Beasley v. Scott, 900 So. 2d 1217, 1221-22 (Miss. Ct. App. 2005).

[239] J.P.M. v. T.D.M., 932 So. 2d 760, 771 (Miss. 2006) (en banc); *see also* Brown v. Crum, 30 So. 3d 1254, 1257

CHILD CUSTODY AND VISITATION   § 12.03[9]

mother had received and retained pornography from her boyfriend was one of several factors that together constituted a material change in circumstances justifying a change in custody.[240] And the factor of moral fitness weighed against a woman who deceived her husband about the paternity of her third child. She told him the child was conceived naturally when in fact, she conceived the child through artificial insemination.[241]

[9] Home, school, and community record of the child. Under this factor, parents have been rated favorably for involvement in a child's activities and for ensuring prompt regular school attendance. A chancellor properly awarded custody to a father based on evidence that his daughters attended school more regularly and were better behaved in his custody.[242] Another father was awarded custody in part because of his involvement in his sons' sports and extracurricular activities.[243] A mother was slightly favored on this factor because her son was doing well in daycare where she lived and had friends in the area.[244] A court rated a mother poorly on this factor based on her child's excessive unexcused absences while in her care.[245] And in a custody action between grandparents, one set of grandparents was favored over the other in part because of the greater educational opportunities their family offered.[246]

The fact that one parent's home is near friends and extended family is sometimes considered under this factor, as well as under the "stability of home environment" factor.[247] In an original custody action, a court may consider that one parent is moving while the other remains where the child's friends and family live.[248] A joint custodial

---

(Miss. Ct. App. 2010) (mother posted photographs of herself with different men, surrounded by people who were intoxicated); Price v. McBeath, 989 So. 2d 444, 456-57 (Miss. Ct. App. 2008) (father who had child out of wedlock favored on this factor over mother whose car smelled of marijuana); Jordan v. Jordan, 963 So. 2d 1235, 1243-44 (Miss. Ct. App. 2007) (mother's excessive use of prescription drugs discussed as factor in awarding custody to father).

[240] Hill v. Hill, 942 So. 2d 207, 211 (Miss. Ct. App. 2006).

[241] Wells v. Wells, 35 So. 3d 1250, 1254 (Miss. Ct. App. 2010) (wife used her physician husband's name to obtain donor sperm, had it mailed to a fictitious clinic and paid for with a credit card set up in the name of the clinic).

[242] *See* Myers v. Myers, 814 So. 2d 833, 835 (Miss. Ct. App. 2002); *see also* Romans v. Fulgham, 939 So. 2d 849, 854 (Miss. Ct. App. 2006) (en banc) (favoring father because child's academic performance improved when she was with him).

[243] *See* Steverson v. Steverson, 846 So. 2d 304, 306 (Miss. Ct. App. 2003); *see also* Owens v. Owens, 950 So. 2d 202, 211 (Miss. Ct. App. 2006) (mother favored because she remained where the boy had lived and attended school, while the father had moved to new location); Hill v. Hill, 942 So. 2d 207, 213 (Miss. Ct. App. 2006) (father who lived near child's sports teams, attended the same church for twenty years, and lived near extended family, rated higher on factor); Marter v. Marter, 914 So. 2d 743, 750 (Miss. Ct. App. 2005) (custody modified to father after mother's move, in part because children did not participate in same activities in new location).

[244] Bass v. Bass, 879 So. 2d 1122, 1125 (Miss. Ct. App. 2004).

[245] *See* Massey v. Huggins, 799 So. 2d 902, 907 (Miss. Ct. App. 2001); *see also* Wheat v. Koustovalas, 42 So. 3d 606, 612 (Miss. Ct. App. 2010) (favoring father who paid for son's daycare), *cert. denied*, 49 So. 3d 106 (Miss. 2010); Brumfield v. Brumfield, 49 So. 3d 138, 146 (Miss. Ct. App. 2010) (favoring father over mother who had no reliable transportation for the children).

[246] *See* Worley v. Jackson, 595 So. 2d 853, 856 (Miss. 1992) (family placed greater emphasis on education; all children graduated from high school).

[247] *See* Jones v. Jones, 19 So. 3d 775, 779 (Miss. Ct. App. 2009) (father who remained in marital home, near his parents, favored); Price v. McBeath, 989 So. 2d 444, 457-58 (Miss. Ct. App. 2008) (father who lived near extended family favored on this factor); Jordan v. Jordan, 963 So. 2d 1235, 1243 (Miss. Ct. App. 2007) (factor weighed in favor of father, who lived in marital home near extended family); Mixon v. Sharp, 853 So. 2d 834, 840 (Miss. Ct. App. 2003) (home, school, and community factor favored mother who lived in community near child's friends; but awarding custody to father).

[248] *See* Sobieske v. Preslar, 755 So. 2d 410, 413 (Miss. 2000); S.B. v. L.W., 793 So. 2d 656, 659-60 (Miss. Ct. App. 2001); *cf.* Benal v. Benal, 22 So. 3d 369, 375-76 (Miss. Ct. App. 2009) (Nebraska mother favored over Mississippi

§ 12.03[10]   MISSISSIPPI FAMILY LAW

father was properly favored on this factor because he planned to remain in the children's hometown of Jackson, while their mother was moving to Memphis.[249] A father was awarded custody in part because the children would remain in the same schools, while the mother would enroll them in different schools.[250] However, a chancellor erred in finding that a mother was more likely to move, simply because she was dating someone who worked in another town. There was no testimony that she planned to marry the man or to move.[251]

The home, school, and community factor also favored a father who kept possession of the marital home where the children had lived.[252] However, a chancellor should not award the marital home to one parent and then find that parent favored on this factor because they retained the marital home.[253]

[10] Preference of a child twelve or older. Until 2006, the Mississippi Code provided that a child of twelve or older "shall have the privilege" of choosing to live with a parent if the choice was in the child's best interests.[254] The statute was amended to provide instead that chancellors "may consider" the preference of a child twelve or older.[255] Today, a child's preference is simply one of many factors for consideration and does not appear to be given substantially greater weight than other *Albright* factors.[256] A court is required, however, to provide findings explaining the reason for rejecting a child's wishes.[257] The amended statute states that a chancellor "shall . . . explain in detail why the wishes of any child were or were not honored."[258] Nonetheless, the court of appeals affirmed a chancellor's award of joint custody over a daughter's expressed wish to live with her father, even in the absence of findings of fact.[259]

A child's wishes have more weight if they appear to be genuinely based on a strong bond with a parent[260] or if custody according to the child's wishes keeps siblings in the

---

father; children lived in Nebraska for all of their lives except the last eight months). In a modification action, however, a custodial parent's relocation is not in itself a material change in circumstances. *See infra* § 12.11[5][b].

[249] Porter v. Porter, 23 So. 3d 438, 447 (Miss. 2009).

[250] Jordan v. Jordan, 963 So. 2d 1235, 1242-43 (Miss. Ct. App. 2007).

[251] Lawrence v. Lawrence, 956 So. 2d 251, 261 (Miss. Ct. App. 2006).

[252] Taylor v. Taylor, 909 So. 2d 1280, 1282 (Miss. Ct. App. 2005).

[253] *See* Jordan v. Jordan, 963 So. 2d 1235, 1243 (Miss. Ct. App. 2007); Horn v. Horn, 909 So. 2d 1151, 1160 (Miss. Ct. App. 2005).

[254] Miss. Code Ann. § 93-5-24 (2004). In one case, a couple agreed in their divorce settlement for the court to reconsider custody when their daughter reached the age to express a preference. Subsequently, the mother petitioned the court to reconsider custody. The child expressed a preference to live with her father, and custody was awarded accordingly. Chroniger v. Chroniger, 914 So. 2d 311, 313 (Miss. Ct. App. 2005).

[255] Miss. Code Ann. § 93-5-24 (Supp. 2010).

[256] *See* Anderson v. Anderson, 961 So. 2d 55, 59 (Miss. Ct. App. 2007); Ferguson v. Ferguson, 639 So. 2d 921, 932 (Miss. 1994) (rejecting father's request for custody based solely on child's expressed wish to live with him); Moore v. Moore, 757 So. 2d 1043, 1050 (Miss. Ct. App. 2000) (child's wish not reflective of best interest).

[257] Polk v. Polk, 589 So. 2d 123, 130 (Miss. 1991); Anderson v. Anderson, 961 So. 2d 55, 59 (Miss. Ct. App. 2007); *cf.* Stribling v. Stribling, 906 So. 2d 863, 868 (Miss. Ct. App. 2005) (court did not err in failing to address custody of twenty-year-old, who was entitled to choose the parent with whom she would live).

[258] Miss. Code Ann. § 93-5-24 (Supp. 2010).

[259] Phillips v. Phillips, 45 So. 3d 684, 693-94 (Miss. Ct. App. 2010), *cert. denied*, 49 So. 3d 636 (Miss. 2010).

[260] Marter v. Marter, 914 So. 2d 743, 750 (Miss. Ct. App. 2005) (custody modified to father in part because thirteen-year-old girl expressed preference to live with him); Taylor v. Taylor, 909 So. 2d 1280, 1282 (Miss. Ct. App. 2005) (custody of fourteen-year-old girl and three-year-old boy awarded to father, based on daughter's strong preference to live with biological father rather than adoptive mother); Cooper v. Ingram, 814 So. 2d 166, 168-69 (Miss. Ct. App. 2002) (twelve-year-old child wanted to live with father, with whom he shared activities); Massey v. Huggins, 799 So. 2d 902,

CHILD CUSTODY AND VISITATION § 12.03[11]

same home.[261] A preference based on a desire to escape discipline[262] or heavily influenced by one parent's hostility to the other will be disregarded.[263] For example, a chancellor properly awarded custody to a mother over her son's wish to live with his father, who allowed him to chew tobacco, ride a four-wheeler, and gave him a .357 magnum.[264] A child's wish to live with a noncustodial parent has been denied in a number of cases because the requested placement would separate the child from other siblings.[265] However, the court of appeals affirmed an award of split custody placing a twelve-year-old boy with his father and a fifteen-year-old girl with her mother, based on their age and sex and the stated preference of each.[266]

[11] Stability of the home environment and employment of each parent

[a] Home environment. Stability of home environment may equal primary caretaking in significance. Courts often emphasize stability of one parent's home as a primary reason for awarding custody. Attributes that contribute to a positive rating on this factor include household routines and activities, location, household composition and the stability of those relationships, personal habits of the parent and other household members, and proximity to extended family. In assessing the suitability of a parent's home, courts have considered whether the parent provides balanced meals and ensures proper hygiene.[267] Courts also examine the extent of family religious and social activities.[268]

The stability of a parent's relationships with other household members is impor-

---

907 (Miss. Ct. App. 2001) (oldest child had "significant emotional bond with father").

[261] *See* Cooper v. Ingram, 814 So. 2d 166, 168-69 (Miss. Ct. App. 2002) (appropriate to transfer custody of twelve-year-old according to wishes, where younger brother would also be living in father's home); Massey v. Huggins, 799 So. 2d 902, 907 (Miss. Ct. App. 2001) (oldest child wanted to live with father, and *Albright* factors favored transferring custody of younger children to father).

[262] *See* Ferguson v. Ferguson, 639 So. 2d 921, 932 (Miss. 1994).

[263] *See* Ellis v. Ellis, 952 So. 2d 982, 997 (Miss. Ct. App. 2006) (child's stated preference to live with mother not controlling; choice likely based upon her mother's attempted alienation); Jernigan v. Jernigan, 830 So. 2d 651, 653 (Miss. Ct. App. 2002).

[264] Ferguson v. Ferguson, 639 So. 2d 921, 932 (Miss. 1994).

[265] *See* Franklin v. Kroush, 622 So. 2d 1256, 1257 (Miss. 1993) (refusing father's request to modify solely on child's preference; modification would separate child from younger siblings); Mixon v. Bullard, 217 So. 2d 28, 30 (Miss. 1968) (court upheld a chancellor's refusal to follow a thirteen-year-old boy's stated desire to live with his father, noting that other factors – such as the resulting separation from his siblings – dictated that he remain in the custody of his mother); Brown v. Brown, 764 So. 2d 502, 505 (Miss. Ct. App. 2000) (father's motion for custody denied; child's preference would separate two boys); Moore v. Moore, 757 So. 2d 1043, 1050 (Miss. Ct. App. 2000) (refusing to modify custody based on older child's request when result would be separation of brothers).

[266] Sandlin v. Sandlin, 906 So. 2d 39 (Miss. Ct. App. 2004); *see also* Magruder v. Magruder, 881 So. 2d 365 (Miss. Ct. App. 2004) (split custody of son and two younger siblings based on older child's preference).

[267] *See* Brumfield v. Brumfield, 49 So. 3d 138, 146 (Miss. Ct. App. 2010) (witnesses characterized mother's home as "messy" and "nasty"); Beasley v. Scott, 900 So. 2d 1217, 1221 (Miss. Ct. App. 2005) (mother's incompetence as housekeeper weighed against her under stability of home environment); Pacheco v. Pacheco, 770 So. 2d 1007, 1010 (Miss. Ct. App. 2000) (father provided a cleaner home and balanced meals).

[268] *See* Montgomery v. Montgomery, 20 So. 3d 39, 46 (Miss. Ct. App. 2009) (father who lived near extended family, took the children to church, and involved them in social activities, favored over a mother who moved several times, did not take the children to church, and lived in a two-bedroom mobile home); Dearman v. Dearman, 811 So. 2d 308, 311 (Miss. Ct. App. 2001) (mother not involved in church or child's school activities); Pacheco v. Pacheco, 770 So. 2d 1007, 1010-11 (Miss. Ct. App. 2000) (father took child to church); *see also* Blevins v. Bardwell, 784 So. 2d 166, 175 (Miss. 2001).

§ 12.03[11][a]   **MISSISSIPPI FAMILY LAW**

tant. A parent who has remarried, with a stable home life and other children in the home, may have an advantage over the other.[269] For example, a remarried father was awarded custody over a mother who had divorced for a second time and was living with her parents.[270] A parent's volatile marriage or relationship negatively affects home environment.[271] A mother's home environment was considered less stable than the father's; she was seeking a divorce from her second husband, who had a drug problem and was subject to a restraining order.[272] And a joint custodial father was favored over a mother based on a stepfather's demeanor and his terminable-at-will employment.[273] The fact that a parent is cohabiting or allows a sexual partner to stay overnight in the home may weigh against them on this factor.[274]

Parental conduct such as gambling,[275] alcohol or drug use,[276] open use of pornography,[277] and even smoking, may negatively affect home environment. A mother's home environment was considered superior to a father's because he lived with his father, who smoked three to four packs of cigarettes a day.[278] A parent's personal-

---

[269] *See* Richardson v. Richardson, 790 So. 2d 239, 242 (Miss. Ct. App. 2001) (custody to father where mother lived for two years with abusive boyfriend, while father was remarried and living in community near family); Stark v. Anderson, 748 So. 2d 838, 842-43 (Miss. Ct. App. 1999) (custody to father; child had good relationship with stepmother).

[270] Mercier v. Mercier, 717 So. 2d 304, 308 (Miss. 1998); *see also* Williams v. Stockstill, 990 So. 2d 774, 777 (Miss. Ct. App. 2008) (favoring married father who owned business over mother who lived with her parents); Stewart v. Stewart, 937 So. 2d 487, 490 (Miss. Ct. App. 2006) (favoring father who lived in an apartment at his workshop over mother who lived with relatives); Parker v. South, 913 So. 2d 339, 342, 349 (Miss. Ct. App. 2005) (moral fitness favored father who was married with children over mother who shared bedroom with two men while children slept on floor or couch); Eason v. Kosier, 850 So. 2d 188, 190 (Miss. Ct. App. 2003) (stability of home environment favored remarried father with child over mother who cohabited with two men).

[271] *See* McSwain v. McSwain, 943 So. 2d 1288, 1291-92 (Miss. 2006) (en banc) (physical violence in custodial mother's second marriage contributed to material change in circumstances adverse to the child); Sullivan v. Beason, 37 So. 3d 706, 712 (Miss. Ct. App. 2010) (modification to father from mother whose second marriage was characterized by violent arguments); Weeks v. Weeks, 989 So. 2d 408, 413 (Miss. Ct. App. 2008) (custody to father over mother whose live-in boyfriend assaulted her in front of children); Brock v. Brock, 906 So. 2d 879, 885 (Miss. Ct. App. 2005) (father's verbal and physical abuse of children's mother a factor in award of custody to mother); White v. Thompson, 822 So. 2d 1125, 1128 (Miss. Ct. App. 2002) (fact that a mother and her current husband had filed and withdrawn divorce pleadings, and evidence of violence in their home were part of the reasons for denying her custody); Richardson v. Richardson, 790 So. 2d 239, 242-43 (Miss. Ct. App. 2001) (mother lived for two years with abusive boyfriend); Stark v. Anderson, 748 So. 2d 838, 842-43 (Miss. Ct. App. 1999) (child afraid of stepfather); *cf.* Pruett v. Prinz, 979 So. 2d 745, 750-51 (Miss. Ct. App. 2008) (mother's violent second marriage a factor in modification).

[272] *See* Massey v. Huggins, 799 So. 2d 902, 907 (Miss. Ct. App. 2001); *see also* Mixon v. Sharp, 853 So. 2d 834, 840 (Miss. Ct. App. 2003) (stability of home environment favored father; mother married three times, was unemployed, arrested, and in abusive relationship).

[273] Porter v. Porter, 23 So. 3d 438, 444 (Miss. 2009) (including use of corporal punishment).

[274] *See* Richardson v. Richardson, 790 So. 2d 239, 242-43 (Miss. Ct. App. 2001) (mother lived for two years with abusive boyfriend); Pacheco v. Pacheco, 770 So. 2d 1007, 1010 (Miss. Ct. App. 2000) (mother dating man who spent several nights a week at her house).

[275] *See* Lowrey v. Lowrey, 25 So. 3d 274, 282-284 (Miss. 2009) (custody of three girls awarded to father over mother who was a compulsive gambler and was largely absent from their lives); Roberson v. Roberson, 814 So. 2d 183, 184 (Miss. Ct. App. 2002).

[276] *See* Johnson v. Gray, 859 So. 2d 1006, 1014 (Miss. 2003) (stability of home environment weighed against mother with alcohol problem).

[277] *See* Brown v. White, 875 So. 2d 1116, 1119 (Miss. Ct. App. 2004) (custody properly modified from mother to father based in part on child's exposure to pornographic tapes). *But cf.* Montgomery v. Montgomery, 20 So. 3d 39, 43-44 (Miss. Ct. App. 2009) (father's use of pornography out of children's presence did not require finding against him on moral fitness).

[278] *See* Blevins v. Bardwell, 784 So. 2d 166, 176 (Miss. 2001); *see also* Boaz v. Boaz, 817 So. 2d 627, 629 (Miss. Ct. App. 2002) (child with respiratory disease). *But cf.* Tritle v. Tritle, 956 So. 2d 369, 274-75 (Miss. Ct. App. 2007) (smoking did not weigh against mother who did not smoke in the house and put the window down in the car).

CHILD CUSTODY AND VISITATION   § 12.03[11][a]

ity traits and behavior may also affect this factor. For example, a mother's home was considered more suitable than the father's because of his temper.[279] Stability of home environment may also be negatively affected by frequent moves from one dwelling to another.[280] It is not, however, affected by the financial value of a parent's home. The supreme court rejected a mother's argument that the marital home awarded to her at divorce was superior to the mobile home in which the father lived: "We cannot hold that the dollar value of a home is determinative for custody purposes."[281] On the other hand, parents who can provide a child with a separate bedroom have been favored on this factor in several cases.[282]

The presence of extended family in the area where one parent lives is a factor favoring that parent.[283] For example, the presence of a father's extended family in Wisconsin overrode the fact that the mother had been the primary caretaker prior to her military assignment in Mississippi.[284] In modification cases, a custodial parent's relocation is not, in itself, a reason to modify custody. Nonetheless, in several cases, custody has been modified to a noncustodial parent who lives in close proximity to extended family and friends.[285] A chancellor did not err in finding for a father who remained in

---

[279] *See* Gable v. Gable, 846 So. 2d 296, 299 (Miss. Ct. App. 2003); *see also* Mabus v. Mabus, 890 So. 2d 806, 817 (Miss. 2003) (factor of mental health weighed slightly against mother because of anger management problems); Benal v. Benal, 22 So. 3d 369, 375-76 (Miss. Ct. App. 2009) (mother favored over father who had minimal ties to Mississippi community, and who threatened to kill himself with a knife in front of children).

[280] *See* Mercier v. Mercier, 717 So. 2d 304, 308 (Miss. 1998); Romans v. Fulgham, 939 So. 2d 849, 854 (Miss. Ct. App. 2006) (en banc) (favoring father because his wife stayed home and he had extended family nearby, while the mother had moved repeatedly); Brock v. Brock, 906 So. 2d 879, 887 (Miss. Ct. App. 2005) (father moved family seven times in eleven years; court rejected argument that treating frequent moves as a negative factor amounted to an impermissible restriction on the right to travel); McCraw v. McCraw, 841 So. 2d 1181, 1184 (Miss. Ct. App. 2003); Jernigan v. Jernigan, 830 So. 2d 651, 652 (Miss. Ct. App. 2002) (five times in seven years); Fletcher v. Shaw, 800 So. 2d 1212, 1215 (Miss. Ct. App. 2001); *cf.* Marshall v. Harris, 981 So. 2d 345, 347 (Miss. Ct. App. 2008) (custody properly awarded to mother who had been primary caregiver over father who divided time between Jackson and Port Gibson).

[281] Lee v. Lee, 798 So. 2d 1284, 1291 (Miss. 2001) (the court noted this was particularly so since the marital home was awarded to the mother as part of the divorce); *see also* Horn v. Horn, 909 So. 2d 1151, 1160 (Miss. Ct. App. 2005) (court erred in finding stability of home environment favored mother over father because court awarded marital home to mother). *But cf.* Montgomery v. Montgomery, 20 So. 3d 39, 46 (Miss. Ct. App. 2009) (father who lived near extended family, took the children to church and had a bedroom for each child, favored over a mother who moved several times, did not take the children to church, and lived in a two-bedroom mobile home); Mayfield v. Mayfield, 956 So. 2d 337, 346 (Miss. Ct. App. 2007) (custody to father who lived in marital home); Taylor v. Taylor, 909 So. 2d 1280, 1282 (Miss. Ct. App. 2005) (court found for father under home environment based on fact that he remained in marital home).

[282] Reed v. Fair, 56 So. 3d 577, 583 (Miss. Ct. App. 2010) (preferring father who could provide bedroom over mother who lived in two bedroom home with a number of people); Marter v. Marter, 914 So. 2d 743, 750 (Miss. Ct. App. 2005) (custody modified to father after mother's move, in part because father's home had separate bedrooms for girls); Bass v. Bass, 879 So. 2d 1122, 1126 (Miss. Ct. App. 2004) (mother slightly favored on factor; son had his own room in her home, while father lived with his parents).

[283] *See, e.g.,* Copeland v. Copeland, 904 So. 2d 1066 (Miss. 2004) (factor favored father who had lived in same location, near extended family, for many years); Jordan v. Jordan, 963 So. 2d 1235, 1243 (Miss. Ct. App. 2007) (custody to father who lived near extended family); Mayfield v. Mayfield, 956 So. 2d 337, 346 (Miss. Ct. App. 2007) (favoring father who lived near parents); Marter v. Marter, 914 So. 2d 743, 749 (Miss. Ct. App. 2005) (custody modified to father after custodial mother's move, in part because father lived near extended family); Brock v. Brock, 906 So. 2d 879, 884 (Miss. Ct. App. 2005) (custody to mother who had family nearby; father's unpredictable work schedule a factor in custody award to mother); Dearman v. Dearman, 811 So. 2d 308, 311 (Miss. Ct. App. 2001) (custody to parent located in school district where child had strong relationships with teachers and friends); Neville v. Neville, 734 So. 2d 352, 356 (Miss. Ct. App. 1999).

[284] *See* Porter v. Porter, 766 So. 2d 55, 57-58 (Miss. Ct. App. 2000).

[285] *See* Sobieske v. Preslar, 755 So. 2d 410, 412 (Miss. 2000) (joint custody modified when mother decided to move to Atlanta); Stark v. Anderson, 748 So. 2d 838, 843 (Miss. Ct. App. 1999) (custody modified when mother moved to Colorado, away from child's family).

§ 12.03[11][b]   MISSISSIPPI FAMILY LAW

Jackson near family over a joint custodial mother moving to Memphis.[286]

[b] Stability of employment. A parent who has steady employment may be rated more favorably on this factor than one who is unemployed or has a history of changing jobs frequently. A father was awarded custody in part because his employment was stable while the mother had disciplinary problems at work.[287] The factor also favored a father who had been employed in the same job for sixteen years, while the mother had worked at her job for only one year.[288] On the other hand, a chancellor properly discounted a guardian ad litem's concern that the father had a work history of low-income jobs – the family was adequately supported and his employment allowed him to spend more time with his daughter. The court rejected the notion that a parent with higher income is entitled to some preference in a custody dispute.[289]

[12] Other relevant factors

[a] Separation of siblings. There is a strong preference for keeping siblings together unless unusual circumstances justify their separation.[290] The court of appeals stated in a 2006 case that it "is assumed to be in the best interest of a child" to keep siblings together. The court also stated, however, that the presumption should not be used to defeat the best interest of a child.[291] The preference, which predates *Albright*, continues to be recognized as an important consideration in custody decisions. For example, the court of appeals reversed an order separating eleven- and twelve-year-old sisters; one daughter's slightly greater attachment to her mother did not justify their separation.[292] And in a case where most factors were equal, a mother was awarded

---

[286] Porter v. Porter, 23 So. 3d 438, 444 (Miss. 2009).

[287] *See* Rinehart v. Barnes, 819 So. 2d 564, 565 (Miss. Ct. App. 2002); *see also* J.P.M. v. T.D.M., 932 So. 2d 760, 774 (Miss. 2006) (en banc) (favoring father who held the same job for three years, while the mother was sporadically employed); Weeks v. Weeks, 989 So. 2d 408, 410-13 (Miss. Ct. App. 2008) (father who lived with parents who owned daycare facility favored over mother); Sumrall v. Sumrall, 970 So. 2d 254, 257-58 (Miss. Ct. App. 2007) (mother steadily employed at Wal-Mart favored over father who was paid $1,000 a month by his parents to run errands for them); DeVito v. DeVito, 967 So. 2d 74, 76 (Miss. Ct. App. 2007) (factor favored father, at same job for several years, over mother who had numerous jobs); Beasley v. Scott, 900 So. 2d 1217, 1221 (Miss. Ct. App. 2005) (factor favored father employed by same company for eleven years over mother who had seven jobs in four years and left without notifying employers).

[288] *See* Pacheco v. Pacheco, 770 So. 2d 1007, 1011 (Miss. Ct. App. 2000); *see also* Brown v. Crum, 30 So. 3d 1254, 1257 (Miss. Ct. App. 2010) (favoring employed father over mother who had no time frame for becoming employed); Webb v. Webb, 974 So. 2d 274, 277-78 (Miss. Ct. App. 2008) (factor favored father who had same job for twenty years and lived three miles from work, over mother who lived in one town and worked in another); Fletcher v. Shaw, 800 So. 2d 1212, 1216-17 (Miss. Ct. App. 2001) (mother held a series of jobs for only several weeks each).

[289] Johnson v. Johnson, 872 So. 2d 92, 95 (Miss. Ct. App. 2004).

[290] *See* Sellers v. Sellers, 638 So. 2d 481, 484 (Miss. 1994) (no separation of siblings in the absence of some unusual and compelling circumstance dictating otherwise).

[291] Owens v. Owens, 950 So. 2d 202, 207 (Miss. Ct. App. 2006) (awarding custody of younger child to mother to avoid separating child from older sister; parents had agreed that mother would have custody of the girl); *see also* Marshall v. Harris, 981 So. 2d 345, 348-50 (Miss. Ct. App. 2008) (denying father's request for custody of older boy, in part to avoid separating him from his younger brother). *But see* C.W.L. v. R.A., 919 So. 2d 267, 273 (Miss. Ct. App. 2005) (court rejected mother's argument that girl should not be separated from her half-brother, stating that "there is no general rule in this state that the best interest of siblings is served by keeping them together").

[292] *See* Sootin v. Sootin, 737 So. 2d 1022, 1026-27 (Miss. Ct. App. 1998); *see also* Sumrall v. Sumrall, 970 So. 2d 254, 259 (Miss. Ct. App. 2007) (mother awarded custody in part to avoid separating child and his half-brother); Taylor v. Taylor, 909 So. 2d 1280, 1282-83 (Miss. Ct. App. 2005) (custody of fourteen-year-old girl and three-year-old boy awarded to father based on daughter's strong preference and emotional bond with father and importance of keeping two

CHILD CUSTODY AND VISITATION §12.03[12][b]

custody to allow a child to remain with his half-brothers and -sisters.[293] In a number of cases, courts have refused to accede to a child's stated preference to live with one parent because the arrangement would separate an older child from siblings.[294] However, the courts have also emphasized that there is no "per se" rule that siblings may not be separated – it is a factor for the chancellor to consider. Awarding custody of a boy to his father was not error, even though the modification separated the child from his half-brother.[295] There is no requirement that a chancellor make a specific finding of fact with regard to this factor.[296] The court of appeals rejected a father's argument that a court must find unusual and compelling circumstances in order to separate siblings.[297]

Cases in which children have been separated often involve unusual and compelling circumstances such as abuse[298] or one child's hostility toward a parent or sibling.[299] Separation of siblings was proper where evidence showed that a boy's relationship with his mother was extremely damaging to him, particularly since the chancellor took care to ensure that the children would be in the same home on weekends.[300]

In a 2007 case, the court of appeals held that the preference for keeping siblings together applies to half-siblings. A chancellor properly awarded custody to a mother in part to avoid separating him from his younger half-brother.[301] In another case, however, the court rejected a mother's argument that the court erred in awarding her husband custody of twins, separating them from her third, nonmarital child. The court held that it would be unfair to deny him custody based on her misconduct and the existence of a child that was not his.[302]

[b] Parental interference. In several cases, custody has been denied to a par-

---

children together).

[293] *See* McWhirter v. McWhirter, 811 So. 2d 397, 399 (Miss. Ct. App. 2001). *But see* Copeland v. Copeland, 904 So. 2d 1066 (Miss. 2004) (custody awarded to father even though award separated boy from his half-sister).

[294] *See* Franklin v. Kroush, 622 So. 2d 1256, 1257 (Miss. 1993) (refusing father's request to modify solely on child's preference; modification would separate child from younger siblings); Mixon v. Bullard, 217 So. 2d 28 (Miss. 1968) (court upheld a chancellor's refusal to follow a thirteen-year-old boy's stated desire to live with his father, noting that other factors – such as the resulting separation from his siblings – dictated that he remain in the custody of his mother); Brown v. Brown, 764 So. 2d 502, 504-05 (Miss. Ct. App. 2000) (father's motion for custody denied; child's preference would separate two boys); Moore v. Moore, 757 So. 2d 1043, 1050 (Miss. Ct. App. 2000) (refusing to modify custody based on older child's request when result would be separation of brothers).

[295] C.A.M.F. v. J.M.B., 972 So. 2d 656, 661 (Miss. Ct. App. 2007); *see also* Montgomery v. Montgomery, 20 So. 3d 39, 42-43 (Miss. Ct. App. 2009) (custody to father even though award separated boys from half-siblings).

[296] C.A.M.F. v. J.M.B., 972 So. 2d 656, 661 (Miss. Ct. App. 2007).

[297] Moorman v. Moorman, 28 So. 3d 670, 671-72 (Miss. Ct. App. 2009).

[298] *See* Carson v. Natchez Children's Home, 580 So. 2d 1248, 1258 (Miss. 1991) (not error to separate siblings where both had been sexually abused and acted out sexually together).

[299] *See* Bowen v. Bowen, 688 So. 2d 1374, 1381-82 (Miss. 1997) (not error to separate siblings where older child was hostile to father and younger was disturbed by rumors of mother's lesbian relationship); Owens v. Owens, 950 So. 2d 202 (Miss. Ct. App. 2006) (reviewing cases); Brawley v. Brawley, 734 So. 2d 237, 241-42 (Miss. Ct. App. 1999) (modifying custody of four-year-old to father with fourteen-year-old remaining with mother; brothers did not get along, and younger brother was not thriving under mother's care).

[300] Holmes v. Holmes, 958 So. 2d 844, 846, 849 (Miss. Ct. App. 2007).

[301] Sumrall v. Sumrall, 970 So. 2d 254, 259 (Miss. Ct. App. 2007). *But cf.* Moorman v. Moorman, 28 So. 3d 670, 672 (Miss. Ct. App. 2009) (rejecting father's argument that half-siblings should have been taken into account in setting visitation schedule).

[302] Wells v. Wells, 35 So. 3d 1250, 1254 (Miss. Ct. App. 2010) (wife conceived by artificial insemination but told husband the child was naturally conceived).

§ 12.03[12][c]   **MISSISSIPPI FAMILY LAW**

ent based on interference with the other's relationship with a child.[303] Awarding custody of a very young girl to her father was not error in light of the mother's interference with the father-daughter relationship.[304] Similarly, a mother's interference with contact between children and their father was one of several reasons supporting a modification of custody.[305] A chancellor also properly modified custody from mother to father because she made numerous unsubstantiated claims of child sexual abuse, encouraged the child to dislike him, and misrepresented facts to agencies and social workers.[306]

[c] Religion. Whether a parent provides religious training cannot be the sole reason for a custody decision.[307] The fact that a parent offers religious training may, however, be considered as a positive aspect of a stable home environment.[308] A custody decision should not be based upon a parent's religious practices or beliefs unless they adversely affect a child. A court erred in modifying custody from a mother based on her church's belief in snake handling; the child was not in danger of being bitten.[309] On the other hand, a chancellor properly awarded custody to a mother primarily because the father lived in an isolated religious community with an unaccredited school and less-than-ideal living conditions.[310]

[d] Military service. The court of appeals refused to adopt a per se rule that a parent's military service may not be considered in a best interests analysis – a parent's work schedule is a proper consideration in determining custody. Accordingly, a chancellor did not err in awarding custody of two girls to their mother. She worked regular hours, while their father was on active duty, on call twenty-four hours a day, and subject to deployment.[311] Similarly, a chancellor properly awarded custody to a father who

---

[303] *See* Ferguson v. Ferguson, 639 So. 2d 921, 932 (Miss. 1994) (father belittled mother and encouraged child to disobey her); *see also* Mabus v. Mabus, 890 So. 2d 806, 818 (Miss. 2003) (mother's interference with children's relationship with father one reason supporting award of legal custody to father).

[304] Masino v. Masino, 829 So. 2d 1267, 1271 (Miss. Ct. App. 2002) (interference and failure to attend parenting classes as ordered negated tender-years factor).

[305] *See* Richardson v. Richardson, 790 So. 2d 239, 242-43 (Miss. Ct. App. 2001) (mother also lived for two years with abusive boyfriend with whom she had a child); *see also* Williams v. Williams, 656 So. 2d 325, 330 (Miss. 1995) (father's coaching children to make negative statements about mother a valid factor in awarding custody to mother); Ellis v. Ellis, 952 So. 2d 982, 986 (Miss. Ct. App. 2006) (custody modified to father; discussing parental alienation syndrome); Parker v. South, 913 So. 2d 339, 346-47 (Miss. Ct. App. 2005) (interference with visitation one of several factors in modifying custody).

[306] Jernigan v. Jernigan, 830 So. 2d 651, 653 (Miss. Ct. App. 2002) (mother failed to provide a stable home, moved frequently, promoted the idea that the father had sexually abused the child, had lived out of wedlock with her current husband, and failed to cooperate with the visitation order); *see also* Potter v. Greene, 973 So. 2d 291, 293-94 (Miss. Ct. App. 2008) (custody modified based on mother's unfounded accusations and interference with visitation); *cf.* T.K. v. H.K., 24 So. 3d 1055, 1064-65 (Miss. Ct. App. 2010) (modification based in part on mother's false allegations of domestic violence).

[307] Messer v. Messer, 850 So. 2d 161, 166 (Miss. Ct. App. 2003).

[308] *See* Davidson v. Coit, 899 So. 2d 904, 911 (Miss. Ct. App. 2005) (chancellor properly factored that father took children to church, while mother did not).

[309] Harris v. Harris, 343 So. 2d 762, 763-64 (Miss. 1977) (snakes were kept in a cage and neither Ms. Harris nor anyone else in church was anointed to handle them).

[310] Muhammad v. Muhammad, 622 So. 2d 1239, 1248 (Miss. 1993) (family lived in one room of a small house in an Islamic community, did not have a refrigerator, had a limited diet, and outside contacts were restricted); *cf.* Forthner v. Forthner, 52 So. 3d 1212, 1220-21 (Miss. Ct. App. 2010) (court did not violate father's religious freedom by commenting on religious practices).

[311] Morris v. Morris, 5 So. 3d 476, 490 (Miss. Ct. App. 2008) (also based on age and sex of children). *See infra* §

362

CHILD CUSTODY AND VISITATION   § 12.04

lived near extended family over a mother on active duty. The court of appeals stated, however, that military service "should not weigh negatively against the stability of a parent's home or employment."[312] A parent's deployment or mobilization may not be considered as a material change for purposes of permanent custody modification.[313]

§ 12.04 JOINT CUSTODY

Until the 1970s, custody between parents generally took the form of sole custody to one parent with visitation awarded to the other. Most of a child's time was spent with the custodial parent, who had decision-making authority with regard to medical care, education, religious training, and other significant aspects of a child's life. Non-custodial parents had limited visitation, typically one or two weekends a month and a few weeks in the summer. As mothers increasingly entered the workforce and fathers became more involved in daily childcare, joint custody emerged as a viable, and some-times preferred, custody arrangement.

Proponents of joint custody point to studies indicating that children who maintain a close relationship with both parents are better adjusted and have higher self-esteem. Joint custody guarantees a child substantial time with each parent and ensures the involvement and support of both parents. On the other hand, several decades of experi-ence with joint custody shows that the arrangement does not work if parents are antago-nistic. In fact, joint custody may exacerbate conflict because of the regular interaction required.[314] In addition, the shift between residences and fluctuation in routine is dis-ruptive to some children and may contribute to a feeling of instability.[315]

In most states, joint custody is simply one option to be considered by a court.[316] In some states, joint custody may be awarded only upon the agreement of the parties.[317] In Mississippi, courts are authorized to order joint custody upon the request of one or both parents, if the arrangement is in the child's best interests.[318] A court did not err in awarding parents alternating weekly custody of two girls.[319] If both parents request joint custody, it is presumed to be in the best interests of the child.[320]

12.11[16] for a discussion of modification based on military service.

[312] Price v. McBeath, 989 So. 2d 444, 458 (Miss. Ct. App. 2008) (father also favored on moral fitness and stability of employment).

[313] *See infra* § 12.11[5][k].

[314] *See* ELROD, *supra* note 3, § 5:01.

[315] *See* ELROD, *supra* note 3, § 5:01 (noting that California and Utah have abandoned a presumption in favor of joint custody).

[316] *See* ELROD, *supra* note 3, § 5:06.

[317] *See, e.g.,* OR. REV. STAT. § 107.169(3) (2009); VT. STAT. ANN. tit. 15, § 665(a) (2011).

[318] MISS. CODE ANN. § 93-5-24(2) (2004) states that in irreconcilable differences divorces joint custody can be awarded to both parents upon an application by both. However, the Mississippi Supreme Court interpreted the statute to allow joint custody awards upon the request of one parent. Crider v. Crider, 904 So. 2d 142, 147 (Miss. 2005) (holding that when parties consent in writing to the court's determination of custody, they are consenting and agreeing to that determination, thus meeting the statutory directive of "joint application" in § 93-5-24(2)); *see also* Hamilton v. Hamilton, 755 So. 2d 528, 530-31 (Miss. Ct. App. 1999) (court awarded joint custody where divorce was granted to husband based on adultery; court of appeals reversed for *Albright* findings).

[319] Phillips v. Phillips, 45 So. 3d 684, 696 (Miss. Ct. App. 2010), *cert. denied*, 49 So. 3d 636 (Miss. 2010).

[320] MISS. CODE ANN. § 93-5-24 (2004).

§ 12.04[1]   **MISSISSIPPI FAMILY LAW**

[1] Forms of joint custody. Parents may share both legal and physical custody. Or, parents may share joint legal custody, with one parent having primary physical custody. Although it is much less common, parents may share physical custody with one parent having sole legal custody.[321]

   [a] Joint legal custody. Joint legal custody gives parents shared decision-making authority with regard to a child's health, education, and welfare. Parents who share joint legal custody are obligated by statute to exchange information related to a child and to confer with each other in making decisions.[322] The Mississippi Supreme Court characterized joint legal custody as approximating the authority in an intact nuclear family.[323] However, a chancellor erred in awarding joint legal custody to allow a mother to keep abreast of her girls' activities. Noncustodial parents are entitled by statute to information and records regarding a minor child. Joint legal custody involves more than information – it gives the parents joint authority over major decisions about their children's lives.[324] A court is not required to make *Albright* findings of fact to support an award of joint legal custody.[325]

   [b] Joint physical custody. Joint physical custody allows each parent to have significant, although not necessarily equal, time with a child. Joint physical custody may be structured in a variety of ways. Time with a child may be divided on a weekly basis[326] or by alternating weeks, months, half-years, or years.[327] An award may simply provide for flexible joint custody to be arranged by the parents, although this arrangement is advisable only between parties who are extremely cooperative.[328] In a few cases, courts have awarded custody to one parent during the school year and the other in the summer as a form of joint custody. The court of appeals referred to one such arrangement as de facto sole custody.[329] In a 2008 case, however, the court of appeals

---

[321] Miss. Code Ann. § 93-5-24 (2004); *see* Mabus v. Mabus, 847 So. 2d 815, 821 (Miss. 2003) (legal custody to father, with physical custody shared equally between parents).

[322] Miss. Code Ann. § 93-5-24 (5)(e) (2004).

[323] Rutledge v. Rutledge, 487 So. 2d 218, 219 (Miss. 1986) ("involves parental consultation and agreement on all major decisions affecting the children") (quoting David J. Miller, *Joint Custody*, 13 Fam. L.Q. 395, 360 (1979)).

[324] Lowrey v. Lowrey, 25 So. 3d 274, 295-96 (Miss. 2009); *see* Miss. Code Ann. § 93-5-24(8) (2004).

[325] Palculict v. Palculict, 22 So. 3d 293, 298 (Miss. Ct. App. 2009).

[326] *See* Elliott v. Elliott, 877 So. 2d 450, 452 (Miss. Ct. App. 2003) (custody to mother three days a week and twenty-four weekends; father two days a week and twenty-eight weekends); Massey v. Huggins, 799 So. 2d 902, 904-05 (Miss. Ct. App. 2001) (father had custody on Wednesdays and weekends during the school year; during summer, children lived with father and spent weekends with mother); Delozier v. Delozier, 724 So. 2d 984, 986 (Miss. Ct. App. 1998) (custody to father during week and mother on weekends).

[327] *See* Mercier v. Mercier, 717 So. 2d 304, 305 (Miss. 1998) (alternating every other week); Morrow v. Morrow, 591 So. 2d 829, 830 (Miss. 1991) (alternating custody of school-aged child every two years); Phillips v. Phillips, 45 So. 3d 684, 691 (Miss. Ct. App. 2010) (alternating weekly), *cert. denied*, 49 So. 3d 636 (Miss. 2010); Elliott v. Elliott, 877 So. 2d 450, 452 (Miss. Ct. App. 2003) (mother to have custody three days a week and twenty-four weekends (57%) and the father two days a week and twenty-eight weekends (43%)); Daniel v. Daniel, 770 So. 2d 562, 567 (Miss. Ct. App. 2000) (alternating every two weeks).

[328] *See* Lackey v. Fuller, 755 So. 2d 1083, 1085 (Miss. 2000) (decree provided that children would spend one-half of their time with each parent, specifying a holiday visitation schedule).

[329] *See* Dearman v. Dearman, 811 So. 2d 308, 314 (Miss. Ct. App. 2001) ("joint custody" where the child was with father during the school year and mother during the summer was really de facto sole custody with visitation); *see also* Floyd v. Floyd, 949 So. 2d 26, 27-28 (Miss. 2007) (child lived with father during week and mother on weekend and in summers); Hamilton v. Hamilton, 755 So. 2d 528, 529 (Miss. Ct. App. 1999) (court awarded joint custody where divorce

364

CHILD CUSTODY AND VISITATION   § 12.04[1][c]

rejected a father's argument that a joint physical custody award was "de facto" sole custody because the mother had custody during the school year, while he had custody in the summer. The court noted that the chancellor designated the father's periods as custodial rather than as visitation, and that joint custody does not require equal custodial periods.[330] In a few cases, Mississippi courts have approved joint physical custody of a child until school age, followed by sole custody in one parent.[331]

[c] Ambiguous custody provisions. Some custody awards or agreements use the term "primary physical custody" as a substitute for the statutory "sole physical custody." In a 2006 case, the supreme court discouraged the use of this term, noting that there is no provision in Mississippi law for "primary" physical custody. The chancellor awarded parents joint legal and physical custody, with primary physical custody, and the bulk of the children's time, to the father. The supreme court remanded for clarification of the ambiguous award, noting that joint physical custody is possible only when both parents have significant periods of custody.[332] In 2009, the Mississippi Supreme Court interpreted an ambiguous agreement as one for joint physical custody. The parents' agreement provided that they would share joint legal and physical custody, with the mother having primary physical custody and the father having secondary physical custody. The agreement defined joint physical custody using the language of the joint custody statute. It did not define "primary" and "secondary." The court noted that there is no provision under the statute for "primary physical custody." Because the agreement used the term joint physical custody, defined as in the statute, the undefined term primary "cannot act to transform such express 'joint physical custody' into de facto sole physical custody."[333]

[2] When joint custody may be awarded

[a] By agreement. There is a presumption that joint custody is in the best interests of a child when both parents request joint custody.[334] No reported appellate case was found in which the parties' agreement for joint custody was denied.

[b] By court order. A court may order joint custody if it is in the children's best interest.[335] In 1999, the court of appeals held that a court may award joint custody in irreconcilable differences divorces only if both parents request an award of joint custody.[336] The court of appeals relied on the language of the applicable statute, which

---

was granted to husband based on adultery; reversed for *Albright* findings).

[330] Collins v. Collins, 20 So. 3d 683, 692-93 (Miss. Ct. App. 2008).

[331] *See* Pierce v. Chandler, 855 So. 2d 455, 459 (Miss. Ct. App. 2003); Daniel v. Daniel, 770 So. 2d 562, 567 (Miss. Ct. App. 2000).

[332] Rush v. Rush, 932 So. 2d 794, 800 (Miss. 2006); *see also* McSwain v. McSwain, 943 So. 2d 1288, 1290 n.2 (Miss. Ct. App. 2006) (no such thing as "primary" physical custody in Miss. Code Ann. § 93-5-24 (2004)).

[333] Porter v. Porter, 23 So. 3d 438, 447 (Miss. 2009).

[334] Miss. Code Ann. § 93-5-24 (4) (2004).

[335] Phillips v. Phillips, 45 So. 3d 684, 696 (Miss. Ct. App. 2010) (affirming award of weekly alternating joint custody), *cert. denied*, 49 So. 3d 636 (Miss. 2010).

[336] Morris v. Morris, 758 So. 2d 1020, 1021 (Miss. Ct. App. 1999) (reversing chancellor's award of joint custody in absence of request by both parents); *see* Grissom v. Grissom, 952 So. 2d 1023, 1028 (Miss. Ct. App. 2007) (rejecting

§ 12.04[3]   **MISSISSIPPI FAMILY LAW**

provides that joint custody in irreconcilable differences divorces is available "upon application of both parents."[337] In 2005, the supreme court held that the language of the statute is capable of more than one interpretation because of the history and chronology of enactment of the divorce and custody statutes. Because the best interest of a child always guides custody decisions, the statute should be interpreted to allow a court to award joint custody in irreconcilable differences or fault-based divorces on the application of one parent.[338]

[3] Factors. As in any custody action, a court should consider the *Albright* factors in making an award of joint custody.[339] A chancellor awarded joint physical custody after analyzing the *Albright* factors and finding that some factors favored the mother and some the father, but that it was in the boy's best interest for the parents to share joint physical custody.[340] No precise test has been articulated to determine when an award of joint rather than sole custody is appropriate. The following considerations are suggested as critical factors in a joint custody award.

[a] Parental fitness. An award of joint custody is necessarily based on a finding that both parents are fit to be custodians of a child.[341] However, parental fitness does not create a presumption that joint custody should be awarded. The Mississippi Supreme Court rejected a mother's argument that because she was awarded shared physical custody – and therefore a fit custodian – she was constitutionally entitled to shared legal custody.[342]

[b] Ability to cooperate. According to a leading national authority on family law, "A rough consensus has developed that where the parents are so antagonistic or hostile toward each other that cooperation in carrying out a joint custody decree is unlikely, such a decree should not be granted."[343] Courts agree that while joint custody may be the ideal post-divorce arrangement, it is unworkable if the parents are "embattled and embittered."[344] The Mississippi Supreme Court stated: "[T]he cardinal criterion for an award of joint custody is the agreement of the parties and their mutual abil-

---

wife's argument that court was not entitled to order joint custody without agreement of parties).

[337] Morris v. Morris, 758 So. 2d 1020, 1021 (Miss. Ct. App. 1999) (reversing chancellor's award of joint custody in absence of request by both parents); *see* MISS. CODE ANN. § 93-5-24(2) (2004).

[338] Crider v. Crider, 904 So. 2d 142, 147 (Miss. 2005).

[339] *See* Hamilton v. Hamilton, 755 So. 2d 528, 530-31 (Miss. Ct. App. 1999) (court awarded joint custody where divorce was granted to husband based on adultery; reversed for *Albright* findings).

[340] Collins v. Collins, 20 So. 3d 683, 692-93 (Miss. Ct. App. 2008) (mother to have custody during the school year and father to have custody during the summer).

[341] *See* ELROD, *supra* note 3, § 5:09.

[342] *See* Mabus v. Mabus, 847 So. 2d 815, 820 (Miss. 2003) (statute explicitly authorizes award of sole legal custody and joint physical custody).

[343] CLARK, JR., *supra* note 43, § 19.5, at 817.

[344] *See* Braiman v. Braiman, 378 N.E.2d 1019, 1021 (N.Y. 1978) ("joint custody is encouraged primarily as a voluntary alternative for relatively stable, amicable parents behaving in a mature civilized fashion"); *see also* Dodd v. Dodd, 403 N.Y.S.2d 401, 405 (N.Y. 1978) ("The most ardent professional proponents of joint custody assume cooperation between parents and agreement about child rearing practices as basic requirements for joint custody."); Vitauts M. Gulbis, Annotation, *Propriety of Awarding Joint Custody of Children*, 17 A.L.R. 4th 1013 (1982) (citing numerous cases holding that joint custody was inappropriate because parents were unable to cooperate).

CHILD CUSTODY AND VISITATION   § 12.04[3][c]

ity to cooperate in reaching shared decisions in matters affecting the child's welfare."[345] The court also noted that in many states, joint custody may not be awarded unless the parties consent.[346]

Ability to cooperate may be even more important in a joint award of legal custody than of physical custody. Physical custody may be structured to minimize contact between parents, while joint legal custody requires regular interaction and cooperation in decisions regarding schooling, medical care, activities, and discipline. The supreme court noted that parents who experience substantial animosity will find it "manifestly impossible" to function under a joint custody award.[347] In one case, the court of appeals approved an award of joint legal custody between parents in conflict, but noted that it may be best to limit joint custody to cases in which the parents can work cooperatively.[348]

[c] Proximity. As a general rule, joint physical custody is feasible only if the parties live in close proximity. Parents may share joint legal custody at a distance. The importance of proximity in joint physical custody is reflected in the fact that appellate courts routinely affirm modification of joint physical custody when one parent moves.[349] In two cases, however, joint custody was approved in spite of distance. The court of appeals affirmed joint custody between parents who lived four hours apart; the child spent the school week with one parent and weekends and summers with the other.[350] Parents were also allowed to share joint custody for two years until a child started school, in part because they had done so prior to the court order. The court of appeals noted, however, that "constantly alternating a child back and forth to each parent is not a habit that should be encouraged."[351]

[d] Domestic violence. Joint custody may not be appropriate in cases involving domestic violence between the parents. In a recent case, a guardian ad litem recommended against joint custody in a case involving domestic violence, stating that the husband's control issues would prevent smooth decision making.[352]

---

[345] Waller v. Waller, 754 So. 2d 1181, 1184 (Miss. 2000) (quoting Vitauts M. Gulbis, Annotation, *Propriety of Awarding Joint Custody of Children*, 17 A.L.R. 4th 1013, 1016 (1982)). The court noted that "[c]ooperation between the parents is paramount even in jurisdictions where there is a presumption that joint custody is in the best interest of the child." *Id. See* Lewis v. Lewis, 974 So. 2d 265, 266 (Miss. Ct. App. 2008) (joint custody not appropriate where parents could not communicate).

[346] *See* Waller v. Waller, 754 So. 2d 1181, 1184 (Miss. 2000).

[347] Rutledge v. Rutledge, 487 So. 2d 218, 220 (Miss. 1986) (case involved sole custody).

[348] *See* Masino v. Masino, 829 So. 2d 1267, 1270-71 (Miss. Ct. App. 2002) (awarding primary physical custody to father, based in part on mother's interference in father-daughter relationship). *But cf.* Phillips v. Phillips, 45 So. 3d 684, 691, 692, 699 (Miss. Ct. App. 2010) (affirming award of joint custody between parents even though the father called DHS on the mother and she cited him for contempt), *cert. denied*, 49 So. 3d 636 (Miss. 2010).

[349] *See infra* § 12.11[7][a].

[350] *See* Delozier v. Delozier, 724 So. 2d 984, 986 (Miss. Ct. App. 1998) (custody to father during week and mother on weekends); *see also* Collins v. Collins, 20 So. 3d 683, 692-93 (Miss. Ct. App. 2008) (awarding joint physical custody between parents living in different towns in North Mississippi; mother to have custody during the school year and father during the summer).

[351] *See* Daniel v. Daniel, 770 So. 2d 562, 567 (Miss. Ct. App. 2000).

[352] Horn v. Horn, 909 So. 2d 1151, 1159-60 (Miss. Ct. App. 2005) (awarding custody to mother in part based on father's violence).

§ 12.04[4]   MISSISSIPPI FAMILY LAW

[4] Joint physical custody vs. sole custody and visitation. It is becoming increasingly common for a noncustodial parent to have extensive visitation, with shared time similar to joint physical custody. When parents live in the same town and are cooperative, the label attached to the agreement may be practically irrelevant. There are, however, significant legal consequences attached to each form of custody. If parents accustomed to joint decision making disagree, the parent with sole legal custody has authority to make unilateral decisions regarding the child. And a move by one of two joint custodians triggers an *Albright* analysis to determine which parent should take sole physical custody. In contrast, when a parent with sole custody relocates, the relocation is not in itself a reason to modify custody.[353]

Parties have argued that courts should look to the substance of a custodial arrangement rather than to the label affixed by court order. However, the Mississippi Supreme Court rejected a father's argument that a custodial arrangement was de facto joint custody because his children spent six of every fourteen days with him.[354]

§ 12.05 RESTRICTIONS AND CONDITIONS ON CUSTODY

A court may impose restrictions or conditions on either parent to prevent harm to a child. Courts have ordered parents to refrain from drinking alcohol in a child's presence[355] and ordered parents to take monthly drug tests.[356] A custodial father was ordered to attend anger management classes, based on evidence that he screamed at his wife in front of the children, and on at least one occasion, at his sons.[357] And courts have prohibited parents from having guests of the opposite sex in their home overnight when children are present.[358] In one case, a chancellor concerned about a custodial parent's home environment ordered the Department of Human Services to make periodic unannounced visits.[359] A court may place restrictions on a custodial parent who interferes with the noncustodial parent's rights of visitation.[360] In the absence of conduct harmful to children, however, a court cannot dictate what would normally be parental decisions about a child's health, education, and welfare. For example, a custodial parent cannot be ordered to live in a particular town or school district or to instruct a child in a certain religion. The court of appeals reversed a chancellor's order that children attend a particular school.[361] However, to avoid harm to a child, a chancellor properly ordered a custodial mother to refrain temporarily from removing the child from the jurisdic-

---

[353] *See infra* § 12.11[7].

[354] *See* Rutledge v. Rutledge, 487 So. 2d 218, 220 (Miss. 1986) ("the claim that joint legal custody and sole custody with liberal visitation rights are indistinguishable is not true") (quoting David J. Miller, *Joint Custody*, 13 FAM. L.Q. 395, 360 (1979)). *But cf.* Dearman v. Dearman, 811 So. 2d 308, 314 (Miss. Ct. App. 2001) (affirming joint custody award deemed actually de facto physical custody to father).

[355] *See* Henderson v. Henderson, 952 So. 2d 273, 276 (Miss. Ct. App. 2006) (both parents ordered to refrain from consuming alcohol while driving the children); Turner v. Turner, 824 So. 2d 652, 657 (Miss. Ct. App. 2002).

[356] *See* McLemore v. McLemore, 762 So. 2d 316, 322 (Miss. 2000).

[357] Gilliland v. Gilliland, 969 So. 2d 56, 63, 71 (Miss. Ct. App. 2007).

[358] *See* Thurman v. Johnson, 998 So. 2d 1026, 1029 (Miss. Ct. App. 2008) (temporary order).

[359] *See* Marascalco v. Marascalco, 445 So. 2d 1380, 1382 (Miss. 1984) (concern over mother's serious drinking problem).

[360] See discussion *infra* § 12.08[5].

[361] *See* Ayers v. Ayers, 734 So. 2d 213, 217 (Miss. Ct. App. 1999).

CHILD CUSTODY AND VISITATION § 12.06

tion. She had moved to Florida to live with the child's abusive father after termination of the father's parental rights.[362] With regard to religious instruction, the supreme court upheld a chancellor's instruction to each parent to take responsibility for the children's church attendance, but noted that the provision should be in the form of a suggestion, rather than a mandatory provision.[363] Visitation restrictions are discussed in detail in Section 12.08[4].

§ 12.06 CUSTODY BETWEEN PARENTS AND THIRD PARTIES

In a custody dispute between a parent and a third party, there is a presumption in favor of the natural parent as custodian. The traditional test for awarding custody to a third party requires a showing of parental unfitness or abandonment. However, recent decisions create several less stringent tests for overcoming the presumption.

[1] Presumption in favor of parents. Biological parents have long been presumed to be the best custodians of their children. The Mississippi Supreme Court held that parents "have a natural right to the nurture, care and custody of their children."[364] The court of appeals emphasized that because of the strong presumption in favor of natural parents, third-party custody should be granted only if there is a clear showing "that the natural parent has relinquished his parental rights, that he has no meaningful relationship with his children, or that the parent's conduct is clearly detrimental to his children."[365]

When a third party seeks custody, the *Albright* best interest analysis does not apply. The traditional test for third-party custody is parental abandonment or unfitness.[366] A child's right to express a preference for one parent as custodian does not apply to disputes between a parent and a third person.[367] Similarly, the preference for keeping siblings together will not override the presumption in favor of a natural parent.[368]

---

[362] Allen v. Williams, 914 So. 2d 254, 258 (Miss. Ct. App. 2005).

[363] *See* McLemore v. McLemore, 762 So. 2d 316, 320 (Miss. 2000). The court approved the following language for such a provision: "Both the mother and father should be vitally interested in seeing that their children get regular and systematic spiritual training. Whether it be by attending Sunday School each Sunday or Church or both is for the parents alone to decide." *Id.*

[364] *See* E.J.M. v. A.J.M., 846 So. 2d 289, 294 (Miss. Ct. App. 2003) (quoting Simpson v. Rast, 258 So. 2d 233, 236 (Miss. 1972)).

[365] *In re* Brown, 902 So. 2d 604 (Miss. Ct. App. 2004); *see also* Allen v. Williams, 914 So. 2d 254, 259 (Miss. Ct. App. 2005) (custody awarded to grandparents in modification proceeding after custodial mother began living with abusive father whose parental rights had been terminated). *But cf.* McCraw v. McCraw, 10 So. 3d 979, 984 (Miss. Ct. App. 2009) (holding that chancellor's *Albright* analysis between child's mother and grandmother "effectively found" that the mother was unfit).

[366] *See* K.D.F. v. J.L.H., 933 So. 2d 971, 980 (Miss. 2006) (father was entitled to custody as against third parties, in the absence of a showing of abandonment or unfitness; court properly declined to conduct *Albright* analysis); Sellers v. Sellers, 638 So. 2d 481, 484 (Miss. 1994); Carter v. Taylor, 611 So. 2d 874, 876 (Miss. 1992); Schonewitz v. Pack, 913 So. 2d 416, 420 (Miss. Ct. App. 2005) (material change in circumstance test not applicable in custody dispute between natural parent and third party); Hillman v. Vance, 910 So. 2d 43, 45-47 (Miss. Ct. App. 2005) (rejecting grandmother's suit for custody based on "unwholesome environment" because mother of child was a stripper); *see also* MISS. CODE ANN. § 93-13-1 (2004) (if one parent dies, the other is the child's legal guardian). *But cf.* Brocato v. Brocato, 731 So. 2d 1138, 1142-43 (Miss. 1999) (court upheld de facto custody in grandmother without a finding that the natural mother was unfit; father had legal custody but child lived with grandmother).

[367] Westbrook v. Oglesbee, 606 So. 2d 1142, 1146 (Miss. 1992).

[368] *See* Sellers v. Sellers, 638 So. 2d 481, 485 (Miss. 1994) (error to place child with aunt so that he could be with

§ 12.06[2]   **MISSISSIPPI FAMILY LAW**

[2] Third parties who may qualify as "parents." Some persons other than biological or adoptive parents are treated as parents for purposes of custody rules. Doctrines such as *in loco parentis*, equitable parent, and intended parent, may elevate a third party's status to that of parent, placing them in equality with biological or adoptive parents.

Mississippi appellate courts have recently revived the common law doctrine of *in loco parentis* to afford parental rights to men who are defrauded about their paternity of a child.[369] The doctrine broadly states that one who has assumed the status and obligations of a parent may have the rights and/or duties of a parent.[370] For example, a mother's husband who believed that he was the father of a child born during their marriage was *in loco parentis*, and had equal rights to custody of the child. The chancellor did not err in conducting an *Albright* analysis and awarding custody to the father.[371]

Although primarily used so far to extend parental rights to defrauded fathers, the doctrine could arguably apply to third parties other than presumed fathers. For example, in a 2009 case the court of appeals affirmed an award of custody to unrelated third parties rather than to a child's father. In addition to finding that the father had abandoned the child, the court noted in support of the decision that the foster parents had acted *in loco parentis*.[372] And the supreme court referred to the doctrine in a 1998 case awarding temporary custody to a stepfather. Although the chancellor found that the mother was unfit, the court also noted that a stepparent who has acted "*in loco parentis*" may be entitled to custody.[373] The scope and application of the doctrine to third parties other than defrauded presumed fathers is not yet clear.

Courts in other states have used similar doctrines, such as de facto, psychological, or equitable parent, to extend parental rights to third parties other than defrauded fathers. In some states, same-sex partners have been accorded rights as intended parents or based on a court's finding that they have acted *in loco parentis* or as a de facto parent. In others, however, courts have denied visitation to same-sex partners, finding that extension of visitation is a matter for the legislature or that the de facto parent doctrine did not apply to same-sex couples.[374]

Designation as "parent" can be even more complicated with regard to a child conceived through assisted reproduction. Usually, the intended parents of an ART child are accorded parental rights. However, other participants in the process may have a claim to parental rights under some circumstances. Assisted reproduction is discussed in detail in Chapter 22.

---

his half-sister).

[369] *See infra* § 11.07[3].

[370] Griffith v. Pell, 881 So. 2d 184 (Miss. 2004).

[371] *See* J.P.M. v. T.D.M., 932 So. 2d 760, 769 (Miss. 2006) (en banc).

[372] *In re* Marriage of Leverock, 23 So. 3d 424, 430-32 (Miss. 2009); *see also* Logan v. Logan, 730 So. 2d 1124, 1127 (Miss. 1998) (discussing stepfather's *in loco parentis* status; also finding mother unfit); Vaughn v. Vaughn, 36 So. 3d 1261, 1262, 1264 (Miss. 2010) (grandmother who cared for child for four years under informal agreement was *in loco parentis*). *But cf.* J.P.M. v. T.D.M., 932 So. 2d 760, 768 (Miss. 2006) (en banc) (distinguishing third-party defrauded father from other third parties against whom natural parent presumption was applied).

[373] *See* Logan v. Logan, 730 So. 2d 1124, 1127 (Miss. 1998). The role of the doctrine is unclear, since the court also found the mother unfit.

[374] *See* discussion of custody rights of same-sex partners Chapter II.

CHILD CUSTODY AND VISITATION § 12.06[3]

[3] Standard for awarding third-party custody. The traditional test for third-party custody required a showing that a parent was unfit or had abandoned a child. Under the traditional test, an otherwise fit parent who had maintained regular contact with a child could resume custody after years of absence without a determination that the transfer was in the child's best interest. In the last decade, Mississippi appellate courts have developed three alternatives to the traditional rule that provide chancellors with some discretion under these circumstances. First, a parent's long absence from a child's daily life may be considered constructive abandonment. Second, the natural parent presumption does not apply if the parent voluntarily relinquishes legal custody of the child. And in 2010, the court of appeals recognized desertion as a basis for third-party custody.

[a] Unfitness and immoral conduct. To award custody to a third party based on parental unfitness, a court must find that a parent engaged in conduct presenting a genuine serious danger to a child. Proof that a parent was occasionally intoxicated or had a past history of drug use was not sufficient to justify third-party custody.[375] A parent who exhibits some undesirable behavior or lacks exemplary parenting skills is not necessarily unfit. Awarding custody to grandparents based on a finding that a father was "unprepared" to take custody as opposed to "unfit" was reversible error.[376] Similarly, a court erred in granting custody to grandparents based primarily on evidence that a father had a "high temper."[377] In contrast, paternal grandparents were properly granted custody of a child who had been sexually abused while in the care of a bipolar, schizophrenic mother who did not take her medication regularly.[378] Similarly, a father who abused alcohol and drugs, was abusive to his son, and failed to report his girlfriend's disappearance was found to be unfit.[379] A mother lost custody to third parties based on evidence that she was unemployed, living in the trailer of her same-sex partner's uncle, used drugs, and exposed the children to nudity.[380]

In a recent third-party custody case, the court of appeals looked to termination of parental rights cases to define "unfitness." Based on these cases, the court held that failure to pay child support may be a factor in determining abandonment, but may not

---

[375] *See* Sellers v. Sellers, 638 So. 2d 481 (Miss. 1994) (use of marijuana discontinued); Westbrook v. Oglesbee, 606 So. 2d 1142, 1145 (Miss. 1992) (past drug habit, occasional intoxication).

[376] Carter v. Taylor, 611 So. 2d 874, 876 (Miss. 1992).

[377] Moody v. Moody, 211 So. 2d 842, 844 (Miss. 1968); *see also* Stoker v. Huggins, 471 So. 2d 1228, 1229-1300 (Miss. 1985) (evidence that father cohabited briefly with current wife and that wife's fifteen-year-old son stayed with children did not support finding of unfitness); *In re* Brown, 902 So. 2d 604 (Miss. Ct. App. 2004) (error to award third-party custody based on father's failure to pay support consistently and inability to visit regularly from Illinois).

[378] E.J.M. v. A.J.M., 846 So. 2d 289, 294 (Miss. Ct. App. 2003); *see also* Loomis v. Bugg, 872 So. 2d 694, 696-97 (Miss. Ct. App. 2004) (custody to child's paternal aunt; mother had history of illegal drug use, unstable employment, frequent moves, and multiple relationships).

[379] *In re* Custody of M.A.G., 859 So. 2d 1001, 1005 (Miss. 2003); *see also* S.C.R. v. F.W.K., 748 So. 2d 693, 701 (Miss. 1999) (presumption of parental fitness rebutted where father instructed young child to lie and fabricate charges of sexual abuse).

[380] White v. Thompson, 569 So. 2d 1181, 1184 (Miss. 1990) (mother admitted smoking marijuana and admitted to adulterous affairs; evidence also showed lack of supervision and care); *see also* McCraw v. McCraw, 10 So. 3d 979, 984 (Miss. Ct. App. 2009) (custody properly awarded to grandmother over mother who exposed child to inappropriate sexual behavior, engaged in drug use prior to her divorce, cohabited with several men, and showed a lack of "thoughtful maturity").

371

§ 12.06[3][b]   **MISSISSIPPI FAMILY LAW**

be a reason to find a parent "otherwise unfit."[381]

[b] Abandonment. Third-party custody may be awarded upon proof that a natural parent abandoned a child. Abandonment is "any course of conduct on the part of a parent evincing a settled purpose to forgo all duties and relinquish all parental claims to the child."[382] It may consist of a single act or a series of actions.[383] Failure to provide financial support for a child is not, in itself, abandonment.[384] Abandonment must be proven by clear and convincing evidence.[385] The supreme court found abandonment by a father who made no contact with a child for seven years and then had occasional contact and provided minimal support for three years.[386] And a father who made no contact with his son for two years had abandoned him, allowing an award of custody to third parties who had cared for the child and his mother prior to her death.[387] However, a child was not abandoned by a parent who left her with relatives for a number of years but maintained contact and visited.[388] Similarly, a mother who left her daughter with grandparents for six out of ten years did not abandon the girl because she visited and sent gifts.[389]

[c] Constructive abandonment. In 2002, the court of appeals held that the natural parent presumption does not apply when a parent "constructively abandons" a child.[390] The catalyst for this doctrine was a custody dispute between grandparents and a mother who left her child with them for eleven years under a temporary custody order. The mother did, however, maintain contact and visit, preventing a finding of actual abandonment. The court of appeals defined constructive abandonment as "voluntary abandonment of parental responsibility" and removal from "active participation in a child's life" for so long that the effect is the same as actual abandonment.[391] A parent who has constructively abandoned a child may regain custody only by showing by clear and convincing evidence that it is in the child's best interests.[392] The court of appeals found no constructive abandonment by a mother who traveled twelve times to Mississippi over a three-year period, trying to locate a child removed from her by the child's father.[393]

[d] Desertion. In a 2010 case, the court of appeals appeared to recognize a new

---

[381] *In re* Brown, 902 So. 2d 604 (Miss. Ct. App. 2004).

[382] Ethredge v. Yawn, 605 So. 2d 761, 764 (Miss. 1992).

[383] Ethredge v. Yawn, 605 So. 2d 761, 764 (Miss. 1992).

[384] Ethredge v. Yawn, 605 So. 2d 761, 765 (Miss. 1992); *In re* Adoption of A Female Child, 412 So. 2d 1175, 1178 (Miss. 1982).

[385] Ethredge v. Yawn, 605 So. 2d 761, 764 (Miss. 1992); *see* Bryant v. Cameron, 473 So. 2d 174, 178-79 (Miss. 1985).

[386] *See* Smith v. Watson, 425 So. 2d 1030, 1034-35 (Miss. 1983).

[387] *In re* Marriage of Leverock, 23 So. 3d 424, 437-38 (Miss. 2009).

[388] Payne v. Payne, 58 So. 2d 377, 378 (Miss. 1952).

[389] Turner v. Turner, 331 So. 2d 903, 905-06 (Miss. 1976).

[390] Hill v. Mitchell, 818 So. 2d 1221, 1226 (Miss. Ct. App. 2002).

[391] Hill v. Mitchell, 818 So. 2d 1221, 1226 (Miss. Ct. App. 2002).

[392] Hill v. Mitchell, 818 So. 2d 1221, 1226 (Miss. Ct. App. 2002) (court noted that constructive abandonment may require a longer period than actual abandonment).

[393] Schonewitz v. Pack, 913 So. 2d 416, 422 (Miss. Ct. App. 2005).

CHILD CUSTODY AND VISITATION   § 12.06[3][e]

circumstance in which a parent forfeits the natural parent presumption – by deserting a child. The court distinguished abandonment and desertion. Abandonment involves relinquishment of rights, while desertion involves inaction or avoidance of a duty. Desertion may involve behavior different from abandonment or constructive abandonment. If a parent is found by clear and convincing evidence to have deserted a child, the court should determine the child's best interest under *Albright*. Applying this test, a father who allowed his daughter to remain with her grandmother for four years, visiting sporadically, deserted her. The court also noted that a chancellor may still consider as a factor in the analysis the interest in preserving the natural parent relationship. [394]

[e] Relinquishment of legal custody. The Mississippi Supreme Court held that the natural parent presumption does not apply when parents "voluntarily relinquish custody of a minor child, through a court of competent jurisdiction."[395] A mother sought to regain custody of children after she and her husband relinquished custody to his parents. The court held that parents who voluntarily relinquish legal custody of their children can reclaim custody only upon showing by clear and convincing evidence that the change in custody is in the child's best interests.[396] In a subsequent application of this exception, the court of appeals held that a chancellor properly refused to modify custody from the paternal grandparents to the natural mother, who voluntarily relinquished custody of a child in divorce proceedings. The mother failed to show that the child's best interest would be served by returning custody to her – the child was thriving in a stable, secure environment.[397] The rule does not apply to parents whose children have been removed from them involuntarily. A father whose children were placed in foster care by the Department of Human Services did not voluntarily relinquish custody.[398] And, a parent who agrees to allow a third party to retain temporary custody pending a trial does not relinquish the natural parent presumption.[399]

[4] Natural parent visitation. When custody is awarded to a third party, the natural parent may be awarded visitation. For example, when custody was awarded to a child's paternal aunt, both the mother and grandparents were awarded visitation.[400] Visitation may be limited or restricted; a mother with a history of drug abuse was restricted to visitation in the presence of the child's grandmother.[401]

---

[394] Vaughn v. Vaughn, 36 So. 3d 1261, 1265-66 (Miss. 2010).

[395] Grant v. Martin, 757 So. 2d 264, 266 (Miss. 2000).

[396] Grant v. Martin, 757 So. 2d 264, 266 (Miss. 2000); *cf.* Ethredge v. Yawn, 605 So. 2d 761, 765 (Miss. 1992) (A father who had alternate weekend visitation with his son and provided some support for him while in grandmother's care did not abandon the child simply because he had signed waiver of process in guardianship proceeding when the child was an infant.); Schonewitz v. Pack, 913 So. 2d 416, 422 (Miss. Ct. App. 2005) (mother did not voluntarily relinquish custody when grandparents were awarded guardianship in a proceeding without notice to her).

[397] Callahan v. Davis, 869 So. 2d 434, 437 (Miss. Ct. App. 2004).

[398] *See* Barnett v. Oathout, 883 So. 2d 563, 569 (Miss. 2004) (requiring proof of material change in circumstances to modify custody).

[399] Vaughn v. Vaughn, 36 So. 3d 1261, 1265-66 (Miss. 2010) (to hold otherwise would discourage cooperative agreements pending trial).

[400] *See* Loomis v. Bugg, 872 So. 2d 694, 696 (Miss. Ct. App. 2004).

[401] Loomis v. Bugg, 872 So. 2d 694, 696 (Miss. Ct. App. 2004).

§ 12.06[5]   MISSISSIPPI FAMILY LAW

[5] Modification of third-party custody. In a case of first impression, the Mississippi Court of Appeals held that a natural parent who seeks to modify court-awarded third-party custody must prove a material change in circumstances in the third-party custodian's home. The fact that the mother had undergone rehabilitation, was working, attending church, and lived in a nice home, was not a basis for modifying custody.[402] The court distinguished the situation in which a parent voluntarily relinquishes custody, in which case the *Grant v. Martin* standard applies.[403] The court analogized the case to one in which DHS has placed a child in the custody of a third party, requiring proof of a material adverse change for the natural parent to regain custody.[404]

§ 12.07 CUSTODY ACTION BETWEEN TWO THIRD PARTIES

Custody is occasionally litigated between two parties neither of whom are the child's natural parents. In an action between third parties, the *Albright* factors apply to determine which of the parties should have custody.[405] For example, in a custody action between a child's maternal and paternal grandparents, the court weighed the relative merits of each family. The mother, who was imprisoned for the murder of the children's father, was not entitled to designate her parents as custodians. It was the court's duty to determine the children's best interests.[406] In an action between a maternal grandmother and paternal aunt, the court of appeals rejected the grandmother's argument that custody should have been awarded to her based on closer kinship. While kinship may be a factor for consideration, there is no rule preferring a third party based on the degree of kinship.[407] Third-party custody disputes may be heard by a chancery court under the general statutory authority to hear cases involving the custody and support of children.[408] Third-party disputes may also be resolved through habeas actions.[409]

§ 12.08 VISITATION

Visitation is the term traditionally used to describe the time a child spends with a noncustodial parent. Frequent ongoing contact is an important right of both parent and child; a noncustodial parent should be awarded substantial unrestricted visitation except in extreme circumstances. Visitation may also be awarded to a child's grandparents, although generally more limited in scope.

Visitation should be substantial, including overnight visits, holidays, and extended summer visits. During visitation, the noncustodial parent should have decision-mak-

---

[402] Adams v. Johnson, 33 So. 3d 551, 554-56 (Miss. Ct. App. 2010).

[403] See discussion *supra* § 12.06[3][a].

[404] Adams v. Johnson, 33 So. 3d 551, 555 (Miss. Ct. App. 2010).

[405] *In re* Guardianship of J.N.T., 910 So. 2d 631, 632-33 (Miss. Ct. App. 2005) (*Albright* factors control custody dispute between best friend of deceased mother and man who believed himself to be child's father); *see* Worley v. Jackson, 595 So. 2d 853, 855 (Miss. 1992) (custody dispute between maternal and paternal grandparents after mother was imprisoned for killing child's father); Loomis v. Bugg, 872 So. 2d 694, 697 (Miss. Ct. App. 2004).

[406] Worley v. Jackson, 595 So. 2d 853, 855 (Miss. 1992).

[407] Loomis v. Bugg, 872 So. 2d 694, 698 (Miss. Ct. App. 2004).

[408] *See* MISS. CODE ANN. § 93-11-65 (2004).

[409] *See* Gladney v. Hopkins, 102 So. 2d 181, 184 (Miss. 1958) (habeas action by maternal grandmother against paternal grandmother).

CHILD CUSTODY AND VISITATION   § 12.08[1]

ing rights regarding the child's activities, schedule, discipline, and religious training. Visitation should be restricted only to prevent harm to a child. Recently, attention has focused on the devastating effects of one parent's attempt to alienate a child from the other parent. Custodial parent interference may result in a finding of contempt, restrictions on the custodial parent, or in some cases, a change of custody.

[1] Noncustodial parent's rights. A noncustodial parent has a right to continued significant contact with a child under circumstances that foster a close relationship.[410] The Mississippi Supreme Court stated the test for awarding visitation as follows: "The best interests of the minor child should be the paramount consideration . . . while respecting the rights of the noncustodial parent and the objective of creating an environment conducive to developing as close and loving a relationship as possible between parent and child."[411] A court erred in awarding custody to one parent without addressing visitation rights of the other.[412]

[2] Scope of visitation. Except in unusual circumstances, a noncustodial parent is entitled to unrestricted and substantial visitation.[413] The Mississippi Supreme Court reversed an award of once-monthly weekend visitation and one week in the summer, holding that "the children at the least are entitled to the company of their mother two full week-ends a month . . . and a five-week period during summer vacation."[414] Visitation orders have been reversed because they provided no summer visitation,[415] no holiday visitation,[416] less than two weekends a month,[417] or only a week of summer visitation.[418] However, a chancellor has substantial discretion in awarding visitation. A court's award of four weeks of summer visitation rather than five was not an abuse of discretion.[419] Nor did a court err in ordering two two-week periods of summer

---

[410] Harrington v. Harrington, 648 So. 2d 543, 545 (Miss. 1994) (error to restrict visitation). The Uniform Marriage and Divorce Act provides that a noncustodial parent is "entitled" to visitation unless the court determines in a hearing that the child's physical or emotional health is in danger. UNIFORM MARRIAGE AND DIVORCE ACT [UMDA] § 407(a).

[411] Chalk v. Lentz, 744 So. 2d 789, 792 (Miss. Ct. App. 1999); *see* Dunn v. Dunn, 609 So. 2d 1277, 1286 (Miss. 1992); White v. Thompson, 569 So. 2d 1181, 1185 (Miss. 1990); Clark v. Myrick, 523 So. 2d 79, 83 (Miss. 1988); Cox v. Moulds, 490 So. 2d 866, 870 (Miss. 1986).

[412] Benal v. Benal, 22 So. 3d 369, 377 (Miss. Ct. App. 2009).

[413] *See* Cassell v. Cassell, 970 So. 2d 267, 272-73 (Miss. Ct. App. 2007) (error to restrict father's visitation based on confrontation with wife as she left marital home); Cox v. Moulds, 490 So. 2d 866, 870 (Miss. 1986) (error to restrict father's overnight visitation with daughter because she had to sleep on the couch).

[414] Crowson v. Moseley, 480 So. 2d 1150, 1153 (Miss. 1985); *see also* Messer v. Messer, 850 So. 2d 161, 167 (Miss. Ct. App. 2003) ("liberal" visitation means two weekends a month until Sunday afternoon, and at least five weeks in the summer); *cf.* Chalk v. Lentz, 744 So. 2d 789, 792 (Miss. Ct. App. 1999) (same). *But cf.* Marshall v. Harris, 981 So. 2d 345, 350-51 (Miss. Ct. App. 2008) (four weeks in summer adequate; chancellor has substantial discretion in awarding visitation); Horn v. Horn, 909 So. 2d 1151, 1162 (Miss. Ct. App. 2005) (chancellor did not err in ordering four weeks of summer visitation rather than five weeks; more limited amount of summer visitation reasonable in light of father's emotional problems).

[415] *See* Fields v. Fields, 830 So. 2d 1266, 1269 (Miss. Ct. App. 2002).

[416] *See* Fields v. Fields, 830 So. 2d 1266, 1269 (Miss. Ct. App. 2002).

[417] *See* Crowson v. Moseley, 480 So. 2d 1150, 1153 (Miss. 1985) (reversing order giving mother one weekend and one night a month and six days in summer).

[418] *See* Crowson v. Moseley, 480 So. 2d 1150, 1153 (Miss. 1985) (reversing order giving mother one weekend and one night a month and six days in summer); Mixon v. Mixon, 724 So. 2d 956, 961 (Miss. Ct. App. 1998).

[419] Marshall v. Harris, 981 So. 2d 345, 350-51 (Miss. Ct. App. 2008).

§ 12.08[2]   **MISSISSIPPI FAMILY LAW**

visitation.[420] Overnight visitation should not be limited unless necessary to protect a child.[421]

Unusual work schedules or substantial distance may justify deviation from the typical every-other-weekend schedule.[422] For example, an order might provide for less frequent but longer visits to avoid disruptive travel. When a custodial mother moved two hundred miles from the father, the court properly granted the father extended weekend visitation.[423] An award of six weeks in the summer and other visitation to be arranged on a flexible schedule was appropriate where the distance between parents was a thirty-two-hour trip.[424] Similarly, a chancellor properly awarded an offshore worker alternate weekends when he was available and ordered the mother to make the children available for visitation outside this schedule.[425]

More limited visitation may be ordered when a child is an infant, depending on the circumstances and parenting skills of the noncustodial parent and the distance between the parties.[426] For example, a court awarded a father limited visitation with an infant living in California, to increase when the child was older. [427] Courts may award more extended visitation if the evidence suggests that additional time with the noncustodial parent is in the child's best interest. A chancellor erred in refusing to extend a mother's weekend visitation through Sunday night when the only evidence presented was a psychologist's report that extended visitation would benefit the children.[428] However, a chancellor did not err in awarding a father standard visitation even though the guardian ad litem recommended liberal visitation. More extensive visitation would require modification when the children started school. The court also pointed out that constantly shifting children back and forth between parents is not in their best interest.[429]

Visitation orders are typically detailed, specifying the dates of visitation and, in some cases, exact times and transfer arrangements. But an order may provide for "reasonable" or "liberal" visitation to be arranged by the parties.[430] Unless parents can work

---

[420] Strange v. Strange, 43 So. 3d 1169, 1172 (Miss. Ct. App. 2010) (rejecting father's argument that he was entitled to "standard" visitation; there is no "standard" visitation).

[421] Wood v. Wood, 579 So. 2d 1271, 1273 (Miss. 1991) (parent presumptively entitled to overnight visitation; no reason to limit father who had regular summer visitation to weekday visitation during the year).

[422] A noncustodial parent in Florida was awarded visitation of one weekend a month rather than two. See Callahan v. Davis, 869 So. 2d 434, 438 (Miss. Ct. App. 2004). But cf. Swiderski v. Swiderski, 18 So. 3d 280, 285-86 (Miss. Ct. App. 2009) (court did not err in awarding a father every-other-weekend visitation while encouraging the mother to work with him to establish visitation that fit his schedule); Fountain v. Fountain, 877 So. 2d 474, 480 (Miss. Ct. App. 2003) (awarding standard visitation to Mississippi father with children in Tampa, Florida).

[423] See Ballard v. Ballard, 843 So. 2d 76, 79-80 (Miss. Ct. App. 2003); see also Stevison v. Woods, 560 So. 2d 176, 181 (Miss. 1990) (suggesting in remand that visitation for entire summer might be appropriate where children lived in Virginia and noncustodial mother in Mississippi).

[424] See Olson v. Olson, 799 So. 2d 927, 930 (Miss. Ct. App. 2001) (court rejected mother's argument that father refused to cooperate in arranging visitation).

[425] See Burge v. Burge, 851 So. 2d 384, 388 (Miss. Ct. App. 2003).

[426] See Balius v. Gaines, 908 So. 2d 791, 795-96 (Miss. Ct. App. 2005) (father of one-year-old child initially awarded holiday visitation and daily weekday visitation, to change to overnight then weekend visitation as child grew older; further, where custodial mother moved to California, father awarded summer, holiday, and weekend visitation, optional holiday visitation, and optional visitation on the third weekend of each month).

[427] See In re Filiation of M.D.B., 914 So. 2d 316, 321 (Miss. Ct. App. 2005).

[428] Wilburn v. Wilburn, 991 So. 2d 1185, 1194-95 (Miss. 2008) (denial was improperly based on mother's conduct at hearing).

[429] Henderson v. Henderson, 952 So. 2d 273, 279 (Miss. Ct. App. 2006).

[430] See Chalk v. Lentz, 744 So. 2d 789, 791 (Miss. Ct. App. 1999).

CHILD CUSTODY AND VISITATION § 12.08[3]

cooperatively, however, a flexible schedule may be an invitation to post-divorce litigation.[431]

[3] Responsibility for transportation. A court may order parents to share responsibility for travel or assign the obligation to one parent. Although no explicit holding to this effect was found, it appears that Mississippi courts historically placed the burden of travel on the noncustodial parent.[432] In 1998, however, the court of appeals rejected a fixed rule that the noncustodial parent bears all transportation expenses. The court held that a custodial parent's obligation to foster a child's relationship with the other parent may require shared responsibility for transportation. In fact, imposing all costs on a noncustodial parent could be error if the expense substantially impairs visitation.[433] Shared responsibility for travel was properly imposed on parents who lived in Michigan and Mississippi. The court ordered the father to deliver the child halfway twice a year, with all other responsibility for travel on the mother.[434] On the other hand, the mere fact that a custodial parent chooses to move does not automatically require shared expenses.[435] A chancellor could reasonably determine that requiring a custodial mother with limited resources to share travel costs would diminish funds needed for the child's support.[436]

[4] Restrictions on visitation. A noncustodial parent has decision-making authority during visitation and broad discretion as to the manner and place for visitation.[437] A court may restrict visitation only if some aspect of visitation is harmful to a child.[438] As the Mississippi Supreme Court explained:

> [V]isitation rights of the non-custodial parent should be tantamount to custody with respect to the place and manner of exercise of same, except in the most unusual circumstances . . . . something approaching actual danger or other substantial detriment to the children – as distinguished from personal inconvenience or possible offense to middle-class sensibilities – is required before a chancellor may restrict visitation.[439]

---

[431] *See* Sistrunck v. McKenzie, 455 So. 2d 768, 770 (Miss. 1984) (modifying order providing for "reasonable" visitation to provide specific visitation in light of custodial parent's refusal to provide visitation).

[432] *See, e.g.,* Hulse v. Hulse, 724 So. 2d 918, 919 (Miss. Ct. App. 1998) (rejecting the chancellor's reliance on *Love v. Barnett*, 611 So. 2d 205, 207 (Miss. 1992), in which the chancellor stated, "we've always pretty well stuck to the visiting parent is responsible for the pick up and delivery of the children"). The *Hulse* court noted that this ruling was not an issue on appeal in *Love. Id.*

[433] *See* Hulse v. Hulse, 724 So. 2d 918, 919 (Miss. Ct. App. 1998).

[434] *See* Olson v. Olson, 799 So. 2d 927, 930 (Miss. Ct. App. 2001); *see also* Balius v. Gaines, 908 So. 2d 791, 798 (Miss. Ct. App. 2005) (custodial mother who moved to California to share expense of summer and holiday visitation; father responsible for optional holiday and monthly visitation).

[435] *See* Ballard v. Ballard, 843 So. 2d 76, 80 (Miss. Ct. App. 2003).

[436] Ballard v. Ballard, 843 So. 2d 76, 80 (Miss. Ct. App. 2003) (rejecting a father's argument that the mother should share visitation travel costs since she chose to move from north to south Mississippi).

[437] Cox v. Moulds, 490 So. 2d 866, 870 (Miss. 1986).

[438] Brocato v. Brocato, 731 So. 2d 1138, 1143 (Miss. 1999) (error to limit mother's visitation with daughter where she was considered fit custodian of son).

[439] Cox v. Moulds, 490 So. 2d 866, 868 (Miss. 1986); *see also* Cassell v. Cassell, 970 So. 2d 267, 272-73 (Miss. Ct. App. 2007) (error to restrict father's visitation based on confrontation with wife as she left marital home). *But cf.* R.L.N. v. C.P.N., 931 So. 2d 620, 626 (Miss. Ct. App. 2005) (visitation restrictions are within chancellor's "sound discretion").

377

§ 12.08[4][a]   MISSISSIPPI FAMILY LAW

Appropriate visitation restrictions often relate to abusive behavior, drug or alcohol abuse, or mental illness. In some cases, restrictions related to a parent's sexual conduct are permissible. Restrictions may include ordering supervised visitation as well as ordering a parent to enter counseling or a treatment program. Parents may be ordered to refrain from using drugs or alcohol, to submit to drug tests, or to refrain from visitation in the presence of certain third parties.

[a] **Abusive behavior.** Restrictions on visitation should be ordered if a parent has physically or sexually abused his or her child or other children.[440] In addition, restrictions may be needed if a child has been abused by someone else while in the parent's care.[441] A court may order a parent's time with a child supervised by a responsible third party or agency, or, in extreme cases, suspend visitation altogether. A chancellor did not err in denying any visitation to a father who sexually abused one of his daughters.[442] When a child had been abused, but it was unclear whether her father was the abuser, denial of all visitation was error. Supervised visitation was appropriate.[443] Restrictions were properly denied when a child's symptoms of abuse were explained by other health problems.[444] A court may also restrict visitation in the presence of others who pose a genuine threat to a child. A chancellor properly ordered that neither parent permit their children to visit unsupervised with the paternal grandmother, who had been abusive to the children.[445]

Allegations of physical or sexual abuse present courts with the daunting task of protecting children from physical danger without allowing a bitter parent to destroy a child's relationship with the other based on false allegations. In any case in which physical or sexual abuse is alleged, the court is required to appoint a guardian ad litem for the child to assist in evaluating the case.[446] Courts may also order that all parties

---

[440] *See* Lewis v. Butler, 794 So. 2d 1015, 1018 (Miss. 2001) (father made sexual advances toward one child; visitation with all denied); *cf.* Craft v. Craft, 32 So. 3d 1232, 1236-38 (Miss. Ct. App. 2010) (affirming supervised visitation for father arrested for sexual battery of a minor even though children testified that they preferred to live with him); Jones v. Jones, 43 So. 3d 465, 480 (Miss. Ct. App. 2009) (court erred in awarding unsupervised visitation to father without appropriate investigation of abuse allegations).

[441] *See* H.L.S. v. R.S.R., 949 So. 2d 794, 800 (Miss. Ct. App. 2006) (court of appeals reversed and remanded for chancellor to reconsider ordering supervised visitation for six-year-old girl who was kissed by teenage half-brother); Doe v. Doe, 644 So. 2d 1199, 1207-08 (Miss. 1994) (unclear who abused child).

[442] *In re* S.C. v. State, 795 So. 2d 526, 532 (Miss. 2001); *see* Lewis v. Butler, 794 So. 2d 1015, 1018 (Miss. 2001) (father made sexual advances toward one child; visitation with all denied); *see also* R.L.N. v. C.P.N., 931 So. 2d 620, 626-27 (Miss. Ct. App. 2005) (court hearing conflicting testimony did not err in finding abuse by father, terminating visitation, and reserving jurisdiction to review case in six months). *But cf. In re* T.A.P., 742 So. 2d 1095, 1104-05 (Miss. 1999) (denying father all visitation or right to work with DHS for reunification was impermissible de facto termination of parental rights).

[443] *See* Doe v. Doe, 644 So. 2d 1199, 1207-08 (Miss. 1994). *But cf.* Suber v. Suber, 936 So. 2d 945, 948 (Miss. Ct. App. 2006) (chancellor properly denied visitation with a father in California after both children testified that the father sexually abused them, even though no other evidence of abuse).

[444] *See* Bratcher v. Surrette, 848 So. 2d 893, 897 (Miss. Ct. App. 2003) (chancellor's finding of no abuse upheld); *see also* Gregory v. Gregory, 881 So. 2d 840, 845-46 (Miss. Ct. App. 2003) (mother's allegations made in good faith, although court found no sexual abuse).

[445] *See* Williams v. Williams, 656 So. 2d 325, 330 (Miss. 1995); *cf.* Harrington v. Harrington, 648 So. 2d 543, 546 (Miss. 1994) (harsh language toward child on two occasions not enough to ban father's girlfriend from children's presence).

[446] MISS. CODE ANN. §§ 93-5-23 (2004), 93-11-65 (2004), 97-5-42 (2006).

378

CHILD CUSTODY AND VISITATION   § 12.08[4][b]

undergo physical or psychological examinations in connection with custody cases.[447] When allegations of abuse are made in custody proceedings, the chancery court must proceed under youth court rules.[448] Parents who make unfounded accusations of abuse must be ordered to pay costs and attorneys' fees associated with the claim.[449]

[b] Family or spousal violence. Time with a parent with a history of family violence may be restricted or supervised. Family violence is defined as a pattern of violence or one incident causing serious injury, directed against a family or household member.[450] If visitation is to be supervised by a member of the noncustodial parent's family, the court must set conditions to be followed during visitation. A parent with a history of violence may be ordered to attend counseling sessions as a condition of visitation or to refrain from alcohol or drug consumption for twenty-four hours prior to visitation.[451] A court has considerable discretion in determining what protections to put in place. A chancellor did not err in refusing to restrict a father's visitation after he was charged with domestic assault. The court ordered him to complete anger management and ordered that visitation exchanges occur at the sheriff's office.[452]

[c] Dangerous conduct. Restrictions may be ordered if a parent engages in conduct that endangers a child. For example, a mother who abused alcohol and had been involved in several wrecks was ordered to refrain from driving with her child in the car.[453] Similarly, a mother with a history of illegal drug use was limited to visitation when the child's grandmother was present.[454] A father who admitted to alcohol and drug problems, tested positive for crystal meth, and failed to take recommended drug tests was properly limited to once-a-week supervised visitation with his young daughter.[455]

[d] Emotional abuse. A court may restrict visitation with a parent who is emotionally abusive.[456] In lieu of restricting visitation or in addition to restrictions, a court may order counseling and set a specific time period to review the case.[457] Furthermore, visitation in the presence of other family members may be restricted if their behavior is emotionally harmful to a child. A chancellor properly restricted the time a child could spend alone with a grandmother who made unfounded accusations of sexual abuse by the mother.[458]

---

[447] *See* Miss. R. Civ. P. 35.

[448] See *infra* § 19.06[5].

[449] Miss. Code Ann. § 93-5-23 (2004).

[450] Miss. Code Ann. § 93-5-24 (9)(a)(i) (2004).

[451] Miss. Code Ann. § 93-5-24 (6)(d) (2004).

[452] Holliday v. Stockman, 969 So. 2d 136, 141 (Miss. Ct. App. 2007).

[453] Johnson v. Gray, 859 So. 2d 1006, 1012 (Miss. 2003).

[454] Loomis v. Bugg, 872 So. 2d 694, 696 (Miss. Ct. App. 2004).

[455] McDuffie v. McDuffie, 21 So. 3d 685, 693 (Miss. Ct. App. 2009).

[456] *See* Elrod, *supra* note 3, § 6:18 (noting that courts carefully review claims of emotional abuse between divorced parents).

[457] *See* Louk v. Louk, 761 So. 2d 878, 882-83 (Miss. 2000) (chancellor did not err in ordering unrestricted visitation with father with explosive temper, subject to continued counseling and review in 180 days).

[458] R.B.S. v. T.M.S., 765 So. 2d 616, 620 (Miss. Ct. App. 2000).

§ 12.08[4][e]   MISSISSIPPI FAMILY LAW

[e] Potential kidnapping. A court should restrict visitation with a parent who has abducted or is likely to abduct children. A father who hid children from their mother for seventeen months was properly restricted to overnight visitation at the grandparents' home for a period of one year.[459] A court did not err in restricting a mother's visitation to once a week in the father's home; she disobeyed a court order modifying custody, abducted the children, and hid them in New Orleans.[460] However, all visitation should not have been denied to a custodial mother who interfered with visitation; she should have been awarded supervised or restricted visitation.[461]

The newly-enacted Uniform Child Abduction Prevention Act authorizes chancellors to take broad protective measures when child kidnapping appears imminent. These include restricting a parent's travel, restricting visitation, prohibiting removal of a child, ordering relinquishment of passports, imposing a bond, and entering an emergency, ex parte custody order.[462] By statute, it is also a crime for a noncustodial parent or other person to remove a child under the age of fourteen from the state with the intention of violating a custody order.[463]

[f] Imprisonment. The Mississippi Supreme Court recently addressed the issue of visitation with an imprisoned parent. The court acknowledged that most courts hold that imprisonment is not, in itself, a reason to deny visitation.[464] In the case at bar, however, the imprisoned father was seeking to modify an order suspending visitation. The court held that visitation should not have been ordered without a showing that modification was in the child's best interest, including specific testimony regarding the effect on a child of visiting in a prison environment.[465]

[g] Mental health. Visitation may be limited or supervised if a parent's mental health or substance abuse presents a danger of physical or emotional harm to a child. A court properly required supervised visitation with a mother who was suicidal, engaged in self-mutilation, had blackouts, and had violent thoughts toward her husband and one child.[466] However, a chancellor did not err in denying a mother's request for a father's mental examination when the record did not support that he presented a danger to the child.[467]

---

[459] *See* Rakestraw v. Rakestraw, 543 So. 2d 174, 176 (Miss. 1989) (also required to post *ne exeat* bond; judgment for $15,000 for mother's cost in locating children).

[460] Newsom v. Newsom, 557 So. 2d 511, 517 (Miss. 1990).

[461] Saint v. Quick, 24 So. 3d 395, 404 (Miss. Ct. App. 2009).

[462] MISS. CODE ANN. § 93-29-15(c) (Supp. 2010).

[463] MISS. CODE ANN. § 97-3-51(3) (Supp. 2010) (punishable by fine of up to $2000 or imprisonment for up to three years); *see also* MISS. CODE ANN. § 97-3-53 (Supp. 2010) (crime punishable by life imprisonment to kidnap child under sixteen).

[464] *See* Christian v. Wheat, 876 So. 2d 341, 346 (Miss. 2004) (denial of visitation usually linked to violent behavior and danger to child).

[465] Christian v. Wheat, 876 So. 2d 341, 345 (Miss. 2004).

[466] *See* Morris v. Morris, 783 So. 2d 681, 693 (Miss. 2001) (lesbian relationship also a factor); *see also* Horn v. Horn, 909 So. 2d 1151, 1162 (Miss. Ct. App. 2005) (chancellor did not err in ordering four weeks of summer visitation rather than five weeks; more limited amount of summer visitation reasonable in light of father's emotional problems). *But cf.* Saunders v. Saunders, 724 So. 2d 1132, 1136 (Miss. Ct. App. 1998) (change from supervised to unsupervised visitation; evidence did not support mother's allegations of father's behavioral problems).

[467] LeBlanc v. Andrews, 931 So. 2d 683, 688 (Miss. Ct. App. 2006).

CHILD CUSTODY AND VISITATION § 12.08[4][h]

[h] Poor parenting or household conditions. Poor parenting skills, short of neglect or abuse, are not ordinarily a reason to limit visitation. However, supervised or restricted visitation may be appropriate with regard to infants. The court of appeals held that a chancellor properly limited a father's overnight visits with an infant daughter to his parents' house, in light of concern about his parenting skills.[468] Overnight visitation should not be denied simply because a noncustodial parent's home is less than ideal for a child. Restricting overnight visitation because a thirteen-year-old girl did not have a separate bedroom and had to sleep on the couch was error.[469]

[i] Sexual conduct. At one time, an unmarried parent's sexual conduct was presumed to have an adverse impact on a child; restrictions on visitation were readily upheld. Today, restrictions based on sexual conduct are permitted only upon a showing of actual adverse effect. Appellate courts are quick to reverse broad restrictions, such as an order barring a mother's visitation in the company of any man who was not a member of her family.[470] Similarly, appellate courts have reversed orders barring fathers from any visitation in the presence of women with whom they had affairs.[471] Overnight visitation restrictions will be affirmed, however, if there is actual evidence of emotional harm to a child.[472] A father was properly ordered to refrain from overnights with his girlfriend present, based on testimony that the child was traumatized by the visits and required treatment for depression.[473]

Restrictions related to a parent's same-sex relationship are subject to the same test. The supreme court held that a chancellor erred in prohibiting a noncustodial father from visiting with his fourteen-year-old son in the presence of his live-in partner.[474] Similarly, the court of appeals reversed an order restricting a lesbian mother to visitation for one hour a week at McDonald's. Emphasizing that parents are ordinarily entitled to overnight visits, the court held that restrictions should be imposed only to prevent harm to a child.[475] But the court of appeals upheld overnight restrictions in light of evidence that a mother's nudity with her partner had an adverse impact on her children.[476]

[j] Activities. Restrictions on other aspects of family life are rarely permitted. For example, the supreme court held that a father should not be prohibited from taking his children flying: "Until a custodial parent can prove that the non-custodial parent demonstrated irresponsible conduct or . . . that the activity would actually endanger or

---

[468] *See* Hill v. Brinkley , 840 So. 2d 778, 780 (Miss. Ct. App. 2003).

[469] Cox v. Moulds, 490 So. 2d 866, 870-71 (Miss. 1986).

[470] *See, e.g.,* Rushing v. Rushing, 724 So. 2d 911, 917 (Miss. 1998).

[471] *See* Dunn v. Dunn, 609 So. 2d 1277 (Miss. 1992); Carr v. Carr, 724 So. 2d 937, 941-42 (Miss. Ct. App. 1998).

[472] Harrington v. Harrington, 648 So. 2d 543, 547 (Miss. 1994) (no proof that father's relationship with live-in girlfriend was detrimental to daughters).

[473] Robison v. Robison, 722 So. 2d 601, 605 (Miss. 1998).

[474] *See* Weigand v. Houghton, 730 So. 2d 581, 587 (Miss. 1999) ("even if Paul is embarrassed, or does not like the living arrangement of his father, this is not the type of harm that rises to the level necessary to place such restrictions on David's visitation"). *But cf.* White v. Thompson, 569 So. 2d 1181, 1185 (Miss. 1990) (upholding third-party custody over custody to lesbian mother; affirming restrictions on visitation in presence of lesbian partner).

[475] *See* Fulk v. Fulk, 827 So. 2d 736, 743 (Miss. Ct. App. 2002).

[476] *See* Lacey v. Lacey, 822 So. 2d 1132, 1138 (Miss. Ct. App. 2002).

§ 12.08[4][k]   **MISSISSIPPI FAMILY LAW**

result in injury to their children, she or he is not authorized to interfere with the former spouse's visitation rights."[477] Similarly, a court had no authority to order a father to refrain from discussing his girlfriend with his children.[478] A custodial parent may not dictate a child's schedule, activities, or exposure to ideas during visitation. For example, a father may decide that a child should not participate in some activities scheduled by the mother during his visitation time.[479]

As a general rule, the constitutional right to freedom of religion prevents courts from ordering a noncustodial parent to take a child to religious services.[480] The Mississippi Supreme Court has held that a chancellor may not order church attendance but may suggest that parents take responsibility for religious training.[481]

[k] Child's wishes. Courts are generally reluctant to limit visitation in response to a child's wishes, which may have been prompted by a custodial parent's influence, a desire to avoid discipline, or dissatisfaction with minor aspects of visitation. Expressing these concerns, the Mississippi Supreme Court stated that a child's wishes are "clearly insufficient as a matter of law" to restrict visitation.[482] A chancellor properly refused to accede to a child's desire not to visit her father; her views were influenced by her mother's ongoing attempts to alienate her from the father.[483] Similarly, a mother was held in contempt for interrupting summer visitation. Her children's complaints that they were not enjoying the visit, did not get enough breakfast, and had to spend too much time at their stepmother's restaurant were not a reason to curtail visitation.[484] In some cases, however, restrictions may be justified by extreme hostility attributable in part to the noncustodial parent. An older child's visitation was properly suspended with her father, who did not make an effort to repair their deteriorated relationship.[485]

[5] Custodial parent interference with visitation. A custodial parent's attempt to interfere with visitation may result in restrictions on the custodial parent. The Mississippi Court of Appeals affirmed an order prohibiting a custodial mother from contacting her child during visitation and requiring that she refrain from scheduling events for the child during visitation.[486] Interference with visitation may also support a finding of

---

[477] Mord v. Peters, 571 So. 2d 981, 986 n.6 (Miss. 1990).

[478] Harrington v. Harringon, 648 So. 2d 543, 546 (Miss. 1994).

[479] *See* Ellis v. Ellis, 840 So. 2d 806, 813 (Miss. Ct. App. 2003).

[480] ELROD, *supra* note 3, § 6:21.

[481] *See* McLemore v. McLemore, 762 So. 2d 316, 320 (Miss. 2000). A chancellor may include a suggestion that parents provide religious training, worded as follows: "Both the mother and father should be vitally interested in seeing that their children get regular and systematic spiritual training. Whether it be by attending Sunday School each Sunday or Church or both is for the parents alone to decide." *Id.*

[482] Cox v. Moulds, 490 So. 2d 866, 870 (Miss. 1986) (children may be "more interested in the desire of the moment than in considering their long range needs for the development of a healthy relationship with both parents").

[483] Ellis v. Ellis, 840 So. 2d 806, 813 (Miss. Ct. App. 2003).

[484] Strain v. Strain, 847 So. 2d 276, 278 (Miss. Ct. App. 2003).

[485] McCracking v. Champaigne, 805 So. 2d 586, 590 (Miss. Ct. App. 2001) (father failed to attend classes as ordered; could still try to repair relationship and resume visitation).

[486] *See* Ellis v. Ellis, 840 So. 2d 806, 813-14 (Miss. Ct. App. 2003); *see also* Cavett v. Cavett, 744 So. 2d 372, 377 (Miss. Ct. App. 1999) (chancellor restricted parents from calling child during time with other parent, except for emergencies); *cf.* Cossitt v. Cossitt, 975 So. 2d 274, 281 (Miss. Ct. App. 2008) (refusing to allow custodial mother to read father's emails to child, but admonishing father not to send daughter inappropriate pictures).

CHILD CUSTODY AND VISITATION   § 12.09

contempt[487] and, in extreme cases, modification of custody.[488] A court may order a custodial parent who denies visitation to provide the noncustodial parent with additional visitation to compensate for lost time with the child.[489]

§ 12.09 THIRD-PARTY VISITATION

Parents have a constitutionally protected right to the custody and control of their children free from interference from the state or others. Traditionally, third parties had no legal right to seek visitation with a child over parents' objections.[490] In recent years, however, legislatures have recognized that children may have a close bond with grandparents and other household members. All states, including Mississippi, now recognize some form of grandparent visitation and some states extend visitation rights to other third parties.[491]

[1] Constitutionality. The validity of third-party visitation statutes was brought into question in 2000 when the United States Supreme Court in *Troxel v. Granville* invalidated Washington's broad third-party visitation statute.[492] The Washington statute allowed courts to award visitation to "any person" at "any time" if visitation would serve the child's best interests.[493] The Supreme Court held the statute unconstitutional. First, parents' wishes were given no weight under the statute; the scheme failed to protect parents' "fundamental constitutional right to make decisions" regarding child-rearing.[494] Second, no consideration was given to the fact that the mother offered to allow the child to visit once a month and on special holidays. The Supreme Court distinguished the Washington statute from state statutes that require a finding that parents unreasonably denied visitation and that visitation would not interfere with the parent-child relationship.[495]

[2] Grandparent visitation in Mississippi

[a] Statutory requirements. The Mississippi statute permits grandparent visitation in two situations. First, when a parent dies, loses custody, or loses parental rights,

---

[487] *See* discussion *infra* § 12.12.

[488] *See infra* § 12.11[12].

[489] *See* Ellis v. Ellis, 952 So. 2d 982, 995-96 (Miss. Ct. App. 2006) (trial court awarded father September visitation to make up for missed summer visit, even though award required that child attend different school); McDonald v. McDonald, 850 So. 2d. 1152, 1155-56 (Miss. Ct. App. 2004) (chancellor found father in contempt for visitation interference; ordered immediate extended visitation for mother). See *infra* § 12.05 for discussion of restrictions on parents in general.

[490] *In re* Adoption of a Minor, 558 So. 2d 854, 856 (Miss 1990).

[491] *See* ELROD, *supra* note 3, § 7:01.

[492] 530 U.S. 57 (2006).

[493] *See* WASH. REV. CODE § 26.10.160(3) (1997). *Troxel* involved a petition for visitation by the paternal grandparents, whose son had committed suicide. Troxel v. Granville, 530 U.S. 57, 60 (2000). The mother of the two children had attempted to limit the grandparents' visitation to one short visit a month. *Id.* The court ordered visitation of one weekend per month, one week during the summer, and four hours on both of the grandparents' birthdays. *Id.* at 75.

[494] Troxel v. Granville, 530 U.S. 57, 70 (2000).

[495] Troxel v. Granville, 530 U.S. 57, 70-71 (2000).

§ 12.09[2][b]   MISSISSIPPI FAMILY LAW

his or her parents may petition for visitation (Type 1).[496] Visitation may be granted if the court finds that it is in the child's best interests.[497] Second, grandparents may petition for visitation if (1) the grandparent had a viable relationship with the child (either of the grandparents provided some financial support for at least six months and had frequent visitation, including overnights, for at least one year); (2) the parent or custodian unreasonably denied visitation; and (3) visitation would be in the child's best interests (Type 2).[498]

[b] Constitutionality. The Mississippi Supreme Court has rejected constitutional challenges to the Mississippi statute under *Troxel*. In contrast to the Washington statute, the Mississippi statute is narrowly drawn.[499] Type 2 visitation requires a finding that the child's parents have unreasonably denied visitation, a factor absent in the Washington statute. Type 1 does not expressly require a finding of unreasonable refusal, leaving it open to a *Troxel* challenge. However, the Mississippi Supreme Court cured any statutory deficiency in Type 1 visitation; the court held in *Zeman v. Stanford* that chancellors may order grandparent visitation only after considering the factors set out in *Martin v. Coop*, which expressly includes parental wishes as a factor.[500]

[3] Additional factors. In addition to finding that a grandparent meets the statutory requirements set out above, a court must consider the factors in *Martin v. Coop* to determine whether visitation is in a child's best interest. These include (1) potential disruption in the child's life; (2) suitability of the grandparents' home; (3) the child's age; (4) the age and physical and mental health of the grandparents; (5) the emotional ties between grandparent and child; (6) the grandparents' moral fitness; (7) physical distance from the parents' home; (8) any undermining of the parents' discipline; (9) the grandparents' employment responsibilities; and (10) the grandparents' willingness not to interfere with the parents' rearing of the child.[501] Visitation awards and denials have been reversed because a chancellor did not consider these factors in determining grandparent visitation.[502]

[4] Application

[a] Type 1 visitation. Type 1 visitation requires a finding that the petition-

---

[496] Miss. Code Ann. § 93-16-3(1) (2004).

[497] Miss. Code Ann. § 93-16-5 (2004).

[498] Miss. Code Ann. §§ 93-16-3(2) to -3(3) (2004); *see* Dearman v. Dearman, 811 So. 2d 308, 314-15 (Miss. Ct. App. 2001) (upholding visitation to grandparents who had custody for six years, based on a viable relationship with child; no express finding that parent unreasonably denied visitation).

[499] Stacy v. Ross, 798 So. 2d 1275, 1279-80 (Miss. 2001) (Mississippi statute narrowly tailored).

[500] *See* Zeman v. Stanford, 789 So. 2d 798, 803 (Miss. 2001) (listing factors in *Martin v. Coop*, 693 So. 2d 912, 916 (Miss. 1997)).

[501] *See* Martin v. Coop, 693 So. 2d 912, 916 (Miss. 1997).

[502] *See* Townes v. Manyfield, 883 So. 2d 93, 97 (Miss. 2004); T.T.W. v. C.C., 839 So. 2d 501, 505 (Miss. 2003) (reversing denial of visitation for failure to consider factors); Morgan v. West, 812 So. 2d 987, 992 (Miss. 2002) (reversing award for failure to consider the amount of potential disruption, the suitability of the grandparents' home and their moral fitness, the distance from the child's home, and whether the grandparents undermined the parents' discipline or interfered with their rearing of the child); Givens v. Nicholson, 878 So. 2d 1073 (Miss. Ct. App. 2004).

CHILD CUSTODY AND VISITATION § 12.09[4][b]

er's child has lost custody rights and that, applying the *Coop* factors, visitation is in the child's best interests. Visitation rights have been readily awarded to grandparents whose child has lost custody[503] or is deceased.[504]

[b] Type 2 visitation. Type 2 visitation, ordered over the objection of a petitioner's own child, requires a greater showing of grandparent involvement in the child's life than Type 1. A petitioner must show that the parents unreasonably denied visitation, that the petitioner had a viable relationship with the child, and that the *Coop* factors indicate visitation would be in the child's best interests.[505]

The Mississippi Supreme Court is protective of parental rights when a petitioner's own child objects to visitation. The court has emphasized that parents have a paramount right to control their children's environment and that only compelling circumstances should override that right.[506] The court reversed an award of unsupervised visitation several hours from a child's home over both parents' objections. The court held that "forced, extensive unsupervised visitation" should not be awarded "absent compelling circumstances which suggest something near unfitness of the custodial parents."[507] A thirteen-year-old girl's monthly Saturday visits with her grandfather were properly discontinued because the visitation was disruptive and the mother's relationship with him was contentious.[508] In one case, however, the court of appeals affirmed grandparent visitation for a fourteen-year-old girl over her mother's objection and even though the child did not want to visit her grandmother.[509] The court refused to accord the same deference to adoptive maternal grandparents who kept a child from its paternal grandparents. The court found visitation in the child's best interests – the paternal grandparents were fit, lived near the child, were willing to cooperate with the maternal grandparents, and had a close relationship with the child.[510]

[5] Scope of visitation. To determine the appropriate amount of grandparent visitation, courts apply the *Martin v. Coop* factors.[511] Except in unusual circumstances, grandparent visitation should not be not the equivalent of noncustodial parent visitation.[512] The supreme court held that grandparent visitation every other weekend, four

---

[503] *See* Zeman v. Stanford, 789 So. 2d 798, 804 (Miss. 2001); Settle v. Galloway, 682 So. 2d 1032, 1034-35 (Miss. 1996).

[504] *See* Martin v. Coop, 693 So. 2d 912, 916 (Miss. 1997); Howell v. Rogers, 551 So. 2d 904, 906 (Miss. 1989).

[505] Conerly v. Davis, 46 So. 3d 858, 859 (Miss. Ct. App. 2010) (Type 2 requires showing of "viable relationship"; Type I does not); Solomon v. Robertson, 980 So. 2d 319, 322 (Miss. Ct. App. 2008) (rejecting mother's argument that paternal grandparents must show "viable relationship" – requirement applicable to Type 2 visitation only).

[506] *See* Stacy v. Ross, 798 So. 2d 1275, 1280 (Miss. 2001) (noting that the determination whether parents have acted unreasonably "is not a contest between equals"); *cf.* Hillman v. Vance, 910 So. 2d 43, 47 (Miss. Ct. App. 2005) (visitation not unreasonably denied; mother willing to allow grandmother visitation if grandmother did not bring boyfriend).

[507] Stacy v. Ross, 798 So. 2d 1275, 1280 (Miss. 2001) (parents were willing to provide more limited visitation).

[508] Vinson v. Vidal, 28 So. 3d 614, 617 (Miss. Ct. App. 2009).

[509] Ferguson v. Lewis, 31 So. 3d 5, 12 (Miss. Ct. App. 2009), *cert. denied*, 29 So. 3d 774 (Miss. 2010).

[510] *See* Woodell v. Parker, 860 So. 2d 781, 785-87 (Miss. 2003) (natural mother had extensive contact with the child, who called her "mother" and called the adoptive grandmother "grandma").

[511] Martin v. Coop, 693 So. 2d 912, 916 (Miss. 1997).

[512] *See* Martin v. Coop, 693 So. 2d 912, 916 (Miss. 1997) ("natural grandparents do not have a right to visit their grandchildren that is as comprehensive as the rights of a parent"); Solomon v. Robertson, 980 So. 2d 319, 321 (Miss. Ct. App. 2008).

§ 12.09[6]   **MISSISSIPPI FAMILY LAW**

weeks in the summer, and various holidays was excessive.[513] However, the court has affirmed more extensive visitation when the noncustodial parent is unable to exercise visitation because of military service[514] or imprisonment.[515] More extensive visitation was also allowed when the child's legal parents were her maternal grandparents.[516] A court that awards grandparent visitation equal to parental visitation must make specific findings on the record to support the award.[517] The court of appeals reversed an award of visitation to the paternal grandparents for failure to make findings of fact.[518] If visitation has been awarded both to grandparents and a noncustodial parent, the parent's visitation should have priority in case of a conflict.[519]

[6] Procedure

[a] Venue. A petition for grandparent visitation should be filed in the county where an order of custody was entered. If no custody order has been entered, venue lies in the county where the child resides or may be found.[520]

[b] Parties. The necessary parties are those persons who would be necessary parties in a custody or termination of parental rights proceeding.[521] A court erred in ordering visitation one weekend a month at the paternal grandparents' home, in a father's modification action to which the grandparents were not parties.[522]

[c] Attorneys' fees. Courts are directed, upon motion of the parents, to order the grandparents to pay reasonable attorneys' fees in advance of any hearing, unless the court finds that the parents will not suffer financial hardship. The grandparents may be ordered to pay fees regardless of the outcome of the petition.[523]

[d] Modification and termination. A court that awards grandparent visitation rights has continuing jurisdiction to modify or terminate visitation "for cause."[524]

[7] Grandparent visitation rights after adoption

---

[513] Martin v. Coop, 693 So. 2d 912, 916 (Miss. 1997).

[514] *See* Settle v. Galloway, 682 So. 2d 1032, 1034-35 (Miss. 1996) (visitation every other weekend and on several holidays appeared to be in lieu of military father's visitation; court did express concern over amount of visitation).

[515] Zeman v. Stanford, 789 So. 2d 798, 804-05 (Miss. 2001) (upholding visitation one weekend every month, alternating holidays, and one week in the summer).

[516] *See* Woodell v. Parker, 860 So. 2d 781, 790 (Miss. 2003) (one weekend a month, five days at Christmas, two weeks in the summer).

[517] Townes v. Manyfield, 883 So. 2d 93, 97 (Miss. 2004).

[518] Conerly v. Davis, 46 So. 3d 858, 860 (Miss. Ct. App. 2010).

[519] Morgan v. West, 812 So. 2d 987, 996 (Miss. 2002).

[520] MISS. CODE ANN. § 93-16-3(4) (2004). Petitions to establish grandparent visitation are governed by Rule 81(d) of the Mississippi Rules of Civil Procedure, which is discussed in detail in Chapter XIX.

[521] MISS. CODE ANN. § 93-16-5 (2004).

[522] Givens v. Nicholson, 878 So. 2d 1073, 1077 (Miss. Ct. App. 2004).

[523] MISS. CODE ANN. § 93-16-3(4) (2004); *see* Vinson v. Vidal, 28 So. 3d 614, 618 (Miss. Ct. App. 2009) (award of $18,226 to a mother in litigation over the paternal grandfather's visitation rights); Solomon v. Robertson, 980 So. 2d 319, 322-23 (Miss. Ct. App. 2008) (affirming award of fees to mother even though grandparents prevailed in action).

[524] MISS. CODE ANN. § 93-16-5 (2004).

CHILD CUSTODY AND VISITATION
§ 12.09[7][a]

[a] Rights of natural grandparents. When a child is adopted, natural grandparents lose visitation rights unless one of the legal parents after adoption is a natural parent[525] or was related to the child by blood or marriage prior to the adoption.[526] Thus, grandparent visitation is permitted if a natural parent's spouse adopts a child or if the child is adopted by relatives such as the child's other grandparents.[527] Unless one of these exceptions applies, natural grandparents' rights cease at adoption, even if a court had previously ordered visitation.[528]

A right to visitation does not give natural grandparents the right to object to an adoption to which the natural parents have consented,[529] even if the objecting grandparent is the guardian of a minor parent who consented to the adoption.[530] Even though grandparents are not necessary parties in an adoption, grandparents who had already filed an independent adoption action should have been joined in an aunt's subsequent adoption action.[531]

[b] Rights of adoptive grandparents. Persons who become grandparents as a result of adoption may petition the court for visitation under the grandparent visitation statute.[532]

[8] Family visitation during military service. In 2008, the Mississippi legislature enacted a statute addressing the rights of parents serving on active duty in the military. The statute provides that when a noncustodial parent is deployed, mobilized, or placed on temporary duty that affects the parent's visitation rights, the court may delegate all or part of the deployed parent's visitation to a family member.[533]

[9] Other third-party visitation. Some states have extended third-party visitation rights to persons other than grandparents. A few states extend the possibility of visitation to any party with a significant relationship with a child. For example, a Virginia

---

[525] Miss. Code Ann. § 93-16-7 (2004). The statute was amended to add this provision after *Olson v. Flinn*, 484 So. 2d 1015, 1017 (Miss. 1986), in which paternal grandparents were denied visitation after their son's death and their grandchild's adoption by his stepfather.

[526] Miss. Code Ann. § 93-16-7 (2004). This provision was added to resolve the dilemma presented in *Muse v. Hutchins*, 559 So. 2d 1031, 1033 (Miss. 1990) (then existing statute barred visitation by maternal grandparents after adoption by paternal grandparents) and *In re Adoption of a Minor*, 558 So. 2d 854, 856 (Miss 1990) (paternal grandparents could not obtain visitation after adoption by maternal grandparents).

[527] *See* Woodell v. Parker, 860 So. 2d 781, 789-90 (Miss. 2003) (paternal grandparents granted visitation after adoption by maternal grandparents); Howell v. Rogers, 551 So. 2d 904, 905-06 (Miss. 1989) (paternal grandparents entitled to visitation after son died and stepfather adopted child).

[528] *See* Olson v. Flinn, 484 So. 2d 1015, 1017 (Miss. 1986).

[529] *In re* Adoption of J.J.G., 736 So. 2d 1037, 1039-40 (Miss. 1999).

[530] *In re* Adoption of D.N.T., 843 So. 2d 690, 713 (Miss. 2003) (concurring opinion suggests that guardian ad litem should be appointed for minor parent).

[531] *In re* Adoption of D.T.H., 748 So. 2d 853, 857 (Miss. Ct. App. 1999). *See infra* § 12.09[2] regarding grandparents' rights of visitation.

[532] Miss. Code Ann. § 93-16-7 (2004).

[533] Miss. Code Ann. § 93-5-34(2)(d) (Supp. 2010) (defining family member as "a person related by blood or marriage including, for purposes of this statute, a step-parent, grandparent, aunt, uncle, adult sibling or other person related by blood or marriage").

§ 12.10   MISSISSIPPI FAMILY LAW

statute permits "any party with a legitimate interest"[534] to seek visitation. Other persons with a close psychological bond with a child might include siblings, stepparents, foster parents, domestic partners, or birth mothers of adopted children.[535] Some statutes limit additional third parties to stepparents and siblings.[536]

The Mississippi Supreme Court has refused to judicially extend visitation to third parties other than grandparents. The supreme court rejected a sister's petition for visitation with her half-brother after their mother died. The court held that the creation of visitation rights is a legislative function.[537] Similarly, a chancellor properly dismissed a stepfather's petition for visitation with his three stepchildren after their mother's death.[538]

Some third parties may be entitled to visitation under doctrines such as *in loco parentis* or de facto parent that accord them parental rights.[539]

§ 12.10 APPOINTMENT OF GUARDIAN AD LITEM

Guardians ad litem have traditionally been appointed in actions involving abused or neglected children. Today, courts also have discretionary power to appoint guardians in contested custody actions. In Mississippi, guardians have usually assisted courts by investigating and making recommendations regarding a child's best interest, acting as an arm of the court. However, guardians may also act as a child's attorney. An appointment of a guardian should clarify the guardian's role as an advocate or arm of the court.

[1] Mandatory appointment. Courts are required to appoint a guardian to protect children whose mental or physical welfare is seriously at risk. In Mississippi, courts are ordered to appoint a guardian in custody cases when allegations of abuse and neglect are made[540] or when parental sexual assault is charged.[541] Failure to appoint a guardian under a mandatory statute requires reversal.[542]

[2] Discretionary appointment. In cases not involving allegations of abuse or neglect, appointment of a guardian ad litem is solely within the chancellor's discretion.[543] Refusal to appoint a guardian ad litem was not error in an uncontested adop-

---

[534] VA. CODE ANN. § 16.1-241(A) (2003) (including, but not limited to, grandparents, stepparents, other blood relatives, and family members).

[535] *See* ELROD, *supra* note 3, §§ 7:12 - 18.

[536] *See, e.g.,* LA. CIV. CODE art. 136 (1999).

[537] *See* Scruggs v. Saterfiel, 693 So. 2d 924, 926 (Miss. 1997).

[538] Pruitt v. Payne, 14 So. 3d 806, 811 (Miss. Ct. App. 2009).

[539] See *supra* § 12.06[2].

[540] MISS. CODE ANN. §§ 93-5-23 (2004), 93-11-65 (2004). Appointment of a guardian is also required in proceedings to terminate parental rights and for adoption, *see id.* § 93-15-107 (2004) (termination), *id.* § 93-17-8 (2004) (contested adoptions), and when a child is involved in youth court proceedings, *see id.* § 43-21-121 (2009); Floyd v. Floyd, 949 So. 2d 26, 29-30 (Miss. 2007) (guardian ad litem required in modification action based on child's allegations of abuse).

[541] MISS. CODE ANN. § 97-5-42 (2006).

[542] *In re* Adoption of E.M.C., 695 So. 2d 576, 581 (Miss. 1997). Appointment of guardians is also mandatory in proceedings in which parental rights will be involuntarily terminated, including contested adoptions. *See infra* § 16.02[2].

[543] *See* Robert K. Downs, *A New Paradigm for the Representation of Children,* 9 DIVORCE LITIGATION 221, 226 (1997) ("The representation of children in divorce-related proceedings is not mandated by any rule of law.").

388

CHILD CUSTODY AND VISITATION   § 12.10[3]

tion proceeding even though overreaching by the adoptive parent was a possibility.[544] Most of the reported custody cases in which guardians were appointed involved serious allegations of adverse circumstances, drug abuse, a parent's mental illness, or intense parental conflict.[545]

[3] Duty of the guardian ad litem. A guardian must be competent, without interests adverse to the child, and adequately informed regarding the duties of a guardian.[546] Guardians ad litem are charged with "an affirmative duty to zealously represent the child's best interest."[547]

[a] Guardian as arm of the court. In cases describing the traditional role of guardians, the Mississippi Supreme Court has stated that a guardian assists the court by investigating and entering a report with recommendations regarding custody.[548] The duty requires at a minimum that the guardian interview the children and their custodians or parents. Adequate representation may also require review of school, medical, and psychological records.[549] One resource notes that:

> Because the best interests standard is extremely broad, the range of information or facts to be explored is nearly endless. The obvious include: interviewing all witnesses such as siblings, parents, relatives, teachers, doctors, neighbors, day care providers; collecting medical, police, court, financial, and school records; and observing the child, the home, and perhaps the interaction of the parents with the children.[550]

The Mississippi Supreme Court has reversed and remanded cases in which a traditional guardian's efforts fell short of this duty. One neglect proceeding was reversed because a guardian did not interview the child in question.[551] Another was reversed because a guardian did not interview the family or make recommendations and

---

[544] *See* C.L.B. v. D.G.B., 812 So. 2d 980, 984 (Miss. 2002); J.C. v. R.Y., 797 So. 2d 209, 215 (Miss. 2001) (no fundamental liberty interest in having a guardian ad litem appointed); *see also In re* Adoption of D.T.H.S.R., 748 So. 2d 853, 855 (Miss. Ct. App. 1999).

[545] *See, e.g.*, McLemore v. McLemore, 762 So. 2d 316, 319 (Miss. 2000) (guardian ad litem appointed in case in which both parents used drugs and care of children was given temporarily to relatives); Passmore v. Passmore, 820 So. 2d 747, 749 (Miss. Ct. App. 2002) (mother had attempted suicide; father suffered from anxiety); Rafferty v. Perkins, 757 So. 2d 992, 994 (Miss. Ct. App. 2000) (guardian ad litem appointed where mother attempted to disestablish paternity of ex-husband and presumed father of children).

[546] *In re* R.D. and B.D, 658 So. 2d 1378, 1383 (Miss. 1995) (proceedings to terminate parental rights).

[547] P.K.C.G. v. M.K.G., 793 So. 2d 669, 674 (Miss. Ct. App. 2001) (quoting D.K.L. v. Hall, 652 So. 2d 184, 188 (Miss. 1995)).

[548] S.N.C. v. J.R.D., Jr., 755 So. 2d 1077, 1082 (Miss. 2000) (termination proceeding); B.S.G. v. J.E.H., 958 So. 2d 259, 268 (Miss. Ct. App. 2007) (guardian acts as representative of the court).

[549] M.J.S.H.S. v. Yalobusha County Dep't of Human Servs., 782 So. 2d 737, 741 (Miss. 2001). *But cf.* R.F. v. Lowndes County Dep't of Human Servs., 17 So. 3d 1133, 1138 (Miss. Ct. App. 2009) (court did not err in terminating rights of mother even though guardian never met with her; guardian made three attempts to visit).

[550] Raven C. Lidman & Betsy R. Hollingsworth, 6 Geo. Mason L. Rev. 255, 276 (1998); *see also* S.G. v. D.C., 13 So. 3d 269, 282 (Miss. 2009) (the guardian should investigate allegations, report all material information, including contradictory and supporting evidence, and then make a recommendation); Symposium, *Guardian Ad Litem Practice*, 63 UMKC L. Rev. 371, 378 (1994) (records from doctors, therapists, schools and other institutions; expert witnesses).

[551] *See* M.J.S.H.S. v. Yalobusha County Dep't of Human Servs., 782 So. 2d 737, 741 (Miss. 2001).

§ 12.10[3][b]   MISSISSIPPI FAMILY LAW

deferred to the parties' briefs.[552] However, the supreme court upheld a custody disposition in which the guardian interviewed the parties and children but did not interview teachers or review school or DHS records; there was no showing that further investigation would have altered the result.[553]

In a 2009 case, the supreme court held that a guardian ad litem, who was not a trained counselor or abuse investigator, was not qualified to offer an opinion regarding abuse. She was not an expert in the area of child sexual abuse and did not engage professionals to provide a factual basis for her opinion. There was no DHS or law enforcement investigation and no testimony by a social worker or trained expert. The court remanded for the chancellor to obtain the assistance of a qualified professional in child sexual abuse.[554]

In a 2010 case, the Mississippi Supreme Court held that a guardian's testimony is subject to the rules of hearsay. A court erred in holding that a guardian's oral report in an emergency hearing, describing conversations with the child's teachers and others, was not governed by the hearsay rules.[555]

[b] Guardian as the child's attorney. In 2009, the Mississippi Supreme Court recognized that guardians may perform in either of two roles. A guardian may serve as an arm of the court, investigating and submitting recommendations, or as a child's attorney, with all the obligations of the attorney-client relationship. However, the guardian may not serve in both roles. The court stated that chancellors should define the role in the order of appointment, setting out the relationship between the guardian and child, the role the guardian is expected to play, and the judge's expectations. Furthermore, the child should be advised of the guardian's role, including whether a confidential relationship exists.[556]

[4] Findings of fact. A chancellor's findings of fact should include a summary of the guardian's qualifications and report.[557] If a court rejects the findings of a mandatory guardian, the court must include its reasons for rejecting the report.[558] When appointment of a guardian is discretionary, these findings are not required.[559]

---

[552] *See In re* D.K.L., 652 So. 2d 184, 191 (Miss. 1995) (neglect proceeding); *see also* Gainey v. Edington, 24 So. 3d 333, 339-40 (Miss. Ct. App. 2009) (guardian who interviewed parties should have provided court with a report).

[553] *See* Scroggins v. Riley, 758 So. 2d 467, 472 (Miss. Ct. App. 2000) (investigation limited because of time constraints); *see also In re* Guardianship of J.N.T., 910 So. 2d 631, 633 (Miss. Ct. App. 2005) (guardian ad litem properly performed her duties by visiting both homes, observing child with both parties, visiting child's school, and reviewing school records).

[554] Jones v. Jones, 43 So. 3d 465 481(Miss. Ct. App. 2009).

[555] McDonald v. McDonald, 39 So. 3d 868, 884 (Miss. Ct. App. 2010) (but distinguishing the guardian's written report). Three justices dissented, stating that providing the court with a report of all information gathered from interviews is an important part of the function of the GAL, and that most of the guardians in the state function in this manner. *Id.* at 889.

[556] S.G. v. D.C., 13 So. 3d 269, 281 (Miss. 2009) (judge may revise the expectation by order "as the need arises" so long as the guardian is not required to breach client confidences or ethical duties).

[557] S.N.C. v. J.R.D., Jr., 755 So. 2d 1077, 1082 (Miss. 2000).

[558] Floyd v. Floyd, 949 So. 2d 26, 29 (Miss. 2007) (reversing and remanding for findings); S.N.C. v. J.R.D., Jr., 755 So. 2d 1077, 1082 (Miss. 2000); *cf.* J.P. v. S.V.B., 987 So. 2d 975, 983 (Miss. 2008) (chancellor adequately explained reasons for rejecting guardian's report).

[559] Porter v. Porter, 23 So. 3d 438, 449 (Miss. 2009); Tanner v. Tanner, 956 So. 2d 1106, 1109 (Miss. Ct. App. 2007) (rejecting mother's argument that chancellor was required to summarize guardian's report; appointment not mandatory);

CHILD CUSTODY AND VISITATION   § 12.10[5]

[5] Weight accorded guardian's report. While a guardian ad litem is useful to the court, particularly in cases involving allegations of abuse and neglect, the court remains the ultimate fact finder and is not required to follow the guardian's recommendations.[560]

[6] Fees. If a court finds that allegations of abuse are unfounded, the alleging party may be ordered to pay costs and reasonable attorneys' fees associated with defending the allegation.[561] The Mississippi Supreme Court held that the statute authorizes an award of guardian ad litem fees against a party who makes unfounded allegations. The court divided the fees between parents who both made unproven allegations.[562] However, an award of fees was not justified when a mother's accusations of abuse, although disproved, were not unfounded; her claims were supported by expert testimony.[563]

§ 12.11 MODIFICATION OF CUSTODY ORDERS

Custody orders are subject to modification, usually upon a showing of a material, adverse change in the custodial parent's home that presents a genuine danger to a child's physical, mental, or emotional well-being. Courts retain continuing jurisdiction over the parties to ensure that a custody order serves a child's best interest. The authority to modify extends to agreed custody orders. The court of appeals rejected a father's argument that modification of his visitation rights amounted to an interference with contract – agreements regarding children implicate the best interests of a child and are subject to modification.[564] Out-of-court agreements to modify are not binding on the parties.

[1] Jurisdiction. Within a state, only the court issuing an original custody order has jurisdiction to modify the order. In interstate cases, jurisdictional disputes are governed by uniform and federal laws.

[a] Modification within the state

[i] Continuing exclusive jurisdiction. A court that enters a custody order has continuing exclusive jurisdiction to modify the decree.[565] The court's jurisdiction "precludes any other court in the same state or sovereignty from thereafter acquiring or

---

Balius v. Gaines, 914 So. 2d 300, 305-06 (Miss. Ct. App. 2005) (court not required to summarize findings or explain failure to follow recommendation of discretionary guardian); Passmore v. Passmore, 820 So. 2d 747, 749 (Miss. Ct. App. 2002).

[560] *See* Hensarling v. Hensarling, 824 So. 2d 583, 587 (Miss. 2002); Passmore v. Passmore, 820 So. 2d 747, 752 (Miss. Ct. App. 2002); S.N.C. v. J.R.D., Jr., 755 So. 2d 1077, 1082 (Miss. 2000); Balius v. Gaines, 914 So. 2d 300, 305-06 (Miss. Ct. App. 2005) (chancellor not required to adopt guardian's findings of fact).

[561] MISS. CODE ANN. § 93-5-23 (2004).

[562] Foster v. Foster, 788 So. 2d 779, 782-83 (Miss. 2001); *cf.* McCraw v. McCraw, 10 So. 3d 979, 985 (Miss. Ct. App. 2009) (court did not err in ordering mother and prevailing grandmother to share guardian ad litem fees).

[563] *See* Gregory v. Gregory, 881 So. 2d 840, 846 (Miss. Ct. App. 2003).

[564] Bittick v. Bittick, 987 So. 2d 1058, 1061 (Miss. Ct. App. 2008).

[565] Reichert v. Reichert, 807 So. 2d 1282, 1286-87 (Miss. Ct. App. 2002); Sanford v. Arinder, 800 So. 2d 1267, 1270 (Miss. Ct. App. 2001).

§ 12.11[1][a][ii]　　　　　**MISSISSIPPI FAMILY LAW**

exercising jurisdiction over the same subject."[566] Even an action to terminate the parental rights of one of the parties is considered a modification of the decree and cannot be filed in another county.[567] However, a court with continuing jurisdiction may transfer a case to the county where the parents or child reside if adjudication in that county would be more efficient.[568]

[ii] Emergency habeas jurisdiction. As a general rule, parents may not use a habeas action to seek custody modification or enforcement in a court without continuing jurisdiction.[569] However, a noncustodial parent may file a habeas action to obtain temporary custody upon a showing that the custodial parent has abandoned the child or has become "altogether unfit" to have custody.[570] Because jurisdiction is temporary, the habeas court's order should include an expiration date giving the parties a reasonable period of time to seek permanent modification in the court with continuing jurisdiction.[571] In addition, a custodial parent may use a habeas corpus petition to enforce an original decree if a noncustodial parent wrongfully retains a child in another county.[572]

[b] Interstate modification. When parents live in different states, more than one state may have jurisdiction to modify custody under traditional jurisdictional rules. These conflicts are now governed by the Uniform Child Custody Jurisdiction Enforcement Act and the Parental Kidnapping Prevention Act, which are covered in detail in Chapter XVIII.

[2] General considerations

[a] Pleadings. A petition to modify custody is governed by rules set out in Rule 81(d) of the Mississippi Rules of Civil Procedure. The petition does not initiate a new action; it is considered a continuation of the original action.[573] A petition to modify custody must properly plead the three-part test for modification of custody.[574] A chancellor properly dismissed a mother's petition for failure to state a claim because the pleadings alleged that the children would be adversely affected unless modification was granted, rather than alleging that a material change in circumstances had occurred that adversely affected the children.[575]

---

[566] Ladner v. Ladner, 206 So. 2d 620, 625 (Miss. 1968) (family court had no authority to modify custody established in Hinds County chancery proceedings).

[567] *See* Tollison v. Tollison, 841 So. 2d 1062, 1066 (Miss. 2003).

[568] Reynolds v. Riddell, 253 So. 2d 834, 837 (Miss. 1971) (transferring custody modification does not conflict with statute barring transfer of divorce case).

[569] *See* Mitchell v. Powell, 179 So. 2d 811 (Miss. 1965); Neal v. Neal, 119 So. 2d 273 (Miss. 1960).

[570] Wade v. Lee, 471 So. 2d 1213, 1215 (Miss. 1985) (father showed mother was intoxicated when she arrived to pick up child, was drug user and emotionally unstable); *see also* Bubac v. Boston, 600 So. 2d 951 (Miss. 1992).

[571] Wade v. Lee, 471 So. 2d 1213, 1217 (Miss. 1985).

[572] *See* Pearson v. Pearson, 458 So. 2d 711, 712 (Miss. 1984) (custodial father filed habeas action to secure return of children wrongfully removed by mother).

[573] *See* discussion of Rule 81 proceedings *infra* § 19.11.

[574] McMurry v. Sadler, 846 So. 2d 240, 244 (Miss. Ct. App. 2002).

[575] McMurry v. Sadler, 846 So. 2d 240, 244 (Miss. Ct. App. 2002).

CHILD CUSTODY AND VISITATION

§ 12.11[2][b]

[b] Findings of fact. Courts are required to make specific findings of fact under the appropriate modification test.[576] Under the traditional test, the court should provide findings with regard to (1) whether a material change has occurred; (2) if so, whether the child was adversely affected; and (3) if so, whether modification is in the child's best interest. If the court finds an adverse material change and proceeds to a best-interests analysis, the court must make findings with respect to the *Albright* factors.[577] Modifications have been reversed because the court did not find an adverse material change before considering a child's best interest.[578] In a 2007 case, the supreme court stated that a finding of a material adverse change is "condition precedent" to a re-weighing of the *Albright* factors.[579] Similarly, appellate courts have reversed modifications when the court found a material change but failed to address the *Albright* factors.[580]

[c] Burden of proof. The burden of proof is on the petitioner to prove that a material change has occurred and that the change is adverse to the child.[581] This burden of proof must be satisfied before the court moves to a best interest analysis under *Albright*.[582]

[d] Evidence of pre-decree conduct. In a proceeding to modify custody, evidence of a custodial parent's conduct prior to the original decree is generally not admissible. The court's prior finding of suitability for custody is res judicata as to those facts.

---

[576] This subsection illustrates the traditional modification test. The necessary fact findings will vary if the court applies the alternate *Riley v. Doerner* modification test. *See infra* § 12.11[18].

[577] *See* C.A.M.F. v. J.M.B., 972 So. 2d 656, 660 (Miss. Ct. App. 2007); Moore v. Cole, 961 So. 2d 737 (Miss. Ct. App. 2007) (three-part test); Anderson v. Anderson, 961 So. 2d 55 (Miss. Ct. App. 2007); Marter v. Marter, 914 So. 2d 743, 746 (Miss. Ct. App. 2005) (chancellor must first identify specific change in circumstances, then analyze *Albright* factors); Parker v. South, 913 So. 2d 339, 347 (Miss. Ct. App. 2005) (describing three-part test for modification); Sturgis v. Sturgis, 792 So. 2d 1020, 1025 (Miss. Ct. App. 2001) (modification reversed because chancellor failed to address each factor).

[578] *See* Ortega v. Lovell, 725 So. 2d 199, 203-04 (Miss. 1998); Pace v. Owens, 511 So. 2d 489, 491 (Miss. 1987) (no findings with regard to material change, adversity, or best interest); Thornell v. Thornell, 860 So. 2d 1241, 1243 (Miss. Ct. App. 2003) (reversing custody modification where court stated material change had occurred but did not provide findings); *cf.* Pruett v. Prinz, 979 So. 2d 745, 750 (Miss. Ct. App. 2008) (court should find material change before determining adverse impact); Powell v. Powell, 976 So. 2d 358, 361-62 (Miss. Ct. App. 2008) (*Albright* factors not reached unless court finds a material change in circumstances); Gray v. Gray, 969 So. 2d 906 (Miss. Ct. App. 2007) (rejecting mother's argument that chancellor should have applied *Albright* factors; no material change in circumstances found); Balius v. Gaines, 914 So. 2d 300, 310 (Miss. Ct. App. 2005) (court properly refused to proceed to *Albright* analysis where petitioner father did not prove material change). *Compare* Floyd v. Floyd, 949 So. 2d 26, 29-30 (Miss. 2007) (remanding for *Albright* findings without discussing need for finding material change), *with* Anderson v. Anderson, 961 So. 2d 55, 58, 60 (Miss. Ct. App. 2007) (chancellor makes *Albright* findings if he or she finds an adverse material change).

[579] Giannaris v. Giannaris, 960 So. 2d 462, 468 (Miss. 2007).

[580] Lowery v. Mardis, 867 So. 2d 1053, 1057 (Miss. Ct. App. 2004) (court found material change but failed to address *Albright* factors).

[581] Lewis v. Lewis, 974 So. 2d 265 (Miss. Ct. App. 2008); Purviance v. Burgess, 980 So. 2d 308 (Miss. Ct. App. 2007) (petitioner mother failed to prove that child was in danger); Duke v. Elmore, 956 So. 2d 244 (Miss. Ct. App. 2006); Marter v. Marter, 914 So. 2d 743, 749 (Miss. Ct. App. 2005) (petitioner has burden of proof in modification proceeding); McCracking v. McCracking, 776 So. 2d 691, 693 (Miss. Ct. App. 2000) (no material change as a result of divorce, some alcohol use and gambling, or leaving child with responsible fourteen-year-old after school); *see also* Sanford v. Arinder, 800 So. 2d 1267, 1272 (Miss. Ct. App. 2001).

[582] McCracking v. McCracking, 776 So. 2d 691, 694 (Miss. Ct. App. 2000) (best-interests question not reached unless chancellor finds adverse material change in circumstance); McGehee v. Upchurch, 733 So. 2d 364, 369 (Miss. Ct. App. 1999) (same).

§ 12.11[3]   MISSISSIPPI FAMILY LAW

Modification must be based on conditions that arise after the decree.[583] For example, a mother's health problems requiring frequent hospitalizations and her smoking were not material changes – both existed at the time of the custody agreement.[584] The defense of res judicata is waived unless the opposing party objects to admission at trial.[585] However, a petitioner who had filed a previous unsuccessful petition to modify is not limited to events occurring since the unsuccessful petition. The court of appeals rejected a mother's argument that the court could only consider evidence dating from a father's first, unsuccessful attempt to modify custody based on her cohabitation. Because the petition sought to modify the divorce decree, the court could hear evidence related to changes occurring since that decree.[586] Similarly, evidence of a mother's interference with visitation since the couple's divorce was considered in the father's third petition for modification.[587]

A noncustodial parent's prior conduct may be a reason to continue to deny custody. When a noncustodial father sought to modify custody, the divorce court's findings that he physically abused his wife and neglected his child were admissible in the modification hearing.[588] The court of appeals has also stated that conduct that seemed minor at the original hearing is admissible if it is relevant when combined with later conduct.[589] And the court of appeals rejected a mother's argument that her post-divorce move was not a new material change since the parties knew at the time of divorce that she might move. The change was the resulting, adverse circumstances in which the girls were living after the move.[590]

In some cases, pre-divorce conduct may be admissible to determine whether post-divorce conduct constitutes a change. A chancellor properly admitted evidence of a couple's frequent moves in order to determine whether the mother's post-divorce moves were a change or the continuation of a pattern that predated divorce.[591]

[3] Maintaining stability. Maintaining stability for children of divorced or separated parents is an important consideration in modification actions. The Mississippi Supreme Court has emphasized that modification is a "jolting, traumatic" experience[592]

---

[583] Lackey v. Fuller, 755 So. 2d 1083, 1086-87 (Miss. 2000); Lewis v. Lewis, 974 So. 2d 265, 267-68 (Miss. Ct. App. 2008) (exposing children to their grandmother's boyfriend was not a material change; he was dating her at the time of the divorce); Moore v. Cole, 961 So. 2d 737, 741 (Miss. Ct. App. 2007) (rejecting mother's request for modification based on father's work schedule, which had actually improved since the original decree); Grissom v. Grissom, 952 So. 2d 1023, 1027-28 (Miss. Ct. App. 2007) (mother sought modification of joint custody based on inability to communicate, but alleged that parties had never been able to communicate; denied because no material change).

[584] Robbins v. Robbins, 40 So. 3d 637, 639-40 (Miss. Ct. App. 2010).

[585] Robison v. Lanford, 850 So. 2d 91, 98 (Miss. Ct. App. 2001).

[586] Savell v. Morrison, 929 So. 2d 414, 417 (Miss. Ct. App. 2006).

[587] Ellis v. Ellis, 952 So. 2d 982, 988 (Miss. Ct. App. 2006) (custody modified to father on third petition).

[588] *See* Herring v. Herring, 571 So. 2d 239, 244 (Miss. 1990) (res judicata would apply if the court had found for the father on these allegations).

[589] *See* Robison v. Lanford, 822 So. 2d 1034, 1040 (Miss. Ct. App. 2002) ("to the extent the conduct appeared relatively minor at the time of the earlier decree, its continuation or worsening since was relevant in the chancellor's consideration"); *cf.* Davidson v. Coit, 899 So. 2d 904, 908 (Miss. Ct. App. 2005) (court rejected mother's argument that lesbian relationships were not a change in circumstances since her sexual preference was known at the time of divorce; mother's exposure of children to relationships after divorce was the material change).

[590] Marter v. Marter, 914 So. 2d 743 (Miss. Ct. App. 2005).

[591] Powell v. Powell, 976 So. 2d 358, 363 (Miss. Ct. App. 2008).

[592] *See* Lambert v. Lambert, 872 So. 2d 679, 684 (Miss. Ct. App. 2003).

CHILD CUSTODY AND VISITATION

§ 12.11[4]

which should not be ordered without serious cause: "[I]t is not in the best interest of a small child to be shifted from parent to parent."[593] Custody should not be modified based on isolated incidents[594] or to punish a parent.[595] Modification should be based only on parental behavior "which clearly poses or causes danger to the mental or emotional well-being of a child."[596] In keeping with this goal, courts will carefully scrutinize modification actions filed shortly after an initial order. A mother's petition to modify joint custody and visitation, filed four months after the order was entered, was rejected – the couple had not given the order time to work.[597]

[4] Effect of nonpayment of child support. The doctrine of clean hands, which bars relief to a party who has failed to comply with other court orders, does not apply to custody modification actions. A chancellor erred in denying the custody modification request of a father who was in arrears in child support; the best interests of the child supported modification.[598]

[5] Test for modification: Adverse material change. The traditional test for modification of custody requires a finding that a material change of circumstances has occurred in the custodial parent's home since the date of the decree, that the change adversely affects the child, and that modification is in the child's best interests, as determined by application of the *Albright* factors. A court may find a material change in circumstances but conclude that a change in custody is not warranted under the *Albright* factors.[599] Courts may apply an alternate test when children have been living in adverse circumstances since the custody order was entered.[600]

[a] Material change. The first prong of the test – a material change in circumstances – requires proof of a serious material change in the home of the custodial parent. A change in the noncustodial parent's home does not satisfy the test.[601] A court erred in finding that a noncustodial father's anticipated move was a material change in circumstances.[602] The material change may not be one that was foreseeable at the

---

[593] Lipsey v. Lipsey, 755 So. 2d 564, 567 (Miss. Ct. App. 2000) (quoting Case v. Stolpe, 300 So. 2d 802, 805 (Miss. 1974)); *see also* Tucker v. Tucker, 453 So. 2d 1294, 1298 (Miss. 1984) ("children do not need to be bounced back and forth between their parents like a volleyball"); Bowden v. Fayard, 355 So. 2d 662, 664 (Miss. 1978) (child is entitled to "the stabilizing influence of knowing where home is").

[594] Tucker v. Tucker, 453 So. 2d 1294, 1297 (Miss. 1984).

[595] Tucker v. Tucker, 453 So. 2d 1294, 1297 (Miss. 1984); Fletcher v. Shaw, 800 So. 2d 1212, 1215-16 (Miss. Ct. App. 2001).

[596] Ballard v. Ballard, 434 So. 2d 1357, 1360 (Miss.1983); *see also* Giannaris v. Giannaris, 960 So. 2d 462, 467 (Miss. 2007); Lambert v. Lambert, 872 So. 2d 679, 684 (Miss. Ct. App. 2003) (only parental conduct that clearly endangers a child's mental or emotional heath is sufficient); *cf.* Williamson v. Williamson, 964 So. 2d 524, 528-29 (Miss. Ct. App. 2007) (denying mother's request for modification in part because of need for stability provided by leaving child with father, who had been her primary caregiver).

[597] Jones v. McGuage, 932 So. 2d 846, 849 (Miss. Ct. App. 2006).

[598] Shelton v. Shelton, 653 So. 2d 283, 288 (Miss. 1995).

[599] *See* Burrus v. Burrus, 962 So. 2d 618 (Miss. Ct. App. 2006); Jones v. McGuage, 932 So. 2d 846 (Miss. Ct. App. 2006); McBride v. Cook, 858 So. 2d 160, 163 (Miss. Ct. App. 2003).

[600] *See infra* § 12.11[18].

[601] *See infra* § 12.11[17].

[602] Giannaris v. Giannaris, 960 So. 2d 462, 466 n.7, 469 (Miss. 2007).

§ 12.11[5][a]   MISSISSIPPI FAMILY LAW

time of the order.[603] A prospective change may constitute a material change in circumstances. A joint custodial mother's planned move from Jackson to Memphis was properly considered as a material change in circumstances.[604]

Whether a material change has occurred depends on the totality of circumstances. Events which would not, alone, be a sufficient material change may in combination provide a basis for modifying custody.[605] A chancellor erred in denying modification on the basis that frequent moves were not a material change – he failed to consider the totality of the circumstances, which included the rape of one child and the mother's reluctance to provide counseling, the mother's unstable cohabitation and sporadic employment, and the children's frequent change of schools.[606]

The material change must present a genuine danger to the child. Conduct that would weigh against a parent in an original custody decision does not necessarily justify custody modification. Courts have rejected claims that modification was required because a parent gambled, used alcohol,[607] or had remarried or divorced.[608] Corporal punishment within the normal range of discipline was not a material change.[609] A change in a custodial parent's work schedule is not a material change in circumstances if the child is well cared for and supervised.[610] The fact that a mother left her children with neighbors several afternoons a week while she worked was not a reason to modify custody – use of daycare services by working parents does not show lack of involvement.[611] A mother's receipt of social services and welfare assistance was not a material change in circumstances.[612] However, a mother's escalating alcohol and drug abuse, resulting in arrests, violent behavior, and automobile accidents was a material change in circumstances.[613]

Ordinarily, modification should not be ordered if a material adverse change has been remedied. A chancellor properly refused modification based on evidence that a child's marijuana-using half-brother had moved out of the home and that the mother's current boyfriend did not sleep over as had her previous boyfriends.[614] In some cases, however, custody may be modified even though the adverse conduct has ended. For

---

[603] Giannaris v. Giannaris, 960 So. 2d 462, 469 (Miss. 2007).

[604] Porter v. Porter, 23 So. 3d 438, 448 (Miss. 2009).

[605] Duke v. Elmore, 956 So. 2d 244 (Miss. Ct. App. 2006); Hill v. Hill, 942 So. 2d 207, 210-11 (Miss. Ct. App. 2006).

[606] Powell v. Powell, 976 So. 2d 358, 361-63 (Miss. Ct. App. 2008).

[607] *See* Lorenz v. Strait, 987 So. 2d 427, 430-34 (Miss. 2008) (father's admitted drinking and DUI while child was with mother not a material change; father was in substance abuse counseling); Robison v. Lanford, 841 So. 2d 1119, 1123-24 (Miss. 2003). Testimony by a mother that the custodial father drank heavily, without evidence of any harm or danger to the child, and evidence that on one occasion he spanked the child hard enough to leave bruises, was not alone sufficient to show a material change in circumstances adverse to the child. *Id. See also* McCracking v. McCracking, 776 So. 2d 691, 693 (Miss. Ct. App. 2000) (no material change as a result of divorce, some alcohol use and gambling, or leaving child with responsible fourteen-year-old after school).

[608] *See* Robison v. Lanford, 841 So. 2d 1119, 1123 (Miss. 2003).

[609] *See* Scroggins v. Riley, 758 So. 2d 467, 471 (Miss. Ct. App. 2000).

[610] Mixon v. Sharp, 853 So. 2d 834, 838 (Miss. Ct. App. 2003).

[611] Staggs v. Staggs, 919 So. 2d 112, 120 (Miss. Ct. App. 2005).

[612] Robinson v. Robinson, 481 So. 2d 855, 857 (Miss. 1986).

[613] Johnson v. Gray, 859 So. 2d 1006, 1014 (Miss. 2003); *see also* Holmes v. Holmes, 958 So. 2d 844, 848 (Miss. Ct. App. 2007) (custody modified based on mother's violent behavior toward son). *But see* Staggs v. Staggs, 919 So. 2d 112, 119 (Miss. Ct. App. 2005) (mother's previous substance abuse not a reason for modification – she had been sober for over two years and was in full compliance with her rehabilitation contract).

[614] Ruth v. Burchfield, 23 So. 3d 600, 606 (Miss. Ct. App. 2009).

CHILD CUSTODY AND VISITATION § 12.11[5][b]

example, a chancellor properly modified custody of a two-year-old based on her mother's drug use, even though she had been drug-free for some months at the time of the hearing.[615]

[b] Adverse effect. Even if a material change is shown, custody should not, ordinarily, be modified unless the change adversely affects the child. A court erred in modifying custody based on a mother's cohabitation that did not adversely affect her children.[616] And a custodial father's move to Alaska, although a material change, did not warrant modification. The move did not adversely affect his disabled child, who was receiving treatment in Alaska.[617] The adverse effect must be linked to the identified "material change." A court erred in finding that a father's move was a material change, and that the child was adversely affected by the mother's attitude toward the child's stepmother.[618]

However, if circumstances in a custodial parent's home create a strong likelihood that a child will be damaged, custody may be modified without a showing that adverse effects have already occurred. The Mississippi Supreme Court has stated that "where a child living in a custodial environment clearly adverse to the child's best interest, somehow appears to remain unscarred by his or her surroundings, the chancellor is not precluded from removing the child for placement in a healthier environment."[619] For example, a chancellor properly modified custody of a teenage girl when her mother cohabited with a man convicted of four counts of sexual assault on a fourteen-year-old, without waiting for proof of injury to the girl.[620] Similarly, it was appropriate to transfer custody of a girl whose new stepfather showed increasing aggression and verbal abuse toward her, without waiting for the girl to suffer injury.[621] A court did not err in modifying custody of a boy whose custodial mother, in a three-year period, moved four times, placed him in three different schools, was involved with at least four men, remarried and divorced, had been arrested, was involved in litigation with her fiancé's former wife, and had received and retained pornographic communications from her fiancé. The child needed a stable home and should not be punished for his resilience.[622]

---

[615] McSwain v. McSwain, 943 So. 2d 1288, 1293 (Miss. 2006) (mother did not complete treatment program and still associated with former drug partner); *see also* Johnson v. Gray, 859 So. 2d 1006, 1014 (Miss. 2003) (mother's treatment for alcoholism and her remarriage did not prevent change of custody; not enough time had passed to determine whether the changes were permanent).

[616] Forsythe v. Akers, 768 So. 2d 943, 948 (Miss. Ct. App. 2000); *see also* Sudduth v. Mowdy, 991 So. 2d 1241, 1244 (Miss. Ct. App. 2008) (mother's relationships and refusal of visitation were material change, but no modification because child was not adversely affected).

[617] Williamson v. Williamson, 964 So. 2d 524, 528-29 (Miss. Ct. App. 2007); *see also* Moore v. Cole, 961 So. 2d 737, 741 (Miss. Ct. App. 2007) (custodial father's second divorce and child's temporary residence with grandparents did not adversely affect child).

[618] Giannaris v. Giannaris, 960 So. 2d 462, 466, 469 (Miss. 2007).

[619] Riley v. Doerner, 677 So. 2d 740, 744 (Miss. 1996); *cf.* Duke v. Elmore, 956 So. 2d 244, 250 (Miss. Ct. App. 2006) (*Riley* does not require the presence of dangerous or illegal behavior such as drug use in order to find an adverse environment).

[620] Burrus v. Burrus, 962 So. 2d 618, 626 (Miss. Ct. App. 2006).

[621] Savell v. Morrison, 929 So. 2d 414, 418 (Miss. Ct. App. 2006); *see also* A.T.K. v. R.M.K.W., 26 So. 3d 1103, 1107 (Miss. Ct. App. 2009) (no need to show adverse impact on girl whose mother married convicted sex offender); C.A.M.F. v. J.M.B., 972 So. 2d 656, 667 (Miss. Ct. App. 2007) (transferring custody of boy whose stepfather was frequently nude and who exposed himself to babysitters, was witnessed choking mother, and had nude photographs taken of child).

[622] Duke v. Elmore, 956 So. 2d 244, 249 (Miss. Ct. App. 2006) (mother married convicted felon, made four moves in two years, and was unemployed for several months); *see also* Graves v. Haden, 52 So. 3d 407, 409 (Miss. Ct. App.

§ 12.11[5][c]   MISSISSIPPI FAMILY LAW

[c] **Child's best interests.** As in all matters related to children, the "polestar consideration" is the best interest of the child, considering the totality of the circumstances.[623] A finding that a material change has adversely affected a child does not always lead to a change in custody. A chancellor properly found that it was not in children's best interest to modify custody, even though their living circumstances had been adversely affected after Hurricane Katrina.[624]

[6] **Combined circumstances as material change.** The court of appeals noted that a court may find a material change based on a totality of circumstances, none of which alone might be sufficient to warrant modification.[625] Cases in which modification is granted often present a combination of adverse circumstances. For example, material adverse changes were found when a custodial mother moved frequently, was unemployed, left her child with friends for a prolonged period, had two children out of wedlock, and exhibited signs of paranoia.[626] In another case, a mother's frequent moves, cohabitation, interference with visitation, and unfounded accusations of sexual abuse justified modification.[627] And custody was modified to a father when the mother threatened suicide, engaged in erratic behavior, and abruptly moved the children 10,000 miles from their home and extended family.[628] A chancellor erred in refusing to modify custody from a father who engaged in questionable sexual activities, neglected the girls' health, and employed a babysitter who was convicted of drug possession.[629]

[7] **Danger of physical or sexual abuse.** Custody has been modified when a child

---

2010) (modifying custody of well-adjusted child based on mother's cohabitation, frequent moves, and relationships; citing *Riley*), *cert. denied*, 50 So. 3d 1003 (Miss. 2011); Betts v. Massey, 40 So. 3d 602, 611 (Miss. Ct. App. 2009), *cert. denied*, 42 So. 3d 24 (Miss. 2010) (not necessary to show that young boy was adversely affected by mother's allowing him to sleep with her and her boyfriend).

[623] Moore v. Cole, 961 So. 2d 737, 740 (Miss. Ct. App. 2007).

[624] Quadrini v. Quadrini, 964 So. 2d 576, 582 (Miss. Ct. App. 2007).

[625] Minter v. Minter, 29 So. 3d 840 (Miss. Ct. App. 2009), *cert. denied*, 29 So. 3d 774 (Miss. 2010) (mother moved five times, had numerous jobs, had a suspended driver's license, and relied on food stamps and family for support; child required to repeat kindergarten because of absences).

[626] *See* Fletcher v. Shaw, 800 So. 2d 1212, 1217 (Miss. Ct. App. 2001); *see also* Betts v. Massey, 40 So. 3d 602, 610 (Miss. Ct. App. 2009), *cert. denied*, 42 So. 3d 24 (Miss. 2010) (material change based on combination of a de facto change in custody, the mother's night work, fact that she was pregnant by her boyfriend of six months, and that the child slept with her and her boyfriend); Pruett v. Prinz, 979 So. 2d 745, 750-51 (Miss. Ct. App. 2008) (modification based on mother's violent second marriage, missed visitation exchanges, cohabitation, coaching child to lie to court); Powell v. Powell, 976 So. 2d 358, 361-63 (Miss. Ct. App. 2008) (modification based on custodial mother's frequent moves, cohabitation, sporadic employment, and the rape of one child and mother's reluctance to provide counseling for her); Parker v. South, 913 So. 2d 339, 345-46 (Miss. Ct. App. 2005) (modification from mother to father based on her cohabitation, attempted interference with visitation, failure to take appropriate steps to protect child from sexual abuse, DUI, and unsuitable home environment); Brown v. White, 875 So. 2d 1116, 1119 (Miss. Ct. App. 2004) (mother lived in ten locations in five states in a four year period; child failed first grade, having attended three different schools in two states).

[627] *See* Jernigan v. Jernigan, 830 So. 2d 651, 652-53 (Miss. Ct. App. 2002); *see also* Newsom v. Newsom, 557 So. 2d 511, 516 (Miss. 1990) (mother's subjecting children to repeated, unwarranted examination to prove sexual abuse by the father constituted a material change in circumstances).

[628] *See* Sanford v. Arinder, 800 So. 2d 1267, 1273 (Miss. Ct. App. 2001).

[629] Gainey v. Edington, 24 So. 3d 333, 335-37 (Miss. Ct. App. 2009) (girls had recurrent ear infections, contracted a staph infection; father married a sex-toy consultant who held "Passion Parties" and maintained a violent and sexually explicit Myspace page); *see also* White v. White, 26 So. 3d 342, 346 (Miss. 2010) (mother removed child from state in violation of a court order, failed to cooperate with the guardian ad litem, and did not properly discipline the child).

CHILD CUSTODY AND VISITATION   § 12.11[8]

was in danger of physical or sexual abuse in the custodial parent's home. Modification was justified because a nine-year-old girl was molested by her mother's friend while in the mother's care.[630] And a court properly awarded sole physical and legal custody to a father and supervised visitation to a mother who was suicidal, engaged in self-mutilation, and had violent thoughts toward her husband and child.[631]

[8] Custodial parent's remarriage. While a parent's remarriage is not in itself a reason to modify custody,[632] a change may be ordered if the stepparent presents a danger to the child's physical or mental health. A chancellor properly modified custody of a ten-year-old girl, based upon evidence that the mother's new husband screamed at the girl daily, using profanity toward her, stated that he thought of "peppering" her with paintballs and duct taping her to a chair, threatened her with a belt, and stated that if he had to, he would go to jail if he "snapped" and whipped her.[633] And a stepfather's presence constituted a material change in circumstances – he was frequently nude, exposed himself to babysitters, and choked the child's mother in his presence.[634] A chancellor erred in holding that a mother's marriage to a convicted sex offender was not a material change because the couple divorced prior to the modification hearing. Evidence showed that they divorced because of the hearing and still spent numerous nights together.[635]

[9] Relocation. Relocation is one of the most difficult issues to resolve in modification actions. Courts and legislatures have struggled to balance custodial parents' need to make reasonable choices about relocation with the rights of noncustodial parents and children to maintain a close relationship. In most states, a move is considered to be a material change in circumstances triggering a best interests evaluation to determine whether custody should be modified.[636] A number of factors have been suggested as guidelines for evaluating whether custody should be modified because of a move: whether the relocation is in good faith; whether the move is in the child's best interests; the extent of a child's involvement with the relocating parent and the nonrelocating parent; the child's preference; the likely impact on the child; and whether the noncustodial parent will realistically be able to maintain a full relationship with the child.[637] In some

---

[630] *See* R.L.S. v. A.R.S., 807 So. 2d 1251, 1261-62 (Miss. Ct. App. 2001); *see also* C.W.L. v. R.A., 919 So. 2d 267, 270 (Miss. Ct. App. 2005) (custody to father; mother continued to expose child to relative who sexually abused her); *cf.* Lorenz v. Strait, 987 So. 2d 427, 431-32 (Miss. 2008) (modification of custody from father not warranted; mother's allegations of abuse unsubstantiated).

[631] Morris v. Morris, 783 So. 2d 681, 693 (Miss. 2001) (lesbian relationship also a factor); *see also* McSwain v. McSwain, 943 So. 2d 1288, 1293 (Miss. 2006) (en banc) (mother's depression and thoughts of suicide a factor in modification action).

[632] Dykes v. McMurray, 938 So. 2d 330, 336 (Miss. Ct. App. 2006) (healthy and well-adjusted child's "occasional unhappiness" after mother's remarriage is not a material change); Jones v. McGuage, 932 So. 2d 846, 849 (Miss. Ct. App. 2006).

[633] Savell v. Morrison, 929 So. 2d 414, 418 (Miss. Ct. App. 2006) (adverse effects presumed) (stepfather's behavior in prior marriages was admissible to show his character and moral fitness).

[634] C.A.M.F. v. J.M.B., 972 So. 2d 656, 665-66 (Miss. Ct. App. 2007); *see also* Sullivan v. Beason, 37 So. 3d 706, 712 (Miss. Ct. App. 2010) (transfer of custody based in part on mother's marriage to and divorce from, a violent husband with whom she had ongoing contact).

[635] A.T.K. v. R.M.K.W., 26 So. 3d 1103, 1107 (Miss. Ct. App. 2009).

[636] *See* ELROD, *supra* note 3, § 7:28.

[637] *See* ELROD, *supra* note 3, § 7:29 (discussing factors used in New Jersey, Missouri, Louisiana, and factors proposed by the American Academy of Matrimonial Lawyers).

§ 12.11[9] MISSISSIPPI FAMILY LAW

states, the burden of proof rests on the noncustodial parent.[638]

Mississippi is in a minority of states in which a custodial parent's move is not, in itself, a material change in circumstances.[639] Something more than the mere fact of relocation must be shown to trigger an *Albright* best interests analysis. For example, a mother's move from Hattiesburg to Batesville three months after divorce was not a material change in circumstances; the fact that mid-week visitation was difficult did not justify modification.[640] In a modification action based on a custodial mother's move to California, the court of appeals stated that a distant move is material, but not necessarily an adverse change, even if the noncustodial parent's visitation rights are curtailed as a result of the move.[641] Furthermore, an agreement between parents that a child will remain in a particular town[642] or that custody will change if the custodial parent moves is unenforceable.[643]

The Mississippi Supreme Court has recognized, however, that a move may present "peculiar or unusual circumstances" that adversely affect children.[644] A mother's move to Alaska with her daughter justified modification because the move separated the girl from her brother.[645] In addition, relocation may be considered as one of several factors which, combined, prove a material change in circumstances.[646] For example, a chancellor properly modified custody when a mother's relocation precipitated an overall adverse change in circumstances – the children were removed from their friends, extended family, and regular activities, were left alone on several occasions as a result of the mother's new job, and stated that they preferred to live with their father.[647]

A parent's good faith in negotiating custody may affect modification based on relocation. Custody was properly transferred to a father based on evidence that the custodial mother agreed to provide the father with extensive visitation even though she

---

[638] *See* ELROD, *supra* note 3, § 7:29.

[639] *See* Bell v. Bell, 572 So. 2d 841, 846 (Miss. 1990); Rutledge v. Rutledge, 487 So. 2d 218, 220 (Miss. 1986); Pearson v. Pearson, 458 So. 2d 711, 714 (Miss. 1984) (rule applies even if parent moves to Alaska or Hawaii); Cheek v. Ricker, 431 So. 2d 1139, 1144 (Miss. 1983); Lambert v. Lambert, 872 So. 2d 679, 685 (Miss. Ct. App. 2003) (mother's move not a material change in circumstances). *But cf.* Gray v. Gray, 969 So. 2d 906, 908 (Miss. Ct. App. 2007) (custodial parent's move not *always* a material change in circumstance (emphasis added)).

[640] Lambert v. Lambert, 872 So. 2d 679, 686 (Miss. Ct. App. 2003) (child's anxiety caused by divorce and subsequent modification litigation rather than relocation); *see also* Gray v. Gray, 969 So. 2d 906, 908 (Miss. Ct. App. 2007) (father's move to Arkansas not a material change in circumstances); Staggs v. Staggs, 919 So. 2d 112, 119 (Miss. Ct. App. 2005) (mother's move to Maryland not material change in circumstances).

[641] Balius v. Gaines, 908 So. 2d 791, 801-02 (Miss. Ct. App. 2005).

[642] *See* Bell v. Bell, 572 So. 2d 841, 845-46 (Miss. 1990) (nor may court prohibit mother from moving without court approval).

[643] *See* McManus v. Howard, 569 So. 2d 1213, 1216 (Miss. 1990) (parents cannot agree that relocation by one parent triggers a change in custody).

[644] *See* Holland v. Spain, 483 So. 2d 318, 321 (Miss. 1986).

[645] Stevison v. Woods, 560 So. 2d 176, 180 (Miss. 1990) (visitation order had allowed children substantial time together).

[646] *See* Stark v. Anderson, 748 So. 2d 838, 843 (Miss. Ct. App. 1999) (frequent moves, cohabitation, relocation to Colorado, stepfather drank excessively and child feared him; emotional problems; failure to provide adequate medical care).

[647] Marter v. Marter, 914 So. 2d 743, 749-50 (Miss. Ct. App. 2005); *see also* Connelly v. Lammey, 982 So. 2d 997, 999-1000 (Miss. Ct. App. 2008) (custody modified upon mother's move to Nevada; based also on child's preference, removal from extended family, and mother's handling of move).

CHILD CUSTODY AND VISITATION § 12.11[10]

planned to move immediately after divorce. The court of appeals affirmed the chancellor's modification of custody one month after divorce because she intentionally concealed her plan to move five hundred miles from the father's home.[648]

[10] Child's choice. A child's preference to shift custody does not in itself constitute an adverse material change in circumstances. The court of appeals reversed a modification based primarily on a child's wishes: "While a child's expression of preference must be afforded weight by the chancellor, this Court is unaware that it has ever held that such an expression, supported by nothing more, constitutes the type of adverse material change in circumstance that would warrant a custody modification."[649] The court did note that a child's preference would support modification if the child "could articulate compelling reasons" to support the request.[650] A seventeen-year-old girl's genuine desire to live with her mother, combined with the custodial father's increasingly controlling behavior, justified modification of custody.[651] A court properly modified custody of a fifteen-year-old from mother to father based on his request as well as evidence that the mother acted violently toward him and that the environment was emotionally destructive to him.[652] In contrast, a court properly ignored the request of a child whose desire to live with his mother was motivated by the lack of discipline in her home.[653]

If a court declines to follow a child's wishes, it must make specific findings explaining the refusal.[654] The Mississippi Supreme Court reversed a denial of modification because the chancellor failed to include reasons for denying a child's election to live with his mother.[655] The court of appeals also held that a chancellor erred in excluding the testimony of children in a mother's suit for modification based on the children's choice to live with her.[656]

---

[648] Pulliam v. Smith, 872 So. 2d 790, 794-95 (Miss. Ct. App. 2004).

[649] Best v. Hinton, 838 So. 2d 306, 308 (Miss. Ct. App. 2002); *see also* Lewis v. Lewis, 974 So. 2d 265, 268 (Miss. Ct. App. 2008) (fact that older girls preferred to live with their father was not in itself a material change in circumstances); Gray v. Gray, 969 So. 2d 906, 908 (Miss. Ct. App. 2007) (affirming denial of modification; child's preference only one factor); Anderson v. Anderson, 961 So. 2d 55, 59-60 (Miss. Ct. App. 2007); Burrus v. Burrus, 962 So. 2d 618, 626 (Miss. Ct. App. 2006) (court did not honor child's preference to live with mother cohabiting with sex offender); Dykes v. McMurray, 938 So. 2d 330, 337 (Miss. Ct. App. 2006) ("child's suggestion of preference, without supporting evidence that there has been a material change . . . adverse to the child's best interests, is not sufficient"); *cf.* Floyd v. Floyd, 949 So. 2d 26, 30 (Miss. 2007) (child's choice alone does not require modification). *But cf.* Chroniger v. Chroniger, 914 So. 2d 311, 313 (Miss. Ct. App. 2005) (parents agreed to allow court to modify custody based on child's choice at the age of twelve).

[650] Best v. Hinton, 838 So. 2d 306, 309 (Miss. Ct. App. 2002); *see also* Connelly v. Lammey, 982 So. 2d 997, 999-1000 (Miss. Ct. App. 2008) (modification based on custodial mother's move and child's preference to be in Mississippi where he could hunt and fish); McKenzie v. McKenzie, 860 So. 2d 316, 317 (Miss. Ct. App. 2003) (no other change since original decree).

[651] Jones v. Jones, 878 So. 2d 1061, 1066 (Miss. Ct. App. 2004).

[652] Holmes v. Holmes, 958 So. 2d 844, 848-49 (Miss. Ct. App. 2007).

[653] White v. White, 26 So. 3d 342, 346 (Miss. 2010) (mother removed child from state in violation of a court order, failed to cooperate with the guardian ad litem, and did not properly discipline the child).

[654] Polk v. Polk, 589 So. 2d 123, 130 (Miss. 1991) (reversing chancellor's refusal to follow child's wish to live with mother); Anderson v. Anderson, 961 So. 2d 55, 59 (Miss. Ct. App. 2007).

[655] Floyd v. Floyd, 949 So. 2d 26, 30 (Miss. 2007). *But see* Phillips v. Phillips, 45 So. 3d 684, 693-94 (Miss. Ct. App. 2010), *cert. denied*, 49 So. 3d 636 (Miss. 2010) (affirming joint custody award over child's preference to live with father; no findings regarding her wishes).

[656] Anderson v. Anderson, 961 So. 2d 55, 59-60 (Miss. Ct. App. 2007).

§ 12.11[11]   MISSISSIPPI FAMILY LAW

[11] Custodial parent's cohabitation or sexual behavior. A custodial parent's cohabitation is a reason for modification only if it adversely affects a child.[657] The court of appeals reversed a modification in which a chancellor stated that a mother's cohabitation with three men after divorce would "in and of itself" constitute a material change.[658] It is also not necessary that a mother "show remorse" for cohabiting with her current husband to allow her to retain custody.[659] On the other hand, cohabitation may be considered as one of several factors that prove a material change in combination with others. Modification was proper based on a mother's cohabitation, frequent moves, relocation to Colorado, failure to provide medical care, and marriage to a man her child feared.[660] A mother's coaching her youngest son to lie to his father and the court about her cohabitation was an important factor in modifying custody to the father. Her conduct had an adverse impact on the child, who was torn between pleasing her and telling the truth.[661]

A parent's sexual conduct may be a factor in modification. A father's marriage to a sex-toy consultant, at least one incident of spouse-swapping, and a violent and sexually explicit Myspace page were part of the reason for modifying custody.[662]

[12] Lack of cooperation by custodial parent. Generally, a custodial parent's lack of cooperation in visitation should be addressed in contempt proceedings rather than through modification. Modification based on a custodial father's interference with visitation over a three-month period was error. The court of appeals recommended instead that courts incarcerate a parent who intentionally denies visitation: "Changing child custody is not appropriate punishment for contempt."[663] Similarly, a mother's accusations and interference with telephone contact did not warrant modification; her conduct did not rise to an extreme level.[664] In some cases, however, interference may justify

---

[657] Forsythe v. Akers, 768 So. 2d 943, 948 (Miss. Ct. App. 2000); *see also* Brown v. Brown, 764 So. 2d 502, 507 (Miss. Ct. App. 2000) (mother's cohabitation with three different men not a material change).

[658] *See* Sullivan v. Stringer, 736 So. 2d 514, 517-18 (Miss. Ct. App. 1999) (while there was evidence of other adverse circumstances, the court did not rely on those); *see also* Kavanaugh v. Carraway, 435 So. 2d 697, 700 (Miss. 1983) (court erred in modifying custody based on mother's brief premarital cohabitation with current husband); Wikel v. Miller, 53 So. 3d 29, 32 (Miss. Ct. App. 2010) (boys did not seem to be adversely affected by stepfather's premarital overnights), *cert. denied*, 53 So. 3d 760 (Miss. 2011); Sudduth v. Mowdy, 991 So. 2d 1241, 1244 (Miss. Ct. App. 2008) (mother's multiple relationships in themselves not a material change; child not adversely affected); Staggs v. Staggs, 919 So. 2d 112, 119-20 (Miss. Ct. App. 2005) (brief cohabitation the week before custodial mother's wedding not a reason to modify custody).

[659] Phillips v. Phillips, 555 So. 2d 698, 702 (Miss. 1989) (reversing chancellor's award of custody to father because mother's boyfriend occasionally spent night at her house and mother "showed no remorse").

[660] See Stark v. Anderson, 748 So. 2d 838, 843 (Miss. Ct. App. 1999); *see also* Sullivan v. Beason, 37 So. 3d 706, 708-09 (Miss. Ct. App. 2010) (custody transfer based on mother's three post-separation relationships, including one with a married man, and domestic violence in the home); Graves v. Haden, 52 So. 3d 407, 409 (Miss. Ct. App. 2010) (modifying custody of well-adjusted child based on mother's cohabitation, frequent moves, and relationships), *cert. denied*, 50 So. 3d 1003 (Miss. 2011); Richardson v. Richardson, 790 So. 2d 239, 243 (Miss. Ct. App. 2001) (mother lived for two years with abusive boyfriend, had child by him, and interfered with children's contact with father).

[661] Pruett v. Prinz, 979 So. 2d 745, 750-51 (Miss. Ct. App. 2008) (also based on violent second marriage and missed visitation exchanges).

[662] Gainey v. Edington, 24 So. 3d 333, 335 (Miss. Ct. App. 2009*). But see* Wikel v. Miller, 53 So. 3d 29, 32 (Miss. Ct. App. 2010) (mother's lapse in judgment – having a sexual relationship with a minor at the high school where she taught – did not harm children), *cert. denied*, 53 So. 3d 760 (Miss. 2011).

[663] *See* Mixon v. Sharp, 853 So. 2d 834, 838 (Miss. Ct. App. 2003).

[664] Bittick v. Bittick, 987 So. 2d 1058, 1061 (Miss. Ct. App. 2008) (interference did not rise to extreme level); *see also* Gilliland v. Gilliland, 984 So. 2d 364, 370 (Miss. Ct. App. 2008) (interference with telephone visitation and volatile

CHILD CUSTODY AND VISITATION   § 12.11[13]

modification. A mother's six-year interference with visitation was a material change justifying an award of primary custody to the father.[665] Modification was proper when a chancellor found that the custodial mother "embarked on a course of conduct designed to isolate the child from his father."[666] Similarly, a chancellor properly modified custody from a mother to the child's legal father based on her interference with the father-child relationship, including denying visitation, interrupting the child's schooling to prevent the father's involvement, engaging the child in disputes with him, and causing the child emotional distress.[667] And, a chancellor who found that a mother's interference was a material change erred in finding for her on the *Albright* factors of continuity of care and emotional ties – her advantage was achieved by interfering with the father's relationship with the girl.[668]

In a 2006 case, the court of appeals affirmed modification of custody based on expert testimony that a mother's interference and daughter's attitude toward her father reflected parental alienation syndrome. Two experts testified that the mother's conduct had resulted in the child's alienation from her father. They stated that the girl suffered from depression, showed an excessive dependency on her mother, and exhibited a "shallow" animosity toward her father and his relatives without being able to explain why – conduct described as consistent with parental alienation syndrome.[669]

[13] Friction between child and custodial parent. Friction between a child and her custodial mother stemming from divorce and the mother's remarriage was not an adverse change warranting modification.[670] Similarly, friction between a child and stepsiblings was not a material change.[671] However, two children's strained relationship with their stepfather, combined with a split custodial arrangement that everyone agreed

---

relationship between parents not a material change); *cf.* Giannaris v. Giannaris, 960 So. 2d 462, 468-69 (Miss. 2007) (mother's attitude toward child's stepmother, and refusal to shift days did not show danger to child); Balius v. Gaines, 914 So. 2d 300, 310 (Miss. Ct. App. 2005) (interference with visitation should be resolved through contempt except in extreme cases); Balius v. Gaines, 908 So. 2d 791, 801-02 (Miss. Ct. App. 2005) (refusal to provide additional visitation, failure to notify father of location for ten-day period, failure to provide diaper bag, and argument over health insurance fell "far short" of the required material adverse change in circumstances); Creel v. Cornacchione, 831 So. 2d 1179, 1183 (Miss. Ct. App. 2002) (no *Albright* consideration required because allegations of father's interference with mother's relationship with children did not show a material change); Lipsey v. Lipsey, 755 So. 2d 564, 566-67 (Miss. Ct. App. 2000) (lack of cooperation between parents not reason to change from sole custody in father to joint custody).

[665] Ash v. Ash, 622 So. 2d 1264, 1266-67 (Miss. 1993) (modification followed ten court hearings and numerous violations by mother; court emphasized that the case was unusual and use of the contempt power a preferable way to protect visitation rights); *see also* T.K. v. H.K., 24 So. 3d 1055, 1064 (Miss. Ct. App. 2010) (modification based in part on mother's removal of child to another state without father's knowledge; he was unable to locate her for two months).

[666] *See* Ferguson v. Ferguson, 782 So. 2d 181, 183 (Miss. Ct. App. 2001) (included forbidding child to speak to father at ball games, installing a blocking device on phone to prevent father's calls, having father forcibly evicted from hospital after he drove a long distance to see child, dismantling child's room after child expressed desire to live with father); *see also* MacDonald v. MacDonald, 876 So. 2d 296, 297-98 (Miss. 2004) (custody temporarily modified to mother based in part on custodial father's interference with visitation).

[667] Thornhill v. Van Dan, 918 So. 2d 725, 733 (Miss. Ct. App.), *cert. granted*, 921 So. 2d 344 (Miss. 2005); *see also* Potter v. Greene, 973 So. 2d 291, 293-94 (Miss. Ct. App. 2008) (mother's unfounded accusations of sexual assault and continued interference with visitation basis for modifying custody); *cf.* Davis v. Davis, 17 So. 3d 114, 118 (Miss. Ct. App. 2009) (custody of a teenage girl modified based upon the mother's interference with visitation and her lack of judgment in writing an intimidating letter to the daughter's friend).

[668] Story v. Allen, 7 So. 2d 3d 295, 298-99 (Miss. Ct. App. 2008).

[669] Ellis v. Ellis, 952 So. 2d 982, 997 (Miss. Ct. App. 2006).

[670] Franklin v. Kroush, 622 So. 2d 1256, 1257 (Miss. 1993).

[671] Mixon v. Sharp, 853 So. 2d 834, 838 (Miss. Ct. App. 2003) (such problems are typical in all families).

§ 12.11[14]   MISSISSIPPI FAMILY LAW

was damaging, warranted modification of joint custody.[672]

[14] Child's behavior. A child's behavioral or emotional problems, or poor school performance under a custodial parent's care may justify a change in custody. However, there must be evidence that the problems are attributable to or exacerbated by circumstances in the custodial home. The fact that a child was experiencing emotional problems since his parents' divorce did not warrant a change in custody – credible evidence was presented that the problems were a result of the divorce and custody battle.[673] Similarly, an otherwise well-adjusted child's precocious sexual knowledge was not a sufficient reason to justify modification.[674] However, a young child's extreme inappropriate behavior in his mother's care was one factor supporting modification.[675] And a chancellor properly found that a mother's frequent moves and relationships had adversely affected a child who suffered from low self-esteem and was doing poorly in school.[676] The fact that a young boy had to repeat kindergarten because of excessive absences was one of several factors supporting modification to a father, in whose temporary custody the child was making good grades and thriving.[677]

[15] De facto change in custody. A custodial parent's voluntary alteration of custody arrangements may constitute a material change in circumstances.[678] A mother's relinquishment of her child's care and custody to her parents for much of the four years after divorce was a material change.[679] And a de facto change in custody was one of several factors supporting a finding of material change – the child spent substantial

---

[672] Breidemeier v. Jackson, 689 So. 2d 770, 776 (Miss. 1997); *see also* Jones v. Jones, 878 So. 2d 1061 (Miss. Ct. App. 2004) (modification based on seventeen-year-old's genuine desire to live with mother, combined with father's increasingly controlling behavior).

[673] Cheek v. Ricker, 431 So. 2d 1139, 1145 (Miss. 1983); *see also* Wikel v. Miller, 53 So. 3d 29, 32 (Miss. Ct. App. 2010) (behavioral problems were linked to the divorce and tension between the parents over visitation), *cert. denied*, 53 So. 3d 760 (Miss. 2011); Lewis v. Lewis, 974 So. 2d 265, 266-67 (Miss. Ct. App. 2008) (conflicts between mother and daughter related to discipline not a reason to change custody; son's learning problems not attributable to mother's parenting); Dykes v. McMurray, 938 So. 2d 330, 336 (Miss. Ct. App. 2006) (child's "occasional unhappiness" after mother's remarriage was not a material change, child was healthy and well-adjusted); Lambert v. Lambert, 872 So. 2d 679, 686 (Miss. Ct. App. 2003) (child's anxiety caused by divorce and subsequent modification litigation rather than relocation); Scroggins v. Riley, 758 So. 2d 467, 471 (Miss. Ct. App. 2000) (son's emotional problems attributable to divorce rather than custodial father's care).

[674] Smith v. Jones, 654 So. 2d 480, 491 (Miss. 1995).

[675] *See* Brawley v. Brawley, 734 So. 2d 237, 241-42 (Miss. Ct. App. 1999) (child used obscene gestures, spit on people, exhibited knowledge of sexual behavior; in addition, house was overcrowded and mother neglected child's hygiene and medical care); *see also* McDonald v. McDonald, 39 So. 3d 868, 880-81 (Miss. Ct. App. 2010) (modification based on boys' disruptive behavior that led to expulsion from daycare programs).

[676] *See* Brown v. White, 875 So. 2d 1116, 1119 (Miss. Ct. App. 2004).

[677] Minter v. Minter, 29 So. 3d 840, 850 (Miss. Ct. App. 2009), *cert. denied*, 29 So. 3d 774 (Miss. 2010).

[678] *See* Brocato v. Brocato, 731 So. 2d 1138, 1143 (Miss. 1999) (custodial father's relinquishment of actual care of both children to relatives was material change). *But cf.* Arnold v. Conwill, 562 So. 2d 97, 99-100 (Miss. 1990) (no material change just because mother requested that child stay temporarily with father immediately after mother moved); Sudduth v. Mowdy, 991 So. 2d 1241, 1242-43 (Miss. Ct. App. 2008) (out-of-court agreement under which daughter lived with noncustodial father for twenty months was not a material change).

[679] McBride v. Cook, 858 So. 2d 160, 162 (Miss. Ct. App. 2003); *see also* Davidson v. Coit, 899 So. 2d 904, 911 (Miss. Ct. App. 2005) (factor in custody modification that mother's partner provided primary care for children). *But see* Keys v. Keys, 930 So. 2d 438, 444 (Miss. Ct. App. 2005) (chancellor erred in transferring custody of college student from father to mother; child had moved her belongings into her mother's house but did not reside with either parent a majority of the time).

CHILD CUSTODY AND VISITATION   § 12.11[16]

time with his father while his mother worked nights at a casino.[680]

[16] Military service. In 2008, the Mississippi legislature enacted a statute providing that a custodial parent's deployment, temporary duty, or mobilization, and the resulting temporary disruption, may not be factors in determining whether a change in circumstances has occurred for purposes of custody modification.[681] The statute also provides that any order of temporary custody shall end ten days after the deployed parent returns.[682]

[17] Improvement in noncustodial parent's circumstances. As a general rule, an improvement in a noncustodial parent's circumstances does not satisfy the traditional test for modification. The test requires a negative change in the custodial parent's home, not a positive change in the noncustodial parent's circumstances. A court erred in modifying custody to a mother based on evidence that she had remarried and established a stable home.[683] Nor does a noncustodial parent's move support modification. The court of appeals reversed a court's custody modification from father to mother; the only change was that the mother moved twenty miles away and could not see the children as often.[684]

Under limited circumstances, however, a noncustodial parent's improved circumstances justify modification. The Mississippi appellate courts have created an alternate test for modification when a child has been living in serious adverse circumstances since entry of the custody decree. [685]

[18] Alternate test for modification: Ongoing adverse circumstances. The traditional test for modification usually achieves a satisfactory balance between protecting children and ensuring the stability of custodial arrangements. However, it hampers courts' ability to protect children in the unfortunate situation in which both parents were questionably fit custodians at the time of divorce. Because the test requires a negative change in the custodial parent, a court is prohibited from transferring custody if the noncustodial parent shows significant improvement.

---

[680] Betts v. Massey, 40 So. 3d 602, 609 (Miss. Ct. App. 2009), *cert. denied*, 42 So. 3d 24 (Miss. 2010) (four judges dissented, stating that considering de facto change in custody as basis for modification would discourage cooperation between parents).

[681] MISS. CODE ANN. § 93-5-34 (Supp. 2010) (providing for expedited hearing on motion of deployed parent and for presentation of evidence by affidavit or electronic means if necessary). *See supra* § 12.09[8] related to visitation for a deployed noncustodial parent.

[682] MISS. CODE ANN. § 93-5-34(3)(b) (Supp. 2010) (but providing for emergency custody hearing upon parent's return based on filing of petition alleging need for emergency custody).

[683] Duran v. Weaver, 495 So. 2d 1355, 1357 (Miss. 1986); *see also* Smith v. Todd, 464 So. 2d 1155, 1158 (Miss. 1985) (noncustodial mother's argument that she could provide better home did not prove material change); Mercier v. Mercier, 11 So. 3d 1283, 1286 (Miss. Ct. App. 2009) (fact that noncustodial mother's home circumstances had improved since decree was irrelevant); McCracking v. McCracking, 776 So. 2d 691, 693 (Miss. Ct. App. 2000) (relative merits of parents is issue for original custody decision; modification requires material adverse change); *cf.* Lewis v. Lewis, 974 So. 2d 265, 267-68 (Miss. Ct. App. 2008) (father's remarriage not a material change in circumstances; change must occur in the custodial parent's home).

[684] Beasley v. Beasley, 913 So. 2d 358, 364 (Miss. Ct. App. 2005); *see also* Giannaris v. Giannaris, 960 So. 2d 462, 469 (Miss. 2007) (court erred in finding that noncustodial father's move to California was material change in circumstances).

[685] *See infra* § 12.11[18].

405

§ 12.11[19]   MISSISSIPPI FAMILY LAW

In 1996, the supreme court in *Riley v. Doerner* addressed this deficiency. The court held that custody may be modified when the environment provided by a custodial parent has been continuously adverse to a child's best interests and the noncustodial parent has changed positively and can provide a more suitable home.[686] Otherwise, "so long as the neglect of the children has been continuous since the earlier grant of custody, the chancellor is without authority to intervene."[687]

The alternate "adverse environment" test applies only when a child is living in genuinely adverse circumstances. For example, the alternate test was properly applied to change custody to a father who showed that the mother had persistently failed to provide proper care for their children and that his home situation had improved since the divorce.[688] Similarly, the *Riley* test was properly applied to modify custody based on evidence that a custodial mother had persistently failed to care for a child's personal hygiene and medical needs.[689] However, the test is not a vehicle for parents to relitigate the *Albright* factors.[690] A chancellor properly applied the traditional test upon finding that a child was properly cared for by her custodial father. The fact that the noncustodial mother had improved her circumstances by remarrying and attending church was not a reason to modify custody.[691] The *Riley* test is not applicable to actions between a third party and natural parent.[692]

[19] Modification of joint custody. Modification of joint custody does not require proof that one of the parents is providing inadequate care. The triggering event is more likely to be a change that makes the arrangement unworkable, such as one parent's relocation or serious parental conflict. Upon finding a material change, a court is to apply the *Albright* factors to determine which parent should have primary custody.[693] A finding of a material change is essential. When a joint custodial mother's work shift changed from night to day, she sought modification to sole custody. The chancellor found that no material adverse change had occurred, but that it was in the child's best interest to modify the joint custody to award primary physical custody to the mother. The court of appeals held that the court erred in modifying joint custody without finding that a material change in circumstances adverse to the child had occurred.[694] As with modification of sole custody, joint custody may be modified based only on events

---

[686] *See* Riley v. Doerner, 677 So. 2d 740, 744 (Miss. 1996) ("A child's resilience and ability to cope with difficult circumstances should not serve to shackle the child to an unhealthy home, especially when a healthier one beckons.") (evidence also showed multiple moves, sporadic employment, and several live-in partners).

[687] Carter v. Carter, 735 So. 2d 1109, 1114 (Miss. 1999) (discussing *Riley* test).

[688] *See* Carter v. Carter, 735 So. 2d 1109, 1114 (Miss. 1999).

[689] *See* Hoggatt v. Hoggatt, 796 So. 2d 273, 274 (Miss. Ct. App. 2001); *see also* Sullivan v. Beason, 37 So. 3d 706, 712 (Miss. Ct. App. 2010) (finding a material change and, alternatively, that child had been in adverse circumstances since decree).

[690] Hoggatt v. Hoggatt, 796 So. 2d 273, 274 (Miss. Ct. App. 2001).

[691] *See* McGehee v. Upchurch, 733 So. 2d 364, 369 (Miss. Ct. App. 1999) (fact that mother remarried and attended church with child was insufficient for modification; no adverse changes occurred in custodial household); *see also* Lewis v. Lewis, 974 So. 2d 265, 268 (Miss. Ct. App. 2008) (*Riley* test not applicable; mother's home environment was not "adverse" to the children).

[692] Hillman v. Vance, 910 So. 2d 43, 45-47 (Miss. Ct. App. 2005) (rejecting grandmother's suit for custody based on "unwholesome environment" because mother was a stripper).

[693] McRree v. McRree, 723 So. 2d 1217, 1220 (Miss. Ct. App. 1998).

[694] Johnson v. Johnson, 913 So. 2d 368, 370 (Miss. Ct. App. 2005).

CHILD CUSTODY AND VISITATION   § 12.11[19][a]

occurring since the original decree. A chancellor erred in modifying joint custody based in part upon a mother's conduct prior to the divorce trial.[695]

[a] One parent's relocation. A move by one joint custodian will almost always be a material change in circumstances warranting a change to sole physical custody in one parent.[696] As the court of appeals recently noted, a "shared custody agreement between parents of a child of school age, living in two different states, would be quite difficult to maintain."[697] A court properly granted a father sole physical and legal custody when the joint custodian mother moved from Mississippi to Arizona without consulting him.[698] A joint custodian father's move from north Mississippi to Memphis, Tennessee was a material change requiring modification. The court awarded him sole custody because he was better able to provide childcare and had greater job stability.[699] And an agreement requiring weekly shared custody was modified when parents moved to different locations.[700] The Court of Appeals affirmed a chancellor's modification from joint physical custody to sole custody in the father when the mother moved eighty miles away. The move required weekly transfers of the four-year-old girl.[701] Similarly, a mother's planned move from Jackson to Memphis was a material change in circumstances warranting transfer of custody to the father, who remained in Jackson.[702] A chancellor may properly find that the factor of stability of environment favors the parent who is not relocating.[703]

[b] Based on inability to cooperate. Parental cooperation is an essential component of joint custody, particularly joint legal custody. Joint custodian parents' estrangement and resulting failure to communicate was a material change in circumstances adverse to their child, warranting modification of custody to the father.[704] Joint custody between combative parents was properly modified based upon proof that the

---

[695] Lackey v. Fuller, 755 So. 2d 1083, 1086-87 (Miss. 2000); *cf.* Pearson v. Pearson, 11 So. 3d 178, 186 (Miss. Ct. App. 2009) (Judge Roberts concurred with a separate opinion joined by Judge Griffis stating that a "material change in circumstances" finding is not required when both parents request a change from joint custody).

[696] *See* Lackey v. Fuller, 755 So. 2d 1083, 1088-89 (Miss. 2000) (mother's move to New York made exchange of custody every two weeks impractical); Sobieske v. Preslar, 755 So. 2d 410, 413 (Miss. 2000) (joint custody modified when mother decided to move to Atlanta); McRree v. McRree, 723 So. 2d 1217, 1219-20 (Miss. Ct. App. 1998) (mother's move to Texas made alternating joint custody impractical).

[697] Elliott v. Elliott, 877 So. 2d 450, 455 (Miss. Ct. App. 2003); *see also* Franklin v. Winter, 936 So. 2d 429, 431 (Miss. Ct. App. 2006) (500 mile move by joint custodial father was material change in circumstances).

[698] Elliott v. Elliott, 877 So. 2d 450, 455-56 (Miss. Ct. App. 2003).

[699] *See* Rinehart v. Barnes, 819 So. 2d 564, 565-66 (Miss. Ct. App. 2002); *see also* Porter v. Porter, 23 So. 3d 438, 447 (Miss. 2009) (mother's relocation from Jackson to Memphis made joint physical custody "impractical" and therefore was a material change in circumstances).

[700] *See* Massey v. Huggins, 799 So. 2d 902, 906 (Miss. Ct. App. 2001) (joint custody requiring four weekly exchanges impractical).

[701] Pearson v. Pearson, 11 So. 3d 178, 182 (Miss. Ct. App. 2009).

[702] Porter v. Porter, 23 So. 3d 438, 447 (Miss. 2009).

[703] *See* Porter v. Porter, 23 So. 3d 438, 448 (Miss. 2009); McRree v. McRree, 723 So. 2d 1217, 1220 (Miss. Ct. App. 1998) (court's consideration of factor was not enforcement of invalid agreement restricting relocation).

[704] *See* Eason v. Kosier, 850 So. 2d 188, 190 (Miss. Ct. App. 2003); *see also* Caples v. Caples, 686 So. 2d 1071, 1073 (Miss. 1996) (modifying joint custody decree where father used decree to file harassing legal proceedings and mother suffered financial hardship as a result). *But cf.* Grissom v. Grissom, 952 So. 2d 1023, 1027-28 (Miss. Ct. App. 2007) (modification denied when mother alleged inability to communicate predating decree; no material change occurring since decree).

§ 12.11[19][c] MISSISSIPPI FAMILY LAW

arrangement was confusing to the child and contributed to his feeling of instability.[705] And joint legal custody was modified based on three years of "acrimony, failure to confer, and failure to communicate."[706] However, a chancellor erred in modifying joint custody to sole custody based on a mother's allegations of lack of communication. The court of appeals distinguished cases in which the parties' behavior showed ongoing, serious acrimony and inability to work together.[707]

[c] Child reaching school age. A joint physical custody arrangement between parents in different locations generally requires modification when the child enters school.[708] However, because parents had agreed to joint custody until the child entered school, followed by primary custody in the father, a court erred in transferring custody to the mother when the child reached school age – no material change had occurred since their agreement.[709]

[d] Disruptive to children. A joint custodial arrangement that is unduly disruptive to children may be modified. The supreme court held that a material change in circumstances occurred when all parties agreed that a split custody arrangement in which children were transferred monthly had an adverse impact on the children.[710]

[e] Modification of joint legal custody. Joint legal custody may be modified upon proof that parents are unable to act cooperatively, and that sole legal custody is in the child's best interest. A chancellor did not err in modifying joint legal custody of an autistic child to sole legal custody in her father – because of the friction between the parties, it was in the child's best interest for one parent to be responsible for determining his medical treatment and education.[711]

[20] Modification of visitation. To modify a visitation order, a petitioner must prove that the visitation order is not working and that it is in the child's best interest to modify the order.[712] It is not necessary to prove a material change in circumstances.[713] Modification of mid-week visitation was permitted when the schedule was disruptive

---

[705] Cavett v. Cavett, 744 So. 2d 372, 377-78 (Miss. Ct. App. 1999).

[706] Cook v. Whiddon, 866 So. 2d 494, 502 (Miss. Ct. App. 2004).

[707] Jones v. McGuage, 932 So. 2d 846, 849 (Miss. Ct. App. 2006).

[708] *See* also Torrence v. Moore, 455 So. 2d 778, 780 (Miss. 1984) (parents in same town agreed that child's entering school was material change and requested change from joint to sole custody).

[709] Pierce v. Chandler, 855 So. 2d 455, 459 (Miss. Ct. App. 2003).

[710] *See* Breidmeir v. Jackson, 689 So. 2d 770, 776 (Miss. 1997).

[711] Purviance v. Burgess, 980 So. 2d 308 (Miss. Ct. App. 2007).

[712] Wilburn v. Wilburn, 991 So. 2d 1185, 1194-95 (Miss. 2008); Jones v. McGuage, 932 So. 2d 846, 850 (Miss. Ct. App. 2006) (test for modifying visitation not met by proof that child made a B on spelling, which she studied at the father's home, while she had As in other subjects); Christian v. Wheat, 876 So. 2d 341, 345 (Miss. 2004); Bittick v. Bittick, 987 So. 2d 1058, 1061 (Miss. Ct. App. 2008); Shepherd v. Shepherd, 769 So. 2d 242, 245 (Miss. Ct. App. 2000).

[713] *See* Sistrunck v. McKenzie, 455 So. 2d 768, 769 (Miss. 1984) (announcing rule); H.L.S. v. R.S.R., 949 So. 2d 794, 797 (Miss. Ct. App. 2006) (father's interference with visitation showed order was not working; *see also* Olson v. Olson, 799 So. 2d 927, 929 (Miss. Ct. App. 2001); Shepherd v. Shepherd, 769 So. 2d 242, 245 (Miss. Ct. App. 2000) (father's desire to spend more time with children not reason to alter schedule); Suess v. Suess, 718 So. 2d 1126, 1130 (Miss. Ct. App. 1998).

CHILD CUSTODY AND VISITATION   § 12.12

to a young child who needed more stability.[714] Similarly, an order was properly modified to eliminate mid-week visitation when a custodial mother moved from Mississippi to Florida.[715] A chancellor properly modified visitation when a noncustodial mother moved from Senatobia to New Albany, based upon a finding that three weekends a month was disruptive to the children's routine.[716] A court erred in refusing to modify a visitation schedule that both parents agreed was not working.[717] However, one parent's dissatisfaction with the arrangement does not necessarily warrant modification.[718]

Custodial parent interference may justify visitation restrictions on the custodial parent. The Mississippi Court of Appeals affirmed a chancellor's order prohibiting a mother from contacting a child during the father's visitation and requiring that she refrain from scheduling events during visitation.[719]

§ 12.12 ENFORCEMENT

A full discussion of contempt as an enforcement mechanism is included in Chapter XIV. This section discusses enforcement issues peculiar to custody cases.

[1] Contempt

[a] Custodial parent. Custodial parents may be held in contempt for failure to comply with court-ordered visitation. A chancellor properly held a mother in contempt for interrupting a father's summer visitation by taking the children back to her home based on their complaints.[720] A custodial parent who removed children from the jurisdiction in violation of a court order was properly held in contempt.[721] Failure to comply with an order is not excused because a custodial parent disagrees with an order or is acting on the advice of counsel or other experts. A mother who claimed to be acting on a psychologist's advice was found in contempt for refusing visitation, scheduling events during visitation, and creating stress by contacting the child during visitation.[722] A custodial father who refused to comply with visitation was found in contempt even though

---

[714] *See* McCracking v. McCracking, 776 So. 2d 691, 695 (Miss. Ct. App. 2000); *see also* McDonald v. McDonald, 39 So. 3d 868, 876-77 (Miss. Ct. App. 2010) (ending mother's Wednesday night visitation; boys exhibited behavioral problems on Thursdays).

[715] *See* Fountain v. Fountain, 877 So. 2d 474, 480-81 (Miss. Ct. App. 2003) (but continuing standard visitation); *see also* Balius v. Gaines, 908 So. 2d 791, 799 (Miss. Ct. App. 2005) (court properly modified visitation order requiring custodial mother in California to share transportation expenses of optional once-a-month visitation; provision imposed an undue financial burden on her).

[716] Mercier v. Mercier, 11 So. 3d 1283, 1287 (Miss. Ct. App. 2009).

[717] Stevison v. Woods, 560 So. 2d 176, 181 (Miss. 1990).

[718] *See* Haddon v. Haddon, 806 So. 2d 1017, 1020 (Miss. 2000).

[719] Ellis v. Ellis, 840 So. 2d 806, 811-12 (Miss. Ct. App. 2003); *see also* Cavett v. Cavett, 744 So. 2d 372, 377 (Miss. Ct. App. 1999) (both parents restricted from calling child during time with other parent).

[720] Strain v. Strain, 847 So. 2d 276, 278 (Miss. Ct. App. 2003) (complaints that they were not fed breakfast, were not having fun, and did not get to see their father enough did not justify interference); *see also* H.L.S. v. R.S.R., 949 So. 2d 794, 797 (Miss. Ct. App. 2006) (father held in contempt for willful failure to permit visitation).

[721] Vockroth v. Vockroth, 200 So. 2d 459, 464 (Miss. 1967); *see also* Faris v. Jernigan, 939 So. 2d 835, 838 (Miss. Ct. App. 2006) (mother held in contempt for refusing to return child after visitation).

[722] Ellis v. Ellis, 840 So. 2d 806, 811-12 (Miss. Ct. App. 2003). *But cf.* Lewis v. Butler, 794 So. 2d 1015, 1016-19 (Miss. 2001) (court did not address contempt against mother who violated order based on father's sexual advances to child).

§ 12.12[1][b]   **MISSISSIPPI FAMILY LAW**

he stated that he was concerned about the mother's mental state and had acted on the advice of counsel; the fact that the defendant had good motives or acted on advice of counsel is relevant only in mitigation.[723] However, there must be some evidence of willful failure to comply. A mother should not have been held in contempt for noncompliance with visitation because her fourteen-year-old daughter refused to visit her father even though the mother encouraged her to visit.[724] A brief failure to comply with visitation orders does not necessarily require a finding of contempt. A court did not err in refusing to hold a mother in contempt for denying visitation for a single weekend after seven years of compliance with the order.[725]

A custodial parent who attempts to block visitation may be held in contempt even though the order does not set specific dates for visitation. A mother was held in contempt for failing to set times for visitation under an order providing for "liberal" visitation to be arranged by the parties. The court noted that liberal visitation provisions are intended to provide flexibility to the parties, but that liberal visitation at a minimum includes two weekends a month and five weeks in the summer.[726]

A court properly ordered a custodial father to pay costs and attorneys' fees associated with a hearing finding him in contempt for violation of visitation orders.[727]

[b] Noncustodial parent violation. The supreme court upheld a chancellor's five-day incarceration of a father who violated an order prohibiting overnight visitation with his girlfriend present; he took the child and his girlfriend on a camping trip.[728]

[c] Joint custodian. A court erred in incarcerating a joint custodian mother for moving to Arizona. The order establishing joint custody did not prohibit the parties from removing the children from the state.[729]

[2] Bond. A parent who has abducted or is likely to abduct children may be required to post a bond. The court of appeals upheld a chancellor's order that a noncustodial mother post a $1,000 bond because she had previously removed the children from the state without consulting their father.[730] A court required a $2,000 bond from

---

[723] Ladner v. Ladner, 206 So. 2d 620, 621 (Miss. 1968).

[724] Goodson v. Goodson, 816 So. 2d 420, 423 (Miss. Ct. App. 2002); *see also* Jones v. Jones, 878 So. 2d 1061, 1064 (Miss. Ct. App. 2004) (mother's communication with child about custody modification technically violated custody order, but conduct was not willful); *cf.* Humphrey v. Martin, 755 So. 2d 551, 555 (Miss. Ct. App. 2000) (noncustodial mother's willful failure to return child to grandparents).

[725] Smith v. Smith, 545 So. 2d 725, 727 (Miss. 1989) (mother denied visitation based on belief that child's father and his partner were not married); *see also* Gregory v. Gregory, 881 So. 2d 840, 846-47 (Miss. Ct. App. 2003) (suggesting the fact that a mother who disobeyed visitation order did so based on evidence of abuse and promptly sought temporary relief, "might be a factor" in the "significance" of the contempt).

[726] *See* Chalk v. Lentz, 744 So. 2d 789, 792 (Miss. Ct. App. 1999).

[727] McDonald v. McDonald, 850 So. 2d 1182, 1193 (Miss. Ct. App. 2002); *see also* H.L.S. v. R.S.R., 949 So. 2d 794, 797 (Miss. Ct. App. 2006) (father held in contempt for willful failure to permit visitation ordered to pay attorneys' fees); Faris v. Jernigan, 939 So. 2d 835, 841 (Miss. Ct. App. 2006) (mother ordered to pay $40,000 of $75,000 expended by father in attempt to recover custody of child).

[728] *See* Dilling v. Dilling, 734 So. 2d 327, 338-39 (Miss. Ct. App. 1999).

[729] Elliott v. Elliott, 877 So. 2d 450, 457 (Miss. Ct. App. 2003).

[730] *See* Ayers v. Ayers, 734 So. 2d 213, 217-18 (Miss. Ct. App. 1999); *see also* Roberts v. Fuhr, 523 So. 2d 20, 19 (Miss. 1987) (father required to post bond for visitation after he had taken child to Germany for months during custody dispute); Rodgers v. Rodgers, 274 So. 2d 671, 673-74 (Miss. 1973) (stating that court may require parent to enter into a

410

CHILD CUSTODY AND VISITATION

§ 12.12[2]

a father who wrongfully removed a child from the mother's home.[731] A chancellor did not err in ordering that a mother post a $40,000 *ne exeat* bond in order to exercise overnight visitation with her daughter outside the State of Mississippi. After an earlier modification of custody based on her interference with visitation rights, the mother refused to return the child from visitation in Georgia, forfeited a $5,000 bond, again made unfounded accusations of abuse, and surrendered the child to Georgia's Child Protective Services.[732]

---

bond to assure its jurisdiction is retained over the child).

[731] Stauffer v. Stauffer, 379 So. 2d 922, 924-25 (Miss. 1980).

[732] Faris v. Jernigan, 939 So. 2d 835, 841 (Miss. Ct. App. 2006).

412

XIII
CHILD SUPPORT

Until recently, a parent's duty to support minor children was policed by the individual states. Judges were authorized to award child support, guided by general standards of need and ability to pay. In the 1980s, national focus on children in poverty prompted federal intervention. Today, state child support laws are the product of Congressional mandates to unify awards and reduce arrearages. Modern child support awards are based on statutory formulas rather than judicial discretion, and a national enforcement mechanism exists to pursue payment of arrearages.

§ 13.01 HISTORY AND OVERVIEW

[1] History

[a] The common law duty of support. The duty of parents to support a child has been recognized and regulated for centuries. Surprisingly, however, the common law basis for support was never well articulated.[1] At different times, the duty has been grounded in morality, linked to custody, and described as an obligation to the state. According to Blackstone, siring a child carried with it a natural law obligation of support.[2] In Elizabethan England, parents' failure to support their children violated a duty to the state, resulting in criminal punishment.[3] American courts in the nineteenth century linked support duties to parents' custodial rights.[4] Ultimately, legislatures removed any lingering uncertainty about the source of parental duties by enacting child support statutes.[5] The modern explanation for the support duty is simply that the obligation serves the best interests of the child and of society.[6]

In 1924, the Mississippi Supreme Court rejected a father's argument that he had no post-divorce support duty to a child in the mother's custody. The court held that a father has a common law duty of support independent of custody or a child's services.[7] The duty is codified in section 93-5-23 of the Mississippi Code: "When a divorce shall be decreed . . . the court may . . . make all orders touching the care, custody, and maintenance of the children of the marriage."[8]

---

[1] *See* H. CLARK, THE LAW OF DOMESTIC RELATIONS IN THE UNITED STATES § 17.1, at 710, n.5 (2d ed. 1987).

[2] *See* FAMILY LAW AND PRACTICE § 33.02[3][a], at 33-37 (Arnold H. Rutkin ed. 1999); Leslie D. Harris et al., *Making and Breaking Connections Between Parents' Duty to Support and Right to Control Their Children*, 69 OR. L. REV. 689, 692-708 (1990).

[3] FAMILY LAW AND PRACTICE, *supra* note 2, § 33.02[1], at 33-35 (citing 43 Eliz 1, c.2 §§ 1. iii (1601) (duty to prevent children from becoming wards of the state)).

[4] Harris et al., *supra* note 2, at 692-708.

[5] *See* Harris et al. *supra* note 2, at 692-708.

[6] Harris et al., *supra* note 2 at 692-708.

[7] *See* Lee v. Lee, 101 So. 345, 346 (Miss. 1924) (noting that, while there was some authority to the contrary, the weight of authority supported the father's continuing obligation).

[8] MISS. CODE ANN. § 93-5-23 (2004). A similar provision was included in the divorce statute as early as 1857. *See* Garland v. Garland, 50 Miss. 694, 705 (1874) (citing art. 13 of the Code of 1857).

§ 13.01[1][b]   MISSISSIPPI FAMILY LAW

[b] Pre-guideline statutes. Until the late 1980s, support obligations were defined in vague terms such as "just" or "reasonable."[9] Support awards were based on general factors such as the child's needs, the parents' resources, the family standard of living, and the noncustodial parent's needs.[10] Awards were enforced through the court's contempt power.

As the divorce rate and the number of nonmarital births increased, national attention focused on the financial plight of single-parent households. Some single parents did not have support awards.[11] Many who did had seriously inadequate awards[12] or awards substantially in arrears.[13] In addition, support awards lacked consistency and predictability even within each state.[14]

Prior to the enactment of guidelines, child support awards in Mississippi were based on general factors established by the Mississippi Supreme Court in 1955 in *Brabham v. Brabham.*[15] Chancellors were to consider the health, income, and earning capacity of both parents; the reasonable needs of the child and custodial parent; the necessary living expenses of the noncustodial parent; tax consequences to both parties; whether the custodial parent had the free use of home, furnishings or automobile; and other relevant facts and circumstances.[16] Trial of a child support case required proof of the income of both parents, their monthly expenses, and the child's reasonable needs. Awards were reversed only upon a showing that the award was an abuse of the court's discretion.

[c] Federal involvement. To address problems of inadequate and inconsistent awards, Congress enacted a series of laws that resulted in an unprecedented federal presence in family law. In 1974, Congress enacted Title IV-D of the Social Security Act, establishing a child support collection system involving federal and state cooperation and funded in part with federal dollars. The Act called for creation of state IV-D agencies responsible for establishing paternity and obtaining and enforcing child support orders. In 1984, the Act was amended to provide for enhanced enforcement of support. Among other provisions, the Act included a mandate that states require income withholding for support in arrears.[17]

---

[9] AMERICAN LAW INSTITUTE, PRINCIPLES OF THE LAW OF FAMILY DISSOLUTION: ANALYSIS AND RECOMMENDATIONS Pt. II, at xxvi (Tentative Draft No. 3, 1988).

[10] *See* CLARK, *supra* note 1, § 18.1, at 360; *see also* UNIF. MARRIAGE AND DIVORCE ACT, 9A U.L.A. §§ 309, 400 (1987).

[11] *See* Nancy Thoennes et al., *The Impact of Child Support Guidelines on Award Adequacy, Award Variability, and Case Processing Efficiency*, 25 FAM. L.Q. 325, 326 (1991) (finding in 1984 that 39% of custodial parents had no child support award).

[12] *See* Lucy Marsh Yee, *What Really Happens in Child Support Cases: An Empirical Study of Establishment and Enforcement of Child Support Orders in the Denver District Court*, 57 DEN. L.J. 21, 36 (1979) (noting that support orders are often lower than car payments).

[13] *See* CENSUS BUREAU, U.S. DEP'T OF COMMERCE, CHILD SUPPORT AND ALIMONY: 1985 (Current Pop. Rep., Series P-23, No. 154, 1989), *cited in* LAURA W. MORGAN, CHILD SUPPORT GUIDELINES: INTERPRETATION AND APPLICATION § 1.01, at 1-4, n.11 (1st ed. 1996 & Supp. 1999). The report estimated that one-quarter of custodial mothers received no support at all and only one-half received the full amount ordered. *Id.*

[14] *See* Kenneth R. White et al., *A Study of Alimony and Child Support Rulings with Some Recommendations*, 10 FAM. L.Q. 75-76, 83 (1976).

[15] 84 So. 2d 147 (Miss. 1955).

[16] Brabham v. Brabham, 84 So. 2d 147, 153 (Miss. 1955).

[17] JOHN DE WITT GREGORY ET AL., UNDERSTANDING FAMILY LAW § 9.06[5], at 345 (2d ed. 2001).

CHILD SUPPORT §13.01[2]

The 1988 Family Support Act addressed the need for increased uniformity in support orders.[18] The Act required that states establish child support guidelines that would set a presumptively correct amount of support.[19] The Family Support Act was the catalyst for a national overhaul of child support standards. In a brief span of time, states discarded the subjective factors of "need" and "ability to pay" for structured guidelines.

Congress again enhanced support enforcement in 1996 when it passed the Personal Responsibility and Work Opportunity Reconciliation Act [PRWORA].[20] The Act provided additional tools for locating absent parents, creating a "new hire" directory and providing state agencies with access to governmental information and records.[21] The Act also required that each state adopt the Uniform Interstate Family Support Act [UIFSA],[22] which provides for expedited and uniform interstate enforcement.

Mississippi adopted statutory child support guidelines in 1989, pursuant to the federal mandate. The legislature adopted the flat percentage method of calculating support, setting support for one child at 17% of a payor's income.[23] The statute was amended the following year to establish lower percentages which remain in effect today.[24]

[2] General considerations

[a] Types of support actions. Child support may be ordered as part of a divorce,[25] annulment,[26] or separate maintenance action.[27] In addition, support may be awarded in an independent action between unmarried parents. Chancery courts are authorized to "entertain suits for the custody, care, support and maintenance of minor children and . . . hear and determine all such matters."[28] A court may also order support in a paternity action.[29]

[b] Jurisdiction and venue. Under the Mississippi Constitution, chancery courts are granted authority over all cases involving divorce and alimony and cases involving minors.[30] Subject matter jurisdiction to award child support is also provided

---

[18] 42 U.S.C. §§ 651-669 (2000).

[19] *See* 42 U.S.C. § 667 (2000) (providing for IV-D agency review and adjustment of support orders at least once every four years). In addition to the federally-mandated guidelines, Congress in 1992 passed the "deadbeat dad" or Child Support Recovery Act, which created criminal liability for a parent who is more than $5,000 in arrears in support or over one year in arrears. 18 U.S.C. § 228 (2004).

[20] 42 U.S.C. §§ 601-615 (2000) (replacing AFDC with Temporary Assistance to Needy Families (TANF) program); 42 U.S.C. § 608(a)(7) (2004) (capping welfare assistance payments to family at five years under programs administered through block grants to states).

[21] GREGORY ET AL., *supra* note 17, § 9.07[g], at 350.

[22] 42 U.S.C. § 666(f) (2004).

[23] *See* Hammett v. Woods, 602 So. 2d 825, 830 (Miss. 1992).

[24] MISS. CODE ANN. § 43-19-101(1) (2004).

[25] *See* MISS. CODE ANN. § 93-5-23 (2004).

[26] *See* MISS. CODE ANN. § 93-7-7 (2004).

[27] *See* Robinson v. Robinson, 554 So. 2d 300, 304-05 (Miss. 1989); Boyett v. Boyett, 119 So. 299, 300-01 (Miss. 1928).

[28] MISS. CODE ANN. § 93-11-65 (2004); *see* Mitchell v. Powell, 179 So. 2d 811 (Miss. 1965) (chancellor erred in modifying habeas order, but treated proceeding as one under new statute); *see also* CLARK, *supra* note 1, § 19.3, at 794 (listing modern statutes and cases providing for civil action).

[29] *See* MISS. CODE ANN. § 93-9-29(2) (2004).

[30] MISS. CONST. art. VI, § 159.

§ 13.01[2][c]   **MISSISSIPPI FAMILY LAW**

by statute in connection with the various actions listed in [a]. A court may not award child support without personal jurisdiction over the defendant, which requires that the defendant have minimum contacts with the state. Personal jurisdiction for purposes of child support is discussed in detail in Sections 18.04 and 18.08[1]. Jurisdiction over interstate child support modification is governed by the Uniform Interstate Family Support Act, discussed in Section 18.08[4].

The appropriate venue for the various actions in which child support may be awarded is discussed in the chapters related to those actions.[31] Venue for an independent child support action lies in the child's county of residence, the county where the party with actual custody resides, or the county in which the defendant resides.[32]

[c] Temporary support. A court may order temporary support during the pendency of a proceeding in which permanent support is sought.[33] Temporary support may be ordered retroactively. A chancellor did not err in awarding one year of back temporary support in a divorce judgment filed one year previously.[34] Temporary support ends when a final judgment is entered.[35] However, a final judgment does not alter a payor's duty to pay past-due temporary support. A judgment may be entered for arrearages of temporary support even if the right to enforce the temporary order was not expressly reserved in the final decree.[36]

[d] Department of Human Services' role. The Department of Human Services [DHS], the Mississippi IV-D agency, plays a critical role in establishing, collecting, and enforcing support orders. DHS is charged with establishing paternity and child support orders for all recipients of public assistance. And for a small fee, DHS may assist anyone in securing support, regardless of receipt of public assistance.[37] Certain tools and remedies for child support collection are available only through DHS.

[i] Assignment of rights. By accepting public assistance, a custodial parent automatically assigns to DHS the right to collect child support. A public assistance recipient is deemed to have assigned to DHS "all rights and interests in any cause of action . . . against . . . the absent or non-supporting parent" and to appoint DHS to collect support and "to [retain] any portion thereof . . . as reimbursement for public assistance

---

[31] *See supra* § 3.07 (annulment); *supra* § 11.02 (paternity); *infra* § 18.03[2] (divorce actions).

[32] Miss. Code Ann. § 93-11-65 (2004). The statute appears to permit service by publication; however, the Mississippi Supreme Court has held that child support may not be awarded in the absence of personal service of process, *See* O'Neill v. O'Neill, 515 So. 2d 1208, 1211 (Miss. 1987).

[33] Miss. Code Ann. § 93-5-17 (2004); *see* Jethrow v. Jethrow, 571 So. 2d 270, 274 (Miss. 1990) (urging attorneys to seek temporary support for clients in need).

[34] Strong v. Strong, 981 So. 2d 1052, 1055 (Miss. Ct. App. 2008) (relying on Miss. Code Ann. § 93-9-11 (paternity), and § 93-11-65 (child support action) as analogous authority for one year of back support).

[35] Bond v. Bond, 355 So. 2d 672, 674-675 (Miss. 1978).

[36] *See* Lewis v. Lewis, 586 So. 2d 740, 742 (Miss. 1991).

[37] Miss. Code Ann. § 43-19-31(c) (2004). The Act was amended to codify the supreme court's ruling in *Department of Human Services v. Shelby.* 802 So. 2d 89, 95 (Miss. 2001) (receipt of public assistance not a prerequisite for DHS involvement in child support). Federal statutes require that state child support agencies must provide child support services to children receiving assistance and to "any other child, if an individual applies for services." 42 U.S.C. § 654(4) (2006).

CHILD SUPPORT

§ 13.01[2][d][ii]

monies."[38] The Mississippi Supreme Court traced the state's right to indemnification for public support to the Elizabethan Poor Law of 1576.[39]

[ii] Scope of DHS litigation. In a suit for child support, DHS attorneys represent the State, not the custodial parent or the child. Consequently, there is no attorney-client relationship between a DHS attorney and any individual party. DHS's authority is limited to establishing paternity and establishing, modifying, and enforcing support orders. Ancillary issues such as custody and visitation are not within the scope of DHS's representation.[40] A custodial parent or custodial third party is not a necessary party in a DHS action for paternity or child support.[41] The DHS claim for support is free of any defenses that a defendant may have against the custodial parent.[42]

[iii] Distribution of support funds. DHS may retain only funds sufficient to reimburse the state for assistance provided to the recipient family.[43] The supreme court rejected DHS' argument that custodial parents waive all claims to support by seeking DHS assistance: "DHS is not nor should it be a 'for profit' enterprise."[44] Funds recovered above the amount of public assistance belong to the custodial parent as fiduciary for the child.[45]

[iv] DHS liability for negligence. In 2010, the court of appeals held that DHS's statutory obligations to collect, account for, and disburse child support payments are ministerial, rather than discretionary. To the extent that DHS fails to exercise ordinary care in the performance of these duties, it may be liable under the Mississippi Tort Claims Act.[46] The court found that the plaintiff in that case was in arrears and therefore DHS was justified in revoking his license, reporting his default to credit agencies, and seizing his bank account. However, the court of appeals found that he presented sufficient credible evidence that DHS's accounting and disbursement was inaccurate to survive a summary judgment motion.[47]

§ 13.02 CHILDREN ENTITLED TO SUPPORT

Outside the protected circle of the intact family, the state will intervene to establish and enforce support. In contrast, the state regulates married parents' duty of support

---

[38] MISS. CODE ANN. § 43-19-35 (1) (2004) (assignment automatic with receipt of benefits; no written assignment necessary); *see* MISS. CODE ANN. § 43-19-31 (2004) (includes "any form of public assistance, including, but not limited to, medical assistance, foster care, food stamps, TANF, or any other program under the federal Social Security Act").

[39] *See* Ivy v. Dep't of Human Servs., 449 So. 2d 779, 781 (Miss. 1994).

[40] *See* MISS. CODE ANN. § 43-19-35(3) (2004).

[41] Thomas v. Byars, 947 So. 2d 375, 379 (Miss. Ct. App. 2007) (third-party custodial grandparents not necessary parties in DHS suit against father).

[42] MISS. CODE ANN. § 43-19-35(4) (2004).

[43] The statute authorizing suit by DHS is governed by the Social Security Act, 42 U.S.C. § 657 (2006), which limits recovery to the amount paid as assistance. *See* MISS. CODE ANN. § 43-19-39 (2004).

[44] Brown v. Dep't of Human Servs., 806 So. 2d 1004, 1008 (Miss. 2000).

[45] Brown v. Dep't of Human Servs., 806 So. 2d 1004, 1008 (Miss. 2000).

[46] Evans v. Dep't of Human Servs., 36 So. 3d 463, 473-74, 77-78 (Miss. Ct. App. 2010).

[47] Evans v. Dep't of Human Servs., 36 So. 3d 463, 473-74, 77-78 (Miss. Ct. App. 2010).

§ 13.02[1]   **MISSISSIPPI FAMILY LAW**

only in the case of extreme neglect.

[1] Children of intact families. Children in an intact family have no legal right to a standard of living above a minimum level of care and no direct cause of action for even this amount of support.[48] The Mississippi Supreme Court held in 1919 that "[t]he moral obligation of a parent to support his child is not directly enforceable, and a court of equity cannot compel this duty."[49] In deference to family privacy,[50] parents' failure to support is sanctioned only if the lack of support rises to the level of neglect.[51]

The common law doctrine of necessaries does provide an indirect source of support for children in intact families.[52] The doctrine, now codified in some states, allows creditors to sue parents for the costs of goods or services provided to children.[53] Mississippi has no similar statute. However, the supreme court in 1995 recognized a closely akin doctrine, imposing liability on parents to third parties who provide their children with reasonable medical care.[54]

[2] Children of separated or divorced parents. When parents separate, the state becomes the guardian of a child's right to support, with ongoing power to modify and enforce support obligations. A court may order payment of child support by a noncustodial parent at divorce[55] or in an annulment action.[56] If a child's parents are separated, a court may award child support with or without an award of separate maintenance.[57] If both are awarded, the separate maintenance allowance and child support should be set out as separate and distinct obligations.[58] If the spouse seeking separate maintenance

---

[48] Comment, *Parent and Child - Child's Right to Sue Parent for Support*, 15 N.C. L. Rev. 67 (1936). The same dichotomy exists between cohabiting spouses and separated spouses. Spouses in an intact household cannot sue each other for support, while a separated spouse may seek separate maintenance in recognition of the spousal duty of support. *See supra* § 1.07.

[49] Rawlings v. Rawlings, 83 So. 146, 146 (Miss. 1919) (suit filed by children against their father, who was living separate and apart from his wife and children).

[50] *See* Lee E. Teitelbaum, *Family History and Family Law*, 1985 Wis. L. Rev. 1135, 1144-45. The writer notes that the state views intrafamily relations as "a private rather than governmental concern" and intervenes only to govern entry into the family (marriage or adoption) and dissolution of the family (divorce or annulment). *Id.*

[51] *See* Miss. Code Ann. § 43-21-105 (2004). A child is defined as neglected when his "parent, guardian or custodian or any person responsible for his care or support, neglects or refuses, when able so to do, to provide for him proper and necessary care or support, or education." *Id.*

[52] The doctrine was originally developed to assist a wife whose husband refused to provide support. In 1993, the Mississippi Supreme Court abolished the husband-wife doctrine of necessaries. *See supra* § 1.07. *But cf.* Miss. Code Ann. § 43-31-25 (2004) ("The father and grandfather, the mother and grandmother, and brothers and sisters, and the descendants of any pauper not able to work, as the board of supervisors shall direct, shall, at their own charge, relieve and maintain such pauper; and, in case of refusal, shall forfeit and pay the county the sum of One Hundred Fifty Dollars ($150.00) per month, for each month they may so refuse, . . . ; and shall be liable to any governmental entity who supplies such poor relative, if abandoned, with necessaries, not exceeding said sum per month.").

[53] *See* Iowa Code Ann. § 675.4 (West 1987 & Supp. 1990); *see also* Harris et al., *supra* note 2, at 692-708.

[54] *See* McGowan v. West Side Bone & Joint Center, 656 So. 2d 119, 122 (Miss. 1995); *see also* Sheppard Pratt Physicians, P.A. v. Sakwa, 725 So. 2d 755, 758 (Miss. 1998) (applying Maryland law but recognizing rule in Mississippi).

[55] *See* Miss. Code Ann. § 93-5-23 (2004) (court may, after divorce decree, change the decree and make new decrees as the case requires).

[56] *See* Miss. Code Ann. § 93-7-7 (2004) (court has power to modify the decree as needed).

[57] *See* Robinson v. Robinson, 554 So. 2d 300, 304-305 (Miss. 1990) (reversing chancellor's award of separate maintenance to wife who substantially contributed to marriage breakup, but permitting award of child support); Boyett v. Boyett, 119 So. 299, 299 (Miss. 1928).

[58] Robinson v. Robinson, 554 So. 2d 300, 305 (Miss. 1990) (stating that child support is a separate and distinct obligation of the father).

418

CHILD SUPPORT   § 13.02[3]

is the noncustodial parent, he or she may still be required to provide child support to the custodial spouse.[59] The statutory child support guidelines govern support awards in separate maintenance actions.[60]

[3] Children of unmarried parents. At least as early as 1906, Mississippi fathers were required by statute to support children born out of wedlock.[61] Today, section 93-9-7 of the Mississippi Uniform Paternity Act provides that the father of a nonmarital child "is liable to the same extent as the father of a child born of lawful matrimony...for the education, necessary support and maintenance, and medical and funeral expenses of the child."[62] The Act also provides for the same continuing jurisdiction to modify and enforce orders as in the case of divorce.[63] A chancellor did not err in ordering a doctor to pay substantial child support for a nonmarital child, including $1,200 a month in basic support, health insurance, all out-of-pocket medical and dental expenses, a life insurance policy of $500,000, and all college expenses.[64]

Despite the statutory language, the obligation is not identical to a married father's duty – the statute authorizes courts to approve lump sum settlements in paternity actions.[65] A mother who settled a 1977 paternity action for $18,000 was barred from bringing a second action against the alleged father. In light of the statutory authorization for lump sum settlements, the rule prohibiting waiver of a child's support right does not apply in paternity actions.[66] The court did note that settlement could be attacked on the basis of fraud or collusion.[67] As the assignee of support rights, the Department of Human Services is a necessary party to settlement of a paternity action by a mother who receives public assistance benefits.[68]

[4] Disabled adult children. Mississippi does not recognize a parental duty to support adult disabled children. In 1925, the Mississippi Supreme Court stated, "Under the common law there is no legal obligation . . . upon the parent to support his adult child."[69] Dicta in recent years suggests, however, that the Mississippi appellate courts may be receptive to a claim for support in a proper case. In a contempt proceeding, the supreme court noted that some states require post-majority support for disabled

---

[59] *See* Steen v. Steen, 641 So. 2d 1167, 1171 (Miss. 1994) (husband who did not want divorce granted a form of separate maintenance; case remanded to determine what child support he should pay to wife who had custody).

[60] *See* Stanford v. Stanford, 734 So. 2d 359, 362 (Miss. 1999).

[61] Section 268, Code of 1906 (Hemingway's Code, § 217) (repealed), required the father to provide support "When any single woman shall be delivered of a bastard," *cited in* Crum v. Brock, 101 So. 704, 705 (Miss. 1924) (holding that a widow was a "single woman" for purposes of the statute).

[62] Miss. Code Ann. § 93-9-7 (2004).

[63] Miss. Code Ann. § 93-9-15 (2004).

[64] Daniels v. Bains, 967 So. 2d 77, 80 (Miss. Ct. App. 2007).

[65] Miss. Code Ann. § 93-9-49 (2004).

[66] Atwood v. Hicks, 538 So. 2d 404, 406 (Miss. 1989) (settlement provided $7,800 to mother for birth expenses and support, $7,200 to her attorney, and $3,000 in the guardianship estate). The court also relied on Miss. Code Ann. § 93-13-59 (2004) (allowing guardians to compromise doubtful claims of wards).

[67] Atwood v. Hicks, 538 So. 2d 404, 408 (Miss. 1989).

[68] Miss. Dep't Human Serv. v. Barnett, 633 So. 2d 430, 436 (Miss. 1993) (chancellor erred in failing to include DHS in settlement negotiations of a paternity case involving an AFDC recipient).

[69] Wright v. Coleman, 102 So. 774, 777 (Miss. 1925).

§ 13.03   MISSISSIPPI FAMILY LAW

children.[70] However, the court held that a contempt proceeding under an existing decree was not the appropriate vehicle to address such a duty.[71] In another case, the court suggested in dicta that parental obligations might extend beyond majority based on "other compelling reasons, such as the mental or physical incapacitation of the child."[72]

Although most parents are not required to support adult disabled children, the legislature has imposed this duty on parents against whom DHS obtains a paternity order. A support award established under this procedure continues past majority "in the case of a child who, upon reaching the age of twenty-one (21) years, is mentally or physically incapable of self-support . . . unless said child is a long-term patient in a facility owned or operated by the State of Mississippi."[73]

§ 13.03 PERSONS RESPONSIBLE FOR SUPPORT

[1] Natural parents. Historically, child support was a father's obligation. A mother was at most secondarily liable.[74] But in 1979, gender-based family law distinctions were declared unconstitutional by the United States Supreme Court in the landmark decision *Orr v. Orr*.[75] Striking down a state law limiting alimony to women, the Court held that gender differences are not justified by preference for a family structure in which the wife plays a dependent role.[76] Most state statutes now provide that parents have equal responsibility for financial support of children.[77]

Section 93-13-1 of the Mississippi Code provides that "father and mother are the joint natural guardians of their minor children and are equally charged with their care, nurture, welfare and education."[78] It is error for a chancellor to fail to award a custodial father support from a noncustodial mother.[79] Similarly, a noncustodial mother's duty

---

[70] Watkins v. Watkins, 337 So. 2d 723, 724-25 (Miss. 1976); *see* Streb v. Streb, 774 P.2d 798, 800 (Alaska 1989) (presumption of emancipation upon attaining majority may be overcome by evidence that adult child is incapable of supporting himself due to physical or mental incapacity); McCauley v. McCauley, 599 So. 2d 1002, 1003 (Fla. Dist. Ct. App. 1992) (duty to pay support ceases when child attains age of majority absent evidence that child suffers from physical or mental incapacities); Monitzer v. Monitzer, 600 So. 2d 575 (Fla. Dist. Ct. App. 1992) (substantial evidence existed that child over age eighteen was dependent due to continued physical or mental incapacity).

[71] Watkins v. Watkins, 337 So. 2d 723, 724-25 (Miss. 1976).

[72] Arthur v. Arthur, 691 So. 2d 997, 1001 (Miss. 1997) (holding that a father's insurance obligation ended at the child's emancipation); *see also* Stokes v. Maris, 596 So. 2d 879, 881-22 (Miss. 1992) (nothing in opinion regarding post-majority support to be construed as deciding issue of whether parent must support adult incapacitated child).

[73] MISS. CODE ANN. § 43-19-33(3) (2004). The statute also provides that a judgment of paternity is res judicata as to the issue of post-majority support. *Id.*

[74] *See* Bass v. Irvin, 170 So. 673, 674 (Miss. 1936) ("father of this child . . . is primarily liable for its support, the mother being liable secondarily"). The court took this position as recently as 1960, in *Pass v. Pass*, 118 So. 2d 769, 772 (Miss. 1960) (stating that the father is primarily charged with providing educational support).

[75] 440 U.S. 268 (1979).

[76] Orr v. Orr, 440 U.S. 268, 280-82 (1979).

[77] CLARK, *supra* note 1, § 17.1, at 710. The Mississippi legislature, in response to *Orr*, amended the divorce statute regarding alimony effective July 1, 1985. *See* MISS. CODE ANN. § 93-5-23 (2004) ("alimony of the wife or husband, or any allowance to be made to her or him").

[78] MISS. CODE ANN. § 93-13-1 (2004).

[79] *See* Bailey v. Bailey, 724 So. 2d 335, 338 (Miss. 1998) (unconstitutional to treat men and women differently for purposes of child support); Chroniger v. Chroniger, 914 So. 2d 311, 316 (Miss. Ct. App. 2005) (child support should be ordered in all but rare circumstances; reversing order relieving noncustodial mother of support pursuant to agreement). *But see* Magruder v. Magruder, 881 So. 2d 365, 368 (Miss. Ct. App. 2004) (chancellor did not err in ordering father with custody of two children to pay 14% of income to mother with custody of one child and declining to order child support

CHILD SUPPORT

§ 13.03[2]

to her children is not affected by her remarriage and the birth of additional children. The supreme court rejected a mother's petition to modify support upon the birth of an additional child, stating "[m]ales and females cannot be treated differently for child-support purposes consistently with the Equal Protection Clause of the United States Constitution."[80]

[2] Adoptive parents. When a child is adopted, the natural parents' rights and obligations are extinguished.[81] The adoptive parents assume all parental rights and duties, including the duty to support their adopted children. The fact that a noncustodial father adopted his wife's natural child only three months before their separation did not diminish his duty of support.[82]

[3] Stepparents. Stepparents have no common law duty to support stepchildren. In a few cases, however, courts have ordered support from divorced stepparents based on the doctrine of equitable estoppel.[83] For example, support was ordered for a child who believed his stepfather's representations that he was the child's father.[84] In other states, stepparent support duties have been grounded in implied or express contract, usually based on a mother's agreement to marry in reliance on a stepfather's express promise to support her children.[85] The Mississippi Supreme Court mentioned in dicta in 1998 that stepparents may be liable for support based on agreement or if support has been provided under circumstances that caused the natural parent to rely detrimentally on the support.[86]

[4] Persons *in loco parentis* to child. The Mississippi Supreme Court has recently extended parental rights to men who were defrauded about their paternity, under the doctrine of *in loco parentis*. The court held that parental rights and duties may apply to a person who assumes the status and obligations of a parent.[87] To date, the doctrine has been used to extend parental rights of custody and visitation to third parties. However,

---

from mother, whose yearly income was $14,000).

[80] Bailey v. Bailey, 724 So. 2d 335, 338 (Miss. 1998) (noncustodial mother's decision to remain home with child of second marriage not a reason to reduce child support).

[81] *See* Miss. Code Ann. § 93-17-13 (2004) (providing that "all parental rights of the natural parent, or parents, shall be terminated, [upon adoption] except as to a natural parent who is the spouse of the adopting parent"). *But cf.* Humphrey v. Pannell, 710 So. 2d 392, 393-94 (Miss. 1998) (enforcing adoptive parents' agreement recognizing visitation rights of biological father and his duty of support).

[82] *See* Adams v. Adams, 467 So. 2d 211, 214 (Miss. 1981).

[83] Miller v. Miller, 478 A.2d 351, 354 (N.J. 1984) (continuing duty may arise from conduct relied on by the mother).

[84] Ross v. Ross, 314 A.2d 623, 626 (N.J. Juv. Ct. 1973).

[85] *See* L. v. L., 497 S.W.2d 840, 841-42 (Mo. Ct. App. 1973) (estoppel requirements met where wife married husband based partly upon promise of support for children); T. v. T., 224 S.E.2d 148, 151 (Va. 1976) (mother moved to another state and married on promise of support for children).

[86] Logan v. Logan, 730 So. 2d 1124, 1126 (Miss. 1998); *see also* Griffith v. Pell, 881 So. 2d 184 (Miss. 2004) (presumed father may have rights and obligations under doctrine of *in loco parentis*). The court of appeals affirmed a chancellor's refusal to enforce a stepfather's divorce settlement agreement to pay "all reasonable expenses of schooling" for his stepdaughter. The court held that the agreement was too vague to be enforced and that enforcement would be unfair. The child accused the stepfather of molestation, a charge from which he was exonerated. Markofski v. Holzhauer, 799 So. 2d 162, 167 (Miss. Ct. App. 2001).

[87] Griffith v. Pell, 881 So. 2d 184, 186 (Miss. 2004).

§ 13.04   MISSISSIPPI FAMILY LAW

in dicta, the court has also noted that one who is *in loco parentis* may be ordered to pay child support.[88]

§ 13.04 CALCULATING SUPPORT UNDER THE GUIDELINES

Child support includes a basic support award calculated under child support guidelines. The award is based upon a percentage applied to adjusted gross income as defined by the guidelines. Deviations from these guidelines may be based upon statutory deviation criteria. A court may also order payment of additional sums for expenses not covered by the basic award, such as health insurance and college expenses.

[1] The Mississippi guidelines. The Mississippi child support guidelines provide that a noncustodial parent should pay the following percentage of adjusted gross income in support of children: 14% for one child, 20% for two children, 22% for three children, 24% for four children, and 26% for five or more children.[89] The Mississippi statute provides that the guidelines are presumptively correct for persons with an adjusted yearly income between $5,000 and $50,000. Within this range, a court may deviate from the statutory percentages only upon a written finding that application of the guidelines would be inappropriate.[90] For persons with income above or below that range, the court must make specific, written findings supporting its award in every case.[91]

[a] Steps in determining basic support. To determine the proper amount of support, a court must first identify a payor's gross income from all sources.[92] Income may be imputed to a payor who is working at less than full capacity or who conceals or diverts income.[93] The payor's gross income is adjusted for taxes, other mandatory deductions, and support for other children.[94] The statutory percentages are then applied to the adjusted gross income to produce the presumptively correct amount of support.[95] A court may then deviate below or above that amount based on statutory criteria for deviation.[96] In addition to the basic support award, a court may order payment of expenses not considered to be covered by the basic award, including health insurance, out-of-pocket medical expenses, life insurance, and college expenses.[97]

[b] Findings of fact. The absence of required findings of fact is the most common reason for reversal of child support awards. Awards have been reversed for lack of findings regarding a payor's adjusted gross income,[98] for failure to apply the statu-

---

[88] Griffith v. Pell, 881 So. 2d 184, 186 (Miss. 2004).

[89] MISS. CODE ANN. § 43-19-101(1) (2004).

[90] MISS. CODE ANN. § 43-19-101(2) (2004).

[91] MISS. CODE ANN. § 43-19-101(4) (2004); *see* Wallace v. Bond, 745 So. 2d 844, 847 (Miss. 1999) (court should first apply guidelines to income over $50,000).

[92] See *infra* § 13.04[2].

[93] See *infra* § 13.04[4].

[94] See *infra* § 13.04[5].

[95] See *infra* § 13.04[6].

[96] See *infra* § 13.05.

[97] See *infra* § 13.07.

[98] *See* Wheat v. Wheat, 37 So. 3d 632, 643-44 (Miss. 2010) (no findings regarding mother's anticipated income;

CHILD SUPPORT § 13.04[1][b]

tory guidelines before deviation,[99] and for failure to explain the reason for deviating from the guidelines.[100] If income is imputed to a payor, the court must provide findings explaining the basis for the amount imputed.[101] An award may be affirmed without specific findings, however, if the record supports the award. In one such case, the supreme court affirmed a chancellor's $600 a month award because the record supported a finding that the father was hiding income and assets.[102]

Findings must be made even in uncontested actions;[103] however, no findings are required when an order is based on the parties' agreement.[104] Findings of fact are required in actions to modify support as well as original actions for support.[105] When a

---

separation package from employer would expire shortly after divorce); Gray v. Gray, 745 So. 2d 234, 237 (Miss. 1999) (reversed for findings to support award of $600 from payor with alleged adjusted gross income of $912); Clausel v. Clausel, 714 So. 2d 265, 267 (Miss. 1998) (award of $750 plus medical insurance from payor with alleged $1,000 per month adjusted gross income reversed because no findings); Morris v. Stacy, 641 So. 2d 1194, 1200 (Miss. 1994) (unable to judge whether increase in modification action warranted because no findings regarding actual income); Brennan v. Brennan, 638 So. 2d 1320, 1325-26 (Miss. 1994) (reversed for findings regarding income); Seghini v. Seghini, 42 So. 3d 635, 639-41 (Miss. Ct. App. 2010) (reversed for findings regarding father's income above amount reported); Ellzey v. White, 922 So. 2d 40, 42 (Miss. Ct. App. 2006) (chancellor's order imputing unreported income to father reversed; no findings to indicate how chancellor arrived at figure). *But see* Clark v. Clark, 754 So. 2d 450, 459 (Miss. 1999) (affirming award based on imputed income without requiring specific findings); Strange v. Strange, 43 So. 3d 1169, 1174 (Miss. Ct. App. 2010) (miscalculation of adjusted gross income was harmless error; four judges dissenting).

[99] *See* Knutson v. Knutson, 704 So. 2d 1331, 1335 (Miss. 1997) (award of 40% of adjusted gross income). *But cf.* Pipkin v. Dolan, 788 So. 2d 834, 837-38 (Miss. Ct. App. 2001) (affirmed even though chancellor did not make specific findings regarding material change; documents relied on were attached to record).

[100] *See* Yelverton v. Yelverton, 961 So. 2d 19, 27 (Miss. 2007) (chancellor failed to make specific finding that the guidelines were unfair); Wallace v. Bond, 745 So. 2d 844, 848 (Miss. 1999) (deviation reversed for findings of fact regarding income and child's needs in modification action); Brocato v. Brocato, 731 So. 2d 1138, 1145 (Miss. 1999) (no support ordered because custody split between parents; reversed for findings to justify); Draper v. Draper, 658 So. 2d 866, 870 (Miss. 1995) (award of $350 rather than $495 under guidelines was error without findings to support); Johnson v. Johnson, 650 So. 2d 1281, 1287-88 (Miss. 1994) (20% basic support ($1,116) plus house note as child support amounted to 39% of payor's adjusted gross income; remanded for findings to support deviation); Dufour v. Dufour, 631 So. 2d 192, 194-95 (Miss. 1994) (award of $800 for one child from payor with alleged $5,000 adjusted gross income error without findings regarding income or child's needs; suggests guidelines produce appropriate amount); Klein v. McIntyre, 966 So. 2d 1252, 1255 (Miss. Ct. App. 2007) (no findings of fact and no transcript of hearing); Chroniger v. Chroniger, 914 So. 2d 311, 316 (Miss. Ct. App. 2005) (chancellor modified custody to father and, pursuant to divorce decree provision, did not order support from mother; reversed for findings of fact supporting deviation); Delozier v. Delozier, 724 So. 2d 984, 987 (Miss. Ct. App. 1998) ($100 support award to father from mother in nursing school with no income was error in the absence of written findings to support deviation); Rakestraw v. Rakestraw, 717 So. 2d 1284, 1289 (Miss. Ct. App. 1998) (no support from father with $180 per month income reversed for findings to support deviation). *But cf.* Peters v. Peters, 906 So. 2d 64, 71-72 (Miss. Ct. App. 2004) (affirming award based on guidelines from payor with income over $50,000, based on chancellor's "rather succinct" statement that he saw "no reason to deviate from the statutory child support guideline").

[101] Gray v. Gray, 745 So. 2d 234, 237 (Miss. 1999); *see* Wheat v. Wheat, 37 So. 3d 632, 643 (Miss. 2010) (rejecting father's argument that chancellor imputed income based on mother's earning capacity; no findings were made regarding her income potential).

[102] *See* Clark v. Clark, 754 So. 2d 450, 459 (Miss. 1999). The court did note, however, that the record supported the award and that the chancellor offered to re-evaluate the figures if the payor would submit more complete financial data; *see also* Morris v. Morris, 5 So. 3d 476, 495 (Miss. Ct. App. 2008) (rejecting high-income payor's argument that award should be reversed for failure to make findings regarding fairness of award; no evidence that amount was inappropriate); Henderson v. Henderson, 952 So. 2d 273, 279 (Miss. Ct. App. 2006) (child support award from payor with high income upheld without extensive findings).

[103] *See* Stinson v. Stinson, 738 So. 2d 1259, 1264 (Miss. Ct. App. 1999) (chancellor must follow statutory guidelines "as rigorously" as in a contested divorce).

[104] Woodfin v. Woodfin. 26 So. 3d 389, 399-400 (Miss. Ct. App. 2010); West v. West. 23 So. 3d 558, 561-62 (Miss. Ct. App. 2009); Williams v. Williams, 810 So. 2d 613, 614-15 (Miss. Ct. App. 2001) (no findings required where parties announced agreement during trial of modification petition).

[105] *See* Gray v. Gray, 909 So. 2d 108, 114 (Miss. Ct. App. 2005); Turner v. Turner, 744 So. 2d 332, 338 (Miss. Ct. App. 1999*). But cf.* Weeks v. Weeks, 29 So. 3d 80, 89 (Miss. Ct. App. 2009) (affirming denial of modification, even

§ 13.04[2]   **MISSISSIPPI FAMILY LAW**

court orders support based on the guidelines for a payor with yearly adjusted income between $5,000 and $50,000, no findings regarding the fairness of the award are required. Only findings with regard to the payor's gross and adjusted gross income are necessary.[106] In a case involving a payor with income above $50,000, the requirement of findings was satisfied when the court detailed both parties' incomes, the number of children in the household, the amount that the guidelines would produce, and stated that "application of the statutory guidelines to the adjusted gross income of each of the parties is reasonable in this case."[107]

[2] Determining gross income. Under the Mississippi guidelines, gross income includes most sources of revenue available to a parent: "wages and salary income; income from self-employment; income from commissions; income from investments, including dividends, interest income and income on any trust account or property; absent parent's portion of any joint income of both parents; workers' compensation, disability, unemployment, annuity and retirement benefits, including an individual retirement account (IRA); any other payments made by any person, private entity, federal or state government or any unit of local government; alimony; any income earned from an interest in or from inherited property; and any other earned income."[108]

[a] Overtime and second jobs. In most states, gross income includes income from overtime and second jobs if the work is consistent and predictable.[109] Courts generally exclude irregular income[110] and income from short-term jobs.[111] A few states exclude income from work that exceeds forty hours a week.[112]

In Mississippi, income from a regular second job was included in gross income,[113] while income from a one-time teaching position was not.[114] A company's one-time buy-out of a father's position was not part of gross income.[115] In contrast, a

---

though court did not list factors considered in determining that no material change had occurred).

[106] McClee v. Simmons, 834 So. 2d 61, 64 (Miss. Ct. App. 2002); *see* Reid v. Reid, 998 So. 2d 1032, 1038 (Miss. Ct. App. 2008) (no findings required as to fairness of guidelines; mother's income below $50,000). *Compare* Bryant v. Bryant, 924 So. 2d 627, 632 (Miss. Ct. App. 2006) (court not required to make findings of fact when applying statutory guidelines) *with* Walton v. Snyder, 984 So. 2d 343 (Miss. Ct. App. 2007) (court properly made findings that application of statutory guidelines to payor with high income was reasonable).

[107] Reid v. Reid, 998 So. 2d 1032, 1038 (Miss. Ct. App. 2008).

[108] Miss. Code Ann. § 43-19-101(3)(a) (2004).

[109] *See, e.g..*Wash. Rev. Code Ann. § 26.19.071(1)(e) (2004).

[110] *See* Wash. Rev. Code Ann. § 26.19.075(1)(b) (West Supp. 2000) (excluding nonrecurring income); State *ex rel.* Smith v. Smith, 631 So. 2d 252, 255 (Ala. Civ. App. 1993); Skipper v. Skipper, 654 So. 2d 1181, 1183 (Fla. Dist. Ct. App. 1995); Price v. Dawkins, 247 S.E.2d 844, 845 (Ga. 1978); Timmons v. Timmons, 605 So. 2d 1162, 1166 (La. Ct. App. 1992); Polen v. Polen, 886 S.W.2d 701, 705 (Mo. Ct. App. 1994) (including sporadic overtime).

[111] *See* Erler v. Erler, 390 N.W.2d 316, 319-20 (Minn. App. 1986) (including father's income from two regular part-time jobs).

[112] N.H. Rev. Stat. Ann. § 458-C:2(IV) (stating income earned for hours over forty hours not considered); Minn. Stat. Ann. § 518.551 (West Supp. 2000) (not including income for work over forty hours per week if work began after divorce action was filed, is an increase in work, and is not required by employer).

[113] *See* Carter v. Carter, 735 So. 2d 1109, 1115-16 (Miss. 1999) (stating that 20% of adjusted gross income includes income from a paper route, in addition to regular employment); *see also* Kay v. Kay, 12 So. 3d 622, 625 (Miss. Ct. App. 2009) (teacher's gross income included regular summer and overload pay).

[114] Johnston v. Johnston, 722 So. 2d 453 (Miss. 1998).

[115] Robertson v. Robertson, 812 So. 2d 998, 1001-02 (Miss. Ct. App. 2001) (but noting that $70,000 payment was a material change in circumstances permitting modification).

CHILD SUPPORT § 13.04[2][b]

regular annual bonus was properly included in income.[116]

[b] Payor's federal and state benefits. Gross income generally includes most federal and state benefits – social security payments,[117] disability payments,[118] veteran's benefits,[119] national guard income,[120] worker's compensation,[121] and unemployment benefits.[122] Means-tested government payments such as Temporary Assistance to Needy Families [TANF], Supplemental Security Income [SSI], or Food Stamps are excluded in some states, since the payments are designed to provide the recipient with a bare minimum level of support.[123]

The Mississippi guidelines specifically include retirement and disability benefits, worker's compensation, and unemployment benefits and provide a catch-all provision for other governmental payments.[124] The statute does not list means-tested benefits such as Supplemental Security Income or Temporary Assistance to Needy Families as income; however, it does state that income includes "any other payments made by any person, private entity, federal or state government or any unit of local government."[125] In a 2010 case, the Mississippi Supreme Court held that, while SSI benefits may not be subject to an income-withholding order,[126] a chancellor has discretion to consider or disregard SSI benefits for purposes of child support.[127] In an earlier appeal by a disabled SSI recipient, the Mississippi Supreme Court recognized that most states exclude SSI benefits from income under child support statutes. However, the court declined to address the issue, since the chancellor's award of sixty-five dollars a month was based in part on his belief that the SSI recipient had the ability to earn additional income.[128]

[c] Federal and state benefits payable to a child. When a child receives benefits based on a payor's retirement or disability, most states reduce support by the amount of the benefit.[129] In keeping with the majority, Mississippi permits a dollar for dollar offset against child support to reflect these benefits.[130] A child's receipt of $900

---

[116] Alderson v. Morgan, 739 So. 2d 465, 467 (Miss. Ct. App. 1999).

[117] *In re* Marriage of Lee, 486 N.W.2d 302, 304-05 (Iowa 1991); *In re* Marriage of Benson, 495 N.W.2d 777, 781 (Iowa Ct. App. 1992); *In re* Marriage of Callaghan, 869 P.2d 240, 241 (Kan. App. 1994); *In re* Marriage of Durbin, 823 P.2d 243, 246 (Mont. 1991).

[118] *In re* Marriage of Briscoe, 949 P.2d 1388, 1390-91 (Wash. 1998).

[119] Rose v. Rose, 481 U.S. 619, 630-31 (1987) (holding that veteran's benefits may be income despite federal law that veterans' benefits are not subject to attachment).

[120] *In re* Marriage of McPheter, 803 P.2d 207 (Kan. App. 1990).

[121] *In re* Marriage of Sullivan, 853 P.2d 1194 (Mont. 1993); Gonsalves v. Roberts, 905 S.W.2d 931 (Tenn. 1995).

[122] *In re* Marriage of Robbins, 510 N.W.2d 844, 846 (Iowa 1994).

[123] *See In re* Marriage of Benson, 495 N.W.2d 777, 782 (Iowa Ct. App. 1992) (stating SSI and AFDC are not income).

[124] Miss. Code Ann. § 43-19-101(3)(a) (2004); *cf.* Crayton v. Burley, 952 So. 2d 957, 960 (Miss. Ct. App. 2006) (payments under private disability policy included in gross income).

[125] Miss. Code Ann. § 43-19-101(3)(a) (2004).

[126] *See infra* § 13.10[3][c].

[127] Barnes v. Dep't of Human Servs., 42 So. 3d 10, 17 (Miss. 2010). Seven justices joined a concurrence stating that chancellors should consider SSI as income for purposes of determining child support. *Id.* at 18.

[128] Lee v. Lee, 859 So. 2d 408, 410 (Miss. Ct. App. 2003) (suggesting payor could find some way to earn money, even if it meant picking up cans).

[129] Cash v. Cash, 353 S.W.2d 348 (Ark. 1962); Perteet v. Sumner, 269 S.E.2d 453 (Ga. 1980); Andler v. Andler, 538 P.2d 649 (Kan. 1975).

[130] Hammet v. Woods, 602 So. 2d 825 (Miss. 1992); Mooneyham v. Mooneyham, 420 So. 2d 1072, 1073 (Miss.

§ 13.04[2][d]   MISSISSIPPI FAMILY LAW

a month in benefits, payable until she was eighteen, allowed suspension of her father's $350 a month obligation for that time period. However, the suspension was only for those months in which she actually received benefits. The father was not entitled to apply a credit for the excess above $350 to his obligation to support her between the ages of eighteen and twenty-one.[131] If a custodial parent fails to apply for benefits available to a child on the payor's account, support should be reduced by the amount the child would have received.[132] On the other hand, support is not reduced to reflect Supplemental Security Income received by a disabled child on his own account.[133]

Based on a 2011 statute, a disabled payor is entitled to offset arrearages when a child receives a lump sum disability payment representing amounts that date back to the date of the disability.[134] The amendment overrides a 2009 court of appeals case.[135]

[d] Alimony and child support. In most states, gross income includes alimony received by a child support payor. In contrast, child support payments for other children living with the payor are not included. Child support payments are held by the payee as a fiduciary and are not considered taxable income to the payee.[136]

The Mississippi definition of gross income includes alimony payments.[137] The statute does not list child support payments as income. Mississippi law is clear that child support payments are held in trust: "Child support benefits belong to the child, and not the parent who, having custody, receives such benefits under a fiduciary duty to hold and use them for the benefit of the child."[138]

[e] Current spouse's income. In the absence of a controlling statute, courts usually disregard income of a child support payor's spouse unless the income directly reduces the payor's expenses.[139] The Mississippi guidelines exclude "any monetary benefits derived from a second household, such as income of the absent parent's current spouse."[140] Nonetheless, a court ordering a father to pay support based on the guidelines did not err in noting that his current wife's high income reduced his living expenses.[141]

1982); *see also* Edmond v. Townes, 949 So. 2d 99, 102 (Miss. Ct. App. 2007) (reducing payor's obligation); Crayton v. Burley, 952 So. 2d 957, 961 (Miss. Ct. App. 2006) (considering benefits received by child in calculating support in modification action).

[131] Keith v. Purvis, 982 So. 2d 1033 (Miss. Ct. App. 2008); *see also* Chapman v. Ward, 3 So. 3d 790, 799 (Miss. Ct. App. 2008) (future support obligation modified based on child's receipt of benefits).

[132] Bradley v. Holmes, 561 So. 2d 1034, 1035-36 (Miss. 1990) (mother did not request benefits based on father's retirement because child could receive higher payments by requesting benefits based on stepfather's retirement).

[133] Hammett v. Woods, 602 So. 2d 825, 830 (Miss. 1992).

[134] Miss. Code Ann § 93-11-71 (6) (2008).

[135] *See* Keith v. Purvis, 982 So. 2d 1033 (Miss. Ct. App. 2008) (father in arrears during period of disability not entitled to credit when child received $7,836 lump sum payment based on his prior disability); *cf.* Chapman v. Ward, 3 So. 3d 790, 796 (Miss. Ct. App. 2008) (payor not entitled to offset against arrearages based on lump sum payment representing benefits due during period of arrearages).

[136] *See* Morgan, *supra* note 13, § 2.01[f].

[137] Miss. Code Ann. § 43-19-101 (2004).

[138] Lawrence v. Lawrence, 574 So. 2d 1376, 1380 (Miss. 1991) (quoting Cumberland v. Cumberland, 564 So. 2d 839, 847 (Miss. 1990)).

[139] Morgan, *supra* note 13, § 2.03[e].

[140] Miss. Code Ann. § 43-19-101 (2004).

[141] Shepherd v. Shepherd, 769 So. 2d 242, 246 (Miss. Ct. App. 2000) (court modified support to statutory amount;

CHILD SUPPORT   **§13.04[2][f]**

[f] **Employment benefits.** Gross income includes non-salary employment benefits, such as the free use of a company car[142] or a housing allowance.[143] Courts in other states have held that military allowances for housing should be included as income for purposes of child support.[144] A court properly included a husband's expense account as part of his income. He was not required to use the account for business expenses, and the amount was reported as income to the IRS.[145]

[g] **Fluctuating income.** With respect to payors with fluctuating income, a court may use an average income for purposes of calculating child support. A chancellor properly averaged the income of a pharmaceutical salesman over a three-year period and found that his average adjusted monthly gross income was $5,326.[146]

[h] **Other income.** Courts will look to all sources of regular income as a basis for child support. The court of appeals held that $60,000 in disability benefits received by a father under a cancer policy should have been included in gross income for purposes of calculating child support.[147] A father's child support was properly based on trust income of $50,000 a year.[148] A court properly looked to a father's total income from ownership in various entities, as well as income from employment, to determine the proper amount of support.[149] And a business owner's gross income included a monthly loan repayment from his business.[150]

[3] **Gross income from self-employment.** Determining adjusted gross income for a salaried payor is fairly simple. Setting a figure for a self-employed payor is significantly more complicated. To determine the proper amount of self-employment income for child support, courts generally look to gross income minus ordinary and reasonable expenses incurred in producing the income.[151]

[a] **Business vs. personal expenses.** Courts generally allow deduction of ex-

---

not error to mention that second wife had high paying job).

[142] Pittman v. Pittman, 791 So. 2d 857, 865-67 (Miss. Ct. App. 2001).

[143] Bustin v. Bustin, 806 So. 2d 1136, 1140 (Miss. Ct. App. 2001) ($1,500 housing allowance met statutory definition of "any other form of earned income").

[144] *See, e.g.*, Rogers v. Sims, 671 So. 2d 714, 716 (Ala. Civ. App. 1995); *In re* Massey, 886 N.Y.S.2d 280, 281-86 (N.Y. App. Div. 2009).

[145] Barnett v. Barnett, 908 So. 2d 833, 844-45 (Miss. Ct. App. 2005).

[146] Roberts v. Roberts, 924 So. 2d 550, 553 (Miss. Ct. App. 2005); *cf.* Hults v. Hults, 11 So. 3d 1273, 1279-80 (Miss. Ct. App. 2009) (upholding a chancellor's decision to deviate below the guidelines based on the difficulty of predicting the father's income which consisted of uncertain overtime pay).

[147] Crayton v. Burley, 952 So. 2d 957, 960 (Miss. Ct. App. 2006).

[148] Owen v. Owen, 22 So. 3d 386, 392 (Miss. Ct. App. 2009).

[149] Tatum v. Tatum, 54 So. 3d 855, 864-65 (Miss. Ct. App. 2010) (adjusted gross income from employment was $42,083, while tax returns showed adjusted income between $131,000 and $161,000).

[150] Lewis v. Lewis, 54 So. 3d 233, 243 (Miss. Ct. App. (2009), *aff'd in part, rev'd in part,* 54 So. 3d 216 (Miss. 2011).

[151] Faerber v. Faerber, 13 So. 3d 853, 864-65 (Miss. Ct. App. 2009). "Gross income" generally includes income retained in a close corporation or partnership. Anderson v. Anderson, 963 S.W.2d 604, 607 (Ark. Ct. App. 1998); Roth v. Roth, 406 N.W.2d 77, 79 (Minn. Ct. App. 1987).

§ 13.04[3][b]   **MISSISSIPPI FAMILY LAW**

penses necessary to the production of income[152] and disallow deduction of expenses viewed as personal – clothing, entertainment, non-business travel and automobile expenses, and leisure activities.[153] A chancellor properly deducted medical malpractice premiums from a physician's income to arrive at adjusted gross income.[154] In contrast, the court of appeals remanded for a trial court to determine whether personal expenses had been deducted from business income, noting that self-employment income is gross income less ordinary and reasonable expenses to produce the income.[155]

[b] Depreciation. Courts vary in their treatment of depreciation as an allowable expense for purposes of child support. Some states disallow all depreciation,[156] some disallow accelerated depreciation,[157] and some leave the question to the discretion of the court.[158] The court of appeals held that a chancellor correctly added depreciation back to a husband's business income to determine child support.[159] One Mississippi case suggests that the supreme court might allow straight-line, but not accelerated, depreciation. The court affirmed a deduction for depreciation, noting that the wife presented no evidence that the depreciation was accelerated.[160]

[c] Tax returns. The Mississippi Supreme Court has stated that tax returns are not determinative of gross income for purposes of child support.[161] For example, a chancellor imputed an additional $500 a month of income to a husband, based on his testimony that he drew $50,302 from the business during the year, even though his tax return showed adjusted gross income of $45,248 and taxable income of $34,398.[162] Nonetheless, the supreme court and court of appeals have approved the use of standard small business tax deductions in calculating gross income. The supreme court held that a chancellor properly based child support on a self-employed father's taxable adjusted gross income of $34,834. The custodial mother argued that deductions for home office expenses, utilities, and depreciation were not legitimate child support deductions. The court stated that "legitimate costs of doing business for a self-employed individual are a proper consideration in determining income available to meet child support

---

[152] *See* Cox v. Cox, 580 N.E.2d 344, 351 (Ind. Ct. App. 1991) (purchase of equipment was necessary and deductible expense).

[153] Coghill v. Coghill, 836 P.2d 921, 927 (Alaska 1992) (holding that party could not deduct clothing as purported business expense); Cahoy v. Darsaklis, 584 N.W.2d 36, 41-42 (Neb. Ct. App. 1998) (stating that cost of housing cannot be deducted as farming expense for purposes of child support).

[154] Henderson v. Henderson, 952 So. 2d 273, 279 (Miss. Ct. App. 2006).

[155] Faerber v. Faerber, 13 So. 3d 853, 864-65 (Miss. Ct. App. 2009); *see also* Sellers v. Sellers, 22 So. 3d 299, 306-307 (Miss. Ct. App. 2009) (personal car expenses added back to business income).

[156] D.C. Code Ann. § 16-916.1 (1997); N.D. Admin. Code § 75-02-04.1; *see* Cox v. Cox, 580 N.E.2d 344, 351 (Ind. Ct. App. 1991); Stewart v. Stewart, 793 P.2d 813, 814-15 (Mont. 1990).

[157] Freking v. Freking, 479 N.W.2d 736, 740 (Minn. Ct. App. 1992) (stating that accelerated depreciation permitted by tax code is not ordinary and necessary expense for purposes of child support; allowing straight line depreciation only).

[158] Tex. Fam. Code Ann. § 154.005[b] (West Supp. 1999).

[159] Sellers v. Sellers, 22 So. 3d 399, 306-07 (Miss. Ct. App. 2009); *see also* Holdeman v. Holdeman, 34 So. 3d 650 , 653-54 (Miss. Ct. App. 2010) (remanding for chancellor to carefully review tax returns, including purpose of large depreciation deductions).

[160] Nix v. Nix, 790 So. 2d 198, 200 (Miss. 2001).

[161] Nix v. Nix, 790 So. 2d 198, 200-01 (Miss. 2001).

[162] Spahn v. Spahn, 959 So. 2d 8, 11 (Miss. Ct. App. 2006).

CHILD SUPPORT

§ 13.04[4]

obligations."[163] In another case, the court of appeals reversed a support award because the chancellor did not deduct items properly allowed under Schedule C in computing a payor's income.[164]

If a self-employed payor's tax returns are not available, a court may determine gross income from other evidence and apply standard tax rates to that amount. A court properly translated nine months of gross income into a yearly amount, then reduced that amount by 30% to reflect standard figures for taxes and Social Security.[165] Where neither party presented evidence of the father's current income, a chancellor did not err in using loan applications to set gross income at $90,000, deducting 25% for taxes, and applying the statutory guidelines.[166] A court may also retain jurisdiction to reexamine support based on additional evidence. A court unable to determine a payor's income properly ordered six months of support and required the payor to provide tax forms at the end of that period for reassessment.[167]

[4] Imputing earning capacity. Under some circumstances, a court may disregard a party's actual income and award support based on a higher, imputed income. An under-employed payor may be required to pay support based on earning capacity rather than income. However, if an income reduction is caused by events beyond a payor's control, such as illness, support should be based on the payor's reduced income.

Imputed income must be adjusted by the same deductions applied to actual income. The Mississippi Court of Appeals reversed a chancellor's award of child support based upon an unemployed father's potential gross earnings rather than potential adjusted gross earnings.[168]

The following rules regarding imputation of income apply in both original actions to award support and modification actions.[169] The rules are also applicable to actions involving spousal support.[170]

[a] Findings of fact. Awards based on imputed income must be supported by findings of fact regarding the payor's earning capacity or true income. The supreme court reversed an award for lack of findings as to the payor's income: "Without having the benefit of the chancellor's findings of fact, it cannot be said that the guidelines were

---

[163] Nix v. Nix, 790 So. 2d 198, 200-01 (Miss. 2001) (court also found no abuse of discretion in part because the issue was not squarely before the court). Judge King's dissenting opinion states that income should not be reduced by home office deductions. *Id.* (King, J., dissenting); *see* Burnham-Steptoe v. Steptoe, 755 So. 2d 1225, 1231 (Miss. Ct. App. 1999) (self-employed payor's earnings were reduced by $12,700 to reflect a one-time draw for business purposes); *see also* Spahn v. Spahn, 959 So. 2d 8, 11 (Miss. Ct. App. 2006) (rejecting wife's argument that automobile expenses and expenses of entertainment should not have been deducted from husband's income; she offered no specific proof of the amount of improper deductions).

[164] Fountain v. Fountain, 877 So. 2d 474, 478-79 (Miss. Ct. App. 2003). Judge Griffis dissented, stating that amounts properly deducted for tax purposes, such as accelerated depreciation and small business write-offs, should not necessarily be deducted for purposes of child support. *Id.* (Griffis, J., dissenting).

[165] Burnham-Steptoe v. Steptoe, 755 So. 2d 1225, 1229-31 (Miss. Ct. App. 1999).

[166] Moore v. Moore. 757 So. 2d 1043, 1050 (Miss. Ct. App. 2000).

[167] James v. James, 756 So. 2d 847, 849-50 (Miss. Ct. App. 2000) (rejecting payor's argument that the six-month review was an impermissible escalation clause).

[168] Osborn v. Osborn, 724 So. 2d 1121, 1125 (Miss. Ct. App. 1998).

[169] See *infra* § 13.11.

[170] See *supra* § 9.09.

§ 13.04[4][b]   MISSISSIPPI FAMILY LAW

either followed or not followed."[171] The court of appeals has recognized, however, that a chancellor's finding with regard to income may be less than exact when a payor has failed to provide the necessary information.[172] A chancellor may also impute income to a payor who is between jobs, based on a reasonable projection of the payor's future income. For example, a chancellor did not err in imputing income of $300,000, the league minimum, to a major league baseball player who was between contracts.[173]

   [b] Good faith/voluntariness test. In many states, the test for imputing income is whether a parent voluntarily chooses to work at less than full earning capacity.[174] Some states require, in addition, that the income reduction be in bad faith – for the purpose of evading child support obligations.[175] Early Mississippi cases imputing income required both voluntariness and bad faith. For example, a 1994 case defined bad faith as "an obligor's action to reduce income or assets for the purpose of *jeopardizing the interests of his children.*"[176] In 1999, the supreme court effectively eliminated the bad faith element by redefining the term for child support purposes as "neglect or refusal to fulfill some duty."[177] Shortly thereafter, the court stated that the true issue in imputing income is whether the income reduction was voluntary.[178] In 2010, however, the court of appeals appeared to return to the bad faith test. The court rejected a custodial father's argument that full-time income should be imputed to a noncustodial mother who reduced her hours to part-time to spend more time with her children. The court held that her actions were not in bad faith, because they were not for the purpose of evading her support obligation.[179] The following sections illustrate application of the test in different contexts.

   [i] Voluntary quit. Income has been imputed to a payor who leaves a job voluntarily, without health-related or other justifiable reasons. A former restaurant manager who quit his job to preach at a monthly salary of $700 was required to pay child support based on his prior income.[180] Similarly, the supreme court rejected a father's request for support modification based upon his decision to leave a construction

---

   [171] Gray v. Gray, 745 So. 2d 234, 237 (Miss. 1999); *see* Ellzey v. White, 922 So. 2d 40, 42 (Miss. Ct. App. 2006) (chancellor's order imputing unreported income to father reversed; no findings to indicate how chancellor arrived at figure). *But cf.* Suber v. Suber, 936 So. 2d 945, 949 (Miss. Ct. App. 2006) (court ordered support above guidelines because father did not produce paystubs; no specific finding regarding imputed income).

   [172] Peters v. Peters, 906 So. 2d 64 (Miss. Ct. App. 2004) (husband who presented conflicting figures and who was less than candid about income "can hardly complain now" of inaccuracies).

   [173] Hackman v. Burkes, 910 So. 2d 1212, 1214 (Miss. Ct. App. 2005) (not error even though player did not secure contract as anticipated; material change, such as failure to enter contract, could be ground for modification).

   [174] Wright v. Wright, 975 S.W.2d 212, 214 (Mo. Ct. App. 1993); *In re* Marriage of Bertram, 981 S.W.2d 820, 829 (Tex. Ct. App. 1998).

   [175] Mich. Child Support Guidelines Manual 7, promulgated by the State Court Admin. Office, *cited in* FAMILY LAW AND PRACTICE, *supra* note 2, § 33.05[2], at 33-42 n.13.

   [176] Parker v. Parker, 645 So. 2d 1327, 1331 (Miss. 1994) (emphasis added); *see also* Lahmann v. Hallmon, 722 So. 2d 614, 622 (Miss. 1998) (stating that payor's lifestyle was a deliberate and voluntary action to reduce child support).

   [177] Bailey v. Bailey, 724 So. 2d 335, 338 (Miss. 1999). *But cf.* Grissom v. Grissom, 952 So. 2d 1023, 1028-29 (Miss. Ct. App. 2007) (using *Parker* definition of bad faith in discussing voluntariness).

   [178] Pullis v. Linzey, 753 So. 2d 480, 484 (Miss. Ct. App. 1999) (reiterating that bad faith is not intentional avoidance, but neglect to fulfill a duty).

   [179] Wells v. Wells, 35 So. 3d 1250, 1260 (Miss. Ct. App. 2010).

   [180] Selman v. Selman, 722 So. 2d 547, 554 (Miss. 1998).

CHILD SUPPORT §13.04[4][b][ii]

job to sing two nights a week in a club.[181] And modification was denied to a payor who voluntarily left employment, providing no evidence to support his explanation that he was offered reduced compensation after an accident.[182] In a related context, the supreme court upheld a chancellor's refusal to modify alimony for a payor who quit work over a dispute with his supervisor and failed to secure employment at a level based on his education and job qualifications.[183]

[ii] **Voluntary unemployment.** Courts have also imputed income to an unemployed parent who is able to work. For example, the court of appeals upheld a support order based on an unemployed father's earning capacity rather than on his unemployment income.[184] And a noncustodial mother who chose to stay at home was properly ordered to pay child support based on her earning capacity as a nurse.[185]

[iii] **Discharge from employment.** A child support payor's discharge from employment is not considered a voluntary income loss if the payor was terminated without fault.[186] If the payor was fired for wrongdoing, some courts base child support on the prior salary, reasoning that the income loss resulted from a voluntary, wrongful act.[187] Others refuse to impute income under those circumstances.[188] In a 1994 case, the Mississippi Supreme Court followed this approach, upholding a support reduction for a payor terminated for alleged sexual misconduct, since his actions were not for the purpose of avoiding child support.[189] The case relied on the "bad faith" test for

---

[181] Lahmann v. Hallmon, 722 So. 2d 614, 622 (Miss. 1998) (concluding that father's lifestyle change was deliberate and voluntary action in order to reduce income and thereby reduce his child support); *see also* Seeley v. Stafford, 840 So. 2d 111, 113-14 (Miss. Ct. App. 2003) (payor who voluntarily left employment not entitled to reduce support); *cf.* Sessums v. Sessums, 12 So. 3d 1146, 1147-48 (Miss. Ct. App. 2009) (denying modification to father who quit job to work for company that paid less but offered more earning potential).

[182] Ballard v. Ballard, 843 So. 2d 76, 78 (Miss. Ct. App. 2003).

[183] Yancey v. Yancey, 752 So. 2d 1006, 1010 (Miss. 1999); *see also* Lane v. Lane, 850 So. 2d 122, 126-27 (Miss. 2002) (no reduction in alimony and child support where payor voluntarily retired); Varner v. Varner, 666 So. 2d 493, 497 (Miss. 1995); Towles v. Towles, 137 So. 2d 182, 184-85 (Miss. 1962) (no reduction where payor voluntarily sold business and continued as employee); Leiden v. Leiden, 905 So. 2d 582 (Miss. Ct. App. 2004) (no modification; payor voluntarily took early retirement from the Navy).

[184] White v. White, 722 So. 2d 731, 734 (Miss. Ct. App. 1999) (basing support on father's educational level, past earning record, and employability); *see* Ballard v. Ballard, 843 So. 2d 76, 79 (Miss. Ct. App. 2003) (payor denied modification without specific proof of attempts to find employment); Osborn v. Osborn, 724 So. 2d 1121, 1126 (Miss. Ct. App. 1998) (approving combined child support, marital debt and alimony constituting 89% of payor's unemployment income); Grice v. Grice, 726 So. 2d 1242 (Miss. Ct. App. 1998).

[185] Bredemeier v. Jackson, 689 So. 2d 770, 777-78 (Miss. 1997) (obligation to children does not decrease just because mother chooses not to work); *see also* Masino v. Masino, 829 So. 2d 1267, 1273-74 (Miss. Ct. App. 2002) (error to abate noncustodial mother's child support obligation based on inability to pay where the mother chose not to seek employment); Creekmore v. Creekmore, 651 So. 2d 513, 516 (Miss. 1995) (unemployed disabled father with drug problem ordered to pay $500 per month, plus health insurance, and one-half of out-of-pocket medical expenses); Smith v. Smith, 614 So. 2d 394, 397 (Miss. 1993) (mother apparently unemployed, but with degree in landscape architecture ordered to pay $224 per month). *But cf.* Wells v. Wells, 35 So. 3d 1250, 1260 (Miss. Ct. App. 2010) (refusing to impute income to noncustodial mother who stopped working full-time to be with children).

[186] *See* Grissom v. Grissom, 952 So. 2d 1023, 1029 (Miss. Ct. App. 2007) (father terminated without fault allowed to reduce child support).

[187] Pope v. Pope, 559 N.W.2d 192, 196 (Neb. 1997).

[188] *In re* Johnson, 950 P.2d 267, 270 (Kan. Ct. App. 1997); Klahold v. Kroh, 649 A.2d 701, 704 (Pa. Super. Ct. 1994).

[189] *See* Parker v. Parker, 645 So. 2d 1327, 1328-31 (Miss. 1994).

§ 13.04[4][b][iv]   **MISSISSIPPI FAMILY LAW**

imputing income.[190] In a 2007 case, the court of appeals affirmed modification of child support after a father was fired from his job, reducing his income from over $300,000 to $114,000. The decision did not discuss the cause for firing.[191]

[iv] Reduced earnings based on illness. When a payor blames income loss on poor health, independent evidence linking income loss to illness or injury may be critical. In one case, support obligations were reduced for a payor who proved that his job required heavy physical labor that he could no longer perform.[192] Similarly, a court erred in denying modification to a payor whose job and income were scaled back as a result of a heart attack.[193] In contrast, income was imputed to a physician who offered only his own testimony that depression and alcoholism prevented him from practicing his specialty.[194] Modification was also denied to a father who chose to resign as a tow boat captain based on job-related stress, in the absence of medical evidence of job-related health problems.[195] And a chancellor's award of more than 20% of a physician father's income as support for two children was based in part on his finding that the father was capable of earning more but chose not to do so.[196]

[v] Resignation to pursue schooling. Some courts refuse to reduce child support when a payor reduces income to return to school.[197] Other courts will reduce support if the additional training will benefit children by increasing the payor's income.[198] The Mississippi Supreme Court indicated in dicta that it would consider reducing support based on a payor's good faith reduction in income to further education.[199]

[vi] Resignation to care for children. A noncustodial parent may seek to reduce an existing support obligation to stay at home with later-born children. The Mississippi Supreme Court rejected a noncustodial mother's request for modification after she quit her job to stay at home with her newborn child. The court held that the birth of additional children does not justify reducing support for earlier-born children.[200] However, the court of appeals held in 2010 that a chancellor was not required to impute full-time earnings to a noncustodial mother who reduced her hours as a nurse to part-

---

[190] See *supra* § 13.04[4][b].

[191] Austin v. Austin, 981 So. 2d 1000 (Miss. Ct. App. 2007).

[192] Kennedy v. Kennedy, 650 So. 2d 1362, 1369-72 (Miss. 1995) (reduction in separate maintenance payments).

[193] McEwen v. McEwen, 631 So. 2d 821, 823-824 (Miss. 1994).

[194] Poole v. Poole, 701 So. 2d 813, 818-19 (Miss. 1997).

[195] Pullis v. Linzey, 753 So. 2d 480, 482 (Miss. Ct. App. 1999) (father testified that he was on the boat 240 days a year, had no personal life, and suffered from work-related stress which affected his health).

[196] Henderson v. Henderson, 952 So. 2d 273, 279 (Miss. Ct. App. 2006) (ordering payment of $2,000 a month support for two children from father with adjusted gross income of $9370 a month).

[197] *See, e.g., In re* Marriage of McNeely, 815 P.2d 1125, 1129-30 (Kan. Ct. App. 1991) (refusing father's request to impute to him a smaller income based on his plans to enter law school); Sabatka v. Sabatka, 511 N.W.2d 107, 111 (Neb. 1994) (denying husband's request to reduce payments when he voluntarily enrolled in school); Schroeder v. Schroeder, 463 S.E.2d 790, 793 (N.C. Ct. App. 1995) (concluding that wife could not claim a change in circumstances because it was "a change that she brought about herself").

[198] *In re* Marriage of Ehlert, 868 P.2d 1168, 1169 (Colo. Ct. App. 1994); *In re* Marriage of Clyatt, 882 P.2d 503, 506 (Mont. 1994).

[199] Tingle v. Tingle, 573 So. 2d 1389, 1393 (Miss. 1990) (but denying modification because the payor knew at the time of the decree that he intended to return to school).

[200] Bailey v. Bailey, 724 So. 2d 335, 336 (Miss. 1998).

CHILD SUPPORT § 13.04[4][b][vii]

time in order to spend more time with her children.[201]

[vii] **Imprisonment.** Some courts treat imprisonment as an involuntary loss of income.[202] Others refuse to reduce support based on imprisonment,[203] particularly if the payor has assets from which support can be provided.[204] The Mississippi Court of Appeals affirmed an order requiring an imprisoned father with assets to pay $225 a month in child support.[205]

[5] Imputing hidden income. Income may also be imputed to a payor who conceals or diverts income or assets. In the absence of direct evidence of concealment, a court may impute income to a payor whose lifestyle is clearly inconsistent with his or her reported income.

[a] Based on transfer of income. Income diverted to family members or employees may be imputed to a payor. A dentist's income was properly recalculated to include the salary, equal to his own, paid to his current wife as office manager.[206] Similarly, a chancellor should have included a payor's mother's paper route in his income. The route was in the payor's name and he performed the work; his mother received the income and made him a monthly "gift" of the proceeds.[207]

[b] Based on transfer of assets. Income was imputed to a payor who transferred substantial business interests to his current wife.[208] Similarly, modification was denied to a payor who voluntarily sold his business but continued as an employee in the business.[209]

[c] Based on inconsistent lifestyle or other evidence. A court may impute income to a payor whose reported income is clearly inadequate to support his or her actual lifestyle. A chancellor properly refused to believe a father's statement of income, based in part on the cost of his various entertainment activities and his inability to corroborate "loans" he received to support his lifestyle.[210] In another case, a chancel-

---

[201] Wells v. Wells, 35 So. 3d 1250, 1260 (Miss. Ct. App. 2010) (noting that there was "no evidence that [the mother] reduced her work hours in bad faith to reduce her child-support obligation").

[202] *See* Jones v. Reed, 705 A.2d 158, 161 (Md. 1998); Wood v. Wood, 964 P.2d 1259, 1266-67 (Wyo. 1998).

[203] *See* Davis v. Vance, 574 N.E.2d 330, 331 (Ind. Ct. App. 1991); *In re* Marriage of Kern, 408 N.W.2d 387, 389-90 (Iowa Ct. App. 1987); Toups v. Toups, 708 So. 2d 849, 850 (La. Ct. App. 1998).

[204] Alred v. Alred, 678 So. 2d 1144, 1146 (Ala. Civ. App. 1996).

[205] Avery v. Avery, 864 So. 2d 1054, 1057 (Miss. Ct. App. 2004) (father in prison had no income but had assets from which support of $225 could be paid).

[206] Stroud v. Stroud, 758 So. 2d 502, 504 (Miss. Ct. App. 2000) (current wife's salary reduced net profits by 60%).

[207] Carter v. Carter, 735 So. 2d 1109, 1115-16 (Miss. 1999).

[208] Grice v. Grice, 726 So. 2d 1242, 1252 (Miss. Ct. App. 1998); *see also* Lane v. Lane, 850 So. 2d 122, 125 (Miss. 2002) (husband's obligation to first wife "paramount to the financial obligations he has as a result of his second marriage"); Turner v. Turner, 744 So. 2d 332, 335-36 (Miss. Ct. App. 1999) (payor transferred assets to current wife but still enjoyed income from assets).

[209] Towles v. Towles, 137 So. 2d 182, 184-85 (Miss. 1962) (no reduction where payor voluntarily sold business and continued as employee); *see also* Suber v. Suber, 936 So. 2d 945, 949 (Miss. Ct. App. 2006) (imputing income to father who failed to produce paystubs).

[210] Dunn v. Dunn, 695 So. 2d 1152, 1157 (Miss. 1997); *see* Clark v. Clark, 754 So. 2d 450, 459 (Miss. 1999) ($600

§ 13.04[5][d]   MISSISSIPPI FAMILY LAW

lor was rightfully skeptical of a father's stated monthly income of $912; he managed twenty-eight apartment units rented at $350 monthly, bought a new truck, and paid his brother-in-law $32,000 during the proceedings.[211] And a chancellor properly imputed income to a father based on deposit slips showing that his income exceeded the amount claimed on his 8.05 financial statement.[212]

[d] Tax returns. Courts are not bound by a payor's declared taxable income in determining income for child support purposes. The court of appeals stated that tax returns are not an appropriate measure of income for a payor who is sheltering income and assets.[213]

[6] Adjustments to gross income. The second step in calculating child support is to determine the payor's adjusted gross income. Application of the statutory percentages to gross income is error.[214] Under the Mississippi guidelines, a payor's gross income is reduced by subtracting legally-mandated deductions and existing child support orders. In addition, courts have discretion to adjust income by an appropriate amount for children living with the payor.

[a] Mandatory deductions. Mandatory deductions include federal, state, and local taxes, Social Security contributions, and mandatory retirement and disability contributions.[215] The court of appeals remanded an award of child support because the chancellor failed to deduct taxes, Social Security, and Medicare.[216]

[b] Voluntary deductions. Gross income should not be reduced to reflect voluntary payments. For example, payments to 401K plans and credit unions may not be deducted for child support purposes.[217] Similarly, a payor's income should not be adjusted by subtracting health insurance payments for the children in question.[218]

---

per month plus medical insurance, one-half of out-of-pocket expenses, and one-half college expenses affirmed where income appeared higher than reported); Poole v. Poole, 701 So. 2d 813, 816 (Miss. 1997) (noted no obvious change in father's lifestyle despite claimed reduction in income); McEachern v. McEachern, 605 So. 2d 809, 813-14 (Miss. 1992) (modification reducing support, but above guidelines not error where court questioned actual income).

[211] Gray v. Gray, 745 So. 2d 234, 237 (Miss. 1999); *see also* Grogan v. Grogan, 641 So. 2d 734, 741-42 (Miss. 1994) (27.5% for two children; question about earnings of father who paid for girlfriend's child's daycare); Ballard v. Ballard, 843 So. 2d 76, 79 (Miss. Ct. App. 2003) (father bought new horses and trailer on alleged income of $6,000 a year).

[212] Swiderski v. Swiderski. 18 So. 3d 280, 287-89 (Miss. Ct. App. 2009), *cert. denied*, 19 So. 3d 82 (2009).

[213] Watkins v. Watkins, 748 So. 2d 808, 811 (Miss. Ct. App. 1999).

[214] Lee v. Stewart, 724 So. 2d 1093, 1097 (Miss. Ct. App. 1998) (reversing child support award because percentages applied to gross income); Osborn v. Osborn, 724 So. 2d 1121, 1125-26 (Miss. Ct. App. 1998) (reversing award based on imputed, prior gross earnings rather than adjusted gross income).

[215] MISS. CODE ANN. § 43-10-101(3)(b) (2004).

[216] Holloway v. Holloway, 31 So. 3d 57, 61 (Miss. Ct. App. 2009), *cert. dismissed*, 29 So. 3d 774 (Miss. 2010). *But see* Strange v. Strange, 43 So. 3d 1169, 1175 (Miss. Ct. App. 2010) (failure to deduct mandatory payments was harmless error; four judges dissenting).

[217] Lee v. Stewart, 724 So. 2d 1093, 1097 (Miss. Ct. App. 1998); *see* Sellers v. Sellers, 13 So. 3d 853 (Miss. Ct. App. 2009) (voluntary retirement payments should not have been deducted from income).

[218] Wells v. Wells. 800 So. 2d 1239, 1247 (Miss. Ct. App. 2001); *see also* Laird v. Blackburn, 788 So. 2d 844, 850 (Miss. Ct. App. 2001) (income not reduced to reflect general household expenses). However, at least one case indicates that payment of health insurance may be considered as a deviation factor. *See* Hults v. Hults, 11 So. 3d 1273, 1279-80 (Miss. Ct. App. 2009) (discussed as deviation, although father's income was above $50,000).

CHILD SUPPORT   § 13.04[6][c]

[c] **Support for other children.** All states agree that court-ordered support for prior children must be considered in calculating child support for later-born children. There is less consensus about adjusting support to reflect expenses for children living with a payor.

[i] **Court-ordered child support.** In most states, existing child support awards are deducted from a payor's gross income.[219] The Mississippi child support guidelines provide that an existing support order is a legally mandated deduction from gross income.[220]

[ii] **Earlier-born children living in payor's home.** The Mississippi guidelines permit courts to adjust income to reflect a payor's support of "another child or other children residing with him."[221] The statute provides that the deduction is discretionary – the court "may" deduct an amount that it deems appropriate.[222] A chancellor did not err in refusing to adjust a payor's income to reflect that an older child lived in the home with him.[223] Similarly, a court did not err in refusing to adjust income for a payor who split custody of three children with his former wife.[224] In some cases, it appears that chancellors have used the statutory percentages as the appropriate figure for adjustment.[225] The provision does not apply to stepchildren living in a payor's home.[226]

[iii] **Later-born children living in the payor's home.** There is considerable disagreement as to whether a payor's income should be adjusted in a modification action to reflect support for later-born children.[227] The Mississippi discretionary adjustment provision does not distinguish between earlier- and later-born children. However, the Mississippi Supreme Court has limited application of the adjustment to earlier-born children. The court rejected a noncustodial mother's argument that her income should be adjusted downward to reflect her in-home support for a new baby – a noncustodial parent may not reduce support obligations to prior children. Otherwise, a parent could "sire himself out of his child support obligation."[228] While the decision appears to limit

---

[219] *See* RUTKIN, *supra* note 2, § 33.05[9], at 33-53.

[220] MISS. CODE ANN. § 43-19-101(3)(b) (2004).

[221] MISS. CODE ANN. § 43-19-101(3)(d) (2004).

[222] MISS. CODE ANN. § 43-19-101(3)(b) (2004).

[223] McClee v. Simmons, 834 So. 2d 61, 65 (Miss. Ct. App. 2002).

[224] *See* Magruder v. Magruder, 881 So. 2d 365, 368 (Miss. Ct. App. 2004) (also rejecting father's argument that ex-wife should have been required to pay support for the two children in his custody).

[225] *See* Grace v. Dep't of Human Servs., 687 So. 2d 1232, 1233 (Miss. 1997) (chancellor apparently reduced payor's income by 14% because an earlier-born child lived in the payor's home); *cf.* Grove v. Agnew, 14 So. 3d 790, 793 (Miss. Ct. App. 2009) (chancellor erred in ordering the father of two children, one living with him, to pay 10% of his adjusted income for child not living with him; the court should subtract proper amount for in-home support and award 14% of AGI for second child).

[226] Kilgore v. Fuller, 741 So. 2d 351, 356-57 (Miss. Ct. App. 1999) (expense of stepson not allowed as deduction).

[227] *See* MORGAN, *supra* note 13, § 3.04[b], at 3-46 to 3-47, table 3-6.

[228] Bailey v. Bailey, 724 So. 2d 335, 336 (Miss. 1998); *see also* Bustin v. Bustin, 806 So. 2d 1136, 1138 (Miss. Ct. App. 2001) (chancellor properly refused to reduce child support on the basis that the payor had added three children to his household since the original order); Turner v. Turner. 744 So. 2d 332, 338 (Miss. Ct. App. 1999) ("addition to a noncustodial parent's family cannot be said to reasonably affect the ability of the parties to abide by the terms of the

---

435

§ 13.04[7]   MISSISSIPPI FAMILY LAW

the discretionary deduction to earlier-born children, several later cases suggest in dicta that the provision may be applied to later-born children.[229]

[7] Applying the statutory percentage. Basic child support is calculated by applying a percentage to adjusted gross income. The percentages vary with the number of children: 14% for one child; 20% for two; 22% for three; 24% for four; and 26% for five or more children.[230] The resulting figure is the presumptively correct amount of basic support for payors with adjusted yearly income between $5,000 and $50,000.

The question has arisen whether "number of children" refers only to the children involved in a particular case or to all children of the payor. The difference in the resulting support order can be substantial. For example, a married father of two children was sued for support of a nonmarital child. He argued that the proper amount of support was one-third of 22%, or $160 a month, rather than 14%, or $305 per month. Focusing on the statutory language, the supreme court held that "number of children" refers to the children for whom support is sought, not the payor's total number of children.[231]

[8] Adjusted gross income above $50,000 or below $5,000. The statutory percentages are presumptively correct for payors with adjusted gross income between $5,000 and $50,000 a year. For payors with income above or below that amount, courts are to make written findings as to whether application of the guidelines is reasonable.[232] Child support awards involving payors with income in this range are discussed in detail in Section 13.06.

§ 13.05 DEVIATION FROM THE GUIDELINES

A court may deviate from the presumptively correct amount of support based on statutory factors. The deviation must be supported by written findings of fact explaining why the presumptively correct amount is inappropriate.[233] In a 2010 case, the court of appeals stated that the guidelines are not a ceiling, but "the floor for what is considered minimally required child support."[234] A chancellor's deviation order should state explicitly that the amount produced by application of the guidelines is "unjust or inap-

---

original divorce decree").

[229] *See* Wallace v. Wallace, 965 So. 2d 737, 742-43 (Miss. Ct. App. 2007) (but affirming chancellor's refusal to adjust income; payor had adequate income to support both families); McClee v. Simmons, 834 So. 2d 61, 65 (Miss. Ct. App. 2002) (not an abuse of discretion to deny payor a deduction for a seventeen-year-old living in the payor's home); Bustin v. Bustin, 806 So. 2d 1136, 1138 (Miss. Ct. App. 2001) (stated that chancellors have discretion while affirming chancellor's refusal to reduce support for later-born children); Shepard v. Shepard, 769 So. 2d 242, 246 n.3 (Miss. Ct. App. 2000) (stating, in cases involving later-born children, that statute gives a chancellor discretion to reduce gross income for children living in the payor's home).

[230] MISS. CODE ANN. § 43-19-101(1) (2004).

[231] Grace v. Dep't of Human Servs., 687 So. 2d 1232, 1235 (Miss. 1997); *see also* Grove v. Agnew, 14 So. 3d 790, 793 (Miss. Ct. App. 2009) (court erred in ordering support for one of two children at 10% of AGI; should have been 14%).

[232] MISS. CODE ANN. § 43-19-101(4) (2004).

[233] Thompson v. Thompson, 894 So. 2d 603 (Miss. Ct. App. 2004); *see* 45 C.F.R. § 302.56(g) (2000) (requiring that states establish deviation criteria).

[234] Strange v. Strange, 43 So. 3d 1169, 1173 (Miss. Ct. App. 2010).

436

CHILD SUPPORT § 13.05[1]

propriate" and refer to the statutory deviation criteria to explain the deviation.[235]

Some payments in excess of the guidelines are not considered deviations. For example, health insurance, payment of out-of-pocket medical expenses, and life insurance may be ordered in addition to basic support without being considered a deviation. In contrast, private school tuition is presumed to be covered in basic support; an order for tuition payments will be treated as a deviation if the tuition plus basic support exceeds the statutory amount.

[1] Deviation criteria. A court may deviate from the statutory guidelines based on (1) a child's extraordinary medical, psychological, dental, or educational expenses; (2) other special needs of the child; (3) shared parenting arrangements; (4) the age of the child; (5) independent income of the child; (6) spousal support to the custodial parent; (7) total available assets of the parents; (8) seasonal variations in income or expenses of one or both spouses; and (9) any other adjustment needed to achieve an equitable result.[236]

[2] Extraordinary medical or educational expenses. A court may deviate from the statutory guidelines based on evidence of unusual medical or educational expenses.

[a] Medical expenses. The supreme court affirmed a chancellor's award slightly above the guidelines based on a finding that two children with asthma had unusual medical expenses.[237]

Courts routinely order noncustodial parents to provide health insurance and to pay one-half of all out-of-pocket medical and other health-related expenses in addition to basic child support. Payment of these expenses is treated as a permissible add-on to basic support, rather than a deviation requiring special findings to support the award.[238] In at least one case, however, a noncustodial parent's payment of health insurance was part of the reason for allowing deviation below the guidelines.[239]

[b] Educational expenses. Courts sometimes order a noncustodial parent to pay tuition for private elementary or secondary school. If the tuition combined with the basic award exceeds the statutory percentages, the award is treated as a deviation that must be supported with findings of fact. The court of appeals reversed a support order requiring payment of the statutory percentage of support, one-half of private school tuition, and the cost of an automobile; the chancellor did not make specific findings of fact to support the deviation.[240] Similarly, an award of basic support plus private school

---

[235] Yelverton v. Yelverton, 961 So. 2d 19, 27 (Miss. 2007).

[236] MISS. CODE ANN. § 43-19-103 (2004).

[237] Grant v. Grant, 765 So. 2d 1263, 1266 (Miss. 2000).

[238] Hoar v. Hoar, 404 So. 2d 1032, 1036 (Miss. 1981) (uninsured medical costs are extraordinary expenses not covered by the basic child support award; chancellor may order payment of one-half of all medical expenses as an addition to regular child support).

[239] Hults v. Hults, 11 So. 3d 1273, 1278-79 (Miss. Ct. App. 2009) (discussed as deviation, although father's income was above $50,000).

[240] Chesney v. Chesney. 828 So. 2d 219, 221 (Miss. Ct. App. 2002), *aff'd in part and rev'd in part*, 849 So. 2d 860

437

§ 13.05[3]   MISSISSIPPI FAMILY LAW

tuition was considered a deviation and reversed for findings even though the parents had agreed before their divorce that the child should attend private school.[241] An award of tuition has been affirmed if the chancellor makes findings justifying the deviation. A chancellor properly ordered a noncustodial parent to pay private school tuition plus basic support; the father had substantial income, the mother had no source of income other than alimony, and the children's special needs included attending the school where their friends and activities were located.[242]

Unusual educational expenses have also been cited as a reason to apply the guidelines to a high-income payor. A payor with monthly income of $19,408 was ordered to pay 14% of his adjusted income for a child who was engaged in extensive extracurricular activities, attended private school, and would benefit from enhanced educational activities.[243]

[3] Shared custody or extensive visitation. Child support guidelines were not designed for shared parenting arrangements. The economic studies used to select guideline percentages were based on the assumption that children spend approximately 20% of their time with noncustodial parents – every other weekend, two weeks in the summer, a day at Christmas and a day at Thanksgiving. In addition, the studies assumed that noncustodial parents do not maintain a duplicate primary residence for the child.[244] When physical time is more evenly divided, a noncustodial parent bears some of the expenses covered in the basic support award. Studies indicate that as visitation approaches 35%, the noncustodial parent typically provides a primary home for the child, duplicating the custodial parent's housing-related costs.[245] This does not mean, of course, that the custodial parent's expenses for housing are reduced. However, with regard to the other high-ticket items – food, entertainment, travel, and childcare – the costs are shifted from the custodial to the noncustodial parent for the time the child spends in the second home.[246]

(Miss. 2002); *see also* Roberts v. Roberts, 924 So. 2d 550, 553-54 (Miss. Ct. App. 2005) (private school tuition ordinarily included in basic support award; affirming refusal to order father to pay private school tuition); *cf.* Laird v. Blackburn, 788 So. 2d 844, 852 (Miss. Ct. App. 2001) (noncustodial father not required to pay for private school tuition where mother did not consult him regarding school transfer).

[241] Southerland v. Southerland, 816 So. 2d 1004, 1006 (Miss. 2002), *aff'd*, 875 So. 2d 204 (Miss. 2004).

[242] Hensarling v. Hensarling. 824 So. 2d 583, 588 (Miss. 2002); *see also* Chesney v. Chesney, 910 So. 2d 1057, 1061-63 (Miss. 2005) (affirming order that noncustodial father pay private school tuition in addition to basic support; father was able to make payment, and child would be harmed by removal from only school she had attended); Southerland v. Southerland, 875 So. 2d 204, 207 (Miss. 2004); Collins v. Collins, 722 So. 2d 596, 599 (Miss. 1998) (rejecting mother's argument that chancellor erred in awarding private school tuition but reducing basic support by that amount); Seymour v. Seymour, 960 So. 2d 513, 517 (Miss. Ct. App. 2006) (affirming order for basic support of 22% for three children plus parochial school tuition; chancellor found that the father had additional, unreported income; the children had always attended the school, and requiring them to attend public school where his girlfriend taught would be stressful); Striebeck v. Striebeck, 911 So. 2d 628, 636-37 (Miss. Ct. App. 2005) (court did not abuse discretion by ordering father to pay one-half of private school tuition even though mother made unilateral decision to enroll child; child was prospering). *But cf.* Roberts v. Roberts, 924 So. 2d 550, 553-54 (Miss. Ct. App. 2005) (affirming chancellor's refusal to require father to pay private school tuition; no special circumstances justifying award).

[243] Smith v. Smith, 25 So. 3d 369, 372-374 (Miss. Ct. App. 2009), *cert. denied*, 24 So. 3d 1038 (Miss. 2010).

[244] *See* MORGAN, *supra* note 13, § 3.03[a], at 3-31, n.91.

[245] *See* AMERICAN LAW INSTITUTE, PRINCIPLES OF THE LAW OF FAMILY DISSOLUTION, ANALYSIS AND RECOMMENDATIONS, Pt. II, Reporter's Notes, at 120-21 (Tentative Draft No. 3, 1988).

[246] One study estimates that expenditures for a child who resides in a household 50% of the time equals approximately 75% of the expenses incurred for a child who lives full-time in the household. *See* Marygold S. Melli. *Guideline*

CHILD SUPPORT § 13.05[3]

Recognizing the shift in expenditures does not lead to a simple solution.[247] The easy case is one in which parents with equal income divide time with their children equally. In that case, no support should be ordered. Calculating appropriate support in arrangements with an uneven split of time, and where incomes are not equal, is a challenge. Some states provide for deviation when visitation reaches a defined percentage of time.[248] Others, including Mississippi, state that shared parenting arrangements are a deviation factor without providing more specific guidance. Most courts require a showing that the additional time spent with the noncustodial parent results in an increase in costs to the noncustodial parent and a corresponding decrease in costs to the custodial parent.[249]

The court of appeals has emphasized that chancellors have considerable discretion in determining whether to deviate from the guidelines based on shared parenting arrangements.[250] Mississippi appellate courts have approved deviations based on shared parenting between parents with equal physical custody[251] and when the noncustodial parent has extensive visitation.[252] When parents shared equal physical custody but the father's income and resources were much higher than the mother's, the court awarded child support to the mother but reduced the amount by 75% during the father's period of custody.[253] And when one of four children began living with a father, the chancellor ordered the mother to pay 14% of her adjusted gross income to the father, ordered the father to pay 22%, and reduced his obligation by the amount owed by the mother.[254] On the other hand, the court of appeals has affirmed a chancellor's award of support based on the statutory guidelines even though the noncustodial mother had visitation 42% of the time.[255] Similarly, when custody was split between a high-income father and low-income mother, the court did not err in ordering support at the statutory level from the father and no support from the mother.[256] Denial of all child support is appropriate

---

Review: Child Support and Time Sharing by Parents, 33 Fam. L.Q. 219, 231 (1999) (citing Edward P. Lazear & Robert. T. Michael, Allocation of Income Within the Household, 165068 (1988)).

[247] For a discussion of alternative approaches, see *1999 Child Support Symposium,* 33 Fam. L. Q. 1 (1999).

[248] Colo. Rev. Stat. § 14-10-115(8) (1999) (stating overnight visitation qualifies for deviation); D.C. Code Ann. § 16-916.1(n) (1981) (stating that 40% of time with one parent qualifies for deviation); Mich. C.S.G. (stating that 128 days qualifies for deviation).

[249] *See* Terpstra v. Terpstra, 588 N.E.2d 592, 595-96 (Ind. Ct. App. 1992); Brazan v. Brazan, 638 So. 2d 1176, 1180 (La. Ct. App. 1994); Hoffman v. Hoffman, 870 S.W.2d 480, 483 (Mo. Ct. App. 1994).

[250] *See* Dunn v. Dunn, 911 So. 2d 591, 600 (Miss. Ct. App. 2005).

[251] Mabus v. Mabus, 890 So. 2d 806, 817-18 (Miss. 2003).

[252] *See* Masino v. Masino, 829 So. 2d 1267, 1273 (Miss. Ct. App. 2002) (reducing noncustodial mother's support by one-half during extensive summer visitation not error); Laird v. Blackburn, 788 So. 2d 844, 849-50 (Miss. Ct. App. 2001) (affirming reduction in support during extensive summer visitation). *But see* Henley v. Jones, 880 So. 2d 382, 383-84 (Miss. Ct. App. 2004) (affirming chancellor's order for support of 20% of adjusted gross income from mother with visitation 42% of time).

[253] Mabus v. Mabus, 890 So. 2d 806, 825 (Miss. 2003)*; see also* Grissom v. Grissom, 952 So. 2d 1023, 1026 (Miss. Ct. App. 2007) (father who shared joint custody originally ordered to pay mother $165 a month in child support); Johnson v. Johnson, 913 So. 2d 368, 369 (Miss. Ct. App. 2005) (no support ordered between employed parents who shared joint custody equally).

[254] Reid v. Reid, 998 So. 2d 1032, 1035 (Miss. Ct. App. 2008).

[255] Henley v. Jones, 880 So. 2d 382, 383-84 (Miss. Ct. App. 2004).

[256] *See* Magruder v. Magruder, 881 So. 2d 365 (Miss. Ct. App. 2004) (also rejecting father's argument that his income should have been reduced to reflect in-home support for two children; court did not discuss shared parenting deviation factor)*; see also* Sellers v. Sellers, 22 So. 3d 299, 301 (Miss. Ct. App. 2009) (split custody of two children; only father was ordered to pay support) *cf.* Dunn v. Dunn, 911 So. 2d 591, 600-01 (Miss. Ct. App. 2005) (father who shared split custody of two children ordered to pay $400 a month in support; had each parent been ordered to pay 14%, mother

§ 13.05[4]   **MISSISSIPPI FAMILY LAW**

when parents of roughly equal income split custody, with each parent having custody of one child.[257]

[4] Reduced visitation. Just as extensive visitation may justify deviation below the guidelines, a noncustodial parent who exercises little or no visitation may be ordered to pay support exceeding the guidelines.[258] For example, a chancellor properly deviated above the guidelines in ordering support from a payor who did not exercise visitation regularly. The court of appeals found it reasonable that a noncustodial parent's failure to exercise visitation would cause the custodial parent's expenses to increase.[259]

[5] Expenses of older children. A support award exceeding the guidelines may be appropriate for older children with increased expenses. The court of appeals upheld an award above the guidelines based upon evidence of the increased educational and extracurricular needs of teenage children.[260] Similarly, a chancellor properly awarded 23% of a payor's adjusted gross income of $67,500 for three teenage children.[261]

[6] Child's income. The Mississippi guidelines list a child's income as a factor that may justify deviation. The cases reflect that chancellors have considerable discretion in whether to deviate from the guidelines based upon a child's income or assets. The court of appeals affirmed a chancellor's deviation below the statutory guidelines based in part on the availability of $34,000 in mutual funds for the children.[262] In contrast, a noncustodial father's support was not reduced even though his disabled son received Supplemental Security Income benefits.[263] The supreme court rejected a wealthy father's argument that he should be relieved from paying college expenses for a daughter with a trust fund. The court held that a parent with sufficient income to support a child is not excused from support because the child has assets of her own.[264] However, a court erred in ordering release of college account funds to a child where the divorce decree clearly established that the funds were for educational purposes.[265]

---

would have received $301 award; upward deviation proper in light of income disparity).

[257] Polk v. Polk, 559 So. 2d 1048, 1050 (Miss. 1990); *see also* Curtiss v. Curtiss, 781 So. 2d 142, 143 (Miss. Ct. App. 2000) (awarding mother, with custody of three children, support for two; father's custody of one of four children offset support for third child). *But cf.* Mitchell v. Mitchell, 767 So. 2d 1037, 1044 (Miss. Ct. App. 2000) (chancellor erred in failing to award child support to father with "fifty percent visitation," where children actually spent little time with father).

[258] *See* Marygold S. Melli. *Guideline Review: Child Support and Time Sharing by Parents*, 33 Fam. L.Q. 219, 224 (1999).

[259] Gray v. Gray, 909 So. 2d 108, 114 (Miss. Ct. App. 2005) ($80 per month over guidelines).

[260] *See* Havens v. Broocks, 728 So. 2d 580, 583 (Miss. Ct. App. 1998) (modification increasing support above guidelines upheld based on specific testimony about increased expenses of older children; also noting impact of inflation on award over ten years old).

[261] Wright v. Stanley, 700 So. 2d 274, 282-83 (Miss. 1997) (23% of payor's income for three children supported by chancellor's finding of children's increased expenses).

[262] Hults v. Hults, 11 So. 3d 1273, 1279 (Miss. Ct. App. 2009).

[263] Hammett v. Woods, 602 So. 2d 825, 830 (Miss. 1992). However, support is reduced dollar for dollar when a child receives benefits on the parent's account, rather than his own. *See supra* § 13.04[2][c]. *See also* Wallace v. Wallace, 965 So. 2d 737, 744 (Miss. Ct. App. 2007) (rejecting father's argument that support should be reduced; not clear that daughter would be able to continue earning $600 a month while attending college).

[264] Saliba v. Saliba, 753 So. 2d 1095, 1099-100 (Miss. 2000).

[265] Keys v. Keys, 930 So. 2d 438, 442-43 (Miss. Ct. App. 2005) (distinguishing *Saliba* on basis that divorce decree made clear that funds in children's names were intended for college support).

CHILD SUPPORT

§ 13.05[7]

[7] Childcare expenses. The Mississippi guidelines do not specifically mention childcare as a deviation factor, although the factors of "extraordinary educational expenses" or "special needs of the child" arguably include childcare.[266] Recognizing that childcare costs often exceed basic child support, many states treat childcare expenses as an add-on to the basic support award.[267] The cost may be divided between the parents equally or in proportion to their incomes or may be borne by one parent alone.[268] The Mississippi Court of Appeals suggested in dicta that deviation based on childcare may be appropriate – the court affirmed an award of 26% of a payor's adjusted gross income for two children, noting that all but ten dollars of the award was consumed by childcare expenses.[269]

[8] Fluctuating income. The Mississippi guidelines lists as a deviation factor "seasonal variations" in a parent's income. The court of appeals affirmed a chancellor's deviation below the statutory guidelines for a payor whose previous year income was based significantly on post-Katrina overtime work. The father's regular gross income was $63,000 a year, but the overtime increased his 2006 annual gross income to approximately $113,000. The deviation was fair, in light of the uncertainty of his income for the upcoming year.[270]

[9] Deviation during college support. In Mississippi, basic support continues until a child reaches the age of twenty-one. However, basic support may be discontinued or reduced for an older child whose food and shelter needs are being provided through college support.[271]

[10] Other. An upward deviation in support may be justified when the noncustodial parent is allowed to claim children as dependents for tax purposes.[272]

[11] Deviations reversed. When deviations are reversed on appeal, the reason for reversal is usually a lack of findings to support the deviation. However, four cases were found in which deviations above the guidelines were reversed as excessive. The supreme court held that a chancellor erred in leaving support at 50% of a payor's income following a substantial decrease in his salary.[273] Similarly, a court erred in ordering aggregate child support and alimony payments of $11,000, which exceeded the payor's net income of $7,300.[274] And an award of 23% of a payor's income for one child was reversed. The court noted that an award of this size would require "extraordinary" cir-

---

[266] *See* MISS. CODE ANN. § 43-19-103 (2004).

[267] *See* MORGAN, *supra* note 13, § 3.02[b], table 3-3.

[268] *See* MORGAN, *supra* note 13, § 3.02[b], at 3-22.

[269] *See* Riley v. Riley, 884 So. 2d 791, 794 (Miss. Ct. App. 2004).

[270] Hults v. Hults, 11 So. 3d 1273, 1279 (Miss. Ct. App. 2009) (discussed as deviation, although father's income was above $50,000).

[271] *See infra* § 13.07[3][g].

[272] *See infra* § 13.08.

[273] McEwen v. McEwen, 631 So. 2d 821, 823 (Miss. 1994).

[274] Tilley v. Tilley, 610 So. 2d 348, 354 (Miss. 1992)*; see also* Cupit v. Cupit, 559 So. 2d 1035, 1037 (Miss. 1990) ($400 plus insurance and one-half out-of-pocket expenses, from $973 adjusted gross income, held excessive).

§ 13.05[12]   MISSISSIPPI FAMILY LAW

cumstances.[275] One deviation below the guidelines was reversed – a mother's estrangement from two of her three daughters was not a reason to award child support of 14%
of her adjusted income.[276]

[12] No order of support. It is generally error for a court to fail to award any child
support from a noncustodial parent.[277] However, a noncustodial parent may be relieved
of child support in unusual circumstances.[278] If a noncustodial parent is unemployed,
courts sometimes order support to begin upon employment.[279] If no support was ordered at divorce, a court may subsequently order support without a showing of a material change in circumstances.[280]

[13] Support from custodial parent. A court may not order a custodial parent
to pay support to a noncustodial parent. The court of appeals reversed an order that
a higher-income custodial father pay support to the low-income mother to assist with
their child's special needs during visitation.[281]

§ 13.06 SUPPORT AWARDS OUTSIDE THE STATUTORY PRESUMPTION

The presumption that the guidelines are correct does not apply to payors with
yearly adjusted income under $5,000 or over $50,000. In any case where adjusted income falls outside this range, a court must make written findings of fact justifying the
award, even if the court applies the statutory percentages. In a number of cases, courts
have applied the statutory percentages to award support from high-income payors.

[1] Yearly adjusted income above $50,000. The statutory percentages have been
applied to award support from payors with monthly adjusted gross incomes of $5,100,[282]
$8,000,[283] and $13,000.[284] The guidelines were applied to a payor's monthly income of

---

[275] Kilgore v. Fuller, 741 So. 2d 351, 357-58 (Miss. Ct. App. 1999).

[276] Lowrey v. Lowrey, 25 So. 3d 274, 293-94 (Miss. 2009).

[277] Brawdy v. Howell, 841 So. 2d 1175, 1179 (Miss. Ct. App. 2003) ("an order that does not require a noncustodial
parent to pay child support should be entered only in rare circumstances").

[278] Brawdy v. Howell, 841 So. 2d 1175, 1179 (Miss. Ct. App. 2003); *see, e.g.*, Forrest v. McCoy, 941 So. 2d 889,
891 (Miss. Ct. App. 2006) (no support ordered at divorce; both parents unemployed).

[279] Chapman v. Ward, 3 So. 3d 790, 792-93 (Miss. Ct. App. 2008) (ordering unemployed father to pay 24% of his
income "due the first month he receives a paycheck").

[280] Forrest v. McCoy, 941 So. 2d 889, 891 (Miss. Ct. App. 2006) (reversing chancellor's denial of subsequent petition for support; petitioner need not show material change).

[281] Rush v. Rush, 932 So. 2d 794, 800 (Miss. 2006) (reversing order that higher-income custodial father pay support to low-income mother to assist with child's special needs during visitation).

[282] Wright v. Stanley, 700 So. 2d 274, 282-83 (Miss. 1997) (23% of payor's income for three children supported
by chancellor's finding of children's increased expenses; adjusted gross income of $67,500); Roberts v. Roberts, 924 So.
2d 550, 553 (Miss. Ct. App. 2005) (statutory child support guidelines produced the proper amount of support from payor
with monthly adjusted income of $5,326); Moore v. Moore, 757 So. 2d 1043, 1050 (Miss. Ct. App. 2000) (awarding 22%
for three children from adjusted gross income of $67,500).

[283] Vaughn v. Vaughn, 798 So. 2d 431, 434-35 (Miss. 2001) (14% of $96,000 adjusted gross income fair in light of
father's substantial income and disparity of mother's income; predivorce standard of living is a valid consideration); *see
also* Palculict v. Palculict, 22 So. 3d 293, 297-98 (Miss. Ct. App. 2009) (award of $980 a month, which was 14% of the
payor's $7,500 monthly income, was not error).

[284] *See* Walton v. Snyder, 984 So. 2d 343 (Miss. Ct. App. 2007) (child support of $2,647 ordered from payor with
adjusted income of $13,267); Russell v. Russell, 733 So. 2d 858, 860 (Miss. Ct. App. 1999) (14% of $13,000 adjusted

442

CHILD SUPPORT

§ 13.06[2]

$19,408, producing child support for one child of $2,717 a month. The child was engaged in extensive extracurricular activities, attended private school, and would benefit from enhanced educational activities.[285] Awards below the percentages have been affirmed for payors with monthly incomes of $13,000,[286] $34,000,[287] and $38,000.[288] An award of $750 for one child was affirmed even though the payor's income would have yielded child support of $1,900 a month under the statutory guidelines.[289] In a case involving a payor with yearly income exceeding one million dollars, the supreme court suggested that the statutory percentages may not be appropriate in cases involving extremely wealthy parents.[290]

[2] Yearly adjusted income below $5,000. Courts have approved deviations above and below the guidelines in awards of support from very low-income parents. A court properly ordered a very low-income noncustodial mother to pay 11% of her income for one child, given the disparity in the parents' incomes and the young age of the child.[291] But a father with fluctuating income that was $759 at the time of divorce was ordered to pay $400 or 22% of income, whichever was greater.[292]

§ 13.07 ADD-ONS TO BASE SUPPORT

Application of the statutory percentages to adjusted gross income produces the basic, or regular, child support award. The basic child support award is intended to cover a child's ordinary living expenses such as food, clothing, and shelter. A parent may also be ordered to pay additional amounts for expenses not covered by the basic award. These include health insurance, out-of-pocket medical and other health-related expenses, life insurance, and expenses of a college education.[293]

---

gross income; $1,250 child support plus $600 in direct expenses); *see also* Henderson v. Henderson, 952 So. 2d 273, 279 (Miss. Ct. App. 2006) (ordering payment of $2,000 a month support for two children from father with adjusted gross income of $9,370 a month, slightly over 20%); Lauro v. Lauro, 924 So. 2d 584, 589 (Miss. Ct. App. 2006) (payor with monthly net income of $9,100 to pay child support under guidelines, $2,001 a month); *cf.* Holloway v. Holloway, 31 So. 3d 57, 62 (Miss. Ct. App. 2009) (noting that some courts apply guidelines to actual income above $50,000), *cert. dismissed*, 29 So. 3d 774 (Miss. 2010).

[285] Smith v. Smith, 25 So. 3d 369, 372-74 (Miss. Ct. App. 2009), *cert. denied*, 24 So. 3d 1038 (Miss. 2010).

[286] Parker v. Dep't of Human Servs., 827 So. 2d 18, 20 (Miss. Ct. App. 2002).

[287] Davis v. Davis, 832 So. 2d 492, 497 (Miss. 2002).

[288] Markofski v. Holzhauer, 799 So. 2d 162, 166 (Miss. Ct. App. 2001) (chancellor did not err in deviating below guidelines, which would require $5,425 per month for one son; $1,500 adequate as agreed at divorce).

[289] Parker v. Dep't of Human Servs., 827 So. 2d 18, 19-20 (Miss. Ct. App. 2002); *see also* Morris v. Morris, 5 So. 3d 476, 495 (Miss. Ct. App. 2008) (award of $1,000; guidelines would have produced award of $1,386); Striebeck v. Striebeck, 911 So. 2d 628, 636-38 (Miss. Ct. App. 2005) (court-ordered child support of $550 a month, including one-half of private school tuition, and college support rather than $2,000 under child support guidelines; guidelines are not presumptively correct for payor earning over $50,000 a year); Staggs v. Staggs, 919 So. 2d 112,123 (Miss. Ct. App. 2005) ($2,500 a month support ordered from payor with monthly income of $52,000).

[290] Moulds v. Bradley, 791 So. 2d 220, 226 (Miss. 2001) (award for one child from extremely high-income payor need not be 14%, but reversing order for consideration of correct income; noting that "the essential purpose of child support remains the support of the child"). *But cf.* Hults v. Hults, 11 So. 3d 1273, 1278-81 (Miss. Ct. App. 2009) (discussing award of $1,000 a month for payor with income of $113,000 as "deviation" from the guidelines).

[291] McGehee v. Upchurch, 733 So. 2d 364, 372 (Miss. Ct. App. 1999).

[292] Cossitt v. Cossitt, 975 So. 2d 274, 277 (Miss. Ct. App. 2008) (also requiring that payor notify court and payee of income change).

[293] Nichols v. Tedder, 547 So. 2d 766, 769 (Miss. 1989); *see* Wallace v. Wallace, 965 So. 2d 737, 744 (Miss. Ct. App. 2007) (court may order, in addition to basic award, health insurance, out-of-pocket medical costs, transportation

§ 13.07[1]   **MISSISSIPPI FAMILY LAW**

[1] Health insurance and medical expenses. The Mississippi child support guidelines were amended in 2004 to state that a court entering a support order must address health insurance needs. If health insurance is not available at a reasonable cost, the court must make specific findings to that effect and must provide for payment of uncovered medical expenses.[294] Even though a father testified that he had always provided health insurance for his wife and daughter, a chancellor erred in failing to order continuance of this arrangement or some other method of providing insurance.[295] Reported cases reflect a range of options for addressing a child's health needs: parents may be ordered to share the cost of health insurance;[296] the noncustodial parent may be ordered to provide health insurance;[297] or the custodial parent may be required to maintain medical insurance.[298] The court of appeals rejected a custodial mother's argument that a chancellor erred in refusing to order the father to provide health insurance.[299]

Payment of health insurance and out-of-pocket medical expenses by a noncustodial parent is typically added to the basic award without treating the cost as an upward deviation. However, the court of appeals noted that while "health, transportation, and college expenses are not included in determining the amount of support . . . such extra obligations could well be considered for a downward departure from the guidelines."[300] The statute provides that if the custodial parent is ordered to provide insurance, that cost should be considered in setting the amount of child support.[301]

Although parents are typically ordered to share out-of-pocket medical expenses, a noncustodial parent may be ordered to bear 100% of these costs.[302] The court of ap-

---

expenses, and support for college); Forrest v. McCoy, 941 So. 2d 889, 891 (Miss. Ct. App. 2006) (support based on the statutory percentage covers the child's basic expenses, including food, clothing, and shelter; court may order also order out-of-pocket medical costs, life insurance, and the costs of college; other expenses such as automobile payments have been ordered); *cf.* Reid v. Reid, 998 So. 2d 1032, 1037 (Miss. Ct. App. 2008) (basic award covers child's share of household expenses as well as direct expenses for child).

[294] *See* MISS. CODE ANN. § 43-19-101 (2004); *see also* Magruder v. Magruder, 881 So. 2d 365 (Miss. Ct. App. 2004) (court may have reduced child support by $58 to account for custodial father's provision of health insurance).

[295] Holdeman v. Holdeman, 34 So. 3d 650, 652 (Miss. Ct. App. 2010) (wife had also testified that she was providing dental insurance for the child).

[296] Sobieske v. Preslar, 755 So. 2d 410, 411 (Miss. 2000) (14% support from noncustodial parent, shared medical insurance).

[297] Mosley v. Mosley, 784 So. 2d 901, 903, 909 (Miss. 2001) (appears to be 20% for two children plus health insurance and one-half out-of-pocket expenses), *aff'd*, Mosley v. Atterberry, 819 So. 2d 1268 (Miss. 2002); Barnett v. Barnett, 908 So. 2d 833, 846 (Miss. Ct. App. 2005) (14% of adjusted gross income for two children, from payor with income over $50,000, plus health, vision, dental insurance, all health insurance co-payments, 60% of out-of-pocket medical, dental, vision, orthodontic, psychological, and prescription drug costs, and one-half of one activity for each child, up to $240 annually per child); Wright v. Wright, 823 So. 2d 586, 587 (Miss. Ct. App. 2002); Wesson v. Wesson, 818 So. 2d 1272, 1272 (Miss. Ct. App. 2002) (14% for one child plus health insurance and one-half out-of-pocket expenses); Burnham-Steptoe v. Steptoe, 755 So. 2d 1225, 1231 (Miss. Ct. App. 1999) (20% plus medical insurance, one-half out-of-pocket medical expenses and life insurance).

[298] Morris v. Stacy, 641 So. 2d 1194, 1195 (Miss. 1994) (noncustodial parent paid $400 monthly in basic support; custodial parent maintained health insurance; parties split out-of-pocket medical costs).

[299] Baldwin v. Baldwin, 788 So. 2d 800, 809 (Miss. Ct. App. 2001) (mother's employer provided group health insurance; case predates amendment).

[300] Kilgore v. Fuller, 741 So. 2d 351, 356 (Miss. Ct. App. 1999); *see also* Barnett v. Barnett, 908 So. 2d 833, 846 (Miss. Ct. App. 2005) (payment of medical costs can be reason to deviate downward from guidelines; case involved payor with adjusted annual income over $50,000. *But see* Johnson v. Johnson, 722 So. 2d 453, 462 (Miss. 1998) (discussing order for payment of health insurance as deviation justified by chancellor's findings sufficient to rebut statutory presumption).

[301] *See* MISS. CODE ANN. § 43-19-101 (2004).

[302] *See* Wells v. Wells, 800 So. 2d 1239, 1247 (Miss. Ct. App. 2001) (14% for one child plus health insurance, 100%

CHILD SUPPORT § 13.07[2]

peals rejected a high-income father's argument that a court erred in making him solely responsible for out-of-pocket medical expenses – he argued that the mother should bear half of the nonreimbursed expenses to promote honesty in medical decision-making.[303]

Whether a noncustodial parent may be ordered to pay a particular medical expense depends upon whether the procedure is considered reasonable and necessary. The court of appeals affirmed a chancellor's finding that one session of counseling was not medically necessary, since no follow-up was ordered. However, orthodontic treatment was medically necessary for a child – the orthodontist testified that braces would reduce the chance of periodontal problems, cavities, and joint problems.[304]

[2] Life insurance. A court may order that a parent maintain life insurance with the children or the custodial parent as beneficiary.[305] Adding the cost of life insurance to the basic award does not appear to be viewed as a deviation.[306] Court-ordered life insurance that is intended to secure child support terminates when the child reaches majority or is emancipated.[307]

Life insurance serves a variety of purposes in divorce proceedings. Termination of an insurance obligation depends on whether the insurance secures child support or alimony or is part of property division. Insurance associated with child support should be designated for that purpose in order to avoid subsequent litigation.

[3] College expenses. The Mississippi Supreme Court held in 1960 that a parent's duty of support includes the cost of a college education if the child is qualified for higher education and the parent is financially able to meet the expenses.[308] An award for college expenses is in addition to the basic support award. Support for college

---

out-of-pocket medical expenses and life insurance); *see also* Grissom v. Grissom, 952 So. 2d 1023, 1026 (Miss. Ct. App. 2007) (father to pay 75% of uncovered medical costs); Barnett v. Barnett, 908 So. 2d 833, 846 (Miss. Ct. App. 2005) (father to pay health insurance, parents split out-of-pocket costs with 60% paid by father); Watkins v. Watkins, 748 So. 2d 808, 810 (Miss. Ct. App. 1999) (father 65%; mother 35% by agreement).

[303] Daniels v. Bains, 967 So. 2d 77, 83 (Miss. Ct. App. 2007).

[304] Wilkerson v. Wilkerson, 955 So. 2d 903, 911 (Miss. Ct. App. 2007) (court of appeals noted that it might have found differently with regard to counseling sessions).

[305] Daniels v. Bains, 967 So. 2d 77, 83 (Miss. Ct. App. 2007) (court did not err in ordering father of nonmarital child to maintain life insurance policy in same amount as for children of marriage, but it was error to order maintenance of policy beyond child's majority); *cf.* Baldwin v. Baldwin, 788 So. 2d 800, 809 (Miss. Ct. App. 2001) (court not required to order maintenance of life insurance).

[306] *See* Wright v. Wright, 823 So. 2d 586, 587 (Miss. Ct. App. 2002); Wells v. Wells. 800 So. 2d 1239, 1247 (Miss. Ct. App. 2001) (14% for one child plus health insurance, 100% out-of-pocket medical expenses and life insurance); Burnham-Steptoe v. Steptoe, 755 So. 2d 1225, 1231 (Miss. Ct. App. 1999) (20% plus medical insurance, one-half out-of-pocket expenses and life insurance); Turner v. Turner, 744 So. 2d 332, 334 (Miss. Ct. App. 1999) (payor to pay medical insurance, $500,000 life insurance, and all private school tuition or day care).

[307] *See infra* § 13.09.

[308] Pass v. Pass, 118 So. 2d 769, 773 (Miss. 1960); *see* Crayton v. Burley, 952 So. 2d 957, 962 (Miss. Ct. App. 2006) (parent may be required to provide college support if child has aptitude, parent has means to pay, and parent's "customary lifestyle will not be affected").

§ 13.07[3][a]   MISSISSIPPI FAMILY LAW

may be ordered by a chancellor[309] or based on the parties' agreement.[310] The order for college support may be entered at the time parties divorce or later in a modification proceeding.

[a] Award at divorce. A court may award college support at divorce for a child who shows the necessary aptitude for higher education. A court did not err in ordering the father of an eight-year-old child to pay for one-half of her future college expenses. The court noted that the father clearly believed that the child would attend college, since he purchased an MPACT certificate for her.[311] The court of appeals has suggested that an award for a very young child might constitute error.[312] However, a chancellor did not err in ordering college support for a young, nonmarital child in a paternity action.[313]

[b] Award in modification proceeding. When parents of a young child divorce, the court or parents may decline to address college support, leaving the issue to be addressed through a modification proceeding. In a modification proceeding, the petitioner must provide proof of the child's aptitude for college and the defendant's ability to pay.[314]

[c] Child's relationship with parents. Support for college is not automatic. It should be ordered if the child has the aptitude for college and maintains a "healthy and caring relationship" with the parent – college education "must be earned by children through respect for their parents, love, affection, and appreciation of parental efforts."[315] However, the deterioration of a father-son relationship caused by the father's unsuccessful paternity challenge did not excuse the father from providing college support.[316]

[d] Aptitude for college. The necessary "aptitude" for college does not require straight A grades. A girl whose first-year grades were "shaky" was entitled to a college education – she was in good standing in her second year and had the ability to "com-

---

[309] *See, e.g.,* Lawrence v. Lawrence, 574 So. 2d 1376, 1382-83 (Miss. 1991) (stating that material change in circumstances may necessitate court order for father to pay child's college expenses); Wray v. Langston, 380 So. 2d 1262, 1264 (Miss. 1980) (holding that it was not error for court to increase child support by $200 per month to defray costs of college). *But see* Harmon v. Yarbrough, 767 So. 2d 1069, 1071 (Miss. Ct. App. 2000) (enforcing father's agreement to provide college support, made when child was three, but noting that court-ordered support for a three-year-old might be too remote to be enforceable).

[310] Harmon v. Yarbrough, 767 So. 2d 1069, 1071 (Miss. Ct. App. 2000).

[311] Striebeck v. Striebeck, 911 So. 2d 628, 637-38 (Miss. Ct. App. 2005) (young age does not necessarily prohibit award of college support).

[312] Harmon v. Yarbrough, 767 So. 2d 1069, 1071 (Miss. Ct. App. 2000) (suggesting that an award for a three-year-old might be error); *cf.* Barnett v. Barnett, 908 So. 2d 833, 847 (Miss. Ct. App. 2005) (court did not err in reserving issue of college support for future adjudication).

[313] Daniels v. Bains, 967 So. 2d 77, 84 (Miss. Ct. App. 2007) (not error to award college support for young child in paternity action; child may not have a relationship with father at all).

[314] See *infra* § 13.11[7].

[315] Barnett v. Barnett, 908 So. 2d 833, 846-47 (Miss. Ct. App. 2005).

[316] Cossey v. Cossey, 22 So. 3d 353, 358 (Miss. Ct. App. 2009) (each parent to pay one-half of college expenses).

CHILD SUPPORT   § 13.07[3][e]

plete her higher education successfully."[317]

[e] **Scope of college support.** Support for a college education includes tuition, books, room and board, necessary living expenses, and necessary educational expenses.[318] With regard to the choice of institution and discretionary costs, a parent's duty may be linked to the family's standard of living. A wealthy father was properly ordered to pay one-half of his daughter's sorority dues, out-of-state tuition, and automobile expenses. The court rejected his argument that college support should be limited to in-state tuition and basic educational expenses; a child of wealthy parents was entitled to an education "commensurate with her parents' station in life."[319] However, when parents agreed that college support would include "any costs as may be necessary" for the children's college education, football tickets, parking tickets, lockout charges, clothing, personal and hair expenses, and sorority dues were not "reasonable and necessary" costs of college education.[320]

[f] **Division of expenses between parents.** If one parent is unemployed or without sufficient income to contribute to college expenses, the other may be ordered to bear all college expenses.[321] Parents with comparable incomes may be ordered to share college expenses equally or to pay expenses in proportion to their incomes.[322] And in one case, a noncustodial parent was ordered to pay all expenses equal to the cost of in-state tuition, room and board, books and supplies; the custodial parent was ordered to pay all expenses exceeding that amount.[323]

[g] **Reduction of basic support during college.** College support is considered an add-on to support, rather than an upward deviation.[324] However, courts have

---

[317] Crayton v. Burley, 952 So. 2d 957, 962 (Miss. Ct. App. 2006); *see also* Wallace v. Wallace, 965 So. 2d 737, 745-46 (Miss. Ct. App. 2007) (no "minimum academic requirements" for ordering support; child improved grades in second year of college).

[318] Wray v. Langston, 380 So. 2d 1262, 1264 (Miss. 1980) ("[t]he duty of a parent to provide a college education contemplates support in addition to tuition and college costs, without which, provision for the college education would be in vain"); *see also* Saliba v. Saliba, 753 So. 2d 1095 (Miss. 2000) (computer may be essential to one student, while lab fees are more important to another).

[319] Saliba v. Saliba, 753 So. 2d 1095, 1103 (Miss. 2000); *see also* Weeks v. Weeks, 29 So. 3d 80, 83 (Miss. Ct. App. 2009) (college support to include tuition, meal plan, books, sorority dues and fees, vehicle and insurance, and health insurance); Striebeck v. Striebeck, 911 So. 2d 628, 637 (Miss. Ct. App. 2005) (ordering payment of one-half of college expenses, described as tuition, room, board, books, fees, sorority, and transportation, including an automobile, insurance, gas, oil, and maintenance).

[320] Cossitt v. Cossitt, 975 So. 2d 274, 280-81 (Miss. Ct. App. 2008).

[321] Lazarus v. Lazarus. 841 So. 2d 181, 185 (Miss. Ct. App. 2003) (affirming order requiring father to pay for costs of college and medical and dental expenses, but no basic support award); *see* Daniels v. Bains, 967 So. 2d 77, 84 (Miss. Ct. App. 2007) (physician father ordered to pay all college support for nonmarital child).

[322] *See* Fancher v. Pell, 831 So. 2d, 1137, 1141-42 (Miss. 2002) (father ordered to pay 70% of college expenses plus all personal expenses, based on higher income); Traxler v. Traxler, 730 So. 2d 1098, 1103 (Miss. 1998) (noncustodial parent ordered to pay 61% of college expense); Cossey v. Cossey, 22 So. 3d 353, 357-58 (Miss. Ct. App. 2009) (each parent to pay one-half of college expenses); Striebeck v. Striebeck, 911 So. 2d 628, 637-38 (Miss. Ct. App. 2005) (higher-income father ordered to pay one-half of college expenses); Baier v. Baier, 897 So. 2d 202, 205-06 (Miss. Ct. App. 2005) (court did not err in requiring lower-income mother to provide one-third of college support; in addition to her salary, she would receive $1,000 a month in alimony, she was awarded most marital assets, and her husband was ordered to pay all debt); Keys v. Keys, 930 So. 2d 438, 440 (Miss. Ct. App. 2005) (parents to share expenses equally).

[323] Morris v. Stacy, 641 So. 2d 1194, 1196 (Miss. 1994).

[324] Fancher v. Pell. 831 So. 2d 1137, 1142 (Miss. 2002); Lawrence v. Lawrence, 574 So. 2d 1376, 1382 (Miss.

§ 13.07[3][h]   MISSISSIPPI FAMILY LAW

discretion to reduce or suspend basic support while a child's living expenses – food
and shelter – are provided in the form of college support. Courts have suspended basic
support during the academic year,[325] reduced basic support by 50%,[326] and suspended
support altogether while a child was in college. [327] In one case, the court awarded child
support of $1,890, but held that basic support would be offset by college support. If
college expenses were less than $1,890 a month, the excess would go to the daughter
during the school year, while the $1,890 was to be paid to the mother during the sum-
mer.[328] In other cases, however, a payor has been ordered to pay basic support plus college expenses. The court of appeals affirmed a chancellor's upward modification of a
seventeen-year-old child's support award to require payment of $907 per month (14%),
medical and dental expenses, one-half of tuition, books, fees, and room and board,
$1,925 toward a vehicle, one-half of license plate and automobile insurance expenses,
and to provide a gas card.[329]

[h] **Performance requirements.** Parents often include a provision that college
support is conditioned upon a child maintaining a certain number of hours per semester
and remaining in good standing. A father's duty of college support was properly terminated when his daughter's grades fell below a 2.0 in her first semester. The parents'
agreement required that she maintain a 2.0 grade point.[330] On the other hand, a chancellor properly denied a father's request that his college support obligation be modified to
require that his children maintain a 2.0 grade point average. The parties' agreement did
not include that requirement. Modification of the agreement requires a material change
in circumstances not foreseeable at the time of the decree.[331]

[i] **College support after majority.** A court may not order a parent to provide
college support for a child who has reached the age of twenty-one.[332] However, parents

---

1991); Wallace v. Wallace, 965 So. 2d 737, 745 (Miss. Ct. App. 2007). *But see* Evans v. Evans, 994 So. 2d 765, 773
(Miss. 2008) (suggesting that chancellor ordering college support that exceeds guidelines must make findings as to why
deviation from the guidelines is necessary).

[325] Fancher v. Pell, 831 So. 2d 1137, 1140 (Miss. 2002) (support payments suspended for oldest while in college;
left in place during June and July); *cf.* Riddick v. Riddick, 906 So. 2d 813 (Miss. Ct. App. 2004) (enforcing agreement
for suspended support while children lived at college and for reduced support if children in college lived with mother).

[326] *See* Traxler v. Traxler, 730 So. 2d 1098, 1103 (Miss. 1998) (noncustodial parent ordered to pay 7% of adjusted
gross income as support for college-age-child during months when child lived for full month with mother, plus 61% of
college expenses).

[327] Lazarus v. Lazarus. 841 So. 2d 181, 183, 185 (Miss. Ct. App. 2003) (affirming order requiring father to pay for
costs of college and medical and dental expenses, but no basic support award); Kirkland v. McGraw, 806 So. 2d 1180,
1183 (Miss. Ct. App. 2002) (recognizing case law allowing reduction of basic support during college); *cf.* Rogers v. Rogers, 919 So. 2d 184, 186 (Miss. Ct. App. 2005) (parents agreed that basic child support would cease when child entered
college, father would then provide support directly to child during college). *But see* Dix v. Dix, 941 So. 2d 913, 918
(Miss. Ct. App. 2006) (denying request for reduction during college; son returned home frequently and mother provided
$400 a month in support).

[328] Weeks v. Weeks, 29 So. 3d 80, 83 (Miss. Ct. App. 2009).

[329] Wallace v. Wallace, 965 So. 2d 737, 741 (Miss. Ct. App. 2007).

[330] Cossitt v. Cossitt, 975 So. 2d 274, 280 (Miss. Ct. App. 2008) (four judges dissenting).

[331] Stigler v. Stigler, 48 So. 3d 547, 556 (Miss. Ct. App. 2009), *cert. denied*, 49 So. 3d 1139 (Miss. 2010).

[332] Stokes v. Maris, 596 So. 2d 879, 882 (Miss. 1992) (court "ha[s] no authority to order child support in any form,
whether regular, college expenses, or otherwise, to continue in effect post majority"); *see also* Crow v. Crow, 622 So.
2d 1226, 1230 (Miss. 1993); Daniels v. Bains, 967 So. 2d 77, 80 (Miss. Ct. App. 2007) (reversing order requiring physician father to pay graduate school support for nonmarital child); Little v. Little, 878 So. 2d 1086, 1089 (Miss. Ct. App.

CHILD SUPPORT § 13.07[3][h][i]

may voluntarily assume an obligation for post-majority college support through an agreement incorporated into a divorce decree,[333] a separate contract,[334] or an agreed modification.[335] Attorneys drafting college support agreements should take care to avoid unintentionally extending support beyond majority.

   [i] Implied agreements for post-majority support. In several cases, the Mississippi Supreme Court has construed a vague support provision as an agreement to pay post-majority college expenses. For example, agreements to pay "all reasonable college expenses"[336] and "all educational expenses of [the children]"[337] were interpreted as agreements for post-majority support. Similarly, a father's agreement to support his child "while in college" required support beyond the age of twenty-one.[338] And an agreed modification assigning a father responsibility for college expenses "of the minor children" required support beyond twenty-one.[339]

   [ii] Scope. The scope of post-majority college support is more limited than college support for minor children. Unless the parties agree otherwise, post-majority college support includes only tuition, room and board, fees, and educational essentials such as a computer. It does not include other living expenses such as clothing and transportation.[340] An agreement expanding the scope of post-majority support was found when a father agreed to pay "$600 per month for the support [of the children] and all reasonable college expenses," plus insurance and property taxes on the home and automobile insurance and tags while the children were in college. The supreme court agreed with the chancellor that this provision extended the $600 payment beyond majority while the children were in college.[341]

   [iii] Duration. The Mississippi Supreme Court has encouraged attorneys drafting college support agreements to specify maximum post-majority support periods and academic performance requirements.[342] In the absence of a time limitation on post-majority support, college support will continue for a reasonable time. Six years was held to be a reasonable period of extended support for a child who worked and went to school part-time.[343]

2004).
   [333] *See* Crow v. Crow, 622 So. 2d 1226, 1230 (Miss. 1993).
   [334] *See* Nichols v. Tedder, 547 So. 2d 766, 770 (Miss. 1989).
   [335] *See* Boleware v. Boleware, 450 So. 2d 92, 93 (Miss. 1984).
   [336] Crow v. Crow, 622 So. 2d 1226, 1227 (Miss. 1993).
   [337] Mottley v. Mottley, 729 So. 2d 1289, 1290 (Miss. 1999).
   [338] Rogers v. Rogers, 662 So. 2d 1111, 1115 (Miss. 1995).
   [339] Boleware v. Boleware, 450 So. 2d 92, 92 (Miss. 1984).
   [340] Meek v. Meek, 726 So. 2d 1292, 1294 (Miss. Ct. App. 1998).
   [341] Rogers v. Rogers, 662 So. 2d 1111, 1115-16 (Miss. 1995); *cf.* Morrison v. Dep't of Human Servs., 852 So. 2d 578, 584 (Miss. Ct. App. 2002) (agreement to pay college expenses did not extend to graduate school unless specified), *aff'd in part and rev'd in part*, 863 So. 2d 948 (Miss. 2004).
   [342] Rogers v. Rogers, 662 So. 2d 1111, 1115 (Miss. 1995).
   [343] Rogers v. Rogers, 662 So. 2d 1111, 1115 (Miss. 1995).

§ 13.07[3][j]   MISSISSIPPI FAMILY LAW

[j] **Education accounts.** The use of accounts established for the purpose of college education should be addressed in divorce proceedings. For example, a court properly ordered a father to establish an education account equal in amount to the account held by the mother and ordered that the parties share college expenses equally after depletion of both accounts.[344] And an investment account in the husband's name, established by the parents for their children's college education, should have been classified as marital property with the stipulation that the funds be used only for the children's college expenses.[345]

Whether a child's account is intended for education should also be clarified at the time of divorce. In a post-divorce petition for an order of college support, the supreme court rejected a wealthy father's argument that accounts in his child's name should be exhausted first for college support. The court held that a parent with sufficient income is not relieved of support because the child has assets of her own.[346] In contrast, a court erred in ordering the release of college account funds to a child where the divorce decree clearly established that the funds were for educational purposes.[347]

[4] **Other.** The supreme court has affirmed a chancellor's order requiring a noncustodial parent to furnish a child with an automobile.[348] A chancellor properly ordered a father to pay for a portion of a daughter's automobile, insurance, tag, and gas costs – she attended college one hundred miles from her mother's home and lived and worked twenty-five miles from the college.[349] Courts have ordered a noncustodial parent to make mortgage payments on the custodial parent's home as part of a child support award.[350] A court has also ordered a noncustodial parent to pay one-half of the cost of one activity per child.[351] However, an order requiring a father to pay one-half of his son's attorney's fees to defend murder charges was beyond the contemplation of the child support statute.[352]

§ 13.08 AWARD OF THE DEPENDENCY EXEMPTION

The Tax Reform Act of 1984 established new rules governing allocation of federal dependency exemptions between divorced parents. Under the Act, the exemption belongs to the custodial parent, who may assign the exemption to the noncustodial parent.

---

[344] Keys v. Keys, 930 So. 2d 438, 442-43 (Miss. Ct. App. 2005) (mother entitled to reimbursement from accounts for out-of-pocket college expenditures).

[345] Barnett v. Barnett, 908 So. 2d 833, 839-40 (Miss. Ct. App. 2005) (noting that parents could petition for release of account if children did not attend college).

[346] Saliba v. Saliba, 753 So. 2d 1095, 1099-00 (Miss. 2000).

[347] Keys v. Keys, 930 So. 2d 438, 443 (Miss. Ct. App. 2005) (distinguishing *Saliba* on basis that divorce decree made clear that funds in children's names were intended for college support).

[348] *See* Chesney v. Chesney, 910 So. 2d 1057, 1060 (Miss. 2005) (noncustodial father ordered to pay $530 a month in basic support, one-half of daughter's private school tuition and activities, an automobile of comparable quality to her contemporaries, and automobile repairs and insurance); Crow v. Crow, 622 So. 2d 1226, 1232 (Miss. 1993); Diamond v. Diamond, 403 So. 2d 129, 131-32 (Miss. 1981).

[349] Wallace v. Wallace, 965 So. 2d 737, 741 (Miss. Ct. App. 2007).

[350] Johnson v. Johnson, 650 So. 2d 1281, 1284 (Miss. 1994) (ordering husband to make mortgage payments until children's majority as form of child support).

[351] Barnett v. Barnett, 908 So. 2d 833, 846 (Miss. Ct. App. 2005).

[352] Edmonds v. Edmonds, 935 So. 2d 980, 988-89 (Miss. 2006).

CHILD SUPPORT

§ 13.08[1]

The custodial parent must execute a written statement that he or she will not claim the exemption for a particular year. The declaration must be attached to the noncustodial parent's tax return for the year in question.[353]

[1] Court-ordered transfer. A court may award the dependency exemption to a noncustodial parent and order the custodial parent to execute the necessary waiver. The custodial parent should be ordered to execute the release on a yearly basis, with yearly execution contingent on the noncustodial parent's full payment of support obligations.[354]

In determining which parent should receive the exemption, courts should consider each parent's income, the value of the exemption to each, the children's age, the percentage of support borne by each parent, and each parent's financial burden under a property settlement.[355] Courts have split exemptions between parents,[356] awarded exemptions to noncustodial parents,[357] and held that the exemption should alternate every other year.[358] A decision that does not address the exemption leaves the deduction with the custodial parent.

[2] Support deviation based on transfer. Award of the dependency exemption to a noncustodial parent may justify an upward deviation in basic child support.[359] For example, the amount of deviation could equal the tax savings to the noncustodial parent. Or, the court could calculate adjusted gross income without the exemption and apply the statutory percentage to the resulting higher adjusted gross income.

§ 13.09 TERMINATION OF THE SUPPORT OBLIGATION

The parental duty of support ends when a child reaches the age of majority. However, courts will enforce a parent's agreement to extend support beyond majority. Support obligations may be terminated prior to majority if the child becomes emancipated or, in extreme cases, when an older child refuses to maintain a relationship with the payor. Parents may not terminate support for a minor child by agreement.

[1] At majority. Although twenty-one is the common law age of majority, statutes in most states lower the age of majority to eighteen. As a result, in most states basic

---

[353] Tax Reform Act, 26 U.S.C. § 152(e) (2008).

[354] Nichols v. Tedder, 547 So. 2d 766, 777 (Miss. 1989).

[355] Louk v. Louk, 761 So. 2d 878, 884 (Miss. 2000); *see* Laird v. Blackburn, 788 So. 2d 844, 852 (Miss. Ct. App. 2001). *But cf.* H.L.S. v. R.S.R., 949 So. 2d 794, 799 (Miss. Ct. App. 2006) (not mandatory that a chancellor address the *Laird* factors related to dependency exemptions).

[356] Morris v. Stacy, 641 So. 2d 1194, 1196 (Miss. 1994).

[357] Davis v. Davis, 832 So. 2d 492, 497-98 (Miss. 2002); Barnett v. Barnett, 908 So. 2d 833, 847 (Miss. Ct. App. 2005) (affirming award of dependency exemption to higher-income father); Fitzgerald v. Fitzgerald, 914 So. 2d 193, 199 (Miss. Ct. App. 2005) (exemption properly awarded to employed husband, rather than unemployed wife, with instructions for reconsideration if she was employed at more than $50,000 annually).

[358] H.L.S. v. R.S.R., 949 So. 2d 794, 799 (Miss. Ct. App. 2006) (parties ordered to alternate dependency exemption each year); Laird v. Blackburn, 788 So. 2d 844, 852 (Miss. Ct. App. 2001).

[359] *See* Hensarling v. Hensarling, 824 So. 2d 583, 588-89 (Miss. 2002) (allowing noncustodial parent to claim the dependency exemption justifies a child support award in excess of the guidelines); Johnston v. Johnston, 722 So. 2d 453, 461-62 (Miss. 1998).

§ 13.09[2]   **MISSISSIPPI FAMILY LAW**

support obligations end when a child is eighteen.[360] However, the Mississippi legislature continues to recognize the common law age of majority.[361] A paternity order terminating support when a child reached sixteen was properly revised years later to provide for support until the age of majority.[362] A court may not order basic child support extending past a child's twenty-first birthday.[363] Nor may a court order that a parent provide add-ons to child support, such as life and health insurance or payment of college expenses, beyond majority.[364] In some states, courts have ordered support for adult disabled children. The Mississippi appellate courts have not yet addressed the issue directly but have suggested in dicta that extended support for disabled adult children may be appropriate.[365]

[2] Upon emancipation. A parent's support duties terminate if a child is emancipated before majority. Emancipation is "the freeing of a child for all the period of its minority from the care, custody, control, and service of its parents; the relinquishment of parental control, conferring on the child the right to its own earnings and terminating the parent's legal obligation to support."[366]

The Mississippi legislature has amended the emancipation statute several times in recent years. Now, a child is emancipated when he or she (1) is twenty-one, (2) marries, (3) is incarcerated for two years or more for committing a felony, or (4) joins the military on a full-time basis. In addition, a court has discretion to determine that a child is emancipated if he or she (1) discontinues full-time education (if eighteen or older and not disabled),[367] (2) voluntarily moves and establishes independent living arrangements, discontinues schooling, and becomes employed full-time, or (3) cohabits with another person without the payor's approval. The statute also provides that child support may be suspended during a period in which an otherwise unemancipated child is incarcerated.[368]

The statutory listing of grounds for emancipation is not exclusive. The supreme court held that the statutory listing adds to, rather than limits, the judicial definition of emancipation as freedom from parental control.[369] For example, an unmarried daughter

---

[360] FAMILY LAW AND PRACTICE, *supra* note 2, § 33.10[1], at 33-79.

[361] MISS. CODE ANN. § 93-11-65(8) (2004). The provisions codified the court's ruling in *Nichols v. Tedder*, 547 So. 2d 766, 770 (Miss. 1989). Prior to *Nichols*, "it [was] common knowledge that . . . the bench and bar have applied the term "children" to offspring who are less than twenty-one." Watkins v. Watkins, 337 So. 2d 723, 724 (Miss. 1976). *See also* Little v. Little, 878 So. 2d 1086, 1089 (Miss. Ct. App. 2004) (twenty-one is age of majority).

[362] Owen v. Wilkinson, 915 So. 2d 493, 495 (Miss. Ct. App. 2005). *But cf.* Stribling v. Stribling, 906 So. 2d 863, 868-69 (Miss. Ct. App. 2005) (chancellor committed harmless error at most in failing to address support for child who was four months from emancipation at time of divorce trial; no indication that child would lack support during four-month period).

[363] Nichols v. Tedder, 547 So. 2d 766, 770 (Miss. 1989); *see also* Little v. Little, 878 So. 2d 1086, 1089 (Miss. Ct. App. 2004).

[364] *See* Stokes v. Maris, 596 So. 2d 879, 882 (Miss. 1992).

[365] *See supra* § 13.02[4].

[366] Rennie v. Rennie, 718 So. 2d 1091, 1093 (Miss. 1998) (citing Caldwell v. Caldwell, 579 So. 2d 543, 549 (Miss. 1991)).

[367] *See* Segree v. Segree, 46 So. 3d 861, 867 (Miss. Ct. App. 2010) (under amended statute, full-time employment is not required for emancipation).

[368] MISS. CODE ANN. § 93-11-65(8) (Supp. 2010).

[369] Rennie v. Rennie, 718 So. 2d 1091, 1093-94 (Miss. 1998) (stating that child "may not now revoke her irresponsible launch into adulthood").

CHILD SUPPORT §13.09[3]

was considered emancipated when she had a child, continued to live with her mother, worked part-time, and received support from her child's father.[370] And a child who had a baby, moved in with the baby's father, and obtained part-time employment was emancipated even though none of the statutory listings fit her circumstances. The court also held that once emancipation occurs, child support is permanently terminated. Support is not renewed when an emancipated child moves back home prior to majority.[371]

On the other hand, a court may find that a child is not emancipated even though the statutory requirements are technically satisfied. A minor must also be freed from the "care, custody, control and service of its parents" for emancipation to occur.[372] An eighteen-year-old son living with his mother met the technical statutory requirements when he left school and began full-time employment. However, because he was unable to support himself on $185 a week, his circumstances did not meet the judicial definition of emancipation.[373] In addition, a parent may not seek to terminate support if a child's employment was forced by the parent's lack of support. A son who left school to work full-time when his father refused to pay for college expenses was not emancipated.[374]

[3] Based on parental agreement. Parents may not curtail the duty of support prior to majority by agreement.[375] A mother's agreement to forego support in return for a transfer of land was void as a matter of public policy; a custodial parent receives support as a fiduciary for the child's benefit.[376] Furthermore, a waiver of the right to support does not prevent a judgment for arrearages. A mother's acceptance of $1,500 as consideration for a waiver of past and future support did not bar her from later obtaining an arrearages award of $89,000 against the father.[377]

[4] Based on interference with visitation. Noncustodial parents have sought to terminate support payments based on a custodial parent's interference with visitation. Courts generally hold that visitation and child support are separate and distinct. Nonpayment of child support does not justify refusing visitation, and interference with

---

[370] Caldwell v. Caldwell, 823 So. 2d 1216, 1221 (Miss. Ct. App. 2002).

[371] Rennie v. Rennie, 718 So. 2d 1091, 1093-94 (Miss. 1998) (stating that child "may not now revoke her irresponsible launch into adulthood").

[372] Andrews v. Williams, 723 So. 2d 1175, 1179 (Miss. Ct. App. 1998).

[373] Andrews v. Williams, 723 So. 2d 1175, 1179 (Miss. Ct. App. 1998); *see also* Carite v. Carite, 841 So. 2d 1148, 1154-55 (Miss. Ct. App. 2002) (no emancipation where child discontinued full-time schooling and became employed full-time but continued to live with his mother who helped support him); Wesson v. Wesson, 818 So. 2d 1272, 1282 (Miss. Ct. App. 2002) (no emancipation where child quit school and moved in with a friend, worked full-time for a month, but was unable to support himself and moved back in with his mother and continued school).

[374] Caldwell v. Caldwell, 579 So. 2d 543, 547-48 (Miss. 1991).

[375] Lawrence v. Lawrence, 574 So. 2d 1376, 1378 (Miss. 1991).

[376] Calton v. Calton, 485 So. 2d 309, 310 (Miss. 1986); *see also* R.K. v. J.K., 946 So. 2d 764, 779-80 (Miss. 2007) (agreement that support would end when daughter no longer lived with mother did not permit termination when child attended boarding school); Chroniger v. Chroniger, 914 So. 2d 311, 316 (Miss. Ct. App. 2005) (agreement that mother would not be required to pay support if custody transferred to father, not binding on chancellor). *But see* Dep't of Human Servs. v. Shelby, 802 So. 2d 89 (Miss. 2001) (agreement to waive child support for property conveyance which was not appealed was not void; decree could not be attacked collaterally, but could be modified based on change in circumstances).

[377] Houck v. Ousterhout, 861 So. 2d 1000, 1002 (Miss. 2003).

§ 13.09[5]   MISSISSIPPI FAMILY LAW

visitation is not a reason to withhold support.[378] However, in a few states, courts have reduced or suspended support based upon refusal of visitation.[379]

In extreme cases, courts have terminated support and even excused arrearages when a custodial parent has hidden a child for a long period of time.[380] The Mississippi Supreme Court refused to award past-due support to a mother who hid children from their father for fourteen years. Relying on the clean hands doctrine, the court held that the mother waived her right to collect support.[381] The court refused to adopt this approach in a less outrageous case, where the father had general knowledge of a child's location and could have taken steps to enforce visitation.[382]

[5] Based on a child's hostility. Courts usually reject attempts to terminate support based on a child's hostility.[383] The Mississippi Supreme Court rejected a father's argument that support should be modified because of his fifteen-year-old's hostility to him – a parent's duty of support is not based upon the amount of love shown by a child.[384] Similarly, a chancellor erred in suspending support for a fourteen-year-old son based on two difficult visits after years of separation from his father.[385]

Under some circumstances, however, a child may forfeit the right to support. A father was not required to continue college support for a nineteen-year-old daughter who refused to visit him for six years and said that she hated him.[386] And a chancellor should have terminated a father's support for an eighteen-year-old daughter who falsely accused him of rape, did not visit him for five years, and stated that she had no interest

---

[378] *See* Clowdis v. Earnest, 629 So. 2d 1044, 1046 (Fla. Dist. Ct. App. 1993) (denial of visitation rights does not warrant reduction in court-ordered support); *In re* Welfare of J.D.N., 504 N.W 2d 54, 57 (Minn. Ct. App. 1993) (failure to allow visitation cannot be factor in terminating or modifying support); Westgate v. Westgate, 887 P.2d 737, 789 (Nev. 1994) (failure to comply with terms of visitation agreement cannot be used as a reason to reduce a child support obligation); Sharpe v. Sharpe, 902 P.2d 210, 216 (Wyo. 1995) (no deviation from guidelines based on denial of visitation).

[379] *See* Schaffer v. Haynes, 847 S.W.2d 814, 819 (Mo. Ct. App. 1992) (court did not err in abating support payment); Welch v. Welch, 519 N.W.2d 262, 271 (Neb. 1994) (court may suspend child support where custodial parent deprives noncustodial parent of visitation); Hiross v. Hiross, 639 N.Y.S.2d 70, 71 (N.Y. App. Div. 1996) (custodial parent's deliberate frustration of visitation rights can warrant suspension).

[380] *See In re* Marriage of Damico, 872 P.2d 126, 129-30 (Cal. 1994) (allowing noncustodial parent to claim active concealment of child as defense to collection of child support arrearages); *In re* Loomis, 587 N.W.2d 427,430 (S.D. 1998) (father did not have to pay retroactive support).

[381] Cole v. Hood, 371 So. 2d 861, 864 (Miss. 1979).

[382] Cunliffe v. Swarzfager, 437 So. 2d 43, 45-46 (Miss. 1983) (father did not see son for five years, but knew generally where his ex-wife lived)*; see* Dep't of Human Servs. v. Marshall, 859 So. 2d 387, 390 (Miss. 2003) (refusing to forgive arrearages based on mother's refusal of visitation for twelve years).

[383] *See* Heath v. Heath, 647 So. 2d 769, 771 (Ala. Civ. App. 1994) (strained relationship did not relieve father of duty to pay); Parker v. Parker, 610 So. 2d 719, 720 (Fla. Dist. Ct. App. 1992) (affirming child support award where child was grossly disrespectful toward father); O'Connell v. O'Connell, 597 A.2d 643, 645 (Pa. 1991) (daughter's willful estrangement from her father did not relieve him of obligation to pay support).

[384] Caldwell v. Caldwell, 579 So. 2d 543, 548 (Miss. 1991).

[385] Dep't of Human Servs. v. Marshall, 859 So. 2d 387, 390 (Miss. 2003) (but refusing to forgive arrearages based on mother's refusal of visitation for twelve years)*; see also* S.S. v. S.H., 44 So. 3d 1054, 1056-57 (Miss. Ct. App. 2010) (reversing termination of child support until child resumed relationship with father; he had been indicted for sexually assaulting her and agreed not to contact her until majority); Dykes v. McMurry, 938 So. 2d 330, 333-34 (Miss. Ct. App. 2006) (son's alienation caused by father's allegations against mother; child's conduct not the "extreme" rejection required to terminate support); Markofski v. Holzhauer, 799 So. 2d 162, 168 (Miss. Ct. App. 2001) (court properly refused to suspend support based on deteriorated relationship with son).

[386] Hambrick v. Prestwood, 382 So. 2d 474, 477 (Miss. 1980) (daughter earned $460 a month and would not be destitute without her father's support). *But see* Rankin v. Bobo, 410 So. 2d 1326, 1329 (Miss. 1982) (father required to pay college support to daughter who "made a greater effort" to continue the relationship than her father).

CHILD SUPPORT

§ 13.09[6]

in a relationship with him.[387]

[6] At adoption or upon termination of parental rights. A parent's support obligation ceases when parental rights are terminated by consent or through a termination action.[388] Similarly, adoption generally terminates a biological parent's duty of support.[389] However, the Mississippi Supreme Court upheld an agreement between a biological father and adopting grandparents granting the biological father visitation rights and providing that he would pay child support.[390]

[7] At payor's death. A parent's duty to support a child ends at the parent's death. A parent's estate is liable for support due and owing at the time of death, but the estate is not liable for continuing support in the absence of an express agreement to that effect.[391] An agreement to provide child support beyond death must be explicit. An agreement for support until each child reached twenty-one, married, died, or was no longer under the mother's supervision did not implicitly extend support beyond the payor's death.[392] And an assignment of ten-year notes as security for support did not mean the father's estate was liable for support if he died within ten years; the notes were simply security for the obligation, which ceased at his death.[393]

[8] Upon parents' remarriage to each other. When parents remarry, child support automatically terminates. Support does not terminate if the parents cohabit without marrying.[394] However, the amount of support due should be offset by direct support provided during cohabitation.[395]

[9] Upon disestablishment of paternity. A payor's obligation for child support may be terminated upon a court's finding that he is not the child's father and disestablishment of his paternity.[396]

§ 13.10 MECHANICS OF THE AWARD

[1] Designation of payee. A court may order payment of support to the custodial parent or to a person designated as trustee for the child. If the child or custodial parent receives public assistance, the court must designate the Department of Human Services

---

[387] Roberts v. Brown, 805 So. 2d 649, 653 (Miss. Ct. App. 2002) (child's actions can result in forfeiture of support in extreme cases).

[388] Grounds for termination of parental rights are set out in MISS. CODE ANN. § 93-15-103 (2004).

[389] *See* MISS. CODE ANN. § 93-17-13 (2004) (providing that "all parental rights of the natural parent, or parents, shall be terminated, [upon adoption] except as to a natural parent who is the spouse of the adopting parent").

[390] Humphrey v. Pannell, 710 So. 2d 392, 393-94 (Miss. 1998).

[391] Smith v. Smith, 349 So. 2d 529, 531 (Miss. 1977); *see* Mahaffey v. First Nat'l Bank, 97 So. 2d 756, 767 (Miss. 1957) (child support duty does not survive death in absence of agreement).

[392] Lewis v. Lewis, 125 So. 2d 286, 290 (Miss. 1960).

[393] Smith v. Smith, 349 So. 2d 529, 531 (Miss. 1977).

[394] FAMILY LAW & PRACTICE, *supra* note 2, § 52.04 [1], at 52-76.

[395] *Cf.* Varner v. Varner, 588 So. 2d 428, 435 (Miss. 1991) (allowing credit where father provided direct support for children who came to live with him).

[396] MISS. CODE ANN. § 93-11-71 (4) (2008). See *supra* § 11.07.

§ 13.10[2]   MISSISSIPPI FAMILY LAW

as trustee for payment.[397] Child support should be paid to the person with actual physical custody of a child. A mother with legal physical custody was not entitled to support for the period of time a child actually lived with his father.[398] A third party who is a child's legal custodian is entitled to receive support from the child's parents. A grandfather with temporary custody of his grandson was entitled to support from both parents if the custody award was continued.[399] Child support may, in some circumstances, be paid directly to an older child.[400] However, a court properly rejected a father's argument that basic support should be paid directly to a nineteen-year-old whose mother still maintained a home for her.[401] A court may order direct payment of support to third-party providers. A chancellor properly directed a noncustodial father to pay a portion of the statutory child support directly to the child's private school.[402]

[2] Escalation clauses. In the face of inflation, child support awards rapidly become inadequate. Unless a noncustodial parent voluntarily agrees to increase an obsolete award, a custodial parent must return to court to obtain an increase in support even to the level required by child support guidelines.[403] Self-adjusting provisions based on a payor's income are permitted in many states. Although the Mississippi Supreme Court has urged lawyers to use escalation clauses, the court rejected attempts to create enforceable escalation agreements until 2005.

[a] Percentage-of-income awards. A number of courts permit use of percentage-of-income escalation provisions. For example, the Georgia Supreme Court enforced an order for payment of $400 per month plus 20% of all earnings over $18,000 per year.[404] The Appellate Court of Illinois upheld a court order requiring a father to pay 40% of his income as child support.[405] The Washington Supreme Court approved a similar award, adding that the provision should also include a maximum amount of support.[406] In contrast, the Indiana Court of Appeals reversed a percentage-of-income award because the child's needs were not factored into the award.[407] Similarly, the Michigan Court of Appeals reversed a percentage award, disapproving of support orders based solely on parental income.[408]

---

[397] MISS. CODE ANN. 93-11-65(1)(a) (2004).

[398] Alexander v. Alexander, 494 So. 2d 365, 368 (Miss. 1986).

[399] *See* Adams v. Adams, 467 So. 2d 211, 215-16 (Miss. 1985).

[400] *See* Bridges v. McCraken, 724 So. 2d 1086, 1087-88 (Miss. Ct. App. 1998) (approving direct payment to older child without discussion of circumstances).

[401] Wallace v. Wallace, 965 So. 2d 737, 749 (Miss. Ct. App. 2007).

[402] Collins v. Collins, 722 So. 2d 596, 598 (Miss. 1998).

[403] *See generally* Annotation, *Validity and Enforceability of Escalation Clause in Divorce Decree Relating to Alimony and Child Support*, 19 A.L.R. 4th 830, 832-33 (1983).

[404] Chandler v. Ratcliffe, 285 S.E.2d 694, 695 (Ga. 1982) (stating that the father's obligation was created by unambiguous and unqualified language of the contract).

[405] Runge v. Kohn, 430 N.E.2d 58, 62 (Ill. App. Ct. 1981) (holding that wife accepted set-sum checks for six years as evidence of an agreement between the parties to modify the initial agreement).

[406] Edwards v. Edwards, 665 P.2d 883, 883-886 (Wash. 1983) (provision requiring father to pay 20% of a bonus or salary increase in addition to set monthly amount in child support).

[407] Hunter v. Hunter, 498 N.E.2d 1278, 1288 (Ind. Ct. App. 1986).

[408] Stanaway v. Stanaway, 245 N.W.2d 723, 724 (Mich. Ct. App. 1976); *see also* Picker v. Vollenhover, 290 P.2d 789, 801 (Or. 1955) (sliding-scale escalation clause based solely on a change in earnings of the father was against the state's policy of considering all surrounding circumstances in setting child support).

CHILD SUPPORT § 13.10[2][b]

[b] Awards tied to child's age. Courts have generally rejected provisions for automatic increases based on a child's age.[409] For example, the Florida District Court of Appeals struck down an escalation clause requiring a father to pay $300 a month until a child turned five, $400 a month until the child turned ten, and $500 a month thereafter.[410]

[c] Mississippi. In 1983, in *Tedford v. Dempsey*, the Mississippi Supreme Court encouraged lawyers to use escalation clauses tying support increases to parents' earnings or an inflation index.[411] But in subsequent cases the court rejected lawyers' attempts to craft escalation clauses, insisting that the clauses factor in a child's needs as well as the payor's income – an almost impossible task. The court has rejected a provision for yearly increases tied to the consumer price index,[412] a provision for a fixed amount of support plus 10% of income over $50,000,[413] and a court-ordered escalation clause increasing support when a child entered kindergarten.[414] The court of appeals also rejected a provision for $300 a month or 25% of adjusted gross income – the clause was an impermissible flat percentage increase that failed to consider the child's needs or the payee's income.[415]

In two cases, the court of appeals approved escalation clauses limited to a one-time adjustment. The court affirmed an order requiring support at the statutory percentage if the noncustodial mother became employed.[416] Similarly, an imminent change in a payor's employment justified a provision increasing support to 14% of the payor's new adjusted gross income. The provision was not an escalation clause because it related to a single anticipated event.[417]

In 2005, the court of appeals altered this approach to agreed escalation clauses, enforcing a father's agreement to pay 14% of his adjusted gross income or $600 a month. The court rejected his argument that the provision was an unenforceable escalation clause, stating that parties "may agree of their own volition to do more than the law requires of them."[418] And in 2009, the court of appeals enforced a father's agreement to pay $1,300 a month or, if his income and bonuses increased, support equal to the

---

[409] *See* McManus v. McManus, 348 N.E.2d 507, 509 (Ill. App. Ct. 1976) (steadily increasing support based on age failed to consider payor's income and child's needs); Larimore v. Larimore, 617 P.2d 892, 894 (Okla. 1980) (error to base increase in child support on one factor).

[410] Penoski v. Patterson, 440 So. 2d 45, 46 (Fla. Dist. Ct. App. 1983); *see also In re* Marriage of Moore, 453 N.E.2d 102, 105 (Ill. App. Ct. 1983) (escalation clause increasing payments by $1,000 per child each year held arbitrary; distinguished clauses tied to income).

[411] Tedford v. Dempsey, 437 So. 2d 410, 419 (Miss. 1983); *see also* Wing v. Wing, 549 So. 2d 944, 947 (Miss. 1989) (recognizing value of escalation clauses to build in support increases).

[412] Wing v. Wing, 549 So. 2d 944, 947-48 (Miss. 1989) (escalation clause must relate to the parents' income and the child's needs, and must establish frequency of adjustment and date of adjustment).

[413] Morris v. Stacy, 641 So. 2d 1194, 1201 (Miss. 1994) (unenforceable because it did not take into account the mother's income, inflation, and the needs of the children).

[414] Gillespie v. Gillespie, 594 So. 2d 620, 623 (Miss. 1992) (support increase must be tied to parent's income and child's needs).

[415] Ligon v. Ligon, 743 So. 2d 404, 407 (Miss. Ct. App. 1999). *But cf.* Carter v. Carter, 735 So. 2d 1109, 1116 (Miss. Ct. App. 1999) (enforcing escalation clause in arrearages action, but admonishing courts against stating award as a percentage of income).

[416] Luckett v. Luckett, 726 So. 2d 1214, 1217 (Miss. Ct. App. 1998).

[417] Robertson v. Robertson, 812 So. 2d 998, 1002 (Miss. Ct. App. 2001).

[418] Rogers v. Rogers, 919 So. 2d 184, 189 (Miss. Ct. App. 2005).

§ 13.10[3]   **MISSISSIPPI FAMILY LAW**

guidelines plus $3,600. The court rejected his argument that an escalation clause must be tied to the *Tedford* factors, ordering him to pay $39,713 in arrearages, interest, and attorneys' fees.[419]

[3] Income withholding. As a result of federal mandates to increase collection of child support, most support orders are now accompanied by an order for income withholding. Requirements for withholding differ depending on whether the custodial parent receives public assistance.

[a] For public assistance recipients. If a custodial parent receives public assistance, child support must be paid through a withholding order designating the Department of Human Services as the payee.[420] The order should state that additional amounts may be withheld upon receipt of an affidavit of delinquency or a notarized record of overdue payments from the department.[421] The order should also state that the amount to be withheld for delinquency should equal 20% of the regular support obligation, subject to the limitations of the Consumer Protection Act.[422] For existing support awards not accompanied by a withholding order, DHS may administratively order income withholding.[423]

[b] In other cases. In cases not brought by the Department of Human Services, income withholding is required for any support order issued, modified, or found to be in arrears after January 1, 1994. A court may dispense with income withholding if one of the parties proves good cause to do so or if both parties agree in writing to an alternative arrangement.[424] The court of appeals held that a chancellor erred in denying a payee's request for a withholding order without finding good cause to forego withholding.[425] An order that is not initially subject to withholding automatically becomes so if the court finds that a support payment is thirty days past due.[426] Under these circumstances, a withholding order may be served by the custodial parent's attorney, DHS, or the court clerk without a hearing.[427]

[c] Limits on wage withholding. The usual limits on wage garnishment[428] do not apply to support orders. Employers may withhold between 50% and 65% of the

---

[419] Stigler v. Stigler, 48 So. 3d 547, 550-54 (Miss. Ct. App. 2009), *cert. denied*, 49 So. 3d 1139 (Miss. 2010). *But cf.* West v. West. 23 So. 3d 558, 561 (Miss. Ct. App. 2009) (stating in dicta that escalation clauses must comply with the requirements of *Tedford*, but holding that appeal was premature because the clause had not yet been triggered), *cert. denied*, 22 So. 3d 1193 (Miss. 2009).

[420] MISS. CODE ANN. § 93-11-103(1) (2004).

[421] MISS. CODE ANN. § 93-11-103(1) (2004).

[422] MISS. CODE ANN. § 93-11-105(2) (2004).

[423] MISS. CODE ANN. § 93-11-105(1) (2004).

[424] MISS. CODE ANN. § 93-11-103(2) (2004).

[425] Meeks v. Meeks, 757 So. 2d 364 (Miss. Ct. App. 2000).

[426] MISS. CODE ANN. § 93-11-103(3) (2004).

[427] Notice may be served "by first class mail or personal delivery on the obligor's payor, superintendent, manager, agent or subsequent payor." MISS. CODE ANN. § 93-11-103(4) (2004).

[428] The usual limits on garnishment are the lesser of 25% of disposable earnings or "the amount by which his disposable earnings for that week exceed thirty (30) times the federal minimum hourly wage." MISS. CODE ANN. § 85-3-4(2) (2004).

458

CHILD SUPPORT § 13.10[3][d]

disposable earnings[429] of an employee pursuant to a support order.[430] If the employee is supporting a spouse or dependent other than the person for whom support is ordered, the maximum withholding is 50% for current regular support payments and 55% for payments more than twelve weeks in arrears.[431] If the employee is not supporting a family, the maximum withholding is 60% for current payments and 65% for payments in arrears.[432]

In a 2010 case, the Mississippi Supreme Court held that the anti-assignment clause of the Social Security Act prohibits using an income-withholding order to collect support from a disabled Supplemental Security Income recipient. In contrast, Social Security disability, which is based on former employment rather than poverty, may be subject to income-withholding.[433]

[d] Priority of child support withholding orders. Child support orders have priority over all wage garnishments. In fact, recent legislation provides that child support orders are not considered garnishments.[434] Employers are directed to withhold support "without regard to any prior or subsequent garnishments, attachments, wage assignments or any other claims of creditors."[435] If an employee is subject to more than one child support order, the orders are paid on a pro rata basis without regard to the order in which they were received.[436]

[4] Security for payment

[a] Bond. A chancery court may require that a payor provide bond or sureties to secure a child support order.[437] If no bond is provided in the initial hearing, bond may later be imposed if payments are thirty days delinquent. The payor is entitled to a hearing prior to imposition of bond.[438] A chancellor erred in failing to require bond from an out-of-state father in arrears who stated that he did not know where his work would take him.[439]

[b] Insurance. One or both parents may agree to maintain insurance to secure child support obligations. The agreement should specify the amount and duration of

---

[429] Disposable earnings are defined in 15 U.S.C. § 1672(b) (2000). "The term 'disposable earnings' means that part of the earnings of any individual remaining after the deduction from those earnings of any amounts required by law to be withheld." *Id.*

[430] *See* Miss. Code Ann. § 85-3-4(3)(b) (2004).

[431] Miss. Code Ann. § 85-3-5 (3)(b)(iii) (2004).

[432] Miss. Code Ann. § 85-3-5 (3)(b)(iii) (2004).

[433] Barnes v. Dep't of Human Servs., 42 So. 3d 10, 13-18 (Miss. 2010) (but chancellor has discretion to consider income as basis for amount of support).

[434] Miss. Code Ann. § 93-11-103(10) (2004).

[435] Miss. Code Ann. § 93-11-111(7) (2004).

[436] Miss. Code Ann. § 93-11-111(8) (2004).

[437] *See* Miss. Code Ann. § 93-5-23 (2004) ("the court may, upon petition of the person to whom such payments are owing, or such person's legal representative, enter an order requiring that bond, sureties or other security be given").

[438] Miss. Code Ann. § 93-11-65(3) (2004).

[439] Bush v. Bush, 451 So. 2d 779, 782 (Miss. 1984) (stating that the circumstances would "make it difficult for Mrs. Bush to locate him and for any court to exercise jurisdiction over him").

459

§ 13.10[5]   MISSISSIPPI FAMILY LAW

the insurance obligation as well as any other requirements.[440] Insurance in the custodial parent's name for the purpose of securing child support does not belong to the custodial parent. An agreement that the husband would provide $70,000 in insurance with the wife as beneficiary did not entitle her to the cash surrender value of a policy. The chancellor properly refused to hold the husband in contempt for cashing in an existing policy and substituting the same amount in term life insurance.[441]

[5] Lump sum payment. As a general rule, child support should not be awarded in lump sum form. In a case involving a void marriage, the court of appeals reversed a chancellor's award of the $26,000 equity in the marital home as a form of lump sum child support.[442] However, Mississippi paternity statutes do permit settlement of a paternity claim in a lump sum.[443]

[6] Definiteness. A child support order must be sufficiently definite for a court to determine whether the payor is in breach of the agreement. An order that an unemployed noncustodial mother pay for her children's clothes in an amount she could afford was too vague to be enforceable.[444] However, a father's agreement to pay 14% of his adjusted gross income or $600 per month was not ambiguous as to whether the $600 figure set a minimum or maximum amount for child support. It clearly anticipated that the father would pay whichever amount was greater.[445]

[7] Source of payments. Courts have rejected payor's arguments that alimony and child support may not be awarded if the only resource available for payment is non-assignable income. For example, support may be ordered even though the payor's only source of income is veteran's disability income.[446] In a 2010 case, the Mississippi Supreme Court held that non-assignable Supplemental Security Income may not be subject to income-withholding orders, but that a chancellor has discretion to consider or disregard the income for purposes of calculating child support.[447]

[8] Qualified domestic relations order. Child support may be paid through a qualified domestic relations order providing for payment of a portion of the noncusto-

---

[440] Johnson v. Johnson, 822 So. 2d 1067 (Miss. Ct. App. 2002). A father who agreed to maintain life insurance to secure his daughter's post-majority college support died after making his new wife the policy beneficiary. At the time of his death, the twenty-one-year-old daughter was not enrolled in college and had not accrued any academic hours. The court of appeals reversed a summary award of the funds to the current wife, holding that a genuine question of fact existed as to the duration, meaning, and effect of the agreement. *Id.*

[441] Alexander v. Alexander, 494 So. 2d 365, 369 (Miss. 1986).

[442] Pittman v. Pittman, 909 So. 2d 148, 153 (Miss. Ct. App. 2005).

[443] *See* § 11.06[2][b].

[444] Lowrey v. Lowrey, 919 So. 2d 1112, 1121 (Miss. Ct. App. 2005); *see also* Rudder v. Rudder, 467 So. 2d 675, 676-77 (Miss. 1985) (order to pay $100 plus "any income or dividend received from any investments in the name of the child" too vague to be enforceable).

[445] Rogers v. Rogers, 919 So. 2d 184, 188-89 (Miss. Ct. App. 2005).

[446] Steiner v. Steiner, 788 So. 2d 771, 777-78 (Miss. 2001) (alimony award).

[447] Barnes v. Dep't of Human Servs., 42 So. 3d 10, 17 (Miss. 2010); *cf.* Bailey v. Fisher, 946 So. 2d 404, 409 (Miss. Ct. App. 2006) (permissible for court to order a father to deposit his Social Security disability benefits into the registry of the court, based on his agreement to do so entered in a prior contempt proceeding).

CHILD SUPPORT § 13.11

dial parent's retirement to the custodial parent or to the child.[448]

§ 13.11 MODIFICATION

Courts retain continuing jurisdiction to modify child support in light of changed circumstances. Many states employ a statutory presumption that support should be modified when an award falls substantially below the child support guidelines. Mississippi uses a factor-based test to determine whether a material change in circumstances has occurred that justifies changing the award.

[1] Role of child support guidelines. After the implementation of uniform child support guidelines in the late 1980s, most states linked requirements for modification directly to application of the guidelines. In Mississippi, the legislature has adopted this approach only with regard to DHS cases. In other cases, courts still apply the factor-based pre-guideline test for modification. However, courts are directed to use the guidelines to determine the proper amount of support upon finding that a material change has occurred based upon these factors.

[a] Presumptions linked to guidelines. In most states, legislatures have created a presumption that support orders that are substantially out of line with the child support guidelines should be modified. The statutes often provide that a material change is presumed to have occurred if an existing order varies by a certain percentage from the amount that would result by applying the state's guidelines to the payor's current income. For example, Alabama law provides: "[T]here is a rebuttable presumption that child support should be modified when the difference between the existing support award and the amount determined by application of the guidelines varies more than 10%."[449] These statutes eliminate the need for evidence of a child's expenses, proof of a custodial parent's resources, or testimony regarding inflation.

[b] Mississippi presumptions. In Mississippi, a modification presumption is in effect for support increases sought by the Department of Human Services for public assistance recipients. Section 43-19-34 of the Mississippi Code provides that every three years, upon the request of a parent or on its own initiative, DHS may seek modification of a support order that differs from the amount that would be required by current application of the guidelines. The statute states that "[no] proof of a material change in circumstances is necessary in the three-year review for adjustment." A parent's preexisting arrearage does not bar modification under this provision.[450]

There is no similar provision for a presumptive increase in private actions to modify support. The Mississippi Supreme Court has stated in several cases that an increase in a payor's income alone does not necessarily constitute a material change.[451] Instead,

---

[448] Carlson v. Matthews, 966 So. 2d 1258, 1261 (Miss. Ct. App. 2007). *See supra* § 7.06[2].

[449] ALA. R. JUD. ADMIN. 32(A)(3)(b) (2009).

[450] MISS. CODE ANN. § 43-19-34(3) (2011).

[451] *See* Pipkin v. Dolan, 788 So. 2d 834, 838-39 (Miss. Ct. App. 2001) ("an increase in income is only one of many factors to be considered in making the determination as to whether a material change in circumstances has occurred");

461

§ 13.11[1][c]   **MISSISSIPPI FAMILY LAW**

courts apply factors set out in pre-guidelines cases to determine whether a material change in circumstances has occurred.[452]

[c] Guidelines determine amount of support. If a court finds that a material change in circumstances has occurred, the statutory guidelines apply to determine the appropriate amount of support. If the court deviates from the presumptively correct amount or if the payor's income level falls outside the presumptive guidelines, the court must make findings of fact to support the award.[453] A chancellor's order increasing support was reversed for failure to apply the statutory guidelines and to make findings of fact to justify deviation from the guidelines.[454]

[2] Aspects of order subject to modification. Most commonly, parents seek to modify basic support awards through petitions to increase support or to reduce support. However, other aspects of support may also be modified. The court of appeals rejected a father's argument that agreements to pay private school tuition are "contractual" and therefore non-modifiable.[455] Support agreements may be modified to provide for college support[456] or to alter arrangements for provision of health insurance. For example, a mother's loss of employer-provided health insurance was a material change in circumstances justifying modification to require the father to provide insurance.[457] An agreed order of support is modifiable in the same manner as court-ordered support.[458]

[3] The material change in circumstances test. In Mississippi, a parent seeking modification of child support in a non-DHS case must show a substantial and material change in the circumstances of the child or parents since the decree awarding support.[459] The change must not have been foreseeable at the time of the award.

[a] Material change. In 1983, the Mississippi Supreme Court set out factors to be considered in determining whether a material change has occurred that warrants modification of support: the increased needs of older children; an increase in expenses;

---

see also Wallace v. Bond, 745 So. 2d 844 (Miss. 1999); Turner v. Turner, 824 So. 2d 652 (Miss. Ct. App. 2002).

[452] See *infra* §13.11[3][a].

[453] *See* MISS. CODE ANN. § 43-19-101(2004) (statute applies to modification actions).

[454] Wallace v. Bond, 745 So. 2d 844 (Miss. 1999) (also reversed because of the custodial parent's failure to prove a material change in circumstances)*; see* Anderson v. Anderson, 692 So. 2d 65 (Miss. 1997) (guidelines produced award of $700; not error to lower child support from $1,000 to $800 based on reduction in father's income, but considering increase in child's needs).

[455] Davis v. Davis, 983 So. 2d 358, 361 (Miss. Ct. App. 2008).

[456] See *infra* § 13.11[7].

[457] H.L.S. v. R.S.R., 949 So. 2d 794, 801-02 (Miss. Ct. App. 2006).

[458] Woodfin v. Woodfin. 26 So. 3d 389, 394-95 (Miss. Ct. App. 2010).

[459] McEwen v. McEwen, 631 So. 2d 821 (Miss. 1994); Gillespie v. Gillespie, 594 So. 2d 620, 623 (Miss. 1992); Weeks v. Weeks, 29 So. 3d 80, 89 (Miss. Ct. App. 2009); Walton v. Snyder, 984 So. 2d 343 (Miss. Ct. App. 2007); Allen v. Allen, 953 So. 2d 279, 282 (Miss. Ct. App. 2007); Austin v. Austin, 981 So. 2d 1000 (Miss. Ct. App. 2007). The court explained the reason for the requirement of a substantial change in *Tedford v. Dempsey*, 437 So. 2d 410, 417 (Miss. 1983). "Matters once finally adjudicated should not be subject to relitigation. . . . It is a rare case where both parents fail to feel a financial pinch. Allowing renewed litigation whenever one begins to feel that pinch would hardly be practicable. Conservation of judicial resources and the desire to hold to a tolerable minimum disruptions in post-divorce domestic tranquility have thus given rise to the rule that there may be no modification in a child support decree absent a substantial or material change in the circumstances of one or more of the interested parties." *Id.*

CHILD SUPPORT

§ 13.11[3][b]

inflation; a child's health and special medical or psychological needs; the parties' relative financial condition and earning capacity; the health and special needs of the parents; the payor's necessary living expenses; each party's tax liability; one party's free use of residence, furnishings, or automobile; and any other relevant facts and circumstances.[460] The Mississippi Supreme Court has stated in several cases that an increase in a payor's income alone does not necessarily constitute a material change.[461] Similarly, the fact that children are older does not, in itself, warrant modification.[462] A chancellor erred in granting modification based on proof that the father's income had increased and that the children were older, without specific proof of the children's increased expenses. The only evidence of increased expenses was a line in the mother's 8.05 financial statement showing that the children were involved in extracurricular activities.[463]

If no child support was ordered at divorce, a later petition for support does not require proof of a material change in circumstances. A chancellor erred in denying a mother's petition to institute child support because she failed to prove a material change in circumstances since the divorce decree.[464]

[b] Occurring since the decree. Modification of support must be based on events since the most recent support order. For example, res judicata barred a husband's attempt to relitigate the issue of emancipation in a second modification petition.[465] In contrast, a court's 2001 finding of no material change did not prevent a payor from seeking subsequent modification based on developments since that date.[466] Modification cannot be used to correct a perceived error in an earlier decree.[467] A chancellor erred in modifying alimony and child support based on his view that the amount of support originally ordered was too high.[468]

[c] Foreseeability. The change must be one that was not foreseeable at the time of the original order.[469] For example, a payor's request to decrease support based on loss of severance pay was denied; he was aware at the time of the decree that the pay

---

[460] Tedford v. Dempsey, 437 So. 2d 410, 422 (Miss. 1983); *see* McEachern v. McEachern, 605 So. 2d 809, 813 (Miss. 1992); Walton v. Snyder, 984 So. 2d 343 (Miss. Ct. App. 2007).

[461] *See* Pipkin v. Dolan, 788 So. 2d 834, 838-39 (Miss. Ct. App. 2001) ("an increase in income is only one of many factors to be considered in making the determination as to whether a material change in circumstances has occurred"); *see also* Wallace v. Bond, 745 So. 2d 844 (Miss. 1999); Turner v. Turner, 824 So. 2d 652 (Miss. Ct. App. 2002).

[462] McNair v. Clark, 961 So. 2d 73, 80 (Miss. Ct. App. 2007).

[463] McNair v. Clark, 961 So. 2d 73, 80 (Miss. Ct. App. 2007).

[464] Forrest v. McCoy, 941 So. 2d 889, 891 (Miss. Ct. App. 2006).

[465] *See* Lane v. Lane, 850 So. 2d 122, 125 (Miss. Ct. App. 2002); *see also* Dix v. Dix, 941 So. 2d 913, 918 (Miss. Ct. App. 2006) (father who agreed at divorce to provide college support not entitled to modify basic support when child enrolled in college; no change had occurred since the decree).

[466] Howard v. Howard, 968 So. 2d 961, 969 (Miss. Ct. App. 2007); *see also* Austin v. Austin, 981 So. 2d 1000 (Miss. Ct. App. 2007) (chancellor properly reduced support based on job loss that occurred after previous unsuccessful petition to modify).

[467] Gresham v. Gresham, 25 So. 2d 760, 761 (Miss. 1946).

[468] Schaeffer v. Schaeffer, 370 So. 2d 240, 241 (Miss. 1979) (amounts were high but not unconscionable; no accident, fraud, or mistake permitting revision of judgment).

[469] *See* Overstreet v. Overstreet, 692 So. 2d 88 (Miss. 1997); Shipley v. Ferguson, 638 So. 2d 1295 (Miss. 1994); Morris v. Morris, 541 So. 2d 1040, 1042-43 (Miss. 1989).

§ 13.11[3][d]　　　　　　　　　　　　　　　MISSISSIPPI FAMILY LAW

would terminate.[470] However, the foreseeability test should not prevent modification to address a child's increased needs or to provide for college expenses, even though it is arguably "foreseeable" that a young child's expenses will increase and that a child may have the aptitude for college. Parties need not anticipate "the natural growth of a child and the inevitable increased expenses" in a toddler's support award.[471]

[d] Circumstances that are not a material change. Changes in a payor's income or expenses resulting from lifestyle choices are not a reason to modify child support. For example, the fact that a support payor has difficulty making payments because of new debt is not a material change in circumstances.[472] Similarly, a payor may not reduce support based on the birth of additional children in a later family.[473]

[4] Limits on modification. Child support may not be modified by an out-of-court agreement. In addition, neither the parties nor a court may modify amounts already due.

[a] Modification of arrearages. Only payments not yet due and owing may be modified. Vested payments of alimony and child support cannot be modified or forgiven by a court.[474] Each payment in arrears "becomes a judgment against the payor."[475] A delinquent parent is also liable for interest on each unpaid support installment from the time it was due.[476]

[b] Modification by private agreement. An out-of-court agreement between parents to modify child support is unenforceable.[477] Child support is paid to the custodial parent in trust for the benefit of the child and may not be altered without court approval.[478] A payor should not rely on an out-of-court agreement to reduce support –

---

[470] Tingle v. Tingle, 573 So. 2d 1389, 1391 (Miss. 1990); *see also* McNair v. Clark, 961 So. 2d 73, 80 (Miss. Ct. App. 2007) (mother failed to prove that children's increased expenses were unforeseeable); Walton v. Snyder, 984 So. 2d 343 (Miss. Ct. App. 2007) (suggesting that increase in private school expenses that predated divorce could not be basis for modification); Dill v. Dill, 908 So. 2d 198, 202-03 (Miss. Ct. App. 2005) (modification based on income reduction denied because both parties were aware at time of divorce that defendant planned to leave Marine Corps); Leiden v. Leiden, 902 So. 2d 582 (Miss. Ct. App. 2004) (husband planned early retirement from the Navy at time of divorce).

[471] Wallace v. Wallace, 965 So. 2d 737, 742 (Miss. Ct. App. 2007) (quoting Kilgore v. Fuller, 741 So. 2d 351, 353 (Miss. Ct. App. 1999)).

[472] Yancey v. Yancey, 752 So. 2d 1006 (Miss. 1999); Magee v. Magee, 754 So. 2d 1275 (Miss. Ct. App. 1999) (personal bills cannot be used as a reason to reduce support).

[473] Bailey v. Bailey, 724 So. 2d 335 (Miss. 1998); Bustin v. Bustin, 806 So. 2d 1136, 1138 (Miss. Ct. App. 2001); Turner v. Turner, 824 So. 2d 652 (Miss. Ct. App. 1999).

[474] Tanner v. Roland, 598 So. 2d 783 (Miss. 1992); Varner v. Varner, 588 So. 2d 428, 432-33 (Miss. 1991); Gregg v. Montgomery, 587 So. 2d 928, 932 (Miss. 1991); Rubisoff v. Rubisoff, 133 So. 2d 534 (Miss. 1961); Pope v. Pope, 803 So. 2d 499 (Miss. Ct. App. 2002) (prospective reduction is proper, but vested payments cannot be altered).

[475] Brand v. Brand, 482 So. 2d 236, 237 (Miss. 1986); Cunliffe v. Swartzfager, 437 So. 2d 43, 45-46 (Miss. 1983); Howard v. Howard, 191 So. 2d 528, 531 (Miss. 1966).

[476] Brand v. Brand, 482 So. 2d 236, 238 (Miss. 1986); *see also* Rubisoff v. Rubisoff, 133 So. 2d 534 (Miss. 1961); Schaffer v. Schaffer, 46 So. 2d 443, 444 (Miss. 1950) (interest on unpaid alimony accrues from the date it was due).

[477] Armstrong v. Armstrong, 618 So. 2d 1278, 1280 (Miss. 1993); Bittick v. Bittick, 987 So. 2d 1058, 1061-62 (Miss. Ct. App. 2008) (out-of-court agreement providing father with relief period from child support to study for bar examination unenforceable).

[478] Armstrong v. Armstrong, 618 So. 2d 1278, 1281 (Miss. 1993); Tanner v. Roland, 598 So. 2d 783, 785 (Miss. 1992); Tillman v. Tillman, 809 So. 2d 767, 770 (Miss. Ct. App. 2002).

CHILD SUPPORT   **§ 13.11[4][c]**

custodial parents have recovered substantial arrearages in spite of their agreement to reduce support. For example, a custodial mother's agreement to accept $1,500 for her waiver of all past and future support was void. She obtained a judgment for $89,000 in arrears in spite of the agreement.[479] However, a payor was relieved of arrearages based on an agreement that both parties understood had been filed with the court and approved.[480]

[c] Modification by payor in arrears: The clean hands doctrine. The clean hands doctrine may bar payors in arrears from seeking prospective modification. The Mississippi Supreme Court stated: "[A] husband may not petition for modification of the original decree without showing either that he has performed it or that his performance has been wholly impossible."[481] Payors in arrears have been denied modification of future payments in spite of a material change in circumstances.[482] For example, a chancellor erred in ordering modification at the request of a payor who failed to prove that he was unable to make prior payments.[483]

In a 1992 case, however, the supreme court stated that a court's entry of judgment for arrearages "cleansed" a payor's hands, allowing him to seek modification.[484] Subsequently, some payors in arrears have been granted modification following the entry of a "cleansing" judgment.[485] For example, the clean hands doctrine did not bar modification by a father who was in arrears, but who sought modification promptly upon losing his job.[486] In other cases, however, the doctrine has been applied to deny modification. The court of appeals held that the doctrine barred modification by a father who promptly filed a modification petition, but failed to pay support after filing. He received $52,000 from unemployment benefits and the sale of a home during that period. The dissenting judge pointed out the contradictory cases and urged that a judgment should cleanse the petitioner's hands to permit modification.[487] The court of appeals explained the follow-

---

[479] Houck v. Ousterhout, 861 So. 2d 1000, 1002 (Miss. 2003) (finding father in arrears in the amount of $89,000). *But see* Dorr v. Dorr, 797 So. 2d 1008 (Miss. Ct. App. 2001) (suggesting in dicta that out-of-court agreements may be honored in some cases, if the child is not adversely affected).

[480] Wright v. Wright, 737 So. 2d 408, 410 (Miss. Ct. App. 1998).

[481] Kincaid v. Kincaid, 57 So. 2d 263 (1952) (payor must show "that he earned all he could, that he lived economically and paid all surplus money above a living on the alimony decreed to the wife); Hooker v. Hooker, 205 So. 2d 276 (Miss. 1967) (citing Ramsay v. Ramsay, 87 So. 491 (1921)).

[482] *See* Mullen v. Mullen, 246 So. 2d 923 (Miss. 1971) (reversing contempt for current inability to pay, but upholding denial of modification based on clean hands doctrine; payor did not show he did all he could to pay arrearages in the past); *see also* Kincaid v. Kincaid, 57 So. 2d 263 (1952).

[483] Taylor v. Taylor, 348 So. 2d 1341, 1342 (Miss. 1977); *see* Bailey v. Bailey, 724 So. 2d 335 (Miss. 1998) (clean hands doctrine prevents modification unless payor proves inability to pay).

[484] Brennan v. Brennan, 605 So. 2d 749, 752 (Miss. 1992) (remanded to consider modification petition).

[485] Lane v. Lane, 850 So. 2d 122, 126 (Miss. 2002); *see also* Andres v. Andres. 22 So. 3d 314, 321 (Miss. Ct. App. 2009) (allowing downward modification for father whose hands were "cleansed" by arrearages judgment); Howard v. Howard, 968 So. 2d 961, 975 (Miss. Ct. App. 2007) (judgment cleansed hands of payor in arrears); Howard v. Howard, 913 So. 2d 1030, 1041-42 (Miss. Ct. App. 2005) (court of appeals disagreed with chancellor's finding that clean hands doctrine barred modification – entry of a judgment of arrearages "cleanses" the hands of a delinquent payor; ruling upheld on other grounds); Brawdy v. Howell, 841 So. 2d 1175 (Miss. Ct. App. 2003) (chancellor did not err in granting a modification even though the father was in contempt for nonpayment, where he misunderstood the agreement and was not in "willful" contempt).

[486] Grissom v. Grissom, 952 So. 2d 1023, 1029-30 (Miss. Ct. App. 2007).

[487] Kelley v. Day, 965 So. 2d 749, 757 (Miss. Ct. App. 2007); *see also* Dill v. Dill, 908 So. 2d 198, 202 (Miss. Ct. App. 2005) (reversing chancellor's grant of modification petition in part because father was in arrears; citing clean hands

§ 13.11[5]   MISSISSIPPI FAMILY LAW

ing year that the doctrine bars modification by payors who are willfully in arrears but allows modification by a payor whose default was not willful.[488]

[5] Petition to increase child support. An increase in support is typically based on a combination of three factors: a substantial increase in the noncustodial parent's income, inflation, and an increase in the costs of raising older children. The supreme court has rejected payors' arguments that modification should be denied because these events are foreseeable. As the supreme court noted, most parents are aware that "children's expenses generally will increase as they get older, that the father and mother's earning capacity will generally increase from year to year, and that inflation will continue at some level." That knowledge does not prevent modification.[489] Similarly, the court of appeals rejected a payor's argument that college expenses were foreseeable and therefore could not be addressed for the first time in a modification petition.[490]

[a] Payor's increase in income. A substantial increase in a payor's income or resources is the most common factor supporting an upward modification of support.[491] A noncustodial father's substantial increase in income was the primary reason for increasing his support obligation from $1,200 to $1,320 a month.[492] Similarly, a father's increased income combined with evidence of the children's increased needs supported modification to the statutory percentage.[493] And a chancellor properly modified a divorce decree to require a recently employed noncustodial mother to pay 22% of her adjusted gross income in child support.[494] However, the court of appeals has stated that an increase in a parent's income alone, without proof of increased expenses, is not a

---

doctrine); Leiden v. Leiden, 902 So. 2d 582 (Miss. Ct. App. 2004) (citing clean hands doctrine; also finding that income reduction was voluntary); Seeley v. Stafford, 840 So. 2d 111 (Miss. Ct. App. 2003) (doctrine barred modification by payor who was $35,000 in arrears).

[488] Hunt v. Asanov, 975 So. 2d 899, 902-03 (Miss. Ct. App. 2008) (doctrine of unclean hands bars payor in willful contempt from seeking downward modification).

[489] Tedford v. Dempsey, 437 So. 2d 410, 419 (Miss. 1983); see also Wallace v. Wallace, 965 So. 2d 737, 742 (Miss. Ct. App. 2007) (parents need not anticipate all expenses in an award for a young child). But see McNair v. Clark, 961 So. 2d 73, 80 (Miss. Ct. App. 2007) (mother failed to prove that older children's increased expenses were unforeseeable).

[490] Lawrence v. Lawrence, 574 So. 2d 1376, 1381 (Miss. 1991).

[491] See Tedford v. Dempsey. 437 So. 2d 410, 418 (Miss. 1983) (father's income doubled from time of original decree) (citing Bracey v. Bracey, 408 So. 2d 1387, 1389 (Miss.1982)).

[492] See Wright v. Stanley, 700 So. 2d 274, 283 (Miss. 1997) (also noting inflation and the increased costs of older children); see also Cox v. Moulds, 490 So. 2d 866, 868-69 (Miss. 1986) (father's income doubled since original decree); Wallace v. Wallace, 965 So. 2d 737, 745 (Miss. Ct. App. 2007) (increase in income combined with proof of child's increased needs); Walton v. Snyder, 984 So. 2d 343 (Miss. Ct. App. 2007) (modification based on 60% increase in father's income and the increased expenses of older children); Staggs v. Staggs, 919 So. 2d 112, 122-23 (Miss. Ct. App. 2005) (support increased from $2,000 a month to $2,500 a month based on increased costs of older children, increase in payors' income, and custodial family's increased costs of living in Maryland); Hopson v. Hopson, 851 So. 2d 397 (Miss. Ct. App. 2003) (support properly modified to 14% of current income where payor's income increased, child's needs increased, and prior support was below guidelines); cf. Kilgore v. Fuller, 741 So. 2d 351, 356 (Miss. Ct. App. 1999) (recognizing increased cost of teenage daughter as material change, but remanding because modification exceeded statutory guidelines without explanation).

[493] Shepherd v. Shepherd, 769 So. 2d 242, 246 (Miss. Ct. App. 2000); see also Hopson v. Hopson, 851 So. 2d 397, 400 (Miss. Ct. App. 2003) (support properly modified to 14% of current income where payor's income increased, child's needs increased, and prior support was below guidelines). But cf. Hammett v. Woods, 602 So. 2d 825, 828 (Miss. 1992) (no increase, even though father's support was below guidelines; child's needs met by child support of $300 and state and federal resources for blind).

[494] Mercier v. Mercier, 11 So. 3d 1283, 1287 (Miss. Ct. App. 2009).

CHILD SUPPORT   **§ 13.11[5][b]**

material change in circumstances supporting modification.[495] A court may disregard slight changes in a payor's income or expenses.[496] For example, a high-income payor's $500 a month increase in income did not justify increasing child support for two children from $2,000 to $2,500 a month.[497]

[b] Increase in costs for older children. Usually, upward modification is also based on a finding that the children's needs have increased. The court of appeals affirmed an increase from $250 to $500 a month based upon evidence of the educational and extracurricular activities of teenage children.[498] An increase was also granted when a custodial parent provided evidence of children's increased expenses based on "age, size, school attendance, participation in community activities and increased medical needs."[499] A custodial parent must offer more than general allegations of increased costs. A chancellor erred in increasing support based upon a custodial mother's general statements that the costs associated with a child had increased. The movant must "show that increased financial obligations have eaten away so significantly at the purchase power" of the award that it no longer meets the child's needs.[500] Similarly, a father's unsupported allegation that a child was older and more expensive did not prove a material change in circumstances.[501] Extravagant or inflated expenses will be disregarded. A court properly refused to increase support of $1,500 a month for one child in spite of the mother's itemization of over $6,000 a month in expenses; the expenses included the cost of a swimming pool and $300 a month for pet care.[502]

[c] Inflation. The decreased value of a child support award due to inflation is a

---

[495] McNair v. Clark, 961 So. 2d 73, 81 (Miss. Ct. App. 2007). *But cf.* Ruth v. Burchfield, 23 So. 3d 600, 608 (Miss. Ct. App. 2009) ("It is well settled in this state that an increase in income constitutes a material change in circumstances.").

[496] *See* Keller v. Keller, 230 So. 2d 808, 809-10 (Miss. 1970). *Keller* deals with modification of alimony, which is also governed by the substantial change in circumstances test. *Id. But see* Robertson v. Robertson, 812 So. 2d 998 (Miss. Ct. App. 2001) (affirming modification of child support by less than two dollars to the statutory 14% as harmless error).

[497] Riddick v. Riddick, 906 So. 2d 813 (Miss. 2004).

[498] Havens v. Broocks, 728 So. 2d 580, 583 (Miss. Ct. App. 1998); *see also* Ruth v. Burchfield, 23 So. 3d 600, 607-08 (Miss. Ct. App. 2009) (child support was properly increased to 14% of payor's current income based on evidence that the child was older and involved in extracurricular activities that increased her expenses).

[499] Shepherd v. Shepherd, 769 So. 2d 242, 246 (Miss. Ct. App. 2000); *see also* Strange v. Strange, 43 So. 3d 1169, 1175-76 (Miss. Ct. App. 2010) (support increased from $360 to $430 based on evidence that child entering school would participate in extracurricular activities); Wallace v. Wallace, 965 So. 2d 737, 742 (Miss. Ct. App. 2007) (mother provided evidence of increased expenses of children); Walton v. Snyder, 984 So. 2d 343 (Miss. Ct. App. 2007) (older children's increased expenses included need for an automobile, extracurricular activities, and an increase in private school tuition); Staggs v. Staggs, 919 So. 2d 112, 122-23 (Miss. Ct. App. 2005) (support increased from $2,000 a month to $2,500 a month based on increased costs of older children, increase in payor's income, and custodial family's increased costs of living in Maryland).

[500] Turner v. Turner, 744 So. 2d 332, 336 (Miss. Ct. App. 1999). In *Wallace v. Bond*, 745 So. 2d 844, 850 (Miss. 1999), the supreme court reversed a chancellor's upward modification of child support from $1,000 to $1,400. The mother's general allegations of increased child support costs, without evidence of the increased costs, were not sufficient to show a material change in circumstances. *Id. See also* McNair v. Clark, 961 So. 2d 73, 80 (Miss. Ct. App. 2007) (no proof of children's increased expenses other than single line in 8.05 financial statement showing that children were involved in extracurricular activities).

[501] Brawdy v. Howell, 841 So. 2d 1175 (Miss. Ct. App. 2003); *see also* Riddick v. Riddick, 906 So. 2d 813 (Miss. 2004) (mother failed to present documentation of children's increased expenses).

[502] Markofski v. Holzhauer, 799 So. 2d 162, 165-66 (Miss. Ct. App. 2001) (noting that $1,500 a month was sufficient support for a teenage boy).

§ 13.11[5][d]   **MISSISSIPPI FAMILY LAW**

factor that supports increasing the amount of an award.[503] The supreme court affirmed a chancellor's order increasing support from $6,000 to $10,000 a year six years after the initial decree. The court noted that the children were older and that "all of their expenses have greatly increased, due in no small measure to an average inflation factor of 8% a year for six years."[504]

[d] Parties' relative financial position. A court should consider the parties' relative financial position at the time modification is requested. A chancellor properly increased child support to 20% of a physician father's adjusted income – the mother was unable to meet the children's needs on her combined income and alimony of $4,000, while the father had adjusted gross income of $13,000 a month.[505]

[e] Other considerations. In one case, the court took into consideration in raising child support that the father had underreported his income in the divorce action, leading to a lower initial award of support.[506]

[6] Petition to reduce support. A payor's involuntary reduction in income may be a reason to reduce the amount of a support award. Support may also be reduced or terminated when a child is emancipated or lives with the noncustodial parent. A payor may not reduce support based on new debt, the remarriage of either party, or the birth of additional children.[507]

[a] Reduction in income. Support may be reduced when a payor loses income. The income reduction must be involuntary, must not have been foreseeable at the time of the decree, and must impact the payor's ability to meet his or her reasonable needs.[508] A chancellor properly reduced child support when a payor was fired from his job and lost two-thirds of his income.[509] A slight decrease in income does not necessarily require an adjustment of support.[510]

A court may disregard a voluntary income reduction and impute income to the payor at a higher earning capacity.[511] For example, the court of appeals affirmed a chancellor's refusal to reduce child support when a father took a job that paid less than he previously made but offered greater advancement opportunity.[512] A court may also

---

[503] Tedford v. Dempsey. 437 So. 2d 410, 419 (Miss. 1983); Wallace v. Wallace, 965 So. 2d 737, 743 (Miss. Ct. App. 2007).

[504] McKee v. McKee, 382 So. 2d 287, 289 (Miss. 1980).

[505] Walton v. Snyder, 984 So. 2d 343 (Miss. Ct. App. 2007).

[506] Walton v. Snyder, 984 So. 2d 343 (Miss. Ct. App. 2007).

[507] *See supra* § 13.11[4].

[508] *See* Grissom v. Grissom, 952 So. 2d 1023, 1029 (Miss. Ct. App. 2007) (support properly reduced when father lost job through no fault of his own). For an unusual case in which support was reduced based on an increase in income, see *Brown v. Brown*, 566 So. 2d 718, 721 (Miss. 1990) (father who agreed to pay one-half of income for one child entitled to modification to statutory guidelines when his income increased).

[509] Austin v. Austin, 981 So. 2d 1000 (Miss. Ct. App. 2007).

[510] *See* Riley v. Riley, 884 So. 2d 791 (Miss. Ct. App. 2004) ($200 per month reduction in support did not require modification).

[511] *See* Leiden v. Leiden, 902 So. 2d 582 (Miss. Ct. App. 2004) (voluntary retirement not a reason to reduce child support).

[512] Sessums v. Sessums, 12 So. 3d 1146, 1147-48 (Miss. Ct. App. 2009) (reduction in income was voluntary, and

CHILD SUPPORT

§ 13.11[6][b]

impute income to a payor who hides or diverts income.[513] A full discussion of imputed income is included in sections 13.04 and 13.05.

A payor who reports a reduction in income must show a corresponding reduction in standard of living. Modification was denied to a payor whose income dropped but who simultaneously purchased an expensive automobile.[514] In contrast, a chancellor erred in refusing to modify support after a payor's 40% drop in pay.[515]

[b] Custodial parent's remarriage. A custodial parent's remarriage is not a reason for the noncustodial parent to reduce support[516] even if the stepparent assists in supporting the children.[517] Both parents are obligated to support children to the extent of their ability; a father's obligation should not be reduced because remarriage assisted a mother to meet her support obligation.[518] In one unusual case, however, the court of appeals approved a modification in child support when the custodial mother remarried.[519] In the divorce proceeding, the father had agreed to pay one-half of his adjusted income as child support. Considering the extremely high level of support, modification upon the mother's remarriage was appropriate.[520]

[c] Emancipation. Whether a payor is entitled to reduce support when a child is emancipated depends in part on the structure of the support award. If the award provides for a certain amount of support per child, support for each child terminates at majority or upon emancipation. A chancellor properly ordered a custodial mother to reimburse a payor for one-third of the payments made after one of three children was emancipated, where the order provided for support of $100 per month per child.[521] A father's $500 per child obligation was modified when one child was emancipated. However, his obligation for the remaining minor child was increased from $500 to $583, 14% of his adjusted income.[522]

If support is provided through a "global" order – a single amount of support for all children – a payor is not necessarily entitled to a reduction when one child is emancipated.[523] The court of appeals upheld a chancellor's refusal to reduce a global support

---

father did not seek to replace part-time job).

[513] *See* discussion of income imputation, *supra* § 13.04[4], [5].

[514] Holcombe v. Holcombe, 813 So. 2d 700 (Miss. 2002) (chancellor's refusal to modify alimony based on reduction in income upheld where husband purchased new automobile with large monthly obligation); *see also* Howard v. Howard, 913 So. 2d 1030, 1042-43 (Miss. Ct. App. 2005) (father's requested reduction in support denied; he paid $1,600 a month in rent, $350 for golf, and contributed $300 a month to charity).

[515] McEwen v. McEwen, 631 So. 2d 821, 823 (Miss. 1994) (reversing chancellor's denial of modification; error to leave support at one-half of income after 40% drop in pay; chancellor did order modification from all of medical to one-half of medical); *see also* McEachern v. McEachern, 605 So. 2d 809 (Miss. 1998) (reduction in income warranted reduction in child support to $750 where payor had $800 after basic expenses and child support was $1,680).

[516] Tedford v. Dempsey, 437 So. 2d 410, 421 (Miss. 1983).

[517] Shipley v. Ferguson, 638 So. 2d 1295, 1298 (Miss. 1994) (fact that mother's income increased by $50 per month also not reason to alter support).

[518] Tedford v. Dempsey, 437 So. 2d 410, 421 (Miss. 1983).

[519] Crist v. Lawrence, 738 So. 2d 267 (Miss. Ct. App. 1999).

[520] Crist v. Lawrence, 738 So. 2d 267, 269 (Miss. Ct. App. 1999).

[521] Ligon v. Ligon, 743 So. 2d 404, 408 (Miss. Ct. App. 1999).

[522] Morris v. Morris, 8 So. 3d 917, 919 (Miss. Ct. App. 2009).

[523] Most of the cases discussing the issue are suits to enforce arrearages; however, the principles should be equally applicable to modification actions. *See* Evans v. Evans, 994 So. 2d 765, 769-70 (Miss. 2008) (father's petition to modify

§ 13.11[6][d]   MISSISSIPPI FAMILY LAW

order for three children when one child moved in with the payor; the child was largely self-supporting and did not impose a significant financial burden on the payor.[524] A chancellor properly modified an $800 a month award for two children to $600 when the older child was emancipated. The chancellor was justified in allocating more than half to the remaining minor child, who required special care.[525]

Mississippi appellate courts have held that global orders should not be reduced on a pro rata basis. For example, the supreme court held that a chancellor erred in reducing arrearages by one-half when one of two children was emancipated; the amount payable for the remaining child or children should be based upon the statutory guidelines.[526] Similarly, the court of appeals held that an order for two children should have been reduced to an amount equaling 14% of the payor's net income when the oldest was emancipated.[527]

[d] Based on a change in custody. A noncustodial parent is entitled to modification of support when custody changes. A father paying $900 per child was entitled to modification when custody of his oldest daughter was transferred to him.[528] However, the fact that a child lived 50% of the time with a father who had joint physical custody was not a reason to modify child support – the decree anticipated shared custody, therefore the arrangement was foreseeable.[529]

Under some circumstances, chancellors may reduce support to reflect a substantial increase in visitation or custodial time by a child support payor.[530] However, a chancellor properly refused to modify child support for a payor whose visitation was increased to alternating weeks – he failed to produce any evidence related to the factors for support modification.[531]

A noncustodial parent is also entitled to a credit on arrearages accrued while there has been a change in custody. In a custodial mother's suit for arrearages, a father was entitled to credit for amounts he actually expended while his two daughters lived with him.[532] And a court erred in awarding a custodial mother arrearages for months when a child lived with his father – the award would unjustly enrich the mother.[533]

---

based on one child's emancipation properly denied; no automatic modification for global order); Dep't of Human Servs. v. Fillingane, 761 So. 2d 869, 872-73 (Miss. 2000) (credit upheld); Wiles v. Williams, 845 So. 2d 709, 712 (Miss. Ct. App. 2003) (chancellor's refusal to allow credit upheld); Caldwell v. Caldwell, 823 So. 2d 1216, 1221 (Miss. Ct. App. 2002) (chancellor's credit for post-arrearage payments upheld); Brown v. Brown, 822 So. 2d 1119, 1124 (Miss. Ct. App. 2002) (refusal to allow credit upheld); Gray v. Pearson, 797 So. 2d 387, 392 (Miss. Ct App. 2001) (credit upheld).

[524] Mark v. Nash, 751 So. 2d 1078 (Miss. Ct. App. 1999).

[525] Gray v. Pearson, 797 So. 2d 387 (Miss. Ct. App. 2001).

[526] *See* Dep't of Human Servs. v. Fillingane, 761 So. 2d 869, 873 (Miss. 2000) (remanded for application of guidelines).

[527] Houck v. Houck, 812 So. 2d 1139, 1143 (Miss. Ct. App. 2002).

[528] Frazier v. Burnett, 767 So. 2d 263, 267-68 (Miss. Ct. App. 2000) (support for two children remaining with mother increased to $1,000); *see also* Reid v. Reid, 998 So. 2d 1032, 1040 (Miss. Ct. App. 2008) (support modified when one of four children came to live with father).

[529] Evans v. Evans, 994 So. 2d 765, 771 (Miss. 2008).

[530] See *supra* § 13.05[3].

[531] Allen v. Allen, 953 So. 2d 279, 282 (Miss. Ct. App. 2007).

[532] Varner v. Varner. 588 So. 2d 428, 434-35 (Miss. 1991).

[533] *See* Alexander v. Alexander, 494 So. 2d 365, 368 (Miss. 1986) (even though no modification petition filed for twenty months). *But see* Formigoni v. Formigoni, 733 So. 2d 868, 870 (Miss. Ct. App. 1999) (appears to award arrearages for two children, even though one child had been living with payor).

CHILD SUPPORT

§ 13.11[7]

[7] Modification related to college expenses. A child's decision to attend college may be a material change in circumstances[534] justifying modification of support in two respects. An existing support order may be modified to require a parent to provide college support. And the basic support obligation may be reduced or suspended during the time a child is in college.

[a] Award of college expenses. The court of appeals rejected a father's argument that a child's attendance at college was an event that was anticipated at the time of divorce and may not be the basis for modification.[535] A petitioner should present evidence of a material change, such as the child's aptitude for college and his or her plans, the anticipated expenses, and the payor's ability to pay college expenses. A court properly modified a child support award to require a father to pay one-half of college costs for his son, who showed aptitude for college by successfully completing one semester.[536] In contrast, the supreme court reversed a chancellor's modification requiring a father to pay 75% of a fifteen-year-old son's college expenses. No proof was presented of his plans to attend college, the associated expenses, or the father's ability to pay.[537] An award of college expenses may be affirmed without proof of exact costs. However, if specific figures are not available, the order should list the expenses to be paid and state the payor's obligation in terms of a percentage of the expenses, rather than ordering a dollar figure for support.[538]

A court may not order payment of college expenses incurred before the filing of a modification petition. However, a chancellor did not err in awarding full support for the fall semester based on a petition filed in September – most of the expenses were incurred after the petition was filed.[539]

[b] Modification of basic support. Courts have broad discretion to grant or deny a payor's request to reduce basic support during a child's college years. A court properly suspended basic child support payments during the academic year.[540] Similarly, a court did not err in ordering a father with an excellent record of providing for his children to pay college and medical expenses only; no regular monthly child support was required.[541]

---

[534] Lawrence v. Lawrence, 574 So. 2d 1376 (Miss. 1991); *see* Webster v. Webster, 17 So. 3d 602, 606-07 (Miss. Ct. App. 2009) (modifying child support to require college support for son who had successfully completed one semester); Wallace v. Wallace, 965 So. 2d 737, 742-43 (Miss. Ct. App. 2007) (rejecting argument that college is a "foreseeable" expense and therefore not proper subject for modification).

[535] Wallace v. Wallace, 965 So. 2d 737, 745 (Miss. Ct. App. 2007).

[536] Webster v. Webster, 17 So. 3d 602, 606-08 (Miss. Ct. App. 2009).

[537] Evans v. Evans, 994 So. 2d 765, 772 (Miss. 2008).

[538] College expenses exceeding the statutory percentage may be a justifiable deviation, if supported by findings. Kirkland v. McGraw, 806 So. 2d 1180 (Miss. Ct. App. 2002).

[539] Crayton v. Burley, 952 So. 2d 957, 962 (Miss. Ct. App. 2006).

[540] Fancher v. Pell, 831 So. 2d 1137, 1142 (Miss. 2002); *see also* Traxler v. Traxler, 730 So. 2d 1098, 1103 (Miss. 1998) (noncustodial parent ordered to pay 61% of college expenses plus basic support during months when child lived with mother); Kirkland v. McGraw, 806 So. 2d 1180, 1183 (Miss. Ct. App. 2002) (recognizing case law allowing reduction of basic support while child in college).

[541] *See* Lazarus v. Lazarus, 841 So. 2d 181 (Miss. Ct. App. 2003). *But see* Wallace v. Wallace, 965 So. 2d 737, 744 (Miss. Ct. App. 2007) (modifying award to require payment of basic support, college expenses, automobile costs, and health insurance); Dix v. Dix, 941 So. 2d 913, 918 (Miss. Ct. App. 2006) (denying request for reduction in basic support

§ 13.11[8]   MISSISSIPPI FAMILY LAW

Parents whose divorce settlement agreement provides for college support may also include a provision reducing basic support during college years. An agreement that basic support would be suspended while the children lived at college and reduced if they lived with the mother during college was enforceable.[542] However, if college support was included in the divorce agreement, the payor may not later seek reduction of basic support. A father who agreed at divorce to provide $2,800 a month for four children, plus pay college expenses, was denied modification of the basic award while his son was in college. No material change in circumstances had occurred to justify altering the agreement.[543]

[8] Amount of modified award. A court's determination of the proper amount of modified support is governed by the child support guidelines.[544] In a number of cases, courts have ordered modified support at the level of the guidelines.[545] In other modification cases, courts have deviated from the guidelines. For example, deviation above the guidelines was proper based on evidence of the increased expenses of older children.[546] However, an award of 23% of a payor's income for one child was not warranted despite evidence of the child's increased needs.[547] Deviation below the guidelines was affirmed when a child's needs were met in part by state and federal payments.[548] Many awards that appear to deviate from the guidelines are not true deviations, but the result of a court's imputation of income to a payor who concealed[549] or voluntarily reduced income.[550]

---

during college; son returned home frequently and mother provided $400 a month in support).

[542] Riddick v. Riddick, 906 So. 2d 813 (Miss. Ct. App. 2004).

[543] Dix v. Dix, 941 So. 2d 913, 918 (Miss. Ct. App. 2006).

[544] *See supra* § 13.11[1][c].

[545] Houck v. Ousterhout, 861 So. 2d 1000 (Miss. 2003) (modification proper when one child was emancipated, but should have been modified to 14% of current income rather than reduced by half); Hopson v. Hopson, 851 So. 2d 397, 400 (Miss. Ct. App. 2003) (properly modified to 14% of current income); Lacey v. Lacey, 822 So. 2d 1132, 1140 (Miss. Ct. App. 2002) (not error to require mother, now employed, to pay 20% of adjusted gross income; employment was a material change in circumstances); Bustin v. Bustin, 806 So. 2d 1136, 1138 (Miss. Ct. App. 2001) (support modified to 20% of adjusted gross income included housing allowance provided by church); Stroud v. Stroud, 758 So. 2d 502, 503-04 (Miss. Ct. App. 2000) (modifying support to 14% of income as agreed in escalation clause); Shepherd v. Shepherd, 769 So. 2d 242, 246 (Miss. Ct. App. 2000) (modified up to 20% of adjusted gross income).

[546] *See* Havens v. Broocks, 728 So. 2d 580, 583 (Miss. Ct. App. 1998) (also noting impact of inflation on award over ten years old)*; see also* Wright v. Stanley, 700 So. 2d 274, 282-83 (Miss. 1997) (23% of payor's income for three children supported by chancellor's finding of children's increased expenses; adjusted gross income of $67,500).

[547] Kilgore v. Fuller, 741 So. 2d 351, 358 (Miss. Ct. App. 1999) (reversing award of 23% of adjusted gross income of $2,000 for one child; chancellor did not support with findings; justifications would need to be "extraordinary" for such a deviation).

[548] Hammett v. Woods, 602 So. 2d 825, 828 (Miss. 1992) (chancellor not justified in raising support based on payor's increased income; even increase to statutory guidelines would have been error where proof showed child's monthly needs of $261 were adequately met by provision of services to deaf).

[549] *See* Dunn v. Dunn, 695 So. 2d 1152, 1156 (Miss. 1997) (affirming chancellor's refusal to modify downward to statutory guidelines, based on skepticism about father's true earnings and reason for reduction in business; child support left at $520 from claimed adjusted gross income of $1,500 per month); Poole v. Poole, 701 So. 2d 813, 818 (Miss. 1997) (noted no obvious change in father's lifestyle despite claimed reduction in income); McEachern v. McEachern, 605 So. 2d 809, 813-14 (Miss. 1992) (modification reducing support, but above guidelines not error where court questioned actual income – $750 a month for five children from alleged $1,500 adjusted gross income); Stroud v. Stroud, 758 So. 2d 502, 503 (Miss. Ct. App. 2000) (payor reduced income in dental practice by 60% by paying wife/manager equal salary); Watkins v. Watkins, 748 So. 2d 808, 811-12 (Miss. Ct. App. 1999) (payor shifted income to his wife and business); Turner v. Turner, 744 So. 2d 332, 336 (Miss. Ct. App. 1999) (income transferred to new wife).

[550] Ballard v. Ballard, 843 So. 2d 76, 79 (Miss. Ct. App. 2003) (father voluntarily left employment; no evidence to

472

CHILD SUPPORT   § 13.11[9]

[9] Effective date of modification. The effective date of a child support modification depends upon whether the modification increases or decreases the award. A
decrease in child support must be made prospectively. The Mississippi Supreme Court
reversed a chancellor's order making a reduction retroactive to the date the petition was
filed. The court held that child support payments that become due while a petition for
modification is pending are vested and cannot be forgiven or modified.[551] When a judgment is appealed and remanded, any resulting modification may be retroactive only to
the date of the judgment.[552]

With regard to an increase in child support, the supreme court has held that modification retroactive to the date of filing is preferable, but that courts have discretion to
order modification prospectively.[553] Modification cannot be made retroactive to a date
prior to the filing. The court of appeals reversed an order for college support for the
year prior to filing.[554] However, a recent amendment to the child support statutes provides that an upward modification "may be ordered back to the date of the event justifying the upward modification."[555] No cases were found interpreting this provision.

§ 13.12 ABATEMENT OF SUPPORT

The emancipation statute provides that child support may be suspended during a
period in which an otherwise unemancipated child is incarcerated.[556] And in at least
one case, the court of appeals affirmed a chancellor's order suspending, but not terminating, support. The trial court suspended a father's obligation to pay child support
for his eighteen-year-old son who was working and no longer attending school. The
chancellor found that he was not emancipated, suspended support while the boy was
out of school, and reserved jurisdiction to reconsider the issue if he became enrolled
in school.[557]

---

support his claim that after accident employer offered him reduced compensation; also, lifestyle did not seem to alter).

[551] Thurman v. Thurman, 559 So. 2d 1014 (Miss. 1990) (payments are vested and unmodifiable); Cumberland v.
Cumberland, 564 So. 2d 839, 847 (Miss. 1990); Howard v. Howard, 968 So. 2d 961, 976 (Miss. Ct. App. 2007); *see also*
MISS. CODE ANN. § 43-19-34(4) (2004).

[552] Howard v. Howard, 968 So. 2d 961, 976 (Miss. Ct. App. 2007).

[553] Lawrence v. Lawrence, 574 So. 2d 1376, 1384 (Miss. 1991); *see* Weeks v. Weeks, 29 So. 3d 80, 89 (Miss. Ct.
App. 2009) (within chancellor's discretion to deny retroactive increase in support); Walton v. Snyder, 984 So. 2d 343
(Miss. Ct. App. 2007); Frazier v. Burnett, 767 So. 2d 263, 268 (Miss. Ct. App. 2000) (error to make support increase to
custodial mother of two of three girls prospective, where reduction to father for support for oldest child, now living with
him, was retroactive).

[554] Kirkland v. McGraw, 806 So. 2d 1180 (Miss. Ct. App. 2002) (reversing an order for college support for the year
predating the petition). *But cf.* Crayton v. Burley, 952 So. 2d 957, 962 (Miss. Ct. App. 2006) (chancellor did not err in
awarding support for the fall semester; most of the expenses were incurred after the petition was filed in September).

[555] MISS. CODE ANN. § 43-19-34(4) (2004). *But cf.* Walton v. Snyder, 984 So. 2d 343 (Miss. Ct. App. 2007) (court
erred in ordering support retroactive to date of divorce decree to remedy father's underreporting of income at divorce).

[556] MISS. CODE ANN. § 93-11-65(8) (Supp. 2010).

[557] Hills v. Hills, 986 So. 2d 354, 355 (Miss. Ct. App. 2008) (three judges dissenting); *see also* MISS. CODE ANN. §
93-11-65 (Supp. 2010) (allowing emancipation when eighteen-year-old stops attending school).

§ 13.13 MISSISSIPPI FAMILY LAW

§ 13.13 EFFECT OF BANKRUPTCY

Child support obligations are not dischargeable in bankruptcy. Furthermore, the automatic stay does not apply to actions to establish or modify an order of child support. In Chapter 7 bankruptcy, the debtor's post-petition income is not part of the bankruptcy estate; thus, arrearages may be collected against future income. In Chapter 13 proceedings, claims for child support are treated as priority claims behind claims of administration but before tax obligations.[558]

---

[558] *See infra* Chapter XXI for a detailed discussion of bankruptcy rules.

XIV
ENFORCEMENT OF DECREES

Chancery courts retain continuing jurisdiction to enforce divorce, child support, and custody decrees. Most frequently, post-judgment petitions are filed to recover unpaid alimony or child support. But courts are also petitioned to enforce custody and visitation orders and to require compliance with property division orders. In an enforcement action, a petitioner typically seeks to establish the defendant's default and to obtain a judgment for unpaid support. In addition, the petitioner usually requests that the court prompt compliance through one or more coercive measures. Contempt, the tool historically used to force compliance with court orders, is now part of an arsenal of remedies for enforcing family support. With the intervention of Congress in child support collection, support recipients may now collect arrearages through wage-withholding orders that exceed usual garnishment limits and by seizing various accounts, tax refunds, and benefits. Payors in arrears may be subject to license revocation, negative credit reports, and in some cases, criminal prosecution. Some of the new tools for support enforcement are available only through the Department of Human Services, while others may be used by any petitioner seeking to enforce support.

§ 14.01 OVERVIEW

[1] Nature of proceeding. A court with jurisdiction to issue an original order of divorce, custody, or support retains continuing jurisdiction over the parties. A petition to enforce an order does not initiate a new action; it is a continuation of the earlier case. Special notice is required to alert the defendant of the renewed litigation, but no independent basis for personal jurisdiction is required.[1] Enforcement proceedings are initiated by petition pursuant to Rule 81 of the Mississippi Rules of Civil Procedure.[2] A full discussion of Rule 81 procedure is included in Chapter XIX.

[2] Interstate enforcement actions. Enforcement of family support orders across state lines is governed by the Uniform Interstate Family Support Act. The Act governs procedures for child support orders, spousal support orders, and paternity orders. To make interstate proceedings more efficient, the Act creates a "two-state" proceeding – an action to enforce an order may be initiated in a payee's home state for prosecution in another state. A full discussion of the Uniform Interstate Family Act is included in Chapter XVIII.[3] Interstate enforcement of custody orders is governed by the Uniform Child Custody Jurisdiction and Enforcement Act, also discussed in Chapter XVIII.[4]

[3] Role of the Department of Human Services. The Department of Human

---

[1] *See* Reichert v. Reichert, 807 So. 2d 1282, 1287 (Miss. Ct. App. 2002) (Rule 81 requires special notice, but personal jurisdiction is not lost).

[2] MISS. R. CIV. P. 81(d).

[3] *See* discussion *infra* § 18.08.

[4] *See* discussion *infra* § 18.09.

475

§ 14.02   MISSISSIPPI FAMILY LAW

Services plays a vital role in actions to enforce support orders, particularly in interstate actions. DHS may assist any person, regardless of receipt of public benefits, in an action to enforce support orders.[5] In addition, DHS is authorized to use certain collection measures not available to private individuals, such as pre-hearing seizure of bank accounts and tax refunds. DHS is also equipped with tools for locating absent support payors.[6]

§ 14.02 ESTABLISHING DEFAULT: NONPAYMENT OF SUPPORT

In an action to recover past-due alimony or child support, a petitioner must establish the amount that is due and owing and reduce that amount to judgment. In some cases, payors may receive credit against arrearages for direct support or for third-party payments.

[1] Proof of arrearage. Courts frequently state that past-due support payments become a final judgment on the date set for payment.[7] However, a creditor spouse typically files a Rule 81 petition to reduce the arrearage to a liquidated sum for enforcement. Payment records need not be complete for a court to find that some amount is in arrears. For example, the supreme court affirmed a judgment for arrearages based primarily on a custodial parent's testimony of her memory of ten years of payments.[8] In another case, the court of appeals upheld an award even though the payor was able to demonstrate at trial that the payee's records contained a number of errors.[9]

For many years, the procedure described above was the only method for obtaining a judgment for arrearages.[10] However, the applicable statute was amended in 1997 to provide that whenever child support is more than thirty days delinquent, "a judgment by operation of law shall arise against the obligor . . . [with] the same effect and . . . fully enforceable as any other judgment entered in this state."[11] This amendment allows the Department of Human Services or a private attorney to enroll the automatic judgment by filing an abstract of the child support order and sworn documentation of the amount of the delinquency.[12] No cases were found discussing enforcement under this statute.

[2] Interest on arrearages. A judgment for arrearages must include interest on overdue payments. It is error as a matter of law for a court to omit an award of interest

---

[5] *See* MISS. CODE ANN. § 43-19-31(c) (2004).

[6] *See infra* § 14.08[4].

[7] Brand v. Brand, 482 So. 2d 236, 237 (Miss. 1986); Cunliffe v. Swartzfager, 437 So. 2d 43, 45-46 (Miss. 1983); Howard v. Howard, 191 So. 2d 528, 531 (Miss. 1966); Dorr v. Dorr, 797 So. 2d 1008, 1015 (Miss. Ct. App. 2001).

[8] Andrews v. Williams, 723 So. 2d 1175, 1178 (Miss. Ct. App. 1998).

[9] Glass v. Glass, 726 So. 2d 1281, 1285 (Miss. Ct. App. 1998) (no manifest error, even though evidence was somewhat vague and indefinite).

[10] *See* MISS. CODE ANN. § 93-11-71 (Supp. 2010).

[11] MISS. CODE ANN. § 93-11-71(1) (Supp. 2010).

[12] MISS. CODE ANN. § 93-11-71(3) (Supp. 2010) (enrollment is not necessary for seizure of certain funds including government payments, unemployment, workers' compensation, lottery and gaming winnings, public and private retirement funds, financial institution deposits, and recovery in civil suits).

ENFORCEMENT OF DECREES

§ 14.02[3]

on a judgment for past-due support:[13] "When a supporting spouse fails timely to make child support payments, he uses the child's money…[d]elay in payment harms the child in a way theoretically irreparable."[14]

Courts have discretion to determine a fair interest rate under the circumstances.[15] Orders setting interest at the legal rate of 8% are usually affirmed.[16] The supreme court affirmed an 8% rate even at a time of low interest rates, in part because the arrearages covered years in which rates were higher.[17] In another case, however, the court suggested that a chancellor reconsider an 8% rate in light of current low rates.[18] And the court of appeals affirmed a 3% interest rate at a time when interest rates were low.[19]

Interest runs from the time each payment was due, rather than from the entry of judgment for arrearages.[20] Payments made on a judgment for arrearages are applied first to aggregate interest, then to the principal amount of the oldest outstanding support obligation.[21]

[3] Temporary support arrearages. The obligation to pay past-due temporary support survives a final judgment, even though the temporary support is replaced by a permanent support order. A payor was properly held in contempt for failure to make temporary child support, alimony, and mortgage payments totaling $2,900.[22]

[4] Credit against amount due. In actions to enforce arrearages, a payor may be credited for some payments made directly to a child or payee.

[a] Credit against property division arrearage. In a former wife's action to recover outstanding property division payments, her ex-husband was credited with over $50,000 in voluntary payments of her expenses.[23]

[b] Credit against alimony arrearages. An alimony payor's arrearages were reduced to reflect voluntary payments to his wife in the form of mortgage, utility, automobile, and insurance payments.[24] Alimony payors are also entitled to credit for

---

[13] Ladner v. Logan, 857 So. 2d 764, 770-71 (Miss. 2003) (chancellor erred in failing to award interest on child support arrearages); Brown v. Gillespie, 465 So. 2d 1046, 1049 (Miss. 1985) (court erred in failing to order interest at legal rate); Walters v. Walters, 383 So. 2d 827, 829 (Miss. 1980); Dorr v. Dorr, 797 So. 2d 1008, 1015 (Miss. Ct. App. 2001).

[14] Brand v. Brand, 482 So. 2d 236, 238 (Miss. 1986); see Cunliffe v. Swartzfager, 437 So. 2d 43, 45-46 (Miss. 1983); Howard v. Howard, 191 So. 2d 528, 531 (Miss. 1966); Rubisoff v. Rubisoff, 133 So. 2d 534, 537 (Miss. 1961) (alimony payments); Schaffer v. Schaffer, 46 So. 2d 443, 444 (Miss. 1950).

[15] Brawdy v. Howell, 841 So. 2d 1175, 1180 (Miss. Ct. App. 2003) (citing MISS. CODE ANN. § 75-17-7 (2009)).

[16] Brand v. Brand, 482 So. 2d 236 (Miss. 1986); see also Adams v. Adams, 591 So. 2d 431 (Miss. 1991); Beasnett v. Arledge, 934 So. 2d 345, 350 (Miss. Ct. App. 2006).

[17] Houck v. Ousterhout, 861 So. 2d 1000, 1003 (Miss. 2003).

[18] Watson v. Watson, 882 So. 2d 95, 111 (Miss. 2004) (interest on property division payments).

[19] Brawdy v. Howell, 841 So. 2d 1175, 1180 (Miss. Ct. App. 2003).

[20] Rubisoff v. Rubisoff, 133 So. 2d 534, 537 (Miss. 1961); Schaffer v. Schaffer, 46 So. 2d 443, 444 (Miss. 1950).

[21] Brand v. Brand, 482 So. 2d 236, 238 (Miss. 1986) (child support payments).

[22] Langdon v. Langdon, 854 So. 2d 485, 496 (Miss. Ct. App. 2003); see also Henderson v. Henderson, 952 So. 2d 273, 280 (Miss. Ct. App. 2006) (payor who failed to pay temporary alimony for seven months properly held in contempt); Baier v. Baier, 897 So. 2d 202, 205 (Miss. Ct. App. 2005) (temporary arrearages may not be forgiven).

[23] Weathersby v. Weathersby, 693 So. 2d 1348, 1353 (Miss. 1997) (down payment on condominium, car payments, utilities, taxes, and bank overdrafts).

[24] McHann v. McHann, 383 So. 2d 823, 825 (Miss. 1980); see also Franklin v. Franklin, 864 So. 2d 970, 978 (Miss.

§ 14.02[4][c]   MISSISSIPPI FAMILY LAW

derivative Social Security payments received by a payee. A court properly credited a former husband with $360 per month to reflect his ex-wife's receipt of benefits based on his employment.[25] But no credit is due for benefits received by an alimony payee based on his or her own employment.[26]

[c] Credit against child support. A child support payor in arrears may receive credit for direct support of a child in his or her custody, for payments made after a child's emancipation, for some third-party payments, and for Social Security benefits based on his or her employment. As a general rule, no credit is allowed for a noncustodial parent's voluntary payment of expenses not ordinarily covered by basic support.

[i] Based on change in custody. Noncustodial parents have been credited with support of children in their custody pursuant to an out-of-court agreement. In a custodial mother's suit for arrearages, a father was entitled to credit for amounts he actually expended while his two daughters lived with him.[27] And a court erred in awarding a custodial mother arrearages for months when a child lived with his father – the award unjustly enriched the mother, who received support for the entire time the child lived with her.[28] Similarly, a father was properly awarded credit against arrearages for a six-month period in which the mother and child both lived with him.[29] However, a father was not entitled to credit based on his oldest child's residence with him; the amount of support ordered was within the guidelines for the remaining two children.[30] In at least one case, a noncustodial father was credited with direct expenditures for a child who spent substantially more time with him than provided in the court's visitation order.[31]

In a 2009 case, the supreme court appeared to establish a new prerequisite to obtaining credit. The court reversed a chancellor's decision crediting a noncustodial mother $14,000 for two years during which a child allegedly lived with her. The court stated that the inquiry does not end with whether the child lived with the mother – she must also prove that she made actual payments for the girl's benefit that she would not otherwise have made.[32]

Ct. App. 2003) (payor should be credited with payments to vendors on ex-wife's behalf).

[25] Spalding v. Spalding, 691 So. 2d 435, 439 (Miss. 1997) (chancellor increased alimony from $250 to $450 per month with a monthly offset of $360); *see also* Brabham v. Brabham, 950 So. 2d 1098, 1103 (Miss. Ct. App. 2007) (husband credited with voluntary payments toward his wife's automobile insurance and medication and with payment of $700 drawn by wife on credit line).

[26] *See* Seale v. Seale, 863 So. 2d 996, 998-99 (Miss. Ct. App. 2004).

[27] Varner v. Varner, 588 So. 2d 428, 434-35 (Miss. 1991).

[28] *See* Alexander v. Alexander, 494 So. 2d 365, 368 (Miss. 1986) (even though no modification petition filed for twenty months). *But see* Formigoni v. Formigoni, 733 So. 2d 868, 870 (Miss. Ct. App. 1999) (appears to award arrearages for two children, even though one child had been living with payor). *But cf.* Dep't of Human Servs. v. Blount, 913 So. 2d 326, 329 (Miss. Ct. App. 2005) (father who failed to petition for modification could not recover child support collected by DHS during years in which children were actually living with him).

[29] Holliday v. Stockman, 969 So. 2d 136, 138-39 (Miss. Ct. App. 2007).

[30] Bosarge v. Bosarge, 879 So. 2d 515 (Miss. Ct. App. 2004) (also finding that payor in arrears did not come to court with clean hands).

[31] Laird v. Blackburn, 788 So. 2d 844 (Miss. Ct. App. 2001); *see also* Crow v. Crow, 622 So. 2d 1226 (Miss. 1993) (noncustodial father given some credit for direct payments to children).

[32] Smith v. Smith, 20 So. 3d 670, 673-74, 676-77 (Miss. 2009).

ENFORCEMENT OF DECREES   § 14.02[4][c][ii]

[ii] For direct expenditures. A noncustodial parent is not entitled to credit for voluntary payments directly to children unless the payment is for items ordinarily covered by basic child support. For example, no credit was allowed to a father who gave his sons cash; the funds were not available to the custodial mother for basic expenses such as food and clothing.[33] Similarly, a noncustodial father was properly denied a credit for purchasing automobiles for his children. The court noted that this was the sort of expenditure that a father should make in addition to court-ordered support, not as a substitute for basic support.[34] A father was also not entitled to credit for private school tuition when the payment was a voluntary undertaking on his part. To allow a noncustodial parent credit for voluntary expenditures would vary the support order and usurp the custodial parent's decision-making rights.[35] However, a father who reduced support for two children when the oldest entered college was properly credited with payments made directly to, or on behalf of the daughter attending college.[36]

Proof of direct support must be clear and convincing. A father's testimony regarding direct support was not sufficient to allow a credit against arrearages in the absence of cancelled checks or other corroborating evidence.[37] A court has discretion to deny credit for direct support. A chancellor did not err in refusing credit against arrearages to a father who provided a rent-free trailer for two of his three children for an unspecified time.[38]

A chancellor properly credited an unmarried father with payments made under a voluntary agreement with the mother prior to the paternity action. The chancellor also properly limited the credit to payments made during the year prior to the filing of the petition, since that was the period for which the order was entered.[39]

[5] Credit for payments after emancipation. A payor may receive credit for support payments made after a child's emancipation. Whether credit is allowed depends in part on whether the support order specifies an amount per child or is undivided.

[a] Per-child order. If a support order specifies a certain amount payable per child, support for each child automatically terminates upon emancipation. A chancellor properly ordered a custodial mother to reimburse a payor for one-third of the payments made after one child was emancipated; the order provided for support of $100 a month

---

[33] Wesson v. Wesson, 818 So. 2d 1272, 1280-81 (Miss. Ct. App. 2002); *cf.* Edwards v. Edwards-Barker, 875 So. 2d 1126, 1129 (Miss. Ct. App. 2004) (payor not entitled to credit against arrearages for amounts allegedly paid in cash, for which he produced no documentary evidence).

[34] Wiles v. Williams, 845 So. 2d 709, 712 (Miss. Ct. App. 2003). *But cf.* Farrior v. Kittrell, 12 So. 3d 20, 23-24 (Miss. Ct. App. 2009) (child support arrearages reduced by $4,400, the value of a vehicle provided to the mother).

[35] Cook v. Whiddon, 866 So. 2d 494, 500-01 (Miss. Ct. App. 2004); *see also* White v. Dep't of Human Servs., 39 So. 3d 986, 990-91 (Miss. Ct. App. 2010) (father properly denied credit for expenditures, including sports equipment, school pictures, and activity fees); *cf.* Farrior v. Kittrell, 12 So. 3d 20, 23 (Miss. Ct. App. 2009) (father should not have been credited against child support with voluntary payments of private school tuition pursuant to an agreement with the mother).

[36] Evans v. Evans, 994 So. 2d 765, 772-73 (Miss. 2008).

[37] Baier v. Baier, 897 So. 2d 202, 204-05 (Miss. Ct. App. 2005); *see* Smith v. Smith, 20 So. 3d 670, 676-77 (Miss. 2009) (chancellor should not have credited mother's arrearages without documentary proof of payments; father testified that he never received the payments).

[38] Strack v. Sticklin, 959 So. 2d 1, 5 (Miss. Ct. App. 2006).

[39] Kelley v. Day, 965 So. 2d 749, 754 (Miss. Ct. App. 2007).

§ 14.02[5][b]   **MISSISSIPPI FAMILY LAW**

for each of three children.[40] Emancipation does not alter a payor's obligation for support payments due prior to emancipation. A payor in arrears at the time of a child's emancipation must continue making payments as ordered until all arrearages are satisfied.[41]

   [b] Undivided order. When support is ordered as a single amount for all children, a chancellor has discretion to allow or refuse credit for payments made after one child's emancipation.[42] If credit is allowed, the payment should not be reduced on a pro rata basis. A chancellor erred in reducing arrearages by one-half when one of two children was emancipated. Instead, the amount due should be calculated under the statutory guidelines for the remaining child or children.[43] Similarly, an order for two children should have been reduced to an amount equaling 14% of the payor's net income at the time the oldest was emancipated.[44] And when the remaining minor child required special care, a court properly reduced an undivided order from $800 to $600 upon the older child's emancipation.[45]

   [6] Credit for third-party payments. Under some circumstances, a child support payor may be credited with payments made by a third party. In one case, a father was credited for sums provided by his parents to his son.[46] On the other hand, a chancellor erred in crediting a father with payments made by a grandfather from an account in the joint names of the child and grandfather. The funds already belonged to the child and could not be used to reduce the father's support obligation.[47]

   [7] Credit for Social Security benefits. In 2008, the court of appeals held that a delinquent payor is not entitled to an offset against arrearages for lump sum Social Security disability benefits. The payor, who was disabled at the time of the divorce, failed to make court-ordered child support payments. Four years later, his children received lump sum payments representing monthly disability benefits from the arrearage period. The court of appeals held that the father was entitled to a prospective reduction in his obligation based on future monthly payments, but that his arrearages could not

---

   [40] Ligon v. Ligon, 743 So. 2d 404, 408 (Miss. Ct. App. 1999).

   [41] MISS. CODE ANN. § 93-11-65(9) (Supp. 2010).

   [42] *See* Burt v. Burt, 841 So. 2d 108, 111 (Miss. 2001) (denying credit to father because daughter was not emancipated); Dep't of Human Servs. v. Fillingane, 761 So. 2d 869, 872-73 (Miss. 2000) (credit upheld); Strack v. Sticklin, 959 So. 2d 1, 6 (Miss. Ct. App. 2006) (within court's discretion whether to recognize emancipation retroactively; father should have brought emancipation to court's attention); Wiles v. Williams, 845 So. 2d 709, 712 (Miss. Ct. App. 2003) (chancellor's refusal to allow credit upheld); Houck v. Houck, 812 So. 2d 1139, 1143 (Miss. Ct. App. 2002) (allowing credit when oldest children emancipated); Caldwell v. Caldwell, 823 So. 2d 1216, 1221 (Miss. Ct. App. 2002) (chancellor's credit for post-arrearage payments upheld); Brown v. Brown, 822 So. 2d 1119, 1124 (Miss. Ct. App. 2002) (refusal to allow credit upheld); Gray v. Pearson, 797 So. 2d 387, 392 (Miss. Ct. App. 2001) (credit upheld).

   [43] *See* Dep't of Human Servs. v. Fillingane, 761 So. 2d 869, 873 (Miss. 2000) (remanded for application of guidelines).

   [44] Houck v. Houck, 812 So. 2d 1139, 1143 (Miss. Ct. App. 2002); *see also* Andres v. Andres, 22 So. 3d 314, 319-20 (Miss. Ct. App. 2009) (father properly credited with payments made after one of two children was emancipated; support amount should have been 14% of adjusted gross income); Bryant v. Bryant, 924 So. 2d 627, 631-32 (Miss. Ct. App. 2006) (award for remaining child based on 14% of payor's income at time of hearing).

   [45] Gray v. Pearson, 797 So. 2d 387, 392 (Miss. Ct. App. 2001).

   [46] Johnston v. Parham, 758 So. 2d 443, 446 (Miss. Ct. App. 2000).

   [47] Mizell v. Mizell, 708 So. 2d 55, 60 (Miss. 1998).

ENFORCEMENT OF DECREES § 14.02[8]

be reduced to reflect the lump sum payments.[48] In 2011, however, the Mississippi legislature amended the child support statutes to provide that a disabled payor is entitled to an offset when a child receives a lump sum disability payment representing amounts that date back to the date of the disability.[49]

As a general rule, a payor is not entitled to prospective credit for payments that a child receives from Social Security because of the child's own disability.[50]

[8] Credit for custodial parent's debt to payor. A noncustodial parent may not offset child support payments by amounts owed to him by the custodial parent. A merchant father should not have reduced child support by the amount of the custodial mother's outstanding account at his store. Child support payments are for the benefit of the child, not the custodial parent, and can only be offset by funds used for the child.[51]

§ 14.03 ESTABLISHING NONCOMPLIANCE WITH OTHER PROVISIONS

Although the majority of enforcement actions involve nonpayment of support, parties may also seek enforcement of property division, custody, visitation, or other orders.

[1] Property division. Parties may be required to take certain post-divorce actions to accomplish property division, such as transferring physical possession of an item or executing a deed to real property. In addition, some aspects of division involve ongoing or deferred payments. A party's failure to comply with property division orders may be enforced through judgment and contempt. An ex-husband who failed to maintain a life insurance policy as part of property division was properly held in contempt.[52] Similarly, an equitable lien was properly imposed to secure payment of property division installments in default.[53] And a husband who failed to make property division payments, deliver his wife's personal property, and put the marital home on the market was properly held in contempt.[54]

[2] Child custody and visitation. A petition for contempt is the proper vehicle for requiring compliance with custody and visitation orders.

[a] Interference with visitation. Custodial parents may be held in contempt for willful failure to comply with court-ordered visitation. A chancellor properly held a

---

[48] Chapman v. Ward, 3 So. 3d 790, 798-99 (Miss. Ct. App. 2008).

[49] MISS. CODE ANN. 93-11-71 (6) (2008).

[50] Hammett v. Woods, 602 So. 2d 825, 828-29 (Miss. 1992).

[51] Laird v. Blackburn, 788 So. 2d 844, 849 (Miss. Ct. App. 2001).

[52] Martin v. Ealy, 859 So. 2d 1034, 1038 (Miss. Ct. App. 2003) (rejecting argument that insurance was to secure child support, rather than part of property division).

[53] *See* Alexander v. Alexander, 494 So. 2d 365, 368 (Miss. 1986) (judgment on husband's indebtedness to wife for her share of home and farm); *see also* Bounds v. Bounds, 935 So. 2d 407, 411 (Miss. Ct. App. 2006) (enforcing provision requiring husband to pay tax lien on home awarded to wife).

[54] Doyle v. Doyle, 55 So. 3d 1097, 1111-13 (Miss. Ct. App. 2010).

§ 14.03[2][b]   MISSISSIPPI FAMILY LAW

mother in contempt for interrupting a father's summer visitation by taking the children back to her home.[55] A custodial parent who removed children from the jurisdiction in violation of a court order was properly held in contempt.[56] Failure to comply with an order is not excused because the custodial parent disagrees with an order or acts on the advice of counsel or other experts.[57] However, there must be some evidence of willful failure to comply. A mother should not have been held in contempt for her fourteen-year-old daughter's refusal to visit her father, when she encouraged the girl to visit him.[58] A brief failure to comply with a visitation order does not necessarily require a finding of contempt. A court did not err in refusing to hold a mother in contempt for denying visitation for a single weekend after seven years of compliance.[59]

A custodial parent who attempts to block visitation may be held in contempt even though the order does not set specific dates for visitation. A mother was held in contempt for failing to cooperate under an order providing for liberal visitation to be arranged by the parties.[60]

[b] Violation of visitation restrictions. A noncustodial parent may be held in contempt for willful violation of court-ordered restrictions on visitation. The supreme court upheld a chancellor's five-day incarceration of a father who took his child and girlfriend on a camping trip in violation of an order prohibiting overnight visitation with his girlfriend present.[61]

[c] Removal of child. A noncustodial parent may be found in contempt for removing a child from the custodial parent. A father who removed a child without the mother's consent was properly held in contempt even though he returned the child prior to the contempt hearing.[62] A court erred, however, in incarcerating a joint custodian mother for moving to Arizona. The order did not prohibit the parents from removing the children from the state.[63]

[3] Other provisions. Enforcement actions are also used to secure compliance with other provisions of a divorce or support decree. An alimony payor was properly held in contempt for failing to provide tax documents as required by an Arkansas

---

[55] Strain v. Strain, 847 So. 2d 276, 278 (Miss. Ct. App. 2003) (complaints that children were not fed enough breakfast, were not having fun, and did not see their father enough were not sufficient to justify removal).

[56] Vockroth v. Vockroth, 200 So. 2d 459, 464 (Miss. 1967).

[57] *See infra* § 14.05[2][i].

[58] *Compare* Goodson v. Goodson, 816 So. 2d 420, 423-24 (Miss. Ct. App. 2002) *with* Humphrey v. Martin, 755 So. 2d 551, 555 (Miss. Ct. App. 2000) (noncustodial mother's willful failure to return child to grandparents).

[59] Smith v. Smith, 545 So. 2d 725, 727 (Miss. 1989) (mother denied visitation based on belief that father and partner were not actually married); *see also* Gilliland v. Gilliland, 984 So. 2d 364, 369 (Miss. Ct. App. 2008) (court did not err in denying contempt, even though there was some evidence that father interfered with telephone visitation).

[60] Chalk v. Lentz, 744 So. 2d 789, 792 (Miss. Ct. App. 1999).

[61] Dilling v. Dilling, 734 So. 2d 327, 338-39 (Miss. Ct. App. 1999); *see also* Henderson v. Henderson, 952 So. 2d 273, 280 (Miss. Ct. App. 2006) (father held in contempt for allowing a girlfriend to spend the night at his house in violation of court order).

[62] Stauffer v. Stauffer, 379 So. 2d 922, 924-25 (Miss. 1980); *see also* Faris v. Jernigan, 939 So. 2d 835, 840-41 (Miss. Ct. App. 2006) (mother properly held in contempt for refusing to return child from visitation in Georgia).

[63] Elliott v. Elliott, 877 So. 2d 450, 457 (Miss. Ct. App. 2003) (non-reversible error).

ENFORCEMENT OF DECREES

§ 14.04

decree.[64] Payors have also been held in contempt for failure to maintain court-ordered health or life insurance.[65]

§ 14.04 DEFENSES TO JUDGMENT FOR DEFAULT

A payor may defend an enforcement action by asserting that the statute of limitations has run or that the claims are barred by res judicata. In rare cases, the clean hands doctrine may bar recovery. It is not a defense to arrearages that the parties informally agreed to modify support. Nor is a custodial parent's interference with visitation or a child's hostility an excuse for default.

[1] Out-of-court modification. Parents may not modify support or forgive arrearages through an out-of-court agreement. An agreement between parents to end a child's support at eighteen was unenforceable.[66] Similarly, a mother's agreement to forego support in return for a transfer of land was void as a matter of public policy; a custodial parent receives support as a fiduciary and cannot waive a child's right to support.[67] Out-of-court modifications of alimony are also unenforceable. A wife's letter stating that she did not seek enforcement of alimony payments was not binding in her subsequent suit for arrearages.[68] However, in a 2006 decision, the court of appeals enforced parents' out-of-court agreement to suspend support when their son came to live with the noncustodial father. The court held that the couple had a valid, extra-judicial agreement, and that the mother would be unjustly enriched by recovering arrearages.[69]

An obligor who reduces support pursuant to an out-of-court agreement risks a later judgment for arrearages. A custodial mother's agreement to accept $1,500 for waiving past and future support was void. She obtained a judgment for $89,000 in spite of the agreement.[70] However, a payor was relieved of arrearages based on an agreement that both parties understood had been filed with the court and approved.[71]

[2] Laches and estoppel. The Mississippi Supreme Court has rejected arguments that petitioners who delay in suing for arrearages are barred by laches. A former wife's

---

[64] Shepherd v. Shepherd, 769 So. 2d 242, 247 (Miss. Ct. App. 2000); *see also* Bounds v. Bounds, 935 So. 2d 407, 411 (Miss. Ct. App. 2006) (enforcing provision requiring husband to pay tax lien on home awarded to wife); *cf.* R.K. v. J.K., 946 So. 2d 764, 777 (Miss. 2007) (suit to enforce agreement not to divulge taped conversations; contempt denied).

[65] *See* Doyle v. Doyle, 55 So. 3d 1097 (Miss. Ct. App. 2010) (failure to provide health insurance); McCardle v. McCardle, 862 So. 2d 1290, 1293 (Miss. Ct. App. 2004) (nonpayment of alimony and life insurance premiums); Langdon v. Langdon, 854 So. 2d 485, 495 (Miss Ct. App. 2003) (failure to maintain insurance); Broome v. Broome, 832 So. 2d 1247, 1254 (Miss. Ct. App. 2002).

[66] Lawrence v. Lawrence, 574 So. 2d 1376, 1378-79 (Miss. 1991).

[67] Calton v. Calton, 485 So. 2d 309, 311 (Miss. 1986); *see also* Strack v. Sticklin, 959 So. 2d 1, 5 (Miss. Ct. App. 2006) (agreement between parties to replace support with in-kind contributions not necessarily binding); *cf.* Kelley v. Day, 965 So. 2d 749, 754 (Miss. Ct. App. 2007) (agreement by unmarried parents with regard to amount of support not binding on court in paternity action). *But cf.* Dep't of Human Servs. v. Shelby, 802 So. 2d 89, 96 (Miss. 2001) (agreement to waive child support for property conveyance which was not appealed was not void; decree could not be attacked collaterally, but could be modified based on change in circumstances).

[68] Gregg v. Montgomery, 587 So. 2d 928, 933 (Miss. 1991).

[69] Bryant v. Bryant, 924 So. 2d 627, 630 (Miss. Ct. App. 2006).

[70] Houck v. Ousterhout, 861 So. 2d 1000, 1002 (Miss. 2003).

[71] Wright v. Wright, 737 So. 2d 408, 410 (Miss. Ct. App. 1998).

§ 14.04[3]   MISSISSIPPI FAMILY LAW

seven-year delay in seeking alimony arrearages did not bar her suit; the delay only worked to her disadvantage.[72] Similarly, an action for child support was not barred by laches even though there was an otherwise inexcusable sixteen-year delay in seeking payment.[73] The court of appeals also held that the defense of laches may not be used unless the statute of limitations has expired.[74]

Defenses based on equitable estoppel have been equally ineffective. A petitioner who delayed twenty years was not equitably estopped from seeking alimony arrearages. Her delay was a reasonable response to her ex-husband's threat to file bankruptcy if she sought to enforce the judgment.[75] Similarly, a payor was not relieved of his obligation to pay medical and orthodontic bills simply because the custodial mother failed to present the bills in a timely fashion.[76] However, a mother was barred from reimbursement for medical bills that she submitted after the right to claim insurance reimbursement expired.[77]

[3] Clean hands doctrine. In rare cases, the equitable doctrine of clean hands may prevent a petitioner from recovering arrearages. A mother who hid children from their father for eight years was barred from recovering support.[78] But arrearages will not be excused if the noncustodial parent had sufficient information to locate a child and enforce visitation. A father who had general information regarding his ex-wife's residence was not relieved of arrearages, even though he did not see his son for five years.[79] A mother in violation of a provision of the couple's divorce decree was not barred by

---

[72] Overstreet v. Overstreet, 692 So. 2d 88, 92 (Miss. 1997).

[73] Glass v. Glass, 726 So. 2d 1281, 1287 (Miss. Ct. App. 1998) (no undue prejudice to the payor, even though bank records prior to 1990 were no longer available to him, since he was well aware that the custodial parent was trying to collect payments); *see also* Beasnett v. Arledge, 934 So. 2d 345, 349-50 (Miss. Ct. App. 2006) (rejecting father's argument that mother's eighteen-year delay caused arrearages to increase from $4,800 to $22,900); Owen v. Wilkinson, 915 So. 2d 493, 495-96 (Miss. Ct. App. 2005) (right to child support not barred by laches based on parent's delay in bringing suit); Durr v. Durr, 912 So. 2d 1033, 1038 (Miss. Ct. App. 2005) (laches did not bar mother's suit for eight years of private school tuition even though suit filed while child was in college).

[74] Brown v. Brown, 822 So. 2d 1119, 1121 (Miss. Ct. App. 2002); *see* Durr v. Durr, 912 So. 2d 1033, 1038 (Miss. Ct. App. 2005) (doctrine of laches does not apply unless statute of limitations has run); Nicholas v. Nicholas, 841 So. 2d 1208, 1211 (Miss. Ct. App. 2001) (alimony arrearage).

[75] Nicholas v. Nicholas, 841 So. 2d 1208, 1211 (Miss. Ct. App. 2001) (but limiting recovery to amounts due within seven years prior to petition). *But cf.* Medders v. Estate of Medders, 458 So. 2d 685, 690 (Miss. 1984) (alimony recipient may be estopped from seeking arrearages from a decedent's estate where she received other support from the decedent for years without objecting to adequacy of the support).

[76] Davis v. Davis, 761 So. 2d 936, 941-42 (Miss. Ct. App. 2000) (but limiting payment for braces to amount charged for standard braces); *see also* Durr v. Durr, 912 So. 2d 1033, 1038 (Miss. Ct. App. 2005) (even if equitable estoppel applied to suits for child support arrearages father could not show how he was harmed by delay).

[77] Milam v. Milam, 509 So. 2d 864, 866 (Miss. 1987); *see* Holloway v. Mills, 872 So. 2d 754, 757 (Miss. Ct. App. 2004) (timely submission required if payor's insurance would have paid the bills).

[78] Cole v. Hood, 371 So. 2d 861, 863 (Miss. 1979); *cf.* Brown v. Brown, 822 So. 2d 1119, 1124-25 (Miss. Ct. App. 2002) (recognizing exception, but finding that payor had information that could have located child).

[79] Cunliffe v. Swartzfager, 437 So. 2d 43, 45-46 (Miss. 1983) (father did not see son for five years, but knew generally where his ex-wife lived); *see* Shelnut v. Dep't of Human Servs., 9 So. 3d 359, 364 (Miss. 2009) (fact that father had not seen child in Canada for twenty years did not excuse arrearages; he knew where the child was located); Dep't of Human Servs. v. Marshall, 859 So. 2d 387, 390 (Miss. 2003) (refusing to forgive arrearages based on mother's refusal of visitation for twelve years); Westmoreland v. Jackson, 401 So. 2d 725, 726 (Miss. 1985) (clean hands doctrine did not bar recovery by mother who refused one weekend of visitation); Patterson v. Patterson, 20 So. 3d 65, 71 (Miss. Ct. App. 2009) (father's obligation was not suspended just because his son was sometimes unavailable for nightly phone visitation); Balius v. Gaines, 908 So. 2d 791, 803 (Miss. Ct. App. 2005) (mother's failure to notify father of her location for a ten-day period was not sufficient to suspend his obligation to pay child support).

ENFORCEMENT OF DECREES

§ 14.04[4]

the clean hands doctrine from seeking an increase in child support.[80] The clean hands doctrine may apply to bar recovery under property division provisions.[81]

[4] Res Judicata. A judgment is res judicata as to all matters that were considered or could have been raised in the action. A wife's request for payment of medical bills was barred by res judicata because the bills were outstanding at the time of a previous contempt petition and were not brought to the court's attention.[82]

[5] Statute of limitations. The statute of limitations for suit on judgments[83] applies to actions to enforce alimony,[84] child support,[85] and property division orders.[86] The statute is seven years for domestic judgments[87] and three years for foreign judgments against Mississippi residents.[88] With respect to child support, the running of the statute of limitations is suspended during the child's minority.

[a] Alimony. The seven-year limitations period runs from the time each alimony payment is due, not from the date of the divorce decree. An action to recover alimony payable over fourteen years was not barred entirely. Only payments due and vested more than seven years prior to the date of filing suit were barred.[89] The court of appeals held in a recent case that the three-year contract statute of limitations applied to a wife's action to enforce an alimony escalation clause.[90]

[b] Child support. The seven-year statute of limitations applies to actions to collect child support arrearages. However, the period does not begin to run until a child reaches the age of twenty-one. The Mississippi savings statute provides that a statute of limitations is tolled if any person entitled to bring the action is "under the disability of infancy."[91]

If the statute of limitations runs on the claim of one of several children covered by a support order, the claim is barred as to that child's pro rata share. A court properly

---

[80] Jurney v. Jurney, 921 So. 2d 372, 377 (Miss. Ct. App. 2005) (support is for the benefit of children).

[81] Morgan v. Morgan, 744 So. 2d 321, 325 (Miss. 1999).

[82] Russell v. Russell, 724 So. 2d 1061, 1064 (Miss. Ct. App. 1999) (chancellor erred in ordering payment of medical bills not included in prior contempt action); *see* Clements v. Young, 481 So. 2d 263, 270 (Miss.1985).

[83] *See* Miss. Code Ann. § 15-1-43 (2003).

[84] Medders v. Estate of Medders, 458 So. 2d 685, 690 (Miss. 1984). *But see* D'Avignon v. D'Avignon, 945 So. 2d 401, 409 (Miss. Ct. App. 2006) (applying three-year statute of limitations to wife's suit to enforce alimony escalation clause).

[85] Glass v. Glass, 726 So. 2d 1281, 1286 (Miss. Ct. App. 1998).

[86] Nicholas v. Nicholas, 841 So. 2d 1208, 1211 (Miss. Ct. App. 2003); Patterson v. Patterson, 915 So. 2d 496, 503 (Miss. Ct. App. 2005) (statute of limitations for enforcing decree is seven-year statute).

[87] *See* Miss. Code Ann. § 15-1-43 (2003).

[88] *See* Miss. Code Ann. § 15-1-45 (2003); *see* Shelnut v. Dep't of Human Servs., 9 So. 3d 359, 365-66 (Miss. 2009) (foreign judgment filed within three years of the child's majority was timely).

[89] Schaffer v. Schaffer, 46 So. 2d 443, 444 (Miss. 1950); *see also* Sides v. Pittman, 150 So. 211, 211-12 (Miss. 1933) (wife's action for alimony, brought eighteen years after she remarried, barred by laches and statute of limitations).

[90] D'Avignon v. D'Avignon, 945 So. 2d 401, 409-10 (Miss. Ct. App. 2006) (increase to be in same percentage as original alimony to husband's income at the time).

[91] Miss. Code Ann. § 15-1-59 (2003); *see* Carlson v. Matthews, 966 So. 2d 1258, 1260 (Miss. Ct. App. 2007) (court permitted to order QDRO to satisfy child support arrearages more than seven years after divorce); Strack v. Sticklin, 959 So. 2d 1, 7 (Miss. Ct. App. 2006) (statute begins to run seven years from the date of the child's emancipation).

485

§ 14.04[5][c]   MISSISSIPPI FAMILY LAW

awarded 25% of a $475 support award for four children; the statute of limitations had run on the claims of all but the youngest child.[92]

Suit may be brought by either the child or the custodial parent within seven years after the child's majority.[93] The supreme court has rejected payors' arguments that the savings clause applies only to a child's action.[94] There is some conflict as to whether custodial parents are required to join emancipated children in a suit for arrearages.[95] In 2003, the Mississippi Supreme Court held that an emancipated child is a necessary party to an arrearages action unless there is proof that the child knowingly waived the right to assert a claim to the funds.[96] However, the court held in 2009 that a child was not a necessary party to an enforcement action, even though she was past the age of majority.[97]

A child may be entitled to seek arrearages even though the custodial parent is not. When a mother failed to appeal a chancellor's denial of arrearages, she was barred from seeking to recover them in a subsequent suit. However, the child was not barred by the mother's failure to appeal.[98]

    [c] Property division. The seven-year statute of limitations also applies to actions to enforce property division provisions. A court properly denied a wife's action, filed more than seven years after divorce, to recover personal property retained by her former husband.[99] In at least one case, however, the court of appeals held that the statute was tolled; a former wife's good faith reliance on statements made by a pension plan administrator led her to delay ten years before seeking her share of her ex-husband's pension.[100]

§ 14.05 CONTEMPT

Contempt is the remedy historically used to enforce court orders. A party may be held in contempt for failure to make child support or alimony payments, failure to

---

[92] Ladner v. Logan, 857 So. 2d 764, 770-71 (Miss. 2003) (distinguishing arrearages when one child is emancipated, but the statute of limitations has not run).

[93] Glass v. Glass, 726 So. 2d 1281, 1286 (Miss. Ct. App. 1998); see Wilson v. Wilson, 464 So. 2d 496, 498-499 (Miss. 1985); White v. Abel, 802 So. 2d 98, 101-02 (Miss. Ct. App. 2001) (statute of limitations ran where mother filed suit more than seven years after emancipation).

[94] Vice v. Dep't of Human Servs., 702 So. 2d 397, 400 (Miss. 1997) (custodial mother permitted to bring an action for past-due support two years after her youngest child reached twenty-one) (rejecting payor's argument that custodial parent would be unjustly enriched).

[95] See Carite v. Carite, 841 So. 2d 1148, 1155-56 (Miss. Ct. App. 2002) (rejecting father's argument that his ex-wife should not have been awarded arrearages).

[96] Ladner v. Logan, 857 So. 2d 764, 770-71 (Miss. 2003) (mother "doggedly sought the unpaid child support on her own behalf"); see also Brown v. Brown, 822 So. 2d 1119, 1122 (Miss. Ct. App. 2002) (holding that mother's claim for support was derivative; mother required to submit daughter's agreement to divide arrearage or prove amount actually expended to compensate for father's failure to provide support). But cf. Strack v. Sticklin, 959 So. 2d 1, 5-6 (Miss. Ct. App. 2006) (parent of an emancipated child may bring an action to collect support arrearages; recovery must be paid to the child with the exception of sums that the custodial parent was obligated to provide over and above their own support obligation).

[97] Shelnut v. Dep't of Human Servs., 9 So. 3d 359, 367 (Miss. 2009).

[98] Forrest v. McCoy, 996 So. 2d 158 (Miss. Ct. App. 2008).

[99] Rubisoff v. Rubisoff, 133 So. 2d 534, 537 (Miss. 1961).

[100] Carite v. Carite, 841 So. 2d 1148, 1152 (Miss. Ct. App. 2002).

ENFORCEMENT OF DECREES § 14.05[1]

comply with property division orders, or disregard of other court orders. A finding of contempt requires that the provision in default be unambiguous and the violation willful. Inability to pay is a defense to a finding of contempt.

[1] Types of contempt. Contempt may be either civil or criminal. The two contempt actions serve different purposes and are governed by different standards. Most petitions for enforcement involve civil contempt.

[a] Civil contempt. The purpose of civil contempt is to secure the defendant's compliance with a court order.[101] A finding of civil contempt may be punished by fines or imprisonment. In either case, the penalty must be lifted when the defendant complies with the order.[102] As a result, civil contempt incarceration is generally ordered for an indefinite period.[103]

A payor's failure to comply with a court order is prima facie evidence of contempt.[104] The burden then shifts to the defendant, who may rebut the prima facie case by proving inability to pay, that the default was not willful, that the provision was ambiguous, or that performance was impossible. Civil contempt must be proved by clear and convincing evidence.[105] The manifest error standard applies to appellate review of civil contempt.[106]

[b] Criminal contempt. The purpose of criminal contempt is to punish a defendant for noncompliance, rather than to secure performance.[107] A court's finding that a custodial mother was in contempt for refusing to allow past visitation was a finding of criminal contempt. The order was based on past behavior rather than future compliance.[108] Incarceration based on criminal contempt is not affected by compliance with prior orders and therefore may be for a fixed period of time.[109] For example, a court's order that a child support payor be incarcerated for ninety days was based on criminal contempt.[110] Criminal contempt must be proved beyond a reasonable doubt.[111] When

---

[101] Moulds v. Bradley, 791 So. 2d 220, 224 (Miss. 2001); Strack v. Sticklin, 959 So. 2d 1, 4 (Miss. Ct. App. 2006) (purpose of contempt is to enforce court's order).

[102] Dennis v. Dennis, 824 So. 2d 604, 608 (Miss. 2002).

[103] Moulds v. Bradley, 791 So. 2d 220, 224 (Miss. 2001); Newell v. Hinton, 556 So. 2d 1037, 1044 (Miss. 1990); *see also* Sappington v. Sappington, 147 So. 2d 494, 498 (Miss. 1962).

[104] Rainwater v. Rainwater, 110 So. 2d 608, 611 (Miss. 1959); *see also* McIntosh v. Dep't of Human Servs., 886 So. 2d 721 (Miss. 2004) (rejecting defendant's argument that DHS had burden of proving ability to pay); Hunt v. Asanov, 975 So. 2d 899, 902 (Miss. Ct. App. 2008); Kelley v. Day, 965 So. 2d 749, 755 (Miss. Ct. App. 2007); Stribling v. Stribling, 960 So. 2d 556, 561 (Miss. Ct. App. 2007); Watkins v. Watkins, 942 So. 2d 224, 230 (Miss. Ct. App. 2006).

[105] Allred v. Allred, 735 So. 2d 1064, 1067 (Miss. Ct. App. 1999).

[106] Dennis v. Dennis, 824 So. 2d 604, 608 (Miss. 2002); Strack v. Sticklin, 959 So. 2d 1, 4 (Miss. Ct. App. 2006) (contempt within chancellor's discretion) (prima facie case made by showing nonpayment); Eades v. Eades, 869 So. 2d 1038, 1039 (Miss. Ct. App. 2003).

[107] *In re* Hampton, 919 So. 2d 949, 954 (Miss. 2006); Moulds v. Bradley, 791 So. 2d 220, 224 (Miss. 2001).

[108] Allred v. Allred, 735 So. 2d 1064, 1068 (Miss. Ct. App. 1999) (reversing because of lack of evidence of willfulness); *see also* Balius v. Gaines, 914 So. 2d 300, 307 (Miss. Ct. App. 2005) (where father sought contempt for mother's alleged past interference with visitation, request was for criminal contempt).

[109] Dennis v. Dennis, 824 So. 2d 604, 608-09 (Miss. 2002). *But see* E.K. v. Hinds County Youth Court, 20 So. 3d 1216, 1218-21 (Miss. 2009) (holding mother in jail for two days to force compliance with order that she allow her thirteen-year-old son to be interviewed by DHS was civil contempt).

[110] Moulds v. Bradley, 791 So. 2d 220, 225 (Miss. 2001).

[111] *In re* Hampton, 919 So. 2d 949, 954 (Miss. 2006); Balius v. Gaines, 914 So. 2d 300, 308 (Miss. Ct. App. 2005)

§ 14.05[2]   **MISSISSIPPI FAMILY LAW**

an order of criminal contempt is appealed the court proceeds *ab initio* to determine whether the defendant is guilty beyond a reasonable doubt.[112]

Criminal contempt may be direct, based on conduct in the court's presence, or constructive, based on conduct outside the courtroom.[113] Direct criminal contempt is punishable by immediate court order.[114] Direct contempt may be punished by the court without notice or a hearing.[115] The supreme court has noted, however, that a judge who is personally attacked should consider waiting until the proceedings end and having another judge handle the contempt hearing.[116]

Contempt based on conduct outside the court's presence is constructive contempt.[117] A defendant charged with constructive criminal contempt must be provided with procedural due process safeguards, including "the nature and cause of the accusation, of his rights to be heard, to counsel, to call witnesses, to an unbiased judge, to a jury trial, and against self-incrimination, and that he is presumed innocent until proven guilty beyond reasonable doubt."[118] A court erred in ordering a child support payor jailed for ninety days without notifying him that he would be charged with criminal rather than civil contempt.[119] However, an attorney charged with criminal contempt waived these rights by participating in the hearing without objecting.[120]

[2] Defenses to contempt. Failure to comply with a court order is not contempt if the defendant was genuinely unable to pay or did not act willfully, if the provision was ambiguous, or if performance was impossible. With regard to civil contempt, payment prior to the hearing is a defense. Defendants have also successfully avoided contempt by proving that he or she was not competent at the time of the default or that the petitioner was partly to blame for the default or otherwise lacked clean hands. It is not a defense, however, that the defendant was acting on the advice of counsel or genuinely believed that the order was wrong.

[a] Inability to pay. A payor may avoid contempt by proving genuine inability to pay the amount ordered. The burden of proof is on the payor[121] who must prove inability to pay with "particularity" and not in general terms.[122]

_____

(burden of proof for criminal contempt beyond a reasonable doubt); Allred v. Allred, 735 So. 2d 1064, 1067 (Miss. Ct. App. 1999).

[112] Dennis v. Dennis, 824 So. 2d 604, 608 (Miss. 2002).

[113] Moulds v. Bradley, 791 So. 2d 220, 224-25 (Miss. 2001) (child support payor in arrears found in constructive criminal contempt). Failure to appear at a hearing is generally constructive contempt, but may be direct contempt when an attorney informs a court officer that he or she does not intend to appear. *In re* Hampton, 919 So. 2d 949, 955 (Miss. 2006).

[114] Dennis v. Dennis, 824 So. 2d 604, 608 (Miss. 2002).

[115] *In re* Hampton, 919 So. 2d 949, 955 (Miss. 2006).

[116] Purvis v. Purvis, 657 So. 2d 794, 798 (Miss. 1994).

[117] *In re* Spencer, 985 So. 2d 330, 346 (Miss. 2008) (holding attorney in contempt for failure to appear and violation of subpoena order was constructive criminal contempt) (judge who initiated criminal contempt should recuse herself from contempt hearing); Purvis v. Purvis, 657 So. 2d 794, 798 (Miss. 1994).

[118] Dennis v. Dennis, 824 So. 2d 604, 609 (Miss. 2002) (service on defendant's attorney rather than defendant was due process violation, but defendant waived violation by appearance).

[119] Moulds v. Bradley, 791 So. 2d 220, 225 (Miss. 2001).

[120] *In re* Spencer, 985 So. 2d 330, 340-42 (Miss. 2008).

[121] Varner v. Varner, 666 So. 2d 493, 496 (Miss. 1995).

[122] McIntosh v. Dep't of Human Servs., 886 So. 2d 721 (Miss. 2004) (defendant who failed to show inability to pay

ENFORCEMENT OF DECREES   § 14.05[2][a][i]

Mere financial difficulty does not excuse nonpayment – contempt may be avoided only on proof that the payor lived economically, paid only bare living expenses, and used all remaining funds to satisfy the support obligation.[123] The fact that a payor could have obtained a modification based on changed circumstances does not excuse arrearages or avoid a finding of contempt.[124] A father who failed to seek modification when his anticipated employment fell through was held in contempt for nonpayment.[125] In contrast, a payor in arrears who petitioned for modification before the payee sought enforcement was liable for arrearages but was not in contempt.[126]

[i] Evidence sufficient. Evidence that a defendant's businesses had been foreclosed, his property sold, and that he had no income was sufficient proof of inability to pay.[127] Similarly, a payor who was hospitalized, living on donations, and without money or property was not in contempt for nonpayment.[128] And a court erred in finding a husband in contempt unless he used his entire income for child support, alimony, and arrearages.[129]

[ii] Evidence insufficient. Default is not justified by payment of debts or expenses other than those necessary to maintain a payor's business or occupation.[130] A child support payor who incurred new debt to purchase an automobile at the same time he failed to pay support was found in contempt.[131] A defendant failed to show inability to pay alimony when he admitting buying and renovating a house with his girlfriend and that he had funds for personal pleasure.[132] And a court did not err in finding a former husband in contempt for nonpayment of alimony even though his income had been

---

properly held in contempt); Morreale v. Morreale, 646 So. 2d 1264, 1267 (Miss. 1994) (proof failed to show inability to pay where payor was not employed but had rental and other income); Seghini v. Seghini, 42 So. 3d 635, 643 (Miss. Ct. App. 2010) (husband's self-generated ledger and incomplete tax return not sufficient proof); Chasez v. Chasez, 957 So. 2d 1031, 1038 (Miss. Ct. App. 2007) (defendant provided no proof of inability to pay; defense rejected).

[123] *See* Lane v. Lane, 850 So. 2d 122, 126 (Miss. 2002) (husband who purchased new pickup and spent surplus funds on himself and second wife did not prove inability to pay); Gregg v. Montgomery, 587 So. 2d 928, 931 (Miss. 1991) (husband failed to show inability to pay); Ramsay v. Ramsay, 87 So. 491, 493 (Miss. 1921) (payor who lived far beyond means did not prove inability to pay).

[124] *See* Duncan v. Duncan, 417 So. 2d 908, 909 (Miss. 1982) (party unable to comply should seek modification; otherwise will be held in contempt); Rainwater v. Rainwater, 110 So. 2d 608, 611 (Miss. 1959) (contempt appropriate where defendant had funds available after meeting basic expenses); Redding v. Redding, 150 So. 776, 776 (Miss. 1933) (simply raising doubts about inability to pay is insufficient).

[125] Barfield v. State, 749 So. 2d 331, 340 (Miss. Ct. App. 1999).

[126] *See* Setser v. Piazza, 644 So. 2d 1211, 1216 (Miss. 1994) (payor who discontinued payments and filed modification petition at same time not in contempt); Thurman v. Thurman, 559 So. 2d 1014, 1016 (Miss. 1990) (payor not in contempt where he filed motion to modify prior to wife's filing contempt motion; still liable for arrearages); *see also* Grissom v. Grissom, 952 So. 2d 1023, 1030 (Miss. Ct. App. 2007) (contempt properly denied; father sought temporary relief three months after losing job). *But cf.* Elliott v. Rogers, 775 So. 2d 1285, 1290 (Miss. Ct. App. 2000) (payor who filed motion to reduce support for reasons other than inability to pay held in contempt for nonpayment during pendency of action); *but see* Kelley v. Day, 965 So. 2d 749, 755 (Miss. Ct. App. 2007) (father who promptly filed petition found in contempt; he had funds with which to pay in spite of job loss).

[127] Hooker v. Hooker, 205 So. 2d 276, 278 (Miss. 1967).

[128] Mullen v. Mullen, 246 So. 2d 923, 924-25 (Miss. 1971) (error to order incarceration).

[129] Davis v. Davis, 268 So. 2d 913, 915-16 (Miss. 1972) (but upholding refusal to modify payments).

[130] Kincaid v. Kincaid, 57 So. 2d 263, 265 (Miss. 1952).

[131] Shelton v. Shelton, 653 So. 2d 283, 287 (Miss. 1995).

[132] Wesson v. Wesson, 818 So. 2d 1272, 1279-81 (Miss. 2002).

§ 14.05[2][a][iii]   **MISSISSIPPI FAMILY LAW**

reduced involuntarily; his savings exceeded the amount of the judgment.[133]

[iii] Inability to pay at time of agreement. Courts are not persuaded by a payor's complaint that he or she agreed to pay an unrealistically high amount of support. An unemployed father who agreed to pay $1,000 a month in child support was properly found in contempt for nonpayment. The court rejected his argument that the agreement was unconscionable and his consent was given at a time when he was desperate. There was no indication that he did not understand the terms of the agreement.[134] Similarly, an unemployed alimony payor was properly incarcerated for failure to make payments under an agreement signed when he was unemployed.[135]

[b] Lack of willfulness. It is a defense to contempt that the default was not willful or deliberate.[136] For example, the court of appeals found no evidence of a husband's willful damage to a barbeque grill and furniture; some of the damage was caused by leaks in a storage unit.[137] Similarly, a husband's failure to transfer an automobile title to his former wife was not willful – he otherwise complied with the order, making payments and maintaining insurance on the vehicle in her possession.[138] A wife who disclosed taped recordings of her husband's conversations in a court action brought against her by her husband's attorney, was not in contempt in spite of an agreement not to reveal the recordings. She had no choice but to make a limited disclosure of the tapes.[139] However, a husband who failed to provide tax records as ordered was in contempt. His reluctance to provide the records because of the confidentiality of his current wife's information did not excuse default.[140] A finding of contempt was proper

---

[133] McCardle v. McCardle, 862 So. 2d 1290, 1293 (Miss. Ct. App. 2004); *see also* Doyle v. Doyle, 55 So. 3d 1097, 1111 (Miss. Ct. App. 2010) (husband complained that he could not pay but did not explain use of $37,000 in savings, nor did bank statements indicate how the funds were spent); Howard v. Howard, 968 So. 2d 961, 976-77 (Miss. Ct. App. 2007) (father who lost income, but bought new home and had substantial cash available, properly found in contempt); Kelley v. Day, 965 So. 2d 749, 755-56 (Miss. Ct. App. 2007) (court properly found father who lost job, but who had $52,000 available to pay support, in contempt); Bounds v. Bounds, 935 So. 2d 407, 411 (Miss. Ct. App. 2006) (evidence that husband lost a business in 1997 due to a fire, and in 2000 due to a tornado, did not establish inability to pay in 2003); Watkins v. Watkins, 942 So. 2d 224, 231 (Miss. Ct. App. 2006) (rejecting father's argument that he was unable to make monthly payments of $500 a month from income of $1,843); Davison v. Mississippi Dep't Human Servs., 938 So. 2d 912, 915-16 (Miss. Ct. App. 2006) (rejecting father's argument that he was disabled; he worked for five years after the accident alleged to cause his disability and spent four days a week at his brother's pool hall performing "employment-like" activities); Bosarge v. Bosarge, 879 So. 2d 515 (Miss. Ct. App. 2004) (contempt proper; injured payor was making $600 per week by time of hearing, and had made no effort to reduce arrearages).

[134] Barfield v. State, 749 So. 2d 331, 340 (Miss. Ct. App. 1999).

[135] Eades v. Eades, 869 So. 2d 1038, 1039-40 (Miss. Ct. App. 2003) (also based on fact that he had transferred property to his new wife).

[136] Westerburg v. Westerburg, 853 So. 2d 826, 828 (Miss. Ct. App. 2003); Weston v. Mounts, 789 So. 2d 822, 826 (Miss. Ct. App. 2001).

[137] Scroggins v. Riley, 758 So. 2d 467, 473 (Miss. Ct. App. 2000); *see also* Cossitt v. Cossitt, 975 So. 2d 274, 279 (Miss. Ct. App. 2008) (husband who genuinely misinterpreted provision for health insurance not in contempt); Powell v. Powell, 976 So. 2d 358, 364 (Miss. Ct. App. 2008) (mother not in contempt for failure to communicate with father about children; her conduct was not willful); Clower v. Clower, 988 So. 2d 441, 445 (Miss. Ct. App. 2008) (husband with income of $1,384 not in willful contempt for failure to pay alimony of $2,000 a month); *cf. In re* Spencer, 985 So. 2d 330, 342-43 (Miss. 2008) (attorney could not be held in contempt for violating vague gag order).

[138] Cooper v. Keyes, 510 So. 2d 518, 519 (Miss. 1987).

[139] R.K. v. J.K., 946 So. 2d 764, 777 (Miss. 2007).

[140] Shepherd v. Shepherd, 769 So. 2d 242, 247 (Miss. Ct. App. 2000); Morris v. Morris, 5 So. 3d 476, 494-95 (Miss. Ct. App. 2008) (contempt proper even though some amounts due were unclear; the defendant was undisputedly

ENFORCEMENT OF DECREES
§ 14.05[2][c]

when a defendant, temporarily occupying her ex-husband's cabin, intentionally tracked oil in the cabin, threw flour on the walls, removed the locks and placed them on the floor, traded his field cultivator to a scrap metal collector, removed the cushions from the cabin couch to cushion her tanning bed during a move, and unplugged the deep freeze, leaving the contents to spoil.[141]

The same standard applies to violation of custody provisions. A mother should not have been held in contempt for her fourteen-year-old daughter's refusal to visit her father, since the mother encouraged her to visit.[142] However, a noncustodial mother's failure to return a child to the custodial grandparents justified a finding of contempt, based on her own testimony that she intended to keep the children when she picked them up.[143] Similarly, a father was incarcerated for contempt for taking his child and girlfriend on a camping trip in violation of an order prohibiting overnight visitation with his girlfriend present.[144]

[c] **Ambiguity.** A party may not be held in contempt for failure to comply with an order that is too vague or ambiguous to be understood. A former husband should not have been held in contempt for failing to transfer home furnishings to his wife. The decree stated only that she was entitled to occupy the home for a certain period, without addressing disposition of furnishings.[145] An agreement to cooperate in filing tax returns did not clearly require joint, rather than separate returns; a wife could not be held in contempt for refusing to execute joint returns.[146] Similarly, a court properly refused to find a spouse in contempt for failure to comply with vague and unclear provisions regarding payment of debt.[147]

However, an award need only be reasonably specific. An order that a wife relinquish personal property to her husband was not too vague to understand, even though it might have been "more artfully drawn."[148] The court of appeals rejected a husband's argument that a decree requiring his wife to pay for all but three specified debts was ambiguous. While the decree did not specifically state that he was to pay the debts,

---

in arrears on other amounts).

[141] Montgomery v. Montgomery, 873 So. 2d 1071, 1072-73 (Miss. Ct. App. 2004).

[142] Goodson v. Goodson, 816 So. 2d 420, 424 (Miss. Ct. App. 2002).

[143] Humphrey v. Martin, 755 So. 2d 551, 555 (Miss. Ct. App. 2000); *see also* Davis v. Davis, 17 So. 3d 114, 120-22 (Miss. Ct. App. 2009) (mother was properly jailed for thirty days for criminal contempt for interference with visitation), *cert. denied*, 17 So. 3d 99 (Miss. 2009); H.L.S. v. R.S.R., 949 So. 2d 794, 801 (Miss. Ct. App. 2006) (contempt for willful failure to permit visitation); Saunders v. Saunders, 724 So. 2d 1132, 1135 (Miss. Ct. App. 1998) (mother in contempt for interference with visitation).

[144] Dilling v. Dilling, 734 So. 2d 327, 338-39 (Miss. Ct. App. 1999).

[145] Martin v. Martin, 254 So. 2d 530, 532-33 (Miss. 1971); *see also* Moses v. Moses, 879 So. 2d 1036, 1040 (Miss. 2004) (error to hold husband in contempt for listing house in newspaper rather than with agent; decree did not specify manner of advertising; Young v. Deaton, 766 So. 2d 819, 821 (Miss. Ct. App. 2000) (wife not in contempt for failing to transfer grandfather clock; decree not sufficiently specific).

[146] Banks v. Banks, 648 So. 2d 1116, 1126 (Miss. 1994).

[147] Jones v. Lee, 754 So. 2d 564, 568 (Miss. Ct. App. 2000); *see also* Hunt v. Asanov, 975 So. 2d 899, 902 (Miss. Ct. App. 2008) (court properly refused to hold father in contempt for failure to comply with contradictory child support orders); Cossitt v. Cossitt, 975 So. 2d 274, 279 (Miss. Ct. App. 2008) (court properly denied contempt; provision regarding health insurance was unclear).

[148] Westerburg v. Westerburg, 853 So. 2d 826, 827-29 (Miss. Ct. App. 2003) (requiring return of "used miter saw, used tools, tackle box, lures, ice chest (60 quart), fishing rods (Shimano and Diawa[sic]), and fish stringers").

§ 14.05[2][d]   **MISSISSIPPI FAMILY LAW**

there was no other possible explanation.[149] Similarly, a father was properly held in contempt for refusing to contribute to his children's college expenses. A provision that the parties would provide the children with a college education "in keeping with the means and ability of Husband and Wife" was not too vague to find him in contempt for refusing to make any payments at all.[150]

[d] Performance impossible. A payor may defend a contempt action by showing that performance was impossible. A wife's argument that she could not transfer jet skis to her husband because they were stolen, if true, was a defense to contempt.[151] However, a payor who claimed inability to obtain life insurance because of heart disease was properly held in contempt in the absence of evidence that he had been denied coverage.[152]

[e] Payment or compliance. A finding of civil contempt is proper only if the defendant is currently in default. A child support payor who paid arrearages prior to the hearing was not in contempt – there were no overdue payments at the time of trial.[153] However, a noncustodial father was properly held in contempt even though he returned a child to his mother prior to the hearing; his conduct cost her $5,000 in fees and costs.[154]

[f] Payee's fault. A defendant may avoid contempt by proving that the petitioner played a role in the default. For example, a payor who failed to provide COBRA health insurance coverage was not in contempt because the petitioner failed to complete forms provided by the insurer.[155] And a father should not be found in contempt for failure to pay medical expenses that the mother did not submit to him until trial.[156]

[g] Clean hands/estoppel. A petitioner may be equitably estopped from seeking a judgment of contempt. A wife who failed to notify her husband of substantial gifts as required by the decree was estopped from obtaining a contempt judgment for his

---

[149] Davis v. Davis, 829 So. 2d 712, 714-15 (Miss. Ct. App. 2002); *see also* Stribling v. Stribling, 960 So. 2d 556, 561-62 (Miss. Ct. App. 2007) (judgment of contempt requiring wife to pay alimony arrearages not vague); Bounds v. Bounds, 935 So. 2d 407, 410-11 (Miss. Ct. App. 2006) (rejecting husband's argument that agreement to pay federal tax lien was vague because it did not specify a monthly payment).

[150] Fancher v. Pell, 831 So. 2d 1137, 1143 (Miss. 2002); *see also* Clements v. Young, 481 So. 2d 263, 271 (Miss. 1985) (father properly held in contempt for failure to pay medically necessary orthodontic bills under agreement to pay reasonable and necessary expenses). *But see* Harmon v. Yarbrough, 767 So. 2d 1069, 1072 (Miss. Ct. App. 2000) (father not in contempt under general provision to pay for college education, where dispute arose over what constituted reasonable expenses).

[151] Ewing v. Ewing, 749 So. 2d 223, 225-26 (Miss. Ct. App. 1999).

[152] Broome v. Broome, 841 So. 2d 1204, 1207 (Miss. Ct. App. 2003).

[153] Strain v. Strain, 847 So. 2d 276, 279 (Miss. Ct. App. 2003); *see also* Jurney v. Jurney, 921 So. 2d 372, 375 (Miss. Ct. App. 2005) (not error to deny contempt petition when defendant mother had complied with decree by time of hearing).

[154] Stauffer v. Stauffer, 379 So. 2d 922, 924-25 (Miss. 1980) (contempt could be purged by paying fees and costs).

[155] Pope v. Pope, 803 So. 2d 499, 502-03 (Miss. Ct. App. 2002) (payor not required to pay resulting medical bills, but was required to reimburse amount that should have been paid for premiums).

[156] Bryant v. Bryant, 924 So. 2d 627, 633 (Miss. Ct. App. 2006); *see also* R.K. v. J.K., 946 So. 2d 764, 778 (Miss. 2007) (wife not in contempt for revealing tapes when husband was partly responsible for events leading to disclosure).

ENFORCEMENT OF DECREES

§ 14.05[2][h]

failure to notify her of retirement income increases.[157] Similarly, a husband who failed to comply with child support and mortgage payment obligations could not hold his wife in contempt for failure to execute joint tax returns.[158] However, a mother in violation of a provision of the couple's divorce decree was not barred by the clean hands doctrine from seeking to enforce payment of child support.[159]

[h] Incompetency. Default by a defendant who is incompetent is not a willful violation of a decree. A chancellor erred in ordering a wife incarcerated for violating a divorce decree provision when she was mentally ill at the time of the default.[160]

[i] Acting on advice of counsel or other authority. The fact that a defendant was acting on the advice of counsel does not excuse failure to abide by a decree, but may be considered in mitigation.[161] A mother who claimed to be acting on a psychologist's advice was found in contempt for refusing visitation, scheduling events during visitation, and creating stress by contacting the child during visitation.[162] A custodial father who refused to comply with visitation was found in contempt even though he was concerned about the mother's mental state and acted on advice of counsel; that the defendant had good motives may be considered in mitigation only.[163] In one case, however, the court of appeals suggested that a mother's good faith could affect the significance of contempt; she disobeyed a visitation order based on evidence of abuse but also promptly sought temporary relief.[164] And a payor's unilateral reduction of child support was not willful contempt when the payor acted on his attorney's advice as well as his own good faith belief that his obligation for college support ended on his son's twenty-first birthday.[165]

[j] Judgment wrong. It is not a defense to contempt that a defendant sincerely believes a court's decision to be wrong. A custodial father who violated a visitation order could not defend against contempt by arguing that the children were in danger

---

[157] Brennan v. Brennan, 605 So. 2d 749, 752 (Miss. 1992).

[158] Banks v. Banks, 648 So. 2d 1116, 1126 (Miss. 1994) (also based on ambiguity of provision); *see also* Cossitt v. Cossitt, 975 So. 2d 274, 279-80 (Miss. Ct. App. 2008) (husband who sent harassing emails not in contempt for violating "respect" provision of decree; both parties used "questionable" language in emails).

[159] Jurney v. Jurney, 921 So. 2d 372, 377 (Miss. Ct. App. 2005) (support is for the benefit of children).

[160] Paxton v. Paxton, 222 So. 2d 834, 837 (Miss. 1969).

[161] Ladner v. Ladner, 206 So. 2d 620, 623 (Miss. 1968) (contempt for violating visitation order), *overruled on other grounds by* Bubec v. Boston, 600 So. 2d 951 (Miss. 1968); Smith v. Little, 843 So. 2d 735, 738 (Miss. Ct. App. 2003).

[162] Ellis v. Ellis, 840 So. 2d 806, 812 (Miss. Ct. App. 2003). *But cf.* Lewis v. Butler, 794 So. 2d 1015 (Miss. 2001) (court did not address contempt against mother who violated order based on father's sexual advances to child).

[163] Ladner v. Ladner, 206 So. 2d 620, 624 (Miss. 1968), *overruled on other grounds by* Bubec v. Boston, 600 So. 2d 951 (Miss. 1968).

[164] *See* Gregory v. Gregory, 881 So. 2d 840, 844-45 (Miss. Ct. App. 2003); *see also* H.L.S. v. R.S.R., 949 So. 2d 794, 801 (Miss. Ct. App. 2006) (suggesting that attorneys' fees might not be appropriate for violations prompted by concern for child).

[165] Gray v. Pearson, 797 So. 2d 387, 395 (Miss. Ct. App. 2001); *see also* R.K. v. J.K., 946 So. 2d 764, 778 (Miss. 2007) (chancellor was within his discretion to find that husband, who relied on his attorney's advice in ceasing to make lump sum payments, was not in contempt); Keys v. Keys, 930 So. 2d 438, 443 (Miss. Ct. App. 2005) (chancellor had discretion to refuse contempt finding where mother who stopped paying child support believed that college student who moved her belongings to mother's house was living with her; acted on advice of attorney).

§ 14.05[2][k]   MISSISSIPPI FAMILY LAW

with their mother, an issue previously heard and decided by the court.[166]

[k] Judgment invalid. It is a defense to a finding of contempt that the underlying decree is void.[167]

§ 14.06 ENTRY OF JUDGMENT

Upon a finding of noncompliance with a decree, a court may enter a judgment for arrearages or otherwise order compliance with the decree. The court may order income withholding, impose a lien, or require the defendant to transfer assets or post a bond. In addition, the court may find the defendant in contempt and require payment of all or a portion of the amount due to purge the contempt. The court may also order the defendant incarcerated.

[1] Judgment for arrearages. In a suit for unpaid support, the court should enter a judgment for the amount owing with interest from the date each payment was due.[168] The court may order immediate payment of the entire amount due. Frequently, however, courts order a payor to satisfy arrearages through installment payments. A chancellor has discretion to order payment over time as a means of curing contempt, but may not prevent the payee from pursuing other means of collecting on the judgment.[169]

[a] Court may not forgive arrearages. A court may not forgive or modify vested payments.[170] Each payment in arrears automatically becomes a judgment against the payor.[171] A court properly rejected a husband's request to reduce alimony arrearages; unexpected circumstances may allow prospective modification but accrued arrearages may not be reduced.[172]

[b] Court may not suspend collection. A petitioner cannot be denied the right to collect a judgment for arrearages through normal collection processes such as garnishment or writ of execution. A chancellor erred in granting a stay of execution on

---

[166] Ladner v. Ladner, 206 So. 2d 620, 623 (Miss. 1968) (contempt for violation of visitation order), *overruled on other grounds by* Bubec v. Boston, 600 So. 2d 951 (Miss. 1968).

[167] Chasez v. Chasez, 957 So. 2d 1031, 1037 (Miss. Ct. App. 2007) (but finding that decree was valid; defendant waived defects by general appearance).

[168] *See supra* § 14.02[2].

[169] Rubisoff v. Rubisoff, 133 So. 2d 534, 538 (Miss. 1961) (chancellor may order payment of alimony arrearages in installments rather than issuing an execution to collect the entire amount); *see* Stigler v. Stigler, 48 So. 3d 547, 554 (Miss. Ct. App. 2009) (father ordered to repay $37,000 in arrearages at the rate of $1,000 a month, even though payment, combined with child support, was half of his disposable income), *cert. denied*, 49 So. 3d 1139 (Miss. 2010).

[170] Tanner v. Roland, 598 So. 2d 783, 786-87 (Miss. 1992); Varner v. Varner, 588 So. 2d 428, 432-33 (Miss. 1991); Gregg v. Montgomery, 587 So. 2d 928, 932 (Miss. 1991); Premeaux v. Smith, 569 So. 2d 681, 685 (Miss. 1990); Thurman v. Thurman, 559 So. 2d 1014, 1016-17 (Miss. 1990); Cumberland v. Cumberland, 564 So. 2d 839, 847 (Miss. 1990); Brand v. Brand, 482 So. 2d 236, 237 (Miss. 1986); Rubisoff v. Rubisoff, 133 So. 2d 534, 537 (Miss. 1961); Baier v. Baier, 897 So. 2d 202, 205 (Miss. Ct. App. 2005) (temporary arrearages may not be forgiven); Pope v. Pope, 803 So. 2d 499, 502 (Miss. Ct. App. 2002) (prospective reduction is proper, but vested payments are judgment and cannot be altered).

[171] Brand v. Brand, 482 So. 2d 236, 237 (Miss. 1986); Cunliffe v. Swartzfager, 437 So. 2d 43, 45-46 (Miss. 1983); Howard v. Howard, 191 So. 2d 528, 531 (Miss. 1966).

[172] Pope v. Pope, 803 So. 2d 499, 502 (Miss. Ct. App. 2002).

ENFORCEMENT OF DECREES   § 14.06[2]

a judgment for past-due child support so long as the defendant paid twenty-five dollars per month.[173] Similarly, a court could not limit a mother's right to collect arrearages by ordering child support reduced if she garnished the payor's wages.[174] And a payor who made monthly arrearages payments for ten years in compliance with a court order could nonetheless be reported to credit bureaus as delinquent.[175]

[2] Income-withholding orders. A court may order income withholding that exceeds the usual limits on garnishment to collect arrearages of child support and to collect alimony arrearages if a child is living with the alimony payee. A court may issue a withholding order directing that, in addition to current support, an employer withhold not less than 15% of the current payment to satisfy arrearages.[176] The amount withheld may not exceed 55% of the disposable income of a payor supporting other dependents[177] or 65% of the disposable income of a payor not supporting other dependents.[178]

Some benefits are protected from assignment or withholding by state or federal law. Under federal law, benefits payable to a veteran cannot be garnished for alimony or child support arrearages.[179] The benefits may be used, however, in calculating child support.[180] Federal law provides for some apportionment of veteran's benefits for a dependent child.[181] The Mississippi Court of Appeals held that even though veterans' benefits are not subject to attachment and cannot be the subject of a withholding order, a chancellor had authority to order a support payor in arrears to voluntarily withhold funds.[182]

In 2010, the Mississippi Supreme Court held that Supplemental Security Income (SSI), payable to very low-income disabled persons, cannot be the subject of an income-withholding order. In contrast, by statute, Social Security disability based on employment may be subject to income-withholding.[183]

[3] Order for asset transfer. A party who fails to comply with provisions for property transfer may be divested of title by court order.[184] A chancellor did not err in ordering the chancery clerk to execute a special commissioner's deed transferring property to a wife when her husband refused to execute quitclaim deeds pursuant to a

---

[173] Walters v. Walters, 383 So. 2d 827, 829 (Miss. 1980); *see also* Brand v. Brand, 482 So. 2d 236, 239 (Miss. 1986).

[174] Peeples v. Yarbrough, 475 So. 2d 1154, 1159 (Miss. 1985).

[175] Dep't of Human Servs. v. St. Peter, 708 So. 2d 83, 85 (Miss. 1998) (but noting that fact that DHS has the statutory right to report the delinquency "does not . . . mean that it is necessary or even advisable for it to do so in the present case").

[176] *See* Miss. Code Ann. § 93-11-103(5) (Supp. 2010).

[177] Miss. Code Ann. § 85-3-4(3)(b)(iii) (1999).

[178] Miss. Code Ann. § 85-3-4(3)(b)(iii) (1999).

[179] 38 U.S.C. § 5301(a)(1) (2006); *see* Rushing v. Rushing, 909 So. 2d 155, 157-58 (Miss. Ct. App. 2005)).

[180] *See supra* § 13.04[2][c].

[181] *See* 38 C.F.R. §§ 3.450 - .461 (2010), *cited in* Rose v. Rose, 481 U.S. 619, 626 (1987).

[182] Rushing v. Rushing, 909 So. 2d 155, 157-58 (Miss. Ct. App. 2005).

[183] Barnes v. Dep't of Human Servs. 42 So. 3d 10, 15-17 (Miss. 2010) (but also holding that chancellors have discretion to consider SSI income in calculating child support).

[184] *See* Miss. R. Civ. P. 70 (when party fails to comply with judgment, court may direct party to act, divest title, order sheriff to deliver possession, and/or find the party in contempt).

§ 14.06[4]   MISSISSIPPI FAMILY LAW

divorce judgment.[185]

[4] Imposition of equitable lien. A court may impress a lien on a defendant's property to secure payment of arrearages[186] even if the original decree did not include an equitable lien[187] and even if the creditor spouse did not request a lien in the pleadings. The lien may secure payments not yet due as well as those in arrears.[188] The supreme court rejected a debtor's argument that impressing a lien to secure future payments was an unconstitutional prejudgment seizure of his property.[189]

[5] Requirement of bond. A defendant may be ordered to post a bond as security for performance.[190] A chancellor erred in failing to require a bond from a defaulting out-of-state father whose future residence was unknown.[191] A parent who has abducted or is likely to abduct children should be required to post a bond. The court of appeals upheld a chancellor's order requiring bond from a noncustodial mother who had previously removed children from the state without consulting their father.[192] Similarly, a court properly required a $2,000 bond prior to visitation from a father who wrongfully removed a child from the mother's home.[193]

[6] Sanctions for contempt. Sanctions for civil contempt include fines, payment of arrearages, prohibition of future conduct, payment of attorney's fees, and/or incarceration.[194] A court erred, however, in barring an attorney defendant from practicing law until he purged himself of contempt.[195]

[a] Plaintiff's right to sanctions. A petitioner is entitled to have the court use its coercive powers to force compliance by a defendant in contempt. A court erred in finding a husband in contempt for failure to transfer title to a van but making no order

---

[185] Ladner v. Ladner, 843 So. 2d 81, 82-83 (Miss. Ct. App. 2003).

[186] Aldridge v. Aldridge, 527 So. 2d 96, 99 (Miss. 1988) (discussing imposition of lien to secure property division payment); Alexander v. Alexander, 494 So. 2d 365, 369 (Miss. 1986); Morgan v. Morgan, 397 So. 2d 894, 896 (Miss. 1981) (discussing lien for future alimony payments).

[187] Cf. Aldridge v. Aldridge, 527 So. 2d 96, 99 (Miss. 1988) (lien does not arise from lis pendens notice; court must find basis for imposing lien independent of filing of lis pendens).

[188] Alexander v. Alexander, 494 So. 2d 365, 368 (Miss. 1986) (stating that where the payment secured reflects a buy-out of the creditor's interest in a marital asset, the lien is actually a purchase money lien on the property secured); see Morgan v. Morgan, 397 So. 2d 894, 895 (Miss. 1981) (discussing lien for future alimony payments).

[189] Morgan v. Morgan, 397 So. 2d 894, 897 (Miss. 1981) (authority under MISS. CODE ANN. § 93-5-23 (2004)).

[190] See MISS. CODE ANN. §§ 93-5-23; 93-11-65(3) (2004) (court may order bond when child support is thirty days in arrears).

[191] Bush v. Bush, 451 So. 2d 779, 782 (Miss. 1984) (stating that the circumstances would "make it difficult for Mrs. Bush to locate him and for any court to exercise jurisdiction over him").

[192] Ayers v. Ayers, 734 So. 2d 213, 217-18 (Miss. Ct. App. 1999); see also Roberts v. Fuhr, 523 So. 2d 20, 27-28 (Miss. 1987) (father required to post bond for visitation after he had taken child to Germany during custody dispute); Rodgers v. Rodgers, 274 So. 2d 671, 673-74 (Miss. 1973) (stating that court may require parent to enter into a bond to assure its jurisdiction is retained over the child); Faris v. Jernigan, 939 So. 2d 835, 839-49 (Miss. Ct. App. 2006) (chancellor did not err in ordering that mother who repeatedly violated visitation order post a $40,000 ne exeat bond in order to exercise visitation outside the state).

[193] Stauffer v. Stauffer, 379 So. 2d 922, 924-25 (Miss. 1980).

[194] MISSISSIPPI CIVIL PROCEDURE § 16A3 (Jeffrey Jackson, ed., 2000).

[195] Rhodes v. Rhodes, 420 So. 2d 759, 761 (Miss. 1982).

ENFORCEMENT OF DECREES

§ 14.06[6][b]

requiring compliance.[196]

[b] Incarceration. A defendant who is currently unable to satisfy a judgment may not be imprisoned for civil contempt.[197] A court erred in incarcerating a defendant who had been injured in an accident, was unable to work, and had no funds with which to pay the judgment.[198] And the supreme court reversed an order jailing a husband who was without funds to pay a judgment even though he had sufficient income when he defaulted.[199] Similarly, a chancellor erred in ordering a payor incarcerated unless payments were made in one week. Destruction of his medical office made immediate satisfaction of the judgment impossible.[200] However, the court of appeals affirmed incarceration of a wife for nonpayment of alimony. Although there was evidence of inability to pay, the court of appeals deferred to the chancellor's finding that the wife misrepresented her financial circumstances.[201] The burden is on the payor to show inability to pay.[202] Proof must be specific and not in general terms.[203]

Courts disagree as to whether a debtor may be imprisoned for default on divorce-related payments.[204] The Mississippi Supreme Court held in 1943 that imprisonment for nonpayment of alimony and child support does not contravene the constitutional prohibition on imprisonment for debt: "[a]limony is not sued on as a debt . . . in the ordinary sense but rather a legal means of enforcing the husband's obligation to his wife and children; . . . It is imposed upon him by virtue of the marriage relation, for reasons of public policy, and not as a debt resulting from some business transaction or other contractual obligation."[205] The decision predated equitable distribution and so does not address incarceration for default on property division payments. The reasoning of the

---

[196] Allred v. Allred, 735 So. 2d 1064, 1069 (Miss. Ct. App. 1999). *But cf.* Balius v. Gaines, 914 So. 2d 300, 307-08 (Miss. Ct. App. 2005) (rejecting father's argument that court erred in failing to sanction mother for disobeying court orders; no authority that court is required to impose sanctions upon finding of criminal contempt).

[197] Lewis v. Lewis, 57 So. 2d 163, 165 (Miss. 1952). The legislature in 2009 amended MISS. CODE ANN. § 93-5-23 to provide that a court has discretion to refer a person incarcerated for contempt for failure to pay child support to a "state, county or municipal restitution, house arrest or restorative justice center or program."

[198] Wilborn v. Wilborn, 258 So. 2d 804, 805-06 (Miss. 1972).

[199] Ramsay v. Ramsay, 87 So. 491, 493 (Miss. 1921); *see* Dickerson v. Horn, 50 So. 2d 368, 369-70 (Miss. 1951) (husband had no property or income except monthly earnings as barber; suffered from kidney stone attacks); Collins v. Collins, 158 So. 914, 915-16 (Miss. 1935) (test for relief from contempt is showing that all surplus was spent on payments; test for incarceration is present ability to pay); *see also* Howard v. Howard, 913 So. 2d 1030, 1039-40 (Miss. Ct. App. 2005) (inability to pay should be determined when order of incarceration is enforced, rather than date order is entered; because chancellor suspended incarceration for twenty-one days, defendant should be permitted to introduce evidence of inability to pay on that date).

[200] Gambrell v. Gambrell, 644 So. 2d 435, 443 (Miss. 1994) (court should have allowed additional reasonable time to pay, without reducing payments).

[201] Stribling v. Stribling, 960 So. 2d 556, 560 (Miss. Ct. App. 2007); *see also* Seghini v. Seghini, 42 So. 3d 635, 642-43 (Miss. Ct. App. 2010) (husband jailed for forty days; evidence of inability to pay not convincing).

[202] Duncan v. Duncan, 417 So. 2d 908, 909-10 (Miss. 1982).

[203] Newell v. Hinton, 556 So. 2d 1037, 1045 (Miss. 1990); Clements v. Young, 481 So. 2d 263, 271 (Miss. 1985); Prestwood v. Hambrick, 308 So. 2d 82, 85 (Miss. 1975); Doyle v. Doyle, 55 So. 3d 1097, 1111-12 (Miss. Ct. App. 2010) (incarceration affirmed; husband alleged inability to pay, but offered no details).

[204] *See In Re* Marriage of Lenger, 336 N.W.2d 191, 194 (Iowa 1983) (permitting imprisonment; property settlement is not "debt" within the meaning of the constitution); McAlear v. McAlear, 469 A.2d 1256, 1272-73 (Md. Ct. App. 1984) (not permitting imprisonment; property division cannot be enforced by contempt),

[205] Felder v. Felder's Estate, 13 So. 2d 823, 827 (Miss. 1943) (imprisonment for contempt for nonpayment of other civil judgments violates the constitutional prohibition against imprisonment for debt); *see* Nichols v. Rutledge, 749 So. 2d 68, 72 (Miss. 1999).

§ 14.06[6][c]   MISSISSIPPI FAMILY LAW

decision would seem equally applicable to property division payments. On the other hand, an argument can be made that property division is distinguishable from support payments. For example, property division payments may be discharged in bankruptcy under some circumstances, while alimony and child support payments may not.[206]

[c] Attorneys' fees. A creditor spouse who successfully prosecutes an action for contempt is entitled to attorneys' fees without a showing of need: "To hold otherwise would cause no peril to those restrained from certain conduct if they violate the orders of a court."[207] A court properly ordered a custodial father to pay costs and attorneys' fees associated with a hearing finding him in contempt for violating visitation orders.[208] No award of attorneys' fees is warranted if a petition for contempt is denied.[209]

§ 14.07 COLLECTION OF JUDGMENT

[1] Execution on judgment. An enrolled judgment becomes a lien on any property of the debtor in the county of enrollment.[210] A petitioner may execute on a judgment for arrearages by any means permitted for collection of judgments,[211] including garnishment,[212] execution of orders by a sheriff,[213] and execution through a sheriff's sale.[214] A creditor spouse may execute an equitable lien on property belonging to a debtor spouse, including homestead property. The home of a debtor and his second wife could be foreclosed to satisfy his first wife's lien securing alimony.[215]

---

[206] Felder v. Felder's Estate, 13 So. 2d 823, 827 (Miss. 1943) (discussing non-dischargeability of alimony and child support).

[207] Smith v. Little, 843 So. 2d 735, 738 (Miss. Ct. App. 2003); *see* Ladner v. Logan, 857 So. 2d 764, 770-71 (Miss. 2003) (custodial parent may be awarded attorneys' fees for prosecuting arrearage action on behalf of children); *see also In re* Hampton, 919 So. 2d 949, 958 (Miss. 2006); *cf.* Jurney v. Jurney, 921 So. 2d 372, 377 (Miss. Ct. App. 2005) (court erred in granting attorneys' fees to defendant mother who violated decree but complied before hearing; award of fees would punish petitioner father for exercising right to bring contempt proceedings, no matter how small amount involved.)

[208] McDonald v. McDonald, 850 So. 2d 1182, 1193 (Miss. Ct. App. 2002); *see* Cook v. Whiddon, 866 So. 2d 494, 501 (Miss. Ct. App. 2004) (plaintiff entitled to attorneys' fees on successful contempt motion); *see also* Kelley v. Day, 965 So. 2d 749, 755 (Miss. Ct. App. 2007) (court properly ordered attorneys' fees); Faris v. Jernigan, 939 So. 2d 835, 841 (Miss. Ct. App. 2006) (chancellor properly ordered mother to pay $40,000 of father's attorneys' fees in contempt proceedings); Watkins v. Watkins, 942 So. 2d 224, 231 (Miss. Ct. App. 2006) (attorneys' fees ordered in successful contempt action); Rushing v. Rushing, 909 So. 2d 155, 158-59 (Miss. Ct. App. 2005) (chancellor properly ordered payment of attorneys' fees in former wife's successful petition for contempt for alimony arrearages).

[209] Varner v. Varner, 666 So. 2d 493, 497 (Miss. 1995) (quoting Cumberland v. Cumberland, 564 So. 2d 839, 845 (Miss. 1990)); Weston v. Mount, 789 So. 2d 822, 826 (Miss. Ct. App. 2001). *But cf.* Holloway v. Holloway, 865 So. 2d 382, 383 (Miss. Ct. App. 2003) (attorneys' fees properly awarded where payor purged of contempt by paying amount due after motion filed, but before hearing); Mixon v. Sharp, 853 So. 2d 834, 841 (Miss. Ct. App. 2003) (upheld award of attorneys' fees in contempt action even though no specific finding of contempt; clear that fees were awarded because of father's interference with court-ordered visitation. *See supra* § 10.03[2].

[210] *See* MISS. CODE ANN. § 11-7-191 (2004).

[211] MISS. R. CIV. P. 69 (providing that the statutory procedures for execution on judgment remain in effect); *see* Rainwater v. Rainwater, 110 So. 2d 608 (Miss. 1959).

[212] *See* MISS. CODE ANN. § 11-5-81 (2002) (garnishment to enforce chancery decrees for money); MISS. CODE ANN. § 11-35-1 (2004) (garnishment procedures).

[213] *See* MISS. CODE ANN. § 11-5-83 (2002) (sheriff to execute decrees).

[214] *See* MISS. CODE ANN. § 13-3-181 (2002) (execution sale by sheriff).

[215] Felder v. Felder's Estate, 13 So. 2d 823, 827 (Miss. 1943).

ENFORCEMENT OF DECREES   § 14.07[2]

When a support order has been in arrears for thirty days, a judgment arises by operation of law. The judgment may be enforced by intercepting payments from government agencies, lottery and gaming winnings that are received in periodic payments, assets held in financial institutions, awards from civil actions, and distributions of retirement funds.[216]

[2] Lien on workers' compensation benefits. Workers' compensation benefits may be impressed with a lien for child support arrearages and for alimony arrearages if a child is living with the alimony payee.[217] The lien is imposed administratively when the payee or Department of Human Services files a notice of the lien with the Executive Director of the Workers' Compensation Commission. The notice must include a certified copy of the court order, a copy of any modification order, and the payee's sworn statement of the amount of arrearages.[218]

[3] Seizure of financial accounts. The Department of Human Services may administratively encumber and seize a delinquent payor's accounts with financial institutions in the state.[219] "Financial institution" is defined to include banks, credit unions, stock brokerages, and public or private entities administering retirement, savings, annuities, life insurance, and/or pension funds.[220] After forty-five days, the encumbered funds are forwarded to DHS.[221] An obligor whose account is seized may petition under Rule 81(d)(2) to have the encumbrance lifted. Issues in the challenge are limited to mistaken identity and mistakes in the amount of overdue support.[222]

[4] Seizure of tax rebates in IV-D cases. The Department of Human Services is authorized to seize state income tax refunds to offset delinquent support.[223] The department may also seize federal tax refunds to satisfy arrearages.[224]

[5] Seizure of retirement funds. Retirement accounts are subject to seizure to satisfy child support arrearages, but only to the extent that the holder "is qualified to receive and receives a lump-sum or periodic distribution from the funds."[225] Federal law specifically provides that Federal Thrift Savings Plans may be seized to satisfy arrearages.[226]

---

[216] MISS. CODE ANN. § 93-11-71 (Supp. 2010).

[217] MISS. CODE ANN. § 71-3-129 (2000) (a lien may also be placed on any workers' compensation benefits to recover arrearages for spousal support payments where a minor child is living with the spouse and maintenance or spousal support is collected in conjunction with child support).

[218] MISS. CODE ANN. § 71-3-129 (2000) (notice should include: name and address of the delinquent obligor, the Social Security number of the obligor, if known, the name of the obligee, and the amount of delinquent child or spousal support).

[219] MISS. CODE ANN. § 43-19-48(1)(b) (2009).

[220] MISS. CODE ANN. § 43-19-48(10)(a) (2009).

[221] MISS. CODE ANN. § 43-19-48(4)(a)(ii) (2009).

[222] MISS. CODE ANN. § 43-19-48(5) (2009).

[223] MISS. CODE ANN. § 43-19-31(h) (2009).

[224] *See* 42 U.S.C. §§ 664(a), 666(a)(3)(A) (2006 & Supp. 2010).

[225] MISS. CODE ANN. § 93-11-71 (2004).

[226] 5 U.S.C. § 8437(e)(3) (Supp. 2010).

§ 14.07[6]   **MISSISSIPPI FAMILY LAW**

[6] Entry of QDRO. A chancellor may order entry of a qualified domestic relations order granting a custodial parent an interest in a delinquent payor's retirement account as a means of satisfying child support arrearages. The court of appeals rejected a father's argument that this constituted a modification of the couple's property settlement agreement.[227]

§ 14.08 OTHER ENFORCEMENT TOOLS

Other indirect measures are available to secure compliance with court-ordered support or to punish willful failure to support, including license revocation, reporting to credit agencies, and criminal prosecution.

[1] License Revocation. In 1996, the Mississippi legislature, pursuant to federal directives, provided for revocation of various licenses as a penalty for nonpayment of child support. The Act applies to business and professional licenses, licenses to sell alcohol, drivers' licenses, and hunting and fishing licenses.[228] License suspension may also be ordered when an individual fails to comply with a subpoena related to paternity or child support proceedings.[229] The order may be stayed for a reasonable time to allow satisfaction of the delinquency.[230]

[2] Report to credit bureau. Section 93-11-69 of the Mississippi Code provides that the Department of Human Services shall report overdue support to credit reporting agencies. The reporting requirement also applies to spousal payments that are collected in conjunction with child support.[231] Furthermore, DHS may report information to a credit bureau even if the payor is complying with a court-ordered payment plan to satisfy arrearages.[232]

[3] Criminal prosecution. A parent may be prosecuted for nonsupport of a child under the Mississippi criminal neglect statute. The statute provides that "[a]ny parent who shall desert or willfully neglect or refuse to provide for the support and maintenance of his or her child or children, . . . shall be guilty of a felony."[233] The Mississippi Supreme Court rejected a defendant's argument that the statute unconstitutionally provides for imprisonment for debt: "[t]his State has a legitimate interest in criminally prosecuting financially able parents who willfully desert or fail to support their children when in destitute or necessitous circumstances."[234] The supreme court affirmed a

---

[227] Carlson v. Matthews, 966 So. 2d 1258, 1261 (Miss. Ct. App. 2007).

[228] MISS. CODE ANN. § 93-11-153(b) (2004).

[229] MISS. CODE ANN. § 93-11-157(15) (2004).

[230] MISS. CODE ANN. § 93-11-163 (2004) (the Act provides that licensing agencies are to respond to court-ordered suspension as an order under the Act).

[231] MISS. CODE ANN. §§ 93-11-69 (1)(d), (2) (2004).

[232] Dep't of Human Servs. v. St. Peter, 708 So. 2d 83, 85 (Miss. 1998).

[233] MISS. CODE ANN. § 97-5-3 (2004) (the penalty for a first offense is a fine of not less than $100 nor more than $500, or a five-year sentence, or both; for a second or subsequent offense, a fine of between $1,000 and $10,000 or imprisonment for two to five years, or both).

[234] Bryant v. State, 567 So. 2d 234, 236 (Miss. 1990); *see also* Martin v. State, 308 So. 2d 925, 926 (Miss. 1975); Williams v. State, 43 So. 2d 389 (Miss. 1949), *overruled in part on other grounds by* Lenoir v. State, 115 So. 2d 731

ENFORCEMENT OF DECREES § 14.08[4]

father's conviction and two-year sentence for failure to support a disabled child whose mother could not care for the child and work.[235]

Federal law criminalizes nonsupport as well. In 1992 Congress passed the Child Support Recovery Act, which created criminal liability for a parent who is in arrears for more than one year or owes more than $5,000.[236]

[4] Parent locator services. In compliance with federal law, the Mississippi Department of Human Services has established a directory of new hires to assist in parent location. Every employer doing business in the state is required to report new hires to the department within fifteen days.[237] DHS has access to similar information in a national new-hire database.

[5] Interstate enforcement. An order issued in one state may be enforced in other states by registering the order through a two-state procedure or by filing directly in the enforcing state to register the order.[238] A court enforcing an order registered from a state with continuing exclusive jurisdiction may not modify the order, forgive arrearages, or entertain defenses.[239] A payee may also send a child support order directly to a payor's employer in another state without first registering the order. The employer must immediately notify the employee and begin withholding as though the order were issued in the employer's state.[240] A payee may also, without registering an order, send the payor's state enforcement agency the order and request that it use any available administrative enforcement mechanisms to collect the amount due.[241]

(Miss. 1959).

[235] Bryant v. State, 567 So. 2d 234, 236 (Miss. 1990); *see also* Knowles v. State, 708 So. 2d 549, 554 (Miss. 1998) (holding that amended statute no longer requires proving that children were destitute).

[236] 18 U.S.C. § 228 (2006). The presumption created in 228(b) has been held unconstitutional in at least two cases. *See* U.S. v. Pillor, 387 F. Supp. 2d 1053, 1056 (N.D. Cal. 2005) (mandatory presumption that defendant had ability to pay violates due process); U.S. v. Morrow, 368 F. Supp. 2d 863, 866 (C.D. Ill. 2005) (same).

[237] Miss. Code Ann. § 43-19-46 (2009).

[238] Procedure for registration is set out in Miss. Code Ann. § 93-25-83 (2004).

[239] Miss. Code Ann. § 93-25-85 (2004).

[240] Miss. Code Ann. § 93-25-69 (2004).

[241] Miss. Code Ann. § 93-25-79 (2004).

502

XV
ASSISTED REPRODUCTION TECHNOLOGY

Co-author Ashley Pittman*

§ 15.01 INTRODUCTION

For most of history, an infertile couple's only option for parenthood was to adopt a child. Today, options for becoming a parent range from old-fashioned procreation to a six-person collaboration involving donated eggs and sperm, a petri dish, and a gestational carrier. The process is nothing short of miraculous, but the attending legal issues are daunting. The legal authority, while developing, is still relatively sparse and varies, sometimes dramatically, from state to state. And in some states, including Mississippi, there is no law on the subject. Judges and practitioners must carefully navigate this patchwork of legal rules. Because agreements regarding parental rights are usually honored, a well-drafted agreement is critical to protect the parties and avoid litigation under unsettled rules.[1]

§ 15.02 TERMINOLOGY AND BASICS

Assisted reproduction refers to a number of advanced techniques used by physicians to aid infertile couples or individuals in achieving pregnancy. The most basic of these techniques is artificial or intrauterine insemination. This involves insemination of a woman with sperm, usually from a donor.[2] A relatively recent development, in vitro fertilization (IVF), has greatly expanded the options available to infertile patients. Through IVF, an embryo is produced by combining an egg and sperm in a laboratory setting. The resulting embryo is then implanted into a woman's uterus. The procedure may be accomplished with the gametes (egg and sperm) of the intended parents or by using donor eggs and/or sperm.[3] And with either of these procedures, a surrogate may be engaged to carry the child.[4]

A host of disputes may arise in the context of assisted reproduction: disputes between surrogates and intended parents over rights and obligations regarding the child, between intended parents over use and disposition of frozen embryos, and, less frequently, between intended parents and donors. Parties may also dispute whether an embryo may be implanted after an intended parent's death, and, if so, whether the

---

* Ashley W. Pittman practices with the law firm of Stubblefield & Yelverton, PLLC, located in Jackson, Mississippi, in the areas of reproductive law and surrogacy law, estate and business planning, probate, asset protection strategies, charitable planning and taxation law.

[1] *See* CHARLES P. KINDREGAN, JR. & MAUREEN MCBRIEN, ASSISTED REPRODUCTIVE TECHNOLOGY (2d ed. 2011) (an excellent treatise, recently released by the American Bar Association).

[2] KINDREGAN, JR., ET AL., *supra* note 1, at § 2.1.

[3] KINDREGAN, JR., ET AL., *supra* note 1, at § 3.1.

[4] *See infra* § 15.07.

§ 15.03   MISSISSIPPI FAMILY LAW

resulting child may inherit from or receive benefits through the deceased.

Surprisingly, many states, including Mississippi, have no law on the topic. An increasing number of states are enacting statutes to address at least some of the issues. But in the absence of statutory or case law, courts are faced with resolving these issues using woefully inadequate contract, property, constitutional, and family law concepts.

§ 15.03 LEGAL STATUS OF THE EMBRYO

The IVF process often produces excess embryos that are cryopreserved, or frozen, for later use. The legal status of frozen embryos is poorly defined and controversial.[5] At one extreme is the right-to-life approach, advocating that life begins at fertilization. Based on this definition, an embryo may not be destroyed, and would enjoy certain rights afforded to persons.[6] At the other extreme is a property approach, which focuses on the rights of the gamete providers (intended parents) to make decisions with regard to embryo disposition.[7] Occupying a place between the two is the special respect approach, which advocates a balancing test that takes into account the rights of all parties.[8] Most courts faced with resolving disputes over embryos have avoided labeling the embryo, opting for a fact-based decision-making framework grounded in contract principles and a balancing of the parties' rights.[9]

To date, Louisiana is the only state to elevate the status of the embryo above the level of personal property and into the realm of semi-human, affording the embryo legally enforceable rights. Louisiana statutes declare that the "in vitro fertilized human ovum is a juridical person which cannot be owned by the in vitro fertilization patients. . ."[10] The statute punishes intentional destruction of embryos, but allows the gamete providers to relinquish rights to embryos for "adoptive implantation" by another couple.[11] The embryo is not considered an heir for inheritance purposes in Louisiana. However, the Louisiana statute provides that the embryo has limited standing to sue and be sued in a court of law.[12]

In the precedential case of *Davis v. Davis,* the Tennessee Supreme Court used the "special respect approach," describing the embryo as "not, strictly speaking, either 'persons' or 'property,' but occupy[ing] an interim category [which] entitles them to special respect because of their potential for human life."[13]

Other courts to address the issue have generally accepted the *Davis* court's char-

---

[5] Angela K. Upchurch, *The Deep Freeze: A Critical Examination of the Resolution of Frozen Embryo Disputes Through the Adversarial Process*, 33 FLA. ST. U. L. REV. 395, 400 (2005).

[6] Mark C. Haut, *Divorce and the Disposition of Frozen Embryos*, 28 HOFSTRA L. REV. 493, 497 (Winter 1999).

[7] At least one court treated embryos as personal property in the context of divorce. *See In re* Marriage of Dahl, 194 P.3d 834, 840-41 (Or. Ct. App. 2008) (contractual right to dispose of embryos is a personal property right; enforcing contract between parties).

[8] *See* Davis v. Davis, 842 S.W.2d 588, 597 (Tenn. 1992); KINDREGAN, JR., ET AL., *supra* note 1, at § 4.4.

[9] See *infra* note 21 and accompanying text.

[10] LA. REV. STAT. ANN. § 9:130 (2010).

[11] LA. REV. STAT. ANN. §§ 9:129, 9:130 (2010). In a dispute over frozen embryos, the courts follow a "best interest of the child" test, instead of focusing on the rights of the parents. *See* LA. REV. STAT. ANN. § 9:131 (2010); *see also* Michael S. Simon, *'Honey, I Froze the Kids': Davis v. Davis and the Legal Status of Early Embryos*, 23 LOY. U. CHI. L.J. 131, 137 (1991) (expressing doubts as to the constitutionality of the statute).

[12] LA. REV. STAT. ANN. §§ 9:124, 9:133 (2010).

[13] *See* Davis v. Davis, 842 S.W.2d 588, 597 (Tenn. 1992).

ASSISTED REPRODUCTION TECHNOLOGY § 15.04

acterization of the embryo as entitled to special consideration, but not affording them the rights and liberties granted to living beings.[14]

As the number of stored embryos grows, the debate over their legal status will become increasingly important. Because the creators of the embryo are generally given authority to determine their disposition,[15] it is important that parties execute agreements spelling out their intent with regard to embryo ownership and disposition during their lives, after their deaths, or in the event of divorce.

§ 15.04 DIVISION OF EMBRYOS AT DIVORCE

Parties who seek in vitro fertilization treatment generally sign a clinic-provided contract that addresses disposition of excess embryos in the event of divorce, death, or other listed circumstances. Courts are divided on the extent to which these contracts are enforceable.

Courts in New York, Oregon, Texas, and Washington (and Tennessee in dicta)[16] have held that a contract providing for disposition of embryos upon divorce is enforceable. The Texas Supreme Court stated "We believe that allowing the parties voluntarily to decide the disposition of frozen embryos in advance of cryopreservation, subject to mutual change of mind, jointly expressed, best serves the existing public policy of this State and the interests of the parties."[17]

In contrast, courts in Iowa, New Jersey, and Massachusetts have held that provisions regarding disposition may not be binding if, due to a change in circumstances such as divorce, one of the parties changes his or her mind.[18] The Iowa Supreme Court proposed that parties should have to give mutual, contemporaneous consent to any use of an embryo.[19]

The ABA Model Act appears to follow the second approach. It encourages agreements, but provides that a party can change his or her earlier instructions by notifying the other intended parent and the clinic.[20]

In the absence of a contract, courts have applied a balancing test in light of the facts and circumstances surrounding the parties at the time of divorce. In *Davis v.*

---

[14] KINDREGAN, JR., ET AL., *supra* note 1, at § 4.4.

[15] *See, e.g.,* Kass v. Kass, 696 N.E.2d 174, 178 (N.Y. 1998); Litowitz v. Litowitz, 48 P.3d 261, 267 (Wash. 2002).

[16] *See* Kass v. Kass, 696 N.E.2d 174, 179 n.4, 182 (N.Y. 1998) (enforcing a couple's contractual agreement to donate frozen embryos for research; but noting that in some cases "changed circumstances" might make a contract unenforceable); *In re* Marriage of Dahl, 194 P.3d 834, 840-41 (Or. Ct. App. 2008) (enforcing contract between parties); Davis v. Davis, 842 S.W.2d 588, 597 (Tenn. 1992) (dictum) (there was no agreement in the case, but the court indicated that an agreement should be honored); Litowitz v. Litowitz, 48 P.3d 261, 268 (Wash. 2002) (en banc) (wife and "intended mother" had equal rights to embryos as the father who contributed sperm).

[17] Roman v. Roman, 193 S.W.3d 40, 49 (Tex. App. 2006).

[18] *In re* Marriage of Witten, 672 N.W. 2d 768 (Iowa 2003); A.Z. v. B.Z., 725 N.E.2d 1051, 1057 (Mass. 2000) (even if husband consented to allow wife to implant, changed circumstances made agreement unenforceable; husband could not be forced to procreate against his will); J.B. v. M.B., 783 A.2d 707, 719 (N.J. 2001) (if one of the parties changed his or her mind about the agreement, court would balance the parties' interests; usually, the party wanting not to procreate would prevail).

[19] *In re* Marriage of Witten, 672 N.W. 2d 768 (Iowa 2003) (contract is enforceable "subject to the right of either party to change his or her mind about disposition up to the point of use or destruction of any stored embryo") (quoting J.B. v. M.B., 783 A.2d 707, 719 (N.J. 2001)).

[20] ABA MODEL ACT GOVERNING ASSISTED REPROD. TECH. §§ 201-202 (2008).

§ 15.05   **MISSISSIPPI FAMILY LAW**

Davis, the husband preferred that the couple's embryos be destroyed at divorce, while his wife opted to donate them to an infertile couple. The Tennessee Supreme Court stated that in the absence of agreement, courts should balance the parents' competing interests. The court found the husband's right not to procreate more compelling than the wife's right to procreate. However, the court noted that if the wife was infertile and the embryos represented her only chance to have children in the future, the decision might be different.[21]

§ 15.05 Use of embryos after death: The posthumously conceived child

Cryopreservation of embryos presents the possibility of implantation after a genetic parent's death, allowing the birth of a person's biological child years after the parent's death. In most states, no law prohibits implantation of an embryo after the death of a genetic parent. A donor's intent is critical in determining whether implantation is permitted. In a well-known case, a California court held that no public policy was violated when a man left his preserved sperm to his girlfriend for use after his death.[22] In two cases, however, parties have been denied access to preserved sperm that donors expressly indicated they wanted destroyed and not used.[23] The technology raises questions of inheritance rights of the posthumously conceived child and the resulting child's right to benefits such as Social Security.

[1] Inheritance. Twelve states specifically address posthumous birth through ART, most requiring written consent in order for a child born through ART to be eligible for inheritance. Some, but not all, set a time period within which implantation or birth must occur.[24]

The Uniform Probate Code, as amended in 2008, provides that the deceased is the parent of a posthumously conceived child if *in utero* not later than 36 months after death, or born not later than 45 months after death.[25] The UPA has been adopted directly in North Dakota, and with some variation in a number of other states.[26] Guidance concerning inheritance rights is also provided in the Uniform Parentage Act (UPA),[27] and Restatement (Third) of Property.[28]

In states without a statute, court decisions have varied, depending upon the wording of the relevant state statute. Some courts have held that posthumously conceived children are not covered by the relevant state intestacy statutes.[29] A New York court,

---

[21] Davis v. Davis, 842 S.W.2d 588, 604 (Tenn. 1992).

[22] Hecht v. Super. Court, 20 Cal. Rptr. 2d 275, 287 (Cal. Ct. App. 1993).

[23] *See In re* Estate of Kievernagel, 83 Cal. Rptr. 3d 311, 317-18 (Cal. Ct. App. 2008); Speranza v. Repro Lab, Inc., 875 N.Y.S.2d 449, 453 (N.Y. App. Div. 2009).

[24] Kindregan, Jr., et al., *supra* note 1, at § 7.7.

[25] Unif. Probate Code 2-120(k) (2010).

[26] N.D. Cent. Code § 14-20-65 (2009); *see* Kindregan, Jr., et al., *supra* note 1, at § 7.7.

[27] Unif. Parentage Act § 707 (2000) (the decedent is the parent if the decedent "consented in a record that if assisted reproduction were to occur after death, the deceased individual would be a parent of the child").

[28] *See* Restatement (Third) of Property § 2.5, Illus. 8 (decedent is considered the parent of a child produced from his or her genetic material through ART if the child is born within a reasonable time after death and circumstances indicate that decedent would have intended to be the child's parent).

[29] Finley v. Astrue, 601 F. Supp. 2d 1092, 1099-1100 (E.D. Ark. 2009) (denying benefits; statute provides for

ASSISTED REPRODUCTION TECHNOLOGY   § 15.05[2]

however, held that children born of new technology should be treated as natural children. The statute in question applied to posthumous children, without limiting inheritance to "posthumously born" children.[30] In Virginia, a posthumously conceived child is in an odd position; a statute provides that he or she is considered the child of a decedent who consented to the conception, but is not entitled to inherit as an heir.[31]

[2] Mississippi. Mississippi intestacy statutes do not specifically address the inheritance status of posthumous children. However, in 1845, the Mississippi Supreme Court recognized the common law rule that a posthumously born child of an intestate inherits the same as other children. The court held that a posthumously born child who was "in existence" at the time of the intestate's death is entitled to inherit.[32] In addition, the Mississippi Code also addresses the rights of a posthumously born child of a person who died with a will. Section 91-5-3 provides that if a testator dies and his wife is "enceinte," the posthumously born child will inherit as if the father had died intestate.[33]

The Ninth Circuit rejected an argument that a posthumously conceived child should be allowed to inherit under a statute allowing inheritance by posthumously "born" children, distinguishing posthumous birth and posthumous conception.[34] Similarly, the Arkansas Supreme Court held that a statute allowing posthumously born children to inherit did not apply to posthumously conceived children; the statute was enacted before IVF was available, and therefore the legislature could not have intended for it to apply to children conceived using this technology.[35]

[3] Social Security. The federal Social Security Act extends benefits to dependent children of a deceased wage earner. Federal courts have reached different conclusions regarding whether posthumously conceived children are entitled to receive Social Security benefits. The wording of the Act is critical to this analysis. Section 416(e) of the Act defines the term "child" as "the child or legally adopted child of an individual."[36] Section 416(h) provides that a "child" for purposes of the Act is one who is entitled to inherit under the intestacy law of the deceased's home state. In the alternative, 416(h) provides that a person is considered the child of a deceased if the deceased acknowledged the child, was judicially declared the child's parent, or was ordered to pay support for the child.[37]

The Third and Ninth Circuits have looked to the definition of child under § 416(e), while the Fourth Circuit has looked to the definition under 416(h), producing directly opposite results. In a Third Circuit case, the commissioner argued that twins conceived

---

posthumously born, but not conceived, children); Khabbaz v. Comm'r, 930 A.2d 1180, 1184 (N.H. 2007) (posthumously conceived child not eligible for inheritance as a "surviving issue" even though father executed a consent agreement that the resulting child would be entitled to inheritance).

[30] *In re* Martin B., 841 N.Y.S.2d 207, 212 (N.Y. Surr. Ct. 2007); *see also* Woodward v. Commissioner of Social Sec., 760 N.E.2d 257 (Mass. 2002).

[31] *See* VA. CODE ANN. § 20-158B (2009).

[32] Harper v. Archer, 12 Miss. 99 (4 S. & M. 99) (Miss. 1845).

[33] MISS. CODE ANN. § 91-5-3 (2010).

[34] Vernoff v. Astrue, 568 F.3d 1102, 1109 (9th Cir. 2009).

[35] Finley v. Astrue, 601 F. Supp. 2d 1092, 1109 (E.D. Ark. 2009).

[36] Social Security Act, 42 U.S.C. §§ 416(e)(1) (2006).

[37] Social Security Act, 42 U.S.C. § 416(h)(3)(C)(i) (2006).

§ 15.06　　　　　　　　　MISSISSIPPI FAMILY LAW

with their deceased father's sperm, and born eighteen months after his death, were not entitled to benefits because, under Florida intestacy law, they would not have been entitled to inherit from him. The court of appeals rejected this argument, holding that § 416(h) (looking to intestacy law) applies only when a child's family status is unclear, as in the case of a nonmarital child. In this case, the children were clearly the deceased's biological children. Thus, the applicable section was § 416(e). Under that section, they were entitled to benefits. The Third Circuit case creates the possibility that a child could be entitled to federal Social Security benefits as an heir of the decedent, while being disallowed inheritance rights under state law.[38] Three months later, the Fourth Circuit Court of Appeals rejected this view, holding that Congress intended for § 416(h) to serve as the basis for determining whether a child was entitled to benefits. Thus, a man's son, born through in vitro fertilization almost seven years after his death, was not entitled to benefits, because he could not inherit under Virginia law. The court also noted that this interpretation serves the basic purpose of the Act – to provide benefits for a child who was financially dependent on the deceased at the time of his death.[39]

§ 15.06 PARENTAL RIGHTS: DONORS AND INTENDED PARENTS

[1] Husband's rights and duties

A number of states have statutes providing that the husband of a woman who undergoes artificial insemination is the resulting child's father if he consented in writing to the procedure. The statutes typically also provide that the donor of sperm has no rights with regard to the child. Most, however, do not address parentage through other procedures such as IVF, and most are limited to artificial insemination of a married woman, excluding cohabitants and same-sex couples.[40] As a result, courts have still had to grapple with identifying the fathers of ART children. The Uniform Parentage Act states that the husband of a woman who gives birth by ART may not challenge paternity more than two years after he learns of the birth and then, only if he did not consent to ART. However, if the husband did not consent, has not cohabited with the mother since conception, and never held the child out as his own, he may challenge paternity at any time.[41]

In the absence of a statute, courts have also found that a husband who consented to or acquiesced in the procedure is the child's legal father. A New York court held that it would violate public policy to accept a wife's argument that her husband was not the

---

[38] Capato v. Comm'r, 631 F.3d 626, 632 (3d Cir. 2011). The Ninth Circuit also rejected the Commissioner's argument that the Act requires a finding of right to inherit under state law, holding that § 416(h) does not apply to one who meets the definition of "child" under § 416(e). However, the Ninth Circuit Court of Appeals looked to Arizona law to determine whether a posthumously conceived child was "legitimate" and therefore dependent on the deceased. Gillett-Netting v. Barnhart, 371 F.3d 593, 598-99 (9th Cir. 2004) (finding that a posthumously conceived child is the legitimate child of his or her natural parents). *But cf.* Vernoff v. Astrue, 568 F.3d 1102, 1107-08 (9th Cir. 2009) (denying benefits to child conceived with deceased's sperm, taken from his body after his death; under California law, man is not the legal father of a posthumously conceived child in the absence of consent).

[39] Schafer v. Astrue, 641 F.3d 49, 58-59 (4th Cir. 2011).

[40] KINDREGAN, JR., ET AL., *supra* note 1, at § 2.9 (noting that states tend to hold that the husband is the father even if the statutory requirements for written consent were not followed).

[41] UNIF. PARENTAGE ACT § 705(b) (2000).

508

ASSISTED REPRODUCTION TECHNOLOGY § 15.06[2]

father of a child conceived through ART during their marriage because he lacked a genetic connection to the child. The court also relied on the presumption that a child born to a married woman is the child of her husband.[42] Similarly, husbands have been found liable for child support in most states, even if they did not sign a written consent to the procedure. A husband was responsible for support of a child born through IVF, based on his oral consent to the procedure.[43] And a husband was obligated to provide support because his knowledge and conduct implied consent to the procedure.[44] In another case, an ex-husband was required to pay child support based on equitable estoppel. He urged his ex-wife to undergo artificial insemination, consented to the procedure, and held the child out as his own for fifteen years.[45] At least one court, however, refused to impose obligations on husbands in the absence of written consent to the procedure.[46]

Mississippi has no statute addressing the rights of a husband whose wife gives birth to a child through ART. However, Mississippi follows the well-established presumption that a man is the father of his wife's child.[47] The presumption could be applied, as in other states, to support a finding that a husband who consents to the procedure is the resulting child's legal father. A recent Mississippi case implies, without directly addressing the issue, that Mississippi follows the general rule. A woman had twins conceived through ART with her husband's consent. Then, she conceived a third child through ART, while telling her husband the child was conceived naturally. The court awarded custody of the twins to the husband without discussion of his parental rights. The court of appeals noted in dicta that the child conceived through ART was not the husband's child.[48]

[2] Unmarried partner's rights and duties. A few cases have addressed the rights of a woman's boyfriend or cohabitant at the time a child was conceived through assisted reproduction. The New York Supreme Court held that a woman's boyfriend who executed a written consent to artificial insemination was not responsible for child support because the statute on which she relied applied only to married women.[49] However, the Illinois Supreme Court held that an umarried woman's partner was the father of a child born through ART under an estoppel theory: "If an unmarried man who biologically causes conception through sexual relations without the premeditated intent of birth is legally obligated to support a child, then the equivalent resulting birth of a child caused by the deliberate conduct of artificial insemination should receive the same treatment in the eyes of the law. Regardless of the method of conception, a child

---

[42] State *ex rel.* H. v. P., 457 N.Y.S.2d 488, 490-91 (N.Y. App. Div. 1982); *see also* Brooks v. Fair, 532 N.E.2d 208, 212-13 (Ohio Ct. App. 1988) (against public policy for ex-wife to disestablish ex-husband's paternity of child conceived by artificial insemination to which they both agreed).

[43] Hill v. Hulet, 881 P.2d 460, 462 (Colo. App. 1994).

[44] *In re* Baby Doe, 353 S.E.2d 877, 878-79 (S.C. 1987).

[45] Levin v. Levin, 645 N.E.2d 601, 604-05 (Ind. 1994).

[46] *In re* Marriage of Witback-Wildhagen, 667 N.E.2d 122, 125 (Ill. App. Ct. 1996); *see also* UNIF. PARENTAGE ACT § 706 (2000) (if divorce occurs before placement of eggs, sperm, or embryo, the former spouse is not a parent unless he or she specifically consented to ART after the divorce).

[47] Rafferty v. Perkins, 757 So. 2d 992, 995 (Miss. 2000).

[48] Wells v. Wells, 35 So. 3d 1250, 1257 (Miss. Ct. App. 2010) (dictum).

[49] Herman v. Lennon, 776 N.Y.S.2d 778, 779 (N.Y. Sup. Ct. 2004).

§ 15.06[3]   **MISSISSIPPI FAMILY LAW**

is born in need of support."[50]

[3] Same-sex partners. Courts have varied with regard to the rights of a same-sex partner of a woman who gives birth through ART. In some states, same-sex partners have been accorded rights as intended parents, or based on a court's finding that they have acted *in loco parentis* or as a de facto parent.[51] In others, courts have denied visitation to same-sex partners, finding that extension of visitation is a matter for the legislature,[52] or that the de facto parent doctrine does not apply to same-sex couples.[53]

[4] Donor's rights

[a] Donors for assisted conception. Donors for physician-assisted conception generally have no rights or duties with regard to a child of ART. A number of states have statutes to this effect, at least with regard to physician-assisted artificial insemination.[54] In addition, persons who donate through clinics typically sign a form waiving all rights to the donated eggs, sperm, or embryos. Thus, ordinarily, they have waived parental rights by contract. There is no requirement that they be notified of adoption[55] or other proceedings related to subsequent children.[56] However, questions about the status of a donor still arise where donation is by a person known to the intended parents.

[b] Known donors. Utilizing a known donor outside the physician-assisted process may create rights in, or against, the donor. A California court held that a donor who contributed sperm for artificial insemination could assert a claim of paternity. The court rejected the mother's argument that she did not intend to allow the donor to have rights with regard to the child, stating that she could have avoided the result by having the donor provide the sperm through a physician.[57] In some cases, known sperm donors have been granted parental rights based upon the donor's contact with the child even though the donor had orally relinquished parental rights at the time of

---

[50] *In re* Parentage of M.J., 787 N.E.2d 144, 152 (Ill. 2003).

[51] *See, e.g.,* Charisma R. v. Kristina S., 44 Cal. Rptr. 3d 332 (Cal. Ct. App 2006) (same-sex partners may have parental rights when a child was received into the home and held out as a natural child); E.N.O. v. L.M.M., 711 N.E.2d 886, 892 (Mass. 1999), *cert. denied,* L.M.M. v. E.N.O., 528 U.S. 1005 (1999) (applying "de facto" parent test); T.B. v. L.R.M., 874 A.2d 34, 38 (Pa. Super. Ct. 2005), *appeal denied,* T.B. v. L.R.M., 890 A.2d 1060 (Pa. 2005) (The trial court erred in denying visitation to former same-sex partner who had *in loco parentis* standing to child.); L.S.K. v. H.A.N., 813 A.2d 872, 878 (Pa. Super. Ct. 2002) (former same-sex partner of biological mother was required to pay child support for five children born through artificial insemination during the relationship); Rubano v. DiCenzo, 759 A.2d 959, 976 (R.I. 2000) (biological mother equitably estopped from denying former same-sex partner parental rights to child born by artificial insemination; de facto parent).

[52] Janis C. v. Christine T., 742 N.Y.S.2d 381, 383 (N.Y. App. Div. 2002), *rev'g* J.C. v. C.T., 711 N.Y.S.2d 295 (N.Y. Fam. Ct. 2000).

[53] Jones v. Barlow, 154 P.3d 808, 813-14 (Utah 2007) (*in loco parentis* standing does not extend to former same-sex partner seeking visitation rights of child conceived by artificial insemination); *In re* Thompson, 11 S.W.3d 913, 923 (Tenn. Ct. App. 1999).

[54] KINDREGAN, JR., ET AL., *supra* note 1, at § 2.1 (similar provisions are included in the UNIF. PARENTAGE ACT and ABA MODEL ACT).

[55] Adoption of Michael, 636 N.Y.S.2d 608, 609 (N.Y. Surr. Ct. 1996).

[56] *In re* E.S., 756 N.E.2d 422, 429-30 (Ill. App. Ct. 2001) (no requirement for notice of juvenile proceeding); *In re* Guardianship of I.H., 834 A.2d 922, 924-25 (Me. 2003) (no requirement for notice of guardianship proceeding).

[57] Jhordan C. v. Mary K., 224 Cal. Rptr. 530, 537-38 (Cal. Ct. App. 1986).

ASSISTED REPRODUCTION TECHNOLOGY   § 15.07

donation.[58] In other cases, however, courts have held that known donors were excluded from parentage under statutes denying parental rights to donors.[59] The Pennsylvania Supreme Court held that a known sperm donor who orally agreed to donate sperm but specifically objected to paying support was not liable for support for the resulting child.[60] And in one case, a court upheld a contract between a same-sex couple and known sperm donor, which stated that the donor would have a significant relationship with the child.[61]

§ 15.07 SURROGACY

The increasing use of a surrogate mother to carry a child to term introduces even more complex issues into the process of conception and birth. In states such as Mississippi that do not address the parental status of surrogate mothers, the surrogate, as the child's birth mother, is considered the child's legal parent.[62] As logic dictates, the surrogate's husband is presumed by law to be the child's father. The main legal issue arising in surrogacy arrangements involves the relinquishment of parental rights by the surrogate and her husband and establishment of parental rights in the intended parents. A few states have enacted statutes addressing the rights of surrogates and intended parents and a number of states have addressed the issues through judicial decisions. An ABA Model Act provides two alternatives that offer guidance on how to proceed.[63]

[1] Types of surrogacy arrangements. There are two generally accepted categories of surrogates: traditional surrogates and gestational surrogates. A traditional surrogate is often artificially inseminated with the intended father's sperm, producing a child genetically related to the surrogate mother and intended father. A gestational surrogacy involves the use of in vitro fertilization to produce an embryo with the egg and/or sperm of the intended parents or of the donors. Because termination of parental rights is less complicated if the surrogate has no genetic connection to the child, there has been a substantial increase in the use of gestational surrogates, rendering the traditional surrogacy arrangement nearly obsolete.

[2] The ABA Model Act. In 2008, the American Bar Association's Section of the Family Law's Committee on Reproductive and Genetic Technology published the

---

[58] L.A.L. v. D.A.L., 714 So. 2d 595, 596-97 (Fla. Dist. Ct. App. 1998) (donor father argued lesbian couple could not preclude him as the child's father without agreed adoption; case settled); Thomas S. v. Robin Y., 618 N.Y.S.2d 356, 362 (N.Y. App. Div. 1995) (lesbian couple allowed donor to have contact with child over six years). *But cf.* Steven S. v. Deborah D., 25 Cal. Rptr. 3d 482, 486 (Cal. Ct. App. 2005) (known donor who provided sperm to physician for AI not entitled to assert paternity; statute provides for non-parentage of donors in physician-assisted AI). For a review of cases, see Meghan Anderson, *K.M. v. E.G., Blurring the Lines of Parentage in the Modern Courts*, 75 U. CIN. L. REV. 275 (2006).

[59] Lamaritata v. Lucas, 823 So. 2d 316, 319 (Fla. Dist. Ct. App. 2002).

[60] Ferguson v. McKiernan, 940 A.2d 1236, 1241-42 (Pa. 2007).

[61] LaChapelle v. Mitten, 607 N.W.2d 151, 157, 168 (Minn. Ct. App. 2000), *cert. denied*, Mitten v. LaChapelle, 531 U.S. 1011 (2000).

[62] KINDREGAN, JR., ET AL., *supra* note 1.

[63] ABA MODEL ACT ALT. A & B (2008); For an excellent article detailing the laws on surrogacy, see Ashley Pittman, *Navigating the Diverse and Evolving Law of Gestational Surrogacy*, 81 MISS. L.J. (forthcoming Aug. 2011).

511

§ 15.07[2][a]   **MISSISSIPPI FAMILY LAW**

Model Act Governing Assisted Reproductive Technology (the ABA Model Act).[64] The Act provides two alternatives to address the rights of surrogates and intended parents. While Alternative A requires at least one court proceeding to validate a gestational agreement, Alternative B[65] sets out guidelines that allow creation of a valid gestational agreement without court involvement.[66]

    [a] Alternative A: Judicially-approved agreement. Section 701 sets out requirements for a valid gestational agreement: All parties (donors, surrogate, her spouse, and intended parents) must enter into the agreement; the gestational carrier must agree to pregnancy through assisted reproduction; all but the intended parents must relinquish parental rights; and the agreement must state that the intended parents are to become the child's parents.[67] The intended parents may agree to pay reasonable consideration to the gestational carrier, but the agreement may not limit her right to make decisions to safeguard her health or that of the embryo or fetus.[68] A petition to validate the agreement may be filed in the state in which the carrier or the intended parents have resided for at least ninety days.[69] After a hearing,[70] the court may issue an order validating the agreement.[71] After the child's birth, the court issues an order confirming parental rights in the intended parents and directing the issuance of a birth certificate to that effect.[72]

    Repeated references in the Act to the "prospective gestational carrier" indicate that the proceeding must take place before implantation.[73] Moreover, the Act provides that if any party wishes to terminate the agreement after a validating order is obtained, the termination must take place before the gestational carrier becomes pregnant.[74]

    If a child is born under a non-validated gestational agreement, the parent-child relationship is determined "as provided under other law."[75] In addition, the intended parents may be held liable for support of the resulting child "under other law."[76]

    [b] Alternative B: Self-executing agreement. This alternative establishes parental rights by virtue of a properly drafted gestational agreement.[77] If all factors are met, the agreement is self-executing and enforceable without court validation. Alternative B recognizes the state law presumption that a birth mother is a child's legal mother,

---

    [64] *See* ABA MODEL ACT, *supra* note 20 (The American Bar Association Model Act Governing Assisted Reproductive Technology was approved by the ABA on February 11, 2008.).

    [65] ABA MODEL ACT ALT. B §§ 701-712 (2008).

    [66] *See* ABA MODEL ACT ALT. A § 702 (2008), *cf.* ABA MODEL ACT ALT. B § 702 (2008).

    [67] ABA MODEL ACT ALT. A § 701 (2008); *see also* UNIF. PARENTAGE ACT § 801 (2002 & Supp. 2010).

    [68] ABA MODEL ACT ALT. A § 701 (2008); *see also* UNIF. PARENTAGE ACT § 801 (2002 & Supp. 2010).

    [69] ABA MODEL ACT ALT. A § 702 (2008); *see also* UNIF. PARENTAGE ACT § 802 (2002).

    [70] ABA MODEL ACT ALT. A § 703 (2008); *see also* UNIF. PARENTAGE ACT § 803 (2002 & Supp. 2010).

    [71] ABA MODEL ACT ALT. A § 703 (2008); *see also* UNIF. PARENTAGE ACT § 803 (2002 & Supp. 2010).

    [72] ABA MODEL ACT ALT. A § 707 (2008); *see also* UNIF. PARENTAGE ACT § 807(a) (2002 & Supp. 2010); TEX. FAM. CODE ANN. § 160.760 (Vernon 2008).

    [73] ABA MODEL ACT ALT. A § 701 (2008).

    [74] ABA MODEL ACT ALT. A § 706 (2008); *see also* UNIF. PARENTAGE ACT § 806 (2002).

    [75] ABA MODEL ACT ALT. A § 709 (2008); *see also* UNIF. PARENTAGE ACT § 809 (2002).

    [76] ABA MODEL ACT ALT. A § 709 (2008); *see also* UNIF. PARENTAGE ACT § 809(c) (2002) (the phrase "under other law" presumes state law).

    [77] ABA MODEL ACT ALT. B §§ 701-712 (2008).

ASSISTED REPRODUCTION TECHNOLOGY § 15.07[3]

but provides a framework to overcome that presumption.[78] A gestational carrier must be twenty-one years old and have given birth to a child.

At least one intended parent must contribute a gamete (sperm or egg) toward the embryo, and the intended mother must have a medical need for the gestational carrier arrangement. Both the gestational carrier and the intended parent(s) must complete a mental health evaluation and be represented by independent legal counsel. The agreement must be in writing, signed by the gestational carrier, her spouse and the intended parent(s), and must be executed before any medical procedures commence.[79] The gestational carrier must retain the right to choose her physician.[80]

The intended parents must accept custody of all resulting children upon birth, and assume sole responsibility for their support.[81] The agreement may allow for compensation to the gestational carrier, as well as reimbursement for reasonable expenses, but is not required to address these topics.[82] If the gestational carrier is to receive compensation, the entire amount must be placed in escrow before commencement of any medical procedure.[83]

The parent-child relationship is established if, prior to or within twenty-four hours of the child's birth, the attorneys for the parties certify in writing that the parties entered into a gestational agreement.[84] If the attorney certification requirements are met, all birth records and the original birth certificate are issued in the name of the intended parent(s).[85]

If any party breaches the agreement or if the agreement fails to meet the requirements of the Act, a court may determine the parties' rights based upon their original intent.[86] The intended parents may not seek specific performance as a remedy for the gestational carrier's breach, if impregnation is the remedy.[87]

[3] State statutes

[a] Recognizing surrogacy. The following states have enacted statutory law allowing a surrogacy arrangement: Arkansas,[88] Florida,[89] Illinois,[90] Nevada,[91] New

---

[78] ABA MODEL ACT ALT. B § 701 (2008). Also note para. 3 of § 701, which addresses the possibility that, due to laboratory error, neither intended parent is genetically related to the intended child. In such case, the intended parents nonetheless enjoy all parental rights otherwise afforded under Alternative B, but allows one or more genetic parents to bring an action to establish parentage within sixty days of the child's birth. *Id.*

[79] ABA MODEL ACT ALT. B § 703(2) (2008).

[80] ABA MODEL ACT ALT. B § 703(3)(c) (2008).

[81] ABA MODEL ACT ALT. B § 703(3)(d) (2008).

[82] ABA MODEL ACT ALT. B § 703(4) (2008).

[83] ABA MODEL ACT ALT. B § 703(2)(e) (2008).

[84] ABA MODEL ACT ALT. B § 705(1) (2008). Section 704(2) requires that the attorney certification forms prescribed by the relevant state agency must be used, in a manner consistent with the state's relevant parentage act, if any. *Id.* at ALT. B § 704(2).

[85] ABA MODEL ACT ALT. B § 705(4) (2008).

[86] ABA MODEL ACT ALT. B § 709(1) (2008).

[87] ABA MODEL ACT ALT. B § 709(2) (2008).

[88] ARK. CODE ANN. § 9-10-201 (2009).

[89] FLA. STAT. ANN. § 63.212 (West 2005 & Supp. 2009); FLA. STAT. ANN. §§ 742.11-16 (West 2010).

[90] Gestational Surrogacy Act, 750 ILL. COMP. STAT. ANN. § 47/1-75 (West 2009).

[91] NEV. REV. STAT. ANN. § 126.045(4)(b) (LexisNexis 2010) (requiring that the intended parents be married at the time they enter into the surrogacy agreement).

§ 15.07[3][b]   **MISSISSIPPI FAMILY LAW**

Hampshire,[92] Texas,[93] Utah,[94] Virginia,[95] and Washington.[96] The most comprehensive of the statutes address qualification of intended parents and surrogates, as well as the terms and validity of the agreement and the proper procedures for establishing parental rights. All statutes, however, address and establish parental rights among the parties to the agreement. Nevada, Virginia, and Washington recognize only uncompensated surrogacy.[97] Several of the statutes recognize only gestational surrogacy,[98] and most apply only to the use of a surrogate by a married couple.[99]

[b] Prohibiting surrogacy. A handful of states prohibit surrogacy arrangements by statute. Arizona prohibits "surrogate parent contracts," which include both traditional and gestational surrogacy agreements.[100] Indiana declares all surrogacy agreements void and unenforceable as against public policy.[101] The District of Columbia and Michigan not only prohibit surrogacy agreements, but impose fines and/or jail time upon those who enter into surrogacy agreements.[102] New York is a hybrid state, with a statute that declares surrogacy agreements void and unenforceable, while also having cases recognizing the rights of intended parents in a surrogacy arrangement.[103]

[c] Indirectly addressing surrogacy. Some states have statutes expressly forbidding a particular type of surrogacy, suggesting that other forms are acceptable. For example, Nebraska prohibits compensated surrogacy without directly addressing uncompensated arrangements.[104] North Dakota statutes prohibit surrogacy, but also provide that intended parents prevail over gestational surrogates.[105] In Kentucky and Louisiana, compensated traditional surrogacy is prohibited, suggesting that gestational and uncompensated surrogacy may not be.[106] In other states, surrogacy may be implic-

---

[92] N.H. Rev. Stat. Ann. §§ 168-B:1 to 32 (LexisNexis 2010).

[93] Tex. Fam. Code Ann. §§ 160.754-762 (Vernon 2008).

[94] Utah Code Ann. §§ 78B-15-801 to -809 (2008).

[95] Va. Code Ann. §§ 20-159 to -160 (2008) (approving uncompensated surrogacy agreements).

[96] Wash. Rev. Code §§ 26.26.101, 26.26.210-260 (West 2005 & Supp. 2009). Only uncompensated surrogacy agreements are enforceable. Compensated agreements are void and unenforceable as against public policy. *Id.* at 26.26.240.

[97] Nev. Rev. Stat. Ann. § 126.045 (LexisNexis 2010); Va. Code Ann. §§ 20-159 to -160 (2008); Wash. Rev. Code § 26.26.240 (West 2005 & Supp. 2009).

[98] See notes 88-96 *supra* (Florida, Massachusetts, North Dakota, Texas, and Utah).

[99] See notes 88-96 *supra* (Florida, Nevada, Utah, and Texas).

[100] Ariz. Rev. Stat. Ann. § 25-218 (2007). *But see* Soos v. Superior Court *ex rel.* County of Maricopa, 897 P.2d 1356 (Ariz. Ct. App. 1994) (finding statutory provision § 25-218, which automatically confers motherhood status to the surrogate, unconstitutional).

[101] Ind. Code Ann. § 31-20-1-1 to -2 (LexisNexis 2007).

[102] D.C. Code Ann. §§ 16-401 to -402 (LexisNexis 2001) (declaring surrogacy agreements unenforceable and imposing a fine of up to $10,000 or imprisonment for up to one year in jail or both); Mich. Comp. Laws Ann. §§ 722.851-861 (West 2002) (declaring surrogacy agreements unenforceable and imposing a fine of up to $50,000, or jail time for up to five years, or both).

[103] N.Y. Dom. Rel. Law § 122 (McKinney 1999); McDonald v. McDonald, 608 N.Y.S.2d 477 (N.Y. App. Div. 1994); Doe v. N.Y. Bd. of Health, 782 N.Y.S.2d 180 (N.Y. Sup. Ct. 2004).

[104] Neb. Rev. Stat. § 25-21,200 (1995) (Compensated surrogacy agreements are void and unenforceable, and custody rights are vested in the biological father and gestational mother in a compensated surrogacy arrangement.).

[105] N.D. Cent. Code § 14-18-05 (2009) (declaring surrogacy agreements void and unenforceable). *But cf.* N.D. Cent. Code § 14-18-08 (2009) (establishing parental rights in the intended parents rather than the gestational carrier or her husband).

[106] Ky. Rev. Stat. Ann. § 1999.590(4) (West 2010); La. Rev. Stat. Ann. § 9:2713 (1991).

ASSISTED REPRODUCTION TECHNOLOGY   § 15.07[4]

itly permitted or prohibited by statutes dealing with other topics. In Connecticut and Wisconsin, birth certificate statutes appear to recognize surrogacy.[107] Iowa, Missouri, Oklahoma, Oregon, and West Virginia statutes dealing with human trafficking also suggest that surrogacy may be permitted.[108] And the adoption statutes of some states may arguably allow uncompensated surrogacy.[109] New Mexico and Delaware have adopted the UPA, which defines surrogacy, but provides that the law "does not authorize or prohibit" surrogacy.[110] And the Tennessee adoption statute, while not expressly permitting surrogacy, provides that adoption is not necessary for a child born through traditional or gestational surrogacy.[111]

[4] Decisional law. A number of states without a controlling statute have addressed the issue through judicial decisions or Attorney General opinions. In California, surrogacy is recognized, but traditional surrogates are accorded greater rights than gestational surrogates.[112] Kentucky and Ohio courts have held that surrogacy does not violate state policies.[113] And in Massachusetts and New Jersey, courts have enforced gestational surrogacy agreements, but treated traditional surrogacy under adoption laws, requiring the surrogate's post-birth consent to adoption.[114] An Oregon decision

---

[107] CONN. GEN. STAT. § 7-48a (2008) (birth certificate statute refers to births "subject to a gestational agreement"); WIS. STAT. ANN. § 69.14(h) (West 2003) (states that a surrogate mother's name is to be placed on the birth certificate of the child until a court determines parental rights, at which time the birth certificate may be changed to reflect the names of the intended parents); cf. R.I. GEN. LAWS §§ 23-16.4-2, -4 (2008). The statute prohibits human cloning but makes an explicit exception for assisted reproductive technologies used in gestational surrogacy. Due to a sunset clause, the prohibition in § 23-16.4-2 expired July 7, 2010. R.I. GEN. LAWS § 23-16.4-4 (2008).

[108] IOWA CODE ANN. § 710.11 (West 2003) (criminalizing the purchase of a human being but specifically excluding surrogate mother arrangements). Missouri has no law on the subject, but the language of the statute addressing child trafficking may exclude compensated surrogacy arrangements. HUMAN RIGHTS CAMPAIGN, MISSOURI SURROGACY LAWS, http://www.hrc.org/issues/parenting/surrogacy/1128.htm (last visited July 10, 2011); see OKLA. STAT. ANN. tit. 10, § 7505-3.2 (West 2007) (compensated surrogacy likely to violate trafficking law); OKLA. STAT. ANN. tit. 21 § 866 (2009) (adoption statute permitting payment of reasonable expenses for birth); Okla. Op. Att'y Gen. No. 83-162 (Sept. 29, 1983); see also OR. REV. STAT. § 163.537 (2009) (prohibiting "buying or selling a person" but exempting "fees for services in an adoption pursuant to a surrogacy agreement"); W. VA. CODE ANN. § 48-22-803(e)(3) (LexisNexis 2009) (prohibits the purchase and sale of a child, but allows "fees and expenses included in any agreement in which a woman agrees to become a surrogate mother").

[109] See N.C. GEN. STAT. § 48-10-102 to -103 (permitting payment of reasonable expenses related to adoption).

[110] DEL. CODE ANN. tit. 13, § 8-103 (2010); N.M. STAT. ANN. § 32A-5-34 (West 2003 & Supp. 2009) (forbidding payment for carrying child, but allowing payment for medical and other similar expenses); see also N.M. STAT. ANN. § 40-11A-801 (2010) (New Mexico UPA "does not authorize or prohibit" surrogacy).

[111] TENN. CODE ANN. § 36-1-102(48) (2010).

[112] Johnson v. Calvert, 851 P.2d 776 (Cal. 1993) (The intended parents in a gestational surrogacy agreement in which the gestational carrier was not the contributor of the egg were recognized as the natural and legal parents of the child.); see also In Re Marriage of Buzzanca, 72 Cal. Rptr. 2d 280 (Cal. Ct. App. 1998) (establishing that parental rights were vested in the intended parents where a surrogate was implanted with an embryo produced by an egg and sperm donated by anonymous donors).

[113] See Surrogate Parenting Ass'n. v. Commonwealth ex rel. Armstrong, 704 S.W.2d 209 (Ky. 1986) (upholding a traditional surrogacy arrangement); see also J.F. v. D.B., 879 N.E.2d 740 (Ohio 2007); cf. OHIO REV. CODE ANN. § 3111.89 (LexisNexis 2008) (addressing artificial insemination but specifically stating it does not deal with surrogate motherhood).

[114] See Culliton v. Beth Israel Deaconess Med. Ctr., 756 N.E.2d 1133 (Mass. 2001) (compensated gestational mother, the biological mother, and the biological father joined in a petition requesting that the court issue the birth certificates of twins born of a gestational arrangement to the biological mother and father); R.R. v. M.H., 689 N.E.2d 790 (Mass. 1998) (stating that two requirements must exist to validate a surrogacy agreement: the surrogate mother's consent must last until four days after the birth, and the surrogate mother must receive no compensation); see also In re Baby M, 537 A.2d 1227 (N.J. 1988) (agreement with traditional surrogate invalid; violated adoption law policy); A.H.W. v. G.H.B., 772 A.2d 948 (N.J. Super. Ct. Ch. Div. 2000); In re Adoption of Two Children by H.N.R., 666 A.2d 535 (N.J.

§ 15.07[5]   MISSISSIPPI FAMILY LAW

permits uncompensated surrogacy.[115] And in Pennsylvania, a court treated a gestational surrogate as a third party and awarded custody to the biological intended father.[116] One case dealing with the rights of same-sex couples indirectly suggested the validity of surrogacy contracts.[117] And in a case involving health insurance, a federal court interpreting South Carolina law held that a gestational surrogate's husband was not the "natural father" of the child.[118] In Alabama and Alaska, rights to a child born through surrogacy have been adjudicated without addressing the validity of surrogacy.[119]

[5] Disputes between intended parents and surrogates. The New Jersey case *In re Baby M* was one of the first widely-publicized cases involving surrogacy.[120] In that case, an infertile couple entered into a traditional surrogacy arrangement, agreeing to pay a woman $10,000 to be inseminated with the husband's sperm and carry the child.[121] The New Jersey Supreme Court declared that the contract was against the State's public policy.[122] However, a majority noted that if the woman agreed to act as a surrogate without compensation, and without agreeing to surrender her parental rights after birth, then the arrangement might be permissible.[123] In the years since, courts have become generally more accepting of surrogacy arrangements, particularly gestational surrogacy.

In the absence of a governing statute, courts have differentiated between traditional surrogacy and gestational surrogacy. Courts tend to hold that a traditional surrogate's agreement to relinquish a child violates state adoption law. In contrast, gestational surrogacy agreements are generally enforced.

[a] Gestational surrogacy. California courts have applied an intent test to

---

Super. Ct. App. Div. 1995); N.D. Cent. Code § 14-18-05 (2009) (declaring surrogacy agreements void and unenforceable); N.D. Cent. Code § 14-18-08 (2009) (establishing parental rights in the intended parents rather than the gestational carrier or her husband).

[115] A compensated surrogacy agreement is unenforceable in Oregon, but uncompensated surrogacy arrangements seem to be allowed. *See In re* the Adoption of Baby A & Baby B, 877 P.2d 107 (Or. Ct. App. 1994) (allowing adoption to which traditional surrogate consented); 46 Ore. Op. Att'y Gen. 221 (April 19, 1989).

[116] Ruth F. v. Robert B., 690 A.2d 1171 (Pa. Super. Ct. 1997) (any exchange of compensation or bargaining over parental rights and duties concerning a child is reprehensible, and an agreement evidencing the same would not be enforceable); J.F. v. D.B, 897 A.2d 1261 (Pa. Super. Ct. 2006), in which the Superior Court of Pennsylvania, reversing a lower court, ruled that the surrogate mother did not have standing to seek custody of the triplets to whom she gave birth.

[117] The groundbreaking case of *Baker v. State*, which led to the acceptance of civil unions in Vermont, listed the goal of minimizing complications in surrogacy agreements in weighing whether to restrict marriage to different-sex couples, which seems to implicitly suggest an acceptance of such agreements. Baker v. State, 744 A.2d 864 (Vt. 1999).

[118] In Mid-South Ins. Co. v. Doe, 274 F. Supp. 2d 757 (D.S.C. 2003), the court gave great deference to the terms of a surrogacy agreement in determining that the child was not covered by the insurance carrier of the surrogate's husband as the child was not considered a "natural child" of the husband.

[119] *See, e.g.,* Brasfield v. Brasfield, 679 So. 2d 1091 (Ala. Civ. App. 1996) (custody of child born through surrogacy awarded to wife; validity of agreement not addressed); *In re* Adoption of T.N.F., 781 P.2d 973 (Alaska 1989) (rejecting claim of surrogate mother based on statute of limitations).

[120] *See* Kimberly D. Krawiec, *Altruism and Intermediation in the Market for Babies,* 66 Wash. & Lee L. Rev. 203, 245 (Winter 2009).

[121] *See* Katherine M. Swift, *Parenting Agreements, The Potential Power of Contract, and the Limits of Family Law,* 34 Fla. St. U. L. Rev. 913, 928 (Spring 2007) (discussion of *In re Baby M).*

[122] *In re* Baby M, 537 A.2d 1227, 1240 (N.J. 1988). Once the child was again in her custody, the surrogate fled with the child from New Jersey to Florida. *Id. See also* Bridget J. Crawford, Symposium, *Taxation, Pregnancy, and Privacy,* 16 Wm. & Mary J. Women & L. 327, 338 (Winter 2010).

[123] *In re* Baby M, 537 A.2d 1227, 1235 (N.J. 1988).

516

ASSISTED REPRODUCTION TECHNOLOGY   § 15.07[5][b]

determine the legal parents of a child born as a result of a gestational surrogacy arrangement.[124] In *Johnson v. Calvert*, the California Supreme Court heard a dispute between a gestational surrogate, or birth mother, and the intended (and genetic) mother of a child.[125] The court held that in a gestational surrogacy, the child's legal mother is the intended mother, rather than the surrogate.[126] California has continued to apply the intent test in gestational surrogacy arrangements post-*Calvert*.[127] For example, in *In re Marriage of Buzzanca*, a California court of appeals required that a divorced man pay child support for a child born to a gestational surrogate even though the child was not genetically his – he had agreed to the surrogacy arrangement.[128] The Ohio Supreme Court held that a contract between intended parents and a gestational surrogate was enforceable and not against public policy: "A written contract defining the rights and obligations of the parties seems an appropriate way to enter into surrogacy agreement. If the parties understand their contract rights, requiring them to honor the contract they entered into is manifestly right and just."[129]

[b] Traditional surrogacy. California courts do not apply *Johnson v. Calvert's* intent-based test in traditional surrogacy arrangements.[130] In *In re Marriage of Moschetta*, a California court of appeals refused to enforce an agreement giving parental rights to intended parents in a traditional surrogacy arrangement. Requiring the child's genetic and birth mother to agree to relinquish parental rights prior to birth was incompatible with the State's adoption and parentage laws.[131] Similarly, the Massachusetts Supreme Court refused to enforce a traditional surrogacy agreement, finding that the agreement violated the state's adoption laws by requiring consent prior to the child's birth.[132] And in the *In re Baby M* case, the New Jersey court reached the same conclusion, holding that the surrogate, as the child's mother, was on equal footing with the intended (and genetic) father in a custody dispute, to be resolved based on the best interests of the child.[133] In contrast, Kentucky and Oregon courts have held that traditional surrogacy does not violate state policies.[134]

---

[124] Ashley E. Bashur, *Whose Baby is it Anyway? The Current and Future Status of Surrogacy Contracts in Maryland*, 38 U. Balt. L. Rev. 165, 168 (Fall 2008).

[125] Johnson v. Calvert, 851 P.2d 776, 782 n.10 (Cal. 1993) (Also, "by voluntarily contracting away any rights to the child, the gestator has, in effect, conceded the best interests of the child are not with her.").

[126] *In re* Marriage of Buzzanca, 72 Cal. Rptr. 2d 280, 293 (Cal. Ct. App. 1998) (rejecting a best interests approach advocated by the dissent).

[127] Carla Spivack, *The Law of Surrogate Motherhood in the United States*, 58 Am. J. Comp. L. 97, 103 (2010).

[128] *In re* Marriage of Buzzanca, 72 Cal. Rptr. 2d 280, 291-92 (Cal. Ct. App. 1998).

[129] J.F. v. D.B., 879 N.E.2d 740, 741-42 (Ohio 2007) (but noting that traditional surrogacy may differ).

[130] Ashley E. Bashur, *Whose Baby is it Anyway? The Current and Future Status of Surrogacy Contracts in Maryland*, 38 U. Balt. L. Rev. 165, 168 (Fall 2008).

[131] 30 Cal. Rptr. 3d 893 (Cal. Ct. App. 1994).

[132] R.R. v. M.H., 689 N.E.2d 790 (Mass. 1998).

[133] *In re* Baby M, 537 A.2d 1227 (N.J. 1988) (agreement with traditional surrogate invalid; violated adoption law policy).

[134] Surrogate Parenting Ass'n. v. Commonwealth ex rel. Armstrong, 704 S.W.2d 209 (Ky. 1986) (upholding a traditional surrogacy arrangement); *see In re* the Adoption of Baby A and Baby B, 877 P.2d 107 (Or. Ct. App. 1994) (allowing adoption to which traditional surrogate consented).

§ 15.08   MISSISSIPPI FAMILY LAW

§ 15.08 EMBRYO DONATION AND ADOPTION

Despite common use of the term "embryo adoption," an embryo is not formally adopted in the way that a child would be adopted. Donors are legally capable of relinquishing rights to an embryo by executing a contract donating the embryo to another hopeful couple.[135] Many states, including California,[136] Connecticut,[137] Florida,[138] Massachusetts,[139] Ohio,[140] Oklahoma,[141] and Texas,[142] have enacted laws requiring that fertility clinics provide patients with information regarding their dispositional options, including donation. And, various groups and organizations across the country have become involved in creating guidelines for embryo donation. In November of 2008, the American Society of Reproductive Medicine (ASRM) and the Society for Assisted Reproduction Technology (SART) jointly issued practice guidelines for donating embryos.[143] Among other requirements, the donors must relinquish all rights to the embryos or any children that may result from the transfer.[144]

In 2009, Georgia was the first state to provide for the formal adoption of an embryo. Georgia's Option of Adoption Act provides a framework by which a donating couple and the embryo recipients (intended parents) may, but are not required to, formally adopt the embryo prior to implantation.[145] The parties may obtain an expedited court order evidencing the donating couple's relinquishment of rights and establishing parental rights in the adoptive couple.

---

[135] These issues are not usually presented in the context of egg or sperm donation, since they do not intend to parent a resulting child. *See* Sarah Terman, *Marketing Motherhood: Rights and Responsibilities of Egg Donors in Assisted Reproductive Technology Agreements*, 3 Nw. U. J.L. & Soc. PoL'y 167, 172 (2008).

[136] CAL. HEALTH & SAFETY CODE § 125315 (West 2004).

[137] CONN. GEN. STAT. § 19a-32g (2010).

[138] FLA. STAT. § 742.17 (2010).

[139] MASS. GEN. LAWS ch. 111L, § 4 (2010).

[140] OHIO REV. CODE ANN. § 3111.97 (West 2010).

[141] OKLA. STAT. tit. 10, § 556 (2010).

[142] TEX. FAM. CODE ANN. § 160.702 (Vernon 2010).

[143] *Am. Soc'y for Reprod. Med. & Soc'y for Asst. Reprod. Tech., 2008 Guidelines for Gamete and Embryo Donation: A Practice Committee Report, on Number of Embryos Transferred, in* 92 FERTILITY AND STERILITY S30, 341-42 (2009).

[144] *Am. Soc'y for Reprod. Med. & Soc'y for Asst. Reprod. Tech., 2008 Guidelines for Gamete and Embryo Donation: A Practice Comm. Report, on Number of Embryos Transferred, in* 92 FERTILITY AND STERILITY S30, 341-42 (2009).

[145] *See* Option of Adoption Act, GA. CODE ANN. §§ 19-8-40 to -43 (2010).

XVI
TERMINATION OF PARENTAL RIGHTS

Few state actions have more grave consequences than the termination of parents' fundamental rights with regard to their children.[1] There is a strong presumption that a parent's rights should be preserved. At some point, however, a child's right "to food, shelter, and opportunity to become a useful citizen outweighs a parent's fundamental right to rear their offspring."[2] Termination proceedings trigger constitutional protections greater than those in most civil proceedings but short of the protections available in criminal proceedings. Petitions to terminate parental rights are frequently brought in connection with a suit for adoption. However, a parent's rights may also be terminated in an independent action.[3] The statutory grounds for termination discussed in this chapter apply in both independent actions and in actions for adoption.[4] However, the adoption statute contains additional grounds for termination that are not available in an independent termination action.[5]

§ 16.01 JURISDICTION AND VENUE

Jurisdiction to terminate parental rights is shared by chancery courts and family and county courts sitting as youth courts.[6] However, a court that has previously exercised jurisdiction over a child has continuing exclusive jurisdiction to hear a petition for termination. For example, a chancery court erred in exercising jurisdiction over foster parents' suit to terminate the rights of a child's parents; the youth court had previously denied a similar petition and entered an order of custody and visitation.[7]

A petition for termination should be filed in the county of the child's or defendant's residence or where an agency with custody of the child is located.[8] If a court has continuing jurisdiction, an action to terminate parental rights should be filed in that court rather than in the child's current county of residence.[9]

---

[1] *See* M.L.B. v. S.L.J., 519 U.S. 102, 118 (1996) (loss is severe and irreversible; requires close and careful scrutiny) (quoting Santosky v. Kramer, 455 U.S. 745, 759 (1982)); S.N.C. v. J.R.D., 755 So. 2d 1077, 1082 (Miss. 2000) ("The grave decision to terminate a parent's fundamental right to be involved in the life of his or her child is among the more difficult decisions a chancellor faces."); *see also In re* T.A.P., 742 So. 2d 1095, 1102 (Miss. 1999).

[2] *In re* A.M.A., 986 So. 2d 999, 1010 (Miss. Ct. App. 2007) (quoting Vance v. Lincoln County Dep't of Pub. Welfare, 582 So. 2d 414 (Miss. 1991)).

[3] *See In re* T.A.P., 742 So. 2d 1095, 1098 (Miss. 1999) (termination proceeding to place child in DHS custody, with authority to place children for adoption).

[4] *See* MISS. CODE ANN. § 93-15-105 (2004).

[5] *See* discussion *infra* § 17.07.

[6] MISS. CODE ANN. § 93-15-105(1) (2004); *see* May v. Harrison County Dep't of Human Servs., 883 So. 2d 74 (Miss. 2004) (termination of parental rights in youth court).

[7] *See* K.M.K. v. S.L.M., 775 So. 2d 115, 118 (Miss. 2000) (holding is limited to counties which have a county court sitting as a youth court, in addition to a chancery court). *But cf. In re* Petition of Beggiani, 519 So. 2d 1208, 1211 (Miss. 1988) (no youth court jurisdiction over adoption in spite of prior order; continuing jurisdiction applicable only to suits of similar nature).

[8] MISS. CODE ANN. § 93-15-105(1) (2004).

[9] Tollison v. Tollison, 841 So. 2d 1062, 1065 (Miss. 2003) (action should be filed in court issuing parties' divorce decree, not in county where mother and child currently lived); C.M. v. R.D.H., 947 So. 2d 1023, 1028 (Miss. Ct. App. 2007) (Hinds County court lacked jurisdiction to hear action to terminate rights; Scott County custody order gave it

519

§ 16.02   MISSISSIPPI FAMILY LAW

§ 16.02 Parties

A petition for termination may be filed by "any person, agency or institution."[10] An action may be prompted by a court order directing the Department of Human Services to initiate termination proceedings. The Mississippi Supreme Court rejected defendant parents' argument that courts lack authority to order that termination proceedings be filed.[11]

[1] Plaintiff and defendant. If a child is in agency custody, the agency should serve as plaintiff.[12] The Department of Human Services should also act as plaintiff when it has legal custody of a child who is in the physical custody of a relative.[13] DHS may bring an action for termination against a minor who is herself under DHS oversight and jurisdiction.[14] The child in question may be made a plaintiff in termination proceedings.[15]

Defendants should include the child's mother, legal father, and known putative father.[16] A natural parent may petition to terminate the rights of the other natural parent.[17]

[2] Guardian ad litem. Appointment of a guardian ad litem is mandatory in actions to terminate parental rights.[18] This includes cases where the action to terminate is pled in the alternative. A chancellor should have appointed a guardian ad litem even though the mother's petition for termination as an alternative to modification was not addressed by the court.[19] Guardians ad litem are charged with "an affirmative duty to zealously represent the child's best interest."[20] A guardian must be competent, without interests adverse to the child, and adequately informed regarding the duties of a guardian.[21] At a minimum, a guardian must interview the children and their custodians or parents. Adequate representation may also require review of school, medical, and psychological records.[22] The supreme court reversed and remanded a termination action in which the guardian cross-examined witnesses but did not testify or provide

---

exclusive jurisdiction).

[10] Miss. Code Ann. § 93-15-105(1) (2004).

[11] *See In re* V.R., 725 So. 2d 241, 245-46 (Miss. 1998) (interpreting Miss. Code Ann. § 43-21-609) (youth court may direct that proceedings be instituted if termination is in the child's best interest); *see also In re* T.T., 427 So. 2d 1382, 1384 (Miss. 1983).

[12] Miss. Code Ann. § 93-15-107(1) (2004).

[13] Miss. Code Ann. § 93-15-107(2) (2004); *see, e.g.*, Lauderdale County Dep't of Human Servs. v. T.H.G, 614 So. 2d 377, 381 (Miss. 1992) (suit filed by DHS based on legal custody of child in foster care).

[14] *In re* C.B.Y., 936 So. 2d 974, 981 (Miss. Ct. App. 2006).

[15] Miss. Code Ann. § 93-15-107(1) (2004).

[16] Miss. Code Ann. § 93-15-107(1) (2004).

[17] *See* M.L.B. v. S.L.J., 806 So. 2d 1023, 1023-24 (Miss. 2000) (suit by father and current wife to terminate mother's rights and for adoption by current wife).

[18] *See* Miss. Code Ann. § 93-15-107(1) (2004); S.N.C. v. J.R.D., 755 So. 2d 1077, 1081 (Miss. 2000).

[19] Heffner v. Rensink, 938 So. 2d 917, 918, 920 (Miss. Ct. App. 2006).

[20] P.K.C.G. v. M.K.G., 793 So. 2d 669, 674 (Miss. Ct. App. 2001) (quoting D.K.L. v. Hall, 652 So. 2d 184, 188 (Miss. 1995)).

[21] *In re* R.D., 658 So. 2d 1378, 1383 (Miss. 1995).

[22] M.J.S.H.S. v. Yalobusha County Dep't of Human Servs., 782 So. 2d 737, 741 (Miss. 2001).

TERMINATION OF PARENTAL RIGHTS

§ 16.03

an independent report.[23] One neglect proceeding was reversed because the guardian did not interview the child.[24] Another was reversed because the guardian did not interview the family or make recommendations and deferred to the parties' briefs.[25]

A chancellor's findings of fact in a termination action should include a summary of the guardian's qualifications and report.[26] The court remains the ultimate fact finder and is not required to follow the guardian's recommendation.[27] However, if the court rejects the guardian's recommendation, the court's findings must include its reasons for rejecting the report.[28] A more complete discussion of the role of the guardian ad litem is found in Section 12.10.

§ 16.03 SERVICE OF PROCESS

Actions to terminate parental rights are governed by Rule 81 of the Mississippi Rules of Civil Procedure, which requires service of a Rule 81 summons on defendants.[29] Resident defendants must be personally served with process. Nonresident defendants or defendants who cannot be located after diligent search may be served by publication.[30] In actions to terminate parental rights, a minor parent may be served as an adult.[31] A parent who has executed a voluntary release of parental rights or release for adoption need not be served with a copy of a summons served on the child.[32]

§ 16.04 GROUNDS FOR INVOLUNTARY TERMINATION

The grounds for involuntary termination of parental rights are statutory. The supreme court has emphasized that the grounds are controlled by the legislature and must be strictly construed. Courts may not add to the enumerated grounds.[33] These grounds apply in adoption actions as well as in independent actions to terminate parental rights.

The statute provides that termination may be ordered when a child cannot be returned to its parents, relatives are not available to care for the child, adoption is in the child's best interest, and one of the following grounds for termination is proved.[34]

---

[23] *See* D.J.L. v. Bolivar County Dep't Human Servs., 824 So. 2d 617, 622-23 (Miss. 2002).

[24] *See* M.J.S.H.S. v. Yalobusha County Dep't of Human Servs., 782 So. 2d 737, 741 (Miss. 2001).

[25] *See In re* D.K.L., 652 So. 2d 184, 191 (Miss. 1995) (neglect proceeding).

[26] S.N.C. v. J.R.D., 755 So. 2d 1077, 1082 (Miss. 2000).

[27] *See* Hensarling v. Hensarling, 824 So. 2d 583, 587 (Miss. 2002); S.N.C. v. J.R.D., 755 So. 2d 1077, 1082 (Miss. 2000); Passmore v. Passmore, 820 So. 2d 747, 751 (Miss. Ct. App. 2002).

[28] S.N.C. v. J.R.D., 755 So. 2d 1077, 1082 (Miss. 2000); *see* Gunter v. Gray, 876 So. 2d 315 (Miss. 2004) (chancellor erred in failing to explain his reasons for not adopting the report of guardian).

[29] *See* discussion of Rule 81 proceedings *infra* § 19.11.

[30] MISS. CODE ANN. § 93-15-105(1) (2004); *see also* C.M. v. R.D.H., 947 So. 2d 1023, 1029 (Miss. Ct. App. 2007) (service of process by publication improper where mother had contacts who knew father's location). A court may waive service of process if a child was adopted in a foreign country and has been legally admitted to the United States. MISS. CODE ANN. § 93-15-105(5) (2004).

[31] MISS. CODE ANN. § 93-15-105(2) (2004).

[32] MISS. CODE ANN. § 93-15-105(3) (2004).

[33] *See* Gunter v. Gray, 876 So. 2d 315 (Miss. 2004) (court erred in terminating rights of imprisoned father; his conduct did not meet any of the enumerated grounds); Hillman v. Vance, 910 So. 2d 43, 45-46 (Miss. Ct. App. 2005) (statutory grounds not met by proof that child's mother was a stripper).

[34] MISS. CODE ANN. § 93-15-103(1) (2004). Termination is not required just because grounds have been proven. *In*

§ 16.04[1]   MISSISSIPPI FAMILY LAW

[1] Desertion or abandonment. Parental rights may be terminated when a parent deserts or abandons a child.[35]

[a] Abandonment. Abandonment has been described by the Mississippi Supreme Court as conduct that shows a "settled purpose to forego all duties and relinquish all parental claims."[36] The test for abandonment is objective, based on the totality of the circumstances.[37] Abandonment may be shown through one event or through a course of conduct.[38] Failure to pay child support does not, in itself, constitute abandonment.[39]

Termination must be based upon affirmative proof of abandonment. A chancellor erred in terminating a mother's rights because she failed to introduce evidence of her involvement with her child.[40] Abandonment requires a showing of extreme disengagement. For example, a father who scheduled visitation during the year preceding the action and sent cards and gifts did not abandon his children.[41] A father's failure to communicate with his children from prison did not constitute abandonment when his only means of communication – telephoning – would have violated a court protective order.[42]

In several cases, the Mississippi Supreme Court has referred to a parent's consent to adoption as abandonment.[43] The court noted that abandonment may result from a single moment in time when a parent signs a consent to adoption. However, the court also emphasized that abandonment by consent to adoption could not occur prior to the three-day waiting period and without meeting the statutory requirements for consent.[44]

---

re Dissolution of Marriage of Leverock & Hamby, 23 So. 3d 424, 428-29 (Miss. 2009) (also noting that child was not "taken" from father and father was willing to provide care).

[35] Miss. Code Ann. § 93-15-103(3)(a) (2004) (abandonment is defined, in reference to Miss. Code Ann. § 97-5-1 (2004), as to "expose such child in any highway, street, field, house, outhouse, or elsewhere, with intent wholly to abandon it").

[36] S.N.C. v. J.R.D., 755 So. 2d 1077, 1081 (Miss. 2000) (quoting Natural Mother v. Parental Aunt, 583 So. 2d 614, 618 (Miss. 1991)); *see also In re* J.D., 512 So. 2d 684, 686 (Miss. 1987) (abandonment is relinquishment of a right); Ainsworth v. Natural Father, 414 So. 2d 417, 420 (Miss. 1982).

[37] S.N.C. v. J.R.D., 755 So. 2d 1077, 1081 (Miss. 2000).

[38] G.Q.A. v. Harrison County Dep't of Human Servs., 771 So. 2d 331, 336 (Miss. 2000).

[39] *See* Carter v. Taylor, 611 So. 2d 874, 877 (Miss. 1992); *In re* Adoption of a Female Child, 412 So. 2d 1175, 1178-79 (Miss. 1982) (failure to pay child support and failure to visit was not abandonment where no visitation was ordered and mother refused to allow father to see child); *In re* Brown, 902 So. 2d 604 (Miss. Ct. App. 2004) (failure to pay support can be factor in abandonment but not a basis for finding parent otherwise unfit); *In re* M.L.W., 755 So. 2d 558, 563 (Miss. Ct. App. 2000).

[40] *See* N.E. v. L.H., 761 So. 2d 956, 964 (Miss. Ct. App. 2000). *But see* Natural Mother v. Paternal Aunt, 583 So. 2d 614, 619 (Miss. 1991) (abandonment by mother who removed herself from children's lives for three and a half years).

[41] S.N.C. v. J.R.D., 755 So. 2d 1077, 1081 (Miss. 2000) (even though defendant's contact with child was minimal, he did remain in contact); *see also* L.O. v. G.V., 37 So. 3d 1248, 1253-54 (Miss. Ct. App. 2010) (mother who visited briefly on weekends with child within six months of filing petition did not abandon her); A.C.W. v. J.C.W., 957 So. 2d 1042, 1045-46 (Miss. Ct. App. 2007) (father who visited child some, and who was current in support, did not abandon child, particularly where mother's family interfered with visitation); *In re* M.L.W., 755 So. 2d 558, 563 (Miss. Ct. App. 2000) (chancellor properly denied termination; father saw child several times during two years after divorce and sent gifts).

[42] Gunter v. Gray, 876 So. 2d 315 (Miss. 2004).

[43] *See In re* Adoption of D.N.T., 843 So. 2d 690, 706-07 (Miss. 2003); Grafe v. Olds, 556 So. 2d 690 (Miss. 1990) (private adoption); Bryant v. Cameron, 473 So. 2d 174, 177 (Miss. 1985); C.C.I. v. Natural Parents, 398 So. 2d 220, 226 (Miss. 1981) (public adoption).

[44] Bryant v. Cameron, 473 So. 2d 174, 178 (Miss. 1985).

TERMINATION OF PARENTAL RIGHTS   § 16.04[1][b]

[b] Desertion. The Mississippi Supreme Court has defined desertion as "forsaking one's duty as well as a breaking away from or breaking off associations with some matter involving a legal or moral obligation."[45] A father who called his children and sent them gifts was not guilty of abandonment or desertion. Furthermore, his failure to pay child support was not, in itself, abandonment or desertion.[46] The court noted, however, that if the conduct continued for a prolonged period, termination would be appropriate.[47]

[2] Failure to contact. Termination may be based on a parent's failure to contact a child under the age of three for six months or a child over the age of three for one year.[48] A chancellor properly refused to terminate a father's rights under this section; evidence showed that he had scheduled visitation during the previous year and sent cards and gifts.[49] However, a court properly terminated the rights of a father who made no contact with his young son for over a year, even though he explained that he was waiting until he finished college and had a job to make contact.[50]

[3] Abuse. Termination may be ordered when a parent "has been responsible for a series of abusive events concerning one or more children."[51] A court did not err in terminating the rights of parents whose eighteen-month-old child was malnourished, severely burned, and not treated for the injury.[52] A mother's rights were properly terminated based on proof that young children had been subjected to numerous incidents of sexual abuse while in her care.[53] Similarly, the rights of both parents were properly terminated based upon evidence that their three-year-old daughter had been sexually abused while in their care, even though both parents denied the abuse – no other person had care of the child and there was no other reasonable explanation.[54] A court properly terminated the rights of a mother who refused to acknowledge her husband's sexual abuse of their daughters and who failed to complete DHS requirements for return of the children to her alone.[55] However, a father's single physical assault on a stepchild did not

---

[45] Petit v. Holifield, 443 So. 2d 874, 878 (Miss. 1984) (citing Ainsworth v. Natural Father, 414 So. 2d 417 (Miss. 1982)).

[46] Petit v. Holifield, 443 So. 2d 874, 878 (Miss. 1984); *see also In re* Adoption of a Female Child, 412 So. 2d 1175, 1178 (Miss. 1982).

[47] Petit v. Holifield, 443 So. 2d 874, 878 (Miss. 1984) (conduct spanning slightly more than one year).

[48] MISS. CODE ANN. § 93-15-103(3)(b) (2004).

[49] S.N.C. v. J.R.D., 755 So. 2d 1077, 1080 (Miss. 2000); *see also In re* A.M.A., 986 So. 2d 999, 1013-14 (Miss. Ct. App. 2007) (error to terminate rights of father incarcerated for seventeen months; he tried to contact children from prison); B.S.G. v. J.E.H., 958 So. 2d 259, 268-69 (Miss. Ct. App. 2007) (court erred in granting termination under the ground of failure to contact; mother awarded supervised visitation with child six months prior to hearing; but affirming termination on other grounds).

[50] W.A.S. v. A.L.G., 949 So. 2d 31, 35 (Miss. 2007); *see also* M.H. v. D.A., 17 So. 3d 610, 617 (Miss. Ct. App. 2009) (termination proper for failure to contact a child for more than one year); R.L. v. G.F., 973 So. 2d 322, 324-25 (Miss Ct. App. 2008) (chancellor properly terminated the rights of a father who made no contact with his four-year-old child for over two years and who paid no child support until the termination proceedings were initiated).

[51] MISS. CODE ANN. § 93-15-103(3)(c) (2004).

[52] G.Q.A. v. Harrison County Dep't of Human Servs., 771 So. 2d 331, 336 (Miss. 2000).

[53] Carson v. Natchez Children's Home, 580 So. 2d 1248, 1257 (Miss. 1991) (holding that statute included sexual abuse even though not explicitly stated).

[54] *In re* D.O., 798 So. 2d 417, 422 (Miss. 2001).

[55] *See* S.R.B.R. v. Harrison County Dep't of Human Servs., 798 So. 2d 437, 442-43 (Miss. 2001); *see also* May v. Harrison County Dep't of Human Servs., 883 So. 2d 74 (Miss. 2004) (mother supported husband in trial for eleven-

§ 16.04[4]   **MISSISSIPPI FAMILY LAW**

constitute a "series of abusive incidents" concerning other children.[56]

[4] Agency custody. Parental rights may be terminated if (1) a child has been in the custody of the Department of Human Services or other agency for a year; (2) the agency has "made diligent efforts to develop and implement a plan for return of the child;" and (3) the parent has failed to exercise visitation with the child or has failed to implement an agreed plan for return of the child.[57] The court properly terminated the rights of a mentally disabled mother for failure to exercise visitation under a DHS plan for reunification. Over six years, she visited the child for a total of 34 one-hour visits, and twice went a year without seeing him.[58]

[5] Ongoing parental behavior. Termination may be based on a parent's ongoing behavior that makes a child's return to the parent impossible. This may include a condition such as alcohol or drug addiction, mental disability or illness, or extreme physical disability that prevents the parent from providing "minimally acceptable" care.[59] In addition, if a childcare agency or court has specified behavior as a barrier to parental custody and has made diligent attempts to assist the parent, the parent's failure to eliminate the identified behavior may be grounds for termination.[60] Termination was proper when parents responsible for a series of abusive incidents refused to acknowledge the abuse and participate in meaningful counseling.[61] Similarly, a court properly terminated the rights of a mother who failed to comply with DHS plans for return of her children – she refused to attend counseling, removed the children from the state, and was arrested for stabbing her husband.[62] The supreme court affirmed termination of the rights of a mother who refused to believe that her daughter was raped by her husband, testified on his behalf, and did not acknowledge the sexual assault until shortly before the termination proceedings.[63]

A chancellor erred, however, in terminating a mother's rights under this provision based on her mental condition; the only evidence was the court's observation of her

---

year-old daughter's rape; testified that child lied). *But cf.* P.K.C.G. v. M.K.G., 793 So. 2d 669, 673 (Miss. Ct. App. 2001) (denying termination; evidence of injuries to child not clearly attributable to alleged abuse by father).

[56] Gunter v. Gray, 876 So. 2d 315 (Miss. 2004); *cf.* S.N.C. v. J.R.D., 755 So. 2d 1077, 1080-81 (Miss. 2000) (a single incident of domestic abuse between a defendant father and petitioner mother did not justify termination of parental rights under this provision).

[57] MISS. CODE ANN. § 93-15-103(3)(d) (2004); *see In re* S.T.M.M., 942 So. 2d 266, 270 (Miss. Ct. App. 2006) (court properly terminated rights of mother who failed to comply with plan for drug testing, counseling, parenting classes and regular visitation). *But cf. In re* A.M.A., 986 So. 2d 999, 1013-14 (Miss. Ct. App. 2007) (error to terminate rights of father whose inability to visit or comply with plan was caused solely by incarceration for seventeen months).

[58] R.F. v. Lowndes County Dep't of Human Servs., 17 So. 3d 1133, 1138 (Miss. Ct. App. 2009).

[59] MISS. CODE ANN. § 93-15-103(3)(e) (2004).

[60] MISS. CODE ANN. § 93-15-103(3)(e)(ii) (2004); *see* B.S.G. v. J.E.H., 958 So. 2d 259, 268-69 (Miss. Ct. App. 2007) (mother continued to use drugs over seven-year period; child was repeatedly removed from her custody); *In re* C.B.Y., 936 So. 2d 974, 979-80 (Miss. Ct. App. 2006) (mother's ongoing behavior included hiding from DHS and failing to visit child for a year in order to avoid DHS contact); *In re* S.T.M.M., 942 So. 2d 266 (Miss. Ct. App. 2006) (court properly terminated rights of mother who failed to comply with plan for drug testing, counseling, parenting classes, and regular visitation).

[61] G.Q.A. v. Harrison County Dep't of Human Servs., 771 So. 2d 331, 337 (Miss. 2000).

[62] *See* K.D.G.L.B.P. v. Hinds County Dep't of Human Servs., 771 So. 2d 907, 913-14 (Miss. 2000).

[63] *See* May v. Harrison County Dep't of Human Servs., 883 So. 2d 74 (Miss. 2004) (termination based on ongoing behavior and on erosion of parent-child relationship).

TERMINATION OF PARENTAL RIGHTS § 16.04[6]

as she sat in the courtroom and a DHS worker's statement that she had some mental difficulty. Termination must be based on competent lay or expert testimony of mental deficiency.[64] In contrast, parents' rights were properly terminated based on expert medical testimony of mental disability that would prevent the father from caring for older children.[65]

Termination under this ground may not be based solely on a parent's incarceration. A court erred in characterizing a father's seventeen-month incarceration as "ongoing behavior" permitting termination.[66] And a mother's rights should not have been terminated for ongoing drug use. Evidence of her rehabilitation and negative drug screens were excluded from evidence.[67]

[6] Extreme antipathy. Termination of parental rights may be based on a child's "extreme and deep-seated antipathy" toward a parent or on a substantial erosion of the parent-child relationship caused in part by serious neglect or abuse or prolonged absence or imprisonment.[68] Termination was proper when a child who was severely injured by her parents' abuse had bonded with her foster parents. The court rejected the parents' argument that the relationship deteriorated because the child was placed in foster care and they were given limited visitation – their conduct caused the removal and resulting erosion.[69] A court properly terminated the rights of a mother who was serving a fifty-four-year prison term for murder – the effect of imprisonment on the parent-child relationship is a proper consideration in a termination action.[70] However, imprisonment is not a per se ground for termination.[71] A court erred in finding a substantial erosion of the parent-child relationship based upon a father's seventeen-month absence while imprisoned.[72]

A court erred in terminating a mother's parental rights based on substantial erosion even though she had married an abusive and alcoholic man, was behind in child support, and had limited contact with her children in the eighteen months since her divorce. Her attempts to visit with her children were, to some extent, thwarted by her ex-husband. In addition, she had made improvements in her circumstances and loved

---

[64] N.E. v. L.H., 761 So. 2d 956, 965 (Miss. Ct. App. 2000); *see also In re* J.J., 31 So. 3d 1271, 1276 (Miss. Ct. App. 2010) (court erred in terminating rights of bipolar mother; though psychiatric reports confirmed disorder, the reports also consistently indicated that the mother's "insight and judgment were good; her attitude was cooperative; and her motivation for ongoing treatment was good. The reports also indicate[d] that her bipolar disorder was being controlled by medication").

[65] *See In re* V.R., 725 So. 2d 241, 247 (Miss. 1998).

[66] *In re* A.M.A., 986 So. 2d 999, 1012 (Miss. Ct. App. 2007) (but distinguishing case in which mother was sentenced to fifty-four years for murder).

[67] A.B. v. Lauderdale County Dep't of Human Servs., 13 So. 3d 1263, 1268-69 (Miss. 2009).

[68] MISS. CODE ANN. § 93-15-103(3)(f) (2004).

[69] G.Q.A. v. Harrison County Dep't of Human Servs., 771 So. 2d 331, 338 (Miss. 2000); *see also In re* C.B.Y., 936 So. 2d 974, 980 (Miss. Ct. App. 2006) (chancellor properly terminated rights of mother who hid from DHS for over a year and whose conduct caused substantial erosion of relationship).

[70] Vance v. Lincoln County Dep't of Pub. Welfare, 582 So. 2d 414, 418 (Miss. 1991) (also rejecting equal protection claim based on fact that a higher percentage of blacks' rights were terminated under the statute than those of whites; no evidence of racially discriminatory purpose or intent).

[71] *See* Gunter v. Gray, 876 So. 2d 315 (Miss. 2004) (imprisonment can be a factor but is not in itself a sufficient basis for termination; length of incarceration is significant).

[72] *In re* A.M.A, 986 So. 2d 999, 1012 (Miss. Ct. App. 2007) (but distinguishing case in which mother was sentenced to fifty-four years for murder).

525

§ 16.04[7]   **MISSISSIPPI FAMILY LAW**

the children. The court noted that "this Court has never allowed termination of parental rights only because others may be better parents."[73] Similarly, a court erred in terminating the rights of a mother who regularly made efforts to maintain a relationship with her children; the welfare department failed to work with the mother, and much of the child's antipathy was the result of third-party interference with the relationship.[74] However, a court properly found substantial erosion caused by a father's failure to have any contact with his young son. The child came to regard his stepfather as his father during that time.[75] And a mother's rights were properly terminated after she stopped exercising regular visitation and did not call her daughter or send gifts for two years, causing the girl to feel rejected and deeply angry with her mother.[76]

[7] Felonious assault or sexual assault. A parent's conviction for sexual assault or exploitation of a child may be a basis for termination of rights with regard to other children. In addition, a conviction for the murder, involuntary manslaughter, or felony assault of another of the defendant's children is grounds for termination.[77] A father's rights with regard to three children were properly terminated based upon his felony abuse of one of the three; it did not matter that the child abused was not his biological child.[78]

[8] Abuse and neglect. Parental rights may be terminated when a court has made a finding of abuse or neglect and provided for foster placement and the court finds that it is not in the child's best interests to be returned to his or her parents.[79] A father's rights were properly terminated under this section, even though he was not personally responsible for the custodial mother's neglect. He alerted DHS of the mother's failure to provide medical treatment for his infant daughter's fractured arm, but did not take steps to care for the children himself and did not oppose their foster care placement.[80] And a mother's rights were properly terminated under this section – she failed to comply with eight of thirteen DHS requirements for reunification, suffered from numerous psychological and physical problems, and was arrested for possession of a controlled substance.[81]

_____

[73] M.L.B. v. S.L.J., 806 So. 2d 1023, 1029 (Miss. 2000).

[74] *See* De La Oliva v. Lowndes County Dep't of Pub. Welfare, 423 So. 2d 1328, 1331-32 (Miss. 1982); *see also In re* V.M.S., 938 So. 2d 829, 837 (Miss. 2006) ("substantial erosion" not shown when mother's failure to visit was based on family court order, and mother sent gifts and wrote child twice a week); *In re* M.L.W., 755 So. 2d 558, 563 (Miss. Ct. App. 2000) (chancellor properly refused to terminate father's rights; mother was part of reason for erosion of relationship).

[75] W.A.S. v. A.L.G., 949 So. 2d 31, 35 (Miss. 2007).

[76] L.O. v. G.V., 37 So. 3d 1248, 1252-53 (Miss. Ct. App. 2010) (mother also abused drugs but was drug-free at the time of trial).

[77] Listed offenses include rape, MISS. CODE ANN. § 97-3-65; sexual battery, *id.* at § 97-3-95(c); touching for lustful purposes, *id.* at § 97-5-23; exploitation, *id.* at § 97-5-31; felonious abuse or battery, *id.* § 97-5-39(2); carnal knowledge of certain children, *id.* at § 97-5-41; and, with regard to another child of the defendant, murder, voluntary manslaughter, conspiracy to commit murder or voluntary manslaughter or felony assault. *See* MISS. CODE ANN. § 93-15-103(3)(g) (2004).

[78] H.D.H. v. Prentiss County Dep't of Human Servs., 979 So. 2d 6, 12 (Miss. Ct. App. 2008).

[79] MISS. CODE ANN. § 93-15-103(3)(h) (2004).

[80] *In re* A.M.A., 986 So. 2d 999, 1015-17 (Miss. Ct. App. 2007).

[81] J.C.N.F. v. Stone County Dep't of Human Servs., 996 So. 2d 768-69 (Miss. 2008).

TERMINATION OF PARENTAL RIGHTS § 16.04[9]

[9] Voluntary relinquishment. Parental rights may be relinquished through a written voluntary release of rights. A minor may execute a valid and enforceable release of parental rights.[82] A discussion of voluntary relinquishment of rights is included in Chapter XVII.[83]

§ 16.05 TRIAL

[1] Time of trial. An action for termination may be tried thirty days after the defendants have been personally served or thirty days after completion of publication for nonresident defendants or defendants who cannot be located.[84] Termination cases in which a child has been sexually abused or suffered serious bodily injury must be given preference "to be determined with all reasonable expedition."[85]

[2] Burden of proof. In *Santosky v. Kramer*, the United States Supreme Court held that the due process clause requires that parental rights be terminated only upon clear and convincing proof of the grounds for termination.[86]

[3] Right to counsel. In *Lassiter v. Department of Social Services*, the United States Supreme Court rejected an argument that indigent parents are entitled to state-provided counsel in all termination proceedings. Instead, the right to counsel should be decided on a case-by-case basis. The Court declined to formulate guidelines for determining when counsel should be appointed. However, the Court found that counsel was not required in the case at bar – the proceeding was not procedurally or substantively difficult, the evidence was so strong that counsel "could not have made a determinative difference," and the petitioner had declined to even attend a hearing.[87] Citing *Lassiter*, the Mississippi Supreme Court held that a mother was not constitutionally entitled to court-appointed counsel in a termination proceeding. She was capable of understanding the proceedings and responding; she had ample time to secure an attorney and did not request a continuance to obtain counsel or ask for court-appointed counsel; and the evidence was so strong that counsel would not have affected the outcome of the trial.[88]

[4] Alternatives to termination. The Mississippi termination statute provides that

---

[82] MISS. CODE ANN. § 93-15-103(2) (2004).

[83] *See infra* § 17.05.

[84] MISS. CODE ANN. § 93-15-105(1) (2004).

[85] MISS. CODE ANN. § 93-15-103(6) (2004).

[86] 455 U.S. 745, 769-70 (1982); *see also* MISS. CODE ANN. § 93-15-109 (2004); S.N.C. v. J.R.D., 755 So. 2d 1077, 1081 (Miss. 2000); Lauderdale County Dep't of Human Servs. v. T.H.G , 614 So. 2d 377, 385 (Miss. 1992) (plaintiff bears the burden of proof); De La Oliva v. Lowndes County Dep't of Pub. Welfare, 423 So. 2d 1328, 1331-32 (Miss. 1982) (reversing termination based on preponderance of the evidence); *In re* A.M.A., 986 So. 2d 999, 1009 (Miss. Ct. App. 2007). *But cf. In re* S.T.M.M., 942 So. 2d 266, 268 (Miss. Ct. App. 2006) (standard of review for a termination decision is whether "reasonable men could not have found as the youth court did beyond a reasonable doubt").

[87] 452 U.S. 18, 32-33 (1981).

[88] *See* K.D.G.L.B.P. v. Hinds County Dep't of Human Servs., 771 So. 2d 907, 911 (Miss. 2000); *see also* J.C.N.F. v. Stone County Dep't of Human Servs., 996 So. 2d 762, 771-72 (Miss. 2008) (mother not entitled to counsel; case did not involve expert testimony or difficult legal issues); Green v. Dep't of Human Servs., 40 So. 3d 660, 664 (Miss. Ct. App. 2010) (presence of counsel would not have altered outcome of case).

§ 16.06   MISSISSIPPI FAMILY LAW

courts should consider permanent alternatives to termination such as placing legal custody with a third party. The court should select these alternatives if continued parental
contact is in a child's best interest and it is possible to provide a permanent placement
and end DHS supervision without termination.[89] However, the supreme court rejected a
mother's argument that a chancellor erred in terminating her parental rights rather than
granting durable legal custody to a relative. While courts may consider durable legal
custody as an alternative, the child's best interest is always the controlling concern.
Furthermore, durable legal custody may be granted only when a child has been in the
custody of the proposed durable legal custodian for one year.[90] Finally, the court noted
that the Adoption and Safe Families Act[91] provides that DHS need not make reasonable efforts to reunite a child with parents who have subjected the child to aggravated
circumstances.[92]

§ 16.06 ORDER OF TERMINATION

A court may terminate both parents' rights with regard to a child. A court may
also terminate one parent's rights alone.[93] In some cases, courts have allowed continued
visitation by a parent whose rights have been terminated.

[1] Placement. Upon termination independent of adoption, a court should award
custody of the child to a suitable person or agency with power to consent to the child's
adoption.[94] While a child may be placed with suitable relatives, the court must make
the placement best suited to the child's needs. The supreme court rejected the argument
of parents whose rights had been terminated that a young girl who had been severely
abused should have been placed with the paternal grandparents along with her three
siblings. The child needed medical care best provided by her foster parents, who were
both nurses.[95]

[2] Parental visitation. In some cases, courts have allowed visitation by natural
parents after termination of their rights and adoption. The supreme court has noted,
however, that such visitation rights are "surplusage" and do not invalidate or alter termination.[96]

---

[89] MISS. CODE ANN. § 93-15-103(4) (2004); *see In re* N.E., 761 So. 2d 956, 961 (Miss. 2000) (alternatives include durable legal custody and third-party guardianship).

[90] May v. Harrison County Dep't of Human Servs., 883 So. 2d 74 (Miss. 2004); *see also In re* Adoption of Minor Child, 931 So. 2d 566, 580 (Miss. 2006) (clear that court carefully considered the only two realistic alternatives, even though no specific findings); B.S.G. v. J.E.H., 958 So. 2d 259, 271 (Miss. Ct. App. 2007) (durable legal custody is not mandatory on courts).

[91] *See* 42 U.S.C. § 671(a) (2006).

[92] May v. Harrison County Dep't of Human Servs., 883 So. 2d 74 (Miss. 2004); *see also In re* Petition of Beggiani, 519 So. 2d 1208, 1211 (Miss. 1988).

[93] MISS. CODE ANN. § 93-15-109 (2004).

[94] MISS. CODE ANN. § 93-15-111 (2004) (after termination, parents are not entitled to notice of adoption proceedings).

[95] G.Q.A. v. Harrison County Dep't of Human Servs., 771 So. 2d 331, 338-39 (Miss. 2000) (foster parents recognized importance of allowing child to visit grandparents and siblings).

[96] *In re* J.E.B., 822 So. 2d 949, 953 (Miss. 2002); *see* discussion *infra* § 17.08[3][a].

TERMINATION OF PARENTAL RIGHTS § 16.06[3]

[3] Inheritance. After termination, a child's natural parents and siblings may not inherit from the child; however, a child may still inherit from his or her natural parents.[97]

[4] Child support. A parent's obligation to pay child support ends upon termination of parental rights. When a mother sought payment of child support arrearages eighteen years after the father signed a voluntary petition for termination, the chancellor properly awarded arrearages until the date of termination. The court emphasized that public policy prohibits allowing a voluntary termination for the purpose of avoiding support. In this case, however, the chancellor considered the effect of termination on support and found that the mother could adequately support the child and that the termination would not adversely affect the child.[98]

§ 16.07 APPEALS

On appeal, a court's findings regarding termination are reviewed under the manifest error/substantial credible evidence test. The issue on appeal is whether there was "credible proof from which a rational trier of fact may have found" grounds for termination.[99]

In *M.L.B. v. S.L.J.*, the United States Supreme Court held that an indigent parent is entitled to a transcript provided by the state in an appeal from an order terminating parental rights.[100] The Mississippi Supreme Court refused to extend the right to a transcript to indigent parents appealing from an adjudication of neglect. The court distinguished a neglect adjudication, which can be altered, from termination, which is irrevocable.[101]

---

[97] MISS. CODE ANN. § 93-17-13 (2004); *see* Alack v. Phelps, 230 So. 2d 789, 792 (Miss. 1970).

[98] Beasnett v. Arledge, 934 So. 2d 345, 347 (Miss. Ct. App. 2006).

[99] S.N.C. v. J.R.D., 755 So. 2d 1077, 1080 (Miss. 2000); H.D.H. v. Prentiss County Dep't of Human Servs., 979 So. 2d 6 (Miss. Ct. App. 2008); *cf. In re* S.T.M.M., 942 So. 2d 266, 268 (Miss. Ct. App. 2006) (standard of review is whether "reasonable men could not have found as the youth court did beyond a reasonable doubt").

[100] 519 U.S. 102, 128 (1996).

[101] J.R.T. v. Harrison County Family Court, 749 So. 2d 105, 109 (Miss. 1999); *see also In re* J.C., 888 So. 2d 456 (Miss. Ct. App. 2004) (right to transcript did not extend to appeal of collateral attack on termination through a circuit court civil rights action).

530

XVII
ADOPTION

Adoption is the legal process through which a new parent-child relationship is created. As a prerequisite to adoption, biological parents' rights with regard to a child must be terminated. Termination may occur in a separate proceeding prior to adoption or as a part of adoption proceedings. The statutory grounds for adoption and involuntary termination must be strictly followed. No action for adoption existed at common law – the proceedings are "purely the creation of statute."[1]

§ 17.01 JURISDICTION AND VENUE

[1] Jurisdiction. Jurisdiction over adoption is vested in Mississippi's chancery courts. Until 2006, jurisdiction was based on an adopting petitioner's residency in the state. The jurisdictional requirements were changed by the legislature to correspond to the Uniform Adoption Act. Under the new provisions, Mississippi has jurisdiction over an adoption action if (1) the child has lived in the state for six months or since birth, with a parent or one acting as a parent (including adopting parents), and there is substantial evidence in the state related to the child's care; (2) the prospective parent has lived in the state for six months and there is substantial evidence in the state related to the child's care; (3) the adoption agency is licensed in Mississippi and jurisdiction is in the child's best interest because of (a) the child and biological parents' connection with Mississippi or the child and adopting parents' connection with the state and (b) substantial evidence in the state related to the child's care; (4) the child and adopting parent are in the state physically and the child has been abandoned or is in danger of mistreatment, abuse, or neglect; or (5) no other state has jurisdiction or the state with jurisdiction has deferred to Mississippi courts.[2]

Although youth courts have concurrent jurisdiction over actions for termination of parental rights,[3] they do not have authority to hear adoption actions. A chancery court properly proceeded with an adoption action in spite of a youth court's outstanding custody order and continuing jurisdiction over a child.[4]

[2] Venue. Suit should be brought in the county in which the petitioner or child resides, the county in which the child was born or found after abandonment or, if the child has been surrendered to a home, in the county in which the home is located.[5]

---

[1] *In re* Adoption of F.N.M, 459 So. 2d 254, 257 (Miss. 1984); *see* N.E. v. L.H., 761 So. 2d 956, 961 (Miss. Ct. App. 2000) (not ground for adoption that adopting parents will be best custodians of child). Statutes authorizing adoptions have been in effect in this state for well over a century. Adams v. Adams, 59 So. 84 (Miss. 1912).

[2] MISS. CODE ANN. § 93-17-3(1) (Supp. 2010).

[3] *See supra* § 16.01.

[4] *In re* Petition of Beggiani, 519 So. 2d 1208, 1211 (Miss. 1988) (continuing jurisdiction applicable only to suits of similar nature); *see also* Neshoba County DHS v. Hodge, 919 So. 2d 1157, 1161 (Miss. Ct. App. 2006) (rejecting DHS's argument that youth court, having taken jurisdiction over the child as an abused child, had exclusive jurisdiction over case).

[5] MISS. CODE ANN. § 93-17-3(1) (2004).

§ 17.01[3]   MISSISSIPPI FAMILY LAW

[3] Relationship to termination proceedings. Parental rights may be terminated apart from adoption in an independent proceeding governed by separate procedural and jurisdictional rules.[6] However, the legal parents' rights may also be terminated as part of an adoption proceeding. When the actions are combined, the jurisdictional requirements and procedures for adoptions apply.[7] For example, a court hearing an adoption petition filed in the petitioner's county of residence had jurisdiction to terminate parental rights even though the termination statute placed venue in the defendant's county of residence.[8]

[4] Jurisdiction in interstate actions. The Uniform Child Custody Jurisdiction and Enforcement Act,[9] which addresses jurisdiction in most proceedings involving custody of children, does not apply to adoptions, in deference to the Uniform Adoptions Act.[10] In 2006, the Mississippi legislature amended the adoption statutes, adding jurisdictional provisions modeled on the Uniform Adoption Act.[11] Even if Mississippi has jurisdiction under one of the five jurisdictional bases of the amended statute, the state may not assume jurisdiction if, at the time of filing, a custody or adoption action regarding the child is pending in another state, in an action that complies with the Uniform Child Custody Jurisdiction Act or the provisions of section 93-17-3(1), unless the action is stayed by the court with initial jurisdiction.[12]

If another state has already issued a custody order concerning a child, Mississippi courts may entertain a petition for adoption of the child only if Mississippi has jurisdiction and the sister state does not have jurisdiction[13] or has declined to exercise jurisdiction.[14]

§ 17.02 PARTIES

[1] Who may adopt. The Mississippi adoption statute provides that "any person" may be adopted. The adopting parent may be an unmarried person or a married person whose spouse joins in the petition.[15] A decree of adoption is void if the adopting parent's spouse was not joined in the petition. In one case, however, an adoption was valid even though the adopting grandmother's husband was not formally joined. He participated in the action as a de facto party, was questioned by the court, and agreed

---

[6] *See supra* § 16.01.

[7] *See* Miss. Code Ann. § 93-17-8(6) (2004) (provisions of termination statute are not applicable except as otherwise provided in adoption statute).

[8] *In re* J.D.H, 734 So. 2d 187, 192-93 (Miss. Ct. App. 1999) (venue proper even though court bifurcated termination and adoption proceedings) (court also had jurisdiction to hear counter-complaint for adoption after petitioner dismissed complaint).

[9] *See* discussion of Act, *infra* § 18.09.

[10] *See* Patricia M. Hoff, *The ABC's of the UCCJEA: Interstate Child-Custody Practice Under the New Act*, 32 Fam. L. Q. 267, 276 (1998).

[11] *See supra* § 17.01[1] .

[12] Miss. Code Ann. § 93-17-3(2) (Supp. 2010).

[13] The sister state's jurisdiction may be continuing jurisdiction under the UCCJA or jurisdiction under an adoption statute similar to Mississippi's. Miss. Code Ann. § 93-17-3(3) (Supp. 2010).

[14] Miss. Code Ann. § 93-17-3(3) (Supp. 2010).

[15] Miss. Code Ann. § 93-17-3(1) (2004); *see In re* Adoption of R.M.P.C., 512 So. 2d 702, 706 (Miss. 1987) (error to fail to include as party husband's spouse, who was not adopting the child).

ADOPTION   § 17.02[2]

to support and care for the child.[16]

The statute prohibits adoption by same-sex couples in Mississippi.[17] However, according to recent federal court decisions, states must recognize same-sex adoption decrees of other states. The Court of Appeals for the Fifth Circuit held that Louisiana could not deny recognition of a New York decree of adoption in favor of same-sex parents.[18]

[2] Necessary parties. Necessary parties to an adoption include the child's parents or another representative of the child, physical and legal custodians of the child, and the child being adopted. Grandparents and foster parents are not necessary parties to an adoption. DHS is not a necessary party unless the child is in DHS custody. Joinder of a necessary party may be accomplished through process or by filing the party's consent to adoption.[19]

[a] Natural parents. A petition for adoption must include as parties the child's parent or parents, including parents who are themselves minors.[20] If the child's parents are not married, the father's rights may be determined in a separate proceeding.[21] Parents whose rights have been previously terminated need not be joined.[22] There is no requirement that the parent or guardian of a minor parent be included as a necessary party.[23] If both parents are dead, two adult relatives within the third degree under the civil law must be made parties.[24] If the child has been abandoned, the petition should allege that the parents cannot be identified after diligent search and inquiry and should include the child's guardian ad litem as a party.[25]

[b] Physical and legal custodians. An adoption action must include anyone with physical or legal custody of a child.[26] A court erred in granting adoption based on a mother's consent, without joining her husband. He lived with the child and was therefore a physical custodian.[27] If a child has been placed in foster care, the agent of the county office responsible for placement must be joined by process or by consent.[28] A petition for adoption of a child in DHS custody should have been dismissed for failure to join DHS as a necessary party.[29] However, foster parents with physical custody

---

[16] *In re* J.D.S., 953 So. 2d 1133, 1138 (Miss. Ct. App. 2007).

[17] Miss. Code Ann. § 93-17-3(2) (2004).

[18] Adar v. Smith, 597 F.3d 697, 719 (5th Cir. 2010), *rev'd in part*, 639 F. 3d 146 (5ᵗʰ Cir. 2010) (en banc) (state must recognize adoption, but need not change child's birth certficate); *see also* Finstuen v. Crutcher, 496 F.3d 1139, 1156 (10th Cir. 2007) (Oklahoma refusal to recognize same-sex adoption violated Full Faith and Credit Clause).

[19] Miss. Code Ann. § 93-17-3(2) (2004).

[20] Miss. Code Ann. § 93-17-5(1) (2004).

[21] *See infra* § 17.06.

[22] Miss. Code Ann. § 93-17-7(1) (2004).

[23] *See In re* Adoption of D.N.T., 843 So. 2d 690, 706-07 (Miss. 2003).

[24] If the child is in the physical custody of a relative within the third degree that relative must join as a petitioner or be made a party to the action. Miss. Code Ann. § 93-17-5(1) (2004).

[25] Miss. Code Ann. § 93-17-5(1) (2004).

[26] Miss. Code Ann. § 93-17-5(1)(ii) (2004).

[27] *In re* J.D.S., 953 So. 2d 1133, 1137 (Miss. Ct. App. 2010).

[28] Miss. Code Ann. § 93-17-5(1)(iii) (2004).

[29] *See In re* Adoption of F.N.M., 459 So. 2d 254 (Miss. 1984) (but finding that DHS waived personal service by

§ 17.02[2][c]   **MISSISSIPPI FAMILY LAW**

are not necessary parties to an adoption action.[30]

[c] Child. A child over fourteen must consent to adoption or be personally served as an adult party.[31] A child under fourteen should be joined in the action through a next friend.[32]

[3] Grandparents. A child's grandparents are not necessary parties to an adoption action, even if they have been granted statutory visitation rights.[33] However, grandparents who had filed a custody action prior to an aunt's petition for adoption should have been joined as necessary parties to protect their interests in the pending action.[34]

§ 17.03 APPOINTMENT OF GUARDIAN AD LITEM

[1] Mandatory appointment. An attorney must be appointed as guardian ad litem in any contested adoption action in which parental rights will be terminated.[35] The guardian acts as a guardian ad litem for the child and not as an attorney in the action. The child's right to a guardian may not be waived by the child or by one acting on the child's behalf.[36] The statute also appears to require appointment of a guardian ad litem when an adoption agency is involved in an uncontested adoption.[37]

[2] Discretionary appointment. In an adoption based on parental consent, a chancellor has discretion to appoint a guardian ad litem.[38] The Mississippi Supreme Court rejected a claim that appointment of a guardian is required because an uncontested adoption has the effect of terminating parental rights. The adoption statute specifically provides that appointment of a guardian is discretionary when the adoption is uncontested and no adoption agency is involved.[39] The supreme court also rejected an argument that a child being adopted has a due process right to a guardian ad litem.[40]

---

entering a general appearance). *But cf. In re* Adoption of Minor Child, 931 So. 2d 566, 574 (Miss. 2006) (DHS was not a necessary party to an adoption action where the child was in the legal custody of third parties, had not been placed in foster care by DHS, and where DHS was no longer involved in the action).

[30] MISS. CODE ANN. § 93-17-5(1)(i) (2004); *cf.* Neshoba County DHS v. Hodge, 919 So. 2d 1157, 1161 (Miss. Ct. App. 2006) (foster parents who sought to adopt had interest in case, but intervention in another party's adoption action was denied because of delay in seeking to intervene).

[31] MISS. CODE ANN. § 93-17-5(4) (2004).

[32] MISS. CODE ANN. § 93-17-5(2) (2004).

[33] *In re* Adoption of J.J.G., 736 So. 2d 1037 (Miss. 1999). *But cf.* Martin v. Putnam, 427 So. 2d 1373 (Miss. 1983) (grandparents who are child's legal custodians are necessary parties, but have no right to object to adoption).

[34] *In re* Adoption of D.T.H., 748 So. 2d 853, 857 (Miss. Ct. App. 1999).

[35] MISS. CODE ANN. § 93-17-8(1)(b) (2004); *id.* at § 93-15-107; *see* E.M.C. v. S.V.M., 695 So. 2d 576, 581 (Miss. 1997); *In re* Adoption of D.T.H, 748 So. 2d 853, 855 (Miss. Ct. App. 1999); *cf.* Neshoba County DHS v. Hodge, 919 So. 2d 1157, 1161-62 (Miss. Ct. App. 2006) (court not required to follow guardian's recommendations but must make findings of fact to explain why recommendation was not followed).

[36] MISS. CODE ANN. § 93-17-8(1)(b) (2004).

[37] *See* MISS. CODE ANN. § 93-17-8(5) (2004) (no guardian required in uncontested action unless chancery judge deems it necessary or an adoption agency is involved). See *supra* § 12.10 for a detailed discussion of the duties of guardians ad litem.

[38] MISS. CODE ANN. § 93-17-8(5) (2004).

[39] *In re* Adoption of D.T.H, 748 So. 2d 853, 855 (Miss. Ct. App. 1999).

[40] J.C. v. Adoption of Minor Child Named Herein, 797 So. 2d 209, 215 (Miss. 2001) (but noting that appointment may have been preferable); *see also* Adoption of C.L.B. v. D.G.B., 812 So. 2d 980, 984 (Miss. 2002).

ADOPTION

§ 17.03[3]

[3] Guardian for minor parent. The supreme court has refused to require the appointment of a guardian ad litem for minor parents whose rights will be terminated by adoption.[41] However, the court has suggested that a guardian should be appointed if the circumstances present an opportunity for overreaching. For example, a guardian would have been preferable to ensure that no overreaching occurred when a minor mother consented to adoption by her parents, in whose home she was living.[42] Similarly, a guardian would have been preferable when a father consented to adoption by his aunt, who was providing him with a place to live.[43]

§ 17.04 PROCEDURE

[1] Rule 81. Actions for adoption are governed by the special procedures set out in Rule 81 of the Mississippi Rules of Civil Procedure. Under Rule 81, an adoption action may be tried thirty days after service of process or, if process is by publication, thirty days after the first publication. Parties must be served with a Rule 81 summons, rather than a summons under Rule 4. Defendants are not required to file a responsive pleading.[44] Procedure in Rule 81 matters is discussed more fully in Chapter XIX.[45]

The adoption statutes provide that in the absence of consent, parties should be served personally. However, a nonresident party or a resident who cannot be located after diligent search and inquiry may be served through publication.[46] Process should be served on the Attorney General as agent for the Department of Human Services.[47]

[2] Consent. It is not necessary to serve a parent or custodian who has executed a sworn or acknowledged consent to adoption. The consent may not be executed prior to seventy-two hours after the child's birth.[48] There is no requirement, however, that the consent be executed after the petition is filed.[49] If the child's physical or legal custodian is an institutional home, an authorized officer or representative of the home may consent to the adoption.[50]

[3] Petition. A petition for adoption must be sworn.[51] The petition must include the certificate of a doctor or nurse practitioner attesting to the child's mental and physical health. If the certificate indicates a medical or physical problem, the petitioners must file an affidavit acknowledging the condition and their willingness to adopt notwith-

---

[41] *See* Adoption of J.M.M. v. New Beginning of Tupelo, Inc., 796 So. 2d 975, 983 (Miss. 2001).

[42] *In re* Adoption of a Minor, 558 So. 2d 854, 857 (Miss. 1990) (but holding chancellor was within discretion in not appointing guardian).

[43] *In re* Adoption of D.T.H, 748 So. 2d 853 (Miss. Ct. App. 1999) (but holding nonetheless that chancellor was within discretion in not appointing guardian).

[44] MISS. R. CIV. P. 81(d).

[45] *See infra* § 19.11.

[46] MISS. CODE ANN. § 93-17-5(4) (2004).

[47] *See* L.W. v. C.W.B., 762 So. 2d 323, 329 (Miss. 2000); MISS. R. CIV. P. 4(d)(5).

[48] MISS. CODE ANN. § 93-17-5(1) (2004).

[49] *In re* Adoption of D.T.H., 748 So. 2d 853, 856 (Miss. Ct. App. 1999).

[50] MISS. CODE ANN. § 93-17-5(2) (2004).

[51] *In re* J.D.H, 734 So. 2d 187, 192-93 (Miss. Ct. App. 1999) (sufficient that petitioners affirmed allegation of petition under oath).

535

§ 17.04[4]   MISSISSIPPI FAMILY LAW

standing the condition.[52] The petition must also be accompanied by a sworn statement describing any property owned by the child.[53]

The statutory requirement of a certificate[54] was not satisfied by a request that the chancellor order the child examined.[55] Similarly, it is not sufficient to state in the adoption petition that the child has no property. The mandatory language of the statute requires a sworn property certificate.[56] However, filing of the certificates is not a jurisdictional prerequisite to suit; the documents may be filed subsequently.[57] A court should not have dismissed an action for lack of subject matter jurisdiction because a certificate was not filed with the petition.[58]

[4] Investigation. A court may order an investigation by a licensed person to determine whether it is in the child's best interest to be adopted and whether the petitioners are suitable parents. The investigation may include a home study of the petitioners, which may be conducted by DHS or by an adoption agency licensed in Mississippi.[59] Courts are required to assess a minimum fee of $350 for each home study conducted by the Department of Human Services. The cost of investigation may be assessed against either or both parties. The court also has discretion to require that DHS bear the expense.[60]

§ 17.05 UNCONTESTED ADOPTIONS

An adoption is uncontested if all parties with a right to object to the adoption consent or if their rights have been previously terminated. Parties with a right to object to adoption include the mother, the child's legal father, and an unmarried father who has established a relationship with the child. A parent's consent, once given, may not be withdrawn in the absence of a showing of fraud, duress, or undue influence.

[1] Parties who must consent

[a] Mother and legal father. No child may be adopted over the objection of a parent unless his or her rights have been terminated. A parent whose rights have been terminated prior to adoption need not be included in the action.[61] "Parent" includes the mother's husband at the time of the child's birth.[62]

---

[52] MISS. CODE ANN. § 93-17-3(1) (2004) ("abnormal mental or physical condition or defect" does not bar adoption, in discretion of chancellor, if adopting parents provide required affidavit).

[53] MISS. CODE ANN. § 93-17-3(1) (2004).

[54] See In re Adoption of D.T.H., 748 So. 2d 853 (Miss. Ct. App. 1999) (physician's letter not sufficient).

[55] In re Adoption of F.N.M, 459 So. 2d 254, 257 (Miss. 1984).

[56] In re Adoption of D.T.H., 748 So. 2d 853, 856-57 (Miss. Ct. App. 1999) (proper certificates should be attached on remand).

[57] See In re J.D.H, 734 So. 2d 187, 192-93 (Miss. Ct. App. 1999) (distinguishing In re Adoption of F.N.M, 459 So. 2d 254, 257 (Miss. 1984)).

[58] See L.W. v. C.W.B., 762 So. 2d 323 (Miss. 2000).

[59] MISS. CODE ANN. § 93-17-11 (Supp. 2010).

[60] MISS. CODE ANN. § 93-17-12 (2004).

[61] MISS. CODE ANN. § 93-17-7(1) (2004); see In re Adoption of Minor Child, 931 So. 2d 566, 570 (Miss. 2006) (petition to terminate mother's rights; father consented to adoption).

[62] See Krohn v. Migues, 274 So. 2d 654 (Miss. 1973); cf. MISS. CODE ANN. § 93-15-107 (2004) (legal father must

ADOPTION § 17.05[1][b]

[b] Unmarried father. Until 2002, an unmarried father had no statutory right to be notified of or to object to an adoption. In 1998, the Mississippi Supreme Court held that the state's adoption statute was unconstitutional as applied to an unmarried father who had established a substantial relationship with his child. The court held that the same rights extend to a father whose diligent attempts to establish a relationship with a child are thwarted by the mother or her family.[63]

The statute was amended in 2002 to reflect the court's decision. Under the amended statute, an unmarried father may not object to adoption unless, within thirty days after the child's birth, he has demonstrated "a full commitment to the responsibilities of parenthood."[64] The statute sets out a separate procedure for determining the rights of an unmarried father.[65]

[c] Child over fourteen. A child over the age of fourteen must consent to adoption in a sworn or acknowledged document or be joined in the action as a party.[66]

[d] Grandparents/other custodians. A child's grandparents have no right to object to adoption. Their consent is not required even if they have been granted statutory visitation rights.[67]

[e] Department of Human Services. DHS's consent is not a prerequisite to adoption. The Mississippi Supreme Court held that a chancellor erred in dismissing an adoption because DHS did not consent – chancery courts are vested with the ultimate responsibility for determining whether adoption is in a child's best interest.[68]

[2] Procedure for consent. The requirements for consent are set out in two separate provisions – one describing consent in connection with surrender of a child to a home, the other referring to the procedure for consent in the termination of parental rights statute.

[a] Surrender of child to home. The adoption statute provides that a parent may surrender a child to a home[69] by a written, acknowledged document giving the home custody of the child, relinquishing all parental rights, authorizing the home to consent to the child's adoption, and waiving process in an adoption proceeding. The surrender must be in writing and executed more than seventy-two hours after the child's birth.[70]

---

be made party defendant in termination proceedings).

[63] Smith v. Malouf, 722 So. 2d 490 (Miss. 1998).

[64] Miss. Code Ann. § 93-17-5(3) (2004).

[65] *See infra* § 17.06.

[66] Miss. Code Ann. § 93-17-5(4) (2004).

[67] *In re* Adoption of J.J.G., 736 So. 2d 1037 (Miss. 1999); *In re* Adoption of D.T.H., 748 So. 2d 853, 857 (Miss. Ct. App. 1999); Martin v. Putnam, 427 So. 2d 1373 (Miss. 1983).

[68] *See* L.W. v. C.W.B., 762 So. 2d 323 (Miss. 2000).

[69] Miss. Code Ann. § 93-17-9 (2004) (a charitable or religious organization or public authority authorized to care for or procure adoption of children).

[70] Miss. Code Ann. § 93-17-9 (2004).

§ 17.05[2][b]   MISSISSIPPI FAMILY LAW

[b] Consent to private adoption. The adoption statute addresses a parent's consent to private adoption indirectly, by reference to the termination statute. The adoption statute provides a list of circumstances under which a child may be adopted over a parent's objection. These include the grounds set out in the termination of parental rights statutes.[71] Those statutes provide that a parent's rights, including the right to object to adoption, may be terminated "by the execution of a written voluntary release, signed by the parent, regardless of the age of the parent."[72]

[3] Requirements. The statutory requirements for consent to terminate parental rights are strictly construed. The agreement must be in writing and must be executed more than seventy-two hours after the child's birth.[73] A mother's oral agreement to allow a couple to adopt her child was not legally binding.[74] In addition, the statute requires that consent to surrender a child to a home must be sworn or acknowledged.[75] A mother's consent to allow a specific couple to adopt her child was not blanket consent to terminate her parental rights. The first adoption did not occur; therefore she retained the right to object to adoption by other parties.[76]

[4] Revocation of consent. Consent to adoption may not be revoked absent clear and convincing proof that the agreement was produced by fraud, duress, or undue influence.[77] The supreme court has rejected arguments that an underage parent's consent to adoption should not be binding. Although minors in Mississippi may not enter into binding contracts, waive certain rights, or choose to have an abortion, the legislature has specifically provided that a minor parent's consent to adoption is valid and binding.[78]

The supreme court rejected a minor mother's attempt to revoke consent to adoption by the couple with whom she lived. She read the document, signed it voluntarily, and understood that she could refuse to consent.[79] The court has also rejected arguments that family pressure or the consenting parent's distress about his or her circumstances amounts to duress. The court has emphasized that "influence exerted by means of advice, arguments, persuasions, solicitation, suggestion, or entreaty is not undue" unless the parent's free will is destroyed.[80]

The same standard applies to attempts to revoke consent prior to the initiation

---

[71] Miss. Code Ann. § 93-17-7(2)(e) (2004).

[72] Miss. Code Ann. § 93-15-103(2) (2004). In several cases, the supreme court has construed a parent's relinquishment of rights as abandonment. *See In re* Adoption of D.N.T., 843 So. 2d 690, 706-07 (Miss. 2003); Grafe v. Olds, 556 So. 2d 690 (Miss. 1990) (private adoption); Bryant v. Cameron, 473 So. 2d 174, 177 (Miss. 1985); C.C.I. v. Natural Parents, 398 So. 2d 220, 226 (Miss. 1981) (public adoption).

[73] Miss. Code Ann. § 93-15-103(2) (2004); *id.* at § 93-17-9.

[74] Bryant v. Cameron, 473 So. 2d 174, 177 (Miss. 1985) (agreements not conforming to the statute are unenforceable).

[75] Miss. Code Ann. § 93-17-9 (2004).

[76] A.D.R. v. J.L.H., 994 So. 2d 177, 183-84 (Miss. 2008).

[77] *In re* Adoption of D.N.T., 843 So. 2d 690 (Miss. 2003); Adoption of J.M.M. v. New Beginnings of Tupelo, Inc., 796 So. 2d 975, 978-79 (Miss. 2001); Grafe v. Olds, 556 So. 2d 690 (Miss. 1990) (private adoption); C.C.I. v. Natural Parents, 398 So. 2d 220, 226 (Miss. 1981) (public adoption).

[78] *See In re* Adoption of D.N.T., 843 So. 2d 690 (Miss. 2003).

[79] *See In* re Adoption of D.N.T., 843 So. 2d 690 (Miss. 2003).

[80] *In re* Adoption of J.M.M., 796 So. 2d 975, 978-79 (Miss. 2001).

538

ADOPTION § 17.06

of adoption proceedings – a minor mother's attempt to withdraw consent three days after agreeing to adoption was properly denied in the absence of a showing of fraud or duress.[81] Several justices of the Mississippi Supreme Court have urged that minor parents who are asked to consent to adoption should be represented by guardians ad litem.[82]

§ 17.06 PETITION FOR DETERMINATION OF FATHER'S RIGHTS

The rights of an unmarried father may be determined in a separate proceeding as a preliminary to an adoption action. After a child is thirty days old, a petition for determination of rights may be filed by an alleged father or by anyone who would be a necessary party to an adoption.[83] The alleged father's right to object to adoption is the sole issue in the proceeding, which may be heard ten days after the completion of process.[84] To be entitled to object to adoption, an unmarried father must prove that, within thirty days of the child's birth, he demonstrated "a full commitment to the responsibilities of parenthood."[85] The necessary commitment may be shown by proof that the father provided financial support during pregnancy and after the child's birth, that he "frequently and consistently" visited the child, and that he is "willing and able to assume legal and physical care" of the child.[86] In the alternative, a father may show that his attempts to support and visit his child were thwarted and that he is ready to assume the child's care.[87] The court may terminate the parental rights of a father who fails to prove a full commitment to fatherhood. If a father who has demonstrated the necessary commitment objects to adoption, the court must set the matter as a contested adoption.[88]

A chancellor properly refused to terminate the rights of an unmarried father who immediately took steps to support and visit his child upon learning of his fatherhood one year after her birth.[89] Similarly, a chancellor properly set aside adoption of a newborn based on the mother's consent. She told the father that the child was not his. He promptly requested a DNA test after the child's birth and notified the adoptive parents that he believed he was the child's father.[90]

§ 17.07 CONTESTED ADOPTION

If a parent whose rights have not been terminated objects to adoption, the proceeding is contested. Adoption may not be ordered unless the court finds by clear and

---

[81] Grafe v. Olds, 556 So. 2d 690 (Miss. 1990).
[82] *See In re* Adoption of D.N.T., 843 So. 2d 690, 712 (Miss. 2003) (Cobb, J., concurring); *In re* Adoption of J.M.M., 796 So. 2d 975, 978-79 (Miss. 2001) (McRae, J., dissenting).
[83] MISS. CODE ANN. § 93-17-6(1) (2004) (prospective adopting parents are not necessary parties).
[84] MISS. CODE ANN. § 93-17-6(1), (2) (2004).
[85] MISS. CODE ANN. § 93-17-5(3) (2004).
[86] MISS. CODE ANN. § 93-17-6(4) (2004).
[87] MISS. CODE ANN. § 93-17-6(4) (2004).
[88] MISS. CODE ANN. § 93-17-6(5), (6) (2004).
[89] K.D.F. v. J.L.H., 933 So. 2d 971, 978-79 (Miss. 2006).
[90] K.B. v. J.G, 9 So. 3d 1124, 1124-27 (Miss. 2009).

§ 17.07[1]   **MISSISSIPPI FAMILY LAW**

convincing evidence that the statutory grounds for termination of parental rights and adoption exist.

[1] Test. Adoption may be ordered over a parent's objection upon proof that the parent abandoned or deserted the child or is "mentally, morally, or otherwise unfit" and if adoption is in the child's best interest.[91] The supreme court has emphasized that the test for adoption is two-fold. First, the court must find that the statutory grounds for termination and adoption have been met. If grounds are proved, the court must then determine whether adoption is in the child's best interest.[92] An order of adoption will be reversed if the court fails to address whether adoption is in the child's best interest – the statute "requires a definite adjudication" that adoption will promote the child's welfare.[93] Similarly, an adoption based solely on the child's best interest, without a finding of parental abandonment or unfitness, will be reversed.[94]

If adoption is not deemed to be in a child's best interest, the fact that a parent surrendered a child for adoption is not evidence of abandonment, desertion, or unfitness.[95]

[2] Enumerated grounds. The adoption statute provides a list of circumstances that meet the "abandoned, deserted, or unfit" test. The list incorporates the separate grounds set out in the statutes governing independent termination of parental rights. There is substantial overlap between the grounds set out in the adoption and termination statutes, but they are not identical.

Termination of parental rights in connection with an adoption may be based on the grounds in either chapter. Therefore, the discussion below should be read in conjunction with the termination grounds set out in Chapter XVI.[96] However, because the termination statute does not incorporate the adoption grounds, it appears that a termination action separate from an adoption may be based only on the grounds in the termination chapter.

[a] Abandonment. Abandonment has been described by the Mississippi Supreme Court as "any conduct by a parent which evinces a settled purpose to forego all duties and relinquish all parental claims to the child."[97] The test for abandonment is objective, based on the "totality of the circumstances."[98] Abandonment may be shown

---

[91] Miss. Code Ann. § 93-17-7(1) (2004); *see* Ainsworth v. Natural Father, 414 So. 2d 417, 419-20 (Miss. 1982).

[92] Miss. Code Ann. § 93-17-8(1)(c) (2004); *see* W.A.S. v. A.L.G., 949 So. 2d 31, 36 (Miss. 2010) (court properly found that adoption by stepfather was in child's best interest); Natural Mother v. Paternal Aunt, 583 So. 2d 614, 618 (Miss. 1991); *see also* Martin v. Putnam, 427 So. 2d 1373 (Miss. 1983).

[93] Ainsworth v. Natural Parent, 414 So. 2d 417, 421 (Miss. 1982); *see* Natural Mother v. Paternal Aunt, 583 So. 2d 614, 618 (Miss. 1991); Martin v. Putnam, 427 So. 2d 1373 (Miss. 1983).

[94] *See* N.E. v. L.H., 761 So. 2d 956, 961 (Miss. Ct. App. 2000) (not ground for adoption that adopting parents will be best custodians of child); *see also In re* Yarber, 341 So. 2d 108, 110 (Miss. 1977) (situation was "regrettable" but did not rise to level of unfitness to support termination).

[95] Miss. Code Ann. § 93-17-8(2) (2004).

[96] *See* discussion *supra* § 16.04.

[97] S.N.C. v. J.R.D., 755 So. 2d 1077, 1081 (Miss. 2000); *see also In re* J.D., 512 So. 2d 684, 686 (Miss. 1987) ("abandonment is relinquishment of a known right"); Ainsworth v. Natural Father, 414 So. 2d 417, 420 (Miss. 1982).

[98] S.N.C. v. J.R.D., 755 So. 2d 1077, 1081 (Miss. 2000).

ADOPTION   **§ 17.07[2][b]**

through one event, such as surrender of a child for adoption, or through a course of conduct.[99] Failure to pay child support does not, in itself, constitute abandonment.[100] The constructive abandonment test for third-party custody, announced in *Hill v. Mitchell*, does not apply in termination actions.[101]

Abandonment is also listed as a ground for termination independent of adoption. The Mississippi cases involving abandonment as a ground for termination, discussed in Chapter XVI, are equally applicable to termination for abandonment in adoption proceedings.[102]

[b] Desertion. The Mississippi Supreme Court has defined desertion as "foresaking one's duty as well as a breaking away from or breaking off associations with some matter involving a legal or moral obligation."[103] Desertion is also listed as a ground for termination independent of adoption. The Mississippi cases involving desertion as a ground for termination, discussed in Chapter XVI, are equally applicable to termination for desertion in adoption proceedings.[104]

[c] Abuse. Adoption may be ordered over the objection of a parent who has (1) inflicted physical or mental injury that caused a child's deterioration; (2) sexually abused a child; or (3) exploited or overworked a child to the point of endangering his or her health or emotional well-being.[105] The related, but not identical, ground under the termination statutes permits termination when a parent "has been responsible for a series of abusive events concerning one or more children."[106] The termination statute also sets out as a ground a parent's conviction for felonious assault or sexual assault on a child.[107]

[d] Failure to provide. Adoption may be ordered when a parent has failed to provide reasonable care for a child, including food, clothing, shelter, and treatment.[108] However, termination on the basis of failure to support was error when the court had suspended the mother's child support obligations.[109]

---

[99] G.Q.A. v. Harrison County Dep't of Human Serv., 771 So. 2d 331, 336 (Miss. 2000).

[100] *See* Carter v. Taylor, 611 So. 2d 874, 877 (Miss. 1992); *In re* Adoption of a Female Child, 412 So. 2d 1175, 1178-79 (Miss. 1982) (failure to pay child support and failure to visit not abandonment where no visitation ordered and mother refused to allow father to see child); *In re* M.L.W., 755 So. 2d 558, 563 (Miss. Ct. App. 2000).

[101] *In re* Adoption of Minor Child, 931 So. 2d 566, 577-78 (Miss. 2006).

[102] *See supra* § 16.04[1].

[103] Petit v. Holifield, 443 So. 2d 874, 878 (Miss. 1984) (citing Ainsworth v. Natural Father, 414 So. 2d 417 (Miss. 1982)).

[104] *See supra* § 16.04[1].

[105] Miss. Code Ann. § 93-17-7(2)(a) (2004).

[106] Miss. Code Ann. § 93-15-103(3)(c) (2004).

[107] Listed offenses include: rape, Miss. Code Ann. § 97-3-65 (2004); sexual battery, *id.* at § 97-3-95(c); touching for lustful purposes, *id.* at § 97-5-23; exploitation, *id.* at § 97-5-33; felonious abuse or battery, *id.* at § 97-5-39(2); carnal knowledge of certain children, *id.* at § 97-5-41. With regard to another child of the defendant, listed offenses include murder, voluntary manslaughter, conspiracy to commit murder or voluntary manslaughter or felony assault, see Miss. Code Ann. § 93-15-103(3)(g) (2004). *See supra* § 16.04[7].

[108] Miss. Code Ann. § 93-17-7(2)(b) (2004).

[109] *In re* Adoption of Minor Child, 931 So. 2d 566, 578 (Miss. 2006).

§ 17.07[2][e]   MISSISSIPPI FAMILY LAW

[e] Condition making parent unable to provide. Adoption may be ordered over the objection of a parent whose illness, disability, mental condition, behavior or conduct disorder, or substance abuse or dependency makes the parent "unable or unwilling to provide an adequate permanent home for the child . . . based upon expert opinion or . . . an established pattern of behavior."[110] A court properly terminated rights of a mother who suffered from bipolar disorder and borderline personality disorder, was hospitalized three times for mental or emotional problems, and had attempted suicide, in spite of evidence of recent positive changes in her life.[111] The termination chapter contains a similar but not identical ground: parental rights may be terminated based on a parent's ongoing behavior that makes a child's return to the parent impossible, including a condition that prevents the parent from providing "minimally acceptable" care for a child.[112]

[f] Conduct posing a substantial risk of harm. Grounds for adoption also include a parent's present or past conduct that poses a substantial risk of harm to a child's physical, mental, or emotional health.[113]

[g] Grounds in termination statute. Adoption may be ordered over a parent's objection if the court finds that any of the grounds set out in the statute governing independent termination of parental rights have been proved.[114] In addition to the grounds discussed in sections 17.07[2][a] - [e], the termination statute includes the following grounds: (1) a parent's failure to contact a child for a specified period of time;[115] (2) a parent's failure to implement a DHS plan for a child's return;[116] (3) a child's "extreme and deep-seated antipathy" toward a parent or "substantial erosion" of the parent-child relationship;[117] and (4) abuse or neglect leading to foster care placement, when it is not in the child's best interest to be returned to his or her parents.[118]

[h] Other unfitness. Courts may find parents unfit based on conduct not specifically enumerated in the statutory listing.[119] However, the catch-all provision has been applied sparingly. Only parental conduct equal in severity to the more specific grounds has been held to be unfitness. For example, a parent's nonmarital cohabitation or adulterous relationship is not unfitness for purposes of adoption.[120] Similarly, a father's conviction for possession of marijuana with intent to distribute did not, in and of itself, make him morally unfit for parenthood.[121] In several cases, the supreme court

---

[110] Miss. Code Ann. § 93-17-7(2)(c) (2004).
[111] *In re* Adoption of Minor Child, 931 So. 2d 566, 581 (Miss. 2006).
[112] Miss. Code Ann. § 93-15-103(3)(e) (2004). *See supra* § 16.04[5].
[113] Miss. Code Ann. § 93-17-7(2)(d) (2004).
[114] Miss. Code Ann. § 93-17-7(2)(e) (2004).
[115] Miss. Code Ann. § 93-15-103(3)(b) (2004). *See supra* § 16.04[2].
[116] Miss. Code Ann. § 93-15-103(3)(d) (2004). *See supra* § 16.04[4].
[117] Miss. Code Ann. § 93-15-103(3)(f) (2004). *See supra* § 16.04[6].
[118] Miss. Code Ann. § 93-15-103(3)(h) (2004). *See supra* § 16.04[8].
[119] Miss. Code Ann. § 93-17-7(2)(f) (2004).
[120] *See In re* J.D., 512 So. 2d 684, 686 (Miss. 1987) (cohabitation); Petit v. Holifield, 443 So. 2d 874 (Miss. 1984) (adultery).
[121] *In re* J.D., 512 So. 2d 684, 686 (Miss. 1987).

ADOPTION

§ 17.07[3]

has stated that a parent's commission of a crime is not, in and of itself, evidence of unfitness.[122] A court erred in finding that a father who shot his children's stepfather four times was morally unfit – the situation was "regrettable" but the stepfather recovered.[123] However, a father who murdered the children's mother and buried her body under the outhouse was morally unfit to have custody of his children.[124]

[3] Procedure

[a] Burden of proof. The petitioner in a contested adoption must prove by clear and convincing evidence that objecting parents have abandoned or deserted a child or are mentally, morally, or otherwise unfit.[125]

[b] Paternity. If paternity is an issue in a contested adoption, the court must order genetic tests, request an expedited report, and hold a hearing on paternity "at the earliest possible time."[126]

[c] Hearings. Hearings are to be scheduled as expeditiously as possible.[127]

§ 17.08 FINAL DECREE

[1] Interlocutory decree. A court's decree of adoption functions as an interlocutory decree for six months, at which time a final decree of adoption may be entered. The six-month interval is not required if (1) the adopting parent is the child's stepparent or related to the child by blood within the third degree or (2) the court determines that the waiting period is not necessary and includes that finding in the decree. In addition, if the child has been living with the adopting parent, the court may reduce the six-month interval by the time of the child's residence with the petitioner.[128]

[2] Provisions and effect. Unless otherwise specifically provided, a decree of adoption affects the rights of the parties as set out below.

[a] Inheritance rights. The final decree should provide that the child will inherit from the adopting parents and their children and that the adopting parents and their children will inherit from the child. In addition, the decree should provide that the child's natural parents and relatives shall not inherit from the child, with the exception

---

[122] *See In re* J.D., 512 So. 2d 684, 686 (Miss. 1987); *In re* Yarber, 341 So. 2d 108 (Miss. 1977) (shooting at children's stepfather).

[123] *In re* Yarber, 341 So. 2d 108, 110 (Miss. 1977) (custody not at issue).

[124] *See* Shoemake v. Davis, 216 So. 2d 420 (Miss. 1968); *see also* Mayfield v. Braund, 64 So. 2d 713 (Miss. 1953) (terminating rights of father sentenced to ten years in penitentiary).

[125] W.A.S. v. A.L.G., 949 So. 2d 31, 36 (Miss. 2007); *In re* Adoption of Minor Child, 931 So. 2d 566, 577 (Miss. 2006) (petitioner for adoption has burden of proving grounds by clear and convincing evidence); Natural Mother v. Paternal Aunt, 583 So. 2d 614, 619 (Miss. 1991) (abandonment by mother who removed herself from children's lives for three and a half years); G.M.R., Sr. v. H.E.S., 489 So. 2d 498, 500 (Miss. 1986).

[126] MISS. CODE ANN. § 93-17-8(1) (2004).

[127] MISS. CODE ANN. § 93-17-8(1)(d) (2004).

[128] MISS. CODE ANN. § 93-17-13 (2004).

§ 17.08[2][b]   MISSISSIPPI FAMILY LAW

of a natural parent whose spouse is adopting the child.[129] However, an adopted child may still inherit from his or her natural family.[130]

[b] Termination of parental rights. The decree should provide that all rights of the natural parents are terminated, with the exception of a natural parent whose spouse is adopting the child.[131] In some instances, however, courts have approved adoptions that recognize some continuing right of visitation in the natural parents.[132]

[c] Grant of parental rights. The decree should provide that the adopting parents and child are vested with all the rights and duties of natural parents and children.[133]

[d] Child's name. The decree may provide for a change in the child's name if the parties so desire.[134]

[e] Grandparent visitation rights. When a child is adopted, natural grandparents lose previously awarded visitation rights unless one of the legal parents after adoption is a natural parent[135] or was related to the child by blood or marriage prior to the adoption.[136] Persons who become grandparents as a result of adoption may petition the court for visitation.[137]

[3] Variations. The Mississippi statute provides that an adoption will have the effects set out above "unless otherwise provided."[138] In several cases, the supreme court has approved non-traditional adoptions deemed to be in a child's best interest.

[a] Natural parent visitation. The supreme court affirmed an agreed order of adoption granting visitation to the natural father and requiring that he pay child support. The court emphasized that intrafamily adoptions may present circumstances in which continued contact with natural parents is appropriate.[139] Subsequently, the court clarified that an adoption provision reserving a father's parental rights and providing for visitation was "mere surplusage" and did not affect the validity of the adoption or

---

[129] MISS. CODE ANN. § 93-17-13 (2004).

[130] *See In re* Estate of Yount, 845 So. 2d 724 (Miss. Ct. App. 2003) (adopted half-brother entitled to share of settlement for wrongful death of natural brother).

[131] MISS. CODE ANN. § 93-17-13 (2004).

[132] *See infra* § 17.08[3][a].

[133] MISS. CODE ANN. § 93-17-13 (2004).

[134] MISS. CODE ANN. § 93-17-13 (2004).

[135] MISS. CODE ANN. § 93-16-7 (2004). The statute was amended to add this provision after *Olson v. Flinn*, 484 So. 2d 1015, 1017 (Miss. 1986), in which paternal grandparents were denied visitation after their son's death and their grandchild's adoption by his stepfather.

[136] MISS. CODE ANN. § 93-16-7 (2004). This provision was added to resolve the dilemma presented in *Muse v. Hutchins*, 559 So. 2d 1031, 1033 (Miss. 1990) (then existing statute barred visitation by maternal grandparents after adoption by paternal grandparents) and *In re Adoption of a Minor*, 558 So. 2d 854, 856 (Miss 1990) (paternal grandparents could not obtain visitation after adoption by maternal grandparents).

[137] MISS. CODE ANN. § 93-16-7 (2004). *See* discussion of grandparent visitation rights *supra* § 12.09.

[138] MISS. CODE ANN. § 93-17-13 (2004).

[139] Humphrey v. Pannell, 710 So. 2d 392, 393-94 (Miss. 1998).

ADOPTION   **§ 17.08[3][b]**

termination of parental rights.[140]

[b] Adoption by unrelated parties. In another unusual case, the supreme court affirmed a chancellor's order allowing adoption by opposing petitioners – the child's maternal grandmother and the deceased mother's former boyfriend, who had lived with and supported the child, believing that she was his biological child. Primary custody was awarded to the grandmother with visitation rights to the boyfriend.[141] In another case, the court permitted a natural father, who had previously consented to adoption by the mother's husband, to adopt his own natural child in a joint petition with the child's mother, even though both were married to others at the time.[142]

[4] Confidentiality. The adoption statute requires that all proceedings be closed to the public and all records maintained as confidential. However, the court in which the proceeding was held may, upon good cause, allow review of the record. The names of the natural parents and the child's original name should not appear in the court's public records. The case should be styled in the names of the petitioners for adoption and indicate that the case is for adoption of a child.[143]

§ 17.09 ACTIONS TO SET ASIDE ADOPTION

A child's natural parents may seek to set aside a decree of adoption on the ground that consent to the adoption was not freely given. Attacks on adoption decrees may also be based on a natural father's challenge to a proceeding to which he was not a party.

[1] Six-month statute of limitations. An action to set aside an adoption must be brought within six months after the final decree is entered.[144] After the six-month statute of limitations has run, a decree may be set aside only for lack of jurisdiction or failure to proceed under the adoption statute.[145] A natural mother's challenge to her consent to adoption nine years earlier was dismissed; claims of coercion and duress may be brought only within six months of adoption.[146] The Mississippi Court of Appeals held that the Illinois Central Railroad's suit to set aside its former employee's adoption of his grandchildren on the basis of fraud was untimely since it was filed one year after the entry of adoption.[147]

---

[140] *In re* Adoption of J.E.B., 822 So. 2d 949 (Miss. 2002).

[141] *In re* Adoption of P.B.H., 787 So. 2d 1268 (Miss. 2001).

[142] *See In re* Adoption of R.M.P.C., 512 So. 2d 702, 706-07 (Miss. 1987).

[143] MISS. CODE ANN. § 93-17-29 (2004). Clerks are directed to maintain a separate confidential index containing the names of all the parties, the date of the adoption, and the name given to the child. The statute provides that the index shall not be examined except by officers of the court, including attorneys, or by court order based on good cause. *Id.* § 93-17-31.

[144] MISS. CODE ANN. § 93-17-15 (2004) (whether by consent, personal service, or publication).

[145] MISS. CODE ANN. § 93-17-17 (2004).

[146] *In re* Adoption of M.D.T., 722 So. 2d 702 (Miss. 1998) (six-month statute is strictly construed to ensure the finality of adoption decrees).

[147] *In re* Adoption of D.C.S., 44 So. 3d 1006, 1009-13 (Miss. Ct. App. 2009) (also holding that the railroad lacked standing to object to the adoption).

545

§ 17.09[2]   MISSISSIPPI FAMILY LAW

[2] Challenge to consent. Within the six-month period following a decree, a natural parent may challenge an uncontested adoption based on fraud, duress, or undue influence. The supreme court rejected a sixteen-year-old mother's claim of duress; she consented after being told by her father that she could live with relatives and keep the child, but could not remain at home. The court held that stressful circumstances do not negate voluntariness: "There is no law to the effect that the surrender of a child is valid only if done without such distress."[148] Similarly, the court rejected a mother's argument that she consented under duress because she was eighteen, suffered from post-partum depression, had attempted suicide, and had recently recovered memories of childhood sexual abuse.[149] And a chancellor properly refused to allow a seventeen-year-old mother to withdraw her consent to adoption, even though she was living with and supported by the adopting couple. Her boyfriend offered to marry her and support the child.[150] The concurrence in this case stressed the need for additional protections for minor parents in adoption actions, suggesting that minors who are not advised by parents should be represented by a guardian ad litem.[151]

Only parents have standing to challenge the validity of an adoption. The Mississippi Supreme Court held that Illinois Central Railroad lacked standing to set aside an adoption by its former employee as fraudulent. The railroad alleged that the dying man's adoption of his grandchildren was a sham to secure decedent's benefits for his grandchildren.[152] Similarly, an executor lacked standing to challenge a deceased's adoption of his stepchildren based on the natural father's lack of consent.[153]

[3] Challenge to jurisdiction. An adoption decree is void if the court lacked subject matter or personal jurisdiction. A decree may be attacked collaterally for lack of jurisdiction after the six-month statute of limitations has expired.[154] Many of the cases attacking jurisdiction involve failure to join a necessary party. For example, an adoption was set aside for failure to join the child's mother. The adopting grandparents represented that she could not be found, concealing the fact that they were in contact with her.[155] Even though she had consented to adoption, a mother's petition to set aside a decree was properly granted based on failure to join her husband. The adopting parent was aware that the mother was married and failed to join her husband.[156] And an adoption was set aside because an unmarried father was not joined in the action. He demonstrated his commitment to parenthood within thirty days of the child's birth by requesting a DNA test and notifying the adoptive parents that he believed he was the child's father.[157] Similarly, a decree was void when service of process was returned to

---

[148] Adoption of J.M.M. v. New Beginnings of Tupelo, Inc., 796 So. 2d 975 (Miss. 2001).

[149] C.L.B. v. D.G.B., 812 So. 2d 980 (Miss. 2002).

[150] *In re* Adoption of D.N.T., 843 So. 2d 690 (Miss. 2003).

[151] *In re* Adoption of D.N.T., 843 So. 2d 690 (Miss. 2003) (Cobb, J., concurring).

[152] *In re* Adoption of D.C.S., 44 So. 3d 1006, 1009-13 (Miss. Ct. App. 2009) (also holding that adoption cannot be set aside for fraud after six-month statute of limitations expires).

[153] Gartrell v. Gartrell, 27 So. 3d 388 (Miss. 2009).

[154] *See In re* Adoption of R.M.P.C., 512 So. 2d 702, 706 (Miss. 1987); Krohn v. Migues, 274 So. 2d 654 (Miss. 1973); *see also* Birindelli v. Egelston, 404 So. 2d 322, 323-24 (Miss. 1981) (void for failure to join father in action).

[155] *See* Naveda v. Ahumada, 381 So. 2d 147, 149 (Miss. 1981).

[156] Krohn v. Migues, 274 So. 2d 654 (Miss. 1973).

[157] K.B. v. J.G, 9 So. 3d 1124, 1128-32 (Miss. 2009).

546

ADOPTION § 17.09[3]

the wrong chancery district.[158]

Procedural defects that are not jurisdictional may be waived. A father was not entitled to set aside an adoption for lack of a doctor's certificate regarding the child's health, lack of a certificate regarding the child's property, failure to join his wife in the action, and failure to have his signature acknowledged.[159]

---

[158] Birindelli v. Egelston, 404 So. 2d 322, 323-24 (Miss. 1981) (also void for failure to join father in action).

[159] *See In re* Adoption of R.M.P.C., 512 So. 2d 702, 706-07 (Miss. 1987) (wife was not child's mother).

548

PART THREE

JURISDICTION, PRACTICE, AND PROCEDURE

XVIII
JURISDICTION

Family law disputes present unique jurisdictional challenges. First, interstate disputes are common, particularly in modification actions, raising questions of conflicting jurisdiction and the requirements of full faith and credit. Second, the requirements for jurisdiction may vary even within a single action. Divorce and custody are adjudications of status, requiring only that a defendant be properly served and before the court, while financial awards – property division, alimony, and child support – require personal jurisdiction based on a defendant's minimum contacts with the forum state. Third, interstate jurisdiction over custody disputes and support orders are now governed by uniform acts that alter traditional jurisdictional rules. Finally, family law issues arise in a variety of actions, including actions for divorce, separate maintenance, annulment, independent support or custody, paternity, termination of parental rights, and adoption.

§ 18.01 COURTS WITH JURISDICTION

[1] Chancery court authority. Chancery courts are vested with jurisdiction over most actions involving family law matters. Section 159 of the Mississippi Constitution provides that the state's chancery courts have full jurisdiction over all cases involving divorce and alimony and cases involving minors.[1] Mississippi chancery courts are also authorized by statute to hear divorce and annulment actions.[2] In these actions, chancellors may address all matters related to custody, child support, alimony[3] and property division.[4] Furthermore, a court that issues a judgment in a family law matter retains continuing jurisdiction to modify and enforce its orders.[5]

Chancery authority to hear suits for separate maintenance is based on the court's equitable power to hear matters related to divorce.[6] Chancery courts are also authorized by statute to hear custody and child support cases apart from divorce.[7] While jurisdiction over adoption is vested exclusively in the chancery courts of Mississippi,[8] jurisdiction to terminate parental rights is granted concurrently to chancery courts and

---

[1] MISS. CONST. art. VI, § 159.

[2] *See* MISS. CODE ANN. § 93-5-7 (2004) (complaints for divorce filed in chancery court); *id.* § 93-7-11 (annulment actions).

[3] *See* MISS. CODE ANN. § 93-5-23 (2004) ("make all orders touching the care, custody and maintenance of the children of the marriage, and also touching the maintenance and alimony of the wife or the husband").

[4] *See* Ferguson v. Ferguson, 639 So. 2d 921, 925 (Miss. 1994) (authorization to provide for maintenance and support includes authority to make equitable distribution of property).

[5] MISS. CODE ANN. § 93-5-23 (2004) ("court may afterwards, on petition, change the decree, and make from time to time such new decrees as the case may require").

[6] *See supra* § 1.14[1].

[7] MISS. CODE ANN. § 93-11-65 (2004) (authority to "entertain suits for the custody, care, support and maintenance of minor children and . . . hear and determine all such matters"); *see* Mitchell v. Powell, 179 So. 2d 811, 817-18 (Miss. 1965) (chancellor erred in modifying habeus order, but treated proceeding as one under new statute); *see also* HOMER H. CLARK, JR., THE LAW OF DOMESTIC RELATIONS IN THE UNITED STATES § 19.3, at 794 (2d ed. 1988) (listing modern statutes and cases providing for civil action for support).

[8] MISS. CODE ANN. § 93-17-3(1) (2004); *see* discussion *supra* § 17.01[1].

551

§ 18.01[2]   MISSISSIPPI FAMILY LAW

to family and county courts sitting as youth courts.[9] Jurisdiction over paternity actions rests in chancery, circuit, and county courts.[10]

[2] Family law exception to federal court jurisdiction. Family disputes are traditionally considered matters within the exclusive province of state courts. Federal court diversity jurisdiction does not extend to domestic relations cases even though requirements for diversity jurisdiction are otherwise met.[11]

The exception does not apply to intra-family actions other than traditional family law matters. For example, federal courts may hear tort actions between former spouses unless the action requires determination of divorce, alimony, or custody matters, or involves state law policies "of substantial public import."[12] Federal courts may also enforce arrearages of support under state court decrees.[13]

[3] Youth court jurisdiction: Abuse and neglect. Cases involving allegations of child abuse create a potential conflict between chancery and youth court jurisdiction. The state's youth courts are vested with exclusive jurisdiction in actions involving abused children, while chancery courts have jurisdiction over custody actions, including those in which abuse or neglect is alleged.[14] A chancery court may take jurisdiction over a custody action based in part on alleged abuse unless there is a prior youth court proceeding concerning the child. The court of appeals rejected a mother's contention that a chancery court lacked jurisdiction over a paternal grandmother's suit for custody based on alleged sexual abuse.[15]

Furthermore, a chancery court with continuing exclusive jurisdiction over an outstanding custody order has jurisdiction to hear a modification petition in which abuse or neglect is alleged. The federal district court for the southern district of Mississippi held that when a chancery court has assumed jurisdiction over a child, youth court jurisdiction is precluded, even if allegations of abuse arise in the chancery court proceeding.[16]

---

[9] MISS. CODE ANN. § 93-15-105(1) (2004); *see* May v. Harrison County Dep't of Human Servs., 883 So. 2d 74 (Miss. 2004) (termination of parental rights in youth court).

[10] MISS. CODE ANN. § 93-9-15 (2004) (defendant must defend the action in the court in which it is filed).

[11] The domestic relations exception to diversity jurisdiction was announced in 1858 in *Barber v. Barber*, 62 U.S. 582, 584 (1858). *See also* Crouch v. Crouch, 566 F.2d 486, 488 (5th Cir. 1978) (domestic relations exception to diversity jurisdiction based on strong state interest and expertise; need to avoid conflicting decisions and congested federal dockets); Davis v. Davis, 558 F. Supp. 485, 486 (N.D. Miss. 1983) (refusing to adjudicate former husband's suit to set aside divorce settlement agreement; assuming jurisdiction over contract claim would amount to modifying divorce decree).

[12] *See* Ankenbrandt v. Richards, 504 U.S. 689, 705-06 (1992) (exercising jurisdiction over a mother's tort action against her former husband based on abuse of their children) (suggesting result might differ if suit filed while divorce was pending).

[13] *See* Jagiella v. Jagiella, 647 F.2d 561, 564 (5th Cir. 1981) (child support arrearages); Crouch v. Crouch, 566 F.2d 486, 488 (5th Cir. 1978) (arrearages under separation agreement).

[14] MISS. CODE ANN. § 43-21-151 (2004); *see In re* L.D.M., 910 So. 2d 522, 524 (Miss. 2005) (en banc) (youth court had no jurisdiction over case filed by mother alleging that one-year-old for which she could not provide care was "child in need of supervision;" petition did not allege neglect or abuse).

[15] E.J.M. v. A.J.M, 846 So. 2d 289, 293 (Miss. Ct. App. 2003); *cf.* Chrissy F. v. Mississippi Dep't of Pub. Welfare, 780 F. Supp. 1104, 1123 (S.D. Miss. 1991) (chancellor has discretion to transfer to youth court).

[16] Chrissy F. v. Miss. Dep't of Pub. Welfare, 780 F. Supp. 1104, 1122 (S.D. Miss. 1991) (but not deciding whether youth court can exercise jurisdiction over child previously under chancery court jurisdiction, where allegations of abuse arise outside context of a custody dispute); *cf.* McDonald v. McDonald, 39 So. 3d 868, 885-86 (Miss. 2010) (chancery court had jurisdiction to hear allegations of abuse; court had issued original custody order two years earlier and petitions for contempt were still pending); Helmert v. Biffany, 842 So. 2d 1287, 1292 (Miss. 2003) (statute abolishing family

JURISDICTION

§ 18.02

However, a chancery court has no jurisdiction to determine custody over a child after the youth court has taken jurisdiction based on abuse or neglect. The court of appeals held that a chancery court lacked jurisdiction to determine custody of a child after the youth court granted temporary custody to the child's maternal grandparents.[17]

The Uniform Rules of Youth Court Practice, effective January 1, 2009, made significant changes in chancery court family law proceedings involving allegations of abuse or neglect of a child. A chancery court hearing allegations of abuse and neglect must follow the rules set out in the Uniform Rules of Youth Court Procedure.[18]

§ 18.02 OVERVIEW OF JURISDICTION

A court's authority to hear a case depends on three types of jurisdiction: jurisdiction of the subject matter of the action, personal jurisdiction over the defendant, and proper service of process on the defendant. Jurisdictional rules in family law cases vary depending on the form of relief sought. For example, a single divorce action typically involves several forms of relief – divorce, property division, alimony, custody, and child support. Personal jurisdiction and service of process requirements for divorce and custody orders are less stringent than for the financial aspects of divorce. In addition, subject matter jurisdiction over custody orders differs from jurisdiction to hear other aspects of a divorce case.

[1] Subject matter jurisdiction. In order to proceed in any action, a court must have jurisdiction over the subject matter of the dispute.[19] In the absence of subject matter jurisdiction, a court's order is void.[20] Lack of subject matter jurisdiction may be raised for the first time on appeal[21] or in a collateral proceeding.[22] Subject matter jurisdiction may not be waived[23] or conferred by agreement of the parties.[24] A court may raise the issue of subject matter jurisdiction on its own motion.[25]

In most family law matters, chancery courts have subject matter jurisdiction based

---

courts and transferring "pending" cases to youth court did not include proceedings to modify final judgments of family court; "pending" referred to cases that had not reached final judgment) (youth court had no jurisdiction over custody and support unrelated to abuse and neglect).

[17] Thomas v. Byars, 947 So. 2d 375, 378 (Miss. Ct. App. 2007).

[18] *See supra* § 12.01[12] .

[19] *See* MISSISSIPPI CIVIL PROCEDURE § 1.1 (Jeffrey Jackson, ed. 2003) (subject matter jurisdiction is "the first step in the court's inquiry").

[20] Roberts v. Roberts, 866 So. 2d 474, 476-77 (Miss. Ct. App. 2003); *see* Evans v. DHS, 36 So. 3d 463, 470 (Miss. Ct. App. 2010) (Mississippi modification of child support void for lack of jurisdiction under UIFSA).

[21] Horton v. Horton, 57 So. 2d 723, 725 (Miss. 1952).

[22] *See* Hunt v. Hunt, 629 So. 2d 548, 551 (Miss. 1992). *But cf.* Adcock v. Van Norman, 917 So. 2d 86, 89 (Miss. 2005) (en banc) (order entered by Mississippi court, in violation of priority jurisdiction rule, must be attacked directly rather than in collateral proceeding).

[23] Harry v. Harry, 856 So. 2d 748, 752 (Miss. Ct. App. 2003) (defendant did not waive subject matter jurisdiction by appearing at the hearing without objection).

[24] Duvall v. Duvall, 80 So. 2d 752, 754 (Miss. 1955) (distinguishing erroneous judgments, which may be reversed on appeal, and judgments lacking subject matter jurisdiction, which are void and may be attacked collaterally); *cf.* Mosley v. Huffman, 481 So. 2d 231, 244 (Miss. 1985) (mother could not agree to give Arizona jurisdiction over custody dispute) ("UCCJA has no provision in it authorizing jurisdiction simply by presence or consent of the adult contestants."); Mitchell v. Mitchell, 767 So. 2d 1078, 1084 (Miss. Ct. App. 2000) (no provision in UCCJA allowing parties to fix jurisdiction by consent).

[25] Duvall v. Duvall, 80 So. 2d 752, 754 (Miss. 1955).

§ 18.02[2]   **MISSISSIPPI FAMILY LAW**

on one party's domicile in the state.[26] With respect to custody of children, however, subject matter jurisdiction is governed by the Uniform Child Custody Jurisdiction and Enforcement Act (UCCJEA), which places jurisdiction in the child's home state.[27] In addition, the traditional continuing exclusive jurisdiction of a court to modify its own orders of custody and support is limited to some extent by the UCCJEA and the Uniform Interstate Family Support Act (UIFSA).[28]

[2] Personal jurisdiction. In most cases, a court must have personal jurisdiction over the parties. The requirements of due process prevent a state from exercising jurisdiction over a nonresident defendant unless he or she has adequate minimum contacts with the state.[29] However, when a court adjudicates status rather than rendering a personal judgment, minimum contacts with the forum state are not required.[30] In these actions, historically referred to as "in rem," the defendant need only be properly served.[31]

Adjudication of marital status and custody are considered to be in rem actions. A court with subject matter jurisdiction may enter a fault-based divorce or custody decree without personal jurisdiction over the defendant.[32] However, in Mississippi, a court may not enter an irreconcilable differences divorce without personal jurisdiction over both parties.[33]

Orders of alimony, child support, and property division are in personam judgments, requiring that the defendant have minimum contacts with the state.[34] An order not based on personal jurisdiction is invalid and subject to attack in a collateral proceeding.[35] However, personal jurisdiction may be waived.[36] A defendant who fails to raise lack of personal jurisdiction in a timely fashion or who makes a general appearance waives the claim.[37] Lack of personal jurisdiction may not be attacked for the first time on appeal or in a collateral action by a defendant who appeared in a proceeding.[38]

[3] Service of process. A court may not exercise jurisdiction over a defendant who has not been properly served with process.[39] A judgment based on inadequate process

---

[26] *See infra* § 18.03[1].

[27] *See infra* § 18.09.

[28] *See infra* §§ 18.08[4], 18.10.

[29] *See* MISSISSIPPI CIVIL PROCEDURE, *supra* note 19, § 2.1; Kolikas v. Kolikas, 821 So. 2d 874, 880 (Miss. Ct. App. 2002).

[30] *See* CLARK, JR., *supra* note 7, § 12.2, at 421 (noting that in rem label simply means that public policy requires allowing a court to adjudicate rights under the given circumstances).

[31] *See* MISSISSIPPI CIVIL PROCEDURE, *supra* note 19, § 2.1; Kolikas v. Kolikas, 821 So. 2d 874, 880 (Miss. Ct. App. 2002).

[32] *See* Brett Turner, *Pursuing the Divisible Divorce: Recent Case Law on State Court Jurisdiction in Divorce Cases*, 12 DIVORCE LITIGATION 125 (July 2000).

[33] *See* MISS. CODE ANN. § 93-5-2(1) (2004).

[34] *See* Fliter v. Fliter, 383 So. 2d 1084, 1087 (Miss. 1980) ("no insurmountable obstacle" that action includes both in rem and in personam components)*;* Lofton v. Lofton, 924 So. 2d 596, 604 (Miss. Ct. App. 2006) (en banc) (Florida court without personal jurisdiction over wife could grant divorce but not address property division and alimony).

[35] *See* Kolikas v. Kolikas, 821 So. 2d 874, 880 (Miss. Ct. App. 2002).

[36] *See* MISSISSIPPI CIVIL PROCEDURE, *supra* note 19, § 1.5.

[37] *See infra* § 18.04[4].

[38] *See* MISSISSIPPI CIVIL PROCEDURE, *supra* note 19, § 1.5; Hamm v. Hall, 693 So. 2d 906, 910-11 (Miss. 1997).

[39] Kolikas v. Kolikas, 821 So. 2d 874, 878 (Miss. Ct. App. 2002).

554

JURISDICTION   § 18.03

or service of process is void unless the defect is waived by the defendant. The defect may be attacked collaterally and is not waived by failure to appear.[40] A defendant may object to service of process through a motion or in a responsive pleading. However, the defense is waived if the defendant appears without raising the objection in the initial pleadings or attached motions.[41]

In divorce and custody matters, a nonresident defendant or a resident who cannot be found after diligent inquiry may be served by publication. However, awards of property division, alimony, or child support must be based upon personal service on the defendant, absent waiver.[42] The requirements for proper service of process are discussed in full in Chapter XIX.[43]

§ 18.03 JURISDICTION OVER DIVORCE

A court has subject matter jurisdiction over an action for divorce if one of the parties is domiciled in the state. Divorce may be granted even though the defendant has no minimum contacts with the state.

[1] Subject matter jurisdiction. An action for divorce is regarded as a form of in rem action, permitting adjudication of rights based on the domicile of one of the parties – and therefore the marriage – in a particular state. According to the United States Supreme Court, "Each state as a sovereign has a rightful and legitimate concern in the marital status of persons domiciled within its borders and . . . can alter within its own borders the marriage status of the spouse domiciled there."[44] Although due process requirements are met if one of the parties is currently domiciled in the state, most states impose additional residency requirements.[45] Courts of a state where neither spouse is domiciled lack jurisdiction to hear a divorce proceeding.[46]

---

[40] Kolikas v. Kolikas, 821 So. 2d 874, 880 (Miss. Ct. App. 2002) (divorce void for failure to mail copy of published summons to physical address) (also finding that wife was not estopped from attacking validity of decree); *see also* Johnson v. Johnson, 191 So. 2d 840, 842-43 (Miss. 1966) (Mississippi defendant not personally served in child support action). *But see* Scribner v. Scribner, 556 So. 2d 350, 353 (Miss. 1990) (wife estopped from attacking Maine divorce decree based on insufficient service of process; she remarried in reliance on validity of decree).

[41] *See* MISS. R. CIV. P. 12(b)(4) (objection to adequacy of summons); *id.* (12)(b)(5) (objection to adequacy of service); *see also* Price v. McBeath, 989 So. 2d 444, 452 (Miss. Ct. App. 2008) (pro se mother waived lack of service of process by appearing and defending without objecting); Chasez v. Chasez, 957 So. 2d 1031, 1037 (Miss. Ct. App. 2007) (defects in service waived by pro se litigant's appearance without objection); Venegas v. Gurganus, 911 So. 2d 562 (Miss. Ct. App. 2005) (defects in service of process waived by failure to assert at trial); *cf.* Hamm v. Hall, 693 So. 2d 906, 908-09 (Miss. 1997) (payment of child support pursuant to an invalid decree did not constitute a waiver).

[42] O'Neill v. O'Neill, 515 So. 2d 1208, 1211 (Miss. 1987); Noble v. Noble, 502 So. 2d 317, 320 (Miss. 1987); *see* CLARK, JR., *supra* note 7, § 12.2, at 421 (service for in rem actions may usually be accomplished by constructive service).

[43] *See infra* § 19.03.

[44] Williams v. North Carolina, 317 U.S. 287, 299 (1942) (service must meet due process requirements). Homer Clark notes, however, that the Supreme Court statements requiring domicile for a state to exercise jurisdiction have been in dicta. CLARK, JR., *supra* note 7, § 12.2, at 428.

[45] *See* CLARK, JR., *supra* note 7, § 12.2, at 413 (from six weeks to two years, with most common time period six months); *cf.* Sosna v. Iowa, 419 U.S. 393, 410 (1975) (upholding one-year residency requirement for divorce).

[46] *See* Hopkins v. Hopkins, 165 So. 414, 415 (Miss. 1936); *cf.* Winters v. Winters, 111 So. 2d 418, 420-21 (Miss. 1959) (Arkansas court without jurisdiction to determine divorce action of two Mississippi residents; their appearance would not create jurisdiction; also finding that wife did not appear voluntarily). *But cf.* JOHN DE WITT GREGORY, PETER N. SWISHER & SHERYL L. WOLF, UNDERSTANDING FAMILY LAW § 8.02, at 228 (2d ed. 2001) (except for dicta, Supreme Court

---

555

§ 18.03[1][a]   MISSISSIPPI FAMILY LAW

Mississippi chancery court jurisdiction over divorce is limited to cases in which one of the parties has been "an actual bona fide resident" for six months prior to commencement of the suit.[47] A court lacked subject matter jurisdiction to adjudicate divorce based on the complaint of a wife who reestablished her domicile in Mississippi only four months prior to filing the complaint.[48] If a member of the United States military is stationed and residing in Mississippi with his or her spouse at the time of separation, both spouses are considered to be domiciled in Mississippi for purposes of divorce jurisdiction.[49]

The Mississippi Supreme Court has held that the statutory term "resident" is synonymous with "domicile."[50] Domicile is typically defined as residence with an intention to remain permanently or indefinitely in a state.[51]

[a] Temporary absence. Temporary absence from one's home state does not affect domicile if the absent spouse intends to return. For example, a wife's extended time in Washington, D.C., did not change her residence from the marital home in Mississippi.[52] Similarly, a husband's residence in Tennessee for training did not constitute an abandonment of his Mississippi domicile.[53] And a wife did not abandon her Mississippi residence by working in California to support her child. She testified that she still regarded Mississippi as her home and intended to return.[54]

Mississippi divorce statutes prohibit a court from taking jurisdiction when proof shows that a plaintiff is residing in the state for the sole purpose of securing a divorce.[55] Similarly, Mississippi courts will not recognize a divorce based on residence in another state for the purpose of obtaining a divorce. A husband did not establish domicile in Arkansas by working in the state, filing for divorce when the state's three-month residency period was met, and then returning to Mississippi. He lived out of suitcases and voted in a Mississippi election during his Arkansas stay.[56]

[b] Change of domicile. A person may have only one domicile at a time.[57] Once a domicile is acquired, it is presumed to continue.[58] A change of domicile must be voluntary and "with the intent to remain at the new home or place of residence without intention of returning to the former domicile."[59] A mere change of residence does

---

has never "squarely held" that domicile is required).

[47] MISS. CODE ANN. § 93-5-5 (2004).

[48] O'Neill v. O'Neill, 515 So. 2d 1208, 1212-13 (Miss. 1987) (rejecting her claim that her domicile never changed from Mississippi, even though she lived in Germany with her husband; wife's domicile is that of husband until she intentionally changes it).

[49] MISS. CODE ANN. § 93-5-5 (2004).

[50] Dunn v. Dunn, 577 So. 2d 378, 380 (Miss. 1991); Bilbo v. Bilbo, 177 So. 772, 776 (Miss. 1938).

[51] *See* GREGORY ET. AL., *supra* note 46, § 7.02[b].

[52] Bilbo v. Bilbo, 177 So. 772, 776 (Miss. 1938).

[53] May v. May, 130 So. 52, 53 (Miss. 1930).

[54] Clay v. Clay, 99 So. 818, 819 (Miss. 1924).

[55] MISS. CODE ANN. § 93-5-5 (2004).

[56] Lynch v. Lynch, 50 So. 2d 378, 380-81 (Miss. 1951).

[57] Newman v. Newman, 558 So. 2d 821, 825 (Miss. 1990).

[58] May v. May, 130 So. 52, 53 (Miss. 1930); *see* Clay v. Clay, 99 So. 818, 818 (Miss. 1924) (wife working in California intended to return to Mississippi).

[59] Bilbo v. Bilbo, 177 So. 772, 776 (Miss. 1938).

JURISDICTION   § 18.03[2]

not in itself constitute a change in domicile.[60] Circumstances indicative of a change in domicile include "[t]he exercise of political rights, admissions, declarations, the acts of purchasing a home and long-continued residency."[61] The party alleging a change of domicile has the burden of proof.[62] The presumption of continued domicile was not rebutted even though a couple purchased a Louisiana residence and lived there for purposes of employment; the husband did not contest his wife's testimony that they intended for Mississippi to remain their home.[63]

[2] Venue. Venue requirements differ for fault-based and irreconcilable differences divorces. Filing in the proper venue is essential – in contrast to most civil actions, proper venue in divorce actions is jurisdictional. The specific provisions regarding venue in annulment, paternity, termination, and adoption actions are addressed in the separate chapters related to those actions.[64]

[a] Venue as jurisdictional. Proper venue is a jurisdictional requirement in Mississippi divorce actions. Proper venue may not be waived by the parties and may be attacked in a collateral proceeding.[65] A wife who improperly filed a suit for fault-based divorce in her county of residence could attack the court's judgment as void, even though she chose the improper venue.[66]

Until recently, a divorce action filed in the wrong county could not be transferred to the proper county.[67] In 2005, however, the legislature amended the venue statute for divorce, adding a provision that "[t]ransfer of venue shall be governed by Rule 82(d) of the Mississippi Rules of Civil Procedure."[68] The amendment did not, however, affect the jurisdictional nature of divorce. In a 2007 case, the court of appeals rejected a wife's argument that her husband waived an objection to venue because he did not object at trial. Venue in divorce cases in Mississippi is jurisdictional, and improper venue makes a divorce decree void.[69]

[b] Location of venue. In fault-based divorces in which the defendant is a Mississippi resident, venue lies in the defendant's county of residence,[70] the county where the defendant may be found,[71] or the county in which the parties resided at the time of

---

[60] Newman v. Newman, 558 So. 2d 821, 825 (Miss. 1990).

[61] Johnson v. Johnson, 191 So. 2d 840, 842 (Miss. 1966).

[62] May v. May, 130 So. 52, 53 (Miss. 1930); *see* Clay v. Clay, 99 So. 818, 818 (Miss. 1924) (wife working in California intended to return to Mississippi).

[63] Johnson v. Johnson, 191 So. 2d 840, 842 (Miss. 1966).

[64] *See supra* § 3.07 (annulment); § 11.02 (paternity); § 16.01 (termination); § 17.01 (adoption). Venue in separate maintenance actions is governed by the general venue statute, MISS. CODE ANN. § 11-15-1 (2004) (in cases not otherwise covered, venue lies in county where any necessary party defendant resides); *see* Dunn v. Dunn, 577 So. 2d 378, 379 (Miss. 1991) (venue is not jurisdictional – court should transfer case to court with proper venue).

[65] *See* Price v. Price, 32 So. 2d 124, 126 (Miss. 1947).

[66] Roberts v. Roberts, 866 So. 2d 474, 476-77 (Miss. Ct. App. 2003) (en banc).

[67] Roberts v. Roberts, 866 So. 2d 474, 477 (Miss. Ct. App. 2003) (en banc).

[68] MISS. CODE ANN. § 93-5-11 (2006).

[69] Hampton v. Hampton, 977 So. 2d 1181 (Miss. Ct. App. 2007).

[70] A temporary absence from the county of residence does not constitute a change in domicile for purposes of venue. *See* Bilbo v. Bilbo, 177 So. 772, 775-76 (Miss. 1938).

[71] Dunn v. Dunn, 577 So. 2d 378, 379 (Miss. 1991) (husband's temporary residence as a guest in Hinds County

§ 18.03[3]   MISSISSIPPI FAMILY LAW

separation, if the plaintiff is still a resident of that county at the time of filing suit. If the defendant is a non-resident or absent, venue for fault-based divorce lies in the county where the plaintiff resides.[72]

In an irreconcilable differences divorce between two Mississippi residents, suit may be filed in either party's county of residence. Otherwise, venue lies in the county in which the resident party lives.[73]

As a general rule, if two courts within a state have concurrent venue over a divorce action, the second action should be abated.[74] Under the doctrine of priority jurisdiction, when a court acquires jurisdiction through filing of an initial pleading, no other court in the state should assume jurisdiction.[75] The rules for determining domicile within a state also apply to determine domicile within a county.[76] For example, Governor Bilbo's temporary four-year residence in Hinds County while seeking the governorship did not change his domicile from Rankin County.[77] However, a wife with a marital home in Hinds County properly filed in Warren County, where she moved after her husband moved to another state. She registered her car in Warren County, was attempting to sell the marital home, and had relocated her residence to Warren County.[78]

[3] Personal jurisdiction. Because divorce is regarded as a form of in rem action, a court may grant divorce even though the defendant does not have the minimum contacts required for personal jurisdiction. In 1942, the United States Supreme Court held that one spouse's domicile in the forum state, combined with proper process, is sufficient to allow a grant of divorce, even in the absence of personal jurisdiction over the defendant.[79] In Mississippi, however, in rem jurisdiction for divorce applies only in fault-based divorces. Because no-fault divorce in Mississippi requires the consent of both spouses, divorce based on irreconcilable differences may be granted only if the court has personal jurisdiction over a defendant who has joined in the action.[80]

[4] Service of process. In Mississippi, a fault-based divorce may be granted even though the defendant was served by publication. Personal service of process is not

---

did not change his residence from Rankin County, where he owned a home, practiced medicine, and voted). The words "may be found" have been interpreted to apply only to non-residents or residents without a fixed residence, *see* Ross v. Ross, 208 So. 2d 194, 196 (Miss. 1968).

[72] Miss. Code Ann. § 93-5-11 (2004); *see* Parks v. Parks, 914 So. 2d 337, 342 (Miss. Ct. App. 2005) (en banc) (where defendant husband was nonresident, venue was proper in county where wife lived).

[73] Miss. Code Ann. § 93-5-11 (2004).

[74] *See* Smith v. Holmes, 921 So. 2d 283, 286 (Miss. 2005) (en banc) (second action between same parties and based on same cause of action should be abated); Lee v. Lee, 232 So. 2d 370, 373 (Miss. 1970) (wife who filed a divorce in Forrest County, then lured her husband to Hancock County under the pretext of reconciliation, could not dismiss the Forrest County action and file in Hancock County) (second action based on the same cause should be abated if case is already pending in court with jurisdiction).

[75] Adcock v. Van Norman, 917 So. 2d 86, 88-89 (Miss. 2005) (en banc) (but stating that lack of jurisdiction should be attacked directly, through post-trial motion or on appeal).

[76] *See* discussion *supra* § 18.03[1].

[77] Bilbo v. Bilbo, 177 So. 772, 775-76 (Miss. 1938).

[78] Hampton v. Hampton, 977 So. 2d 1181 (Miss. Ct. App. 2007).

[79] Williams v. North Carolina, 317 U.S. 287, 299 (1942) (service must meet due process requirements); *see also* Estin v. Estin, 334 U.S. 541, 549 (1948); *see, e.g.*, Pierce v. Pierce, 42 So. 3d 658, 659 (Miss. Ct. App. 2010) (Washington court granted divorce to military husband against Mississippi wife, but lacked jurisdiction to divide property).

[80] *See* Miss. Code Ann. § 93-5-2(1) (2004).

558

JURISDICTION §18.04

required so long as the statutory requirements for service of process are met.[81] In contrast, divorce based upon irreconcilable differences may be granted "only upon the joint complaint of the husband and wife or a complaint where the defendant has been personally served with process or where the defendant has entered an appearance by written waiver of process."[82]

§ 18.04 JURISDICTION OVER FINANCIAL AWARDS

One party's domicile in the forum state is sufficient to provide subject matter jurisdiction over financial matters related to dissolution of a marriage. In contrast to a grant of divorce, however, financial aspects of divorce may not be addressed unless the court has personal jurisdiction over the parties. Minimum contacts with the state are not necessary if the defendant is personally served in the state, makes a general appearance, or waives the right to object to lack of jurisdiction.

[1] Subject matter jurisdiction. A chancery court in divorce actions may make all orders relating to maintenance, alimony, and support of children.[83] Although the statute does not specifically address property division, the Mississippi Supreme Court has held that the power to order maintenance includes the power to make an equitable distribution of assets at divorce.[84]

[2] Personal jurisdiction: Minimum contacts. To order property division, alimony, or child support, a court must have personal jurisdiction over the parties.[85] In 1948, the United States Supreme Court held that a husband's ex parte divorce validly dissolved his marriage but could not affect his ex-wife's property and support rights in the absence of personal jurisdiction over her.[86] Subsequently, the Supreme Court applied the same rule to an action for child support, rejecting a mother's argument that her domicile in California provided jurisdiction for a child support modification action against her former husband.[87] A defendant's contacts with the forum state "must amount to something more than . . . casual, isolated contact with an in-state resident . . . . [T]he non-resident defendant [must] have continuous and systematic general contacts with this state."[88] Applying this rule, the Mississippi Court of Appeals held that a Florida divorce decree was not res judicata with respect to financial awards because Florida did not have personal jurisdiction over the wife, a Mississippi resident. She had

---

[81] O'Neill v. O'Neill, 515 So. 2d 1208, 1211 (Miss. 1987); Noble v. Noble, 502 So. 2d 317, 320 (Miss. 1987); *see* CLARK, JR., *supra* note 7, § 12.2, at 421 (service for in rem actions may usually be accomplished by constructive service). *See* discussion of service of process *infra* § 19.03.

[82] MISS. CODE ANN. § 93-5-2(1) (2004).

[83] MISS. CODE ANN. § 93-5-23 (2004).

[84] Ferguson v. Ferguson, 639 So. 2d 921, 927 (Miss. 1994).

[85] *See* Int'l Shoe Corp. v. Washington, 326 U.S. 310, 316 (1945) (replacing physical presence test for personal jurisdiction).

[86] Estin v. Estin, 334 U.S. 541, 549 (1948).

[87] Kulko v. Superior Court of Cal., 436 U.S. 84, 98 (1978).

[88] *See* McDaniel v. Ritter, 556 So. 2d 303, 309 (Miss. 1989) (wrongful death action). *But see* Petters v. Petters, 560 So. 2d 722, 725 (Miss. 1990) (personal jurisdiction to determine division of military pension must be based on the serviceperson's residence, domicile, or consent).

§ 18.04[2][a]   MISSISSIPPI FAMILY LAW

never lived in Florida, did not appear in the action, and was not served in the state.[89] Similarly, Mississippi did not have personal jurisdiction to order child support from a Louisiana resident who had never lived or worked in the state and who had almost no contact with the state.[90]

If a defendant objects to personal jurisdiction, the burden of proving minimum contacts rests on the plaintiff.[91] A judgment against a nonresident without minimum contacts with the state is void absent waiver by the defendant.[92]

[a] Contacts sufficient. One authority suggests that the most likely indicator of minimum contacts is whether the forum state was the couple's last marital residence. As a general rule, minimum contacts exist if the couple last lived together in the forum state; at the other extreme, minimum contacts are unlikely to exist if the couple never lived in the forum state.[93] Fact patterns that fall between these two examples are more difficult to predict. Mississippi cases appear to follow this pattern. The Mississippi Supreme Court held that a court had personal jurisdiction over a nonresident defendant who resided in Mississippi at the time the parties separated.[94] Similarly, a defendant living in California was subject to personal jurisdiction; he was married to the plaintiff (twice) in Mississippi, the couple lived in the state, and his wife and three children remained in Mississippi.[95] A husband who lived with his family in Vicksburg and practiced medicine across the river in Louisiana was subject to personal jurisdiction in Mississippi even after he moved his domicile to Louisiana.[96]

[b] Contacts insufficient. The minimum contacts test is not satisfied by proof that a defendant's spouse or children reside in the forum state or that the couple married in the state. The United States Supreme Court held that a couple's marriage in California did not, in itself, provide personal jurisdiction over the husband, who never lived in the state. Nor was personal jurisdiction conferred because he consented to the presence of his children in California.[97] The Mississippi Court of Appeals agreed that neither marriage within the state nor payment of child support to a resident is sufficient to meet the minimum contacts test.[98] A defendant who was married, domiciled, and

---

[89] Lofton v. Lofton, 924 So. 2d 596, 602-03 (Miss. Ct. App. 2006) (en banc) (Mississippi court converted separate maintenance award to periodic alimony); *see also* Pierce v. Pierce, 42 So. 3d 658, 659 (Miss. Ct. App. 2010) (Washington court granted divorce to military husband against Mississippi wife, but lacked jurisdiction to divide property).

[90] Richardson v. Stogner, 958 So. 2d 235, 238 (Miss. Ct. App. 2007).

[91] *See* Mississippi Civil Procedure, *supra* note 19, § 2.11.

[92] *See* Mississippi Civil Procedure, *supra* note 19, § 2.5.

[93] *See* Turner, *supra* note 32, at 125 (noting also that if the couple lived in the forum state, but not as their most recent residence, cases are mixed regarding whether minimum contacts exist).

[94] Hussey v. Hussey, 82 So. 2d 442, 444 (Miss. 1955) (husband personally served in state was subject to personal jurisdiction; parties lived in Washington County at the time of separation); *see also* Fliter v. Fliter, 383 So. 2d 1084, 1088 (Miss. 1980) (jurisdiction proper over defendant who married and lived in Mississippi and left wife and children in state).

[95] Penton v. Penton, 539 So. 2d 1036, 1038 (Miss. 1989).

[96] Chenier v. Chenier, 573 So. 2d 699, 702 (Miss. 1990).

[97] Kulko v. Superior Court of Cal., 436 U.S. 84, 84-85 (1978); *cf.* Nelson v. Nelson, 891 So. 2d 317, 322-23 (Ala. Civ. App. 2004) (residence in Alabama for one month prior to marriage not sufficient contacts for personal jurisdiction).

[98] McCubbin v. Seay, 749 So. 2d 1127, 1128-29 (Miss. Ct. App. 1999).

560

JURISDICTION

§ 18.04[3]

divorced in Ohio was not subject to personal jurisdiction in Mississippi even though his former wife and child lived in the state.[99]

[3] Personal jurisdiction: Defendant served in state. Even in the absence of minimum contacts, a court has personal jurisdiction over a defendant who is served while physically present in the forum state. In 1990, the Supreme Court confirmed that the traditional basis for personal jurisdiction – physical presence – is sufficient even if a defendant does not have minimum contacts with the forum state.[100] However, a defendant who is in the state under subpoena to testify on an unrelated matter may not be served while in the state for that purpose.[101]

[4] Waiver of personal jurisdiction. A defendant who objects to personal jurisdiction may fail to appear and, if a default judgment is obtained, attack the judgment in collateral proceedings. Or, the defendant may appear and make a timely objection to jurisdiction.

A defendant's general appearance without preserving an objection to personal jurisdiction constitutes a waiver of the objection.[102] Objections to jurisdiction must be preserved by including the defense in a responsive pleading or motion attached to the pleading.[103] A defendant who answers a complaint without preserving the objection waives the right to contest jurisdiction.[104] However, a husband's application for a stay of proceedings under the Soldiers' and Sailors' Relief Act was not a general appearance.[105] And an attorney did not waive his client's objection to personal jurisdiction by agreeing to set a Rule 81 hearing date and appearing at the hearing to object to jurisdiction.[106] A defendant who chooses to appear and contest jurisdiction is bound by the court's finding with regard to jurisdiction. If no appeal is taken, res judicata bars relitigation of the issue in a collateral proceeding.[107]

---

[99] *See* Carpenter v. Allen, 540 So. 2d 1334, 1336-37 (Miss. 1989); *see also* Richardson v. Stogner, 958 So. 2d 235, 238 (Miss. Ct. App. 2007) (no personal jurisdiction over Louisiana resident who had never lived or worked in Mississippi); Lofton v. Lofton, 924 So. 2d 596, 602 (Miss. Ct. App. 2006) (en banc) (Florida lacked personal jurisdiction over Mississippi resident who never lived in state).

[100] *See* Burnham v. Superior Court, 495 U.S. 604, 619 (1990); *see also* Lofton v. Lofton, 924 So. 2d 596, 602-03 (Miss. Ct. App. 2006) (en banc).

[101] *See* Chenier v. Chenier, 573 So. 2d 699, 702 (Miss. 1990) (but finding exception applies only to defendants not otherwise subject to personal jurisdiction of court; not applicable to husband with minimum contacts with Mississippi).

[102] Chenier v. Chenier, 573 So. 2d 699, 702 (Miss. 1990); Lofton v. Lofton, 924 So. 2d 596, 602-03 (Miss. Ct. App. 2006) (en banc) (Florida lacked personal jurisdiction over Mississippi resident who never lived in state, did not appear in action, and was not served in the state).

[103] Jones v. Chandler, 592 So. 2d 966, 969 (Miss. 1991); *cf.* Scaife v. Scaife, 880 So. 2d 1089, 1094 (Miss. Ct. App. 2004) (jurisdiction was not waived when a father answered generally but, with leave of court, amended answer to object to personal jurisdiction). Objection to personal jurisdiction may be made in the answer or a 12(b)(2) motion, *see* Miss. R. Civ. P. 12.

[104] Miller v. Miller, 512 So. 2d 1286, 1288 (Miss. 1987) (pro se answer responding on the merits without objecting to jurisdiction constitutes appearance); Brown v. Brown, 493 So. 2d 961, 963 (Miss. 1986) (California resident who filed three responsive pleadings was subject to personal jurisdiction in Mississippi); *cf.* Pace v. Pace, 16 So. 3d 734, 737-38 (Miss. Ct. App. 2009) (rejecting a father's argument that a decree was void for lack of service of process; he appeared in numerous hearings without objecting).

[105] O'Neill v. O'Neill, 515 So. 2d 1208, 1211 (Miss. 1987).

[106] Richardson v. Stogner, 958 So. 2d 235, 238-39 (Miss. Ct. App. 2007).

[107] Dep't of Human Servs. v. Shelnut, 772 So. 2d 1041, 1049 (Miss. 2000) (defendant who failed to appeal order finding Canadian court had jurisdiction was barred from attacking jurisdiction in Mississippi action to enforce Canadian

§ 18.04[5]   MISSISSIPPI FAMILY LAW

[5] Jurisdiction over property located in state. As a general rule, a court must have personal jurisdiction to divide a couple's property at divorce. However, a court may have in rem jurisdiction to determine rights with regard to property located in the state. A Missouri Court had in rem jurisdiction over real property located in the state in connection with a divorce action; the court of appeals stated that in rem jurisdiction over property is appropriate where the claim to property (equitable distribution) is inextricably linked to the actual controversy.[108] Similarly, a Georgia court had in rem jurisdiction to divide property located in the state and belonging to a husband who moved to Georgia and filed for divorce.[109] The Mississippi Supreme Court suggested in dicta that service by publication in a divorce action would be sufficient to adjudicate not only divorce and custody, but rights to property located within the state.[110]

[6] Jurisdiction to divide military pensions. Minimum contacts are not sufficient to provide jurisdiction to divide military pensions. The state in which a serviceperson is presently domiciled or resides has exclusive jurisdiction to divide military pensions, unless he or she waives the requirement through a general appearance in an action.[111]

[7] Jurisdiction to award child support. The Uniform Interstate Family Support Act (UIFSA), which governs awards of child support, provides expanded bases for personal jurisdiction with regard to child support orders, including some that arguably require less than minimum contacts. The Mississippi Supreme Court has indicated, however, that it will continue to apply traditional requirements of minimum contacts in child support actions in spite of the expanded provisions of UIFSA.[112] A full discussion of UIFSA provisions governing initial child support awards is set out in Section 18.08.

§ 18.05 JURISDICTION TO DETERMINE CUSTODY

The Uniform Child Custody Jurisdiction and Enforcement Act (UCCJEA), which governs custody awards, places jurisdiction over most custody disputes in a child's home state. Determination of custody of a child does not require personal jurisdiction over the defendant. A full discussion of the UCCJEA bases for jurisdiction, the defenses to jurisdiction, and the requirements for notice are included in Section 18.09.

[1] Subject matter jurisdiction. Historically, jurisdiction to determine child cus-

---

order); *see also* Shelnut v. Dep't of Human Servs., 9 So. 3d 359, 363-64 (Miss. 2009) (reaffirming holding in *Shelnut I*; rejecting father's argument that he appeared only in a temporary hearing and not in the action itself).

[108] *In re* Marriage of Breen, 560 S.W.2d 358, 363 (Mo. Ct. App. 1977).

[109] Abernathy v. Abernathy, 482 S.E.2d 265, 266-68 (Ga. 1997). *But see* Hoffman v. Hoffman, 821 S.W.2d 3, 5 (Tex. App. 1992) (rejecting in rem jurisdiction over property).

[110] *See* O'Neill v. O'Neill, 515 So. 2d 1208, 1211 (Miss. 1987).

[111] 10 U.S.C. § 1408(c)(4) (2006); *see* Southern v. Glenn, 568 So. 2d 281, 284 (Miss. 1990). *See* discussion of military pensions *supra* § 7.07[1][b].

[112] *See* McCubbin v. Seay, 749 So. 2d 1127, 1129 (Miss. Ct. App. 1999).

JURISDICTION § 18.05[2]

tody was based on a child's presence in the state.[113] A custody order entered by a state without jurisdiction based on physical presence was void.[114] The UCCJEA creates a preference for jurisdiction in a child's home state. Courts in other states may exercise jurisdiction only if the child has no home state, the home state has declined to exercise jurisdiction, or on a temporary basis because of an emergency.[115] As a result, a court with jurisdiction to determine divorce and financial matters may lack jurisdiction to determine custody.

[2] Personal jurisdiction. Under the UCCJEA and the decisions of most courts, custody actions are regarded as an adjudication of status similar to an adjudication of divorce. Personal jurisdiction over the child and the defendant is not required.[116]

[3] Service of process. The UCCJEA requires that notice and an opportunity to be heard be given to parents whose rights have not been previously terminated, persons with physical custody of a child, and any persons entitled to notice in a child custody proceeding.[117] Although service must be "reasonably calculated to give actual notice," service may be by publication if other means cannot be used.[118] No notice is required if a party submits to the jurisdiction of the court.[119]

§ 18.06 INTERSTATE CONFLICTS OVER INITIAL DIVORCE ORDERS

If two states have jurisdiction over an action for divorce, the first decree entered is controlling. States must, as a general rule, accord full faith and credit to an order issued by a sister state with jurisdiction. With regard to custody and support orders, these rules are altered to some extent by the UCCJEA and UIFSA.

[1] Concurrent actions in two states. Because jurisdiction for divorce is based on domicile, two states may have concurrent jurisdiction over a divorce. The Full Faith and Credit Clause does not prohibit a state from proceeding with a divorce action over which it has jurisdiction simply because a similar proceeding is pending in another

---

[113] *See* Cole v. Cole, 12 So. 2d 425, 425 (Miss. 1943) ("general rule is that in order that a decree or judgment awarding the custody of children shall be valid, the child or children must be within the territorial jurisdiction of the court").

[114] Kincaid v. Kincaid, 43 So. 2d 108 (Miss. 1949) (Mississippi court could not award custody of children living with mother in Louisiana, even though she filed suit in Mississippi; *see also* Montgomery v. Walker, 86 So. 2d 502 (Miss. 1956) (Mississippi court had no jurisdiction to award custody of children living in Texas with defendant mother); Hawkins v. Hawkins, 45 So. 2d 271 (Miss. 1950).

[115] MISS. CODE ANN. § 93-27-201(1) (2004).

[116] MISS. CODE ANN. § 93-27-201(3) (2004); *see* Yearta v. Scroggins, 268 S.E.2d 151 (Ga. 1980); Gay v. Morrison, 511 So. 2d 1173 (La. Ct. App. 1987). Under the UCCJA, which did not expressly address personal jurisdiction, an early case appeared to require personal jurisdiction. *See* Mississippi Dep't of Human Servs. v. Marquis, 630 So. 2d 331, 335 (Miss. 1993) (Mississippi lacked personal jurisdiction to modify a Colorado custody order where mother objected to jurisdiction and had lived continuously in Colorado with the children). However, a subsequent decision stated that personal jurisdiction existed if the state had significant connections to the case. White v. Thompson, 822 So. 2d 1125, 1127 (Miss. Ct. App. 2002); *cf.* Jackson v. Terrill, 562 So. 2d 1271 (Miss. 1990) (discussing and following Indiana law that personal jurisdiction is not required).

[117] MISS. CODE ANN. § 93-27-205 (2004).

[118] MISS. CODE ANN. § 93-27-108(1) (2004).

[119] MISS. CODE ANN. § 93-27-108(3) (2004).

§ 18.06[2]   **MISSISSIPPI FAMILY LAW**

state.[120] The first judgment of divorce entered is entitled to recognition.[121] The Mississippi Supreme Court has held that the pendency of an action in another state does not bar a Mississippi court from proceeding to hear a case.[122] A resident husband's divorce action was not barred by his previously filed divorce action in Pennsylvania, where he resided before moving to Mississippi.[123]

Under the doctrine of forum non conviens, however, a court may decline to exercise jurisdiction. Courts should consider "the presence or absence of exigent circumstances, the legitimate needs and conveniences of the parties, and considerations of interstate comity and the need to avoid unseemly forum shopping."[124] A chancellor properly applied this doctrine to dismiss a resident husband's divorce action in deference to his wife's previously filed action in Illinois, where the couple lived until their separation.[125]

With respect to child support orders, however, UIFSA limits the right of a state to act in the face of concurrent proceedings. A state may not take jurisdiction to enter a child support order if the defendant files a similar proceeding in the child's home state before the time for challenging jurisdiction in the first state expires and if the defendant properly challenges the exercise of jurisdiction.[126] Otherwise, the first state to properly take jurisdiction over a support action acquires exclusive jurisdiction. A Mississippi court erred in taking jurisdiction over a child support action after proceedings had been filed in Louisiana.[127]

Similarly, the UCCJEA limits the right of a state to proceed with a custody determination in the face of concurrent proceedings. If another action is pending, a court is prohibited from taking jurisdiction if the first proceeding "substantially" complies with the UCCJEA. However, a court may take jurisdiction if the first state stays the proceeding because the second state is a more appropriate forum.[128]

[2] Full faith and credit. The Full Faith and Credit Clause of the United States Constitution requires that states recognize divorce decrees valid in another state.[129] Until the mid-twentieth century, states often refused to recognize sister state divorces. In 1942, the United States Supreme Court held that an ex parte divorce based on proper jurisdiction in one state, and with adequate notice to satisfy due process, must

---

[120] Sallis v. Sallis, 860 So. 2d 824, 826 (Miss. Ct. App. 2003) (court has discretion to stay or continue action, considering exigent circumstances, the parties' needs, and prevention of forum shopping).

[121] See Turner, supra note 32, at 125.

[122] Brown v. Brown, 493 So. 2d 961, 963 (Miss. 1986).

[123] Cox v. Cox, 108 So. 2d 422, 424 (Miss. 1959) (husband moved with child to Mississippi and established domicile).

[124] Brown v. Brown, 493 So. 2d 961, 963 (Miss. 1986).

[125] Sallis v. Sallis, 860 So. 2d 824, 825 (Miss. Ct. App. 2003); see also Brown v. Brown, 493 So. 2d 961, 964 (Miss. 1986) (chancellor properly stayed divorce action filed by serviceman stationed in Mississippi, pending the outcome of proceedings filed by his wife in California, where the couple were domiciled).

[126] MISS. CODE ANN. § 93-25-15 (2004).

[127] Richardson v. Stogner, 958 So. 2d 235, 240 (Miss. Ct. App. 2007).

[128] MISS. CODE ANN. § 93-27-206(1) (2004); see Caples v. Caples, 686 So. 2d 1071, 1073 (Miss. 1996) (Texas had continuing jurisdiction under UCCJA but waived jurisdiction in favor of Mississippi); Richardson v. Stogner, 958 So. 2d 235, 240-41 (Miss. Ct. App. 2007) (Mississippi court erred in taking jurisdiction over custody action after proceedings initiated in Louisiana).

[129] U.S. CONST. art. IV, § 1.

JURISDICTION § 18.06[3]

be given full faith and credit.[130] A state may not disregard an otherwise valid decree on the basis that the granting state's policies differ substantially from those of the reviewing state. However, if the divorce was not based on personal jurisdiction, a state may independently review the facts to determine whether the granting state's jurisdictional requirements were met.[131] But if the defendant appeared and defended on the merits, the reviewing court must accept the granting state's finding of jurisdiction.[132] After an Ohio court denied a wife's petition to set aside a divorce and property division for lack of personal jurisdiction, a Mississippi court properly refused to hear a collateral attack on Ohio jurisdiction. Res judicata and the full faith and credit clause required that Mississippi recognize the foreign state's adjudication of jurisdiction on the merits.[133]

The Mississippi Supreme Court held that a court was bound by a Florida divorce decree rendered after a husband left Mississippi and established his domicile in Florida.[134] However, the Full Faith and Credit Clause did not require recognition of a divorce decree obtained in another state under duress. The husband forced his wife to move with him to Alabama, where they obtained a divorce before returning to Mississippi.[135] Similarly, the Mississippi Supreme Court was not bound by a divorce granted by an Arkansas court based on a husband's temporary residence there for the purpose of obtaining a divorce.[136]

A sister state's judgment of divorce, while entitled to full faith and credit, does not bar subsequent determination of alimony and property division if these issues were not decided on the merits in the foreign court.[137] A husband's ex parte divorce in Virginia did not prevent a Mississippi court from converting a Mississippi separate maintenance award to alimony or from considering property division.[138]

UIFSA, which governs full faith and credit for child support orders, requires that states recognize child support orders entered by a state with jurisdiction under the Act.[139] Similarly, the UCCJEA, which governs full faith and credit with regard to custody orders, requires recognition of custody orders that substantially comply with the Act.[140]

[3] Foreign decrees. The Full Faith and Credit Clause does not apply to decrees

---

[130] *See* Williams v. North Carolina, 317 U.S. 287, 302 (1942) (Nevada divorce assumed valid because no evidence that parties were not domiciled there for required six-week period).

[131] Williams v. North Carolina, 325 U.S. 226, 227 (1945) (North Carolina court found that husband was not, in fact, domiciled in Nevada under Nevada law).

[132] *See* Sherrer v. Sherrer, 334 U.S. 343, 352 (1948).

[133] Swaney v. Swaney, 962 So. 2d 105, 110 (Miss. Ct. App. 2007).

[134] Anglin v. Anglin, 51 So. 2d 781, 783 (Miss. 1951).

[135] Hopkins v. Hopkins, 165 So. 414, 415 (Miss. 1936).

[136] Lynch v. Lynch, 50 So. 2d 378, 380-81 (Miss. 1951).

[137] *See* Weiss v. Weiss, 579 So. 2d 539, 541 (Miss. 1991) (Louisiana divorce was not res judicata as to alimony and property division in Mississippi where the wife resided).

[138] Chapel v. Chapel, 876 So. 2d 290 (Miss. 2004); *see also* Vanderbilt v. Vanderbilt, 354 U.S. 416, 418 (1957) (wife allowed to proceed with alimony claim in New York in spite of husband's ex parte Nevada divorce; personal claim cannot be adjudicated without personal jurisdiction); Lofton v. Lofton, 924 So. 2d 596, 602-03 (Miss. Ct. App. 2006) (en banc) (Florida divorce decree did not bar Mississippi court from converting separate maintenance to alimony; Florida court lacked personal jurisdiction over wife).

[139] MISS. CODE ANN. § 93-25-85 (2004).

[140] MISS. CODE ANN. § 93-27-303(1) (2004).

565

§ 18.07   MISSISSIPPI FAMILY LAW

from courts outside the United States. The principle of comity governs recognition of foreign decrees – the principle is similar to full faith and credit, but application rests in the trial judge's discretion.[141] Courts generally will not recognize a foreign divorce decree unless one of the parties was domiciled in the foreign country. A husband who traveled to the Dominican Republic for two days was not a bona fide domiciliary of that country – he admitted that the sole purpose of the trip was to obtain a divorce.[142]

§ 18.07 JURISDICTION TO MODIFY

Awards of custody, child support, and some forms of alimony may be modified upon a showing of a material change in circumstances since the initial decree. A court issuing an award of support or custody has continuing subject matter jurisdiction over the case and continuing personal jurisdiction over the parties to modify these orders.[143] A court that enters a family support order is authorized by statute to "afterwards, on petition, change the decree, and make from time to time such new decrees as the case may require."[144] The power to modify is also part of the inherent power of chancery courts.[145] Historically, however, a state could assert jurisdiction to modify another state's award based on a party's subsequent domicile in the modifying state.[146] Today, jurisdiction to modify outstanding orders related to custody and support has been substantially altered by the Uniform Child Custody Jurisdiction and Enforcement Act and the Uniform Interstate Family Support Act.

[1] Modification within a state. A petition to modify or enforce a divorce decree or custody or support order must be filed in the court that issued the decree. As between the parties to the original action, the issuing court's jurisdiction is exclusive, precluding any other court in the state from exercising jurisdiction over the case.[147] For example, a petition to modify custody was not properly filed in the county where the child resided at the time of the modification petition.[148] Similarly, a petition to terminate a father's parental rights was not properly filed in the county where the child currently resided, when custody of the child had been determined in divorce proceedings in another

---

[141] Laskosky v. Laskosky, 504 So. 2d 726, 729 (Miss. 1987); Asanov v. Hunt, 914 So. 2d 769, 772 (Miss. Ct. App. 2005) (en banc) (court properly recognized Russian court's judgment of divorce, custody, and child support based on comity); Kolikas v. Kolikas, 821 So. 2d 874, 880 (Miss. Ct. App. 2002).

[142] Carr v. Carr, 724 So. 2d 937, 940 (Miss. Ct. App. 1998).

[143] *See* Campbell v. Campbell, 357 So. 2d 129, 131 (Miss. 1978) (jurisdiction to modify child support even though both parties moved from state). *But cf.* Rothschild v. Hermann, 542 So. 2d 264, 265 (Miss. 1989) (suggesting that court might not have jurisdiction over contempt action where neither party had lived in Mississippi for many years; appellee failed to respond to issue).

[144] MISS. CODE ANN. § 93-5-23 (2004).

[145] Campbell v. Campbell, 357 So. 2d 129, 130 (Miss.1978).

[146] *See* CLARK, Jr., *supra* note 7, §12.5, at 458.

[147] Ladner v. Ladner, 206 So. 2d 620, 624-25 (Miss. 1968) (family court had no authority to modify custody established in Hinds County chancery proceedings); *cf.* C.M. v. R.D.H., 947 So. 2d 1023 (Miss. Ct. App. 2007) (Hinds County lacked jurisdiction to terminate parental rights; Scott County issued divorce and custody decree and had exclusive jurisdiction); Allen v. Williams, 914 So. 2d 254, 258 (Miss. Ct. App. 2005) (court that entered order terminating father's rights and granting custody to mother and visitation to grandparents had continuing jurisdiction to hear grandparents' petition to modify custody).

[148] Reynolds v. Riddell, 253 So. 2d 834, 837 (Miss. 1971).

JURISDICTION § 18.07[2]

county.[149] However, if an issuing court finds that adjudication in another court would be more efficient, jurisdiction may be transferred to that court.[150]

[2] Interstate modification. Modification of custody and support are governed by the UCCJEA and UIFSA. Both acts recognize the traditional continuing jurisdiction of courts to modify and enforce decrees, but limit continuing jurisdiction when all parties have moved from the state.

[a] Modification of child support. Under UIFSA, a court that issued a child support order has continuing exclusive jurisdiction to modify the order so long as the payor, the payee, or the child continue to live in the state. The parties may, however, jointly request that the court agree to transfer jurisdiction to another court for the purpose of modifying the order.[151] A full discussion of modification jurisdiction under UIFSA is set out in Section 18.08[4].

[b] Modification of alimony. UIFSA provides that a court issuing a spousal support order has permanent exclusive jurisdiction to modify the order. No other state may modify an alimony order, even if both parties have moved from the issuing state.[152] The Act does not address whether spouses may consent to jurisdiction in another state. The drafters' comments note that this issue is left to the individual states to determine.[153]

[c] Modification of custody. Under the UCCJEA, the court issuing an initial custody decree has continuing exclusive jurisdiction to modify the order. The court loses its continuing jurisdiction when both parties and the child have moved from the state.[154] However, if the issuing state determines that it no longer has a significant connection with the case, or that another state would be a more appropriate forum for the modification, a second state may proceed.[155] In either case, a court may not modify another state's custody order unless the modifying court would have jurisdiction under the Act to make an initial award.[156] A full discussion of modification jurisdiction under the UCCJEA is included in Section 18.10.

---

[149] Tollison v. Tollison, 841 So. 2d 1062, 1065 (Miss. 2003) (statute permitting filing of termination action in county where child resides applies only if no previous custody ruling).

[150] Reynolds v. Riddell, 253 So. 2d 834, 837 (Miss. 1971) (transferring custody modification does not conflict with statute barring transfer of divorce case).

[151] MISS. CODE ANN. § 93-25-17(a)(2) (2004).

[152] MISS. CODE ANN. § 93-25-26.1 (2004).

[153] *See* UNIFORM INTERSTATE FAMILY SUPPORT ACT § 205, cmt., 9C U.L.A. (2001); *see also* Kurtis A. Kemper, *Construction and Application of Uniform Interstate Family Support Act*, 90 A.L.R. 5th 1, § 21(b) (2001).

[154] MISS. CODE ANN. § 93-27-202(1) (2004); *cf.* Bridges v. Bridges, 910 So. 2d 1156, 1158-59 (Miss. Ct. App. 2005) (Arkansas had jurisdiction over modification of Louisiana custody decree; mother moved to Arkansas with children; father moved to Mississippi). For a discussion of application of the Act to military families, see generally Joseph W. Booth, *A Guide for Assisting Military Families with the Uniform Interstate Family Support Act*, 43 FAM. L. Q. 203 (2009) (discussing problems of residency and domicile).

[155] MISS. CODE ANN. § 93-27-203(a) (2004).

[156] MISS. CODE ANN. § 93-27-203(b) (2004).

§ 18.08   MISSISSIPPI FAMILY LAW

§ 18.08 THE UNIFORM INTERSTATE FAMILY SUPPORT ACT

The Uniform Interstate Family Support Act (UIFSA) provides jurisdictional and procedural rules governing actions to recover spousal or child support. These rules apply whether support is sought in a suit for divorce, an independent action for child support, or a paternity action. The Act governs initial orders for support as well as petitions to modify support. UIFSA was designed to facilitate interstate establishment and enforcement of support and paternity orders. The Act creates a two-state procedure that allows a petitioner to proceed in another state by filing a petition in his or her home state. In addition, the Act sets out the procedure for registering an order in another state. To reduce interstate conflicts over modification jurisdiction, the Act creates a uniform system for modification, recognizing continuing exclusive jurisdiction in the issuing court while any party or the child remains in the issuing state.

[1] Personal jurisdiction. Under the Act, any state with personal jurisdiction over a defendant may enter an initial child support order or order of paternity. The Act provides for personal jurisdiction over a non-resident based on (1) personal service in the state; (2) consent, general appearance, or waiver;[157] (3) the defendant's residence with the child in the state; (4) the defendant's residence in the state and provision of prenatal support for the child; (5) sexual intercourse in the state leading to the child's conception; (6) assertion of parentage in the state's registry; (7) the child's residence in the state as a result of the individual's acts or directives; or (8) any other basis for jurisdiction consistent with constitutional concerns.[158]

The UIFSA provisions for jurisdiction are extremely broad and may be subject to attack for failure to meet due process requirements of minimum contacts with the forum state. Even the drafters of UIFSA noted that several of the sections, if applied literally, could offend due process.[159] For example, the provision for jurisdiction based on a nonresident's "acts or directives" may be overbroad as applied – the United States Supreme Court held that a father's acquiescence in his child's presence in California by purchasing a plane ticket and allowing her to remain there with her mother was not a sufficient minimum contact to confer personal jurisdiction.[160] Some courts have held that domestic abuse that causes a spouse to flee to another state qualifies as "acts or directives" sufficient to provide personal jurisdiction for purposes of child support. For example, a husband's course of conduct intended to terrorize his wife was an act that forced her to flee her home state for Colorado, giving Colorado personal jurisdiction over him.[161]

---

[157] *See* Peters v. Peters, 744 So. 2d 803, 806 (Miss. Ct. App. 1999) (court had jurisdiction because defendant mother made general appearance in Mississippi, but declining jurisdiction because Virginia had continuing exclusive jurisdiction); *see also* Scaife v. Scaife, 880 So. 2d 1089, 1094 (Miss. Ct. App. 2004) (jurisdiction was not waived when a father answered generally but, with leave of court, amended answer to object to personal jurisdiction).

[158] MISS. CODE ANN. § 93-25-9 (2004).

[159] *See* UNIFORM INTERSTATE FAMILY SUPPORT ACT § 201, cmt., 9C U.L.A. (2001).

[160] Kulko v. Superior Court of Cal., 436 U.S. 84, 87 (1978).

[161] 163 *In re* Marriage of Malwitzal, 99 P.3d 56, 61 (Colo. 2004); *see also* Sneed v. Sneed, 842 N.E.2d 1095, 1101 (Ohio Ct. App. 2005) (Ohio had jurisdiction to determine child support for wife who fled from husband's abuse in Texas); *cf.* Jill S. v. Steven S., 842 N.Y.S.2d 401, 402 (N.Y. App. Div. 2007) (whether abuse caused parent to flee is question of fact; expert opinion not required).

568

JURISDICTION

§ 18.08[2]

The Mississippi Supreme Court has emphasized that it will follow traditional requirements of minimum contacts notwithstanding the broad wording of the Act. For example, a nonresident father's support for a child living in Mississippi was not sufficient to confer personal jurisdiction. Nor was jurisdiction provided by the fact that the couple married in Mississippi or that the child was domiciled in Mississippi.[162] However, an unmarried nonresident father whose child was conceived while he attended school in Mississippi was subject to personal jurisdiction. The court held that jurisdiction was provided under the Mississippi long-arm statute, but also noted that statutory authority to exercise personal jurisdiction over nonresidents is not required.[163]

[2] The two-state procedure. If a petitioner's home state does not have personal jurisdiction over a defendant, so that suit in the defendant's home state is required, the petitioner may use a two-state filing procedure or may file suit directly in the defendant's home state.[164] Using the two-state procedure, a petition for support or modification is filed in the petitioner's home state (the "initiating state") to be forwarded to the defendant's state of residence (the "responding state").[165] The petition must contain the information and accompanying documents listed in Section 93-25-47 of the Mississippi Code, must specify the relief sought, and must comply substantially with the federal forms mandated for use by state enforcement agencies.[166] Addresses and other identifying information may be withheld if disclosure would put a child at risk.[167]

A proceeding initiated in one state and forwarded to a responding state is based on the law of the responding state. The responding state applies its procedural and substantive law, including its child support guidelines and other laws regarding the duty of support.[168] A responding state may order support or determine parentage, but may not condition support upon compliance with a visitation order.[169]

A court using the two-state procedure is required to permit testimony by telephone.[170] The procedure also permits admission of testimony through affidavits if the

---

[162] *See* McCubbin v. Seay, 749 So. 2d 1127, 1129 (Miss. Ct. App. 1999); *see also* Richardson v. Stogner, 958 So. 2d 235, 238 (Miss. Ct. App. 2007) (no jurisdiction over Louisiana resident who had no contacts with Mississippi).

[163] *See* Jones v. Chandler, 592 So. 2d 966, 971 (Miss. 1991) (begatting a child analogized to a quasi-contractual relationship; failing to support the child analogized to a tort committed in the state); *see also* Venegas v. Gurganus, 911 So. 2d 562, 563, 566 (Miss. Ct. App. 2005) (jurisdiction over unmarried father's paternity suit against Louisiana resident who attended school in Mississippi when child was conceived). The long-arm statute, MISS. CODE ANN. § 13-3-57 (2002) provides: "Any nonresident person . . . who shall make a contract with a resident of this state to be performed in whole or in part by any party in this state, or who shall commit a tort in whole or in part in this state against a resident or nonresident of this state . . . shall by such act or acts be deemed to be doing business in Mississippi . . ."

[164] MISS. CODE ANN. § 93-25-27 (2004).

[165] MISS. CODE ANN. § 93-25-27 (2004). The initiating court forwards the petition to the appropriate court or, if the appropriate court is not known, to the responding state's enforcement agency. *Id.* § 93-25-33. The responding state's enforcement agency must attempt to locate the individual, identify the proper court, and forward the pleadings to that court. *Id.* § 93-25-39; *see also id.* § 93-25-41 (attorney general may order agency to perform its duties under the act or may provide the services directly).

[166] MISS. CODE ANN. § 93-25-47 (2004). The forms required for an interstate proceeding are provided by the federal Office of Child Support Enforcement and are available at http://www.acf.dhhs.gov/programs/cse under "Policy documents."

[167] MISS. CODE ANN. § 93-25-49 (2004).

[168] MISS. CODE ANN. § 93-25-31 (2004).

[169] MISS. CODE ANN. § 93-25-35(4) (2004).

[170] MISS. CODE ANN. § 93-25-57(6) (2004).

§ 18.08[3]   **MISSISSIPPI FAMILY LAW**

substance of the testimony would not be hearsay if given in person.[171] A petitioner may not be required to pay a filing fee or other costs in connection with a UIFSA proceeding.[172] A support obligor may be ordered to pay a successful petitioner's attorneys' fees, expenses, and costs. However, an unsuccessful petitioner may not be ordered to pay fees except as otherwise provided by law.[173]

[3] Retroactive application. Courts have differed as to whether UIFSA may be applied retroactively. Some state statutes include a provision specifically making application retroactive. In the absence of an explicit provision, some courts have held that UIFSA affects only procedural rights and therefore may be applied retroactively. The Mississippi Supreme Court adopted this approach in dicta, stating that UIFSA applies to cases that arose prior to the statute's effective date.[174] Other courts have found that since the language of UIFSA does not expressly or implicitly permit retroactive application, the Act does not retroactively apply to support orders.[175]

[4] Modification under UIFSA. Under UIFSA, a state issuing a child support order retains continuing exclusive jurisdiction to modify the order while any party or a child continues to reside in the state. However, the parties may consent to a transfer of jurisdiction to another state. When all parties have moved from the issuing state, jurisdiction to modify is determined by the defendant's residence. With regard to alimony, however, an issuing court retains permanent exclusive jurisdiction.

[a] Modification of child support

[i] Continuing exclusive jurisdiction. A court that issued a child support order has continuing exclusive jurisdiction if the payor, an individual payee, or the child continue to live in the state.[176] No other state may modify the order, even though the second state has personal jurisdiction over the parties and the order is registered and enforced in that state.[177] A North Carolina court lacked jurisdiction to modify a Mississippi child support order while the mother and child continued to reside in Mississippi.[178] Similarly, Mississippi lacked jurisdiction to modify a Virginia order even

---

[171] MISS. CODE ANN. § 93-25-57(2) (2004).

[172] MISS. CODE ANN. § 93-25-51 (2004).

[173] MISS. CODE ANN. § 93-25-51 (2004).

[174] *See* Dep't of Human Servs. v. Shelnut, 772 So. 2d 1041, 1050 (Miss. 2000) (finding that the argument was barred because not raised at trial; statement about retroactivity dicta); *see also* Dep't of Human Servs. v. Jacoby, 975 P.2d 939, 943 (Utah Ct. App. 1999) (applying UIFSA retroactively even though a shorter statute of limitations applied).

[175] Georgia Dept. of Human Resources v. Deason, 520 S.E.2d 712, 714-715 (Ga. App. 1999) (finding that the Act affected substantive rights; therefore, in the absence of legislative intent, the Act only applied prospectively). *See generally* 90 A.L.R.5th 1, § 3[b] (2011).

[176] MISS. CODE ANN. § 93-25-17 (2004); *see* Evans v. DHS, 36 So. 3d 463, 469 (Miss. Ct. App. 2010).

[177] MISS. CODE ANN. § 93-25-9 (2004).

[178] Thrift v. Thrift, 760 So. 2d 732, 735 (Miss. 2000) (father moved to North Carolina and procured modification); *see also* Peddar v. Peddar, 683 N.E.2d 1045, 1048 (Mass. App. Ct. 1997) (Georgia, not Massachusetts, had jurisdiction to modify a Georgia decree while father remained in Georgia); Carr v. Carr, 724 So. 2d 937, 940 (Miss. Ct. App. 1998) (father obtained foreign divorce after Mississippi court issued child support order for mother and child in Tennessee; foreign judgment was not entitled to recognition; Mississippi had continuing exclusive jurisdiction because father continued to reside in Mississippi); *In re* Witaschek, 276 B.R. 668, 677 (Bankr. N.D. Okla. 2002).

570

JURISDICTION § 18.08[4][a][ii]

though the father resided in Mississippi; the mother continued to reside in Virginia.[179] And Mississippi lacked jurisdiction to modify a Louisiana child support decree while the mother remained in Louisiana, even though DHS agreed to the Mississippi modification.[180] If another state attempts to modify an order while the issuing state has continuing exclusive jurisdiction, the authority of the issuing state is unaffected.[181]

[ii] Consent to transfer jurisdiction. Parties may file a written consent with the court that has continuing exclusive jurisdiction requesting that another court assume jurisdiction for the purpose of modifying a support order.[182] The court assuming jurisdiction must have jurisdiction over at least one party or must be in the child's state of residence.[183] UIFSA requires that the parties obtain permission from the issuing state to proceed in another state.[184] However, the Mississippi Supreme Court appeared to permit jurisdiction by consent without compliance with the UIFSA approval procedures. Although a mother's petition to increase support should have been filed in the father's home state of Maryland, he consented to jurisdiction in Mississippi by signing an agreed temporary order stating that the court assumed jurisdiction over all aspects of the case, including support.[185] On the other hand, Mississippi did not gain jurisdiction to modify a Louisiana decree just because the Louisiana-based mother provided an affidavit stating that the father was not in arrears.[186]

[iii] Assumption of jurisdiction after all parties have moved. If all parties have moved from the issuing state, another state may take jurisdiction based on the child's residence or personal jurisdiction over one of the parties. The issuing state may no longer modify the order if all parties have moved and a second state has properly assumed jurisdiction to modify. However, if all parties consent to modification in the is-

---

[179] Peters v. Peters, 744 So. 2d 803, 805 (Miss. Ct. App. 1999); *see also* Gowdey v. Gowdey, 825 So. 2d 67, 69 (Miss. Ct. App. 2002) (no jurisdiction in Mississippi to modify Texas support order while mother and child remained in Texas); Watkins v. Watkins, 802 So. 2d 145, 147 (Miss. Ct. App. 2001) (Georgia, not Mississippi, was the proper forum for modification of a Georgia child support order where the noncustodial payor mother remained in Georgia while the custodial father and the child moved to Mississippi).

[180] Evans v. DHS, 36 So. 3d 463, 469-70 (Miss. Ct. App. 2010).

[181] *See* Wallace v. Delaney, 962 P.2d 187, 191 (Alaska 1998) (Washington modification did not deprive Alaska of jurisdiction; mother still resided in Alaska); Hartman v. Hartman, 712 N.E.2d 367, 372 (Ill. App. Ct. 1999) (Illinois did not lose jurisdiction where Florida did not modify, but enforced the Illinois support order); Loden v. Loden, 740 N.E.2d 865, 872 (Ind. Ct. App. 2000).

[182] Miss. Code Ann. § 93-25-17(2)(a) (2004).

[183] Miss. Code Ann. § 93-25-17(2)(a) (2004).

[184] Miss. Code Ann. § 93-25-17(2)(a) (2004); *see* McCarthy v. McCarthy, 785 So. 2d 1138, 1140 (Alaska Civ. App. 2000) (consent must be filed in state with jurisdiction, not in state to which transfer is sought); Daknis v. Burns, 719 N.Y.S.2d 134, 135-36 (N.Y. App. Div. 2000) (New York court should not have modified Pennsylvania order even though parties proceeded in New York; Pennsylvania still had jurisdiction because mother remained there); Link v. Alvarado, 929 S.W.2d 674, 676 (Tex. App. 1996) (registering state may proceed only if the parties have followed UIFSA procedure for consent to transfer). *But cf.* Linn v. Del. Child Support Enforcement, 736 A.2d 954, 960 (Del. 1999) (if all parties have left the issuing state, that state no longer has continuing exclusive jurisdiction; parties may not seek consent to transfer in that state).

[185] *See* Nelson v. Halley, 827 So. 2d 42, 51 (Miss. Ct. App. 2002) (declining to decide whether father's Mississippi petition to modify custody was consent to Mississippi jurisdiction over child support).

[186] Evans v. DHS, 36 So. 3d 463, 470-71 (Miss. Ct. App. 2010) (nor did her later affidavit that she had orally agreed to try the case in Mississippi satisfy the requirement of written consent).

§ 18.08[4][a][iii]   MISSISSIPPI FAMILY LAW

suing state, a court of that state may modify the order.[187] When the parties have moved from the issuing state but no other state has yet assumed jurisdiction, most courts hold that the issuing state retains jurisdiction to enforce the order but not to modify the order.[188]

An issuing state that loses jurisdiction to modify may nonetheless continue to enforce the order.[189] However, if the order has been modified in another state, the modified order must be registered in the state that issued the original order before it may be enforced. A Mississippi court lacked jurisdiction to enforce a Georgia child support order. The original Mississippi order was modified in Georgia after the payor moved to that state. The mother sought enforcement of the modified order in Mississippi. Because she failed to register the Georgia order in Mississippi, the Mississippi court had no authority to enforce the judgment under the Uniform Interstate Family Support Act.[190]

If all parties move to the same state, that state may take continuing exclusive jurisdiction and modify the original order.[191] If the parties move to different states, the payor must seek modification in the payee's state of residence. The payee must seek modification in the payor's state of residence.[192] For example, California no longer had exclusive jurisdiction to modify after a mother and child moved to Mississippi and the father to Maryland. Maryland, not Mississippi, was the state with jurisdiction to hear the mother's petition to increase child support.[193] And jurisdiction to hear a Mississippi mother's petition to modify a New Hampshire child support order was in California, where the father lived, not Mississippi.[194] However, a party may consent to jurisdiction in the state where the other resides. Virginia properly modified a Mississippi order at the mother's request, after she moved to Virginia, since the father consented to amend the order there.[195] In any action to modify, the original order must first be registered in the state assuming jurisdiction.[196]

A court assuming jurisdiction to modify another state's order may not modify any aspect of the order that was not modifiable under the law of the issuing state, including the duration of payments and other obligations of support.[197] For example, a Missis-

---

[187] MISS. CODE ANN. § 93-25-101 (2004).

[188] Lattimore v. Lattimore, 991 So. 2d 239, 244 (Ala. Civ. App. 2008) (noting that most states to consider the issue have taken this position); Linn v. Delaware Child Support Enforcement, 736 A.2d 954, 962-64 (Del. 1999); Lunceford v. Lunceford, 204 S.W.3d 699, 703 (Mo. Ct. App. W.D. 2006).

[189] MISS. CODE ANN. § 93-25-103 (2004); Linn v. Del. Child Support Enforcement, 736 A.2d 954, 962 (Del. 1999) (agreeing with comments of National Conference of Commissioners on Uniform State Laws); see also In re Marriage of Abplanalp, 7 P.3d 1269, 1271 (Kan. Ct. App. 2000); Jurado v. Brashear, 782 So. 2d 575, 580 (La. 2001) (Louisiana had power to enforce order even though all parties left the state, but could not modify the order); Youssefi v. Youssefi, 744 A.2d 662, 668 (N.J. Super. Ct. App. Div. 2000); Dep't. Social Servs. v. Richter, 475 S.E.2d 817, 820 (Va. Ct. App. 1996).

[190] Williams v. Smith, 915 So. 2d 1114, 1116-17 (Miss. Ct. App. 2005); see also McLean v. Kohnle, 940 So. 2d 975, 979-80 (Miss. Ct. App. 2006) (Mississippi court lacked jurisdiction to enforce Mississippi order that had been modified by Virginia court until Virginia order registered in Mississippi).

[191] MISS. CODE ANN. § 93-25-107 (2004).

[192] The statute provides that a state may take jurisdiction if the petitioner is a nonresident and the state has personal jurisdiction over the defendant. MISS. CODE ANN. § 93-25-101 (2004).

[193] Nelson v. Halley, 827 So. 2d 42, 48 (Miss. Ct. App. 2002) (but finding that father consented to jurisdiction in Mississippi).

[194] Patterson v. Patterson, 20 So. 3d 65, 69-71 (Miss. Ct. App. 2009).

[195] McLean v. Kohnle, 940 So. 2d 975, 979 (Miss. Ct. App. 2006).

[196] MISS. CODE ANN. § 93-25-97 (2004).

[197] MISS. CODE ANN. § 93-25-101(3) (2004).

JURISDICTION **§ 18.08[4][b]**

sippi court could not modify a California order to require support until a child was twenty-one. Under California law, court-ordered support terminates at nineteen.[198] However, a modifying state applies its own law regarding requirements, procedures, and defenses applicable to modification of child support.[199] This includes the child support guidelines of the modifying state. Most courts to consider the issue have held that once a state acquires jurisdiction to modify another state's order, the child support guidelines of the modifying state should be applied to determine the proper amount of support.[200] In one case, a court applied California child support guidelines to a child support modification even though the original Idaho child support settlement provided that Idaho law would govern the agreement.[201]

[b] Modification of alimony. A court issuing an alimony order has permanent exclusive jurisdiction to modify the order.[202] No other court may modify an alimony order, even though all parties have moved from the state. Courts in other states have enforced this provision in spite of inconvenience to the parties. For example, a Florida court lacked jurisdiction to modify a Massachusetts alimony award even though the plaintiff sued the defendant alimony recipient in Florida where she was domiciled. The court noted that the statute distinguishes child support orders and spousal support orders for purposes of continuing exclusive jurisdiction – a state issuing a spousal support order retains continuing exclusive jurisdiction for the life of the order.[203] Similarly, a New Jersey award of alimony could not be modified by a Pennsylvania court, even though the husband had moved to that state and his former wife sought enforcement there. Suit could be filed only in New Jersey, even if it was an inconvenient forum for both parties.[204] The Act does not address whether spouses may consent to jurisdiction in another state. The drafters' comments note that this issue is left to the individual states to determine.[205] No Mississippi case was found discussing modification of alimony under UIFSA.

[5] Enforcement under UIFSA. An order issued in one state may be enforced in other states by (1) registering the order through the two-state proceeding (filing a peti-

---

[198] Nelson v. Halley, 827 So. 2d 42, 51 (Miss. Ct. App. 2002).

[199] MISS. CODE ANN. § 93-25-101(2) (2004).

[200] State of Alaska v. Bromely, 987 P. 2d 183, 190 (Alas. 1999) (applying Alaska child support guidelines in modification); Crosby v. Grooms, 10 Cal Rptr. 3d 146, 151 (Cal. App. 2004); Groseth v. Groseth, 600 N.W. 2d 159, 170 (Neb. 1999) (guidelines of issuing state apply in actions for enforcement only, but when issuing state loses jurisdiction, guidelines of modifying state apply); Cooney v. Cooney, 946 P. 2d 345, 348 (Or. Ct. App. 1997) (applying Oregon law to determine amount of support, but Nevada law to determine duration).

[201] *In re* Marriage of Crosby & Grooms, 10 Cal. Rptr. 3d 146, 149-53 (Cal. Ct. App. 2004). The court found that once California assumed continuing exclusive jurisdiction, California law applied, and the settlement provision did not change this result under California's choice-of-law provisions. *Id.* at 151-53. *See also In re* Scott, 999 A.2d 229, 236-38 (N.H. 2010) (New Hampshire law applied in determining whether a father had to pay college expenses even though a Massachusetts divorce decree provided that Massachusetts law would govern).

[202] MISS. CODE ANN. § 93-25-26.1 (2004).

[203] *See* Spalding v. Spalding, 886 So. 2d 1075, 1077 (Fla. Dist. Ct. App. 2004).

[204] *See* Hibbitts v. Hibbitts, 749 A.2d 975 (Pa. Super. Ct. 2000); *see also* Kurtis A. Kemper, *Construction and Application of Uniform Interstate Family Support Act,* 90 A.L.R. 5th 1, § 21(a) (2001).

[205] *See* UNIFORM INTERSTATE FAMILY SUPPORT ACT § 205, cmt., 9C U.L.A. (2001). *See generally* Kurtis A. Kemper, *Construction and Application of Uniform Interstate Family Act,* 90 A.L.R. 5th 1, § 21[a] (2001).

§ 18.08[5][a]   **MISSISSIPPI FAMILY LAW**

tion in the home state for transfer to the registering state); (2) proceeding directly to register the order in the other state; (3) sending an order directly to an employer without registering the order; and (4) sending an order directly to a state enforcement agency without registering the order.

[a] Registration. Registration is the procedure for entering a support order as a foreign judgment in an enforcing state. Registration is accomplished by sending a letter of transmittal with two copies of the order, including one certified copy, a sworn statement of arrearages, the obligor's name, address, and Social Security number, the obligor's employer's name and address, any other source of income, and a description and the location of non-exempt property of the obligor.[206] A state may not enforce an order that has not been registered in the enforcing state.[207]

Upon registration, the registering court notifies the respondent, who has twenty days to request a hearing to contest the order.[208] An obligor may contest registration only on the grounds that (1) the issuing court lacked personal jurisdiction; (2) there was fraud in obtaining the judgment; (3) the order has been vacated, suspended, modified, or stayed; (4) there is a defense under the law of the registering state to the particular remedy sought; (5) full or partial payment has been made; (6) the statute of limitations has run; or (7) another state's order is controlling.[209]

[b] Registering state's authority. A court enforcing another state's order may not modify the order unless the requirements for modification jurisdiction are met.[210] Registration does not affect the continuing exclusive jurisdiction of the issuing state.[211] The law of the issuing state governs the amount and duration of payments and the computation and payment of arrearages and accrual of interest on the arrearages.[212] However, the statute of limitations to enforce arrearages is the longer of the statute in the issuing state or the registering state.[213] The procedures for enforcement and remedies for enforcing support orders are governed by the law of the enforcing state.[214]

[c] Income withholding and administrative enforcement. A payee may send a child support order directly to a payor's employer in another state without first registering the order.[215] The employer must immediately notify the employee and begin

---

[206] MISS. CODE ANN. § 93-25-83 (2004).

[207] Williams v. Smith, 915 So. 2d 1114, 1117 (Miss. Ct. App. 2005) (Mississippi court erred in enforcing Georgia modification of Mississippi order; modified order was not registered in Mississippi).

[208] MISS. CODE ANN. § 93-25-89 (2004).

[209] MISS. CODE ANN. § 93-25-93 (2004).

[210] MISS. CODE ANN. § 93-25-85 (2004); *see* Patterson v. Patterson, 20 So. 3d 65, 68-71 (Miss. Ct. App. 2009) (Mississippi lacked jurisdiction to modify New Hampshire order, but could enforce order).

[211] MISS. CODE ANN. § 93-25-85 (2004).

[212] MISS. CODE ANN. § 93-25-87 (2004).

[213] MISS. CODE ANN. § 93-25-87(2) (2004).

[214] MISS. CODE ANN. § 93-25-85(3) (2004); *see* Ferrari v. Ferrari, 2000 WL 1196505 (Conn. Super. Ct. 2000) (Connecticut could enforce Texas order even though Texas law would have required filing with six months of child's majority); Judith S. v. John M., 701 N.Y.S.2d 880 (N.Y. Fam. Ct. 1999) (Florida order registered in New York subject to New York enforcement procedures; contempt not an available remedy in New York).

[215] MISS. CODE ANN. § 93-25-67 (2004).

JURISDICTION   § 18.09

withholding as though the order were issued in the employer's state.[216] The employee may challenge the withholding order as if the order were issued in the enforcing state or through the Act's registration process.[217] A payee may also, without first registering an order, send the order to the state enforcement agency in the payor's state of residence. The agency may use its administrative enforcement mechanisms for enforcement and income-withholding.[218]

§ 18.09 THE UNIFORM CHILD CUSTODY JURISDICTION ENFORCEMENT ACT

Jurisdiction over interstate custody disputes is governed by the relatively new Uniform Child Custody Jurisdiction and Enforcement Act [UCCJEA][219] and the Parental Kidnapping Prevention Act [PKPA], a federal full faith and credit act.[220] The UCCJEA governs jurisdiction over custody issues in divorce as well as independent custody actions and other proceedings related to children.

The predecessor of the Act, the UCCJA, was promulgated in 1968 to create uniformity in state decisions and to limit forum shopping by custody litigants.[221] Because some states were slow to adopt the Act, Congress in 1980 passed the PKPA, which contains requirements almost, but not quite, identical to the UCCJA. Although the two Acts were intended to ensure uniformity in interstate custody decisions, the differences between the two led to confusion. The UCCJEA, promulgated in 2001, was intended to resolve these conflicts. In addition, the UCCJEA creates an interstate enforcement mechanism similar to that provided for support orders. The Act was adopted in Mississippi in 2004. This section discusses the provisions of the UCCJEA as well as Mississippi cases interpreting UCCJA provisions that were not substantially altered in the new Act.

[1] Scope of the UCCJEA. The UCCJEA applies to initial custody actions, modifications, permanent orders, and temporary orders.[222] It also applies to actions dealing solely with visitation.[223] In addition to custody orders in divorce and independent custody actions, the Act applies to proceedings involving separation, guardianship, neglect, abuse and dependency, paternity, termination of parental rights, and protection from domestic violence.[224] The Act does not apply to proceedings involving juvenile delinquency, petitions for adoption, or authorization for a child's emergency medical

---

[216] MISS. CODE ANN. § 93-25-69 (2004).

[217] MISS. CODE ANN. § 93-25-77 (2004).

[218] MISS. CODE ANN. § 93-25-79 (2004) (agency must register order if the payor contests the validity or enforcement of the order).

[219] UNIFORM CHILD CUSTODY JURISDICTION AND ENFORCEMENT ACT, 9B U.L.A. (2001).

[220] 28 U.S.C. § 1738A (2006).

[221] *See* MISS. CODE ANN. § 93-25-1 (repealed).

[222] MISS. CODE ANN. § 93-27-102(c) (2004); *see* Walters v. Walters, 519 So. 2d 427, 428 (Miss. 1988) (UCCJA covers custody actions under the general petition for custody, MISS. CODE ANN. § 93-11-65 (2004)).

[223] MISS. CODE ANN. § 93-27-102(d) (2004); *see* Roberts v. Fuhr, 523 So. 2d 20, 23 (Miss. 1987) (custodial father's petition to restrict mother's visitation governed by UCCJA). *But cf.* Stewart v. Evans, 136 P.3d 524, 528 (Mont. 2006) (grandparent's petition for contact with the child not governed by UCCJEA).

[224] MISS. CODE ANN. § 93-27-102(d) (2004); *see In re* Matter of Guardianship of Z.J., 804 So. 2d 1009, 1017 (Miss. 2002) (UCCJA applied to grandparents' guardianship petition; court should determine whether Alabama, where grandparents planned to take child, was more convenient forum).

575

§ 18.09[2]   MISSISSIPPI FAMILY LAW

care.[225]

To the extent that custody of a child is governed by the Indian Child Welfare Act, the UCCJEA does not apply; the tribe is treated as a state for purposes of the Act, and a tribe's custody determination is given full faith and credit if in substantial conformity with the Act.[226] In international custody disputes, a foreign country's custody determination should be treated as the determination of a state, receiving recognition if the decision is in substantial conformity with the jurisdictional standards of the Act.[227]

[2] UCCJEA affidavit. The Act requires that in any proceeding to determine custody, each party must provide information related to the child's present location and residence for the last five years. Each party must also indicate whether he or she has participated in an action concerning the child's custody or is aware of any proceeding that could affect the action, including actions related to domestic violence, protective orders, termination, or adoption. The affidavit must include the names and addresses of any persons with physical custody of the child or who claim legal custody, physical custody, or a right to visitation.[228] The Mississippi Supreme Court held that a party's failure to file an affidavit does not deprive a court of jurisdiction. The Act provides that the court *may* stay the action if the information is not provided.[229]

[3] Interstate cooperation. The Act provides for cooperation between courts in different states. A court may assist a court in a sister state by holding hearings, ordering parties to appear at hearings, ordering the production of evidence or home studies, or taking testimony for forwarding to the forum state.[230]

[4] Subject matter jurisdiction. As a general rule, the Act places jurisdiction in a child's home state. Another state may assume jurisdiction only if the child has no home state, the home state declines jurisdiction, or the court takes temporary jurisdiction in an emergency.

[a] Child's home state. A court has home state jurisdiction over a child who lived in the state with a parent or "person acting as a parent" for at least six consecutive months preceding the action or, if the child is under six months old, since birth. Temporary absences during the six-month period are counted as part of the six months.[231] A court has home state jurisdiction if (1) this definition is met on the date the proceeding commences or (2) the state was the child's home state within the last six months

---

[225] MISS. CODE ANN. § 93-27-102(d), -103 (2004). Under the UCCJA, which did not explicitly exempt adoption actions, the Mississippi Supreme Court held that the Act did not apply to consensual adoptions, Adoption of C.L.B. v. D.G.B., 812 So. 2d 980, 983 (Miss. 2002). *But cf. In re* Adoption of D.N.T., 843 So. 2d 690, 697-99 (Miss. 2003) (suggesting that UCCJA might have some applicability in contested adoptions).

[226] MISS. CODE ANN. § 93-27-104 (2004).

[227] MISS. CODE ANN. § 93-27-105 (2004); *see* Laskosky v. Laskosky, 504 So. 2d 726, 729-30 (Miss. 1987) (applying similar UCCJA provision to custody dispute between parties in Canada and Mississippi).

[228] MISS. CODE ANN. § 93-27-209 (2004).

[229] White v. White, 26 So. 3d 342, 347 (Miss. 2010).

[230] MISS. CODE ANN. §§ 93-27-110, -111, -112 (2004).

[231] MISS. CODE ANN. § 93-27-102(g) (2004); *see also* Waltenburg v. Waltenburg, 270 S.W.3d 308, 316-18 (Tex. Ct. App. 2008) (UCCJEA does not apply to unborn children).

JURISDICTION   **§ 18.09[4][b]**

and a parent remains in the state.[232] In effect, if one parent moves with a child from the family's home state, the parent who remains has six months to exercise home state jurisdiction.

A child's home state is not necessarily the same as legal domicile, which refers to the parents' legal residence. For example, Mississippi was the home state of a child attending school in Mississippi, even though it was not clear that the child's parents had permanently moved their domicile from California to Mississippi.[233]

[b] Significant connections. A court may exercise jurisdiction under the significant connections test if no state has home state jurisdiction or if the child's home state declines to exercise jurisdiction. A court has significant connections jurisdiction if (1) the child and at least one contestant have a significant connection with the state other than "mere physical presence" and (2) substantial evidence related to the action is available in the state.[234] This provision is a significant change from the UCCJA, which gave equal weight to significant connections jurisdiction and home state jurisdiction, creating the possibility that two states could claim jurisdiction.

[c] Emergency jurisdiction. A state may exercise temporary emergency jurisdiction over a child who is physically present in the state and who has been abandoned or needs protection because of an emergency related to mistreatment or abuse of the child or a sibling or parent of the child.[235] Because the emergency provision includes abuse of a parent, a court may award emergency custody in a proceeding for protection from domestic violence, even if home state jurisdiction lies in another state. If there is an outstanding custody order, or custody proceedings have begun in a court with jurisdiction under the Act, the emergency order must specify a period of time within which the petitioner must obtain an order from the state with jurisdiction.[236]

[d] No other state has jurisdiction. The UCCJEA default provision states that a court may exercise jurisdiction if no other state has jurisdiction or if all courts with jurisdiction have declined to exercise jurisdiction.[237]

[5] Defenses to initial jurisdiction. A court with jurisdiction to enter an initial order may nonetheless decline to exercise jurisdiction. Parties may urge the court to decline jurisdiction because the state is not the most convenient forum or because of a party's wrongful conduct.

---

[232] MISS. CODE ANN. § 93-27-201(1) (2004).

[233] Jundoosing v. Jundoosing, 826 So. 2d 85, 87 (Miss. 2002) (interpreting UCCJA, court noted that the father sent money to the family in Mississippi, indicating that Mississippi was their home state); *see also* Carter v. Carter, 758 N.W.2d 1, 8-9 (Neb. 2008) (two-year military assignment was not a temporary absence from the child's home state, even though parents may not have changed domicile; place of assignment became child's home state).

[234] MISS. CODE ANN. § 93-27-201(1)(b) (2004).

[235] MISS. CODE ANN. § 93-27-204(1) (2004); *see In re* Adoption of D.N.T., 843 So. 2d 690, 704 (Miss. 2003) (Mississippi had jurisdiction to issue initial order under UCCJA emergency provision, even though Arizona was the child's home state; mother's consent to an adoption in Mississippi constituted abandonment).

[236] MISS. CODE ANN. § 93-27-204(3) (2004). If there is no outstanding order and no order is subsequently sought, the temporary order may become permanent. *Id.* § 93-27-204(2).

[237] MISS. CODE ANN. § 93-27-201(1)(c), (d) (2004).

§ 18.09[5][a]   **MISSISSIPPI FAMILY LAW**

[a] Inconvenient forum defense. The UCCJEA provides that a court may decline jurisdiction if it is an inconvenient forum and another court is a more appropriate forum.[238] In making this determination a court is to act in the child's best interest, considering (1) whether domestic violence is involved; (2) the length of time the child has resided outside the state; (3) the distance between the two states; (4) the parties' financial circumstances; (5) agreements regarding jurisdiction; (6) the location of evidence, including the child's testimony; (7) each court's ability to decide the issue expeditiously; and (8) each court's familiarity with the issues.[239] A court that declines custody jurisdiction may still retain jurisdiction over other aspects of a pending action such as divorce.[240]

The forum non conveniens defense, like improper venue, is waived by failure to raise it before trial. A chancellor properly refused to hear a party's forum non conveniens argument under the UCCJA, since she failed to appear and assert the issue at trial.[241]

[b] Petitioner's conduct. The Act provides that courts should refuse to hear cases in which jurisdiction is based on a petitioner's "unjustifiable conduct," unless (1) all parties consent to jurisdiction, (2) the proper court to have jurisdiction determines that the court is a more appropriate forum, or (3) no other state has jurisdiction.[242] Under the UCCJA, courts were required to decline jurisdiction if a petitioner had "wrongfully taken the child from another state or engaged in similar reprehensible conduct."[243] Interpreting this provision, the Mississippi Supreme Court held that Mississippi did not become the home state of children brought to Mississippi in violation of a Utah court order.[244] The court also held that a grandmother's removal of a child from her mother was wrongful, and could not confer jurisdiction on an Arizona court.[245]

When no custody order is outstanding, one parent's removal of a child may be, but is not necessarily, a wrongful taking. The Mississippi Supreme Court noted that both mother and father have equal right to custody prior to a court order.[246] Under the UCCJA, courts distinguished between removal for legitimate purposes and removal to avoid jurisdiction, forum shop, or to separate the child from the other parent. For example, a mother who moved from Canada to Mississippi in breach of an informal agreement wrongfully brought the child to Mississippi.[247]

[6] Waiver of subject matter jurisdiction. Under the UCCJA, courts disagreed as to whether parties could consent to jurisdiction in a state that did not otherwise have

---

[238] Miss. Code Ann. § 93-27-207 (2004).

[239] Miss. Code Ann. § 93-27-207(2) (2004).

[240] Miss. Code Ann. § 93-27-207(4) (2004).

[241] Hunt v. Hunt, 629 So. 2d 548, 554 (Miss. 1992).

[242] Miss. Code Ann. § 93-27-208(1) (2004). If a court declines or stays jurisdiction on this basis, it should assess fees and expenses against the wrongdoer unless he or she proves that assessment is clearly inappropriate. *Id.*

[243] Miss. Code Ann. § 93-23-15 (1) (repealed).

[244] Curtis v. Curtis, 574 So. 2d 24, 29 (Miss. 1990); *see also* Mitchell v. Mitchell, 767 So. 2d 1078, 1082 (Miss. Ct. App. 2000) (state cannot become a child's home state if child is wrongfully retained after visitation).

[245] Mosley v. Huffman, 481 So. 2d 231, 242-43 (Miss. 1985).

[246] Mosley v. Huffman, 481 So. 2d 231, 242-43 (Miss. 1985).

[247] Laskosky v. Laskosky, 504 So. 2d 726, 731 (Miss. 1987).

578

JURISDICTION § 18.09[7]

subject matter jurisdiction.[248] The Mississippi Supreme Court took the position that parties may not confer subject matter jurisdiction by agreement. For example, the court held that a mother could not consent to give Arizona jurisdiction which it did not have under law.[249] Similarly, a Connecticut court had no jurisdiction over a child wrongfully retained in the state after visitation, even though the custodial father appeared with counsel in the Connecticut proceeding.[250]

[7] Concurrent actions in two states. If an action is pending in another state, a court is prohibited from taking jurisdiction if the first proceeding substantially complies with the UCCJEA. However, if the first state stays the proceeding because the forum state is more appropriate, the court may take jurisdiction.[251]

Furthermore, a second state can proceed if the first state's assumption of jurisdiction or proceeding does not comply with the UCCJEA.[252] States have proceeded in spite of a pending action when the first state lacked jurisdiction,[253] the proceeding did not comply with UCCJA notice procedures,[254] or the child was brought wrongfully into the first state.[255] For example, Mississippi had jurisdiction over a mother's custody suit even though her husband had obtained a temporary custody order in California. She did not receive notice of the action.[256] Similarly, Mississippi had jurisdiction in spite of proceedings in Arizona; the child was abducted by her grandparents and taken there.[257] However, a Mississippi court erred in taking jurisdiction of a mother's custody petition. A custody action filed several years earlier in Louisiana, the child's home state, was still pending.[258]

[8] Personal jurisdiction. Custody is regarded as an adjudication of status similar to a divorce action. Personal jurisdiction over the child and the parties is not required.[259] The UCCJEA requires that notice and an opportunity to be heard be given to parents whose rights have not been previously terminated, persons with physical custody of a

---

[248] *Compare* Lutes v. Alexander, 421 S.E.2d 857, 863 (Va. Ct. App. 1992) (having chosen to litigate in Tennessee, father could not complain that it lacked jurisdiction) *with* Joliff v. Joliff, 829 P.2d 34, 36 (Okla. 1992) (parties may not confer subject matter jurisdiction under UCCJA) and *In re* Marriage of Arnold v. Cully, 271 Cal. Rptr. 624, 626 (Cal. Ct. App. 1990) (appellant's consent did not confer subject matter jurisdiction).

[249] Mosley v. Huffman, 481 So. 2d 231, 244 (Miss. 1985) ("UCCJA has no provision in it authorizing jurisdiction simply by presence or consent of the adult contestants.")

[250] Mitchell v. Mitchell, 767 So. 2d 1078, 1084 (Miss. Ct. App. 2000) (no provision in UCCJA allowing parties to fix jurisdiction by consent).

[251] Miss. Code Ann. § 93-27-206(1) (2004); *see* Caples v. Caples, 686 So. 2d 1071, 1073 (Miss. 1996) (Texas had continuing jurisdiction under UCCJA but waived jurisdiction in favor of Mississippi); Richardson v. Stogner, 958 So. 2d 235, 240-41 (Miss. Ct. App. 2007) (Mississippi court erred in taking jurisdiction after Louisiana action began); *cf.* C.M. v. R.D.H., 947 So. 2d 1023 (Miss. Ct. App. 2007) (Hinds County lacked jurisdiction to terminate parental rights; Scott County issued divorce and custody decree and had exclusive jurisdiction).

[252] *See* Miss. Code Ann. § 93-27-202 (2004).

[253] *See* Davis v. Davis, 281 S.E.2d 411, 415-17 (N.C. Ct. App. 1981) (disagreeing with California court's interpretation of "significant connections").

[254] Houtchens v. Houtchens, 488 A.2d 726, 732 (R.I. 1985).

[255] Mosley v. Huffman, 481 So. 2d 231, 243 (Miss. 1985).

[256] Jundoosing v. Jundoosing, 826 So. 2d 85, 90 (Miss. 2002).

[257] Mosley v. Huffman, 481 So. 2d 231, 243 (Miss. 1985).

[258] Richardson v. Stogner, 958 So.2d 235, 240-41 (Miss. Ct. App. 2007).

[259] Miss. Code Ann. § 93-27-201(3) (2004); *see* Yearta v. Scroggins, 268 S.E.2d 151 (Ga. 1980); Gay v. Morrison, 511 So. 2d 1173 (La. Ct. App. 1987).

§ 18.10   MISSISSIPPI FAMILY LAW

child, and any persons entitled to notice in a child custody proceeding.[260] At least one court has held that a biological father whose paternity had not been legally determined was not entitled to notice of custody proceedings initiated by a child's grandparents under the UCCJEA.[261] Service on out-of-state parties may be made under Mississippi law or the law of the state in which service is made. Although service must be "reasonably calculated to give actual notice," service may be by publication if other means cannot be used.[262] No notice is required if a party submits to the jurisdiction of the court.[263] Inadequate service is waived by the defendant's failure to object at trial[264] or by entry of a general appearance.[265] However, a party's appearance in the state to participate in a child custody proceeding does not, in and of itself, subject the party to personal jurisdiction on other matters.[266]

§ 18.10 JURISDICTION TO MODIFY CUSTODY

Prior to the promulgation of uniform custody acts, it was not unusual for courts in more than one state to assert jurisdiction to modify custody. One state might assert continuing jurisdiction to modify its own order, while another state might assert jurisdiction based on a party's current residence. Under the UCCJEA, only one court may assert jurisdiction after an initial custody order has been entered.

[1] Continuing exclusive jurisdiction. Under the UCCJEA, a court issuing an initial decree has continuing subject matter jurisdiction over the action and continuing personal jurisdiction over the parties. No other court may modify the decree.[267] Interpreting a similar provision under the UCCJA, the Mississippi Supreme Court held that Mississippi lacked jurisdiction to modify a Utah decree while the mother and child still lived in Utah.[268] However, even if one party remains in the state, a second state may modify the order if the issuing court finds that the parties no longer have a significant connection with the state and that substantial evidence is no longer available in the state. Only the issuing state may make this determination.[269] The issuing state no longer has continuing jurisdiction when the child and both parents have moved from the state.[270]

---

[260] MISS. CODE ANN. § 93-27-205 (2004).

[261] *In re* Sophia G.L., 890 N.E. 2d 470, 484 (Ill. 2008) (even though grandparents assumed he was the father).

[262] MISS. CODE ANN. § 93-27-108(1) (2004).

[263] MISS. CODE ANN. § 93-27-108(3) (2004).

[264] *See* Dep't of Human Servs. v. Marquis, 630 So. 2d 331, 335 (Miss. 1993) (while in personam jurisdiction may be waived, defendant preserved the objection); Mitchell v. Mitchell, 767 So. 2d 1078, 1085 (Miss. Ct. App. 2000) (whether a person may raise personal jurisdiction as an issue "depends entirely on when it was raised").

[265] *See* Peters v. Peters, 744 So. 2d 803, 807 (Miss. Ct. App. 1999) (Virginia mother who entered a general appearance in a Mississippi divorce action submitted to personal jurisdiction for purposes of child support and custody issues).

[266] MISS. CODE ANN. § 93-27-109(1) (2004).

[267] MISS. CODE ANN. § 93-27-202(1) (2004).

[268] Curtis v. Curtis, 574 So. 2d 24, 30 (Miss. 1990); *see also* White v. White, 26 So. 3d 342, 348 (Miss. 2010) (Mississippi court had jurisdiction to modify decree even though mother lived in Texas; father remained in Mississippi).

[269] MISS. CODE ANN. § 93-27-202(1) (2004).

[270] MISS. CODE ANN. § 93-27-202(1) (2004) (parent includes person acting as a parent).

JURISDICTION § 18.10[2]

[2] Modification in second state. A court may not modify another state's custody order unless the modifying court would have jurisdiction to make an initial award under the Act and all parties, including the child, have moved from the issuing state.[271] After all parties have moved from the issuing state, jurisdiction lies in the child's home state unless the home state declines jurisdiction[272] or the child has no home state.[273] A court without home state jurisdiction may also exercise jurisdiction to enter temporary orders in emergencies.[274] A state may also modify another state's order that was not entered in compliance with the Act.[275] For example, under the UCCJA, a Texas order was not entitled to full faith and credit because the court did not have jurisdiction to enter the order under that Act.[276]

[a] Inconvenient forum. A court with continuing jurisdiction may decline to modify custody if another court is a more appropriate forum.[277] Under the UCCJA, a Mississippi court had continuing jurisdiction to modify its decree; however, Alabama was a more convenient forum, since the children lived there and evidence regarding custody was more readily available there.[278] Similarly, Texas was a more appropriate forum than Mississippi, even though Mississippi had continuing jurisdiction, since the children lived in Texas and evidence relevant to the case was there.[279] In contrast, the supreme court held that Mississippi should exercise continuing jurisdiction under the UCCJA even though the child and mother lived in Texas; Mississippi was the home state of another child in the custody dispute.[280]

[b] Emergency. Even though another state has continuing exclusive jurisdiction, a chancellor may exercise temporary jurisdiction under the UCCJEA emergency provisions.[281] However, the emergency order must specify a period of time within

---

[271] Miss. Code Ann. § 93-27-203(b) (2004).

[272] *See* Caples v. Caples, 686 So. 2d 1071, 1073 (Miss. 1996) (under UCCJA, Mississippi court could modify Texas decree when Texas, as child's home state, waived jurisdiction in favor of Mississippi); Bridges v. Bridges, 910 So. 2d 1156, 1159 (Miss. Ct. App. 2005) (jurisdiction to modify Louisiana custody decree rested in Arkansas, where custodial mother lived with children for more than six months; father's residence in Mississippi did not provide jurisdiction); *cf.* Scaife v. Scaife, 880 So. 2d 1089, 1093 (Miss. Ct. App. 2004) (under UCCJA, Mississippi did not have jurisdiction to modify Washington state custody order with regard to child who lived with custodial father in California; mother and siblings' residence in Mississippi did not provide jurisdiction)*; see also* Shadden v. Shadden, 11 So. 3d 761, 763 (Miss. Ct. App. 2009) (Mississippi did not have jurisdiction to modify a California custody award in an action filed five months after the mother moved from California to Mississippi).

[273] A preference is created for home state jurisdiction in initial awards. *See* Miss. Code Ann. § 93-27-102 (2004).

[274] *See* Miss. Code Ann. § 93-27-204 (2004).

[275] *See* Miss. Code Ann. § 93-27-202 (2004).

[276] Mosley v. Huffman, 481 So. 2d 231, 239 (Miss. 1985) (no jurisdiction because child was wrongfully taken into state).

[277] Miss. Code Ann. §§ 93-27-203(a), -207 (2004).

[278] Stowers v. Humphrey, 576 So. 2d 138, 141-42 (Miss. 1991).

[279] Siegel v. Alexander, 477 So. 2d 1345, 1347 (Miss. 1985); *see also* Ortega v. Lovell, 725 So. 2d 199 (Miss. 1998) (chancellor should decline jurisdiction to modify a Mississippi decree when child lived in California and none of the parties had ever resided in Mississippi); Hobbs v. Hobbs, 508 So. 2d 677, 680 (Miss. 1987) (court should consider whether Mississippi should decline jurisdiction in favor of child's home state); Yeager v. Kittrell, 35 So. 3d 1221, 1225-26 (Miss. Ct. App. 2009) (chancellor did not err in finding that Texas was a more convenient forum than Mississippi to modify visitation; children had lived in Texas for over a year and their school and medical records were located there), *cert. denied*, 36 So. 3d 455 (Miss. 2010).

[280] Hunt v. Hunt, 629 So. 2d 548, 552 (Miss. 1992).

[281] *See* Miss. Code Ann. § 93-27-204 (2004). *See* discussion *supra* § 18.09[4][c].

§ 18.10[2][c]   MISSISSIPPI FAMILY LAW

which the petitioner must obtain an order from the state with jurisdiction.[282]

[c] No significant connection. A state may modify another state's order even though one party remains in the issuing state if the issuing court determines that the state has no continuing significant connection with the parties and that substantial evidence related to the child is not available in the state. This determination may be made only by the state issuing the order.[283]

§ 18.11 INTERSTATE ENFORCEMENT OF CUSTODY DECREES

[1] Registration. The UCCJEA added provisions for enforcement and registration of custody orders. One state's custody order may be registered in another state by sending a request and two copies of the order to the chancery clerk's office, accompanied by an affidavit that, to the best of the petitioner's knowledge, the order has not been modified. The request must also include the name and address of the petitioner and of any parent or person with custody or visitation.[284] The respondent is notified that he or she may contest the order's validity within twenty days.[285] If a hearing is not requested within twenty days of service of notice, the order is confirmed, precluding further contest with respect to issues that could have been asserted at that time. Grounds for contest include a claim that the issuing court lacked jurisdiction, that the order has been modified or stayed, or that the contestor did not receive required notice of the proceedings in which the order was entered.[286]

[2] Enforcement. The Act provides for expedited enforcement of registered orders, allowing a parent entitled to custody or visitation to obtain a hearing on the next judicial day after service "unless that date is impossible."[287] The order for appearance must state the time and place of the hearing and that the petitioner may take immediate custody of the child at the hearing, unless the respondent proves that an order has not been registered, and that the issuing court lacked jurisdiction, the order has been modified or stayed, or that the contestor did not receive required notice of the proceedings in which the order was entered.[288] At the hearing, the court may order that the petitioner be given immediate physical custody.[289] A court may also issue a warrant to take physical custody of a child prior to the hearing if the court finds that the child is in imminent danger of serious physical harm or removal from the state.[290] Furthermore, a court without jurisdiction to modify a custody order may nonetheless issue a temporary

---

[282] MISS. CODE ANN. § 93-27-204(3) (2004). If there is no outstanding order and no order is subsequently sought, the temporary order may become permanent. *Id.* § 93-27-204(2).

[283] MISS. CODE ANN. §§ 93-27-202, -203 (2004).

[284] MISS. CODE ANN. § 93-27-305 (2004).

[285] MISS. CODE ANN. § 93-27-305(2) (2004).

[286] MISS. CODE ANN. § 93-27-305(4) (2004).

[287] MISS. CODE ANN. § 93-27-311 (2004).

[288] MISS. CODE ANN. § 93-27-308(2004).

[289] MISS. CODE ANN. § 93-27-310 (2004).

[290] MISS. CODE ANN. § 93-27-311 (2004); *cf.* Blake v. Wilson, 962 So. 2d 705, 708-09 (Miss. Ct. App. 2007) (dismissing civil suit filed by father against Rankin county officials who enforced Virginia order by picking up children on same day order filed in Mississippi).

JURISDICTION

§ 18.12

order enforcing visitation, even if the order does not include a specific visitation schedule. The court should provide a specific reasonable period for the petitioner to obtain an order from the court with jurisdiction.[291]

§ 18.12 OTHER JURISDICTIONAL ACTS

Jurisdiction over children residing on tribal lands is governed by the Indian Child Welfare Act. International child abductions are addressed under the Hague Convention on the Civil Aspects of International Child Abduction and the International Child Abductions Remedies Act.[292]

---

[291] MISS. CODE ANN. § 93-27-304 (2004).
[292] *See supra* § 12.01[7].

584

XIX
PROCEDURE

Domestic relations cases are governed primarily by specific statutes set out in Title 93 of the Mississippi Code. To the extent that an issue is not specifically addressed by these statutes, the Mississippi Rules of Civil Procedure apply as in any other action.[1] In addition, certain rules specific to family law matters are set out in the Uniform Rules of Chancery Court Practice. The procedural rules for family law cases vary to some extent depending upon the type of action. For example, suits for divorce are governed by the rules generally applicable to initiating a civil suit. Independent suits for custody and support and actions related to paternity, termination of parental rights, adoption, and grandparent visitation are governed by Rule 81 of the Mississippi Rules of Civil Procedure, which provides special rules for service, timing, and pleading. Petitions to modify and enforce family law orders and for temporary relief are also governed by Rule 81. Chancery court proceedings involving allegations of abuse and neglect are governed by the Uniform Rules of Youth Court Procedure, which specify procedures for summons, subpoenas, time of service, and other matters unique to these proceedings.[2]

§ 19.01 PARTIES TO THE ACTION

As a general rule, only a husband and wife are proper parties to an action for divorce, property division, and alimony. In some cases, however, it may be proper to join third parties who have an interest in property involved in the suit. In actions involving children, third parties with custody or visitation rights may be necessary or proper parties to the action. And in some support and paternity actions, the Department of Human Services may be a necessary party.

[1] Divorce. Third parties are not allowed to intervene in divorce actions except in unusual circumstances. In 1928, the Mississippi Supreme Court held that men named as correspondents in a divorce based on a wife's adultery had no right to intervene to defend the allegations against them.[3] The court reaffirmed the general rule in 1999, but found that the case at bar was a rare exception – a man's second wife should have been permitted to intervene in his former wife's action to set aside their divorce. The intervenor, who was separated from the defendant, had substantial marital and property rights at stake that were not adequately protected by her estranged husband.[4]

[2] Property division. A third party with an interest in property owned by a

---

[1] MISS. R. CIV. P. 81(a)(9); *see* Crowe v. Crowe, 641 So. 2d 1100, 1103 (Miss. 1994); Queen v. Queen, 551 So. 2d 197, 199-200 (Miss. 1989); Mayoza v. Mayoza, 526 So. 2d 547 (Miss. 1988).

[2] *See supra* § 12.01[12].

[3] *See* Hulett v. Hulett, 119 So. 581, 586 (Miss. 1928).

[4] *See* Cohen v. Cohen, 748 So. 2d 91 (Miss. 1999); *see also* MISS. R. CIV. P. 24 (providing for intervention of right if petitioner can show an interest in the subject matter, that disposition may impair his ability to protect his interest, and that his interest is not adequately protected by other parties).

585

§ 19.01[2][a]   **MISSISSIPPI FAMILY LAW**

spouse may in some cases be a proper or necessary party in a divorce action. However, a third party's joint ownership with a spouse does not necessarily require joinder.

[a] Joint ownership with third party. Equitable distribution may be accomplished without joining a third party who jointly owns property with a divorcing spouse. The divorcing owner's interest may be included in the marital estate without affecting the legal rights of other owners.[5] If, however, a spouse seeks division of an interest belonging to a third party, that person is a necessary party. A court may not divide assets owned by a third party in his or her absence.[6] On the other hand, an alleged third-party owner is not a necessary party if the court finds that the spouse is the sole owner of the asset. The Mississippi Supreme Court rejected a husband's argument that a chancellor should not have proceeded without joining a third party who allegedly was the beneficial owner of stock titled in the husband's name. The court properly found that the stock belonged to the husband.[7]

[b] Transfer of assets to third party. A third party to whom a spouse has transferred marital assets must be joined if the non-owning spouse seeks to set aside the transfer.[8] For example, a wife attempting to set aside a transfer joined two corporations and her husband's brother, to whom he sold the corporations the day before a restraining order prohibiting sale became effective.[9]

[c] Third-party interest. A party with a claim against property of divorcing spouses may be a proper party to a divorce action. A court properly consolidated the complaint of a divorcing wife's mother against her daughter and son-in-law with their divorce action. She was granted an equitable lien on the marital home to secure a $50,000 loan related to the home.[10]

[3] Custody. Custody proceedings are governed by the Uniform Child Custody Jurisdiction Enforcement Act (UCCJEA), which replaces the Uniform Child Custody Jurisdiction Act (UCCJA). The Act applies to adjudications of custody in divorce and in Rule 81 actions.[11] The Act requires notice to any person entitled to notice in a

---

[5] *See* MacDonald v. MacDonald, 698 So. 2d 1079, 1085 (Miss. 1997) (court also found that business actually belonged entirely to husband; partner/father never participated in business or benefitted from business); *see also* discussion of third-party joint ownership *supra* § 6.09.

[6] *See* Skinner v. Skinner, 509 So. 2d 867, 870 (Miss. 1987) (error to award wife property titled in corporation without joining corporation); East v. East, 493 So. 2d 927, 933 (Miss. 1986) (error to modify wife's employment contract with husband's corporation without joining corporation). *But cf.* Burns v. Burns, 789 So. 2d 94, 100 (Miss. Ct. App. 2000) (not necessary to join third party claimed by husband to be equitable owner of stocks titled in husband's name; chancellor found that stocks belonged to husband).

[7] Burns v. Burns, 789 So. 2d 94, 100 (Miss. Ct. App. 2000) (also stating that the third party was aware of the proceedings and could have intervened); *see also* Shaw v. Shaw, 603 So. 2d 287, 294-95 (Miss. 1992) (rejecting wife's claim that her father, who deeded property to her, should have been joined to protect his interest); *cf.* Smith v. Holmes, 921 So. 2d 283, 285 (Miss. 2005) (en banc) (denial of party's motion to intervene is an appealable final order).

[8] *See* discussion of fraudulent conveyances *supra* § 6.10.

[9] Grogan v. Grogan, 641 So. 2d 734, 739 (Miss. 1994).

[10] Dudley v. Light, 586 So. 2d 155 (Miss. 1991); *cf.* Neyland v. Neyland, 482 So. 2d 228, 230-31 (Miss. 1986) (parents of wife granted equitable lien against marital home of divorcing daughter and son-in-law in separate action).

[11] *See* discussion *supra* § 18.09.

PROCEDURE

§ 19.01[4]

custody proceeding under state law,[12] to parents whose rights have not been terminated, and to any person with physical custody of a child.[13] No Mississippi case was found describing the parties entitled to notice in a custody action. In addition to parents and physical custodians, a third-party legal custodian of a child should certainly be included in the action.[14] In a 1961 case, the supreme court held that a couple who had physical custody of a one-year-old since her birth were *in loco parentis* to the child and were entitled to notice of custody proceedings regarding her.[15] Grandparents with physical custody of a child were proper, but not necessary parties to a custody hearing; however, the court's award of custody to the father was not binding on the grandparents in their absence.[16]

Although they are directly affected by a custody dispute, children are not parties to a divorce or independent custody action.[17] In some actions, however, courts are required to appoint a guardian ad litem to protect a child's interest. And in all family law matters affecting children, courts have discretion to appoint a guardian.[18]

Parties other than parents or custodians may be proper parties or parties entitled to intervene in a custody action. For example, grandparents with visitation rights with a child may be proper parties to a custody action involving the child.[19] And, in a case involving alleged sexual abuse of a child whose mother fled with her, the chancellor erred in denying her grandmother's petition to intervene.[20]

[4] Child support. The Mississippi Department of Human Services is charged with establishing paternity and child support orders for all recipients of public assistance. A public assistance recipient is deemed to have assigned to DHS all rights against the noncustodial parent.[21] Because of the assignment of rights, DHS should be a necessary party in any action for child support on behalf of a recipient of public assistance.[22] The custodial parent is not a necessary party to the DHS action for support. Similarly, a court properly found paternity and ordered a father to pay child support even though the custodial grandparents were not parties to the suit initiated by

---

[12] MISS. CODE ANN. §§ 93-27-102, -103 (2004) (defining custody proceedings to include custody and visitation; proceedings for divorce, separation, neglect, abuse, dependency, guardianship, paternity, termination of parental rights, and protection from domestic violence; but not including proceedings involving juvenile delinquency or adoption).

[13] MISS. CODE ANN. § 93-27-205(1) (2004) (duty to join parties and rights to intervene governed by state law).

[14] In suits for adoption, necessary parties include persons with physical or legal custody. *See supra* § 17.02[2][b].

[15] Farve v. Medders, 128 So. 2d 877, 879-80 (Miss. 1961); *see also* Sinquefield v. Valentine, 132 So. 81, 82 (Miss. 1931) (parents entitled to notice); *cf.* Smith v. Watson, 425 So. 2d 1030, 1033-34 (Miss. 1983) (en banc) (custody award in suit between parents not binding on grandparents with physical custody of child, although they were not necessary parties to action as between parents).

[16] Thomas v. Byars, 947 So. 2d 375, 379 (Miss. Ct. App. 2007).

[17] HOMER H. CLARK, JR., THE LAW OF DOMESTIC RELATIONS IN THE UNITED STATES § 14.2, at 533 (2d ed. 1988).

[18] *See* discussion *supra* § 12.10.

[19] *See* discussion of visitation rights *supra* § 12.09.

[20] S.G. v. D.C., 13 So. 3d 269, 278-79 (Miss. 2009).

[21] MISS. CODE ANN. § 43-19-35(1) (2004) (assignment automatic with receipt of benefits; no written assignment necessary); *see also* MISS. CODE ANN. § 43-19-31 (2004) (Assistance includes "any form of public assistance, including, but not limited to, medical assistance, foster care, food stamps, TANF, or any other program under the federal Social Security Act.").

[22] *Cf.* Dep't of Human Servs. v. Barnett, 633 So. 2d 430, 436 (Miss. 1993) (error to deny DHS intervention in action for lump sum settlement of support in paternity action until after settlement negotiated).

§ 19.01[5]   **MISSISSIPPI FAMILY LAW**

DHS.[23] The Mississippi Supreme Court noted in one action that, although a complaint was styled in the name of a child's mother, DHS and the child were the real parties in interest.[24]

[5] Married minors. A married minor is treated as an adult in actions involving divorce, support, property division, custody, and support of children. Suit need not be brought by a next friend or guardian ad litem; a judgment is effective as if the minor were an adult.[25] However, a court may appoint a guardian ad litem for a minor defendant.[26]

[6] Mentally incompetent spouse. A guardian for a mentally incompetent spouse may file suit for fault-based divorce on behalf of the incompetent spouse.[27] In addition, a guardian may be appointed for a mentally incompetent defendant.[28] For example, a chancellor ordered a psychological examination and appointed a guardian ad litem for a mentally incompetent wife upon the petition of her attorney, after she terminated his representation and signed an agreement that he believed to be unfair.[29] However, a court has no duty to inquire into mental competence unless the issue is raised at trial – parties are presumed to be mentally capable of entering into a contract.[30]

[7] Pro se parties. There is no constitutional right to state-provided counsel in civil matters. The supreme court rejected a defendant's argument that a chancellor should not have heard a petition for contempt without appointing counsel to represent him.[31] In matters involving termination of parental rights[32] and in contempt proceedings[33] parties may be entitled to counsel depending on the circumstances of the case.

Parties have a constitutional right to appear pro se in civil actions, including family law matters.[34] A pro se litigant "is bound by the same rules of practice and procedure as an attorney."[35] However, an unrepresented party is not necessarily held to the same standard in drafting pleadings and presenting arguments on appeal.[36] Nonetheless, a

---

[23] Thomas v. Byars, 947 So. 2d 375, 379 (Miss. Ct. App. 2007).

[24] Lee v. Stewart, 724 So. 2d 1093, 1095 (Miss. Ct. App. 1998).

[25] MISS. CODE ANN. § 93-5-9 (2004).

[26] MISS. CODE ANN. § 93-5-13 (2004).

[27] MISS. CODE ANN. § 93-5-15 (2004).

[28] MISS. CODE ANN. § 93-5-13 (2004).

[29] Rush v. Rush *ex rel.* Mayne, 914 So. 2d 322, 324 (Miss. Ct. App. 2005) (en banc).

[30] Parks v. Parks, 914 So. 2d 337, 341 (Miss. Ct. App. 2005) (en banc) (court had no obligation to take special steps to determine whether husband, who claimed on appeal to be under mental disability, understood agreement).

[31] Goodin v. Dep't of Human Servs., 772 So. 2d 1051, 1055 (Miss. 2000); *see also* Parker v. Bliven, 59 So. 3d 619, 621 (Miss. Ct. App. 2010) (rejecting father's argument that he was denied due process in child support enforcement proceeding because he could not afford counsel); *cf.* J.C.N.F. v. Stone County Dep't Human Servs., 996 So. 2d 762, 770 (Miss. 2008) (parents in termination proceedings not entitled to automatic appointment of counsel, but must be considered on case-by-case basis).

[32] See *supra* § 16.05[3].

[33] See *supra* § 14.06[6][b].

[34] *See* MISS. CONST. art. III, § 25 (no person barred from prosecuting or defending suit pro se or through counsel).

[35] Bullard v. Morris, 547 So. 2d 789, 790 (Miss. 1989); *see also* Ellzey v. White, 922 So. 2d 40 (Miss. Ct. App. 2006), *overruled on other grounds by* Daniels v. Bains, 967 So. 2d 77 (Miss. Ct. App. 2007); Chasez v. Chasez, 935 So. 2d 1058, 1062 (Miss. Ct. App. 2005).

[36] *See* Goodin v. Dep't of Human Servs., 772 So. 2d 1051, 1055 (Miss. 2000); Chasez v. Chasez, 957 So. 2d 1031, 1035 (Miss. Ct. App. 2007) (pro se parties may be "offered some leeway"); Asanov v. Hunt, 914 So. 2d 769, 771 (Miss.

PROCEDURE   § 19.01[8]

chancellor was not required to modify child support for a pro se litigant who did not petition for modification.[37]

[8] Prisoners. A prisoner has a constitutional right of access to court to obtain a divorce. However, it is within the trial court's discretion whether to allow a prisoner to attend a hearing. The court of appeals held that a chancellor was within her discretion to deny a prisoner's motion to attend trial, but erred in denying the divorce based on lack of personal appearance.[38]

§ 19.02 PLEADINGS

Requirements for pleadings in family law matters vary depending on the nature of the action. Actions for divorce are initiated by a complaint and require an answer from the defendant. Actions involving paternity, termination, adoption, custody and support apart from divorce, grandparent's visitation, and modification actions are governed by Rule 81. These actions are initiated by petition and service of a Rule 81 summons. No answer is required.[39]

[1] Complaint or petition. The sufficiency of petitions and complaints in domestic relations cases are tested under the notice pleading requirements of Rule 8 of the Mississippi Rules of Civil Procedure. Claims may be stated in general terms and relief may be based on a general request, so long as the defendant will not be surprised or prejudiced by the award.[40] This section discusses the degree of specificity required to address divorce, custody, and financial matters in a complaint, petition, counter-complaint or counter-petition. These rules are generally applicable regardless of the type of proceeding.

[a] Request for divorce. An action for divorce is initiated by a complaint in chancery.[41] The complaint must name the parties, state when the parties were married, and provide the number and names of the couple's living minor children born of the

---

Ct. App. 2005) (en banc) (court may "credit a poorly drafted appeal" to preserve meritorious claim); Caudill v. Caudill, 811 So. 2d 407, 409 (Miss. Ct. App. 2001) (pleadings). *But see* Jacobs v. Jacobs, 918 So. 2d 795, 797 (Miss. Ct. App. 2005) (pro se party on appeal is bound by same rules of procedure as attorney; failure to cite authority for alleged error barred consideration).

[37] Caudill v. Caudill, 811 So. 2d 407, 409 (Miss. Ct. App. 2001) (court is not required to be a mind-reader).

[38] Fisher v. Fisher, 944 So. 2d 134, 137 (Miss. Ct. App. 2006) (inmate entitled to divorce based on deposition testimony).

[39] *See* discussion of Rule 81 proceedings *infra* § 19.11.

[40] *See* Smith v. Smith, 607 So. 2d 122, 127 (Miss. 1992) (rules govern divorce proceedings in the absence of specific statute); *see also* Crowe v. Crowe, 641 So. 2d 1100, 1103-04 (Miss. 1994) (Rule 8 requires only notice, not a statement of facts); Bryant v. Bryant, 924 So. 2d 627, 631 (Miss. Ct. App. 2006) (father's petition to terminate child support sufficient notice of alternate request to modify child support); Jones v. Jones, 917 So. 2d 95, 102-03 (Miss. Ct. App. 2005) (wife's request for funds to "allow her to repair and maintain" property sufficient notice to include past and future repairs); *cf.* D'Avignon v. D'Avignon, 945 So. 2d 401, 407-08 (Miss. Ct. App. 2006) (court properly ordered enforcement of alimony escalation clause contained in agreement attached to wife's petition to modify alimony, even though she did not request enforcement).

[41] MISS. CODE ANN. § 93-5-7 (2004).

§ 19.02[1][a][i]   MISSISSIPPI FAMILY LAW

marriage.[42]

        [i] Grounds for fault-based divorce. In a complaint for divorce based on fault, the plaintiff may allege a single ground or multiple grounds for divorce.[43] Fault-based divorce is adequately pled by using only the statutory language describing the ground.[44] A complaint for divorce based on fault may also include in the alternative a request for divorce based on irreconcilable differences[45] or request for separate maintenance.[46] Except in a complaint for divorce based on irreconcilable differences alone, the complaint must be accompanied by an affidavit stating that there is no collusion between the parties for the purpose of obtaining a divorce.[47] The affidavit must be provided by the complainant and not his or her attorney.[48]

        [ii] Irreconcilable differences divorce. Divorce may be requested by a joint complaint, by one party's complaint for irreconcilable differences divorce alone, or as an alternative to fault-based grounds.[49] A court may not grant a divorce on the grounds of irreconcilable differences unless one of the parties' pleadings includes a request for divorce on that ground.[50] A court erred in granting a divorce to a couple who agreed to an irreconcilable differences divorce on the day set for trial of a fault-based divorce, when neither had requested a no-fault divorce.[51]

        [b] Request for property division, alimony or child support. A request for an award of property, alimony, or child support must be included in the pleadings unless the issue is tried by the parties without objection.

        [i] Request for alimony. Failure to make a request for support or maintenance bars an award of alimony.[52] A court erred in granting alimony to a wife who answered her husband's complaint for divorce without filing a cross-complaint requesting alimony and child support.[53] However, all that is needed is a request sufficient to provide the defendant with notice. A wife's request for a "reasonable sum to be paid periodically by the counter-defendant as permanent support and maintenance"

---

    [42] MISS. CODE ANN. § 93-5-33 (2004).

    [43] MISS. CODE ANN. § 93-5-1 (2004).

    [44] MISS. CODE ANN. § 93-5-7 (2004); *cf.* Lawson v. Lawson, 821 So. 2d 142, 145 (Miss. Ct. App. 2002) (rejecting claim that divorce was improperly granted because complaint did not use the statutory language; parties tried issue by implied consent; but suggesting that better practice is to use language of statute).

    [45] MISS. CODE ANN. § 93-5-7 (2004).

    [46] Lakey v. Lakey, 67 So. 2d 711, 712 (Miss. 1953).

    [47] MISS. CODE ANN. § 93-5-7 (2004); *see* Keller v. Keller, 763 So. 2d 902 (Miss. Ct. App. 2000) (court did not lack jurisdiction because wife's affidavit of no collusion was notarized but not signed; chancellor properly allowed amendment of the pleadings to include a signed affidavit).

    [48] Vance v. Vance, 20 So. 2d 825, 827 (Miss. 1945).

    [49] MISS. CODE ANN. § 93-5-2 (2004).

    [50] Alexander v. Alexander, 493 So. 2d 978, 980 (Miss. 1986).

    [51] Perkins v. Perkins, 787 So. 2d 1256 (Miss. 2001). For a complete discussion of requirements for ID divorce, *see supra* § 4.04.

    [52] Scott v. Scott, 69 So. 2d 489, 495-96 (Miss. 1954).

    [53] Diamond v. Diamond, 403 So. 2d 129, 131 (Miss. 1981).

PROCEDURE § 19.02[1][b][ii]

was sufficient to allow an award of lump sum alimony as well as periodic alimony.[54] And listing the "equity position of the parties" as an issue for submission to the chancellor was sufficient notice that alimony could be considered.[55] A court properly ordered a husband to pay his former wife an amount equal to unpaid insurance premiums even though her pleadings did not request that specific relief, when the parties knew that insurance under COBRA was an issue before the court.[56]

[ii] Child support. Child support may not be awarded unless it is requested in the pleadings, tried by consent, or the court notifies the parties that the issue will be addressed. A court erred in awarding child support to a mother who did not request child support in a pleading.[57] Similarly, a mother should not have been ordered to pay child support in a custody action; her petition requested child support, but the father's petition did not.[58] A request for child support includes all matters related to support, including insurance, medical support, schooling, and other child-related costs.[59] For example, a chancellor properly considered college support based upon a mother's request for an increase in child support in general; submission of child support to the court includes "all matters touching on that subject."[60] A mother's request for child support was sufficient to allow a chancellor to award a tax dependency exemption.[61]

A mother was allowed to recover support that became due after her petition for enforcement was filed; the court of appeals rejected the defendant's argument that she was required to amend her pleadings to include arrearages that accrued during the proceedings. Evidence of the amounts due was introduced at trial.[62]

[iii] Form of support. Rule 54 of the Mississippi Rules of Civil Procedure provides that a court shall grant the relief to which a plaintiff is entitled "even if the party has not demanded such relief in his pleading."[63] If a complaint requests alimony and division of marital assets, a general request for relief is sufficient to allow the court to grant an equitable lien to secure the award.[64] Similarly, a request for support and an assertion of an interest in the marital home was sufficient to support a court's order of partition without a specific request for partition.[65] And a court properly ordered

---

[54] *See* Crowe v. Crowe, 641 So. 2d 1100, 1103-04 (Miss. 1994).

[55] Rhodes v. Johnston, 722 So. 2d 453 (Miss. 1998).

[56] Pope v. Pope, 803 So. 2d 499 (Miss. Ct. App. 2002).

[57] Fortenberry v. Fortenberry, 338 So. 2d 806 (Miss. 1976); *see also* Overstreet v. Overstreet, 692 So. 2d 88 (Miss. 1997) (modification action); *cf.* Miller v. Miller, 512 So. 2d 1286, 1288 (Miss. 1987) (but waived by failure to appeal; husband could not attack decree collaterally).

[58] Massey v. Huggins, 799 So. 2d 902 (Miss. Ct. App. 2001); *see also* Purviance v. Burgess, 980 So. 2d 308 (Miss. Ct. App. 2007) (error to increase noncustodial mother's child support in her action to modify custody).

[59] Stinson v. Stinson, 738 So. 2d 1259, 1263 (Miss. Ct. App. 1999).

[60] Evans v. Evans, 994 So. 2d 765, 772 (Miss. 2008).

[61] Johnston v. Johnston, 722 So. 2d 453, 463 (Miss. 1998); *see also* Peters v. Ridgely, 797 So. 2d 1020, 1024 (Miss. Ct. App. 2001) (court did not err in awarding tax exemption for two children to mother, even though pleadings only requested award with regard to one child); *cf.* Bryant v. Bryant, 924 So. 2d 627, 631 (Miss. Ct. App. 2006) (father's petition to terminate child support sufficient notice of alternate request to modify child support).

[62] Watkins v. Watkins, 748 So. 2d 808, 812 (Miss. Ct. App. 1999).

[63] Miss. R. Civ. P. 54(c) (but judgment may not be entered in an amount greater than that requested).

[64] Smith v. Smith, 607 So. 2d 122, 127 (Miss. 1992), *rev'g* Holleman v. Holleman, 527 So. 2d 90, 93 (Miss. 1988).

[65] *See* Johnson v. Johnson, 550 So. 2d 416, 419 (Miss. 1989) (overruled on other grounds).

§ 19.02[1][c]   MISSISSIPPI FAMILY LAW

enforcement of an alimony escalation clause in the divorce agreement attached to a wife's petition to modify alimony, even though she requested modification rather than enforcement of the escalation clause.[66]

[c] Custody. A court may address and award custody of children even if the parties do not address custody in the pleadings. A court did not err in awarding custody of children to a father and his parents, even though the father did not request an award of custody in a cross-complaint.[67]

[d] Trial by consent/failure to object. Prior to adoption of the rules of civil procedure, a court could not award alimony or child support unless a specific request was included in the pleadings. Under the rules of civil procedure, however, issues not raised in the pleadings but tried by the consent of the parties are treated as if they were raised in the pleadings. A husband's failure to object to the admission of evidence related to alimony was a waiver of his wife's failure to request alimony in the pleadings.[68] Similarly, a father's failure to object to DHS's evidence related to past-due child support waived the objection that the complaint did not request past-due support.[69]

[e] Attorneys' fees. Attorneys' fees must be requested in the pleadings. A wife was barred from seeking fees – the pleadings did not request fees, the agreement to submit issues to the court did not mention fees, and the issue was not tried by implicit consent.[70]

[2] Responsive pleadings. Responsive pleadings are required in some, but not all, family law actions. An answer is required in a suit for divorce, but not in actions governed by Rule 81.[71] A defendant in a divorce action need not answer under oath. Furthermore, admissions in the answer are not to be taken as evidence.[72] A defendant in a divorce matter has thirty days to respond.[73] Objections to personal jurisdiction or service of process must be raised prior to or simultaneously with the answer. Affirmative defenses must also be raised in the answer.

[a] Preserving objections to jurisdiction. A court with subject matter jurisdiction may enter a fault-based divorce or custody decree without personal jurisdiction over a defendant.[74] In contrast, orders of alimony, child support, and

---

[66] D'Avignon v. D'Avignon, 945 So. 2d 401, 408 (Miss. Ct. App. 2006).

[67] Dickerson v. Dickerson, 148 So. 2d 510, 512 (Miss. 1963).

[68] Queen v. Queen, 551 So. 2d 197, 199-200 (Miss. 1989).

[69] Lee v. Stewart, 724 So. 2d 1093 (Miss. Ct. App. 1998); *see also In re* Adoption of Minor Child, 931 So. 2d 566, 573 (Miss. 2006) (en banc) (deficiencies in pleadings cured by the pre-trial order listing additional grounds for termination, without objection from defendant).

[70] Wideman v. Wideman, 909 So. 2d 140, 144-46 (Miss. Ct. App. 2005).

[71] *See* discussion *infra* § 19.11.

[72] Miss. Code Ann. § 93-5-7 (2004).

[73] Miss. R. Civ. P. 12(a).

[74] *See* Brett Turner, *Pursuing the Divisible Divorce: Recent Case Law on State Court Jurisdiction in Divorce Cases,* 12 Divorce Litig. 125 (July 2000).

PROCEDURE § 19.02[2][b]

property division are in personam judgments, requiring that the defendant have minimum contacts with the state.[75] Although subject matter jurisdiction may not be waived,[76] a defendant who responds without raising lack of personal jurisdiction in the answer or a motion waives the claim.[77] Similarly, the defense of improper service of process is waived when a defendant appears without raising the objection in the initial pleadings or attached motions.[78] For example, a court had jurisdiction over a mother whose attorney answered a complaint, introduced evidence on her behalf, and did not challenge jurisdiction.[79]

[b] Affirmative defenses. Affirmative defenses must be raised in the pleadings.[80] A noncustodial father's defense of laches was properly excluded because it was not raised in the pleadings or tried by consent of the parties.[81] However, waiver occurs only if a responsive pleading is required. Affirmative defenses are not waived in Rule 81 actions – a defendant payor did not waive the affirmative defense of statute of limitations when he responded to a contempt petition without including the defense.[82]

[c] Failure to answer. No judgment by default may be granted in divorce proceedings.[83] A defendant who fails to provide a required answer is not entitled to notice of subsequent proceedings in the action. The supreme court rejected a husband's attempt to set aside an uncontested divorce granted to his wife; he did not enter an appearance and was not entitled to notice of the subsequent hearing on her complaint.[84] However, a defendant who fails to provide a required response may nonetheless appear and offer proof in rebuttal of the plaintiff's case. No evidence may be offered of affirmative defenses or counterclaims.[85]

---

[75] *See* Fliter v. Fliter, 383 So. 2d 1084, 1087 (Miss. 1980) ("no insurmountable obstacle" that action includes both in rem and in personam components). *See* discussion *supra* §§ 18.03 - .05.

[76] Harry v. Harry, 856 So. 2d 748, 752 (Miss. Ct. App. 2003) (defendant did not waive subject matter jurisdiction by appearing at the hearing without objection).

[77] *See* Miller v. Miller, 512 So. 2d 1286, 1288 (Miss. 1987) (husband who answered complaint by letter to Chancery Court waived defense by responding on the merits); MISSISSIPPI CIVIL PROCEDURE, § 1.5 (Jeffrey Jackson ed., 2003); *see supra* § 18.04[4].

[78] *See* MISS. R. CIV. P. 12(b)(4) (objection to adequacy of summons); MISS. R. CIV. P. 12 (b)(5) (objection to adequacy of service); *see also* Venegas v. Gurganus, 911 So. 2d 562 (Miss. Ct. App. 2005) (defects in service of process waived by failure to assert at trial; motion objecting to personal jurisdiction did not raise issue of insufficiency of process); *cf.* Scaife v. Scaife, 880 So. 2d 1089, 1094 (Miss. Ct. App. 2004) (jurisdiction was not waived when a father answered generally but, with leave of court, amended answer to object to personal jurisdiction); Hamm v. Hall, 693 So. 2d 906, 908-09 (Miss. 1997) (payment of child support pursuant to an invalid decree did not constitute a waiver). *See* discussion *supra* § 18.04[4].

[79] Isom v. Jernigan, 840 So. 2d 104 (Miss. 2003); *see also* Rains v. Gardner, 731 So. 2d 1192, 1197 (Miss. 1999) (objection may be filed prior to or simultaneously with answer).

[80] MISS. R. CIV. P. 8(c).

[81] Andrews v. Williams, 723 So. 2d 1175 (Miss. Ct. App. 1998); *see also* Ashburn v. Ashburn, 970 So. 2d 204, 213 (Miss. Ct. App. 2007) (court erred in denying divorce based on condonation when defense not raised in pleadings).

[82] Dep't of Human Servs. v. Guidry, 830 So. 2d 628 (Miss. 2002).

[83] *See infra* § 19.05[2].

[84] *See* Stinson v. Stinson, 738 So. 2d 1259, 1263 (Miss. Ct. App. 1999); *see also* Lindsey v. Lindsey, 818 So. 2d 1191, 1194 (Miss. 2002) (wife who failed to respond could not attack grant of divorce); Carlisle v. Carlisle, 11 So. 3d 142, 145-46 (Miss. Ct. App. 2009) (husband who failed to respond not entitled to notice of hearing).

[85] Rawson v. Buta, 609 So. 2d 426, 430 (Miss. 1992).

§ 19.02[3]   MISSISSIPPI FAMILY LAW

[3] Rule 8.05 financial statement. Rule 8.05 of the Uniform Chancery Rules requires each party in a domestic case involving economic issues to provide a statement of income, expenses, assets, and liabilities, using the form set out in the rules. In addition, the parties must provide copies of income tax returns for the previous year and a statement of employment history and earnings from the date of the marriage or divorce, depending on the nature of the action.[86] A party filing sensitive information and data may file an unredacted document under seal or file a reference list under seal. The reference list must contain the complete personal data and information required by the Rule.[87] The court of appeals emphasized the importance of filing a financial statement in a 2004 case, stating that disclosure is "mandatory" unless excused by court order. The court held that a chancellor should have held a husband in contempt and set aside a divorce decree for his failure to disclose substantial lottery winnings.[88]

In later cases, however, the court of appeals stated that failure to file a financial statement does not, in the absence of fraud, require that an agreement be set aside. For example, the court of appeals refused to set aside a property settlement agreement based on the absence of 8.05 financial statements, where no concealment of assets was alleged.[89] In a 2007 case, the court of appeals held that a husband's underreporting of income at divorce, even if fraudulent, would have been a fraud on the party, rather than a fraud on the court. Fraud on a party must be addressed within six months of a judgment under Rule 60(b), while fraud on the court may be addressed at any time.[90] This issue was resolved by the Mississippi Supreme Court in 2010. The court held that a party's intentional, substantial misrepresentation on a Rule 8.05 financial statement is fraud on the court, and must be addressed within a reasonable time, rather than within the six-month limit.[91]

The court of appeals has held that a chancellor was within his discretion to dispense with Rule 8.05 financial statements in an uncontested divorce proceeding in which the husband did not appear. The court also noted that the husband waived the objection by failing to appear.[92]

[4] UCCJEA affidavit. The initial pleading or response in any action involving custody of a child must include an affidavit stating the child's present address, the places where the child has lived during the last five years, and the names and present addresses of the persons with whom the child lived during that period. The pleading or affidavit must also identify any other custody or visitation proceedings in which the party has participated. In addition, the affidavit or pleading must state whether the

---

[86] MISS. UNIF. CHANC. CT. RULE 8.05; *cf.* Ghoston v. Ghoston, 979 So. 2d 719 (Miss. Ct. App. 2007) (rejecting husband's argument that he was injured by wife's failure to provide 8.05 prior to trial; he also failed to provide disclosure until the date of trial).

[87] MISS. UNIF. CHANC. CT. RULE 8.05.

[88] Kalman v. Kalman, 905 So. 2d 760 (Miss. Ct. App. 2004); *see also infra* § 19.08[2][c][iii] for a discussion of failure to provide a financial statement as fraud on the party or on the court.

[89] Kalman v. Kalman, 905 So. 2d 760, 764 (Miss. Ct. App. 2004).

[90] Walton v. Snyder, 984 So. 2d 343, 350-351 (Miss. Ct. App. 2007).

[91] Trim v. Trim, 33 So. 3d 471, 479 (Miss. 2010).

[92] Luse v. Luse, 992 So. 2d 659, 664 (Miss. Ct. App. 2008).

PROCEDURE

§ 19.03

party knows of any proceeding that could affect the current action, or knows the names and addresses of any person who has physical custody of the child or who claims rights of legal or physical custody of, or visitation with, the child.[93] Under the predecessor act to the UCCJEA, the supreme court held that although the required affidavit is a jurisdictional requirement, failure to file a UCCJA affidavit does not defeat jurisdiction if the failure is cured by amendment.[94] In 2010, however, the Mississippi Supreme Court held that a party's failure to file an affidavit does not deprive a court of jurisdiction. The Act provides that the court *may* stay the action if the information is not provided.[95]

§19.03 SERVICE OF PROCESS

The requirements for service of process depend upon the type of action. In suits for divorce, service of process is governed by Rule 4 of the rules of civil procedure. In other family law matters – petitions for custody or support, paternity, termination, adoption, and grandparent visitation – and in actions to modify or enforce a decree, service of process is governed by Rule 81(d).[96] Rule 81(d) prescribes the form of summons to be used; however, the method of service is governed by Rule 4.

[1] Form of summons. The proper form of summons for divorce is governed by Rule 4 of the Rules of Civil Procedure.[97] A divorce action was set aside because the defendant, who did not appear, was served with a Rule 81 summons rather than a Rule 4 summons.[98] The summons should include the name of the court and parties; be directed to the defendant; and state the name and address of the plaintiff's attorney, the time required to appear and defend, and that failure to appear will result in judgment by default.[99] It should be noted that true default judgments may not be granted in divorce; if a defendant fails to appear the matter is uncontested, but the plaintiff is nonetheless required to put on proof.[100]

[2] Manner of service

[a] On resident defendant. A resident defendant may be served by delivering a copy of the complaint and summons to the defendant personally.[101] If personal delivery cannot be made "with reasonable diligence" service may be made by leaving process at the defendant's "usual place of abode" with a family member over the age

---

[93] MISS. CODE ANN. § 93-27-209 (2004).

[94] Marr v. Adair, 841 So. 2d 1195, 1201 (Miss. Ct. App. 2003); Robison v. Lanford, 822 So. 2d 1034 (Miss. Ct. App. 2002) (requirement was waived because the appellant did not object to the failure to file an affidavit, where no other proceedings were actually pending).

[95] White v. White, 26 So. 3d 342, 347 (Miss. 2010).

[96] *See* discussion of Rule 81 matters *infra* § 19.11.

[97] Sanghi v. Sanghi, 759 So. 2d 1250, 1252 (Miss. Ct. App. 2002).

[98] Clark v. Clark, 43 So. 3d 496, 500-501 (Miss. Ct. App. 2010) (requirements for the two summons are substantially different; reversing property division, alimony, custody and child support awards).

[99] MISS. R. CIV. P. 4(b).

[100] *See infra* § 19.05[2].

[101] MISS. R. CIV. P. 4(d)(1)(A) (by leaving copy with defendant or agent).

§ 19.03[2][b]   MISSISSIPPI FAMILY LAW

of sixteen willing to receive process and by then mailing a copy to the defendant at the address of delivery by first-class mail.[102]

Service may also be made by mailing the resident defendant a copy of the summons and complaint, two copies of a notice and acknowledgment form, and a return envelope, postage prepaid, addressed to the sender. The defendant has twenty days to respond. If an acknowledgment is not received within twenty days of mailing, service may be made by any other method permitted by the rule.[103] Service by certified mail, as permitted for nonresidents, is not a valid method of service on resident defendants.[104]

Service may be made by publication on a resident defendant who cannot be found.[105] Process by publication does not provide personal jurisdiction to address issues of property division, alimony, or child support.[106]

[b] On nonresident defendants. A nonresident defendant may be served in any manner available for service on a resident defendant. In addition, a nonresident defendant may be served by mailing a copy of the summons and complaint by certified mail, return receipt requested. For service on an individual, the envelope must be marked "restricted delivery."[107] A nonresident defendant may be served by publication. However, the court will not have jurisdiction to address property division, alimony, or child support.[108] Furthermore, personal service of process on a nonresident defendant will not confer personal jurisdiction over a defendant who lacks the minimum contacts with the state necessary to satisfy due process requirements.[109]

[c] Service by publication. Service in family law matters may be made by publication on nonresident defendants or on a resident defendant who cannot be found after "diligent inquiry."[110] The request for publication must be made in a sworn complaint, petition, or affidavit, and must provide the defendant's post office address or state that the address is unknown after diligent inquiry.[111] If the post office address is stated, the defendant's street address must also be provided unless the affidavit or complaint states that the street address cannot be ascertained after diligent inquiry.[112] Publication must be made once a week for three successive weeks in a public newspaper

---

[102] Miss. R. Civ. P. 4(d)(1)(A).

[103] Miss. R. Civ. P. 4(c)(3)(A), (B). The notice and acknowledgment must be executed under oath. Miss. R. Civ. P. 4(c)(3)(D).

[104] Triple C Transport, Inc. v. Dickens, 870 So. 2d 1195 (Miss. 2004).

[105] Miss. R. Civ. P. 4(c)(4)(A).

[106] O'Neill v. O'Neill, 515 So. 2d 1208, 1211 (Miss. 1987) (adjudication requires personal service or general appearance).

[107] Miss. R. Civ. P. 4(c)(5). Service is considered complete on the date of delivery as shown by the return receipt or returned envelope marked refused. *Id.*

[108] O'Neill v. O'Neill, 515 So. 2d 1208, 1211 (Miss. 1987) (adjudication of other matters requires personal service or general appearance).

[109] *See supra* § 18.04[2].

[110] Miss. R. Civ. P. 4(c)(4)(A).

[111] Miss. R. Civ. P. 4(c)(4)(A). If the petition is filed by one other than the plaintiff, the petition should state that the address is unknown after diligent inquiry by the affiant, and that the affiant believes it is unknown to the plaintiff after diligent inquiry. Miss. R. Civ. P. 4(c)(4)(A).

[112] Miss. R. Civ. P. 4(c)(4)(B).

PROCEDURE   **§ 19.03[2][d]**

of the county in which the action is pending.[113] Service by publication in a custody matter is improper if the petitioner misrepresented his or her inability to locate the defendant.[114]

If a defendant is served by publication, the court may adjudicate marital status and custody, and may determine the disposition of property located within the state. The court may not award alimony, child support, or divide property not located within the state.[115] A court properly granted divorce and reserved jurisdiction to determine financial matters when service of process on a nonresident husband was by publication and mailing a copy to his last known address. Service through certified mail, return receipt requested, would have provided jurisdiction to award alimony and child support.[116] Similarly, a court did not have personal jurisdiction to order payment of child support by a resident defendant served by publication.[117]

[d] Service on mentally incompetent party. If a defendant is mentally incompetent but not institutionalized, or is unable to manage his or her estate "by reason of advanced age, physical incapacity or mental weakness," service should be made on both the defendant and a caretaker.[118] If the incompetent party is institutionalized by judicial order, service should be made on the party and the guardian, unless the superintendent of the institution certifies that the party is mentally incapable of responding to process. If the confined party has no guardian or conservator, the court should appoint a guardian ad litem.[119]

[e] Waiver of process. Rule 4(e) of the Rules of Civil Procedure provides that a defendant may waive service and enter an appearance through a sworn or acknowledged writing dated and signed by the defendant. The waiver must be executed after the date on which the complaint was filed.[120] A wife's motion to set aside a judgment of divorce entered eight months earlier should have been granted for failure to comply with the statute; the waiver was signed on the day of filing and post-dated for the following day.[121]

[3] Inadequate process or service of process. A court does not have jurisdiction over a defendant unless the requirements for service of process have been strictly followed. The contents of the summons, the complaint for service by publication, the

---

[113] Miss. R. Civ. P. 4(c)(4)(B). If there is no newspaper in the county, notice should be posted at the courthouse door and also published in the newspaper of an adjoining county or of the state capital. Miss. R. Civ. P. 4(c)(4)(B).

[114] C.M. v. R.D.H., 947 So. 2d 1023, 1028 (Miss. Ct. App. 2007) (mother alleged inability to locate even though she knew that her mother had been in touch with defendant; the court suggested that order could be set aside under Rule 60(b) more than one year after judgment).

[115] O'Neill v. O'Neill, 515 So. 2d 1208, 1211 (Miss. 1987) (adjudication of other matters requires personal service or general appearance).

[116] Noble v. Noble, 502 So. 2d 317, 320 (Miss. 1987).

[117] Johnson v. Johnson, 191 So. 2d 840, 842 (Miss. 1996); *see also* Hamm v. Hall, 693 So. 2d 906, 908-09 (Miss. 1997) (payment of child support pursuant to an invalid decree did not constitute a waiver).

[118] Miss. R. Civ. P. 4(d)(2)(B).

[119] Miss. R. Civ. P. 4(d)(2)(C).

[120] Miss. R. Civ. P. 4(e); *see also* Rogers v. Rogers, 290 So. 2d 631, 634 (Miss. 1974) (decree void; wife incompetent at time of signing waiver).

[121] Peterson v. Peterson, 648 So. 2d 54 (Miss. 1994).

§ 19.03[4]   MISSISSIPPI FAMILY LAW

necessary attachments, and the method of service must strictly conform to the statute.[122] For example, a divorce rendered against a North Carolina defendant was void for lack of jurisdiction; notice was published but no copy mailed to the provided physical address as required by Rule 4(c).[123] Similarly, service was ineffective when a complainant provided only the absent defendant's post office address, and did not allege that "after diligent search and inquiry" the street address could not be ascertained.[124]

Actual notice of the proceedings is not sufficient to cure defective service of process.[125] A judgment based on inadequate process or service of process is void unless the defect is waived by the defendant. The defect may be attacked collaterally and is not waived by failure to appear.[126] When a defendant claims lack of service, the burden is on the plaintiff to prove service by filing a return acknowledgment, affidavit of service, or return receipt for a certified letter. In the absence of proof of service, the presumption of jurisdiction is rebutted and the court lacks personal jurisdiction over the matter.[127]

[4] Preserving objections to process. A court may not exercise jurisdiction over a defendant who has not been properly served with process.[128] However, the defense is waived if a defendant appears in an action without raising the objection in the initial pleadings or attached motions.[129] Objections may be made through a Rule 12(b) motion to dismiss prior to filing an answer or by raising the defense in the answer.[130] Although a defendant in a Rule 81 action need not file a responsive pleading, a general appearance without objecting to jurisdiction is a waiver of that objection.[131] However, contact with a court administrator to discuss a date for a hearing was not a waiver of defective service of process.[132]

---

[122] Caldwell v. Caldwell, 533 So. 2d 413 (Miss. 1988) (plaintiff's counsel's failure to make diligent inquiry regarding address of wife invalidates service of process).

[123] Kolikas v. Kolikas, 821 So. 2d 874, 880 (Miss. Ct. App. 2002) (also resulting in husband's subsequent, bigamous marriage).

[124] McDuff v. McDuff, 173 So. 2d 419, 423-24 (Miss. 1965).

[125] See Brown v. Riley, 580 So. 2d 1234, 1237 (Miss. 1991) (citing Mosby v. Gandy, 375 So. 2d 1024 (Miss. 1979)).

[126] Johnson v. Johnson, 191 So. 2d 840, 842 (Miss. 1966) (Mississippi defendant not personally served in child support action); Kolikas v. Kolikas, 821 So. 2d 874, 880 (Miss. Ct. App. 2002) (divorce void for failure to mail copy of published summons to physical address) (finding wife not estopped from attacking validity of decree).

[127] Morrison v. Dep't of Human Servs., 863 So. 2d 948, 952-53 (Miss. 2004).

[128] Kolikas v. Kolikas, 821 So. 2d 874, 878 (Miss. Ct. App. 2002); see also Clark v. Clark, 43 So. 3d 496, 501 (Miss. Ct. App. 2010); cert. denied, 49 So. 3d 106 (Miss. 2010).

[129] Chasez v. Chasez, 957 So. 2d 1031, 1037 (Miss. Ct. App. 2007) (defects in service waived by pro se litigant's appearance without objection); Venegas v. Gurganus, 911 So. 2d 562 (Miss. Ct. App. 2005) (defects in service of process waived by failure to assert at trial).

[130] See Miss. R. Civ. P. 12(b)(4) (objection to adequacy of summons); Miss. R. Civ. P. 12(b)(4) 12(b)(5) (objection to adequacy of service).

[131] See Isom v. Jernigan, 840 So. 2d 104 (Miss. 2003) (defendant was properly before the court; her attorney appeared and presented evidence on her behalf without objecting to process); Dennis v. Dennis, 824 So. 2d 604 (Miss. 2002) (defendant waived his procedural rights by appearing voluntarily at the hearing and defending, without objecting to service of process); Saddler v. Saddler, 556 So. 2d 344, 345-46 (Miss. 1990); Reichert v. Reichert, 807 So. 2d 1282 (Miss. Ct. App. 2002); Sanghi v. Sanghi, 759 So. 2d 1250, 1255 (Miss. Ct. App. 2000).

[132] Sanghi v. Sanghi, 759 So. 2d 1250, 1255 (Miss. Ct. App. 2000); cf. Hamm v. Hall, 693 So. 2d 906, 908-09 (Miss. 1997) (payment of child support pursuant to an invalid decree did not constitute a waiver).

PROCEDURE   § 19.04

§ 19.04 PRE-TRIAL PROCEEDINGS

[1] Temporary orders. Chancellors have authority to provide for temporary custody of children and temporary financial support in family law matters.[133] In addition, courts may order parties to refrain from disposing of property or enter restraining orders during the pendency of proceedings. For example, a court entered a temporary order granting custody of children to a wife and ordering her husband to pay temporary alimony and child support, to make mortgage payments, to continue medical insurance for his wife and children, and restraining him from transferring assets.[134]

Courts may also restrain the parties from discussing the litigation with their children and restrain a spouse from having children in the presence of a romantic partner during the litigation.[135] Under some circumstances, a court may enter an ex parte temporary order of custody.[136]

A request for temporary support is a Rule 81 matter triable seven days after service of process or thirty days after service by publication.[137] Rule 81 provides that in temporary hearings in pending divorce, custody, or support actions, Rule 5(b) notice – notice on a party's attorney – is sufficient if the defendant has been served in the action.[138] However, some attorneys and judges question whether this provision applies if a request for temporary relief was not included in the complaint. Furthermore, some judges require service of both a Rule 4 and Rule 81 summons when a complaint requests temporary relief.

Temporary orders are enforceable by contempt.[139] The duty to pay temporary support terminates upon final judgment,[140] but a judgment does not extinguish arrearages of temporary support.[141] A chancellor erred in reinstating a wife's temporary support pending her appeal of the couple's divorce action – temporary support ends with the grant of divorce.[142] A temporary order is not a final judgment and is not an appealable order.[143]

---

[133] MISS. CODE ANN. § 93-5-17 (2004).

[134] *See* Langdon v. Langdon, 854 So. 2d 485, 487 (Miss. Ct. App. 2003); *see also* Rush v. Rush *ex rel.* Mayne, 914 So. 2d 322, 324 (Miss. Ct. App. 2005) (en banc) (court entered temporary order to prevent husband's sale of assets pending divorce; wife filed lis pendens notice to prevent third party from exercising option to purchase marital property). For discussion of temporary alimony, see *supra* § 9.01[5][b], for temporary custody, see *supra* § 12.01[8], and for temporary child support, see *supra* § 13.01[2][c].

[135] Burrus v. Burrus, 962 So.2d 618, 625-26 (Miss. Ct. App. 2006) (restraining wife from having children in presence of boyfriend).

[136] *See* discussion *supra* § 12.01[8][9].

[137] *See* discussion of Rule 81 *infra* § 19.11.

[138] MISS. R. CIV. P. 81(d)(6); *see* Allen v. Williams, 914 So. 2d 254, 259 (Miss. Ct. App. 2005) (proper to serve Rule 81 petition on defendant's attorney to notice contempt hearing during pendency of modification action).

[139] Langdon v. Langdon, 854 So. 2d 485, 496 (Miss. Ct. App. 2003).

[140] *See* Bond v. Bond, 355 So. 2d 672, 674-75 (Miss. 1978). In an unusual case, a chancellor denied a wife's petition for separate maintenance but awarded her temporary support, even though no divorce action was pending. The issue was not appealed. Miley v. Daniel, 37 So. 3d 84, 86 (Miss. Ct. App. 2009), *cert. denied*, 36 So. 3d 455 (Miss. 2010); *cf.* Clark v. Clark, 43 So. 3d 496, *cert. denied*, 43 So. 3d 496, 502-503 (Miss. Ct. App. 2010) (divorce based on service under Rule 81 set aside for lack of jurisdiction, but temporary support allowed to stand).

[141] *See* Lewis v. Lewis, 586 So. 2d 740, 742 (Miss. 1991).

[142] McIntosh v. McIntosh, 977 So. 2d 1257, 1272-73 (Miss. Ct. App. 2008).

[143] MacDonald v. MacDonald, 876 So. 2d 296, 298 (Miss. 2004) (no jurisdiction to hear appeal of temporary custody order).

599

§ 19.04[2]   MISSISSIPPI FAMILY LAW

[2] Discovery. The rules of discovery apply in family law matters governed by Title 93.[144] The statutes governing divorce provide that a defendant is entitled to discover "any matter, not privileged, which is relevant to the issues raised."[145] Appellate courts have enforced the rules of discovery in family law cases as in other civil actions. For example, in a divorce case based on habitual drug use, a chancellor erred in allowing a wife to testify with regard to information that should have been provided as a supplement to discovery.[146] And, the supreme court reversed a chancellor's ruling limiting a wife's discovery to depositions; she was entitled to production of corporate documents related to "loans" to her husband. The court noted that "in contentious proceedings involving complex finances of such great magnitude, it is not sufficient to simply tell one party to rely on the self-interested assertions of their opponent and his witnesses."[147]

The rules regarding failure to respond to requests for admissions apply in family law actions. However, a chancellor properly refused to decide custody based on a mother's failure to respond to requests for admissions. The court of appeals rejected her argument that admissions may not relate to the ultimate issue in a case, but held that "no right-minded chancellor" would allow custody to be decided solely on the basis of a failure to respond to admissions requests.[148] Similarly, the court of appeals rejected a wife's argument that her husband's failure to respond to a request for admissions established habitual, cruel, and inhuman treatment as a matter of law. The court did deem the matters admitted, but they did not go to the ultimate issue in the case.[149]

A chancellor has considerable latitude in determining whether to impose sanctions for a party's conduct in regard to discovery.[150] However, the supreme court held that a chancellor erred in failing to impose sanctions against a wife for lying about the beginning date of an affair and for destroying evidence requested in discovery. The court stated that her conduct in resisting discovery "must not go unpunished." Courts must "consider sanctions that are severe enough to deter others."[151]

---

[144] *See* Miss. Code Ann. § 93-5-19 (2004) ("depositions may be taken . . . as in other cases").

[145] Miss. Code Ann. § 93-5-7 (2004).

[146] *See* Ladner v. Ladner, 436 So. 2d 1366, 1370 (Miss. 1983) (but holding that error was not reversible; other testimony adequate to support divorce); *see also* Klink v. Brewster, 986 So. 2d 1060, 1064-65 (Miss. Ct. App. 2008) (chancellor did not err in excluding witnesses where party did not provides list of witnesses until two days before trial); Pool v. Pool, 989 So. 2d 920, 924-25 (Miss. Ct. App. 2008) (chancellor properly denied last-minute motion to compel discovery, when documents had been available for inspection for a year).

[147] West v. West, 891 So. 2d 203, 218 (Miss. 2004).

[148] Gilcrease v. Gilcrease, 918 So. 2d 854, 858-59 (Miss. Ct. App. 2005) (mother should have filed motion asking chancellor to withdraw admission); *see also In re* Dissolution of Marriage of Leverock and Hamby, 23 So. 3d 424, 433 (Miss. 2009) (chancellor erred in refusing to deem requests for admission admitted; however, admissions that go to the heart of custody cannot be dispositive of the issue); Cockrell v. Watkins, 936 So. 2d 970, 972 (Miss. Ct. App. 2006) (when father failed to respond to request to admit that he was not a fit parent, chancellor properly treated the matter as admitted without allowing the admission to be dispositive of the case).

[149] Kumar v. Kumar, 976 So. 2d 957, 963-64 (Miss. Ct. App. 2008) (matters deemed admitted, but did not go to ultimate issue).

[150] Jones v. Jones, 995 So. 2d 706, 711 (Miss. 2008) (appellate court reviews chancellor's decisions regarding discovery for abuse of discretion).

[151] Jones v. Jones, 995 So. 2d 706, 710 (Miss. 2008) (wife took chisel and hatchet, hacked up a computer, put the pieces in a metal box, poured gas over the box and burned it, put the remains in a plastic bag and dumped it in a bayou).

PROCEDURE

§ 19.04[3]

[3] Continuances. In divorce proceedings, a chancellor is authorized to continue a case even though the parties have not complied with the requirements for obtaining a continuance in other civil actions.[152] The grant or denial of a continuance is within the trial court's discretion and will not be reversed in the absence of manifest injustice.[153] However, a per se rule that continuances will not be granted in contempt matters was reversible error – an attorney's prior trial commitment should have been considered as a reason for continuance.[154] In Rule 81 matters, continuances must be granted by an order entered on the date originally set for hearing, or new process must issue.[155]

[4] Motions

[a] Motion to recuse. A judge may not preside over a case involving parties to whom he or she is related, a case in which the judge has an interest, or a case in which the judge has served as counsel, except with the consent of the parties.[156] In addition, a judge may be disqualified from hearing a case if "a reasonable person, knowing all the circumstances, would harbor doubts about his impartiality."[157] A chancellor should have recused herself from hearing a contempt matter against an attorney because the contempt proceeding was initiated by the chancellor rather than by a party or the guardian ad litem.[158] Judges are presumed to be impartial; a judge's denial of a recusal motion will be reversed only if there has been a manifest abuse of discretion.[159] A judge

---

[152] MISS. CODE ANN. § 93-5-7 (2004); *see* Stuart v. Stuart, 956 So. 2d 295, 300 (Miss. Ct. App. 2006) (rejecting husband's argument that he was denied due process because of delays; continuances were justifiable; right to speedy trial applies only to criminal defendants). *But cf. In re* Profilet, 826 So. 2d 91 (Miss. 2002) (court did not err in refusing continuance to attorney who requested continuance three days prior to trial; also procedurally barred).

[153] Irby v. Estate of Irby, 7 So. 3d 223, 228-30 (Miss. 2009) (chancellor did not err in refusing to grant a continuance to allow a wife to introduce 1700 pages of documents produced two days before trial, with no explanation for delay); J.C.N.F. v. Stone County Dep't Human Serv., 996 So. 2d 762, 772 (Miss. 2008) (court did not err in denying continuance in termination hearing; mother had five months to obtain an attorney); Rogers v. Rogers, 290 So. 2d 631, 634 (Miss. 1974) (chancellor did not err in denying continuance); Sullivan v. Sullivan, 43 So. 3d 536, 539 (Miss. Ct. App. 2010) (chancellor did not err in denying continuance requested by husband on morning of trial, three weeks after his attorney was dismissed); Pace v. Pace, 16 So. 3d 734, 740 (Miss. Ct. App. 2009) (continuance properly denied to husband who provided no verification that he was required to take a family member to the hospital); Bougard v. Bougard, 991 So. 2d 646, 649 (Miss. Ct. App. 2008) (chancellor did not err in denying husband's motion to continue temporary support hearing; he had forty-three days to secure counsel); Carroll v. Carroll, 976 So. 2d 880, 885-86 (Miss. Ct. App. 2007) (court did not err in refusing to grant continuance when husband's attorney withdrew six weeks prior to trial); Henderson v. Henderson, 952 So. 2d 273, 277 (Miss. Ct. App. 2006) (en banc) (court did not err in refusing to grant husband's three requests for continuances; suit was pending for over a year and he changed attorneys four times); *cf.* J.N.W.E. v. W.D.W., 922 So. 2d 12, 18-19 (Miss. Ct. App. 2005) (en banc) (mother's action for custody modification was dismissed with prejudice one year after petition was filed, when she failed to obtain new attorney within ten days of her attorney's removal for conflict).

[154] Leonard v. Leonard, 486 So. 2d 1240, 1241-42 (Miss. 1986); *cf.* Cannon v. Cannon, 571 So. 2d 976, 980 (Miss. 1990) (court erred in holding trial in absence of defendant and attorney when attorney had prior trial setting; not justified by fact that attorney's notice was one day prior to trial).

[155] *See infra* § 19.11[5].

[156] MISS. CONST. art. 6, § 165; *see* MISS. CODE ANN. § 9-1-11 (2006).

[157] J.N.W.E. v. W.D.W., 922 So. 2d 12, 14 (Miss. Ct. App. 2005) (en banc).

[158] *In re* Spencer, 985 So. 2d 330, 344 (Miss. 2008).

[159] Henderson v. Henderson, 952 So. 2d 273, 278 (Miss. Ct. App. 2006) (en banc); J.N.W.E. v. W.D.W., 922 So. 2d 12, 14-15 (Miss. Ct. App. 2005) (en banc) (appellant presented no evidence of court's allegedly biased statements); *see also* Shelnut v. Dep't of Human Servs., 9 So. 3d 359, 368 (Miss. 2009) (judge's description of defendant's testimony as self-serving did not exhibit bias). *But cf.* Schmidt v. Bermudez, 5 So. 3d 1064, 1074 (Miss. 2009) (en banc) (chancellor's conduct toward a mother in a custody modification hearing was "so combative, antagonistic, discourteous, and adversarial" that "no reasonable person" would conclude that she was afforded a fair trial).

§ 19.04[4][b]   **MISSISSIPPI FAMILY LAW**

must rule on a motion for recusal within thirty days.[160] Denial of the motion must be appealed within fourteen days after the thirty days for ruling expires.[161]

[b] Motion for summary judgment. Summary judgment is rarely granted in family law matters, since most matters involve issues of fact. For example, a court erred in granting partial summary judgment to a defendant husband on his wife's claim of adultery – she presented an affidavit disputing his claim that she condoned the adultery.[162] In contrast, summary judgment was appropriate to deny a mother's claim for child support arrearages from a father whose parental rights were terminated eighteen years earlier. As a matter of law, his obligation to pay child support ended when his parental rights were terminated.[163]

[c] Dismissal under Rule 41(b). Under Rule 41(b) of the Mississippi Rules of Civil Procedure, a chancellor may grant a defendant's motion to dismiss for failure to prove a right to relief at the close of the plaintiff's case. A chancellor did not err in dismissing a mother's modification petition at the conclusion of her evidence, finding that she had not proven a material change in circumstances. The court of appeals noted that under Rule 41(b), a chancellor sitting without a jury does not have to consider the evidence in the light most favorable to the plaintiff or give her the benefit of reasonable inferences in order to dismiss.[164]

§ 19.05 TRIAL

[1] Proceedings. Title 93 provides that proceedings for divorce must be held in open court.[165] However, courts have discretion to exclude persons other than the court, attorneys, parties, and testifying witness.[166] Parties can execute a knowing and intelligent waiver of the rights inherent in a hearing. The supreme court rejected a wife's argument that a hearing should have been conducted even though she agreed to forego the hearing.[167] In a case involving a prison inmate, the court of appeals noted that there is no statutory requirement that parties appear in a fault-based divorce.[168] In contrast, an attorney may not disregard a court order setting a matter for hearing. An attorney's failure to appear at a court hearing, even at the client's direction, is punishable as contempt of court.[169]

---

[160] UNIF. CHANC. R. 1.11.

[161] MISS. R. APP. P. 48; *see* Parks v. Parks, 914 So. 2d 337, 342 (Miss. Ct. App. 2005) (en banc).

[162] Lawrence v. Lawrence, 956 So. 2d 251, 256-57 (Miss. Ct. App. 2006) (summary judgment may be granted if the pleadings and depositions "on file" establish no genuine issue of material fact).

[163] Beasnett v. Arledge, 934 So. 2d 345, 347 (Miss. Ct. App. 2006).

[164] Gilliland v. Gilliland, 984 So. 2d 364, 366 (Miss. Ct. App. 2008).

[165] MISS. CODE ANN. § 93-5-17 (2004); *see* Luse v. Luse, 992 So. 2d 659, 663 (Miss. Ct. App. 2008). *But cf.* Ory v. Ory, 936 So. 2d 405, 410 (Miss. Ct. App. 2006) (en banc) (even if divorce not rendered in open court, issue was not raised at trial and could not be considered on appeal).

[166] MISS. CODE ANN. § 93-5-21 (2004).

[167] Louk v. Louk, 761 So. 2d 878, 884-85 (Miss. 2000); *see also* Duncan v. Duncan, 915 So. 2d 1124, 1126 (Miss. Ct. App. 2005) (en banc) (parties agreed to submit evidence of contribution to marital home to chancellor in form of documentation, receipts, and affidavits).

[168] Fisher v. Fisher, 944 So. 2d 134, 137 (Miss. Ct. App. 2006) (inmate entitled to divorce based on deposition testimony).

[169] *In re* Hampton, 919 So. 2d 949, 954 (Miss. 2006); *see also In re* Spencer, 985 So. 2d 330, 340-42 (Miss. 2008)

PROCEDURE

§ 19.05[2]

[2] No default; requirement of proof. No divorce may be taken by default.[170] Rule 55 of the Mississippi Rules of Civil Procedure prohibits judgment in a divorce action "unless the claimant establishes his claim or rights to relief by evidence."[171] Even if a defendant fails to answer and defend a suit, the plaintiff must prove the elements of the case to the court's satisfaction.[172] For example, a wife whose husband failed to appear was required to provide proof of habitual, cruel, and inhuman treatment.[173] Similarly, in Rule 81 matters, petitions "shall not be taken as confessed."[174] However, the court of appeals has held that in uncontested proceedings a chancellor may dispense with financial statements and *Ferguson* findings of fact. Nor is there a requirement of a transcript in an uncontested proceeding.[175]

A joint complaint of husband and wife for divorce solely on the ground of irreconcilable differences is taken as proved and judgment may be entered without proof or testimony regarding divorce.[176] The procedures for divorce based on irreconcilable differences are set out in detail in Chapter IV.[177]

[3] Limits on testimony. Courts have authority under Rule 611 of the rules of evidence to limit the time for trial in a manner that does not infringe on the litigants' rights to a full hearing on the issues.[178] A court's limitation of time will not be reversed unless the complaining party can demonstrate harm. For example, a court did not err in limiting a divorce trial to one day; the complaining husband offered no proof to show that he was adversely affected by the ruling.[179] However, a court erred in refusing to allow a defendant in a contempt proceeding to present any of his witnesses or testimony – parties are entitled to a full and complete hearing, with an opportunity to be heard and to call witnesses.[180]

[4] Stipulations. Stipulations made by the parties at trial may be set aside based on material mistake of fact, misrepresentation, or inadvertence. The court of appeals rejected a husband's argument that a chancellor should have enforced a stipulation that the parties would divide the husband's stock in a family corporation as part of property

---

(court did not err in holding attorney in contempt for failure to appear at a hearing, even though the attorney's failure to appear was not "willful").

[170] Miss. Code Ann. § 93-5-7 (2004).

[171] Miss. R. Civ. P. 55; *see* Miss. Code Ann. § 93-5-17 (2004).

[172] *See* Lindsey v. Lindsey, 818 So. 2d 1191, 1194 (Miss. 2002); Rawson v. Buta, 609 So. 2d 426, 430-31 (Miss. 1992) (complainant's proof requirement does not become lighter because the defendant fails to answer); Luse v. Luse, 992 So. 2d 659, 661 (Miss. Ct. App. 2008).

[173] *See* Mayoza v. Mayoza, 526 So. 2d 547, 549 (Miss. 1988).

[174] Miss. R. Civ. P. 81(d)(3).

[175] Luse v. Luse, 992 So. 2d 659, 662 (Miss. Ct. App. 2008).

[176] Miss. Code Ann. § 93-5-2(4) (2004) (also applicable if defendant has been personally served or entered appearance by waiver of process).

[177] *See supra* § 4.04.

[178] *See* Miss. R. Evid. 611 (court should exercise control over presentation of witnesses to ascertain truth and to avoid unnecessary consumption of time).

[179] Moore v. Moore, 757 So. 2d 1043, 1047 (Miss. Ct. App. 2000).

[180] Weeks v. Weeks, 556 So. 2d 348, 349 (Miss. 1990). *But cf.* Wilburn v. Wilburn, 991 So. 2d 1185 (Miss. 2008) (mother did not offer to present witnesses, provide offer of proof, or object that she was denied right to present witnesses); Klink v. Brewster, 986 So. 2d 1060 (Miss. Ct. App. 2008) (chancellor did not err in excluding witnesses where party did not provide list of witnesses until two days before trial).

§ 19.06   **MISSISSIPPI FAMILY LAW**

division. The parties later learned that he did not have authority to transfer the stock. The stipulation was unenforceable and was therefore invalid.[181]

§ 19.06 EVIDENCE

The Mississippi Rules of Evidence apply in domestic relations cases as in other civil actions. This section highlights issues that arise frequently in family law matters. Evidentiary issues regarding the testimony of children and introduction of medical and psychological records are discussed below. Evidentiary issues related to valuation of assets and businesses are discussed in Chapters VI and VIII.[182] Admissibility of electronic mail and recorded telephone conversations are discussed in Chapter XX.[183] The sufficiency of the evidence with regard to a particular claim or issue is discussed in the chapter related to that issue.

[1] Testimony of children. There is no per se rule prohibiting the testimony of a child in a divorce or custody action. The Mississippi Supreme Court has encouraged parties and attorneys to refrain from calling children as witnesses except in exigent cases, but has noted that parents cannot be precluded from doing so. A court may exclude a child's testimony only on the basis of lack of competency, evidentiary defects, or for the child's protection. The supreme court has instructed chancellors to hold an in-camera interview with the child to determine whether the child is competent to testify, the evidence is relevant and competent, and the child's best interests will be served by allowing the testimony.[184] The court of appeals held that a chancellor erred in excluding the testimony of older children in a mother's suit to modify custody based on their expressed preference to live with her.[185]

Under some circumstances, witnesses may be allowed to testify regarding a child's out-of-court statements to them. In addition, a child's testimony regarding sexual abuse may be offered through closed-circuit television in some cases.

[a] Tender years exception. The tender years exception to the hearsay rule provides that statements made by a child of tender years describing sexual contact are admissible if: (a) the court finds that "the time, content, and circumstances of the statement provide substantial indicia of reliability;" and (b) the child testifies or is deemed unavailable as a witness. Under Rule 804(a)(6), a child is deemed unavailable if there is a substantial likelihood that testifying would impair the child's emotional or

---

[181] Seymour v. Seymour, 960 So. 2d 513, 518 (Miss. Ct. App. 2006).

[182] *See supra* § 6.07 (evidence of asset value) and § 8.04 (valuation of businesses).

[183] *See infra* § 20.09.

[184] Jethrow v. Jethrow, 571 So. 2d 270, 274 (Miss. 1990) (also noting that essential matters should be placed on record and that court should make findings regarding decision); *see* Brent v. State, 632 So. 2d 936, 942 (Miss. 1994) (en banc) (A trial judge should determine "that the child has ability to perceive and remember events, to understand and answer questions intelligently and to comprehend and accept the importance of truthfulness.") (quoting Mohr v. State, 584 So. 2d 426, 431 (Miss. 1991)); Frei v. State, 934 So. 2d 318, 322 (Miss. Ct. App. 2006) (en banc) (court did not err in admitting four-year-old's testimony regarding sexual abuse; court conducted a competency hearing, determined that she remembered the incident and knew the importance of telling the truth). In light of *Robison v. Lanford*, 841 So. 2d 1119 (Miss. 2003), it may be necessary for a court reporter to record the interview. *See infra* § 19.06[1][f].

[185] Anderson v. Anderson, 961 So. 2d 55, 60 (Miss. Ct. App. 2007).

604

PROCEDURE § 19.06[1][b]

psychological health.[186] If the testimony is offered by a third party because the child is deemed unavailable, there must be corroborating evidence of the act.[187]

To prove unavailability, a proponent must show that testimony would traumatize a child, that the trauma would exceed "mere nervousness," and that no less traumatic means of testimony are available. A court erred in admitting a child's statements to a social worker when the proponent failed to show that there were no alternatives to admission such as testimony before closed-circuit television.[188] However, a three-year-old girl's statements to a social worker were admissible under the tender years exception, based on the court's finding that her statements were sufficiently reliable. The court noted that children under twelve are presumed to be "of tender years."[189]

[b] Statement for purpose of medical diagnosis. Rule 803(4) of the Rules of Evidence permits admission of out-of-court statements "made for purposes of medical diagnosis or treatment," including statements regarding medical history, symptoms, pain, and sensation. The exception also applies to statements regarding the cause of a condition if "reasonably pertinent" to the diagnosis and treatment.[190] A three-year-old child's statements to a court-appointed psychologist regarding abuse were admissible under this exception; the statements were used by the doctor in his diagnosis and treatment.[191]

[c] Other hearsay exceptions. Testimony regarding a child's out-of-court statements have also been admitted in family law actions under the present sense impression,[192] excited utterance,[193] and existing mental, emotional, or physical condition[194] exceptions to the hearsay rule. For example, the Mississippi Supreme Court required admission of a wife's testimony regarding her six-year-old daughter's statements about her fear of her father and related stomach pains. The testimony was

---

[186] MISS. R. EVID. 804(a)(6).

[187] MISS. R. EVID. 803(25).

[188] J.L.W.W. v. Clarke County Dep't Human Servs., 759 So. 2d 1183, 1186 (Miss. 2000) (proponent has burden of proving child is unavailable, including a showing that closed-circuit television testimony is not an option) (citing Griffith v. State, 584 So. 2d 383, 387 (Miss. 1991)); *cf.* C.A.M.F. v. J.B.M., 972 So. 2d 656, 662 (Miss. Ct. App. 2007) (error to admit testimony about child's statement with no discussion of unavailability).

[189] B.R.C. v. State, 795 So. 2d 526, 529 (Miss. 2001) (reviewing factors set out in comments to Rule 803(25)); *cf.* McGowan v. State, 742 So. 2d 1183, 1186 (Miss. Ct. App. 1999) (tender years judged by child's age at time of incident); *see also* Hobgood v. State, 926 So. 2d 847, 851-52 (Miss. 2006) (en banc) (court properly admitted testimony of a mother, babysitter, social worker, psychologist, and physician regarding a four-year-old boy's statements about sexual abuse by his mother's boyfriend; psychologist testified that the child would be re-traumatized and his mental health impaired if he was required to testify); Frei v. State, 934 So. 2d 318, 322-23 (Miss. Ct. App. 2006) (en banc) (court properly admitted testimony of a social worker and forensic interviewer regarding child's hearsay statements; shown to have sufficient indicia of reliability under MISS. R. EVID. 803(25)); E.J.M. v. A.J.M, 846 So. 2d 289, 295 (Miss. Ct. App. 2003) (chancellor did not err in allowing expert witnesses to testify about child's credibility regarding out-of-court statements). Most of the cases interpreting the tender years exception are criminal cases. See cases cited in the annotations to MISS. R. EVID. 803(25), 804(a)(6).

[190] MISS. R. EVID 803(4) (court must find statements trustworthy).

[191] B.R.C. v. State, 795 So. 2d 526, 530 (Miss. 2001) (noting two-part test for admission: "(1) the declarant's motive in making the statement must be consistent with purposes of promoting treatment; and, (2) the content of the statement must be such as is reasonably relied on by the physician").

[192] MISS. R. EVID. 803(1).

[193] MISS. R. EVID. 803(2).

[194] MISS. R. EVID. 803(3).

§ 19.06[1][d]   **MISSISSIPPI FAMILY LAW**

admissible under all three exceptions because the statements were made as the stomach pain and fear occurred.[195] A boy's statement to his grandmother, as he ran from his house to her car, that his stepfather was choking his mother, was properly admitted as an excited utterance.[196] In contrast, statements made to family members regarding incidents several days earlier were not admissible under the present sense impression and excited utterance exceptions.[197]

[d] Testimonial statements. Admission of a child's "testimonial" statements – statements given in connection with prosecution – is error. A court erred in admitting the testimony of investigating police officers regarding a boy's statements about abuse. However, his statements to his mother, babysitter, social worker, and doctors for the purpose of treatment and not prosecution were admissible.[198]

[e] Testimony through closed-circuit television. Testimony of a child under the age of sixteen regarding a sexual offense may be taken and shown by closed-circuit television upon motion of any party or the court. The court must find that there is a substantial likelihood that the victim will "suffer traumatic emotional or mental distress" as a result of testifying in open court.[199]

[f] In-chambers interview with child. Chancellors may conduct an in-chambers interview with a child in actions related to custody. The Mississippi Supreme Court held in 2003 that an in-chamber interview must be recorded by a court reporter who is physically present during the interview. The court has discretion to order the transcription sealed.[200]

[2] Expert testimony. Expert testimony in family law cases must meet the requirements of Rule 702 of the Mississippi Rules of Evidence and the standards set out by the United States Supreme Court in *Daubert v. Merrell Dow Pharmecueticals*. Rule 702 provides that expert testimony may be admitted if the evidence will assist the trier of fact, the witness is qualified as an expert, and the opinion is based upon "sufficient facts or data," is "the product of reliable principles and methods" and the witness "has applied the principles and methods reliably."[201] The *Daubert* factors for determining reliability include: whether the theory can or has been tested, whether it is subject to peer review, whether there is a high possibility of error, whether there are standards that govern the techniques used, and whether the theory or technique is generally

---

[195] Holladay v. Holladay, 776 So. 2d 662, 675 (Miss. 2000). *But see* Limbaugh v. Limbaugh, 749 So. 2d 1244, 1247-48 (Miss. Ct. App. 1999) (father's testimony regarding child's statement about mother's conduct was inadmissible hearsay; but held harmless error because not a determining factor in custody decision).

[196] C.A.M.F. v. J.B.M., 972 So. 2d 656, 664 (Miss. Ct. App. 2007).

[197] *In re* C.B., 574 So. 2d 1369, 1372 (Miss. 1990); *see also* Mayfield v. Mayfield, 956 So.2d 337, 348 (Miss. Ct. App. 2007) (child's statement did not qualify under excited utterance exception because made in response to questioning).

[198] Hobgood v. State, 926 So. 2d 847, 852 (Miss. 2006) (en banc).

[199] Miss. R. Evid. 617.

[200] Robison v. Lanford, 841 So. 2d 1119, 1125 (Miss. 2003) (may be unsealed for appellate review).

[201] Miss. R. Evid. 702.

606

PROCEDURE § 19.06[3]

accepted by the relevant scientific community.[202]

In a 2007 case, the Mississippi Supreme Court reversed a custody judgment based on expert testimony that did not satisfy these requirements. A social worker testified that her training consisted of five weeks of training and one year of working with children; that she had done five or six interviews for custody actions; and that her conclusions were not based on science, but largely on instinct and training. Her conclusions were based on unrecorded interviews with the child, for which she had no notes.[203] In contrast, a counselor with a Master's Degree in counseling and special training in marriage and family therapy was properly allowed to testify regarding impact of the marriage on the wife's physical and mental health.[204]

[3] Medical testimony: Physician/patient privilege. Parents' and children's physical and mental states may be relevant in actions for divorce, custody, adoption, termination of parental rights, and visitation. Parties may seek to introduce testimony of professionals such as physicians, psychologists, or marriage counselors, raising questions of privilege. In addition, courts may order mental or physical examinations of one or both parties or a child.

[a] Scope of privilege. Rule 503 of the Mississippi Rules of Evidence provides that a patient may prevent disclosure of confidential communications to a physician or psychotherapist regarding treatment.[205] The Rule 503 privilege is limited to physicians, psychotherapists and persons under their direction.[206] The privilege includes "confidential communications made for the purpose of diagnosis or treatment . . . among himself . . . and persons who are participating in the diagnosis or treatment under the direction of the physician or psychotherapist, including members of the patient's family."[207] The extent to which the testimony of other therapists may be admitted has not been clearly addressed. For example, the statutes governing marriage and family therapists provide that a therapist who has counseled both spouses may not testify in an alimony, custody, or divorce action.[208] However, the Mississippi Supreme Court noted in dicta that this statute potentially conflicts with the rules of evidence. Rule 1103 repeals all statutes inconsistent with the rules of evidence.[209]

---

[202] Daubert v. Merrell Dow Pharm., Inc., 509 U.S. 579, 593 (1993).

[203] Giannaris v. Giannaris, 960 So. 2d 462, 470-71 (Miss. 2007); *see also* Minter v. Minter, 29 So. 3d 840, 852-53 (Miss. Ct. App. 2009), *cert. denied*, 29 So. 3d 774 (Miss. 2010) (court-appointed expert properly allowed to testify; he was qualified and testified regarding the procedures and diagnostic techniques he used); *cf.* DeVito v. DeVito, 967 So. 2d 74, 76 (Miss. Ct. App. 2007) (chancellor properly refused to consider a wife's allegations regarding the husband's use of pornography; proper procedures were not used to allow the experts to identify the user responsible for the images).

[204] Jones v. Jones, 43 So. 3d 465, 484 (Miss. Ct. App. 2009) (noting that the Fifth Circuit has held that the *Daubert* safeguards are not as essential when a judge sits as the trier of fact), *cert. denied*, 49 So. 3d 106 (Miss. 2010).

[205] Miss. R. Evid. 503(b) (psychotherapist includes physician or licensed psychologist). The rule limited the scope of the previous statutory privilege, see Miss. Code Ann. § 13-1-21 (2002) (extending privilege to "physician, osteopath, dentist, hospital, nurse, pharmacist, podiatrist, optometrist or chiropractor").

[206] Miss. R. Evid. 503.

[207] Miss. R. Evid. 503(b); *cf.* Ramon v. State, 387 So. 2d 745, 750 (Miss. 1980) (emergency room nurse's testimony admitted; privilege does not apply to nurse who is not assisting a physician); Suber v. Suber, 936 So. 2d 945, 950 (Miss. Ct. App. 2006) (court properly admitted journal kept by father in connection with a support group).

[208] Miss. Code Ann. § 73-54-39 (2004).

[209] Mabus v. Mabus, 890 So. 2d 806, 811 (Miss. 2003); *cf.* Miss. R. Evid. 1103 (all inconsistent rules "whether by

§ 19.06[3][b]   MISSISSIPPI FAMILY LAW

[b] Waiver of privilege. A patient may expressly waive his or her medical privilege. The testimony of a licensed psychotherapist was properly admitted in a divorce and custody action when both spouses signed written waivers.[210] Rule 503 provides that the privilege is also waived if a party places his or her physical, mental, or emotional condition in issue. Arguably, a parent who contests custody or seeks visitation, or a spouse who seeks divorce based on habitual, cruel, and inhuman treatment puts his or her condition in issue in the proceeding. The rules of evidence provide that the privilege may be waived in custody actions. [211] But litigating divorce based on cruelty does not put one's mental condition in issue.

[i] By parent in proceedings involving children. One of the factors for determining custody is a parent's physical and mental health.[212] However, prior to 2003, the Mississippi appellate courts held that the Rule 503 medical privilege is not waived by a parent's participation in proceedings involving custody.[213] Rule 503(d)(4), added in 2003, creates an exception to the privilege in actions in which a party's condition is relevant to custody, visitation, adoption, or the termination of parental rights.[214] However, waiver is not automatic; the court must determine in an in-chambers hearing that the need for the information outweighs the patient's right to privacy. The comments to the rule state that courts should consider the following factors in making this determination: whether "(1) the treatment was recent enough to be relevant; (2) substantive independent evidence of serious impairment exists; (3) sufficient evidence is unavailable elsewhere; (4) court-ordered evaluations are an inadequate substitute; and (5) given the severity of the alleged disorder, communications made in the course of treatment are likely to be relevant."[215]

[ii] By party alleging habitual, cruel, and inhuman treatment. A party who seeks divorce based on habitual, cruel, and inhuman treatment arguably raises the issue of physical and mental health. To obtain divorce on that ground, a plaintiff must show that the defendant's conduct caused him or her physical or emotional harm.[216]

---

statute, court decision, or court rule" repealed); Whitehurst v. State, 540 So. 2d 1319, 1324 (Miss. 1989) (not error to admit blood tests barred by statute; statute conflicted with rules); *see also* Touchstone v. Touchstone, 682 So. 2d 374, 380 (Miss. 1996) (testimony of licensed social worker not covered by Rule 503 privilege).

[210] Mabus v. Mabus, 890 So. 2d 806, 812 (Miss. 2003) (testimony of psychologist properly admitted; both parties waived privilege); *see also* Talbert v. Talbert, 759 So. 2d 1105, 1109-10 (Miss. 1999) (wife waived privilege when she showed husband letters written at her psychologist's request; court erred in excluding letters relevant to the issues of cruelty and adultery).

[211] Miss. R. Evid. 503.

[212] *See supra* § 12.03[6]; *see also* Sandlin v. Sandlin, 699 So. 2d 1198, 1205 (Miss. 1997) (rejecting mother's argument that testimony regarding her mental state was not raised by the pleadings; a petition requesting custody "inherently" includes notice that testimony will address mental and physical health).

[213] *See* Belding v. Belding, 736 So. 2d 425, 431 (Miss. Ct. App. 1999) (citing Lauderdale County Dep't Human Servs. v. T.H.G., 614 So. 2d 377, 383 (Miss. 1992) (termination proceedings)). *But cf.* Blevins v. Bardwell, 784 So. 2d 166, 173-74 (Miss. 2001) (chancellor did not err in finding for mother on issue of health, when parties mutually agreed to release records and father then refused to do so).

[214] Miss. R. Evid. 503(d)(4) (condition includes physical, mental, or emotional health or drug or alcohol condition).

[215] Miss. R. Evid. 503, cmt. 8.

[216] Bias v. Bias, 493 So. 2d 342, 345 (Miss. 1986) ("proximate cause of harm to the health and physical well being of the plaintiff"); *see* Faries v. Faries, 607 So. 2d 1204, 1209 (Miss. 1992); Peters v. Peters, 906 So. 2d 64, 69-70 (Miss.

PROCEDURE   **§ 19.06[3][b][iii]**

Although not discussing the issue directly, the supreme court implicitly agreed that the privilege is not automatically waived in a divorce action based on cruelty. The court held that a trial court should have admitted records based on a wife's waiver of the privilege, suggesting that the records would not have been admissible otherwise.[217] Similarly, a chancellor properly excluded documents from a couple's joint counseling sessions as evidence of abuse. The records could not be introduced over her husband's objection.[218]

      [iii] By child. A difficult question arises when one parent seeks disclosure of a child's privileged medical or psychological records. Rule 503 provides that the privilege and the right to waive it belong to the patient or his guardian.[219] In the absence of a custody order, however, both parents have equal rights as custodians of a child.[220] The Mississippi Supreme Court held that a chancellor properly granted a mother's motion to exclude the testimony of a psychologist who counseled children at their father's request. The communications were protected by the doctor-patient privilege.[221] When parents disagree over waiver, some courts appoint a guardian ad litem to represent the child in determining whether the privilege should be waived.[222]

[4] Medical records

      [a] HIPAA. Release of medical records by health care providers[223] is governed by the Health Insurance Portability and Accountability Act of 1996 (HIPAA). Regulations promulgated under the Act provide standards for disclosure of medical records in judicial proceedings.[224] A health care provider may release records in response to a court order.[225] Only the information expressly authorized may be released.[226]

The regulations also provide for the release of records in response to a subpoena or discovery request if the requesting party offers the provider satisfactory evidence that he or she has sought to notify the patient in a manner permitting time for objection or has obtained a qualified protective order.[227] This provision should not apply to

---

Ct. App. 2004); Rakestraw v. Rakestraw, 717 So. 2d 1284, 1288 (Miss. Ct. App. 1998); *see* discussion *supra* § 4.02[8] [b].

[217] Talbert v. Talbert, 759 So. 2d 1105, 1109-10 (Miss. 1999).

[218] Brabham v. Brabham, 950 So. 2d 1098, 1102 (Miss. Ct. App. 2007).

[219] Miss. R. Evid. 503(c).

[220] *See* Miss. Code Ann. § 93-13-1 (2004) (parents are "the joint natural guardians of their minor children and are equally charged with their care, nurture, welfare and education, and the care and management of their estates").

[221] Hensarling v. Hensarling, 824 So. 2d 583, 588 (Miss. 2002).

[222] *See* Gerard F. Glynn, *Multi-Disciplinary Representation of Children: Conflicts over Disclosures of Client Communications,* 27 J. Marshall L. Rev. 617 (1994).

[223] Health care providers are broadly defined to include providers of medical or health care services and "any other person or organization who furnishes, bills, or is paid for health care in the normal course of business." 45 C.F.R. § 160.103 (2009).

[224] For a discussion of HIPAA, *see* Tamela J. White & Charlotte A. Hoffman, *The Privacy Standards Under the Health Insurance Portability and Accountability Act: A Practical Guide to Promote Order and Avoid Potential Chaos,* 106 W. Va. L. Rev. 709, 740 (2004).

[225] 45 C.F.R. § 164.512(e)(1)(i) (2009).

[226] 45 C.F.R. § 164.512(e)(1)(i) (2009).

[227] *See* 45 C.F.R. § 164.512(e)(1)(ii)(A), (B) (describing proof required to show satisfactory efforts; describing

§ 19.06[4][b]   **MISSISSIPPI FAMILY LAW**

physicians' and psychologists' records in custody proceedings, which should be released only through a court order as required by Rule 503. HIPAA does not preempt state law to the extent that it is more restrictive than the Act.[228] However, records that are not privileged under state law may be sought through subpoena if the necessary proof of notice is provided.

[b] Procedure for determining privilege. When document release is challenged based on privilege, the court must conduct an in camera, document-by-document review, stating the rule or exception applicable to each item. A blanket statement regarding admissibility is not sufficient. In addition, the party objecting to release must be given a reasonable time to review the order and file an appeal before the documents are released. Issuance of a protective order is not sufficient to protect the objecting party's rights. Release of the documents should be stayed pending appeal.[229]

[c] Authentication of records. A husband's records for treatment of gambling addiction were properly admitted under Rule 803(6) of the Rules of Evidence, as the admission of records kept in the course of a regularly conducted business activity.[230]

[5] Court-ordered mental or physical examination. Until recently, courts in Mississippi could not order a party to undergo a mental or physical examination.[231] In 2003, the supreme court adopted Rule 35 of the Rules of Evidence, which provides that a court may order an examination when the mental or physical condition of a party or person in the custody of a party is in controversy. An examination may be ordered upon motion "for good cause shown." The person to be examined and all parties must be notified of the hearing. The rule states that in family law matters, the examinations may be ordered "in the discretion of the Chancery Judge."[232] The court of appeals rejected a mother's argument that the testimony of a court-appointed expert was unreliable because he only interviewed her once. He was a professional counselor and social worker. He testified regarding the interviewing techniques and diagnostic procedures he used. He had the skill, experience and education to assist the trier of fact and the interviews were an appropriate and reliable method of gathering information. [233]

[6] Priest/penitent privilege. Rule 505 of the Mississippi Rules of Evidence creates a privilege for confidential communications to a clergyman in his or her professional capacity as a spiritual advisor. The rule defines clergyman as a "minister, priest, rabbi or other similar functionary of a church, religious organization, or religious

---

qualified protective order).

[228] *See* White & Hoffman, *supra* note 224, at 716; 45 C.F.R. § 160.203 (2009).

[229] Brown v. Miss. United Methodist Conference, 911 So. 2d 478, 481-82 (Miss. 2005) (priest-penitent privilege).

[230] Jones v. Jones, 43 So. 3d 465, 483-84 (Miss. Ct. App. 2009).

[231] *See* Belding v. Belding, 736 So. 2d 425, 431-32 (Miss. Ct. App. 1999).

[232] Miss. R. Evid. 35; *see* Reed v. Seay, 42 So. 3d 474, 495 (Miss. 2010) (circuit court in damages action did not err in denying request for mental and physical examination; no showing that medical records and testimony of physician were inadequate); LeBlanc v. Andrews, 931 So. 2d 683, 687-88 (Miss. Ct. App. 2006) (chancellor did not err in refusing to order mental examination of a father; record did not support that the father presented a danger to the child).

[233] Minter v. Minter, 29 So. 3d 840, 852-53 (Miss. Ct. App. 2009), *cert. denied*, 29 So. 3d 774 (Miss. 2010).

PROCEDURE **§ 19.06[7]**

denomination."[234] The privilege extends to communications to the clergyman's "secretary, stenographer, or clerk." Rule 505 does not include an exception similar to the Rule 503 exception for matters involving custody of children. A chancellor properly excluded testimony of a wife's minister about confidential conversations between them. Rule 503(d)(4), allowing medical and psychological testimony relevant to child custody, does not apply to priest-penitent confidential communications.[235]

[7] Guardian ad litem testimony. In a 2009 case, the supreme court held that a guardian ad litem, who was not a trained counselor or abuse investigator, was not qualified to offer an opinion regarding abuse. She was not an expert in the area of child sexual abuse and did not engage professionals to provide a factual basis for the opinion. There was no DHS or law enforcement investigation and no testimony by a social worker or trained expert. The Court remanded for the chancellor to obtain the assistance of a professional qualified in child sexual abuse.[236]

[8] Journals. In a non-family law case, the supreme court held that journals maintained by various family members at a relative's nursing home room were admissible even though they contained entries made by a deceased family member. The journals fell under the present sense impression exception to the hearsay rule. The entries were spontaneous, and were made contemporaneously with the events described.[237]

§ 19.07 JUDGMENT

[1] Findings of fact and conclusions of law. Rule 52(a) of the Mississippi Rules of Civil Procedure provides that courts in non-jury cases shall make findings of fact and conclusions of law when required or upon the request of any party.[238] The court's ruling must be written or entered into the record. The Court of Appeals reversed and remanded an appeal because of the lack of a record of the proceedings – a chancellor's oral ruling must be transcribed for the record.[239] In addition, the Mississippi Supreme Court has set out factors related to various aspects of family law. Chancellors are required to make specific findings of fact related to these factors.

[a] Required findings. In family law cases, courts must provide specific findings of fact based on factors for custody determinations,[240] property division,[241] alimony,[242] child support,[243] grandparent visitation,[244] and awards of attorneys' fees.[245]

---

[234] MISS. R. EVID. 505(a).
[235] Suber v. Suber, 936 So. 2d 945, 950 (Miss. Ct. App. 2006).
[236] Jones v. Jones, 43 So. 3d 465 (Miss. Ct. App. 2009), *cert. denied*, 49 So. 3d 106 (Miss. 2010).
[237] Mariner Health Care, Inc. v. Estate of Edwards, 964 So. 2d 1138 (Miss. 2007).
[238] MISS. R. CIV. P. 52(a).
[239] Daley v. Daley, 909 So. 2d 106, 107-08 (Miss. Ct. App. 2005).
[240] *See supra* § 12.03[1].
[241] *See supra* § 6.08[1][g].
[242] *See supra* § 9.04.
[243] *See supra* § 13.01[3][b].
[244] *See supra* § 12.09[3].
[245] *See supra* § 10.02.

§ 19.07[1][b]   MISSISSIPPI FAMILY LAW

Specific findings are also required with regard to the tests for modification of custody[246] and support,[247] and with regard to adultery as a ground for divorce.[248] In irreconcilable differences divorce, courts are required to make on-the-record findings approving agreements.[249] A court is not, however, required to make specific findings of fact in uncontested actions.[250] A failure to make the required findings may result in reversal. On the other hand, cases are occasionally affirmed even in the absence of specific findings. The separate chapters on these topics discuss the required degree of specificity in findings of fact.

[b] Requested findings. In addition to the required findings, a chancellor must make special findings of fact and conclusions of law upon the request of any party.[251] The supreme court remanded a chancellor's custody order for failure to make findings of fact as requested. However, the court also stated that a ruling may be affirmed without findings of fact if the underlying facts are undisputed, there are no credibility issues to be resolved, and the record does not permit a different finding.[252] A chancellor's findings may be dictated into the record or written.[253]

[c] Adoption of one party's proposed findings and conclusions. When a court adopts one party's findings of fact and conclusions of law verbatim, the appellate court will view the findings with a "more critical eye." The case is not reviewed de novo, but the appellate court accords less deference to the chancellor's findings of fact.[254] However, an appellate court does not afford less deference to a chancellor's opinion simply because one party's attorney drafted an order based on the court's bench ruling. While less deference is required when a court adopts one party's proposed findings verbatim, the same is not true simply because one attorney is charged with memorializing the chancellor's ruling.[255]

[2] Time of decision. Rule 15 of the Mississippi Rules of Appellate Procedure provides that when a trial court has taken a motion or request for relief that would dispose of substantive issues and has not rendered an opinion in sixty days, the parties are to submit a proposed order to the judge within fourteen days. A copy should be sent to the Administrative Office of Courts. If the AOC does not receive a written decision

---

[246] *See supra* § 12.11[2][b].

[247] *See supra* § 13.11[1][c].

[248] *See supra* § 4.02[3][a].

[249] *See supra* § 4.04.

[250] Perkins v. Perkins, 787 So. 2d 1256, 1265 n.4 (Miss. 2001).

[251] Miss. R. Civ. P. 52(a); *see also* Unif. Chanc. Ct. R. 4.01 (findings upon request in writing, filed or dictated into record, and called to Chancellor's attention); *cf.* Farrior v. Kittrell, 12 So. 3d 20, 24-25 (Miss. Ct. App. 2009) (absence of specific findings in a contempt action did not require reversal; there was no written request for findings).

[252] Patout v. Patout, 733 So. 2d 770 (Miss. 1999); *see also* Lowery v. Lowery, 657 So. 2d 817 (Miss. 1995) (but reversing for findings; evidence not so overwhelming as to remove need for findings pursuant to request).

[253] Davis v. Davis, 829 So. 2d 712 (Miss. Ct. App. 2002).

[254] Dep't of Human Services v. Murphy, 997 So. 2d 983 (Miss. Ct. App. 2008); *cf.* Balius v. Gaines, 908 So. 2d 791, 797 (Miss. Ct. App. 2005) (no lessened deference where uncertain whether court adopted almost verbatim mother's proposed findings); Wilson v. Wilson, 811 So. 2d 342 (Miss. Ct. App. 2001); Stark v. Anderson, 748 So. 2d 838 (Miss. Ct. App. 1999).

[255] Balius v. Gaines, 914 So. 2d 300, 304-05 (Miss. Ct. App. 2005).

612

PROCEDURE

§ 19.07[3]

in six months, notice is forwarded to the supreme court, which treats the notice as an application for mandamus.[256]

[3] Consent judgments. A settlement agreement incorporated into a divorce decree becomes a part of the final decree "for all legal intents and purposes."[257] The provisions are viewed as if they had been awarded by the court after a contested trial.[258] For example, property division provisions of a consent judgment are not modifiable, while custody, child support, and alimony provisions are modifiable to the same extent as if awarded by a court.[259]

Although agreements are usually approved and accepted, courts are not bound by parties' agreements with respect to custody, child support, and alimony.[260] In contrast, property division provisions should not be altered by courts in the absence of fraud, duress, or unconscionability.[261] A court may not vary a term of an agreement without holding a hearing.[262] There must be evidence of the parties' agreement, either through a transcript that shows agreement was announced in open court, or through their signatures on the agreement. The court of appeals reversed a consent judgment based on a pro se appellant's assertion that she did not consent – there was no transcript of the hearing, and her attorney signed the agreed order as to form only.[263]

[4] Retention of jurisdiction. A court may retain jurisdiction over issues not ripe for adjudication. For example, reservation of jurisdiction over alimony is appropriate if a wage-earner spouse is currently unemployed or otherwise unable to pay alimony, if alimony is not feasible because of substantial post-marital debt, or if both spouses are currently employed but one has medical problems that create a likelihood of unemployment.[264] Similarly, certain marital assets such as unvested pensions,[265] attorneys' contingent fees,[266] or future benefits[267] may not be ripe for division at the time of trial. Reserved jurisdiction may also be appropriate when assets cannot be valued and classified because of pending bankruptcy proceedings.[268] And a chancellor properly retained jurisdiction to determine income pending an audit of the parties'

---

[256] MISS. R. APP. P. 15.

[257] Switzer v. Switzer, 460 So. 2d 843, 845 (Miss. 1984).

[258] Switzer v. Switzer, 460 So. 2d 843, 845 (Miss. 1984) (also rejecting argument that property settlements could not be enforced as a judgment because they were not modifiable); *see also* Tedford v. Dempsey, 437 So. 2d 410, 417 (Miss. 1983) (child support provisions of agreement incorporated into decree are enforceable as if court-ordered; subject to modification based on changed circumstances); *see infra* § 23.10.

[259] *See* discussion of separation agreements *infra* §§ 23.08 - .13.

[260] *See* Reno v. Reno, 176 So. 2d 58, 61 (Miss. 1965) (distinguishing agreement regarding property rights and those related to alimony, custody, and child support, which must be approved by the court; fault-based divorce).

[261] Barton v. Barton, 790 So. 2d 169, 172 (Miss. 2001).

[262] Palmere v. Curtis, 789 So. 2d 126 (Miss. Ct. App. 2001) (court-approved agreement, drafted by father's attorney, inserted visitation provision not included in the agreement dictated into the record).

[263] Klein v. McIntyre, 966 So. 2d 1252, 1258 (Miss. Ct. App. 2007).

[264] *See* discussion of cases reserving jurisdiction over alimony *supra* § 9.08[2].

[265] *See* discussion *supra* § 7.12.

[266] *See* discussion *supra* § 6.06[5].

[267] Wesson v. Wesson, 818 So. 2d 1272, 1278 (Miss. Ct. App. 2002).

[268] Heigle v. Heigle, 654 So. 2d 895, 898 (Miss. 1995) (chancellor erred in dividing assets of husband's business while bankruptcy involving the business was pending).

§ 19.07[5]   MISSISSIPPI FAMILY LAW

business.[269]

[5] Specific provisions. Discussion of specific provisions related to property division, alimony, custody, and child support are discussed in the chapters related to those topics. In addition, Chapter XXIII includes a discussion of prohibited provisions in consent judgments.[270]

[6] Modification of bench opinion. A court's bench opinion is not final and may be modified or amended prior to final judgment. A chancellor did not err in amending an oral opinion to decrease the amount of alimony awarded – a court's decision and the final judgment are not synonymous.[271]

[7] Finality. A judgment is final and appealable only when it is entered by the clerk of the court. A chancellor's bench opinion is not a final judgment,[272] nor is the filing of a judgment with the clerk. Instead, the clerk's entry of an order pursuant to Rule 58 is the act that creates a final and appealable judgment.[273] In the case of conflict between a bench opinion and judgment, the judgment is controlling.[274]A judgment addressing one of several issues is not a final, appealable judgment. A court's entry of judgment of divorce that reserved property division issues for a later hearing was not a final judgment.[275]

[8] Death of spouse before entry of judgment. A spouse's death before the court's adjudication of divorce ends the action. However, the decree need not have been formally entered. A court properly entered a judgment nunc pro tunc when a husband died several days after the court rendered a bench opinion granting divorce.[276]

[9] Offer of judgment. The "costs" due to a party under Rule 68 do not include attorneys' fees. A divorcing wife submitted an offer of judgment to the court, which was sealed until the court's judgment. Because the judgment was less favorable than the offer, the court ordered the husband to pay attorneys' fees incurred by her after the offer was rejected. The court of appeals held that the court erred in awarding attorneys' fees as part of costs under Rule 68.[277]

---

[269] Black v. Black, 741 So. 2d 299, 300 (Miss. Ct. App. 1999).

[270] *See infra* § 23.14.

[271] *See* Banks v. Banks, 511 So. 2d 933, 935 (Miss. 1987) (citing Rule 54 of the Rules of Civil Procedure); *see also* Hinson v. Hinson, 877 So. 2d 547, 548 (Miss. Ct. App. 2004).

[272] Banks v. Banks, 511 So. 2d 933, 935 (Miss. 1987).

[273] *See* MISS. R. CIV. P. 52, cmt.

[274] Hill v. Hill, 942 So. 2d 207, 209 (Miss. Ct. App. 2006) (judgment awarding sole physical custody controlled over bench opinion awarding sole legal and physical custody).

[275] Walters v. Walters, 956 So. 2d 1050, 1053 (Miss. Ct. App. 2007). For a discussion of appealable orders, see § 19.09[1].

[276] *See* White v. Smith, 645 So. 2d 875 (Miss. 1994); *see also* Thrash v. Thrash, 385 So. 2d 961, 964 (Miss. 1980) (decree signed by a chancellor the day prior to the death of one of the spouses, but dated two days later, was valid and binding as of the date of judgment by the court, prior to filing with the clerk of court).

[277] Harbit v. Harbit, 3 So. 3d 156, 158, 162-64 (Miss. Ct. App. 2009) (but finding award of fees appropriate on other grounds).

PROCEDURE

§ 19.07[10]

[10] Entry of judgment nunc pro tunc. A court may enter a judgment nunc pro tunc to correct omissions in the record. The judgment is effective at the earlier date. The nunc pro tunc order "constitutes the later evidence of a prior effectual act." [278]

§ 19.08 POST-JUDGMENT MOTIONS

Parties have several options for seeking relief from a judgment. For ten days following the entry of judgment, a party may request, or the court may initiate, the reopening of a judgment. In addition, relief may be granted for a period of six months for conduct such as fraud. And in unusual cases, relief may be granted more than six months after entry of judgment. Clerical errors may be corrected at any time.

[1] Reopening judgment within ten days. Rule 59 of the Mississippi Rules of Civil Procedure permits a court to reopen a judgment and take additional testimony, make new findings of fact and conclusions of law, and enter a new judgment. A Rule 59 motion must be filed by a party or initiated by the court within ten days of the entry of judgment. [279] The court of appeals reversed a chancellor's order amending a judgment to require payment of attorneys' fees two months after entry of judgment. Courts must also comply with Rule 59, which requires action within ten days, notice to the parties, and an opportunity to be heard. [280] However, a party's failure to object to untimeliness will waive the ten-day requirement. A mother's request for reconsideration, filed 11 days after the court's judgment, was properly heard. The father did not object to untimeliness and could not raise the issue on appeal. [281]

A motion filed prematurely is nonetheless effective. The court of appeals rejected a mother's argument that a father's motion to reconsider was not timely because it was filed before entry of final judgment. Finding this to be an issue of first impression in Mississippi, the court looked to federal authority, which states that Rule 59 sets a maximum, rather than a minimum, time for filing. [282]

Chancellors have substantial discretion in reopening judgments within the ten-day period. A chancellor properly reopened a judgment awarding custody to a father in an uncontested hearing, to allow the mother to present testimony on the *Albright* factors. [283] However, a father's motion to reopen based on the mother's post-trial conduct was properly treated as a motion for modification. [284] A chancellor erred in refusing to reopen a divorce action to consider the husband's post-trial assertion that his wife was responsible for tax on $14,305 of income from the previous year. The evidence was

---

[278] Henderson v. Henderson, 27 So. 3d 462, 464 (Miss. Ct. App. 2010).

[279] *See* Miss. R. Civ. P. 52.

[280] Ford v. Ford, 795 So. 2d 600 (Miss. Ct. App. 2001); *cf.* Scally v. Scally, 802 So. 2d 128 (Miss. Ct. App. 2001) (untimely motion to amend judgment cannot be attacked for that reason on appeal unless appellant objected to the untimeliness in the court below); *see also* Sullivan v. Sullivan, 942 So. 2d 305, 307 (Miss. Ct. App. 2006) (when mobile home awarded to wife burned shortly after trial, chancellor properly amended judgment to award wife insurance proceeds).

[281] Wilburn v. Wilburn, 991 So. 2d 1185, 1191 (Miss. 2008).

[282] Street v. Street, 936 So. 2d 1002, 1008-09 (Miss. Ct. App. 2006) (motion for reconsideration treated as Rule 59(e) motion to amend judgment).

[283] Wade v. Wade, 967 So. 2d 682, 684 (Miss. Ct. App. 2007).

[284] Gilcrease v. Gilcrease, 918 So. 2d 854, 859-60 (Miss. Ct. App. 2005).

§ 19.08[2]   MISSISSIPPI FAMILY LAW

relevant under the *Ferguson* factor of "tax consequences," the omission was excusable, since the taxes were not completed at the time of trial, and the absence of the evidence could result in an injustice.[285]

A timely motion for reconsideration will extend the time period for filing an appeal; however, if the motion is not timely, the appeal period is not extended.[286]

[2] Relief from judgment

[a] Clerical mistakes. Rule 60(a) of the Rules of Civil Procedure permits correction of clerical mistakes and errors in a judgment.[287] For example, a chancellor properly corrected a five-year-old divorce judgment to conform to the court's memorandum opinion. The judgment characterized pension payments to the wife as alimony rather than part of property division as intended and as provided in the memorandum opinion. The supreme court noted that Rule 60(a) places no time limit on a court's correction of a clerical error.[288] Similarly, a chancellor had authority to clarify that lump sum alimony was awarded as spousal support and not as part of property division.[289] However, a husband was not entitled to relief under this provision to reform a settlement agreement regarding division of retirement benefits. The correction he requested was language in an earlier draft of the proposed agreement that had been subsequently edited and revised – it was not a mere clerical error.[290]

[b] Misconduct, mistake, newly discovered evidence. Rule 60(b) provides that a party may be relieved from final judgment based on fraud, misrepresentation or other misconduct, accident or mistake, or newly discovered evidence that could not have been discovered in time to make a Rule 59 motion. The motion must be made within six months after judgment.[291] Rule 60(b) may not be used to relitigate matters argued and resolved in the proceeding.[292] A wife's discovery that she could not withdraw from her retirement account without penalty was not "newly discovered evidence" – the information was available at the time of trial.[293] Furthermore, an attorney's

---

[285] Dunn v. Dunn, 911 So. 2d 591, 601-03 (Miss. Ct. App. 2005).

[286] Wilburn v. Wilburn, 991 So. 2d 1185, 1191 (Miss. 2008). See *infra* § 19.09.

[287] Miss. R. Civ. P. 60(a).

[288] Townsend v. Townsend, 859 So. 2d 370, 379 (Miss. 2003).

[289] Seymour v. Seymour, 869 So. 2d 1035, 1037 (Miss. Ct. App. 2004) (A court may not use Rule 60(a) to change a judgment, but may "correct an order that failed accurately to reflect the judge's original decision."); *see also* Wilkerson v. Wilkerson, 955 So. 2d 903, 907 (Miss. Ct. App. 2007) (court clarified whether judgment ordered payment of interest on lump sum amount).

[290] Pratt v. Pratt, 977 So. 2d 386 (Miss. Ct. App. 2007) (also holding that husband waived argument by waiting eighteen months after learning of discrepancy to bring to court's attention).

[291] Miss. R. Civ. P. 60(b); *see* Pratt v. Pratt, 977 So. 2d 386 (Miss. Ct. App. 2007) (husband barred from seeking relief; waited eighteen months after learning of discrepancy to seek reformation); Salemi v. Salemi, 972 So. 2d 1, 5 (Miss. Ct. App. 2007) (rejecting husband's motion to reform agreement nine years after judgment on basis that he did not understand provision); *cf.* Klein v. McIntyre, 966 So. 2d 1252, 1257 (Miss. Ct. App. 2007) (pro se mother's appeal on grounds that she did not agree to consent order construed as Rule 60(b) motion and remanded to trial court).

[292] Askew v. Askew, 699 So. 2d 515, 520 (Miss. 1997); *see also* Montgomery v. Montgomery, 759 So. 2d 1238 (Miss. 2000) (Rule 60(b) may not be used to relitigate matters already settled; relief denied, based on litigant's unsubstantiated claim that her settlement agreement was coerced by her attorney).

[293] Weeks v. Weeks, 29 So. 3d 80, 91-92 (Miss. Ct. App. 2009).

PROCEDURE   **§ 19.08[2][c]**

alleged negligence is not a proper basis to set aside a decree under Rule 60(b).[294]

To warrant reopening a judgment for misrepresentation, the statement must have been intended to influence the trier of fact and must have in fact been relied upon by the trier of fact. A father's testimony, in a modification hearing, that his current wife was trained and certified in speech therapy did not warrant reversal, even though she was not in fact certified. It was her training and experience that was relevant to the court's decision.[295] An agreement may also be set aside based on duress and overreaching as "other misconduct" under Rule 60(b).[296]

Whether a party is limited to six months to seek relief based on fraud depends upon whether the misconduct is considered fraud on a party, which requires action within six months, or fraud on the court, which must be addressed within a reasonable time.[297]

[c] Relief from judgment after six months. Rule 60(b) provides that a court may at any time set aside a decree for voidness or for fraud on the court. Under the rule's catch-all provisions, decrees may also be set aside "for any other reason justifying relief from the judgment."[298] In order to set aside a judgment for voidness, fraud, or under the catch-all provision, the petition must be filed within a reasonable time. A wife's petition to set aside a property settlement agreement, filed five years after the judgment, was not filed within a reasonable time.[299]

[i] Void provisions. A void provision may be set aside even years after entry of a decree. The court of appeals stated that a void judgment "may be attacked directly or collaterally, anywhere, and at any time" as a nullity.[300] For example, an agreed provision that custody would automatically change if a custodial mother moved was void and contrary to public policy. The court refused to enforce the provision seven years later.[301] Similarly, an agreement providing for termination of child support when a child reached the age of eighteen was void and not enforceable in an action five years later.[302]

[ii] Any other reason justifying relief. The supreme court noted that the catch-all phrase in Rule 60(b) "is designed for cases of extreme hardship not covered under any of the other subsections."[303] Orders of child support have been set aside under

---

[294] Buie v. Buie, 772 So. 2d 1079 (Miss. Ct. App. 2000) (attorney neglect or incompetence not a reason to set aside a final decree of divorce; chancellor properly refused to set aside a divorce granted when the wife's attorney failed to show up for hearing or present properly supported motion for continuance).

[295] Williamson v. Williamson, 964 So. 2d 524, 529-30 (Miss. Ct. App. 2007).

[296] Lowrey v. Lowrey, 919 So. 2d 1112, 1119 (Miss. Ct. App. 2005).

[297] *See infra* § 19.08[2][c][iii].

[298] Miss. R. Civ. P. 60(b).

[299] *In re* Dissolution of the Marriage of De St. Germain, 977 So. 2d 412, 416-17 (Miss. Ct. App. 2008).

[300] Cobb v. Cobb, 29 So. 3d 145, 148 (Miss. Ct. App. 2010) (rejecting wife's argument that previously dismissed appeal precluded court from hearing appeal of Rule 60(b) motion to set aside).

[301] McManus v. Howard, 569 So. 2d 1213, 1216 (Miss. 1990).

[302] Lawrence v. Lawrence, 574 So. 2d 1376, 1381 (Miss. 1991).

[303] Burkett v. Burkett, 537 So. 2d 443, 447 (Miss. 1989) (chancellor did not err in granting relief from default based on husband's petition filed seven months after decree, where he had good defense and wife suffered no prejudice).

§ 19.08[2][c][iii]   **MISSISSIPPI FAMILY LAW**

the catch-all provision years after entry, when it was learned that a support payor was not in fact the child's father. The court held that the issue was properly addressed through a Rule 60(b)(6) motion for relief.[304]

A court noted in dicta that a father's petition to set aside a year-old order terminating his parental rights might constitute "other reasons" to set aside a judgment. He alleged that the mother served him by publication even though he had returned from prison to his hometown, and even though she knew her mother had been in touch with him.[305] However, a man was not entitled to relief under this provision to reform an agreement providing his wife with retirement benefits that he did not realize were included in the agreement.[306] And a joint custodial mother was not entitled to set aside a custody modification based upon her planned moved from Jackson to Memphis, even though her husband lost his Memphis job shortly after the modification. The chancellor found that the parents no longer worked cooperatively, and that the mother might plan to move again if her husband acquired another job.[307]

[iii] Fraud on the court. Whether a party's concealment of or misrepresentation regarding assets constitutes fraud on a party or on the court was unclear in Mississippi until 2010. In 2002, the court of appeals held that a husband's false responses regarding assets in discovery and on his 8.05 financial statement, although fraudulent, were not a basis to set aside a decree two and a half years later. The court distinguished fraud on a party, which must be addressed within six months of a judgment, and fraud on the court, which is not time-limited.[308] In 2004, however, the supreme court held that a judgment should have been set aside two years after a divorce decree was entered. The court characterized the husband's failure to disclose substantial lottery winnings as "perpetuating a fraud on the court by failing to disclose accurate financial information." The case was also based upon the court's finding that his failure to file an 8.05 financial statement was contempt.[309]

The issue was resolved in 2010 when the Mississippi Supreme Court held that a party's intentional misrepresentation of a substantial matter constitutes fraud on the court. When a couple divorced in 2000, the husband testified that his 49% interest in a closely held corporation was worth $100,000. One year after the divorce, in litigation with his partner, the husband's expert valued his interest at slightly over $1,000,000. The court of appeals held that, even if the husband committed fraud, it was fraud on a party, not on the court, and had to be brought to the court's attention within six months of judgment. The Supreme Court reversed, stating that, while "mere nondisclosure" of facts to an adverse party is not fraud on the court, "the intentional filing of a substan-

---

[304] M.A.S. v. Miss. Dep't of Human Servs., 842 So. 2d 527, 530-31 (Miss. 2003) (rejecting court of appeals reasoning that petitioner delayed unreasonably in seeking relief); *see also* Williams v. Williams, 843 So. 2d 720, 723 (Miss. 2003) (divorced husband not required to continue paying support for child he later discovered was not his).

[305] C.M. v. R.D.H., 947 So. 2d 1023, 1026 (Miss. Ct. App. 2007).

[306] Pratt v. Pratt, 977 So. 2d 386 (Miss. Ct. App. 2007) (provision was not "inequitable"; Rule 60(b)(6) reserved for exceptional circumstances); *see also* Salemi v. Salemi, 972 So. 2d 1, 5 (Miss. Ct. App. 2007) (rejecting husband's motion to reform agreement nine years after judgment on basis that he did not understand provision).

[307] Porter v. Porter, 23 So. 3d 438 (Miss. 2009).

[308] Brown v. Johnson, 822 So. 2d 1072 (Miss. Ct. App. 2002); *see also* Walton v. Snyder, 984 So. 2d 343 (Miss. Ct. App. 2007); Shaw v. Shaw, 985 So. 2d 346 (Miss. Ct. App. 2007).

[309] Kalman v. Kalman, 905 So. 2d 760 (Miss. Ct. App. 2004).

PROCEDURE § 19.09

tially false Rule 8.05 statement is misconduct that rises above mere nondisclosure of material facts to an adverse party" and is fraud upon the court. [310]

§ 19.09 APPEALS

The Mississippi Rules of Appellate Procedure apply to appeals from family law matters. The discussion below highlights family law cases discussing appellate procedure. It is not intended as a general review of the rules of appellate practice.[311]

[1] Appealable orders. As a general rule, appeals may be taken only from the entry of final judgment in a case.[312] A final judgment is "one which resolves all issues, and requires no further action by the court."[313] Appellate courts may not hear an appeal from a temporary order[314] or a chancellor's bench ruling.[315] An order denying a motion to intervene is an appealable order.[316] A judgment on some but not all of the issues in a case is not a final judgment. For example, when a chancellor bifurcated trial on grounds for divorce and on financial and custody issues, his written judgment on grounds for divorce was an interlocutory order.[317] Similarly, when a court ruled on visitation but reserved issues of child support, appeal from the visitation ruling was dismissed as premature.[318] And a judgment is not final until the court has ruled on pending post-trial motions.[319]

Interlocutory appeals may be taken under Rule 5 of the Rules of Appellate Procedure upon a showing that "there is a substantial basis for a difference of opinion" on a question of law, and that an immediate appeal will avoid expense, protect a party from irreparable injury, or resolve an issue significant to the administration of justice.[320] Under Rule 54 of the Rules of Civil Procedure, a party who wishes to appeal a judgment on fewer than all claims in an action must request the court to enter judgment on those issues, based upon an "expressed determination that there is no just reason for delay."[321] The court of appeals lacked jurisdiction to hear the appeal of a judgment of divorce based on constructive desertion. The court entered judgment on divorce, reserving the

---

[310] Trim v. Trim, 33 So. 3d 471, 472-74, 478-79 (Miss. 2010).

[311] For an excellent treatise on appellate practice, see LUTHER MUNFORD, MISSISSIPPI APPELLATE PRACTICE (1997).

[312] *See* MISS R. APP. P. 4(a).

[313] Scally v. Scally, 802 So. 2d 128 (Miss. Ct. App. 2001).

[314] Michael v. Michael, 650 So. 2d 469, 471 (Miss. 1995) (temporary custody order); *cf.* Quadrini v. Quadrini, 964 So. 2d 576, 580 (Miss. Ct. App. 2007) (temporary order converted to permanent by passage of time was appealable).

[315] Banks v. Banks, 511 So. 2d 933, 935 (Miss. 1987); *see* Hinson v. Hinson, 877 So. 2d 547, 548 (Miss. Ct. App. 2004).

[316] Smith v. Holmes, 921 So. 2d 283, 285 (Miss. 2005) (en banc); *cf.* S.G. v. D.C., 13 So. 3d 269, 278 (Miss. 2009) (appeal may be filed immediately but not required to be filed prior to final judgment).

[317] Scally v. Scally, 802 So. 2d 128, 130 (Miss. Ct. App. 2001).

[318] Cameron v. Burns, 802 So. 2d 1069, 1071 (Miss. Ct. App. 2001).

[319] Wilson v. Mallett, 28 So. 3d 669, 669-70 (Miss. Ct. App. 2009) (appeal filed before disposition of post-trial motions is ineffective to appeal until the last motion is heard and judgment entered), *cert. denied,* 27 So. 3d 404 (Miss. 2010); Beamer v. Beamer, 22 So. 3d 430, 431 (Miss. Ct. App. 2009) (appeal dismissed as premature because chancellor never ruled on pending Rule 59 motion).

[320] MISS. R. APP. P. 5(a); *see* Boutwell v. Boutwell, 829 So. 2d 1216 (Miss. 2002) (interlocutory appeal rarely granted from discovery disputes, with the exception of privilege issues); Cameron v. Burns, 802 So. 2d 1069, 1071 (Miss. Ct. App. 2001) (appeal dismissed; no request for interlocutory appeal within required fourteen-day period).

[321] MISS. R. CIV. P. 54(b).

§ 19.09[2]   MISSISSIPPI FAMILY LAW

issue of property division for later, but failed to include the required finding that "there is no just reason for delay."[322]

[2] Time of appeal. An appeal must be perfected by filing a notice of appeal within thirty days after entry of judgment in a case.[323] The court of appeals dismissed a mother's appeal of a custody award filed one day late. The court lacked jurisdiction to hear the appeal.[324]

An appeal filed prematurely may be dismissed.[325] However, a notice of appeal filed prematurely becomes effective upon entry of a final judgment.[326] Notice of appeal should be filed with the trial court. However, filing with the supreme court is sufficient to confer jurisdiction for the appeal.[327] The opposing party has fourteen days to file a cross-appeal after the first notice is filed.[328]

The filing of certain post-trial motions delays the running of the appeal period until an order is entered on the motion.[329] The tolling does not apply, however, if a Rule 59 or 60(b) motion is untimely.[330] A court's sua sponte entry of an amended order correcting non-substantive provisions of a judgment does not toll the appeal period.[331]

The appeal period may be extended for good cause by a motion filed within the appeal period or for excusable neglect by a motion filed after the appeal period. The court may grant an extension for the longer of thirty days from the original appeal period or ten days from the date of the extension order, whichever is later.[332]

Rule 4(h) specifically addresses extension of the time to appeal when a party has not received notice of the judgment. By motion made within 180 days of entry of judgment or within seven days of notice, whichever is earlier, the appeal period may be reopened for fourteen days.[333] The court of appeals lacked jurisdiction to hear a father's appeal of termination of his parental rights. The youth court granted the father an additional thirty days to appeal; however, the court had no authority to expand the fourteen-

---

[322] Walters v. Walters, 956 So. 2d 1050, 1053 (Miss. Ct. App. 2007).

[323] MISS. R. APP. P. 4.

[324] Dudley v. Harris, 979 So. 2d 692, 693 (Miss. Ct. App. 2008).

[325] Wilson v. Mallett, 28 So. 3d 669, 669-70 (Miss. Ct. App. 2009) (appeal filed before disposition of post-trial motions is ineffective to appeal until the last motion is heard and judgment entered), *cert. denied*, 27 So. 3d 404 (Miss. 2010).

[326] Phelps v. Phelps, 937 So. 2d 974, 977 (Miss. Ct. App. 2006) (husband's notice of appeal filed before the disposition of all motions).

[327] Dudley v. Harris, 979 So. 2d 692, 692 (Miss. Ct. App. 2008).

[328] MISS. R. APP. P. 4(c).

[329] *See* MISSISSIPPI CIVIL PROCEDURE § 17:17 (Jeffrey Jackson ed., 2003).

[330] Anderson v. Anderson, 8 So. 3d 264, 270-71 (Miss. Ct. App. 2009) (thirty-day appeal period was not tolled by chancellor's grant of untimely motion for specific findings of fact); *In re* A.M.A., 986 So. 2d 999, 1007 (Miss. Ct. App. 2007) (motions filed forty-two days after entry of judgment did not toll running of appeal period). *But cf.* Wilburn v. Wilburn, 991 So. 2d 1185, 1191 (Miss. 2008) (mother's motion for reconsideration was untimely, making appeal untimely, but father did not object and could not raise matter on appeal).

[331] Penton v. Penton, 2010 WL 1444537 (Miss. Ct. App. April 13, 2010) (husband's notice of appeal, filed forty-nine days after judgment but twenty-nine days after judgment clarifying instructions to the clerk, was untimely).

[332] M.R.A.P. 4(g); *see In re* A.M.A., 986 So. 2d 999, 1007 (Miss. Ct. App. 2007) (court lacked jurisdiction where notice was filed 113 days after judgment and 30 days after order granting extension); *cf.* Penton v. Penton, 2010 WL 1444537, 4-5 (Miss. Ct. App. April 13, 2010) (untimely notice of appeal did not operate as request for extension of time).

[333] M.R.A.P. 4(h).

620

PROCEDURE

§ 19.09[3]

day period.[334]

Attorneys should exercise caution in identifying the relevant period for appeal. An appeal filed thirty days after a Rule 60 motion that restated grounds in a previous Rule 59 motion was not timely; a second, redundant motion for reconsideration does not toll the running of the time period.[335] In addition, care should be taken in determining the period for filing when both parties have filed petitions for modification or enforcement. In one case, the supreme court noted that a wife's motion for contempt in response to her husband's motion for modification could have been either a counter-claim or a separate petition. Because the chancellor treated it as a counter-claim, her notice of appeal was properly filed within thirty days after the court's ruling on her husband's motion. Had the court treated it as a separate petition, she would have been required to file within thirty days of the court's earlier ruling on her motion.[336]

[3] Stay pending appeal. A party may obtain a stay of a money judgment by filing a supersedeas bond as required by Rule 8 of the Rules of Appellate Procedure. A stay of other orders should be sought from the trial court.[337] When a money judgment is appealed, the bond should be 125% of the amount of the judgment. For other judgments, the court may order security in an amount it deems proper. The court of appeals held that a wife should have been ordered to post a 125% bond to secure payment of a lump sum in the appeal of a divorce action. With regard to appeal of an order requiring her to transfer land to her husband, the court of appeals held that the chancellor should set the bond in an amount sufficient to prevent her husband from loss of the property during appeal. The court noted that a chancellor may look to the practices set out in repealed statutes to determine an appropriate amount of bond to secure non-money judgments.[338] A chancellor erred in granting a stay without requiring that the wife post a supersedeas bond.[339]

A chancellor allowed a defendant to obtain a stay of a judgment for alienation of affection by providing a bank letter of credit in the required amount, in lieu of a bond.[340] However, providing a bond or other security does not entitle the appellant to a release of the judgment lien pending appeal.[341] In the absence of a supersedeas bond, either party can enforce the judgment. A court did not err in allowing a wife who appealed the court's division of marital assets to enforce the property division pending appeal; her husband did not seek supersedeas.[342] The court of appeals rejected a defendant's argument that a third order of contempt was improper because he had appealed

---

[334] *In re* A.M.A., 986 So. 2d 999, 1006 (Miss. Ct. App. 2007).

[335] Bresler v. Bresler, 824 So. 2d 641 (Miss. Ct. App. 2002); *see also* Carter v. Carter, 735 So. 2d 1109, 1113 (Miss. Ct. App. 2001).

[336] Carter v. Carter, 735 So. 2d 1109, 1113 (Miss. Ct. App. 1999) (also noting that parties should use term "petition" rather than "motion").

[337] Miss. R. App. P. 8 (stay of nonmonetary aspects of a judgment must be requested in the trial court).

[338] Deal v. Wilson, 922 So. 2d 24, 29-31 (Miss. Ct. App. 2005) (citing Miss. Code Ann. §§ 11-51-35 (double one year of rent in ejectment action) and § 11-51-41 (double the value of real estate)).

[339] McIntosh v. McIntosh, 977 So. 2d 1257, 1273 (Miss. Ct. App. 2008).

[340] Fitch v. Valentine, 946 So. 2d 780, 784 (Miss. Ct. App. 2007) ($943,000 letter of credit).

[341] Fitch v. Valentine, 946 So. 2d 780, 785 (Miss. Ct. App. 2007) (lien may be removed only by an endorsement by the judgment creditor that the lien has been satisfied).

[342] Ladner v. Ladner, 843 So. 2d 81, 82-83 (Miss. Ct. App. 2003).

§ 19.09[4]   MISSISSIPPI FAMILY LAW

a second order of contempt with supersedeas. The supersedeas stayed only the amount due at the time of the second order. It did not stay the payments due in the six months between the second and third contempt orders.[343]

Parties should be aware of the consequences of reversal on appeal. When an alimony award was reversed, a chancellor properly ordered the wife to reimburse her husband for payments received during the period of appeal.[344]

[4] Standard of review. Chancellors are accorded great discretion in resolving disputed questions of fact; awards will not be reversed on appeal unless the chancellor was manifestly in error in the findings of fact[345] and the decision is "so oppressive, unjust or grossly inadequate as to evidence an abuse of discretion."[346] The supreme court has noted that "[o]ur job is not to reweigh the evidence . . . . The chancellor, by his presence in the courtroom, is best equipped to listen to the witnesses, observe their demeanor, and determine the credibility of the witnesses and what weight ought to be ascribed to the evidence given by those witnesses."[347] In contrast, questions of law are reviewed de novo. Appellate courts will reverse if a chancellor applied an incorrect legal standard.[348] Issues related to jurisdiction are reviewed de novo on appeal.[349] With limited exceptions, an issue that was not raised at trial may not be considered on appeal.[350]

[5] Appeal of consent judgment. Consent judgments may be appealed; however, review is limited to a consideration of whether circumstances exist that would justify setting a judgment aside under Rule 60(b), such as fraud or misrepresentation.[351] Parties may not appeal as error a judgment to which they agreed. However, an irreconcilable differences divorce based on consent will be reversed unless the statutory requirements were strictly followed. In several cases, a grant of divorce has been reversed because the parties' agreement was presented orally or dictated into the court record rather than presented in writing.[352]

---

[343] Chasez v. Chasez, 957 So. 2d 1031, 1037 (Miss. Ct. App. 2007).

[344] Henderson v. Henderson, 757 So. 2d 285, 294 (Miss. 2000).

[345] Powers v. Powers, 568 So. 2d 255, 257 (Miss. 1990); Carpenter v. Carpenter, 519 So. 2d 891, 894-95 (Miss. 1988); McNally v. McNally, 516 So. 2d 499, 501 (Miss. 1987); Richardson v. Richardson, 912 So. 2d 1079, 1081 (Miss. Ct. App. 2005) (standard of review of custody award is abuse of discretion).

[346] Voda v. Voda, 731 So. 2d 1152 (Miss. 1999); Armstrong v. Armstrong, 618 So. 2d 1278 (Miss. 1993); Martin v. Martin, 271 So. 2d 391, 394 (Miss. 1972).

[347] Carter v. Carter, 735 So. 2d 1109, 1113 (Miss. Ct. App. 1999); Murphy v. Murphy, 631 So. 2d 812, 815 (Miss. 1994).

[348] Brown v. Miss. Dep't of Human Servs., 806 So. 2d 1004 (Miss. 2000); Marter v. Marter, 914 So. 2d 743, 746 (Miss. Ct. App. 2005) (court reviews de novo whether chancellor applied correct test for modification; as to whether test was properly applied to facts, chancellor will be reversed only for abuse of discretion); Sanghi v. Sanghi, 759 So. 2d 1250, 1252 (Miss. Ct. App. 2000); Carter v. Carter, 735 So. 2d 1109 (Miss. Ct. App. 1999).

[349] Thomas v. Byars, 947 So. 2d 375, 378 (Miss. Ct. App. 2007); In re A.M.A., 986 So. 2d 999, 1009 (Miss. Ct. App. 2007); Williams v. Smith, 915 So. 2d 1114, 1116 (Miss. Ct. App. 2005).

[350] See, e.g., Ory v. Ory, 936 So. 2d 405, 410 (Miss. Ct. App. 2006) (en banc) (refusing to consider husband's argument on appeal that he failed to prove his case at trial).

[351] Rushing v. Rushing, 724 So. 2d 911, 916 (Miss. 1998); see discussion infra § 23.11.

[352] See, e.g., Cassibry v. Cassibry, 742 So. 2d 1121, 1125 (Miss. 1999).

PROCEDURE § 19.09[6]

[6] Briefs on appeal

[a] Appellee's failure to file brief. An appellee's failure to file a brief is the equivalent of confession of error.[353] If an issue has been thoroughly briefed by an appellant who makes an apparent case of error, or when a case is complicated, the judgment should be reversed. If the case is not complicated and the brief does not make a case of apparent error, the court may proceed to examine the record.[354] The court of appeals has noted "this is all the more important in domestic cases that raise issues regarding children."[355]

[b] Lack of citation. A court is not required to address issues on appeal that are not supported by authority. The court of appeals refused to address a father's argument that a final order improperly reduced his visitation from that provided in a temporary order; he offered no support for his argument.[356]

[c] Untranscribed proceedings. If the proceeding below was not transcribed, the appellant should prepare a statement of evidence from the best means available, including recollection. If the parties disagree regarding what occurred, the disagreement should be submitted to the chancellor for clarification.[357] In one case, an attorney's representation of facts in his unopposed brief and oral argument was accepted as a stipulation of the parties pursuant to Mississippi Rule of Appellate Procedure 10.[358]

[d] Waiver. A wife who did not appear at the divorce trial appealed the court's division of assets, failure to award alimony, and custody award. The Court of Appeals held that she was procedurally barred from raising the issues on appeal. They were not presented to the court at trial and did not constitute plain error.[359] The court of appeals refused to consider a husband's argument that a chancellor erred in ordering him to pay temporary support. The issue was not raised at trial and therefore not preserved for

---

[353] Hayes v. Hayes, 994 So. 2d 246, 248 (Miss. Ct. App. 2008) (A husband/appellee's failure to file brief could be taken as confession of error if "the record is complicated or the case has been briefed and makes a clear case of error."); Ashburn v. Ashburn, 970 So. 2d 204, 206 (Miss. Ct. App. 2007) (reversing; appellee failed to file brief; court could not say with confidence that no error occurred); Engel v. Engel, 920 So. 2d 505, 509-10 (Miss. Ct. App. 2006) (case should be reversed when appellee fails to file brief, unless court can say with confidence that there was no error); Williams v. Smith, 915 So. 2d 1114, 1116 (Miss. Ct. App. 2005) (failure of appellee to file brief equivalent of confession of error); Allred v. Allred, 735 So. 2d 1064, 1067 (Miss. Ct. App. 1999); cf. Parker v. Parker, 929 So. 2d 940, 945 (Miss. Ct. App. 2005) (failure to cite authority forfeits consideration of issue by appellate court).

[354] Sullivan v. Sullivan, 942 So. 2d 305, 307 (Miss. Ct. App. 2006).

[355] Clark v. Clark, 739 So. 2d 440, 442 (Miss. Ct. App. 1999); see J.P.M. v. T.D.M., 932 So. 2d 760, 765 (Miss. 2006) (en banc) (appellate court makes a special effort to review the record in child custody and support cases).

[356] Mitchell v. Mitchell, 823 So. 2d 568, 572 (Miss. Ct. App. 2002); see also Edmonds v. Edmonds, 935 So. 2d 980, 988 (Miss. 2006) (father's request to make payments directly to his son not supported by authority); J.P.M. v. T.D.M., 932 So. 2d 760, 779 (Miss. 2006) (en banc) (mother who failed to cite authority for argument was procedurally barred from raising issue); cf. Boutwell v. Boutwell, 829 So. 2d 1216 (Miss. 2002) (but reviewing claim on merits nonetheless); Forrest v. McCoy, 996 So. 2d 158, 160 (Miss. Ct. App. 2008) (failure to cite authority precludes consideration of issue on appeal; addressing merits nonetheless); Asanov v. Hunt, 914 So. 2d 769, 772 (Miss. Ct. App. 2005) (en banc) (failure to cite authority obviates need to review issue; jurisdictional claim reviewed nonetheless).

[357] Luse v. Luse, 992 So. 2d 659, 662 (Miss. Ct. App. 2008).

[358] Anderson v. Anderson, 961 So. 2d 55, 58 n.1 (Miss. Ct. App. 2007).

[359] Henrichs v. Henrichs, 32 So. 3d 1202, 1205-06 (Miss. Ct. App. 2009), cert. denied, 31 So. 3d 1217 (Miss. 2010).

§ 19.09[7]   MISSISSIPPI FAMILY LAW

appeal.[360]

[7] Reversal

[a] Reversal of divorce. When a grant of divorce is reversed, all matters related to divorce, including property settlement, are null and void.[361] When a divorce decree was set aside for use of the wrong summons, the court also vacated property division, alimony, custody, and child support awards.[362]

[b] Reversal of financial award. Financial awards in divorce – property division, alimony, child support, and attorneys' fees – are linked. Reversal of property division requires reversal of permanent and lump sum alimony, child support, and attorneys' fees.[363] Similarly, reversal of a substantial alimony award required reversal of the court's division of marital assets.[364] The supreme court has held, however, that reversal of property division does not require reversal of rehabilitative alimony. It is not awarded as "an equalizer" and is not linked to other awards.[365] And in one case, a court's reversal of property division required reversal of alimony and child support, but not of attorneys' fees.[366]

When payment of financial awards are not stayed pending appeal, repayment may be required. After alimony was reversed on appeal, a chancellor properly ordered a wife to reimburse her husband for alimony payments received during the period of appeal.[367]

[c] Remand. The supreme court held that on remand of property valuation the chancellor should value the marital assets as of the date of the divorce hearing. In contrast, the court was to determine the appropriate amount of alimony and child support

---

[360] Common v. Common, 42 So. 3d 59, 62 (Miss. Ct. App. 2010); *see also* Parker v. Bliven, 59 So. 3d 619, 622 (Miss. Ct. App. 2010) (father waived issues of contempt and support modification by failing to present them to court in final hearing).

[361] Peterson v. Peterson, 797 So. 2d 876, 877 (Miss. 2001).

[362] Clark v. Clark, 43 So. 3d 496 (Miss. Ct. App. 2010).

[363] Faerber v. Faerber, 13 So. 3d 853, 863-64 (Miss. Ct. App. 2009) (reversal of property division required reversal of lump sum alimony, denial of attorneys' fees, and award of child support); Daniels v. Daniels, 950 So. 2d 1044, 1046-47 (Miss. Ct. App. 2007) (rehabilitative and permanent alimony awards reversed and remanded because division of assets remanded); Long v. Long, 928 So. 2d 1001, 1004 (Miss. Ct. App. 2006) (reversing periodic alimony award because property division reversed); Fitzgerald v. Fitzgerald, 914 So. 2d 193, 199 (Miss. Ct. App. 2005) (reversing allocation of tax liability and award of dependency exemption upon reversal of property division); Gray v. Gray, 909 So. 2d 108, 115 (Miss. Ct. App. 2005) (child support award should be revisited on remand of property division award); Thompson v. Thompson, 894 So. 2d 603, 607 (Miss. Ct. App. 2004); Hankins v. Hankins, 866 So. 2d 508, 511-12 (Miss. Ct. App. 2004); *see also* Lauro v. Lauro, 847 So. 2d 843, 849 (Miss. 2003) (rule not applicable to rehabilitative alimony); *cf.* Yelverton v. Yelverton, 961 So. 2d 19, 30 (Miss. 2007) (on remand of child support and alimony award, court could reconsider attorneys' fees even though not requested by appellant).

[364] *See* Duncan v. Duncan, 815 So. 2d 480, 484 (Miss. Ct. App. 2002).

[365] Lauro v. Lauro, 847 So. 2d 843, 849 (Miss. 2003); *see also* Lauro v. Lauro, 924 So. 2d 584, 588 (Miss. Ct. App. 2006) (reversal of property division requires reversal of periodic alimony, but not rehabilitative). *But cf.* Clark v. Clark, 43 So. 3d 496, 502 (Miss. Ct. App. 2010) (rehabilitative alimony reversed when grant of divorce was reversed for lack of jurisdiction). *But see* Daniels v. Daniels, 950 So. 2d 1044, 1046-47 (Miss. Ct. App. 2007) (rehabilitative and permanent alimony awards reversed and remanded because division of assets remanded).

[366] Segree v. Segree, 46 So. 3d 861, 869 (Miss. Ct. App. 2010) (opinion supported by finding of inability to pay).

[367] Henderson v. Henderson, 757 So. 2d 285, 294 (Miss. 2000).

PROCEDURE § 19.09[7][d]

based upon circumstances existing at the time of the remand hearing.[368] And in the remand of a child custody determination, the court was to consider the child's circumstances at the time of remand, rather than at the time of the hearing three years earlier.[369] Similarly, on remand of an award of child support entered three years earlier, the chancellor should base support on the mother's income and circumstances at the time of remand.[370]

[d] Harmless error. No reversal is necessary if a court's error is minor or harmless. For example, a court's division of marital assets was affirmed – misstatement of two facts did not affect the court's holding.[371]

[8] Certiorari to Mississippi Supreme Court. Many family law cases are assigned to the court of appeals. A party who seeks supreme court review of a court of appeals decision must file a petition for rehearing in the court of appeals as a prerequisite to seeking certiorari.[372] A motion for rehearing must be received within fourteen days after the court of appeals announces its decision.[373] The motion for certiorari must be filed within fourteen days of the court of appeals' decision on the petition for rehearing.[374]

[9] Agreement not to appeal. A divorcing couple may enter into a binding agreement not to appeal a chancellor's decision. The supreme court held that a husband's appeal should be dismissed in light of his agreement not to pursue an appeal in exchange for his wife's agreement to release certain claims.[375]

[10] Attorneys' fees on appeal. An appellate court may award a successful party on appeal attorneys' fees equal to one-half of the amount awarded in the trial court.[376] An exception is made when the appellant has been awarded alimony or marital assets in an amount sufficient to pay the fees.[377] Fees may not be awarded on appeal if they were not granted or requested at the trial level.[378]

[11] Right to appeal *in forma pauperis*. As a general rule, an indigent party is not entitled to a waiver of fees and transcript costs on appeal. However, an indigent parent is entitled to a transcript provided by the state in an appeal from an order terminating

---

[368] Yelverton v. Yelverton, 26 So. 3d 1053, 1057 (Miss. 2010) (husband filed motion for reconsideration alleging change in circumstances affecting alimony and child support).

[369] Vaughn v. Davis, 36 So. 3d 1261, 1267 (Miss. 2010).

[370] Wheat v. Wheat, 37 So. 3d 632, 643 (Miss. 2010).

[371] Berryman v. Berryman, 907 So. 2d 944, 948 (Miss. 2005) (en banc).

[372] M.R.A.P. 17, 40(a).

[373] M.R.A.P. 40(a).

[374] M.R.A.P. 17(b).

[375] Nobile v. Nobile, 535 So. 2d 1385, 1388 (Miss. 1988).

[376] Grant v. Grant, 765 So. 2d 1263, 1268 (Miss. 2000); Williams v. Williams, 164 So. 2d 898 (Miss. 1964); Broome v. Broome, 832 So. 2d 1247, 1256 (Miss. Ct. App. 2002); Black v. Black, 741 So. 2d 299 (Miss. Ct. App. 1999).

[377] McKee v. McKee, 418 So. 2d 764, 767 (Miss. 1982); *cf.* Riddick v. Riddick, 906 So. 2d 813 (Miss. Ct. App. 2004) (suggesting that an appellant may be required to deplete assets for attorneys' fees on appeal even though attorneys' fees were awarded based on need in trial).

[378] Rankin v. Bobo, 410 So. 2d 1326, 1329 (Miss. 1982).

§ 19.09[12]   MISSISSIPPI FAMILY LAW

parental rights.[379] The Mississippi appellate courts have refused to extend this right to parents appealing an adjudication of neglect[380] or to the appeal of a custody action.[381]

[12] Dismissal of appeal

[a] Fugitive dismissal rule. The fugitive dismissal rule allows an appellate court to dismiss the appeal of a fugitive from justice. Applying the rule, the court of appeals dismissed a father's appeal of a criminal contempt conviction. During the pendency of a custody action between the father and the child's maternal grandmother, the father took the child. Their location remained unknown at the time of appeal.[382]

[b] Dismissal for mootness. An appeal should only be heard if an actual controversy exists at the time of the appeal. Appellate review should not be used for "abstract or academic" questions. The court of appeals dismissed a mother's appeal of a habeas order giving the father custody of their son. The couple resolved their dispute after the appeal was filed.[383] However, if the matter is one of significant public interest, the court may address the issue even though the underlying controversy is moot.[384]

§ 19.10 PETITIONS FOR MODIFICATION AND ENFORCEMENT

Chancery courts retain continuing jurisdiction to modify and enforce decrees. Awards of custody, child support, and some forms of alimony remain modifiable based on a material change of circumstances. In addition, courts may be asked to enforce various aspects of a family law decree. The court's subject matter and personal jurisdiction in family law matters continues after the final decree, even if the parties have relocated so that the court would not have original jurisdiction.[385] Special notice is required to notify the defendant of the renewed litigation, but no independent basis for personal jurisdiction is required.[386] However, a court's continuing jurisdiction is limited to some extent by uniform acts addressing interstate jurisdiction in custody and support actions. Petitions to modify or enforce decrees are governed by Rule 81(d), with procedural requirements that vary to some extent from ordinary rules of civil procedure.[387]

The substantive law governing modification of custody and support is discussed in

---

[379] M.L.B. v. S.L.J., 519 U.S. 102, 123-24 (1996).

[380] J.R.T. v. Harrison Cnty. Family Court, 749 So. 2d 105, 109-10 (Miss. 1999).

[381] Schonewitz v. Pack, 913 So. 2d 416, 423 (Miss. Ct. App. 2005).

[382] Weaver v. Parks, 947 So. 2d 1009, 1013-14 (Miss. Ct. App. 2006) (appeal to be reinstated if child returned within thirty days of order); *see also* D.C. v. D.C., 988 So. 2d 359, 364 (Miss. 2008) (appeal of mother who fled with children dismissed).

[383] Wilson v. Mallett, 50 So. 3d 366, 368 (Miss. Ct. App. 2010).

[384] Alford v. Mississippi Div. of Medicaid, 30 So. 3d 1212, 1214 (Miss. 2010) (addressing whether chancery court has jurisdiction to increase Medicaid community spouse support even though husband's death made issue moot), *cert. denied*, 131 S. Ct. 224 (2010).

[385] Reichert v. Reichert, 807 So. 2d 1282 (Miss. Ct. App. 2002); *see also* Sanford v. Arinder, 800 So. 2d 1267 (Miss. Ct. App. 2001).

[386] Reichert v. Reichert, 807 So. 2d 1282, 1287 (Miss. Ct. App. 2002) (Rule 81 requires special notice, but personal jurisdiction is not lost).

[387] *See infra* § 19.11.

PROCEDURE

§ 19.11

the Chapters on custody,[388] alimony[389], and child support.[390] Enforcement actions are covered in Chapter XIV, and jurisdiction in modification and enforcement actions is discussed in Chapter XVIII.[391]

§ 19.11 RULE 81(d) PROCEDURES

[1] Scope of rule. Rule 81(d) of the Mississippi Rules of Civil Procedure provides special procedural rules applicable primarily to family law cases and matters involving estates. Actions involving paternity, adoption, termination of parental rights, grandparents' visitation, and independent custody and support may be tried thirty days after service.[392] The Act also applies to temporary relief in divorce, separate maintenance, custody, and support matters; to actions to modify custody, support or alimony; and to actions for contempt. These matters may be tried seven days after service of process.[393]

[2] Pleadings

[a] Initial pleading. An action under Rule 81(d) is initiated by filing a petition or complaint. The supreme court has advised attorneys that these pleadings should not be designated as motions.[394] However, mislabeling is a matter of form and does not affect a court's authority to act on the matter.[395] The requirements for pleading discussed earlier in this chapter apply to Rule 81(d) petitions as well,[396] including the requirement that the petitioner provide a UCCJEA affidavit in actions related to children.[397]

[b] Responsive pleadings. A defendant is not required to file a pleading in response to a Rule 81 petition. Because no responsive pleading is required, a defendant may raise affirmative defenses at the hearing.[398] A court may, however, order a response to clarify issues in the case. A defendant who fails to comply with an order to respond may not present evidence on the issue.[399] Furthermore, a defendant who seeks affirmative relief must file a counter-petition. The supreme court rejected a father's argument that child support should have been modified in a mother's action to collect child support. Modification was not properly before the court, since he did not file a

---

[388] *See supra* § 12.11.

[389] *See supra* § 9.09.

[390] *See supra* § 13.11.

[391] *See* discussion of modification jurisdiction *supra* § 18.07.

[392] MISS. R. CIV. P 81(d)(1) (also applicable to other matters, including birth certificate correction, name change, legitimation, and matters involving wills and decedent's estates).

[393] MISS. R. CIV. P 81(d)(2) (also including actions to remove minority, and other estate and wards' business).

[394] *See* Jones v. Lee, 754 So. 2d 564, 565 (Miss. Ct. App. 2000); Magee v Magee, 754 So. 2d 1275, 1281 (Miss. Ct. App. 1999); Suess v. Suess, 718 So. 2d 1126, 1128 (Miss. Ct. App. 1998).

[395] Sanghi v. Sanghi, 759 So. 2d 1250, 1255 (Miss. Ct. App. 2000).

[396] *See supra* § 19.02[1][b], [c].

[397] *See supra* § 19.02[4].

[398] Mississippi Dep't Human Servs. v. Guidry, 830 So. 2d 628 (Miss. 2002) (defendant did not waive statute of limitations defense by omitting defense from answer, because answer was elective).

[399] MISS. R. CIV. P. 81(d)(4).

§ 19.11[3]   MISSISSIPPI FAMILY LAW

counter petition for modification.[400]

Attorneys should be careful in calculating time limits for post-trial motions and appeals from Rule 81 judgments. When a Rule 81 defendant responds with a petition or "motion" seeking affirmative relief, a chancellor may treat the response as a counterclaim to the first petition or as a separate petition. The court's characterization of the response may affect the timeliness of later filings.[401] When a defendant's request for relief is treated as a counterclaim, no additional Rule 81 summons is required. A father was properly found in contempt on a mother's petition filed as a counterclaim to his petition to modify. There was no requirement that he be notified of the hearing by a Rule 81 summons.[402]

[3] Service of process. In a number of cases, Rule 81 judgments have been reversed for failure to meet the requirements for service of process. The rule requires service of a specific type of summons, which must be served on the defendant rather than his or her attorney. In addition, continuances must strictly comply with the requirements of the rule, or summons must be reissued.

The Mississippi appellate courts have traditionally required strict compliance with the requirements of Rule 81(d). However, in a 2006 case, the court of appeals appeared to abandon this position, stating that "[w]e further withdraw the conclusion in *Floyd* that 'Rule 81 requires strict compliance.' "[403]

[a] Form of summons. Rule 81 requires use of a special summons, which commands that the defendant appear and defend at a specific time and place set by order of the court and informs him or her that no answer is necessary.[404] In addition, the petition should be attached to the summons.[405] Use of a Rule 4 summons, typically used to initiate a case, does not provide adequate service of process; the Rule 4 summons requires a defendant to answer within thirty days, rather than to appear and defend on a certain date.[406] Similarly, service of a notice of pleading – commonly used in post-trial motions – is insufficient process.[407] A notice of hearing was defective service of process in a Rule 81(d) matter; it did not state that the defendant need not answer in writing.[408] However, a Rule 81 summons is not required to notice a hearing on a

---

[400] Goodin v. Dep't Human Servs., 772 So. 2d 1051 (Miss. 2000).

[401] Carter v. Carter, 735 So. 2d 1109, 1113 (Miss. 1999) (where the chancellor has not made a clear statement on the issue, counsel should be "wary of relying on the result in this case").

[402] Carlson v. Matthews, 966 So. 2d 1258, 1260 (Miss. Ct. App. 2007).

[403] Bailey v. Fischer, 946 So. 2d 404, 408 (Miss. Ct. App. 2006) (quoting Floyd v. Floyd, 870 So. 2d 677, 680 (Miss. Ct. App. 2004)); *see also* M.H. v. D.A., 17 So. 3d 610, 616 (Miss. Ct. App. 2009) (strict compliance with Rule 81(d) no longer required).

[404] *See* Miss. R. Civ. P. 81, cmt. (Section (d)(5) "recognizes that since no answer is required of a defendant/respondent, then the summons issued shall inform him of the time and place where he is to appear and defend.").

[405] Sanghi v. Sanghi, 759 So. 2d 1250, 1253 (Miss. Ct. App. 2000) (noting that the form requires attachment although Rule 81 does not; petition is necessary to notify defendant of substance).

[406] Powell v. Powell, 644 So. 2d 269, 274 (Miss. 1994) (modification based on Rule 4 summons reversed); Saddler v. Saddler, 556 So. 2d 344, 346 (Miss. 1990); *cf.* Clark v. Clark, 43 So. 3d 496 (Miss. Ct. App. 2010) (divorce action served with Rule 81 summons void for lack of jurisdiction).

[407] Serton v. Serton, 819 So. 2d 15 (Miss. Ct. App. 2002) (service of motion on defendant); Sanghi v. Sanghi, 759 So. 2d 1250 (Miss. Ct. App. 2000) (service of a court administrator's notice of hearing).

[408] Chasez v. Chasez, 935 So. 2d 1058, 1061 (Miss. Ct. App. 2005).

628

PROCEDURE § 19.11[3][b]

defendant's counterclaim in a Rule 81 matter.[409] The rules of civil procedure provide a sample form for initiating Rule 81 actions; the supreme court noted that, while the form is not mandatory, its use "removes any question of sufficiency under the Rules."[410]

[b] Manner of service. A Rule 81 summons must be served on the defendant. Service of process was defective when notice was served on a defendant's attorney, rather than the defendant in a contempt proceeding.[411] Rule 81 does not address the means of service, so actual service on the defendant can be accomplished as in actions under the provisions of Rule 4.[412]

[c] Waiver of service of process. A court does·not have jurisdiction over a defendant unless the requirements for service of process are met. A defendant's knowledge of a proceeding does not cure defective service of process.[413] The defect may be attacked collaterally and is not waived by failure to appear.[414] However, defects are waived if the defendant or the defendant's attorney enters a general appearance in the action. For example, a defendant whose attorney appeared and presented evidence on her behalf without objecting to process was properly before the court.[415] In contrast, contact with a court administrator to discuss another date for a hearing did not waive defective service of process.[416]

[d] Service in contempt proceedings in pending action. Rule 81(d)(2)(6) provides that "Rule 5(b) notice shall be sufficient as to any temporary hearing in a pending divorce, separate maintenance, custody or support action provided the defendant has been summoned to answer the original complaint."[417] In a 2007 case, the court of appeals held that Rule 81(d) notice was not required to find a husband in contempt

---

[409] Carlson v. Matthews, 966 So. 2d 1258, 1260 (Miss. Ct. App. 2007) (hearing on mother's counterclaim for contempt did not require Rule 81 summons).

[410] The recommended form may be found in Miss. R. Civ. P. App. A, Form 1D.

[411] Dennis v. Dennis, 824 So. 2d 604 (Miss. 2002).

[412] Sanghi v. Sanghi, 759 So. 2d 1250 (Miss. Ct. App. 2000); *see* discussion of manner of service under Rule 4 *supra* § 19.03[2].

[413] Reichert v. Reichert, 807 So. 2d 1282 (Miss. Ct. App. 2002) (Rule 81 summons is mandatory; judgment is void without proper service).

[414] Johnson v. Johnson, 191 So. 2d 840, 842 (Miss. 1966) (Mississippi defendant not personally served in child support action); Kolikas v. Kolikas, 821 So. 2d 874, 880 (Miss. Ct. App. 2002) (divorce void for failure to mail copy of published summons to physical address) (finding wife not estopped from attacking validity of decree).

[415] Isom v. Jernigan, 840 So. 2d 104 (Miss. 2003); *see also In re* Adoption of Minor Child, 931 So. 2d 566, 575 (Miss. 2006) (en banc) (mother's attorney agreed to new hearing date without objecting to failure to comply with Rule 81); Dennis v. Dennis, 824 So. 2d 604 (Miss. 2002) (defendant waived his procedural rights by appearing voluntarily at the hearing and defending, without objecting to service of process); M.H. v. D.A., 17 So. 3d 610, 615-16 (Miss. Ct. App. 2009) (failure to serve Rule 81(d) summons waived when father participated in custody proceedings without objection); Ellzey v. White, 922 So. 2d 40, 43 (Miss. Ct. App. 2006) (continuance order not entered on date set for hearing; defect waived by appearance without objection), *overruled on other grounds by* Daniels v. Bains, 967 So. 2d 77 (Miss. Ct. App. 2007); Bailey v. Fischer, 946 So. 2d 404, 408 (Miss. Ct. App. 2006) (defects waived by appearance); Chasez v. Chasez, 935 So. 2d 1058, 1062 (Miss. Ct. App. 2005) (waiver by failure to assert at first opportunity).

[416] Sanghi v. Sanghi, 759 So. 2d 1250, 1255 (Miss. Ct. App. 2000); *see also* Hamm v. Hall, 693 So. 2d 906, 908-09 (Miss. 1997) (payment of child support pursuant to an invalid decree did not constitute a waiver); Venegas v. Gurganus, 911 So. 2d 562 (Miss. Ct. App. 2005) (defects in service of process waived by failure to assert at trial).

[417] Miss. R. Civ. P. 81(d)(2)(6).

§ 19.11[4]   **MISSISSIPPI FAMILY LAW**

for nonpayment of temporary support.[418] In 2011, however, the Mississippi Supreme Court reversed a chancellor's contempt order in post-divorce proceedings, holding that "[a] chancery court's continuing jurisdiction to enforce a judgment does not waive the requirement for a Rule 81 summons in contempt actions."[419]

[4] Hearing. Rule 81(d) petitions for temporary relief, for contempt, or for modification may be heard seven days after personal service of process or thirty days after the first publication.[420] Petitions for paternity, adoption, termination of parental rights, or grandparent visitation, or for custody or support may be tried thirty days after personal service of process or the first publication.[421] No default judgment is available in Rule 81(d) matters; the petition "shall not be taken as confessed."[422]

[5] Continuance. Rule 81(d)(5) provides that if an action is not heard on the day specified in the summons, it "may by order signed on that day be continued to a later day for hearing without additional summons."[423] In a number of cases, Rule 81(d) judgments have been reversed because a hearing was continued by an order that was not signed on the day set for hearing or by one that continued the action indefinitely. For example, the supreme court held that when a defendant appeared on the date originally set for hearing and the proceedings were continued indefinitely, a new rule 81 summons was required to notify the defendant of the new hearing date.[424]

[6] Continuance by order of chancery clerk. Rule 81(d)(5) also provides that continuance may be by an order signed by the chancery clerk. However, continuance by a court administrator is not authorized by Rule 81.[425]

§ 19.12 MEDIATION

Parties are increasingly using mediation as an alternative to litigated resolution of divorce, custody, and support actions. Parties may voluntarily choose to mediate a dispute or may be referred to mediation by a court. Mediation in domestic cases is governed by the Court Annexed Mediation Rules for Civil Litigation. Under the rules, communications made in mediation are confidential and cannot be used as evidence in the case. No record is made in mediation and the mediator may not be required to

---

[418] Carroll v. Carroll, 976 So. 2d 880, 885 (Miss. Ct. App. 2007).

[419] Hanshaw v. Hanshaw, 55 So. 3d 143 (Miss. 2011).

[420] MISS. R. CIV. P. 81(d)(2).

[421] MISS. R. CIV. P. 81(d)(1).

[422] MISS. R. CIV. P. 81(d)(3).

[423] MISS. R. CIV. P. 81(d)(5).

[424] Caples v. Caples, 686 So. 2d 1071 (Miss. 1996), *see also* Vincent v. Griffin, 872 So. 2d 676 (Miss. 2004); *cf.* Bailey v. Fischer, 946 So. 2d 404, 407-08 (Miss. Ct. App. 2006) (continuance not signed on date of hearing; defects waived by appearance); Ellzey v. White, 922 So. 2d 40, 43 (Miss. Ct. App. 2006) (continuance order not entered on date set for hearing; defect waived by appearance without objection), *overruled on other grounds by* Daniels v. Bains, 967 So. 2d 77 (Miss. Ct. App. 2007).

[425] MISS. R. CIV. P. 81(d)(5); *cf.* Bailey v. Fischer, 946 So. 2d 404, 408 (Miss. Ct. App. 2006) (continuance order signed by court administrator rather than chancery clerk; defects waived by appearance).

PROCEDURE § 19.13

testify or disclose information revealed in the process.[426] A written agreement reached in mediation is enforceable in the same manner as any other settlement agreement, and may be incorporated into the court's decree.[427]

§ 19.13 EFFECT OF BANKRUPTCY PROCEEDINGS

The Bankruptcy Abuse Prevention and Consumer Protection Act of 2005, which took effect in October of 2005, substantially altered bankruptcy treatment of domestic support and property obligations. The prior rules and the changes implemented by the 2005 Act are discussed in detail in Chapter XXI.

§ 19.14 SERVICEMEMBERS CIVIL RELIEF ACT

A defendant who is in active military service may in some circumstances obtain a stay of proceedings under the Servicemembers Civil Relief Act,[428] adopted in 2003. The Act revised the Soldiers' and Sailors' Relief Act to provide expanded protection for members of the United States military. The Act's provisions apply to members of the National Guard on active duty.[429]

[1] Appearance by defendant. A servicemember who receives notice of a proceeding may obtain a ninety-day stay by sending a written communication to the court (1) explaining how military duty materially affects the defendant's ability to appear and (2) giving a date on which he or she will be able to appear. The letter must be accompanied by a commanding officer's letter stating that military duty prevents the defendant from appearing, and that at the time of the letter, leave is not authorized for the defendant.[430] The servicemember's letter may also request an additional stay beyond the ninety days. The Act provides that if the court refuses the request for additional stay, counsel must be appointed to represent the servicemember.[431] An application for stay does not constitute an appearance; the request does not waive jurisdictional or procedural defects.[432]

[2] Defendant does not appear. The Act provides a different set of procedures for actions in which a defendant does not appear. Before a default judgment may be entered in a civil action, courts are required to inquire whether the defendant is in active military duty.[433] The plaintiff must submit an affidavit stating whether or not the

---

[426] MISS. R. MEDIATION CIV. LIT. § VII (B).

[427] MISS. R. MEDIATION CIV. LIT. § VIII(A)-(B); *see infra* § 23.09 discussing enforceability of consent decrees.

[428] 50 U.S.C. § 501 (2006).

[429] 50 U.S.C. § 511(2)(A)(ii) (2006).

[430] 50 U.S.C. § 522(b)(2)(A)-(B) (2006).

[431] 50 U.S.C. § 522(d)(1)-(2) (2006). Commentators have expressed concern over the lack of provision for payment of counsel or explanation of how appointed counsel will proceed with the defense. *See* Mark E. Sullivan, *A Brief Overview of the New Servicemembers Civil Relief Act*, 16 DIVORCE LITIG. 3 (March 2004).

[432] 50 U.S.C. § 522(c) (2006).

[433] 50 U.S.C. app. § 521(a) (2006 & Supp. 2010) (requirement applies "to any civil action or proceeding, including any child custody proceeding, in which the defendant does not make an appearance").

631

§ 19.14[2]   **MISSISSIPPI FAMILY LAW**

defendant is in military service or that the plaintiff is unable to determine the defendant's military status. If the defendant is an active servicemember, the court may stay the action[434] or must appoint an attorney to represent the defendant.[435]

---

[434] 50 U.S.C. app. § 521(b), (d)(1)-(2) (2006) (minimum stay of ninety days should be granted if court finds that the servicemember may have a defense or counsel has been unable to contact defendant to determine whether there is a valid defense).

[435] 50 U.S.C. app. § 521(b)(2) (2006).

XX
ETHICAL ISSUES IN FAMILY LAW PRACTICE

This chapter highlights ethical issues that family law practitioners are likely to encounter. It is not intended to provide a comprehensive overview of the rules of professional responsibility. Ethical issues related to dual representation, third-party payment of fees, and the use of electronic surveillance are common in divorce actions. In addition, fee arrangements in divorce actions are subject to limitations that are not applicable in most civil cases.

§ 20.01 CONFLICTS OF INTEREST

Attorneys are ethically barred from representing both parties in a suit for divorce. In addition, prior representation of one or both spouses may create a conflict with regard to divorce representation. Similarly, representation of one spouse at divorce may create a conflict with regard to subsequent representation of the other spouse.

[1] Dual representation. An attorney may not represent both spouses in an action for divorce, even if they have agreed to an uncontested irreconcilable differences divorce. The Rules of Professional Conduct provide that "A lawyer shall not represent a client if the representation of that client will be directly adverse to another client..."[1] Dual representation of divorcing parties is considered an automatic violation of this rule. As the Mississippi Ethics Committee noted, the interests of divorcing parties are conflicting and inconsistent "no matter what the parties themselves, as laymen, may believe."[2]

[2] Avoiding the appearance of dual representation. An attorney should exercise caution to dispel any impression of dual representation, particularly when the opposing spouse is unrepresented. Rule 4.3 provides, "In dealing on behalf of a client with a person who is not represented by counsel, a lawyer shall not state or imply that the lawyer is disinterested. When the lawyer knows or reasonably should know that the unrepresented person misunderstands the lawyer's role in the matter, the lawyer shall make reasonable efforts to correct the misunderstanding."[3] Rule 4.3 was amended in 2005 to add, "The lawyer shall not give legal advice to an unrepresented person, other than the advice to secure counsel, if the lawyer knows or reasonably should know that the interests of such a person are or have a reasonably [sic] possibility of being in conflict with the interests of the client."[4]

---

[1] MISS. R. PROF. CONDUCT 1.7(a).

[2] *See* M.S.B. Ethics Op. 80 (March 25, 1983) ("Common representation entails parallel duties to both parties; and the lawyer, therefore, cannot place the interests of one client above the interests of the other.").

[3] MISS. R. PROF. CONDUCT 4.3. *But cf.* Parks v. Parks, 914 So. 2d 337, 340 (Miss. Ct. App. 2005) (wife's attorney did not owe unrepresented husband duty beyond duty to advise that he retain his own counsel; rejecting husband's argument that wife's lawyer had duty to consider husband's alleged mental disability in communications with him).

[4] MISS. R. PROF. CONDUCT. 4.3.

§ 20.01[3]   **MISSISSIPPI FAMILY LAW**

A divorce attorney should not perform any services for a nonclient spouse that could be interpreted as representation. For example, Rule 4.3 was violated when an attorney for one spouse told the adverse party to disregard a summons and then took a default judgment when she failed to respond.[5]

An unrepresented spouse should be advised in writing to seek independent counsel. In addition, a settlement agreement should include a provision that the unrepresented party was advised to obtain representation and declined to do so. However, a written disclaimer may be ineffective if the lawyer or lawyer's staff has performed any services for the adverse party that could have been misinterpreted. The Mississippi Supreme Court held that an attorney's actions of post-dating waivers of process for an adverse party raised a jury question as to the existence of an attorney-client relationship in spite of explicit disclaimers.[6] It is also important that a divorce attorney meet with his or her client separately from the adverse party. In finding a jury question of dual representation, the supreme court considered it significant that the attorney never met separately with his client.[7]

[3] Prior representation. Prior representation of an opposing party spouse or both spouses may bar representation at divorce. Rule 1.9 of the Rules of Professional Conduct provides: "A lawyer who has formerly represented a client in a matter shall not thereafter: (a) represent another in the same or a substantially related matter in which that person's interests are materially adverse to the interests of the former client unless the former client consents after consultation."[8] The test for determining whether prior representation creates a conflict consists of two parts: (1) "Does the former representation have a substantial relationship to the matters involved in the present representation?" and (2) "Does the attorney have information from the former representation that can be used in the new matter against the former client?"[9]

In some cases, prior family representation on matters such as drafting wills, providing estate planning, or incorporating a family business could arm an attorney with information that could be used against an opposing spouse at divorce. However, an attorney who represented a couple in probate proceedings, preparation of their wills, and business litigation was not barred from representing the wife in divorce proceedings. The information obtained previously was "the kind that should be disclosed by each side in the present case."[10] An attorney who represented a wife in a personal injury action was not ethically barred from representing her husband in a divorce action against her two years later: "[T]he Committee can foresee no reasonable probability that the requesting attorney would possess confidences and secrets of the wife which could be utilized against her in the present action."[11]

---

[5] *See* Attorney Q v. Miss. Bar, 587 So. 2d 228, 233 (Miss. 1991).

[6] *See* Winstead v. Berry, 556 So. 2d 321, 324 (Miss. 1989).

[7] *See* Winstead v. Berry, 556 So. 2d 321, 324 (Miss. 1989).

[8] Miss. R. Prof. Conduct 1.9.

[9] M.S.B. Ethics Op. 106 (September 13, 1985) (citing Spragins v. Huber Farm Service, Inc., 542 F. Supp. 166, 172 (N.D. Miss. 1982); Duncan v. Merrill Lynch, Pierce, Fenner & Smith, 646 F.2d 1020, 1027-28 (5th Cir. 1981)). Further, the burden is on the former client to show the substantial relationship. *Id.*

[10] Shorter v. Shorter, 740 So. 2d 352, 355 (Miss. Ct. App. 1999) (no information not already available to wife).

[11] M.S.B. Ethics Op. 128 (December 5, 1986) (opining that "Lawyer A may ethically represent the husband in the

634

ETHICAL ISSUES § 20.01[4]

[4] Subsequent representation. A lawyer may be asked to represent a person whose interests are adverse to a former divorce client. The applicable conflicts test is the Rule 1.9 test discussed above – a conflict exists if there is a substantial relationship between the two matters or if the lawyer received confidential information that could be used against the former client. Any post-divorce proceedings such as alimony, child custody, or child support modification proceedings are "substantially related" to the former action. Representation of the other spouse in those proceedings is clearly inappropriate.[12]

[5] Prior participation as judge. An attorney may not participate as counsel in a case if he or she substantially participated in the case as a judge.[13] An attorney who had previously entered a temporary custody order with respect to a child while serving as chancellor was disqualified from representing the mother in a modification action. However, the court did not err in refusing to disqualify the husband's attorney, who had served as a specially appointed youth court judge during a period when allegations similar to the instant case were pending in youth court. He had no involvement in the case, never saw the file, and testified that he only had access to files of cases assigned to him as judge.[14]

[6] Participation as a mediator. Rule 1.12 provides that a lawyer is barred from representing anyone in connection with a case in which the lawyer participated substantially as a mediator or other third-party neutral, unless written informed consent is given by all parties.[15]

§ 20.02 CONFIDENTIALITY

Rule 1.6 provides that a lawyer must preserve a client's confidences unless the client gives informed consent to the disclosure. The Rule permits disclosure if the lawyer reasonably believes disclosure is necessary to prevent death or serious bodily harm, if disclosure will prevent the commission of a crime or fraud that will produce substantial injury and in which the client has used the lawyer's services, to obtain legal advice about compliance with the rules, in a controversy between the lawyer and client, and to comply with a court order or other law.[16]

---

subsequent divorce action filed by the wife.").

[12] See M.S.B. Ethics Op. 88 (September 23, 1983) (lawyer who represented wife in irreconcilable differences divorce should not represent former husband in child support modification proceeding).

[13] MISS. R. PROF. CONDUCT 1.12.

[14] J.N.W.E. v. W.D.W., 922 So. 2d 12, 16-18 (Miss. Ct. App. 2005) (ruling on temporary custody constituted "substantial participation" in related litigation); *see also* James v. Mississippi Bar, 962 So. 2d 528 (Miss. 2007) (rejecting attorney's argument that divorce matter was not the same "case" as the previous emergency custody and visitation matter, which was tried in a different county); *see* MISS. R. PROF. CONDUCT 1.12.

[15] MISS. R. PROF. CONDUCT 1.12.

[16] MISS. R. PROF. CONDUCT 1.6.

§ 20.03   MISSISSIPPI FAMILY LAW

§ 20.03 ATTORNEYS' FEES

[1] Fees. An attorney may not charge a fee in a domestic relations case that is contingent upon securing a divorce or upon the amount of alimony, support, or property division obtained in the action.[17] Attorneys may, however, charge contingency fees for recovery of vested arrearages of child support and alimony. The Mississippi Ethics Committee explained that the reason for prohibiting contingent fees for divorce – the public policy favoring reconciliation – does not exist with respect to arrearages.[18]

An attorney's fee must be reasonable, considering factors set out in Rule 1.5, including the time and effort involved, the novelty of the questions, the customary local fee, the lawyer's skill and experience, and the time limits involved.[19]

[2] Retainers. Retainers may be classified as general, special, or advance payment. All retainers are subject to the requirement of reasonableness.

[a] General retainers. A general or classic retainer is paid as consideration for an attorney's acceptance of a case. The general retainer is considered to be earned at the moment of payment. The client retains no interest in the funds – the fee need not be segregated in a trust account or any portion returned if the representation is terminated.[20]

[b] Special retainers. A special retainer is a fee paid at the beginning of representation with the understanding that the attorney's hourly rate will be charged against the retainer. The comments to Rule 1.5 of the Mississippi Rules of Professional Conduct recognize that attorneys may charge a special retainer, but require that any unearned portion of the retainer must be returned to the client.[21] A special retainer is a client pledge to secure the payment of fees and should be segregated in a trust account and held for the client's benefit.[22]

[c] Advance payment retainer. In 2002, the Ethics Committee of the Mississippi Bar released an opinion discussing non-refundable retainers that are also used to pay an attorney's hourly fee. The committee stated that a potential ethical dilemma arises when an attorney takes a hybrid retainer that is both non-refundable and used as

---

[17] MISS. R. PROF. CONDUCT 1.5(d)(1); *see* Avant v. Whitten, 253 So. 2d 394, 396 (Miss. 1971) (void as against public policy); Ownby v. Prisock, 138 So. 2d 279, 280-81 (Miss. 1962) (attorney who charged contingency fee in divorce entitled to recover reasonable fee under quantum meruit).

[18] M.S.B. Ethics Op. 88 (Sept. 23, 1983) (attorney may ethically enter into a contingent fee contract to collect past due support).

[19] MISS. R. PROF. CONDUCT Rule 1.5(1), (3), (5), (7).

[20] *See In re* Viscount Furniture Corporation, 133 B.R. 360, 364 (Bankr. N.D. Miss. 1991); M.S.B. Ethics Op. 244 (September 11, 1998).

[21] MISS. R. PROF. CONDUCT 1.5, cmt.; *see also* MISS. R. PROF CONDUCT Rule 1.16(d) (upon termination, a lawyer must refund any unearned payment).

[22] *See In re* Viscount Furniture Corporation, 133 B.R. 360, 365 (Bankr. N.D. Miss. 1991) (describes "security retainer" in which hourly fees are charged against retainer, and advance payment retainer in which title passes to attorney at time of payment, with hourly fees to be charged against payment; suggests that attorney must return any unearned portion, and that retainer must be placed in client trust fund until applied to hourly fees.); M.S.B. Ethics Op. No. 219 (June 3, 1994) (requires that attorneys refund any advance fee payment that has not been earned).

636

ETHICAL ISSUES   **§ 20.04**

a special retainer. The committee noted that these retainers are not per se prohibited. However, if representation is terminated, an attorney must refund "any advance payment that has not been earned," including any unreasonable portion of a non-refundable retainer. Furthermore, the committee noted that the fee arrangement should be in writing and should specifically state the amount of the fee that is non-refundable.[23]

§ 20.04 ATTORNEY LIENS

Attorneys' fees may be secured by liens on client assets unrelated to pending litigation unless the lien is adverse to the client or interferes with the conclusion of the case. In addition, two common law liens arise by operation of law, allowing an attorney to retain property and funds related to litigation under some circumstances.

[1] Consensual liens. An attorney may secure payment of fees by a lien on client property unrelated to the litigation for which the attorney has been retained.[24] Rule 1.8 provides, however, that an attorney may not take an interest in property that is the subject matter of the litigation.[25] The Mississippi Ethics Committee stated that a client's conveyance of his one-half interest in the marital home to his divorce lawyer was ethically barred, since the home was part of the subject matter of the divorce litigation. Furthermore, the attorney's joint ownership with his client's wife could create a situation in which the attorney's interests were adverse to those of his client.[26]

[2] Judgment liens. An attorney may proceed to judgment and obtain a judgment lien to recover unpaid fees. However, an attorney may not impose a lien on property if the interest is adverse to the client or interferes with the conclusion of the case. For example, this rule was violated when an attorney filed a lis pendens notice against his client's home on the same day that a divorce decree was entered ordering sale of the home.[27]

[3] Common law liens. An attorney lien may also arise by operation of law. Common law recognizes two attorney liens on client property in an attorney's possession – the retaining lien and the charging lien. The retaining lien attaches to client property held by an attorney pursuant to representation. The attorney may retain the property until all fees are paid. The charging lien entitles an attorney to recover fees from the proceeds of a case at its conclusion. While some cases suggest that the proceeds must actually come into the lawyer's hands, the lien has also been enforced on proceeds in the possession of third parties. For example, the Mississippi Supreme Court held in 1976 that an attorney's lien could be imposed on funds owed to his client.[28] Further-

---

[23] M.S.B. Ethics Op. 250 (June 25, 2002) (citing Rule 1.16(d)).

[24] *See In re* Viscount Furniture Corp., 133 B.R. 360, 364 (Bankr. N.D. Miss. 1991) (retainer may be held as security for payment of fees).

[25] MISS. R. PROF. CONDUCT 1.8(i).

[26] M.S.B. Ethics Op. 152 (June 2, 1988).

[27] M.S.B. Ethics Op. 244 (Sept. 11, 1998) (lis pendens notice interfered with the court-ordered sale obtained by the attorney).

[28] *See* Indianola Tractor Co. v. Tankesly, 337 So. 2d 705, 706 (Miss. 1976) (attorney's lien imposed on garnished

§ 20.04[4]   MISSISSIPPI FAMILY LAW

more, a chancery court may impose an attorney's lien against the personal property of a client for unpaid fees. The common law lien may not be imposed against real property.[29]

[4] Client files. The retaining lien also allows an attorney to retain client files until all fees are paid. Rule 1.16(d) provides, "Upon termination of representation, a lawyer shall take steps to the extent reasonably practicable to protect a client's interest, such as . . . surrendering papers and property to which the client is entitled and refunding any advance payment that has not been earned. The lawyer may retain papers relating to the client to the extent permitted by other law."[30] However, the Ethics Committee has warned that an attorney may not retain client files if retention would prevent the client from obtaining other representation or interfere with an ongoing case. The committee also noted that the client "file" consists of client papers and property delivered to the lawyer, the lawyer's end work product such as pleadings, and lawyer correspondence. The client file does not include the lawyer's other work product such as notes and internal memoranda.[31]

§ 20.05 THIRD-PARTY FEE PAYMENT

It is not unusual for an attorney's fees to be paid by a divorce client's parents or other family member. Rule 1.8(f) provides that a lawyer "shall not accept compensation for representing a client from one other than the client unless: (1) the client consents after consultation; (2) there is no interference with the lawyer's independence of professional judgment or with the client-lawyer relationship; and (3) information relating to representation of a client is protected as required by Rule 1.6."[32]

§ 20.06 LIMITED REPRESENTATION

Divorcing parties often have limited funds available for legal fees. Attorneys may be asked to provide limited representation such as drafting and presenting a settlement agreement without rendering more extensive legal advice. The request for limited representation can create a genuine dilemma. The assistance may be a valuable service to a client with limited resources. On the other hand, in some cases limited representation may violate an attorney's duty to provide thorough and competent representation. Rule 1.1 provides that a "lawyer shall provide competent representation to a client. Competent representation requires the . . . thoroughness and preparation reasonably necessary for the representation."[33] Rule 1.2(c) provides, "A lawyer may limit the objectives of the representation if the client gives informed consent."[34] In 2011, comments were added

---

funds owed to client).
[29] *See* Tuggle v. Williamson, 450 So. 2d 93, 95 (Miss. 1984).
[30] MISS. R. PROF. CONDUCT 1.16(d).
[31] M.S.B. Ethics Op. 144 (March 11, 1998).
[32] MISS. R. PROF. CONDUCT 1.8(f).
[33] MISS. R. PROF. CONDUCT 1.1.
[34] MISS. R. PROF. CONDUCT 1.2(c).

ETHICAL ISSUES § 20.07

to Rule 1.2 to clarify that limited scope representation in all forms is encouraged, but that attorneys must (1) determine that limited representation is reasonable under the circumstances, (2) explain to the client any disadvantages involved in limited representation, and (3) obtain the client's informed consent.[35]

§ 20.07 NON-LEGAL ADVICE

In emotionally charged matters such as divorce and child custody, effective representation may call for advice incorporating non-legal considerations. The Rules of Professional Conduct permit a lawyer to provide advice other than legal advice: "In rendering advice, a lawyer may refer not only to law but to other considerations such as moral, economic, social and political factors, that may be relevant to the client's situation."[36] For example, family law attorneys may recommend that clients seek counseling for themselves or for their children or may encourage clients to seek mediation as an alternative to litigation.[37]

§ 20.08 CONDUCT DURING REPRESENTATION

An attorney may not make false statements of law or fact, assist a client in future criminal conduct, or use evidence obtained in violation of wiretapping laws.

[1] False Statements. Rule 4.1 provides that a lawyer may not knowingly "make a false statement of material fact or law to a third person."[38] An attorney who lured a party into Mississippi by pretending to schedule a deposition to obtain service of process violated Rule 4.1.[39]

[2] Client's criminal or fraudulent behavior. Divorce clients may conceal assets, make fraudulent transfers of assets, or divert income to alter the financial outcome of divorce. Divorcing parents may refuse to send children on court-ordered visitation or attempt to remove or conceal children from the other parent. Knowledge of a client's criminal conduct requires an attorney to negotiate conflicting ethical obligations: Rule 1.6 provides that a lawyer shall not reveal confidential client information.[40] Rule 1.2 provides that a lawyer must not assist a client in criminal or fraudulent conduct.[41] Rule 3.4 provides that a lawyer shall not counsel or assist a client to "alter, destroy or conceal a document or other material having potential evidentiary value" or to testify falsely.[42] With regard to the rules of ethics, knowledge of client criminal behavior can

---

[35] MISS R. PROF. CONDUCT 1.2, cmt.

[36] MISS R. PROF. CONDUCT 2.1.

[37] *See* MISS. R. PROF. CONDUCT 2.1, cmt. ("Family matter can involve problems within the professional competence of psychiatry, clinical psychology or social work.").

[38] MISS. R. PROF. CONDUCT 4.1.

[39] *See* Mississippi Bar v. Robb, 684 So. 2d 615, 623 (Miss. 1996).

[40] MISS R. PROF. CONDUCT 1.6.

[41] MISS. R. PROF. CONDUCT 1.2; *see also* MISS. R. PROF. CONDUCT 4.1 (lawyer may not fail to disclose fact if disclosure is necessary to prevent assisting client with criminal or fraudulent conduct).

[42] MISS. R. PROF. CONDUCT 3.4(a), (b).

§ 20.08[2][a]   MISSISSIPPI FAMILY LAW

be grouped into three categories: (1) knowledge of past criminal behavior; (2) knowledge or belief that a client will commit a crime in the future; and (3) knowledge that the lawyer's actions will assist a client in criminal behavior.

[a] Past conduct. In 2006, the Rules of Professional Conduct were amended to provide that, under certain circumstances, a lawyer *may* reveal a client's past conduct. A lawyer may reveal confidential client information "to the extent the lawyer reasonably believes necessary . . . to prevent, mitigate or rectify substantial injury to the financial interests or property of another that is reasonably certain to result or has resulted from the client's commission of a crime or fraud in furtherance of which the client has used the lawyer's services." [43] The comments note that this permissive disclosure is allowed when the lawyer believes disclosure will "enable the affected persons to prevent or mitigate reasonably certain losses or to attempt to recoup their losses."[44]

[b] Future conduct. In 2006, the Rules of Professional Conduct were amended to provide that, under certain circumstances, a lawyer may reveal a client's intended conduct "to prevent reasonably certain death or substantial bodily harm," or "to prevent the client from committing a crime or fraud that is reasonably certain to result in substantial injury to the financial interest or property of another and in furtherance of which the client has used or is using the lawyer's services."[45]

[c] Assisting future conduct. A lawyer may not provide representation in a manner that assists a client in conduct that the lawyer knows is criminal or fraudulent.[46] Nor may an attorney knowingly present false evidence or make false statements of law or fact.[47] The Mississippi Supreme Court held that an attorney who did not reveal the known location of children in a domestic case violated Rule 3.3.[48] When continued representation of a client would result in violation of the rules, an attorney should withdraw from representation in a manner that complies with Rule 1.16.[49]

[d] Mandatory reporting. Under Mississippi's mandatory reporting statute, attorneys are required to report suspected child abuse and neglect to the Department of Human Services even though the information was acquired in an attorney-client relationship.[50]

§ 20.09 SURVEILLANCE

Wire and electronic surveillance occur frequently in connection with family law actions. Today, interception of electronic mail poses legal and ethical issues previously

---

[43] MISS R. PROF. CONDUCT 1.6(b)(3).
[44] MISS R. PROF. CONDUCT 1.6, cmt.
[45] MISS R. PROF. CONDUCT 1.6(b)(1), (2).
[46] MISS. R. PROF. CONDUCT 1.2(d).
[47] MISS. R. PROF. CONDUCT 3.3.
[48] Harrison v. Mississippi Bar, 637 So. 2d 204, 223 (Miss. 1994).
[49] MISS. R. PROF. CONDUCT 1.16.
[50] *See* MISS. CODE ANN. § 43-21-353 (2004) (upon "reasonable cause" to suspect abuse).

ETHICAL ISSUES § 20.09[1]

limited to telephonic wiretapping. It is critical that attorneys understand the extent to which information gained through wire and electronic surveillance may be used in divorce and custody proceedings. Unfortunately, the legality of a spouse's recovery and use of electronic communications is unclear.

The 1968 Federal Wiretap Act, Title III of the Omnibus Crime Control and Safe Streets Act, governs the legality of interceptions of wire and oral communications.[51] The Act was amended in 1986 by the Electronics Communications Privacy Act (Stored Communications Act) to address interception of electronic communications.[52]

[1] Interspousal wiretapping. The Wiretap Act prohibits interception of a wire communication by "any person."[53] Although the Act does not explicitly exclude spouses, the Fifth Circuit and the Mississippi Supreme Court have adopted a minority rule that interspousal wiretapping does not violate the Act.[54] Similarly, the Mississippi Supreme Court held that a custodial parent is not prohibited from recording a child's conversations with a noncustodial parent from a telephone in the home where the custodial parent and child live.[55] However, the interspousal exemption applies only to interceptions of conversations in the marital home.[56] For example, the Fifth Circuit held that the exemption did not protect a man who hid under his girlfriend's house and intercepted telephone calls; he was not a part of the household and had no legal right to be on the premises.[57] The exemption does not cover interceptions by third parties. The few courts to consider the issue have held that the exception does not apply when third parties tape a spouse's conversation.[58]

It should be noted that the Eleventh Circuit recently overruled the 1974 Fifth Circuit case that created the exception, noting that since the decision, "an overwhelming majority of [courts] have refused to imply an exception to Title III liability for interspousal wiretapping." Furthermore, the court applied its ruling retroactively, in part because interspousal wiretapping currently is criminalized under the statutes of all states of the Eleventh Circuit.[59]

---

[51] *See* 18 U.S.C. § 2510 (2006).

[52] *See* 18 U.S.C. §§ 2510-2711 (2006 & Supp. 2008, 2009, 2010). For an excellent overview of the two acts, see Richard K. Turkington, *Protection for Invasions of Conversational and Communication Privacy by Electronic Surveillance in Family, Marriage, and Domestic Disputes under Federal and State Wiretap and Store Communications Acts and the Common Law Privacy Intrusion Tort*, 82 Neb. L. Rev. 693 (2004).

[53] 18 U.S.C. § 2511 (2006).

[54] *See* Simpson v. Simpson, 490 F. 2d 803 (5th Cir. 1974); Stewart v. Stewart, 645 So. 2d 1319 (Miss. 1994); *see also* Title III of the Omnibus Crime Control and Safe Streets Act of 1968, 18 U.S.C. § 2510 (2006).

[55] *See* Wright v. Stanley, 700 So. 2d 274, 277-79 (Miss. 1997) (child custody modification proceeding between former spouses).

[56] *See* Simpson v. Simpson, 490 F. 2d 803, 810 (5th Cir. 1974) ("[T]he locus in quo does not extend beyond the marital home of the parties.").

[57] United States v. Schrimsher, 493 F.2d 848, 850-51 (5th Cir. 1974); *see also* Gaubert v. Gaubert, No. Civ.A. 97-1673, 1999 WL 10384, at *1 (E.D. La. January 7,1999) (no interspousal immunity where husband moved out of the marital home prior to attaching a wiretapping device).

[58] *See* United States v. Rizzo, 583 F.2d 907, 909 (7th Cir. 1978), *cert. denied*, 440 U.S. 908 (1979) (investigator either installed the electronic device or instructed the spouse in installing the device; no immunity for "third-party intrusion into the marital home, even if instigated by one spouse"); White v. Weiss, 535 F.2d 1067, 1071 (8th Cir. 1976) ("no sound rationale . . . to insulate a private detective from the reach of the civil penalties contained in the statute"); *see also* Turkington, *supra* note 52, at 705.

[59] *See* Glazner v. Glazner, 347 F.3d 1212, 1221 (11th Cir. 2003) (allowing wife's civil action for damages against husband who taped her conversations during divorce proceedings).

641

§ 20.09[2]   **MISSISSIPPI FAMILY LAW**

[2] Attorney use of and advice regarding wiretapping. In Mississippi, an attorney does not violate ethical rules by advising a client to tape a spouse's conversations in the marital home or by using evidence obtained in that manner. However, advice to proceed in a manner that violates the Wiretap Act for any of the reasons discussed above would constitute an ethical violation.[60] The Wiretap Act excludes use of any illegally intercepted communication in legal proceedings.[61]

The Mississippi Supreme Court has also held that a lawyer does not violate ethical rules by surreptitiously taping a conversation to which the attorney is a party. However, the court noted its distaste for the tactic, which "falls below the standards of professional conduct expected of lawyers."[62] On the other hand, using a taped conversation to threaten or blackmail a party may constitute an ethical violation.[63] And, surreptitious taping may amount to fraudulent concealment under some circumstances.[64] Furthermore, an attorney who falsely denies that he is taping a conversation violates Rules 4.1 and 8.4 of the Rules of Professional Conduct.[65]

[3] Interception of electronic mail. There is little caselaw addressing the legality of e-mail interception. Whether a spouse's recovery of the other's email violates the law depends in part on whether e-mails are intercepted in transit or retrieved from a computer hard drive.

The Fifth Circuit held, in a criminal law case, that stored e-mails are governed exclusively by the Stored Communications Act.[66] This Act prohibits "unauthorized" retrieval of e-mails in "electronic storage."[67]

[a] Use of common computer. Spouses may argue that use of a common computer satisfies the requirement of authorized use. The Fourth Circuit rejected this argument, holding that joint use of a household computer does not in itself authorize access to password-protected files.[68] In contrast, the New Jersey Supreme Court held that a wife did not violate the Act by retrieving her husband's stored e-mails from a joint computer hard drive. She was an authorized user of the machine and did not use her husband's private password to access the file.[69]

---

[60] *See* M.S.B. Ethics Op. 203 (October 30, 1992).

[61] 18 U.S.C. § 2515 (2006).

[62] *See* Attorney M v. Miss. Bar, 621 So. 2d 220, 224 (Miss. 1992); *see also* Attorney LS v. Miss. Bar, 649 So. 2d 810, 813 (Miss. 1995).

[63] Attorney M v. Miss. Bar, 621 So. 2d 220, 224 (Miss. 1992).

[64] *See* Mabus v. St. James Episcopal Church, 884 So. 2d 747, 762-63 (Miss. 2004) (priest and husband failed to reveal taping of confrontation with wife regarding her affair).

[65] *See* Miss. Bar v. Attorney ST, 621 So. 2d 229, 233 (Miss. 1993) ("When asked point-blank whether he is mechanically reproducing a conversation, his answer must be truthful.").

[66] Steve Jackson Games, Inc. v. United States Secret Service, 36 F.3d 457, 464 (5th Cir. 1994).

[67] 18 U.S.C. § 2701 (2006).

[68] Trulock v. Freeh, 275 F.3d 391, 403 (4th Cir. 2001); *see also* Potter v. Havlicke, 2007 WL 539534 (S.D. Ohio 2007) (rejecting argument in dicta).

[69] *See* White v. White, 781 A.2d 85, 90-91 (N.J. Super Ct. Ch. Div. 2001).

ETHICAL ISSUES   § 20.09[3][b]

[b] Stored emails. At least one court has held that e-mails that have been sent and stored are not covered by the Act at all. The New Jersey court adopted a technical definition of "electronic storage" that excludes e-mails that have been sent and stored. The court held that "electronic storage" refers to storage during transmission. Based on this narrow definition, a spouse who retrieves stored e-mails from a home computer is not in violation of the Act.[70]

[c] Exclusion from evidence. The Stored Communications Act does not contain an exclusionary rule comparable to the Wiretap Act prohibition. Thus, even illegally obtained stored e-mails could arguably be used in court proceedings.[71] On the other hand, a Florida court held that illegally obtained e-mails were properly excluded from evidence even though the Florida wiretap statute did not specifically prohibit their use.[72]

[d] Use of spyware. Spouses may also install devices that attempt to capture an e-mail in the process of transmission. For example, a wife installed a program on the family computer that periodically took snapshots of the computer screen, providing her with a record of her husband's chat room conversations and ingoing and outgoing e-mails. Interpreting the Florida wiretap statute, the court held that her actions were an illegal interception of an electronic communication. The court distinguished between spyware that retrieves information already stored, and a program that copies a communication in transmission.[73]

§ 20.10 NO DUTY OF CONTINUING REPRESENTATION

A judgment of divorce does not always end litigation between former spouses. Parties may subsequently petition the court to modify or enforce orders related to support, custody, or visitation. The court retains continuing jurisdiction to resolve these matters. However, absent an agreement to that effect, an attorney has no general duty to represent a client in post-divorce litigation. The Mississippi Ethics Committee rendered an opinion stating that a lawyer who represented a wife in a divorce action was not required to represent her in subsequent litigation between the parties.[74]

---

[70] *See* White v. White, 781 A.2d 85, 89-90 (N.J. Super Ct. Ch. Div. 2001).

[71] Turkington, *supra* note 52, at 735-36.

[72] *See* O'Brien v. O'Brien, 899 So. 2d 1133, 1137 (Fla. Dist. Ct. App. 2005) (trial court had discretion to exclude illegally obtained evidence).

[73] *See* O'Brien v. O'Brien, 899 So. 2d 1133, 1136-37 (Fla. Dist. Ct. App. 2005); *see also* Bailey v. Bailey, 2008 WL 324156 (E.D. Mich. 2008).

[74] M.S.B. Ethics Op. 166 (June 23, 1989).

644

XXI
BANKRUPTCY AND FAMILY LAW

*Co-author John M. Czarnetzky**

Family law practitioners must have a basic familiarity with the provisions of the Bankruptcy Code. A bankruptcy filed before or during the pendency of divorce will trigger an automatic stay that may affect parts of the divorce action, particularly property division. The financial strain of divorce may push a former spouse to file bankruptcy, potentially affecting divorce-related payments of alimony, child support, and property division. If the debtor is in arrears on these payments, the support creditor's collection of arrearages and enforcement of liens may be limited. The practitioner should consider these effects when crafting a divorce settlement if circumstances suggest that bankruptcy may be filed later.

The Bankruptcy Reform Act of 2005,[1] effective October 17, 2005, made significant changes in the Code's provisions related to family law. However, because the Act does not apply to petitions filed prior to the effective date, practitioners must also be familiar with the former Code provisions.

§ 21.01 BANKRUPTCY BASICS

Obligations to children, spouses, and former spouses are accorded greater protections in bankruptcy than ordinary unsecured debts. Alimony and child support obligations are provided the most complete protection. Property division payments receive greater protection under the 2005 amendments than under prior law but are still subject to limitations not applicable to spousal and child support. This chapter discusses the provisions affecting family law obligations under Chapters 7 and 13, the most commonly used forms of personal bankruptcy.

[1] Liquidation. Chapter 7 affords debtors a fresh start as of the date of filing bankruptcy. In a Chapter 7 proceeding, the debtor's nonexempt, pre-petition assets become the property of the bankruptcy estate.[2] The property is sold by the bankruptcy trustee and the proceeds distributed to pre-petition creditors in accordance with bankruptcy priority rules.[3] The debtor is discharged from debts that are not satisfied by the sale, with the exception of certain nondischargeable debts.[4] Income earned after the

---

* Professor of Law, University of Mississippi. B.S., Massachusetts Institute of Technology; J.D., University of Virginia.

---

[1] Bankruptcy Abuse Prevention and Consumer Protection Act of 2005, Pub. Law 109-8, 119 Stat. 23 (codified as amended in scattered sections of 11 U.S.C.).

[2] 11 U.S.C. § 541(a)(1) (Supp. 2010) (estate includes "all legal or equitable interests of the debtor in property as of the commencement of the case").

[3] 11 U.S.C. § 704(a)(1) (Supp. 2010) (duties of the trustee include the duty to "collect and reduce to money the property of the estate for which such trustee serves"). Priority rules for Chapter 7 proceedings can be found at 11 U.S.C. § 507 (Supp. 2010) and rules for distribution of property at 11 U.S.C. § 726 (Supp. 2010).

[4] 11 U.S.C. § 523(a) (Supp. 2010) (list of debts that are not dischargeable in bankruptcy); *see also id.* § 524 (effect of discharge), *id.* § 727 (provision for discharge).

§ 21.01[2]   **MISSISSIPPI FAMILY LAW**

petition is filed remains the property of the debtor and is available for payment of support obligations.[5]

[2] Reorganization. Chapter 13 provides for debt restructuring, allowing the debtor to retain his or her property while making payments from post-petition income. The debtor must submit a payment plan that provides for debt repayment over a three- to five-year period.[6] When all plan payments have been made, the debtor is discharged from all but certain specified debts. If a general unsecured creditor or the trustee objects to a proposed plan that otherwise meets the mandatory provisions contained in the code, the debtor must devote all of his or her "disposable income" – defined as income above "reasonable living expenses" – to paying creditors.[7] If the debtor fails to complete payments under an approved Chapter 13 plan, the debtor may still be discharged provided that the debtor has, among other things, paid each unsecured creditor an amount equal to that they would have received in a Chapter 7 case.[8]

[3] The automatic stay. The filing of a bankruptcy petition is accompanied by an automatic stay that arises by operation of law, without prior notice to creditors. The stay stops all actions against the debtor in connection with pre-petition obligations. The stay applies to judicial proceedings, non-judicial attempts to collect pre-petition debts or to exercise control over the debtor's property, and actions to establish or enforce liens against the debtor.[9]

§ 21.02 THE BANKRUPTCY REFORM ACT OF 2005: AN OVERVIEW

The 2005 amendments made several significant changes that affect domestic relations orders and proceedings. These include the creation of a new, expanded designation for family law obligations, exemption of most obligations from the automatic stay of bankruptcy, and creation of a new priority for family support obligations.

[1] The "domestic support obligation". The 2005 amendments introduce a new term of art, the "domestic support obligation" or DSO, to describe family support obligations entitled to special protection. A domestic support obligation is defined as a debt that accrues before or after filing, including interest, "owed to or recoverable by a spouse, former spouse, or child of the debtor or such child's parent, legal guardian or responsible relative; or a governmental unit; in the nature of alimony, maintenance, or support, . . . without regard to whether such debt is expressly so designated," established before or after the bankruptcy filing under a separation agreement, court order,

---

[5] *See* 11 U.S.C. § 541(a)(5) (Supp. 2004) (amended 2005) (excluding from property of the estate "earnings from services performed by an individual debtor after the commencement of the case").

[6] 11 U.S.C. § 1322(d) (Supp. 2010) (containing the formula a court must apply to determine whether repayment plan will be three or five years).

[7] 11 U.S.C. § 1325(b)(1)-b(2) (Supp. 2010).

[8] 11 U.S.C. § 1328(b)(2) (Supp. 2004) (amended 2005); 11 U.S.C. § 1325(a)(4) (plan should be confirmed if value of property to be distributed is at least equal to amount that would be paid to unsecured creditors under liquidation).

[9] 11 U.S.C. § 362(a) (Supp. 2010).

BANKRUPTCY AND FAMILY LAW

§ 21.02[2]

or government agency determination.[10] Thus, the definition includes alimony and child support accruing before or after the petition as well as alimony and child support established by a post-petition order. The definition also includes support payable through a state's IV-D agency, such as the Department of Human Services. It does not include property division payments or arrearages.

[2] The automatic stay. Under prior law, most family law proceedings were technically subject to the automatic stay. Now, most family law proceedings other than property division are excluded from the automatic stay.[11]

[3] Dischargeability. The amendments expand the nondischargeability of domestic relations obligations. Under prior law, alimony, maintenance, and child support were nondischargeable, but nondischargeability of property division payments was decided under a balancing test. Under the amendments, property division obligations are nondischargeable in Chapter 7 proceedings. In Chapter 13, however, a debtor may be allowed to pay less than the full amount owed in property division.[12]

[4] Priority. Under prior law, alimony and child support obligations were not a first priority among creditors. The amendments give domestic support obligations first priority over all other debts except expenses of the bankruptcy proceeding.[13]

[5] Effective date. The amendments do not apply to petitions filed before October 17, 2005. Thus, for a period of time, practitioners must be familiar with both prior law and the new amendments.[14]

§ 21.03 THE AUTOMATIC STAY AND FAMILY LAW OBLIGATIONS

The 2005 amendments made significant changes in application of the automatic stay to family law matters. Family law matters affected by bankruptcy may include original orders for divorce; orders of custody, paternity, visitation, alimony, child support, or domestic violence protective orders; orders to modify custody, alimony, or child support; actions to establish property division as part of a divorce action; actions to collect currently due support under an outstanding order; and actions to collect or enforce arrearages in support or property division. Whether a particular action is stayed depends upon the nature of the action, whether the bankruptcy is a liquidation or reorganization, and whether the petition was filed before or after October 17, 2005.

[1] Original orders. Under prior law, the stay did not apply to actions to establish paternity or to establish or modify alimony, maintenance, or child support.[15] The

---

[10] 11 U.S.C. § 101(14A)(A) (Supp. 2010) (defining disposable income).

[11] *See infra* § 21.03.

[12] *See infra* § 21.04.

[13] 11 U.S.C. § 507(a)(1)(A)-(B) (Supp. 2010).

[14] 11 U.S.C. § 1501 (2006).

[15] 11 U.S.C. § 362(b)(2)(A)(i)-(ii) (2000) (amended 2005).

§ 21.03[2]   **MISSISSIPPI FAMILY LAW**

stay did apply to actions for divorce, custody, property division, and protection from domestic violence. In order to proceed with one of the latter actions, a petitioner was required to seek an order from the bankruptcy court granting relief from the stay.[16] Failure to obtain a stay technically resulted in a void or voidable decree. In contrast to some courts, the Fifth Circuit has held that orders obtained in violation of the stay are voidable rather than void, particularly if the bankruptcy court subsequently lifts the stay.[17] With respect to a petition filed prior to October 17, 2005, it is still necessary to obtain relief from the stay to commence or continue a family law matter other than child support or paternity actions.

Under the 2005 amendments, most actions to establish or modify a domestic relations order other than property division may proceed without regard to the stay. For actions filed after October 17, 2005, the stay does not apply to actions for divorce, paternity, custody, visitation, or protective orders. It does not apply to actions to establish or modify domestic support obligations (DSO), which include alimony, maintenance, and child support, including child support collected by the Department of Human Services.[18]

[2] Modification of custody, alimony, or support. An action to modify custody, alimony, or child support is not stayed by the defendant's bankruptcy filing, whether the petition for modification is filed before or after the bankruptcy petition.[19]

[3] Property division. Family law and bankruptcy become most entangled when property division and bankruptcy coincide. A state court hearing a divorce action has the power to divide marital property equitably without regard to who holds title to the property.[20] However, in Mississippi, a spouse has no interest in property owned by the other until a court judgment classifies the property as marital and orders a transfer of property or a lump sum payment as part of equitable distribution. In contrast to community property, no right or interest arises as a result of the marriage, nor does the filing of a divorce action alter title to the property.[21] When bankruptcy and divorce occur simultaneously, marital property may include assets that are, or will become, property of the bankruptcy estate.

The effect of the automatic stay on property division is the same under both prior law and the 2005 amendments – division of marital assets is subject to the automatic stay.[22] A state court may not classify and divide marital property without permission of the bankruptcy court. However, a spouse who files a divorce action seeking property division is asserting a claim against assets held by the debtor spouse and arguably at the moment of filing divorce becomes a creditor with an unliquidated claim against the estate. The spouse may file a claim in bankruptcy and seek relief from the stay for the

---

[16] 11 U.S.C. § 362(d) (2000) (amended 2005).

[17] *See* Chunn v. Chunn, 106 F.3d 1239, 1242 n.6 (5th Cir. 1997).

[18] 11 U.S.C. § 362(b)(2) (Supp. 2010); *see* 11 U.S.C. § 101(14A) (Supp. 2010) (defining domestic support order).

[19] 11 U.S.C. § 362(b)(2) (Supp. 2010).

[20] Ferguson v. Ferguson, 639 So. 2d 921 (Miss. 1994) (marital property includes any asset acquired by the efforts of one of the parties during the marriage).

[21] Ferguson v. Ferguson, 639 So. 2d 921 (Miss. 1994).

[22] 11 U.S.C. § 362(b)(2)(A)(iv) (Supp. 2010).

648

BANKRUPTCY AND FAMILY LAW

§ 21.03[4]

state court to determine the share of assets to which he or she would be entitled outside of bankruptcy. Or, the state court may chose to proceed with the divorce and other aspects of the proceeding and reserve jurisdiction to divide property after the bankruptcy is concluded.[23]

[4] Collection of support payments. Alimony, child support, and sometimes property division, require ongoing payments by the obligor. When the debtor files bankruptcy, questions arise with regard to collection of these obligations. In addition, the support creditor may seek to collect arrearages in payments by obtaining a judgment for arrearages, executing on the judgment, seizing tax refunds, or seeking to have the debtor held in contempt.[24] Child support and alimony recipients may also have the debtor's driver's, professional, or recreational licenses suspended or report the delinquency to a credit reporting agency as a means of encouraging payment.[25] The 2005 amendments enhance a support recipient's ability to pursue payment and collection without regard to the automatic stay.

[a] Currently-due payments. Under prior law, efforts to collect alimony, maintenance, and child support from a Chapter 7 debtor's post-petition earnings were not stayed.[26] With respect to Chapter 13 proceedings, however, the support creditor was required to seek payment under the reorganization plan or to obtain relief from the stay.[27] As under prior law, a support recipient may seek payment of alimony or child support from a Chapter 7 debtor's post-petition earnings, which are not part of the bankruptcy estate.[28] It should be noted that the expanded definition of domestic support obligations under the amendments also allows governmental units such as DHS to collect support from post-petition earnings.[29]

The amendments expand a support creditor's ability to collect current support in Chapter 13 proceedings without obtaining relief from the stay. Under the amendments, the stay does not apply to income-withholding orders even though the debtor's post-petition income is property of the estate.[30] Thus, an outstanding income-withholding order for alimony or child support continues in effect without regard to bankruptcy filing.

[b] Collection of arrearages. The 2005 amendments made only slight changes in the effect of the automatic stay on collection of arrearages. Arrearages in

---

[23] WILLIAM HOUSTON BROWN, BANKRUPTCY AND DOMESTIC RELATIONS MANUAL, § 10:8 (2005).

[24] *See supra* §§ 14.02, 14.05, 14.07; 11 U.S.C. § 362(b)(2)(A)–(G) (2006) (specifying actions not stayed in relation to DSO's and their enforcement).

[25] *See supra* § 14.08[1], [2]; 11 U.S.C. § 362(b)(2)(D)-(F) (Supp. 2010) (automatic stay not applicable).

[26] 11 U.S.C. § 362(b)(2)(B) (2000) (amended 2005).

[27] Under prior law, no provision similar to 11 U.S.C. § 362(b)(2)(C) (2006) (enforcement of existing DSO) existed, thus preventing enforcement in a pending Chapter 13 case without lifting the stay. The support creditor could seek payment under the plan by filing a claim against the estate pursuant to 11 U.S.C. § 501 (2000) (amended 2005) or seek relief from the automatic stay under 11 U.S.C. § 362(d) (2000) (amended 2005).

[28] 11 U.S.C. §§ 541(a)(6), 1304(a)(2) (Supp. 2004) (amended 2005).

[29] 11 U.S.C. § 101(14A)(A)(ii) (Supp. 2010) (defining DSO's to include obligations owed to a governmental unit).

[30] 11 U.S.C. § 362(b)(2)(C) (Supp. 2010).

§ 21.03[5]   MISSISSIPPI FAMILY LAW

alimony or child support may be sought from a Chapter 7 debtor's post-petition income under prior law as well as under the amendments.[31] Under the 2005 amendments, this includes collection by DHS. Arrearages in property division must be collected through the bankruptcy proceedings.

In Chapter 13 proceedings, arrearages in support must be sought through the bankruptcy court whether the petition was filed before or after the effective date of the amendments. The reorganization plan must provide for repayment of all domestic support obligations.[32]

[5] Enforcement of judicial liens. A divorce decree may provide a former spouse with an equitable lien on pre-petition assets to secure payments of alimony, child support, or property division. Execution of an equitable or other judicial lien is subject to the stay in bankruptcy in either a Chapter 7 or Chapter 13 proceeding under prior law and the amendments.[33] However, the judicial lien provides the spouse with the status of a secured creditor, with respect to either support or property obligations. It should also be noted that the 2005 amendments provide that assets exempt from the bankruptcy estate are subject to the claims of domestic support order creditors even if the property is exempt from the claims of creditors under state law.[34]

[6] Contempt actions. Contempt is one of the tools commonly used to enforce a domestic relations order. Upon finding a debtor in contempt, a court may order incarceration, enter a judgment for arrearages, and order the debtor to pay the petitioner's attorneys' fees.[35] Contempt proceedings are not exempted from the automatic stay. Relief from the stay should be sought from the bankruptcy court to proceed with an action for contempt.[36]

[7] Other enforcement tools. Child support and alimony collection have been enhanced by a number of additional remedies for nonpayment, including proceedings to suspend the debtor's driver's, professional, or recreational licenses, reporting delinquencies to credit reporting agencies, intercepting tax refunds, and collection of medical insurance support through withholding orders. Under the 2005 amendments, these additional remedies are not affected by the automatic stay.[37]

§ 21.04 DISCHARGEABILITY

Under both Chapters 7 and 13, a debtor receives a discharge from most debts. The 2005 amendments expand the extent to which family law obligations are nondischarge-

---

[31] 11 U.S.C. § 362(b)(2)(B) (Supp. 2010).

[32] 11 U.S.C. § 1322(a)(2) (Supp. 2010).

[33] 11 U.S.C. § 362(a)(4) (Supp. 2010).

[34] 11 U.S.C. § 522(c)(2) (2006). The Fifth Circuit had held in *In re David*, 170 F.3d 475 (5th Cir. 1999) that property released from bankruptcy but exempt under state law could not be reached by support creditors.

[35] *See supra* §§ 14.05, 12.03[2].

[36] MICHAELA M. WHITE, MARIANNE B. CULHANE, & NATHALIE MARTIN, WHEN WORLDS COLLIDE: BANKRUPTCY AND ITS IMPACT ON DOMESTIC RELATIONS AND FAMILY LAW, at 17 (American Bankruptcy Institute 3d ed. 2005).

[37] 11 U.S.C. § 362(b)(2)(D)-(F) (Supp. 2010).

BANKRUPTCY AND FAMILY LAW §21.04[1]

able in bankruptcy.

[1] Alimony and child support. Alimony and child support are nondischargeable under both the old and new provisions of the Act, but the definition of family support is broader under the amendments. Under prior law, bankruptcy did not discharge a debtor from a debt to a spouse, former spouse, or child for alimony, maintenance or support under a separation agreement or court order. The exception did not apply to support payments made to a governmental entity such as the Department of Human Services.[38] Under the amendments, "domestic support obligations" (DSO) are nondischargeable in Chapter 7[39] and Chapter 13 proceedings.[40]

[2] Property division. Whether a property division transfer or payment is dischargeable may depend on whether the debtor's petition was filed before October 17, 2005. In Chapter 7 proceedings under prior law, dischargeability of property division payments was determined by a balancing test. The obligation could be discharged if the debtor lacked the ability to pay the debt or if the benefit to the debtor of discharging the debt outweighed the harm to the creditor.[41] In Chapter 13 proceedings, the debt could be discharged if all plan payments were made.[42] One of the most significant changes made by the amendments was to make property division payments nondischargeable in Chapter 7 proceedings. The ability-to-pay and balancing tests are no longer applicable.[43] In Chapter 13 proceedings, property settlement debts will be discharged if the debtor makes all the required plan payments and has paid all domestic support obligations that are due.[44]

[3] Payment of debts. A divorce decree may include a provision that the debtor spouse pay certain joint debts and hold the other spouse harmless for the nonpayment of those debts. These provisions are typically part of property division. In some cases, however, payment of debt may be part of an award of alimony.[45] Whether the obligation can be discharged, leaving the former spouse solely liable, will depend on whether the obligation is classified as alimony or property division. Payment of debt as part of alimony will be nondischargeable. The dischargeability of property division debts will depend on when the bankruptcy petition was filed and whether the proceeding is under Chapter 7 or 13.[46]

[4] Attorneys' fees. In family law proceedings in Mississippi, a court may order one spouse to pay the other's attorneys' fees based on the beneficiary's inability to pay.

---

[38] 11 U.S.C. § 523(a)(5) (2000) (amended 2005).

[39] 11 U.S.C. §§ 523(a)(5), 727(b) (2006).

[40] 11 U.S.C. § 1328(c)(2) (2006).

[41] 11 U.S.C. § 523(a)(5) (2000) (amended 2005).

[42] 11 U.S.C. § 1328(a) (2000) (amended 2005).

[43] 11 U.S.C. § 523(a)(5) (Supp. 2010).

[44] 11 U.S.C. § 1328(a) (2006).

[45] *See supra* § 9.07.

[46] *See supra* § 21.04[2]. *Compare* 11 U.S.C. § 523(a)(15) (property division debts dischargeable in Chapter 7) *with* 11 U.S.C. § 1328(a)(2)(omitting § 523(a)(15) from the list of Chapter 7 nondischargeable debts that are also nondischargeable in Chapter 13).

651

§ 21.05   MISSISSIPPI FAMILY LAW

Because attorneys' fees are awarded based upon need, they are likely to be deemed "in the nature of support" and nondischargeable.[47]

§ 21.05 DISTINGUISHING PROPERTY DIVISION PAYMENTS AND SUPPORT

Whether a payment is alimony or part of property division has important consequences in bankruptcy. The distinction is less critical under the 2005 amendments for Chapter 7 proceedings. But it retains significance in a Chapter 13 proceeding. Property division payments are not necessarily paid in full, while domestic support obligations must be completely satisfied. The question of whether a particular payment is support is determined by reference to federal bankruptcy law, although the court may look to state law for assistance in making the determination. The court will consider whether the obligation ends with death or remarriage, whether it is intended to reduce an income disparity between the parties, whether the payments are installments or a lump sum, whether the obligation is modifiable, whether there was a need for support, and whether there was a division of property and debt.[48] Under both the old and new provisions, the bankruptcy court is not bound by the labels used by the state court or the parties to describe a payment.[49]

§ 21.06 ASSETS OF THE NONDEBTOR SPOUSE AND THE BANKRUPTCY ESTATE

[1] Bankruptcy filed during marriage. Property owned solely by the nondebtor spouse is not included in the bankruptcy estate in equitable distribution states such as Mississippi. With regard to jointly owned property, only the debtor's interest is included in the estate.[50] It should be noted, however, that under some circumstances, the bankruptcy court may order a sale of jointly owned assets to the extent that creditors could reach the debtor's interest under state law.[51] In Mississippi, property owned in joint tenancy or tenancy in common can be sold to satisfy the claims of creditors, but property held as tenants by the entirety cannot be reached by one spouse's creditors.[52]

[2] Bankruptcy filed during pending divorce. When bankruptcy is filed after a divorce petition is filed but before the judgment of divorce, all assets titled in the name of the debtor spouse become a part of the bankruptcy estate. The state court action is stayed with respect to property division. In Mississippi, a spouse has no property interest in assets titled in the other's name until a judgment of divorce and equitable

---

[47] *See In re* Joseph, 16 F.3d 86 (5th Cir. 1994).

[48] *See In re* Davidson, 104 B.R. 788 (Bankr. N.D. Tex. 1989), *rev'd on other grounds*, 947 F.2d 1294 (5th Cir. 1991). On appeal, the Fifth Circuit held that the payor was estopped from claiming that payments were dischargeable property division payments, after he deducted them as alimony for tax purposes. 947 F.2d at 1297.

[49] 11 U.S.C. § 101(14A)(B) (Supp. 2010).

[50] BROWN, *supra* note 23, § 10:6.

[51] BROWN, *supra* note 23, § 10:6.

[52] Burns v. Burns, 518 So. 2d 1205, 1216 (Miss. 1988) ("marriage has many protective attributes not available to others including . . . the right to hold property free from assault by a spouse's individual creditors as tenants by the entirety").

652

BANKRUPTCY AND FAMILY LAW § 21.06[3]

distribution.[53] Under these circumstances, the nondebtor spouse becomes an unsecured creditor in the bankruptcy with regard to assets titled in the debtor's name.[54]

[3] Bankruptcy filed after judgment of divorce. As a general rule, property in the debtor's name awarded to the nondebtor spouse in divorce does not become a part of the bankruptcy estate in a subsequently-filed bankruptcy, even if the actual transfer has yet to take place.[55] Similarly, property of the nondebtor spouse awarded to the debtor in a pre-bankruptcy decree should be included in the bankruptcy estate.[56]

[4] Joint debts. A nondebtor spouse is entitled to some protection from liability for joint debt assigned to the debtor spouse. In Chapter 13 reorganizations, a creditor is stayed from proceedings against a co-debtor with regard to payment of a debt provided for in the repayment plan unless the debt was incurred in the ordinary course of the co-debtor's business or the co-debtor received the consideration for the debt.[57] After the plan payments are completed and the Chapter 13 case ended, however, the stay is lifted and creditors may pursue the co-debtor for any remaining debt.

§ 21.07 THE TRUSTEE'S AVOIDANCE POWER

A trustee may set aside a pre-bankruptcy transfer by the debtor intended to defraud creditors of available assets. Under prior law, transfers within one year of bankruptcy, for less than a reasonably equivalent value, could also be set aside.[58] The 2005 amendments change the look-back period to two years, effective April, 2006.[59] A transfer between spouses intended to defraud creditors may be set aside under these provisions.

---

[53] *See* Ferguson v. Ferguson, 639 So. 2d 921 (Miss. 1994).

[54] BROWN, *supra* note 23, § 10:9 ("claim" includes contingent, unmatured, disputed, or unliquidated claims).

[55] *Contra* W.R. HABEEB, Annotation, *Obligation Under Property Settlement Agreement Between Spouses as Dischargeable in Bankruptcy*, 74 A.L.R. 2d 758 (1960). 11 U.S.C. § 541(d) (property in which debtor has mere legal title and another has equitable title does not become property of the bankruptcy estate); *see In re* Erwin, 25 B.R. 363 (Bankr. D. Minn. 1982) (property granted to debtor, but encumbered by lien to satisfy former wife's property settlement, not part of bankruptcy estate, to extent of wife's equitable interest).

[56] BROWN, *supra* note 23, § 10:6.

[57] 11 U.S.C. § 1301(a) (Supp. 2004) (amended 2005).

[58] 11 U.S.C. § 548 (2000) (amended 2005).

[59] 11 U.S.C. § 548(a)(1) (2006).

653

654

XXII
TAX EFFECTS
OF PAYMENTS AND TRANSFERS PURSUANT TO DIVORCE

A judgment of divorce may order several payments or property transfers between spouses. These may include child support, four types of alimony, transfers or payments pursuant to property division, payment of debts or attorneys' fees, or payment of monthly expenses such as mortgages or utilities. Understanding the tax effects of these payments is critical to the evaluation of settlement proposals and to ensure proper tax reporting. Failure to consider tax implications can result in serious over- or under-valuing an agreement's worth to a client. Improper post-divorce treatment of payments or transfers can create substantial tax liability and generate litigation over which of the parties should bear the loss.

This chapter discusses in detail the tax effects of the most common divorce-related payments or transfers – child support, alimony, and basic property transfers. In addition, the chapter explains the allocation of a number of common tax deductions between divorcing parties, without a full discussion of the deductions themselves. The chapter also notes potential tax problems related to more complex dissolution transactions.

§ 22.01 Alimony

Payments that meet the Internal Revenue Code (Code)[1] definition of alimony are taxable income to the payee[2] and an adjustment to income for the payor.[3] The label alimony may be misleading – alimony classification under state law includes transactions that do not qualify as alimony under the Code.

[1] Code requirements for alimony. The Code defines alimony as a payment in cash received by or on behalf of a spouse under a divorce or separation instrument, which is not designated as non-alimony and is not for child support, paid when the parties are not members of the same household, and for which there is no liability after the payee's death.[4]

[a] Payment in cash. To qualify as alimony, payments must be in cash or by check. A transfer of services or property does not qualify as alimony.[5]

[b] Payment to a spouse or on behalf of a spouse. A divorce decree may re-

---

[1] Unless otherwise indicated, all references to the "Code" are to the Internal Revenue Code.

[2] I.R.C. § 71(a) (2006). A spouse who makes alimony payments to a non-resident alien is required to withhold 30% of the payment for taxes. I.R.C. §§ 871, 1441 (2006).

[3] I.R.C. § 215(a) (2006) ("[T]here shall be allowed as a deduction an amount equal to the alimony or separate maintenance payments paid during such individual's taxable year.").

[4] I.R.C. § 71(b)(1) (2006).

[5] Treas. Reg. § 1.71-1T(A-5) (1984).

655

§ 22.01[1][b][i]　　　　　　　　　**MISSISSIPPI FAMILY LAW**

quire one spouse to make post-divorce payments to a third party on behalf of the other. For example, one spouse may be required to pay the other's mortgage, property taxes or insurance, rent, utility bills, medical insurance, or medical expenses. A party may be ordered to provide a life insurance policy for the benefit of the other. As a general rule, these qualify as payments made "on behalf of a spouse" and are deductible to the payor and income to the payee if the other requirements of Code § 71 are met.[6] Third-party payments related to a residence or to life insurance premiums are subject to additional requirements.

[i] Payment of life insurance premiums. Life insurance premiums on a taxpayer's life are deductible if the policy is owned by the other spouse and if the other requirements of Code § 71 are met. The payee must declare the payments as income. If, however, the payee spouse may be removed as a policy beneficiary, the payments are not deductible.[7]

[ii] Payments related to residence. Divorce decrees frequently require a spouse to pay mortgage payments, taxes, or insurance for a home occupied by the other spouse. Whether these payments qualify as deductible alimony depends on post-divorce ownership of the home. If the payee occupant owns the home, the payments are deductible to the payor and income to the payee. If the payor spouse owns the home, the payments may not be deducted as alimony and are not income to the occupant spouse.[8] If ownership is joint, the payor may deduct as alimony a percentage of the payments that corresponds to the payee's percentage of ownership.[9]

[c] Pursuant to a divorce decree or separation agreement. To qualify as alimony, a payment must be made pursuant to a "divorce or separation instrument," which includes a divorce or separate maintenance decree, a written separation agreement, or a court-ordered decree for temporary support.[10] Support payments made by a spouse during separation but before divorce may be treated as alimony if the payments are court-ordered or established in a written, signed agreement.[11] The payments must meet the alimony requirements set out above.[12] Payments made voluntarily, including those in excess of an agreed amount, are not deductible.[13] A spouse who files a joint return may not claim a deduction for support payments paid during that year.[14]

[d] Not designated as non-alimony. The Code permits parties to elect to treat otherwise deductible alimony as nondeductible by including a provision to that effect in

---

[6] Treas. Reg. § 1.71-1T (1984).

[7] Treas. Reg. § 1.71-1T(A-6) (1984).

[8] Treas. Reg. § 1.71-1T(A-6) (1984).

[9] Treas. Reg. §§ 1.71-1T(A-6), (A-7) (1984); Zinsmeister v. Comm'r, 80 T.C.M. (CCH) 774 (2006); Rev. Rul. 67-420, 1967-2 C.B. 63.

[10] I.R.C. § 71(b)(2) (2006).

[11] I.R.C. § 71(b)(2) (2006) (describing divorce or separation instrument as "a written separation agreement" or "a decree . . . requiring a spouse to make payments for the support or maintenance of the other").

[12] The agreement should provide that the payments will cease upon the payee's death.

[13] *See* Bishop v. Comm'r, 46 T.C.M. (CCH) 15 (1983); Ellis v. Comm'r, 60 T.C.M. (CCH) 593 (1990).

[14] I.R.C. § 71(e) (2006).

TAX EFFECTS

§ 22.01[1][e}

a divorce decree or settlement agreement. The reverse is not true. Parties may not convert nondeductible child support or property transfers into alimony by agreement.[15]

[e] While the parties are not members of the same household. Payments made while the parties occupy the same residence do not qualify as alimony, even if the other requirements of Code § 71 are met. This is true even though the spouses have entered into a separation agreement and are physically living apart in the residence.[16]

[f] Not for the support of a child. Payments designated as alimony, but which terminate or are reduced upon child-related events (graduation, majority, marriage, or death of a child) will be treated as child support.[17] The regulations create two presumptions that apply to specific child-related events. First, reductions in payments within six months of a child's eighteenth or twenty-first birthday create a presumption that the payment is for child support.[18] Second, if a couple has two or more children and an alimony award is reduced at least twice, the payment is presumed to be child support if both reductions occur within one year of the children reaching an age between eighteen and twenty-four.[19] The presumption may be rebutted by a showing that the time of reduction was unrelated to the children.[20] The Mississippi Court of Appeals reversed a chancellor's award of $700 a month in alimony until the wife's daughter from a previous marriage graduated from high school, noting that the IRS would classify the payment as child support.[21] Occasionally a decree, usually for temporary support, will order payment of a designated amount of "family support" without distinguishing spousal and child support. If no designation of individual amounts is made and the temporary order does not specifically state that payments terminate upon the spouse's death, the payment is nondeductible child support.[22]

[g] Does not survive the death of the payee. To qualify as alimony under the Code, payments may not survive a payee's death. An alimony provision that provides for substitute payments to be made in the event of the payee's death will also be treated as non-alimony.[23] Most alimony provisions meet the other requirements of the Code; this requirement is the most likely to prevent tax classification as alimony. Under Mississippi law, some forms of alimony survive the payee's death and therefore do not satisfy the Code requirements.

---

[15] I.R.C. § 71(b)(1)(B) (2006); Treas. Reg. § 1.71-1T(A-8) (1984) (requirements for enforceable provision electing non-alimony treatment).

[16] Treas. Reg. § 1.71-1T(A-9) (1984) (exception if one spouse is preparing to leave and actually does leave within one month).

[17] I.R.C. § 71(c)(2) (2006).

[18] Treas. Reg. § 1.71-1T(A-18) (1984).

[19] Treas. Reg. § 1.71-1T(A-18) (1984).

[20] Treas. Reg. § 1.71-1T(A-18) (1984) (rebutted by showing that payments terminate after six years of alimony payments or at time normally recognized in state law for alimony termination).

[21] Pierce v. Pierce, 42 So. 3 658, 663 (Miss. Ct. App. 2010) (remanding for clarification).

[22] See Lovejoy v. Comm'r, 293 F. 3d 1208 (10th Cir. 2002) (unallocated payments were to continue until further order of the court); Gilbert v. Comm'r, 85 T.C.M. (CCH) 1087 (2003) (state law did not address whether temporary unallocated payment terminated upon spouse's death).

[23] Treas. Reg. § 1.71-1T(A-14) (1984). For examples of substitute payments, see I.R.S. Pub. No. 504 (2009).

§ 22.01[2]   MISSISSIPPI FAMILY LAW

[2] Relationship to state law on alimony. Understanding the tax consequences of alimony is complicated by the fact that many states recognize multiple forms of alimony. Some qualify as alimony for tax purposes and some do not. Mississippi recognizes four distinct forms of alimony – periodic, lump sum, rehabilitative, and reimbursement. In addition, spouses in Mississippi may create hybrid forms of alimony with characteristics of more than one of the traditional forms of alimony. As a result, each alimony provision in an agreement should be separately analyzed using the Code definition.

[a] Traditional forms of alimony. Traditional periodic alimony is not vested until payable, can be modified, terminates on the payee's remarriage or death, and does not survive the payor's death. In contrast, lump sum alimony is a fixed, vested payment that cannot be modified and does not terminate upon the death of either party or the recipient's remarriage. Like periodic alimony, rehabilitative alimony is not vested until payable, can be modified, terminates upon the payee's death, and does not survive the payor's death. Rehabilitative alimony differs from periodic alimony in that the payments are for a definite, fixed period of time rather than continuing indefinitely. Reimbursement alimony, designed to compensate a spouse for investment in the other's career, is generally a fixed, vested amount that cannot be modified and does not terminate upon the death of either party or the recipient's remarriage.[24]

Assuming that a particular award meets other Code requirements, periodic and rehabilitative alimony qualify as alimony for tax purposes because they terminate at the payee's death, while lump sum alimony and reimbursement alimony do not. Note, however, that the Code permits the parties to provide by agreement that otherwise taxable alimony will be treated as nontaxable and nondeductible.

[b] Hybrid alimony. Recent Mississippi cases recognize hybrid forms of alimony that blur the lines between the traditional forms. For example, the Mississippi Supreme Court has approved agreements to pay lump sum alimony that survives the payor's death but not the payee's death. Similarly, the court has approved lump sum alimony that is reduced but not terminated upon the payee's remarriage.[25] This area of the law is still developing. The extent to which parties or courts may alter the traditional forms is not yet clear. A hybrid award that meets the Code definition of alimony appears to qualify for alimony tax treatment, but attorneys should consult a tax specialist with regard to deductibility of a particular provision.[26]

[3] Problem areas

[a] Front-loaded alimony payments. If payments under an alimony award decrease significantly in the first three years, the payor may be subject to additional taxes under the recapture rule of Code § 71. A good rule of thumb to follow is that

---

[24] *See* discussion of forms of alimony *supra* § 9.02.
[25] *See* cases discussed *supra* § 9.03.
[26] No case was found ruling on the alimony designation of such an award.

658

TAX EFFECTS   **§ 22.01[3][b]**

the recapture rules are not triggered if alimony payments are ordered for at least three years and payments for the first three years are equal.[27]

[b] Underpayment of support. If a payor is obligated to pay both spousal and child support and pays less than the required amount, the Service will consider that child support is paid in full first. For example, if a payor owes $1,000 in alimony and $600 in child support, and pays only $500, the entire amount will be deemed child support and will not be considered deductible.[28]

§ 22.02 CHILD SUPPORT PAYMENTS AND RELATED DEDUCTIONS

Awards of child support may include a base support award payable to the custodial parent, payment of medical insurance premiums and out-of-pocket medical expenses, and add-ons such as college expenses, automobile insurance, or life insurance. These payments typically are designated in the divorce decree as child support and, in Mississippi, terminate when a child reaches the age of twenty-one. Child support payments are not taxable income to a payee and are not deductible by a payor.[29] Some of the payments, such as medical and educational support, may be deductible under other provisions of the Code.

[1] Code requirements. A payment will be classified as child support under the Code if the decree or document "fixes" the payment as a sum payable for a child's support.[30] Furthermore, a payment designated as alimony, but which terminates upon a child-related event, will be treated as child support.[31]

[2] Child-related deductions. The Code contains several deductions and credits related to children or dependents. The dependency exemption, child tax credit, and educational credits belong to the custodial parent but may be waived. The childcare credit belongs to the custodial parent and cannot be waived. The medical expense deduction may be claimed by either parent.

[a] Dependency exemptions. Taxpayers are allowed a dependency exemption for children under nineteen or for dependent students under twenty-four.[32] In the case of divorced parents, the default rule provides that the custodial parent is entitled to the dependency exemption. A "custodial parent" is defined as the parent who has custody for the greater part of the year.[33] The custodial parent may waive the rule through use

---

[27] I.R.C. § 71(f) (2006). The recapture rule applies only to fixed payments, not to provisions which order the payor to pay a certain percentage of profits or income as alimony. I.R.C. § 71(f)(5)(C) (2006). No recapture occurs as a result of reduction due to the payee's death or remarriage. I.R.C. § 71(f)(5)(A) (2006).

[28] I.R.C. § 71(c)(3) (2006); Treas. Reg. § 1.71-1 (1984).

[29] Treas. Reg. § 1.71-1T(A-15) (1984).

[30] I.R.C. § 71(c) (2006).

[31] *See supra* § 22.01[1][f].

[32] I.R.C. § 151(c) (2006).

[33] I.R.C. § 152(e)(1) (2006) (provisions applicable only if child receives over half of his support from parents and lives with one or both parents for over half of year).

659

§ 22.02[2][b]   MISSISSIPPI FAMILY LAW

of IRS Form 8332.[34] State courts disagree as to whether a divorce court may order a custodial parent to execute a waiver. In Mississippi, a court may order waiver by the custodial parent.[35] A court did not err in ordering an unemployed mother to waive the dependency exemption in favor of the father until she was earning at least $50,000 a year.[36]

It may be unclear who qualifies as the custodial parent in a joint custody arrangement. If a custody arrangement involves a flexible and unstructured schedule, it is important for the parties to agree who is entitled to claim the exemption and to provide for execution of the necessary waivers.

[b] Child tax credit. A credit against taxes is available to taxpayers with school-age children.[37] The credit is available to the parent who can claim the child as a dependent. Thus, the custodial parent is entitled to the credit unless a waiver has been executed in favor of the noncustodial parent.[38]

[c] Educational credits. The Hope Scholarship and Lifetime Learning Credits, which provide a credit for post-secondary education expenses, are available to the taxpayer who claims the student as a dependent.[39] Thus, these credits are available only to the custodial parent unless a waiver is executed transferring the dependency exemption to the noncustodial parent.[40]

[d] Childcare credit. A taxpayer who maintains a household for a dependent can claim a credit for qualifying childcare expenses necessary for employment.[41] In the case of divorced parents, only the custodial parent may claim the credit.[42]

[e] Medical expense deductions. Either parent may claim any available medical expense deduction for medical payments made on a child's behalf.[43]

§ 22.03 TRANSFERS OF PROPERTY

At divorce, property classified as marital is divided equitably between the parties regardless of title. Division of marital property may entail transfer of title from one party to the other, a lump sum payment or installment payments from one spouse to the other, or assumption of debt by one spouse. A portion of one spouse's retirement ac-

---

[34] I.R.C. § 152(e)(2) (2006); IRS Form 8332 Release/Revocation of Release of Claim to Exemption for Child by Custodial Parent (OMB No. 1545-0074) (2010).

[35] Nichols v. Tedder, 547 So. 2d 766, 777 (Miss. 1989).

[36] Fitzgerald v. Fitzgerald, 914 So. 2d 193, 199 (Miss. Ct. App. 2005) (award of tax exemption reversed and remanded when property division remanded; financial awards are linked).

[37] I.R.C. § 24(a) (2006).

[38] I.R.C. § 24(a) (2006) (child qualifies for credit to taxpayer who takes § 151 deduction); *see* Bramante v. Comm'r, 84 T.C.M. (CCH) 299 (2002).

[39] I.R.C. § 25A(g)(3)(A) (2006).

[40] *See supra* § 22.02[2][a].

[41] I.R.C. § 21(a)(1) (2006).

[42] I.R.C. § 21(e)(5) (2006).

[43] I.R.C. § 213 (2006).

TAX EFFECTS § 22.03[1]

count may be transferred to a separate account or part of future benefits assigned to the non-owner. Property division may also involve the transfer of interests in a business, partnership, or corporation or an agreement to transfer future income from an asset.

[1] Code treatment of transfers

[a] **Non-recognition of gain or loss.** Property division "incident to divorce" does not result in income to the recipient or permit a deduction by the payor and does not produce taxable gain or loss for either spouse.[44] A transfer is deemed incident to divorce if it is made (1) within one year of the date of divorce or (2) is "related to the cessation of the marriage." A transfer made pursuant to a divorce decree or separation agreement and within six years of the date of divorce is presumed to be related to the cessation of the marriage. Transfers more than a year after divorce but not pursuant to an agreement, or more than six years after divorce, may qualify for non-recognition if the parties can prove that the transfer was to accomplish the division of property owned prior to divorce.[45]

[b] **Transferee's basis in property.** The transferor's adjusted basis carries over to the recipient spouse[46] even if the property is later sold at a loss.[47] The impact of the adjusted basis can dramatically affect the value of property division. For example, if a wife is awarded real property titled in her husband's name, valued at $100,000 with an adjusted basis of $10,000, and her husband is awarded property also valued at $100,000, but with an adjusted basis of $40,000, the husband's "equal" award is significantly more valuable.

[2] Property division payments as deductible alimony. After the 1986 Tax Reform Act, installment payments as part of property division may qualify as alimony under the provisions of Code § 71. Prior to the Act, a payment that was part of property division could not qualify as deductible alimony. The Tax Reform Act eliminated this distinction. Now, a payment that otherwise meets Code requirements – a cash payment to a spouse pursuant to a divorce decree, which terminates at the payee's death and is neither child support nor designated as non-alimony – is deductible. Thus, a property division buy-out that specifically states that the obligation ceases upon the payee's death may be deductible.[48]

[3] Specific types of transfers

[a] **Marital residence.** Transfer of the marital residence from one spouse to the other pursuant to divorce qualifies for non-recognition under § 1041. If the parties con-

---

[44] I.R.C. § 1041(a)(2) (2006).

[45] Treas. Reg. § 1.1041-1T(b)(A-7) (1984). The provisions of § 1041 do not apply to transfers to nonresident aliens. I.R.C. § 1041(d) (2006).

[46] I.R.C. § 1041(b) (2006).

[47] I.R.C. § 1015(e) (2006).

[48] The drafter should be careful not to trigger the recapture provisions of I.R.C. § 71 (2006).

661

§ 22.03[3][b]   **MISSISSIPPI FAMILY LAW**

template sale of the marital home, the principal residence gain exclusion provisions of § 121 must be considered as well. That provision allows homeowners to exclude the first $250,000 of gains on the sale of a principal residence ($500,000 for married taxpayers filing jointly).[49] Divorcing spouses may contemplate a future sale of the home, with one spouse occupying the home until sale. The non-occupying spouse may continue to own the home jointly with the occupant or hold title alone. An owner who does not live in the home may qualify for § 121 non-recognition so long as the other spouse has occupied the house pursuant to a divorce decree.[50] If, however, the decree provides for sole title in the name of the occupant, with a portion of the proceeds of sale to be paid to the former spouse, only the owning spouse may claim the exclusion.[51]

[b] **Pensions and IRAs.** One spouse's retirement account may be divided between the parties pursuant to divorce. Transfers pursuant to a Qualified Domestic Relations Order (QDRO) are exceptions to the general anti-assignment rule applicable to plans governed by the Employee Retirement Income Security Act.[52] If division is through a transfer to a separate retirement account, the recipient is not taxed on the distribution if it is transferred within sixty days to a qualified retirement plan.[53] If division is accomplished by designating the non-owning spouse as an alternate payee under the plan, the non-owning spouse is taxed as distributions are made.[54] If the documents do not meet the requirements for a QDRO or other required order,[55] distributions to an alternate payee spouse will be taxed to the participant spouse.[56] A transfer of an IRA by one spouse to the other pursuant to a divorce or separate maintenance agreement does not give rise to tax liability on the part of the owning spouse.[57]

[c] **Assignment of asset income.** One spouse may be instructed to pay the other a part of future income from a particular asset that remains in the ownership of the payor. Until recently, the IRS applied the assignment of income doctrine to these arrangements, creating potentially unexpected tax consequences. The IRS allocated taxable income to a former spouse who rendered a service[58] or owned an asset[59] that generated income, even if the divorce decree assigned that income to his or her former spouse. For example, if one spouse was awarded a share of an unliquidated legal claim of the other, the litigant spouse would be liable for all taxes on the judgment, a result that the parties may not have expected.[60] Similarly, an attorney was taxed on the entire amount of the fee from a case, even though he was required by the terms of his divorce

---

[49] I.R.C. § 121 (2006).
[50] I.R.C. § 121(d)(3)(B) (2006).
[51] *See* Suhr v. Comm'r, 81 T.C.M. (CCH) 1114 (2001).
[52] I.R.C. § 414(p) (2006).
[53] I.R.C. §§ 402(c), (e)(1)(B) (2006).
[54] I.R.C. § 402(e)(1)(A) (2006).
[55] *See supra* Chapter VII.
[56] Rodoni v. Comm'r, 105 T.C. 29 (1995).
[57] I.R.C. § 408(d)(6) (2006).
[58] Lucas v. Earl, 281 U.S. 111 (1930).
[59] Helvering v. Horst, 311 U.S. 112 (1940).
[60] Rev. Rul. 87-112, 1987-2 C.B. 207; Treas. Reg. § 1.454-1(a) (as amended in 1967); I.R.S. Priv. Ltr. Rul. 91-43-050 (July 26, 1991).

TAX EFFECTS § 22.03[3][d]

decree to pay 50% of the award to his former wife.[61] However, the Service appears to have reversed this position by the issuance of Revenue Ruling 2002-22. The ruling applies only to income from stock options and nonqualified deferred compensation. However, the comments to the Ruling state broadly that, "applying the assignment of income doctrine in divorce cases to tax the transferor spouse when the transferee spouse ultimately receives income from the property transferred in the divorce would frustrate the purpose of § 1041 with respect to divorcing spouses."[62] Drafters should carefully examine tax treatment of any transfer of future income to determine the tax consequences.

[d] Interest on installment payments. One spouse may be ordered to make installment payments to the other as part of equitable distribution. Any interest payable on the amount due is income to the recipient.[63] The interest payment may be deductible by the payor if it otherwise qualifies for a principal residence or business interest deduction.[64]

[e] Closely held corporations. If both spouses have an interest in a closely held business, the business is typically awarded to one spouse, who may be ordered to purchase the other's interest. If the transaction involves payments from a corporation or partnership entity rather than the individual spouse, the transfer may trigger dividend income or taxable gain. For example, when a divorce decree required that a husband purchase his wife's stock in a corporation, the corporation's redemption of her stock was treated as a constructive dividend to the husband.[65]

§ 22.04 PAYMENTS RELATED TO LITIGATION

In addition to support and property division payments, a divorce decree may order payment of attorneys' and expert fees, costs of mediation, and costs of court. Each party may be ordered to bear his or her own expenses or one party may be ordered to pay some or all of the other's fees. As a general rule, a spouse's attorneys' and expert fees for divorce are not deductible; the expenses are regarded as personal, not business. However, fees are deductible to the extent that they are paid for advice or assistance in determining the tax effects of alimony, child support, or property division.[66] In addition, an alimony recipient may deduct legal or expert fees to the extent that the services were for the purpose of securing alimony.[67] A spouse who is ordered to pay the other's legal or expert fees may not deduct those fees even though the other spouse could have

---

[61] Kochansky v. Comm'r, 67 T.C.M. (CCH) 2665 (1994), *aff'd in part, rev'd in part,* 92 F.3d 957 (9th Cir. 1996); *see also* Rev. Rul. 87-112, 1987-2 C.B. 207 (husband, required by decree to transfer bonds to wife, had to recognize accrued interest as income).

[62] Rev. Rul. 2002-22, 2002-19 I.R.B. 849.

[63] Gibbs v. Comm'r, 73 T.C.M. (CCH) 2669 (1997).

[64] *See* I.R.C. § 163(h) (2006).

[65] *See* Hayes v. Comm'r, 101 T.C. 593 (1993).

[66] I.R.C. § 212(3) (2006).

[67] I.R.C. § 212(1) (2006) (expenses for the production of income).

663

§ 22.05 MISSISSIPPI FAMILY LAW

deducted portions of the fee.[68]

§ 22.05 OTHER DIVORCE-RELATED TAX CONSIDERATIONS

[1] Filing status. Marital status on the last day of the taxable year determines a taxpayer's filing status. If spouses divorce on or before December 31, they must each file as single or head of household for that year. If the divorce is not final by year end, spouses must file as a married couple for that calendar year.[69]

[a] During separation. Spouses must file a joint or separate return as a married couple unless separate maintenance has been ordered or the abandoned spouse rule applies. If a court has issued a separate maintenance order, spouses file as single even though they are still legally married.[70] However, neither a temporary support order pending divorce nor an agreement to live separately allows a spouse to file as a single taxpayer.[71] A married taxpayer may file as head of household if he or she pays more than half the cost of maintaining a household where a dependent child lives for more than six months of the year, but only if they have been separated from their spouse for the last six months of the year.[72]

[b] After divorce. If divorce occurs by the last day of the taxable year, the parties must file as single or head of household. Only one party may claim head-of-household status, which requires that the taxpayer maintain the principal residence of a child for over half the taxable year and must pay over half the expenses of maintaining the home.[73]

[2] Tax refunds. The parties may provide by agreement for the allocation of a refund on a joint tax return. If this issue is not addressed by agreement, a refund belongs to the spouse whose income and tax payments created the refund.[74] A formula is provided by the Service for calculating ownership of a joint filing refund between spouses.[75]

[3] Tax liability. A court may order one spouse to assume liability for tax debts, or may require that tax liability be shared between divorcing spouses. A chancellor did not err in finding that tax liability for a couple's last year of marriage was a marital debt, ordering the wife to sign a joint return to reduce the amount owed, and directing

---

[68] *See* U.S. v. Davis, 370 U.S. 65 (1962).

[69] I.R.C. § 7703(a) (2006); *cf.* Fitzgerald v. Fitzgerald, 914 So. 2d 193, 198-99 (Miss. Ct. App. 2005) (chancellor did not err in ordering wife to sign joint return for year prior to divorce; no evidence that return was inaccurate and joint return would reduce tax liability).

[70] I.R.C. § 6013(d)(2) (2006).

[71] I.R.C. § 7703(a)(2) (2006); *see* Boyer v. Comm'r, 732 F.2d 191 (D.C. Cir. 1984); Johnson v. Comm'r, 39 T.C.M. (CCH) 868 (1980).

[72] I.R.C. § 7703(b) (2006).

[73] I.R.C. § 2(b) (2006).

[74] Rev. Rul. 74-611, 1974-2 C.B. 399.

[75] Rev. Rul. 80-7, 1980-1 C.B. 296.

664

TAX EFFECTS § 22.05[4]

the wife to pay 10% and the husband 90% of the amount due.[76]

[4] Innocent spouse relief. A divorced spouse may seek relief from paying pre-divorce jointly owed taxes under Code § 6013. If the IRS seeks recovery of a tax under-payment, a spouse may be entitled to one of three types of relief: (1) relief from liability for a substantial understatement resulting from a former spouse's "grossly erroneous" item, if the innocent spouse had no knowledge or reason to know of the error;[77] (2) elective proportioning of liability;[78] or (3) discretionary relief.[79]

[5] Estate and gift tax consequences. Most divorce-related payments and trans-fers are excluded from gift taxes pursuant to Code § 2516. This section provides that transfers made for child support or to a spouse in satisfaction of marital or property rights is not considered a gift if the transfer is pursuant to a written agreement made within two years before divorce or one year after divorce.[80]

If one spouse dies after divorce, any remaining divorce-related obligations may constitute deductible expenses to the estate. Code § 2043 provides that any payment or transfer which meets the gift tax exclusion requirements of Code § 2516 is considered to be a payment for "adequate and full consideration" for purposes of Code § 2053 estate expenses.[81] If a divorce decree requires that alimony payments continue after the payor's death, the actuarial value of the payments is a deduction to the estate.[82]

---

[76] Fitzgerald v. Fitzgerald, 914 So. 2d 193, 198-99 (Miss. Ct. App. 2005) (allocation reversed when property divi-sion reversed; financial awards are linked); *see also* Irby v. Estate of Irby, 7 So. 3d 223, 234 (Miss. 2009) (federal taxes of $104,130 from the husband's business classified as marital debt; wife ordered to pay 25% of the debt); A & L, Inc. v. Grantham, 747 So. 2d 832, 841 (Miss. 1999) (court did not err in ordering husband to assume responsibility for 80% of potential; unclear tax liability).

[77] I.R.C. § 6015(b) (2006).

[78] I.R.C. § 6015(c) (2006).

[79] I.R.C. § 6015(f) (2006).

[80] I.R.C. § 2516 (2006).

[81] I.R.C. § 2043(b)(2) (2006).

[82] I.R.C. § 2053 (2006); *see* Rev. Rul. 60-247, 1960-2 C.B. 272 (death or remarriage of payee shortly after payor's death may reduce value).

XXIII
MARITAL AGREEMENTS

Most family law matters are settled rather than litigated.[1] Settlement agreements address the dissolution of a marriage and division of the parties' assets and debts. Many agreements must also anticipate and provide for an ongoing relationship with regard to custody of children and continuing support obligations. Drafting a separation agreement requires knowledge of general contract principles as well as rules peculiar to domestic relations law. Freedom to contract is more limited in domestic matters than in most civil actions – courts have ultimate authority to determine matters related to custody and support of children.

Spouses may also address financial matters and property rights in premarital agreements. Persons who plan to marry are increasingly using premarital agreements to provide in advance for disposition of assets and support duties upon death or at divorce. Although less common, spouses may also enter postmarital agreements addressing property and support rights even if divorce is not anticipated. While general principles of contract law also govern these agreements, courts scrutinize pre- and postmarital agreements more carefully than arm's-length contracts.[2]

§ 23.01 Marital agreements

As used in this chapter, the term "marital agreements" includes agreements in contemplation of marriage (premarital agreements) and those executed during marriage (postmarital agreements). The term does not include agreements in anticipation of divorce. The term "settlement agreement" is used to refer to agreements to resolve divorce, custody, or support actions.[3]

[1] **History.** Agreements altering spouses' property rights during marriage or at death have long been recognized as legitimate family planning devices. Courts have approved pre- and postmarital agreements dealing with interspousal transfers of property, waiver of inheritance rights, execution of wills, and provision of insurance. Until the 1970s, however, agreements purporting to resolve financial matters at divorce were considered void as against public policy;[4] they were viewed as encouraging divorce.[5]

With the increase in divorce and second marriages, courts recognized the utility

---

[1] Laura W. Morgan & Brett R. Turner, Attacking and Defending Marital Agreements § 1.02 (2001) (survey of *Divorce Litigation* subscribers showed 75% settlement rate).

[2] *See* discussion *infra* § 23.02.

[3] See *infra* §§ 23.07 through 23.14 for a discussion of settlement agreements.

[4] *See* Brian Bix, *Bargaining in the Shadow of Love: The Enforcement of Premarital Agreements and How We Think About Marriage*, 40 Wm. & Mary L. Rev. 145, 150 (1998) (agreements regulating rights at divorce considered to encourage divorce); J.W. Bunkley & W.E. Morse, Amis on Divorce & Separation in Mississippi § 10.02, at 240 (1957) (agreement in anticipation of divorce is void).

[5] Karen Servidea, *Reviewing Premarital Agreements to Protect the State's Interest in Marriage*, 91 Va. L. Rev. 535, 537 (2005).

§ 23.01[2]   **MISSISSIPPI FAMILY LAW**

of premarital agreements resolving property rights at divorce.[6] The Uniform Premarital Agreements Act, promulgated in 1983, has been adopted by more than half of the states. Under this Act, a premarital agreement is enforceable if it was entered voluntarily and is not unconscionable.[7] Some states analyze premarital agreements under a more stringent test, requiring that the agreement be fair and conscionable both at the time of execution and, to some extent, at the time of enforcement.[8]

[2] Mississippi. As early as the mid-1800s, the Mississippi Supreme Court approved the use of premarital agreements regarding property rights upon a spouse's death.[9] Similarly, the Mississippi Supreme Court has long approved postnuptial agreements fixing property and support rights upon death.[10] And in 1995, the supreme court adopted the modern approach to premarital agreements affecting rights at divorce, holding that these agreements are "enforceable like any other contract."[11] A court erred in awarding a wife one-half of the value of cattle owned by her husband rather than one-third, as provided in the couple's premarital agreement.[12] The few decisions to date place Mississippi among the states with the least stringent test for validity of marital agreements. Parties must disclose their assets, enter the agreement voluntarily, and the agreement must be fair in its execution.[13] The supreme court has declined to consider the substantive fairness of premarital agreements.[14] However, the court set aside a postmarital agreement based on unconscionability.[15]

§ 23.02 REQUIREMENTS

In most states, pre- and postmarital agreements are subject to the same requirements.[16] In Mississippi, an agreement must be entered voluntarily; the parties must

---

[6] *See* Posner v. Posner, 233 So. 2d 381, 384 (Fla. 1970) (many prospective spouses may desire to privately structure property and alimony in the event of divorce).

[7] UNIF. PREMARITAL AGREEMENT ACT § 6, 9 U.L.A. 38 (1983).

[8] *See* Servidea, *supra* note 5, at 541 (some states require fairness at the time of divorce, particularly with regard to alimony).

[9] *See* Gorin v. Gordon, 38 Miss. 205, 1859 WL 3681, at *3 (Miss. 1859) ("Antenuptial marriage settlements, fairly made, are, under all circumstances, favored and supported by courts of equity."); *see also* Watson v. Duncan, 37 So. 125, 127 (Miss. 1904) (enforcing husband's prenuptial agreement to forego spousal rights at wife's death); Stevenson v. Renardet, 35 So. 576 (Miss. 1904) (prenuptial contract is "like any other" and can be rescinded by agreement of the parties).

[10] *See In re* Sadler's Estate, 98 So. 2d 863, 866 (Miss. 1957) (mutual promises to relinquish right of renunciation or will are adequate consideration for agreement); Wiley v. Gray, 36 Miss. 510 (Miss. 1858) (postnuptial agreements to transfer property for consideration enforceable against creditors and purchasers); *see also* Roberts v. Roberts, 381 So. 2d 1333, 1335 (Miss. 1980) (general principles of contract law apply; court is to construe document as a whole); *cf.* Kirby v. Kent, 160 So. 569, 572 (Miss. 1935) (settlement agreement did not waive rights at death prior to divorce); Wyatt v. Wyatt, 32 So. 317, 318 (Miss. 1902) (family settlements for fair and adequate consideration are enforceable); *In re* Estate of Burns, 31 So. 3d 1227, 1231 (Miss. Ct. App. 2009) (premarital agreement waiving rights of inheritance did not bar a husband from participating in a wrongful death settlement stemming from his deceased wife's accident).

[11] Smith v. Smith, 656 So. 2d 1143, 1147 (Miss. 1995).

[12] Richardson v. Richardson, 912 So. 2d 1079, 1081-82 (Miss. Ct. App. 2005) (agreement to divide marital assets with two-thirds to husband and one-third to wife; complete waiver of wife's claim to husband's logging business).

[13] Smith v. Smith, 656 So. 2d 1143, 1147 (Miss. 1995).

[14] *See* Mabus v. Mabus, 890 So. 2d 806 (Miss. 2003).

[15] *In re* Johnson, 351 So. 2d 1339, 1341-42 (Miss. 1977).

[16] AMERICAN LAW INSTITUTE, PRINCIPLES OF THE LAW OF FAMILY DISSOLUTION: ANALYSIS AND RECOMMENDATIONS § 7.01 cmt. at 953 (2002) [ALI PRINCIPLES] (but noting that different problems are presented by each).

MARITAL AGREEMENTS § 23.02[1]

make full and fair disclosure of their assets; the agreement must be fair in the execution; and the agreement must not be unconscionable. However, a postmarital agreement requires some consideration in addition to the marriage itself.

[1] Consideration. No independent consideration is necessary for a premarital agreement; the agreement to marry is sufficient consideration.[17] With regard to postmarital agreements, however, the traditional view is that an agreement altering existing marital rights must be supported by independent consideration. The Mississippi Supreme Court applied this rule, examining a postmarital agreement to determine whether a wife's renunciation of inheritance rights was supported by consideration.[18] Mutual promises to relinquish inheritance rights are adequate consideration for a postmarital agreement.[19] The modern trend is to dispose of the consideration requirement in postmarital agreements.[20]

[2] Voluntariness. Each party must enter the agreement voluntarily. Voluntariness may be negated by a showing of fraud, misrepresentation,[21] or duress.[22] The Mississippi Supreme Court rejected a wife's argument that she did not voluntarily sign an agreement presented by her husband the night before their wedding. The wife had assets that she wished to protect by agreement, and she had indicated several times prior to signing that she intended to execute a premarital agreement.[23]

[3] Full and fair disclosure. The Mississippi Supreme Court has stated that the duty to disclose assets "is of paramount importance" in a premarital agreement.[24] However, a spouse's knowledge of the other's assets and income may satisfy the requirement in the absence of a detailed financial statement. A premarital agreement was properly enforced even though no financial statement was attached; the wife handled financial matters for her husband-to-be and, according to testimony, had worked with him to develop financial statements in support of the agreement.[25]

[4] The role of independent counsel. While independent counsel is not a requirement in most states, the existence of counsel is nonetheless an important factor in de-

---

[17] *See* UNIF. PREMARITAL AGREEMENT ACT § 5, 9 U.L.A. 372 (1983) (no consideration required).

[18] *In re* Johnson's Will, 351 So. 2d 1339, 1341-42 (Miss. 1977).

[19] *See In re* Sadler's Estate, 98 So. 2d 863, 866 (Miss. 1957); J. THOMAS OLDHAM, DIVORCE, SEPARATION & THE DISTRIBUTION OF PROPERTY § 4.03[2][g], at 3-11 (2001) (mutual waiver of property rights sufficient consideration to support a postnuptial agreement).

[20] *See* ALI PRINCIPLES, *supra* note 16, § 7.01, at 948 (adopting trend).

[21] MORGAN & TURNER, *supra* note 1, § 10.05, at 404.

[22] *See* Casto v. Casto, 508 So. 2d 330, 334-35 (Fla. 1987) (agreement invalidated based on husband's threats). However, threats to cancel a wedding are generally rejected as proof of duress. *See, e.g., Ex parte* Walters, 580 So. 2d 1352, 1354 (Ala. 1991); *In re* Marriage of Adams, 729 P.2d 1151, 1158 (Kan. 1986); *see also* MORGAN & TURNER, *supra* note 1, § 10.053, at 407.

[23] Mabus v. Mabus, 890 So. 2d 806, 819 (Miss. 2003); *see also* Ware v. Ware, 7 So. 3d 271, 276-77 (Miss. Ct. App. 2008) (upholding validity of agreement signed two days before wedding, and which wife did not read); Kitchens v. Kitchens, 850 So. 2d 215, 217-18 (Miss. Ct. App. 2003) (husband signed agreement voluntarily and without coercion).

[24] Hensley v. Hensely, 524 So. 2d 325, 328 (Miss. 1988).

[25] Mabus v. Mabus, 890 So. 2d 806, 819 (Miss. 2003).

§ 23.02[5]   MISSISSIPPI FAMILY LAW

termining the validity of an agreement.[26] For example, a wife's execution of a premarital agreement was binding in part because she obtained independent advice.[27] However, an agreement may be valid even though one party to the contract was unrepresented.[28] The court of appeals rejected a wife's argument that a premarital agreement that she did not read was invalid because the agreement incorrectly stated that she had consulted an attorney. A contracting party may not complain of misrepresentations that could have been discovered by reading a document.[29]

[5] Procedural fairness. An agreement must be fair "in the execution,"[30] which requires procedural, not substantive, fairness. The timing of an agreement is an important element of procedural fairness. This includes both the time at which the parties first discussed executing a premarital agreement and the time the actual agreement was available for review.[31] Other factors affecting procedural fairness include the availability of independent counsel, whether the complaining spouse had adequate time to review the document, the relative education and sophistication of the parties, and whether the terms of the agreement were explained.

No Mississippi case was found in which a premarital agreement was set aside for procedural unfairness. However, the Mississippi Supreme Court found procedural unfairness in the execution of a postmarital agreement. A wife was asked to sign an agreement with no advance warning or discussion, no explanation of the terms, no opportunity to obtain independent counsel, and no real opportunity to review the agreement.[32] In contrast, a premarital agreement was fairly executed when the husband's attorney explained the terms, the wife obtained independent advice, and the parties dealt honestly and fairly with each other.[33] The court of appeals rejected a wife's argument that a premarital agreement executed two days before the wedding was invalid because she did not have an opportunity to read the document or to consult an attorney. The court also rejected her argument that she was misled because her husband told her the provisions applied only at death.[34]

[6] Substantive fairness and unconscionability. Some states require that an agreement be substantively fair at the time of enforcement as well as at the time of execution. Other states require substantive fairness only at the time of execution. And in states with the least stringent test, courts decline to address substantive fairness at

---

[26] HOMER H. CLARK, JR., THE LAW OF DOMESTIC RELATIONS IN THE UNITED STATES § 1.1, at 4-5 (2d ed. 1988). Comments to Section 6 of the UPAA state that while independent counsel is not required, absence of independent counsel may affect the determination of unconscionability. UNIF. PREMARITAL AGREEMENT ACT § 6 cmt., 9B U.L.A. 369 (1983).

[27] Hensley v. Hensely, 524 So. 2d 325, 327-28 (Miss. 1988) (factor in enforcing agreement that wife obtained independent advice); *In re* Sadler's Estate, 98 So. 2d 863, 866 (Miss. 1957) (mutual promises to relinquish right of renunciation are adequate consideration for agreement).

[28] Mabus v. Mabus, 890 So. 2d 806, 821 (Miss. 2003).

[29] Ware v. Ware, 7 So. 3d 271, 276 (Miss. Ct. App. 2008).

[30] Mabus v. Mabus, 890 So. 2d 806, 821 (Miss. 2003); Smith v. Smith, 656 So. 2d 1143, 1147 (Miss. 1995).

[31] MORGAN & TURNER, *supra* note 1, § 10.02, at 397.

[32] *In re* Johnson, 351 So. 2d 1339, 1342 (Miss. 1977).

[33] Hensley v. Hensley, 524 So. 2d 325, 327 (Miss. 1988).

[34] Ware v. Ware, 7 So. 3d 271, 276-77 (Miss. Ct. App. 2008) (party may not complain of misrepresentations that could have been discovered by reading document.

MARITAL AGREEMENTS §23.02[7]

all, applying the more lenient test of unconscionability at the time of execution.[35] The Mississippi Supreme Court has adopted the latter approach. The court has declined to address the substantive fairness of an agreement, even at the time of execution. Rejecting a wife's argument that an agreement was unfair, the court stated that a "claim that the estates of the parties are so disparate that it questions fundamental fairness is of no consequence."[36] Similarly, the court has stated that it "will not relieve a party" of a premarital agreement "which becomes more onerous than had originally been anticipated."[37] Applying the unconscionability test, the supreme court refused to enforce a postmarital agreement in which a wife waived all rights of inheritance in return for the "purely speculative" benefit of retaining a life estate in homestead if she should remarry. The court defined an unconscionable agreement as one "that no wife in her senses and not under a delusion would agree to and no fair-minded husband would propose."[38]

[7] Interpretation of agreements. The Court of Appeals held that an agreement stating that "all property now separately owned by each [spouse] . . . shall remain the separate property of each [spouse]" included property that was commingled during marriage, property used for family purposes, and property that appreciated during marriage as a result of one spouse's work. The wife's separate property certificate of deposit, which was used to secure a loan for the marital home, remained her separate property. Proceeds from the husband's separate home, used to build the marital home, remained his separate property.[39] And a postmarital agreement transferring corporate stock from a husband to his wife, but providing that the transfer would be ineffective in the event of divorce, was enforceable. The wife had no greater rights than she would otherwise have had under equitable distribution.[40]

§23.03 STATUTE OF FRAUDS

An agreement "in consideration of marriage" must be in writing and signed by the party denying enforcement of the agreement.[41] Thus, a premarital agreement must be in writing if part of the consideration is the agreement to marry.[42] Some states, including Mississippi, recognize an exception to the writing requirement if marriage is not part of the agreed consideration.[43] The Mississippi Supreme Court in a 1904 case enforced

---

[35] *See* MORGAN & TURNER, *supra* note 1, § 12.02.

[36] Mabus v. Mabus, 890 So. 2d 806, 821 (Miss. 2003).

[37] Kitchens v. Kitchens, 850 So. 2d 215, 217-218 (Miss. Ct. App. 2003) (quoting Hensley v. Hensley, 524 So. 2d 325, 328 (Miss. 1996)).

[38] *In re* Johnson, 351 So. 2d 1339, 1342 (Miss. 1977).

[39] Long v. Long, 928 So. 2d 1001, 1002-04 (Miss. Ct. App. 2006).

[40] Fleishhacker v. Fleishhacker, 39 So. 3d 904, 909-10 (Miss. Ct. App. 2009).

[41] *See* MISS. CODE ANN. § 15-3-1(b) (2003) (no action on "any agreement made upon consideration of marriage, mutual promises to marry excepted" unless in writing); Pardue v. Ardis, 58 So. 769, 769 (Miss. 1912) (oral prenuptial unenforceable); Hankins v. Hankins, 866 So. 2d 508, 511-12 (Miss. Ct. App. 2004) (refusing to enforce wife's oral agreement recognizing husband's property as separate).

[42] CLARK, JR., *supra* note 26, § 1.1, at 2. Clark notes that most courts refuse to apply the doctrine of part performance to enforce an oral prenuptial agreement. *Id.* at 3.

[43] *See* W. M. Moldoff, Annotation, *What Constitutes Promise Made in or upon Consideration of Marriage within Statute of Frauds*, 75 A.L.R. 2d 633 (1961).

671

§ 23.04   MISSISSIPPI FAMILY LAW

an oral agreement altering marital property rights at death because the agreement was made after the couple had agreed to marry. The court distinguished agreements "in consideration" of marriage from those "in contemplation of marriage," which need not be in writing.[44] No Mississippi case addresses whether a postmarital agreement must be in writing to be enforceable.

§ 23.04 SCOPE OF ENFORCEABLE AGREEMENTS

Freedom to alter marital property rights by contract is limited to financial obligations between the parties. Agreements attempting to regulate behavior during marriage or rights and obligations with regard to children are generally unenforceable.[45] Courts have refused to enforce pre- and postmarital agreements specifying the amount of support required during marriage, attempting to regulate sexual relationships, or limiting the spouses' right to seek divorce.[46]

§ 23.05 SETTLEMENT AGREEMENTS AS POSTMARITAL AGREEMENTS

An agreement originally intended as a settlement agreement may become an enforceable postmarital contract even if the parties do not divorce. Whether a settlement agreement survives reconciliation depends on the wording of the contract. An agreement which specifically stated that it was "not contingent upon divorce" was enforceable upon the death of one spouse two days later,[47] while an agreement to resolve property rights "in order that [a divorce complaint] may be later filed" was not enforceable upon the husband's death.[48]

§ 23.06 BREACH

One party's breach of a marital agreement does not invalidate the entire agreement unless the breach relates to an essential term, involves a substantial part of the contract, or defeats the purpose of the agreement. The court of appeals rejected a husband's argument that a premarital agreement should be set aside because his wife failed to make mortgage payments as required by the agreement. The court noted that cancellation is an extreme remedy; the husband was made whole by a refund of payments that he

---

[44] Steen v. Kirkpatrick, 36 So. 140, 141 (Miss. 1904) ("[T]o fall within . . . [the statute of frauds], the agreement must be strictly in consideration of marriage, and not merely made in contemplation of marriage, as in the case before us, after the mutual promises to marry had been made and become binding."). The court seemed to recognize the continuing validity of this distinction in *Flechas v. Flechas*, 791 So. 2d 295, 300 (Miss. Ct. App. 2001), finding an alleged oral agreement unenforceable for lack of specificity, whether in consideration or contemplation of marriage.

[45] *See* Bix, *supra* note 4, at 148.

[46] CLARK, JR., *supra* note 26, § 1.1, at 15-17.

[47] *See* Roberts v. Roberts, 381 So. 2d 1333, 1335 (Miss. 1980) (agreement stating it was not contingent on divorce, but was "final and binding, not only while they lived, but, also, in the event of the death of one of the parties whether a divorce was obtained or not"); *see also* Crosby v. Peoples Bank, 472 So. 2d 951, 954-56 (Miss. 1985) (enforcing agreement that contemplated divorce or living separate and apart).

[48] Johnson v. Collins, 419 So. 2d 1029, 1031 (Miss. 1982) (transfer of certificates of deposit pursuant to agreement contingent on divorce did not constitute enforceable gift when husband died prior to divorce).

672

MARITAL AGREEMENTS   § 23.07

made while his wife was unemployed.[49] A premarital agreement is ordinarily enforced upon divorce or the death of one of the spouses. However, the Mississippi Supreme Court has noted in dicta that remedies may be available for breach of the agreement outside these settings.[50]

The Mississippi Supreme Court imposed a constructive trust to enforce a wife's premarital agreement waiving any claim to her husband's estate. Under federal law, benefits were paid to her under a policy through the Federal Employees Group Life Insurance Act (FEGLIA). FEGLIA regulations required payment of undesignated funds to the insured's widow. Although she agreed that her husband intended the benefits to go to his children, she claimed the agreement was preempted by federal law. The supreme court noted that while federal courts have tended to find state law preempted by FEGLIA regulations, a majority of state courts have held to the contrary. The court held that imposition of a constructive trust under state law was a proper method of enforcing the agreement.[51]

§ 23.07 WAIVER

Under some circumstances, courts have held that a spouse's conduct may constitute a modification or waiver of a marital agreement.[52]

§ 23.08 SETTLEMENT AGREEMENTS

A settlement agreement is an agreement between spouses in settlement of divorce, custody, or child support actions. Upon incorporation into a court decree, it becomes part of the court's judgment and is enforceable as any other decree. Freedom to contract is more limited than in ordinary contracts. Provisions related to property division may be binding on a court, while agreements related to alimony, child support, and custody are not. In Mississippi, different requirements apply to settlement agreements in fault-based and irreconcilable differences divorces.

[1] Nature of agreement. A settlement agreement is governed by the general law of contracts,[53] with some exceptions peculiar to domestic relations law. The Mississippi Supreme Court has stated that a divorce agreement is "no different from any other contract, and the mere fact that it is between a divorcing husband and wife, and incorporated into a divorce decree, does not change its character."[54] The supreme court has

---

[49] Doster v. Doster, 853 So. 2d 147, 150-151 (Miss. Ct. App. 2003).

[50] Smith v. Smith, 656 So. 2d 1143, 1147 (Miss. 1995).

[51] McCord v. Spradling, 830 So. 2d 1188 (Miss. 2002).

[52] See 5 FAMILY LAW AND PRACTICE, ch. 59, § 59.05[23], at 59-35 (Arnold Rutkin ed.). *But cf.* Richardson v. Richardson, 912 So. 2d 1079, 1081-82 (Miss. Ct. App. 2005) (agreement to submit property division issues to court was not waiver of couple's premarital agreement).

[53] *In re* Hodges, 807 So. 2d 438, 445 (Miss. 2002).

[54] East v. East, 493 So. 2d 927, 931-32 (Miss. 1986); *see also* Harris v. Harris, 988 So. 2d 376, 378 (Miss. 2008) (property settlement agreement is a contract); *In re* Dissolution of the Marriage of De St. Germain, 977 So. 2d 412, 418-20 (Miss. Ct. App. 2008) (agreements enforceable as any other; may be set aside for overreaching); Kelley v. Kelley, 953 So. 2d 1139, 1143 (Miss. Ct. App. 2007) (court may not modify agreement absent fraud or mutual mistake in drafting); Beezley v. Beezley, 917 So. 2d 803, 807 (Miss. Ct. App. 2005) (agreement between divorcing parties to be interpreted

§ 23.08[2]   **MISSISSIPPI FAMILY LAW**

also emphasized that when a chancellor has approved an agreement, "we will enforce it, absent fraud or overreaching, and we take a dim view of efforts to modify it just as we do when persons seek relief from improvident contracts."[55] Courts will not rewrite marital contracts "to satisfy the desires of either party."[56]

[2] Requirements. Parties to a settlement agreement must have the capacity to contract[57] and must enter the agreement freely and voluntarily.[58] There must be a showing that the parties intended to be bound by the agreement. For example, no agreement was reached in a case in which the parties exchanged several versions of a contract but the wife never signed the agreement.[59] As with all contracts, a settlement agreement must be sufficiently specific to be enforced.[60]

[3] Formalities. In most states, settlement agreements are not explicitly covered by the general statute of frauds. However, certain provisions that commonly appear in divorce settlement agreements, such as provisions for transfer of real property, must be in writing. Many states, however, require that all settlement agreements be in writing, because of the unique circumstances surrounding execution of these agreements.[61] In Mississippi, different requirements are imposed for fault-based and irreconcilable differences divorce agreements.

[a] In general. A settlement agreement in a fault-based divorce action or modification action is binding only if the agreement is reduced to writing or dictated into the court record. Rule 5.03 of the Mississippi Uniform Chancery Court Rules requires that all consent judgments must be signed by counsel before being presented to a chancellor.[62] Based on this provision, the Mississippi Supreme Court reversed a court's entry of judgment in a modification action based on the parties' alleged oral agreement during trial. The agreement was never reduced to writing and signed, nor was it dictated into the court record.[63] In contrast, an agreement dictated into the record is binding if the parties intended to be bound. For example, the supreme court rejected a former husband's argument that an agreement dictated into the record was not binding until he

---

as any other agreement).

[55] Bell v. Bell, 572 So. 2d 841, 844 (Miss. 1990); *see* West v. West, 891 So. 2d 203, 210-11 (Miss. 2004).

[56] McManus v. Howard, 569 So. 2d 1213, 1215 (Miss. 1990); *see also* Morris v. Morris, 541 So. 2d 1040, 1043 (Miss. 1989) (alimony provision based on agreement should not be modified without "close scrutiny").

[57] MORGAN & TURNER, *supra* note 1, § 2.02 (spouse must show how mental impairment affected ability to understand agreement); *see* Parks v. Parks, 914 So. 2d 337, 341 (Miss. Ct. App. 2005) (en banc) (burden of proof on spouse seeking to set aside agreement based on lack of capacity; law presumes parties are mentally capable of entering contract).

[58] JOHN DE WITT GREGORY, PETER N. SWISHER & SHERYL L. WOLFE, UNDERSTANDING FAMILY LAW § 4.05, at 106 (2d ed. 1993) ("freely and understandingly" signed).

[59] Rennie v. Rennie, 718 So. 2d 1091, 1094 (Miss. 1998).

[60] *See* Wing v. Wing, 549 So. 2d 944, 948 (Miss. 1989) (child support provision with escalation clause not sufficiently specific; did not specify consumer price index to be used).

[61] MORGAN & TURNER, *supra* note 1, § 2.06.

[62] MISS. UNIF. CH. CT. R. 5.03.

[63] Samples v. Davis, 904 So. 2d 1061, 1065-66 (Miss. 2004); *see also* MORGAN & TURNER, *supra* note 1, § 2.06 (substantial number of states refuse to enforce oral settlement agreements).

MARITAL AGREEMENTS §23.08[3][b]

signed a document embodying the terms of the agreement.[64]

[b] Irreconcilable differences divorce. Agreements in irreconcilable differences divorce actions must be in writing; dictation into the record is not sufficient. In several cases, the appellate courts have reversed a grant of divorce because the parties' agreement was presented orally or dictated into the court record rather than in writing.[65] Similarly, the supreme court has refused to approve an oral modification to a previously submitted written agreement in an irreconcilable differences divorce.[66] The agreement must be signed by both parties, state that the parties consent to court decision on unresolved issues, list the unresolved issues, and state that the parties understand that the court's decision will be binding.[67]

§ 23.09 ENFORCEABILITY: BINDING EFFECT ON PARTIES

In many states, agreements in family law matters are binding on the parties prior to court approval. In Mississippi, there is no clear caselaw to this effect. A reading of the cases suggests that this is the rule, although there is also dicta that suggests otherwise.

[1] General rule. According to leading authorities on family law, a voluntary agreement regarding property division, custody, child support, or alimony is binding on the parties in the absence of a defense of fraud, duress, or unconscionability.[68] A settlement agreement is a "binding legal document that cannot be destroyed by either party alone."[69] An otherwise valid agreement "will not be rejected merely because a party had a 'change of heart' after the agreement was executed."[70]

[2] Mississippi: Withdrawal of consent to no-fault divorce. In Mississippi, an agreement in an irreconcilable differences divorce becomes void if one spouse withdraws consent to the divorce in a timely manner.[71] The supreme court rejected a wife's attempt to enforce a settlement agreement entered in contemplation of irreconcilable differences divorce after she decided to pursue divorce based on adultery. The court noted that parties bargain for a no-fault divorce as a package deal: "It would be

---

[64] McDonald v. McDonald, 850 So. 2d 1182, 1189 (Miss. Ct. App. 2002).

[65] Cassibry v. Cassibry, 742 So. 2d 1121, 1125 (Miss. 1999). *But see* Heatherly v. Heatherly, 914 So. 2d 754, 758 (Miss. Ct. App. 2005) (en banc) (suggesting that party in irreconcilable differences divorce would be bound by agreement dictated into record).

[66] *See* Cook v. Cook, 725 So. 2d 205, 207 (Miss. 1998).

[67] Massengill v. Massengill, 594 So. 2d 1173, 1178 (Miss. 1992); *see also* Cook v. Cook, 725 So. 2d 205, 206 (Miss. 1998). *See* discussion *supra* § 4.04[4].

[68] *See* CLARK, JR., *supra* note 26, § 18.2, at 761 (spouses may attack agreement during divorce proceedings based on fraud, duress, or other inequitable conduct); GREGORY, ET AL., *supra* note 58, § 4.05, at 106; *see also* MORGAN & TURNER, *supra* note 1, § 3.07, at 47 (agreement to pay child support binding prior to court approval); Pittman v. Pittman, 909 So. 2d 148, 152 (Miss. Ct. App. 2005) (en banc) (agreement executed in connection with ending of void marriage was binding).

[69] MORGAN & TURNER, *supra* note 1, § 4.04, at 76 (one party "cannot simply change his or her mind and walk away).

[70] GREGORY ET AL., *supra* note 58, § 4.05, at 106.

[71] *See* MISS. CODE ANN. § 93-5-32 (2004); *see* discussion *supra* § 4.04.

§ 23.09[3]   MISSISSIPPI FAMILY LAW

fundamentally unfair to hold either of the parties to portions of the package after the foundation of the bargain is removed."[72] The court did note, however, that parties could include in the agreement a specific provision indicating that they intended to be bound whether or not divorce occurred.[73]

[3] Mississippi: Withdrawal of consent to other agreements. Although the case-law is not entirely clear on this point, it appears that Mississippi follows the general rule that parties may not withdraw their consent to agreements other than those for irreconcilable differences divorces. In an action to modify custody and visitation, the supreme court held that a father could not withdraw consent to his agreement announced in open court. Noting that a consent judgment is in the nature of a contract, the court stated, "Whether contracting parties are bound by an informal agreement prior to the execution of a contemplated formal writing is a matter of intention to be determined by the surrounding facts and circumstances of each particular case."[74]

With respect to irreconcilable differences divorce, it appears that parties may not withdraw consent to an agreement unless they are also withdrawing consent to divorce based on irreconcilable differences. For example, the supreme court noted in dicta that "a properly drafted agreement may be binding vis-a-vis the parties" even though the chancellor has discretion to alter its terms.[75] Similarly, in reviewing a couple's settlement agreement addressing property division, custody and support, the supreme court stated, "although a no-fault divorce may not be granted without the parties having made provisions by written agreement for custody and . . . property rights . . . it does not delay the effective date of a separation agreement."[76] It should be noted, however, that there is disagreement among lawyers and judges regarding this issue, based on language to the effect that an agreement for irreconcilable differences divorce is not enforceable until approved by the court.[77] In any case, parties may provide in an agreement that it is not binding until approved by the court.

§ 23.10 COURT APPROVAL AND INCORPORATION INTO DECREE

Even though a voluntarily executed agreement may be binding on the parties, the agreement must be approved by the chancery court and incorporated into the divorce decree. Freedom of contract is limited to some extent in domestic matters. Courts are

---

[72] Grier v. Grier, 616 So. 2d 337, 339 (Miss. 1993); *see also* McCleave v. McCleave, 491 So. 2d 522, 523 (Miss. 1986); Ash v. Ash, 877 So. 2d 458, 460 (Miss. Ct. App. 2003) (agreement not binding if one party withdraws consent to irreconcilable differences divorce).

[73] Grier v. Grier, 616 So. 2d 337, 341 (Miss. 1993) (contract should indicate "with particularity" the parties' intention to be bound in fault-based divorce as well as irreconcilable differences divorce).

[74] McDonald v. McDonald, 850 So. 2d 1182, 1189 (Miss. Ct. App. 2002).

[75] Grier v. Grier, 616 So. 2d 337, 340 (Miss. 1993).

[76] Crosby v. People's Bank of Indianola, 472 So. 2d 951, 955 (Miss. 1985) (irreconcilable differences divorce; agreement also indicated intent to be bound in absence of divorce).

[77] *See* Ash v. Ash, 877 So. 2d 458, 460 (Miss. Ct. App. 2003) (agreement unenforceable if one party withdraws consent); *see also* Barton v. Barton, 790 So. 2d 169, 172 (Miss. 2001) (child support, custody, and alimony subject to modification and approval by court after sixty-day waiting period). The author interprets these comments as referring to the fact that agreements are not binding on the court, rather than that the agreement is not binding vis-à-vis the parties. However, there is support for both positions.

MARITAL AGREEMENTS

§ 23.10[1]

charged with oversight of the welfare and support of children – parties may not by agreement bind the court to provisions related to children. In Mississippi, this principle also extends to spousal support. Thus, an agreement for property division may be binding on the court in the absence of fraud, duress, or unconscionability, while agreements with respect to alimony, custody, and child support are subject to the court's review and modification.

[1] Court approval

[a] Property division. Provisions for property division should not be altered by courts in the absence of fraud, duress, or unconscionability.[78] In a case of first impression, the supreme court held in 2005 that a court may also set aside an agreement based on overreaching.[79] The court noted that while other provisions remain subject to alteration by the court, provisions related to property division are "permissible subjects of a contractual agreement."[80] Similarly, the court stated that property division agreements are enforced with "few, if any, exceptions."[81]

[b] Child custody and support. In contrast, parties cannot by agreement deprive a court of its authority to review provisions for support and custody.[82] A court may alter or modify the parties' agreement with respect to these matters, even if the parties intended to be bound by the agreement regardless of court approval.[83] The Mississippi Supreme Court noted that while agreements are generally enforced, the best interest of children may override an agreement.[84] For example, a father's petition for custody was treated as an original custody action even though he had privately agreed that the mother would have custody of the child.[85] Similarly, a couple's postnuptial agreement giving the father custody upon separation was void as against public policy.[86] Most authorities note, however, that in spite of courts' authority to disregard custody and child support agreements, courts do in fact recognize and adopt most agreements, particu-

---

[78] CLARK, JR., *supra* note 26, § 18.5 at 775; *see* Woodfin v. Woodfin, 26 So. 3d 389, 395 (Miss. Ct. App. 2010) (chancellor erred in modifying a couple's property division agreement without a finding of fraud, duress, or unconscionability); *cf. In re* Filiation of M.D.B., 914 So. 2d 316, 319 (Miss. Ct. App. 2005) (en banc) (custody agreement set aside on basis of duress).

[79] Lowrey v. Lowrey, 919 So. 2d 1112, 1119-22 (Miss. Ct. App. 2005) (setting aside property settlement agreement).

[80] Barton v. Barton, 790 So. 2d 169, 172 (Miss. 2001).

[81] McManus v. Howard, 569 So. 2d 1213, 1215 (Miss. 1990).

[82] GREGORY ET AL., *supra* note 58, § 4.05, at 109; MORGAN & TURNER, *supra* note 1, § 6.041, at 284, § 6.066, at 325.

[83] *See* Reno v. Reno, 176 So. 2d 58, 61 (Miss. 1965) (distinguishing agreement regarding property rights and those related to alimony, custody, and child support, which must be approved by the court; fault-based divorce).

[84] McManus v. Howard, 569 So. 2d 1213, 1215 (Miss. 1990); *see* Lowrey v. Lowrey, 919 So. 2d 112, 119-22 (Miss. Ct. App. 2005) (court may override agreement on financial matters only upon showing of overreaching or fraud, but reviews custody agreement in light of child's best interests); Chroniger v. Chroniger, 914 So. 2d 311, 316 (Miss. Ct. App. 2005) (agreement that mother would not be required to pay support if custody transferred to father not binding on chancellor); *see also* Bittick v. Bittick, 987 So. 2d 1058, 1061 (Miss. Ct. App. 2008) (rejecting father's argument that court's modification of visitation agreement was interference with contract).

[85] *See* White v. Thompson, 822 So. 2d 1125, 1128 (Miss. Ct. App. 2002).

[86] *See* McKee v. Flynt, 630 So. 2d 44, 50 (Miss. 1993); *see also* McManus v. Howard, 569 So. 2d 1213, 1216 (Miss. 1990) (parents cannot agree that relocation by one parent triggers a change in custody).

§ 23.10[1][c]   MISSISSIPPI FAMILY LAW

larly those in which the parties were represented by counsel.[87]

[c] **Alimony.** In many states, agreements for spousal support are treated in the same manner as property division agreements – they are matters between the spouses and will not be altered by a court absent fraud, duress, or unconscionability.[88] In Mississippi, however, agreements for alimony are treated in the same manner as child support provisions; they are subject to the court's review and approval.[89]

[2] **Out-of-court agreements.** While parties have freedom to contract with respect to property division, agreements must be reviewed and incorporated into the court's decree. A court will not enforce an agreement between spouses that was not submitted for approval. A written agreement that a husband would receive certain property in return for making mortgage payments was not enforceable, because the couple did not include their contract in the settlement agreement presented to the court. However, the husband was entitled to an amount that would put him in the position he would have been without the contract.[90] Similarly, an out-of-court agreement for the transfer of three assets from a wife to her husband was not enforceable.[91] And a wife's agreement to terminate alimony was not enforceable absent court approval.[92] In one case, however, a payor was relieved of arrearages based on an agreement that both parties understood had been filed with the court and approved.[93]

[3] **Incorporation into decree.** A settlement agreement incorporated into a divorce decree becomes a part of the final decree "for all legal intents and purposes," whether the agreement is copied into the decree, attached as an exhibit, incorporated by reference, or on file with the clerk of the court.[94] The provisions are treated as if they had been awarded by the court after a contested trial.[95]

§ 23.11 DEFENSES TO ENFORCEMENT

Settlement agreements are scrutinized more carefully than contracts negotiated at arm's length. Prior to judgment, agreements may be set aside based on fraud, duress, overreaching, or unconscionability. These contract law defenses are more likely to be applied to agreements between spouses than to ordinary commercial contracts. Courts must balance spouses' freedom to contract with the state's interest in the terms of mar-

---

[87] *See* CLARK, JR., *supra* note 26, § 18.5, at 772-73.

[88] GREGORY ET AL., *supra* note 58, § 4.05, at 109.

[89] *See* Barton v. Barton, 790 So. 2d 169, 172 (Miss. 2001); Roberts v. Roberts, 381 So. 2d 1333, 1335 (Miss. 1980); Stone v. Stone, 385 So. 2d 610, 614 (Miss. 1980).

[90] Sullivan v. Pouncey, 469 So. 2d 1233, 1234 (Miss. 1985); *see also* Dorr v. Dorr, 797 So. 2d 1008, 1015 (Miss. Ct. App. 2001) (out-of-court agreement not enforceable, but former wife should not benefit from agreement).

[91] Traub v. Johnson, 536 So. 2d 25, 27 (Miss. 1988) (irreconcilable differences divorce); Morgan v. Morgan, 744 So. 2d 321 (Miss. Ct. App. 1999) (also noting that court could deny relief under clean-hands doctrine).

[92] Gregg v. Montgomery, 587 So. 2d 928, 933 (Miss. 1991).

[93] Wright v. Wright, 737 So. 2d 408, 410 (Miss. Ct. App. 1998).

[94] Switzer v. Switzer, 460 So. 2d 843, 845 (Miss. 1984).

[95] *See infra* § 23.12.

MARITAL AGREEMENTS

§ 23.11[1]

riage dissolution.[96]

Some authorities note that, after a decree has been entered, the parties should be able to challenge agreements only on grounds generally available for reopening a judgment.[97] For example, Professor Homer Clark states that post-decree attacks should be limited to matters traditionally allowed for setting aside a judgment, such as mistake, fraud, newly discovered evidence, or excusable neglect. He notes, however, that courts often do not distinguish defenses used to set aside agreements prior to divorce from defenses available to attack judgments. He suggests that this may reflect courts' greater oversight of agreements between divorcing spouses.[98] Some Mississippi cases reflect this tendency. For example, unconscionability, which is not a ground for setting aside a judgment, was discussed as a defense in an action to set aside a divorce decree.[99]

[1] Fraud, misrepresentation, or concealment. A settlement agreement may be set aside before or after judgment based on one spouse's fraud, misrepresentation, or concealment.[100] A divorce decree was reopened several years after judgment because a husband failed to disclose his $2.6 million lottery winnings in divorce proceedings.[101] However, a decree will not be set aside if the complaining spouse had personal knowledge of the other's assets. The supreme court rejected a former wife's argument that a property settlement agreement should be set aside because her husband concealed his financial worth – she had signed joint tax returns during the marriage, was represented by counsel, and acknowledged at the time of divorce that the agreement was fair.[102] Similarly, a wife was not entitled to set aside an agreement for fraud based on her husband's failure to list his pension on a financial statement under retirement accounts. He testified that he did not understand the document, and so listed it in the margin under deductions from income.[103]

It was unclear until recently whether a spouse's concealment or misrepresentation of assets was fraud on a party – which must be raised within six months of judgment – or fraud on the court, which must be raised within a reasonable time. The issue was resolved by the Mississippi Supreme Court, which held that a party's intentional, significant misrepresentation is fraud on the court and not subject to the six-month limitation period.[104]

[2] Duress, undue influence, or overreaching. A settlement agreement may be set aside before or after judgment based on duress or overreaching. A petition to set

---

[96] CLARK, JR., *supra* note 26, § 58.2, at 759.

[97] MORGAN & TURNER, *supra* note 1, § 4.02, at 67.

[98] CLARK, JR., *supra* note 26, § 18.2, at 760.

[99] *See* Warren v. Warren, 815 So. 2d 457, 461 (Miss. Ct. App. 2002) (but finding no unconscionability). *See supra* § 19.08 for a discussion of post-judgment motions.

[100] *See* CLARK, JR., *supra* note 26, § 18.2, at 760; GREGORY ET AL, *supra* note 58, § 4.05 at 106 (agreement binding in absence of fraud, duress, concealment, overreaching, or unconscionability).

[101] Kalman v. Kalman, 905 So. 2d 760, 764 (Miss. Ct. App. 2004).

[102] Craft v. Craft, 478 So. 2d 258, 262 (Miss. 1985) (also rejecting her argument that the parties were in a fiduciary relationship); *see also* Warner v. Warner, 167 So. 615 (Miss. 1936) (finding no evidence of fraud).

[103] Shaw v. Shaw, 985 So. 2d 346 (Miss. Ct. App. 2007).

[104] Trim v. Trim, 33 So. 3d 471, 479 (Miss. 2010).

§ 23.11[3]   MISSISSIPPI FAMILY LAW

aside on these grounds must be filed within six months of judgment.[105] To prove duress, a party must show that his or her consent to the agreement was the result of the other spouse's wrongful conduct.[106] For example, a custody agreement was properly set aside on the basis of duress – a child's father held him for nine days and threatened to abscond to Mexico unless the mother signed the agreement.[107] The closely related defense of undue influence allows cancellation of an agreement when one spouse so dominates the other that an agreement is not voluntary.[108]

The Mississippi Supreme Court held in 2005 that a party may also set aside a divorce settlement agreement based on overreaching. The court distinguished between fraud and overreaching, stating that overreaching does not require proof of the elements of fraud. Instead, overreaching occurs when one party takes unfair advantage of another, which may occur through abuse of superior bargaining power. An agreement may be one-sided or unfair without rising to the level of overreaching. The complaining party must show that he or she "had no meaningful choice."[109] An agreement in which the husband received all marital assets, agreed to pay all marital debts, and was to have custody of their son, was enforceable. There was no showing of a lack of bargaining power or other circumstances that robbed the wife of meaningful choice. An agreement will not be set aside "simply because [it] is not necessarily in one's best interest."[110] A husband who agreed to pay $1,500 in child support, $4,500 in alimony, and $3,000 in household expenses was not entitled to set aside a property settlement agreement for overreaching. The court of appeals rejected his argument that he was "in the unfortunate position of having a pregnant girlfriend and a hostile wife" and had no choice but to sign the agreement. [111]

[3] Unconscionability. A settlement agreement may clearly be set aside before judgment based on unconscionability.[112] Rule 60(b) does not include unconscionability as a ground for setting aside a judgment.[113] Although no Mississippi case was found setting aside a judgment on this basis, the appellate courts have entertained unconscionability arguments as a basis for setting aside a judgment. The court of appeals stated that "[w]hile a properly drafted agreement may be binding on the parties, the chancellor is within his discretion to modify the terms in a divorce decree . . . . [T]he courts are not used as tools 'for implementing unconscionable contracts which are not fair to either party.'"[114] The court defined an unconscionable agreement as one that no person in his

---

[105] *See infra* § 19.08[2].

[106] MORGAN & TURNER, *supra* note 1, § 4.05, at 8.

[107] *In re* Filiation of M.D.B., 914 So. 2d 316, 318-19 (Miss. Ct. App. 2005) (en banc).

[108] MORGAN & TURNER, *supra*, note 1, § 4.051; *cf.* King v. King, 946 So. 2d 395, 402 (Miss. Ct. App. 2006) (court in divorce action set aside deed executed by wife under undue influence from husband).

[109] Lowrey v. Lowrey, 919 So. 2d 1112, 1119-22 (Miss. Ct. App. 2005) (overreaching may be asserted under MISS. R. CIV. P. 60(b) as "other misconduct").

[110] *In re* Dissolution of the Marriage of De St. Germain, 977 So. 2d 412, 420 (Miss. Ct. App. 2008) (husband also gave wife a portion of the sale proceeds of one asset).

[111] Pace v. Pace, 24 So. 3d 325, 329-30 (Miss. Ct. App. 2009).

[112] *See* Clark, Jr., *supra* note 26, at 418.

[113] *See supra* § 19.08[2].

[114] Warren v. Warren, 815 So. 2d 457, 461 (Miss. Ct. App. 2002) (petition to modify judgment) (quoting Grier v. Grier, 616 So. 2d 337, 340 (Miss. 1993)).

MARITAL AGREEMENTS   § 23.11[4]

senses would accept and no honest person would propose.[115] In each case, however, the courts have found no unconscionability. The supreme court rejected a former husband's argument that his agreement to pay his wife 50% of his earnings before taxes was unconscionable – he was a sophisticated businessman who was represented by counsel. The terms, although "less than desirable," could not be characterized as terms that no spouse in his or her right mind would accept.[116] Similarly, a husband's agreement to pay his wife $900 a month in alimony, although high, was not unconscionable. He was able to make the payments, understood the terms of the contract, and voluntarily entered into the agreement.[117]

[4] Agreement void as against public policy. A court may at any time refuse to enforce a provision that is void as against public policy. For example, an agreed provision that custody would automatically change if a custodial mother moved was void and contrary to public policy. The court refused to enforce the provision seven years later.[118] Similarly, an agreement providing for termination of child support when a child reached the age of eighteen was void and not enforceable.[119]

[5] Clarification. Courts may clarify ambiguous orders.[120] For example, a court did not err in extending the time for one party's performance under a settlement agreement when there was a good-faith misunderstanding between the parties regarding the meaning of the agreement.[121]

[6] Mistake. A settlement agreement may be reformed as any other contract based on a mutual mistake of fact or an error in drafting. A court had authority to reform a contract that erroneously provided for payments by a wife instead of, as intended, by her husband.[122] However, an agreement could not be reformed based on the parties' misunderstanding of the tax consequences of their alimony agreement – the mistake was in the making of the contract, not in the drafting.[123] Similarly, a court erred in modifying a couple's agreement that they would share expenses related to the marital home during the wife's occupancy. When the couple discovered extensive foundation problems, the court ordered the husband to provide the necessary repairs. The court of appeals held that their lack of knowledge of the problems was not the kind of "mutual

---

[115] Warren v. Warren, 815 So. 2d 457, 461 (Miss. Ct. App. 2002) (but finding no unconscionability).

[116] West v. West, 891 So. 2d 203, 214 (Miss. 2004).

[117] Steiner v. Steiner, 788 So. 2d 771, 777 (Miss. 2001) (fact that husband made a bad deal "does not relieve him of his duty to live up to his bargain").

[118] *See* McManus v. Howard, 569 So. 2d 1213, 1216 (Miss. 1990).

[119] Lawrence v. Lawrence, 574 So. 2d 1376, 1381 (Miss. 1991); *see also* R.K. v. J.K., 946 So. 2d 764, 779-80 (Miss. 2007) (agreement to terminate support if child no longer lived with mother did not allow termination when child attended boarding school).

[120] MORGAN & TURNER, *supra* note 1, § 6.028, at 253.

[121] Dalton v. Dalton, 852 So. 2d 586, 589 (Miss. Ct. App. 2002); *see also* Crisler v. Crisler, 963 So. 2d 1248, 1254 (Miss. Ct. App. 2007) (clarifying provision for sale of property).

[122] Dilling v. Dilling, 734 So. 2d 327, 335 (Miss. Ct. App. 1999) (also holding that even if mistake was not mutual, husband's conduct was inequitable).

[123] Ivison v. Ivison, 762 So. 2d 329, 335 (Miss. 2000) (alimony provisions of contract were clear; parties had different understandings of tax consequences).

§ 23.11[7]   MISSISSIPPI FAMILY LAW

mistake" contemplated by this exception.[124] And a wife's assumption that her husband would retire at sixty-five was not a mistake of fact allowing revision of an agreement that she would receive one-half of his retirement.[125]

[7] Frustration of purpose. Courts may fashion an equitable remedy if unforeseen circumstances frustrate the purpose of a provision. For example, when a car on which the husband was to make payments was destroyed and his obligation satisfied with insurance proceeds, the court should have required him to make similar payments on another automobile.[126]

[8] Equitable principles. A court may use equitable principles to reform an agreement in unusual circumstances. The court of appeals affirmed a chancellor's use of equitable principles to modify a liquidated damages provision that a wife would forfeit alimony if she revealed the contents of taped recordings. The wife, who was sued by her husband's attorney for making the tapes, was placed in a position of "extreme hardship" by the suit – one that her husband assisted in creating. In light of his lack of clean hands and the hardship placed on her, limiting the provision to provide for actual damages was an equitable solution.[127]

§ 23.12 ENFORCEMENT AND MODIFICATION

Consent decrees may be modified and enforced in the same manner as if ordered by a court.[128]

[1] Enforcement. A decree based on the parties' agreement may be enforced as any other judgment. The supreme court rejected a husband's argument that a property settlement agreement was a contract that could not be enforced through contempt proceedings.[129]

[2] Modification of consent decree. Modification of consent decree provisions is governed by the rules applicable to modification of court-ordered provisions. A property settlement agreement incorporated into a divorce decree may not be modified.[130] For example, a husband's agreement to provide a $150,000 life insurance policy for his wife as part of a property settlement rather than alimony was not modifiable.[131] In

---

[124] Kelley v. Kelley, 953 So. 2d 1139, 1143 (Miss. Ct. App. 2007).

[125] Lestrade v. Lestrade, 49 So. 3d 639, 644-45 (Miss. Ct. App. 2010) (no requirement that husband stop working at sixty-five).

[126] Morgan v. Morgan, 744 So. 2d 321, 325-26 (Miss. 1999).

[127] R.K. v. J.K., 946 So. 2d 764, 773 (Miss. 2007).

[128] East v. East, 493 So. 2d 927, 931 (Miss. 1986).

[129] Switzer v. Switzer, 460 So. 2d 843, 845 (Miss. 1984) (also rejecting argument that property settlements could not be enforced as a judgment because they were not modifiable); *see also* Tedford v. Dempsey, 437 So. 2d 410, 417 (Miss. 1983) (child support provisions of agreement incorporated into decree are enforceable as if court-ordered; subject to modification based on changed circumstances).

[130] East v. East, 493 So. 2d 927, 931 (Miss. 1986); Stone v. Stone, 385 So. 2d 610, 614 (Miss. 1980); Lestrade v. Lestrade, 49 So. 3d 639, 644-45 (Miss. Ct. App. 2010); Hopson v. Hopson, 851 So. 2d 397, 399 (Miss. Ct. App. 2003).

[131] Weathersby v. Weathersby, 693 So. 2d 1348, 1352 (Miss. 1997); *see also* Geiger v. Geiger, 530 So. 2d 185, 187

MARITAL AGREEMENTS §23.13

contrast, agreements regarding child support, permanent alimony, and custody can be modified based upon a material change in circumstances since the decree.[132] The Mississippi Supreme Court rejected an argument that an agreed provision for permanent alimony was not modifiable – agreements pursuant to irreconcilable differences divorce may be modified in the same manner as those pursuant to fault-based divorce.[133] The court has also stated, however, that an alimony provision based upon the parties' agreement should not be modified without close scrutiny.[134] With regard to financial matters between spouses "the parties should be allowed broad latitude."[135]

§23.13 CONSTRUCTION

The rules generally applicable to construction of written contracts apply to settlement agreements; the intent of the parties is determined by viewing the document as a whole.[136] Intent is tested by an objective standard - whether the language is clear, not whether the parties disagree about the meaning of the language.[137] The supreme court has stated that the typical three-tiered approach used in interpreting contracts should also be used to interpret divorce settlement agreements. First, the court looks to the language of the agreement. If it is clear and unambiguous, the court will enforce the contract as written.[138] The words used by the parties are "by far the best resource for ascertaining intent and assigning meaning with fairness and accuracy."[139] If the language of the contract is not clear, the court must, if possible, "harmonize the provisions in accord with the parties' apparent intent."[140] If the parties' intent remains uncertain, the court should resort to rules generally applicable to construction of contracts.[141] Finally, the court may consider parole or extrinsic evidence if necessary.[142] A chancel-

---

(Miss. 1988) (dicta).

[132] Barton v. Barton, 790 So. 2d 169, 172 (Miss. 2001); Switzer v. Switzer, 460 So. 2d 843, 845 (Miss. 1984).

[133] Taylor v. Taylor, 392 So. 2d 1145, 1148 (Miss. 1981) (rejecting argument that alimony was to be treated differently because irreconcilable differences divorce statute does not mention alimony).

[134] Morris v. Morris, 541 So. 2d 1040, 1043 (Miss. 1989).

[135] Weathersby v. Weathersby, 693 So. 2d 1348, 1351 (Miss. 1997).

[136] Roberts v. Roberts, 381 So. 2d 1333, 1335 (Miss. 1980); Beezley v. Beezley, 917 So. 2d 803, 807-08 (Miss. Ct. App. 2005) (agreement between divorcing parties interpreted as any other agreement and construed more strongly against drafter); cf. Mason v. Mason, 919 So. 2d 200, 204 (Miss. Ct. App. 2005) (en banc) (ambiguous agreement construed more strongly against wife, whose attorney drafted agreement).

[137] Ivison v. Ivison, 762 So. 2d 329, 335 (Miss. 2000) (alimony provisions of contract were clear; parties disagreed as to their understanding of tax consequences).

[138] West v. West, 891 So. 2d 203, 210-11 (Miss. 2004); D'Avignon v. D'Avignon, 945 So. 2d 401, 409 (Miss. Ct. App. 2006); Beezley v. Beezley, 917 So. 2d 803, 807 (Miss. Ct. App. 2005) (if document is clear, court is not concerned with parties' intent but with document language).

[139] Newell v. Hinton, 556 So. 2d 1037, 1042 (Miss. 1990).

[140] West v. West, 891 So. 2d 203, 210-11 (Miss. 2004); Newell v. Hinton, 556 So. 2d 1037, 1042 (Miss. 1990) (ambiguous because contract referred to car which neither party owned at time of signing; parties could not have intended to contract with regard to previously owned car).

[141] See Wood v. Wood (In re Dissolution of Marriage of Wood), 35 So. 3d 507, 513 (Miss. 2010) (agreement construed against wife, whose attorney drafted agreement); Owen v. Gerity, 422 So. 2d 284, 288 (Miss. 1982) (agreement must be construed more strongly against party whose attorney drafted it); D'Avignon v. D'Avignon, 945 So. 2d 401, 409 (Miss. Ct. App. 2006) (same).

[142] West v. West, 891 So. 2d 203, 210-11 (Miss. 2004); see Beezley v. Beezley, 917 So. 2d 803, 807-08 (Miss. Ct. App. 2005) (when contract is ambiguous, court considers parole evidence to determine intent of parties; text interpretation subject to de novo review); cf. Weeks v. Weeks, 29 So. 3d 80, 84-85 (Miss. Ct. App. 2009) (in dispute over meaning of provision, court adopted the interpretation supported by the chancellor who wrote the provision)

§ 23.14   MISSISSIPPI FAMILY LAW

lor properly admitted extrinsic evidence to determine the meaning of the term "debt" in an agreement, when the canons of construction did not resolve the ambiguity.[143] Parole evidence was not admissible to determine whether parties intended to release a wife's tort claim against her husband; the agreement clearly released all claims.[144] The parties' conduct in regard to a provision may be evidence of the meaning of their agreement. The supreme court rejected a former husband's argument that provisions of a settlement agreement regarding income from his business were ambiguous, in large part because he had complied with the provision for almost ten years.[145] A court is not bound to accept a construction that common sense suggests no one would agree to. Under a husband's proposed construction of a provision for sale of 42 acres and division of the proceeds, he could sell all but one acre of the property, receive almost all of the value, and still have no obligation to make a payment to his former wife.[146]

§ 23.14 Specific provisions

Specific provisions related to property division, alimony, custody, and child support are discussed in the chapters on each of these topics. This section does not fully address all cases involving specific provisions of marital and settlement agreements. It highlights certain provisions that are unenforceable.

[1] Custody of children. Parents may not by agreement define future circumstances that will constitute a material change in circumstances supporting a change in custody. Agreements providing that a child will remain in a particular town[147] or that custody will change if a custodial parent moves are unenforceable.[148]

[2] Child support. Parents may not agree to curtail the duty of support prior to a child's majority.[149] They may, however, agree to extend support beyond majority[150] or to continue support after death.[151]

[3] Alimony. Divorcing spouses have some flexibility to create alimony that does

---

[143] Harris v. Harris, 988 So. 2d 376, 379 (Miss. 2008) (if ambiguous, interpretation is question of fact); *see also* Wood v. Wood (*In re* Dissolution of Marriage of Wood), 35 So. 3d 507, 513-15 (Miss. 2010) (court properly looked to extrinsic evidence to determine intent regarding ambiguous agreement awarding each party a specific sum from a retirement account of estimated value).

[144] Martinez v. Martinez, 860 So. 2d 1247, 1251 (Miss. Ct. App. 2003); *see also* D'Avignon v. D'Avignon, 945 So. 2d 401, 410 (Miss. Ct. App. 2006) (alimony escalation clause clear and unambiguous).

[145] West v. West, 891 So. 2d 203, 211 (Miss. 2004); *see also* Crisler v. Crisler, 963 So. 2d 1248, 1253 (Miss. Ct. App. 2007) (husband's transfer of funds to wife upon sale of each lot was proof that she was to be paid as sales occurred rather than when all property was sold).

[146] Crisler v. Crisler, 963 So. 2d 1248, 1253 (Miss. Ct. App. 2007).

[147] *See* Bell v. Bell, 572 So. 2d 841, 845-846 (Miss. 1990) (nor may agreement prohibit mother from moving without court approval).

[148] *See* McManus v. Howard, 569 So. 2d 1213, 1216 (Miss. 1990) (parents cannot agree that relocation by one parent triggers a change in custody); *see* discussion *supra* § 12.11[5][b].

[149] Lawrence v. Lawrence, 574 So. 2d 1376, 1378 (Miss. 1991). See discussion *supra* § 13.09[3].

[150] Nichols v. Tedder, 547 So. 2d 766, 770 (Miss. 1989).

[151] Mahaffey v. First Nat'l Bank, 97 So. 2d 756, 767 (Miss. 1957) (child support duty does not survive death in absence of agreement). *See* discussion *supra* § 13.09[7].

684

MARITAL AGREEMENTS   § 23.14[4]

not fit the traditional forms. Parties may alter permanent alimony to survive the payor's death[152] but may not agree that it is nonmodifiable.[153] Parties may also create lump sum alimony that terminates at the death of either party or remarriage.[154] Parties or courts may provide that rehabilitative alimony terminates at remarriage.[155] Beyond these approved variations, parties should proceed with caution in creating hybrid forms of alimony.[156] Spouses may agree to self-adjusting alimony based on an escalation clause tied to a cost-of-living index.[157]

An order that one spouse pay the other's future medical expenses must be expressed in terms of a maximum amount. An order requiring a husband to pay one-half of all of his wife's future medical expenses was unenforceable.[158] Similarly, a court may not require payment of a spouse's health insurance unless the costs are known.[159] In contrast, an order that a husband pay 25% of his wife's future medical expenses up to $250 a month was definite and enforceable.[160]

Parties may agree that alimony will cease if the recipient cohabits, without a showing of mutual support between the alimony recipient and cohabitant.[161]

[4] Property division. Parties may agree that one spouse will inherit from the other. A divorce agreement providing that an incompetent wife would inherit from her former husband was an enforceable agreement; she was entitled to a child's share of his estate.[162] If an agreement between divorcing spouses does not address the continued validity of an existing will, it is a question of fact whether the spouses intended to revoke prior wills by implication. A will was not revoked when proof showed that an ex-husband continued to assist his former wife in business affairs, stated that he would always see to her welfare, expressed continued feelings for her, left her as signatory on his checking account, and kept the will in his desk drawer.[163]

Parties may agree to divide assets that would otherwise be nonmarital. The court of appeals rejected a husband's request, twenty years after his divorce, to limit his wife's share of his retirement to the marital portion. The agreement provided that she would receive "one-half of his retirement," not one-half of the marital portion.[164]

Clarity in drafting provisions involving retirement accounts is particularly important. A significant number of post-divorce property division disputes center around these provisions. For example, the supreme court reversed a chancellor's decision that

---

[152] *See In re* Estate of Kennington, 204 So. 2d 444, 449 (Miss. 1967).

[153] Taylor v. Taylor, 392 So. 2d 1145, 1147 (Miss. 1981); *see* McDonald v. McDonald, 683 So. 2d 929, 931 (Miss. 1996) (permanent alimony modifiable "regardless of any intent expressed by the parties to the contrary"). *See* discussion *supra* § 9.02[1][e].

[154] *See* Elliott v. Rogers, 775 So. 2d 1285, 1289-90 (Miss. Ct. App. 2000).

[155] *See* Waldron v. Waldron, 743 So. 2d 1064, 1065 (Miss. Ct. App. 1999).

[156] *See* discussion *supra* § 9.03[3].

[157] Speed v. Speed, 757 So. 2d 221, 223 (Miss. 2000).

[158] *See* Tillman v. Tillman, 791 So. 2d 285, 288 (Miss. Ct. App. 2001).

[159] Duncan v. Duncan, 815 So. 2d 480, 484 (Miss. Ct. App. 2002).

[160] Tillman v. Tillman, 791 So. 2d 285, 287 (Miss. Ct. App. 2001).

[161] Weathersby v. Weathersby, 693 So. 2d 1348, 1351 (Miss. 1997) (clause terminated alimony, which could not later be reinstated through modification). *See* discussion *supra* § 9.11[2][c].

[162] Burnett v. Burnett, 362 So. 2d 828, 830 (Miss. 1978).

[163] Hinders v. Hinders, 828 So. 2d 1235 (Miss. 2002).

[164] Lestrade v. Lestrade, 49 So. 3d 639, 643 (Miss. Ct. App. 2010).

§ 23.14[5]   MISSISSIPPI FAMILY LAW

a provision awarding the wife retirement survivor benefits "otherwise accorded her by law" included military survivor benefits. Military law made the choice optional by the servicemember and therefore not "accorded her by law." Four justices dissented, interpreting "by law" to refer to state marital property law.[165]

[5] Jurisdiction. Parties may not agree to jurisdiction in a court that lacks subject matter jurisdiction.[166] However, parties may waive personal jurisdiction.[167]

[6] General release and waiver. Most settlement agreements include a provision to the effect that the parties release each other from all claims and causes of action. A general waiver will release claims for torts committed during the marriage. The Mississippi Supreme Court held that a wife's general release in a divorce action barred a subsequent tort action against her husband for physical violence during the marriage.[168]

§ 23.15 DEATH OF A SPOUSE

In several cases, the Mississippi Supreme Court has addressed the validity of a settlement agreement when one of the spouses dies prior to divorce. An agreement that is contingent on court review or divorce is not binding when death occurs before divorce. However, parties may agree to be bound by property division provisions whether or not divorce occurs.

[1] Agreements not contingent on divorce. An agreement intended to be binding immediately is binding upon death with regard to property division. An agreement executed one week before a couple filed for divorce was enforceable when the husband died a few days later. The agreement provided that it was not contingent upon obtaining a divorce.[169] In 2001, the supreme court addressed this issue more explicitly in *Barton v. Barton*, holding that while provisions for support and custody are clearly subject to alteration and approval by the court after the sixty-day waiting period, "such a period

---

[165] Williams v. Williams, 37 So. 3d 1171, 1176-78 (Miss. 2010) (Kitchens, J., dissenting); *see also* Wood v. Wood (*In re* Dissolution of Marriage of Wood), 35 So. 3d 507, 513-515 (Miss. 2010) (provision for specific amounts to be awarded from "estimated" value of retirement account was ambiguous; court looked to extrinsic evidence); Lestrade v. Lestrade, 49 So. 3d 639, 644-645 (Miss. Ct. App. 2010) (reversing chancellor's modification of unambiguous retirement provision based on wife's "assumption" that husband would retire at sixty-five); Pratt v. Pratt, 977 So. 2d 386, 389 (Miss. Ct. App. 2007) (husband not entitled to revision of property settlement agreement to conform to his understanding of pension division); Salemi v. Salemi, 972 So. 2d 1, 5 (Miss. Ct. App. 2007) (husband time-barred from seeking clarification of agreement to divide pension nine years after judgment); Rogers v. Rogers, 919 So. 2d 184, 187-88 (Miss. Ct. App. 2005) (provision that the wife was to receive "one-half of the husband's 401k in the approximate sum of $69,000.00" meant $69,000 at the time of the divorce hearing, not when the qualified domestic relations order was entered several years later); Chroniger v. Chroniger, 914 So. 2d 311, 315 (Miss. Ct. App. 2005) (husband's obligation to pay wife one-half of his military retirement was part of property division and did not terminate upon cohabitation).

[166] Duvall v. Duvall, 80 So. 2d 752, 754 (Miss. 1955) (distinguishing erroneous judgments, which may be reversed on appeal, from judgments lacking subject matter jurisdiction, which are void and may be attacked collaterally). *See* discussion *supra* § 18.02[1].

[167] *See* discussion *supra* § 18.04[4].

[168] *See* Martinez v. Martinez, 860 So. 2d 1247, 1250 (Miss. Ct. App. 2003).

[169] Roberts v. Roberts, 381 So. 2d 1333, 1335 (Miss. 1980).

MARITAL AGREEMENTS § 23.15[2]

does not exist for provisions dealing with property." The agreement, which stated that it was binding as of the date of signing, was not contingent on the parties' obtaining an irreconcilable differences divorce. The property settlement agreement was enforceable when the husband died during the sixty-day period.[170]

[2] Agreements contingent on divorce. An agreement that is contingent on divorce is not binding on the parties upon death. For example, a husband's agreement to transfer certificates of deposit to his wife, made in contemplation of an irreconcilable differences divorce, was not enforceable when he died before the divorce was finalized. In contrast to the *Barton* contract, the agreement did not state that it was binding on the date of execution.[171] Similarly, a property settlement agreement stating that it would be null and void in the event the parties did not divorce was not enforceable upon the husband's death.[172]

§ 23.16 RECONCILIATION

In the absence of a provision to the contrary, most courts hold that the parties' reconciliation terminates the unexecuted provisions of a settlement agreement.[173]

---

[170] Barton v. Barton, 790 So. 2d 169, 171 (Miss. 2001).

[171] Johnson v. Collins, 419 So. 2d 1029, 1031 (Miss. 1982).

[172] Rennie v. Rennie, 718 So. 2d 1091, 1094 (Miss. 1998) (also stating that property settlement agreements entered in anticipation of irreconcilable differences divorce must be approved by court to be enforceable).

[173] GREGORY ET AL., *supra* note 58, § 4.05, at 109.

687

688

TABLE OF CASES

A

Abernathy v. Abernathy, 482 S.E.2d 265, 266-68 (Ga. 1997) 562
Abernethy v. Fishkin, 699 So. 2d 235, 236 (Fla. 1997) 213
A.B. v. Lauderdale County Dep't of Human Servs., 13 So. 3d 1263, 1268-69 (Miss. 2009) 525
Ackley v. Ackley, 472 N.Y.S.2d 804, 806 (N.Y. App. Div. 1984) 139
A.C.W. v. J.C.W., 957 So. 2d 1042, 1045-46 (Miss. Ct. App. 2007) 522
Adair v. Adair, 735 So. 2d 383, 384 (Miss. 1999) 167
Adams v. Adams, 59 So. 84 (Miss. 1912) 531
Adams v. Adams, 357 So. 2d 881 (La. Ct. App. 1978) 76
Adams v. Adams, 467 So. 2d 211, 215-16 (Miss. 1985) 421, 456
Adams v. Adams, 591 So. 2d 431 (Miss. 1991) 303, 477
Adams v. Johnson, 33 So. 3d 551, 554-56 (Miss. Ct. App. 2010) 374
Adar v. Smith, 597 F.3d 697, 719 (5th Cir. 2010) 54, 533
Adcock v. Van Norman, 917 So. 2d 86, 88-89 (Miss. 2005) 553, 558
Adoption of C.L.B. v. D.G.B., 812 So. 2d 980, 983 (Miss. 2002). 534, 576
Adoption of J.M.M. v. New Beginnings of Tupelo, Inc., 796 So. 2d 975, 983 (Miss. 2001) 535, 538, 546
A.D.R. v. J.L.H., 994 So. 2d 177, 183-84 (Miss. 2008) 538
A.H.W. v. G.H.B., 772 A.2d 948 (N.J. Super. Ct. Ch. Div. 2000) 515
Ainsworth v. Natural Father, 414 So. 2d 417, 419-20 (Miss. 1982) 522, 540, 541
Air Comfort Sys., Inc. v. Honeywell, Inc., 760 So. 2d 43, 47 (Miss. Ct. App. 2000) 126
Alack v. Phelps, 230 So. 2d 789, 792 (Miss. 1970) 529
Albright v. Albright, 437 So. 2d 1003, 1005 (Miss. 1983) 122, 329, 330, 331, 339, 342, 345
Alderson v. Alderson, 810 So. 2d 627, 629 (Miss. Ct. App. 2002) 341
Alderson v. Morgan, 739 So. 2d 465, 467 (Miss. Ct. App. 1999) 425
Aldridge v. Aldridge, 27 So. 2d 884, 885-86 (Miss. 1946) 226, 247, 273
Aldridge v. Aldridge, 77 So. 150, 150-51 (Miss. 1918) 4, 47, 63
Aldridge v. Aldridge, 527 So. 2d 96, 99 (Miss. 1988) 496
Alexander v. Alexander, 493 So. 2d 978, 980 (Miss. 1986) 105, 106, 590
Alexander v. Alexander, 494 So. 2d 365, 368 (Miss. 1986) 194, 456, 460, 470, 478, 481, 496
Alexander v. Daniel, 904 So. 2d 172, 179-80 (Miss. 2005) 15
Alexis v. Tarver, 879 So. 2d 1078, 1080 (Miss. Ct. App. 2004) 297, 298
Alford v. Alford, 653 So. 2d 133, 135-36 (La. Ct. App. 1995) 201
Alford v. Mississippi Div. of Medicaid, 30 So. 3d 1212, 1214 (Miss. 2010) 626
A & L, Inc. v. Grantham, 747 So. 2d 832, 837 (Miss. 1999) 140, 141, 142, 144, 160,
        164, 178, 187, 217, 219, 220, 221, 226, 227, 245, 271, 281, 305, 307, 665
Alldread v. Bailey, 626 So. 2d 99, 102-03 (Miss. 1993) 26
Allen v. Allen, 953 So. 2d 279, 282 (Miss. Ct. App. 2007) 462, 470
Allen v. Williams, 914 So. 2d 254, 258 (Miss. Ct. App. 2005) 369, 566, 599
Allred v. Allred, 735 So. 2d 1064, 1067 (Miss. Ct. App. 1999) 487, 488, 497, 623
Almond v. Almond, 850 So. 2d 104, 107 (Miss. Ct. App. 2002) 200
Alred v. Alred, 678 So. 2d 1144, 1146 (Ala. Civ. App. 1996) 433
Alston v. Alston, 629 A.2d 70, 74 (Md. 1993) 160
Alwell v. Alwell, 471 N.Y.S.2d 899, 901-02 (N.Y. App. Div. 1984) 149
Amacker v. Amacker, 33 So. 3d 493, 495-96 (Miss. Ct. App. 2009) 137, 174, 266, 267, 275, 276
Amer v. Akron City Hosp., 351 N.E.2d 479, 484 (Ohio 1976) 26
Ammons v. Ammons, 109 So. 795, 795 (Miss. 1926) 100
Am. Nat'l Ins. Co. v. Hogue, 749 So. 2d 1254, 1262 (Miss. Ct. App. 2000) 25, 26
Anciaux v. Anciaux, 666 So. 2d 577, 578 (Fla. Dist. Ct. App. 1996) 212
Andersen v. Andersen, 200 So. 726, 728 (Miss. 1941) 87, 88, 119
Anderson-Tully Co. v. Wilson, 74 So. 2d 735, 737 (Miss. 1954) 4
Anderson v. Anderson, 8 So. 3d 264, 270-71 (Miss. Ct. App. 2009) 620
Anderson v. Anderson, 54 So. 3d 850, 851 (Miss. Ct. App. 2010) 85, 88, 91, 92, 95
Anderson v. Anderson, 162 So. 2d 853 (Miss. 1956) 301
Anderson v. Anderson, 200 So. 726, 727 (Miss. 1941) 71
Anderson v. Anderson, 692 So. 2d 65, 72 (Miss. 1997) 297, 462
Anderson v. Anderson, 961 So. 2d 55, 58, 60 (Miss. Ct. App. 2007) 356, 393, 401, 604, 623
Anderson v. Anderson, 963 S.W.2d 604, 607 (Ark. Ct. App. 1998) 427
Andler v. Andler, 538 P.2d 649 (Kan. 1975) 425
Andres v. Andres, 22 So. 3d 314, 319-20 (Miss. Ct. App. 2009) 465, 480
Andrews v. Williams, 723 So. 2d 1175, 1178 (Miss. Ct. App. 1998) 453, 476, 593
Angel v. Angel, 562 S.W.2d 661, 664 (Ky. Ct. App. 1978) 139

689

TABLE OF CASES

Anglin v. Anglin, 51 So. 2d 781, 783 (Miss. 1951)..565
Ankenbrandt v. Richards, 504 U.S. 689, 705-06 (1992)...552
Anon. v. Anon., 126 N.Y.S. 149, 149 (N.Y. Sup. Ct. 1910) 63
Antoine v. Antoine, 96 So. 305, 306 (Miss. 1923) 64
Armstrong v.Armstrong, 32 Miss. 279, 289 (1856)..101, 103, 120, 237, 243
Armstrong v. Armstrong, 618 So. 2d 1278, 1280 (Miss. 1993) 35, 240, 242, 246,
    247, 254, 255, 261, 262, 270, 271, 287, 290, 464, 622
Armstrong v. Armstrong, 836 So. 2d 794, 797-98 (Miss. Ct. App. 2002)....................................207
Arnold v. Conwill, 562 So. 2d 97, 99-100 (Miss. 1990)...404
Aron v. Aron, 832 So. 2d 1257, 1258-59 (Miss. Ct. App. 2002) 136, 161
Arthur v. Arthur, 691 So. 2d 997, 1001 (Miss. 1997)...........................75, 134, 138, 144, 199, 420
Asanov v. Hunt, 914 So. 2d 769, 771 (Miss. Ct. App. 2005)...................................566, 588, 623
Ashburn v. Ashburn, 970 So. 2d 204, 206 (Miss. Ct. App. 2007).........82, 83, 101, 102, 103, 593, 623
Ashley v. Ashley, 990 S.W.2d 507, 509 (Ark. 1999)..213
Ash v. Ash, 622 So. 2d 1264, 1266-67 (Miss. 1993) 403
Ash v. Ash, 877 So. 2d 458, 460 (Miss. Ct. App. 2003)..109, 676
Askew v. Askew, 699 So. 2d 515, 520 (Miss. 1997)..616
Askins v. Askins, 704 S.W.2d 632, 635-36 (Ark. 1986)..203
Atkinson v. Atkinson, 11 So. 3d 172, 174 (Miss. Ct. App. 2009) 76, 89, 117, 149, 171, 179
Atkinson v. Atkinson, 408 N.W. 2d 516, 519 (Mich. 1987)...323
A.T.K. v. R.M.K.W., 26 So. 3d 1103, 1107 (Miss. Ct. App. 2009) 397, 399
Attorney LS v. Miss. Bar, 649 So. 2d 810, 813 (Miss. 1995)...642
Attorney M v. Miss. Bar, 621 So. 2d 220, 224 (Miss. 1992)..642
Attorney Q v. Miss. Bar, 587 So. 2d 228, 233 (Miss. 1991)..634
Atwood v. Hicks, 538 So. 2d 404, 406 (Miss. 1989) 321, 419
Aubert v. Aubert, 529 A.2d 909, 911-12 (N.H. 1987)..125
Aufort v. Aufort, 49 P.2d 620, 620 (Cal. Dist. Ct. App. 1935) 10
Austin v. Austin, 100 So. 591, 592 (Miss. 1924) 13
Austin v. Austin, 766 So. 2d 86, 89 (Miss. Ct. App. 2000)...290, 292, 293
Austin v. Austin, 981 So. 2d 1000, 1003-04 (Miss. Ct. App. 2007) 241, 287, 288, 293, 295,
    296, 432, 462, 463, 468
Autrey v. Parson, 864 So. 2d 294 (Miss. Ct. App. 2003) 319
Avant v. Whitten, 253 So. 2d 394, 396 (Miss. 1971) 636
Avery v. Avery, 864 So. 2d 1054 (Miss. Ct. App. 2004).....................................77, 191, 245, 275, 433
Ayers v. Ayers, 734 So. 2d 213, 214-16 (Miss. Ct. App. 1999)...........69, 95, 96, 333, 368, 410, 496
Ayers v. Petro, 417 So. 2d 912, 913 (Miss. 1982)..17, 18
A.Z. v. B.Z., 725 N.E.2d 1051, 1057 (Mass. 2000)..505

B

Baby Doe, 353 S.E.2d 877, 878-79 (S.C. 1987) 509
Baehr v. Lewin, 852 P.2d 44, 47 (Haw. 1993)..6
Baehr v. Miike, No. 91-1394, 1996 WL 694235, at *21 (Haw. Cir. Ct. Dec. 3, 1996) 6
Baier v. Baier, 897 So. 2d 202, 204-05 (Miss. Ct. App. 2005) 447, 477, 479, 494
Bailey v. Bailey, 724 So. 2d 335, 336 (Miss. 1998) 291, 420, 421, 430, 432, 435, 464, 465
Bailey v. Bailey, 2008 WL 324156 (E.D. Mich. 2008)..643
Bailey v. Fischer, 946 So. 2d 404, 408 (Miss. Ct. App. 2006)...........................460, 628, 629, 630
Baker, Donelson, Bearman, Caldwell & Berkowitz, P.C. v. Seay, 42 So. 3d 474, 487-89 (Miss. 2010)...............28
Baker v. Baker, 807 So. 2d 476, 480 (Miss. Ct. App. 2001)...199, 266, 275
Baker v. Baker, 861 So. 2d 351, 353 (Miss. Ct. App. 2003) 200
Baker v. State, 744 A.2d 864, 886 (Vt. 1999)...49, 516
Baker v. Williams, 503 So. 2d 249, 252 (Miss. 1987)..........................314, 315, 316, 322, 323, 324
Baldwin v. Baldwin, 788 So. 2d 800, 809 (Miss. Ct. App. 2001)......................................444, 445
Balius v. Gaines, 908 So. 2d 791, 795-96 (Miss. Ct. App. 2005)...........376, 377, 400, 402, 409, 484, 612
Balius v. Gaines, 914 So. 2d 300, 304-05 (Miss. Ct. App. 2005) 308, 390, 391, 393, 402, 487, 497, 612
Ballard v. Ballard, 434 So. 2d 1357, 1360 (Miss.1983)...395
Ballard v. Ballard, 843 So. 2d 76, 78 (Miss. Ct. App. 2003)...................376, 377, 431, 434, 472
Ball v. Ball, 335 So. 2d 5, 7 (Fla. Dist. Ct. App. 1976) 149
Baneck v. Baneck, 455 So. 2d 766, 767-68 (Miss. 1984) 342
Banks v. Banks, 511 So. 2d 933, 935 (Miss. 1987)...614, 619
Banks v. Banks, 648 So. 2d 1116, 1126 (Miss. 1994) 491, 493
Barbee v. Pigott, 507 So. 2d 77, 83-85 (Miss. 1987) 23, 24

TABLE OF CASES

Barber v. Barber, 62 U.S. 582, 584 (1858) 552
Barbour v. Barbour, 464 A.2d 915, 921 (D.C. Cir. 1983) 203
Barfield v. State, 749 So. 2d 331, 340 (Miss. Ct. App. 1999) 489, 490
Barker v. Barker, 996 So. 2d 161 (Miss. Ct. App. 2008) 255, 267, 275, 276, 280
Barkley v. Barkley, 694 N.E.2d 989, 992 (Ohio Ct. App. 1997) 201
Barnes v. Barnes, 820 P.2d 294, 297 (Alaska 1991) 202
Barnes v. Dep't of Human Servs., 42 So. 3d 10, 13-18 (Miss. 2010) 425, 459, 460, 495
Barnett v. Barnett, 908 So. 2d 833, 837-38 (Miss. Ct. App. 2005) 144, 170, 177, 182,
    183, 186, 199, 257, 258, 259, 261, 262, 275, 278, 283, 427, 444, 445, 446, 450, 451
Barnett v. Oathout, 883 So. 2d 563, 566 (Miss. 2004) 338, 373
Barrett v. United States, 74 F.3d 661, 665 (5th Cir. 1996) 252
Barton v. Barton, 790 So. 2d 169, 172 (Miss. 2001) 613, 676, 677, 678, 683, 687
Barton v. State, 143 So. 861, 862 (Miss. 1932) 9, 42
Bascomb v. Bascomb, 25 N.H. 267, 1852 WL 2138 (1852) 73
Bass v. Bass, 879 So. 2d 1122, 1124 (Miss. Ct. App. 2004) 343, 345, 348, 355, 359
Bass v. Irvin, 170 So. 673, 674 (Miss. 1936) 420
Bates v. Bates, 755 So. 2d 478, 482 (Miss. Ct. App. 1999) 173, 301, 302
Beamer v. Beamer, 22 So. 3d 430, 431 (Miss. Ct. App. 2009) 619
Beasley v. Beasley, 518 A.2d 545, 555 (Pa. Super. Ct. 1986) 155
Beasley v. Beasley, 913 So. 2d 358, 363 (Miss. Ct. App. 2005) 337, 405
Beasley v. Scott, 900 So. 2d 1217, 1220 (Miss. Ct. App. 2005) 343, 345, 350, 352, 353, 354, 357, 360
Beasnett v. Arledge, 934 So. 2d 345, 347 (Miss. Ct. App. 2006) 477, 484, 529, 602
Becker v. Becker, 639 So. 2d 1082, 1084 (Fla. Dist. Ct. App. 1994) 144, 150
Beddingfield v. Beddingfield, 11 So. 3d 780, 783-784 (Miss. Ct. App. 2009) 258, 266, 275
Beeks v. Beeks, 63 So. 444, 445 (Fla. 1913) 11
Beezley v. Beezley, 917 So. 2d 803, 806 (Miss. Ct. App. 2005) 240, 241, 247, 248, 250, 252, 254, 285, 673, 683
Belding v. Belding, 736 So. 2d 425, 428 (Miss. Ct. App. 1999) 151, 159, 174, 349, 608, 610
Belk v. State Dep't of Pub. Welfare, 473 So. 2d 447, 451 (Miss. 1985) 314
Bellais v. Bellais, 931 So. 2d 665, 671 (Miss. Ct. App. 2006) 351
Bell v. Bell, 572 So. 2d 841, 844 (Miss. 1990) 290, 400, 674, 684,
Benal v. Benal, 22 So. 3d 369, 373 (Miss. Ct. App. 2009) 344, 355, 359, 375
Benson v. Benson, 608 So. 2d 709, 711 (Miss. 1992) 80
Berryman v. Berryman, 907 So. 2d 958, 959-60 (Miss. Ct. App. 2004) 160, 174, 625
Berry v. Berry, 647 S.W.2d 945, 946-47 (Tex. 1983) 204, 205
Best v. Hinton, 838 So. 2d 306, 308 (Miss. Ct. App. 2002) 401
Beth R. v. Donna M., 853 N.Y.S. 2d 501 (N.Y. Sup. Ct. 2008) 52
Betts v. Massey, 40 So. 3d 602, 609 (Miss. Ct. App. 2009) 397, 398, 404
Bias v. Bias, 493 So. 2d 342, 344 (Miss. 1986) 83, 85, 86, 87, 104, 118, 608
Biggs v. Roberts, 115 So. 2d 151, 154 (Miss. 1959) 19
Bilbo v. Bilbo, 177 So. 772, 775-76 (Miss. 1938) 32, 301, 556, 557, 558
Birindelli v. Egelston, 404 So. 2d 322, 323-24 (Miss. 1981) 546, 547
Bishop v. Bishop, 308 N.Y.S.2d 998, 1000-01 (N.Y. Sup. Ct. 1970) 12
Bishop v. Comm'r, 46 T.C.M. (CCH) 15 (1983) 656
Bissell v. Bissell, 117 A. 252, 254 (N.J. Ch. 1922) 73
Bittick v. Bittick, 987 So. 2d 1058, 1061 (Miss. Ct. App. 2008) 391, 402, 408, 464, 677
Black v. Black, 741 So. 2d 299, 300 (Miss. Ct. App. 1999) 192, 211, 309, 614, 625
Blake v. Wilson, 962 So. 2d 705, 708-09 (Miss. Ct. App. 2007) 582
Blalack v. Blalack, 938 So. 2d 909, 911-12 (Miss. Ct. App. 2006) 256, 275, 278
Bland v. Bland, 620 So. 2d 543, 545 (Miss. 1993) 86, 94, 118
Bland v. Hill, 735 So. 2d 414, 418 (Miss. 1999) 27, 28
Blase v. Blase, 704 So. 2d 741, 742 (Fla. Dist. Ct App. 1998) 201, 202
Blevins v. Bardwell, 784 So. 2d 166, 170-71 (Miss. 2001) 331, 336, 343, 357, 358, 608
Blount v. Blount, 95 So. 2d 545, 552 (Miss. 1957) 187, 192, 309
Boaz v. Boaz, 817 So. 2d 627, 629 (Miss. Ct. App. 2002) 353, 358
Bodne v. King, 835 So. 2d 52, 55 (Miss. 2003) 85, 93, 95
Boemio v. Boemio, 994 A.2d 911, 917 (Md. 2010) 236
Boleware v. Boleware, 450 So. 2d 92, 92 (Miss. 1984) 449
Bonderer v. Robinson, 502 So. 2d 314, 316 (Miss. 1986) 252
Bond v. Bond, 355 So. 2d 672, 674-75 (Miss. 1978) 416, 599
Boone v. Downey, 259 So. 2d 710, 711 (Miss. 1972) 77, 334
Bosarge v. Bosarge, 879 So. 2d 515 (Miss. Ct. App. 2004) 478, 490
Bougard v. Bougard, 991 So. 2d 646, 649 (Miss. Ct. App. 2008) 108, 169, 601

TABLE OF CASES

Bounds v. Bounds, 935 So. 2d 407, 411 (Miss. Ct. App. 2006) 305, 307, 481, 483, 490, 492
Boutwell v. Boutwell, 829 So. 2d 1216, 1220 (Miss. 2002) 72, 76, 93, 147, 148, 159, 219, 619, 623
Bowden v. Fayard, 355 So. 2d 662, 664 (Miss. 1978) 394
Bowen v. Bowen, 688 So. 2d 1374, 1376-78 (Miss. 1997) 38, 90, 91, 95, 118, 361
Bowen v. Bowen, 982 So. 2d 385, 392-93 (Miss. 2008) 142, 147, 191, 221, 239, 265, 266, 274, 277, 280
Bower v. Bower, 758 So. 2d 405, 411-12 (Miss. 2000) 350, 351
Bowe v. Bowe, 557 So. 2d 793, 795 (Miss. 1990) 241, 252
Box v. Box, 622 So. 2d 284, 288-89 (Miss. 1993) 260, 284
Boyce v. Boyce, 541 A.2d 614, 615 (D.C. 1988) 152
Boyce v. Boyce, 694 S.W.2d 288, 290 (Mo. Ct. App. 1985) 147
Boyett v. Boyett, 119 So. 299, 300-01 (Miss. 1928) 38, 333, 415, 418
Boykin v. Boykin, 445 So. 2d 538, 539 (Miss. 1984) 180
Boykin v. Boykin, 565 So. 2d 1109, 1112-13 (Miss. 1990) 190, 200, 210
Brabham v. Brabham, 84 So. 2d 147, 153 (Miss. 1955) 35, 186, 237, 240, 254, 289, 414
Brabham v. Brabham, 950 So. 2d 1098, 1102 (Miss. Ct. App. 2007) 167, 173, 175, 176, 183,
  265, 268, 274, 275, 276, 478, 609
Bracey v. Bracey, 408 So. 2d 1387, 1389 (Miss.1982) 466
Bradley v. Holmes, 561 So. 2d 1034, 1035-36 (Miss. 1990) 426
Bradley v. Jones, 949 So. 2d 802, 805 (Miss. Ct. App. 2006) 352
Bradley v. Somers, 322 S.E.2d 665, 666-67 (S.C. 1984) 29
Bradley v. State, 1 Miss. (Walker) 156 (1824) 111
Brady v. Brady, 14 So. 3d 823, 826 (Miss. Ct. App. 2009) 248, 249, 274, 280
Brahan v. Meridian Light & Ry. Co., 83 So. 467, 467 (Miss. 1919) 25
Braiman v. Braiman, 378 N.E.2d 1019, 1021 (N.Y. 1978) 366
Bramante v. Comm'r, 84 T.C.M. (CCH) 299 (2002) 660
Brame v. Brame, No. 98-CA-00502-COA, 2000 Miss. App. LEXIS 142, at *9 (Miss. Ct. App. 2000) 147
Brandt v. Brandt, 167 So. 524, 525 (Fla. 1936) 10
Brand v. Brand, 482 So. 2d 236, 237 (Miss. 1986) 290, 464, 476, 477, 494, 495
Brasfield v. Brasfield, 679 So. 2d 1091 (Ala. Civ. App. 1996) 516
Bratcher v. Surrette, 848 So. 2d 893, 897 (Miss. Ct. App. 2003) 378
Brawdy v. Howell, 841 So. 2d 1175, 1179 (Miss. Ct. App. 2003) 291, 442, 465, 467, 477
Brawley v. Brawley, 734 So. 2d 237, 241-42 (Miss. Ct. App. 1999) 346, 361, 404
Brazan v. Brazan, 638 So. 2d 1176, 1180 (La. Ct. App. 1994) 439
B.R.C. v. State, 795 So. 2d 526, 529 (Miss. 2001) 605
Bredemeier v. Jackson, 689 So. 2d 770, 777-78 (Miss. 1997) 304, 408, 431
Brehm v. Brehm, 762 So. 2d 1259, 1264 (La. Ct. App. 2000) 145, 150
Brekeen v. Brekeen, 880 So. 2d 280, 285-86 (Miss. 2004) 345, 352
Breland v. Breland, 920 So. 2d 510, 512 (Miss. Ct. App. 2006) 106
Brennan v. Brennan, 605 So. 2d 749, 752 (Miss. 1992) 291, 465, 493
Brennan v. Brennan, 638 So. 2d 1320 (Miss. 1994) 259, 275, 423
Brennan v. Ebel, 880 So. 2d 1058, 1063 (Miss. Ct. App. 2004) 275, 295
Brent v. State, 632 So. 2d 936, 942 (Miss. 1994) 604
Bresler v. Bresler, 824 So. 2d 641 (Miss. Ct. App. 2002) 621
Bresnahan v. Bresnahan, 818 So. 2d 1113, 1119 (Miss. 2002) 146, 161, 163, 167, 173, 219
Brewer v. Brewer, 919 So. 2d 135, 138 (Miss. Ct. App. 2005) 71, 74, 77, 103, 343, 346
Bridges v. Bridges, 217 So. 2d 281, 281 (Miss. 1968) 64, 242
Bridges v. Bridges, 330 So. 2d 260, 262 (Miss. 1976) 34, 37
Bridges v. Bridges, 910 So. 2d 1156, 1158-59 (Miss. Ct. App. 2005) 567, 581
Bridges v. McCracken, 724 So. 2d 1086, 1087 (Miss. Ct. App. 1998) 250, 260, 456
Brinkman v. Brinkman, 966 S.W.2d 780, 783 (Tex. Ct. App. 1998) 125
Brister v. Dunaway, 115 So. 36, 38 (Miss. 1927) 28
Brocato v. Brocato, 731 So. 2d 1138, 1142-43 (Miss. 1999) 369, 377, 404, 423
Brock v. Brock, 906 So. 2d 879, 887-88 (Miss. Ct. App. 2005) 122, 144, 146, 148, 151, 159,
  345, 348, 352, 358, 359
Brooks v. Brooks, 652 So. 2d 1113, 1116 (Miss. 1995) 71, 74, 75, 260, 275, 278
Brooks v. Brooks, 757 So. 2d 301, 304 (Miss. Ct. App. 1999) 143
Brooks v. Fair, 532 N.E.2d 208, 212-13 (Ohio Ct. App. 1988) 509
Broome v. Broome, 832 So. 2d 1247, 1256 (Miss. Ct. App. 2002) 309, 483, 625
Broome v. Broome, 841 So. 2d 1204, 1207 (Miss. Ct. App. 2003) 492
Brown v. Brown, 14 S.W.3d 704, 707 (Mo. Ct. App. 2000) 202
Brown v. Brown, 493 So. 2d 961, 963 (Miss. 1986) 561, 564
Brown v. Brown, 507 A.2d 1223, 1225-26 (Pa. Super. Ct. 1986) 149

TABLE OF CASES

Brown v. Brown, 566 So. 2d 718, 721 (Miss. 1990) 468
Brown v. Brown, 574 So. 2d 688, 691 (Miss. 1990) 167, 171, 198
Brown v. Brown, 724 So. 2d 874, 877 (Miss. 1998) 282
Brown v. Brown, 764 So. 2d 502, 504-05 (Miss. Ct. App. 2000).................357, 361, 401
Brown v. Brown, 792 A.2d 463 (N.J. App. Div. 2002) 224
Brown v. Brown, 797 So. 2d 253, 256 (Miss. Ct. App. 2001) 140
Brown v. Brown, 817 So. 2d 588, 590 (Miss. Ct. App. 2002)......................33, 34, 35, 86, 95
Brown v. Brown, 822 So. 2d 1119, 1121 (Miss. Ct. App. 2002)...............470, 480, 486, 484
Brown v. Brown, 962 S.W.2d 810, 812-13 (Ark. 1998)..203, 204, 206
Brown v. Crum, 30 So. 3d 1254, 1257 (Miss. Ct. App. 2010).............339, 340, 349, 354, 360
Brown v. Dep't of Human Servs., 806 So. 2d 1004, 1008 (Miss. 2000)..........................417
Brown v. Gillespie, 465 So. 2d 1046, 1049 (Miss. 1985)..477
Brown v. Johnson, 822 So. 2d 1072 (Miss. Ct. App. 2002) 618
Brown v. Miss. Dep't of Human Servs., 806 So. 2d 1004 (Miss. 2000)..........................622
Brown v. Miss. United Methodist Conference, 911 So. 2d 478, 481-82 (Miss. 2005) 610
Brown v. Riley, 580 So. 2d 1234, 1237 (Miss. 1991)...598
Brown v. White, 875 So. 2d 1116, 1119 (Miss. Ct. App. 2004)...................345, 358, 398, 404
Brumfield v. Brumfield, 49 So. 3d 138, 142-43 (Miss. Ct. App. 2010)...............331, 346, 353, 355, 357
Bryant v. Bryant, 924 So. 2d 627, 630 (Miss. Ct. App. 2006).........307, 424, 480, 483, 492, 589, 591
Bryant v. Cameron, 473 So. 2d 174, 177 (Miss. 1985) 522, 538
Bryant v. State, 567 So. 2d 234, 236 (Miss. 1990) 20, 500, 501
B.S.G. v. J.E.H., 958 So. 2d 259, 268-69 (Miss. Ct. App. 2007)...............389, 523, 524, 528
Bubec v. Boston, 600 So. 2d 951 (Miss. 1968)...334, 392, 493, 494
Buckley v. Buckley, 815 So. 2d 1260, 1263 (Miss. Ct. App. 2002) 171, 172, 178, 258, 264, 265, 269, 275, 276
Buie v. Buie, 772 So. 2d 1079 (Miss. Ct. App. 2000)..617
Bulicek v. Bulicek, 800 P.2d 394, 399 (Wash. Ct. App. 1990).......................................203
Bullard v. Morris, 547 So. 2d 789, 790 (Miss. 1989)..109, 588
Bullock v. Bullock, 699 So. 2d 1205, 1209 (Miss. 1997)..................85, 93, 151, 159, 160, 170, 174
Bullock v. Bullock, 733 So. 2d 292, 298-99 (Miss. Ct. App. 1998)................................163
Bumpous v. Bumpous, 770 So. 2d 558, 559 (Miss. Ct. App. 2000)....... 171, 175, 179, 226, 261, 262, 275, 276, 280
Bunyard v. Bunyard, 828 So. 2d 775, 777 (Miss. 2002)...135
Burcham v. Burcham, 869 So. 2d 1058 (Miss. Ct. App. 2004) 274, 279
Burdine v. Burdine, 112 So. 2d 522, 523 (Miss. 1959)..98
Burgess v. Burgess, 710 P.2d 417, 420-21 (Alaska 1985) 147
Burge v. Burge, 851 So. 2d 384 (Miss. Ct. App. 2003) 182, 269, 275, 279, 376
Burkett v. Burkett, 537 So. 2d 443, 447 (Miss. 1989) 617
Burks v. Moody, 106 So. 528, 529 (Miss. 1926)..23
Burnette v. Burnette, 271 So. 2d 90, 93 (Miss. 1973) 71
Burnett v. Burnett, 362 So. 2d 828, 830 (Miss. 1978)...685
Burnett v. Burnett, 792 So. 2d 1016, 1019 (Miss. Ct. App. 2001)................................321
Burnham-Steptoe v. Steptoe, 755 So. 2d 1225, 1231 (Miss. Ct. App. 1999)...............170, 180, 182, 183,
224, 265, 274, 277, 280, 304, 429, 444, 445
Burnham v. Superior Court, 495 U.S. 604, 619 (1990) 561
Burns v. Burns, 31 So. 3d 1227, 1232 (Miss. Ct. App. 2009)...26
Burns v. Burns, 518 So. 2d 1205, 1208-10 (Miss. 1988) 25, 124, 125, 652
Burns v. Burns, 789 So. 2d 94, 100 (Miss. Ct. App. 2000)...................................185, 586
Burns v. Burns, 847 S.W.2d 23, 26 (Ark. 1993)...216
Burrus v. Burrus, 962 So. 2d 618, 620 (Miss. Ct. App. 2006)...............297, 298, 337, 395, 397, 401, 599
Burt v. Burt, 841 So. 2d 108, 111 (Miss. 2001)..480
Burwell v. Burwell, 44 So. 3d 421 (Miss. Ct. App. 2010)......................................293, 296
Bush v. Bush, 451 So. 2d 779, 782 (Miss. 1984)..459, 496
Bustin v. Bustin, 806 So. 2d 1136, 1138 (Miss. Ct. App. 2001)...............427, 435, 436, 464, 472
Butler v. Butler, 663 A.2d 148, (Pa. 1995)..155
Butler v. Hinson, 386 So. 2d 716, 717 (Miss. 1980) 247
Byars v. Byars, 850 So. 2d 147, 148-49 (Miss. Ct. App. 2003)....................................298
Byrd v. Matthews, 571 So. 2d 258, 260 (Miss. 1990)...26

C

Cahoy v. Darsaklis, 584 N.W.2d 36, 41-42 (Neb. Ct. App. 1998).................................428
Cain v. Cain, 795 So. 2d 614, 616 (Miss. Ct. App. 2001) 72, 74, 104
Caldwell v. Caldwell, 533 So. 2d 413 (Miss. 1988) 598

TABLE OF CASES

Caldwell v. Caldwell, 579 So. 2d 543, 547-48 (Miss. 1991)..452, 453, 454
Caldwell v. Caldwell, 823 So. 2d 1216, 1221 (Miss. Ct. App. 2002) 453, 470, 480
Callahan v. Callahan, 381 So. 2d 178, 179 (Miss. 1980) 63
Callahan v. Davis, 869 So. 2d 434, 437 (Miss. Ct. App. 2004)... 373, 376
Calloway v. Calloway, 832 S.W.2d 890, 892-93 (Ky. Ct. App. 1992) 139
Calton v. Calton, 485 So. 2d 309, 310 (Miss. 1986) 453, 483
Cameron v. Burns, 802 So. 2d 1069, 1071 (Miss. Ct. App. 2001).. 619
C.A.M.F. v. J.B.M., 972 So. 2d 656, 662 (Miss. Ct. App. 2007)...............361, 393, 397, 399, 605, 606
Campbell v. Campbell, 19 So. 2d 354, 354 (Ala. 1944) 78
Campbell v. Campbell, 339 S.E.2d 591, 593 (Ga. 1986) 152
Campbell v. Campbell, 357 So. 2d 129, 130 (Miss.1978)..566
Camp v. Robert, 462 So. 2d 726, 726 (Miss. 1985)... 28
Cannon v. Cannon, 571 So. 2d 976, 980 (Miss. 1990) 601
Capato v. Comm'r, 631 F.3d 626, 632 (3d Cir. 2011) 508
Caples v. Caples, 686 So. 2d 1071, 1073 (Miss. 1996) 407, 564, 579, 581, 630
Carite v. Carite, 841 So. 2d 1148, 1152 (Miss. Ct. App. 2002)..210, 453, 486
Carlisle v. Allen, 40 So. 3d 1252, 1255-61 (Miss. 2010)... 110
Carlisle v. Carlisle, 11 So. 3d 142, 145-46 (Miss. Ct. App. 2009) 593
Carlson v. Matthews, 966 So. 2d 1258, 1260 (Miss. Ct. App. 2007)...............461, 485, 500, 628, 629
Carnathan v. Carnathan, 722 So. 2d 1248 (Miss. 1998)..................162, 262, 275, 279, 280
Carney v. McGilvray, 119 So. 157, 160 (Miss. 1928) 29
Carpenter v. Allen, 540 So. 2d 1334, 1336-37 (Miss. 1989) 561
Carpenter v. Carpenter, 519 So. 2d 891 (Miss. 1988)..304, 305, 622
Carroll v. Carroll, 976 So. 2d 880, 887 (Miss. Ct. App. 2007) 165, 241, 242, 247, 254, 256, 303, 601, 630
Carroll v. Carroll, No. 2009-CA-00328-COA, 2010 WL 5093660, at *3 (Miss. Ct. App. Dec. 14, 2010)........... 188
Carrow v. Carrow, 642 So. 2d 901, 907 (Miss. 1994) 121, 134, 140, 141, 143, 168, 176, 219, 220, 237, 268
Carr v. Carr, 480 So. 2d 1120, 1123 (Miss. 1985).. 48, 352, 353
Carr v. Carr, 724 So. 2d 937, 940 (Miss. Ct. App. 1998) 381, 566, 570
Carr v. Carr, 784 So. 2d 227, 230 (Miss. Ct. App. 2000) 28
Carson v. Natchez Children's Home, 580 So. 2d 1248, 1257 (Miss. 1991)..................... 361, 523
Carter v. Carter, 97 So. 2d 529 (Miss. 1957) 78
Carter v. Carter, 419 A.2d 1018, 1022 (Me. 1980)... 149
Carter v. Carter, 735 So. 2d 1109, 1113 (Miss. Ct. App. 1999) 406, 424, 433, 457, 621, 622, 628
Carter v. Carter, 758 N.W.2d 1, 8-9 (Neb. 2008)... 577
Carter v. Taylor, 611 So. 2d 874, 876 (Miss. 1992)....................................369, 371, 522, 541
Case's Will v. Case, 150 So. 2d 148, 151 (Miss. 1963)... 64
Case v. Case, 150 So. 2d 148, 153 (Miss. 1963)..62, 63
Case v. Stolpe, 300 So. 2d 802, 805 (Miss. 1974) 394
Cash v. Cash, 353 S.W.2d 348 (Ark. 1962) 425
Cassell v. Cassell, 970 So. 2d 267, 271 (Miss. Ct. App. 2007) 72, 73, 84, 85, 87, 90, 92, 93, 375, 377
Cassibry v. Cassibry, 742 So. 2d 1121, 1125 (Miss. 1999)....................................108, 622, 675
Casto v. Casto, 508 So. 2d 330, 334-35 (Fla. 1987)..669
Caswell v. Caswell, 763 So. 2d 890, 893 (Miss. Ct. App. 2000).. 345, 349
Caudill v. Caudill, 811 So. 2d 407, 409 (Miss. Ct. App. 2001) 589
Cavett v. Cavett, 744 So. 2d 372, 377 (Miss. Ct. App. 1999)........................348, 382, 407, 409
C.C.I. v. Natural Parents, 398 So. 2d 220, 226 (Miss. 1981)...522, 538
Cerniglia v. Cerniglia, 679 So. 2d 1160, 1164 (Fla. 1996) 125
Cerutti-O'Brien v. Cerutti-O'Brien, 928 N.E.2d 1002 (Mass. Ct. App. 2010) 52
Chaffin v. Chaffin, 437 So. 2d 384, 386 (Miss. 1983) 102, 103, 120
Chalk v. Lentz, 744 So. 2d 789, 792 (Miss. Ct. App. 1999)..........................375, 376, 410, 482
Chambers v. Ormiston, 935 A. 2d 956 (R.I. 2007) 52
Chamblee v. Chamblee, 637 So. 2d 850, 860 (Miss. 1994).............................71, 87, 119, 171
Chandler v. Ratcliffe, 285 S.E.2d 694, 695 (Ga. 1982) 456
Chapel v. Chapel, 700 So. 2d 593 (Miss. 1997)..........................267, 270, 274, 275, 277
Chapel v. Chapel, 876 So. 2d 290, 295 (Miss. 2004) 39, 565
Chapman v. Ward, 3 So. 3d 790, 792-93 (Miss. Ct. App. 2008).........................426, 442, 481
Chapman v. White Sewing-Mach. Co., 28 So. 735, 736 (Miss. 1900)................................... 16
Charisma R. v. Kristina S., 44 Cal. Rptr. 3d 332 (Cal. Ct. App 2006) 54, 510
Chasez v. Chasez, 935 So. 2d 1058, 1062 (Miss. Ct. App. 2005) 307, 588, 628, 629
Chasez v. Chasez, 957 So. 2d 1031, 1037 (Miss. Ct. App. 2007)...............489, 494, 555, 588, 598, 622
Cheatham v. Cheatham, 537 So. 2d 435, 438 (Miss. 1988) 101, 103, 243, 246, 271, 272
Cheeks v. Herrington, 523 So. 2d 1033, 1035 (Miss. 1988) 19

TABLE OF CASES

Cheek v. Ricker, 431 So. 2d 1139, 1144 (Miss. 1983) 400, 404

Chenier v. Chenier, 573 So. 2d 699, 702 (Miss. 1990) 560, 561

Cherry v. Cherry, 593 So. 2d 13, 17-18 (Miss. 1991)......................92, 94, 100, 101, 102

Chesney v. Chesney, 828 So. 2d 219 (Miss. Ct. App. 2002) 265, 274, 276, 437

Chesney v. Chesney, 849 So. 2d 860, 863 (Miss. 2002)...306

Chesney v. Chesney, 910 So. 2d 1057, 1060 (Miss. 2005) 438, 450

Children's Medical Group v. Philips, 940 So. 2d 931 (Miss. 2006) 27

Childs v. Childs, 806 So. 2d 273, 275 (Miss. Ct. App. 2000) 171, 177, 179

Chisolm v. Eakes, 573 So. 2d 764, 766 (Miss. 1990) 318

Chmelicek v. Chmelicek, 51 So. 3d 1000, 1008 (Miss. Ct. App. 2010)...............169, 256

Choctaw, Inc. v. Wichner, 521 So. 2d 878, 879 (Miss. 1988)...................................25, 26

Chrismond v. Chrismond, 52 So. 2d 624, 630 (Miss. 1951)...44

Chrissy F. v. Miss. Dep't of Pub. Welfare, 780 F. Supp. 1104, 1122 (S.D. Miss. 1991)........552

Christian v. Wheat, 876 So. 2d 341, 345 (Miss. 2004)..380, 408

Christopher v. Christopher, 766 So. 2d 119, 122 (Miss. Ct. App. 2000) 166

Chroniger v. Chroniger, 914 So. 2d 311, 313 (Miss. Ct. App. 2005)..........193, 241, 242, 247, 252,
   297, 356, 401, 420, 423, 453, 677, 686

Chunn v. Chunn, 106 F.3d 1239, 1242 (5th Cir. 1997) 648

Clark v. Clark, 43 So. 3d 496, 500-501 (Miss. Ct. App. 2010)...........238, 595, 598, 599, 624, 628

Clark v. Clark, 293 So. 2d 447, 449 (Miss. 1974)..243

Clark v. Clark, 739 So. 2d 440, 442 (Miss. Ct. App. 1999)..623

Clark v. Clark, 754 So. 2d 450, 459 (Miss. 1999) 258, 423, 433

Clark v. Jeter, 486 U.S. 456, 463-64 (1988)...313

Clark v. Myrick, 523 So. 2d 79, 83 (Miss. 1988)...375

Clausel v. Clausel, 714 So. 2d 265, 267 (Miss. 1998)..423

Clauson v. Clauson, 831 P.2d 1257, 1264 (Alaska 1992)...213

Clay v. Clay, 99 So. 818, 818 (Miss. 1924)..556, 557

Clay v. Clay, 837 So. 2d 215, 217-18 (Miss. Ct. App. 2003)..............................345, 350,351

C.L.B. v. D.G.B., 812 So. 2d 980, 984 (Miss. 2002)..388, 546

Clements v. Young, 481 So. 2d 263, 271 (Miss. 1985)..........................485, 492, 497

Cleveland v. Cleveland, 600 So. 2d 193, 196-97 (Miss. 1992).....................240, 243, 252

Clowdis v. Earnest, 629 So. 2d 1044, 1046 (Fla. Dist. Ct. App. 1993) 454

Clower v. Clower, 988 So. 2d 441, 443, 445 (Miss. Ct. App. 2008).......267, 286, 291, 293, 302, 490, 296

C.M. v. R.D.H., 947 So. 2d 1023, 1026 (Miss. Ct. App. 2007) 335, 337, 519, 521, 566, 579, 597, 618

Cobb v. Cobb, 29 So. 3d 145, 148 (Miss. Ct. App. 2010) 106, 107, 617

Cochran v. Cochran, 912 So. 2d 1086, 1089 (Miss. Ct. App. 2005)..........71, 85, 87, 118, 119

Cockrell v. Watkins, 936 So. 2d 970, 973 (Miss. Ct. App. 2006)...............122, 331, 600

Coggin v. Coggin, 837 So. 2d 772, 775 (Miss. Ct. App. 2003)....................................178

Coghill v. Coghill, 836 P.2d 921, 927 (Alaska 1992) 428

Cohen v. Cohen, 748 So. 2d 91 (Miss. 1999)...585

Cole v. Cole, 12 So. 2d 425, 425 (Miss. 1943)...563

Cole v. Hood, 371 So. 2d 861, 863 (Miss. 1979)...454, 484

Collins v. Collins, 20 So. 3d 683, 692-93 (Miss. Ct. App. 2008)...............365, 366, 367

Collins v. Collins, 158 So. 914, 915-16 (Miss. 1935)...497

Collins v. Collins, 722 So. 2d 596, 599 (Miss. 1998) 167, 191, 225, 438, 456

Common v. Common, 42 So. 3d 59 (Miss. Ct. App. 2010) 166, 189, 624

Conerly v. Davis, 46 So. 3d 858, 859 (Miss. Ct. App. 2010)...............................385, 386

Coney v. Coney, 503 A.2d 912, 917 (N.J. Super. Ct. Ch. Div. 1985) 135

Conley v. Conley, 14 Ohio Supp. 22, available at 1943 WL 6289, at *3 (Ohio Com. Pl. May 1, 1943)................12

Connelly v. Lammey, 982 So. 2d 997, 999-1000 (Miss. Ct. App. 2008)...............400, 401

Conn v. Boutwell, 58 So. 105, 106 (Miss. 1912)...16

Cook v. Cook, 725 So. 2d 205, 207 (Miss. 1998) 108, 675

Cook v. Whiddon, 866 So. 2d 494, 499 (Miss. Ct. App. 2004) 291, 407, 479, 498

Cooney v. Cooney, 946 P. 2d 345, 348 (Or. Ct. App. 1997) 573

Cooper v. Ingram, 814 So. 2d 166 (Miss. Ct. App. 2002) 347, 356, 357

Cooper v. Keyes, 510 So. 2d 518, 519 (Miss. 1987)..490

Copeland v. Copeland, 904 So. 2d 1066 (Miss. 2004) 343, 346, 348, 353, 359, 361

Cork v. Cork, 811 So. 2d 427 (Miss. Ct. App. 2001) 171, 204, 275, 278, 284

Cosentino v. Cosentino, 912 So. 2d 1130, 1132-33 (Miss. Ct. App. 2005) 169, 239, 255

Cosentino v. Cosentino, 986 So. 2d 1065, 1068 (Miss. Ct. App. 2008)...............255, 264, 274, 275

Cosgrove v. Cosgrove, 217 N.E.2d 754, 756 (Mass. 1966) 100

Cossey v. Cossey, 22 So. 3d 353, 356-57 (Miss. Ct. App. 2009).............107, 137, 163, 446, 447

695

TABLE OF CASES

Cossitt v. Cossitt, 975 So. 2d 274, 277 (Miss. Ct. App. 2008) 382, 443, 447, 448, 490, 491, 493
Cotton v. Cotton, 44 So. 3d 371, 373-76 (Miss. Ct. App. 2010) 44, 47, 63
Cott v. Cott, 98 So. 2d 379, 380 (Fla. Ct. App. 1957)... 73
Countrywide Home Loans v. Parker, 975 So. 2d 233, 234 (Miss. 2008)... 15
Cox v. Cox, 108 So. 2d 422, 424 (Miss. 1959)... 564
Cox v. Cox, 580 N.E.2d 344, 351 (Ind. Ct. App. 1991) 428
Cox v. Cox, 882 P.2d 909, 920 (Alaska 1994) 215
Cox v. Moulds, 490 So. 2d 866, 868-69 (Miss. 1986)...............................375, 377, 381, 382, 466
Craft v. Craft, 32 So. 3d 1232, 1244 (Miss. Ct. App. 2010) 258, 268, 269, 378
Craft v. Craft, 478 So. 2d 258, 262 (Miss. 1985)... 679
Craft v. Craft, 825 So. 2d 605, 608-09 (Miss. 2002)...................................... 140, 141, 142, 177, 217, 219, 220, 245,
      258, 267, 268, 271, 275, 277, 279, 280, 281
Crayton v. Burley, 952 So. 2d 957, 960 (Miss. Ct. App. 2006)................... 425, 426, 427, 445, 447, 471, 473
Creekmore v. Creekmore, 651 So. 2d 513, 515-18 (Miss. 1995)........................... 246, 247, 252, 253, 268,
      270, 272, 273, 274, 275, 277 431
Creel v. Cornacchione, 831 So. 2d 1179, 1183 (Miss. Ct. App. 2002).. 402
Crenshaw v. Crenshaw, 767 So. 2d 272, 275 (Miss. Ct. App. 2000)...................... 33, 34, 35, 37, 91, 95, 301
Crider v. Crider, 904 So. 2d 142, 147 (Miss. 2005)... 363, 366
Crisler v. Crisler, 963 So. 2d 1248, 1252 (Miss. Ct. App. 2007)..................................... 193, 684, 681
Crist v. Lawrence, 738 So. 2d 267 (Miss. Ct. App. 1999)... 469
Criswell v. Criswell, 182 So. 2d 587, 589 (Miss. 1966)... 78, 79
Croft v. Croft, 634 So. 2d 76, 77 (La. Ct. App. 1994)... 206
Crosby v. Crosby, 434 So. 2d 162, 163 (La. Ct. App. 1983) 32, 81
Crosby v. Grooms, 10 Cal Rptr. 3d 146, 151 (Cal. App. 2004) 573
Crosby v. Hatten, 56 So. 2d 705, 706 (Miss. 1952) 104
Crosby v. People's Bank of Indianola, 472 So. 2d 951, 955 (Miss. 1985)................................ 672, 676
Crouch v. Crouch, 410 N.E.2d 580, 582 (Ill. App. Ct. 1980).. 135
Crouch v. Crouch, 566 F.2d 486, 488 (5th Cir. 1978)... 552
Crowe v. Crowe, 641 So. 2d 1100, 1102-03 (Miss. 1994)............................ 244, 245, 246, 266, 271, 273, 275, 278,
      280, 304, 585, 589, 591
Crowson v. Moseley, 480 So. 2d 1150, 1153 (Miss. 1985) 375
Crow v. Crow, 622 So. 2d 1226, 1230 (Miss. 1993) 448, 449, 478
Crum v. Brock, 101 So. 704, 705 (Miss. 1924).. 48, 419
Crutcher v. Crutcher, 38 So. 337 (Miss. 1905) 76, 92, 94
Cuevas v. Cuevas, 191 So. 2d 843, 846 (Miss. 1966)... 16, 17
Culliton v. Beth Israel Deaconess Med. Ctr., 756 N.E.2d 1133 (Mass. 2001)................................ 515
Culver v. Culver, 383 So. 2d 817, 817-18 (Miss. 1980) 82, 91
Cumberland v. Cumberland, 564 So. 2d 839, 847 (Miss. 1990) 296, 426, 473, 494, 498
Cunliffe v. Swartzfager, 437 So. 2d 43, 45-46 (Miss. 1983)........................... 454, 464, 476, 477, 484, 494
Cunningham v. Lanier, 589 So. 2d 133, 137 (Miss. 1991) 252
Cupit v. Cupit, 559 So. 2d 1035, 1037 (Miss. 1990)... 441
Curry v. Curry, 45 So. 3d 724, 727-28 (Miss. Ct. App. 2010)...................................... 160, 174, 182
Curry v. McDaniel, 37 So. 3d 1225, 1227-30 (Miss. Ct. App. 2010) 340, 350
Curtiss v. Curtiss, 781 So. 2d 142, 143 (Miss. Ct. App. 2000) 440
Curtis v. Curtis, 574 So. 2d 24, 29 (Miss. 1990) 578, 580
Curtis v. Curtis, 796 So. 2d 1044, 1049 (Miss. Ct. App. 2001) 74, 75, 180, 190, 266, 275, 278
Curtis v. Firth, 850 P. 2d 749 (Idaho 1993)... 125, 126
C.W.L. v. R.A., 919 So. 2d 267, 270 (Miss. Ct. App. 2005) 122, 331, 340, 346, 347, 360, 398

D

Daigle v. Daigle, 626 So. 2d 140, 147 (Miss. 1993)..36, 37, 95, 301, 303
Daknis v. Burns, 719 N.Y.S.2d 134, 135-36 (N.Y. App. Div. 2000).. 571
Dale Polk Construction Co. v. White, 287 So. 2d 278 (Miss. 1973)... 4, 47, 97
Daley v. Carlton, 19 So. 3d 781, 783 (Miss. Ct. App. 2009) 193
Daley v. Daley, 909 So. 2d 106, 107-08 (Miss. Ct. App. 2005).. 611
Dalton v. Dalton, 852 So. 2d 586, 589 (Miss. Ct. App. 2002)... 193, 681
Daniels v. Bains, 967 So. 2d 77, 80 (Miss. Ct. App. 2007)..... 301, 320, 322, 419, 445, 446, 447, 448, 588, 629, 630
Daniels v. Daniels, 950 So. 2d 1044 (Miss. Ct. App. 2007)... 169, 624
Daniel v. Daniel, 770 So. 2d 562, 567 (Miss. Ct. App. 2000) 364, 365, 367
Daubert v. Merrell Dow Pharm., Inc., 509 U.S. 579, 593 (1993) 607
Daughdrill v. Daughdrill, 178 So. 106 (Miss. 1938) 70, 77

TABLE OF CASES

Davidson v. Coit, 899 So. 2d 904, 908 (Miss. Ct. App. 2005)..354, 362, 394, 404

David v. David, 954 S.W.2d 611, 616 (Mo. Ct. App. 1997) 215

D'Avignon v. D'Avignon, 945 So. 2d 401, 404 (Miss. Ct. App. 2006) ..284, 288, 295, 296, 485, 589, 592, 683, 684

Davison v. Mississippi Dep't Human Servs., 938 So. 2d 912, 915-16 (Miss. Ct. App. 2006)............................490

Davis v. Davis, 12 So. 2d 435, 436 (Miss. 1943) 333

Davis v. Davis, 17 So. 3d 114, 118 (Miss. Ct. App. 2009) 347, 351, 403, 491

Davis v. Davis, 175 A. 574, 577 (Conn. 1934) 12

Davis v. Davis, 268 So. 2d 913, 915-16 (Miss. 1972) 489

Davis v. Davis, 281 S.E.2d 411, 415-17 (N.C. Ct. App. 1981) 579

Davis v. Davis, 558 F. Supp. 485, 486 (N.D. Miss. 1983) 552

Davis v. Davis, 638 So. 2d 1288 (Miss. 1994) 170, 172

Davis v. Davis, 643 So. 2d 931, 936 (Miss. 1994) 43, 45, 46

Davis v. Davis, 761 So. 2d 936, 941-42 (Miss. Ct. App. 2000)...484

Davis .v Davis, 775 S.W.2d 942, 944 (Ky. Ct. App. 1989) 157

Davis v. Davis, 829 So. 2d 712, 714-15 (Miss. Ct. App. 2002) 492, 612

Davis v. Davis, 832 So. 2d 492, 494-95, 498-500 (Miss. 2002)...170, 175, 180, 245, 246,
     266, 271, 272, 278, 280, 451, 443

Davis v. Davis, 842 S.W.2d 588, 597 (Tenn. 1992) 504, 505, 506

Davis v. Davis, 983 So. 2d 358, 361 (Miss. Ct. App. 2008) 462

Davis v. Vance, 574 N.E.2d 330, 331 (Ind. Ct. App. 1991)..433

Day v. Day, 28 So. 3d 672, 677 (Miss. Ct. App. 2010) 193, 307

Day v. Day, 501 So. 2d 353, 355 (Miss. 1987) 39, 79, 80, 81, 87

Day v. Day, 663 S.W.2d 719, 722 (Ark. 1984)...202

D.C. v. D.C., 988 So. 2d 359, 364 (Miss. 2008) 626

Deal v. Wilson, 922 So. 2d 24, 28 (Miss. Ct. App. 2005).............................136, 173, 174, 176, 179, 183, 621

Dean v. Kavanaugh, 920 So. 2d 528, 534-35 (Miss. Ct. App. 2006) 46

Dearman v. Dearman, 811 So. 2d 308, 311 (Miss. Ct. App. 2001) 357, 359, 364, 368, 384

Deen v. Deen, 856 So. 2d 736 (Miss. Ct. App. 2003)..80, 304

De La Oliva v. Lowndes County Dep't of Pub. Welfare, 423 So. 2d 1328, 1331-32 (Miss. 1982).............526, 527

Delfino v. Delfino, 35 N.Y.S.2d 693, 693 (N.Y. Sup. Ct. 1942) 12

Delk v. Delk, 41 So. 3d 738, 740-41 (Miss. Ct. App. 2010) 143, 148, 149, 151, 159, 173

Delozier v. Delozier, 724 So. 2d 984, 986 (Miss. Ct. App. 1998) 364, 367, 423

De Marco v. De Marco, 24 So. 2d 358, 359 (Miss. 1946) 291

Dennis v. Dennis, 824 So. 2d 604 (Miss. 2002) 487, 488, 598, 629

Department of Human Services and Child Welfare Agency Review Bd. v. Howard, 238 S.W.3d 1 (Ark. 2006) 54

Department of Human Services v. Shelby. 802 So. 2d 89, 95 (Miss. 2001) 416

Dep't of Human Services v. Murphy, 997 So. 2d 983 (Miss. Ct. App. 2008) 612

Dep't of Human Servs. v. Barnett, 633 So. 2d 430, 436 (Miss. 1993) 587

Dep't of Human Servs. v. Blount, 913 So. 2d 326, 329 (Miss. Ct. App. 2005) 478

Dep't of Human Servs. v. Fillingane, 761 So. 2d 869, 872-73 (Miss. 2000)...470, 480

Dep't of Human Servs. v. Guidry, 830 So. 2d 628 (Miss. 2002) 593

Dep't of Human Servs. v. Helton, 741 So. 2d 240, 243-44 (Miss. 1999)...320

Dep't of Human Servs. v. Jacoby, 975 P.2d 939, 943 (Utah Ct. App. 1999)..570

Dep't of Human Servs. v. Jones, 627 So. 2d 810, 812 (Miss. 1993)...316

Dep't of Human Servs. v. Marquis, 630 So. 2d 331, 335 (Miss. 1993) 563, 580

Dep't of Human Servs. v. Marshall, 859 So. 2d 387, 390 (Miss. 2003)...454, 484

Dep't of Human Servs. v. Molden, 644 So. 2d 1230, 1231 (Miss. 1994)...320

Dep't of Human Servs. v. Murphy, 997 So. 2d 983, 990 (Miss. Ct. App. 2008) 326

Dep't of Human Servs. v. Shelby, 802 So. 2d 89 (Miss. 2001) 308, 453, 483

Dep't of Human Servs. v. Shelnut, 772 So. 2d 1041, 1049 (Miss. 2000)..561, 570

Dep't of Human Servs. v. Smith, 627 So. 2d 352, 353 (Miss. 1993)...316, 318

Dep't of Human Servs. v. St. Peter, 708 So. 2d 83, 85 (Miss. 1998)...495, 500

Dep't. Social Servs. v. Richter, 475 S.E.2d 817, 820 (Va. Ct. App. 1996)..572

Desfosses v. Desfosses, 815 P.2d 1094, 1099 (Idaho Ct. App. 1991)..205, 207

Detrio v. Boylan, 190 F.2d 40, 43 (5th Cir. 1951) 22

Devereaux v. Devereaux, 493 So. 2d 1310, 1312 (Miss. 1986) 72, 87, 88, 89, 110, 117

DeVito v. DeVito, 967 So. 2d 74, 76 (Miss. Ct. App. 2007)...348, 353, 360, 607

Devore v. Devore, 725 So. 2d 193, 196-97 (Miss. 1998)...149

De Vries v. De Vries, 195 Ill. App. 4, 5-6 (1915)...12

Dexter v. Dexter, 661 A.2d 171, 174-75 (Md. Ct. Spec. App. 1995) 213

Diamond v. Diamond, 403 So. 2d 129, 131 (Miss. 1981) 450, 590

Dickerson v. Dickerson, 34 So. 3d 637, 642-43 (Miss. Ct. App. 2010)....... 72, 76, 100, 169, 170, 176, 183, 246, 306

TABLE OF CASES

Dickerson v. Dickerson, 148 So. 2d 510, 512 (Miss. 1963) 592
Dickerson v. Horn, 50 So. 2d 368, 369-70 (Miss. 1951) 497
Dickerson v. Thompson, 897 N.Y.S. 2d 298 (N.Y. App. Div. 2010) 52
Diefenthaler v. Diefenthaler, 580 N.E.2d 477, 483 (Ohio Ct. App. 1989) 207
Diehl v. Diehl, 29 So. 3d 153, 156 (Miss. Ct. App. 2010) 33, 35, 36, 238
Dilling v. Dilling, 734 So. 2d 327, 338-39 (Miss. Ct. App. 1999) 410, 482, 491, 681
Dillon v. Dillon, 498 So. 2d 328, 330 (Miss. 1986) 74, 75, 171, 301
Dill v. Dill, 908 So. 2d 198, 202-03 (Miss. Ct. App. 2005) 297, 464, 465
Divers v. Divers, 856 So. 2d 370, 374 (Miss. Ct. App. 2003) 341, 345, 350
Dixon v. Dixon, 919 P.2d 28, 30-31 (Okla. Civ. App. 1996) 157
Dix v. Dix, 941 So. 2d 913, 916 (Miss. Ct. App. 2006) 288, 289, 293, 295, 448, 463, 471, 472
D.J.L. v. Bolivar County Dep't Human Servs., 824 So. 2d 617, 622-23 (Miss. 2002) 521
D.K.L. v. Hall, 652 So. 2d 184, 188 (Miss. 1995) 389, 520
Dobbs v. Dobbs, 912 So. 2d 491, 492-93 (Miss. Ct. App. 2005) 152, 167, 174, 275
Dochelli v. Dochelli, 6 A.2d 324, 325-26 (Conn. 1939) 100
Dodd v. Dodd, 403 N.Y.S.2d 401, 405 (N.Y. 1978) 366
Dodson v. Dodson, 955 P.2d 902, 909-10 (Alaska 1998) 202
Dodson v. Singing River Hosp. Sys., 839 So. 2d 530 (Miss. 2003) 247
Doe v. Doe, 644 So. 2d 1199, 1207-08 (Miss. 1994) 378
Doe v. N.Y. Bd. of Health, 782 N.Y.S.2d 180 (N.Y. Sup. Ct. 2004) 514
Donati v. Church, 80 A.2d 633, 634 (N.J. Super. Ct. App. Div. 1951) 61
Doran v. Beale, 63 So. 647, 648 (Miss. 1913) 17
Dorman v. Dorman, 737 So. 2d 426, 429-30 (Miss. Ct. App. 1999) 74
Dorr v. Dorr, 797 So. 2d 1008, 1015 (Miss. Ct. App. 2001) 307, 465, 476, 477, 678
Dorsey v. Dorsey, 972 So. 2d 48, 51-52 (Miss. Ct. App. 2008) 132, 138, 141, 147, 150,
151, 218, 219, 225, 255, 258, 264, 302, 304
Doss v. State, 126 So. 197, 198-99 (Miss. 1930) 5, 58
Doster v. Doster, 853 So. 2d 147, 150-151 (Miss. Ct. App. 2003) 673
Dotsko v. Dotsko, 583 A.2d 395, 400 (N.J. Super. Ct. App. Div. 1990) 139
Douglas v. Douglas, 766 So. 2d 68, 71 (Miss. Ct. App. 2000) 306, 307
Doyle v. Doyle, 55 So. 3d 1097, 1107-08 (Miss. Ct. App. 2010) 136, 148, 150, 182, 202, 497, 481, 483, 490
Draper v. Draper, 627 So. 2d 302, 306 (Miss. 1993) 199, 200
Draper v. Draper, 658 So. 2d 866, 870 (Miss. 1995) 423
Driste v. Driste, 738 So. 2d 763, 765 (Miss. Ct. App. 1998)121, 125, 170, 176, 237, 245, 246, 266, 268, 269, 270, 272,
275, 277, 279, 280, 281
Drumheller v. Drumheller, 972 A.2d 176, 190 (Vt. 2009) 224
Drummonds v. Drummonds, 156 So. 2d 819, 822 (Miss. 1963) 37
Drumright v. Drumright, 812 So. 2d 1021, 1025-26 (Miss. Ct. App. 2001) 125, 159, 161,
174, 180, 190, 274, 277, 279, 280
Ducharme v. Ducharme, 535 N.Y.S.2d 474, 476 (N.Y. App. Div. 1988) 135
Dudley v. Harris, 979 So. 2d 692, 692 (Miss. Ct. App. 2008) 620
Dudley v. Light, 586 So. 2d 155 (Miss. 1991) 185, 586
Dufour v. Dufour, 631 So. 2d 192, 195 (Miss. 1994) 252, 423
Duke v. Elmore, 956 So. 2d 244, 249 (Miss. Ct. App. 2006) 393, 396, 397
Dunaway v. Dunaway, 749 So. 2d 1112, 1114-15 (Miss. Ct. App. 1999) 162, 165, 177, 178, 183, 190, 223, 225
Duncan v. Duncan, 417 So. 2d 908, 909-10 (Miss. 1982) 489, 497
Duncan v. Duncan, 815 So. 2d 480, 484 (Miss. Ct. App. 2002) 170, 275, 278, 282, 624, 685
Duncan v. Duncan, 915 So. 2d 1124, 1126 (Miss. Ct. App. 2005) 148, 159, 169, 191, 302, 304, 602
Duncan v. Merrill Lynch, Pierce, Fenner & Smith, 646 F.2d 1020, 1027-28 (5th Cir. 1981) 634
Dunn v. Dunn, 125 So. 562, 563 (Miss. 1930) 100
Dunn v. Dunn, 577 So. 2d 378, 379 (Miss. 1991) 556, 557
Dunn v. Dunn, 609 So. 2d 1277, 1286 (Miss. 1992) 375, 381
Dunn v. Dunn, 695 So. 2d 1152, 1156 (Miss. 1997) 433, 472
Dunn v. Dunn, 811 S.W.2d 336, 338-39 (Ark. Ct. App. 1991) 154
Dunn v. Dunn, 911 So. 2d 591, 595-96 (Miss. Ct. App. 2005) 165, 168, 169, 223, 224, 439, 616
Dunn v. Grisham, 157 So. 2d 766, 768 (Miss. 1963) 48, 313
Duran v. Weaver, 495 So. 2d 1355, 1357 (Miss. 1986) 405
Durr v. Durr, 912 So. 2d 1033, 1038 (Miss. Ct. App. 2005) 307, 309, 484
Duvall v. Duvall, 80 So. 2d 752, 754 (Miss. 1955) 37, 553, 686
D v. C, 221 A.2d 763, 765-66 (N.J. Ch. 1966) 63
Dycus v. State, 396 So. 2d 23, 28 (Miss. 1981) 30
Dye v. Dye, 22 So. 3d 1241, 1244-45 (Miss. Ct. App. 2009) 138, 144, 185, 199, 282

TABLE OF CASES

Dykes v. McMurray, 938 So. 2d 330, 336 (Miss. Ct. App. 2006) 399, 401, 404, 454

E

Eades v. Eades, 869 So. 2d 1038, 1039-40 (Miss. Ct. App. 2003) 487, 490
Eason v. Kosier, 850 So. 2d 188, 190-91 (Miss. Ct. App. 2003) 353, 358, 407
East v. East, 493 So. 2d 927, 929, 932-33 (Miss. 1986)... 185, 192, 218, 242, 247, 253, 254, 287, 290, 586, 673, 682
East v. East, 775 So. 2d 741, 744-45 (Miss. Ct. App. 2000).... 161, 189, 244, 246, 266, 267, 271, 275, 278, 280, 303
Edmonds v. Edmonds, 935 So. 2d 980, 988-89 (Miss. 2006).. 450, 623
Edmond v. Townes, 949 So. 2d 99, 102 (Miss. Ct. App. 2007) 426
Edwards v. Edwards, 665 P.2d 883, 883-886 (Wash. 1983) 456
Edwards v. Edwards-Barker, 875 So. 2d 1126, 1129 (Miss. Ct. App. 2004) 479
E.J.M. v. A.J.M, 846 So. 2d 289, 293 (Miss. Ct. App. 2003) 337, 369, 371, 552, 605
E.K. v. Hinds County Youth Court, 20 So. 3d 1216, 1218-21 (Miss. 2009) 487
Elam v. Hinson, 932 So. 2d 76, 78-79 (Miss. Ct. App. 2006) 141, 220, 257, 261, 270, 272, 275, 278, 283
Elliott v. Elliott, 11 So. 3d 784, 786-787 n.5 (Miss. Ct. App. 2009) 257, 275
Elliott v. Elliott, 621 S.W.2d 305, 307-08 (Mo. Ct. App. 1981) 139
Elliott v. Elliott, 877 So. 2d 450, 452 (Miss. Ct. App. 2003) 364, 407, 410, 482
Elliott v. Rogers, 775 So. 2d 1285, 1287-88 (Miss. Ct. App. 2000) 253, 254, 285, 489, 685
Ellis v. Comm'r, 60 T.C.M. (CCH) 593 (1990) 656
Ellis v. Ellis, 119 So. 304, 305 (Miss. 1928) 7, 58, 62
Ellis v. Ellis, 651 So. 2d 1068, 1072 (Miss. 1995) 241, 286, 297
Ellis v. Ellis, 840 So. 2d 806, 811-12 (Miss. Ct. App. 2003) 382, 409, 493
Ellis v. Ellis, 952 So. 2d 982, 986 (Miss. Ct. App. 2006)...................... 338, 341, 343, 347, 357, 362, 383, 394, 403
Ellzey v. Ellzey, 253 So. 2d 249, 250 (Miss. 1971) 90, 117
Ellzey v. White, 922 So. 2d 40, 42 (Miss. Ct. App. 2006) 423, 430, 588, 629, 630
E.M.C. v. S.V.M., 695 So. 2d 576, 581 (Miss. 1997) 534
Engel v. Engel, 920 So. 2d 505, 509-10 (Miss. Ct. App. 2006) 105, 106, 108, 623
Enis v. State, 408 So. 2d 486, 488 (Miss. 1981) 8, 62
E.N.O. v. L.M.M., 711 N.E.2d 886, 892 (Mass. 1999) 54, 510
Ensminger v. Campbell, 134 So. 2d 728, 732 (Miss. 1961) 24, 124
Ensminger v. Ensminger, 77 So. 2d 308, 309 (Miss. 1955) 24, 124
Erickson v. Erickson, 48 N.Y.S.2d 588, 589 (N.Y. Sup. Ct. 1944) 12
Ericson v. Tullos, 876 So. 2d 1038 (Miss. Ct. App. 2004) 262, 265, 266, 275, 277
Erler v. Erler, 390 N.W.2d 316, 319-20 (Minn. App. 1986) 424
Erp v. Erp, 976 So. 2d 1237-38 (Fla. Dist. Ct. App. 2008) 224
Ervin v. Bass, 160 So. 568, 569 (Miss. 1935) 58
Estate of Alexander, 445 So. 2d 836, 839 (Miss. 1984) 46, 47
Estate of Burns, 31 So. 3d 1227, 1231 (Miss. Ct. App. 2009) 668
Estate of Childress, 588 So. 2d 192, 197 (Miss. 1991) 17, 18
Estate of Ellis, 23 So. 3d 589, 599-00 (Miss. Ct. App. 2009) 32
Estate of Hodges, 807 So. 2d 438, 443 (Miss. 2002) 242
Estate of Kennington, 204 So. 2d 444, 449 (Miss. 1967) 242, 254, 685
Estate of Kievernagel, 83 Cal. Rptr. 3d 311, 317-18 (Cal. Ct. App. 2008) 506
Estate of Marshall, 138 So. 2d 482, 483-84 (Miss. 1962) 19
Estate of Patterson v. Patterson, 798 So. 2d 347, 349-50 (Miss. 2001) 313
Estate of Reaves v. Owen, 744 So. 2d 799, 802 (Miss. Ct. App. 1999) 6, 46, 53
Estate of Yount, 845 So. 2d 724 (Miss. Ct. App. 2003) 544
Estin v. Estin, 334 U.S. 541, 549 (1948) 558, 559
Etheridge v. Webb, 50 So. 2d 603, 606 (Miss. 1951) 15, 39, 81
Ethredge v. Yawn, 605 So. 2d 761, 765 (Miss. 1992) 372, 373
Eureka Block Coal Co. v. Wells, 147 N.E. 811, 812 (Ind. App. 1925) 64
Evans v. Dep't of Human Servs., 36 So. 3d 463, 473-74, 77-78 (Miss. Ct. App. 2010) 417, 571, 570
Evans v. Evans, 994 So. 2d 765, 769-70 (Miss. 2008) 448, 469, 470, 471, 479, 591
Everett v. Everett, 919 So. 2d 242, 246 (Miss. Ct. App. 2005) 132, 138, 175, 179, 221
Ewing v. Ewing, 749 So. 2d 223, 225-26 (Miss. Ct. App. 1999) 492

F

Faerber v. Faerber, 13 So. 3d 853, 859-60 (Miss. Ct. App. 2009) 141, 148, 150, 157, 162, 165, 247, 254, 427, 428, 624
Fancher v. Pell. 831 So. 2d 1137, 1140 (Miss. 2002)... 447, 448, 471, 492
Fanning v. State, 497 So. 2d 70, 74 (Miss. 1986) 30

699

TABLE OF CASES

Faries v. Faries, 607 So. 2d 1204, 1208 (Miss. 1992) 72, 83, 85, 87, 88, 118, 119, 333, 608
Faris v. Jernigan, 939 So. 2d 835, 838 (Miss. Ct. App. 2006) 307, 308, 409, 410, 411, 482, 496, 498
Farmer v. Farmer, 398 So. 2d 723, 726 (Ala. Civ. App. 1981) 149
Farrior v. Kittrell, 12 So. 3d 20, 23-24 (Miss. Ct. App. 2009) 479, 612
Farve v. Medders, 128 So. 2d 877, 879-80 (Miss. 1961) 587
Fed. Credit Co. v. Scoggins, 130 So. 153, 154 (Miss. 1930) 23
Felder v. Felder's Estate, 13 So. 2d 823, 827 (Miss. 1943) 236, 497, 498
Feltmeier v. Feltmeier, 798 N.E.2d 75 (Ill. 2003) 125
Ferguson v. Ferguson, 639 So. 2d 921, 925 (Miss. 1994)15, 33, 72, 74, 94, 132, 133, 134, 138, 139, 140, 161, 166, 167,
         168, 174, 177, 184, 186, 189, 200, 202, 219, 225, 232, 237, 239, 263, 356, 357, 362, 551, 559, 648, 653
Ferguson v. Ferguson, 782 So. 2d 181, 183 (Miss. Ct. App. 2001) 403
Ferguson v. Ferguson, 947 So. 2d 1015, 1017 (Miss. Ct. App. 2007) 39
Ferguson v. Lewis, 31 So. 3d 5, 12 (Miss. Ct. App. 2009) 385
Ferguson v. McKiernan, 940 A.2d 1236, 1241-42 (Pa. 2007) 511
Ferrara v. Walters, 919 So. 2d 876, 882-83 (Miss. 2005) 17
Ferrari v. Ferrari, 2000 WL 1196505 (Conn. Super. Ct. 2000) 574
Ferro v. Ferro, 871 So. 2d 753 (Miss. Ct. App. 2004) 94, 256, 260, 262, 274, 280
Fid. & Deposit Co. v. Lovell, 108 F. Supp. 360, 363-64 (S.D. Miss. 1952) 24
Fields v. Fields, 830 So. 2d 1266, 1269 (Miss. Ct. App. 2002) 375
Finley v. Astrue, 601 F. Supp. 2d 1092, 1099-1100 (E.D. Ark. 2009) 506, 507
Finstuen v. Crutcher, 496 F. 2d 1139 (10th Cir. 2007) 54, 533
First Nat'l Bank in Grand Forks v. N.D. Workmen's Comp. Bureau, 68 N.W.2d 661, 664 (N.D. 1955) 64
Fisher v. Fisher, 771 So. 2d 364, 369 (Miss. 2000) 94, 169, 283
Fisher v. Fisher, 944 So. 2d 134, 137 (Miss. Ct. App. 2006) 77, 589, 602
Fisher v. State, 690 So. 2d 268, 272 (Miss. 1996) 30
Fitch v. Valentine, 946 So. 2d 780, 784 (Miss. Ct. App. 2007) 621
Fitch v. Valentine, 959 So. 2d 1012 (Miss. 2007) 27, 28
Fitzgerald v. Fitzgerald, 914 So. 2d 193, 197 (Miss. Ct. App. 2005) 135, 182, 239, 451, 624, 660, 664, 665
Flechas v. Flechas, 724 So. 2d 948, 951-52 (Miss. Ct. App. 1998) 245, 246, 248, 249,
         255, 270, 272, 275, 277, 279, 280
Flechas v. Flechas, 791 So. 2d 295, 298 (Miss. Ct. App. 2001) 142, 218, 221, 245, 672
Fleishhacker v. Fleishhacker, 39 So. 3d 904, 913 (Miss. Ct. App. 2009) 136, 142, 164, 221, 671
Fleming v. Fleming, 56 So. 2d 35, 39 (Miss. 1952) 72, 97
Fletcher v. Shaw, 800 So. 2d 1212, 1215-16 (Miss. Ct. App. 2001) 348, 350, 359, 360, 395, 398
Flight Line, Inc. v. Tanksley, 608 So. 2d 1149, 1169 (Miss. 1992) 26
Fliter v. Fliter, 383 So. 2d 1084, 1087 (Miss. 1980) 554, 560, 593
Floyd v. Floyd, 870 So. 2d 677, 680 (Miss. Ct. App. 2004) 628
Floyd v. Floyd, 949 So. 2d 26, 27-28 (Miss. 2007) 364, 388, 390, 393, 401
Fogarty v. Fogarty, 922 So. 2d 836, 840 (Miss. Ct. App. 2006) 136, 148, 152, 159, 174, 181,
         190, 225, 275, 279, 280
Folsom v. Pearsall, 245 F.2d 562, 567 (9th Cir. 1957) 64
Fondi v. Fondi, 802 P.2d 1264, 1267 (Nev. 1990) 203
Ford v. Ford, 766 P.2d 950, 952 (Okla. 1988) 141
Ford v. Ford, 795 So. 2d 600 (Miss. Ct. App. 2001) 171, 271, 275, 280, 281, 615
Formigoni v. Formigoni, 733 So. 2d 868, 870 (Miss. Ct. App. 1999) 341, 470, 478
Forney v. Minard, 849 P.2d 724, 729 (Wyo. 1993) 212
Forrest v. McCoy, 941 So. 2d 889, 891 (Miss. Ct. App. 2006) 442, 444, 463
Forrest v. McCoy, 996 So. 2d 158, 160 (Miss. Ct. App. 2008) 486, 623
Forsythe v. Akers, 768 So. 2d 943, 948 (Miss. Ct. App. 2000) 397, 401
Forsythe v. Forsythe, 558 S.W.2d 675, 679 (Mo. Ct. App. 1977) 139
Fortenberry v. Fortenberry, 338 So. 2d 806 (Miss. 1976) 591
Forthner v. Forthner, 52 So. 3d 1212, 1220-21 (Miss. Ct. App. 2010) 34, 362
Foster v. Foster, 788 So. 2d 779, 782-83 (Miss. 2001) 308, 391
Fountain v. Fountain, 877 So. 2d 474, 478-79 (Miss. Ct. App. 2003) 376, 408, 429
Fournet v. Fournet, 481 So. 2d 326, 327 (Miss. 1985) 85, 96
Frank G.W. v. Carol M.W., 457 A.2d 715, 717-19 (Del. 1983) 137
Franklin v. Franklin, 864 So. 2d 970, 976 (Miss. Ct. App. 2003) 170, 172, 183, 257, 341, 477
Franklin v. Kroush, 622 So. 2d 1256, 1257 (Miss. 1993) 357, 361, 403
Franklin v. Winter, 936 So. 2d 429, 431 (Miss. Ct. App. 2006) 407
Franks v. Franks, 759 So. 2d 1164, 1165 (Miss. 1999) 140, 171, 176, 245, 246, 281
Franks v. Franks, 873 So. 2d 135, 139 (Miss. Ct. App. 2004) 122, 348, 349
Frazier v. Burnett, 767 So. 2d 263, 267-68 (Miss. Ct. App. 2000) 470, 473

TABLE OF CASES

Freed v. Killman, 6 So. 2d 909, 909-10 (1942) 29
Freeman v. Freeman, 497 S.W.2d 97, 100 (Tex. Civ. App. 1973) 202
Frei v. State, 934 So. 2d 318, 322-23 (Miss. Ct. App. 2006) 604, 605
Freking v. Freking, 479 N.W.2d 736, 740 (Minn. Ct. App. 1992) 428
Frerichs v. Frerichs, 704 S.W.2d 258, 261-62 (Mo. Ct. App. 1986) 145
Friedman v. Friedman, 965 S.W.2d 319, 328 (Mo. Ct. App. 1998) 145, 150
Fulk v. Fulk, 827 So. 2d 736, 739-40 (Miss. Ct. App. 2002) 341, 354, 381
Fulton v. Fulton, 36 Miss. 517, 525, 1858 WL 4618 (1858) 79
Fulton v. Fulton, 218 So. 2d 866 (Miss. 1969) 335
Fulton v. Fulton, 918 So. 2d 877, 879-80 (Miss. Ct. App. 2006) 71, 87, 88, 89, 101, 117, 119
Funderburk v. Funderburk, 909 So. 2d 1241, 1243 (Miss. Ct. App. 2005) 340
F.W.H. v. R.J.H., 666 S.W.2d 910, 912 (Mo. Ct. App. 1984) 135

G

Gaber v. Gaber, 32 P.3d 921, 925 (Or. Ct. App. 2001) 125
Gable v. Gable, 846 So. 2d 296, 299 (Miss. Ct. App. 2003) 170, 256, 275, 279, 359
Gabriel v. Gabriel, 79 N.Y.S.2d 823, 825 (N.Y. App. Div. 1948) 63
Gaillard v. Gaillard, 23 Miss. 152, 153 (1851) 77
Gainey v. Edington, 24 So. 3d 333, 335-37 (Miss. Ct. App. 2009) 389, 398, 402
Galachiuk v. Galachiuk, 691 N.Y.S.2d 828, 829 (N.Y. App. Div. 1999) 158
Gallagher v. Gallagher, 539 N.W. 2d 479, 481 (Iowa 1995) 323, 325
Gallaspy v. Gallaspy, 459 So. 2d 283, 284 (Miss. 1984) 84, 96, 105
Galtney v. Wood, 115 So. 117, 121 (Miss. 1928) 13
Gambrell v. Gambrell, 644 So. 2d 435, 443 (Miss. 1994) 497
Gambrell v. Gambrell, 650 So. 2d 517, 519-20 (Miss. 1995) 263, 302
Gantenbein v. Gantenbein, 852 So. 2d 63, 65-66 (Miss. Ct. App. 2002) 345, 348
Gardner v. Gardner, 618 So. 2d 108, 114 (Miss. 1993) 71, 87, 88, 106, 119
Garland v. Garland, 50 Miss. 694, 705 (1874) 21, 33, 333, 413
Garrett v. Garrett, 683 P.2d 1166, 1170 (Ariz. Ct. App. 1983) 156
Garriga v. Garriga, 770 So. 2d 978, 982-83 (Miss. Ct. App. 2000) ..72, 76, 89, 93, 94, 118, 177, 178, 180, 190, 226, 301, 306
Gartrell v. Gartrell, 27 So. 3d 388 (Miss. 2009) 546
Gatlin v. Gatlin, 161 So. 2d 782, 783 (Miss. 1964) 248, 290
Gatlin v. Gatlin, 234 So. 2d 634, 635 (Miss. 1970) 87, 90, 117
Gaubert v. Gaubert, No. Civ.A. 97-1673, 1999 WL 10384, at *1 (E.D. La. January 7,1999) 641
Gay v. Morrison, 511 So. 2d 1173 (La. Ct. App. 1987) 563, 579
G.B.W. v. E.R.W., 9 So. 3d 1200, 1205 (Miss. Ct. App. 2009) 34, 85
Geiger v. Geiger, 530 So. 2d 185, 187 (Miss. 1988) 192, 682
Gemma v. Gemma, 778 P.2d 429, 431 (Nev. 1989) 200, 206
George v. George, 22 So. 3d 424, 428 (Miss. Ct. App. 2009) 257, 266, 275
George v. George, 389 So. 2d 1389, 1390 (Miss. 1980) 3, 8, 42, 51
Georgia Dept. of Human Resources v. Deason, 520 S.E.2d 712, 714-715 (Ga. App. 1999) 570
Ghoston v. Ghoston, 979 So. 2d 719 (Miss. Ct. App. 2007) 255, 594
Giannaris v. Giannaris, 960 So. 2d 462, 466, 469 (Miss. 2007) 393, 395, 397, 402, 405, 607
Gibbs v. Comm'r, 73 T.C.M. (CCH) 2669 (1997) 663
Gilbert v. Comm'r, 85 T.C.M. (CCH) 1087 (2003) 657
Gilbert v. Gilbert, 442 So. 2d 1330, 1332 (La. Ct. App. 1983) 154
Gilcrease v. Gilcrease, 918 So. 2d 854, 858-59 (Miss. Ct. App. 2005) 600, 615
Gillespie v. Gillespie, 506 P. 2d 775 (N. Mex. 1973) 143
Gillespie v. Gillespie, 594 So. 2d 620, 623 (Miss. 1992) 457, 462
Gillett-Netting v. Barnhart, 371 F.3d 593, 598-99 (9th Cir. 2004) 508
Gilliland v. Gilliland, 969 So. 2d 56, 61-62 (Miss. Ct. App. 2007) 122, 124, 343, 349, 350, 368
Gilliland v. Gilliland, 984 So. 2d 364, 366 (Miss. Ct. App. 2008) 402, 482, 602
Gill v. Office of Personnel Management, 699 F. Supp. 2d 374 (D. Mass. 2010) 51
Gilman v. Gilman, 526 S.E.2d 763, 770 (Va. Ct. App. 2000) 156
Giovine v. Giovine, 663 A. 2d 109 (N.J. Super Ct. App. Div. 1995) 125, 126
Givens v. Nicholson, 878 So. 2d 1073 (Miss. Ct. App. 2004) 384, 386
Gladney v. Hopkins, 102 So. 2d 181 (Miss. 1958) 334, 374
Glass v. Glass, 726 So. 2d 1281, 1285 (Miss. Ct. App. 1998) 476, 484, 485, 486
Glass v. Glass, 857 So. 2d 786, 789 (Miss. Ct. App. 2003) 168, 182, 282
Glaze v. Glaze, 46 Va. Cir. 333, 334 (Va. Cir. Ct. 1998) 76

TABLE OF CASES

Glazner v. Glazner, 347 F.3d 1212, 1221 (11th Cir. 2003) 641
G.M.R., Sr. v. H.E.S., 489 So. 2d 498, 500 (Miss. 1986) 543
Godwin v. Godwin, 758 So. 2d 384, 386-87 (Miss. 1999) 33, 135, 136, 170, 256, 281
Goellner v. Goellner, 11 So. 3d 1251, 1257 (Miss. Ct. App. 2009) 89, 92, 93, 117, 173, 274, 280, 282
Goldstein v. Goldstein, 414 S.E.2d 474, 475 (Ga. 1992) 155
Gomez v. Perez, 409 U.S. 535, 537-38 (1973) 313
Gondouin v. Gondouin, 111 P. 756, 756 (Cal. Dist. Ct. App. 1910) 10
Gonsalves v. Roberts, 905 S.W.2d 931 (Tenn. 1995) 425
Gonzalez v. Green, 831 N.Y.S. 2d 856 (N.Y. Sup. 2006) 52
Goode v. Goode, 396 S.E.2d 430, 435-36 (W. Va. 1990) 43
Goode v. Goode, 692 S.W.2d 757, 759 (Ark. 1985) 153
Goodin v. Department of Human Services, 772 So. 2d 1051, 1057 (Miss. 2000) 291, 588, 628
Goodson v. Goodson, 816 So. 2d 420, 423-24 (Miss. Ct. App. 2002) 169, 410, 482, 491
Goodson v. Goodson, 910 So. 2d 35, 37-38 (Miss. Ct. App. 2005) 136, 162, 225
Gorin v. Gordon, 38 Miss. 205, 1859 WL 3681, at *3 (Miss. 1859) 668
Gorman v. McMahon, 792 So. 2d 307, 313 (Miss. Ct. App. 2001) 27
Gottlieb v. Gottlieb, 448 S.E.2d 666, 670 (Va. Ct. App. 1994) 78
Govan v. Medical Credit Servs., Inc., 621 So. 2d 928, 930-31 (Miss. 1993) 21
Gowdey v. Gowdey, 825 So. 2d 67, 69 (Miss. Ct. App. 2002) 571
G.Q.A. v. Harrison County Dep't of Human Servs., 771 So. 2d 331, 336 (Miss. 2000) 522, 523, 524, 525, 528, 541
Grace v. Dep't of Human Servs., 687 So. 2d 1232, 1233 (Miss. 1997) 435, 436
Grafe v. Olds, 556 So. 2d 690 (Miss. 1990) 522, 538, 539
Graham v. Graham, 767 So. 2d 277, 280-81 (Miss. Ct. App. 2000) 136, 261, 268, 269, 274, 276
Graham v. Graham, 948 So. 2d 451, 453-54 (Miss. Ct. App. 2006) 175, 226, 279, 280
Grant v. Grant, 765 So. 2d 1263, 1266 (Miss. 2000) 80, 309, 437, 625
Grant v. Martin, 757 So. 2d 264, 266 (Miss. 2000) 373
Graves v. Graves, 41 So. 384, 384 (Miss. 1906) 78
Graves v. Haden, 52 So. 3d 407, 409 (Miss. Ct. App. 2010) 49, 397, 402
Gray v. Gray, 83 So. 725 (Miss. 1920) 334
Gray v. Gray, 484 So. 2d 1032, 1033 (Miss. 1986) 33, 36
Gray v. Gray, 745 So. 2d 234, 237 (Miss. 1999) 192, 423, 430, 434
Gray v. Gray, 909 So. 2d 108, 110-11 (Miss. Ct. App. 2005) 168, 239, 255, 302, 309, 423, 440, 624
Gray v. Gray, 969 So. 2d 906, 908 (Miss. Ct. App. 2007) 393, 400, 401
Gray v. Pearson, 797 So. 2d 387, 392 (Miss. Ct App. 2001) 470, 480, 493
Great N. Ry. Co. v. Johnson, 254 F. 683, 684-85 (8th Cir. 1918) 9
Green v. Dep't of Human Servs., 40 So. 3d 660, 664 (Miss. Ct. App. 2010) 527
Green v. Ribicoff, 201 F. Supp. 721, 723-24 (S.D. Miss. 1961) 8
Gregg v. Gregg, 31 So. 3d 1277, 1280-81 (Miss. Ct. App. 2010) 135, 138, 141, 173, 174, 202, 219, 220
Gregg v. Montgomery, 587 So. 2d 928, 931 (Miss. 1991) 290, 464, 483, 489, 494, 678
Gregory v. Gregory, 881 So. 2d 840, 844-45 (Miss. Ct. App. 2003) 86, 91, 308, 378, 391, 410, 493
Gresham v. Gresham, 25 So. 2d 760, 761 (Miss. 1946) 463
Grice v. Grice, 726 So. 2d 1242, 1245 (Miss. Ct. App. 1998) 241, 286, 292, 293, 305, 431, 433
Grier v. Grier, 616 So. 2d 337, 340 (Miss. 1993) 106, 109, 206, 676, 680
Griffin v. Griffin, 42 So. 2d 720, 722 (Miss. 1949) 80
Griffin v. Griffin, 579 So. 2d 1266, 1268 (Miss. 1991) 308
Griffith v. Pell, 881 So. 2d 184, 186 (Miss. 2004) 316, 324, 370, 421, 422
Griffith v. State, 584 So. 2d 383, 387 (Miss. 1991) 605
Grisham v. Britfield, 391 So. 2d 107, 108 (Miss. 1980) 319
Grisham v. Grisham, 407 A.2d 9, 11-12 (Me. 1979) 137
Grishman v. Grishman, 407 A.2d 9, 11-12 (Me. 1979) 135
Grissom v. Grissom, 952 So. 2d 1023, 1026 (Miss. Ct. App. 2007) 365, 393, 407, 430, 431, 439
        445, 465, 468, 489
Grogan v. Grogan, 641 So. 2d 734, 739 (Miss. 1994) 185, 218, 283, 434, 586
Groseth v. Groseth, 600 N.W.2d 159, 170 (Neb. 1999) 573
Gross v. Gross, 8 S.W.3d 56, 57 (Ky. Ct. App. 1999) 215
Groves v. Slaton, 733 So. 2d 349, 353 (Miss. Ct. App. 1999) 318
Grove v. Agnew, 14 So. 3d 790, 793 (Miss. Ct. App. 2009) 435, 436
Gudelj v. Gudelj, 259 P.2d 656, 661 (Cal. 1953) 156
Guess v. Smith, 56 So. 166, 167 (Miss. 1911) 237, 246
Gunter v. Gray, 876 So. 2d 315 (Miss. 2004) 521, 522, 524, 525
Gurley v. Gorman, 102 So. 65, 66 (Miss. 1924) 104
Gutierrez v. Bucci, 827 So. 2d 27, 31-32 (Miss. Ct. App. 2002) 147, 150, 343, 344, 347, 351

TABLE OF CASES

Guy v. Guy, 736 So. 2d 1042, 1044 (Miss. 1999) 155, 238, 250, 251, 387

H

Hackman v. Burkes, 910 So. 2d 1212, 1214 (Miss. Ct. App. 2005) 430
Haddon v. Haddon, 806 So. 2d 1017, 1020 (Miss. 2000) 409
Hambrick v. Prestwood, 382 So. 2d 474, 477 (Miss. 1980) 454
Hamilton v. Hamilton, 755 So. 2d 528, 530-31 (Miss. Ct. App. 1999) 341, 346, 363, 364, 366
Hammett v. Woods, 602 So. 2d 825, 828-29 (Miss. 1992) 415, 425, 426, 440, 466, 472, 481
Hammonds v. Hammonds, 597 So. 2d 653, 655 (Miss. 1992) 237, 240, 268
Hammond v. Hammond, 641 So. 2d 1216 (Miss. 1994) 296
Hamm v. Hall, 693 So. 2d 906, 908-09 (Miss. 1997) 554, 555, 593, 597, 598, 629
Hampton v. Hampton, 977 So. 2d 1181 (Miss. Ct. App. 2007) 557, 558
Hancock v. Watson, 962 So. 2d 627 (Miss. Ct. App. 2007) 28
Handshoe v. Handshoe, 560 So. 2d 182, 184 (Miss. 1990) 80
Hand v. Berry, 154 S.E. 239, 240 (Ga. 1930) 12
Haney v. Haney, 788 So. 2d 862, 865-66 (Miss. Ct. App. 2001) 141, 285
Haney v. Haney, 881 So. 2 862, 866 (Miss. Ct. App. 2003) 255, 271
Haney v. Haney, 907 So. 2d 948, 952 (Miss. 2005) 245
Hankins v. Hankins, 729 So. 2d 1283, 1285 (Miss. 1999) 139, 141, 172, 180, 302, 303
Hankins v. Hankins, 866 So. 2d 508, 511-12 (Miss. Ct. App. 2004) 141, 142, 144, 148, 157, 159, 219, 220,
   239, 624, 671
Hanshaw v. Hanshaw, 55 So. 3d 143 (Miss. 2011) 630
Hanson v. Hanson, 191 N.E. 673, 674 (Mass. 1934) 12
Haralson v. Haralson, 362 So. 2d 190, 191 (Miss. 1978) 7, 61, 96
Harbit v. Harbit, 3 So. 3d 156, 158, 162-64 (Miss. Ct. App. 2009) 182, 305, 614
Harkins v. Fletcher, 499 So. 2d 773, 775 (Miss. 1986) 318
Harmon v. Harmon, 757 So. 2d 305, 308 (Miss. Ct. App. 1999) 72, 74, 97, 100, 102, 120, 345
Harmon v. Yarbrough, 767 So. 2d 1069, 1071 (Miss. Ct. App. 2000) 446, 492
Harper v. Archer, 12 Miss. 99 (4 S. & M. 99) (Miss. 1845) 507
Harper v. Fears, 151 So. 745, 747 (Miss. 1934) 4, 59
Harper v. Harper, 448 A.2d 916, 918 (Md. 1982) 137
Harrell v. Harrell, 231 So. 2d 793, 797 (Miss. 1970) 256
Harrington v. Harrington, 648 So. 2d 543, 546 (Miss. 1994) 375, 378, 381, 382
Harrison v. Mississippi Bar, 637 So. 2d 204, 223 (Miss. 1994) 640
Harris v. Harris, 343 So. 2d 762, 763-64 (Miss. 1977) 362
Harris v. Harris, 988 So. 2d 376, 378 (Miss. 2008) 673, 684
Harris v. Harris, 991 P.2d 262, 266 (Ariz. Ct. App. 1999) 213
Harris v. State, 14 So. 266 (Miss. 1894) 111
Harris v. Ventura, 582 S.W.2d 853, 855 (Tex. Civ. App. 1979) 145, 156
Harry v. Harry, 856 So. 2d 748, 752 (Miss. Ct. App. 2003) 553, 593
Hartman v. Hartman, 712 N.E.2d 367, 372 (Ill. App. Ct. 1999) 571
Harvey v. Harvey, 918 So. 2d 837, 839 (Miss. Ct. App. 2005) 106
Hassett v. Hassett, 690 So. 2d 1140, 1143 (Miss. 1997) 71, 72, 75, 87, 90, 119, 343
Hatcher v. Hatcher, 343 N.W.2d 498, 503 (Mich. Ct. App. 1983) 216
Havens v. Broocks, 728 So. 2d 580, 583 (Miss. Ct. App. 1998) 440, 467, 472
Hawkins v. Hawkins, 45 So. 2d 271 (Miss. 1950) 563
Hawkins v. Hawkins, 45 So. 3d 1212, 1216-17 (Miss. Ct. App. 2010) 181
Hayes v. Comm'r, 101 T.C. 593 (1993) 663
Hayes v. Hayes, 994 So. 2d 246, 248 (Miss. Ct. App. 2008) 623
Hayes v. Rounds, 658 So. 2d 863, 865 (Miss. 1995) 48, 340
Hazard v. Hazard, 833 S.W.2d 911, 914 (Tenn. Ct. App. 1991) 155, 156, 225
H.D.H. v. Prentiss County Dep't of Human Servs., 979 So. 2d 6, 12 (Miss. Ct. App. 2008) 526, 529
Heatherly v. Heatherly, 914 So. 2d 754, 757 (Miss. Ct. App. 2005) 87, 106, 675
Heath v. Heath, 647 So. 2d 769, 771 (Ala. Civ. App. 1994) 454
Hecht v. Super. Court, 20 Cal. Rptr. 2d 275, 287 (Cal. Ct. App. 1993) 506
Heffner v. Rensink, 938 So. 2d 917, 918, 920 (Miss. Ct. App. 2006) 520
Heigle v. Heigle, 654 So. 2d 895, 897 (Miss. 1995) 151, 192, 613
Heigle v. Heigle, 771 So. 2d 341, 346-47 (Miss. 2000) 161, 163, 164, 165, 169
Heinrich v. Heinrich, 609 So. 2d 94, 95-96 (Fla. Dist. Ct. App. 1992) 158
Helmert v. Biffany, 842 So. 2d 1287, 1292 (Miss. 2003) 314, 552
Helmsley v. Helmsley, 639 So. 2d 909, 912 (Miss. 1994) 168, 236

TABLE OF CASES

Helvering v. Horst, 311 U.S. 112 (1940)..662
Hemingway v. Scales, 42 Miss. 1, 13 (Miss. 1868) 16
Hemsley v. Hemsley, 639 So. 2d 909, 912-13 (Miss. 1994)...........................132, 134, 170, 171, 211, 221, 255, 266, 275, 278, 284, 303
Henderson v. Henderson, 27 So. 3d 462, 464 (Miss. Ct. App. 2010).....................................615
Henderson v. Henderson, 43 So. 2d 871, 872 (Miss. 1950)..13, 19, 20
Henderson v. Henderson, 703 So. 2d 262, 264-65 (Miss. 1997)...................150, 151, 159, 255
Henderson v. Henderson, 757 So. 2d 285, 290-91 (Miss. 2000)..... 139, 164, 170, 260, 263, 275, 279, 280, 622, 624
Henderson v. Henderson, 952 So. 2d 273, 279 (Miss. Ct. App. 2006) 338, 342, 368, 376, 423, 428, 432, 443, 477, 482, 601
Hendry v. Hendry, 300 So. 2d 147, 149 (Miss. 1974) 15
Henley v. Jones, 880 So. 2d 382, 383-84 (Miss. Ct. App. 2004) 439
Hennefeld v. Township of Montclair, 22 N.J. Tax 166, 2005 WL 646650 (2005)...................53
Hennessey v. Hennessey, 551 So. 2d 597, 598 (Fla. Dist. Ct. App. 1989) 216
Henrichs v. Henrichs, 32 So. 3d 1202, 1205-06 (Miss. Ct. App. 2009) 342, 623
Hensarling v. Hensarling, 824 So. 2d 583, 588-89 (Miss. 2002) 74, 135, 136, 137, 163, 170, 171, 221, 275, 276, 280, 306, 307, 341, 391, 438, 451, 521, 609
Hensley v. Hensley, 524 So. 2d 325, 327-28 (Miss. 1988)....................................669, 670, 671
Herman v. Lennon, 776 N.Y.S.2d 778, 779 (N.Y. Sup. Ct. 2004) 509
Herring v. Herring, 571 So. 2d 239, 244 (Miss. 1990) 394
Herron v. Herron, 936 So. 2d 956, 958 (Miss. Ct. App. 2006) 179, 188, 190
Hesington v. Hesington's Estate, 640 S.W.2d 824, 826 (Mo. Ct. App. 1982)..........................3
Hewitt v. Hewitt, 394 N.E.2d 1204, 1211 (Ill. 1979) 43
Hibbitts v. Hibbitts, 749 A.2d 975 (Pa. Super. Ct. 2000) 573
Hibner v. Hibner, 64 So. 2d 756, 756, 758 (Miss. 1953)...91
Hicks v. Hicks, 27 Cal. Rptr. 307, 313 (Cal. Dist. Ct. App. 1962)................................ 150, 156
Hillman v. Vance, 910 So. 2d 43, 45-46 (Miss. Ct. App. 2005)..................369, 385, 406, 521
Hills v. Hills, 986 So. 2d 354, 355 (Miss. Ct. App. 2008)..473
Hill v. Brinkley, 840 So. 2d 778, 780 (Miss. Ct. App. 2003)...321, 381
Hill v. Hill, 398 N.E.2d 1048, 1052-53 (Ill. App. Ct. 1979) 10
Hill v. Hill, 942 So. 2d 207, 209 (Miss. Ct. App. 2006)...................348, 353, 355, 396, 614
Hill v. Hulet, 881 P.2d 460, 462 (Colo. App. 1994) 509
Hill v. Mitchell, 818 So. 2d 1221, 1226 (Miss. Ct. App. 2002) 372
Hill v. United Timber & Lumber Co., 68 So. 2d 240 (Miss. 1953)..71
Hinders v. Hinders, 828 So. 2d 1235 (Miss. 2002)...685
Hinson v. Hinson, 877 So. 2d 547, 548 (Miss. Ct. App. 2004) 614, 619
Hinton v. Hinton, 179 So. 2d 846, 848 (Miss. 1965) 72, 101, 130, 230
Hiross v. Hiross, 639 N.Y.S.2d 70, 71 (N.Y. App. Div. 1996) 454
Hisgen v. Hisgen, 554 N.W.2d 494, 497-98 (S.D. 1996)..213
H.L.S. v. R.S.R., 949 So. 2d 794, 797 (Miss. Ct. App. 2006) 378, 408, 409, 410, 451, 462, 491, 493
Hoar v. Hoar, 404 So. 2d 1032, 1036 (Miss. 1981) 437
Hobbs v. Hobbs, 508 So. 2d 677, 680 (Miss. 1987) 581
Hobgood v. State, 926 So. 2d 847, 851-52 (Miss. 2006)...605, 606
Hockaday v. Hockaday, 644 So. 2d 446, 450 (Miss. 1994)...295
Hodges v. Hodges, 346 So. 2d 903, 904 (Miss. 1977)..215
Hodges v. Hodges, 807 So. 2d 438, 442-44 (Miss. 2002) 285
Hodge v. Hodge, 186 So. 2d 748, 751 (Miss. 1966).. 75
Hodge v. Hodge, 837 So. 2d 786, 788 (Miss. Ct. App. 2003).................................... 86, 87, 93
Hoebelheinrich v. Hoebelheinrich, 600 S.E.2d 152, 156 (Va. Ct. App. 2004)......................224
Hoffman v. Hoffman, 676 S.W.2d 817, 825-26 (Mo. 1984) 143
Hoffman v. Hoffman, 821 S.W.2d 3, 5 (Tex. App. 1992) 562
Hoffman v. Hoffman, 870 S.W.2d 480, 483 (Mo. Ct. App. 1994)...439
Hoggatt v. Hoggatt, 766 So. 2d 9 (Miss. Ct. App. 2000) 259, 275, 277, 279, 280
Hoggatt v. Hoggatt, 796 So. 2d 273, 274 (Miss. Ct. App. 2001)....................................346, 406
Holcombe v. Holcombe, 813 So. 2d 700, 705 (Miss. 2002) 294, 469
Holdeman v. Holdeman, 34 So. 3d 650, 652 (Miss. Ct. App. 2010)...................... 163, 428, 444
Holden v. Frasher-Holden, 680 So. 2d 795, 796 (Miss. 1996)... 75
Holden v. Holden, 520 S.E.2d 842, 843 (Va. Ct. App. 1999) 145
Holden v. State, 399 So. 2d 1343, 1345 (Miss. 1981)... 29
Holladay v. Holladay, 776 So. 2d 662, 665-66 (Miss. 2000) 85, 87, 89, 94, 117, 118, 606
Holland v. Holland, 759 So. 2d 1271, 1272 (Miss. Ct. App. 2000) 344
Holland v. Spain, 483 So. 2d 318, 321 (Miss. 1986)..400

TABLE OF CASES

Holleman v. Holleman, 527 So. 2d 90, 92 (Miss. 1988)..242, 591
Holley v. Holley, 892 So. 2d 183, 186 (Miss. 2004) 248, 255, 269, 279
Holley v. Holley, 969 So. 2d 842, 843-44 (Miss. 2007)................241, 257, 259, 261, 262, 265, 269, 275
Holliday v. Holliday, 651 A.2d 12, 15 (N.H. 1994) 160
Holliday v. Stockman, 969 So. 2d 136, 138-39 (Miss. Ct. App. 2007)...379, 478
Holloman v. Holloman, 691 So. 2d 897, 899-900 (Miss. 1996)...........................200, 202, 207, 210
Hollon v. Hollon, 784 So. 2d 943, 948 (Miss. 2001)..349, 354
Holloway v. Holloway, 31 So. 3d 57, 61 (Miss. Ct. App. 2009) 434, 443
Holloway v. Holloway, 865 So. 2d 382, 383 (Miss. Ct. App. 2003)...........................302, 306, 307, 498
Holloway v. Mills, 872 So. 2d 754, 757 (Miss. Ct. App. 2004)..484
Hollyfield v. Hollyfield, 618 So. 2d 1303, 1305 (Miss. 1993)..211
Holmes v. Holmes, 958 So. 2d 844, 846, 849 (Miss. Ct. App. 2007) 361, 396, 401
Honea v. Honea, 888 So. 2d 1192 (Miss. Ct. App. 2004)...35
Hooker v. Hooker, 205 So. 2d 276, 278 (Miss. 1967)...290, 465, 489
Hopkins v. Hopkins, 165 So. 414, 415 (Miss. 1936)..555, 565
Hopkins v. Hopkins, 379 So. 2d 314, 315 (Miss. 1980)..290
Hopkins v. Hopkins, 703 So. 2d 849, 850 (Miss. 1997)..133
Hopson v. Hopson, 851 So. 2d 397, 399 (Miss. Ct. App. 2003) 192, 466, 472, 682
Horn v. Horn, 909 So. 2d 1151, 1156-57 (Miss. Ct. App. 2005) 85, 86, 87, 89, 92, 118, 122,
    123, 132, 161, 162, 182, 221, 342, 344, 347, 351, 356, 359, 367, 375, 380
Horton v. Boatright, 97 So. 2d 637, 641 (Miss. 1957)..22
Horton v. Horton, 57 So. 2d 723, 725 (Miss. 1952)..553
Horton v. Horton, 480 So. 2d 258, 259 (Fla. Dist. Ct. App. 1986) 156
Hoskins v. Hoskins, 21 So. 3d 705, 708-10 (Miss. Ct. App. 2009).......................80, 85, 86, 87, 119
Houck v. Houck, 812 So. 2d 1139, 1143 (Miss. Ct. App. 2002)...470, 480
Houck v. Ousterhout, 861 So. 2d 1000, 1002 (Miss. 2003)..........................453, 465, 472, 477, 483
Houska v. Houska, 512 P.2d 1317, 1319 (Idaho 1973)..145
Houtchens v. Houtchens, 488 A.2d 726, 732 (R.I. 1985) 579
Howard v. Howard, 191 So. 2d 528, 531 (Miss. 1966)...464, 476, 477, 494
Howard v. Howard, 913 So. 2d 1030, 1039-40 (Miss. Ct. App. 2005)................................465, 469, 497
Howard v. Howard, 968 So. 2d 961, 969 (Miss. Ct. App. 2007)..................303, 305, 307, 309, 463, 465, 473, 490
Howell v. Howell, 523 S.E.2d 514, 518 (Va. Ct. App. 2000)..155, 224
Howell v. Rogers, 551 So. 2d 904, 905-06 (Miss. 1989)..385, 387
Hubbard v. Hubbard, 603 P.2d 747, 750 (Okla. 1979)...155
Hubbard v. Hubbard, 656 So. 2d 124, 128-29 (Miss. 1995) 238, 241, 242, 247, 248, 249, 265, 286, 287
Hubbard v. Miss. Conference of the United Methodist Church, 138 F. Supp. 780, 780 (S.D. Miss. 2001)..........126
Hudson v. Allen, 313 So. 2d 401, 402-03 (Miss. 1975) 23
Hughes v. Hahn, 46 So. 2d 587, 590 (Miss. 1950)...15
Hughes v. Hughes, 438 So. 2d 146, 149 (Fla. Dist. Ct. App. 1983)...155
Hulett v. Hulett, 119 So. 581, 586 (Miss. 1928)...74, 75, 585
Hulse v. Hulse, 724 So. 2d 918, 919 (Miss. Ct. App. 1998)..377
Hults v. Hults, 11 So. 3d 1273, 1277, 1282-83 (Miss. Ct. App. 2009)...................136, 177, 181, 258, 259,
    263, 268, 275, 276, 280, 303, 427, 434, 437, 440, 441, 443
Humber v. Humber, 68 So. 161, 163 (Miss. 1915) 83
Humphrey v. Martin, 755 So. 2d 551, 555 (Miss. Ct. App. 2000)....................................410, 482, 491
Humphrey v. Pannell, 710 So. 2d 392, 393-94 (Miss. 1998)..421, 455, 544
Humphries v. Humphries, 904 So. 2d 192, 197-98 (Miss. Ct. App. 2005)................176, 182, 183, 226
Hunter v. Hunter, 498 N.E.2d 1278, 1288 (Ind. Ct. App. 1986)..456
Hunt v. Asanov, 975 So. 2d 899, 902-03 (Miss. Ct. App. 2008) 167, 191, 218, 226, 466, 487, 491
Hunt v. Hunt, 161 So. 119, 120 (Miss. 1935)...5, 8, 10
Hunt v. Hunt, 629 So. 2d 548, 551 (Miss. 1992)...553, 578, 581
Hunt v. Hunt, 952 S.W.2d 564, 567 (Tex. Ct. App. 1997) 145
Hurt v. Hurt, 433 S.E.2d 493, 498 (Va. Ct. App. 1993)..145
Husband v. Wife, 262 A.2d 656, 657 (Del. Super. Ct. 1970)...10
Hussey v. Hussey, 82 So. 2d 442, 444 (Miss. 1955)...560
Hyer v. Hyer, 636 So. 2d 381, 383-84 (Miss. 1994)...72, 100
Hyslop v. Hyslop, 2 So. 2d 443, 445 (Ala. 1941) 10

I

Indianola Tractor Co. v. Tankesly, 337 So. 2d 705, 706 (Miss. 1976) 637
Inman v. Inman, 648 S.W.2d 847, 852 (Ky. 1982) 155

TABLE OF CASES

Irby v. Estate of Irby, 7 So. 3d 223, 228-30 (Miss. 2009)...................................... 107, 150, 162, 164, 182, 601, 665
Isom v. Jernigan, 840 So. 2d 104 (Miss. 2003) 593, 598, 629
Israel v. Allen, 577 P.2d 762, 764 (Colo. 1978).. 2
Ivison v. Ivison, 762 So. 2d 329, 335 (Miss. 2000).. 681, 683
Ivy v. Dep't of Human Servs., 449 So. 2d 779, 781 (Miss. 1994) 417
Ivy v. Harrington, 644 So. 2d 1218, 1221 (Miss. 1994) 315, 316, 322, 323, 324
Ivy v. Ivy, 863 So. 2d 1010, 1014 (Miss. Ct. App. 2004) 345, 348, 353

J

Jackson v. Hall, 460 So. 2d 1290, 1291 (Ala. 1984) 125
Jackson v. Jackson, 765 S.W.2d 561, 563 (Ark. 1989) 137
Jackson v. Jackson, 922 So. 2d 53, 56 (Miss. Ct. App. 2006).................. 84, 87, 92, 93, 94, 148, 166, 177, 179, 265
Jackson v. Terrill, 562 So. 2d 1271 (Miss. 1990)... 563
Jagiella v. Jagiella, 647 F.2d 561, 564 (5th Cir. 1981)... 552
James v. James, 724 So. 2d 1098, 1102-03 (Miss. Ct. App. 1998) 151, 289, 291, 296
James v. James, 736 So. 2d 492, 494-95 (Miss. Ct. App. 1999)... 173, 429
James v. Mississippi Bar, 962 So. 2d 528 (Miss. 2007) 635
Janis C. v. Christine T., 742 N.Y.S.2d 381, 383 (N.Y. App. Div. 2002)... 54, 510
J.B. v. M.B., 783 A.2d 707, 719 (N.J. 2001)... 505
J.C.N.F. v. Stone County Dep't Human Serv., 996 So. 2d 762, 772 (Miss. 2008).................526, 527, 588, 601
J.C. v. C.T., 711 N.Y.S.2d 295 (N.Y. Fam. Ct. 2000)... 54, 510
J.C. v. R.Y., 797 So. 2d 209, 215 (Miss. 2001) 388
Jellenc v. Jellenc, 567 So. 2d 847, 847-48 (Miss. 1990) 333
Jenkins v. Jenkins, 55 So. 3d 1094, 1095-97 (Miss. Ct. App. 2010)...93, 100
Jenkins v. Jenkins, 278 So. 2d 446, 449 (Miss. 1973)..243, 283
Jernigan v. Jernigan, 697 So. 2d 387 (Miss. 1997).. 45
Jernigan v. Jernigan, 830 So. 2d 651, 652-53 (Miss. Ct. App. 2002) 353, 357, 359, 362, 398
Jerome v. Stroud, 689 So. 2d 755, 757 (Miss. 1997)..346
Jethrow v. Jethrow, 571 So. 2d 270, 274 (Miss. 1990).. 101, 102, 416, 604
J.F. v. D.B., 879 N.E.2d 740, 741-42 (Ohio 2007) 517
J.F. v. D.B., 897 A.2d 1261 (Pa. Super. Ct. 2006) 516
Jhordan C. v. Mary K., 224 Cal. Rptr. 530, 537-38 (Cal. Ct. App. 1986) 510
Jill S. v. Steven S., 842 N.Y.S.2d 401, 402 (N.Y. App. Div. 2007)..568
J.L.W.W. v. Clarke County Dep't Human Servs., 759 So. 2d 1183, 1186 (Miss. 2000) 605
J.N.W.E. v. W.D.W., 922 So. 2d 12, 14-15 (Miss. Ct. App. 2005) 601, 635
Joe T. Dehmer Distribs., Inc. v. Temple, 826 F.2d 1463, 1467 (5th Cir. 1987) 15
Johnson v. Calvert, 851 P.2d 776, 782 n.10 (Cal. 1993)..515, 517
Johnson v. Collins, 419 So. 2d 1029, 1031 (Miss. 1982).. 672, 687
Johnson v. Comm'r, 39 T.C.M. (CCH) 868 (1980)..664
Johnson v. Gray, 859 So. 2d 1006, 1012 (Miss. 2003).. 341, 351, 358, 379, 396
Johnson v. Johnson, 17 So. 2d 805, 806 (Miss. 1944) 8
Johnson v. Johnson, 21 So. 3d 694, 697 (Miss. Ct. App. 2009)... 106
Johnson v. Johnson, 191 So. 2d 840, 842 (Miss. 1966) 555, 557, 597, 598, 629
Johnson v. Johnson, 550 So. 2d 416, 420 (Miss. 1989)..148, 190, 591
Johnson v. Johnson, 650 So. 2d 1281, 1284 (Miss. 1994) 146, 150, 151, 181, 237, 257, 264, 282, 423, 450
Johnson v. Johnson, 722 So. 2d 453, 462 (Miss. 1998) 444
Johnson v. Johnson, 822 So. 2d 1067 (Miss. Ct. App. 2002) 460
Johnson v. Johnson, 823 So. 2d 1156, 1160 (Miss. 2002).. 168, 169
Johnson v. Johnson, 852 So. 2d 681 (Miss. Ct. App. 2003) 170, 263, 276
Johnson v. Johnson, 872 So. 2d 92, 95 (Miss. Ct. App. 2004)..360
Johnson v. Johnson, 877 So. 2d 485, 491-92 (Miss. Ct. App. 2003)218, 220, 240, 259, 262, 264, 268, 270, 275, 279
Johnson v. Johnson, 913 So. 2d 368, 369 (Miss. Ct. App. 2005) 406, 439
Johnston v. Johnston, 179 So. 853, 853-54 (Miss. 1938).. 37, 38, 301, 333
Johnston v. Johnston, 722 So. 2d 453, 457 (Miss. 1998) 108, 162, 244, 275, 280, 424, 451, 591
Johnston v. Parham, 758 So. 2d 443, 446 (Miss. Ct. App. 2000)..480
Johns v. Johns, 57 Miss. 530, 1879 WL 6488 (1879) 330
Joiner v. Joiner, 739 So. 2d 1043, 1045 (Miss. Ct. App. 1999).. 108
Jones v. Barlow, 154 P.3d 808, 813-14 (Utah 2007) 54, 510
Jones v. Chandler, 592 So. 2d 966, 969 (Miss. 1991) 561, 569
Jones v. Fluor Daniel Servs. Corp., 32 So. 3d 417, 423 (Miss. 2010).. 126
Jones v. Jones, 19 So. 3d 775, 779-80 (Miss. Ct. App. 2009)..353, 355

TABLE OF CASES

Jones v. Jones, 43 So. 3d 465, 476-79 (Miss. Ct. App. 2009)................92, 93, 94, 378, 390, 607, 610, 611

Jones v. Jones, 55 So. 361, 361 (Miss. 1911) 22

Jones v. Jones, 532 So. 2d 574, 576 (Miss. 1988)..93

Jones v. Jones, 780 P.2d 581, 583 (Haw. Ct. App. 1989)...213

Jones v. Jones, 878 So. 2d 1061, 1064 (Miss. Ct. App. 2004) 401, 403, 410

Jones v. Jones, 904 So. 2d 1143 (Miss. Ct. App. 2004).................157, 162, 173, 178, 180, 202, 275

Jones v. Jones, 917 So. 2d 95, 99-100 (Miss. Ct. App. 2005)...............255, 282, 288, 289, 295, 302, 303, 589,

Jones v. Jones, 995 So. 2d 706, 710 (Miss. 2008)............ 151, 156, 167, 171, 173, 175, 177, 178, 179, 600

Jones v. Lee, 754 So. 2d 564, 565 (Miss. Ct. App. 2000)..491, 627

Jones v. McGuage, 932 So. 2d 846, 849 (Miss. Ct. App. 2006) 395, 399, 408

Jones v. Reed, 705 A.2d 158, 161 (Md. 1998)...433

Jones v. Somerville, 28 So. 940, 940 (Miss. 1900) 14, 19

Jordan v. Jordan, 510 So. 2d 131, 132 (Miss. 1987)..72, 74

Jordan v. Jordan, 963 So. 2d 1235, 1242-43 (Miss. Ct. App. 2007)...............148, 159, 171, 343, 345, 347,
        348, 351, 355, 356, 359

Joy v. Miles, 199 So. 771, 771 (Miss. 1941)...62

J.P.M. v. T.D.M., 932 So. 2d 760, 765 (Miss. 2006) 347, 350, 351, 354, 360, 370, 623

J.P. v. S.V.B., 987 So. 2d 975, 980-83 (Miss. 2008)..123, 332, 390

J.R.T. v. Harrison County Family Court, 749 So. 2d 105, 109 (Miss. 1999) 529, 626

Judith S. v. John M., 701 N.Y.S.2d 880 (N.Y. Fam. Ct. 1999) 574

Judkins v. Judkins, 441 S.E.2d 139, 140 (N.C. Ct. App. 1994)..211

Jundoosing v. Jundoosing, 826 So. 2d 85, 87 (Miss. 2002) 577, 579

Jurado v. Brashear, 782 So. 2d 575, 580 (La. 2001) 572

Jurek v. Jurek, 606 P.2d 812, 814 (Ariz. 1980) 152

Jurney v. Jurney, 921 So. 2d 372, 377 (Miss. Ct. App. 2005).........................485, 492, 493, 498

Justus v. Justus, 3 So. 3d 141 (Miss. Ct. App. 2009)..289, 291, 293

J.V. v. Barron, 332 N.W.2d 796, 799 (Wis. 1983)...334

K

Kalman v. Kalman, 905 So. 2d 760, 763-64 (Miss. Ct. App. 2004).............160, 194, 594, 618, 679

Kambur v. Kambur, 652 So. 2d 99, 102-03 (La. Ct. App. 1995)...157

Karenina v. Presley, 526 So. 2d 518, 522 (Miss. 1988) 314, 315, 322, 323, 324

Kass v. Kass, 696 N.E.2d 174, 178 (N.Y. 1998) 505

Kavanaugh v. Carraway, 435 So. 2d 697, 700 (Miss. 1983)..402

Kay v. Kay, 12 So. 3d 622, 625 (Miss. Ct. App. 2009)..182, 262, 424

K.B. v. J.G, 9 So. 3d 1124, 1124-27 (Miss. 2009)...539, 546

K.D.F. v. J.L.H., 933 So. 2d 971, 978-79 (Miss. 2006)..369, 539

K.D.G.L.B.P. v. Hinds County Dep't of Human Servs., 771 So. 2d 907, 911 (Miss. 2000);................524, 527

Keith v. Purvis, 982 So. 2d 1033 (Miss. Ct. App. 2008) 426

Keller v. Keller, 230 So. 2d 808, 809-10 (Miss. 1970) 288, 467

Keller v. Keller, 763 So. 2d 902, 904 (Miss. Ct. App. 2000) 85, 89, 93, 94, 118, 590

Kelley v. Day, 965 So. 2d 749, 755-56 (Miss. Ct. App. 2007).........301, 321, 322, 465, 479, 483, 487, 489, 490, 498

Kelley v. Kelley, 953 So. 2d 1139, 1143 (Miss. Ct. App. 2007)....................................192, 673, 682

Kelln v. Kelln, 515 S.E.2d 789, 796 (Va. Ct. App. 1999) 158

Kelly v. Kelly, 702 A.2d 999, 1004 (Md. Ct. Spec. App. 1997)...206

Kemp v. Kemp, 723 S.W.2d 138, 140 (Tenn. Ct. App. 1986) 125

Kennedy v. DuPont Sav. and Inv. Plan, 129 S. Ct. 865, 869-70 (2009)...201

Kennedy v. Kennedy, 650 So. 2d 1362, 1367 (Miss. 1995)...33, 39, 432

Kennedy v. Kennedy, 662 So. 2d 179, 181 (Miss. 1995)..36, 37

Kergosian v. Kergosian, 471 So. 2d 1206, 1208 (Miss. 1985) 34, 70, 84, 85, 95, 96

Kerrigan v. Comm'r of Pub. Health, 957 A.2d 407 (Conn. 2008) 50

Keyes v. Keyes, 171 So. 2d 489, 490 (Miss. 1965) 230, 236, 330, 352

Keys v. Keys, 930 So. 2d 438, 440 (Miss. Ct. App. 2005)........................404, 440, 447, 450, 493

Khabbaz v. Comm'r, 930 A.2d 1180, 1184 (N.H. 2007)..507

Kibler v. Kibler, 24 S.W.2d 867, 868 (Ark. 1930)..61

Kilgore v. Fuller, 741 So. 2d 351, 353 (Miss. Ct. App. 1999)...............435, 442, 444, 464, 466, 472

Killen v. Killen, 54 So. 3d 869, 871-72, 874 (Miss. Ct. App. 2010)...................................... 33, 35, 95

Kilpatrick v. Kilpatrick, 732 So. 2d 876, 880 (Miss. 1999). 134, 156, 200, 237, 246, 275

Kincaid v. Kincaid, 43 So. 2d 108, 109 (Miss. 1949)...99, 563

Kincaid v. Kincaid, 57 So. 2d 263, 265 (Miss. 1952)...290, 465, 489

King v. King, 152 So. 2d 889, 890 (Miss. 1963)..34

707

TABLE OF CASES

King v. King, 191 So. 2d 409, 410-11 (Miss. 1966)..230, 236, 352
King v. King, 481 A.2d 913, 915 (Pa. Super. Ct. 1984)..135
King v. King, 719 So. 2d 920, 923 (Fla. Dist. Ct. App. 1998) 202
King v. King, 760 So. 2d 830, 836 (Miss. Ct. App. 2000) 147, 159, 161, 171, 172
King v. King, 862 So. 2d 1287 (Miss. Ct. App. 2004) 172
King v. King, 946 So. 2d 395, 400-01, 404 (Miss. Ct. App. 2006) 121, 127, 166, 177, 178, 182, 189, 680
Kirby v. Kent, 160 So. 569, 572 (Miss. 1935)..668
Kirkland v. McGraw, 806 So. 2d 1180, 1183 (Miss. Ct. App. 2002)...........................448, 471, 473
Kirk v. Koch, 607 So. 2d 1220, 1224 (Miss. 1992) 27
Kitchens v. Kitchens, 850 So. 2d 215, 217-18 (Miss. Ct. App. 2003).................................669, 671
Klahold v. Kroh, 649 A.2d 701, 704 (Pa. Super. Ct. 1994) 431
Klauser v. Klauser, 865 So. 2d 363, 365 (Miss. Ct. App. 2003) 170, 173, 175, 256, 259, 275
Klein v. McIntyre, 966 So. 2d 1252, 1255 (Miss. Ct. App. 2007) 423, 613, 616
Klink v. Brewster, 986 So. 2d 1060, 1063-64 (Miss. Ct. App. 2008) 344, 345, 353, 600, 603
Klumb v. Klumb, 194 So. 2d 221, 224 (Miss. 1967) 266
K.M.K. v. S.L.M., 775 So. 2d 115, 118 (Miss. 2000)..519
Knowles v. State, 708 So. 2d 549, 552 (Miss. 1998)..20, 501
Knutson v. Knutson, 704 So. 2d 1331, 1335 (Miss. 1997)..............................262, 275, 278, 423
Kochansky v. Comm'r, 67 T.C.M. (CCH) 2665 (1994) 663
Kolar v. Chicago, 299 N.E.2d 479, 482 (Ill. App. Ct. 1973)...26
Kolikas v. Kolikas, 821 So. 2d 874, 880 (Miss. Ct. App. 2002)...............554, 555, 566, 598, 629
Kozich v. Kozich, 580 A.2d 390, 393 (Pa. Super. Ct. 1990) 152
Kramer v. Kramer, 567 N.W.2d 100, 113 (Neb. 1997) 213
Krohn v. Migues, 274 So. 2d 654 (Miss. 1973) 536, 546
Kulko v. Superior Court of Cal., 436 U.S. 84, 84-85 (1978) 559, 560, 568
Kumar v. Kumar, 976 So. 2d 957, 960-63 (Miss. Ct. App. 2008)...73, 84, 85, 87, 88, 89, 92, 94, 102, 117, 120, 600

L

Labella v. Labella, 722 So. 2d 472, 473-74 (Miss. 1998) 88, 89, 117
Lacey v. Lacey, 822 So. 2d 1132, 1138 (Miss. Ct. App. 2002)...381, 472
LaChapelle v. Mitten, 607 N.W.2d 151, 157, 168 (Minn. Ct. App. 2000)....................................511
Lackey v. Fuller, 755 So. 2d 1083, 1085 (Miss. 2000)...................................352, 364, 394, 406, 407
Ladner v. Ladner, 49 So. 3d 669, 672 (Miss. Ct. App. 2010) 88, 119, 267, 268, 302
Ladner v. Ladner, 206 So. 2d 620, 621 (Miss. 1968)...................................391, 409, 493, 494, 566
Ladner v. Ladner, 436 So. 2d 1366, 1370 (Miss. 1983) 82, 83, 600
Ladner v. Ladner, 843 So. 2d 81, 82-83 (Miss. Ct. App. 2003) 496, 621
Ladner v. Logan, 857 So. 2d 764, 770-71 (Miss. 2003)...477, 486, 498
Ladnier v. Estate of Ladnier, 109 So. 2d 338, 342 (Miss. 1959) 8
Lahmann v. Hallmon, 722 So. 2d 614, 622 (Miss. 1998)...............................301, 305, 430, 431
Laird v. Blackburn, 788 So. 2d 844, 849-50 (Miss. Ct. App. 2001) 434, 438, 439, 451, 478, 481
Lakey v. Lakey, 67 So. 2d 711, 712 (Miss. 1953)...590
L.A.L. v. D.A.L., 714 So. 2d 595, 596-97 (Fla. Dist. Ct. App. 1998)..511
Lamaritata v. Lucas, 823 So. 2d 316, 319 (Fla. Dist. Ct. App. 2002)..511
Lambert v. Lambert, 872 So. 2d 679, 684 (Miss. Ct. App. 2003)...............................394, 395, 400, 404
Lambert v. Powell, 24 So. 2d 773, 775 (Miss. 1946)...96
Landrum v. Landrum, 498 So. 2d 1299, 1299 (Miss. 1986) 38
Landwehr v. Landwehr, 545 A.2d 738, 742-43 (N.J. 1988) 152
Lane v. Lane, 850 So. 2d 122, 124 (Miss. Ct. App. 2002) 291, 293, 431, 433, 463, 465, 489
Langdon v. Langdon, 854 So. 2d 485, 487 (Miss. Ct. App. 2003)............88, 89, 102, 117, 120, 153, 157,
    183, 219, 275, 279, 477, 483, 599
Lannamann v. Lannamann, 89 A.2d 897, 897 (Pa. Super. Ct. 1952)..12
Larimore v. Larimore, 617 P.2d 892, 894 (Okla. 1980)...457
Larney v. Record, 908 So. 2d 171, 174-75 (Miss. Ct. App. 2005)................... 265, 266, 275, 277
Larue v. Larue, 969 So. 2d 99, 105 (Miss. Ct. App. 2007) 140, 175, 177, 181, 182, 183, 257, 266,
    267, 270, 275, 278, 303
Laskosky v. Laskosky, 504 So. 2d 726, 729-30 (Miss. 1987) 566, 576, 578
Last Will and Testament of Sheppard, 757 So. 2d 173, 175 (Miss. 2000) 242
Lattimore v. Lattimore, 991 So. 2d 239, 244 (Ala. Civ. App. 2008)..572
Lauderdale County Dep't of Human Servs. v. T.H.G., 614 So. 2d 377, 381 (Miss. 1992).............. 520, 527, 608
Laurel Oil & Fertilizer Co. v. Horne, 57 So. 624, 625-26 (Miss. 1912).......................................23
Lauro v. Lauro, 847 So. 2d 843, 846-47 (Miss. 2003) 169, 239, 269, 309, 624

TABLE OF CASES

Lauro v. Lauro, 924 So. 2d 584, 586, 589 (Miss. Ct. App. 2006) 169, 174, 175, 177, 239, 260, 269,
    270, 274, 277, 279, 302, 303, 306, 307, 309, 443, 624
Lawrence v. Lawrence, 574 So. 2d 1376, 1378-79 (Miss. 1991)426, 446, 447, 453, 466, 471, 473, 483, 617, 681, 684
Lawrence v. Lawrence, 956 So. 2d 251, 253 (Miss. Ct. App. 2006).............. 101, 102, 103, 332, 346, 353, 356, 602
Lawrence v. Texas, 539 U. S. 558 (2003)...43
Lawson v. Lawson, 821 So. 2d 142, 145 (Miss. Ct. App. 2002)..82, 83, 351, 590
Lawton v. Lawton, 905 So. 2d 723 (Miss. Ct. App. 2004)..267, 269, 270, 274, 279
Law v. Page, 618 So. 2d 96, 101 (Miss. 1993)..48, 335
Lazarus v. Lazarus. 841 So. 2d 181, 183, 185 (Miss. Ct. App. 2003) 447, 448, 471
LeBlanc v. Andrews, 931 So. 2d 683, 686-87 (Miss. Ct. App. 2006)....................248, 274, 279, 281, 283, 380, 610
Lee v. Lee, 12 So. 3d 548 (Miss. Ct. App. 2009)...326
Lee v. Lee, 101 So. 345, 346 (Miss. 1924)...413
Lee v. Lee, 232 So. 2d 370, 373 (Miss. 1970)... 102, 120, 558
Lee v. Lee, 798 So. 2d 1284, 1288 (Miss. 2001)..340, 343, 349, 351, 359
Lee v. Lee, 859 So. 2d 408, 410 (Miss. Ct. App. 2003)..425
Lee v. Stewart, 724 So. 2d 1093, 1095 (Miss. Ct. App. 1998) 434, 588, 592
Leiden v. Leiden, 902 So. 2d 582 (Miss. Ct. App. 2004).. 431, 464, 466, 468
Leisure v. Leisure, 605 N.E.2d 755, 759 (Ind. 1993)..214
Lemon v. Lemon, 537 N.E.2d 246, 249 (Ohio Ct. App. 1988)..216
Lenherr's Estate, 314 A.2d 255, 258 (Pa. 1974)..3
Lenoir v. Lenoir, 611 So. 2d 200, 204 (Miss. 1992) 18
Leonard v. Leonard, 486 So. 2d 1240, 1241-42 (Miss. 1986)..601
Lestrade v. Lestrade, 49 So. 3d 639, 643 (Miss. Ct. App. 2010)....................... 192, 193, 204, 682, 685, 686
Leszinske v. Poole, 798 P.2d 1049, 1054 (N.M. Ct. App. 1990)..3
Levin v. Levin, 645 N.E.2d 601, 604-05 (Ind. 1994) 509
Levy v. Levy, 34 N.E.2d 650, 652 (Mass. 1941)..10
Levy v. Louisiana, 391 U.S. 68, 71-72 (1968)...313
Lewis v. Butler, 794 So. 2d 1015, 1016-19 (Miss. 2001).. 378, 409, 493
Lewis v. Lewis, 54 So. 3d 233, 238-40 (Miss. Ct. App. 2009) 143, 150, 151, 162, 164, 166, 427
Lewis v. Lewis, 57 So. 2d 163, 165 (Miss. 1952)..497
Lewis v. Lewis, 125 So. 2d 286, 290 (Miss. 1960)...455
Lewis v. Lewis, 586 So. 2d 740, 742 (Miss. 1991) 416, 599
Lewis v. Lewis, 602 So. 2d 881, 883 (Miss. 1992) 91
Lewis v. Lewis, 974 So. 2d 265, 266-67 (Miss. Ct. App. 2008) 367, 393, 401, 404, 405, 406
Ligon v. Ligon, 743 So. 2d 404, 408 (Miss. Ct. App. 1999)..457, 469, 480
Limbaugh v. Limbaugh, 749 So. 2d 1244, 1246-47 (Miss. Ct. App. 1999)........................341, 344, 606
Lindsey v. Lindsey, 612 So. 2d 376, 379-80 (Miss. 1992)..192
Lindsey v. Lindsey, 749 So. 2d 77, 79-80 (Miss. 1999).. 160, 174, 267, 275, 276
Lindsey v. Lindsey, 818 So. 2d 1191, 1194 (Miss. 2002)..71, 103, 593, 603
Lindsey v. Sears Roebuck & Co., 846 F. Supp. 501, 507 (S.D. Miss. 1993)...26
Link v. Alvarado, 929 S.W.2d 674, 676 (Tex. App. 1996)...571
Linn v. Delaware Child Support Enforcement, 736 A.2d 954, 962-64 (Del. 1999)........................571, 572
Lipsey v. Lipsey, 755 So. 2d 564, 566-67 (Miss. Ct. App. 2000) 395, 403
Lister v. Lister, 981 So. 2d 340, 344-45 (Miss. Ct. App. 2008) 74, 75, 76
Litowitz v. Litowitz, 48 P.3d 261, 267 (Wash. 2002)..505
Little v. Collier, 759 So. 2d 454, 458 (Miss. Ct. App. 2000)...125
Little v. Little, 878 So. 2d 1086, 1089 (Miss. Ct. App. 2004) 448, 452
Little v. Streater, 452 U.S. 1, 9-10 (1981) 317
L.M.M. v. E.N.O., 528 U.S. 1005 (1999)... 54, 510
Lockert v. Lockert, 815 So. 2d 1267, 1269-70 (Miss. Ct. App. 2002)........................ 148, 160, 171, 173
Loden v. Loden, 740 N.E.2d 865, 872 (Ind. Ct. App. 2000)...571
Lofton v. Lofton, 924 So. 2d 596, 602-03 (Miss. Ct. App. 2006)...........................39, 554, 560, 561, 565
Lofton v. Secretary of the Department of Children and Family Services, 35877 F. 3d 8041275 (11th Cir., 2004)54
Logan v. Logan, 730 So. 2d 1124, 1126 (Miss. 1998)...370, 421
Logan v. Rankin, 94 So. 2d 330, 335 (Miss. 1957) 334
Logue v. Logue, 106 So. 2d 498, 500 (Miss. 1958) 192, 282
Long v. Long, 13 S.E.2d 349, 350 (Ga. 1941)..73
Long v. Long, 135 So. 204, 204 (Miss. 1931) 100
Long v. Long, 734 So. 2d 206, 207, 209-10 (Miss. Ct. App. 1999)............................. 244, 245, 246, 264, 265, 267,
    271, 272, 275, 281
Long v. Long, 928 So. 2d 1001, 1004 (Miss. Ct. App. 2006)..239, 624, 671
Loomis v. Bugg, 872 So. 2d 694, 696-97 (Miss. Ct. App. 2004)..371, 373, 374, 379

709

TABLE OF CASES

Lorenz v. Strait, 987 So. 2d 427, 430-34 (Miss. 2008) 396, 399
Loughridge v. Bowland, 52 Miss. 546, 558 (Miss. 1876) 23
Louk v. Louk, 761 So. 2d 878, 882-83 (Miss. 2000) 169, 180, 379, 451, 602
Lovejoy v. Comm'r, 293 F. 3d 1208 (10th Cir. 2002) 657
Love v. Love, 687 So. 2d 1229, 1232 (Miss. 1997) 171, 173, 264, 275, 277
L.O. v. G.V., 37 So. 3d 1248, 1252-53 (Miss. Ct. App. 2010) 522, 526
Loving v. Virginia, 388 U.S. 1, 12 (1967) 2
Lowdermilk v. Lowdermilk, 825 P.2d 874, 878 (Alaska 1992) 141
Lowery v. Lowery, 657 So. 2d 817 (Miss. 1995) 612
Lowery v. Mardis, 867 So. 2d 1053, 1057 (Miss. Ct. App. 2004) 393
Lowrey v. Lowrey, 25 So. 3d 274, 282-284 (Miss. 2009) 161, 164, 178, 182, 205, 345, 358, 364, 442
Lowrey v. Lowrey, 919 So. 2d 112, 119-22 (Miss. Ct. App. 2005) 127, 338, 460, 617, 677, 680
Loyacono v. Loyacono, 618 So. 2d 896, 897 (La. Ct. App. 1993) 141
L.S.K. v. H.A.N., 813 A.2d 872, 878 (Pa. Super. Ct. 2002) 54, 510
Lucas v. Earl, 281 U.S. 111 (1930) 662
Luckett v. Luckett, 726 So. 2d 1214, 1217 (Miss. Ct. App. 1998) 457
Lunceford v. Lunceford, 204 S.W.3d 699, 703 (Mo. Ct. App. W.D. 2006) 572
Luse v. Luse, 992 So. 2d 659, 661 (Miss. Ct. App. 2008) 71, 169, 594, 602, 603, 623
Lutes v. Alexander, 421 S.E.2d 857, 863 (Va. Ct. App. 1992) 579
L. v. L., 497 S.W.2d 840, 841-42 (Mo. Ct. App. 1973) 421
L.W. v. C.W.B., 762 So. 2d 323 (Miss. 2000) 535, 536, 537
Lyman v. Lyman, 97 A. 312, 315 (Conn. 1916) 10
Lynam v. Gallagher, 526 A.2d 878, 884 (Del. 1987) 149
Lynch v. Lynch, 50 So. 2d 378, 380-81 (Miss. 1951) 556, 565
Lynch v. Lynch, 63 So. 2d 657, 662-63 (Miss. 1953) 78, 79, 80, 101
Lynch v. Lynch, 522 A.2d 234, 235 (Vt. 1987) 158
Lynch v. Lynch, 616 So. 2d 294, 296 (Miss. 1993) 34, 80
Lynch v. Lynch, 665 S.W.2d 20, 24 (Mo. Ct. App. 1983) 203, 206

M

Mabus v. Mabus, 847 So. 2d 815, 820 (Miss. 2003) 364, 366
Mabus v. Mabus, 890 So. 2d 806, 811 (Miss. 2003) 138, 141, 171, 176, 177, 200, 202, 205,
    215, 258, 261, 263, 264, 267, 268, 274, 275, 276, 359, 362, 439, 607, 608, 668, 669, 670, 671
Mabus v. Mabus, 910 So. 2d 486, 489-91 (Miss. 2005) 305, 307
Mabus v. St. James Episcopal Church, 884 So. 2d 747, 762-63 (Miss. 2004) 642
MacDonald v. MacDonald, 559 A.2d 780, 781 (Me. 1989) 141
MacDonald v. MacDonald, 683 So. 2d 929, 932 (Miss. 1996) 253
MacDonald v. MacDonald, 698 So. 2d 1079, 1080 (Miss. 1997) 163, 184, 217, 218, 226, 244, 285, 586
MacDonald v. MacDonald, 876 So. 2d 296, 297-98 (Miss. 2004) 336, 403, 599
Mace v. Mace, 818 So. 2d 1130, 1134 (Miss. 2002) 155, 164, 165
Madden v. Rhodes, 626 So. 2d 608, 618 (Miss. 1993) 148
Magee v. Magee, 661 So. 2d 1117, 1124 (Miss. 1995) 134, 278
Magee v. Magee, 724 So. 2d 1034 (Miss. Ct. App. 1998) 262, 275, 278
Magee v. Magee, 754 So. 2d 1275, 1279 (Miss. Ct. App. 1999) 288, 289, 291, 293, 295, 464, 627
Magruder v. Magruder, 881 So. 2d 365, 368 (Miss. Ct. App. 2004) 357, 420, 435, 439, 444
Mahaffey v. First Nat'l Bank, 97 So. 2d 756, 767 (Miss. 1957) 455, 684
Maher v. Maher, 533 N.Y.S.2d 961, 961-62 (N.Y. App. Div. 1988) 139
Mahoney v. Mahoney, 453 A.2d 527, 533-34 (N.J. 1982) 250
Main v. Main, 74 So. 138, 141 (Miss. 1917) 11
Malmquist v. Malmquist, 792 P.2d 372, 381 (Nev. 1990) 145
Malone v. Odom, 657 So. 2d 1112, 1117 (Miss. 1995) 45, 47
Manning v. Manning, 133 So. 673, 674 (Miss. 1931) 102, 120
Mann v. Mann, 778 P.2d 590, 591 (Alaska 1989) 215
Mann v. Mann, 904 So. 2d 1183, 1183-84 (Miss. Ct. App. 2004) 333
Mansell v. Mansell, 490 U.S. 581, 588-92 (1989) 213
Marascalco v. Marascalco, 445 So. 2d 1380, 1382 (Miss. 1984) 368
Marble v. Marble, 457 So. 2d 1342, 1343 (Miss. 1984) 79, 84, 96
Maricle v. Maricle, 378 N.W.2d 855, 857 (Neb. 1985) 152
Markofski v. Holzhauer, 799 So. 2d 162, 165-66 (Miss. Ct. App. 2001) 421, 443, 454, 467
Mark v. Nash, 751 So. 2d 1078 (Miss. Ct. App. 1999) 470
Marriage of Arnold v. Cully, 271 Cal. Rptr. 624, 626 (Cal. Ct. App. 1990) 579

TABLE OF CASES

Marr v. Adair, 841 So. 2d 1195, 1201 (Miss. Ct. App. 2003) 595
Marshall v. Harris, 981 So. 2d 345, 347 (Miss. Ct. App. 2008) 344, 359, 360, 375
Marshall v. Marshall, 979 So. 2d 699 (Miss. Ct. App. 2007) 135, 165, 167
Marsh v. Marsh, 437 S.E.2d 34, 36 (S.C. 1993) 152
Marsh v. Marsh, 868 So. 2d 394, 398 (Miss. Ct. App. 2004) 239, 256, 263, 274, 276
Marsh v. Whittington, 40 So. 326, 326 (Miss. 1906) 11, 61
Marter v. Marter, 914 So. 2d 743, 746 (Miss. Ct. App. 2005) 343, 347, 348, 355, 356, 359, 393, 394, 400, 622
Martinez v. County of Monroe, 850 N.Y.S. 2d 740 (N.Y. App. Div. 2008) 53
Martinez v. Martinez, 860 So. 2d 1247, 1250 (Miss. Ct. App. 2003) 126, 684, 686
Martin v. Coop, 693 So. 2d 912, 916 (Miss. 1997) 384, 385
Martin v. Ealy, 859 So. 2d 1034, 1038 (Miss. Ct. App. 2003) 194, 481
Martin v. First Nat'l Bank, 164 So. 896, 899-900 (Miss. 1936) 22
Martin v. Martin, 254 So. 2d 530, 532-33 (Miss. 1971) 491
Martin v. Martin, 271 So. 2d 391, 394 (Miss. 1972) 622
Martin v. Martin, 566 So. 2d 704, 706 (Miss. 1990) 72, 74
Martin v. Martin, 751 So. 2d 1132, 1135 (Miss. Ct. App. 1999) 292, 294, 298
Martin v. Martin's Estate, 63 So. 2d 827, 830 (Miss. 1953) 9, 42
Martin v. Putnam, 427 So. 2d 1373 (Miss. 1983) 534, 537, 540
Martin v. State, 308 So. 2d 925, 926 (Miss. 1975) 500
Martin v. State, 773 So. 2d 415, 417-18 (Miss. Ct. App. 2000) 30
Marvin v. Marvin, 176 Cal. Rptr. 555, 558-59 (Cal. Ct. App. 1981) 47
Marvin v. Marvin, 557 P.2d 106, 122 (Cal. 1976) 43
Masino v. Masino, 829 So. 2d 1267, 1271-72 (Miss. Ct. App. 2002) 258, 262, 275, 277, 301, 362, 367, 431, 439
Maslowski v. Maslowski, 655 So. 2d 18, 23 (Miss. 1995) 150, 151, 159, 173
Mason v. Mason, 895 S.W.2d 513, 520 (Ark. 1995) 158
Mason v. Mason, 919 So. 2d 200, 204 (Miss. Ct. App. 2005) 683
Massachusetts v. U.S. Dep't of Health and Human Serv., 698 F. Supp. 2d 234 (D. Mass. 2010) 51
Massengill v. Massengill, 594 So. 2d 1173, 1175 (Miss. 1992) 105, 106, 108, 675
Massey v. Huggins, 799 So. 2d 902, 904-05 (Miss. Ct. App. 2001) 123, 348, 352, 353, 355, 356,
357, 358, 364, 407, 591
Massey v. Massey, 475 So. 2d 802, 806 (Miss. 1985) 308
M.A.S. v. Miss. Dep't of Human Servs., 842 So. 2d 527, 528 (Miss. 2003) 325, 326, 618
Maxcy v. Estate of Maxcy, 485 So. 2d 1077, 1078 (Miss. 1986) 242, 247, 252, 253
Maxey v. Maxey, 120 So. 179, 180 (Miss. 1929) 39
Maxwell v. Maxwell, 796 P.2d 403, 406 (Utah Ct. App. 1990) 212
Mayes v. Stewart, 11 S.W.3d 440, 457 (Tex. App. 2000) 160
Mayfield v. Braund, 64 So. 2d 713 (Miss. 1953) 543
Mayfield v. Mayfield, 956 So. 2d 337, 343 (Miss. Ct. App. 2007) 348, 349, 352, 354, 359, 606
Mayoza v. Mayoza, 526 So. 2d 547, 549 (Miss. 1988) 585, 603
May v. Harrison County Dep't of Human Servs., 883 So. 2d 74 (Miss. 2004) 519, 523, 524, 528, 552
May v. May, 130 So. 52, 53 (Miss. 1930) 556, 557
May v. May, 589 S.E.2d 536 (W. Va. 2003) 224
McAdory v. McAdory, 608 So. 2d 695, 699 (Miss. 1992) 48, 73, 74, 76, 352
McAlear v. McAlear, 469 A.2d 1256, 1272-73 (Md. Ct. App. 1984) 497
McAllum v. Spinks, 91 So. 694, 697 (Miss. 1922) 4
McBride v. Cook, 858 So. 2d 160, 162 (Miss. Ct. App. 2003) 395, 404
McBride v. Jones, 803 So. 2d 1168, 1169-70 (Miss. 2002) 326
McBroom v. McBroom, 58 So. 2d 831, 831 (Miss. 1952) 94
McCardle v. McCardle, 862 So. 2d 1290, 1293 (Miss. Ct. App. 2004) 241, 483, 490
McCarrell v. McCarrell, 19 So. 3d 168, 170 (Miss. Ct. App. 2009) 259, 275, 277, 280, 303
McCarthy v. McCarthy, 785 So. 2d 1138, 1140 (Alaska Civ. App. 2000) 571
McCarty v. McCarty, 453 U.S. 210, 232-35 (1981) 210
McCauley v. McCauley, 599 So. 2d 1002, 1003 (Fla. Dist. Ct. App. 1992) 420
McCleave v. McCleave, 491 So. 2d 522, 523 (Miss. 1986) 106, 676
McClee v. Simmons, 834 So. 2d 61, 64-65 (Miss. Ct. App. 2002) 321, 424, 435, 436
McCollum v. State Dep't of Pub. Welfare, 447 So. 2d 650, 653 (Miss. 1984) 315, 321, 335
McCord v. Spradling, 830 So. 2d 1188 (Miss. 2002) 673
McCorkle v. McCorkle, 811 So. 2d 258, 264 (Miss. Ct. App. 2001) 126
McCoy v. Colonial Baking Co., 572 So. 2d 850, 853-54 (Miss. 1990) 25, 26
McCoy v. Cook, 419 N.W.2d 44, 46 (Mich. Ct. App. 1988) 125
McCracking v. Champaigne, 805 So. 2d 586, 590 (Miss. Ct. App. 2001) 382
McCracking v. McCracking, 776 So. 2d 691, 693 (Miss. Ct. App. 2000) 393, 396, 405, 408

711

TABLE OF CASES

McCraw v. Buchanan, 10 So. 3d 979, 985-86 (Miss. Ct. App. 2009) 301, 369, 371, 391
McCraw v. McCraw, 759 So. 2d 519, 521 (Miss. Ct. App. 2000)...295
McCraw v. McCraw, 841 So. 2d 1181, 1184 (Miss. Ct. App. 2003) 350, 352, 359
McCrory v. Donald, 80 So. 643, 645 (Miss. 1919) 23
McCubbin v. Seay, 749 So. 2d 1127, 1129 (Miss. Ct. App. 1999) 560, 562, 569
McCulloch v. McCulloch, 435 N.W.2d 564, 568 (Minn. Ct. App. 1989)....................................147
McCullough v. McCullough, 52 So. 3d 373, 380-81 (Miss. Ct. App. 2009) 346, 353
McDaniels v. Carlson, 738 P. 2d 254, 261 (Wash. 1987)...323
McDaniel v. Ritter, 556 So. 2d 303, 309 (Miss. 1989) 559
McDannell v. United States Office of Personnel Mgmt., 716 F.2d 1063, 1065-66 (5th Cir. 1983) 200, 210
McDermott v. McDermott, 986 S.W.2d 843, 848 (Ark. 1999) 156
McDonald v. McDonald, 39 So. 3d 868, 872, 882 (Miss. Ct. App. 2010)...............344, 347, 351, 390, 404, 408, 552
McDonald v. McDonald, 608 N.Y.S.2d 477 (N.Y. App. Div. 1994).. 514
McDonald v. McDonald, 683 So. 2d 929, 931-33 (Miss. 1996)..............241, 246, 247, 253, 286, 287, 685
McDonald v. McDonald, 850 So. 2d 1182, 1189 (Miss. Ct. App. 2002) 383, 410, 498, 675, 676
McDougal v. McDougal, 545 N.W.2d 357, 363 (Mich. 1996)...156
McDuffie v. McDuffie, 21 So. 3d 685, 689 (Miss. Ct. App. 2009) 108, 162, 148, 190, 306, 379
McDuff v. McDuff, 173 So. 2d 419, 423-24 (Miss. 1965)..598
McEachern v. McEachern, 605 So. 2d 809, 813-14 (Miss. 1992) 261, 434, 463, 469, 472
McEwen v. McEwen, 631 So. 2d 821, 823-824 (Miss. 1994)............................. 432, 441, 462, 469
McGee v. McGee, 726 So. 2d 1220, 1222-23 (Miss. Ct. App. 1998).................. 149, 184, 185, 192
McGehee v. McGehee, 85 So. 2d 799, 804 (Miss. 1956). 22
McGehee v. Upchurch, 733 So. 2d 364, 369 (Miss. Ct. App. 1999) 393, 406, 443
McGinley v. McGinley, 565 A.2d 1220, 1225 (Pa. Super. Ct. 1989)......................................158
McGlaston v. Cook, 576 So. 2d 1268, 1269 (Miss. 1991) 320
McGowan v. State, 742 So. 2d 1183, 1186 (Miss. Ct. App. 1999)..605
McGowan v. West Side Bone & Joint Center, 656 So. 2d 119, 122 (Miss. 1995)........................... 418
McGuire v. McGuire, 59 N.W.2d 336, 342 (Neb. 1953)...20
McHann v. McHann, 383 So. 2d 823, 826 (Miss. 1980) 230, 296, 477
McIlwain v. McIlwain, 815 So. 2d 476 (Miss. Ct. App. 2002)..................................... 275, 278
McIntosh v. Dep't of Human Servs., 886 So. 2d 721 (Miss. 2004)..............................317, 487, 488
McIntosh v. McIntosh, 117 So. 352, 352 (Miss. 1928)..61, 97, 99
McIntosh v. McIntosh, 977 So. 2d 1257, 1259, 1271 (Miss. Ct. App. 2008) 33, 34, 35, 85, 86, 92,
93, 95, 133, 194, 248, 268, 276, 303, 599, 621
McIver v. McIver, 374 S.E.2d 144, 149-51 (N.C. Ct. App. 1988)..............................135, 137
McKay v. McKay, 8 S.W.3d 525 (Ark. 2000) 150
McKee v. Flynt, 630 So. 2d 44, 48-49 (Miss. 1993).......................... 72, 87, 88, 338, 677
McKee v. McKee, 382 So. 2d 287, 288 (Miss. 1980)...288, 468
McKee v. McKee, 418 So. 2d 764, 767 (Miss. 1982) 304, 305, 309, 625
McKenzie v. McKenzie, 860 So. 2d 316, 317 (Miss. Ct. App. 2003)......................................401
McKissack v. McKissack, 45 So. 3d 716, 718-22 (Miss. Ct. App. 2010)........ 138, 144, 147, 219, 239, 260, 264, 265
McKnight v. McKnight, 951 So. 2d 594, 596 (Miss. Ct. App. 2007) 162
McLarty v. McLarty, 433 S.W.2d 722, 724 (Tex. Civ. App. 1968).. 61
McLaurin v. McLaurin, 853 So. 2d 1279 (Miss. Ct. App. 2003) 265, 274, 276
McLean v. Kohnle, 940 So. 2d 975, 979-80 (Miss. Ct. App. 2006)......................................572
McLemore v. McLemore, 163 So. 500, 501 (Miss. 1935) 79
McLemore v. McLemore, 762 So. 2d 316, 319 (Miss. 2000) 368, 369, 382, 389
McLemore v. Riley's Hosp., 20 So. 2d 67, 68-69 (Miss. 1944) 21
McManus v. Howard, 569 So. 2d 1213, 1216 (Miss. 1990).....................338, 400, 617, 674, 677, 681, 684
McManus v. McManus, 348 N.E.2d 507, 509 (Ill. App. Ct. 1976)..457
M.C.M.J. v. C.E.J., 715 So. 2d 774, 776-77 (Miss. 1998)...342
McMurry v. Sadler, 846 So. 2d 240, 244 (Miss. Ct. App. 2002)..392
McNair v. Clark, 961 So. 2d 73, 80 (Miss. Ct. App. 2007).....................463, 464, 466, 467
McNally v. McNally, 516 So. 2d 499, 501 (Miss. 1987)...........................285, 290, 622
McNaughton v. McNaughton, 538 A.2d 1193, 1197 (Md. Ct. Spec. App. 1988)............................143
McNeal v. Adm'r of Estate of McNeal, 254 So. 2d 521, 522-23 (Miss. 1971)...........................24, 124
McNeill v. McNeill, 87 So. 645, 646 (Miss. 1921) 84
McNeil v. McNeil, 607 So. 2d 1192, 1195 (Miss. 1992)...187, 188
McRree v. McRree, 723 So. 2d 1217, 1220 (Miss. Ct. App. 1998) 406, 407
McSwain v. McSwain, 943 So. 2d 1288, 1293 (Miss. 2006) 123, 350, 351, 358, 365, 396, 399
McWhirter v. McWhirter, 811 So. 2d 397, 399 (Miss. Ct. App. 2001) 361
Meador v. Meador, 44 So. 3d 411, 419-21 (Miss. Ct. App 2010)....................260, 262, 264, 266, 269

TABLE OF CASES

Means v. Indus. Comm'n, 515 P.2d 29, 32 (Ariz. 1973) 64
Medders v. Estate of Medders, 458 So. 2d 685, 690 (Miss. 1984) 484, 485
Meek v. Meek, 726 So. 2d 1292, 1294 (Miss. Ct. App. 1998)...................................449
Merch. Nat'l Bank v. Se. Fire Ins. Co., 751 F.2d 771, 777 (5th Cir. 1985) 16
Mercier v. Mercier, 11 So. 3d 1283, 1287 (Miss. Ct. App. 2009).....................405, 409, 466
Mercier v. Mercier, 717 So. 2d 304, 307 (Miss. 1998).............343, 346, 347, 364, 358, 359
Meredith v. Shakespeare, 122 S.E. 520, 526 (W. Va. 1924) 12
Messer v. Messer, 850 So. 2d 161, 167-70 (Miss. Ct. App. 2003) 134, 150, 151, 162, 191, 343, 344, 362, 375
Metzner v. Metzner, 446 S.E.2d 165, 173 (W. Va. 1994) 156
M.H. v. D.A., 17 So. 3d 610, 615-16 (Miss. Ct. App. 2009) 523, 628, 629
Michael v. Michael, 650 So. 2d 469, 471 (Miss. 1995) 92, 337, 619
Mid-South Ins. Co. v. Doe, 274 F. Supp. 2d 757 (D.S.C. 2003) 516
Milam v. Milam, 509 So. 2d 864, 866 (Miss. 1987)...484
Miley v. Daniel, 37 So. 3d 84, 86 (Miss. Ct. App. 2009)............................35, 37, 599
Millar v. Millar, 167 P. 394, 396 (Cal. 1917)..10
Miller-Jenkins v. Miller-Jenkins, 912 A.2d 951 (Vt. 2006).......................................55
Miller v. Lucks, 36 So. 2d 140, 142 (Miss. 1948)...3
Miller v. Miller, 159 So. 112, 119-20 (Miss. 1935)........................236, 237, 240, 246
Miller v. Miller, 298 So. 2d 704, 707 (Miss. 1974)..13, 19
Miller v. Miller, 478 A.2d 351, 354 (N.J. 1984)...421
Miller v. Miller, 512 So. 2d 1286, 1288 (Miss. 1987)..............................561, 591, 593
Miller v. Miller, 617 A.2d 375, 376-78 (Pa. Super. Ct. 1992)..................................213
Miller v. Miller, 838 So. 2d 295, 298 (Miss. Ct. App. 2002)....................................18
Miller v. Miller, 874 So. 2d 469, 472 (Miss. Ct. App. 2004)...................................268
Mills v. Mills, 279 So. 2d 917, 924 (Miss. 1973) 19
Minor v. Higdon, 61 So. 2d 350, 357 (Miss. 1952)..62
Minter v. Minter, 29 So. 3d 840, 852-53 (Miss. Ct. App. 2009) 398, 404, 607, 610
Miss. Bar v. Attorney ST, 621 So. 2d 229, 233 (Miss. 1993) 642
Miss. Dep't of Human Servs. v. Barnett, 633 So. 2d 430, 436 (Miss. 1993) 321, 319
Miss. Dep't of Human Servs. v. Gaddis, 730 So. 2d 1116, 1118 (Miss. 1998)...................315
Miss. Dep't of Human Servs. v. Sanford, 850 So. 2d 86, 89 (Miss. 2003) 315, 320
Mississippi Bar v. Robb, 684 So. 2d 615, 623 (Miss. 1996)......................................639
Mississippi Dep't Human Servs. v. Guidry, 830 So. 2d 628 (Miss. 2002) 627
Mississippi Dep't of Human Servs. v. Marquis, 630 So. 2d 331, 335 (Miss. 1993)...............563
Mitchell v. Mitchell, 732 P.2d 208, 211-12 (Ariz. 1987)....................................155, 224
Mitchell v. Mitchell, 767 So. 2d 1037, 1041 (Miss. Ct. App. 2000) 69, 75, 95, 96, 440, 553, 578, 579, 580
Mitchell v. Mitchell, 823 So. 2d 568, 571 (Miss. Ct. App. 2002) 85, 623
Mitchell v. Powell, 179 So. 2d 811 (Miss. 1965)....................................334, 392, 415, 551
Mitten v. LaChapelle, 531 U.S. 1011 (2000)...511
Mixon v. Bullard, 217 So. 2d 28, 30 (Miss. 1968)..357, 361
Mixon v. Mixon, 724 So. 2d 956, 960 (Miss. Ct. App. 1998) 89, 118, 301, 308, 375
Mixon v. Sharp, 853 So. 2d 834, 838 (Miss. Ct. App. 2003)..........123, 343, 348, 355, 358, 396, 402, 403, 498
Mizell v. Mizell, 708 So. 2d 55, 60 (Miss. 1998)...185, 480
M.J.S.H.S. v. Yalobusha County Dep't of Human Servs., 782 So. 2d 737, 741 (Miss. 2001) 389, 520, 521
M.L.B. v. S.L.J., 519 U.S. 102, 118 (1996)...519, 626
M.L.B. v. S.L.J., 806 So. 2d 1023, 1023-24 (Miss. 2000) 520, 526
Moak v. Moak, 631 So. 2d 196, 197 (Miss. 1994) 48, 344, 348, 352
Mobley v. Mobley, 16 So. 2d 5, 7 (Ala. 1943)..10
Moe v. Dinkins, 669 F.2d 67, 68 (2d Cir. 1982)...2
Mohr v. State, 584 So. 2d 426, 431 (Miss. 1991) 604
Monitzer v. Monitzer, 600 So. 2d 575 (Fla. Dist. Ct. App. 1992)...............................420
Monroe v. Monroe, 612 So. 2d 353, 358-59 (Miss. 1992) 266
Monroe v. Monroe, 745 So. 2d 249 (Miss. 1999) 244, 271, 275, 279
Montgomery v. Montgomery, 20 So. 3d 39, 41-45 (Miss. Ct. App. 2009).......343, 346, 349, 353, 357, 358, 359, 361
Montgomery v. Montgomery, 759 So. 2d 1238 (Miss. 2000) 616
Montgomery v. Montgomery, 873 So. 2d 1071, 1072-73 (Miss. Ct. App. 2004)...................491
Montgomery v. Walker, 86 So. 2d 502 (Miss. 1956)..563
Moody v. Moody, 211 So. 2d 842, 844 (Miss. 1968)......................................333, 371
Mooneyham v. Mooneyham, 420 So. 2d 1072, 1073 (Miss. 1982)..............................425
Moon v. Moon, 790 P.2d 52, 57 (Utah Ct. App. 1990)..156
Moon v. Moon, 795 S.W.2d 511, 514 (Mo. Ct. App. 1990).......................................213
Moore v. Cole, 961 So. 2d 737, 740 (Miss. Ct. App. 2007)...............................393, 397, 398

TABLE OF CASES

Moore v. Moore, 757 So. 2d 1043, 1047 (Miss. Ct. App. 2000)............85, 88, 89, 118, 356, 357, 361, 442, 429, 603
Moore v. Moore, 803 So. 2d 1214, 1219 (Miss. Ct. App. 2001) 258, 275
Moorman v. Moorman, 28 So. 3d 670, 671-72 (Miss. Ct. App. 2009).. 361
Moorman v. State, 93 So. 368, 368 (Miss. 1922)..20
Mord v. Peters, 571 So. 2d 981, 986 n.6 (Miss. 1990) 382
Morgan v. Morgan, 397 So. 2d 894, 895 (Miss. 1981) 285, 496
Morgan v. Morgan, 744 So. 2d 321, 325 (Miss. 1999).. 193, 485, 678, 682
Morgan v. Sauls, 413 So. 2d 370, 375 (Miss. 1982)..23
Morgan v. West, 812 So. 2d 987, 992 (Miss. 2002)...384, 386
Morreale v. Morreale, 646 So. 2d 1264, 1267 (Miss. 1994)... 188, 307, 489
Morrison v. Dep't of Human Servs., 852 So. 2d 578, 584 (Miss. Ct. App. 2002) 449
Morrison v. Dep't of Human Servs., 863 So. 2d 948, 952-53 (Miss. 2004) 598
Morrison v. Morrison, 692 S.W.2d 601, 603 (Ark. 1985)...154
Morris v. Morris, 5 So. 3d 476, 487-90 (Miss. Ct. App. 2008) 169, 173, 349, 362, 442, 443, 490
Morris v. Morris, 8 So. 3d 917, 919 (Miss. Ct. App. 2009) 289, 294, 469
Morris v. Morris, 541 So. 2d 1040, 1043 (Miss. 1989)..463, 674, 683
Morris v. Morris, 758 So. 2d 1020, 1021 (Miss. Ct. App. 1999) 365, 366
Morris v. Morris, 783 So. 2d 681, 687-88 (Miss. 2001) 76, 85, 86, 90, 93, 94, 100, 350, 380, 399
Morris v. Morris, 804 So. 2d 1025, 1029 (Miss. 2002) 90, 95, 96
Morris v. Morris, 894 S.W.2d 859, 861-62 (Tex. Ct. App. 1995) 211
Morris v. Stacy, 641 So. 2d 1194, 1195 (Miss. 1994) 423, 444, 447, 451, 457
Morrow v. Morrow, 591 So. 2d 829, 830 (Miss. 1991) 364
Mortenson v. Trammell, 604 S.W.2d 269, 276 (Tex. App. 1980)... 156
Mosby v. Gandy, 375 So. 2d 1024 (Miss. 1979) 598
Mosby v. Mosby, 962 So. 2d 119, 124 (Miss. Ct. App. 2007) 181
Moses v. Moses, 879 So. 2d 1036, 1040 (Miss. 2004)...87, 95, 491
Mosley v. Atterberry, 819 So. 2d 1268 (Miss. 2002)..353, 444
Mosley v. Huffman, 481 So. 2d 231, 239 (Miss. 1985) 553, 578, 579, 581
Mosley v. Mosley, 784 So. 2d 901, 903, 909 (Miss. 2001) 244, 246, 271, 275, 280, 347, 444
Mottley v. Mottley, 729 So. 2d 1289, 1290 (Miss. 1999)..449
Moulds v. Bradley, 791 So. 2d 220, 225 (Miss. 2001) 443, 487, 488
Mount v. Mount, 476 A.2d 1175, 1181 (Md. Ct. Spec. App. 1984).. 157
Mount v. Mount, 624 So. 2d 1001, 1004 (Miss. 1993)...192, 282, 307
Muhammed v. Muhammed, 622 So. 2d 1239, 1241-42, 1250 (Miss. 1993) 93, 362
Mullen v. Mullen, 246 So. 2d 923, 924-25 (Miss. 1971) 465, 489
Murdoch v. Murdoch, [1975] 1 S.C.R. 423 (Can.)..130
Murphy v. Murphy, 631 So. 2d 812, 815 (Miss. 1994) 622
Murphy v. Murphy, 797 So. 2d 325, 329-30 (Miss. Ct. App. 2001)............................ 199, 200, 214, 215, 341, 342
Muse v. Hutchins, 559 So. 2d 1031, 1033 (Miss. 1990)...387, 544
Myers v. Myers, 741 So. 2d 274, 279 (Miss. Ct. App. 1998).......................................74, 104, 153, 187, 306
Myers v. Myers, 814 So. 2d 833, 835 (Miss. Ct. App. 2002)...341, 347, 355
Myers v. Myers, 881 So. 2d 180, 183 (Miss. 2004) 18, 33, 38
Myrick v. Myrick, 739 So. 2d 432, 434 (Miss. Ct. App. 1999) 149, 151

N

Nash v. Mobile & O.R. Co., 116 So. 100, 101-02 (Miss. 1928) 25
Nash v. Nash, 388 N.W.2d 777, 781 (Minn. Ct. App. 1986)...150
Nash v. Overholser, 757 P.2d 1180, 1180-81 (Idaho 1988) 125, 126
Natural Mother v. Paternal Aunt, 583 So. 2d 614, 619 (Miss. 1991)... 522, 540, 543
Naveda v. Ahumada, 381 So. 2d 147, 149 (Miss. 1981)...335, 546
Neal v. Neal, 119 So. 2d 273, 275-76 (Miss. 1960) 334, 335, 392
Neely v. Neely, 52 So. 2d 501 (Miss. 1951)..238
Nell v. Nell, 560 N.Y.S.2d 426, 426 (N.Y. App. Div. 1990)... 141
Nelson v. Halley, 827 So. 2d 42, 51 (Miss. Ct. App. 2002)..571, 572, 573
Nelson v. Nelson, 891 So. 2d 317, 322-23 (Ala. Civ. App. 2004) 560
Neshoba County DHS v. Hodge, 919 So. 2d 1157, 1161 (Miss. Ct. App. 2006) 531, 534
Neville v. Neville, 734 So. 2d 352, 353, 357-58 (Miss. Ct. App. 1999).................. 135, 237, 250, 252, 359
N.E. v. L.H., 761 So. 2d 956, 961 (Miss. Ct. App. 2000) 522, 525, 531 540
Newell v. Hinton, 556 So. 2d 1037, 1042 (Miss. 1990) 487, 497, 683
Newman v. Newman, 558 So. 2d 821, 823 (Miss. 1990) 133, 211, 556, 557
Newsom v. Newsom, 557 So. 2d 511, 516 (Miss. 1990) 380, 398

TABLE OF CASES

Neyland v. Neyland, 482 So. 2d 228, 230-31 (Miss. 1986) 185, 586
Nicholas v. Nicholas, 841 So. 2d 1208, 1210 (Miss. Ct. App. 2003)......................283, 484, 485
Nichols v. Funderburk, 881 So. 2d 266, 271 (Miss. Ct. App. 2003) 46, 185
Nichols v. Nichols, 31 Vt. 328, 331 (1858) 99
Nichols v. Nichols, 254 So. 2d 726, 727 (Miss. 1971) 295
Nichols v. Rutledge, 749 So. 2d 68, 72 (Miss. 1999)...497
Nichols v. Sauls, 165 So. 2d 352, 358 (Miss. 1964)...8
Nichols v. Tedder, 547 So. 2d 766, 769 (Miss. 1989)..................443, 449, 451, 452, 660, 684
Niles v. Niles, 550 N.Y.S.2d 208, 209 (N.Y. App. Div. 1990) 139
Nix v. Nix, 790 So. 2d 198, 200-01 (Miss. 2001) 428, 429
Nobile v. Nobile, 535 So. 2d 1385, 1388 (Miss. 1988)...625
Noble v. Noble, 502 So. 2d 317, 320 (Miss. 1987)..555, 559, 597
Nolden v. Nolden, 448 N.W.2d 892, 893-94 (Minn. Ct. App. 1989)...139
Norman v. Bucklew, 684 So. 2d 1246, 1248 (Miss. 1996)..126
Norman v. Norman, 962 So. 2d 718, 721-22 (Miss. Ct. App. 2007)..342
Norton v. Norton, 742 So. 2d 126, 129-31 (Miss. 1999)...247, 283, 287

O

Oberlin v. Oberlin, 29 So. 2d 82, 83 (Miss. 1947).. 74, 100
O'Brien v. O'Brien, 489 N.E.2d 712, 716-19 (N.Y. 1985) 154
O'Brien v. O'Brien, 899 So. 2d 1133, 1136-37 (Fla. Dist. Ct. App. 2005)..............................643
O'Connell v. O'Connell, 597 A.2d 643, 645 (Pa. 1991) 454
Odle v. Eastman, 453 S.E.2d 598, 602 (W. Va. 1994) 157
Oliver v. Oliver, 812 So. 2d 1128, 1134-35 (Miss. Ct. App. 2002).........................146, 151, 159
Olson v. Flinn, 484 So. 2d 1015, 1017 (Miss. 1986) 387, 544
Olson v. Olson, 445 N.W.2d 1, 11 (N.D. 1989) 215
Olson v. Olson, 799 So. 2d 927, 930 (Miss. Ct. App. 2001)..376, 377, 408
O'Neal v. O'Neal, 17 So. 3d 572, 575-78 (Miss. 2009) 107
O'Neal v. O'Neal, 703 S.W.2d 535, 538 (Mo. Ct. App. 1985) 139
O'Neill v. O'Neill, 515 So. 2d 1208, 1211 (Miss. 1987)...............416, 555, 556, 559, 561, 562, 596, 597
Orr v. Orr, 440 U.S. 268, 279 (1979)...................................... 5, 14, 32, 33, 81, 231, 330, 420
Ortega v. Lovell, 725 So. 2d 199, 203-04 (Miss. 1998)...393, 581
Ory v. Ory, 936 So. 2d 405, 410 (Miss. Ct. App. 2006) 141, 152, 153, 159, 174, 191, 602, 622
Osborn v. Osborn, 724 So. 2d 1121, 1125-26 (Miss. Ct. App. 1998) 261, 275, 276, 279, 280, 429, 431, 434
Osguthorpe v. Osguthorpe, 804 P.2d 530, 535-36 (Utah Ct. App. 1990)................................ 139
Oster v. Oster, 876 So. 2d 428, 431-32 (Miss. Ct. App. 2004) 249, 250, 287
Oswalt v. Oswalt, 981 So. 2d 993, 995-96 (Miss. Ct. App. 2007) 87, 88, 90, 93, 118, 140, 144, 146, 148, 150, 151, 219
Outlaw v. State, 43 So. 2d 661, 664 (Miss. 1949)..29
Ouzts v. Carroll, 199 So. 76, 77-78 (Miss. 1940) 32
Overberg v. Lusby, 727 F. Supp. 1091, 1094 (E.D. KY 1990)...125
Overstreet v. Merlos, 570 So. 2d 1196, 1198 (Miss. 1990)...28
Overstreet v. Overstreet, 692 So. 2d 88, 90 (Miss. 1997)..............190, 249, 250, 287, 302, 463, 484, 591
Owens v. Owens, 274 S.E.2d 484, 485-86 (Ga. 1981)...76
Owens v. Owens, 950 So. 2d 202, 207 (Miss. Ct. App. 2006)...............133, 172, 175, 179, 183, 349, 355, 360, 361
Owen v. Gerity, 422 So. 2d 284, 287 (Miss. 1982)... 74, 296, 683
Owen v. Owen, 12 So. 3d 603, 606-07 (Miss. Ct. App. 2009)...167, 179
Owen v. Owen, 22 So. 3d 386, 389-90 (Miss. Ct. App. 2009) 158, 303, 427
Owen v. Owen, 419 S.E.2d 267, 270-71 (Va. Ct. App. 1992)... 213
Owen v. Owen, 798 So. 2d 394, 399-400 (Miss. 2001)..............................168, 170, 172, 199, 207
Owen v. Wilkinson, 915 So. 2d 493, 495-96 (Miss. Ct. App. 2005)......................................452, 484
Ownby v. Prisock, 138 So. 2d 279, 280-81 (Miss. 1962) 636

P

Pace v. Owens, 511 So. 2d 489, 491 (Miss. 1987)..346, 393
Pace v. Pace, 16 So. 3d 734, 737-38 (Miss. Ct. App. 2009)...94, 561, 601
Pace v. Pace, 24 So. 3d 325, 329-30 (Miss. Ct. App. 2009) 680
Pacheco v. Pacheco, 770 So. 2d 1007, 1010-11 (Miss. Ct. App. 2000) 256, 301, 302, 303, 304, 357, 358, 360
Palculict v. Palculict, 22 So. 3d 293, 297 (Miss. Ct. App. 2009) 241, 245, 263, 266, 271, 272, 274, 277, 279, 342, 364, 442

715

TABLE OF CASES

Palmere v. Curtis, 789 So. 2d 126 (Miss. Ct. App. 2001) 613
Palmer v. Clarksdale Hosp., 57 So. 2d 476, 478 (Miss. 1952)..25, 26
Palmer v. Palmer, 654 So. 2d 1, 4 (Miss. 1995)... 186
Palmer v. Palmer, 841 So. 2d 185, 188-89 (Miss. Ct. App. 2003) 169, 256, 260, 261, 275, 278
Pardue v. Ardis, 58 So. 769, 769 (Miss. 1912)... 671
Parker v. Bliven, 59 So. 3d 619, 621 (Miss. Ct. App. 2010)... 588, 624
Parker v. Miss. Dep't of Human Servs., 827 So. 2d 18, 20 (Miss. Ct. App. 2002)...................... 321, 443
Parker v. Parker, 14 So. 459, 459 (Miss. 1893)... 301
Parker v. Parker, 55 N.W.2d 183, 186 (Iowa 1952).. 78
Parker v. Parker, 519 So. 2d 1232, 1234 (Miss. 1988) 85, 100
Parker v. Parker, 610 So. 2d 719, 720 (Fla. Dist. Ct. App. 1992) 454
Parker v. Parker, 641 So. 2d 1133, 113 (Miss. 1994).................................... 199, 200, 202, 207, 208
Parker v. Parker, 645 So. 2d 1327, 1328-31 (Miss. 1994) 430, 431
Parker v. Parker, 929 So. 2d 940, 944 (Miss. Ct. App. 2005) 133, 138, 144, 157, 176, 178, 191, 623
Parker v. Parker, 934 So. 2d 359, 360 (Miss. Ct. App. 2006)...................................261, 264, 275, 278
Parker v. Parker, 980 So. 2d 323, 327 (Miss. Ct. App. 2008)............... 142, 147, 162, 165, 178, 190, 221, 303
Parker v. South, 913 So. 2d 339, 342-43, 349-50 (Miss. Ct. App. 2005) 343, 347, 348, 351, 353, 358, 362, 393, 398
Parkinson v. Mills, 159 So. 651, 654 (Miss. 1935)..7, 61, 63 96, 97
Parks v. Parks, 914 So. 2d 337, 339-40, 343 (Miss. Ct. App. 2005)..................................173, 588, 602, 633, 674
Parsons v. Parsons, 678 So. 2d 701, 702 (Miss. 1996)................................ 170, 260, 261, 267, 270, 274, 277, 279
Passmore v. Passmore, 820 So. 2d 747, 749 (Miss. Ct. App. 2002) 342, 345, 347, 350, 389, 390, 391, 521
Pass v. Pass, 118 So. 2d 769, 772 (Miss. 1960) 420, 445
Patout v. Patout, 733 So. 2d 770 (Miss. 1999) 612
Patterson v. Patterson, 20 So. 3d 65, 68-71 (Miss. Ct. App. 2009).................................. 484, 572, 574
Patterson v. Patterson, 915 So. 2d 496, 499 (Miss. Ct. App. 2005).............................. 242, 285, 485
Patterson v. Patterson, 917 So. 2d 111, 119 (Miss. Ct. App. 2005) 175, 183, 269, 275, 278
Paxton v. Paxton, 222 So. 2d 834, 837 (Miss. 1969) 493
Payne v. Payne, 58 So. 2d 377, 378 (Miss. 1952)... 372
Pearson v. Hatcher, 279 So. 2d 654, 656 (Miss. 1973) 301, 307
Pearson v. Pearson, 11 So. 3d 178, 182 (Miss. Ct. App. 2009)............................ 341, 350, 406, 407
Pearson v. Pearson, 458 So. 2d 711, 712-13 (Miss. 1984)................................ 334, 335, 392, 400
Pearson v. Pearson, 761 So. 2d 157, 160 (Miss. 2000) 16, 20, 141, 147, 149, 219, 244, 246, 262, 263, 265, 267, 269, 274, 277, 281
Peddar v. Peddar, 683 N.E.2d 1045, 1048 (Mass. App. Ct. 1997) 570
Peeples v. Yarbrough, 475 So. 2d 1154, 1159 (Miss. 1985).. 495
Pellegrin v. Pellegrin, 478 So. 2d 306, 307 (Miss. 1985).. 342
Pender v. Pender, 945 S.W.2d 395, 397 (Ark. Ct. App. 1997) 211
Penoski v. Patterson, 440 So. 2d 45, 46 (Fla. Dist. Ct. App. 1983)... 457
Penton v. Penton, 539 So. 2d 1036, 1038 (Miss. 1989)... 560
Penton v. Penton, 2010 WL 1444537, 4-5 (Miss. Ct. App. April 13, 2010) 620
Pereira v. Pereira, 103 P. 488, 491 (Cal. 1909)... 143
Perkins v. Perkins, 787 So. 2d 1256, 1263-64 (Miss. 2001)......................... 107, 109, 590, 612
Perteet v. Sumner, 269 S.E.2d 453 (Ga. 1980).. 425
Peterson v. Peterson, 648 So. 2d 54 (Miss. 1994) 597
Peterson v. Peterson, 797 So. 2d 876, 877 (Miss. 2001)... 624
Peters v. Peters, 744 So. 2d 803, 805 (Miss. Ct. App. 1999)................................... 568, 571, 580
Peters v. Peters, 906 So. 2d 64 (Miss. Ct. App. 2004) 72, 84, 85, 87, 90, 93, 94, 95, 118, 423, 430, 608
Peters v. Ridgely, 797 So. 2d 1020, 1024 (Miss. Ct. App. 2001)... 591
Petit v. Holifield, 443 So. 2d 874, 878 (Miss. 1984) 523, 541, 542
Petschel v. Petschel, 406 N.W.2d 604, 607 (Minn. Ct. App. 1987)... 206
Petters v. Petters, 560 So. 2d 722, 726 (Miss. 1990)...211, 212, 559
Phelps v. Bing, 316 N.E.2d 775, 776-77 (Ill. 1974).. 5
Phelps v. Phelps, 937 So. 2d 974, 976-77 (Miss. Ct. App. 2006)...................... 170, 185, 275, 278, 620
Philan v. Turner, 13 So. 2d 819, 821 (Miss. 1943) 15
Phillips v. Phillips, 45 So. 3d 684, 688 (Miss. Ct. App. 2010)......... 121, 176, 179, 354, 356, 363, 364, 365, 367, 401
Phillips v. Phillips, 555 So. 2d 698, 702 (Miss. 1989)..402
Phillips v. Phillips, 904 So. 2d 999 (Miss. 2004)... 133, 138, 180, 215
Pickens v. Pickens, 490 So. 2d 872, 875 (Miss. 1986) 45, 47
Picker v. Vollenhover, 290 P.2d 789, 801 (Or. 1955) 456
Pierce v. Chandler, 855 So. 2d 455, 459 (Miss. Ct. App. 2003) 365, 408
Pierce v. Cook, 992 So. 2d 612, 615 (Miss. 2008)... 27
Pierce v. Pierce, 42 So. 3d 658, 663 (Miss. Ct. App. 2010)................... 169, 209, 239, 254, 257, 309, 558, 560, 657

TABLE OF CASES

Pierce v. Pierce, 267 So. 2d 300 (Miss. 1972) 285
Pierce v. Pierce, 648 So. 2d 523, 526 (Miss. 1994) 199, 200, 211
Pigford Brothers Construction Co. v. Evans, 83 So. 2d 622, 625 (Miss. 1955)..................2, 4, 97
Pipkin v. Dolan, 788 So. 2d 834, 837-38 (Miss. Ct. App. 2001) 307, 423, 461, 463
Pittman v. Pittman, 791 So. 2d 857, 861-62 (Miss. Ct. App. 2001)........ 134, 136, 147, 178, 220, 266, 275, 276, 427
Pittman v. Pittman, 909 So. 2d 148, 150, 152 (Miss. Ct. App. 2005) 9, 44, 460, 675
P.K.C.G. v. M.K.G., 793 So. 2d 669, 674 (Miss. Ct. App. 2001)..........................389, 520, 524
Planned Parenthood v. Casey, 505 U.S. 833, 893-94 (1992) 31
Planned Parenthood v. Casey, 510 U.S. 1309 (1994) 31
Planned Parenthood v. Danforth, 428 U.S. 52, 70 (1976) 31
P.M. v. T.D.M., 932 So. 2d 760, 785 (Miss. 2006)...324
Poe v. Poe, 711 S.W.2d 849, 857 (Ky. Ct. App. 1986)...216
Polen v. Polen, 886 S.W.2d 701, 705 (Mo. Ct. App. 1994) 424
Polk v. Polk, 559 So. 2d 1048, 1050 (Miss. 1990)..440
Polk v. Polk, 589 So. 2d 123, 130 (Miss. 1991)..356, 401
Poole v. Poole, 701 So. 2d 813, 816 (Miss. 1997) 432, 434, 472
Pool v. Pool, 989 So. 2d 920, 923, 929 (Miss. Ct. App. 2008) 33, 35, 36, 37, 71, 75, 76, 74,
    303, 304, 305, 309, 600
Pope v. Pope, 559 N.W.2d 192, 196 (Neb. 1997) 431
Pope v. Pope, 803 So. 2d 499, 502-03 (Miss. Ct. App. 2002) 290, 298, 464, 492, 494, 591
Porter v. Porter, 23 So. 3d 438, 444 (Miss. 2009)..................356, 358, 360, 365, 390, 395, 407, 618
Porter v. Porter, 195 P.2d 132, 134 (Ariz. 1948)...145, 150, 156
Porter v. Porter, 526 N.E.2d 219, 227 (Ind. Ct. App. 1988)...202
Porter v. Porter, 766 So. 2d 55, 57-58 (Miss. Ct. App. 2000)..359
Portuondo v. Portuondo, 570 So. 2d 1338, 1340 (Fla. Dist. Ct. App. 1990) 139
Posner v. Posner, 233 So. 2d 381, 384 (Fla. 1970) 668
Potter v. Greene, 973 So. 2d 291, 293-94 (Miss. Ct. App. 2008)..........................338, 362, 403
Potter v. Havlicke, 2007 WL 539534 (S.D. Ohio 2007) 642
Potts v. Potts, 700 So. 2d 321, 322 (Miss. 1997)...86, 95
Powell v. Ayars, 792 So. 2d 240 (Miss. 2001) 341
Powell v. Powell, 644 So. 2d 269, 276 (Miss. 1994)..305, 308, 628
Powell v. Powell, 976 So. 2d 358, 361-62 (Miss. Ct. App. 2008) 393, 394, 396, 398, 490
Powers v. Powers, 568 So. 2d 255, 257 (Miss. 1990) 622
Pratt v. Pratt, 977 So. 2d 386, 389 (Miss. Ct. App. 2007)........................193, 616, 618, 686
Premeaux v. Smith, 569 So. 2d 681, 685 (Miss. 1990)..494
Prescott v. Prescott, 736 So. 2d 409, 413-14 (Miss. Ct. App. 1999)............. 138, 144, 182, 207, 238, 264,
    274, 275, 277, 302, 307
Prestwood v. Hambrick, 308 So. 2d 82, 85 (Miss. 1975)..497
Price v. Dawkins, 247 S.E.2d 844, 845 (Ga. 1978)..424
Price v. McBeath, 989 So. 2d 444, 452 (Miss. Ct. App. 2008) 343, 345, 346, 347, 355, 363, 555
Price v. Price, 5 So. 3d 1151 (Miss. Ct. App. 2009) 288
Price v. Price, 22 So. 3d 331, 332 (Miss. Ct. App. 2009) 87, 89, 93
Price v. Price, 32 So. 2d 124, 126 (Miss. 1947)...557
Price v. Price, 179 So. 855, 857-58 (Miss. 1938)...100
Price v. Price, 355 S.E.2d 905, 909 (Va. Ct. App. 1987)..135
Price v. Price, 480 S.E.2d 92, 93-94 (S.C. Ct. App. 1996)..213
Pro-Choice Miss. v. Fordice, 716 So. 2d 645, 655-58 (Miss. 1998) 31
Pruett v. Prinz, 979 So. 2d 745, 750-51 (Miss. Ct. App. 2008)..................348, 358, 393, 398, 402
Pruitt v. Payne, 14 So. 3d 806, 811 (Miss. Ct. App. 2009) 388
Pucylowski v. Pucylowski, 741 So. 2d 998, 1000-01 (Miss. Ct. App. 1999).......................76, 86
Pulliam v. Smith, 872 So. 2d 790, 794-95 (Miss. Ct. App. 2004) 400
Pullis v. Linzey, 753 So. 2d 480, 482 (Miss. Ct. App. 1999) 430, 432
Purdon v. Locke, 807 So. 2d 373, 377 (Miss. 2001)...26
Purviance v. Burgess, 980 So. 2d 308 (Miss. Ct. App. 2007)...........................393, 408, 591
Purvis v. Purvis, 657 So. 2d 794, 798 (Miss. 1994) 488
Putt v. Ray Sewell Co., 481 So. 2d 785, 786 (Miss. 1985) 20

Q

Quadrini v. Quadrini, 964 So. 2d 576, 580-81 (Miss. Ct. App. 2007)....................337, 398, 619
Queen v. Queen, 551 So. 2d 197, 199-200 (Miss. 1989)...585, 592

TABLE OF CASES

R

Rafferty v. Perkins, 757 So. 2d 992, 993 (Miss. 2000) 315, 317, 322, 323, 324, 389, 509
Rains v. Gardner, 731 So. 2d 1192, 1197 (Miss. 1999) 593
Rainwater v. Rainwater, 110 So. 2d 608, 611 (Miss. 1959) 487, 489, 498
Rakestraw v. Rakestraw, 543 So. 2d 174, 176 (Miss. 1989) 380
Rakestraw v. Rakestraw, 717 So. 2d 1284, 1285-86 (Miss. Ct. App. 1998) 85, 92, 93, 118, 423, 609
Ramon v. State, 387 So. 2d 745, 750 (Miss. 1980) 607
Ramsay v. Ramsay, 87 So. 491, 493 (Miss. 1921) 290, 465, 489, 497
Rankin v. Bobo, 410 So. 2d 1326, 1329 (Miss. 1982) 309, 454, 625
Raven C. Lidman & Betsy R. Hollingsworth, 6 Geo. Mason L. Rev. 255, 276 (1998) 389
Rawlings v. Rawlings, 83 So. 146, 146 (Miss. 1919) 418
Rawson v. Buta, 609 So. 2d 426, 430-31 (Miss. 1992) 70, 71, 88, 90, 117, 603
Rayburn v. Rayburn, 749 So. 2d 185, 189 (Miss. Ct. App. 1999) 301
R.B.S. v. T.M.S., 765 So. 2d 616, 620 (Miss. Ct. App. 2000) 379
Reddell v. Reddell, 696 So. 2d 287, 288 (Miss. 1997) 133
Redding v. Redding, 150 So. 776, 776 (Miss. 1933) 489
Redd v. Redd, 774 So. 2d 492, 494-95 (Miss. Ct. App. 2000) 134, 161, 166, 171, 172, 177
Reed v. Fair, 56 So. 3d 577, 583 (Miss. Ct. App. 2010) 340, 344, 359
Reed v. Reed, 37 So. 642, 642 (Miss. 1905) 47
Reed v. Reed, 177 S.W.2d 26, 27 (Tenn. Ct. App. 1943) 73
Reed v. Reed, 839 So. 2d 565, 567 (Miss. Ct. App. 2003) 71, 86, 87, 90, 118, 119
Reed v. Seay, 42 So. 3d 474, 495 (Miss. 2010) 610
Reeves v. Reeves, 410 So. 2d 1300, 1302-03 (Miss. 1982) 243
Regan v. Regan, 507 So. 2d 54, 56-57 (Miss. 1987) 152, 181, 190
Reichert v. Reichert, 807 So. 2d 1282, 1286-87 (Miss. Ct. App. 2002) 391, 475, 598, 626, 629
Reid v. Reid, 998 So. 2d 1032, 1035 (Miss. Ct. App. 2008) 294, 424, 439, 444, 470
Rennie v. Rennie, 718 So. 2d 1091, 1093-94 (Miss. 1998) 211, 452, 453, 674, 687
Reno v. Reno, 176 So. 2d 58, 61 (Miss. 1965) 613, 677
Rester v. Rester, 5 So. 3d 1132 (Miss. Ct. App. 2008) 297
Retzer v. Retzer, 578 So. 2d 580, 590 (Miss. 1990) 236, 237, 243
R.E. v. C.E.W., 752 So. 2d 1019, 1020-21 (Miss. 1999) 316, 320, 321, 322, 324, 326
Reynolds v. Reynolds, 85 Mass. 605, 607 (1862) 10, 11
Reynolds v. Reynolds, 755 So. 2d 467, 468 (Miss. Ct. App. 1999) 75, 214
Reynolds v. Riddell, 253 So. 2d 834, 837 (Miss. 1971) 392, 566, 567
R.F. v. Lowndes County Dep't of Human Servs., 17 So. 3d 1133, 1138 (Miss. Ct. App. 2009) 389, 524
R.G.M. v. D.E.M., 410 S.E.2d 564, 566-67 (S.C. 1991) 76
Rhodes v. Johnston, 722 So. 2d 453 (Miss. 1998) 591
Rhodes v. Rhodes, 420 So. 2d 759, 761 (Miss. 1982) 496
Richardson v. Miller, 48 Miss. 311 (1873) 17
Richardson v. Richardson, 790 So. 2d 239, 242-43 (Miss. Ct. App. 2001) 49, 123, 346, 353, 358, 362, 402
Richardson v. Richardson, 856 So. 2d 426, 430-31 (Miss. Ct. App. 2003) 85
Richardson v. Richardson, 912 So. 2d 1079, 1081-82 (Miss. Ct. App. 2005) 161, 190, 341, 622, 668, 673
Richardson v. Stogner, 958 So. 2d 235, 238-39 (Miss. Ct. App. 2007) 560, 561, 564, 569, 579
Richard v. Richard, 711 So. 2d 884, 888 (Miss. 1998) 86, 91, 93, 94
Richey v. Richey, 185 So. 2d 431, 432 (Miss. 1966) 78
Rickenbach v. Kosinksi, 32 So. 3d 732, 735-36 (Fla. Dist. App. 2010) 249, 287
Riddick v. Riddick, 906 So. 2d 813 (Miss. 2004) 303, 309, 448, 467, 472, 625
Riechers v. Riechers, 679 N.Y.S.2d 233 (N.Y. Sup. Ct. 1998) 158
Riley v. Doerner, 677 So. 2d 740, 744 (Miss. 1996) 397, 406
Riley v. Riley, 884 So. 2d 791, 793 (Miss. Ct. App. 2004) 38, 39, 441, 468
Rindlaub v. Rindlaub, 125 N.W. 479 (N.D. 1910) 83
Rinehart v. Barnes, 819 So. 2d 564, 565 (Miss. Ct. App. 2002) 348, 360, 407
R.K. v. J.K., 946 So. 2d 764, 777 (Miss. 2007) 453, 483, 490, 492, 493, 681, 682
R.L.N. v. C.P.N., 931 So. 2d 620, 626-27 (Miss. Ct. App. 2005) 377, 378
R.L.S. v. A.R.S., 807 So. 2d 1251, 1261-62 (Miss. Ct. App. 2001) 398
R.L. v. G.F., 973 So. 2d 322, 324-25 (Miss Ct. App. 2008) 523
Roach v. Lang, 396 So. 2d 11, 13 (Miss. 1981) 335
Robbins v. Berry, 57 So. 2d 576, 579-80 (Miss. 1952) 15
Robbins v. Robbins, 40 So. 3d 637, 639-40 (Miss. Ct. App. 2010) 394
Roberson v. Roberson, 814 So. 2d 183, 184 (Miss. Ct. App. 2002) 358
Roberson v. Roberson, 949 So. 2d 866, 869 (Miss. Ct. App. 2007) 255, 258, 259, 265, 275, 278

TABLE OF CASES

Robertson v. Robertson, 812 So. 2d 998, 1001-02 (Miss. Ct. App. 2001) 424, 457, 467

Roberts v. Brown, 805 So. 2d 649, 653 (Miss. Ct. App. 2002) 455

Roberts v. Fuhr, 523 So. 2d 20, 19 (Miss. 1987) 410, 496, 575

Roberts v. Roberts, 381 So. 2d 1333, 1335 (Miss. 1980) 668, 672, 678, 683, 686

Roberts v. Roberts, 395 So. 2d 1035, 1037 (Ala. Civ. App. 1981) 288

Roberts v. Roberts, 866 So. 2d 474, 476-77 (Miss. Ct. App. 2003) 553, 557

Roberts v. Roberts, 924 So. 2d 550, 553-54 (Miss. Ct. App. 2005) 239, 248, 258, 259, 275,
   277, 279, 280, 427, 438, 442

Robinson v. Robinson, 72 So. 923, 923 (Miss. 1916) 236, 237, 240

Robinson v. Robinson, 481 So. 2d 855, 856 (Miss. 1986) 337, 396

Robinson v. Robinson, 554 So. 2d 300, 303 (Miss. 1989) 14, 21, 34, 35, 36, 38, 95, 96, 333, 415, 418

Robison v. Lanford, 822 So. 2d 1034, 1040 (Miss. Ct. App. 2002) 595, 394

Robison v. Lanford, 841 So. 2d 1119, 1123-24 (Miss. 2003) 396, 604, 606

Robison v. Lanford, 850 So. 2d 91, 98 (Miss. Ct. App. 2001) 394

Robison v. Robison, 722 So. 2d 601, 602, 604-05 (Miss. 1998) 85, 89, 92, 93, 94, 244, 246,
   271, 272, 275, 278, 280, 381

Rodgers v. Rodgers, 274 So. 2d 671, 673-74 (Miss. 1973) 333, 410, 496

Rodoni v. Comm'r, 105 T.C. 29 (1995) 662

Rodriguez v. Rodriguez, 2 So. 3d 720, 724-725 (Miss. Ct. App. 2009) 72, 74, 161, 177, 178,
   179, 180, 263, 267, 275, 303

Rogers v. Morin, 791 So. 2d 815, 819 (Miss. 2001) 170, 258, 264, 275, 277, 308

Rogers v. Rogers, 118 So. 619 (Miss. 1928) 11

Rogers v. Rogers, 290 So. 2d 631, 634 (Miss. 1974) 597, 601

Rogers v. Rogers. 662 So. 2d 1111, 1115-16 (Miss. 1995) 449

Rogers v. Rogers, 919 So. 2d 184, 186 (Miss. Ct. App. 2005) 193, 209, 448, 457, 460, 686

Rogers v. Sims, 671 So. 2d 714, 716 (Ala. Civ. App. 1995) 427

Roland v. State, 882 So. 2d 262, 265-66 (Miss. Ct. App. 2004) 30

Rollings v. Rosenbaum, 148 So. 384, 385 (Miss. 1933) 23

Romans v. Fulgham, 939 So. 2d 849, 852-53 (Miss. Ct. App. 2006) 340, 346, 353, 355, 359

Roman v. Roman, 193 S.W.3d 40, 49 (Tex. App. 2006) 505

Rosengarten v. Downes, 802 A. 2d 170 (Conn. 2002) 52

Rose v. Rose, 481 U.S. 619, 626 (1987) 425, 495

Ross v. Ross, 208 So. 2d 194, 196 (Miss. 1968) 558

Ross v. Ross, 314 A.2d 623, 626 (N.J. Juv. Ct. 1973) 421

Rothschild v. Hermann, 542 So. 2d 264, 265 (Miss. 1989) 566

Roth v. Roth, 406 N.W.2d 77, 79 (Minn. Ct. App. 1987) 427

Rounsaville v. Rounsaville, 732 So. 2d 909, 911 (Miss. 1999) 108

R.R. v. M.H., 689 N.E.2d 790 (Mass. 1998) 515, 517

Rubano v. DiCenzo, 759 A.2d 959, 976 (R.I. 2000) 54, 510

Rubin v. Rubin, 527 A.2d 1184, 1187 (Conn. 1987) 158

Rubisoff v. Rubisoff, 133 So. 2d 534, 537 (Miss. 1961) 290, 464, 477, 486, 494

Rudder v. Rudder, 467 So. 2d 675, 676-77 (Miss. 1985) 460

Runge v. Kohn. 430 N.E.2d 58, 62 (Ill. App. Ct. 1981) 456

Rush ex rel. Mayne, 914 So. 2d 322, 327 (Miss. Ct. App. 2005) 257, 258, 275, 279

Rushing v. Rushing, 724 So. 2d 911, 914 (Miss. 1998) 72, 74, 104, 285, 291, 294, 307, 342, 381, 495, 498, 622

Rush v. Rush, 360 So. 2d 1240, 1244 (Miss. 1978) 19

Rush v. Rush, 914 So. 2d 322, 324 (Miss. Ct. App. 2005) 94, 165, 168, 169, 175, 190,
   257, 258, 261, 266, 279, 302, 588, 599

Rush v. Rush, 932 So. 2d 794, 800 (Miss. 2006) 365, 442

Rush v. Rush, 932 So. 2d 800, 803 (Miss. Ct. App. 2005) 165, 184, 179, 189, 192, 217, 225, 226, 268, 275, 279

Russell v. Russell, 128 So. 270, 272 (Miss. 1930) 84

Russell v. Russell, 241 So. 2d 366, 367 (Miss. 1970) 236

Russell v. Russell, 724 So. 2d 1061, 1064 (Miss. Ct. App. 1999) 485

Russell v. Russell, 733 So. 2d 858, 860 (Miss. Ct. App. 1999) 170, 174, 244, 261, 270, 271,
   272, 275, 278, 306, 442

Ruth F. v. Robert B., 690 A.2d 1171 (Pa. Super. Ct. 1997) 516

Ruth v. Burchfield, 23 So. 3d 600, 606 (Miss. Ct. App. 2009) 396, 467

Rutland v. Pridgen, 493 So. 2d 952, 954-55 (Miss. 1986) 334

Rutledge v. Rutledge, 487 So. 2d 218, 220 (Miss. 1986) 364, 367, 368, 400

Ryder v. Ryder, 28 A. 1029, 1030 (Vt. 1892) 73

Rylee v. Rylee, 108 So. 2d 161, 162 (Miss. 1926) 81

719

TABLE OF CASES

S

Sabatka v. Sabatka, 511 N.W.2d 107, 111 (Neb. 1994)..432
Sabia v. Sabia, 84 A.2d 559, 561 (N.J. 1951) 78
Saddler v. Saddler, 556 So. 2d 344, 345-46 (Miss. 1990) 598, 628
Sadler's Estate, 98 So. 2d 863, 866 (Miss. 1957) 668, 669, 670
Saint v. Quick, 24 So. 3d 395, 404 (Miss. Ct. App. 2009) 380
Salemi v. Salemi, 972 So. 2d 1, 5 (Miss. Ct. App. 2007)..................193, 200, 204, 616, 618, 686
Saliba v. Saliba, 753 So. 2d 1095, 1099-00 (Miss. 2000).....................................440, 447, 450
Sallis v. Sallis, 860 So. 2d 824, 825 (Miss. Ct. App. 2003) 564
Samples v. Davis, 904 So. 2d 1061, 1065-66 (Miss. 2004)...674
Sanderson v. Sanderson, 824 So. 2d 623, 624 (Miss. 2002) 147, 244, 263, 264, 265, 270,
    271, 272, 275, 276, 281,   332
Sandifer v. Sandifer, 61 So. 2d 144, 144 (Miss. 1952)..........................85, 89, 92, 93, 117
Sandlin v. Sandlin, 699 So. 2d 1198, 1203 (Miss. 1997)...............................165, 169, 608
Sandlin v. Sandlin, 906 So. 2d 39 (Miss. Ct. App. 2004) 179, 257, 268, 274, 276, 343, 357
Sanford v. Arinder, 800 So. 2d 1267, 1270 (Miss. Ct. App. 2001).....................391, 393, 398, 626
Sanford v. Sanford, 749 So. 2d 353, 356 (Miss. Ct. App. 1999).....................................106
Sanghi v. Sanghi, 759 So. 2d 1250, 1252 (Miss. Ct. App. 2000) 595, 598, 622, 627, 628, 629
Santosky v. Kramer, 455 U.S. 745, 759 (1982)..519
Sappington v. Sappington, 147 So. 2d 494, 498 (Miss. 1962)..487
Sarda v. Sarda, 153 A.2d 305, 308 (D.C. 1959) 63
Sarphie v. Sarphie, 177 So. 358, 358 (Miss. 1937) 73, 91
Sartin v. Sartin, 405 So. 2d 84, 86 (Miss. 1981)...181, 190
Sarver v. Sarver, 687 So. 2d 749, 753-54 (Miss. 1997) 16, 149, 192, 244, 246, 265, 267,
    269, 272, 275, ,276, 281, 304
Saucier v. Saucier, 830 So. 2d 1261, 1263-64 (Miss. Ct. App. 2002) 163, 258
Sauls v. Rainey, 919 So. 2d 182, 183-84 (Miss. Ct. App. 2005) 322, 351
Saunders v. Alford, 607 So. 2d 1214, 1215 (Miss. 1992)......................................27, 28, 42
Saunders v. Saunders, 724 So. 2d 1132, 1135 (Miss. Ct. App. 1998).............................380, 491
Savelle v. Savelle, 650 So. 2d 476, 478 (Miss. 1995) 171, 200
Savell v. Morrison, 929 So. 2d 414, 417 (Miss. Ct. App. 2006).............................394, 397, 399
Savell v. Savell, 240 So. 2d 628, 629 (Miss. 1970)...92, 93
S.B. v. L.W., 793 So. 2d 656, 659-60 (Miss. Ct. App. 2001) 340, 354, 355
S.B. v. S.J.B., 609 A.2d 124, 126 (N.J. Super. Ct. Ch. Div. 1992) 76
Scaife v. Scaife, 880 So. 2d 1089, 1094 (Miss. Ct. App. 2004)...........................561, 568, 581, 593
Scalchunes v. Scalchunes, 520 N.Y.S.2d 812 (N.Y. App. Div. 1997) 166
Scally v. Scally, 802 So. 2d 128 (Miss. Ct. App. 2001)...........................90, 94, 615, 619
Schaeffer v. Schaeffer, 370 So. 2d 240, 241 (Miss. 1979)...463
Schafer v. Astrue, 641 F.3d 49, 58-59 (4th Cir. 2011)..508
Schaffer v. Haynes, 847 S.W.2d 814, 819 (Mo. Ct. App. 1992)......................................454
Schaffer v. Schaffer, 46 So. 2d 443, 444 (Miss. 1950)..464, 477, 485
Schanck v. Schanck, 717 P.2d 1, 3 (Alaska 1986)..135
Scharwath v. Scharwath, 702 So. 2d 1210, 1211 (Miss. 1997).......................................297
Schibi v. Schibi, 69 A.2d 831, 833 (Conn. 1949) 12
Schilling v. Schilling, 452 So. 2d 834, 835-36 (Miss. 1984).....................................243
Schinker v. Schinker, 68 N.Y.S.2d 470, 472 (N.Y. App. Div. 1947)..................................11
Schmidt v. Bermudez, 5 So. 3d 1064, 1074 (Miss. 2009) 601
Schonewitz v. Pack, 913 So. 2d 416, 420 (Miss. Ct. App. 2005) 369, 372, 373, 626
Schroeder v. Schroeder, 463 S.E.2d 790, 793 (N.C. Ct. App. 1995) 432
Scott v. Scott, 19 So. 589, 589 (Miss. 1896) 15
Scott v. Scott, 69 So. 2d 489, 494 (Miss. 1954) 86, 102, 118, 120, 590
Scott v. Scott, 835 So. 2d 82, 86-87 (Miss. Ct. App. 2002) 161, 163, 179, 180, 181
Scribner v. Scribner, 556 So. 2d 350, 353 (Miss. 1990) 555
Scroggins v. Riley, 758 So. 2d 467, 471 (Miss. Ct. App. 2000) 307, 390, 396, 404, 490
Scruggs v. Saterfiel, 693 So. 2d 924, 926 (Miss. 1997) 388
S.C.R. v. F.W.K., 748 So. 2d 693, 701 (Miss. 1999)..371
Scurlock v. Purser, 985 So. 2d 362, 364-65 (Miss. Ct. App. 2008) 304
S.C. v. State, 795 So. 2d 526, 532 (Miss. 2001) 378
Seale v. Seale, 863 So. 2d 996, 998-99 (Miss. Ct. App. 2004) 275, 293, 294, 295, 478
Seeley v. Stafford, 840 So. 2d 111, 113-14 (Miss. Ct. App. 2003) 431, 466
See v. See, 415 P.2d 776, 779-80 (Cal. 1966)...145

TABLE OF CASES

Seghini v. Seghini, 42 So. 3d 635, 639-40 (Miss. Ct. App. 2010)...................................169, 188, 256, 423, 489, 497

Segree v. Segree, 46 So. 3d 861, 865-66 (Miss. Ct. App. 2010)...................................169, 239, 309, 624

Self v. King, 87 So. 489, 490 (Miss. 1921)...................................23

Sellers v. Sellers, 13 So. 3d 853 (Miss. Ct. App. 2009)...................................434

Sellers v. Sellers, 22 So. 3d 299, 301 (Miss. Ct. App. 2009)...................................107, 257, 264, 276, 428, 439

Sellers v. Sellers, 638 So. 2d 481, 484 (Miss. 1994)...................................339, 360, 369, 371

Selman v. Selman, 722 So. 2d 547 (Miss. 1998)...................................170, 181, 274, 276, 430

Serio v. Serio, 94 So. 2d 799, 802 (Miss. 1957)...................................32, 81

Serton v. Serton, 819 So. 2d 15, 18 (Miss. Ct. App. 2002)...................................89, 117, 628

Sessums v. Sessums, 12 So. 3d 1146, 1147-48 (Miss. Ct. App. 2009)...................................431, 468

Sessums v. Vance, 12 So. 3d 1146, 1149 (Miss. Ct. App. 2009)...................................302

Setser v. Piazza, 644 So. 2d 1211, 1216 (Miss. 1994)...................................301, 489

Settle v. Galloway, 682 So. 2d 1032, 1034-35 (Miss. 1996)...................................385, 386

Seymour v. Seymour, 869 So. 2d 1035, 1037 (Miss. Ct. App. 2004)...................................616

Seymour v. Seymour, 960 So. 2d 513, 517, 520 (Miss. Ct. App. 2006)...................................135, 142, 166, 175, 176, 221, 258, 262, 269, 275, 278, 303, 438, 604

S.G. v. D.C., 13 So. 3d 269, 278-79 (Miss. 2009)...................................389, 390, 587, 619

Shadden v. Shadden, 11 So. 3d 761, 763 (Miss. Ct. App. 2009)...................................581

Shaeffer v. Shaeffer, 370 So. 2d 240, 242 (Miss. 1979)...................................288

Sharpe v. Sharpe, 902 P.2d 210, 216 (Wyo. 1995)...................................454

Sharplin v. Sharplin, 465 So. 2d 1072, 1072-73 (Miss. 1985)...................................252, 253

Shavers v. Shavers, 982 So. 2d 397, 404-05 (Miss. 2008)...................................87

Shaw v. Shaw, 603 So. 2d 287, 294-95 (Miss. 1992)...................................586

Shaw v. Shaw, 985 So. 2d 346 (Miss. Ct. App. 2007)...................................194, 618, 679

Shearer v. Shearer, 540 So. 2d 9, 12 (Miss. 1989)...................................296

Shelley v. Westbrooke, 37 Eng. Rep 850 (1817)...................................329

Shell v. State, 554 So. 2d 887, 893 (Miss. 1989)...................................30

Shell v. State, 595 So. 2d 1323 (Miss. 1992)...................................30

Shelnut v. Dep't of Human Servs., 9 So. 3d 359, 363-64 (Miss. 2009)...................................484, 485, 486, 562, 601

Shelton v. Shelton, 477 So. 2d 1357 (Miss. 1985)...................................71

Shelton v. Shelton, 653 So. 2d 283, 287 (Miss. 1995)...................................395, 489

Shepard v. Shepard, 769 So. 2d 242, 246 n.3 (Miss. Ct. App. 2000)...................................436

Shepherd v. Shepherd, 336 So. 2d 497, 499 (Miss. 1976)...................................17, 18

Shepherd v. Shepherd, 769 So. 2d 242, 245 (Miss. Ct. App. 2000)...................................408, 426, 466, 467, 472, 483, 490

Sheppard Pratt Physicians, P.A. v. Sakwa, 725 So. 2d 755, 758 (Miss. 1998)...................................418

Sherrer v. Sherrer, 334 U.S. 343, 352 (1948)...................................565

Sherrod v. Sherrod, 709 So. 2d 352, 356 (La. Ct. App. 1998)...................................202

Shipley v. Ferguson, 638 So. 2d 1295, 1298 (Miss. 1994)...................................463, 469

Shoemake v. Davis, 216 So. 2d 420 (Miss. 1968)...................................543

Shoffner v. Shoffner, 909 So. 2d 1245, 1248 (Miss. Ct. App. 2005)...................................138, 167, 178, 182, 183

Shorter v. Shorter, 740 So. 2d 352, 354 (Miss. Ct. App. 1999)...................................34, 37, 39, 72, 80, 81, 91, 634

Sides v. Pittman, 150 So. 211, 211-12 (Miss. 1933)...................................242, 485

Siegel v. Alexander, 477 So. 2d 1345, 1347 (Miss. 1985)...................................581

Simmons v. Simmons, 724 So. 2d 1054, 1059-60 (Miss. Ct. App. 1998)...................................149, 185, 186

Simmons v. Simmons, 773 P.2d 602, 604-05 (Colo. Ct. App. 1988)...................................125

Simpson v. Poindexter, 133 So. 2d 286, 288 (Miss. 1961)...................................25

Simpson v. Rast, 258 So. 2d 233, 236 (Miss. 1972)...................................369

Simpson v. Simpson, 490 F. 2d 803 (5th Cir. 1974)...................................641

Sims v. Sims, 85 So. 73, 74 (Miss. 1920)...................................8, 47

Sinclair v. Sinclair, 86 N.Y.S. 539 (App. Div. 1904)...................................329

Singley v. Singley, 846 So. 2d 1004, 1008 (Miss. 2002)...................................150, 155, 159, 165, 170, 176, 225

Sinquefield v. Valentine, 132 So. 81, 82 (Miss. 1931)...................................587

Sistrunk v. McKenzie, 455 So. 2d 768, 769 (Miss. 1984)...................................377, 408

Skehan v. Davidson Co., 145 So. 247, 248 (Miss. 1933)...................................20, 21

Skelton v. Skelton, 111 So. 2d 392, 393 (Miss. 1959)...................................96

Skinner v. Skinner, 509 So. 2d 867, 870 (Miss. 1987)...................................185, 217, 218, 284, 586

Skipper v. Skipper, 654 So. 2d 1181, 1183 (Fla. Dist. Ct. App. 1995)...................................424

Skokos v. Skokos, 968 S.W.2d 26, 31 (Ark. 1998)...................................158

Smithston v. Smithston, 74 So. 149, 151 (Miss. 1916)...................................83

Smith v. Bell, 876 So. 2d 1087 (Miss. Ct. App. 2004)...................................313

Smith v. Holmes, 921 So. 2d 283, 285 (Miss. 2005)...................................558, 586, 619

Smith v. Jones, 654 So. 2d 480, 491 (Miss. 1995)...................................404

TABLE OF CASES

Smith v. Little, 834 So. 2d 54, 58-59 (Miss. Ct. App. 2002) 252, 253, 282
Smith v. Little, 843 So. 2d 735, 738 (Miss. Ct. App. 2003) 493, 498
Smith v. Malouf, 722 So. 2d 490 (Miss. 1998) 49, 537
Smith v. Smith, 20 So. 3d 670, 673-74, 676-77 (Miss. 2009) 478, 479
Smith v. Smith, 25 So. 3d 369, 372-74 (Miss. Ct. App. 2009) 165, 275, 278, 303, 438, 443
Smith v. Smith, 40 So. 2d 156 (Miss. 1949) 102, 103, 120
Smith v. Smith, 47 Miss. 211, 216 (1872) 7, 96
Smith v. Smith, 229 S.W. 398, 398-99 (Mo. Ct. App. 1921) 73
Smith v. Smith, 293 So. 2d 466 (Miss. 1974) 285
Smith v. Smith, 349 So. 2d 529, 530-31 (Miss. 1977) 242, 455
Smith v. Smith, 530 So. 2d 1389, 1390 (Ala. 1988) 125
Smith v. Smith, 545 So. 2d 725, 727 (Miss. 1989) 410, 482
Smith v. Smith, 607 So. 2d 122, 127 (Miss. 1992) 242, 589, 591
Smith v. Smith, 614 So. 2d 394, 395-96 (Miss. 1993) 93, 94, 302, 431
Smith v. Smith, 631 So. 2d 252, 255 (Ala. Civ. App. 1993) 424
Smith v. Smith, 656 So. 2d 1143, 1147 (Miss. 1995) 668, 670, 673
Smith v. Smith, 856 So. 2d 717, 719 (Miss. Ct. App. 2003) 133, 255
Smith v. Smith, 994 So. 2d 882, 886 (Miss. Ct. App. 2008) 89, 117, 141, 147, 150, 169, 177, 191
Smith v. Todd, 464 So. 2d 1155, 1158 (Miss. 1985) 405
Smith v. Watson, 425 So. 2d 1030, 1032 (Miss. 1983) 334, 372, 587
Smith v. Weir, 387 So. 2d 761, 763 (Miss. 1980) 2, 5, 97
S.N.C. v. J.R.D., 755 So. 2d 1077, 1080-81 (Miss. 2000) 380, 390, 391, 519, 520, 521,
   522, 523, 524, 527, 529, 540
Sneed v. Sneed, 842 N.E.2d 1095, 1101 (Ohio Ct. App. 2005) 568
Sobeiske v. Preslar, 755 So. 2d 410, 411-12 (Miss. 2000) 341, 355, 359, 407, 444
Sobol v. Sobol, 150 N.Y.S. 248, 250-51 (N.Y. Sup. Ct. 1914) 11
Solomon v. Robertson, 980 So. 2d 319, 321 (Miss. Ct. App. 2008) 385, 386
Sootin v. Sootin, 737 So. 2d 1022, 1026-27 (Miss. Ct. App. 1998) 360
Sosna v. Iowa, 419 U.S. 393, 410 (1975) 555
Southerland v. Southerland, 816 So. 2d 1004, 1006 (Miss. 2002) 438
Southerland v. Southerland, 875 So. 2d 204, 207 (Miss. 2004) 438
Southern v. Glenn, 568 So. 2d 281, 284 (Miss. 1990) 211, 562
Spahn v. Spahn, 959 So. 2d 8, 10, 15 (Miss. Ct. App. 2006) 132, 135, 140, 150, 168, 169,
   219, 220, 275, 282, 428, 303, 429
Spalding v. Spalding, 691 So. 2d 435, 439 (Miss. 1997) 294, 478
Spalding v. Spalding, 886 So. 2d 1075, 1077 (Fla. Dist. Ct. App. 2004) 573
Speed v. Speed, 757 So. 2d 221, 223 (Miss. 2000) 284, 685
Spence v. Spence, 930 So. 2d 415, 418-19 (Miss. Ct. App. 2005) 74, 75, 76, 95
Speranza v. Repro Lab, Inc., 875 N.Y.S.2d 449, 453 (N.Y. App. Div. 2009) 506
Spradling v. Spradling, 362 So. 2d 620, 624 (Miss. 1978) 288, 292, 295
Spragins v. Huber Farm Service, Inc., 542 F. Supp. 166, 172 (N.D. Miss. 1982) 634
Sproles v. Sproles, 782 So. 2d 742, 745 (Miss. 2001) 72, 74, 82, 87, 89, 93, 94, 117, 168, 174, 177
S.R.B.R. v. Harrison County Dep't of Human Servs., 798 So. 2d 437, 442-43 (Miss. 2001) 523
S. Ry. Co. v. Baskette, 133 S.W.2d 498, 502-03 (Tenn. 1939) 64
S.S. v. S.H., 44 So. 3d 1054, 1056-57 (Miss. Ct. App. 2010) 454
Stacy v. Ross, 798 So. 2d 1275, 1279-80 (Miss. 2001) 384, 385
Staggs v. Staggs, 919 So. 2d 112, 119-20 (Miss. Ct. App. 2005) 396, 400, 402, 443, 466, 467
Stainback v. Stainback, 396 S.E.2d 686, 689-90 (Va. Ct. App. 1990) 139
Stallings v. Stallings, 393 N.E.2d 1065, 1067 (Ill. App. Ct. 1979) 135
Stanard v. Bolin, 565 P.2d 94, 97-98 (Wash. 1977) 28
Stanaway v. Stanaway, 245 N.W.2d 723, 724 (Mich. Ct. App. 1976) 456
Stanford v. Stanford, 734 So. 2d 359, 360 (Miss. Ct. App. 1999) 21, 33, 36, 38, 419
Stanley v. Stanley, 29 So. 2d 641, 644-45 (Miss. 1947) 62
Stanton v. Stanton, 421 U.S. 7, 14 (1975) 5
Stark v. Anderson, 748 So. 2d 838, 843 (Miss. Ct. App. 1999) 49, 346, 358, 359, 400, 402, 612
Starr v. Starr, 39 So. 2d 520, 522-23 (Miss. 1949) 32, 81, 103
State of Alaska v. Bromely, 987 P. 2d 183, 190 (Alas. 1999) 573
State v. Guzman, 842 P.2d 660 (Idaho 1992) 125
State v. Jenkins, 3 A.3d 806 (Conn. 2010) 6, 50
State v. Saunders, 381 A.2d 333, 339 (N.J. 1977) 43
State v. Winslow, 45 So. 2d 574, 576 (Miss. 1950) 4, 59
Stauffer v. Stauffer, 379 So. 2d 922, 924-25 (Miss. 1980) 410, 482, 492, 496

TABLE OF CASES

Steen v. Kirkpatrick, 36 So. 140, 141 (Miss. 1904)..672

Steen v. Steen, 641 So. 2d 1167, 1169 (Miss. 1994)......................21, 34, 38, 90, 95, 118, 333, 419

Stegienko v. Stegienko, 295 N.W. 252, 254 (Mich. 1940)...10

Steiner v. Steiner, 788 So. 3d 771, 776 (Miss. 2001)......................255, 285, 289, 294, 460, 681

Stein v. Stein, 11 So. 3d 1288, 1292 (Miss. Ct. App. 2009)...............86, 89, 93, 94, 117, 118, 178

Stennis v. Stennis, 464 So. 2d 1161, 1161 (Miss. 1985)...71, 95

Steve Jackson Games, Inc. v. United States Secret Service, 36 F.3d 457, 464 (5th Cir. 1994)...........642

Stevenson v. Renardet, 35 So. 576 (Miss. 1904)...668

Steven S. v. Deborah D., 25 Cal. Rptr. 3d 482, 486 (Cal. Ct. App. 2005).......................................511

Stevens v. Stevens, 924 So. 2d 645, 649 (Miss. Ct. App. 2006).....245, 246, 255, 264, 269, 270, 271, 272, 275, 278

Steverson v. Steverson, 846 So. 2d 304, 306 (Miss. Ct. App. 2003)................................343, 352, 355

Stevison v. Woods, 560 So. 2d 176, 180 (Miss. 1990)..376, 400, 409

Stewart v. Evans, 136 P.3d 524, 528 (Mont. 2006)..575

Stewart v. Stewart, 2 So. 3d 770, 773-74 (Miss. Ct. App. 2009)..................142, 148, 150, 221, 222, 303

Stewart v. Stewart, 645 So. 2d 1319 (Miss. 1994)...641

Stewart v. Stewart, 793 P.2d 813, 814-15 (Mont. 1990)..428

Stewart v. Stewart, 864 So. 2d 934, 937-38 (Miss. 2003)...147, 159, 160

Stewart v. Stewart, 937 So. 2d 487, 489 (Miss. Ct. App. 2006)...347

Stigler v. Stigler, 48 So. 3d 547, 550-54 (Miss. Ct. App. 2009).....................................448, 458, 494

Stinson v. Stinson, 738 So. 2d 1259, 1263 (Miss. Ct. App. 1999)...................................423, 591, 593

Stockton v. Stockton, 203 So. 2d 806, 807 (Miss. 1967)...92, 94

Stoker v. Huggins, 471 So. 2d 1228, 1229-1300 (Miss. 1985)...371

Stokes v. Maris, 596 So. 2d 879, 882 (Miss. 1992)...420, 448, 452

Stone v. Stone, 32 So. 2d 278, 279 (Fla. 1947)...12

Stone v. Stone, 385 So. 2d 610, 614 (Miss. 1980)...678, 682

Stone v. Stone, 824 So. 2d 645, 647 (Miss. Ct. App. 2002)..92, 93, 136

Story v. Allen, 7 So. 2d 3d 295, 298-99 (Miss. Ct. App. 2008)...403

Stouffer v. Stouffer, 867 P.2d 226, 227 (Haw. Ct. App. 1994)..204, 206

Stowers v. Humphrey, 576 So. 2d 138, 141-42 (Miss. 1991)...581

Strack v. Sticklin, 959 So. 2d 1, 4 (Miss. Ct. App. 2006)...............479, 480, 483, 485, 486, 487

Strain v. Strain, 847 So. 2d 276, 278 (Miss. Ct. App. 2003)............................382, 409, 482, 492

Strange v. Strange, 43 So. 3d 1169, 1172 (Miss. Ct. App. 2010)...........376, 423, 434, 436, 467

Streb v. Streb, 774 P.2d 798, 800 (Alaska 1989)...420

Street v. Street, 936 So. 2d 1002, 1008-09 (Miss. Ct. App. 2006)...............255, 262, 343, 347, 615

Stribling v. Stribling, 215 So. 2d 869, 870 (Miss. 1968...102

Stribling v. Stribling, 215 So. 2d 869, 870 (Miss. 1968)...120

Stribling v. Stribling, 906 So. 2d 863, 868-69 (Miss. Ct. App. 2005).....102, 178, 179, 231, 255, 266, 307, 356, 452

Stribling v. Stribling, 960 So. 2d 556, 561-62 (Miss. Ct. App. 2007)..............................487, 492, 497

Striebeck v. Striebeck, 5 So. 3d 450, 452 (Miss. Ct. App. 2008)..137, 156

Striebeck v. Striebeck, 911 So. 2d 628, 632-33 (Miss. Ct. App. 2005)....................132, 134, 136, 137, 156,
174, 176, 179, 239, 263, 438, 443, 446, 447

Stringer v. Stringer, 46 So. 2d 791, 791-92 (Miss. 1950)...95

Strong v. Strong, 981 So. 2d 1052, 1055 (Miss. Ct. App. 2008)......................................178, 184, 416

Stroud v. Stroud, 758 So. 2d 502, 503-04 (Miss. Ct. App. 2000).......................................433, 472

Stuart v. Stuart, 421 N.W. 2d 505, 507 (Wis. 1988)...125

Stuart v. Stuart, 956 So. 2d 295, 298-99 (Miss. Ct. App. 2006).....................261, 263, 266, 275, 278, 303, 306, 601

Studdard v. Studdard, 894 So. 2d 615 (Miss. Ct. App. 2004)...162

Sturgis v. Sturgis, 792 So. 2d 1020, 1025 (Miss. Ct. App. 2001)...393

Stutts v. Estate of Stutts, 194 So. 2d 229, 231 (Miss. 1967)...8, 64

Suber v. Suber, 936 So. 2d 945, 948 (Miss. Ct. App. 2006)........................378, 430, 433, 607, 611

Sudduth v. Mowdy, 991 So. 2d 1241, 1244 (Miss. Ct. App. 2008)...................................397, 402, 404

Suess v. Suess, 718 So. 2d 1126, 1128 (Miss. Ct. App. 1998)...........................305, 307, 408, 627

Sullivan v. Beason, 37 So. 2d 706 (Miss. Ct. App. 2010)..................49, 123, 358, 399, 402, 406

Sullivan v. Pouncey, 469 So. 2d 1233, 1234 (Miss. 1985)...109, 678

Sullivan v. Stringer, 736 So. 2d 514, 517-18 (Miss. Ct. App. 1999)...402

Sullivan v. Sullivan, 43 So. 3d 536, 539 (Miss. Ct. App. 2010)......................................169, 304, 601

Sullivan v. Sullivan, 942 So. 2d 305, 307 (Miss. Ct. App. 2006)....................................166, 193, 615, 623

Sullivan v. Sullivan, 990 So. 2d 783, 786 (Miss. Ct. App. 2008)...................137, 163, 175, 176, 177, 179, 268, 304

Sumrall v. Sumrall, 970 So. 2d 254, 257-58 (Miss. Ct. App. 2007)....................345, 349, 354, 360, 361

Surrogate Parenting Ass'n. v. Commonwealth ex rel. Armstrong, 704 S.W.2d 209 (Ky. 1986)...................515, 517

Suter v. Suter, 16 So. 673, 674 (Miss. 1894)...81

Swaney v. Swaney, 962 So. 2d 105, 110 (Miss. Ct. App. 2007)...565

TABLE OF CASES

Swartzfager v. Derrick, 942 So. 2d 255, 259 (Miss. 2006) 336
Swiderski v. Swiderski, 18 So. 3d 280, 285-86 (Miss. Ct. App. 2009) 376, 434
Switzer v. Switzer, 460 So. 2d 843, 845 (Miss. 1984) 613, 678, 682, 683

T

Tacchi v. Tacchi, 195 N.Y.S.2d 892, 894-95 (N.Y. Sup. Ct. 1959) 11
Tackett v. Tackett, 967 So. 2d 1264, 1267 (Miss. Ct. App. 2007) 34, 36, 69, 84, 95
Talbert v. Talbert, 759 So. 2d 1105, 1108 (Miss. 1999) 69, 74, 75, 76, 86, 95, 118, 608, 609
Tanner v. Roland, 598 So. 2d 783, 785 (Miss. 1992) 290, 464, 494
Tanner v. Tanner, 956 So. 2d 1106, 1108-09 (Miss. Ct. App. 2007) 349, 390
T.A.P., 742 So. 2d 1095, 1104-05 (Miss. 1999) 378
Tatum v. Tatum, 54 So. 3d 855, 860-62 (Miss. Ct. App. 2010) 172, 174, 257, 259, 265, 269, 302, 427
Taylor v. Taylor, 108 So. 2d 872, 873-74 (Miss. 1959) 95
Taylor v. Taylor, 317 So. 2d 422, 423 (Miss. 1975) 47
Taylor v. Taylor, 348 So. 2d 1341, 1342 (Miss. 1977) 290, 465
Taylor v. Taylor, 392 So. 2d 1145, 1147 (Miss. 1981) 241, 286, 290, 683, 685
Taylor v. Taylor, 736 S.W.2d 388, 391 (Mo. 1987) 135
Taylor v. Taylor, 909 So. 2d 1280, 1281 (Miss. Ct. App. 2005) 342, 356, 359, 360
T.B. v. L.R.M., 874 A.2d 34, 38 (Pa. Super. Ct. 2005) 54, 510
T.B. v. L.R.M., 890 A.2d 1060 (Pa. 2005) 54, 510
Tedford v. Dempsey, 437 So. 2d 410, 417 (Miss. 1983) 457, 462, 463, 466, 468, 469, 613, 682
Tedford v. Tedford, 856 So. 2d 753 (Miss. Ct. App. 2003) 86, 90, 93, 94
Terpstra v. Terpstra, 588 N.E.2d 592, 595-96 (Ind. Ct. App. 1992) 439
Tevis v. Tevis, 400 A.2d 1189, 1196 (N.J. 1979) 125
Thames v. Thames, 100 So. 2d 868, 870 (Miss. 1958) 68, 91, 101, 102, 119, 120
Thibodeaux v. Thibodeaux, 712 So. 2d 1024, 1028 (La. Ct. App. 1998) 215
Thomas S. v. Robin Y., 618 N.Y.S.2d 356, 362 (N.Y. App. Div. 1995) 511
Thomas v. Byars, 947 So. 2d 375, 379 (Miss. Ct. App. 2007) 417, 553, 587, 588, 622
Thomas v. Thomas, 4 S.W.3d 517, 524-25 (Ark. Ct. App. 1999) 201, 203, 204
Thomas v. Thomas, 377 S.E.2d 666, 669 (Ga. 1989) 137
Thompson v. Clay, 82 So. 1, 2 (Miss. 1919) 8
Thompson v. Thompson, 527 So. 2d 617, 621-22 (Miss. 1988) 34, 35, 36, 37
Thompson v. Thompson, 576 So. 2d 267, 269 (Fla. 1991) 155, 224
Thompson v. Thompson, 799 So. 2d 919, 924 (Miss. Ct. App. 2001) 336
Thompson v. Thompson, 815 So. 2d 466, 468 (Miss. Ct. App. 2002) 168, 170, 175, 176, 181
Thompson v. Thompson, 816 So. 2d 417, 419 (Miss. Ct. App. 2002) 179, 256
Thompson v. Thompson, 894 So. 2d 603 (Miss. Ct. App. 2004) 133, 158, 168, 436, 624
Thoms v. Thoms, 928 So. 2d 852, 854-55 (Miss. 2006) 324
Thornell v. Thornell, 860 So. 2d 1241, 1243 (Miss. Ct. App. 2003) 393
Thornhill v. Van Dan, 918 So. 2d 725, 733 (Miss. Ct. App.) 403
Thrasher v. Thrasher, 91 So. 2d 543, 544 (Miss. 1956) 79
Thrash v. Thrash, 385 So. 2d 961, 964 (Miss. 1980) 614
Thrift v. Thrift, 760 So. 2d 732, 735 (Miss. 2000) 570
Thurman v. Johnson, 998 So. 2d 1026, 1028-30 (Miss. Ct. App. 2008) 352, 368
Thurman v. Thurman, 559 So. 2d 1014, 1016-17 (Miss. 1990) 473, 489, 494
Thweatt v. Thweatt, 4 So. 3d 1085, 1090 (Miss. Ct. App. 2009) 18
Tilley v. Tilley, 610 So. 2d 348, 352 (Miss. 1992) 272, 441
Tillman v. Tillman, 716 So. 2d 1090, 1095 (Miss. 1998) 134, 174, 244, 275, 278
Tillman v. Tillman, 791 So. 2d 285, 287 (Miss. Ct. App. 2001) 282, 685
Tillman v. Tillman, 809 So. 2d 767, 770 (Miss. Ct. App. 2002) 290, 294, 297, 464
Timmons v. Timmons, 605 So. 2d 1162, 1166 (La. Ct. App. 1992) 424
Tingle v. Tingle, 573 So. 2d 1389, 1391 (Miss. 1990) 288, 432, 464
Tiser v. McCain, 74 So. 660, 661 (Miss. 1917) 19
T.K. v. H.K., 24 So. 3d 1055, 1064-65 (Miss. Ct. App. 2010) 127, 362, 403
Tollison v. Tollison, 841 So. 2d 1062, 1065 (Miss. 2003) 392, 519, 567
Torrence v. Moore, 455 So. 2d 778, 780 (Miss. 1984) 352, 408
Torwich v. Torwich, 660 A.2d 1214, 1214 (N.J. Super. Ct. App. Div. 1995) 213
Touchstone v. Touchstone, 682 So. 2d 374, 380 (Miss. 1996) 608
Toups v. Toups, 708 So. 2d 849, 850 (La. Ct. App. 1998) 433
Towles v. Towles, 137 So. 2d 182, 184-85 (Miss. 1962) 288, 293, 431, 433
Townes v. Manyfield, 883 So. 2d 93, 97 (Miss. 2004) 384, 386

TABLE OF CASES

Townsend v. Townsend, 859 So. 2d 370, 379 (Miss. 2003)..................................616
Tramel v. Tramel, 740 So. 2d 286, 289-91 (Miss. 1999) 153
Trammel v. United States, 445 U.S. 40, 44 (1980) 30
Traub v. Johnson, 536 So. 2d 25, 27 (Miss. 1988) 678
Travers v. Reinhardt, 205 U.S. 423, 437 (1907)..2
Travis v. Travis, 795 P.2d 96, 100 (Okla. 1990)..155, 225
Traxler v. Traxler, 730 So. 2d 1098, 1102-03 (Miss. 1998)...........157, 215, 262, 275, 278, 447, 448, 471
Tribble v. Gregory, 288 So. 2d 13, 16-17 (Miss. 1974)..................................25, 26
Trigg v. Trigg, 498 So. 2d 334, 336 (Miss. 1986) 18
Trim v. Trim, 33 So. 3d 471, 472-74, 478-79 (Miss. 2010) 194, 594, 619, 679
Triple C Transport, Inc. v. Dickens, 870 So. 2d 1195 (Miss. 2004)...................596
Tritle v. Tritle, 956 So. 2d 369, 274-75 (Miss. Ct. App. 2007)...........255, 269, 275, 278, 332, 349, 351, 353, 358
Trovato v. Trovato, 649 So. 2d 815, 817-18 (Miss. 1995) 181
Troxel v. Granville, 530 U.S. 57, 60 (2000)..383
Trulock v. Freeh, 275 F.3d 391, 403 (4th Cir. 2001)...642
T.T.W. v. C.C., 839 So. 2d 501, 505 (Miss. 2003)...384
Tucker v. Tucker, 19 So. 955, 956 (Miss. 1896)..27
Tucker v. Tucker, 453 So. 2d 1294, 1297 (Miss. 1984)...............................394, 395
Tuggle v. Williamson, 450 So. 2d 93, 95 (Miss. 1984).......................................638
Turner v. Avery, 113 A. 710, 710-11 (N.J. Ch. 1921) 10
Turner v. Turner, 331 So. 2d 903, 905-06 (Miss. 1976).....................................372
Turner v. Turner, 744 So. 2d 332, 334 (Miss. Ct. App. 1999) 305, 423, 433, 435, 445, 467, 472
Turner v. Turner, 824 So. 2d 652, 657 (Miss. Ct. App. 2002)..............368, 462, 463, 464
Turnley v. Turnley, 726 So. 2d 1258, 1266 (Miss. Ct. App. 1998).........179, 249, 255, 259, 268, 270, 275, 276, 280
Turpin v. Turpin, 699 So. 2d 560, 563 (Miss. 1997)...177
Tutor v. Tutor, 494 So. 2d 362, 363 (Miss. 1987) 243, 284
T. v. T., 224 S.E.2d 148, 151 (Va. 1976)...421
Tynes v. Tynes, 860 So. 2d 325, 330-31 (Miss. Ct. App. 2003).....................153, 168, 214, 301, 302, 305
Tyrone v. Tyrone, 32 So. 3d 1206, 1212-14 (Miss. Ct. App. 2009) 107

U

Uglem v. Uglem, 831 So. 2d 1175, 1177-78 (Miss. Ct. App. 2002) 159, 191
Ullah v. Ullah, 555 N.Y.S.2d 834, 835-36 (N.Y. App. Div. 1990) 160
United States v. Diogo, 320 F.2d 898, 909 (2d Cir. 1963) 12
United States v. Lutwak, 195 F.2d 748, 753 (7th Cir. 1952)...............................12
United States v. Rizzo, 583 F.2d 907, 909 (7th Cir. 1978) 641
United States v. Schrimsher, 493 F.2d 848, 850-51 (5th Cir. 1974) 641
U.S. v. Pillor, 387 F. Supp. 2d 1053, 1056 (N.D. Cal. 2005)...........................501

V

Van Camp v. Van Camp, 199 P. 885, 888-89 (Cal. 1921) 143
Vance v. Lincoln County Dep't of Pub. Welfare, 582 So. 2d 414, 418 (Miss. 1991) 525
Vance v. Vance, 20 So. 2d 825, 827 (Miss. 1945)..590
Vanderbilt v. Vanderbilt, 354 U.S. 416, 418 (1957)..565
Van Norman v. Van Norman, 38 So. 2d 452, 454 (Miss. 1949) 81
Varner v. Varner, 588 So. 2d 428, 432-33 (Miss. 1991)..........455, 464, 470, 478, 494
Varner v. Varner, 666 So. 2d 493, 497 (Miss. 1995) 285, 291, 305, 431, 488, 498
Varnum v. Brien, 763 N.W.2d 862 (Iowa 2009)...6, 50
Vaughn v. Davis, 36 So. 3d 1261, 1267 (Miss. 2010) 625
Vaughn v. Vaughn, 16 So. 2d 23, 24 (Miss. 1943)..5
Vaughn v. Vaughn, 36 So. 3d 1261, 1262, 1264 (Miss. 2010) 346, 370, 373
Vaughn v. Vaughn, 118 So. 2d 620, 622 (Miss. 1960)...17
Vaughn v. Vaughn, 798 So. 2d 431, 434-35 ....170, 221, 258, 275, 278, 442
Venegas v. Gurganus, 911 So. 2d 562 (Miss. Ct. App. 2005) 555, 569, 593, 598, 629
Vernoff v. Astrue, 568 F.3d 1102, 1107-08 (9th Cir. 2009).........................507, 508
Vetrano v. Gardner, 290 F. Supp. 200, 205 (N.D. Miss. 1968) 8
Vice v. Dep't of Human Servs., 702 So. 2d 397, 400 (Miss. 1997)....................486
Villasenor v. Villasenor, 657 P.2d 889, 892 (Ariz. Ct. App. 1982) 154
Vincent v. Griffin, 872 So. 2d 676 (Miss. 2004) 630
Vinson v. Vidal, 28 So. 3d 614, 617 (Miss. Ct. App. 2009).......................385, 386

TABLE OF CASES

Vockroth v. Vockroth, 200 So. 2d 459, 464 (Miss. 1967) 409, 482
Voda v. Voda, 731 So. 2d 1152 (Miss. 1999) 170, 256, 275, 277, 622
Vogel v. Vogel, 549 N.Y.S.2d 438, 440 (N.Y. App. Div. 1989) 139
Vronsky v. Presley, 526 So. 2d 518, 522 (Miss. 1988) 316

W

Wade v. Lee, 471 So. 2d 1213, 1215 (Miss. 1985) 335, 392
Wade v. Wade, 967 So. 2d 682, 684 (Miss. Ct. App. 2007) 615
Wadlow v. Wadlow, 491 A.2d 757, 762 (N.J. Super. Ct. App. Div. 1985) 145
Waggoner v. Waggoner, 531 N.E.2d 1188, 1189 (Ind. Ct. App. 1988) 135
Waldron v. Waldron, 743 So. 2d 1064, 1065 (Miss. Ct. App. 1999) 248, 249, 250, 254, 287, 685
Walker v. Matthews, 3 So. 2d 820, 824 (Miss. 1941) 2, 3, 8, 42, 62, 97
Walker v. Walker, 36 So. 3d 483, 490-91 (Miss. Ct. App. 2010) 183
Walker v. Walker, 105 So. 753, 756 (Miss. 1925) 99
Wallace v. Bond, 745 So. 2d 844, 847 (Miss. 1999) 422, 423, 462, 463, 467
Wallace v. Delaney, 962 P.2d 187, 191 (Alaska 1998) 571
Wallace v. Wallace, 12 So. 3d 572 (Miss. Ct. App. 2009) 297, 299
Wallace v. Wallace, 965 So. 2d 737, 741 (Miss. Ct. App. 2007) 436, 440, 443, 447, 448,
    450, 456, 464, 466, 467, 468, 471
Waller v. Waller, 754 So. 2d 1181, 1181 (Miss. 2000) 333, 367
Wallmark v. Wallmark, 863 So. 2d 68, 71 (Miss. Ct. App. 2003) 170, 275, 276
Waltenburg v. Waltenburg, 270 S.W.3d 308, 316-18 (Tex. Ct. App. 2008) 576
Walters v. Walters, 383 So. 2d 827, 829 (Miss. 1980) 477, 495
Walters v. Walters, 519 So. 2d 427, 428 (Miss. 1988) 334, 575
Walters v. Walters, 956 So. 2d 1050, 1053 (Miss. Ct. App. 2007) 614, 620
Walter v. Wilson, 228 So. 2d 597, 598 (Miss. 1969) 27, 28
Walther v. Walther, 709 P.2d 387, 388 (Utah 1985) 125
Walton v. Snyder, 984 So. 2d 343 (Miss. Ct. App. 2007) 424, 442, 462, 463, 464, 466, 467, 468, 473, 594, 618
Walton v. Walton, 25 So. 166, 168 (Miss. 1899) 78
Ward v. Dulaney, 23 Miss. 410, 414 (1852) 71
Ward v. Ward, 453 N.W.2d 729, 732 (Minn. Ct. App. 1990) 152
Ward v. Ward, 825 So. 2d 713, 718 (Miss. Ct. App. 2002) 161, 162
Ware v. Ware, 7 So. 3d 271, 273-74 (Miss. Ct. App. 2008) 100, 102, 669, 670
Waring v Waring, 722 So. 2d 723, 725-26 (Miss. Ct. App. 1998) 141, 189
Waring v. Waring, 747 So. 2d 252 (Miss. 1999) 142, 221
Warner v. Warner, 167 So. 615 (Miss. 1936) 679
Warner v. Warner, 651 So. 2d 1339, 1340 (La. 1995) 212
Warren v. Joeckel, 656 P. 2d 329, 332 (Or. Ct. App. 1982) 323
Warren v. Warren, 563 N.E.2d 633, 634-35 (Ind. Ct. App. 1990) 212
Warren v. Warren, 815 So. 2d 457, 460 (Miss. Ct. App. 2002) 200, 215, 679, 680, 681
Waskam v. Waskam, 31 Miss. 154, 155 (1856) 81
W.A.S. v. A.L.G., 949 So. 2d 31, 35 (Miss. 2007) 523, 526, 540, 543
Watkins v. Watkins, 337 So. 2d 723, 724-25 (Miss. 1976) 420, 452
Watkins v. Watkins, 748 So. 2d 808, 810 (Miss. Ct. App. 1999) 305, 434, 445, 472, 591
Watkins v. Watkins, 802 So. 2d 145, 147 (Miss. Ct. App. 2001) 571
Watkins v. Watkins, 942 So. 2d 224, 228-29 (Miss. Ct. App. 2006) 39, 487, 490, 498
Watkins v. Watkins, 957 So. 2d 440, 443-44 (Miss. Ct. App. 2007) 39
Watson v. Duncan, 37 So. 125, 127 (Miss. 1904) 668
Watson v. Watson, 143 S.W.2d 349, 350 (Mo. Ct. App. 1940) 10
Watson v. Watson, 724 So. 2d 350 (Miss. 1998) 267, 274, 277, 279, 302
Watson v. Watson, 882 So. 2d 95, 105-06 (Miss. 2004) 139, 155, 165, 177, 223, 225, 477
Watts v. Watts, 405 N.W.2d 303, 310-11 (Wis. 1987) 43
Watts v. Watts, 854 So. 2d 11, 13 (Miss. Ct. App. 2003) 343, 344, 345, 349, 351
Weakley v. Weakley, 731 S.W.2d 243, 246 (Ky. 1987) 152
Weathersby v. Weathersby, 693 So. 2d 1348, 1351 (Miss. 1997) 194, 242, 298, 477, 682, 683, 685
Weaver v. Parks, 947 So. 2d 1009, 1013-14 (Miss. Ct. App. 2006) 626
Webb v. Webb, 974 So. 2d 274, 277-78 (Miss. Ct. App. 2008) 343, 348, 349, 353, 360
Webster v. Webster, 17 So. 3d 602, 606-07 (Miss. Ct. App. 2009) 471
Weeks v. Weeks, 29 So. 3d 80, 83 (Miss. Ct. App. 2009) 282, 288, 289, 292, 303, 305,
    423, 447, 448, 462, 473, 616, 683
Weeks v. Weeks, 556 So. 2d 348, 349 (Miss. 1990) 603

TABLE OF CASES

Weeks v. Weeks, 654 So. 2d 33, 35 (Miss. 1995) 4, 59, 62, 98
Weeks v. Weeks, 832 So. 2d 583, 586 (Miss. Ct. App. 2002) 170, 172, 175, 240, 244,
255, 259, 266, 267, 275, 276
Weeks v. Weeks, 989 So. 2d 408, 410-11 (Miss. Ct. App. 2008) 123, 342, 353, 358, 360
Weigand v. Houghton, 730 So. 2d 581, 586-87 (Miss. 1999) 354, 381
Weilmunster v. Weilmunster, 858 P. 2d 766, 771 (Idaho Ct. App. 1993) 145, 150
Weisfeld v. Weisfeld, 513 So. 2d 1278, 1280-81 (Fla. Dist. Ct. App. 1987) 153
Weiss v. Weiss, 579 So. 2d 539, 541-42 (Miss. 1991) 37, 39, 565
Welch v. Welch, 519 N.W.2d 262, 271 (Neb. 1994) 454
Welch v. Welch, 755 So. 2d 6, 9 (Miss. Ct. App. 1999) 173, 175, 176, 263, 269, 275
Welder v. Welder, 794 S.W.2d 420, 426 (Tex. App. 1990) 145, 156
Wells v. Talham, 194 N.W. 36, 37, 40 (Wis. 1923) 11
Wells v. Wells, 35 So. 3d 1250, 1252 (Miss. Ct. App. 2010) 136, 178, 221, 261, 264, 265,
303, 322, 346, 348, 355, 361, 430, 431, 433, 509
Wells v. Wells, 800 So. 2d 1239, 1241 (Miss. Ct. App. 2001) 165, 167, 172, 175, 256,
269, 283, 284, 303, 305, 434, 444, 445
Wesson v. Wesson, 818 So. 2d 1272, 1272 (Miss. Ct. App. 2002) 153, 192, 260, 267, 275,
276, 279, 282, 444, 453, 479, 489, 613
Westbrook v. Oglesbee, 606 So. 2d 1142, 1145 (Miss. 1992) 369, 371
Westbrook v. Westbrook, 364 S.E.2d 523, 527 (Va. Ct. App. 1988) 147
Westerburg v. Westerburg, 853 So. 2d 826, 827-29 (Miss. Ct. App. 2003) 490, 491
Westgate v. Westgate, 887 P.2d 737, 789 (Nev. 1994) 454
Westmoreland v. Jackson, 401 So. 2d 725, 726 (Miss. 1985) 484
Weston v. Mounts, 789 So. 2d 822, 826 (Miss. Ct. App. 2001) 180, 282, 490, 498
West v. West. 23 So. 3d 558, 561-62 (Miss. Ct. App. 2009) 423, 458
West v. West, 891 So. 2d 203, 210-11 (Miss. 2004) 188, 227, 252, 253, 284, 600, 674, 681, 683, 684
Wheat v. Koustovalas, 42 So. 3d 606, 608 (Miss. Ct. App. 2010) 332, 344, 350, 355
Wheat v. Wheat, 37 So. 3d 632, 639 (Miss. 2010) 137, 141, 207, 422, 423, 625
Whitehead v. Kirk, 64 So. 658, 658 (Miss. 1914) 19
Whitehurst v. State, 540 So. 2d 1319, 1324 (Miss. 1989) 608
White v. Abel, 802 So. 2d 98, 101-02 (Miss. Ct. App. 2001) 486
White v. Dep't of Human Servs., 39 So. 3d 986, 990-91 (Miss. Ct. App. 2010) 479
White v. Smith, 645 So. 2d 875, 876 (Miss. 1994) 108, 614
White v. Thompson, 569 So. 2d 1181, 1184 (Miss. 1990) 354, 371, 375, 381
White v. Thompson, 822 So. 2d 1125, 1128 (Miss. Ct. App. 2002) 123, 337, 338, 358, 563, 677
White v. Weiss, 535 F.2d 1067, 1071 (8th Cir. 1976) 641
White v. White, 26 So. 3d 342, 346 (Miss. 2010) 398, 401, 576, 580, 595
White v. White, 722 So. 2d 731, 734 (Miss. Ct. App. 1999) 431
White v. White, 781 A.2d 85, 89-90 (N.J. Super Ct. Ch. Div. 2001) 642, 643
White v. White, 868 So. 2d 1054, 1056 (Miss. Ct. App. 2004) 133, 245, 275
White v. White, 913 So. 2d 323, 325-26 (Miss. Ct. App. 2005) 256, 266, 269, 275, 278
White v. Williams, 132 So. 573, 575 (Miss. 1931) 7, 62
Whitman v. Whitman, 41 So. 2d 22, 25 (Miss. 1949) 4, 97
W.H.W. v. J.J., 735 So. 2d 990, 992 (Miss. 1999) 316
Wideman v. Wideman, 909 So. 2d 140, 144-46 (Miss. Ct. App. 2005) 592
Wikel v. Miller, 53 So. 3d 29, 32 (Miss. Ct. App. 2010) 402, 404
Wilborn v. Wilborn, 258 So. 2d 804, 805-06 (Miss. 1972) 497
Wilbourne v. Wilbourne, 748 So. 2d 184, 186 (Miss. Ct. App. 1999) 21, 33, 34, 36, 38, 69, 90, 95, 96, 118
Wilburn v. Wilburn, 991 So. 2d 1185, 1191 (Miss. 2008) 338, 376, 408, 603, 615, 616, 620
Wiles v. Williams, 845 So. 2d 709, 712 (Miss. Ct. App. 2003) 470, 479, 480
Wiley v. Gray, 36 Miss. 510 (Miss. 1858) 668
Wilkerson v. Wilkerson, 955 So. 2d 903, 907-08 (Miss. Ct. App. 2007) 189, 193, 445, 616
Wilkins v. Wilkins, 432 S.E.2d 891, 897 (N.C. Ct. App. 1993) 202
Williamson v. Williamson, 964 So. 2d 524, 528-29 (Miss. Ct. App. 2007) 395, 397, 617
Williams v. Johnston, 114 So. 733, 734 (Miss. 1927) 62
Williams v. Mason, 556 So. 2d 1045, 1049 (Miss. 1990) 46
Williams v. North Carolina, 317 U.S. 287, 299 (1942) 555, 558, 565
Williams v. North Carolina, 325 U.S. 226, 227 (1945) 565
Williams v. Smith, 915 So. 2d 1114, 1116-17 (Miss. Ct. App. 2005) 374, 574, 622, 623
Williams v. State, 43 So. 2d 389 (Miss. 1949) 500
Williams v. Stockstill, 990 So. 2d 774, 776 (Miss. Ct. App. 2008) 340, 354, 358
Williams v. Williams, 37 So. 3d 1171, 1175-76 (Miss. 2010) 193, 686

TABLE OF CASES

Williams v. Williams, 164 So. 2d 898 (Miss. 1964)...309, 625
Williams v. Williams, 528 So. 2d 296, 297-98 (Miss. 1988)..36, 37
Williams v. Williams, 656 So. 2d 325, 330 (Miss. 1995)...336, 362, 378
Williams v. Williams, 810 So. 2d 613, 614-15 (Miss. Ct. App. 2001)...............................423
Williams v. Williams, 843 So. 2d 720, 721 (Miss. 2003)..316, 325, 618
Wilson v. Ake, 354 F. Supp. 2d 1298 (M.D. Fla. 2005)..51, 52
Wilson v. Dabo, 461 N.E.2d 8, 9 (Ohio Ct. App. 1983)...29
Wilson v. Mallett, 28 So. 3d 669, 669-70 (Miss. Ct. App. 2009) 619, 620
Wilson v. Mallett, 50 So. 3d 366, 368 (Miss. Ct. App. 2010)...626
Wilson v. Wilson, 22 So. 2d 161, 163 (Miss. 1945) 39, 78
Wilson v. Wilson, 32 So. 2d 686, 688 (Miss. 1947) 81
Wilson v. Wilson, 61 So. 453, 454 (Miss. 1913) 97
Wilson v. Wilson, 464 So. 2d 496, 498-499 (Miss. 1985)..486
Wilson v. Wilson, 547 So. 2d 803, 804-05 (Miss. 1989)..................................84, 95, 96, 105
Wilson v. Wilson, 741 S.W.2d 640, 647 (Ark. 1987) 155, 224
Wilson v. Wilson, 810 So. 2d 615, 616-17 (Miss. Ct. App. 2002) 282, 295
Wilson v. Wilson, 811 So. 2d 342, 346 (Miss. Ct. App. 2001)......................136, 161, 162, 612
Wilson v. Wilson, 820 So. 2d 761, 763 (Miss. Ct. App. 2002)...................................148, 159
Wilson v. Wilson, 975 So. 2d 261, 264 (Miss. Ct. App. 2007) 162, 167, 260, 261, 275
Winfield v. Winfield, 35 So. 2d 443, 444 (Miss. 1948)..................................230, 236, 352
Wing v. Wing, 549 So. 2d 944, 947-48 (Miss. 1989) 457, 674
Winkler v. Winkler, 61 So. 1, 2 (Miss. 1913)...236
Winner v. Winner, 177 N.W. 680, 682 (Wis. 1920) 10
Winstead v. Berry, 556 So. 2d 321, 324 (Miss. 1989)...634
Winters v. Winters, 111 So. 2d 418, 420-21 (Miss. 1959)...555
Wires v. Wires, 297 So. 2d 900, 901-02 (Miss. 1974)...71, 84
Wise v. Wise, 37 So. 3d 95, 98 (Miss. Ct. App. 2010)...225, 226
Wolcott v. Wolcott, 184 So. 2d 381, 382 (Miss. 1966) 13, 18, 19
Wolfe v. Wolfe, 42 So. 2d 438, 439 (Miss. 1949)..16, 17
Wolfe v. Wolfe, 49 So. 3d 650 (Miss. Ct. App. 2010)...113, 115
Wolfe v. Wolfe, 766 So. 2d 123, 126 (Miss. Ct. App. 2000) 171, 177, 235, 249, 259, 275, 277, 279, 280, 287
Woodell v. Parker, 860 So. 2d 781, 785-87 (Miss. 2003) 385, 386, 387
Woodfin v. Woodfin. 26 So. 3d 389, 394-95 (Miss. Ct. App. 2010)....................261, 423, 462, 677
Woodham v. Woodham, 17 So. 3d 153, 156 (Miss. Ct. App. 2009).................343, 348, 350, 353
Wood v. Wood, 35 So. 3d 507, 515 (Miss. 2010) 193, 194, 200, 683, 684, 686
Wood v. Wood, 495 So. 2d 503, 505 (Miss. 1986) 101, 103
Wood v. Wood, 579 So. 2d 1271, 1273 (Miss. 1991) 376
Wood v. Wood, 964 P.2d 1259, 1266-67 (Wyo. 1998)...433
Woodward v. Commissioner of Social Sec., 760 N.E.2d 257 (Mass. 2002)...............................507
Woolbert v. Lee Lumber Co., 117 So. 354, 359 (Miss. 1928)...21
Woolridge v. Woolridge, 856 So. 2d 446, 452 (Miss. Ct. App. 2003) 45
Workman v. Workman, 418 S.E.2d 269, 272-74 (N.C. Ct. App. 1992).......................................203
Worley v. Jackson, 595 So. 2d 853, 855 (Miss. 1992) 355, 374
Woy v. Woy, 737 S.W.2d 769, 774 (Mo. Ct. App. 1987) 10
Wray v. Langston, 380 So. 2d 1262, 1264 (Miss. 1980)..446, 447
Wray v. Wray, 394 So. 2d 1341, 1344-45 (Miss. 1981)..247, 252, 253
Wright v. Coleman, 102 So. 774, 775 (Miss. 1925)...19, 419
Wright v. Stanley, 700 So. 2d 274, 277-79 (Miss. 1997) 302, 440, 442, 466, 472, 641
Wright v. Wright, 2 Miss. Dec. 67, 1883 WL 6853, at *4 (1883)..81
Wright v. Wright, 737 So. 2d 408, 410 (Miss. Ct. App. 1998) 465, 483, 678
Wright v. Wright, 779 S.W.2d 183, 184 (Ark. Ct. App. 1989) 157
Wright v. Wright, 823 So. 2d 586, 587 (Miss. Ct. App. 2002)....................................89, 118, 444, 445
Wright v. Wright, 975 S.W.2d 212, 214 (Mo. Ct. App. 1993) 430
Wyatt v. Wyatt, 32 So. 317, 318 (Miss. 1902) 22, 668

Y

Yancey v. Yancey, 752 So. 2d 1006, 1010 (Miss. 1999)................ 144, 157, 291, 293, 431, 464
Yates v. Yates, 284 So. 2d 46, 47 (Miss. 1973)...352
Yazoo Lumber Co. v. Clark, Jr.,48 So. 516, 517 (Miss. 1909)..15
Yeager v. Kittrell, 35 So. 3d 1221, 1225-26 (Miss. Ct. App. 2009) 581
Yearta v. Scroggins, 268 S.E.2d 151 (Ga. 1980)..563, 579

TABLE OF CASES

Yelverton v. Yelverton, 26 So. 3d 1053, 1057 (Miss. 2010)... 164, 625
Yelverton v. Yelverton, 961 So. 2d 19, 25 n.6 (Miss. 2007)....................225, 245, 261, 275, 279, 309, 423, 437, 624
Young v. Deaton, 766 So. 2d 819, 821 (Miss. Ct. App. 2000).. 307, 491
Youssefi v. Youssefi, 744 A.2d 662, 668 (N.J. Super. Ct. App. Div. 2000) 572

Z

Zablocki v. Redhail, 434 U.S. 374, 386 (1978) 2
Zeigler v. Zeigler, 164 So. 768, 769 (Miss. 1935).. 11
Zeman v. Stanford, 789 So. 2d 798, 803 (Miss. 2001) 384, 385, 386
Zemke v. Zemke, 860 P.2d 756, 762-64 (N. Mex. Ct. App. 1993).. 145
Zinsmeister v. Comm'r, 80 T.C.M. (CCH) 774 (2006)... 656
Zoglio v. Zoglio, 157 A.2d 627, 629 (D.C. 1960)... 10

730

INDEX

A

Abortion, 30
Abuse, *see also Domestic Violence*
    adoption grounds, 541, 544
    allegations, 338
    grounds for termination of parental rights, 523, 526
    grounds for divorce, 83-91
    mandatory reporting, 640
Adoption, See Generally Chapter XVII
    actions to set aside, 545
    burden of proof, 543
    child's name, 544
    confidentiality, 544
    consent to,
        child, 537
        Department of Human Services, 537
        grandparents, 537
        legal father, 536
        mother, 536
        procedure, 537
        requirements, 538
        revocation of, 538
        unmarried father, 537
    grandparent visitation rights after, 544
    grounds for,
        abandonment, 540
        abuse, 541
        conduct posing substantial risk, 542
        desertion, 541
        failure to provide, 541
        other, 542
        parent's condition, 542
        standard, 540
        termination statute grounds, 542
    guardian ad litem,
        discretionary, 534
        for minor parent, 535
        mandatory, 534
    hearings, 543
    inheritance after, 543
    interlocutory decree, 543
    interstate actions, 532
    judgment of adoption, 543
    jurisdiction, 531
    natural parent visitation, 544
    parties,
        child, 534
        custodians, 533
        grandparents, 534
        necessary, 533
        parents, 533
    petition for, 535
    procedure, 535
    termination of parental rights, 532, 544
    uncontested, 536
    venue, 531
Alienation of affection, 27
Alimony, See Generally Chapter IX
    bond to secure, 286
    cohabitants, 46

equitable liens to secure, 285
escalation clauses, 284
factors, 255
    age, 267
    assets, 263
    children, 262
    deductions from income, 257
    dissipation of assets, 269
    earning capacity, 259
    expenses, 260
    fault, 268
    foregone opportunities, 270
    health, 266
    home or car, use of, 261
    income, 257
    marriage length, 264
    obligations, 262
    standard of living, 259
    support during school, 270
    tax effects, 270
fault as factor, 268
findings of fact, 254
forms of, 283
guidelines for awards, 233
history, 229
hybrid alimony, 251
jurisdiction, 238, *see Jurisdiction, financial awards,*
life insurance to secure, 285
lump sum alimony, 243
    analysis of awards, 280
    factors, 245, 272-73
    history, 243
    installment payments, 247
    modification, 247
    purpose, 244
    termination, 247
    vesting, 246
men as recipients, 230
modification, 286
    arrearages, 290
    effective date, 296
    forseeability, 288
    lump sum alimony, 247, 287
    out-of-court agreements, 290
    permanent alimony, 241, 286
    petition to increase alimony, 291
    petition to reduce alimony, 293
    rehabilitative alimony, 249, 287
    reimbursement alimony, 287
    remarriage, effect of, 291
    restrictions, 289
    Social Security benefits, effect on, 294
    test for modification, 288
    third-party payments, 287
permanent alimony, 240
    amount, 241
    analysis of awards, 273
    amount, 277
    marriages over twenty years, 276
    marriages ten to nineteen years, 276
    marriages under ten years, 277
    conversion to rehabilitative, 241

INDEX

factors, 240
modification, 241
purpose, 240
termination, 241
vesting, 241
property division, relationship to, 232, 239
rehabilitative alimony, 248
analysis of awards, 279
amount, 280
length, 280
conversion to permanent, 249
extension, 249
factors, 248
modification, 249
purpose, 248
termination, 250
vesting, 249
reimbursement alimony, 250
amount, 251
characteristics, 251
factors, 251
purpose, 250
reserved jurisdiction, 284
security for, 285
source of payments, 285
specificity, 286
temporary alimony, 238
termination, 296
cohabitation, 296
de facto marriage, 298
effective date, 298
material change, 296
theories of, 232
third-party payments as, 281
medical expenses, 281
mortgage payments, 282
types, 231
Annulment, See Generally Chapter III
defenses to,
estoppel, 62
laches, 61
ratification, 61
statute of limitations, 61
effect of on,
alimony, 63
children, 64
property rights, 63
grounds for,
age, 60
bigamy, 59
impotency, 60
kinship, 59
lack of consent, 60
mental capacity, 60
no license, 60
physical capacity, 60
wife's pregnancy by another, 60
history of, 57
jurisdiction, 64
parties, 62
procedure, 64
retroactivity, 64

void marriages, 58
voidable marriages, 58
Appeals
agreement not to appeal, 625
appealable orders, 619
attorneys' fees, 625
briefs,
failure to file, 623
lack of citation, 623
lack of transcript, 623
waiver of issue, 623
certiorari, 625
consent judgments, 622
dismissal,
fugitive dismissal, 626
mootness, 626
harmless error, 625
in forma pauperis appeals, 625
reversal on appeal,
divorce, 624
financial awards, 624
remand, 624
standard of review, 622
stay pending appeal, 621
time of appeal, 620
Arrearages, *see Enforcement of Decrees*
Artificial insemination, *see Assisted Reproduction*
Assisted reproduction, See Generally Chapter XV
Embryos, 503
adoption of, 518
division at divorce, 504
donation, 518
legal status of, 504
posthumous implantation, 506
parental rights of,
donors, 510
husband of birth mother, 508
unmarried partner of birth mother, 509
posthumous conception,
inheritance rights, 506
Social Security benefits, 507
surrogacy,
ABA Model Act, 511
judicial decisions, 515-517
state statutes, 513-14
types of surrogacies, 511
Attorneys' fees, See Generally Chapter X
amount of award, 304
appeals, 309, 625
based on defendant conduct, 306
contempt actions, 307, 498
dilatory tactics, 306
frivolous litigation, 308
unfounded accusations, 308
ethical issues, 636
fault as factor, 304
findings of fact, 302
grandparents' visitation actions, 386
inability to pay, 302
need, 302
notice of hearing, 308
paid to litigant, 308

732

INDEX

proof, 304
reversed with property division, 309
separate maintenance actions, 37

B

Bankruptcy, See Generally Chapter XXI
  automatic stay of
    collection of support, 649
    contempt actions, 650
    judicial lien enforcement, 650
    modification, 648
    original orders, 647
    property division, 648
  dischargeability of
    alimony, 651
    attorneys' fees, 651
    child support, 651
    debts, 651
    property division, 651
  domestic support obligation, 646
  joint debts, 653
  liquidation, 645
  nondebtor spouse's assets, 652
  priority, 647
  reorganization, 646
Bigamy, 4, 59, 97
Breach of promise to marry, 28
Businesses, Property Division, See Generally
Chapter VIII
  burden of proof, 221
  equitable distribution,
    jointly owned businesses, 226
    lump sum award, 225
  forms of ownership, 217
  fraudulent transfers, 227
  joinder of entity, 217
  marital property classification, 218
  mixed asset classification, 220
  piercing corporate veil, 227
  separate property classification, 219
  valuation of, 222
    discounts, 224
    goodwill, 224
    Revenue Ruling 59-60, 222
    valuation methods, 222

C

Child Support, See Generally Chapter XIII
  Abatement, 473
  adjustments to income, 434
    child support as adjustment, 435
    children in home, 435
    mandatory deductions, 434
    voluntary deductions, 434
  adoptive parents, 421
  bankruptcy, effect of, *see Bankruptcy*
  bond to secure, 459
  college expenses, 445
    after majority, 448
    aptitude of child, 446

basic support during college, 447
between parents, 447
child's relationship with parent, 446
education accounts, 450
performance requirements, 448
scope of college support, 447
time of award, 446
custodial parent support, 442
Department of Human Services role, 416
deviation from guidelines, factors, 436
  child's income, 440
  childcare expenses, 440
  college support, 441
  criteria for, 437
  educational expenses of child, 437
  extensive visitation, 438
  fluctuating income, 440
  medical expenses, 437
  older children, 440
  reduced visitation, 440
  reversed deviations, 441
  shared custody, 438
disabled adult children, support for, 419
escalation clauses, 456
gross income, amounts included,
  alimony payments, 426
  child support, 426
  employment benefits, 427
  federal benefits, 425
  fluctuating income, 427
  overtime, 424
  second jobs, 424
  self-employment income, 427
  spouse's income, 426
  state benefits, 425
guidelines for support,
  findings of fact, 422
  income outside guidelines, 436, 442-443
  percentages of income, 436
  steps in applying guidelines, 422
health insurance, 444
history, 413
imprisonment, 433
imputed income, 429-433
  asset transfers, 433
  findings of fact, 429
  good faith test, 430
  hidden income, 433
  income transfers, 433
  resignation from job, 430
  tax returns as evidence of income, 433
  unemployment, 431
  voluntariness test, 430
in loco parentis as basis for, 421
income withholding, 458
jurisdiction, *see Jurisdiction, financial awards*
life insurance to secure, 445, 459
lump sum payment, 460
medical expenses, 444
modification, *see Modification of child support*
no support ordered, 442
payee, 455

INDEX

Qualified Domestic Relations Order, 460
security for payment, 459
separate maintenance actions, 38
separated parents, 418
source of payments, 460
stepparents, 421
temporary support, 416
termination based on
adoption, 455
agreement, 453
child's hostility, 453
dissestablishment of paternity, 455
emancipation, 451
majority, 451
parents' remarriage, 455
payor's death, 455
termination of parental rights, 455
types of actions, 415
unmarried parents, 419
venue, 415
Closely held businesses, *see Businesses*
Cohabitation, See Generally Chapter II
alimony awards, 46
between former spouses, 44-45
crime of, 42
property rights, 43-46
putative spouse doctrine, 44
Social Security benefits, 47
void marriages, 44
workers' compensation benefits, 47
Common law marriage, 8, 42
Conflicts of law, 3
Contempt actions, *see Enforcement of Decrees*
Continuances, 602
Contracts
between spouses, 22
pre and postmarital agreements, *see Marital Agreements*
settlement agreements, *see Marital Agreements*
Conveyances between spouses, 22
Credit bureau reports, 500
Criminal conversation, 28
Custody of children, See Generally Chapter XII
abuse and neglect allegations, 338
appeals, 338
best interest test factors, 340-362
age of parent, 351
age, health and sex of child, 342
alcohol or drug use, 351
bond between parent and child, 352
child's home and school record, 355
child's preference, 356
childcare capacity, 348
continuing care, 344
employment responsibilities, 348
findings of fact regarding, 341
home environment, 357
mental health, 350
military service, 362
moral fitness, 352
parent's health and age, 349
parental interference, 361

parenting skills, 346
physical health of parent, 349
religion, 361
separation of siblings, 360
custody proceedings, types, 333-336
adoption, 334
annulment, 333
custody petition, 333
divorce, 333
habeas actions, 334
paternity, 334
protection orders, 334
separate maintenance, 333
youth court , 334
emergency custody, 337
history, 329
joint custody
agreed, 365
ambiguous awards, 365
court-ordered, 365
forms, 364
joint legal custody, 364
joint physical custody, 364
presumption regarding, 332
relocation, effect of, 368
joint custody factors, 366
cooperation, 366
domestic violence, 367
parental fitness, 366
proximity, 367
jurisdiction, *see Jurisdiction, custody*
out-of-court agreements, 337
presumptions regarding custody, 330-332
domestic violence presumption, 332
joint custody presumption, 332
natural parent presumptions, 331
parental equality, 330
restrictions on custody, 369
temporary custody, 335
third-party custody, 369-374
abandonment, 372
between third parties, 374
constructive abandonment, 372
desertion, 372
immoral conduct, 371
in loco parentis, 370
legal custody relinquishment, 373
modification of, 374
natural parent presumption, 369
third-parties as parents, 370
unfitness, 371
visitation, 373
types of custody, 332

D

Death of spouse
before entry of judgment, 614
effect on agreements, 686
Default judgments, 70, 602
Default, *see Enforcement of Decrees*
Defense of Marriage Act, 50

734

INDEX

Discovery, 600
Divorce , See Generally Chapter IV
    burden of proof, 70
    corroboration, 70
    default judgments, 70
    defenses to divorce,
        collusion, 103
        condonation, 101
        connivance, 103
        knowledge, 99
        mental illness, 99
        ratification, 99
        recrimination, 100
        reformation, 101
        res judicata, 103
    fault-based grounds,
        adultery, 73
        bigamy, 97
        constructive desertion, 80
        desertion, 77
        habitual cruelty, 83-95
        habitual drug use, 81
        habitual drunkenness, 81
        impotency, 73
        imprisonment, 77
        kinship, 98
        mental illness, 96, 98
        wife's pregnancy by another, 97
    findings of fact, 72
    history, 67
    irreconcilable differences, 105
        consent, 106
        jurisdiction, 105
        requirements for, 106
    jurisdiction, *see Jurisdiction, divorce*
    revocation of, 109
    standard of review, 73
Doctrine of necessaries, 20
Domestic violence, See Generally Chapter V
    custody,
        custody factors, 122
        joint custody, 123
        presumptions against award to violent
            parent, 121
        visitation restrictions, 123
    false allegations of, 127
    firearms prohibitions, 116
    grounds for divorce, 116
    mediation, 124
    property division, 121
    protection orders,
        attorneys' fees, 115
        child support, 114
        custody orders, 114
        emergency orders, 114
        enforcement, 115
        findings of fact, 115
        interstate enforcement, 115
        judgments, 114
        jurisdiction, 112
        modification, 115
        mutual orders, 114

        notice, 113
        parties, 112
        permanent orders, 114
        petition, 113
        procedure, 113
        temporary orders, 114
    safety assessments, 116
    tort actions based on domestic violence,
        causes of action, 125
        immunity, 124
        relationship to divorce, 125
        statute of limitations, 126

E

Enforcement of Decrees, See Generally Chapter XIV
    Arrearages, 476-481, 494
        interest on, 476
        proof, 476
        temporary support arrearages, 477
    bond, 496
    collection, 494
        execution on judgment, 499
        lien on worker's compensation awards, 499
        Qualified Domestic Relations Order, 500
        retirement funds, 499
        seizure of accounts, 499
        tax rebates, 499
    contempt,
        civil, 486
        criminal, 487
    defenses to contempt,
        advice of counsel, 493
        ambiguity, 491
        clean hands doctrine, 492
        estoppel, 492
        inability to pay, 488
        invalid judgment, 494
        lack of willfulness, 490
        mental illness, 493
        payee's fault, 492
        payment, 492
        performance impossible, 492
        sanctions for,
            attorneys' fees, 498
            incarceration, 497
    credits against arrearages, 477
        alimony, 477
        child support, 477
        custodial parent's debt, 481
        payments after emancipation, 479
        property division, 477
        Social Security benefits, 480
        third-party payments, 480
    criminal prosecution for arrearages, 500
    defenses to noncompliance with decree, 482-486
        clean hands, 484
        estoppel, 483
        laches, 483
        private agreement, 483
        res judicata, 485

INDEX

statute of limitations, 485
Department of Human Services role, 475
    equitable lien, 496
    forgiveness, 494
    income withholding, 495
    interstate actions, 475
    license revocation, 500
    noncompliance with orders
        child custody, 481
        property division, 481
        removal of child, 482
        visitation restrictions, 482
        visitation, 481
Equitable distribution, *see Property division*
Ethical issues, See Generally Chapter XX
    fee arrangements,
        attorneys' fees, 636
        attorneys' liens, 637-638
        retainers, 636
    client behavior,
        criminal conduct, 639
        future conduct, 640
        past conduct, 640
    client files, 638
    confidentiality, 635
    conflicts of interest,
        dual representation, 633
        judges, 635
        mediators, 635
        prior representation, 634
        subsequent representation, 635
    continuing representation, 643
    false statements, 639
    limited representation, 638
    mandatory reporting of abuse, 640
    nonlegal advice, 639
    surveillance, *see Surveillance and Wiretapping*
    third-party fee payment, 638
Evidence
    competency, 29
    hearsay exceptions, 605
    HIPAA, 609
    Journals, 611
    medical records, 609
    mental examination, 610
    physical examination, 610
    privileges,
        marital, 29
        physician/patient, 607
        priest/penitent, 610
    testimony,
        children, 604
        closed-circuit television, 606
        expert, 606
        guardian ad litem, 611
        limits on, 603
        medical, 607

F

Financial statements, 594
Fraud

Businesses, 227
    marriage, 10
Fraudulent conveyances, 186

G

Goodwill, 224
Guardians ad litem, See Generally Chapter XXII, 388-391
    discretionary appointment, 388
    duties, 389
    fees, 391
    findings of fact regarding, 390
    mandatory appointment, 388
    report, weight accorded, 391

H

Healthcare directives, 31
Heart balm actions,
    alienation of affection, 27
    breach of promise to marry, 28
    criminal conversation, 28
Homestead property, 15

I

In loco parentis doctrine, 370, 421
In vitro fertilization, see *Assisted Reproduction*
Inheritance rights between spouses, 18
Interest on arrearages, 476
Intestacy, 18
Irreconcilable differences divorce, 105

J

Judgments, See Generally Chapter XIX, 611-615
    consent judgments, 613
    finality, 614
    findings of fact, 611
    modification, 614
    nunc pro tunc, 615
    offer of judgment, 614
    requested findings, 612
    required findings, 611
    retained jurisdiction, 613
    time of decision, 612
Jurisdiction, See Generally Chapter XVIII
    adoption, 531
    alimony, see *Jurisdiction, financial awards*
    annulment, 64
    chancery courts, 551
    child support, see *Jurisdiction, financial awards*
    custody awards,
        interstate actions, see *Uniform Child Custody Jurisdiction and Enforcement Act*
        personal jurisdiction, 563
        service of process, 563
        subject matter jurisdiction, 562
    divorce,
        absence from state, 556
        domicile, change of, 556

INDEX

personal jurisdiction, 558
service of process, 558
subject matter, 555
venue, 557
federal courts, 552
financial awards in divorce,
    child support, 562
    interstate actions, see *Uniform Interstate Family*
Support Act
    military pensions, 562
    personal jurisdiction, 559
    property in state, 562
    subject matter jurisdiction, 559
    waiver of jurisdiction, 561
interstate actions, divorce, 563
military pensions, 562
modification of alimony, 567
modification of child support, 567
modification of custody, 567
modification within state, 566
personal jurisdiction, generally, 554
property division, see *financial awards*
service of process, generally, 554
subject matter jurisdiction, generally, 553
youth courts, 552

L

Legitimacy, annulled marriage, 64
License revocation, 500
Locator services, 501
Loss of consortium, 25

M

Marital Agreements, See Generally Chapter XXIII
alimony provisions, 684
child support provisions, 684
clarification, 681
construction, 683
custody provisions, 684
defenses to enforcement,
    against public policy, 681
    duress or undue influence, 679
    equitable principles, 682
    fraud or misrepresentation, 679
    frustration of purpose, 682
    mistake, 681
    unconscionability, 680
    voidness, 680
enforcement, 682
general release, 686
history, 667
jurisdiction provisions, 686
modification, 682
premarital agreements,
    breach, 672
    consideration, 669
    disclosure, 669
    fairness, 670
    independent counsel, 669
    interpretation, 671

    scope, 672
    settlement agreements as, 672
    statute of frauds, 671
    voluntariness, 669
    waiver, 673
property division provisions, 685
reconciliation, effect on, 687
settlement agreements,
    alimony provisions, 678
    child support provisions, 677
    court approval, 676
    custody provisions, 677
    enforceability, 675
    formalities, 674
    incorporation into judgment, 678
    nature of, 673
    out-of-court agreements, 678
    property division provisions, 677
    requirements, 674
Marital rape, 30
Marriage, See Generally Chapter I
conflicts of law, 3
consent to, 10
duress, 11
eligibility to marry,
    age, 4
    bigamy, 4
    kinship, 3
    mental capacity, 6
    physical capacity, 6
    same sex, 5
for limited purpose, 11
fraud, 10
in jest, 12
presumptions regarding, 2
requirements form
    ceremony, 8
    common law marriage, 8
    failure to comply, 9
    license, 9
Married Women's Property Acts, 13
Mediation, 630
Modification of Child Support, See Generally
Chapter XIII 461-473
arrearages, 464
clean hands doctrine, 465
college expenses, 471
    award of college expenses, 472
    basic support, 473
decrease in support, 468
    change in custody, 470
    emancipation, 469
    reduction in income, 468
    remarriage, 469
guidelines, 461
increase in support, 466
    expenses of older children, 467
    inflation, 467
limits on, 464
material changes test,
    examples, 464
    foreseeability, 463

INDEX

material change, 462
timing of change, 462
out-of-court agreement, 464
Modification of custody, See Generally Chapter XII, 391-408
bond to secure, 408
burden of proof, 393
child support, nonpayment, 395
contempt, 408
enforcement, 408
evidence, 393
findings of fact, 392
joint custody modification, 406
disruption as basis, 408
inability to cooperate, 407
relocation, 407
joint legal custody, 408
jurisdiction, 391
material change in circumstances test,
adverse effect, 397
behavior of child, 404
child's best interest, 398
child's choice, 401
cohabitation, 402
de facto custody change, 404
friction between child and parent, 403
lack of cooperation, 402
material change in circumstances, 395
military service, 405
noncustodial parent improvement, 405
relocation, 399
remarriage as basis, 399
totality of circumstances, 398
pleadings, 392
stability as factor, 394
visitation modification, 408
Motions
dismissal , 602
recusal, 601
relief from judgment, 616
reopen, motion to, 615
set aside judgment, motion to, 615-618
summary judgment, 602
Parties, See Generally Chapter XIX, 585-589
adoption, 533-34
annulment, 62
child support actions, 587
custody actions, 586
divorce, 585
mentally incompetent parties, 588
minors, 588
pro se parties, 589
property division, parties to, 585

P

Partition, 18, 190
between spouses, 18
separate maintenance actions, 38
Paternity, See Generally Chapter XI
acknowledgment, 314
appeals, 318

burden of proof, 318
defenses to action, 319
collateral estoppel, 320
laches, 320
res judicata, 320
statute of limitations, 319
disestablishing paternity, 322-326
estoppel, 326
presumption of legitimacy, 322
suit by mother child or biological father, 323
suit by presumed father, 325
genetic tests, 316
challenge to report, 317
costs, 317
expert testimony, 317
presumption of paternity, 317
refusal to cooperate, 316
testing facility, 316
guardian ad litem, 316
history, 313
judgment, 320
child support award, 321
costs, 322
custody, 321
security, 322
visitation, 321
jurisdiction, 314
jury trial, 316
parties,
child, 315
Department of Human Services, 315
father, biological, 315
father, legal, 315
paternity fraud, 326
service of process, 316
time of trial, 316
venue, 314
witnesses, 318
Pleadings, See Generally Chapter XIX, 589-594
affirmative defenses, 592
complaint, 589
child support, 590
custody, 592
divorce, 589
property division, 590
responsive pleadings, 592
Property division, See Generally Chapter VI
annulment, 63
attorneys' fees, 155
businesses, 159, *see Businesses*
clarification of, 193
classification of assets,
appreciation, 140
beginning date, 134
commingled assets, 144, 149
conversion to marital, 146
ending date, 134
exchanges of property, 143
failure to classify, 133
gifts, 139
income from assets, 140
inheritances, 139

738

INDEX

joint titling, 148
   marital property defined, 134
   separate property, 138
   tracing, 144
cohabitants, 44-45
community property, 130
constructive trust, 192
debt, assignment of, 181
disability benefits, 153
division factors,
   agreement, 177
   contribution by homemaker, 171
   contribution to stability, 174
   contribution to education, 174
   dissipation of assets, 177
   elimination of alimony, 176
   emotional attachment to asset, 179
   fault, 176
   financial contribution, 173
   need, 175
   separate estate, 175
   tax consequences, 180
enforcement, 194
equitable credit, 191
equitable distribution, 131
factors, 133
frustration of purpose, 195
intellectual property, 156
life insurance, 156
loan proceeds, 156
lottery winnings, 159
lump sum award, 189
marital home, 159, 180
marital property division,
   basic principles, 166
   findings of fact, 168
   relationship to alimony, 168
   standard of review, 168
modification of, 192
partition, 190
personal injury awards, 152
presumption in favor of marital property, 132
professional degrees, 154
reserved jurisdiction, 192
retirement benefits, 159
sale of assets, 189
security for, 192
separate maintenance actions, 37
steps in division, 132
third-party interests,
   children's assets, 186
   constructive trust, 185
   corporate entities, 186
   equitable liens, 184
   joinder, 184
title system, 130
title, transfer of, 189
trusts, 157
waiver, 194
worker's compensation awards, 153

Property rights between spouses
   Homestead, 15
   joint ownership, 16
   ownership, 14
   partition, 17
Putative spouse doctrine, 44

R

Residence, choice of, 32
Retirement benefits, See Generally Chapter VII
   classification, 199
   defined benefit plans, 203-207
   defined contribution plans,
      classification, 201
      division, 202
      taxes, 202
      valuation, 201
   definitions,
      alternate payee, 198
      deferred distribution, 198
      defined benefit, 197
      defined contribution, 197
      immediate offset, 198
      mature, 198
      participant, 197
      vested, 198
   division, 200
   equitable distribtution, 198
   federal regulation, 208
   federal retirement benefits, 214
   IRAs, 214
   military benefits, 210
      disability, 213
      division, 212
      jurisdiction, 211
   Qualified Domestic Relations Order, 208
   Social Security benefits, 215
   state benefits, 215
   unvested pensions, 216
   valuation, 199
Rule 81(d), See Generally Chapter XIX, 627-630
   continuances, 630
   hearings, 630
   pleadings,
      initial, 627
      responsive, 627
   scope, 627
   service of process,
      contempt proceedings, 629
      form, 628
      manner of service, 628
      waiver of service, 629

S

Same-sex partners, See Generally Chapter II
   adoption, 54
   custody and visitation, 54
   divorce actions, 52
   federal law, 50
   interstate recognition, 51-53

INDEX

marriage banned, 50
marriage rights, 49
state benefits, 53
Separate maintenance, See Generally Chapter I
  attorneys' fees, 37
  basis for award, 34
  child support, 38
  factors, 35
  history, 33
  lump sum payments, 37
  modification, 38
  partition, 38
  property division, 37
  scope, 34
  temporary support, 37
  termination, 38
  third-party payments, 36
Service of process, See Generally Chapter XIX, 595
  inadequate process, 597
  mentally incompetent party, 597
  nonresident defendants, 596
  publication, 596
  resident defendants, 595
  waiver, 597
Servicemembers Civil Relief Act, 104, 631
Social Security
  alimony modification, 294
  cohabitants, 47
  credit against arrearages, 480
  property division, 216
Spousal support, *see Alimony*
Stipulations, 603
Surrogacy, *see Assisted Reproduction*
Surveillance,
  electronic mail, 642
  interspousal, 641
  spyware, 643
  use by attorney, 642

T

Tax Effects, See Generally Chapter XXII
  alimony, 655
    code requirements, 655
    problem areas, 658
    state law impact, 658
  child support,
    child tax credit, 660
    child-related deductions, 659
    childcare credit, 660
    code requirements, 659
    dependency deductions, 659
    educational credits, 660
    medical expense deductions, 660
  estate and gift tax, 665
  filing status, 664
  innocent spouse relief, 665
  litigation-related payments, 663
  property transfers, 660
    as alimony, 661
    assignment of asset income, 662
    closely held corporations, 663

    code requirements, 661
    interest on installment payments, 663
    marital residence, 661
    pensions, 662
  tax liability, 664
  tax refunds, 664
Temporary support
  alimony, 239
  arrearages, 477
  child support, 416
  custody, 336
  protection orders, 114
  separate maintenance, 37
Termination of parental rights, See Generally
Chapter XVI
  alternatives to termination, 527
  appeals, 529
  burden of proof, 527
  child support effect on, 529
  grounds,
    abandonment, 522
    abuse, 523, 526
    agency custody, 524
    assault, 526
    desertion, 523
    extreme antipathy, 525
    failure to contact, 523
    neglect, 526
    parental behavior, 524
    voluntary relinquishment, 526
  guardian ad litem, 520
  inheritance rights, 529
  judgment, 528
  jurisdiction, 519
  parties, 520
  right to counsel, 527
  service of process, 521
  time of trial, 527
  venue, 519
Tort actions, *see also Heart Balm actions*
  domestic violence, 24
  immunity, 24

U

Undue influence, 186
Uniform Child Custody Jurisdiction Enforcement
Act, See Generally Chapter XVIII, 575-582
  affidavit, 576
  enforcement, 582
  modification jurisdiction,
    continuing exclusive jurisiction, 580
    emergency jurisdiction, 581
    second state modification, 581
  personal jurisdiction, 579
  registration of orders, 582
  scope, 575
  subject matter jurisdiction,
    concurrent actions, 578
    defenses to, 577-578
    emergency jurisdiction, 577
    home state, 576

740

INDEX

no state with jurisdiction, 577
significant connections, 576
waiver of, 578
Uniform Interstate Family Support Act, See Generally Chapter XVIII, 568-574
enforcement,
income withholding, 574
registration, 574
modification,
alimony, 573
child support, 570
personal jurisdiction, 568
two-state procedure, 569
Unmarried partners, *See Cohabitants*

V

Valuation, 174
burden of proof, 162
businesses, 166, 222-224
date of valuation, 163
findings of fact, 161
proof of value,
buy-sell agreements, 166
expert testimony, 164
financial statements, 165
parties' testimony, 165
retirement benefits, 166
Visitation, See Generally Chapter XII, 374-387
grandparent visitation, 383-387
adoption, effect on, 386, 544
attorneys' fees, 386
constitutionality, 383
modification, 386
parties, 386
scope, 385
statutory requirements, 383
types, 384
venue, 386
guardian ad litem, *see Guardian ad litem*
military service, family visitation, 387
noncustodial parent rights, 375
restrictions on, 377
abusive behavior, 378
activities, 381
child's wishes, 382
custodial parent interference, 382
emotional abuse, 379
family violence, 379
household conditions, 381
imprisonment, 380
kidnapping, 380
mental health, 380
poor parenting, 381
sexual conduct, 381
scope, 375
third-party visitation, 387
transportation, 375
Void marriage, 44, 57

W

Wills, 19
Wrongful death, 26
alimony awards, 284
annulled marriage, 63

ABOUT THE AUTHOR

Deborah Hodges Bell is a Professor of Law at the University of Mississippi and the Mississippi Defense Lawyers Association Distinguished Lecturer in Law. She is the founder of the school's Civil Legal Clinic and its director until 2009. In 2011, she became director of the Law School Pro Bono Initiative. Professor Bell graduated from the University of Mississippi School of Law in 1979. She served as Editor-in-Chief of the *Mississippi Law Journal*. After graduating, she clerked for Judge Elbert Tuttle, Sr., of the United States Fifth Circuit Court of Appeals. After working as an attorney for the Atlanta Legal Aid Society, Professor Bell joined the faculty at the University of Mississippi. In her tenure at the law school, she has taught Property, Real Estate Sales, Negotiable Instruments, Secured Transactions, Sales, Housing Law, Poverty Law, Family Law, and Lawyering Skills. She was a visiting professor at Ohio State University School of Law and Emory University School of Law. From 1988-89, she was a research fellow at Harvard University School of Law. Professor Bell is a frequent speaker on family law in Mississippi. She also offers a yearly, day-long continuing legal education program on family law, provides annual training for the state's chancellors and judicial clerks on family law issues, and offers mediation services for parties in divorce.

Made in the USA
Middletown, DE
08 January 2019